T5-BSG-344

Cleveland
Cuyahoga, Geauga, Lake, and portions of Lorain County

street guide

TELL US — response form in back — WHAT YOU THINK

CONTENTS

NAVTECH ON BOARD ®

LEGEND

- **123** Insterstate Highway
- **BUS 123** Interstate (Business) Highway
- **123** U.S. Highway
- **123** State/Provincial Highway
- **123** Secondary State/Provincial Highway/County Highway
- **1** Trans-Canada Highway
- **123** Canadian Autoroute
- **123** Mexican Highway
- **123** Other Highway Designation
- **456** Exit Number
- Free Limited Access Highway (with Tunnel)
- Toll Limited Access Highway Toll Plaza
- Interchange
- Ramp
- Highway
- Primary Road
- Secondary Road
- Minor Road, Unpaved Road
- Walkway, Trail

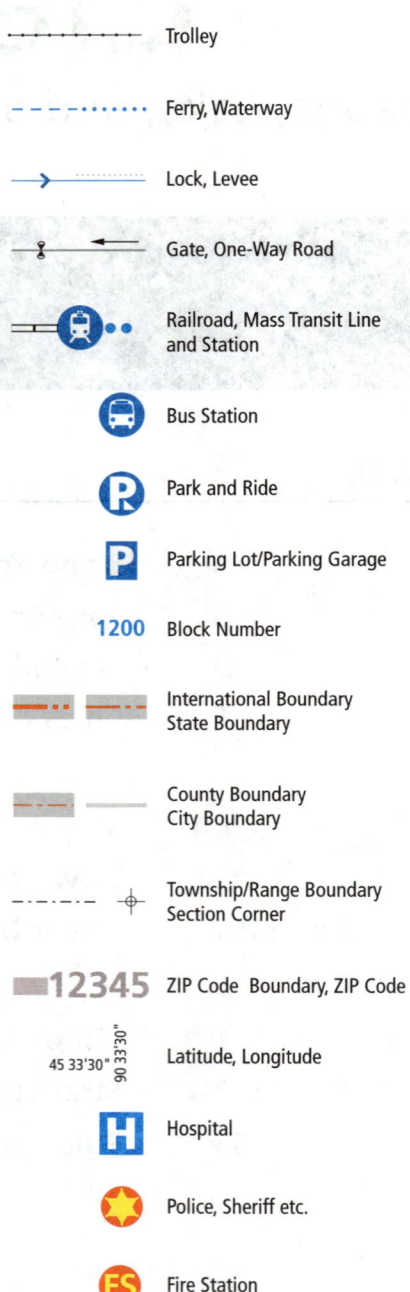

- Trolley
- Ferry, Waterway
- Lock, Levee
- Gate, One-Way Road
- Railroad, Mass Transit Line and Station
- Bus Station
- Park and Ride
- Parking Lot/Parking Garage
- **1200** Block Number
- International Boundary State Boundary
- County Boundary City Boundary
- Township/Range Boundary Section Corner
- **12345** ZIP Code Boundary, ZIP Code
- 45 33'30" 90 33'30" Latitude, Longitude
- **H** Hospital
- Police, Sheriff etc.
- **FS** Fire Station
- **?** Information/Visitor Center/ Welcome Center

- City/Town/Village Hall
- Courthouse
- Post Office
- **Lib** Library
- Museum
- School
- University or College
- Service Area
- Rest Area
- Border Crossing or Port of Entry
- Golf Course
- Other Point of Interest

VICINITY MAP

LAKE ERIE

0   3.0   6.0   9.0   12.0 miles

1 in. = 9.5 mi.

CITIES & COMMUNITIES

Community Name	Abbr.	County	ZIP Code	Map#
* Amherst	AMHT	Lorain	44001	2872
Amherst Township	AhtT	Lorain	44035	2873
* Aquilla	AQLA	Geauga	44024	2505
-- Ashtabula County	AshC			
Auburn Center		Geauga	44023	2893
Auburn Corners		Geauga	44021	2893
Auburn Township	AbnT	Geauga	44023	2893
* Aurora	AURA	Portage	44202	3156
* Avon	AVON	Lorain	44011	2618
* Avon Lake	AVLK	Lorain	44012	2488
Axtel		Erie	44089	2869
Bainbridge		Geauga	44023	2891
Bainbridge Township	BbgT	Geauga	44023	2891
* Bay Village	BYVL	Cuyahoga	44140	2620
* Beachwood	BHWD	Cuyahoga	44122	2628
Beacon Hill		Geauga	44023	2891
Beartown		Geauga	44023	3023
* Bedford	BDFD	Cuyahoga	44146	2887
* Bedford Heights	BDHT	Cuyahoga	44146	2887
Bennetts Corners		Cuyahoga	44133	3147
* Bentleyville	BTVL	Cuyahoga	44022	2889
* Berea	BERA	Cuyahoga	44017	2880
* Boston Heights	BSHT	Summit	44236	3153
Boston Township	BosT	Summit	44141	3153
* Bratenahl	BTNH	Cuyahoga	44108	2496
* Brecksville	BKVL	Cuyahoga	44141	3016
Brentwood		Lake	44060	2251
Brentwood Lake		Lorain	44044	3006
* Broadview Heights	BWHT	Cuyahoga	44147	3014
* Brooklyn	BKLN	Cuyahoga	44144	2753
* Brooklyn Heights	BNHT	Cuyahoga	44131	2755
* Brook Park	BKPK	Cuyahoga	44142	2881
Brown		Geauga	44024	2380
Brownhelm		Lorain	44001	2871
Brownhelm Township	BhmT	Lorain	44001	2742
* Brunswick	BNWK	Medina	44212	3146
Brunswick Hills Twp	BHIT	Medina	44212	3146
Bundysburg		Geauga	44062	2898
* Burton	BURT	Geauga	44021	2766
Burton Lake		Geauga	44021	2765
Burton Station		Geauga	44021	2637
Burton Township	BtnT	Geauga	44024	2635
Carlisle Township	CrlT	Lorain	44050	3005
* Chagrin Falls	CNFL	Cuyahoga	44022	2761
Chagrin Falls Park		Geauga	44023	2890
Chagrin Falls Township	CFIT	Cuyahoga	44022	2761
* Chardon	CRDN	Geauga	44024	2380
Chardon Township	CdnT	Geauga	44024	2379
Chester Center		Geauga	44026	2502
Chesterland		Geauga	44026	2502
Chester Township	CsTp	Geauga	44026	2502
Claridon		Geauga	44024	2506
Claridon Township	ClrT	Geauga	44024	2506
Clearview		Lorain	44052	2745
* Cleveland	CLEV	Cuyahoga	44114	2624
* Cleveland Heights	CVHT	Cuyahoga	44118	2497
Coffee Corners		Trumbull	44062	2769
Columbia Center		Lorain	44028	3009
Columbia Hills Corners		Lorain	44028	3010
Columbia Station		Lorain	44028	3010
Columbia Township	ClbT	Lorain	44028	3009
Concord		Lake	44077	2254
Concord Township	CcdT	Lake	44077	2254
-- Cuyahoga County	CyhC			
* Cuyahoga Heights	CHHT	Cuyahoga	44125	2755
Driftwood		Ashtabula	44041	1844
East Bass Lake		Geauga	44024	2504
* Eastlake	ETLK	Lake	44095	2250
East Carlisle		Lorain	44035	3006
East Claridon		Geauga	44021	2506
* East Cleveland	ECLE	Cuyahoga	44112	2497
Eaton		Lorain	44044	3007
Eaton Estates		Lorain	44044	3008
Eaton Township	EatT	Lorain	44044	3007
* Elyria	ELYR	Lorain	44035	2875
Elyria Township	EyrT	Lorain	44035	2874
-- Erie County	EreC			
* Euclid	EUCL	Cuyahoga	44123	2373
* Fairport Harbor	FTHR	Lake	44077	2039
* Fairview Park	FWPK	Cuyahoga	44126	2751
Farmington Township	FnTp	Trumbull	44062	2769
Florence Township	FrnT	Erie	44889	2870
Footville		Ashtabula	44084	2259
Fowlers Mill		Geauga	44024	2503
Freedom Township	FdmT	Portage	44234	3161
Fullertown		Geauga	44072	2633
* Garfield Heights	GDHT	Cuyahoga	44125	2885
* Garrettsville	GTVL	Portage	44234	3161
* Gates Mills	GSML	Cuyahoga	44040	2500
-- Geauga County	GegC			
Geauga Lake		Portage	44202	3021
* Geneva	GNVA	Ashtabula	44041	1944
* Geneva On The Lake	GOTL	Ashtabula	44041	1844
Geneva Township	GnvT	Ashtabula	44041	1943
Genung Corners		Lake	44057	1942
* Glenwillow	GNWL	Cuyahoga	44139	3019
* Grafton	GFTN	Lorain	44044	3142
Grafton Township	GftT	Lorain	44028	3143
* Grand River	GDRV	Lake	44045	2039
Hambden		Geauga	44024	2381
Hambden Township	HmbT	Geauga	44024	2381
Hardscrabble		Medina	44280	3144
Harpersfield Township	HpfT	Ashtabula	44041	2151
Hartsgrove Township	HgvT	Ashtabula	44099	2384
Hayes Corners		Geauga	44062	2768
Henrietta Township	HetT	Lorain	44889	2870
* Highland Heights	HDHT	Cuyahoga	44143	2499
* Highland Hills	HIHL	Cuyahoga	44128	2758
Hinckley Township	HkyT	Medina	44233	3147
* Hiram	HRM	Portage	44234	3161
Hiram Rapids		Portage	44234	3026
Hiram Township	HrmT	Portage	44234	3027
* Hudson	HDSN	Summit	44236	3156
* Hunting Valley	HGVL	Cuyahoga	44022	2630
* Hunting Valley	HGVL	Geauga	44073	2631
Huntsburg		Geauga	44046	2508
Huntsburg Township	HtbT	Geauga	44046	2508
* Independence	INDE	Cuyahoga	44131	2884
Jeddoe		Portage	44234	3161
* Kirtland	KTLD	Lake	44094	2376
* Kirtland Hills	KDHL	Lake	44060	2252
Lagrange Township	LrgT	Lorain	44050	3139
-- Lake County	LkeC			
* Lakeline	LKLN	Lake	44095	2249
Lake Lucerne		Geauga	44023	2891
* Lakewood	LKWD	Cuyahoga	44107	2623
Lane		Lake	44081	2041
LaPorte		Lorain	44035	3006
Leroy Center		Lake	44077	2148
Leroy Township	LryT	Lake	44077	2148
* Linndale	LNDL	Cuyahoga	44135	2753
Little Mountain		Lake	44077	2253
Liverpool Township	LvpT	Medina	44280	3144
* Lorain	LORN	Lorain	44052	2614
-- Lorain County	LrnC			
* Lyndhurst	LNHT	Cuyahoga	44124	2499
* Macedonia	MCDN	Summit	44056	3153
* Madison	MDSN	Lake	44057	2044
Madison On The Lake		Lake	44057	1941
Madison Township	MadT	Lake	44057	1942
* Mantua	MNTU	Portage	44255	3159
Mantua Center		Portage	44255	3159
Mantua Corners		Portage	44255	3159
Mantua Township	ManT	Portage	44255	3159
Maple Grove		Geauga	44231	3026
* Maple Heights	MPHT	Cuyahoga	44137	2886
* Mayfield	MAYF	Cuyahoga	44143	2500
* Mayfield Heights	MDHT	Cuyahoga	44124	2499
McFarlands Corners		Geauga	44023	2891
-- Medina County	MdnC			
* Mentor	MNTR	Lake	44060	2144
* Mentor On The Lake	MONT	Lake	44060	2143
Mesopotamia Twp	MstT	Trumbull	44062	2769
* Middleburg Heights	MDBH	Cuyahoga	44130	2881
* Middlefield	MDFD	Geauga	44062	2767
Middlefield Township	MdfT	Geauga	44062	2768
Montville		Geauga	44064	2383
Montville Township	MtlT	Geauga	44064	2383
* Moreland Hills	MDHL	Cuyahoga	44022	2759
Mulberry Corners		Geauga	44026	2502
Munson Township	MsnT	Geauga	44024	2504
Nelson Township	NsnT	Portage	44491	3028
New Russia Township	NRsT	Lorain	44074	3003
* Newburgh Heights	NBGH	Cuyahoga	44105	2755
Newbury		Geauga	44065	2764
Newbury Township	NbyT	Geauga	44065	2764
North Eaton		Lorain	44028	3008
* Northfield	NHFD	Summit	44067	3018
Northfield Center		Summit	44067	3152
Northfield Center Twp	NCtT	Summit	44067	3152
North Madison		Lake	44057	1942
* North Olmsted	NOSD	Cuyahoga	44070	2750
* North Perry	NPRY	Lake	44081	1940
* North Randall	NRDL	Cuyahoga	44128	2758
* North Ridgeville	NRDV	Lorain	44039	2877
* North Royalton	NRYN	Cuyahoga	44133	3013
Novelty		Geauga	44072	2632
* Oakwood	OKWD	Cuyahoga	44146	3018
* Oberlin	OBLN	Lorain	44074	3138
* Olmsted Falls	ODFL	Cuyahoga	44138	2879
Olmsted Township	OmsT	Cuyahoga	44138	2879
* Orange	ORNG	Cuyahoga	44022	2759
* Painesville	PNVL	Lake	44077	2146
Painesville on the Lake		Lake	44077	2040
Painesville Township	PnvT	Lake	44077	2145
Parkman		Geauga	44062	2896
Parkman Township	PkmT	Geauga	44234	3027
* Parma	PRMA	Cuyahoga	44129	2882
* Parma Heights	PMHT	Cuyahoga	44130	2882
Pecks Corners		Lake	44094	2377
Penfield Junction		Lorain	44052	2745
* Pepper Pike	PRPK	Cuyahoga	44124	2629
* Perry	PRRY	Lake	44081	2042
Perry Township	PryT	Lake	44081	1941
Pittsfield Township	PtfT	Lorain	44074	3139
-- Portage County	PtgC			
Redbird		Lake	44057	1941
* Reminderville	RMDV	Summit	44202	3020
* Richfield	RHFD	Summit	44286	3150
Richfield Township	RchT	Summit	44141	3151
* Richmond Heights	RDHT	Cuyahoga	44143	2498
* Rocky River	RKRV	Cuyahoga	44116	2621
Russell Center		Geauga	44072	2762
Russell Township	RslT	Geauga	44072	2762
Sagamore Hills		Cuyahoga	44141	3016
Sagamore Hills Twp	SgHT	Summit	44067	3017
Scotland		Geauga	44026	2501
* Seven Hills	SVHL	Cuyahoga	44131	2884
* Shaker Heights	SRHT	Cuyahoga	44120	2627
Shalersville Township	ShvT	Portage	44255	3157
* Sheffield	SFLD	Lorain	44054	2616
* Sheffield Lake	SDLK	Lorain	44054	2616
Sheffield Township	ShfT	Lorain	44055	2745
Shoreland		Lake	44077	2040
* Solon	SLN	Cuyahoga	44139	2889
* South Amherst	SAHT	Lorain	44001	2872
* South Euclid	SELD	Cuyahoga	44121	2498
Southington Township	StnT	Trumbull	44491	3029
South Lorain		Lorain	44055	2745
South Madison		Lake	44057	2150
South Newbury		Geauga	44065	2764
* South Russell	SRSL	Geauga	44073	2762
Spring Valley		Geauga	44023	3022
* Streetsboro	STBR	Portage	44241	3157
* Strongsville	SGVL	Cuyahoga	44136	3011
-- Summit County	SmtC			
Sunnyside		Lorain	44089	2741
Taborville		Geauga	44023	3023
Thompson		Geauga	44086	2150
Thompson Township	TpnT	Geauga	44086	2150
* Timberlake	TMLK	Lake	44095	2249
Troy Township	TroT	Geauga	44021	2895
-- Trumbull County	TmbC			
Trumbull Township	TmbT	Ashtabula	44086	2151
* Twinsburg	TNBG	Summit	44087	3019
Twinsburg Township	TwbT	Summit	44087	3020
Unionville		Lake	44057	1943
* University Heights	UNHT	Cuyahoga	44118	2628
* Valley View	VLVW	Cuyahoga	44125	2885
* Vermilion	VMLN	Lorain	44089	2741
* Vermilion	VMLN	Erie	44089	2740
Vermilion Township	VmnT	Erie	44089	2740
Vincent		Lorain	44055	2746
* Waite Hill	WTHL	Lake	44094	2376
* Walton Hills	WNHL	Cuyahoga	44146	3017
* Warrensville Heights	WVHT	Cuyahoga	44128	2758
Welshfield		Geauga	44234	2895
West Bass Lake		Geauga	44024	2504
* West Farmington	WFAR	Trumbull	44491	2898
West View		Cuyahoga	44138	3010
* Westlake	WTLK	Cuyahoga	44145	2749
* Wickliffe	WKLF	Lake	44092	2374
* Willoughby	WLBY	Lake	44094	2250
* Willoughby Hills	WBHL	Lake	44094	2375
* Willowick	WLWK	Lake	44095	2249
Windsor Township	WndT	Ashtabula	44099	2509
* Woodmere	WDMR	Cuyahoga	44122	2759
Yates Corner		Geauga	44072	2763

*Indicates incorporated city

Downtown Cleveland

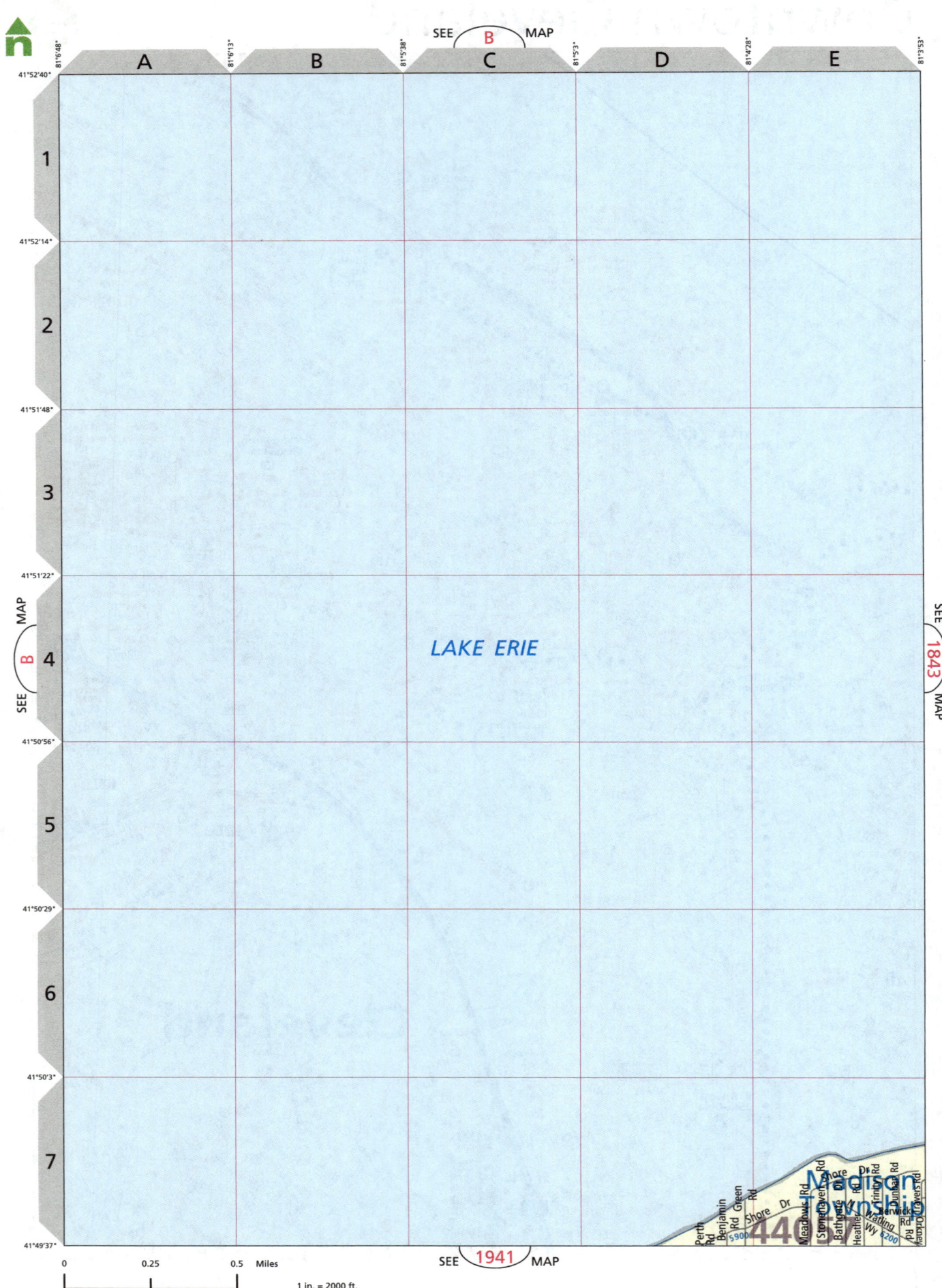

MAP 1842

N

A   B   C   D   E

SEE B MAP

41°52'40"
81°6'48"

1

41°52'14"
81°6'13"

2

41°51'48"
81°5'38"

3

41°51'22"
81°5'3"

SEE B MAP

4

LAKE ERIE

SEE 1843 MAP

41°50'56"
81°4'28"

5

41°50'29"
81°3'53"

6

41°50'3"

7

41°49'37"

Madison Township

440

Perth Rd
Benjamin Rd
Green Rd
5900
Shore Dr
Meadows Rd
Stonehaven Rd
Shore Dr
Bathe
Heather
Firing Rd
Wading Wy 4200
Traverse Rd
Berwick
Dunant Rd
Orkney Rd

SEE 1941 MAP

0   0.25   0.5   Miles

1 in. = 2000 ft.

MAP 1843

SEE B MAP

SEE 1842 MAP

SEE 1844 MAP

A   B   C   D   E

81°3'53"   81°3'18"   81°2'44"   81°2'29"   81°1'34"   81°0'59"

41°52'43"

1

41°52'17"

2

41°51'51"

3

41°51'25"

4

41°50'58"

5

41°50'32"

6

41°50'6"

7

41°49'40"

LAKE ERIE

Lake Shore Blvd

Atwater Dr
Division Dr
Bank Rd
Shoreacre Dr
Cloverleigh Dr
Maple Av
Grand Av

Hearn Dr

7300

LAKE   RD   E

White Sands Blvd
Bennett Rd

Arthur Ct

Cleveland Av

Anthony Ct

MADISON TOWNSHIP PARK

Swetland Rd
Hubbard Rd
Belleair Av
Avalon Av
Manatee Av
Cumings Blvd

Beach Dr
Circle Dr

LAKE   RD

Dorchester Dr
Oxford Dr
E
Dr

Claymoor Dr

7000

Dunedin Av
Ormond Av
Sebring Av

Amity
Oxford Dr
Argyle Dr

RD

Erieview Dr

ERIE SHORES GOLF COURSE

1300

Roe

Av
Blvd

Erie Av
Huron Av

Park Av
Av

Parkview Av

Av
Chapman Av

Ansonia Av

Ornelda Av

Oldsmar Av

Davista Av

Ornelda Av

Argyle Av

1400

HUBBARD RD

Mohawk Dr
Ottawa Dr

Cumings Blvd 00E

Deermont Dr
Cumings Dr

Madison Av

BENNETT RD

Earl Av
Hall Av
Haywood Av
Easton Av
Park Av
Av

Yale Av
Rosena Av
Lakeview Av
Hazel Av

6600

6500

Seneca

Dave   Dr

Indianola
Tarbell Dr
Av

Magnolia Dr

1500

6900

1500

Madison Township

44057

Devon St
Scotland Dr
Berwick

Red Bird Rd

W

LAKE RD

RED BIRD RD

St. John Dr
Grove Av
Glenview Av

Fairkirk Rd
Stirling

1600

RED BIRD Rd

6500

SEE 1942 MAP

Miles 0   0.25   0.5

1 in. = 2000 ft.

MAP 1844-1938

LAKE ERIE

SEE B MAP

SEE 1843 MAP

SEE B MAP

Driftwood

Lake Rd W 6500

Lake Rd

ARCOLA CREEK PARK

Lake Rd

GENEVA STATE PARK

Geneva On The Lake

Lake Rd W

Lake Rd W

Padanarum Rd

6200

LAKE RD

Edgewood Av

Lake Shore Blvd

900

Dock Rd

Dr

7600

Norton Av

Ashview Dr

Dock Ln

Forest Rd

Elm Av

Angela Ln

Travis Ct

Madison Township

LAKE CO

ASHTABULA CO

44041

Geneva Township

LAKE RD E

Marilyn Av

Martha Av

Eddie Rd

Vrooman Rd

County Line Rd

1000

Arcola Creek

1200

Wheeler Creek

4200

Wheeler Creek Rd

PADANARUM RD

44057

DOCK RD

Arcola Creek

3900

4000

0   0.25   0.5   Miles

1 in. = 2000 ft.

MAP 1939

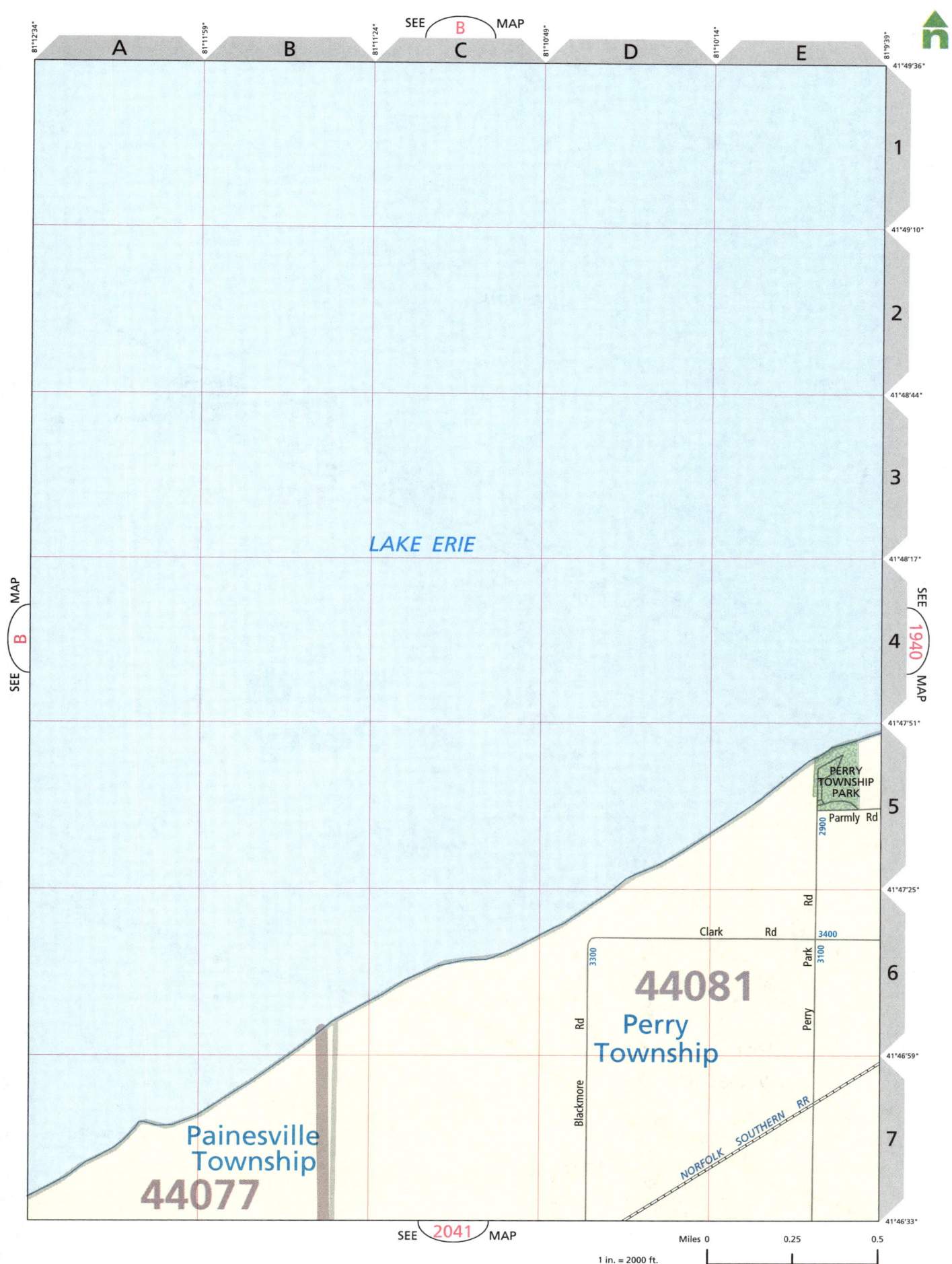

LAKE ERIE

SEE B MAP

SEE B MAP

SEE 1940 MAP

PERRY
TOWNSHIP
PARK

2900 Parmly Rd

Rd

Clark   Rd   3400

3300

44081
Perry
Township

Park   3100

Perry

Blackmore   Rd

NORFOLK SOUTHERN RR

Painesville
Township
44077

SEE 2041 MAP

Miles 0   0.25   0.5

1 in. = 2000 ft.

81°12'34"   81°11'59"   81°11'24"   81°10'49"   81°10'14"   81°9'39"

41°49'36"
41°49'10"
41°48'44"
41°48'17"
41°47'51"
41°47'25"
41°46'59"
41°46'33"

A   B   C   D   E

1   2   3   4   5   6   7

MAP 1940

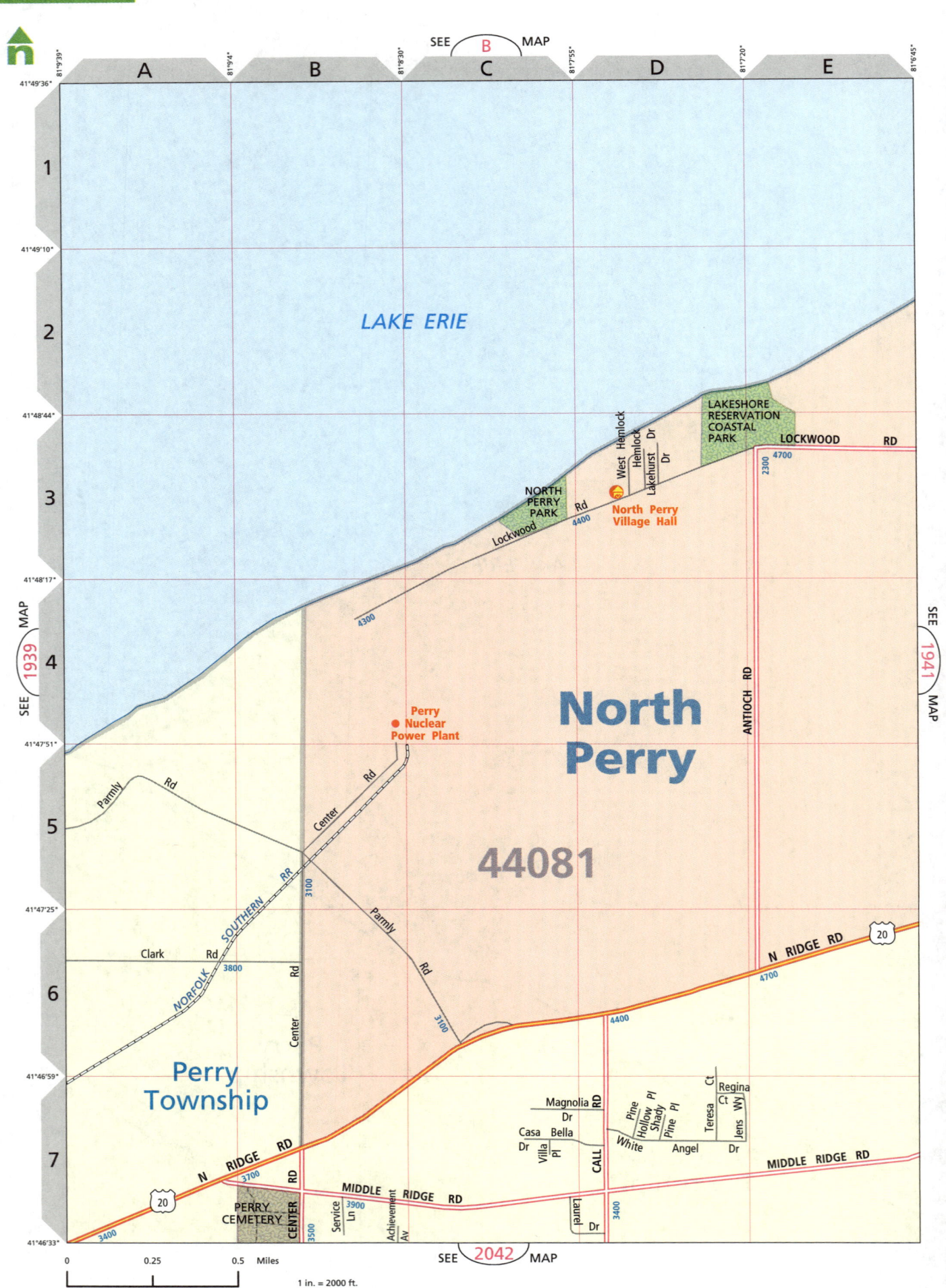

SEE B MAP

LAKE ERIE

LAKESHORE RESERVATION COASTAL PARK

LOCKWOOD RD

West Hemlock
Hemlock Dr
Lakehurst Dr

NORTH PERRY PARK

Lockwood Rd
4400

North Perry Village Hall

SEE 1939 MAP

SEE 1941 MAP

Perry Nuclear Power Plant

North Perry

ANTIOCH RD

44081

Center Rd

Parmly Rd

Parmly Rd

NORFOLK SOUTHERN RR

3100

Clark Rd
3800

Center Rd

N RIDGE RD 20

4700

4400

3100

Perry Township

N RIDGE RD 20

3700

CALL RD

Magnolia Dr

Casa Bella Dr

Villa Pl

White

Pine Hollow Pl
Shady Pine Pl

Angel

Teresa Ct

Regina Ct
Jens Wy

Dr

PERRY CEMETERY

CENTER RD
3500

Service Ln

Achievement Av

MIDDLE RIDGE RD
3900

Laurel Dr

3400

MIDDLE RIDGE RD

20
3400

SEE 2042 MAP

0   0.25   0.5 Miles

1 in. = 2000 ft.

MAP 1941

SEE 1842 MAP

LAKE ERIE

Madison On The Lake

Redbird

North Perry

44081

44057

Madison Township

Perry Township

Madison

MADISON COUNTRY CLUB

SEE 1940 MAP

SEE 1942 MAP

SEE 2043 MAP

Miles 0   0.25   0.5

1 in. = 2000 ft.

MAP 1942

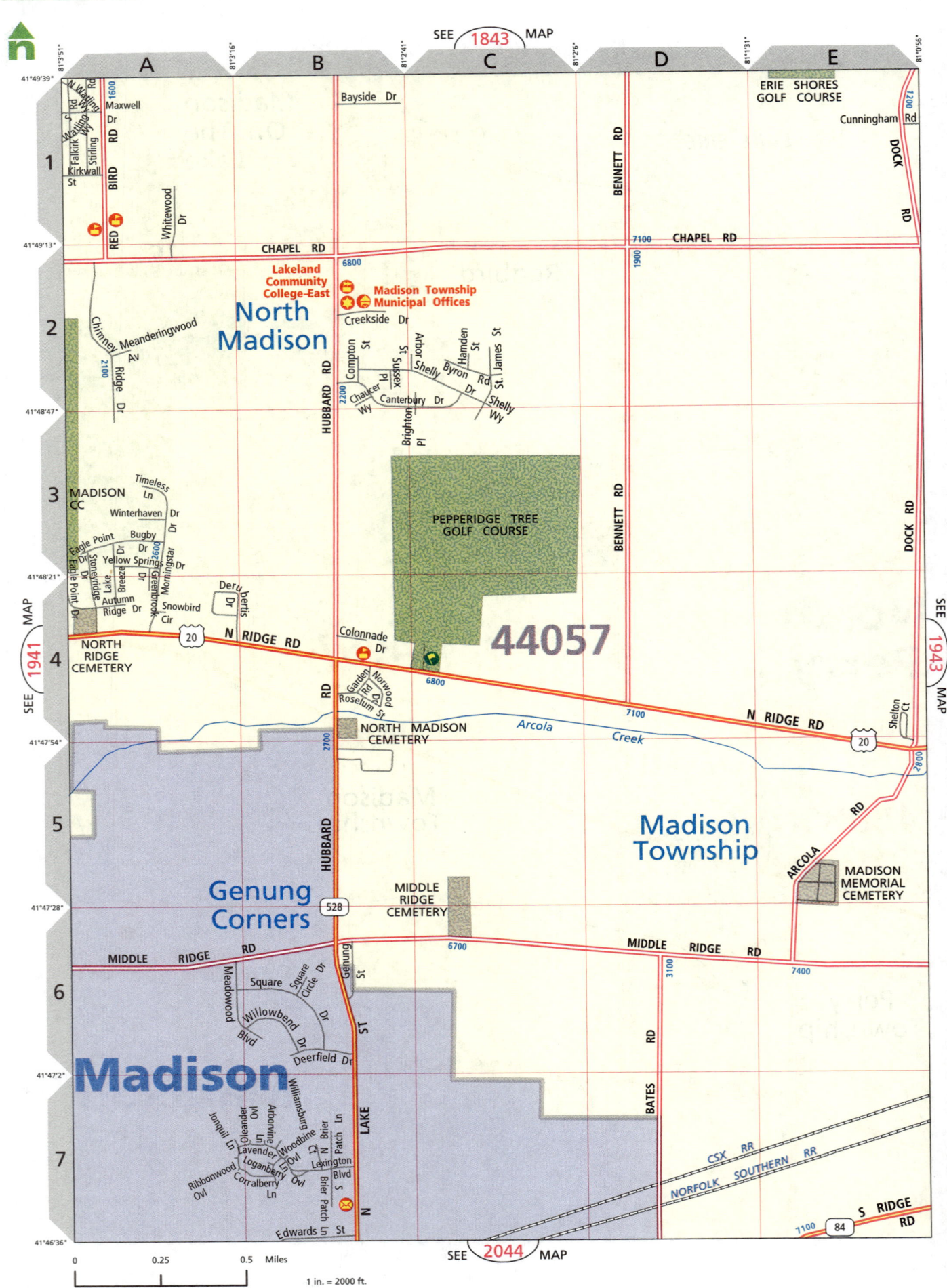

SEE 1843 MAP

A   B   C   D   E

ERIE SHORES GOLF COURSE

Cunningham Rd

Bayside Dr

Maxwell Dr

BENNETT RD

DOCK RD

Whitewood Dr

1600

N Walling Rd
S Walling Rd
Stirling
Kirkwall St
Falkirk St

BIRD RD
RED RD

CHAPEL RD

CHAPEL RD

7100
1900

Lakeland Community College-East

6800

Madison Township Municipal Offices

Creekside Dr

North Madison

Chimney Ridge Dr
Meanderingwood Av

2100

HUBBARD RD

2200

Compton St
Chaucer Wy
Sussex Pl
Canterbury Dr
Arbor St
Shelly Dr
Byron Dr
Hamden St
St. James St
Shelly Wy

Brighton Pl

MADISON CC

Timeless Ln
Winterhaven Dr

PEPPERIDGE TREE GOLF COURSE

BENNETT RD

Eagle Point Dr
Bugby Dr
Yellow Springs
Stoneyridge
Lake Breeze Dr
Autumn Ridge Dr
Morningstar Dr
Greenbrook
Snowbird Cir

2600

Deruberts Dr

44057

NORTH RIDGE CEMETERY

20

N RIDGE RD

Colonnade Dr

6800

Garden Dr
Norwood Dr
Roselum St

7100

N RIDGE RD

20

Shelton Ct

DOCK RD

2700

NORTH MADISON CEMETERY

Arcola Creek

2800

SEE 1941 MAP
SEE 1943 MAP

Madison Township

HUBBARD RD

ARCOLA RD

MADISON MEMORIAL CEMETERY

Genung Corners

528

MIDDLE RIDGE CEMETERY

MIDDLE RIDGE RD

6700

MIDDLE RIDGE RD

7400

3100

BATES RD

Genung St

Meadowood
Square Dr
Square Circle Dr
Willowbend Blvd
Deerfield Dr

Madison

LAKE ST

Williamsburg Ln
Arborvine Ovl
Lavender Ln
Jonquil Ln
Oleander Ovl
Loganberry Ovl
Ribbonwood Ovl
Corralberry Ln
Woodbine Ovl
N Brier Patch Ln
Lexington Ln
N Brier Patch Blvd
S

CSX RR
NORFOLK SOUTHERN RR

Edwards Ln

S RIDGE RD

1100
84

SEE 2044 MAP

0   0.25   0.5   Miles

1 in. = 2000 ft.

MAP 1943

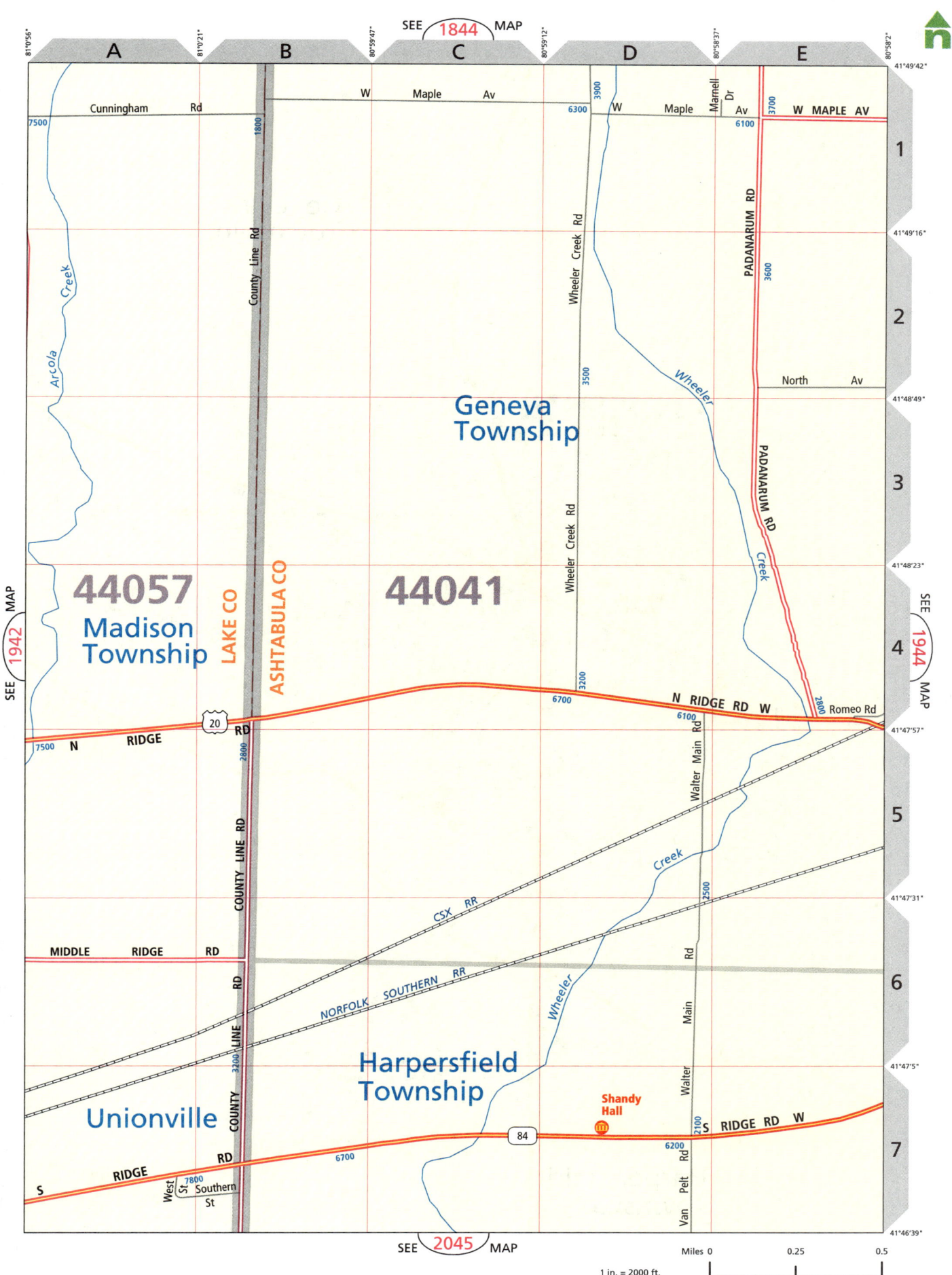

SEE 1844 MAP

A   B   C   D   E

81°0'56"   81°0'21"   80°59'47"   80°59'12"   80°58'37"   80°58'2"

41°49'42"

Cunningham Rd

W Maple Av

W Maple Marnell Dr Av

W MAPLE AV

7500

1800

6300

6100

3900

3700

PADANARUM RD

3600

Arcola Creek

County Line Rd

Wheeler Creek Rd

1

41°49'16"

2

41°48'49"

North Av

Geneva
Township

3500

Wheeler

3

41°48'23"

44057

Madison
Township

LAKE CO

ASHTABULA CO

44041

Wheeler Creek Rd

PADANARUM RD

Creek

SEE 1942 MAP

SEE 1944 MAP

4

41°47'57"

3200

6700

N RIDGE RD W

6100

2800

Romeo Rd

20

N RIDGE RD

7500

Walter Main Rd

5

41°47'31"

CSX RR

Creek

2500

MIDDLE RIDGE RD

6

41°47'5"

COUNTY LINE RD

3200

NORFOLK SOUTHERN RR

Wheeler

Main Rd

Harpersfield
Township

Shandy
Hall

S RIDGE RD W

2100

Unionville

84

6200

Walter Pelt Rd

Van Pelt Rd

7

41°46'39"

S RIDGE RD

6700

West St

7800 Southern St

SEE 2045 MAP

Miles 0   0.25   0.5

1 in. = 2000 ft.

MAP 1944 2036

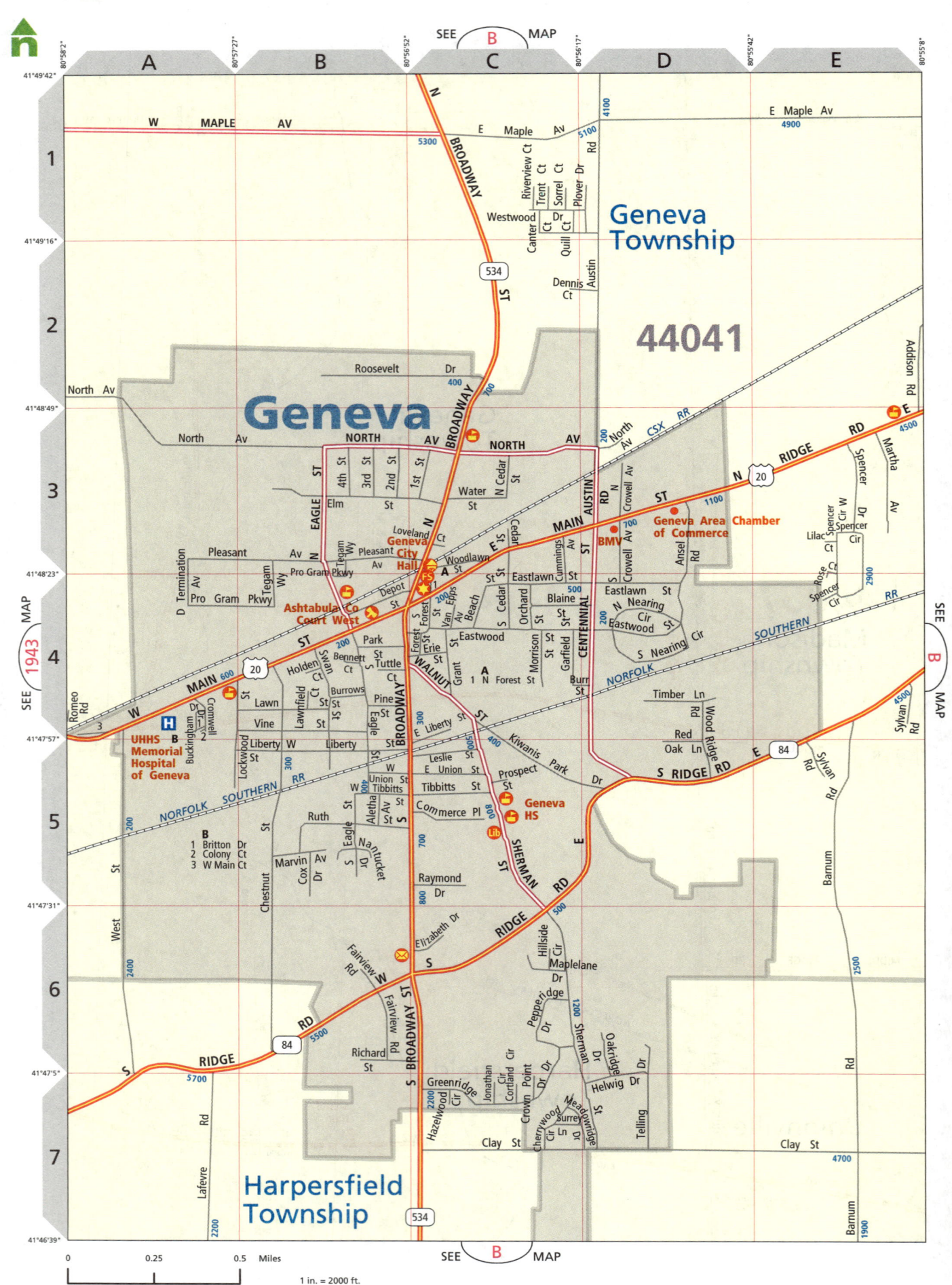

SEE B MAP

A B C D E

W MAPLE AV

E Maple Av

BROADWAY
534 ST

N

5300
5100
4100
4900

E Maple Av

Riverview Ct
Trent Ct
Sorrel Ct
Plover Dr
Canter Ct
Quill Ct
Westwood Ct

Geneva
Township

Dennis Ct
Austin

44041

Roosevelt Dr
400
700

Addison Rd

North Av

Geneva

North Av
NORTH AV
NORTH AV
North Av

4th St
3rd St
2nd St
1st St
EAGLE ST
ELM St

Water St
N Cedar St

200
CSX RR
N RIDGE RD
US 20

4500

Martha Av
Spencer Dr W
Spencer Cir
Spencer Cir
Lilac Dr
Spencer Cir
Rose Ct
Spencer Cir

Loveland Ct
Geneva City Hall
Pleasant Av
Woodlawn Ct
Pleasant Av
N Tegam Wy
Pro Gram Pkwy
Tegam Wy
D Termination Av
Pro Gram Pkwy

Cedar St
AUSTIN RD
CROWELL ST
Crowell Av
MAIN St
700
BMV
Geneva Area Chamber of Commerce
1100
Ansel Rd

S Forest
Van Epps
S Beach
S Cedar St
S Orchard St
Blaine St
Eastlawn St
S Crowell St
Eastlawn St
N Nearing Cir
Eastwood St
S Nearing Cir

Depot
1
A St
200
Eastlawn St
Ashtabula Co Court West
Park St
Bennett Ct
S Tuttle
Eastwood St
S Grant
S Morrison St
Garfield St
CENTENNIAL ST
500
200
Burr St

Erie St
A
1 N Forest St

Holden St
Swan St
Lawnfield St
Burrows St
Pine St
WALNUT ST
BROADWAY

NORFOLK SOUTHERN RR

Timber Ln
Wood Ridge Rd
4500
Sylvan Py
Sylvan Rd

Lawn St
Vine St
Liberty W
Lockwood St
Liberty W
Eagle St

E Liberty St
300
Red Oak Ln
S RIDGE RD
84 E

UHHS Memorial Hospital of Geneva
H
B
Cromwell Dr 1 2
Buckingham Dr

Romeo Rd
3
W MAIN ST
600
20

Leslie St
E Union St
Kiwanis Park Dr
400
SHERMAN RD

200
NORFOLK SOUTHERN RR
300
W 100t
Union St
Tibbitts
W Aletha St
S Eagle St
Tibbitts St
Commerce Pl
800
Geneva HS
Lib
Prospect

B
1 Britton Dr
2 Colony Ct
3 W Main Ct

Ruth St
Marvin
Cox Dr
S Nantucket Dr

Raymond Dr
800
700

West St
2400
Chestnut St

Elizabeth Dr
RIDGE RD
500
Hillside Cir
Maplelane Dr
Pepperidge Dr
1200
Sherman Dr
Oakridge Dr
Helwig Dr

Fairview Rd W
S
BROADWAY ST
Fairview Rd

84
5500

Richard St

Greenridge Cir
Jonathan Cir
Cortland Cir
Crown Point
Meadowridge Dr
Telling St

Barnum Rd

2500

Lafevre Rd
RIDGE RD
5700
S
2200

Hazelwood Cir
2200
Cherrywood Cir
Surrey Ln
Clay St

Clay St
4700

Harpersfield
Township

534

Barnum
1900

0 0.25 0.5 Miles

1 in. = 2000 ft.

SEE B MAP

41°49'42"
41°49'16"
41°48'49"
41°48'23"
41°47'57"
41°47'31"
41°47'5"
41°46'39"

80°58'2"
80°57'27"
80°56'52"
80°56'17"
80°55'42"
80°55'08"

SEE 1943 MAP

SEE B MAP

MAP 2037

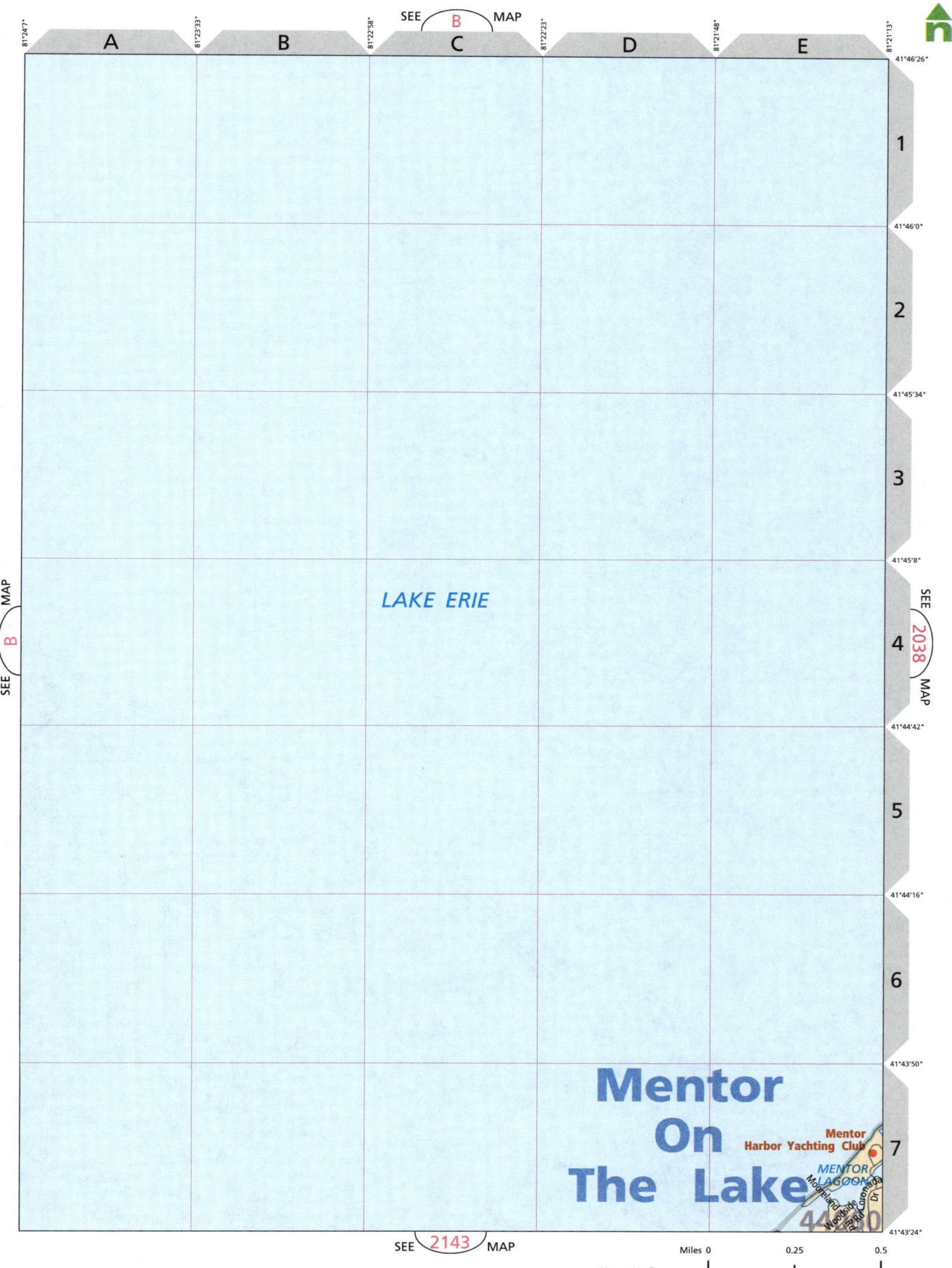

SEE B MAP

A 81°24'7" B 81°23'33" C 81°22'58" D 81°22'23" E 81°21'48" 81°21'13"

41°46'26"
41°46'0"
41°45'34"
41°45'8"
41°44'42"
41°44'16"
41°43'50"
41°43'24"

1
2
3
4
5
6
7

LAKE ERIE

SEE B MAP

SEE 2038 MAP

SEE 2143 MAP

Mentor
On
The Lake

Mentor
Harbor Yachting Club

MENTOR LAGOON

Woodside Dr

Morningside

Corona Dr

4440

Miles 0   0.25   0.5

1 in. = 2000 ft.

MAP 2038

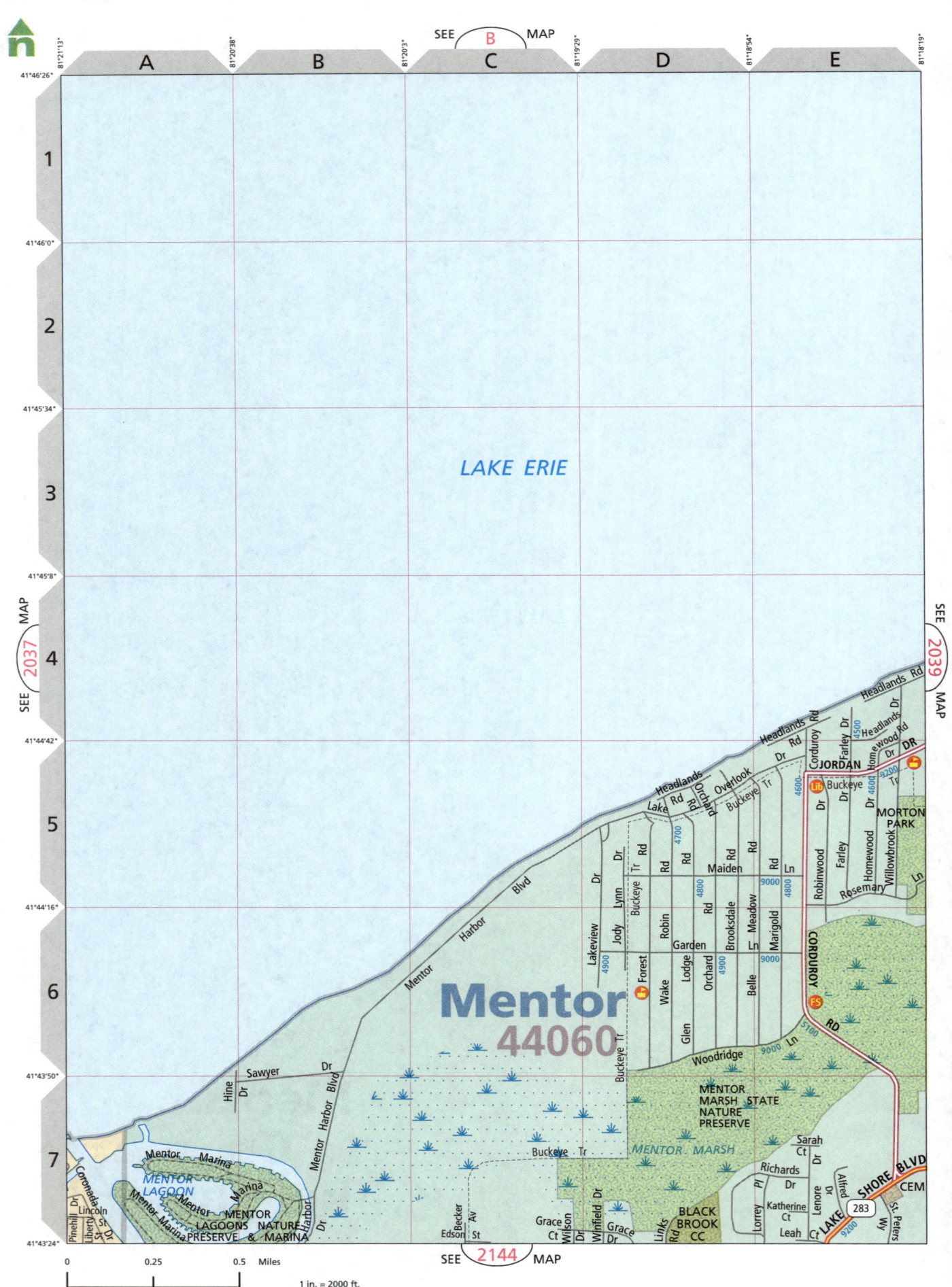

SEE B MAP

A · 81°21'13" · 81°20'38" B · 81°20'3" C · 81°19'29" · D · 81°18'54" E · 81°18'19"

41°46'26"

1

41°46'0"

2

41°45'34"

LAKE ERIE

3

SEE 2037 MAP

41°45'8"

SEE 2039 MAP

4

Headlands Rd

41°44'42"

Headlands Rd

Corduroy Rd

Farley Dr

4500 Homewood Dr Headlands Rd

Headlands Dr JORDAN DR

Overlook

Headlands Lake Rd Orchard Rd Buckeye Tr

5

Lib Buckeye Dr

4600 Tr

MORTON PARK

Mentor Harbor Blvd

Lakeview Dr

Jody Lynn Dr

Buckeye Tr Rd

4700 Robin Rd

Rd Maiden Rd

9000 Rd Ln

4800 Robinwood Dr

Farley Dr

Homewood Dr

Willowbrook Ln

Rosemary

41°44'16"

4900

Forest

Wake Lodge

Garden Rd

Orchard

4900 Brooksdale

Belle Ln

Meadow Ln

9000 Marigold

CORDUROY RD

6

Mentor
44060

Glen

Buckeye Tr

Woodridge 9000 Ln

5100 RD

FS

41°43'50"

Hine Dr

Sawyer Dr

Mentor Harbor Blvd

Buckeye Tr

MENTOR MARSH STATE NATURE PRESERVE

Mentor Marsh

Sarah Ct

Richards Dr

7

Mentor Marina

Coronada Dr

MENTOR LAGOON

Mentor Marina

Mentor Harbor Dr

MENTOR LAGOONS NATURE PRESERVE & MARINA

Becker Av

Edson St

Grace Ct

Wilson

Winfield Dr

Grace Dr

Links Rd

BLACK BROOK CC

Lorrey Pl

Katherine Ct

Leah

Lenore Dr

Alfred

LAKE 283 SHORE BLVD

9200 St Peters

CEM

Wy

Pinehill Dr

Liberty St

Lincoln

41°43'24"

SEE 2144 MAP

0   0.25   0.5   Miles

1 in. = 2000 ft.

MAP 2039

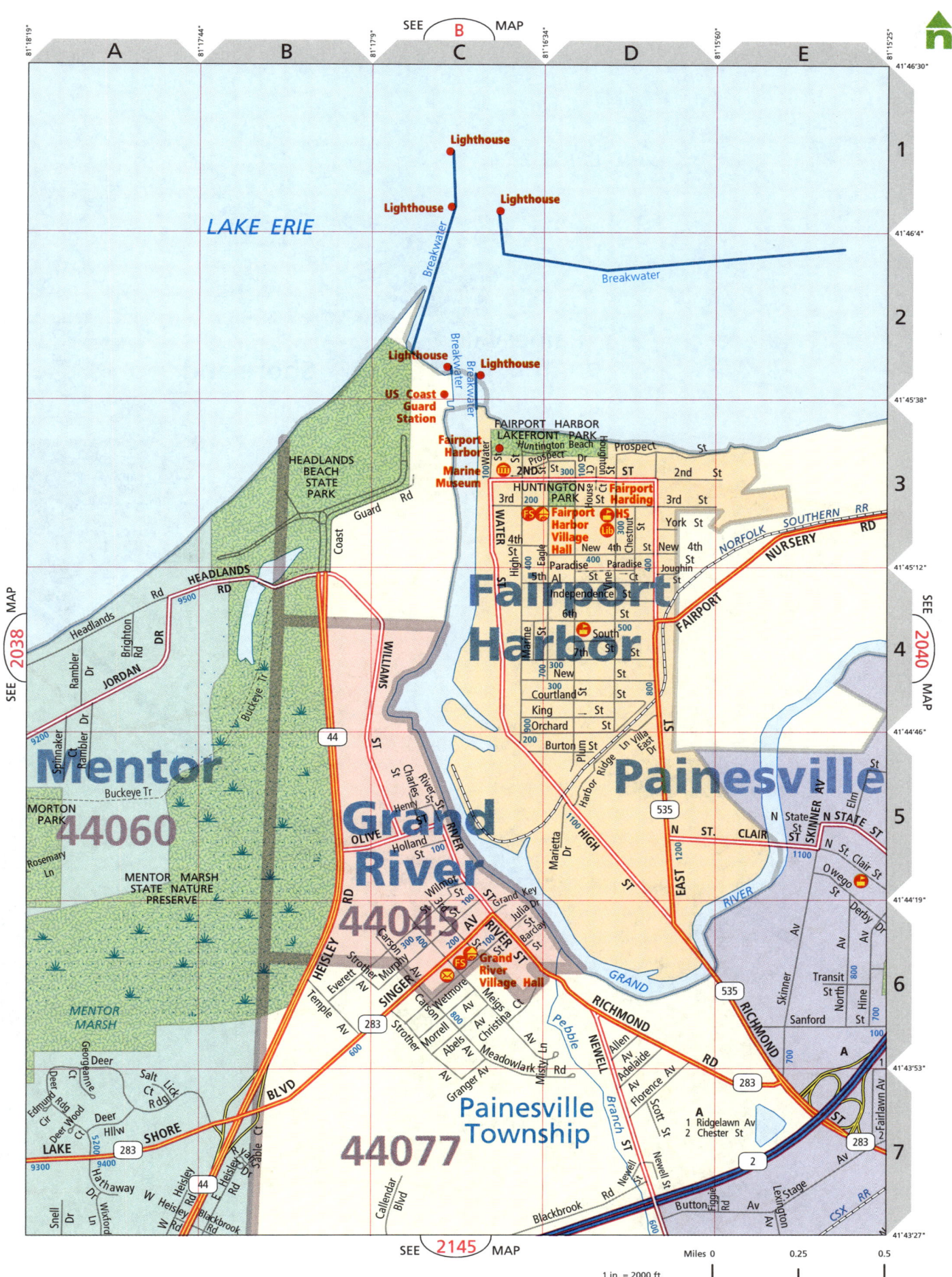

SEE B MAP

A   B   C   D   E

81°18'19"   81°17'44"   81°17'9"   81°16'34"   81°15'60"   81°15'25"

41°46'30"

1

Lighthouse

LAKE ERIE

Lighthouse   **Lighthouse**

41°46'4"

Breakwater

Breakwater

2

Breakwater

Lighthouse **Lighthouse**

41°45'38"

US Coast Guard Station

FAIRPORT HARBOR LAKEFRONT PARK

Fairport Harbor Marine Museum

Huntington Beach

Prospect   St

Water St   Prospect   St   300

2ND   St   ST   2nd   St

HUNTINGTON PARK   **Fairport Harding**   3rd   St

3rd   200   House   Ct

Fairport Harbor Village Hall   HS   Chestnut   York St

FS   Lib   300

4th   St   New   4th   New   4th   St   St

High   Eagle   Paradise   St   Paradise   Ct   400   Joughin

5th   St   400   Vine   St   St

Al   Independence   St

6th   St

Marine   St   South   500   St

7th   St   700   St

New   300   St

Courtland   800   St

King   St   —   St

900   Orchard   St

200   Burton   St   Plum St

Harbor   Ridge   Ln Villa   East   St

3

41°45'12"

41°44'46"

Fairport Harbor

Painesville

Mentor
44060

Grand River
44045

WILLIAMS   ST

Charles   St   River   St

Henry   St

OLIVE   St   Holland   St   100

Wilmot   St

3rd   St   100

Carson   300 400   Grand Key

Murphy   200   Julia Dr   Barclay

SINGER   AV   RIVER ST   100

Grand River Village Hall   FS

Calson   Wetmore   Meigs Ct

283   Morrell   Av   Christina Ct

Strother   Abels   Av   Meadowlark   Ln

Av   Granger Av   Misty   Rd

HEISLEY   RD

Everett   Av

Strother   Av

Temple   Av

HEADLANDS   RD

9500

Headlands   Rd

Brighton   Rd

JORDAN   DR

Rambler   Dr

Spinnaker   Ct   Rambler

9200

Buckeye Tr

MENTOR MARSH STATE NATURE PRESERVE

MORTON PARK

Rosemary   Ln

MENTOR MARSH

HEADLANDS BEACH STATE PARK

Coast   Guard   Rd

Buckeye Tr

44

FAIRPORT   RD

NORFOLK   SOUTHERN   RR

NURSERY   RD

535

N   ST.   CLAIR

EAST   1200   ST   CLAIR

HIGH   ST

Marietta   Dr

1100

535

N   State   N State St   Elm

N   St   SKINNER AV

RIVER

N St. Clair St

Owego   1100   Derby Dr   St

Av

Av

Skinner   Transit   800   St

Sanford   Hine   St   700

100

4

5

6

Painesville Township

44077

RICHMOND   RD

Allen   Av

Adelaide   Av   Florence   Av

NEWELL   Scott   St

BRANCH   ST

283   535   RICHMOND   RD   700   283

Pebble   GRAND   RIVER

A   1 Ridgelawn Av   2 Chester St

2

7

41°44'19"

41°43'53"

41°43'27"

LAKE

283

SHORE   BLVD

Deer   Georgeanne   Ct   Hllw

Edmund   Rdg   Cir   Deer Wood Ct

Salt Lick Ct Rdg

Deer

9300   9400

Snell   Dr   Wixford

W Heisley Rd   Blackbrook   Rd

Heisley   Rd

44   Hathaway   Callendar   Blvd

Blackbrook   Rd

Figgie   Rd   Button   Av

Newell   St

2   Lexington   Stage   CSX   RR

283   ST   Fairlawn Av

SEE 2038 MAP

SEE 2040 MAP

SEE 2145 MAP

Miles   0   0.25   0.5

1 in. = 2000 ft.

MAP 2040

SEE B MAP

A B C D E

LAKE ERIE

1

Painesville
on the Lake   Shoreland

2

PAINESVILLE
TOWNSHIP
PARK

FAIRWAY
PINES
GOLF COURSE

NORFOLK SOUTHERN RR

FAIRPORT NURSERY RD

3

Painesville
Township

Painesville
Speedway

Post Rd

Greenside

535

SEE 2039 MAP

44077

Painesville

Red   Creek

FAIRPORT NURSERY RD

Blase

SEE 2041 MAP

4

20

5

Huntington
Rd

N RIDGE RD

RR

Red   Creek

2

CSX

6

ROTARY
PARK

E ERIE ST

GRAND   RIVER

PAINESVILLE CITY
KIWANIS
REC PARK

CASEMENT
CLUB
GOLF
COURSE

Terminal

Casement
Airport

Avery
Dennison

7

EVERGREEN
CEMETERY

Lake
County
General
Health
District

Branch   Av

A
1 N Park Pl
2 S Park Pl
3 Hillside Dr
4 Joughin Al
5 Police Al
6 Phelps St
7 Main St

283

RICHMOND ST

Lake
Co Jail
Lake
Co Ct
Hse

86

SEE 2146 MAP

MADISON   AV

0   0.25   0.5   Miles

1 in. = 2000 ft.

MAP 2041

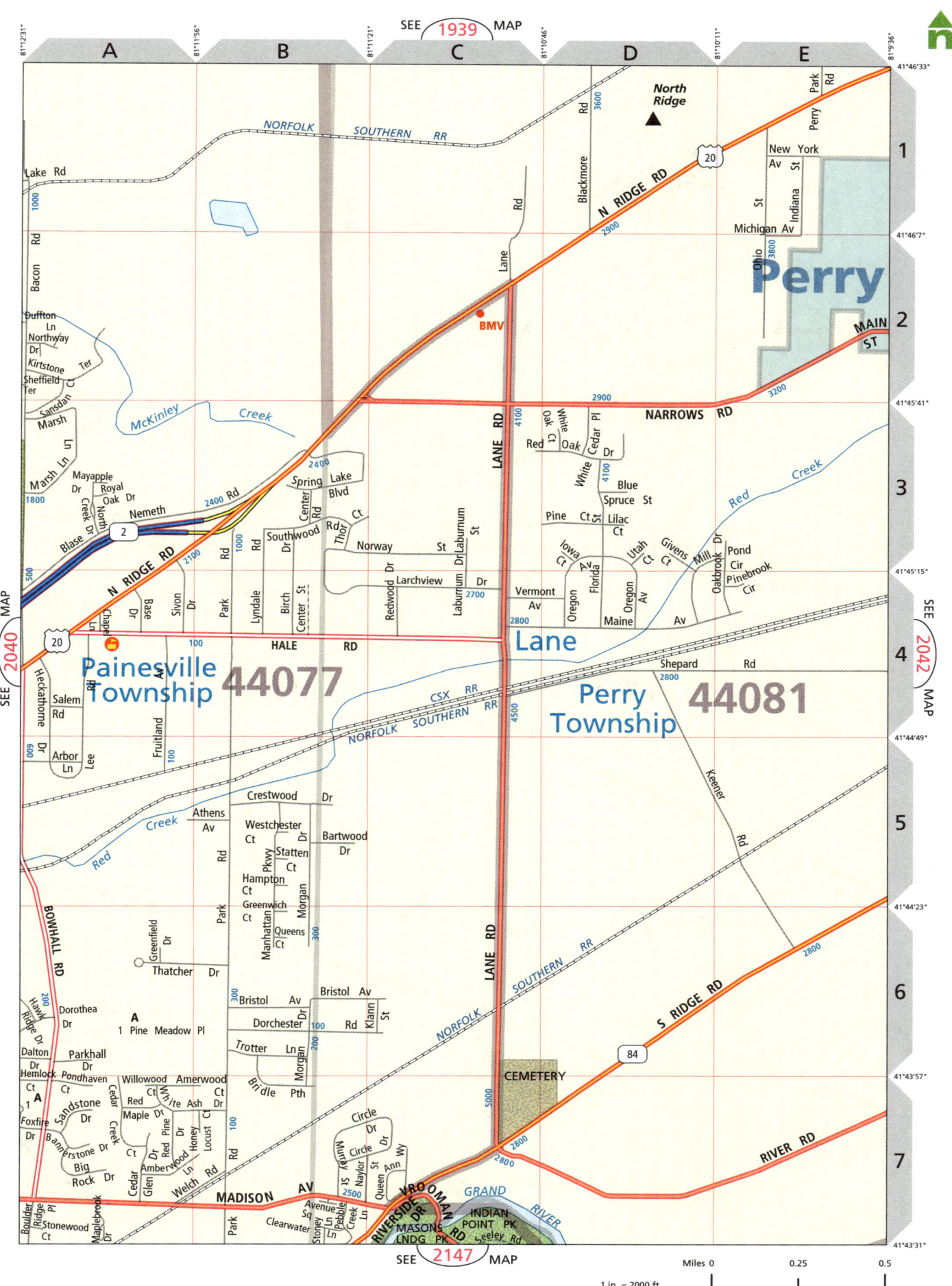

SEE 1939 MAP

SEE 2040 MAP

SEE 2042 MAP

SEE 2147 MAP

North Ridge

Perry

Painesville Township 44077

Perry Township 44081

Miles 0   0.25   0.5

1 in. = 2000 ft.

MAP 2042

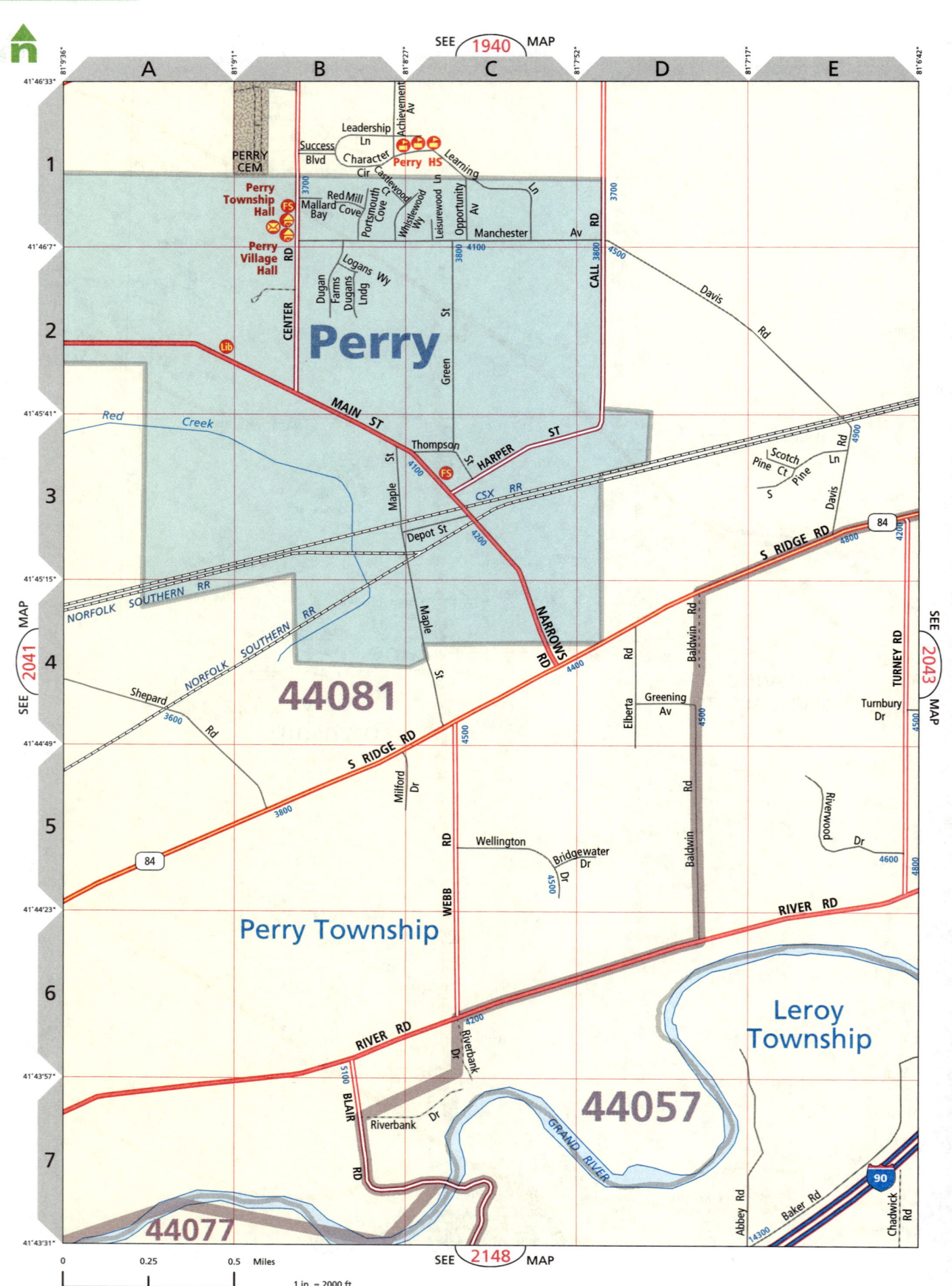

SEE 1940 MAP

A   B   C   D   E

41°46'33"
1
41°46'7"
2
41°45'41"
3
41°45'15"
4
41°44'49"
5
41°44'23"
6
41°43'57"
7
41°43'31"

81°9'36"   81°9'1"   81°8'27"   81°7'52"   81°7'17"   81°6'42"

PERRY CEM

Perry Township Hall
Perry Village Hall

Leadership Ln
Success Blvd
Character Cir
Achievement Av
Perry HS
Learning

Red Mill Cove
Mallard Bay
Portsmouth Cove
Castlewood Cove
Whistlewood Wy
Leisurewood Ln
Opportunity Av
Manchester Av

CENTER RD
CALL RD

Logans Wy
Dugan Farms
Dugans Lndg

Perry

Green St

Lib

Red Creek

MAIN ST

Thompson St
HARPER ST
FS
CSX RR

Maple St

Davis Rd
Scotch Ln
Pine Ct
Pine S
Davis Rd

84
S RIDGE RD

Depot St

NORFOLK SOUTHERN RR

Maple St

Shepard Rd

NARROWS RD

44081

S RIDGE RD

Milford Dr

WEBB RD

Wellington
Bridgewater Dr

Elberta Rd
Greening Av

Baldwin Rd
Baldwin Rd

TURNEY RD

Turnbury Dr

Riverwood Dr

84

RIVER RD

Perry Township

RIVER RD

Riverbank Dr

BLAIR RD

Riverbank Dr

GRAND RIVER

Leroy Township

44057

44077

Abbey Rd
Baker Rd
Chadwick Rd

90

SEE 2041 MAP
SEE 2043 MAP
SEE 2148 MAP

0   0.25   0.5   Miles

1 in. = 2000 ft.

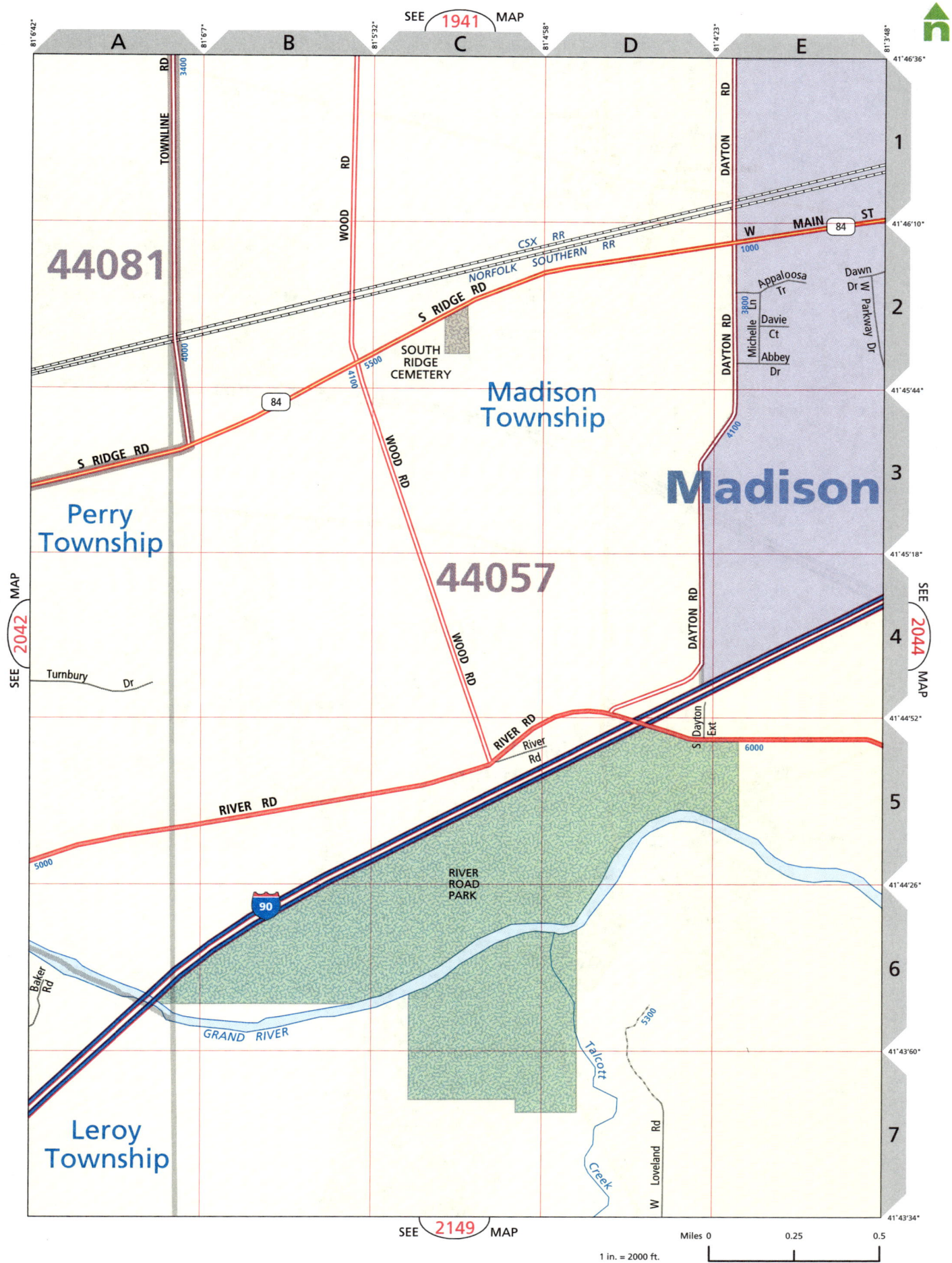

MAP 2043

MAP 2044

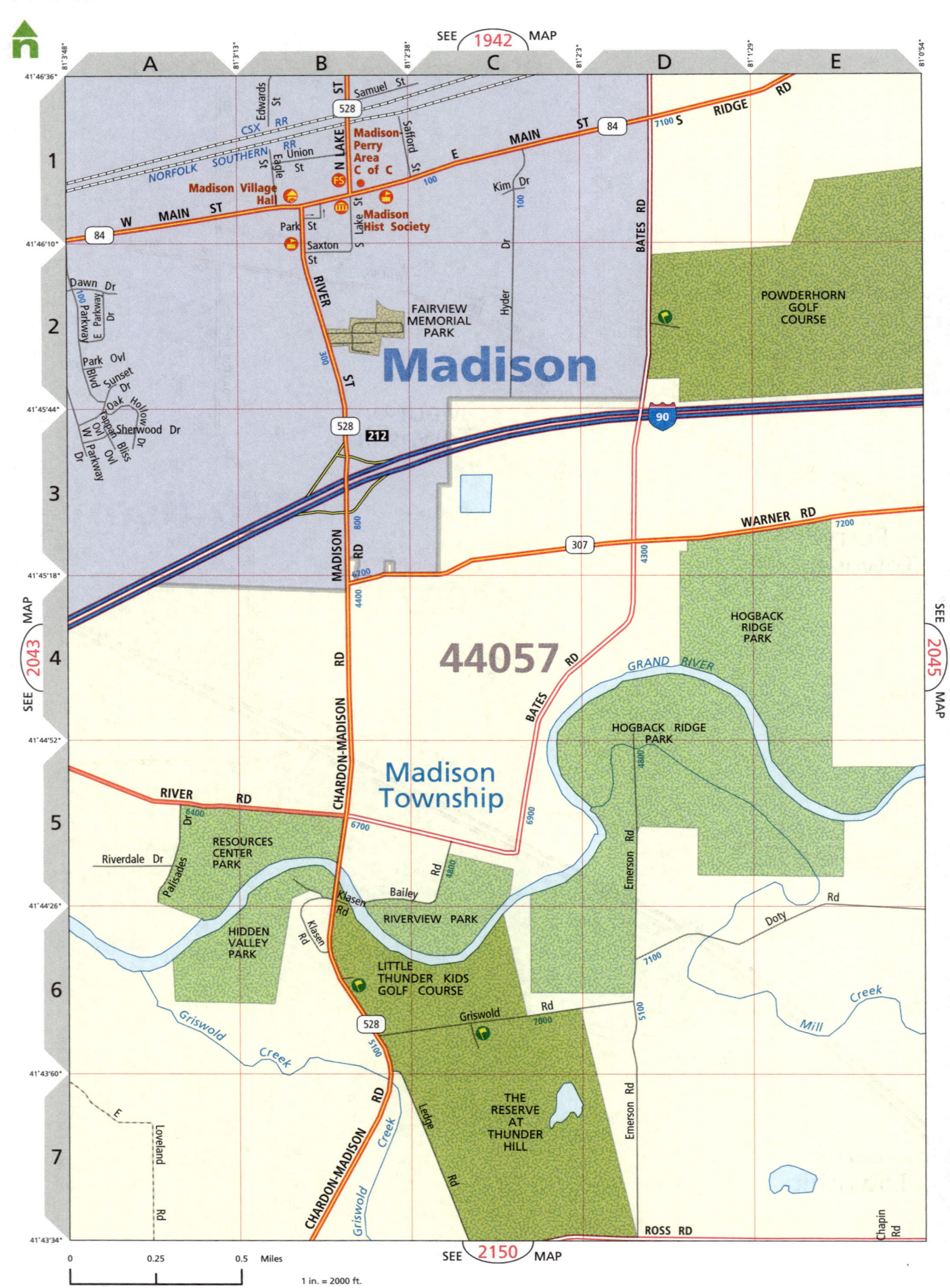

SEE 1942 MAP

N

A   B   C   D   E

81°3'48"   81°3'13"   81°2'38"   81°2'23"   81°1'29"   81°0'54"

41°46'36"

SEE RIDGE RD

7100 S

Edwards St

Samuel St

528

CSX RR

Safford St

MAIN ST   84

NORFOLK SOUTHERN RR

Madison-Perry Area C of C

Madison Village Hall

E MAIN ST

Kim Dr

100

Eagle St   Union St

N LAKE ST

FS

Madison Hist Society

BATES RD

41°46'10"

84   W MAIN ST

Park St

Saxton St

S Lake St   100

Hyder Dr

Dawn Dr

E Parkway Dr

100 Parkway

RIVER ST

FAIRVIEW MEMORIAL PARK

300

POWDERHORN GOLF COURSE

1

2

Park Blvd Ovl

Sunset Dr

Oak Hollow Dr

Sherwood Dr

Vernon Ovl

Bliss Dr

W Parkway Dr

Owl Ovl

Madison

41°45'44"

528   212

I-90

3

800

MADISON RD

WARNER RD   7200

307

4300

41°45'18"

SEE 2043 MAP

6700

6400

44057

BATES RD

6900

HOGBACK RIDGE PARK

SEE 2045 MAP

4

GRAND RIVER

HOGBACK RIDGE PARK

4800

41°44'52"

RIVER RD

6700

CHARDON-MADISON RD

Madison Township

Emerson Rd

5

Riverdale Dr

Palisades Dr

RESOURCES CENTER PARK

Klasen Rd

Bailey

Rd

4800

RIVERVIEW PARK

Rd

Doty   Rd

7100

Mill   Creek

41°44'26"

HIDDEN VALLEY PARK

Klasen Rd

LITTLE THUNDER KIDS GOLF COURSE

Griswold   Rd

5100

6

528

Griswold Rd   7000

5100

41°43'60"

E

Loveland

Griswold   Creek

528

Ledge Rd

THE RESERVE AT THUNDER HILL

Emerson Rd

Chapin Rd

7

CHARDON-MADISON RD

Griswold Creek

Rd

41°43'34"

SEE 2150 MAP

ROSS RD

0   0.25   0.5   Miles

1 in. = 2000 ft.

MAP 2045-2141

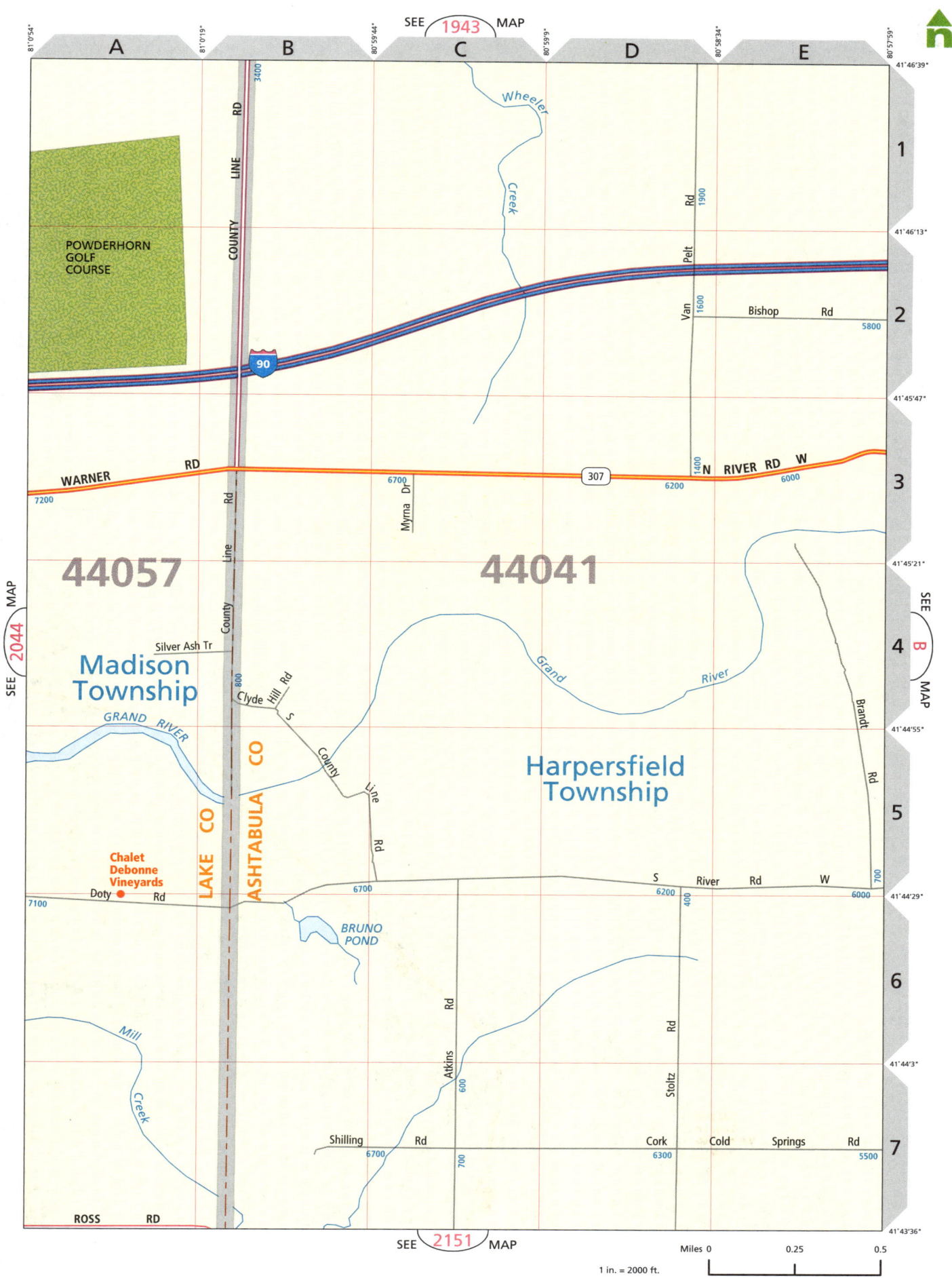

SEE 1943 MAP

A B C D E

81°0'54" 81°0'19" 80°59'44" 80°59'9" 80°58'34" 80°57'59"

41°46'39"

1

Wheeler

Creek

3400

COUNTY LINE RD

POWDERHORN GOLF COURSE

41°46'13"

Rd 1900

Pelt

2

Van 1600

Bishop Rd 5800

90

41°45'47"

WARNER RD

7200

6700

Myrna Dr

307

1400 N RIVER RD W

6200 6000

3

SEE 2044 MAP

44057

44041

41°45'21"

SEE B MAP

Line Rd County

800

Silver Ash Tr

Madison Township

Clyde Hill Rd

S County Line Rd

Grand River

Harpersfield Township

Brandt Rd

4

41°44'55"

GRAND RIVER

LAKE CO

ASHTABULA CO

5

Chalet Debonne Vineyards

Doty Rd
7100

6700

BRUNO POND

S River Rd W

6200 400 6000 700

41°44'29"

Mill

Creek

Atkins Rd 600

Stoltz Rd

6

41°44'3"

Shilling Rd 6700 700

Cork Cold Springs Rd
6300 5500

7

ROSS RD

41°43'36"

SEE 2151 MAP

Miles 0   0.25   0.5

1 in. = 2000 ft.

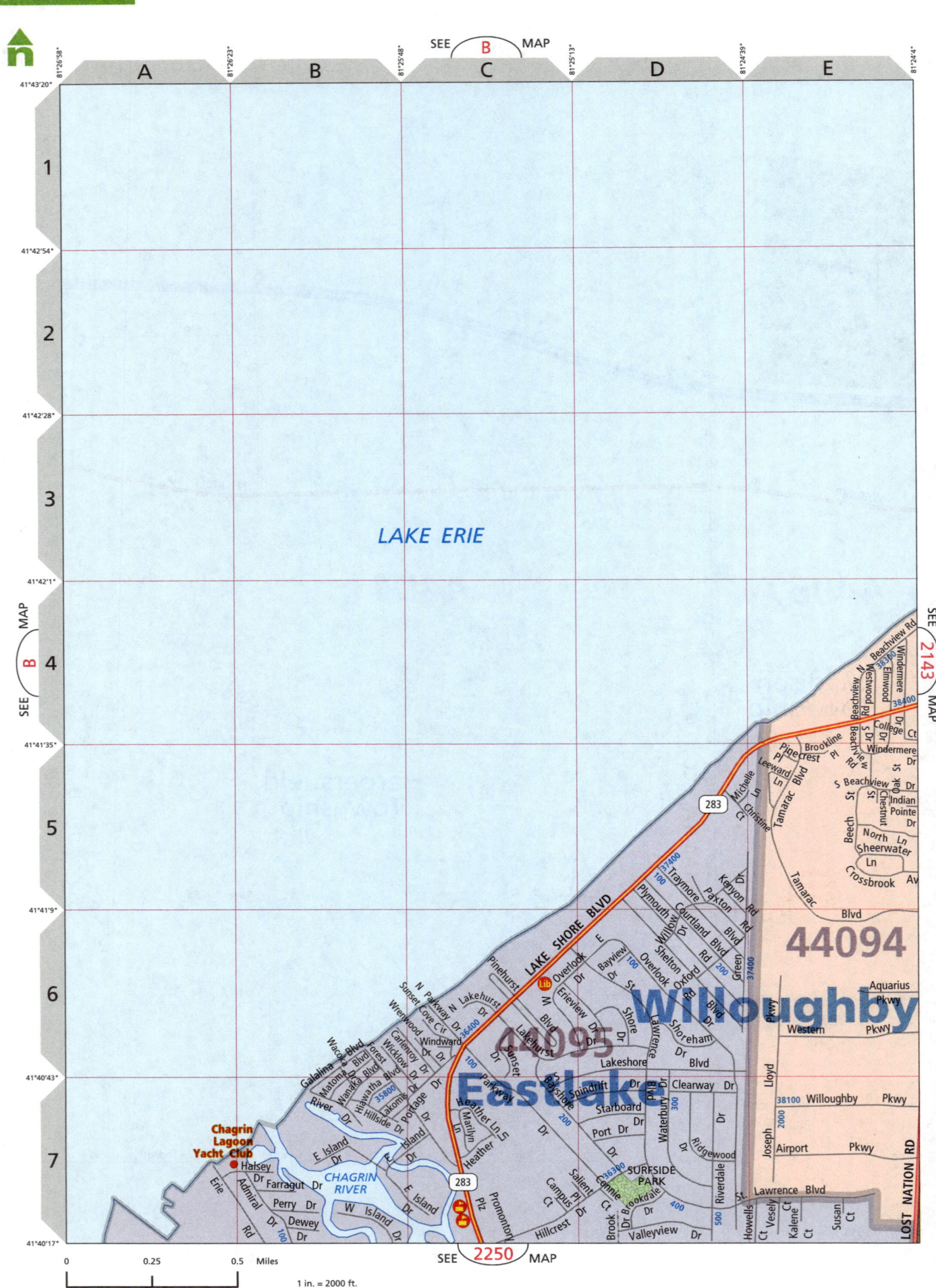

MAP 2142

SEE B MAP

SEE 2143 MAP

LAKE ERIE

Beachview Rd
Windermere
Westwood Rd
Elmwood
38300
College Dr
S Dr
Windermere Dr
Pinecrest
Brookline
Beachview Rd
38400
Leeward Ln
Tamarac Blvd
S Beachview
Oak
Indian Pointe Dr
St
Chestnut
Beech
St
St
North Sheerwater Ln
Ln
Crossbrook Av
Tamarac
Blvd

Michelle
Christine
Ct
283
Kenyon Rd
Paxton Rd
Traymore
100
37400
Courtland Blvd
Plymouth
Shelton
Oxford Rd
200
Green
37400

44094

Willoughby

Aquarius Pkwy
Western Pkwy
Lloyd Dr
38100 Willoughby Pkwy
2000
Joseph Airport Pkwy
Lawrence Blvd

LAKE SHORE BLVD
37000
Pinehurst
Lib
Overlook Dr
Bayview
100
Ereview Dr
Overlook
St
Shore
Dr
Lawrence
Shoreham Dr
N Pakway Dr
Sunset Cove Cir
N Lakehurst Dr
36400
Blvd Dr
Lakehurst
Dr
Lakeshore Blvd
Clearway Dr
Wrenwood
Galenroy Dr
Windward
Wicklow Dr
Dr
Sunset
Heather Ln
Spindrift
200
Ridgewood Dr
Howells

Waco Blvd
Galalina Blvd
Matoma Blvd
Forest Dr
Wanaka Blvd
Hiawatha Blvd
35800
Lakonis Dr
Hillside Dr
Portage
Island Dr
Marilyn
Ln
Heather
283
Parkway
Bayshore Blvd
Starboard Dr
Port Dr
Waterbury Blvd
300
River Dr
E Island Dr
E Island Dr
W Island Dr
CHAGRIN RIVER

44095
Eastlake

Campus Ct
Salient Ct
36300
Gennie
SURFSIDE PARK
Brookdale
400
500
Riverdale St
Lawrence Blvd
St Vesely Ct
Kalene Ct
Susan Ct

Chagrin Lagoon Yacht Club
Halsey
Dr
Admiral
Farragut Dr
Perry
Dr
Dewey
Dr
Erie
Rd
100
Promontory
Plz
Hillcrest
Brook Dr
Valleyview Dr
283

LOST NATION RD

SEE 2250 MAP

0   0.25   0.5   Miles

1 in. = 2000 ft.

MAP 2143

SEE 2037 MAP

A B C D E

LAKE ERIE

MENTOR LAGOON

B
1 Coronada Dr
2 Pinehill Dr
3 Cherry St

MENTOR BEACH PARK

OVERLOOK BEACH PARK

Mentor On The Lake

Mentor On The Lake Village Hall

JOHN R McMINN MEM PARK

LAKE SHORE BLVD

283

ANDREWS RD

LAKEWAY BLVD

PLAINS RD

MUNSON RD

615

WILLOUGHBY MUN PARK

PLAINS ROAD CEM

LAKE SHORE BLVD

283

44060

Willoughby 44094

Woodbridge Condominiums

Mentor Radio

Lost Nation Municipal Airport

Jet Center Terminal

BELLFLOWER PARK

Lake Catholic HS

A
1 College Ct
2 Windermere Ct
3 S Beachview Ct
4 North Ln

BELLFLOWER RD

306

REYNOLDS RD

HODGSON RD

LOST NATION RD

HODGSON PARK

LOST NATION MUNICIPAL GOLF COURSE

PRESIDENTS PARK

LAKELAND FRWY

2

TYLER BLVD

Mentor

SEE 2142 MAP

SEE 2144 MAP

SEE 2251 MAP

Miles 0   0.25   0.5

1 in. = 2000 ft.

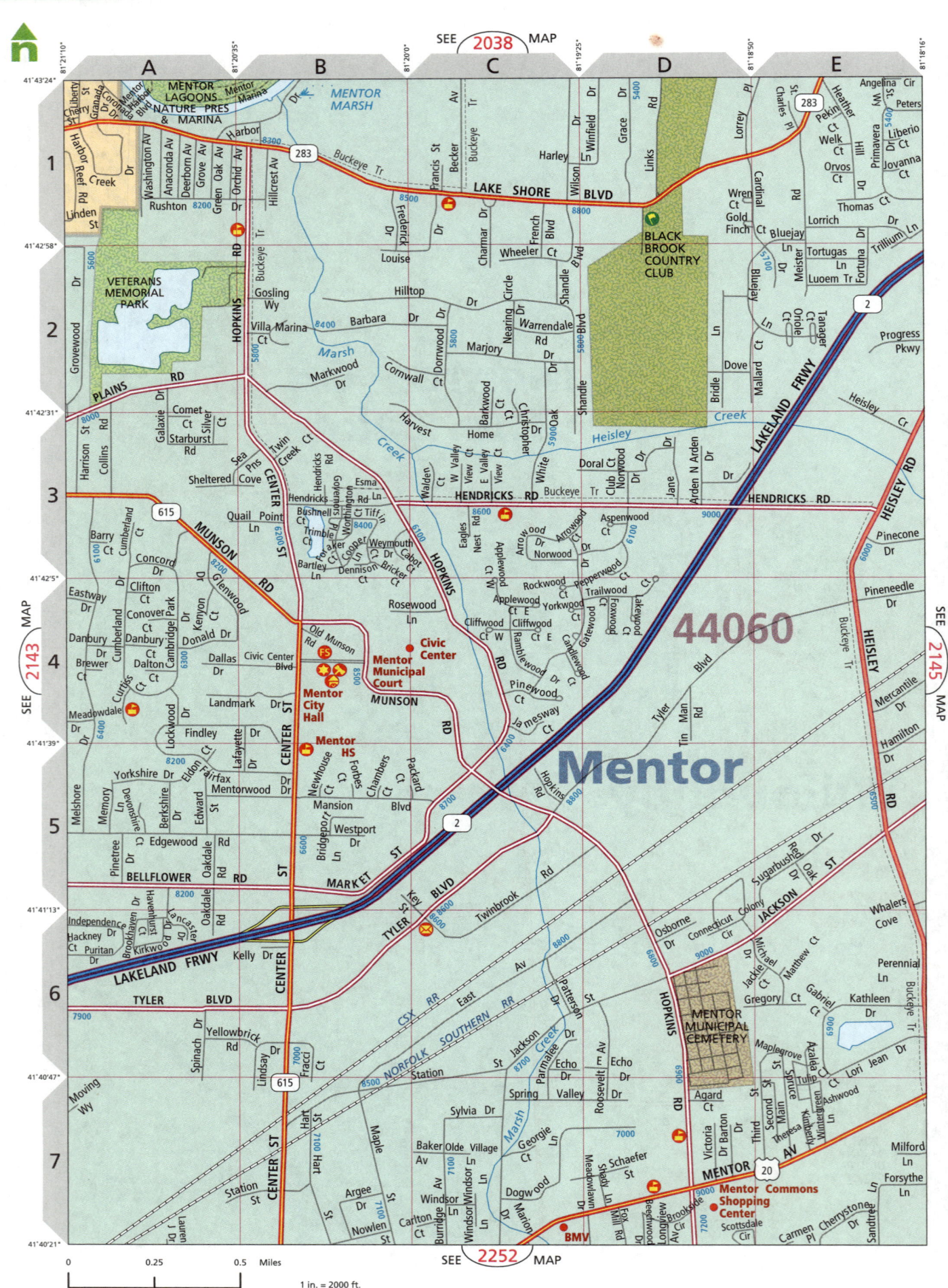

MAP 2144

SEE 2038 MAP

A   B   C   D   E

1

2

3

4

5

6

7

MENTOR LAGOONS NATURE PRES & MARINA

MENTOR MARSH

Mentor Marina Dr

Harbor

283

Buckeye Tr

LAKE SHORE BLVD

8300

8500

8800

BLACK BROOK COUNTRY CLUB

283

2

Progress Pkwy

VETERANS MEMORIAL PARK

5600

5700

5800

5900

HOPKINS RD

PLAINS RD

Marsh

6200

Creek

Heisley Creek

HENDRICKS RD

HENDRICKS RD

LAKELAND FRWY

HEISLEY RD

615

MUNSON RD

8000

8200

8400

8600

9000

6000

6100

44060

CENTER ST

Civic Center

Mentor Municipal Court

Mentor City Hall

MUNSON RD

HOPKINS RD

6300

8500

6100

la mesway

Tin Man Rd

Mentor

Mentor HS

8200

8700

8800

6400

2

6600

MARKET ST

TYLER BLVD

Key Rd

8600

LAKELAND FRWY

TYLER BLVD

7900

8200

9000

JACKSON ST

Sugarbush Rd

MENTOR MUNICIPAL CEMETERY

7000

HOPKINS RD

CSX RR

NORFOLK SOUTHERN RR

8500

8700

9000

8800

6960

6069

615

7000

7100

7200

MENTOR AV

20

Mentor Commons Shopping Center

BMV

SEE 2252 MAP

SEE 2143 MAP

SEE 2145 MAP

0   0.25   0.5 Miles

1 in. = 2000 ft.

81°21'10"   81°20'35"   81°20'0"   81°19'25"   81°18'50"   81°18'16"

41°43'24"
41°42'58"
41°42'31"
41°42'5"
41°41'39"
41°41'13"
41°40'47"
41°40'21"

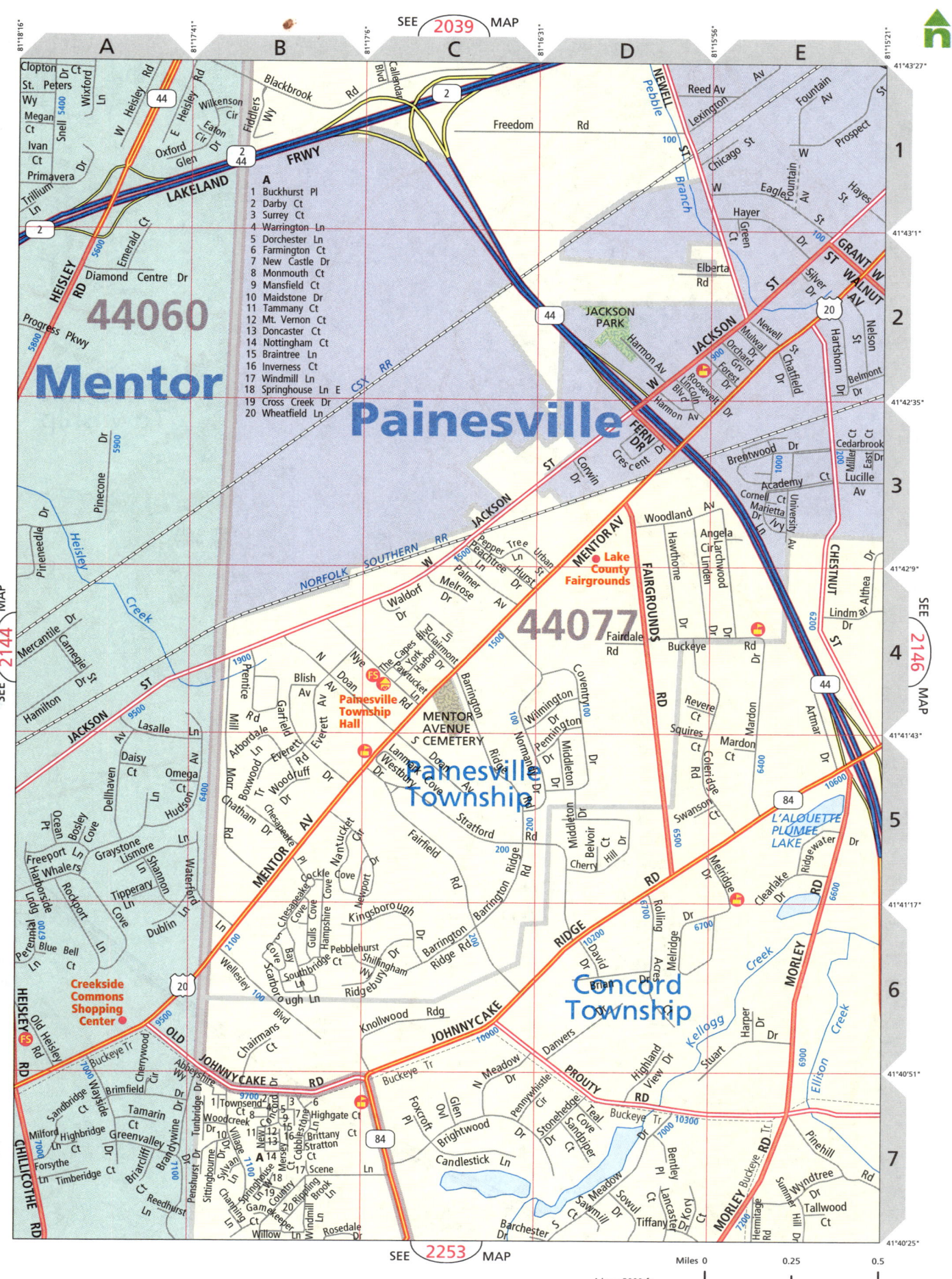

MAP 2145

SEE 2039 MAP

A | B | C | D | E

A
1 Buckhurst Pl
2 Darby Ct
3 Surrey Ct
4 Warrington Ln
5 Dorchester Ln
6 Farmington Ct
7 New Castle Dr
8 Monmouth Ct
9 Mansfield Ct
10 Maidstone Dr
11 Tammany Ct
12 Mt. Vernon Ct
13 Doncaster Ct
14 Nottingham Ct
15 Braintree Ln
16 Inverness Ct
17 Windmill Ln
18 Springhouse Ln E
19 Cross Creek Dr
20 Wheatfield Ln

44060

Mentor

Painesville

44077

Painesville Township

Concord Township

Lake County Fairgrounds

MENTOR AVENUE CEMETERY

Painesville Township Hall

Creekside Commons Shopping Center

L'ALOUETTE PLUMEE LAKE

SEE 2144 MAP

SEE 2146 MAP

SEE 2253 MAP

Miles 0   0.25   0.5

1 in. = 2000 ft.

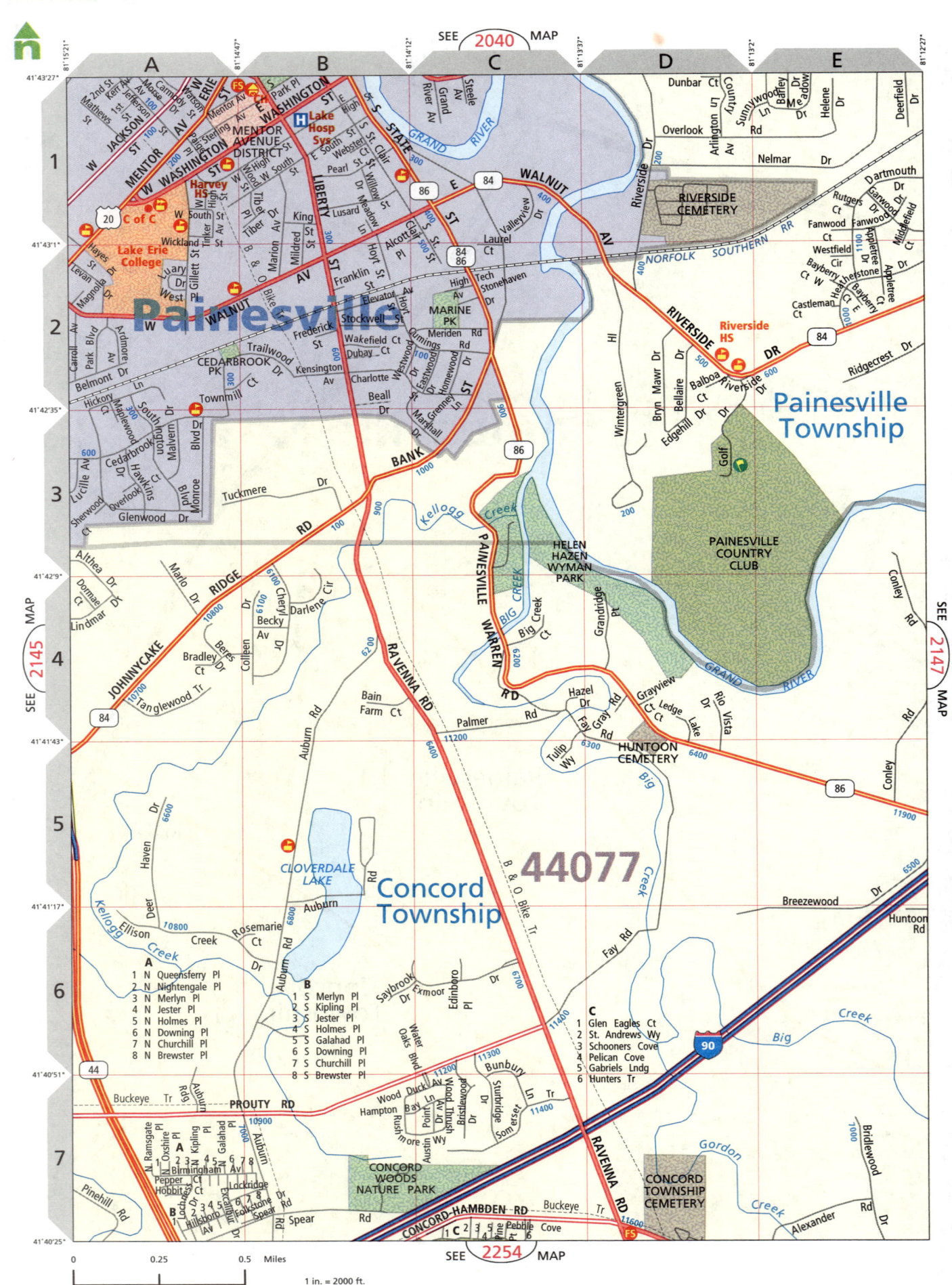

MAP 2146

SEE 2040 MAP

SEE 2145 MAP

SEE 2147 MAP

Painesville

Painesville Township

Concord Township

44077

Lake Erie College

MENTOR AVENUE DISTRICT

Harvey HS

Lake Hosp Sys

C of C

Marine PK

CEDARBROOK PK

RIVERSIDE CEMETERY

Riverside HS

NORFOLK SOUTHERN RR

PAINESVILLE COUNTRY CLUB

HELEN HAZEN WYMAN PARK

HUNTOON CEMETERY

CLOVERDALE LAKE

CONCORD WOODS NATURE PARK

CONCORD TOWNSHIP CEMETERY

Kellogg Creek

Big Creek

GRAND RIVER

Gordon Creek

A
1 N Queensferry Pl
2 N Nightengale Pl
3 N Merlyn Pl
4 N Jester Pl
5 N Holmes Pl
6 N Downing Pl
7 N Churchill Pl
8 N Brewster Pl

B
1 S Merlyn Pl
2 S Kipling Pl
3 S Jester Pl
4 S Holmes Pl
5 S Galahad Pl
6 S Downing Pl
7 S Churchill Pl
8 S Brewster Pl

C
1 Glen Eagles Ct
2 St. Andrews Wy
3 Schooners Cove
4 Pelican Cove
5 Gabriels Lndg
6 Hunters Tr

SEE 2254 MAP

0   0.25   0.5 Miles

1 in. = 2000 ft.

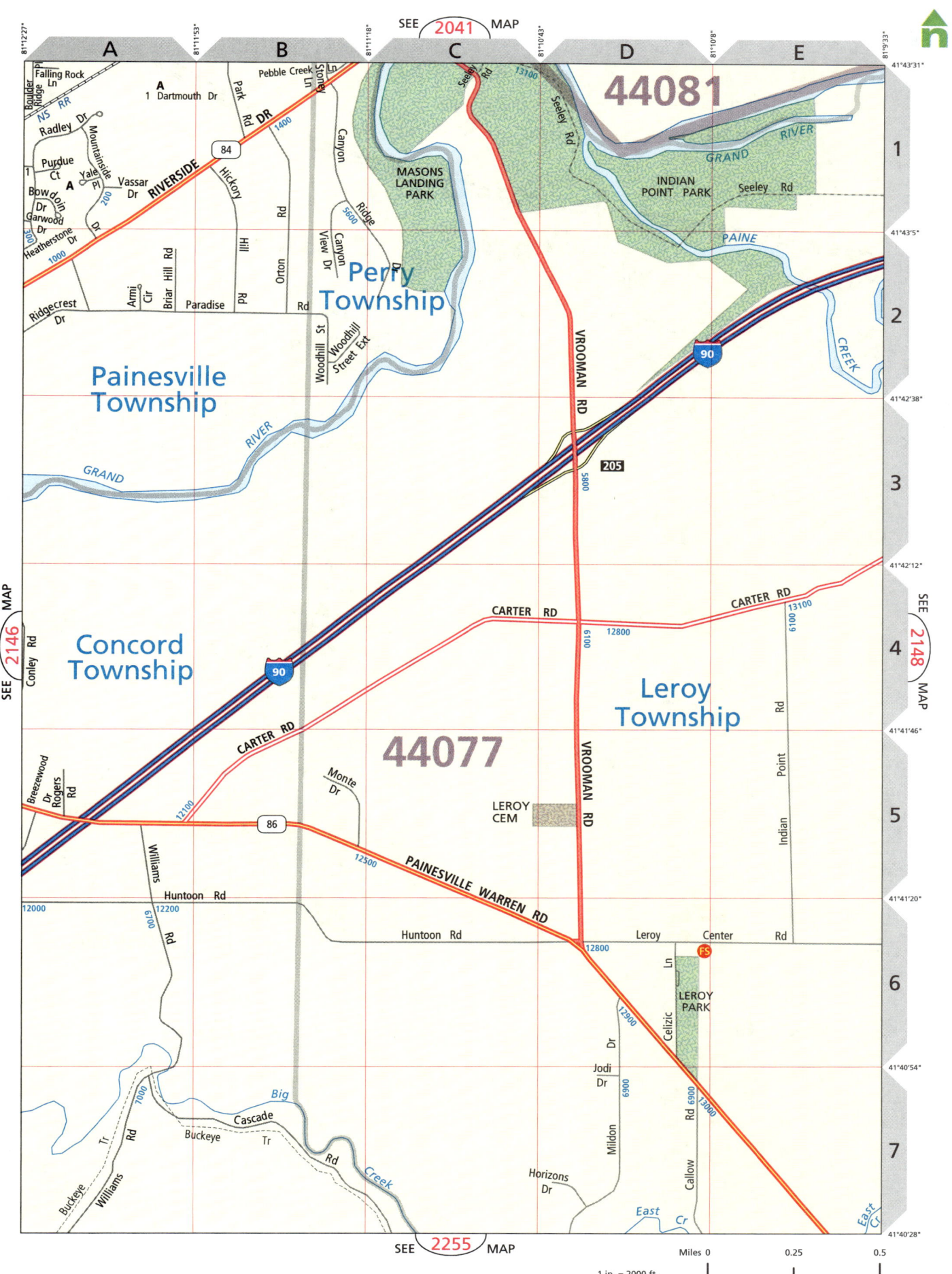

MAP 2147

MAP 2148

SEE 2042 MAP

A   B   C   D   E

Perry
Township

GRAND RIVER

Baker   Rd

Chadwick Rd

FORD   RD

14100

Abbey
Rd

FORD   RD

BLAIR   RD

5400

13500

I-90

1

Seeley   Rd

13300

14300

Trask   Rd   5400

PAINE FALLS
PARK

44057

2

PAINE   CREEK

Taylor   Rd

5700

Leroy
Township

Balch   Rd

14400

PAINE

5800

Paine

Trask Rd

5800

CARTER   RD

13100

3

Paine   Rd

6100

Piney Hllw

Maggie
Ln

Taylor   Rd

Creek

HELL   HOLLOW
WILDERNESS
AREA

Trask   Rd

SEE 2147 MAP

SEE 2149 MAP

6200

4

Shirley   Park   Dr

6200

44077

Paine   Rd

5

Taylor   Rd

Paine

Brockway   Rd

6600

Leroy
Town Hall

Leroy   Center Rd

13200

Leroy   Center   Rd

13600

Leroy   Center   Rd

13900

Kniffen   Rd

6700

Leroy   Center   Rd

6

Leroy
Center

Brakeman   Rd

6700

44086

7

East

Creek

0   0.25   0.5   Miles

1 in. = 2000 ft.

SEE 2256 MAP

MAP 2149

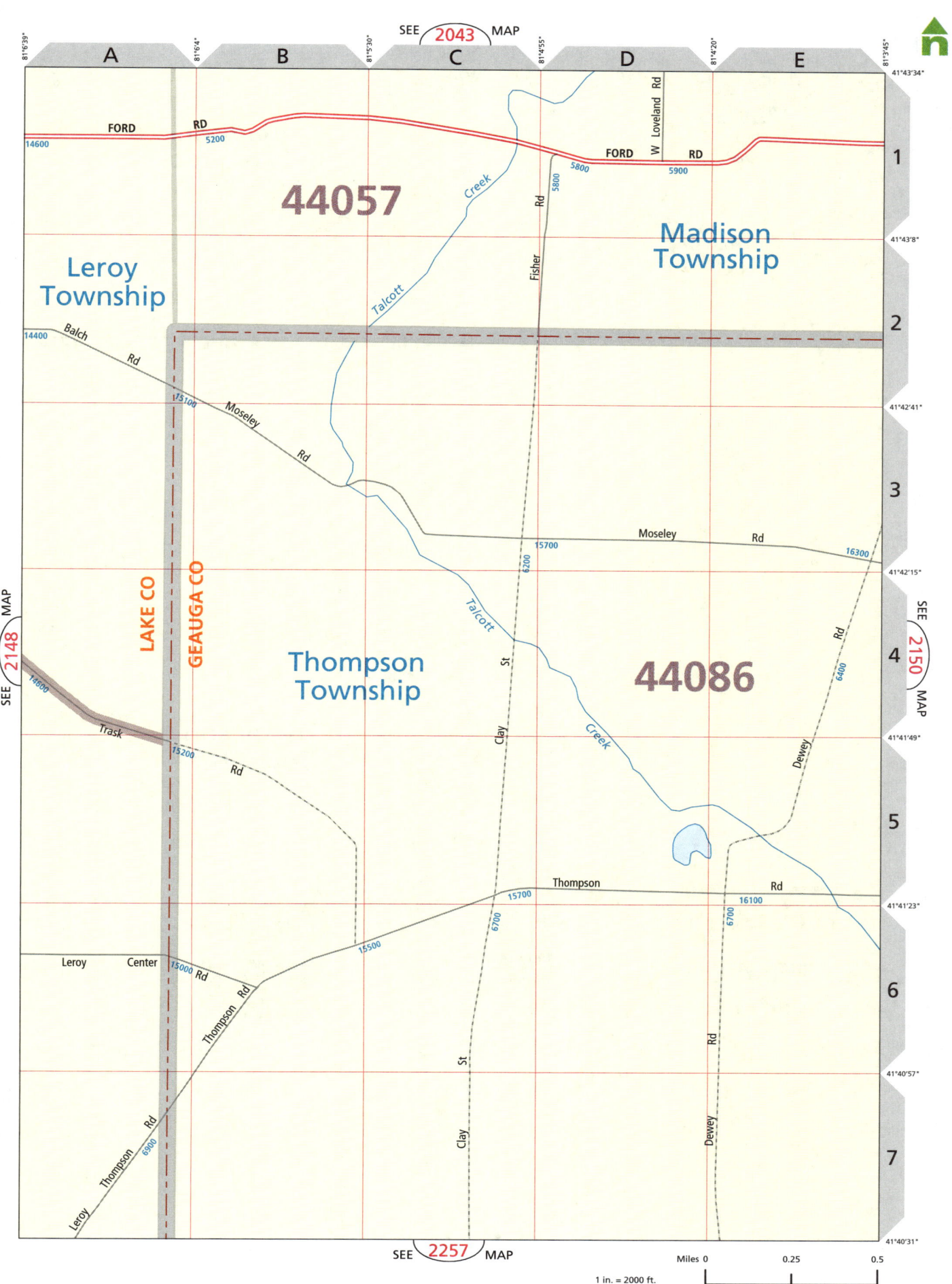

SEE 2043 MAP

A   B   C   D   E

81°6'39"   81°6'4"   81°5'30"   81°4'55"   81°4'20"   81°3'45"

41°43'34"

FORD   RD

14600   5200

W Loveland Rd

FORD   RD

5800   5900

1

44057

41°43'8"

Leroy
Township

Madison
Township

Creek

Talcott

Fisher Rd

5800

2

Balch   Rd

14400

15100

Moseley

Rd

41°42'41"

LAKE CO   GEAUGA CO

3

Moseley   Rd

15700   16300

41°42'15"

Talcott

6200

Thompson
Township

44086

Rd

6400

Dewey

Trask

14600

Rd

15200

Clay   St

Creek

4

41°41'49"

SEE 2148 MAP

SEE 2150 MAP

5

Thompson   Rd

15700   16100

41°41'23"

Leroy   Center

15000   Rd

Thompson Rd

15500

6700

6700

Dewey   Rd

6

41°40'57"

Clay   St

7

Leroy

Thompson   Rd

6900

41°40'31"

SEE 2257 MAP

Miles 0   0.25   0.5

1 in. = 2000 ft.

MAP 2150

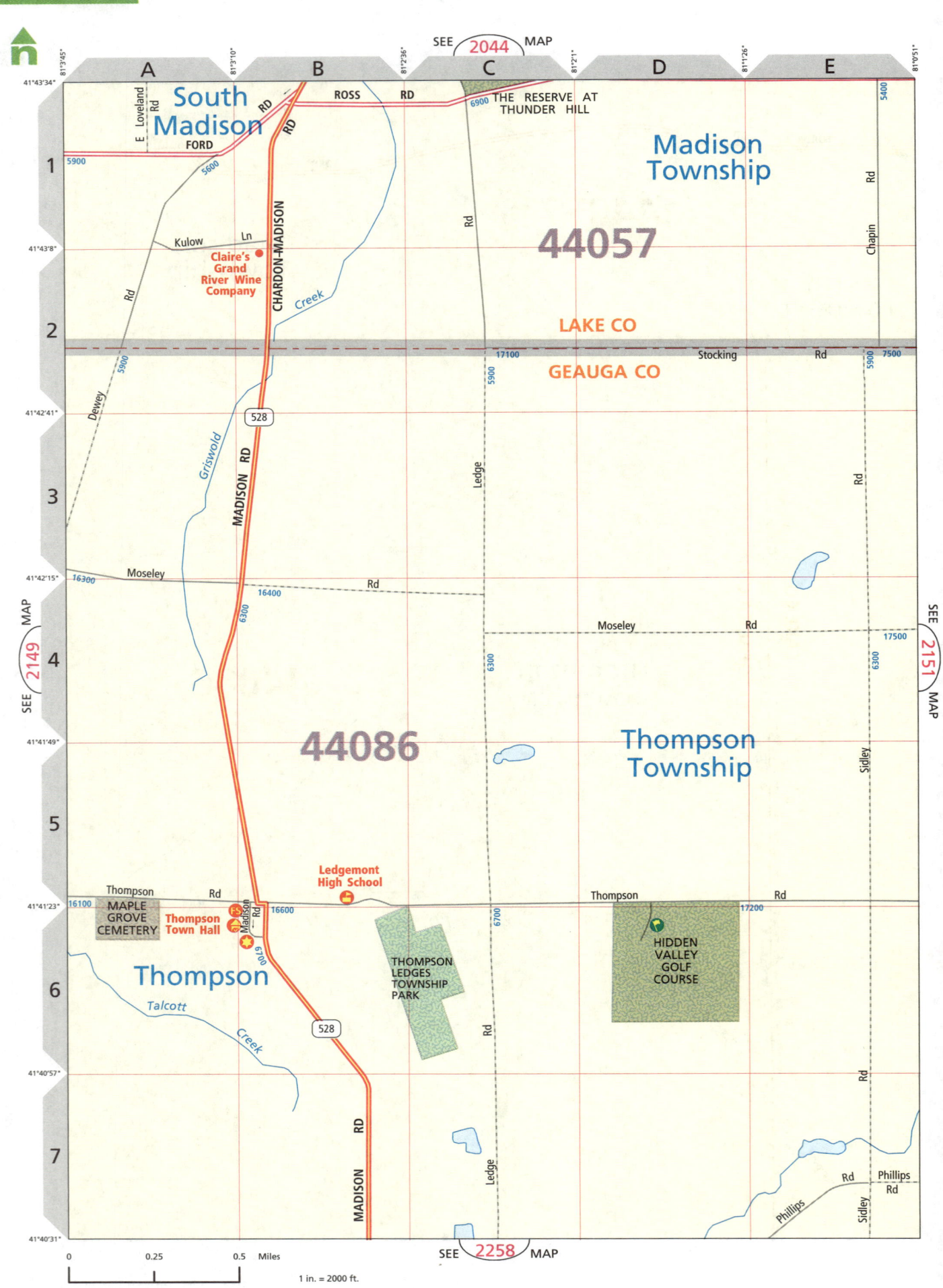

SEE 2044 MAP

SEE 2149 MAP

SEE 2151 MAP

SEE 2258 MAP

South Madison

Madison Township

44057

THE RESERVE AT THUNDER HILL

LAKE CO

GEAUGA CO

44086

Thompson Township

Ledgemont High School

MAPLE GROVE CEMETERY

Thompson Town Hall

Thompson

THOMPSON LEDGES TOWNSHIP PARK

HIDDEN VALLEY GOLF COURSE

Claire's Grand River Wine Company

E Loveland Rd
FORD
ROSS RD
Kulow Ln
CHARDON-MADISON RD
Creek
Dewey Rd
Griswold
528
MADISON RD
Moseley Rd
Chapin Rd
Stocking Rd
Ledge Rd
Moseley Rd
Sidley Rd
Thompson Rd
Thompson Rd
Talcott Creek
528
MADISON RD
Ledge Rd
Phillips Rd
Phillips Rd
Sidley

0   0.25   0.5   Miles
1 in. = 2000 ft.

MAP 2151-2247

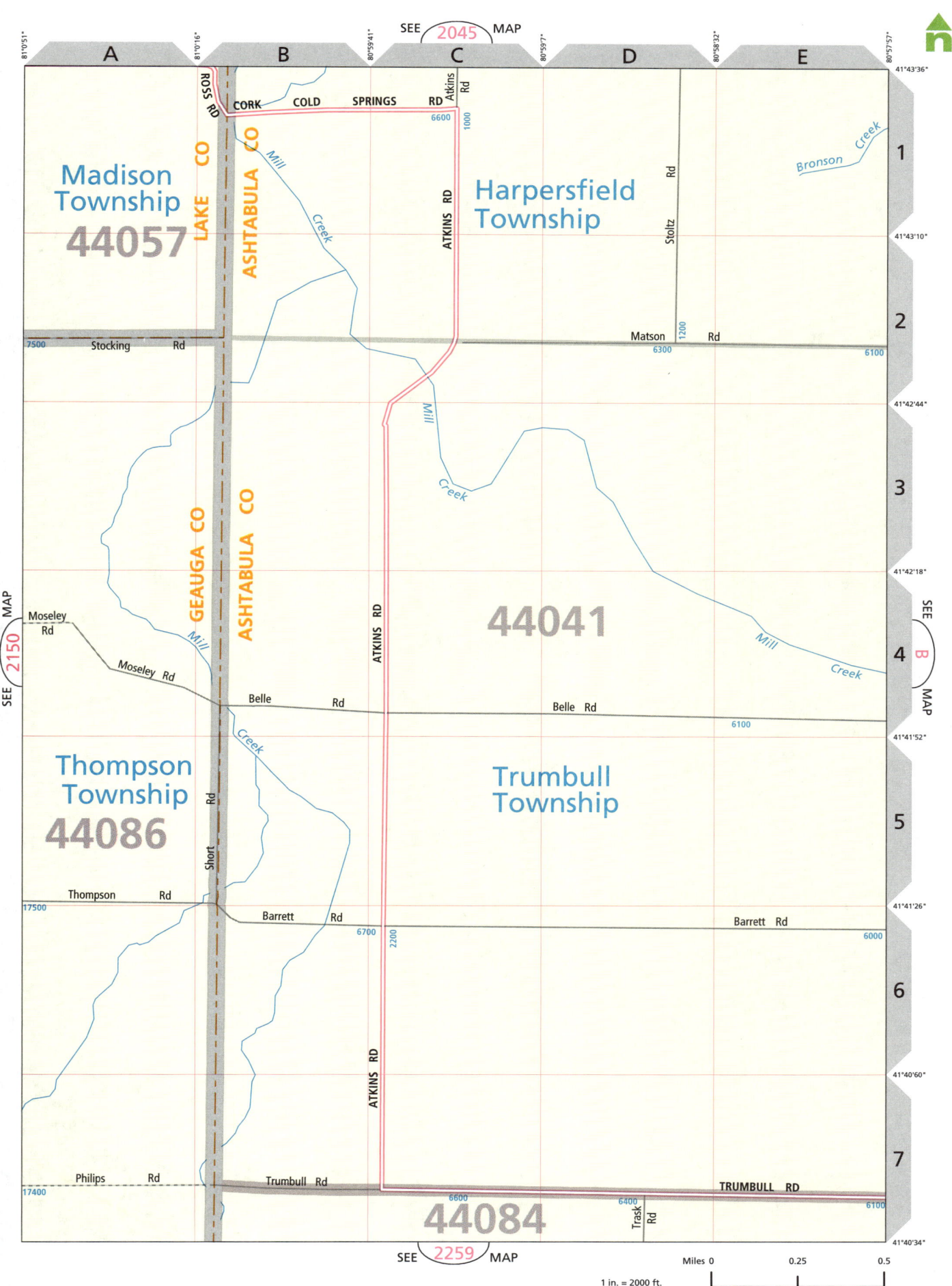

SEE 2045 MAP

A   B   C   D   E

Madison
Township
44057

LAKE CO

ASHTABULA CO

Mill Creek

CORK   COLD   SPRINGS   RD   Atkins Rd
6600

1000

ATKINS RD

Harpersfield
Township

Bronson Creek

Stoltz Rd

1

2

Stocking   Rd
7500

GEAUGA CO

ASHTABULA CO

Matson   Rd
6300   1200   6100

Mill Creek

41°43'36"
41°43'10"
41°42'44"

SEE 2150 MAP

Moseley
Rd

Moseley   Rd

44041

Atkins RD

Mill Creek

3

4

41°42'18"

SEE B MAP

Belle   Rd   Belle Rd
6100

Thompson
Township
44086

Short Rd

Creek

Trumbull
Township

41°41'52"

5

Thompson   Rd
17500

Barrett   Rd   Barrett Rd
6700 2200   6000

6

41°41'26"

41°40'60"

Atkins RD

7

Philips   Rd   Trumbull Rd   TRUMBULL RD
17400   6600   6400   6100

44084

Trask Rd

41°40'34"

SEE 2259 MAP

Miles 0   0.25   0.5

1 in. = 2000 ft.

MAP 2248

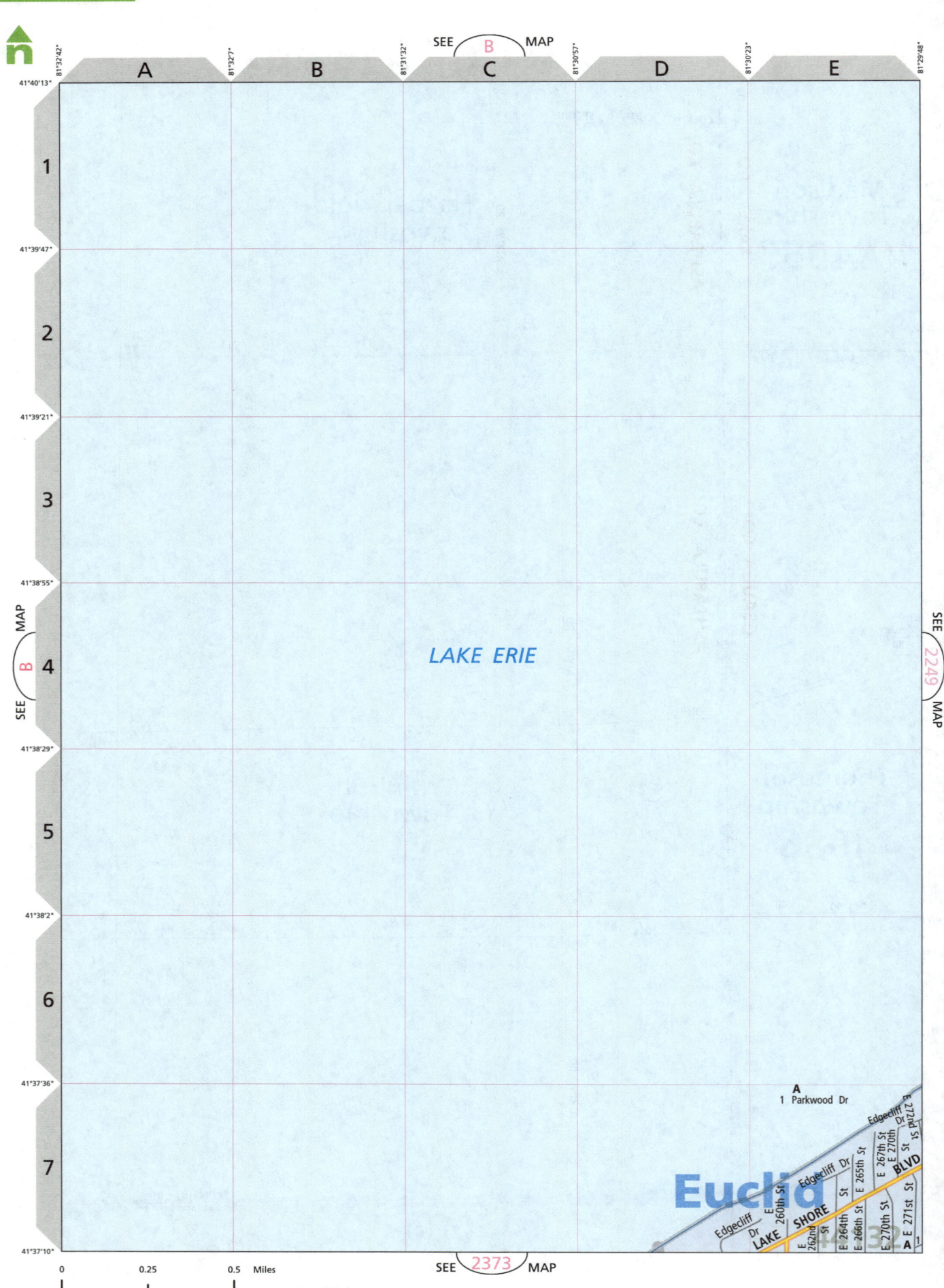

LAKE ERIE

SEE B MAP

SEE 2249 MAP

SEE B MAP

SEE 2373 MAP

A B C D E

1 2 3 4 5 6 7

81°32'42" 81°32'7" 81°31'32" 81°30'57" 81°30'23" 81°29'48"

41°40'13"
41°39'47"
41°39'21"
41°38'55"
41°38'29"
41°38'2"
41°37'36"
41°37'10"

A
1 Parkwood Dr

Euclid

Edgecliff Dr
Edgecliff Dr
Edgecliff Dr
E 272nd St
E 271st St
E 270th St
E 267th St
E 266th St
E 265th St
E 264th St
E 262nd St
E 260th St
LAKE SHORE BLVD

2433
A

0   0.25   0.5   Miles

1 in. = 2000 ft.

MAP 2249

SEE B MAP

A B C D E

SEE 2248 MAP

SEE 2250 MAP

1
2
3
4
5
6
7

Timberlake

Timberlake Village Hall

Lakeline

Lakeline Village Hall

Eastlake

LAKE ERIE

A
1 Oakridge Dr
2 Douglas Rd
3 Mapledale Rd

BMV

Willowick Chamber of Commerce

Willowick City Hall

Shoregate Shopping Ctr

44095
Willowick

Euclid

Wickliffe

Industrial Park

MANRY PARK

DUDLEY PARK

BAYRIDGE BLVD

44094

44092

LAKE SHORE BLVD

VINE ST

640

283

LAKELAND BLVD

CURTIS FRWY

EUCLID AV

20

JINDRA PK

SEE 2374 MAP

Miles 0   0.25   0.5

1 in. = 2000 ft.

MAP 2250

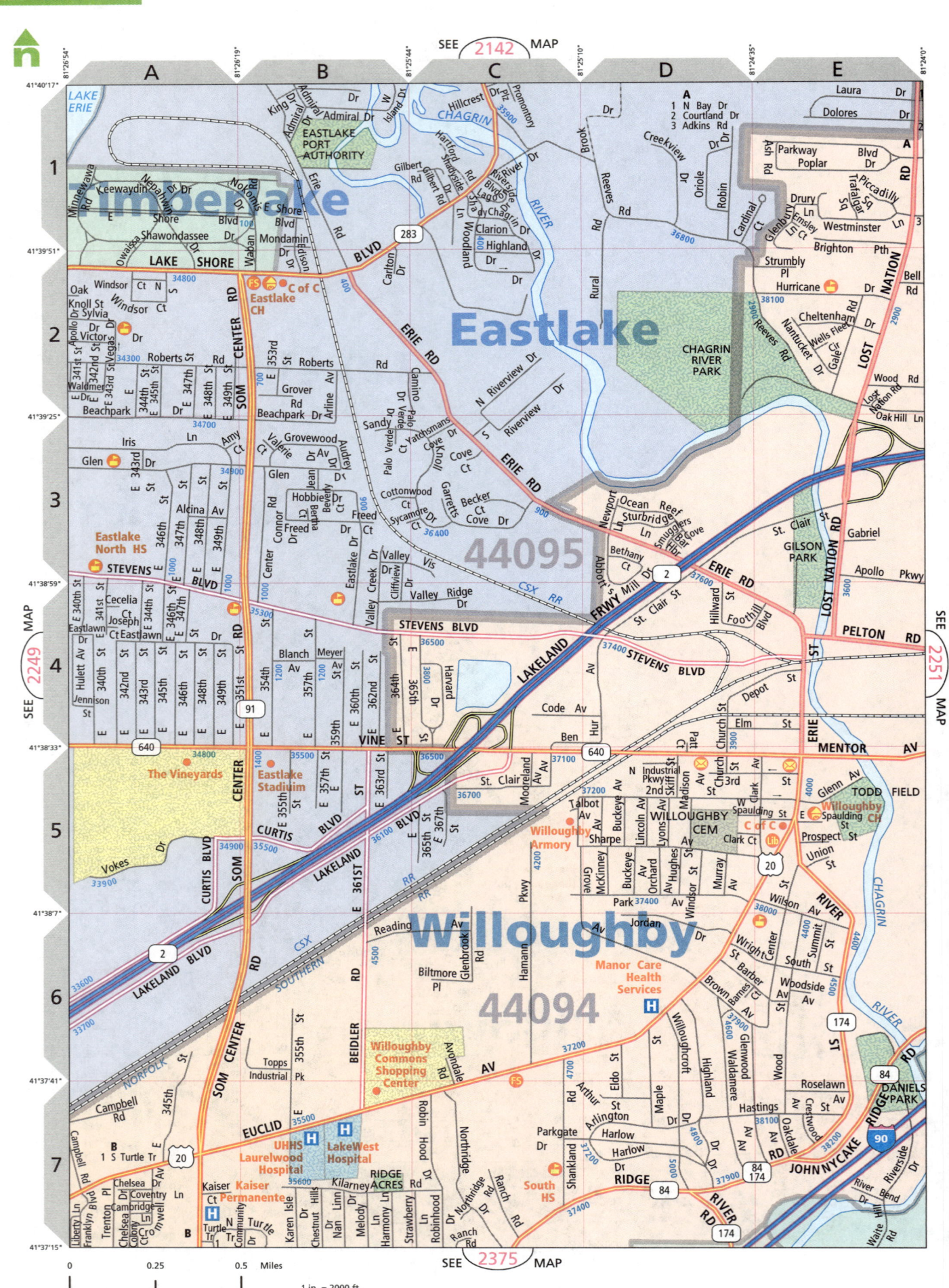

SEE 2142 MAP
SEE 2249 MAP
SEE 2251 MAP
SEE 2375 MAP

LAKE ERIE

Timberlake

Eastlake

44095

Willoughby

44094

CHAGRIN RIVER PARK

GILSON PARK

TODD FIELD

DANIELS PARK

EASTLAKE PORT AUTHORITY

Eastlake North HS

The Vineyards

Eastlake Stadium

Willoughby Commons Shopping Center

Willoughby Armory

WILLOUGHBY CEM

Manor Care Health Services

UHHS Laurelwood Hospital

LakeWest Hospital

Kaiser Permanente

RIDGE ACRES

South HS

0   0.25   0.5 Miles

1 in. = 2000 ft.

MAP 2251

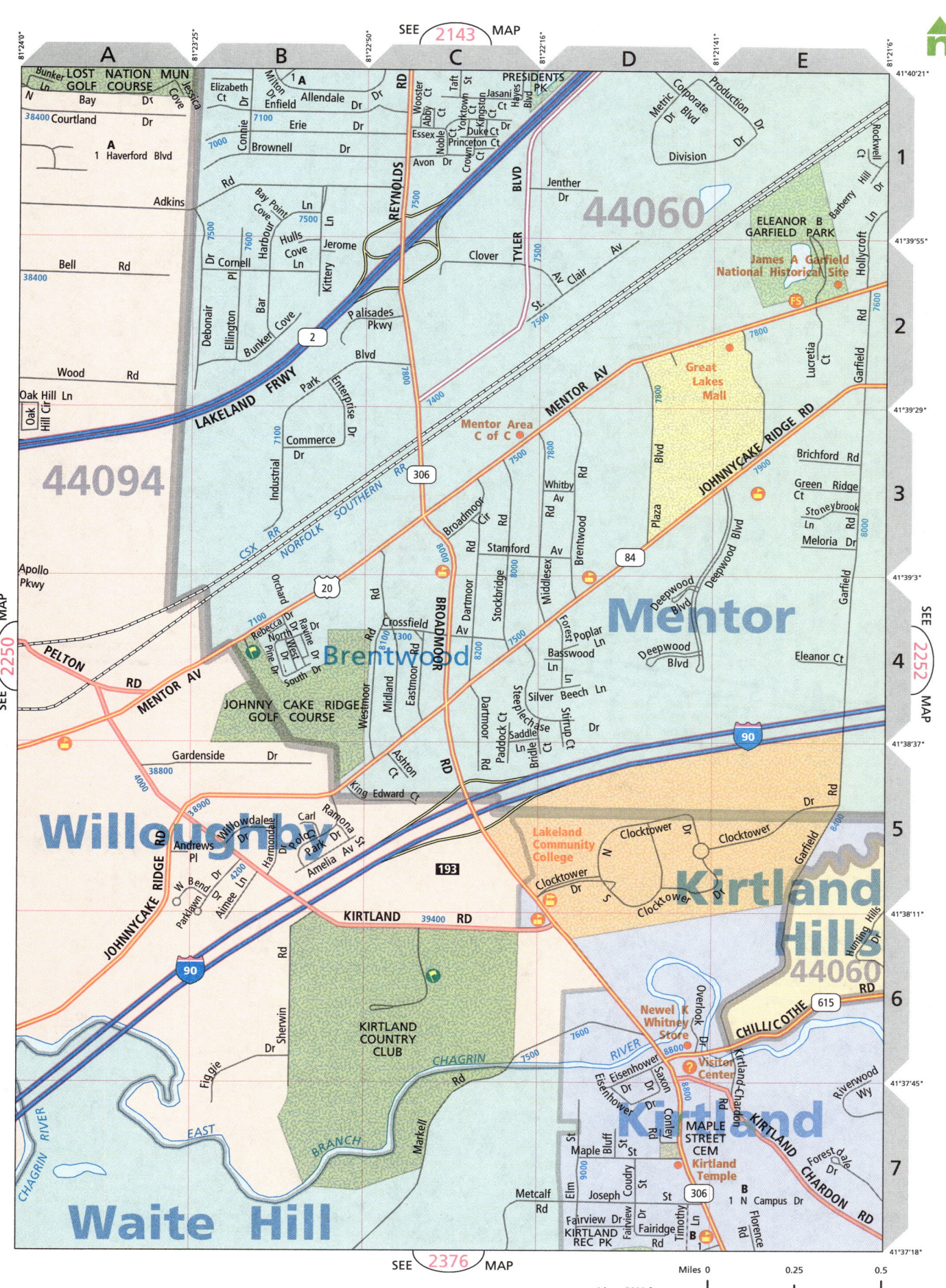

SEE 2143 MAP

A   B   C   D   E

1

2

3

4

5

6

7

SEE 2250 MAP

SEE 2252 MAP

SEE 2376 MAP

LOST NATION MUN GOLF COURSE
Bunker Ln
Jessica Cove
Bay Dr
38400 Courtland Dr
A
1 Haverford Blvd
Adkins
Bell Rd
38400
Wood Rd
Oak Hill Ln
Oak Hill Cir
44094

Elizabeth Ct
Milton Dr
Enfield
Allendale Dr
1 A
Conlie Dr
Erie Dr
7100
Brownell Dr
7000
Rd
Bay Point Cove
Ln
7500
7600
Hulls Cove Ln
Kittery Ln
Jerome
Debonair Dr
Cornell Pl
Bar
Harbour
Bunker Cove
Ellington
Palisades Pkwy
Blvd
2
Park
Enterprise Dr
7100
Commerce Dr
Industrial
LAKELAND FRWY
REYNOLDS RD
7500
7600
7800

Wooster
Abby Ct
Taft St
Yorktown Ct
Jasani Dr
Hayes Blvd
Essex
Noble
Crown Ct
Duke Ct
Princeton Ct
Avon
PRESIDENTS PK
TYLER BLVD
Jenther Dr
Clover
Clair
St
44060
7500
7500
7400

Metric Dr
Corporate Blvd
Production Dr
Division
ELEANOR B GARFIELD PARK
James A Garfield National Historical Site
FS
Rockwell Ct
Hill
Baberry Ln
Hollycroft
Garfield Rd
7600
7800
41°40'21"
41°39'55"
41°39'29"

Great Lakes Mall
Lucretia Ct
Garfield
Brichford Rd
Green Ridge Ct
Stoneybrook Ln
Meloria Dr
JOHNNYCAKE RIDGE RD
7900
8000

Mentor Area C of C
MENTOR AV
Whitby Av
Brentwood Rd
Plaza Blvd
84
Mentor
Deepwood Blvd
Deepwood Blvd
Eleanor Ct
7500
7800
7800
7800

306
Broadmoor Rd
Broadmoor Cir
Stamford
Dartmoor
Stockbridge
Middlesex Av
Forest
Poplar
Basswood
Silver Beech Ln
Steeplechase
Saddle Ct
Bridle Ln
Paddock Ln
Dartmoor
BROADMOOR RD
Ashton
King Edward Ct
8000
8000
8200
7500

Orchard Rd
Rebecca Dr
North
West
Pine Dr
Ravine Ln
South
Crossfield
Westmoor
Midland
Eastmoor
JOHNNY CAKE RIDGE GOLF COURSE
Brentwood
7100
8100
1300

Apollo Pkwy
PELTON RD
MENTOR AV
Gardenside Dr
38800
38900
4000
JOHNNYCAKE RIDGE RD
Willoughby
Willowdale
Andrews Pl
W Bend Dr
Parklawn
Aimee Ln
4200
Carl
Polc Dr
Hammonds
Ramona St
Park
Amelia Av
193
KIRTLAND RD
39400
I-90

Stirrup Ct
Dr
90
Dr
Rd
Clocktower Dr
Clocktower
N
Clocktower
Clocktower
Lakeland Community College
Garfield
Kirtland Hills
44060
Hunting Hills Dr
8400
CHILLICOTHE RD
615
41°39'3"
41°38'37"
41°38'11"
41°37'45"

KIRTLAND COUNTRY CLUB
Rd
Sherwin Dr
Figgie Dr
Markell Rd
CHAGRIN
RIVER
EAST BRANCH
7500
7600
CHAGRIN RIVER
Newel K Whitney Store
Visitor Center
Overlook Dr
Eisenhower Dr
Eisenhower Dr
Saxon Dr
Conley Rd
Kirtland-Chardon Rd
KIRTLAND CHARDON RD
Maple Bluff St
Maple St
Elm St
Joseph St
Coudry St
Fairview Dr
Fairview Rd
Fairridge Rd
Timothy
Metcalf Rd
KIRTLAND REC PK
MAPLE STREET CEM
Kirtland Temple
306
Kirtland
Florence Rd
Forest dale Dr
Riverwood Wy
B
1 N Campus Dr
B
8800
8800
9000
41°37'18"

Waite Hill

Miles 0   0.25   0.5
1 in. = 2000 ft.

MAP 2252

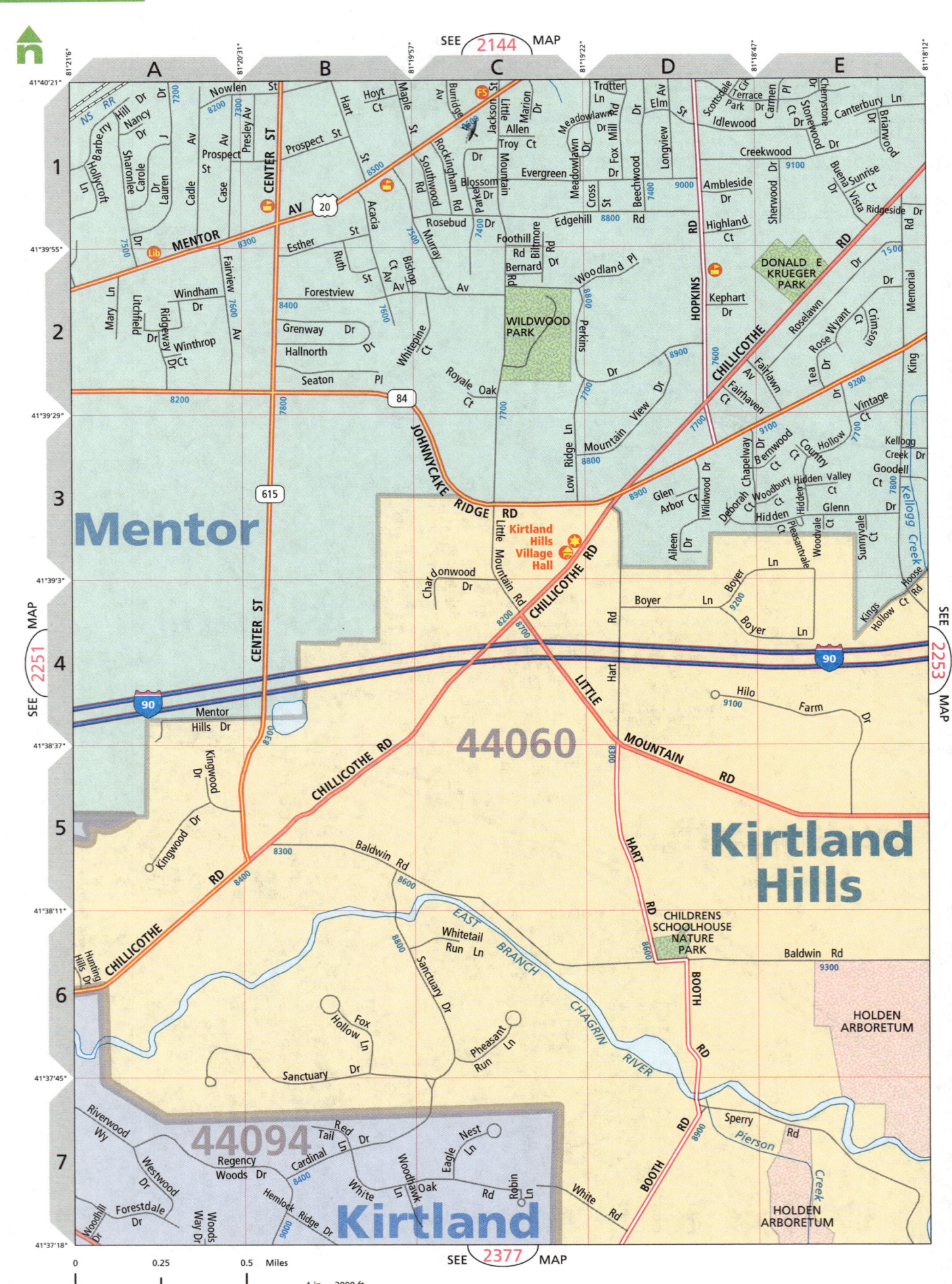

SEE 2144 MAP

A   B   C   D   E

Mentor

Kirtland
Hills

44060

44094

Kirtland

Holden
Arboretum

Holden
Arboretum

SEE 2251 MAP

SEE 2253 MAP

SEE 2377 MAP

0   0.25   0.5   Miles

1 in. = 2000 ft.

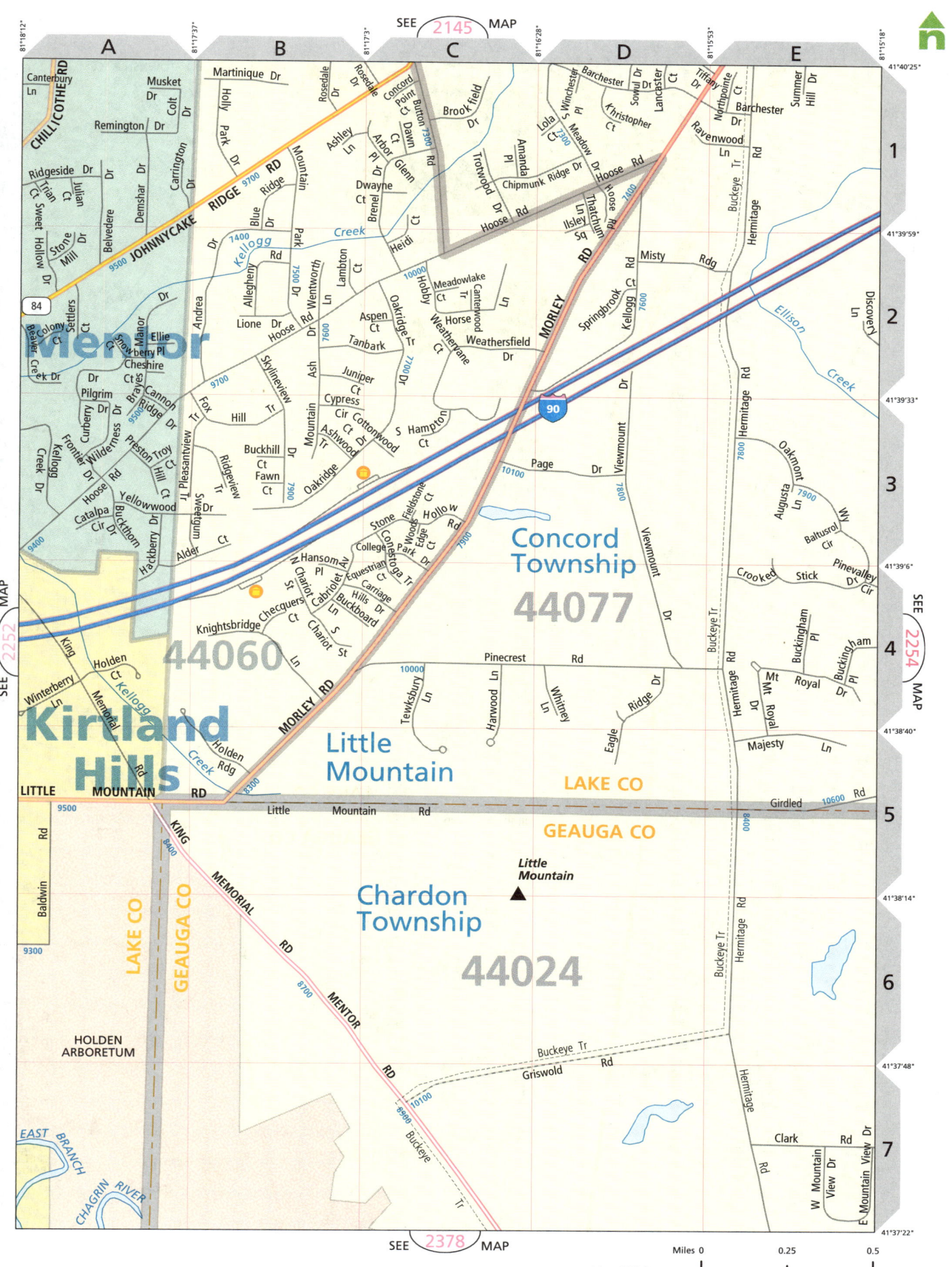

MAP 2253

A **B** **C** **D** **E**

Mentor

Kirtland Hills

LITTLE MOUNTAIN RD

Little Mountain

Concord Township
44077

44060

Chardon Township
44024

Little Mountain

LAKE CO
GEAUGA CO

HOLDEN ARBORETUM

EAST BRANCH CHAGRIN RIVER

LAKE CO
GEAUGA CO

SEE 2145 MAP
SEE 2252 MAP
SEE 2254 MAP
SEE 2378 MAP

Miles 0   0.25   0.5

1 in. = 2000 ft.

MAP 2254

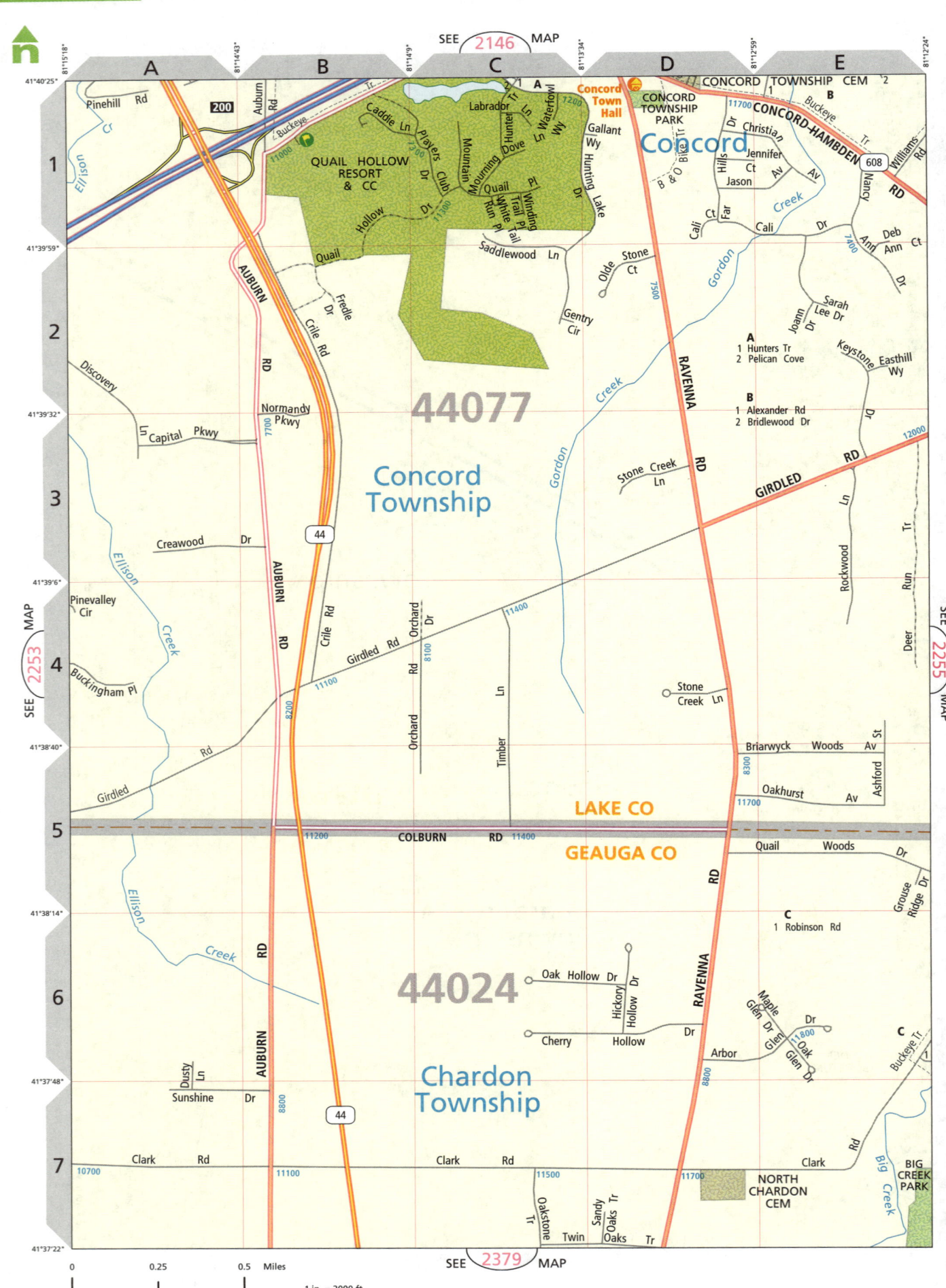

SEE 2146 MAP

SEE 2253 MAP

SEE 2255 MAP

SEE 2379 MAP

81°15'18"   81°14'43"   81°14'9"   81°13'34"   81°12'59"   81°12'24"

41°40'25"
41°39'59"
41°39'32"
41°39'6"
41°38'40"
41°38'14"
41°37'48"
41°37'22"

A   B   C   D   E
1   2   3   4   5   6   7

Pinehill Rd
200
Auburn Rd
Ellison Cr

CONCORD TOWNSHIP CEM
Buckeye Tr
CONCORD-HAMBDEN RD
11700
Concord Town Hall
CONCORD TOWNSHIP PARK
Concord
608
Williams Rd
Nancy

Caddie Ln
Buckeye Tr
QUAIL HOLLOW RESORT & CC
11000
Players Club Dr
7300
Mountain
Mourning Dove
Hunter Ln
Labrador Ln
Waterfowl Wy
7200
Gallant Wy
Hunting Lake Dr

B & O Bike Tr
Christian Dr
Hills Dr
Jennifer Ct
Jason Av
Cali Ct
Far Ct
Cali Dr
Deb Ann Ct
Ann Dr

Hollow
11300
Quail Run
White Tail Pl
Winding Trail Pl
Pl
Saddlewood Ln

Olde Stone Ct
7500
Gordon Creek
7000
Sarah Lee Dr
Joann Dr
Keystone Dr
Easthill Wy

Quail
Fredie Dr
Crile Rd

Gentry Cir

A
1 Hunters Tr
2 Pelican Cove

B
1 Alexander Rd
2 Bridlewood Dr

AUBURN RD

Discovery
Capital Pkwy
Normandy Pkwy
7700

44077

Gordon Creek

RAVENNA RD

Stone Creek Ln

GIRDLED RD
12000
Rockwood Ln
Deer Run Tr

Concord Township

Creawood Dr
44
AUBURN RD
Crile Rd

Ellison Creek

Pinevalley Cir
Buckingham Pl
Girdled Rd
8200
11100
Orchard Rd
Girdled Rd
Orchard Dr
8100
11400
Timber Ln

Stone Creek Ln

Briarwyck Woods Av St
8300
Oakhurst Av
Ashford Av

LAKE CO
11700

GEAUGA CO
11200
COLBURN RD
11400
RAVENNA RD

Quail Woods Dr
Grouse Ridge Dr

Ellison Creek

44024

C
1 Robinson Rd

Oak Hollow Dr
Hickory Hollow Dr
Cherry Hollow Dr
Arbor Dr
8800
Maple Glen Dr
Glen Dr
Oak Glen Dr
11800
Buckeye Tr

Dusty Ln
Sunshine Dr
8800
44
AUBURN RD

Chardon Township

Clark Rd
10700
11100
Clark Rd
11500
Clark Rd
11700
NORTH CHARDON CEM
Clark Rd
Big Creek
BIG CREEK PARK

Oakstone Tr
Sandy Oaks Tr
Twin Oaks Tr

0   0.25   0.5   Miles

1 in. = 2000 ft.

MAP 2255

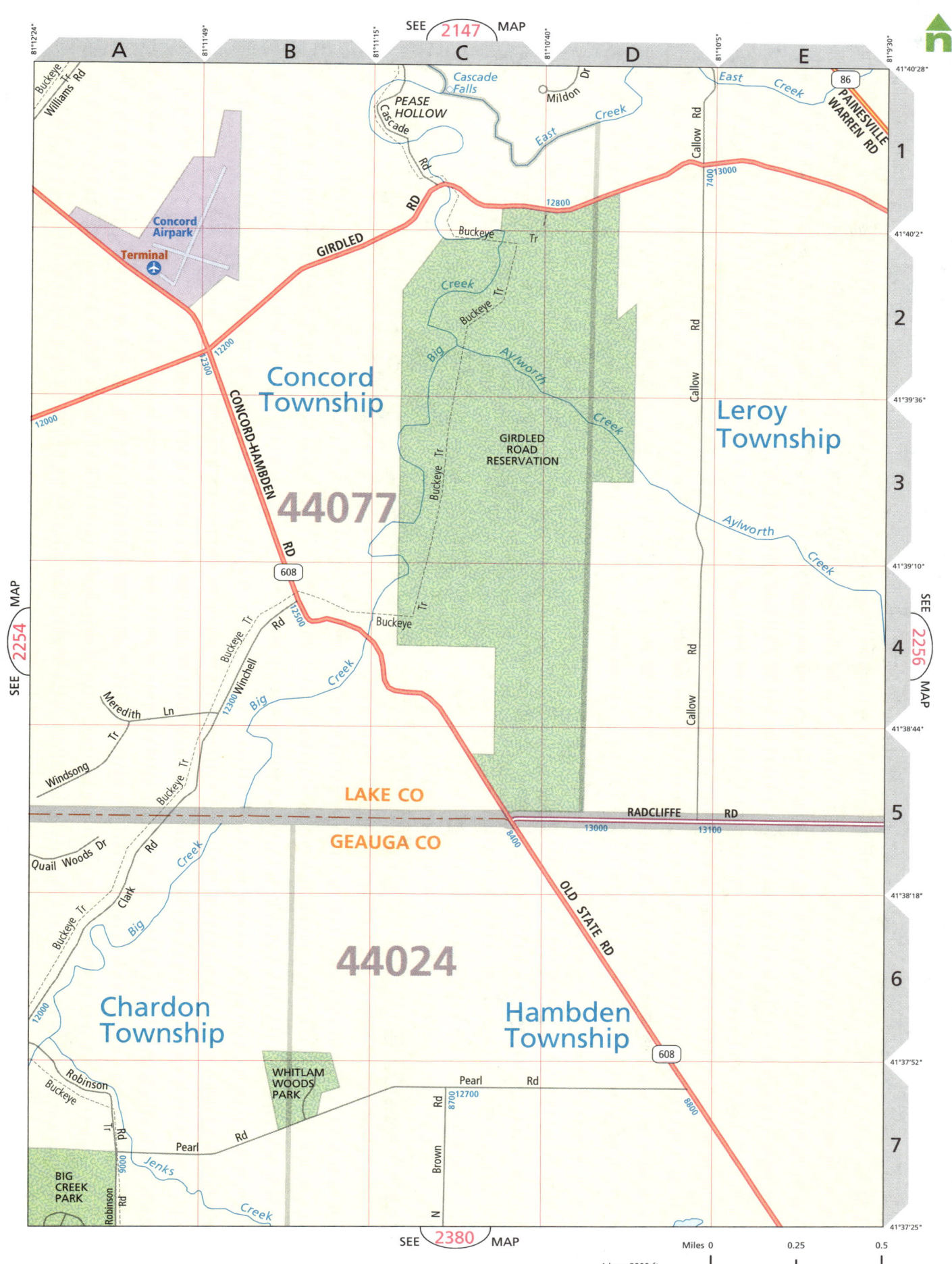

SEE 2147 MAP

A   B   C   D   E

Concord
Airpark

Terminal

PEASE
HOLLOW

Cascade
Falls

Cascade

Mildon

East   Creek

Callow   Rd

PAINESVILLE
WARREN RD

86

East   Creek

GIRDLED   RD

Buckeye   Tr

12800

13000

7400

1

41°40'28"

41°40'2"

CONCORD-HAMBDEN   RD

Concord
Township

44077

608

Creek

Buckeye   Tr

Big

Aylworth   Creek

GIRDLED
ROAD
RESERVATION

Buckeye   Tr

Leroy
Township

Callow   Rd

41°39'36"

2

3

Buckeye   Tr

Buckeye   Tr

Aylworth   Creek

41°39'10"

SEE 2254 MAP

12200

12300

12000

12500

Buckeye   Tr

Winchell   Rd

12300

Meredith   Ln

Big   Creek

Buckeye

Callow   Rd

SEE 2256 MAP

41°38'44"

4

Windsong   Tr

Buckeye   Tr

LAKE CO

GEAUGA CO

RADCLIFFE   RD

13000   13100

8400

5

41°38'18"

Quail Woods Dr

Clark   Rd

Buckeye   Tr

Big   Creek

44024

Chardon
Township

Hambden
Township

OLD   STATE   RD

608

6

12000

Robinson

Buckeye

WHITLAM
WOODS
PARK

Pearl   Rd

Brown   Rd

8700   12700

Pearl   Rd

8800

41°37'52"

7

BIG
CREEK
PARK

Buckeye   Tr   Rd

9000

Robinson   Rd

Pearl   Rd

Jenks   Creek

N   Brown   Rd

41°37'25"

SEE 2380 MAP

Miles 0   0.25   0.5

1 in. = 2000 ft.

MAP 2256

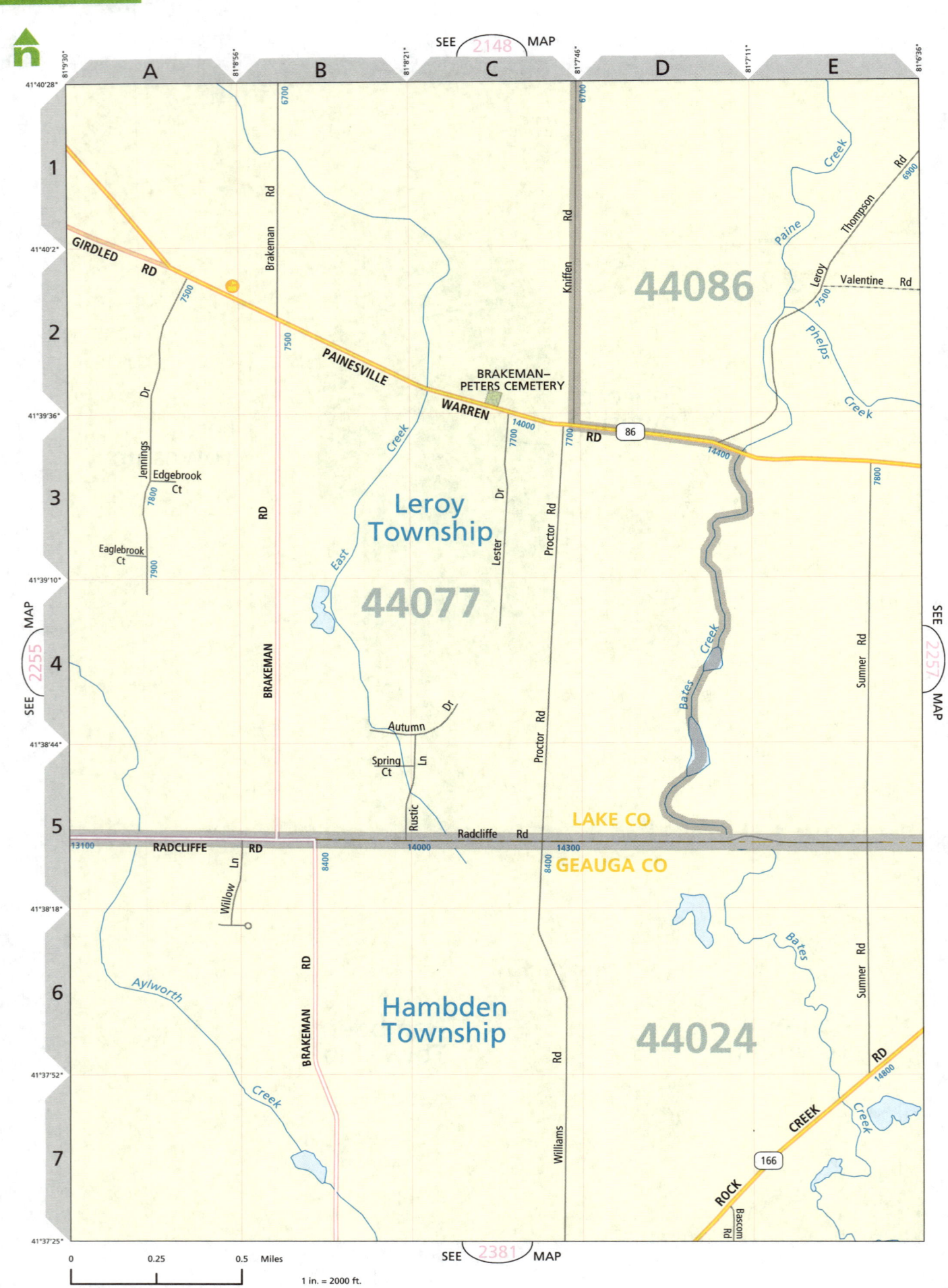

SEE 2148 MAP

A B C D E

GIRDLED RD

Brakeman Rd

Kniffen Rd

44086

Creek

Thompson Rd

6900

Leroy

Valentine Rd

7500

PAINESVILLE

7500

Phelps

Creek

Jennings Dr

Edgebrook Ct

7800

BRAKEMAN-PETERS CEMETERY

WARREN

14000

7700

7700

RD

86

14400

7800

Eaglebrook Ct

7900

RD

Leroy
Township

44077

Lester Dr

Proctor Rd

East Creek

Bates Creek

Sumner Rd

SEE 2255 MAP

BRAKEMAN

Autumn Dr

Proctor Rd

SEE 2257 MAP

Spring Ct

Ln

Rustic

LAKE CO

13100

RADCLIFFE RD

8400

14000

Radcliffe Rd

14300

8400

GEAUGA CO

Willow Ln

Aylworth

BRAKEMAN RD

Hambden
Township

Williams Rd

44024

Bates

Sumner Rd

RD

14800

Creek

Creek

ROCK CREEK RD

166

Bascom Rd

SEE 2381 MAP

0   0.25   0.5   Miles

1 in. = 2000 ft.

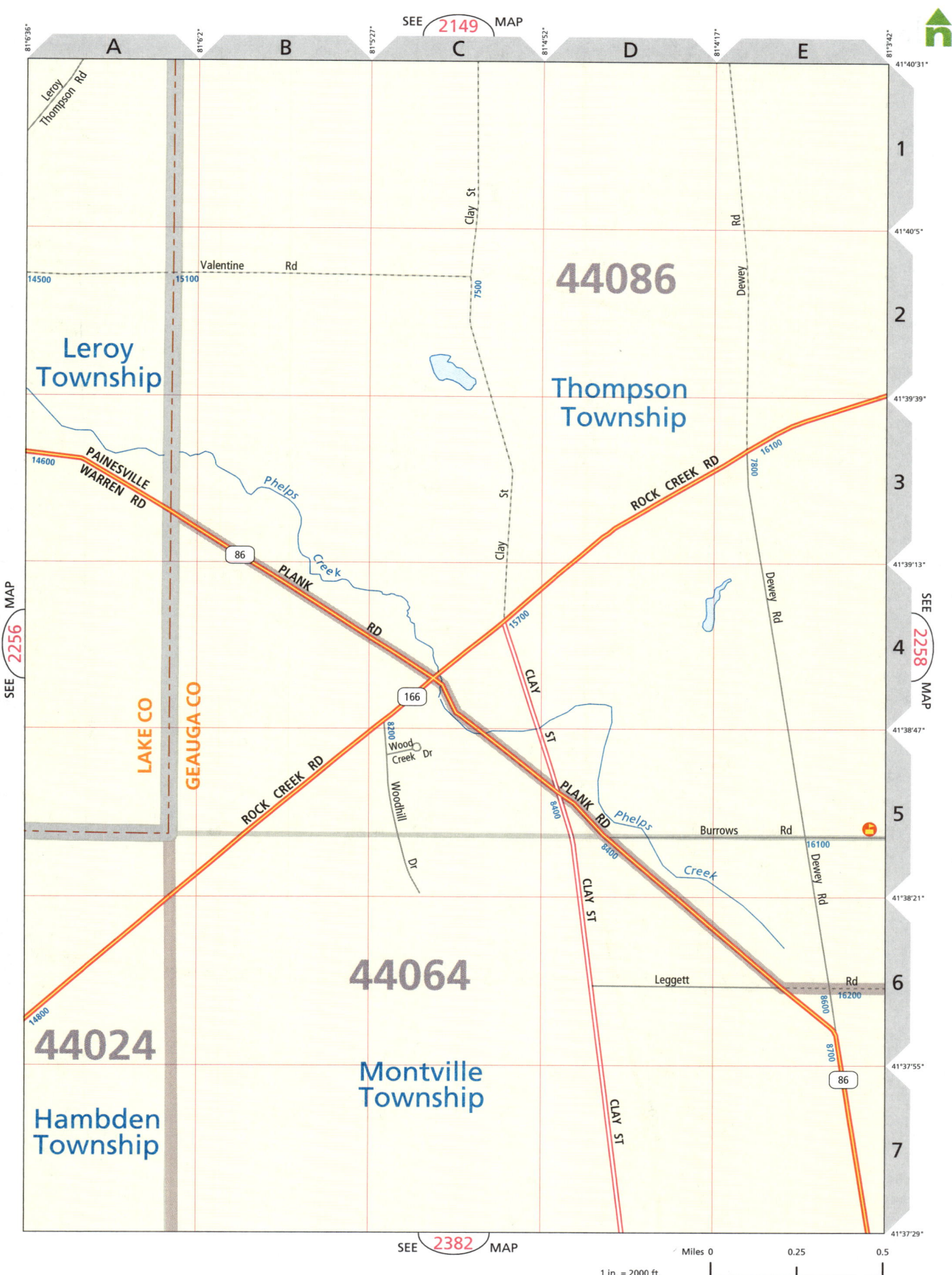

MAP 2257

SEE 2149 MAP

A   B   C   D   E

81°6'36"   81°6'2"   81°5'27"   81°4'52"   81°4'17"   81°3'42"

41°40'31"

1

Leroy
Thompson Rd

Clay St

Rd

41°40'5"

Valentine   Rd

14500   15100   7500

44086

Dewey

2

Leroy
Township

Thompson
Township

41°39'39"

PAINESVILLE

WARREN RD

Phelps

ROCK CREEK RD

16100

7800

14600

3

86

PLANK

Creek

St

Dewey Rd

SEE 2256 MAP

41°39'13"

RD

Clay

15700

SEE 2258 MAP

4

166

CLAY

LAKE CO

GEAUGA CO

8200

ST

41°38'47"

Wood
Creek Dr

PLANK RD

Phelps

5

ROCK CREEK RD

Woodhill

8400

Burrows   Rd

Dewey Rd

Creek

16100

Dr

8400

41°38'21"

Leggett   Rd

6

44064

CLAY ST

8600   16200

14800

8700

41°37'55"

44024

Montville
Township

86

7

Hambden
Township

CLAY ST

41°37'29"

SEE 2382 MAP

Miles 0   0.25   0.5

1 in. = 2000 ft.

MAP 2258

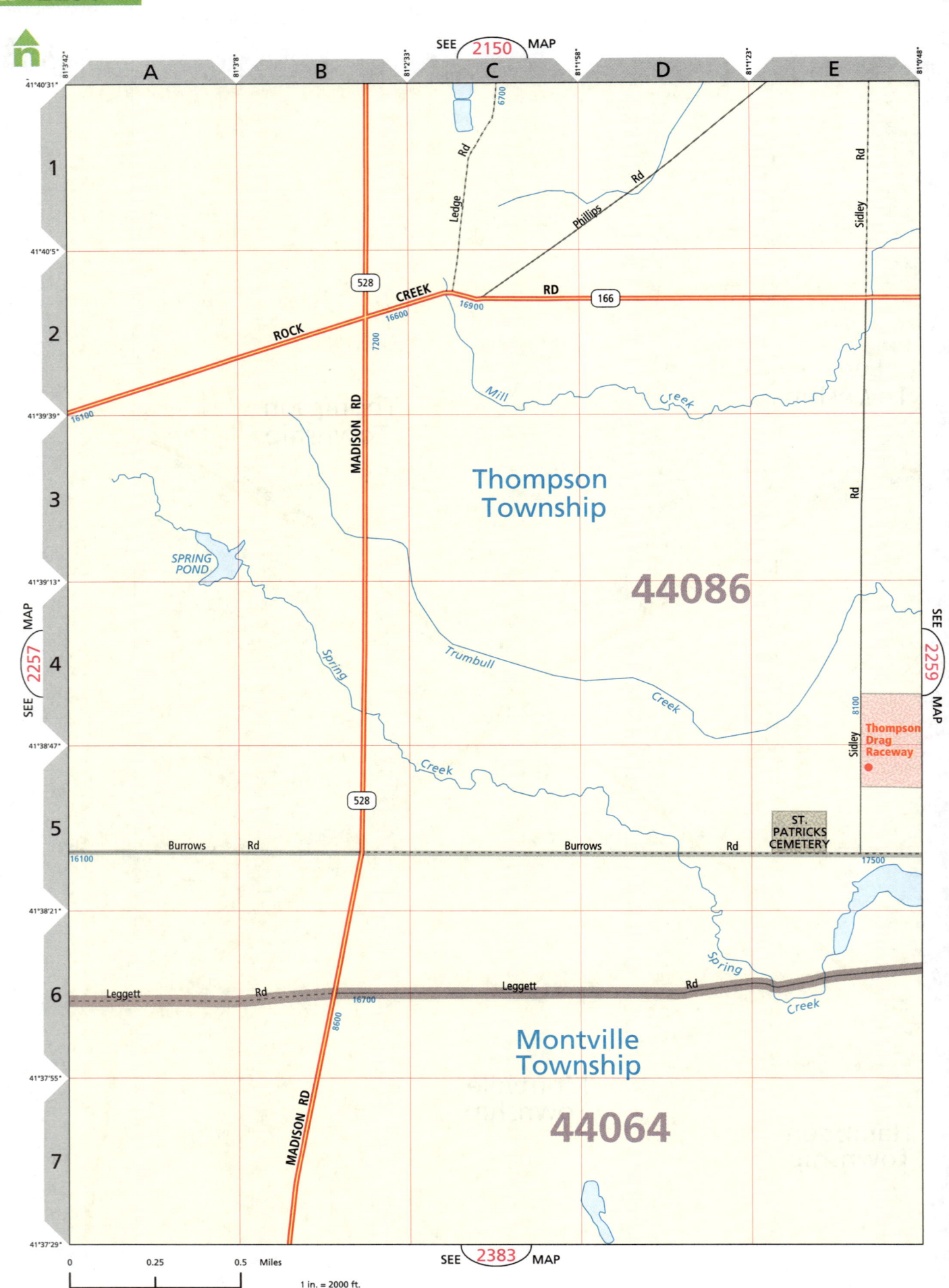

SEE 2150 MAP

A   B   C   D   E

81°3'42"   81°3'8"   81°2'33"   81°1'58"   81°1'23"   81°0'48"

41°40'31"

1

Ledge Rd
6700

Phillips Rd
Sidley Rd

41°40'5"

528

2

ROCK   CREEK   RD   166

16600   16900

7200

16100

41°39'39"

Mill   Creek

3

Thompson
Township

SPRING
POND

44086

41°39'13"

SEE 2257 MAP

4

Spring

Trumbull   Creek

Sidley Rd

8100

Thompson
Drag
Raceway

SEE 2259 MAP

41°38'47"

Creek

5

Burrows   Rd   Burrows   Rd

16100   17500

ST.
PATRICKS
CEMETERY

41°38'21"

528

6

Leggett   Rd   Leggett   Rd

16700

8600

Spring   Creek

Montville
Township

41°37'55"

44064

7

MADISON RD

MADISON RD

41°37'29"

SEE 2383 MAP

0   0.25   0.5   Miles

1 in. = 2000 ft.

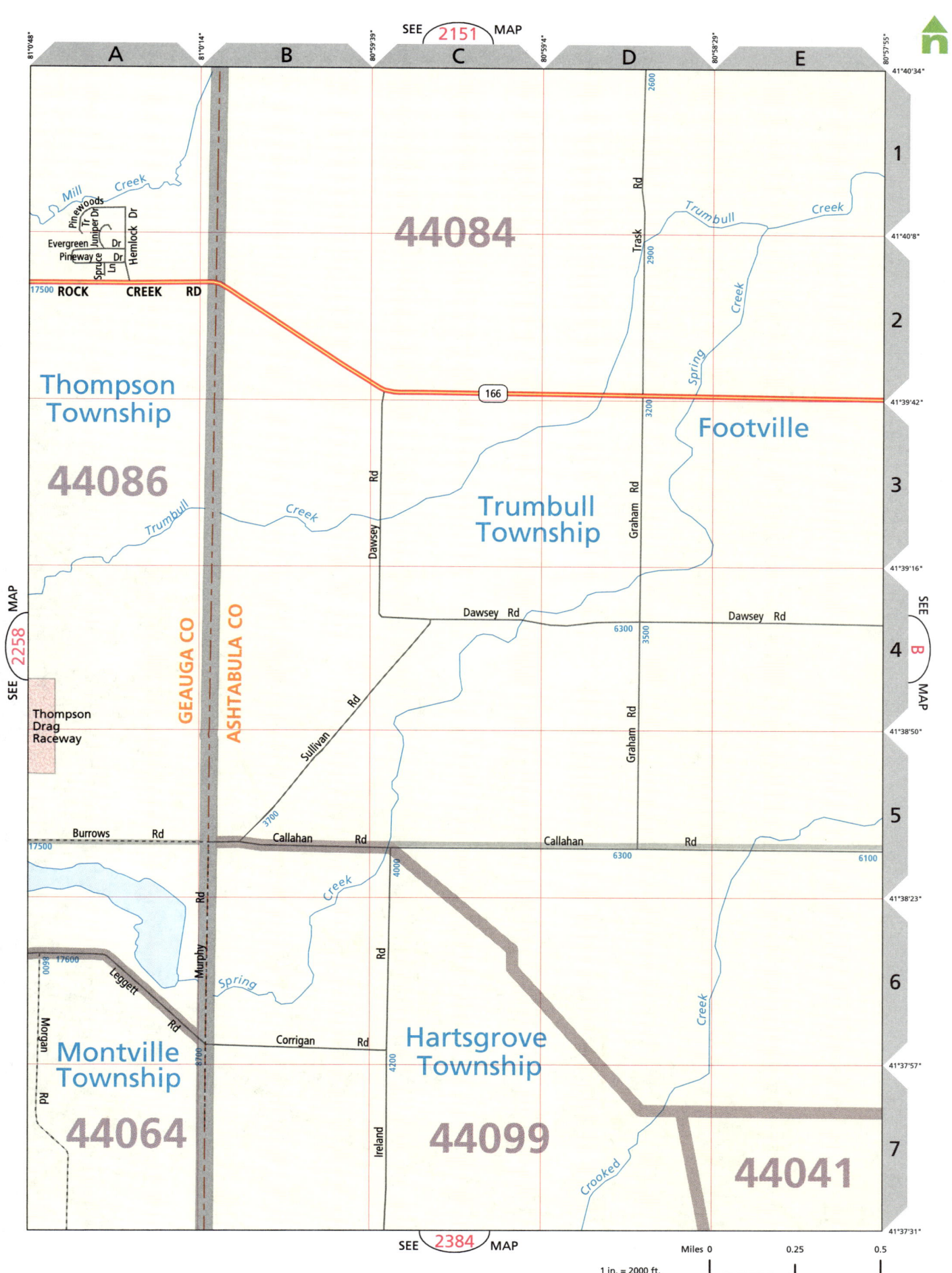

MAP 2259-2371

SEE 2151 MAP

A   B   C   D   E

1

44084

2

ROCK   CREEK   RD
17500

Thompson
Township

44086

Footville

Trumbull
Township

3

Dawsey Rd   Dawsey Rd

4

SEE 2258 MAP

SEE B MAP

Thompson
Drag
Raceway

GEAUGA CO

ASHTABULA CO

Trumbull   Creek

Spring

Sullivan   Rd

Graham Rd

Trask Rd

5

Burrows   Rd

Callahan   Rd   Callahan   Rd

17500

Murphy   Rd

Creek

Graham Rd

6

Leggett   Rd

Spring

Morgan   Rd

Montville
Township

44064

Corrigan   Rd

Hartsgrove
Township

44099

Ireland   Rd

44041

Crooked   Creek

SEE 2384 MAP

Miles 0   0.25   0.5

1 in. = 2000 ft.

MAP 2372

SEE B MAP

A B C D E

1

2

LAKE ERIE

3

SEE B MAP

Euclid Hospital
Villa Angela-St. Joseph HS

Euclid
44119

BEACHWOOD PK

SEE 2373 MAP

D 1 Neff Rd

4

C
1 Center St
2 Lincoln Dr
3 Maple St
4 Poplar Av
5 Surrey Ln
6 Washington Blvd
7 Winchester Av

WILDWOOD PARK

5

CLEVELAND LAKEFRONT STATE PARK

A
1 E 157th St
2 E 158th St
3 E 162nd St
4 E 165th St

B
1 Evergreen Pl
2 Villa Beach Dr

NOTTINGHAM RD

Euclid

VILLAVIEW RD

6

Northeast Yacht Club

HUMPHREY PARK

Cleveland
44110

EUCLID CREEK PARK

7

WHITE CITY PARK

Cleveland

WATERLOO RD

90
2

SEE 2497 MAP

0   0.25   0.5 Miles
1 in. = 2000 ft.

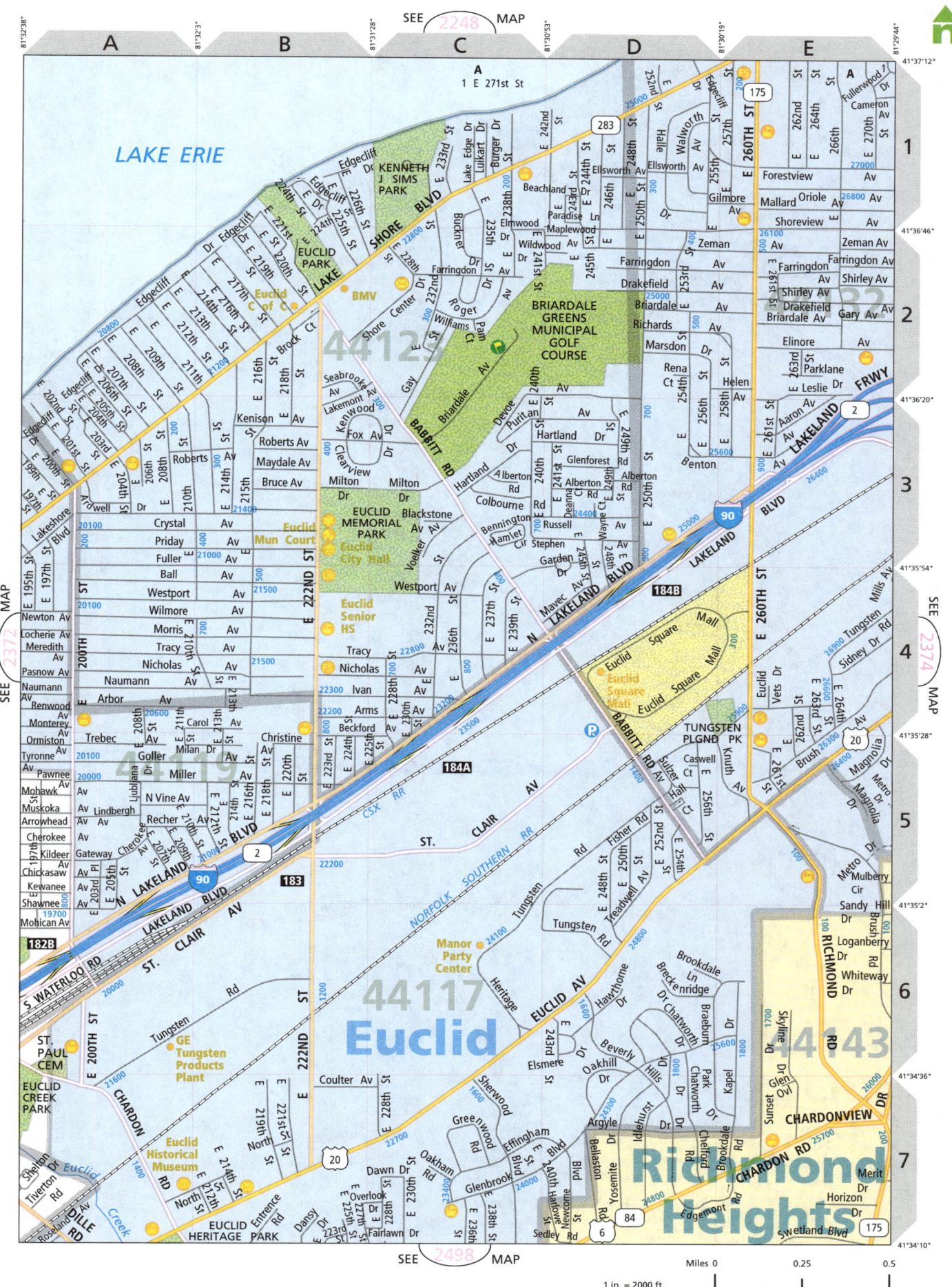

MAP 2373

SEE 2248 MAP

A 1 E 271st St

LAKE ERIE

A B C D E

KENNETH J SIMS PARK

EUCLID PARK

44129

BRIARDALE GREENS MUNICIPAL GOLF COURSE

EUCLID MEMORIAL PARK

Euclid Mun Court

Euclid City Hall

Euclid Senior HS

44119

Euclid Square Mall

TUNGSTEN PLGND PK

184B

184A

184

CSX RR

ST. CLAIR AV

NORFOLK SOUTHERN RR

Manor Party Center

44117
Euclid

GE Tungsten Products Plant

ST. PAUL CEM

EUCLID CREEK PARK

Euclid Historical Museum

44143

RICHMOND RD

CHARDONVIEW

Richmond Heights

EUCLID HERITAGE PARK

DILLE RD

SEE 2372 MAP

SEE 2374 MAP

SEE 2498 MAP

Miles 0   0.25   0.5

1 in. = 2000 ft.

MAP 2374

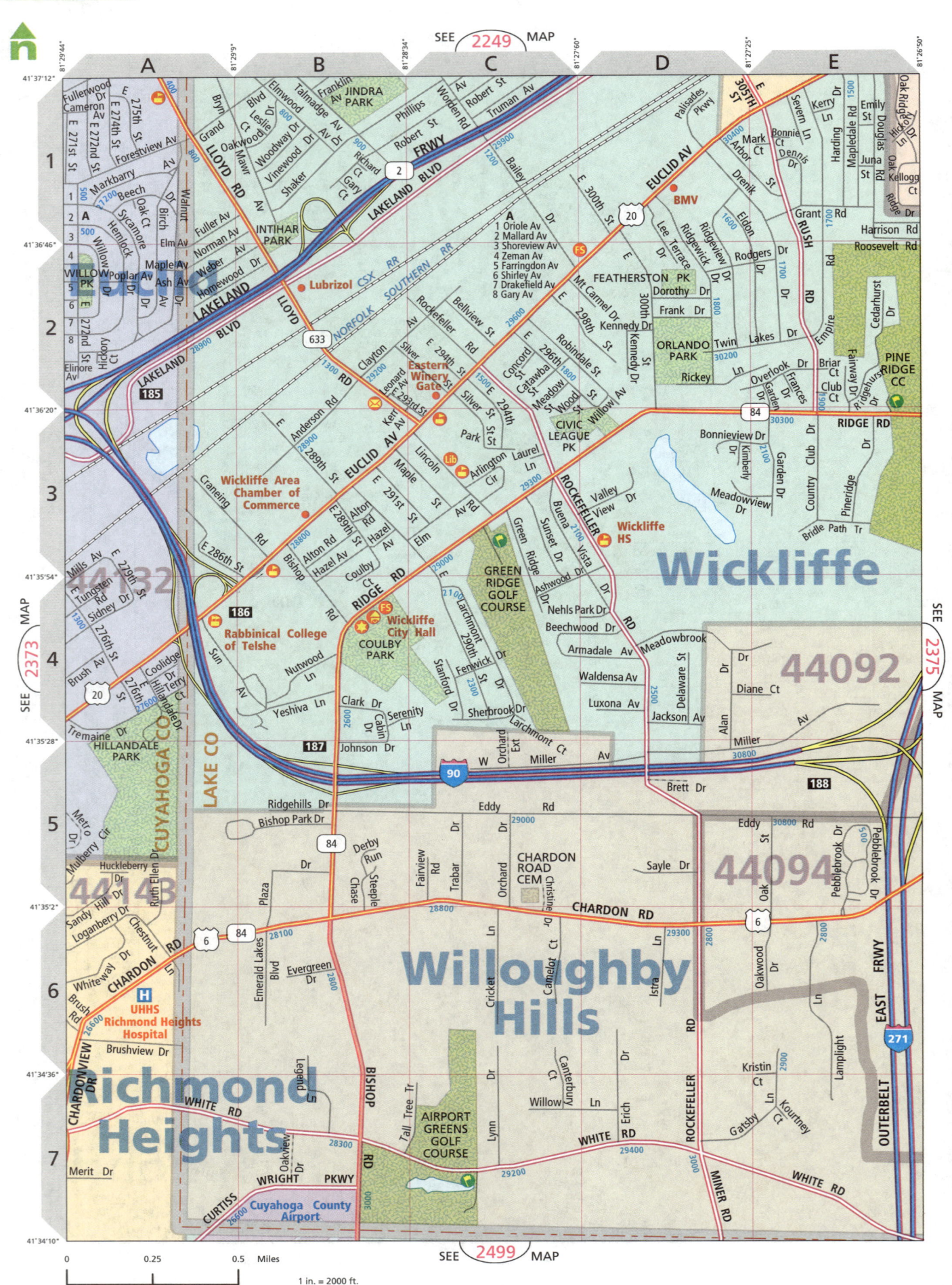

SEE 2249 MAP

SEE 2373 MAP

SEE 2375 MAP

SEE 2499 MAP

A
1 Oriole Av
2 Mallard Av
3 Shoreview Av
4 Zeman Av
5 Farringdon Av
6 Shirley Av
7 Drakefield Av
8 Gary Av

Wickliffe

Willoughby Hills

Richmond Heights

44092
44094
44143
44132

0   0.25   0.5   Miles

1 in. = 2000 ft.

MAP 2375

SEE 2250 MAP

N

A   B   C   D   E

Willoughby

91

Turtle Tr

Community Dr

Oaktree Dr

Aspenwood Ln

Chelsea
Colony Ct
Trenton Ct
Liberty Ln
Franklyn Blvd

Oak Ridge Dr
Wildwood
Red
Sierra Dr
Haven Ct
Cascade Ct
Milwood Ln
Canyon Ct

Weston
Harrison Rd

Bramble Ct
Roosevelt Rd
Harold Ct
York
Grand
Colonial
Delta
Royal
Noble
Forest Dr
Edgewood Dr
Atwood Pl
Beacon Dr
Halle Dr
Halle
Farm Dr

Halle
Par Ln

84

189

Mary
Hills

Isle
Karen Dr
Chestnut
Nan
Linn
Dale
Melody
Skytop

Clairidge Dr
Ericson Ln
Ridgeway
Boyd Ln
Fawn Ridge
Timber Ln
Deercreek Dr
Deer Hill Pl

Harmony
Strawberry St
Robinhood Dr
Ranch Rd
Ranch Dr

35800
36300

84

90

Northridge Dr

A
1 Hampton Ct
2 Crown Ct
3 Marble Ln
4 Pineview Ln

174

RIVER RD

Waite Hill
Rd
Drury Ln

Waite
Hill

CHAGRIN   RIVER

Jennie Ln
Somrack Dr

MAPLEGROVE   RD

36000

Sherwood
Ln Dr

Parsons Dr
Hanna

Mapleview

35600
35500

MAPLE
GROVE CEMETERY

Riviera Ridge Rd

EAGLE   RD

Tralland
Glengate Rd Dr

Mayfriars Dr   Dr

EAGLE MILLS
RD

Smith Rd

Kennilw Dr
Chagrin Dr

37300
2400

Fox Pass
Red

Dodd Rd

MANAKIKI
GOLF
COURSE

Donald Ross Dr

Timberline Dr

Glen
Kyle Ln

Eddy Rd

35700

Bates Ln

Deer Run Ln

Eddy Rd

36100

44094

RIVER   RD

36700

Beech   Hills

Dr

Dodd's Hill Rd

Milann Dr
Milann Dr
Dodd Rd
2600

Rd

HACH-
OTIS
STATE
NATURE
PRESERVE

Valley Rd

Morningstar Ct

Eddy Rd

34900

Willoughby Hills
Mayors Court

Willoughby Hills
City Hall

CHARDON   RD

35800

Skyline   Dr

2700

36700

Pleasant

Valley

CHARDON RD

37200

6

Willoughby
Hills

6

Hondros
College
Cleveland
East

ROEMISCH
FIELDS
PARK

35200

91

Eddy
Fowler Dr
Stark Dr

2700

Dixon   Rd

Martin   Rd

Strawberry

Valley Pkwy

Forest Ln

Buttermilk Falls Pkwy

174

CHAGRIN   RIVER

Loreto Dr

34900

Squires Castle

2800
2900

Hayes Dr

Rosewood   Tr

SOM CENTER   RD

3000

NORTH
CHAGRIN
METROPOLITAN
PARK

RIVER RD

Hunters
Woods
Ln

Sleepy Hollow Dr
Windy Hill Tr
Hemlock Dr

Mill
Gate Dr

Valley Brook Dr

Rogers Dr
37000
Buckeye
Rogers Dr
Rogers Rd

7

Marcum
Parkview   Blvd
Rd

44092

SEE 2500 MAP

1
2
3
4
5
6
7

SEE 2374 MAP
271
90

SEE 2376 MAP

41°37'17"
41°36'50"
41°36'24"
41°35'58"
41°35'32"
41°35'6"
41°34'40"
41°34'14"

81°26'50"
81°26'15"
81°25'41"
81°25'6"
81°24'31"
81°23'56"

PINE
RIDGE
CC

Miles 0   0.25   0.5

1 in. = 2000 ft.

MAP 2376

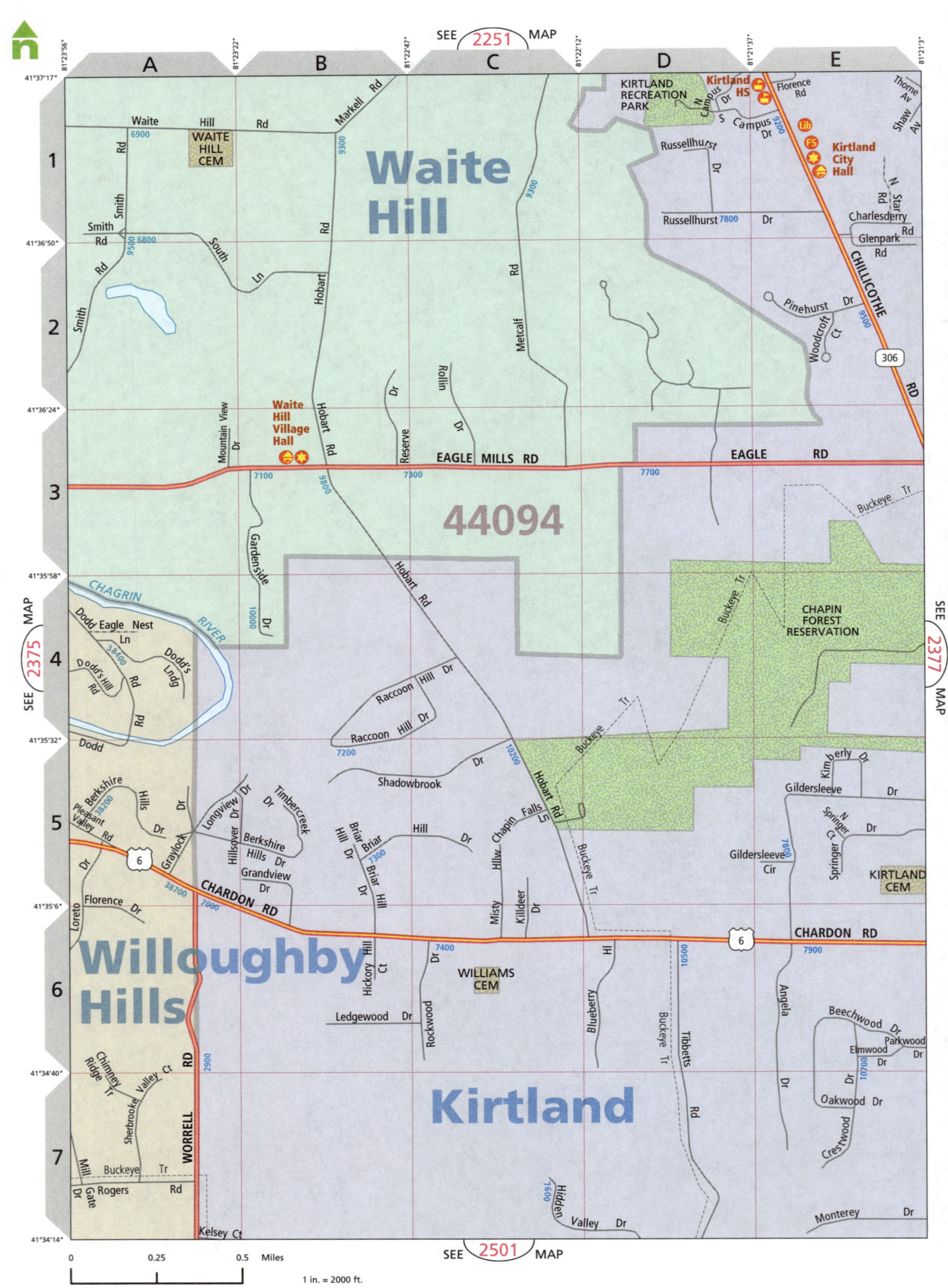

SEE 2251 MAP

A B C D E

1 2 3 4 5 6 7

41°37'17"
41°36'50"
41°36'24"
41°35'58"
41°35'32"
41°35'6"
41°34'40"
41°34'14"

81°23'56" 81°23'22" 81°22'47" 81°22'12" 81°21'37" 81°21'3"

Waite Hill Rd
WAITE HILL CEM
6900

Waite Hill

Markell Rd
9300

Smith Rd
6900
Smith Rd
9500 6800
Smith Rd

South Ln

Hobart Rd

Hobart Rd
9800

Metcalf Rd

Rollin Dr
Reserve Dr

KIRTLAND RECREATION PARK
Kirtland HS
N Campus Dr
S Campus Dr
9200
Florence Rd
Lib
FS
Kirtland City Hall

Russellhurst Dr
Russellhurst 7800 Dr

Thorne Av
Shaw Av

N Star Rd
Charlesderry Rd
Glenpark Rd

CHILLICOTHE RD

Pinehurst Dr
9500
Woodcroft Ct

306

Waite Hill Village Hall
EAGLE MILLS RD
7100 7300 7700
EAGLE RD

44094

Gardenside Dr
10000

CHAGRIN RIVER

Dodd Eagle Nest Ln
38400
Dodd's Lndg
Dodd's Hill Rd
Rd
Dodd

Hobart Rd

Raccoon Hill Dr
Raccoon Hill Dr
7200

Shadowbrook Dr

Hobart Rd
10200

Buckeye Tr

Buckeye Tr

CHAPIN FOREST RESERVATION

Buckeye Tr

SEE 2375 MAP
SEE 2377 MAP

Berkshire Hills Dr
38200
Pleasant Valley Rd
Graylock Dr
Longview Dr
Timbercreek Dr
Hillsover Dr
Berkshire Hills Dr
Grandview Dr

Briar Hill Dr
7300
Briar Hill Dr

Hill Dr

Chapin Falls Ln
Misty Hllw

Buckeye Tr

Kimberly Dr
Gildersleeve Dr
Springer Ct
N Springer Dr
Gildersleeve Cir
7800
KIRTLAND CEM

6
CHARDON RD
38700
7000
Loreto Dr
Florence Dr

Willoughby Hills

Hickory Hill Ct
Rockwood Dr
7400
WILLIAMS CEM
Ledgewood Dr

Killdeer Dr

IH

Blueberry Dr
10500
10501

Buckeye Tr
Tibbetts Rd

6 CHARDON RD
7900

Angela Dr

Kimberly Dr
Beechwood Dr
Parkwood Dr
Elmwood Dr
10700
Oakwood Dr
Crestwood Dr

Kirtland

Chimney Ridge Tr
Sherbrooke Valley Ct
WORRELL RD
2900
Buckeye Tr
Mill Gate Dr
Rogers Rd
Kelsey Ct

Hidden Valley Dr
1600

Monterey Dr

SEE 2501 MAP

0   0.25   0.5 Miles
1 in. = 2000 ft.

MAP 2377

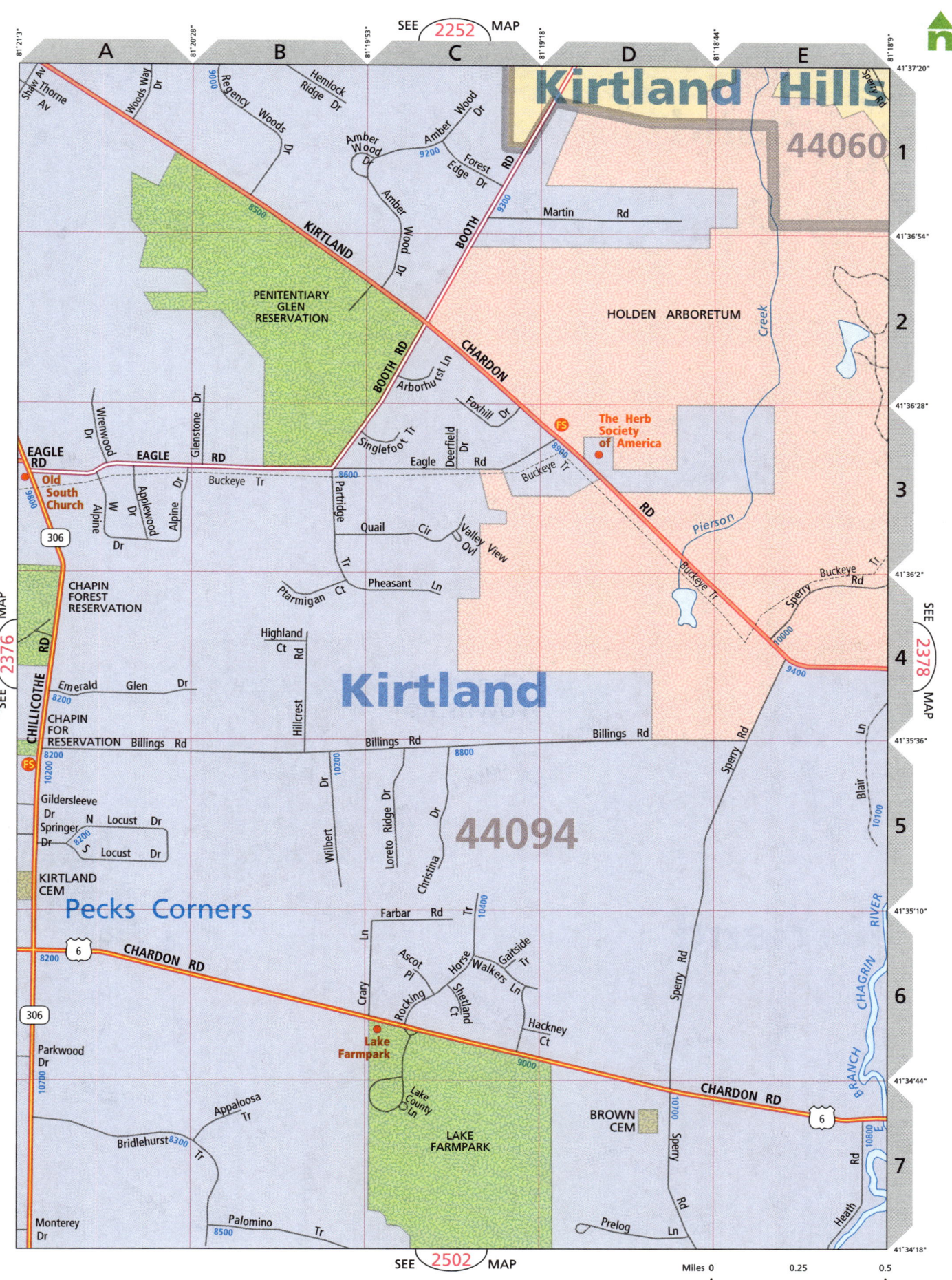

SEE 2252 MAP

SEE 2376 MAP

SEE 2378 MAP

SEE 2502 MAP

Kirtland Hills

44060

Kirtland

44094

Pecks Corners

HOLDEN ARBORETUM

PENITENTIARY GLEN RESERVATION

CHAPIN FOREST RESERVATION

CHAPIN FOR RESERVATION

KIRTLAND CEM

The Herb Society of America

Lake Farmpark

LAKE FARMPARK

BROWN CEM

Old South Church

Miles 0   0.25   0.5

1 in. = 2000 ft.

MAP 2378

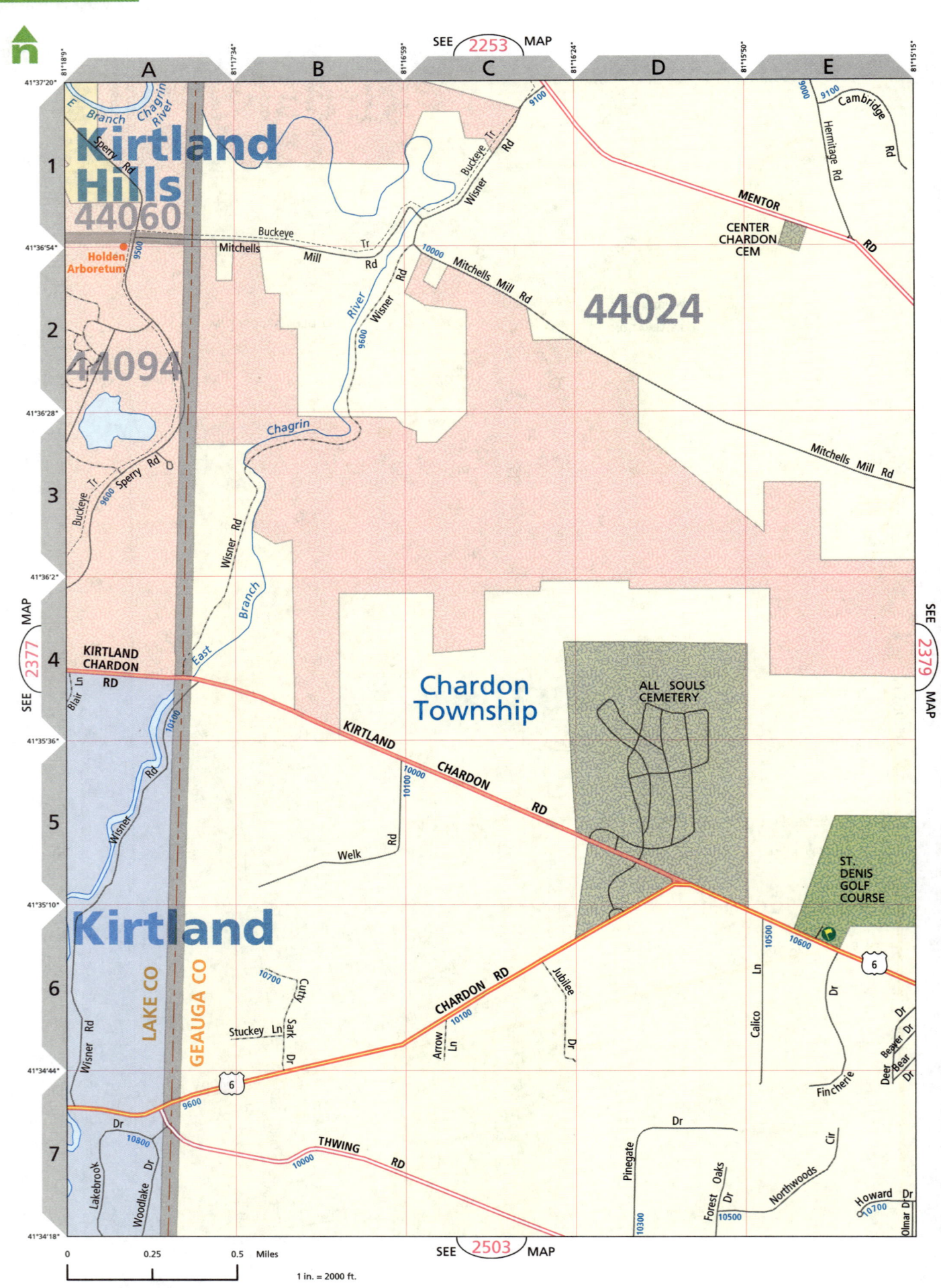

SEE 2253 MAP

A   B   C   D   E

Kirtland
Hills
44060

E Branch Chagrin River

Sperry Rd

9500

Holden
Arboretum

Buckeye Tr

Mitchells Mill Rd

Wisner Rd

River

Chagrin

9600

44094

Buckeye Tr

9600 Sperry Rd

Wisner Rd

East Branch

9100

Wisner Rd

Buckeye Tr Rd

10000

Mitchells Mill Rd

9000 9100

Cambridge Rd

Hermitage Rd

MENTOR RD

CENTER
CHARDON
CEM

44024

Mitchells Mill Rd

SEE 2377 MAP

KIRTLAND
CHARDON
RD

Blair Ln

Wisner Rd

10100

Chardon
Township

KIRTLAND   CHARDON   RD

10000

10100

ALL SOULS
CEMETERY

ST.
DENIS
GOLF
COURSE

SEE 2379 MAP

Kirtland

LAKE CO   GEAUGA CO

Wisner Rd

Welk Rd

10700

Cutty

Sark

Dr

Stuckey Ln

Dr
10800

Lakebrook Dr

Woodlake Dr

6

9600

CHARDON RD

10100

Arrow Ln

Jubilee

Dr

Dr

THWING RD

10000

Pinegate

10300

Dr

Forest Oaks Dr

10500

Northwoods Cir

Calico Ln

10500

10600

Dr

Fincherie

Deer Dr

Beaver Dr

Bear Dr

6

Howard Dr

10700

Olmar Dr

0   0.25   0.5   Miles

1 in. = 2000 ft.

SEE 2503 MAP

41°37'20"
41°36'54"
41°36'28"
41°36'2"
41°35'36"
41°35'10"
41°34'44"
41°34'18"

81°18'9"
81°17'34"
81°16'59"
81°16'24"
81°15'50"
81°15'15"

MAP 2379

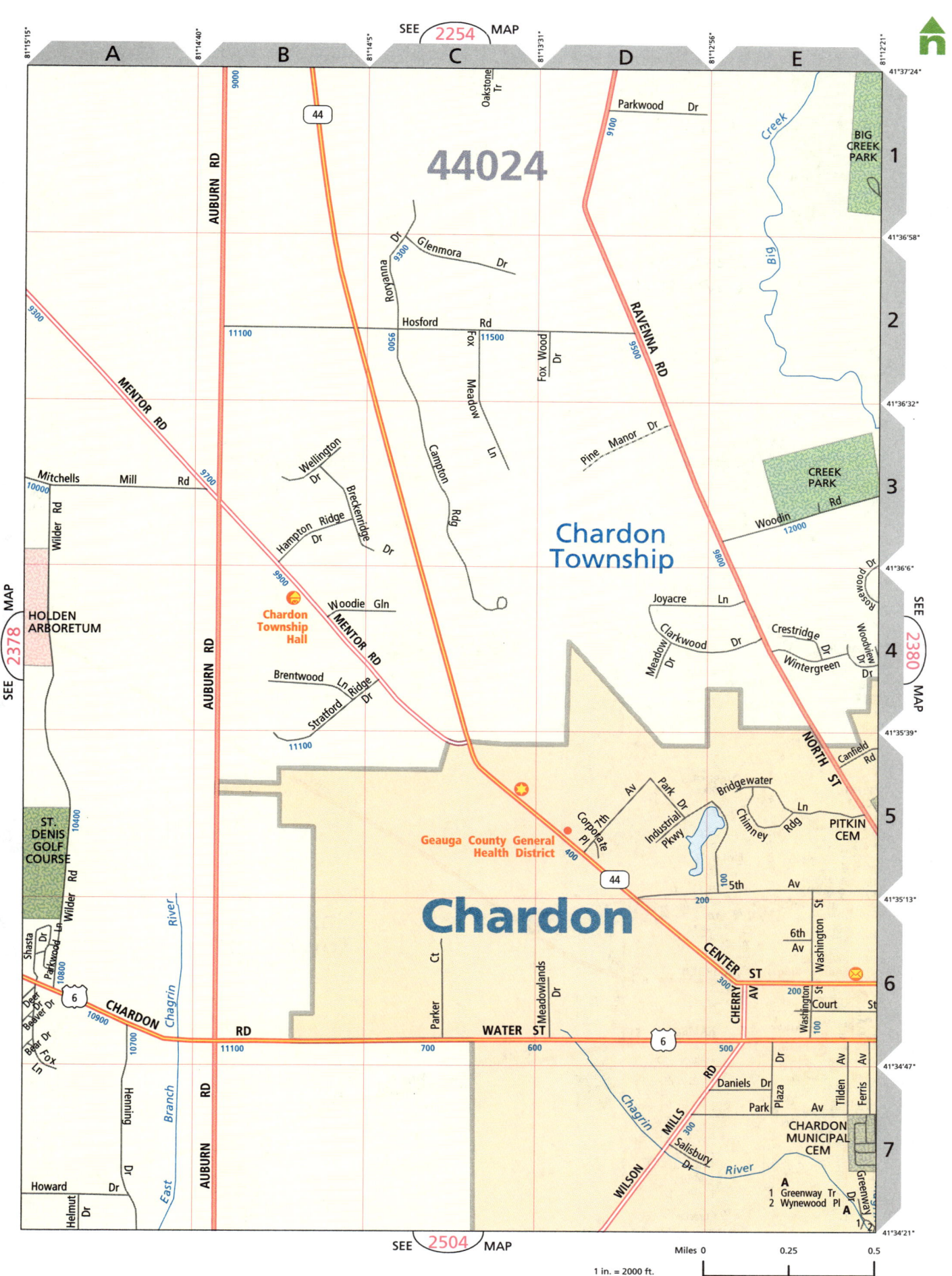

SEE 2254 MAP

44024

Chardon
Township

Chardon

BIG CREEK PARK

CREEK PARK

PITKIN CEM

CHARDON MUNICIPAL CEM

HOLDEN ARBORETUM

ST. DENIS GOLF COURSE

Chardon Township Hall

Geauga County General Health District

SEE 2378 MAP

SEE 2380 MAP

SEE 2504 MAP

Miles 0   0.25   0.5

1 in. = 2000 ft.

1 Greenway Tr
2 Wynewood Pl

MAP 2380

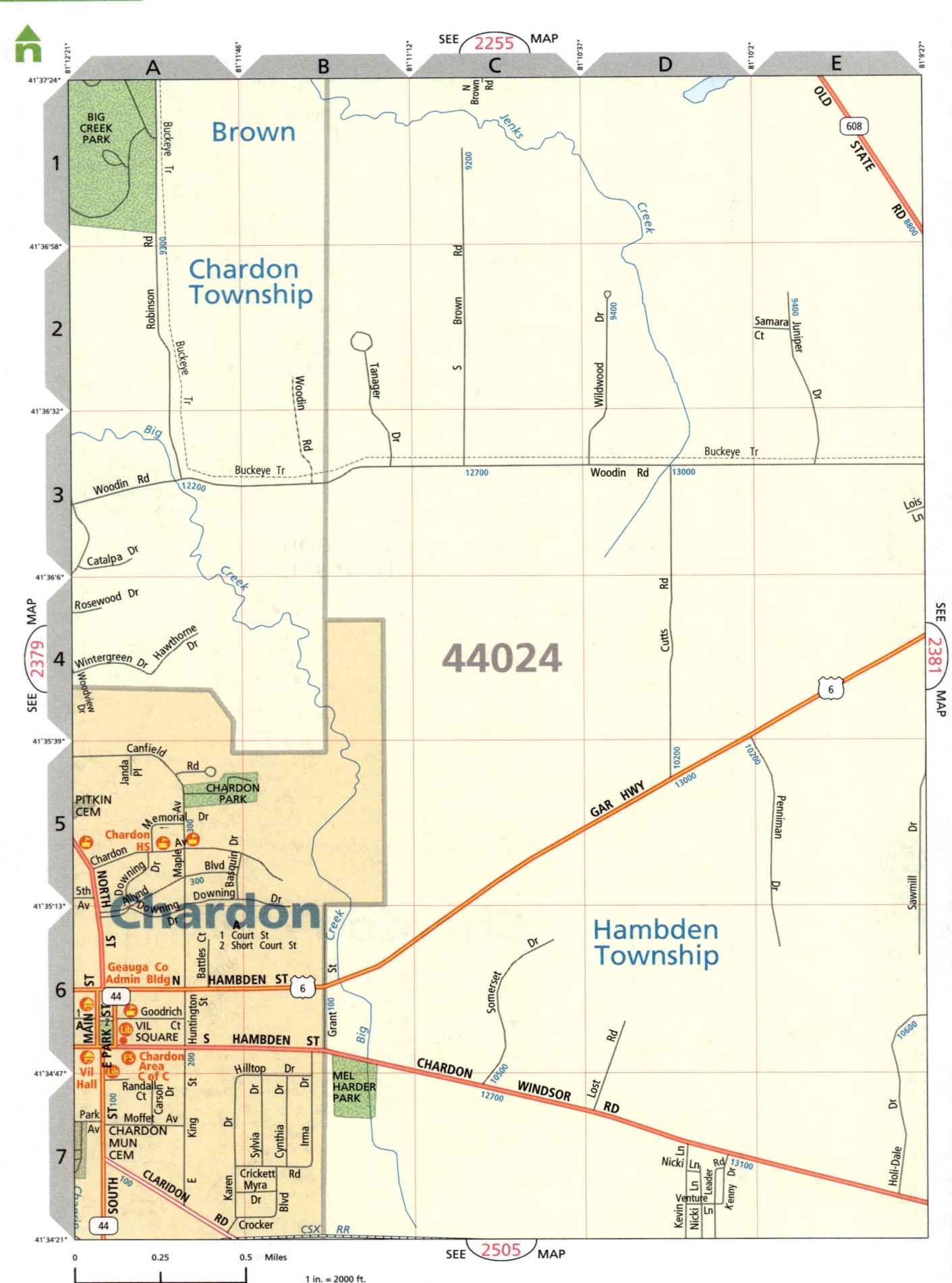

N

A B C D E

SEE 2255 MAP

81°12'21" 81°11'46" 81°11'12" 81°10'37" 81°10'2" 81°9'27"

41°37'24"

Big Creek Park

Brown

Chardon Township

OLD STATE RD

608

8800

1

41°36'58"

Robinson Rd

Buckeye Tr

9300

Brown Rd

Jenks Creek

9200

Chardon Township

Wildwood Dr

9400

Samara Ct

Juniper Dr

9400

2

41°36'32"

Buckeye Tr

Woodin Rd

Big Creek

Tanager Dr

S Brown Rd

3

41°36'6"

Woodin Rd

12200

Buckeye Tr

12700

Woodin Rd

13000

Lois Ln

Catalpa Dr

Creek

Cutts Rd

44024

SEE 2379 MAP

4

41°35'39"

Rosewood Dr

Hawthorne Dr

Wintergreen Dr

Woodview Dr

6

13000

10200

SEE 2381 MAP

Penniman Dr

Sawmill Rd

5

Janda Pl

Canfield Rd

Chardon Park

PITKIN CEM

Memorial Av

Chardon HS

Maple Av

Chardon Dr

Downing Dr

Allyng Dr

300

Blvd

Basquin Dr

Downing Dr

10200

13000

GAR HWY

Hambden Township

6

41°35'13"

Chardon

North St

Downing

A

1 Court St
2 Short Court St

Battles Ct

Creek St

Somerset Dr

Lost Rd

Rd

41°35'39"

Geauga Co Admin Bldg

N

HAMBDEN ST

6

Grant St

100

44

Main St

E Park St

Goodrich

VIL SQUARE

Lib

Huntington St

S HAMBDEN ST

Big Creek

10500

10600

6

41°34'47"

Vil Hall

Lib

Chardon Area C of C

FS

Randall Ct

Carson Dr

King St

Hilltop Dr

Dr

Dr

CHARDON WINDSOR RD

12700

10500

Lost Rd

7

Park Av

Moffet Av

CHARDON MUN CEM

E

Sylvia Dr

Cynthia Dr

Irma Dr

MEL HARDER PARK

Nicki Ln

Leader Rd

Kenny Dr

13100

Holi-Dale Dr

South St

100

CLARIDON RD

Crickett Dr

Myra Blvd

Karen Dr

Crocker Rd

Kevin Ln

Nicki Ln

Venture Ln

44

CSX RR

41°34'21"

SEE 2505 MAP

0   0.25   0.5 Miles

1 in. = 2000 ft.

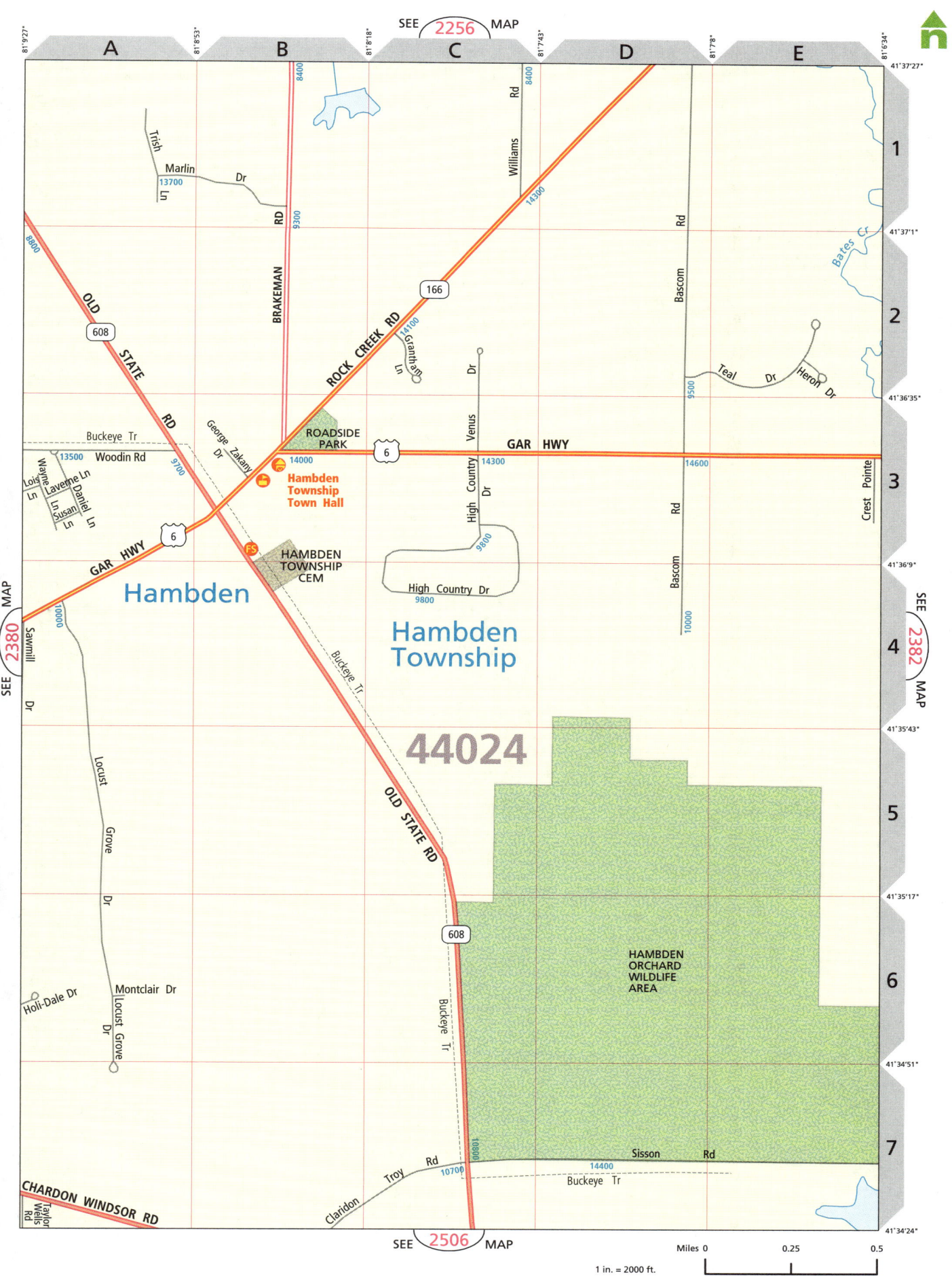

MAP 2381

SEE 2256 MAP

A   B   C   D   E

1

2

3

4

5

6

7

Trish

Marlin   Dr
13700
Ln

BRAKEMAN   RD
8400
9300

Williams   Rd
8400

OLD   STATE   RD
608
8800

166

14300

ROCK CREEK RD
14100
Grantham   Ln

Bascom   Rd
9500

Teal   Dr   Heron Dr

Bates Cr

Buckeye Tr
13500
Wayne   Woodin Rd
9700
George Zakany Dr
ROADSIDE PARK
14000
US 6
Venus Dr
GAR   HWY
High Country Dr   14300
14600
Crest Pointe

Lois   Laverne Ln   Daniel Ln
Ln   Susan Ln

Hambden
Township
Town Hall

Hambden

GAR   HWY
6
10000

FS
HAMBDEN TOWNSHIP CEM

High Country Dr
9800

High Country Dr
9800

Bascom   Rd
10000

Sawmill   Dr

Hambden
Township

44024

Buckeye Tr

Locust   Grove   Dr

OLD STATE RD

608

HAMBDEN
ORCHARD
WILDLIFE
AREA

Holi-Dale Dr   Montclair Dr
Locust Grove Dr

Buckeye Tr
10800

Sisson   Rd
14400
Buckeye Tr

CHARDON WINDSOR RD
Taylor Wells Rd

Troy   Rd
10700
Claridon

SEE 2506 MAP

SEE 2380 MAP

SEE 2382 MAP

81°9'27"   81°8'53"   81°8'18"   81°7'43"   81°7'8"   81°6'34"

41°37'27"
41°37'1"
41°36'35"
41°36'9"
41°35'43"
41°35'17"
41°34'51"
41°34'24"

Miles 0   0.25   0.5

1 in. = 2000 ft.

MAP 2382

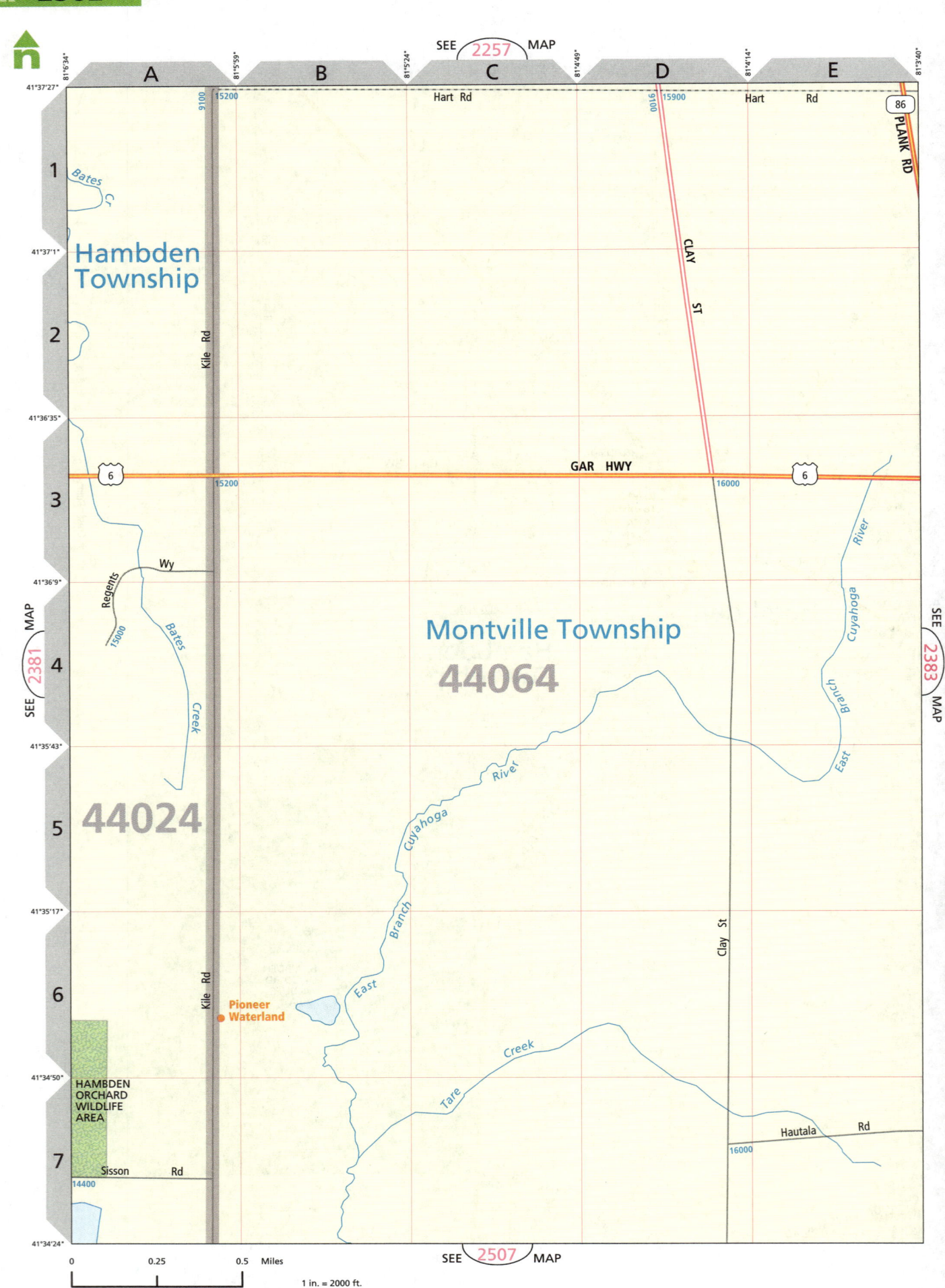

SEE 2257 MAP

A · B · C · D · E

Hart Rd · Hart Rd

Hambden Township

Kile Rd

CLAY ST

PLANK RD
86

GAR HWY
6 · 6

Wy

Regents

Bates Creek

Montville Township

44064

Cuyahoga River

East Branch

SEE 2381 MAP

SEE 2383 MAP

44024

Cuyahoga River

East Branch

Clay St

Kile Rd

Pioneer Waterland

Creek

Tare

HAMBDEN ORCHARD WILDLIFE AREA

Hautala Rd

Sisson Rd

SEE 2507 MAP

0 · 0.25 · 0.5 Miles

1 in. = 2000 ft.

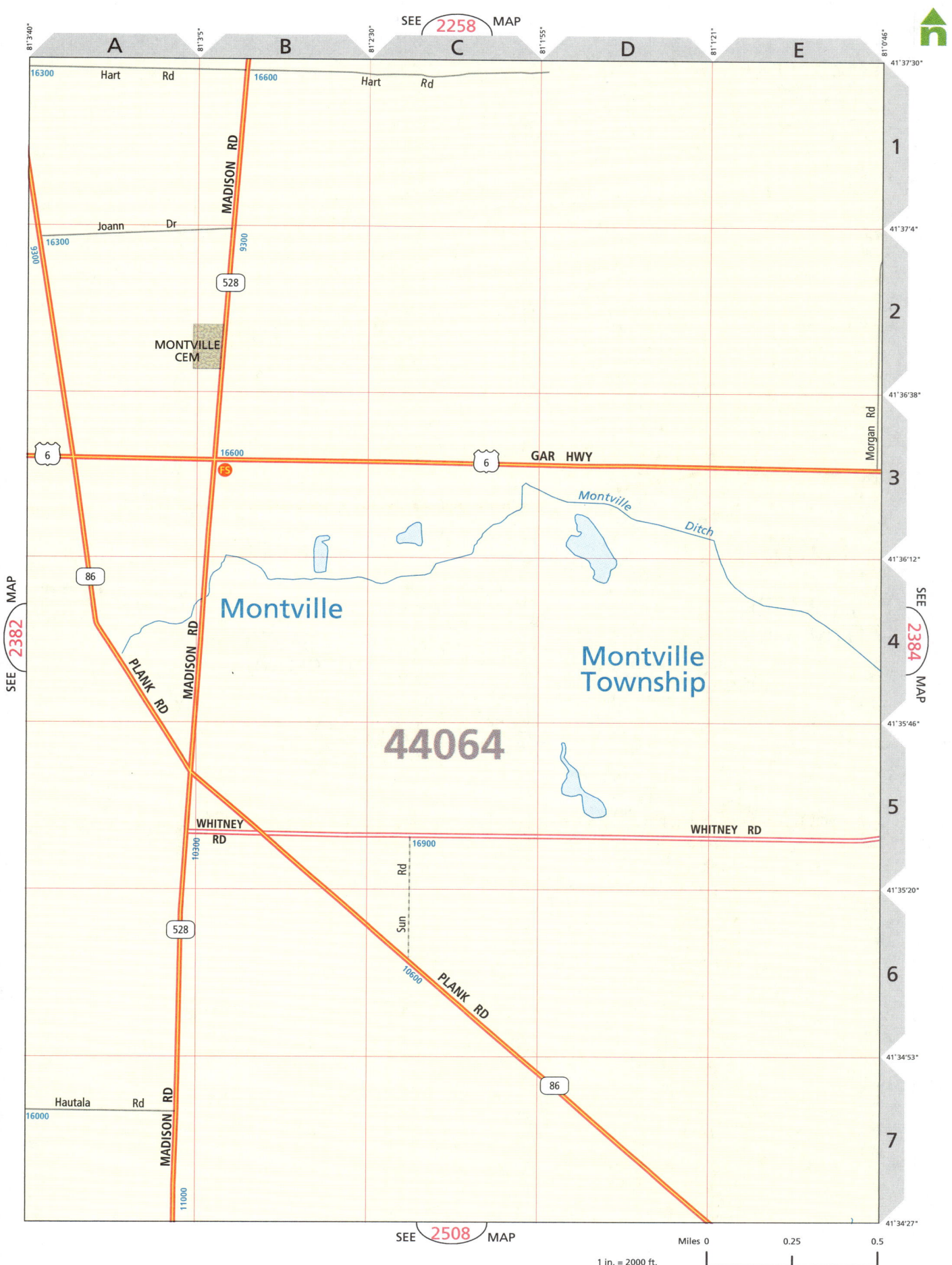

MAP 2383

SEE 2258 MAP

A   B   C   D   E

81'3'40"   81'3'5"   81'2'30"   81'1'55"   81'1'21"   81'0'46"

41'37'30"

16300   Hart   Rd   16600   Hart   Rd

MADISON RD

1

Joann   Dr   41'37'4"

9300   16300   9300

528

2

MONTVILLE
CEM   41'36'38"

6   16600   6   GAR   HWY

FS   41'36'12"

Montville
Ditch

86

Montville   41'36'12"

SEE 2382 MAP

PLANK RD   MADISON RD   Montville
Township   SEE 2384 MAP

4

44064   41'35'46"

5

WHITNEY
RD   WHITNEY   RD

10300   16900

528   41'35'20"

Sun   Rd

6

10600   PLANK   RD

41'34'53"

86

Hautala   Rd

MADISON RD   7

16000

41'34'27"

11000

SEE 2508 MAP

Miles 0   0.25   0.5

1 in. = 2000 ft.

MAP 2384-2486

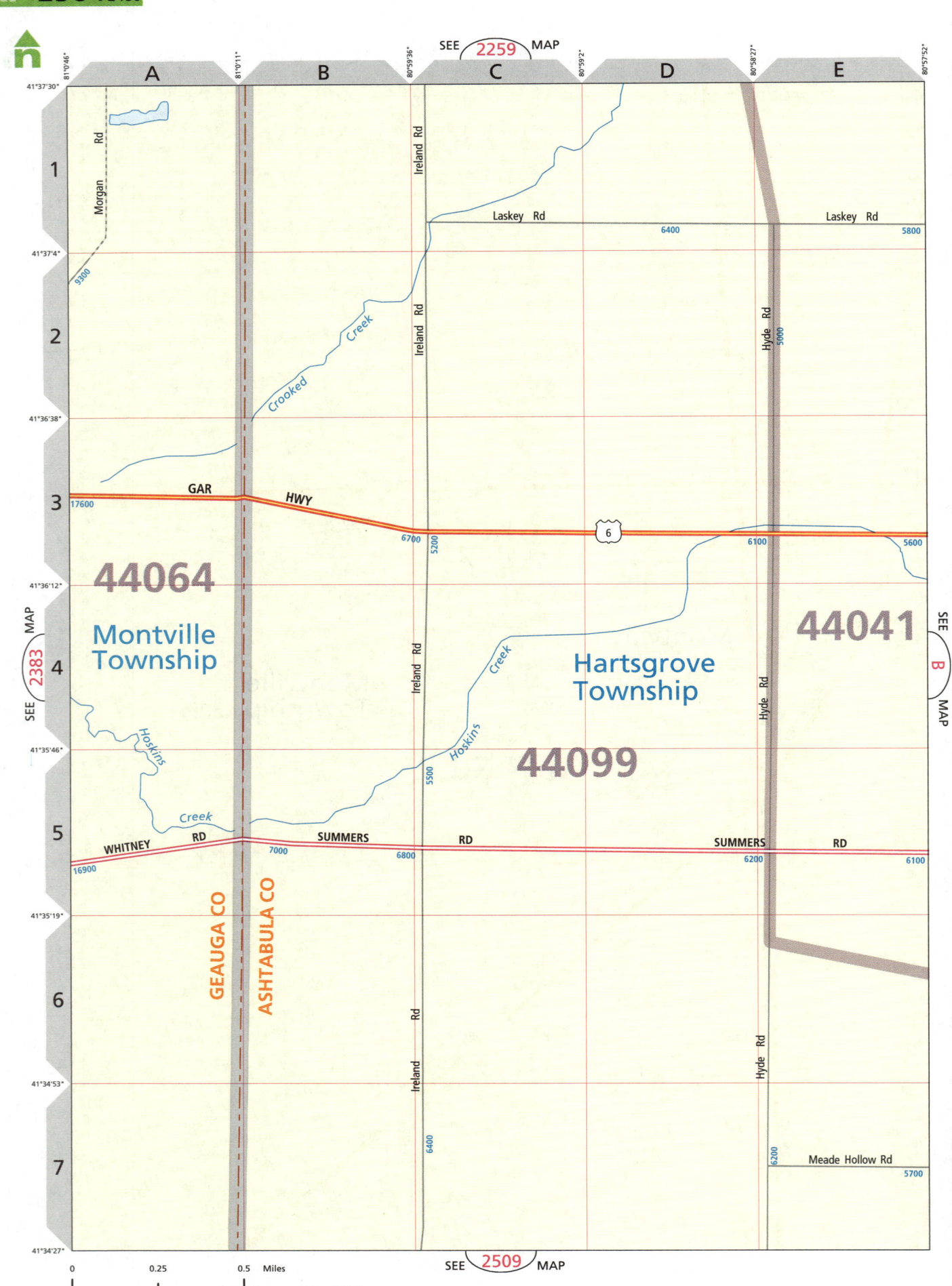

SEE 2259 MAP

A 81°0'46" B 80°59'36" C 80°59'2" D 80°58'27" E 80°57'52"

41°37'30"

1

Morgan Rd

9300

41°37'4"

Ireland Rd

Laskey Rd

Laskey Rd

6400

5800

2

Crooked Creek

Ireland Rd

Hyde Rd

5000

41°36'38"

3

GAR HWY

17600

6700

5200

6

6100

5600

41°36'12"

44064

Montville Township

44041

4

Ireland Rd

Creek

Hartsgrove Township

Hyde Rd

Hoskins

44099

41°35'46"

Hoskins

5500

Creek

5

WHITNEY RD

SUMMERS RD

SUMMERS RD

16900

7000

6800

6200

6100

41°35'19"

GEAUGA CO ASHTABULA CO

6

Ireland Rd

Hyde Rd

41°34'53"

7

Ireland Rd

6400

6200

Meade Hollow Rd

5700

41°34'27"

SEE 2509 MAP

0   0.25   0.5 Miles

1 in. = 2000 ft.

MAP 2487

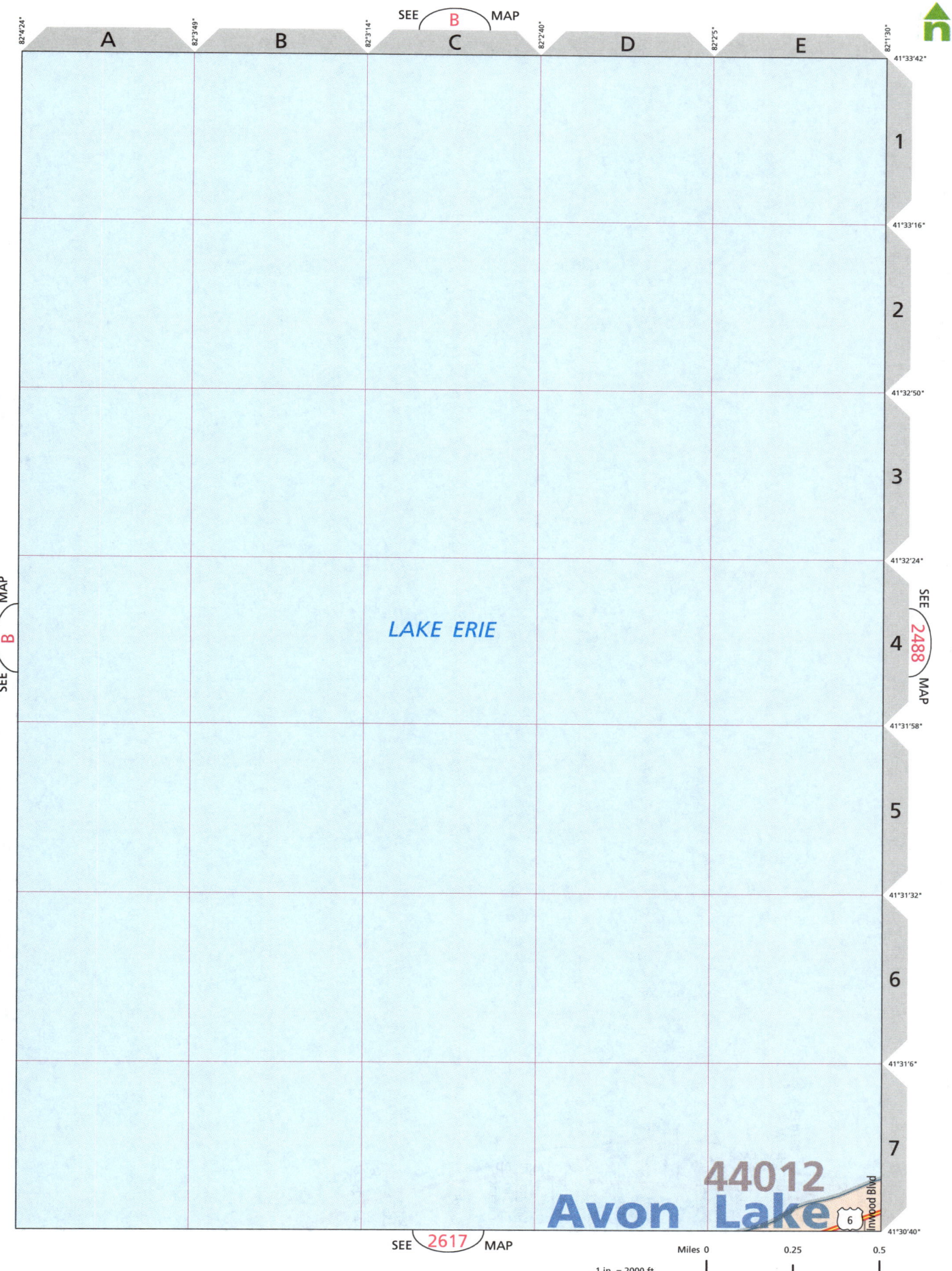

SEE B MAP

| A | B | C | D | E |

82°4'24" 82°3'49" 82°3'14" 82°2'40" 82°2'5" 82°1'30"

41°33'42"

1

41°33'16"

2

41°32'50"

3

41°32'24"

SEE B MAP

LAKE ERIE

SEE 2488 MAP

4

41°31'58"

5

41°31'32"

6

41°31'6"

7

41°30'40"

44012
Avon Lake
Inwood Blvd
6

SEE 2617 MAP

Miles 0   0.25   0.5

1 in. = 2000 ft.

MAP 2488-2494

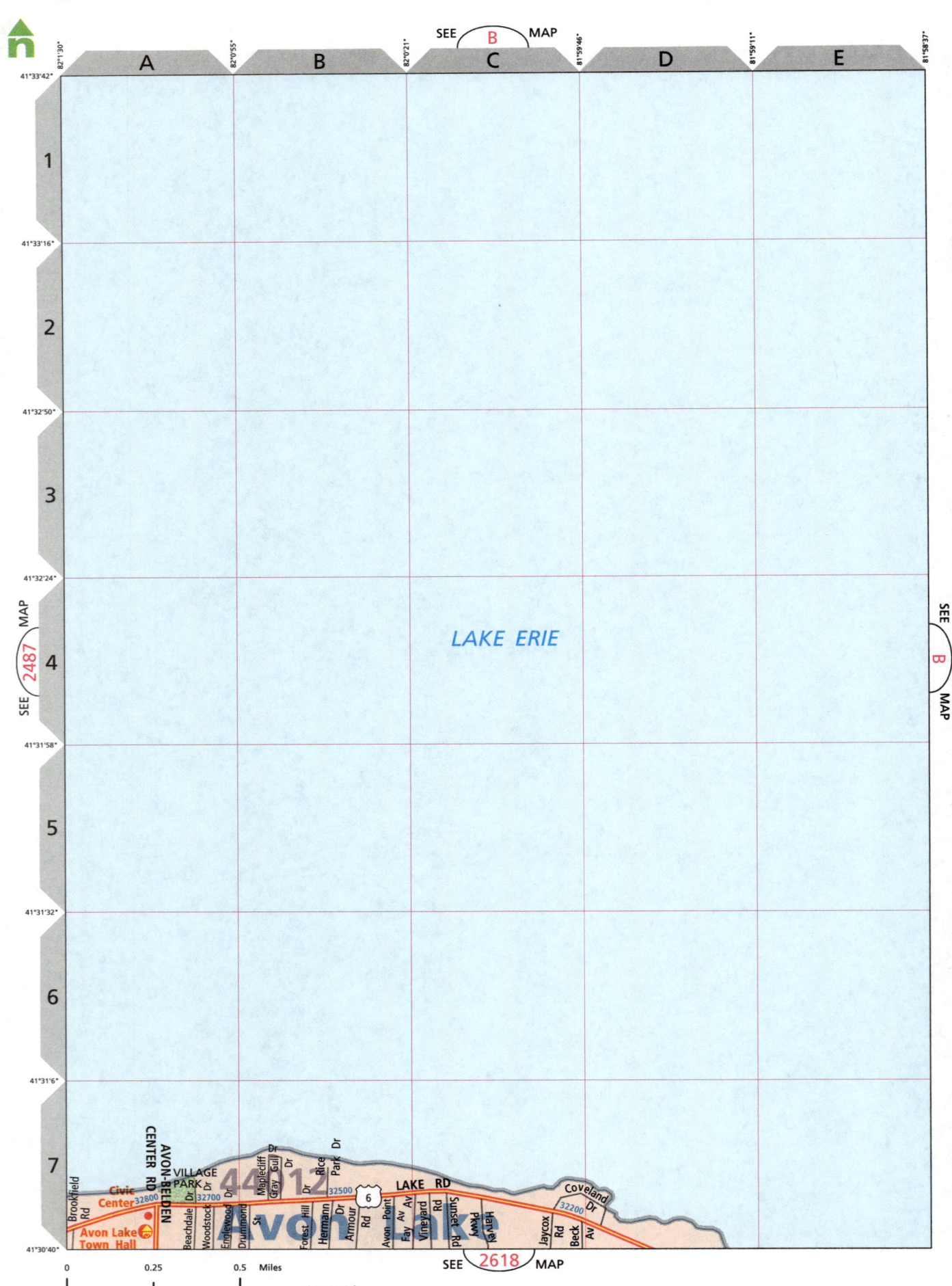

SEE B MAP

A 82°1'30"   82°0'55"   B   82°0'21"   C   81°59'46"   D   81°59'11"   E 81°58'37"

41°33'42"

1

41°33'16"

2

41°32'50"

3

41°32'24"

SEE 2487 MAP

4

LAKE ERIE

SEE B MAP

41°31'58"

5

41°31'32"

6

41°31'6"

7

Brookfield Rd   Civic Center   32800   AVON-BELDEN CENTER RD   VILLAGE PARK   Beachdale Dr   Woodstock   Englewood Dr   32700   Drummond   Maplecliff   Gray St   Gull Dr   Dr   Rice Dr   Park Dr   32500   44012   LAKE RD   6   Forest Hill   Hermann Dr   Armour Rd   Avon Point Av   Fay Av   Vineyard Rd   Sunset   Harvey Pkwy   Rd   Coveland Dr   32200   Jaycox Rd   Beck Av

Avon Lake Town Hall

Avon Lake

41°30'40"

SEE 2618 MAP

0   0.25   0.5   Miles

1 in. = 2000 ft.

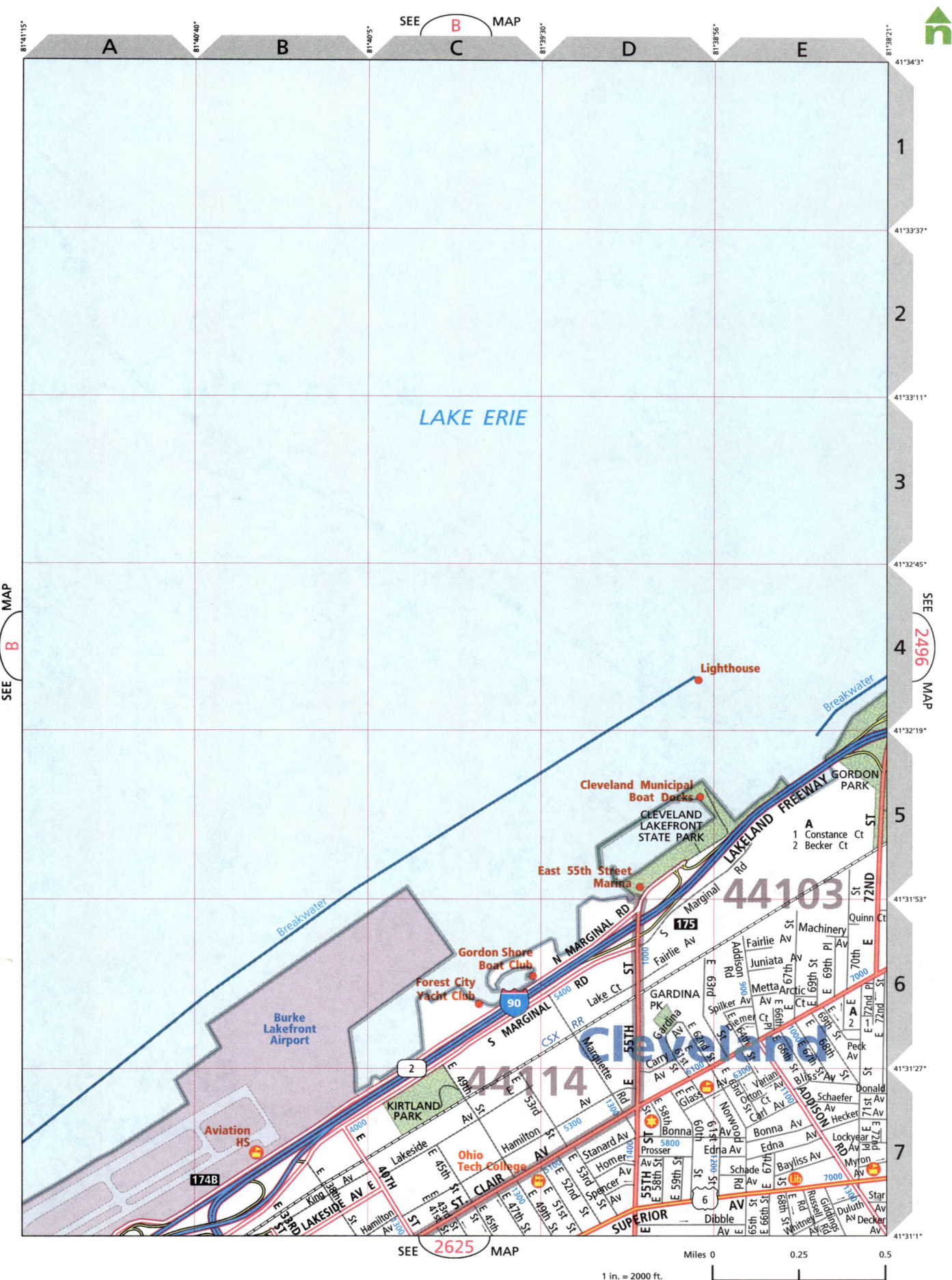

MAP 2495

A   B   C   D   E

SEE B MAP

81°41′15″   81°40′40″   81°40′5″   81°39′30″   81°38′56″   81°38′21″

41°34′3″

1

41°33′37″

2

LAKE ERIE

41°33′11″

3

41°32′45″

SEE 2496 MAP

4

Lighthouse

Breakwater

41°32′19″

Cleveland Municipal Boat Docks

CLEVELAND LAKEFRONT STATE PARK

LAKELAND FREEWAY   GORDON PARK

E 72ND ST

A
1 Constance Ct
2 Becker Ct

5

East 55th Street Marina

Marginal Rd

44103

Quinn Ct

41°31′53″

Breakwater

N MARGINAL RD

175

Fairlie Av   Machinery Av

Fairlie Av

Addison Rd   Juniata Av

E 63rd St   E 67th Av   E 69th Pl   E 69th St   E 70th St

S Marginal Rd

Gordon Shore Boat Club

Forest City Yacht Club

I-90   5400   Lake Ct

GARDINA PK

Gardina

Spilker Av   Metta Av   Arctic Av   E 72nd St

A
2

6

Burke Lakefront Airport

S MARGINAL RD

CSX RR

Cleveland

Marquette Av

Carry St   E 63rd St   Bliss Av   Peck Av

41°31′27″

2

44114

Glass Av   Varian Av   Otton Ct   Carl Av   E 67th St   E 71st Av   Donald Av   Schaefer Av

E 49th St   E 53rd St

Hamilton Av

Bonna Av   Norwood   Bonna Av   Hecker Av   Lockyear Av   Myron Av

KIRTLAND PARK

E 58th St   E 60th   E 61st St   Edna Av   Edna

E 65th   E 67th St   E 71st

Prosser

Aviation HS

Lakeside   Av

Ohio Tech College

E 45th St   E 52nd St   Homer Av   Spencer Av

Schade Av   Russell Rd   Bayliss Av   Duluth Av

7

King Av   E 48th St

Lakeside Av

Hamilton   E 47th   E 49th St   Stanard Av

5300   E 53rd St

E 55TH ST   E 59th Av

6

Schade   E 67th St   Giddings Rd   Whitney Av   Decker Av

174B

E 33RD   E 38th   LAKESIDE AVE   40TH   ST

Hamilton Av   E 45th St

ST CLAIR   AV

SUPERIOR   AV

Dibble   E 65th   Russell Rd   Star Av

41°31′1″

SEE 2625 MAP

Miles 0   0.25   0.5

1 in. = 2000 ft.

MAP 2496

MAP 2497

SEE 2372 MAP
SEE 2496 MAP
SEE 2498 MAP
SEE 2627 MAP

Miles 0   0.25   0.5

1 in. = 2000 ft.

MAP 2498

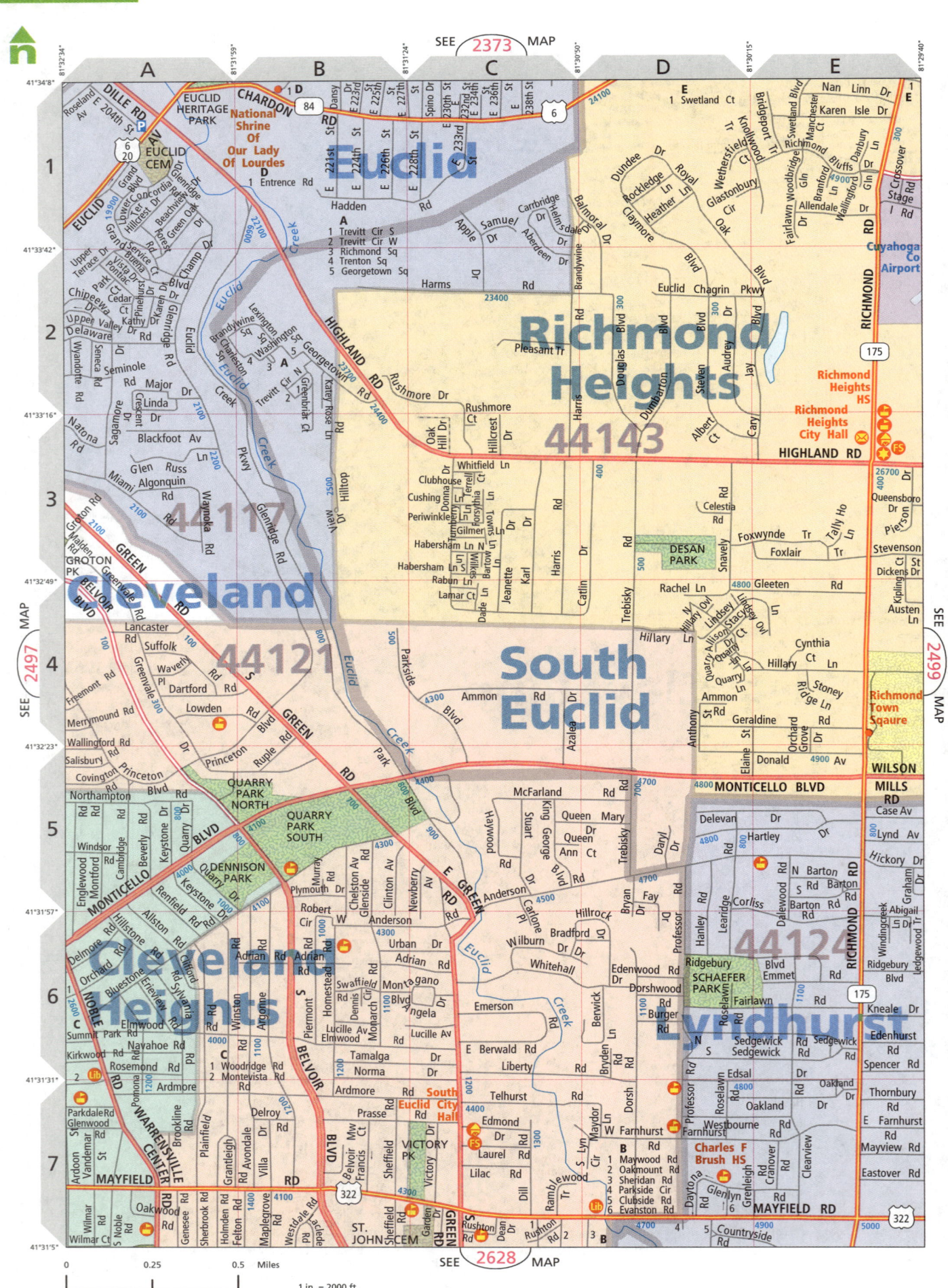

SEE 2373 MAP

SEE 2497 MAP

SEE 2499 MAP

SEE 2628 MAP

Euclid

Richmond Heights
44143

Cleveland
44117

South Euclid
44121

Cleveland Heights

Mayfield

Lyndhurst
44124

0   0.25   0.5 Miles

1 in. = 2000 ft.

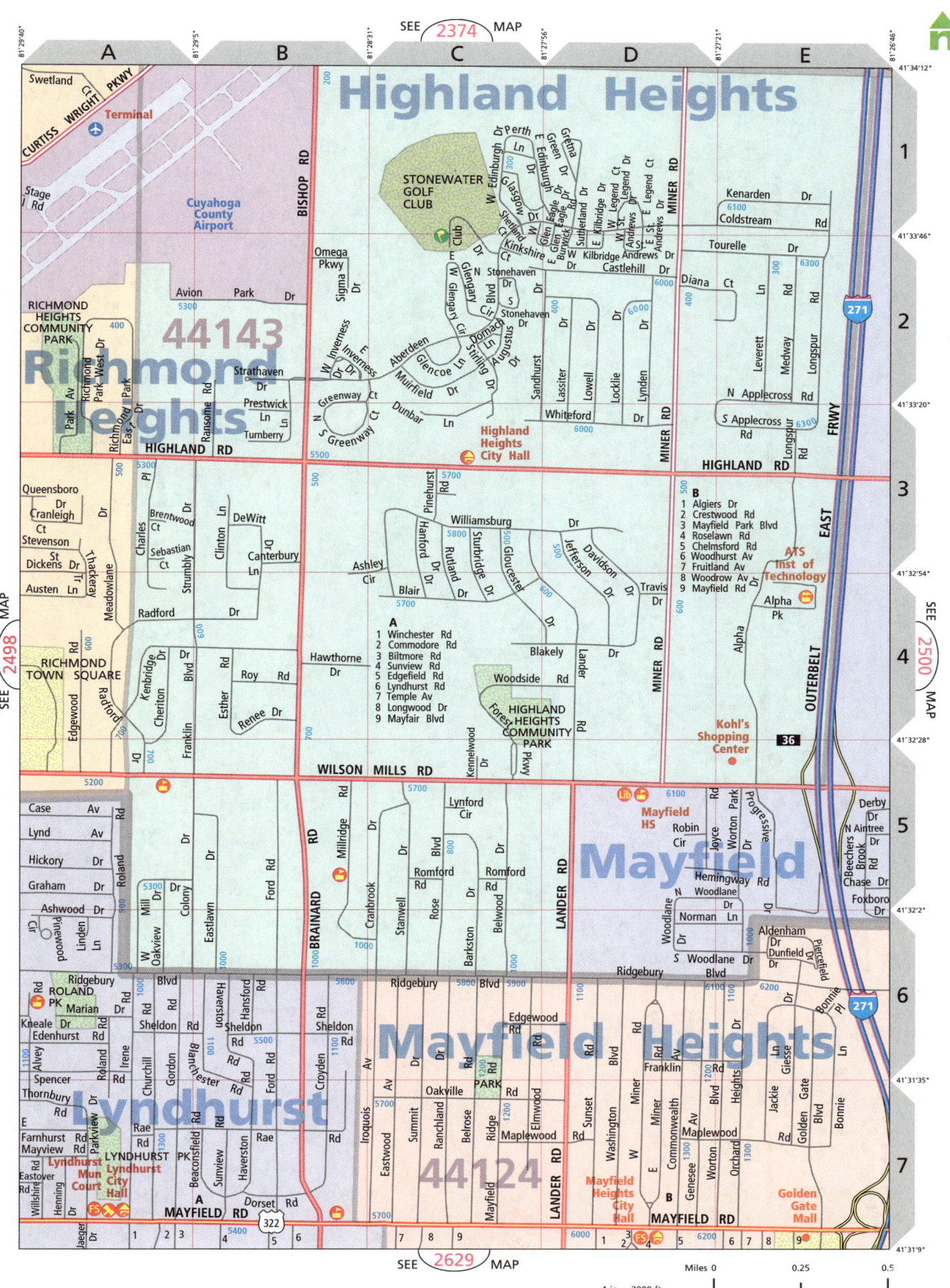

MAP 2499

SEE 2374 MAP

SEE 2498 MAP

SEE 2500 MAP

SEE 2629 MAP

Highland Heights

STONEWATER GOLF CLUB

RICHMOND HEIGHTS COMMUNITY PARK

44143

Richmond Heights

Cuyahoga County Airport

Terminal

Highland Heights City Hall

HIGHLAND RD

RICHMOND TOWN SQUARE

A
1 Winchester Rd
2 Commodore Rd
3 Biltmore Rd
4 Sunview Rd
5 Edgefield Rd
6 Lyndhurst Rd
7 Temple Av
8 Longwood Rd
9 Mayfair Blvd

B
1 Algiers Dr
2 Crestwood Rd
3 Mayfield Park Blvd
4 Roselawn Rd
5 Chelmsford Rd
6 Woodhurst Dr
7 Fruitland Av
8 Woodrow Av
9 Mayfield Rd

ATS Inst of Technology

Alpha Pk

HIGHLAND COMMUNITY PARK

WILSON MILLS RD

Kohl's Shopping Center

Mayfield HS

Mayfield

Lib

Mayfield Heights

Lyndhurst

Lyndhurst Mun Court

Lyndhurst City Hall

ROLAND PK

Ridgebury

44124

Mayfield Heights City Hall

Golden Gate Mall

MAYFIELD RD

322

1 in. = 2000 ft.

Miles 0   0.25   0.5

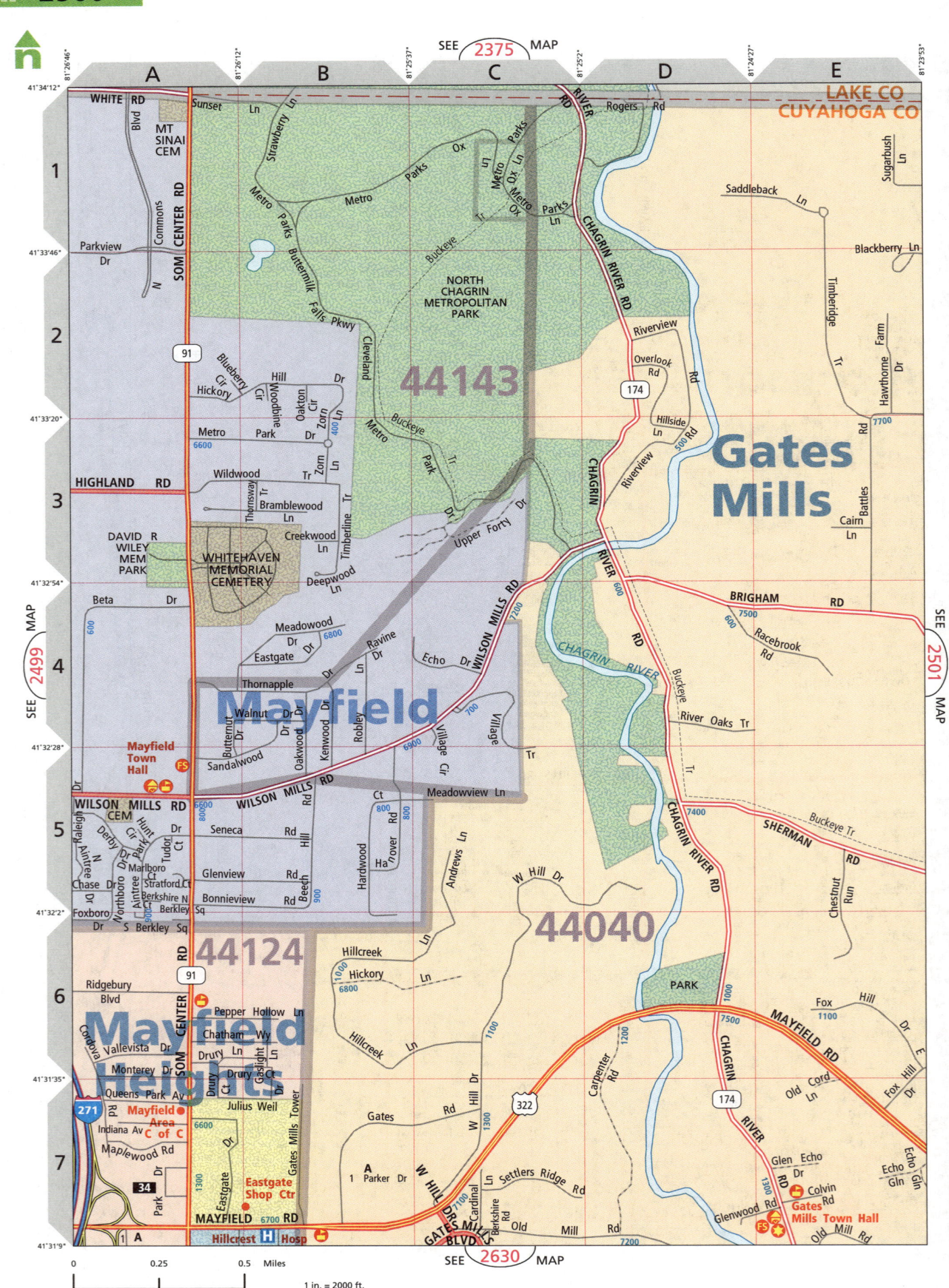

MAP 2500

SEE 2375 MAP

LAKE CO
CUYAHOGA CO

WHITE RD

MT SINAI CEM

SOM CENTER RD

Sunset Ln

Strawberry Ln

Metro Parks

Ox

Metro Ox Ln

Parks Ln

Rogers Rd

CHAGRIN RIVER RD

Saddleback Ln

Sugarbush Ln

Blackberry Ln

Parkview Dr

Commons N

Metro Parks

Buttermilk Falls Pkwy

Buckeye

NORTH CHAGRIN METROPOLITAN PARK

44143

Riverview

Overlook Rd

174

Hillside Ln

Riverview Rd

Timberidge Tr

Hawthorne Farm Dr

Blueberry Cir

Hill Dr

Hickory Cir

Woodbine

Oakton Cir

Zorn 400

Metro Park 6600

Zorn Ln

CHAGRIN RIVER RD

500 Rd

Riverview

Gates Mills

Battles

Cairn Ln

7700

HIGHLAND RD

Wildwood

Thornsway Tr

Bramblewood Ln

Creekwood Ln

Timberline Tr

Zorn Tr

Buckeye Park Tr

Metro

Upper Forty Dr

CHAGRIN RIVER RD

600

CHAGRIN RIVER

BRIGHAM RD
7500

Racebrook Rd
600

DAVID R WILEY MEM PARK

WHITEHAVEN MEMORIAL CEMETERY

Deepwood Ln

Beta Dr

600

Meadowood Dr 6800

Eastgate Dr

Ravine Dr

Echo Dr

WILSON MILLS RD
7200

Buckeye Tr

River Oaks Tr

SEE 2501 MAP

Thornapple

Mayfield

Walnut Dr

Butternut Dr

Oakwood

Kenwood

Robley

Village

700

Village Cir

800

Meadowview Ln

SEE 2499 MAP

Mayfield Town Hall FS

Sandalwood

6600

WILSON MILLS RD

6900

Tr

SHERMAN RD

Chestnut Run

7400

WILSON MILLS CEM

Raleigh Dr
Derby Cir
Hunt Dr
Tudor Ct

Aintree N
Marlboro Ct
Aintree Ct
Stratford Ct
Berkshire N

Chase Dr

Northboro Dr

Seneca Rd

Hill Rd

Hardwood

Hoover Rd 800

800

Andrews Ln

W Hill Dr

44040

Glenview Rd

Bonnieview Rd

Beech

900

Foxboro Dr
Berkley Sq
S Berkley Sq

44124

91

SOM CENTER RD

Ridgebury Blvd

Hillcreek Ln
1000
6800

Hickory Ln

Hillcreek Ln

1100

PARK

7500

Fox Hill 1100

MAYFIELD RD

Old Cord Ln

Mayfield Heights

Cordova
Vallevista Dr

Monterey Dr

Queens Park Av

Pepper Hollow Ln

Chatham Wy

Drury Ln

Gaslight Ct

Drury Ct

Gates Mills Tower

W Hill Dr

1300

322

Carpenter Rd
1200

CHAGRIN RIVER RD

174

Fox Hill Dr

Fox Hill E

271

Indiana Av

Mayfield Area C of C

Julius Weil

6600

Gates Rd

W Hill Dr

Glen Echo Dr

Echo Gln

Echo Gln

Maplewood Rd

34

Park Dr

Eastgate

1300

Eastgate Shop Ctr

MAYFIELD RD
6700

A 1 Parker Dr

Settlers Ridge Rd

Old Mill Rd
7200

Cardinal Rd

Berkshire Rd

Old Mill Rd

Glenwood Rd
1300

Colvin Rd

Gates Mills Town Hall FS

Old Mill Rd

1 A

Hillcrest H Hosp

GATES MILLS BLVD

SEE 2630 MAP

0   0.25   0.5   Miles

1 in. = 2000 ft.

MAP 2501

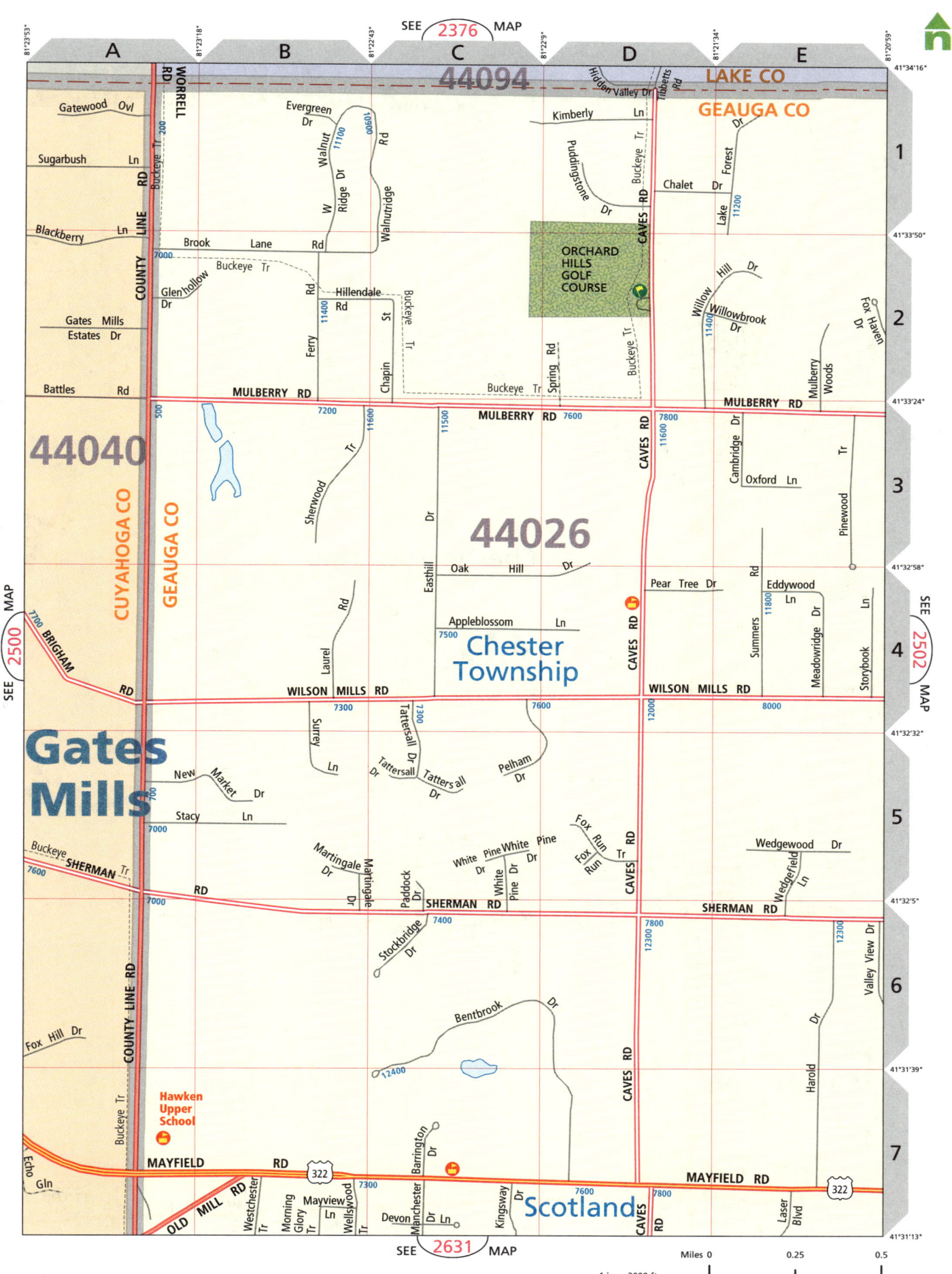

SEE 2376 MAP

44094

Hidden Valley Dr

LAKE CO
GEAUGA CO

A   B   C   D   E

WORRELL RD

Gatewood Ovl
Sugarbush Ln
Blackberry Ln

Buckeye Tr   200

COUNTY LINE   RD

Gates Mills
Estates Dr

Battles Rd

44040

CUYAHOGA CO
GEAUGA CO

SEE 2500 MAP

BRIGHAM   RD
7700

Gates
Mills

COUNTY LINE   RD

Buckeye Tr

Buckeye   SHERMAN   Tr
7600
RD
7000

Fox Hill Dr

Echo Gln

Evergreen Dr
W   Walnut   Ridge   Dr   10900   11100
Walnutridge

Brook   Lane   Rd
7000
Glen hollow   Buckeye Tr   Rd
Dr
Hillendale   Rd
11400
Ferry   Rd   Chapin   St   Buckeye   Tr

MULBERRY RD   7200   11600
Sherwood   Tr   11500   MULBERRY RD

Easthill   Dr
Oak   Hill   Dr

Laurel   Rd
Appleblossom   Ln
7500

WILSON MILLS RD
7300   7300   7600
Surrey   Ln   Tattersall Dr   Tatters all   Dr   Pelham   Dr

New   Market   Dr
Stacy   Ln
7000   700

Martingale   Dr   Martingale   Dr   Paddock   Dr   White Pine White   Dr   Pine   Dr
SHERMAN   RD   White   Pine   Dr
7000   7400

Stockbridge   Dr

Bentbrook   Dr
12400

Hawken
Upper
School

Buckeye Tr

MAYFIELD   RD   322
OLD   MILL   RD   Westchester Tr   Morning Glory Tr   Mayview Ln   Wellswood Tr   7300   Manchester Dr   Devon Dr   Ln
Barrington   Dr   Kingsway   Dr

SEE 2631 MAP

Kimberly   Ln
Forest   Dr
Chalet   Dr
Lake   11200

Puddingstone   Dr

CAVES   RD
Buckeye Tr

ORCHARD
HILLS
GOLF
COURSE

Willow   Hill   Dr
Willowbrook   Dr   11400

Fox Haven   Dr

Mulberry   Woods

Spring   Rd
Buckeye   Tr

MULBERRY   RD
7600   7800

CAVES   RD

MULBERRY   RD

Cambridge   Dr
Oxford   Ln   Pinewood   Tr   11600

44026

Pear Tree   Dr
Rd

Eddywood   Ln   11800
Summers   Meadowridge   Dr   Stonybook   Ln

CAVES   RD

Chester
Township

WILSON MILLS RD
12000   8000

Fox   Run   Tr
Fox   Run   CAVES   RD

Wedgewood   Dr
Wedgefield   Ln

SHERMAN   RD   SHERMAN   RD
7800   1300   1300
12300

CAVES   RD

Valley   View   Dr

Harold   Dr

MAYFIELD   RD   322
Scotland   7600   7800   CAVES   RD   Laser   Blvd

SEE 2502 MAP

Miles 0   0.25   0.5

1 in. = 2000 ft.

81°23'53"   81°23'18"   81°22'43"   81°22'9"   81°21'34"   81°20'59"
41°34'16"
41°33'50"
41°33'24"
41°32'58"
41°32'32"
41°32'5"
41°31'39"
41°31'13"

MAP 2502

SEE 2377 MAP

A   B   C   D   E

LAKE CO   44094

GEAUGA CO

Lake Farmpark

Dewey   Rd

Sharp   Ln

8200

1

Kirkwood

Spruce Dr

Cranwood   Dr

8300   8600

11100

Windingbrook

Cliff View Ln

Sperry Rd

Heath Rd

East Branch

2

Fox Haven Dr

Deer Haven Dr

WESTERN RESERVE MEMORIAL GARDENS

11300

Kristine Dr

Spruce Dr

Rust

Peach Tree Dr

Pine Acres Ln

Mulberry Rd

9000

Blackberry Ln

11300

Chagrin

44024

MULBERRY   RD

Mulberry   Rd

8500

8700

Briarwood Rd

Lyman Rd

11600

8300

Mulberry Corners

3

Legend Creek Dr

Clearview

Merrie   Ln

8200

11600

FS

Chester Township

Sperry Rd

Hervie Dr

SEE 2501 MAP

44026

4

WILSON   MILLS   RD

Oakwood Ln

WILSON MILLS RD

Africa Acres Dr

Parker Dr

9000

WILSON MILLS RD

11900 9300

Sandgate Dr

SEE 2503 MAP

Ln

8500

12000

8600

5

Privacy Ln

306

Red Oak Dr

W Shiloh Dr

Bardwell Dr

Shiloh

N Shiloh Dr

Shiloh Dr

E Shiloh Dr

Sperry Rd

Shadow Hill Tr

Woodchuck Hllw

Norton Dr

Whiting Dr

Reserve Ln

CHESTER TOWNSHIP CEM

Chester Center

Sherman Rd

12100

Sherman Rd

8900

Sherman Rd

12300

Sherman Rd

9200

SHERMAN   RD

8500

6

Lincoln Dr

Northward Dr

Falcon Ridge Rd

CHILLICOTHE RD

Pointe

Maple Dr

View Dr

12500

12500

Seminary Ln

Seminary Ln

Parkview Ln

Hovey Dr

Herrick Dr

Barfield

12600

Chesterfield Ln

Sperry Rd

7

Chesterland

Valley

Buckeye

Woodside

Ward

Woodside Dr

CENTER WOODSIDE CEM

CHESTERLAND CITY PK

AAA

?

Chester Township Hall

FS

Parkside Dr

Opalocka Dr

8600

8900

Vincent Dr

322

Cassie Ln

9400

OLD SETTLERS CEM

Lynn Dr

S Woodside Dr

MAYFIELD   RD

Opalocka Dr

SPERRY RD

MAYFIELD   RD

SEE 2632 MAP

0   0.25   0.5   Miles

1 in. = 2000 ft.

41°34'16"

41°33'50"

41°33'24"

41°32'58"

41°32'32"

41°32'5"

41°31'39"

41°31'13"

81°20'59"

81°20'24"

81°19'50"

81°19'15"

81°18'40"

81°18'11"

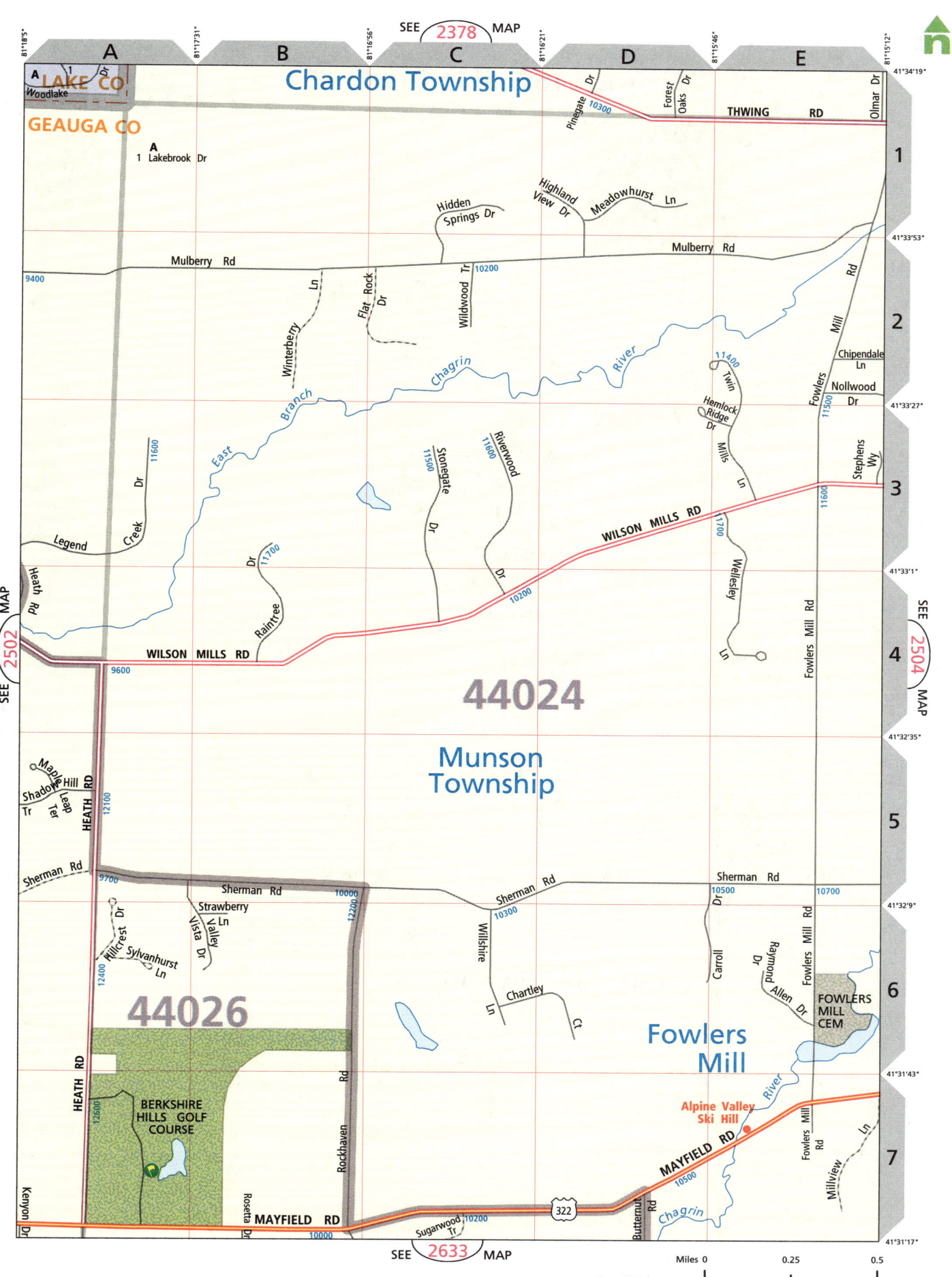

MAP 2503

MAP 2504

SEE 2379 MAP

Chardon Township

Chardon

A | B | C | D | E

Wynewood Pl

Helmut Dr
Henning Dr
THWING RD
Chagrin River
11100
11200
THWING RD

Fowlers Mill Rd

1

East Branch Chagrin

Winchester Dr
Pinehurst Dr

LEGEND LAKE GOLF COURSE

Wilson Mills RD
11600

Dr 11100

CHARDON LAKES GOLF COURSE

AUBURN RD
11100

Tall Pines Dr
11600

Beechnut

Chipendale Ln

2

WOODIEBROOK RD
11400
11300

Clearfield Ln
11800

200

Nollwood Dr

Wexford Dr
Upper Chelsea Dr
11500

WILSON MILLS RD

Linden Way Dr
Gate Post Ln
Boxwood Cir
Orchard Rd

Forest View Dr

WILSON MILLS RD

Lower Chelsea Dr

11200
11500

Wilbert Rd

Parkside

Parkway

Forest Rd
1500
Fenway Dr
Rockside Rd

Dr

Chagrin River

11600

Britton Ln

3

Oriole Pl
Springway Rd
Sycamore Rd
Basswood Rd
Edgewood
Chestnutdale Rd
Maplewood Rd
Overlook Rd

3

Rd

Lake

11400

GEAUGA PARK WILDLIFE PRES

Wood Hollow Dr
Brookside

Sun Ridge Cir

West Bass Lake

Bass Lake Club

East Bass Lake

Summit Rd

4

Burlington Rdg
11900

44024

Lake Rd

SEE 2503 MAP

Glen Dr
Epping Tr

11900

Lake Rd

SEE 2505 MAP

11600

Burlington Dr

River Rd

BASS LAKE

Lake Rd

Quartermane Cir

Pheasant Ct

Munson Township Hall
FS

Falls Rd

Heron Tr

Blue

5

KAWALEC RECREATIONAL FIELDS

River

Sherman Rd

Sherman Rd
11700

Sherman Rd

Sherman Rd
10700

AUBURN RD
12200
11100

Chagrin River

Beaver Creek

Heather Hill Hospital
H

BASS LAKE RD
12200

6

Munson Township

MAYFIELD RD
12500
12500

322

11500 Ashton Tr

Windy Hill Dr
12500
11800

7

Klatka Dr

Gwendolyn Farms Dr

Gray Friar Wy

SEE 2634 MAP

0   0.25   0.5   Miles

1 in. = 2000 ft.

41°34'19"
41°33'53"
41°33'27"
41°33'1"
41°32'35"
41°32'9"
41°31'43"
41°31'17"

81°15'12"
81°14'37"
81°14'2"
81°13'27"
81°12'53"
81°12'18"

MAP 2505

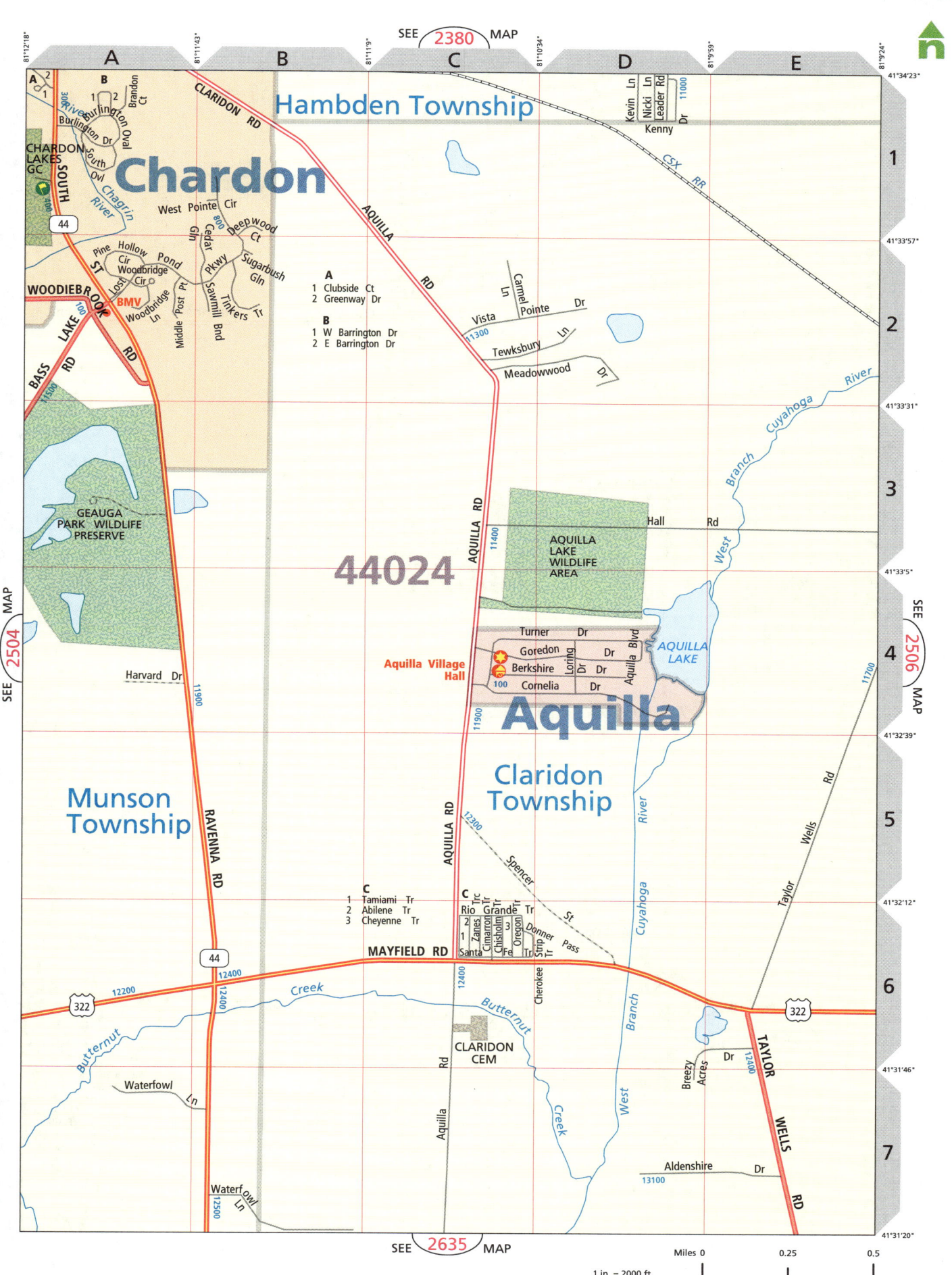

Chardon

Aquilla

44024

Hambden Township

Munson Township

Claridon Township

GEAUGA PARK WILDLIFE PRESERVE

AQUILLA LAKE WILDLIFE AREA

AQUILLA LAKE

CHARDON LAKES GC

Aquilla Village Hall

CLARIDON CEM

A
1 Clubside Ct
2 Greenway Dr

B
1 W Barrington Dr
2 E Barrington Dr

C
1 Tamiami Tr
2 Abilene Tr
3 Cheyenne Tr

CLARIDON RD
AQUILLA RD
RAVENNA RD
MAYFIELD RD
TAYLOR RD
WELLS RD
BASS LAKE RD
SOUTH ST
Chagrin River

Kevin Ln
Nicki Ln
Leader Rd
Kenny Dr
CSX RR

Camel Ln
Vista
Pointe Dr
Tewksbury Ln
Meadowwood Dr

Hall Rd
West Branch Cuyahoga River

Turner Dr
Goredon Dr
Berkshire Dr Loring Dr
Cornelia Dr
Aquilla Blvd

West Branch Cuyahoga River

Spencer St

Rio Grande Tr
Zanes Tr
Santa Fe Tr
Cimarron Tr
Chisholm Tr
Oregon Tr
Donner Tr
Strip Tr
Pass

Cherokee

Butternut Creek

Waterfowl Ln

Harvard Dr

West Pointe Cir
Deep Wood Ct
Cedar Gln
Sugarbush Gln
Pine Hollow Cir
Lost Pond
Woodbridge Cir
Woodbridge Ln
Middle Post Pt
Sawmill Bnd
Tinkers Tr
Pkwy

Brandon Ct
Burlington Oval
Burlington Dr
River Oval

BMV

Butternut Creek
Waterfowl Ln

Breezy Acres Dr
Aldenshire Dr

Taylor Rd

44
322
US 322

12200
12400
12500
11900
11300
100
800
300
11400
11300
12300
11900
13100
12400
11700
12400
100
11000

SEE 2504 MAP
SEE 2506 MAP
SEE 2380 MAP
SEE 2635 MAP

A B C D E
1 2 3 4 5 6 7

81°12'18" 81°11'43" 81°11'9" 81°10'34" 81°9'59" 81°9'24"

41°34'23"
41°33'57"
41°33'31"
41°33'5"
41°32'39"
41°32'12"
41°31'46"
41°31'20"

Miles 0   0.25   0.5
1 in. = 2000 ft.

MAP 2506

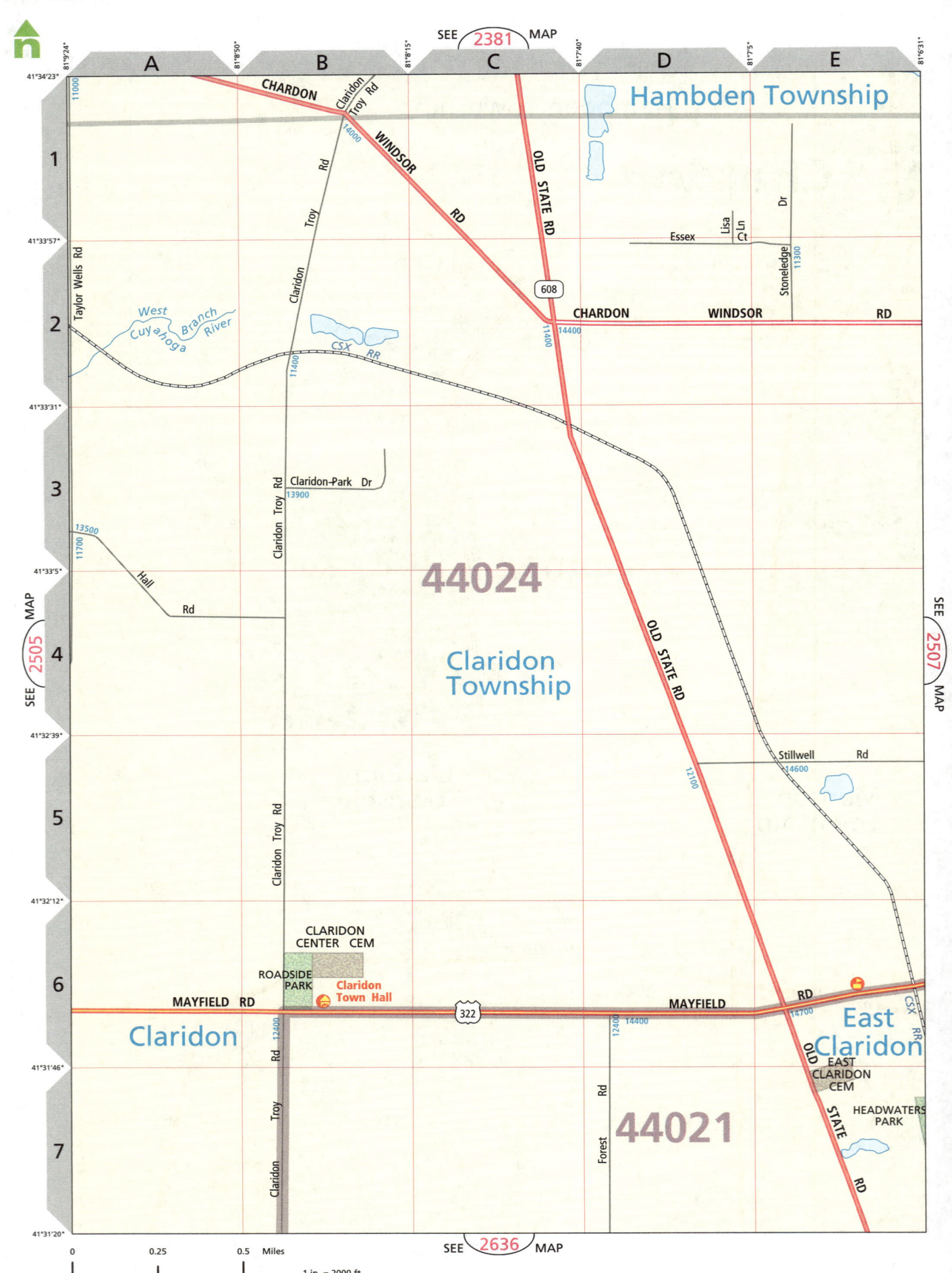

SEE 2381 MAP

Hambden Township

A   B   C   D   E

CHARDON   Claridon Troy Rd

WINDSOR RD

OLD STATE RD

Taylor Wells Rd

Essex   Lisa Ct   Ln   Stoneledge   Dr

11300

608

CHARDON   WINDSOR   RD

West Cuyahoga Branch River

Troy   Rd

11400   14400

Claridon   Troy   Rd

CSX   RR

11400

Claridon-Park   Dr
13900

44024

SEE 2505 MAP

13500
11700

Hall   Rd

Claridon   Township

OLD STATE RD

SEE 2507 MAP

Stillwell   Rd
14600

12100

Claridon   Troy   Rd

CLARIDON CENTER CEM

ROADSIDE PARK   Claridon Town Hall

MAYFIELD   RD   322   MAYFIELD   RD   14700

CSX   RR

East Claridon

Claridon   12400   12400 14400

EAST CLARIDON CEM

Troy   Rd   Forest   Rd   44021   STATE   RD   HEADWATERS PARK

Claridon

SEE 2636 MAP

0   0.25   0.5   Miles

1 in. = 2000 ft.

MAP 2507

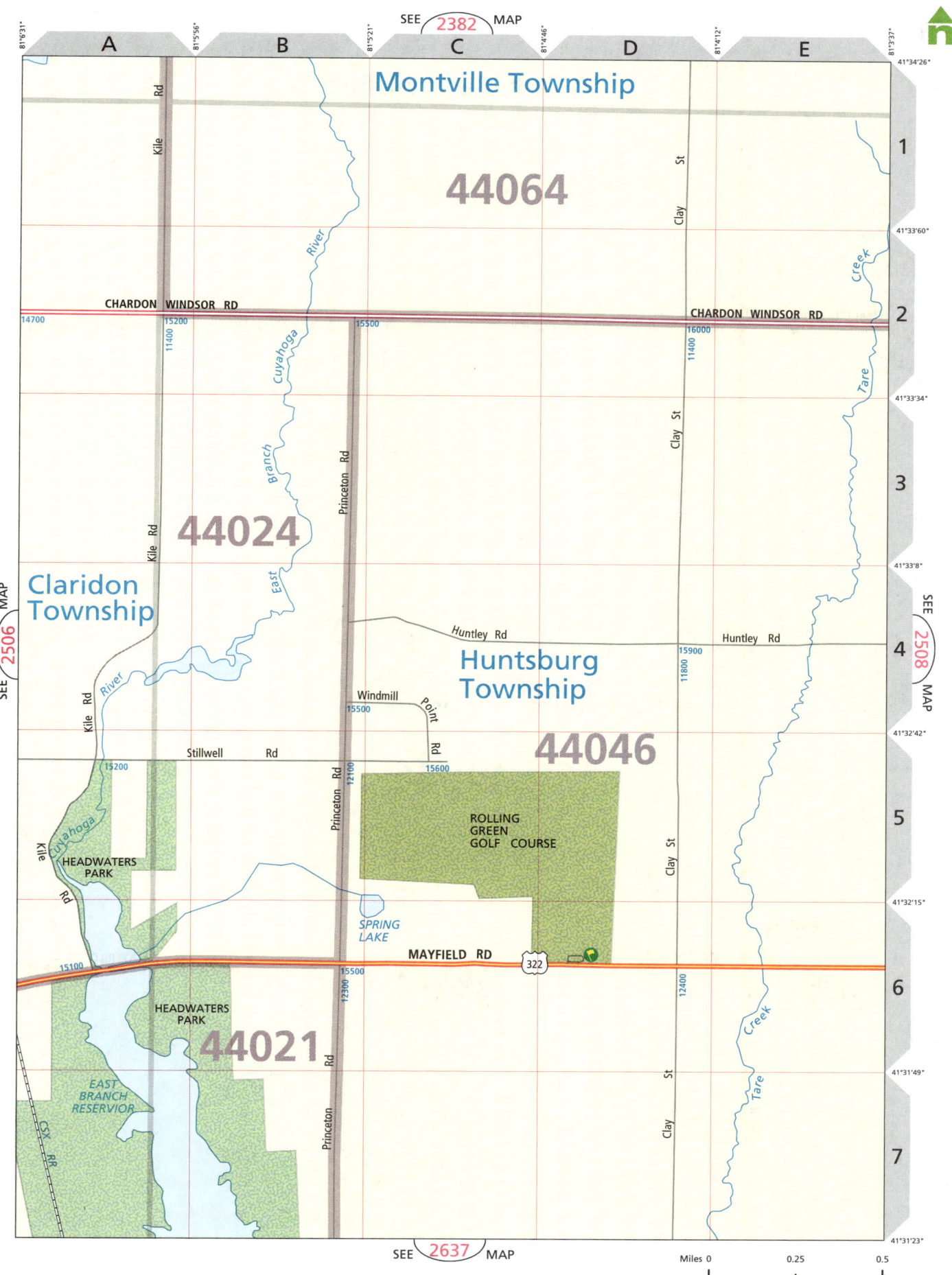

SEE 2382 MAP

A   B   C   D   E

81°6'31"   81°5'56"   81°5'21"   81°4'46"   81°4'12"   81°3'37"

41°34'26"

Montville Township

44064

1

41°33'60"

Kile Rd

Clay St

Creek

CHARDON WINDSOR RD

CHARDON WINDSOR RD

14700   15200   15500   16000   11400   2

11400

41°33'34"

Cuyahoga

Clay St

Tare

3

East   Branch   River

Princeton Rd

44024

41°33'34"

Kile Rd

41°33'8"

SEE 2506 MAP

Claridon Township

River

Kile Rd

Huntley Rd   Huntley Rd

15900

11800

Huntsburg Township

4

41°32'42"

SEE 2508 MAP

Windmill   Point   Rd

15500

44046

Stillwell   Rd

15200

Princeton Rd   12100   15600

HEADWATERS PARK

Kile Rd

Cuyahoga

ROLLING GREEN GOLF COURSE

Clay St

5

41°32'15"

SPRING LAKE

15100   MAYFIELD RD   322

15500   12300

Clay St

Tare   Creek

6

41°31'49"

HEADWATERS PARK

44021

Princeton Rd

EAST BRANCH RESERVOIR

Clay St

7

CSX RR

41°31'23"

SEE 2637 MAP

Miles 0   0.25   0.5

1 in. = 2000 ft.

MAP 2508

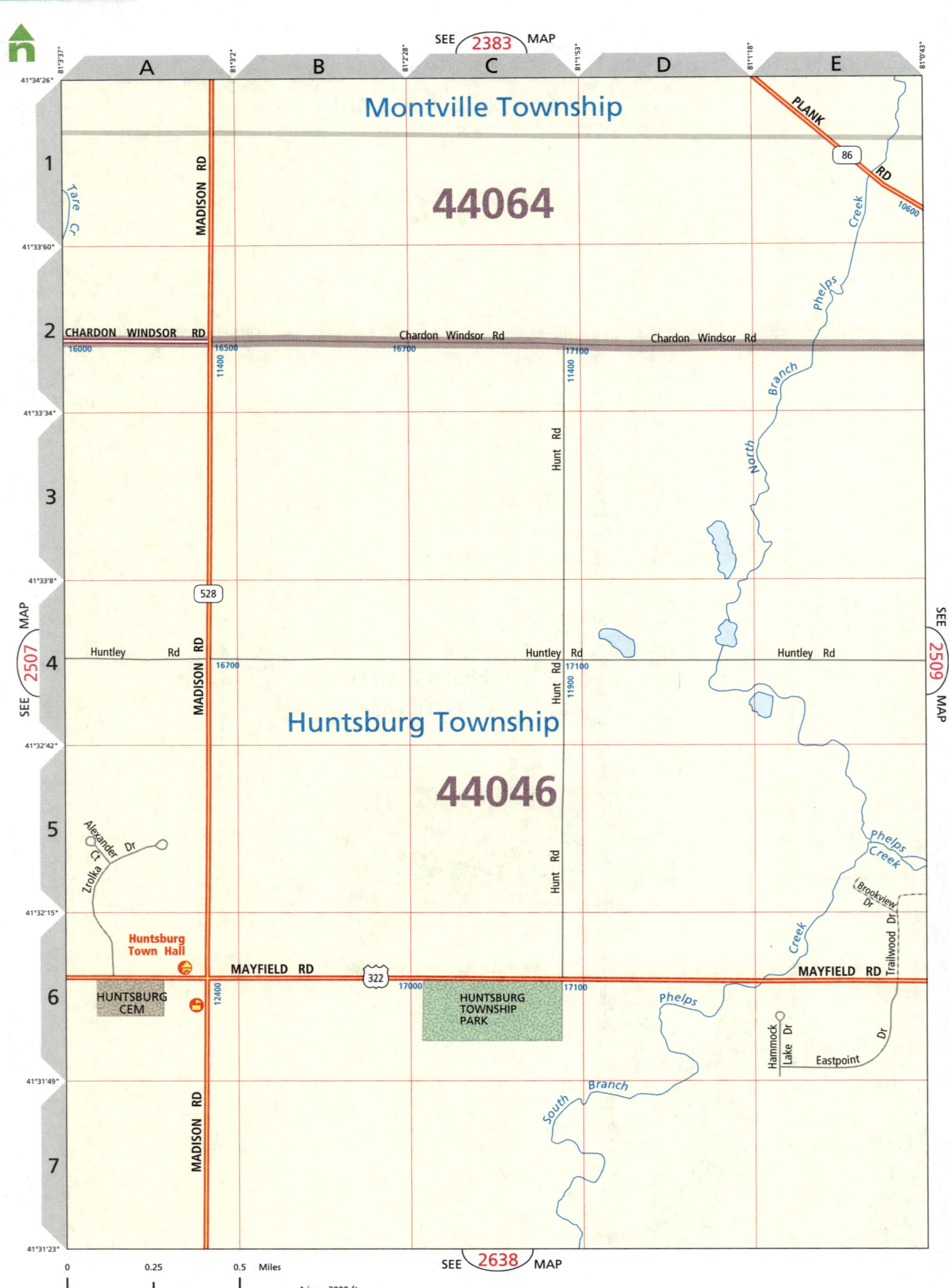

SEE 2383 MAP

Montville Township

44064

Huntsburg Township

44046

SEE 2507 MAP

SEE 2509 MAP

CHARDON WINDSOR RD

Chardon Windsor Rd

Chardon Windsor Rd

Huntley Rd

Huntley Rd

Huntley Rd

MADISON RD

Hunt Rd

Tare Cr

North Branch

Phelps Creek

Phelps Creek

Creek

Phelps

South Branch

Brookview Dr

Trailwood Dr

Hammock Lake Dr

Eastpoint Dr

MAYFIELD RD

MAYFIELD RD

Huntsburg Town Hall

HUNTSBURG CEM

HUNTSBURG TOWNSHIP PARK

Alexander Dr

Ct

Zrolka

PLANK RD

86

10600

16000

11400

16500

16700

11400

17100

16700

17100

11900

12400

17000

17100

528

322

SEE 2638 MAP

0   0.25   0.5 Miles

1 in. = 2000 ft.

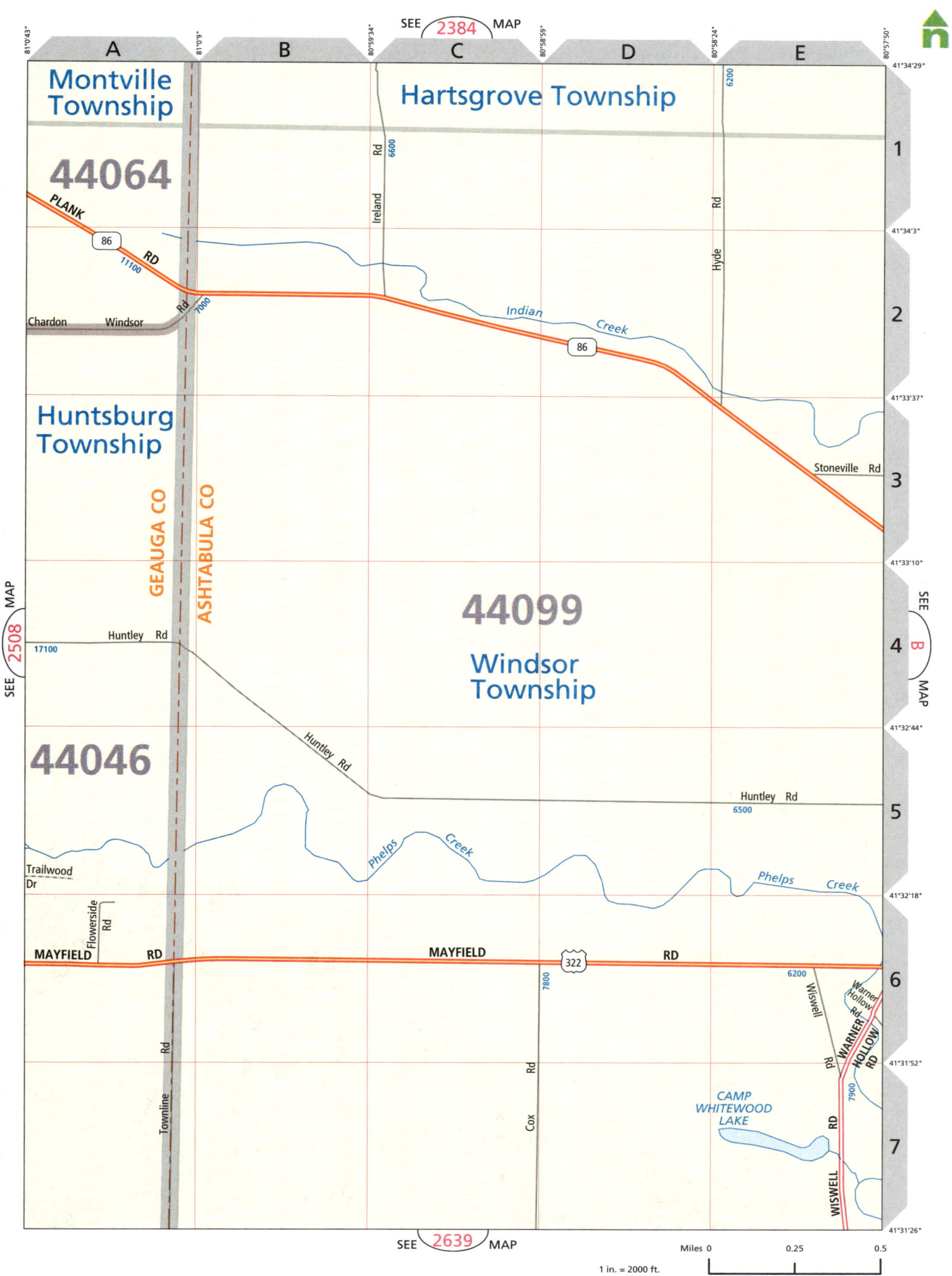

MAP 2509-2613

Montville
Township

44064

Hartsgrove Township

SEE 2384 MAP

Ireland Rd 6600

Hyde Rd

6200

PLANK
86 RD
11100

Rd 7000

Chardon   Windsor

Indian   Creek
86

Stoneville   Rd

Huntsburg
Township

44099

Windsor
Township

GEAUGA CO

ASHTABULA CO

Huntley Rd
17100

Huntley Rd

Huntley   Rd
6500

44046

Trailwood
Dr

Phelps   Creek

Phelps   Creek

Flowerside Rd

MAYFIELD   RD   MAYFIELD   RD
322

Townline Rd

Cox   Rd
7800

6200

Wiswell

Warner
Hollow
Rd

WARNER   HOLLOW   RD
7900

CAMP
WHITEWOOD
LAKE

Rd

WISWELL   RD

SEE 2639 MAP

SEE 2508 MAP

SEE B MAP

41°34'29"
41°34'3"
41°33'37"
41°33'10"
41°32'44"
41°32'18"
41°31'52"
41°31'26"

81°0'43"
81°0'9"
80°59'34"
80°58'59"
80°58'24"
80°57'50"

A   B   C   D   E

1 2 3 4 5 6 7

Miles 0   0.25   0.5

1 in. = 2000 ft.

MAP 2614

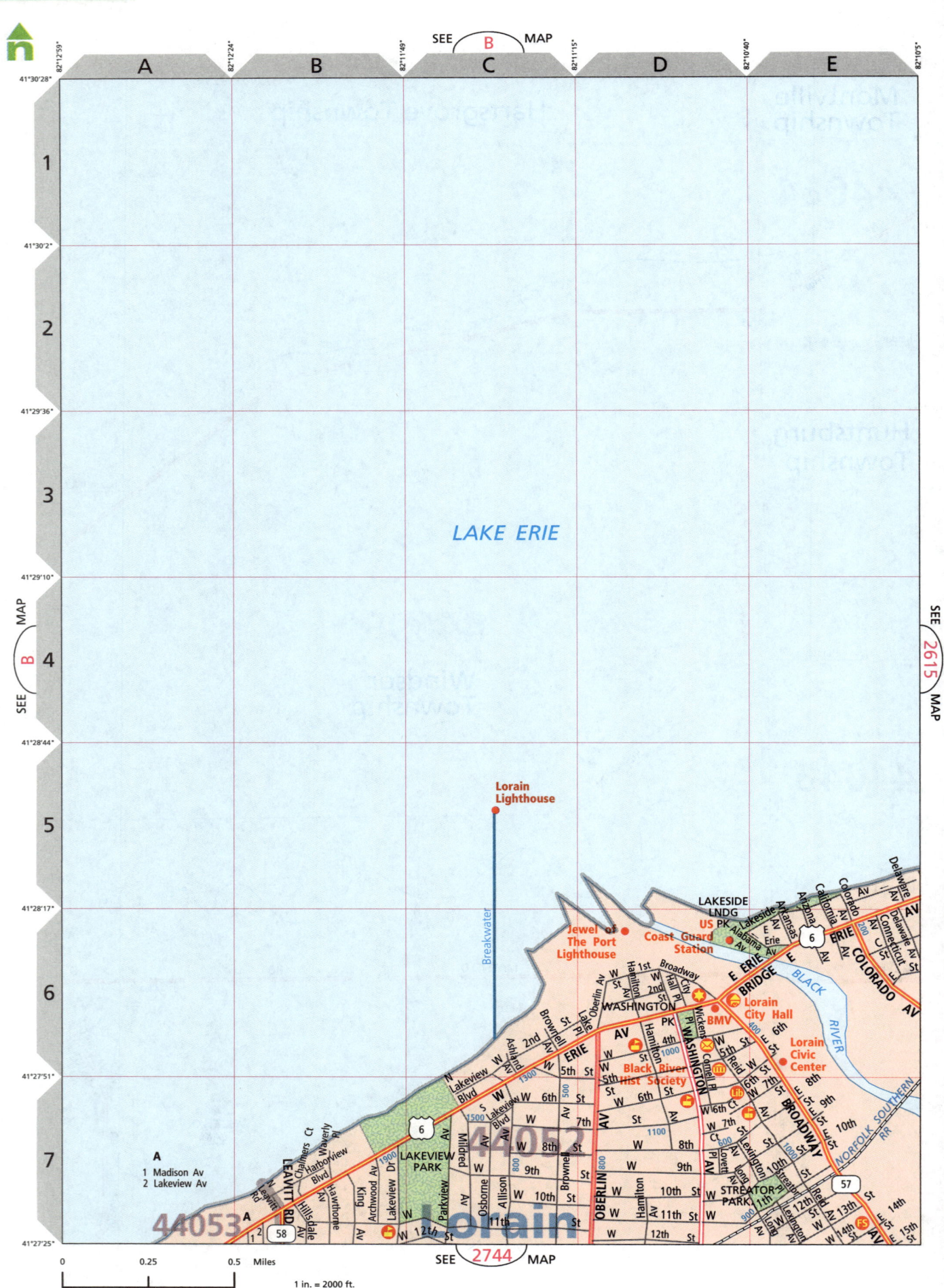

LAKE ERIE

Lorain Lighthouse

Breakwater

Jewel of The Port Lighthouse

Coast Guard Station

LAKESIDE LNDG

US PK

Lakeside

E Erie

Alabama Av

Arkansas

Arizona

California

Colorado Av

Delaware Av

Connecticut St

C St

D St

E St

ERIE

COLORADO AV

E ERIE

BRIDGE

BLACK

RIVER

NORFOLK SOUTHERN RR

1st

Broadway

Oberlin Av

Hamilton

2nd

Lake

Brownell

Camel

Hall

Wicken

City

PK

3rd

WASHINGTON

AV

Lorain City Hall

BMV

Lorain Civic Center

Ashland St

Brownell

N

Lakeview Blvd

ERIE

AV

W 4th

W 5th

W 5th St

W 6th

W 6th St

St

Reid

5th

6th

7th

8th

Black River Hist Society

Lib

BROADWAY

9th

10th

W 2nd

1500

Lakeview Blvd

W 6th

1000

Hamilton

W 5th

1100

W 7th

Lexington

10th

Long

Reid

W

6

1900

1500

500

W 7th St

W 8th

800

500

Oberlin Av

8th

STREATOR PARK

Lovett

57

9th

10th

11th

13th

14th

FS

15th

LAKEVIEW PARK

Mildred

Osborne

Allison

Parkview

W 9th

W 10th

W 11th

W 12th

W 9th St

9th

10th

11th

12th

Hamilton

W 10th

W 11th

W 12th

44052

Lorain

44053

A

1 Madison Av
2 Lakeview Av

Chalmers Ct

Harborview Blvd

Waverly Pl

Hawthorne

King

Archwood Dr

Lakeview

LEAVITT RD

Hillsdale Av

A

58

Lorain

SEE B MAP

SEE B MAP

SEE 2615 MAP

SEE 2744 MAP

0   0.25   0.5   Miles

1 in. = 2000 ft.

MAP 2615

SEE B MAP

A 82°10'5"   B 82°9'31"   82°8'56"   C 82°8'21"   D 82°7'46"   E 82°7'12"

41°30'34"

1

41°30'8"

2

LAKE ERIE

41°29'42"

3

A
1 Maple Grove Dr

LAKEWOOD
BEACH
PARK

SEE 2614 MAP

RD A   41°29'16"

LAKE

Tennyson Av
Tennyson Av
Devonshire Av
Hawthorne Dr
Ferndale Dr
Forestlawn Av
Warwick Av
West Av

Devonshire Dr
Dillewood Dr
Beach Dr

Sheffield

3500

6

Mariners Wy

Anchor Dr
Abbotsford Dr
Pembridge
Latimer Ct
Lakewood Ct
South Av

Lake

SEE 2616 MAP

4

41°28'50"

PARK

E ERIE AV

Day Blvd
Cleveland Dr
Haddam Dr
Concord Dr
Atlas Blvd
Root Rd

3200

3300

CENTURY
PARK

6

B
1 Andress Ct

Maine Av
Massachusetts
Michigan
Montana Blvd
Mississippi
Cleveland Dr
Nebraska
Jefferson Blvd
Jefferson

STREET
PK

Grant

Pin Oak Dr
Dakota Av
Vermont Av
Blossom Dr
Sterling Rd

Georgia Av
Idaho
Georgia Av
Kentucky Av
Augusta
Louisiana
Alexander
Longfellow
Pkwy
**LONGFELLOW
PARK**

GARFIELD
PK
Blvd
Garfield
St
Lincoln Dr
Sterling Rd

McKinley St
Energy
1000

500

800

1800

2700

2600

2700

5

41°28'24"

Illinois
Iowa
Indiana
Danley
N Sq
Danley
St
Fillmore Cir
Fillmore Av
Adams
Michigan
Wilson St
Larkmoor
New Mexico St
Lincoln
Wilson St

Cedar Dr
Dakota Rd
Maple Av

44054

B
Georgia
Idaho
Florida
Ct St
Delaware Av
E Av
F Av
700
G Av
H St
Jackson
Eastlawn St
Crehore
Crehore St
Monroe
Nebraska Av
New Jersey St
Nevada Av
New St
New Mexico
Euclid St

MAPLE
HEIGHTS
PARK

Root Rd

Sheffield

1300

2600

2700

6

41°27'58"

HIGHVIEW
PK
Dorado
Hancock St
Randall
Fillmore
Paine St
Randall St

Pennsylvania Ct
Ohio Av

HENDERSON DR
Kansas Av
Augusta Av
Iowa Av
Lehigh
Maine
Maryland
Fillmore

1500

COLORADO AV
2500

611

Cedar Dr
3500

1700

Georgia Av
Iowa Av
Idaho
Bridge Dr
H St
1900
300

New Jersey Av
Cromwell Dr
River
Industrial Rd
CROMWELL
PARK
Pennsylvania Rd
River Industrial Rd
3400

7

41°27'31"

Black River

Lorain

44052

Black River
Old Colorado Av
44052

SEE 2745 MAP

Miles 0   0.25   0.5

1 in. = 2000 ft.

MAP 2616

SEE ⒷMAP

A B C D E

LAKE ERIE

C
1 Sheffield Edgewater Dr
2 Cedar
3 Abbe Rd
4 Willow Ln

ERIE SHORES PARK

Edgewater Dr

SHELL COVE PARK

WALKER RD

A
1 Maple Grove Dr
2 Beach St
3 Lake Breeze Rd

Civic Center

COMMUNITY PARK

LAKE RD

Edgewater RD

Tennyson Av

WESTSHORE PARK

Hawthorne Av

Madison

Richelieu Blvd

LINCOLN PARK

Northwood Dr

Pinewood Dr

Richelieu

Walker

Maple

Woodruff Dr

Mapleview Av

Lakeview Av

Pleasantview Av

Beach Av

Cove

MEMORIAL PARK

Sheffield Lake City Hall

Saddlewood Dr

Redwood Dr

Rosewood Dr

Ivanhoe Av

Beachwood Dr

Greenwood Dr

Ferndale Dr

Elmwood Dr

Southwood Dr

Oster Dr

Irving Rd

Schumaker Ditch

ABBE RD

Sheffield Lake

B
1 Brookside Rd
2 Monroe Ct
3 June Av
4 Page Ct

Forestlawn Av

NORFOLK SOUTHERN RR

44054

HARRIS RD

Brookside HS

LAKE BREEZE RD

Sheffield

301

ST. TERESA CEM

COLORADO AV 611

Old Colorado Av

French Creek

ABBE RD

FRENCH CREEK RESERVATION

COLORADO AV

Sheffield Village Hall

Marcus Dr

Old Colorado Av

Orchard Ct

Ph Oak Cir

Barkwood Dr

E RIVER RD

0   0.25   0.5   Miles

1 in. = 2000 ft.

MAP 2617

SEE 2487 MAP

A   B   C   D   E

LAKE ERIE

103rd Ohio
Volunteer
Infantry
Memorial
Foundation

MILLER
ROAD
PARK

LAKE RD

Electric

AQUA
MARINE
GOLF
COURSE

WARREN
GUENTHER
PARK

Hawthorne Av

Lynne Dr
Gayle Dr
Thelma Dr
Blvd
Erieview

Durrell Av

Clinton Av

Elberston Av
Avondale Av
Clinton Av

Durrell Av

Caldwell Blvd

Woodruff Av

York St
Burton St
June St

Karen Dr
Charleston Av
Chelsea Av
Chatham Dr

MOORE RD

Geon Ct

Colony Dr
W Shore Rd
Avalon Dr
Moore Rd
Bonnieview Dr

Parkland Dr
Rosewood Dr
Edgewood Dr

LAKE RD

Electric

Dr
Ashwood
Durrell
Moreland
Belmar
Av

Duff

Prebblebrook Ct

Belmar

Clearbrook Dr

Blvd

Artsdale
Curtis
Laurel Av

Fernwood
Canterbury

Richland Av
Robinwood Av

Crestwood Dr
Vinewood
Moorewood

Waterside Ct

Cascade Dr

Crestwood

Rosewood
Parkwood Dr
Beechwood Av
Fairfield Av
Berkshire Av
Inwood
Brookfield Rd

Redwood

Dellwood

Maplewood Cir

Dr

Durrell Av
Bellaire Av

INWOOD
PARK

BMV

WALKER   RD

44012

**Avon
Lake**

Miller Rd

MOORE RD

Brookcrest Ct

Bayberry Ct

Whitaker Cove

Waterford Ct
Crossings Wy
Fawnhaven Wy
Ambleside
Dr

Webber Rd

Klingshirn
Winery

WEISS PARK

Chappel
Titus
Hill
Deer Run
Ln
Ln

Pin   Oak   Pkwy   Pin   Oak   Pkwy

NORFOLK   SOUTHERN   RR

MOORE RD

Freemon Pl

Avon

44011

Shadetree Tr
Wood Ln
Ledgewood Ls
Acorn Ct

Miller Rd

Chester Industrial Pkwy

COLORADO AV

CHESTER   RD

Chester Rd   Chester Rd

Moore Rd

Barkwood
Dr

Kline Ditch
French Creek

Moore Rd
Windmill Wy N
Windmill Wy E
Windmill Wy S
Windmill Wy W
Windmill Ct
Windmill Wy

Doovys St
Caroline Dr
Lorie Blvd
Lake Dr

Eaton Dr
Eaton Dr
Julia Av
Miriam Av
Sandalwood Dr
Candlewood Dr

Ridgeland Dr
Reserve Cir N
Reserve Cir S
Reserve Ct
Clifton Dr
Lake Pointe Dr
Reserve Wy
Reserve Cir E
Healthway Dr

SEE 2616 MAP

SEE 2618 MAP

SEE 2747 MAP

1
2
3
4
5
6
7

41°30'40"
41°30'14"
41°29'48"
41°29'22"
41°28'56"
41°28'30"
41°28'3"
41°27'37"

82°4'18"
82°3'44"
82°3'9"
82°2'34"
82°1'59"
82°1'25"

Miles 0   0.25   0.5

1 in. = 2000 ft.

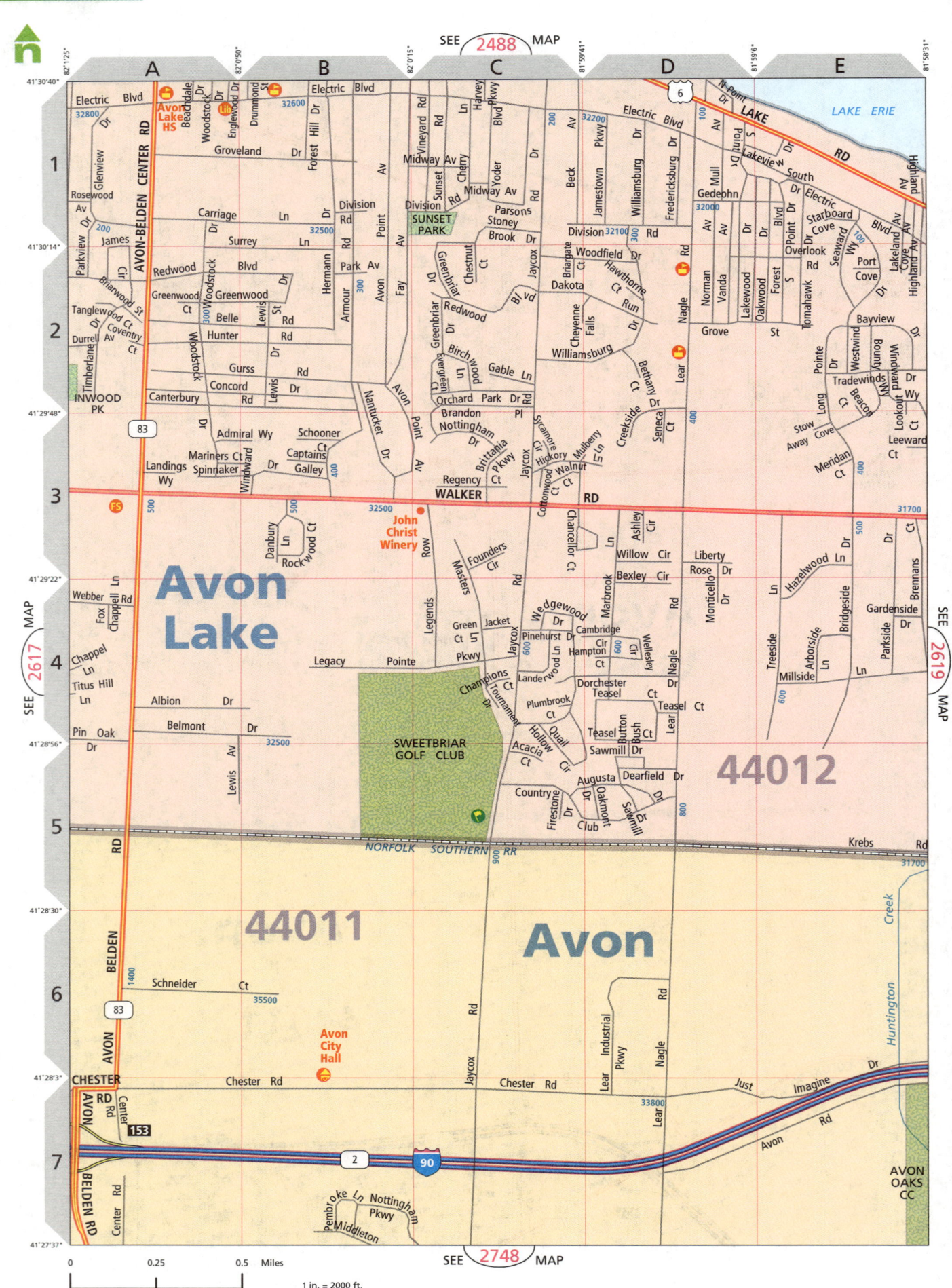

MAP 2618

SEE 2488 MAP

LAKE ERIE

A   B   C   D   E

Avon Lake

INWOOD PK

SUNSET PARK

John Christ Winery

Avon Lake HS

SWEETBRIAR GOLF CLUB

44012

WALKER RD

NORFOLK SOUTHERN RR

Krebs Rd

44011

Avon

Avon City Hall

CHESTER   Chester Rd

BELDEN RD

AVON OAKS CC

SEE 2748 MAP

SEE 2617 MAP

SEE 2619 MAP

0   0.25   0.5   Miles

1 in. = 2000 ft.

MAP 2619

A   B   C   D   E

SEE — B — MAP

N

1
2
3
4
5
6
7

41°30'46"
41°30'19"
41°29'53"
41°29'27"
41°29'1"
41°28'35"
41°28'9"
41°27'43"

81°58'31"   81°57'57"   81°57'22"   81°56'47"   81°56'12"   81°55'38"

LAKE ERIE

Electric
RESATAR PARK
Brunswick Dr
Salem Dr
Newbury Ct
Compass Cove Dr
Commodore Cove
Driftwood Ct
Sailors Cove
Maritime Ct
Regatta Ct
Tradewinds
Anchors Away
Leeward Ct
Newport
Windward Wy

Avon Lake

31700
100

Anna
Kensington Cir
Eagle Cliff Dr
Huntington Park Dr
Woods Dr
Roxbury Cove
Manchester Ln
Narragansett
Nantucket
Arlington Pkwy
Cir

Plymouth   100
30800

44140

LAKE RD
30300

Webster Rd
Winston Dr
Salem Dr
Manhasset Dr
Saddler Rd   200
Breezewood Dr
Bayview Dr

Ruth St
Florence St
Gate St
Chelsea Dr
US 6
Electric
Foote Rd
Rye Dr
Goulders Grn
Northfield Rd
Westwood Rd
Pinewood
Northfield Rd
Longbeach Park Pkwy

LAKESIDE CEM
Huntington Playhouse

c   1 Rose Hill Ln

Rose Hill Cahoon Homestead Mus

LAKE RD

WALKER RD   31200

Plymouth Dr   31200
Bexley Dr
Carlton Dr
Carlton Dr
Fairwin Dr
Bar
Harbor Dr
Clarewood
Drake Dr
Tuttle Dr
Powell Dr
Pellett Dr
Wolf Rd
Aldrich Dr
Dr

LORAIN CO   CUYAHOGA CO
BRADLEY RD   300

Timber Ln
Appleblossom Dr
Tanglewood Ln
Winsor Rd
Saddler Rd   300
Applewood Dr
Ednil Dr
Tanglewood Ln
Westlawn Dr
Saddler Rd

Foote Rd
Edgewood
Wayside Ln
Huntington Park Dr
Northfield Rd

CLEVELAND METRO PARK

CAHOON MEM PARK
C   1
400

Bates Dr
Brownstone Cir

Hurst
Walmar
Kimberly Dr
Kimberly Cir
Marvis Dr
Roberta Dr
Walmar Dr
Clinton Dr
Perry Dr
Brooke Ln
Jonathan Ln
500

Maple Dr
Willow Wy
Sherwood Dr   30400
Meadowlane Dr
Crestview Dr
Ashton Dr
Crestview Dr
Provincetown Dr
Wildbrook
Yarmouth
29900

BRADLEY PARK
Huntington

BASSETT RD   400
WOLF RD
Creek
Inverness Dr
Cowles Dr
W Oakland Rd
Bracken Dr
Turnbridge Dr
Osborn Rd
Beach Rd
Oakland Rd
Woodpark Rd
W Oakland Rd
Sutcliffe Dr   400
Sites Rd

Bay HS

Lake Erie Nature & Science Center
WOLF RD
FS

Bay Village

44012

Krebs Rd
Naigle Dr
30800
Cambridge Dr
1 2 3
Wellfleet Dr
Chatham Point Dr

Lindford Dr
Marygate Dr
Lisaview Dr
Norfolk Dr
W Lincoln Rd   28900
Welshire Dr
Debbington Dr
Buchanan Rd
Millard Dr
N Lincoln Dr
Dwight Dr
Revere Dr   W
Forest Dr
Oviatt Rd
Lincoln Rd   28100
Rexford Rd
Aberdeen Rd
Av

Glendening Dr

A   1 Cambridge Ct W   2 Cambridge Ct E   3 Cambridge Cir

Knickerbocker   28100

NORFOLK SOUTHERN RR   700

Caroline Cir

44011
Avon

Viking Pkwy
Pkwy   30800

CROCKER RD   600

Hillard Rd
Bell Dr
Batey Dr
Lavandef
Payne

Bassett Rd
Ranney Rd
RANNEY PARK PKWY   28000
Westchester Pkwy
Westchester Pkwy
Bryandale Dr
Whitehill Cir
27700

Clemens Rd
30100

Clemens Rd
Mildred Av   1200
44145

Creekwood Dr   Cr   200

Cahoon Rd
Dellwood Dr

Just Imagine Dr
2
90   NORTHWEST FRWY
Avon Rd   31200

AVON OAKS CC
Huntington Creek

Logan Blvd
Glen Ct
Lyon Dr
Durham Dr
Falkirk Dr
Barclay Dr
Kilgour Dr
Cedarwood Dr
Alder Ln
Juniper Dr
Crossings Pkwy
Crossings Pkwy
Wood Cir
BRADLEY RD   30600
B   1 Savannah Pkwy

156
Bobby Ln   1300
Patti Pk
Westford Cir
Westford Cir
Westford Cir
254
Ridge Ln
Trotters
Saddle Brook Ln
Hunters Chase Dr
Weymouth Cir
Bassett Rd   1600
29600

Westlake

CEM
DETROIT RD   27800
Settlers
Reserve Rd
Sperrys Forge Tr
Coes Post Run
Halls Carriage Pth
Roanoke Wy
Winchester Dr
Remington Dr   500
Winchester Ct
Remington Dr
Farrs Garden
Holdens Arbor Run

SEE 2618 MAP
SEE 2620 MAP
SEE 2749 MAP

Miles 0   0.25   0.5
1 in. = 2000 ft.

MAP 2620

LAKE ERIE

SEE 2619 MAP

SEE 2621 MAP

44140

Bay Village

Westlake
44145

CAHOON MEM PK

BAY VILLAGE PARK

Bay Village City Hall

SEE B MAP

SEE 2750 MAP

0   0.25   0.5   Miles

1 in. = 2000 ft.

MAP 2621

MAP 2622

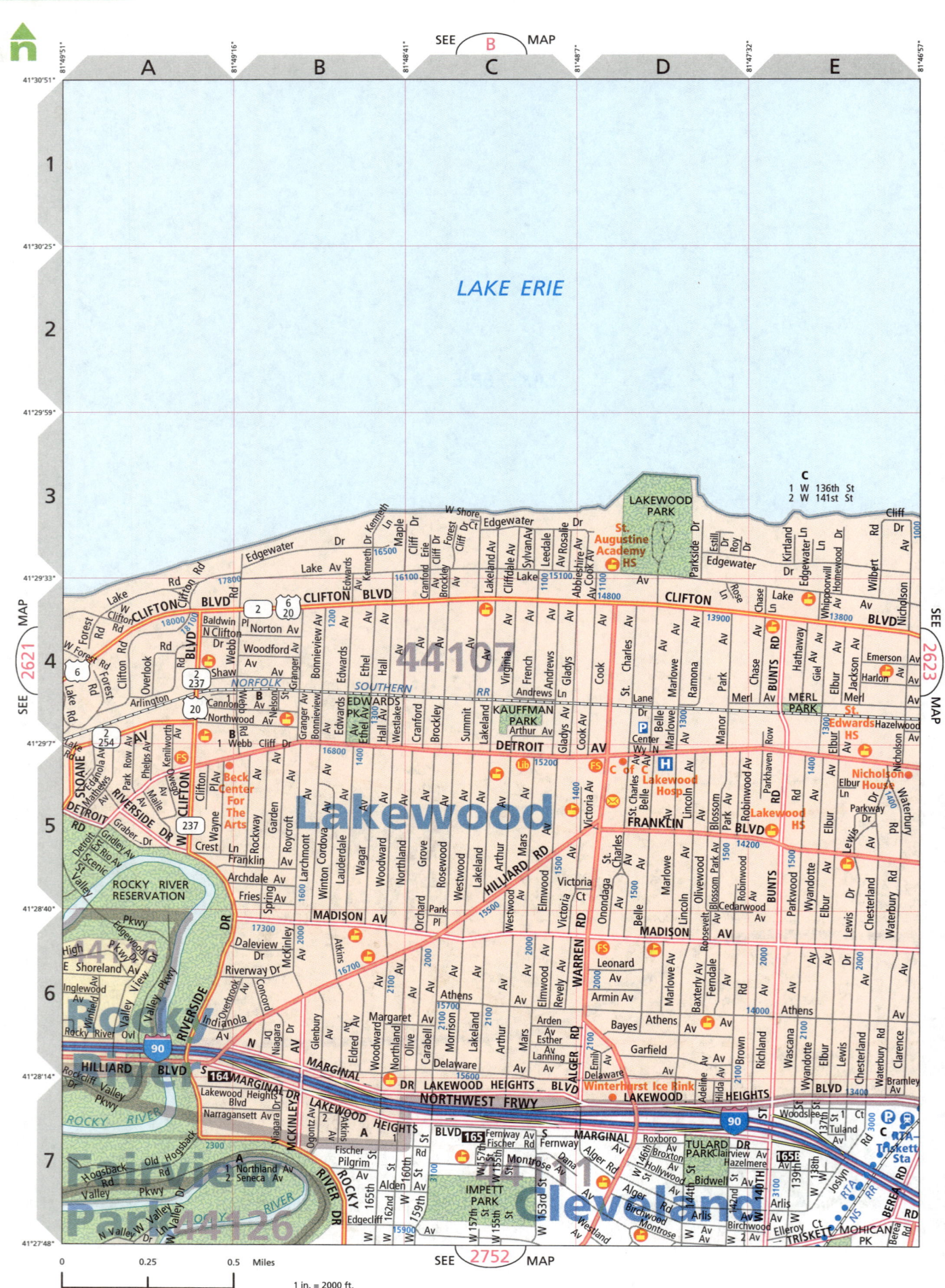

LAKE ERIE

SEE 2752 MAP

MAP 2623

MAP 2624

SEE B MAP

SEE 2623 MAP
SEE 2625 MAP

SEE 2754 MAP

LAKE ERIE

44114

44113
Cleveland

44102

B
1 Walnut Av
2 E 3rd St
3 E 2nd St
4 Center Ct
5 Ontario St
6 Central Viaduct
7 Commercial Rd

C
1 Elton Ct
2 W 68th St
3 W 68th Pl

A
1 Vermont Av
2 Superior Viaduct
3 Leonard St
4 West Av

0   0.25   0.5 Miles

1 in. = 2000 ft.

MAP 2625

SEE 2495 MAP
SEE 2624 MAP
SEE 2626 MAP
SEE 2755 MAP

Miles 0   0.25   0.5

1 in. = 2000 ft.

MAP 2626

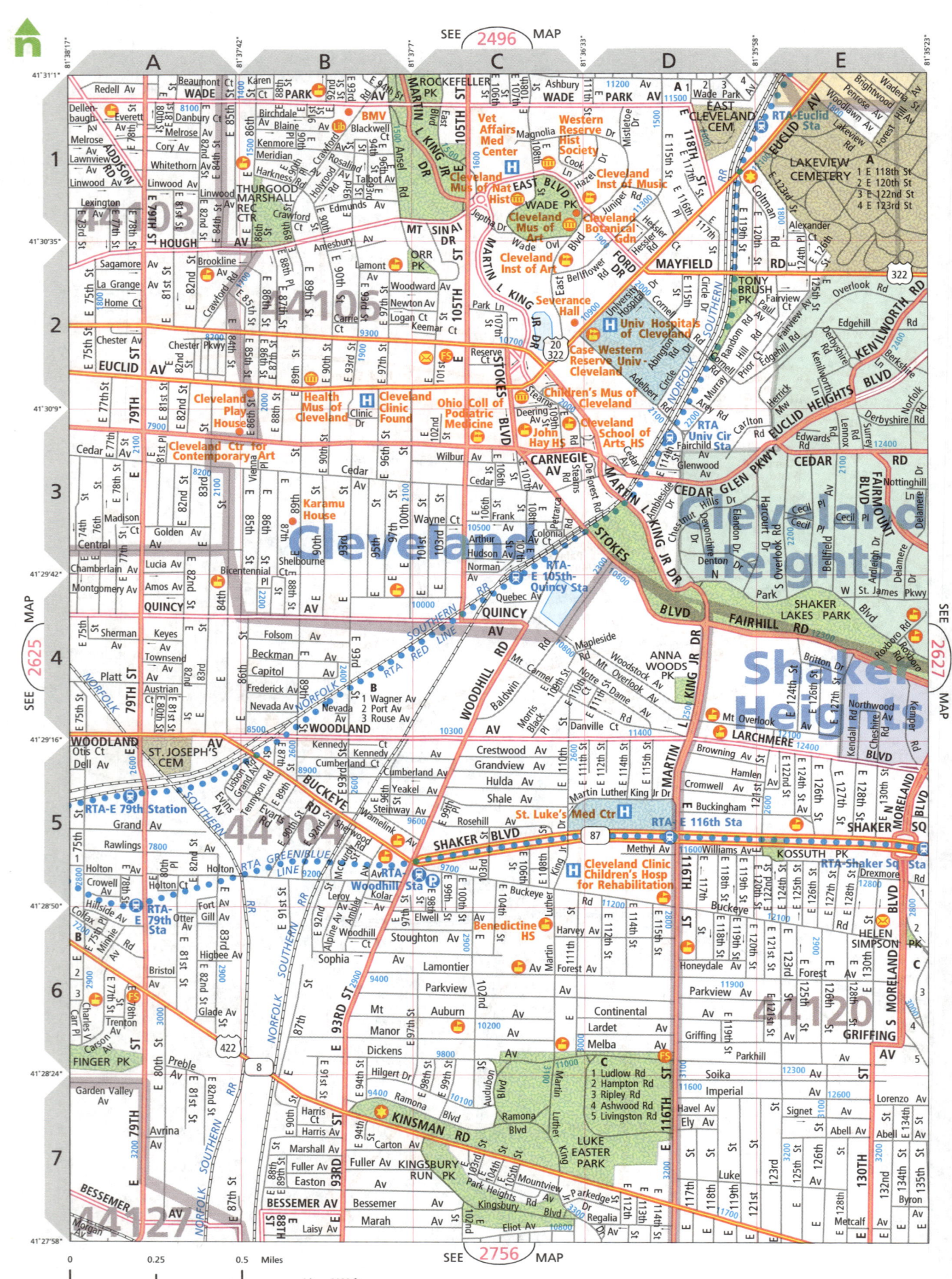

SEE 2496 MAP
SEE 2625 MAP
SEE 2627 MAP
SEE 2756 MAP

0   0.25   0.5   Miles

1 in. = 2000 ft.

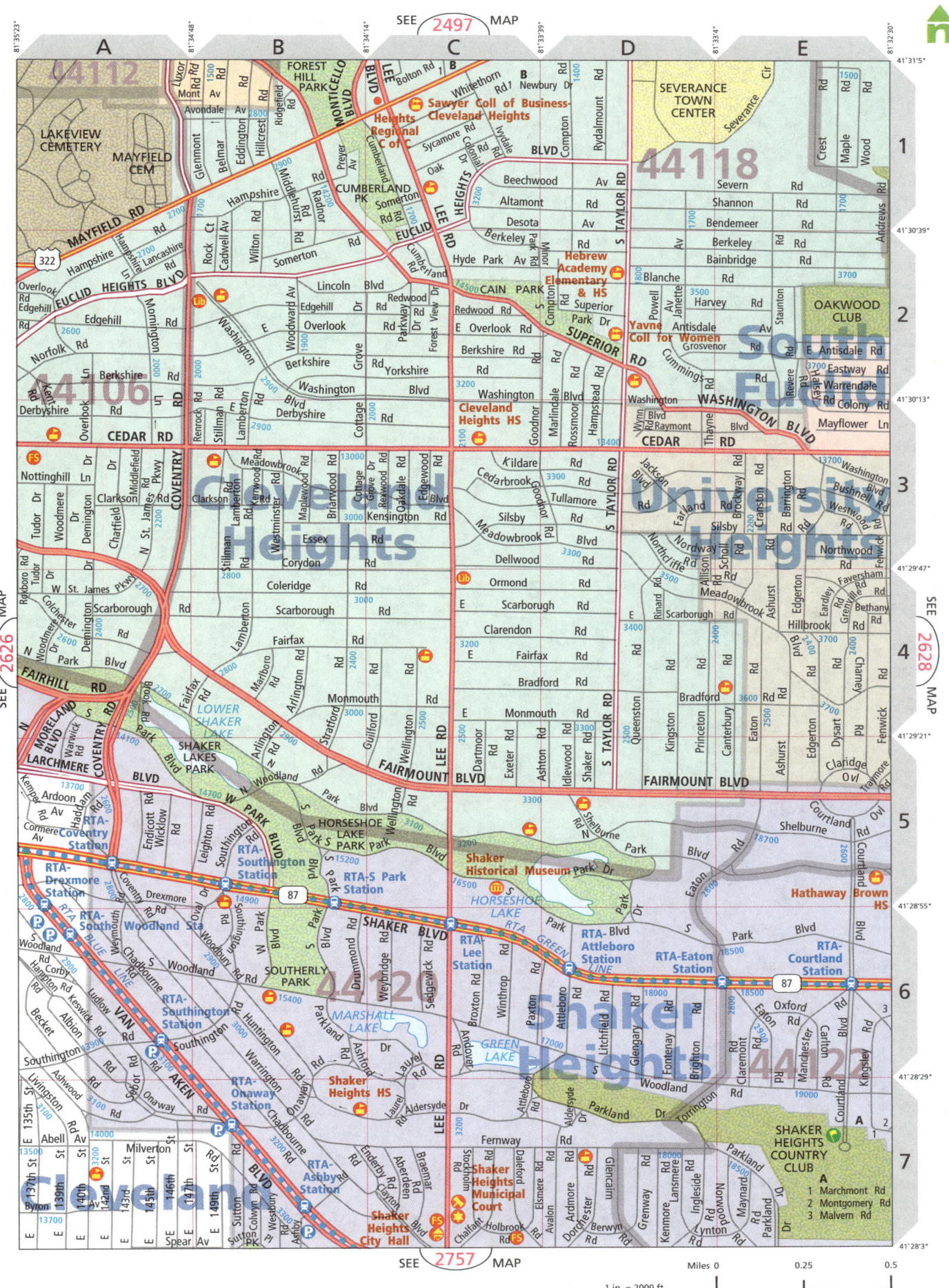

MAP 2627

SEE 2497 MAP

SEE 2626 MAP

SEE 2628 MAP

Miles 0   0.25   0.5

1 in. = 2000 ft.

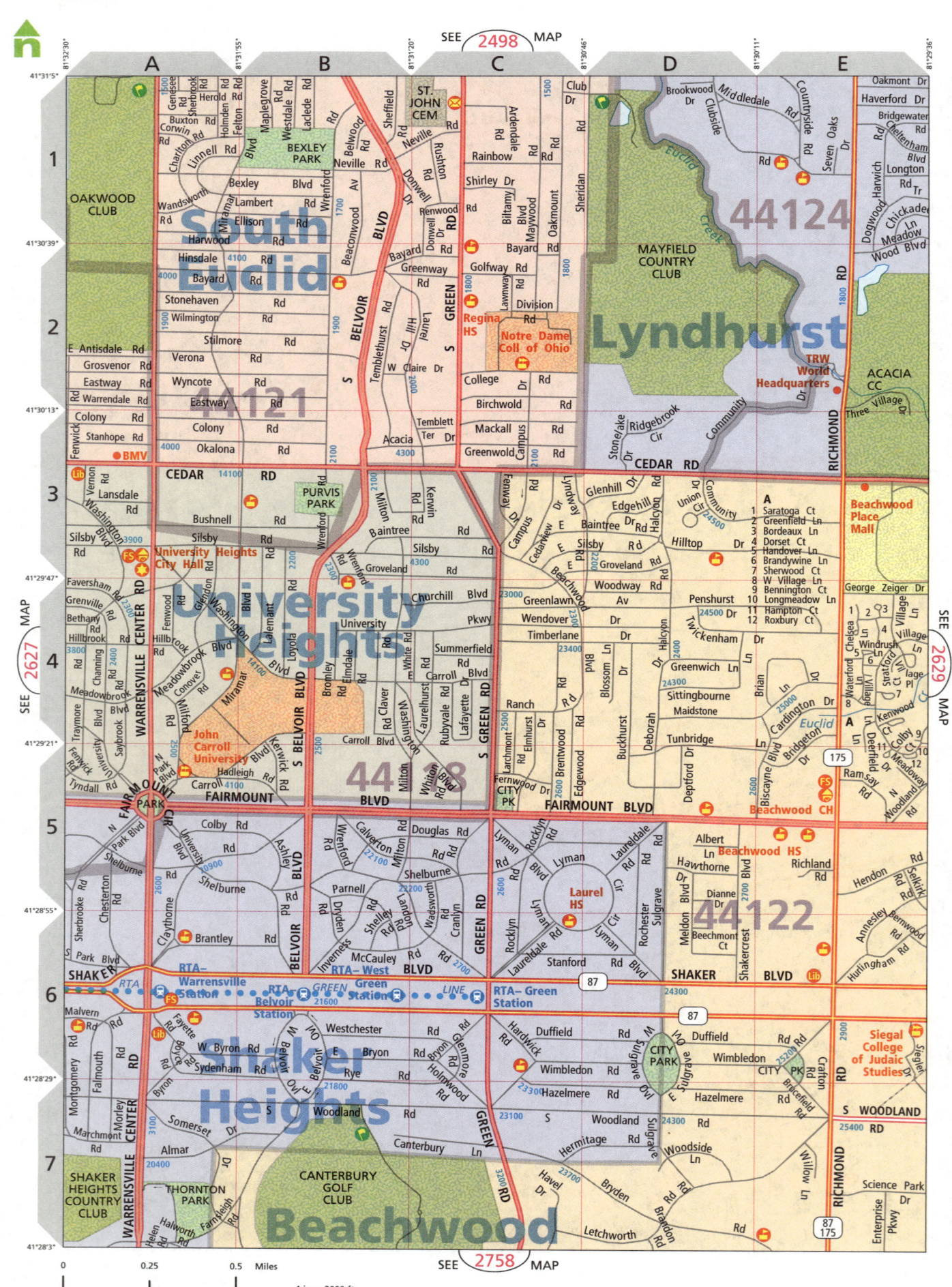

MAP 2628

SEE 2498 MAP

SEE 2627 MAP

SEE 2629 MAP

SEE 2758 MAP

OAKWOOD CLUB

South Euclid

44121

Lyndhurst

44124

MAYFIELD COUNTRY CLUB

ACACIA CC

TRW World Headquarters

BEXLEY PARK

ST. JOHN CEM

Regina HS

Notre Dame Coll of Ohio

Beachwood Place Mall

University Heights

University Heights City Hall

PURVIS PARK

John Carroll University

44118

FAIRMOUNT

FAIRMOUNT BLVD

Beachwood CH

44122

Beachwood HS

Laurel HS

SHAKER BLVD

RTA–West Green Station
RTA–Warrensville Station
RTA–Belvoir Station
RTA–Green Station

GREEN LINE

Shaker Heights

Siegal College of Judaic Studies

SHAKER HEIGHTS COUNTRY CLUB

THORNTON PARK

CANTERBURY GOLF CLUB

Beachwood

A 1 Saratoga Ct
2 Greenfield Ln
3 Bordeaux Ln
4 Dorset Ct
5 Handover Ln
6 Brandywine Ln
7 Sherwood Ct
8 W Village Ln
9 Bennington Ct
10 Longmeadow Ln
11 Hampton Ct
12 Roxbury Ct

0   0.25   0.5   Miles
1 in. = 2000 ft.

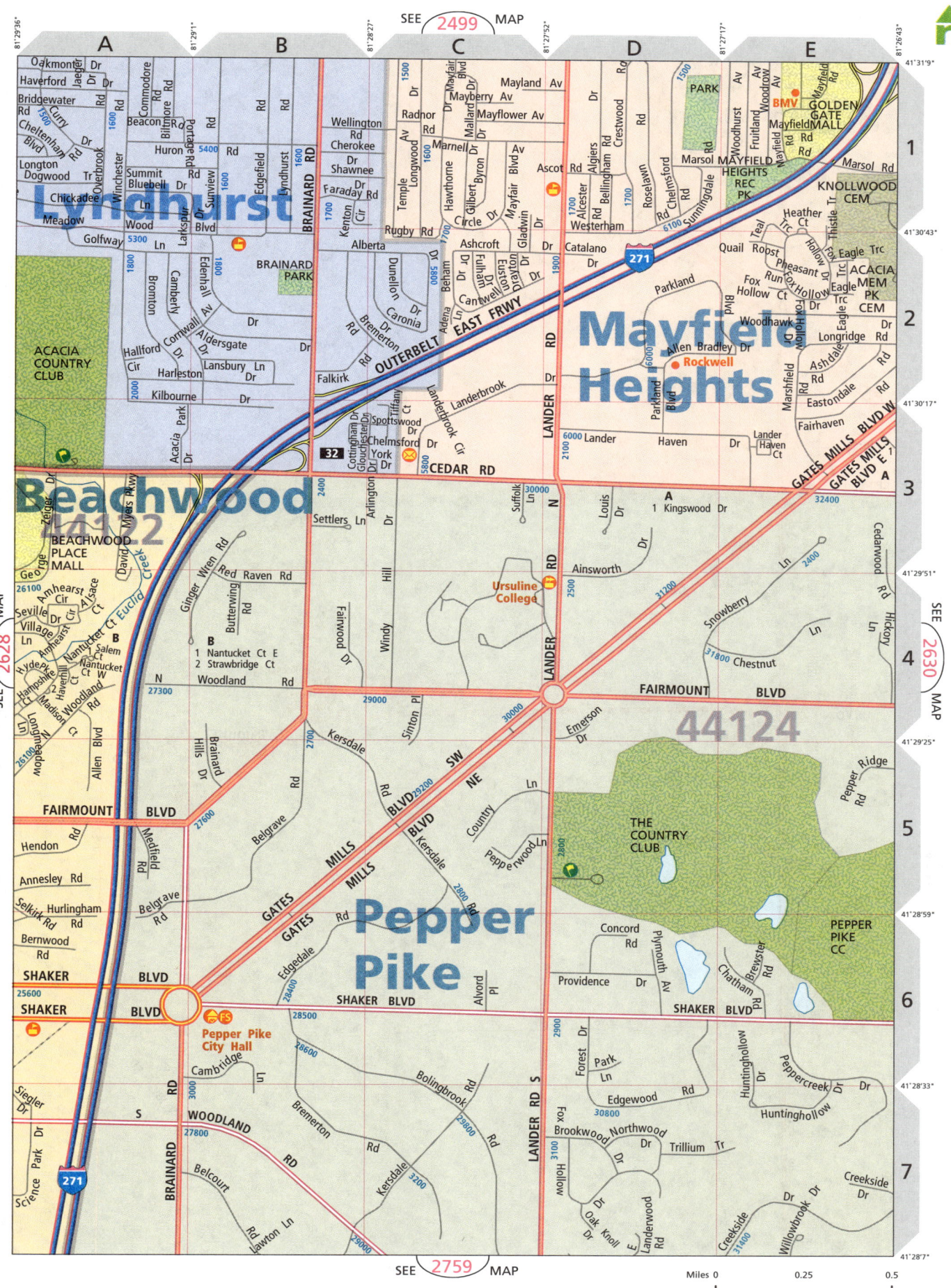

MAP 2629

MAP 2630

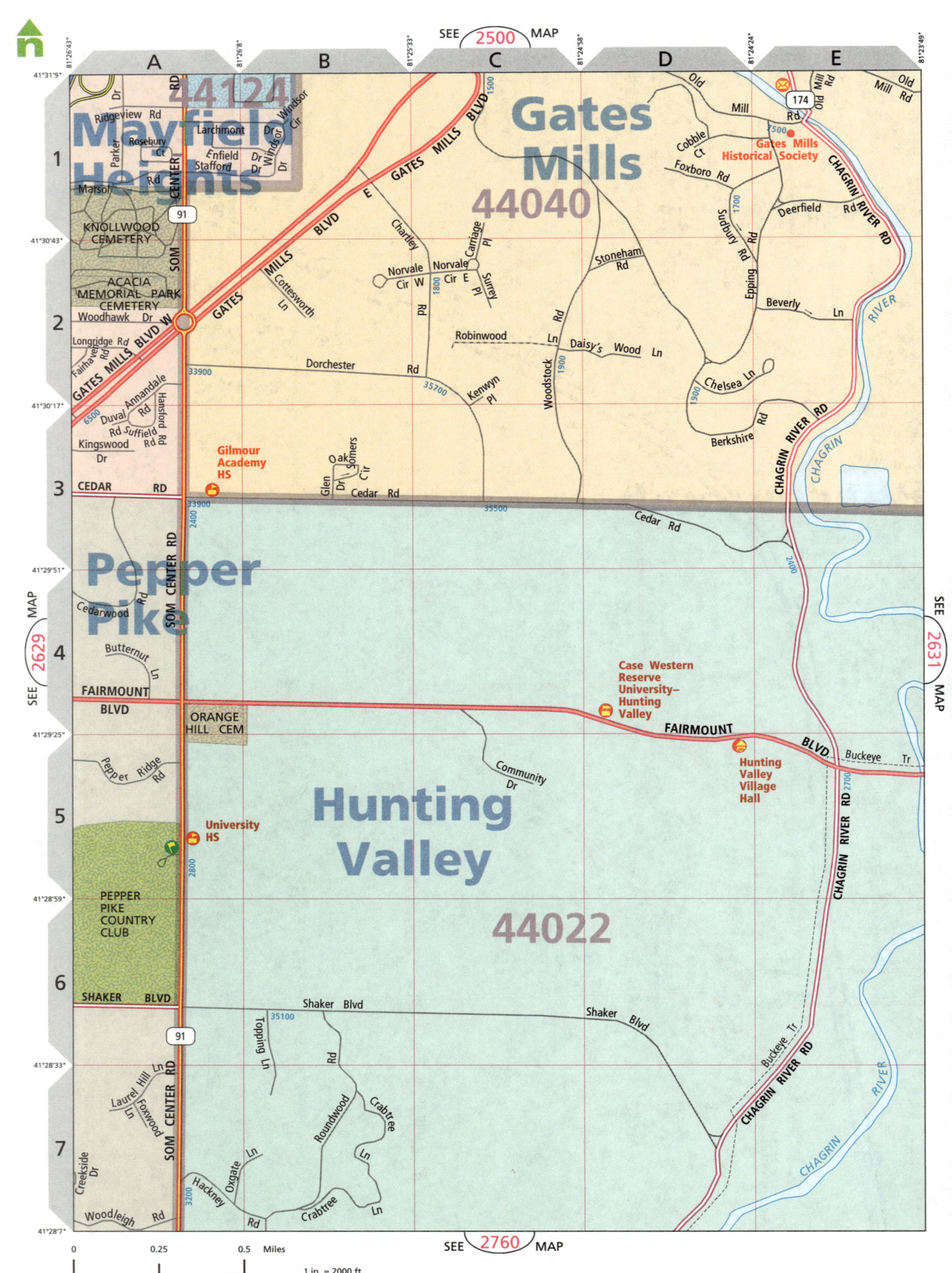

SEE 2500 MAP

44124

Mayfield Heights

Gates Mills 44040

Gates Mills Historical Society

Pepper Pike

SEE 2629 MAP

SEE 2631 MAP

Hunting Valley 44022

Case Western Reserve University– Hunting Valley

Hunting Valley Village Hall

Gilmour Academy HS

University HS

Pepper Pike Country Club

ORANGE HILL CEM

KNOLLWOOD CEMETERY

ACACIA MEMORIAL PARK CEMETERY

0   0.25   0.5   Miles

1 in. = 2000 ft.

SEE 2760 MAP

MAP 2631

SEE 2501 MAP

A B C D E

SEE 2630 MAP

SEE 2632 MAP

81°23'49"
81°23'14"
81°22'40"
81°22'5"
81°21'30"
81°20'56"

41°31'13"
41°30'47"
41°30'21"
41°29'55"
41°29'29"
41°29'3"
41°28'37"
41°28'11"

1
2
3
4
5
6
7

Old Mill Rd
Buckeye Tr
12800
1600
Hillcrest Ln
Westchester Tr
12900
13000
W
Cedarcrest
Geauga Tr
Birdland Tr
Springblossom Tr
Woodcrest
Morning Glory Tr
Wellswood Tr
Steelwood Ln
Warwick
Avon Ln
Manchester Dr
Greenfield 7400 Tr
Stratford
Drury Ln
Fairfield Tr
Kingsway Dr
Woodlands Tr
7700
Cherry Ln
Cherry Ln
Laser Blvd
Birchwood Dr
Griswold Creek

44040
Gates Mills

Chester Township

44026

1900
7100
Cedar Rd
7400
Foxmoor Tr
13300
Ledges Ln
Fox Ledges Ln
Gray Eagle Chase

7800
Caves Rd
13200
Cedar Rd
8100
BESSIE BENNER METZENBAUM PARK
13200
Green Rd
Hickory St S
Shady Ln

Chesterbrook Rd
Glenhill Dr
Maple Grove
Dr

Ledgebrook Ln
COUNTY LINE RD
Buckeye Tr
Buckeye Tr

44022
Hunting Valley

CHAGRIN RIVER

Griswold Creek
Caves Rd
Sunrise
Wildflower Ln
Cir
13600
Braeburn Ln
Braeburn Ln
Hill
Fox
Dr
Bell Vernon Dr
13500

Buckeye Tr
Buckeye Tr BLVD
FAIRMOUNT
39000
Quail Ln
Partridge Ln
Partridge Ln
Pheasant Ln
44073
Calley Ln
14000
Wharton Dr
Griswold Creek
Fox Hollow Dr
13800
Sweetbriar Ln
James Dr
Benner Dr
13800
Caves Rd
FAIRMOUNT RD
7500
W Willard Rd
Willard Rd
E Willard
14000
7900
W
River Dr
Russell Township

CUYAHOGA CO
GEAUGA CO
CHAGRIN RIVER
COUNTY LINE RD
100
7300
14300
Ravencrest Dr
Stump Hollow Ln
14500
Thistle Ln
DINES RD
7500
Hartwell Tr
14300
Hunting Hills Dr
Squire Ln
7600
44072
DINES RD
7800
Woodsway Ln
Thornapple Ln
Ridge Ln
W Ridge Dr
River Glen Dr
Deerbrook Dr
Caves Rd
14400
7800
Whispering Pines Dr
Silver Cr
Chagrin River
Russell Ln

Mather Ln
45000
Whisperwood Ln

SEE 2761 MAP

Miles 0   0.25   0.5

1 in. = 2000 ft.

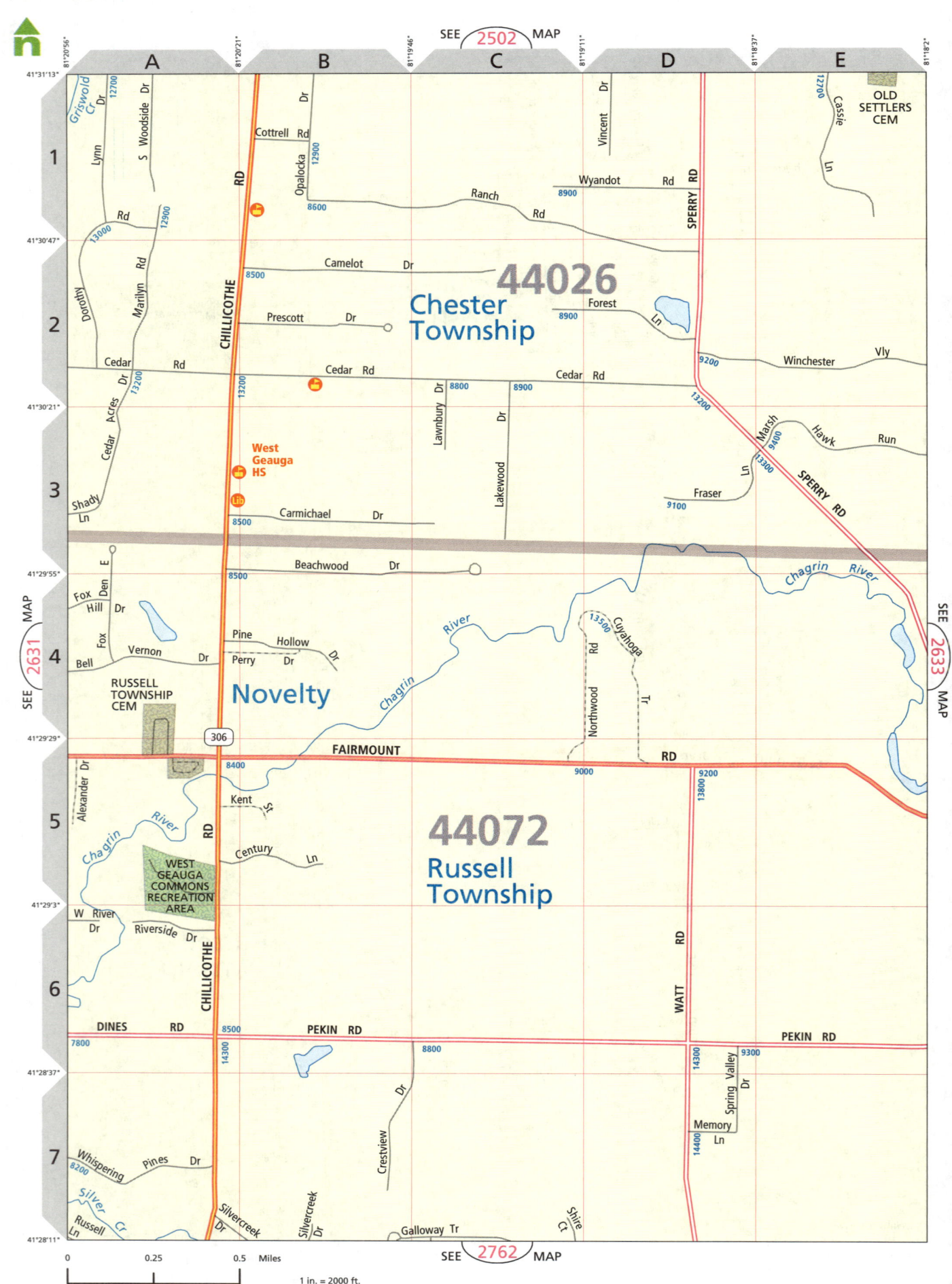

MAP 2632

SEE 2502 MAP

A   B   C   D   E

1

44026

Chester Township

Cottrell Rd

Opalocka 12900

8600

Ranch Rd

Wyandot Rd

8900

Vincent Dr

SPERRY RD

OLD SETTLERS CEM

12700

Cassie Ln

Griswold Cr 12700

Lynn

S Woodside Dr

2

Rd 12900

13000

Dorothy

Marilyn Rd

Camelot Dr

8500

Prescott Dr

Forest

8900

Ln

Winchester Vly

Cedar Rd

Cedar Acres Dr 13200

CHILLICOTHE RD 13200

Cedar Rd

Lawnbury Dr 8800

Lakewood Dr 8900

Cedar Rd

13200

Marsh Ln 9400

Hawk Run

9200

3

Shady Ln

West Geauga HS

Lib

8500

Carmichael Dr

Fraser 9100

SPERRY RD 13300

Beachwood Dr

8500

Chagrin River

4

Fox Hill Den E Dr

Fox Bell

Vernon Dr

Pine Hollow Dr

Perry Dr

Novelty

Chagrin River

Cuyahoga Rd 13500

Northwood Rd

Tr

2631 MAP SEE

RUSSELL TOWNSHIP CEM

306

FAIRMOUNT RD

8400

9000

9200

13800

SEE 2633 MAP

5

Alexander Dr

Chagrin River

WEST GEAUGA COMMONS RECREATION AREA

Kent St

Century Ln

44072

Russell Township

6

W River Dr

Riverside Dr

CHILLICOTHE RD

WATT RD

DINES RD

7800

8500

PEKIN RD

14300

8800

PEKIN RD

14300

9300

Spring Valley Dr

7

Whispering Pines Dr

8200

Silver Cr

Russell Ln

Silvercreek Dr

Silvercreek Dr

Crestview Dr

Galloway Tr

Shire Ct

Memory Ln 14400

SEE 2762 MAP

41°31'13"
41°30'47"
41°30'21"
41°29'55"
41°29'29"
41°29'3"
41°28'37"
41°28'11"

81°20'56"   81°20'21"   81°19'46"   81°19'11"   81°18'37"   81°18'2"

0   0.25   0.5   Miles

1 in. = 2000 ft.

MAP 2633

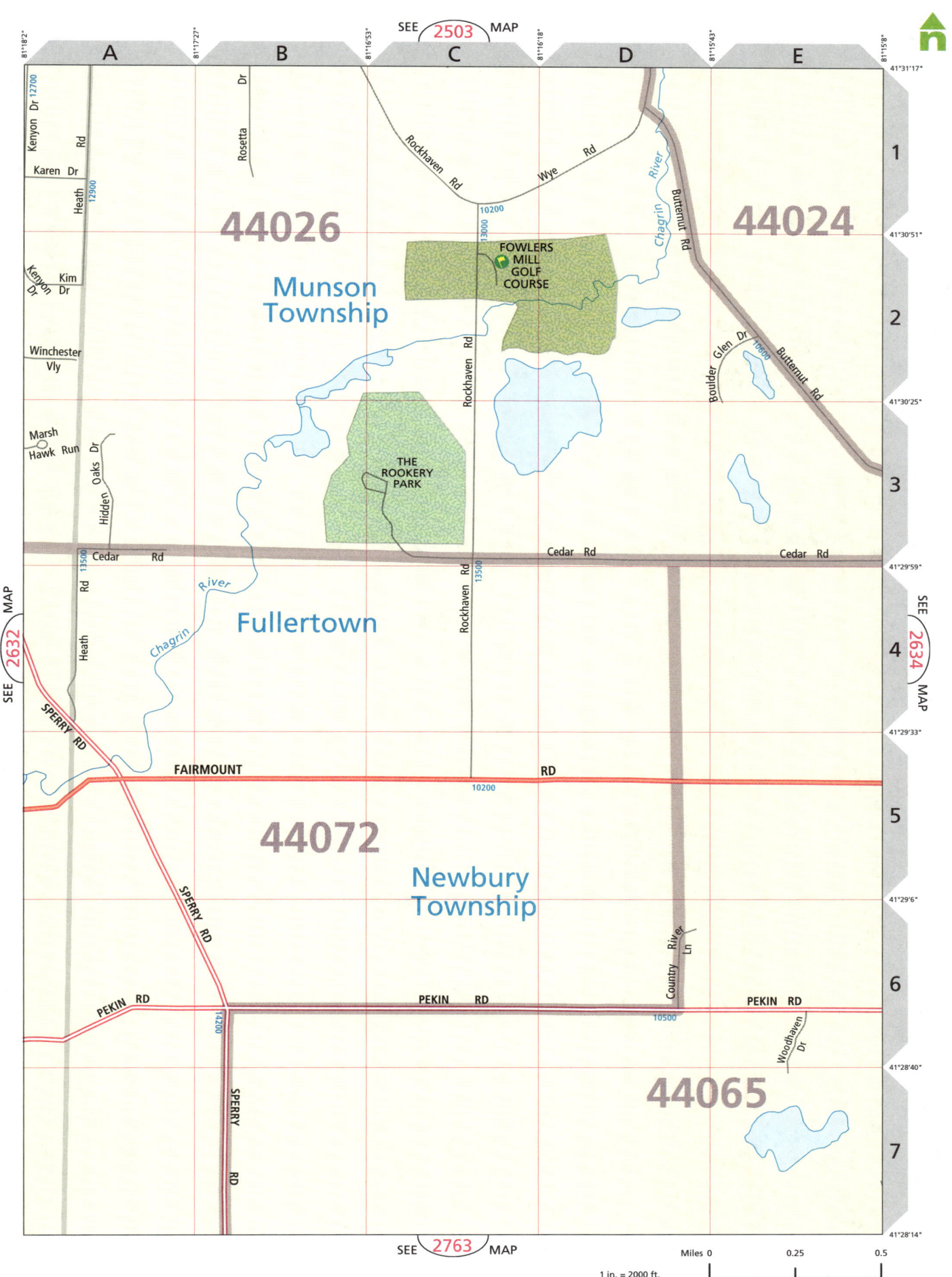

SEE 2503 MAP

A   B   C   D   E

81°18'2"   81°17'27"   81°16'53"   81°16'18"   81°15'43"   81°15'8"

41°31'17"

Kenyon Dr 12700

Karen Dr

Heath Rd

12900

44026

Rosetta Dr

Rockhaven Rd

Wye Rd

Chagrin River

Butternut Rd

44024

41°30'51"

Kenyon Dr

Kim Dr

Munson Township

10200

13000

FOWLERS MILL GOLF COURSE

1

2

Winchester Vly

Rockhaven Rd

Boulder Glen Dr   10600   Butternut Rd

41°30'25"

Marsh Hawk Run

Hidden Oaks Dr

THE ROOKERY PARK

3

13500   Cedar Rd

Cedar Rd

Cedar Rd

41°29'59"

SEE 2632 MAP

13500   Cedar Rd

Heath Rd

Chagrin River

Fullertown

Rockhaven Rd

SEE 2634 MAP

4

41°29'33"

Sperry Rd

FAIRMOUNT   RD

10200

41°29'6"

44072

Newbury Township

5

SPERRY RD

Country River Ln

6

PEKIN RD

14200

PEKIN RD

10500

PEKIN RD

Woodhaven Dr

41°28'40"

SPERRY RD

44065

7

41°28'14"

SEE 2763 MAP

Miles 0   0.25   0.5

1 in. = 2000 ft.

MAP 2634

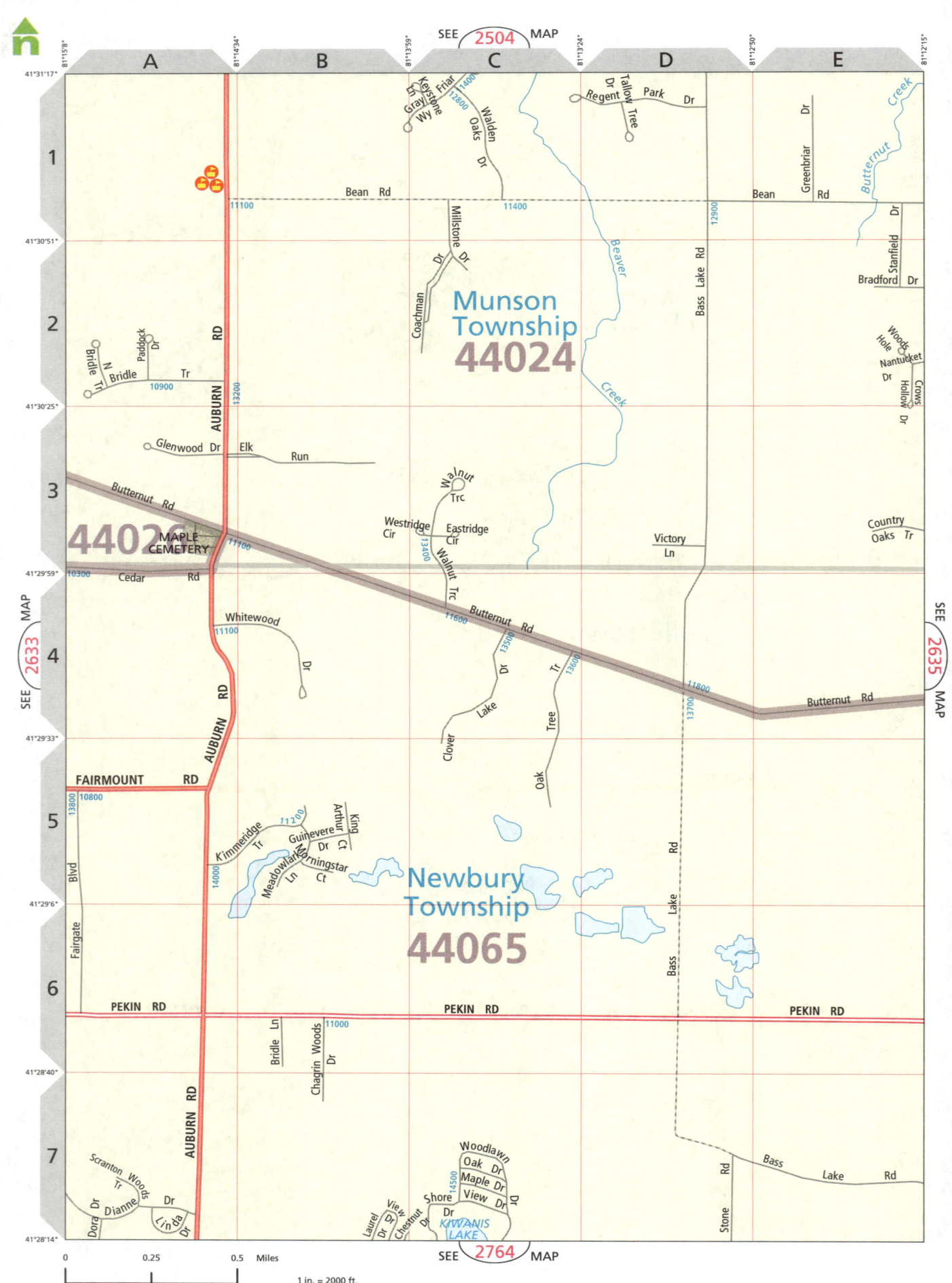

SEE 2504 MAP

A　B　C　D　E

41°31'17"

1

Keystone Wy
Gray Friar
Walden Oaks Dr

Regent Dr
Tallow Tree Park Dr

Greenbriar Dr

Butternut Creek

Bean Rd 11100

Bean Rd 11400

Bean Greenbriar Rd

41°30'51"

12900

2

Munson Township 44024

Coachman Dr

Millstone Dr

Bass Lake Rd

Beaver Creek

Stanfield Dr
Bradford Dr

Bridle Tr N
Bridle Tr
Paddock Dr 10900

AUBURN RD 13200

Woods Hole
Nantucket Dr
Crows Hollow Dr

41°30'25"

3

Glenwood Dr
Elk Run

Walnut Trc

Westridge Cir
Eastridge Cir 13400

Victory Ln

Country Oaks Tr

Butternut Rd

44026

MAPLE CEMETERY 11100

41°29'59"

Cedar Rd 10300

Walnut Trc

Butternut Rd 11600

SEE 2635 MAP

SEE 2633 MAP

4

Whitewood Dr 11100

Lake Dr 13500

Tree Tr 13600

Butternut Rd 11800

Butternut Rd

13700

Clover

Oak

41°29'33"

FAIRMOUNT RD

AUBURN RD

5

Blvd 13800 10800

Kimmeridge Tr
Meadowlark Ln 11200
Guinevere Dr
Morningstar Ct
Arthur Ct
King

Bass Lake Rd

14000

Newbury Township 44065

Fairgate

41°29'6"

6

PEKIN RD

PEKIN RD

PEKIN RD

Bridle Ln
Chagrin Woods Dr 11000

41°28'40"

7

AUBURN RD

Scranton Woods Tr
Dianne Dr
Linda Dr

Woodlawn Dr
Oak Dr
Maple Dr
View Dr
Shore Dr 14500

Bass Lake Rd

Stone Rd

Dora Dr

Laurel Dr
View Dr
Chestnut Dr

KIWANIS LAKE

41°28'14"

SEE 2764 MAP

0　0.25　0.5　Miles

1 in. = 2000 ft.

MAP 2635

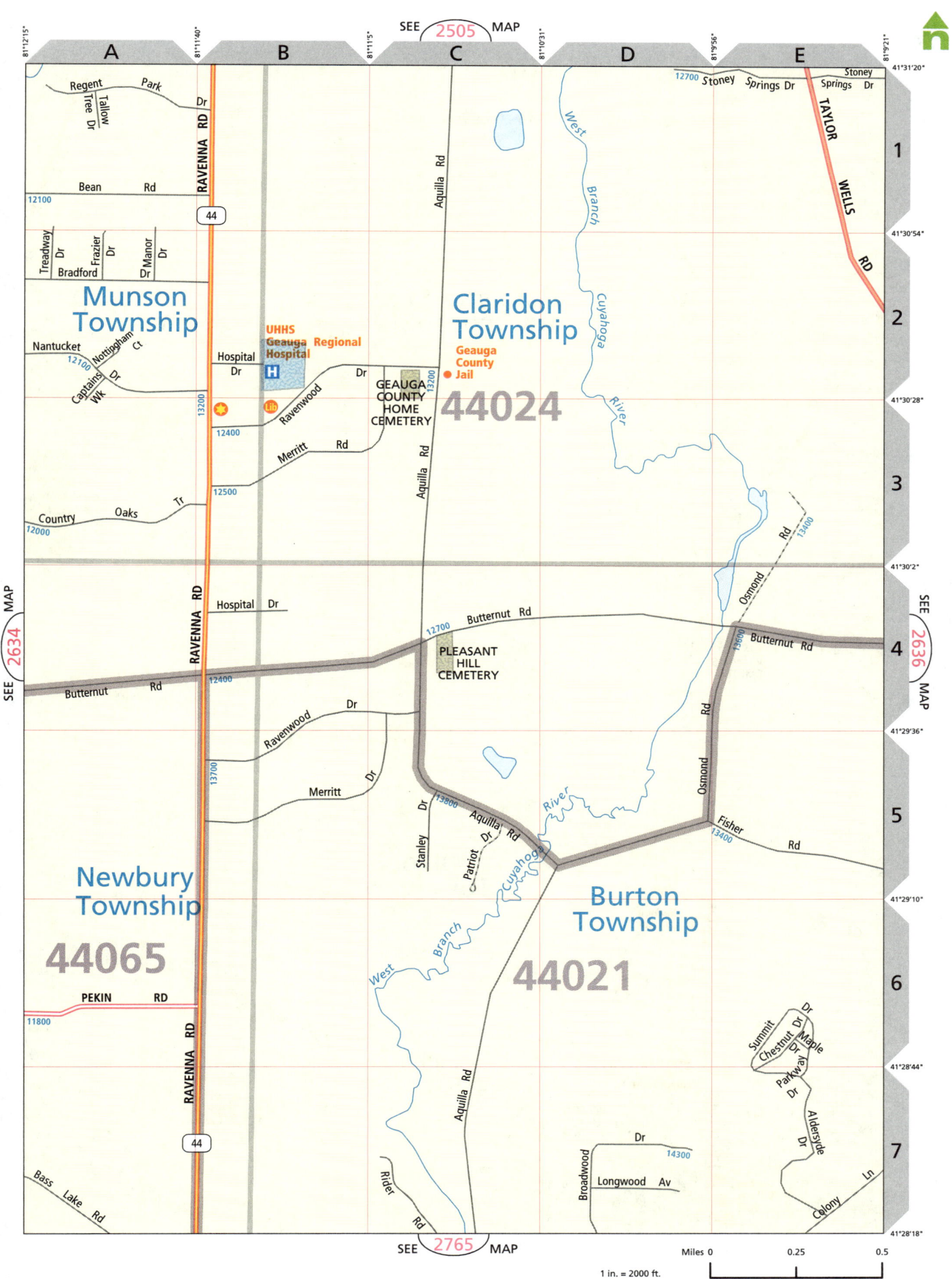

SEE 2505 MAP

A   B   C   D   E

81°12'15"   81°11'40"   81°11'15"   81°10'31"   81°9'56"   81°9'21"

Stoney Springs Dr   Stoney Springs Dr   41°31'20"   1

12700

Regent   Park

Tallow   Tree   Dr

Bean   Rd

12100   41°30'54"

TAYLOR   WELLS   RD

Treadway   Dr   Frazier   Dr Manor Dr

Bradford   Dr

Munson Township   **Claridon Township**   2

Nantucket   Nottingham Ct

12100

Captains   Wk   Dr

Hospital   Dr

UHHS   **Geauga Regional**   Hospital   H   **Geauga County Jail**   **44024**   41°30'28"

RAVENNA   RD   44

13200

Ravenwood   Dr   **GEAUGA COUNTY HOME CEMETERY**   13200

Lib

12400

Merritt   Rd

12500

Country   Oaks   Tr   Aquilla Rd

12000   41°30'2"   3

West   Branch   Cuyahoga   River

Osmond   Rd   13400

Hospital   Dr   41°30'2"

SEE 2634 MAP

SEE 2636 MAP

RAVENNA   RD

Butternut   Rd   12700   Butternut Rd   13600   Butternut Rd   4

12400   **PLEASANT HILL CEMETERY**

Butternut   Rd

13700   Ravenwood   Dr   41°29'36"

Merritt   Dr   Osmond   Rd

Stanley Dr   13800   Fisher   Rd   5

Aquilla   Rd   13400

Newbury Township   Patriot   Dr   Cuyahoga   River   41°29'10"

44065   **Burton Township**   6

44021

PEKIN   RD   West   Branch   Summit Dr   Chestnut Dr   Maple Dr

11800   Parkway Dr   41°28'44"

Aquilla   Rd   Aldersyde Dr

RAVENNA   RD   44   Dr   14300   Colony Ln   7

Broadwood   Longwood   Av

Bass   Lake   Rd   Rider   Rd   41°28'18"

SEE 2765 MAP

Miles 0   0.25   0.5

1 in. = 2000 ft.

MAP 2636

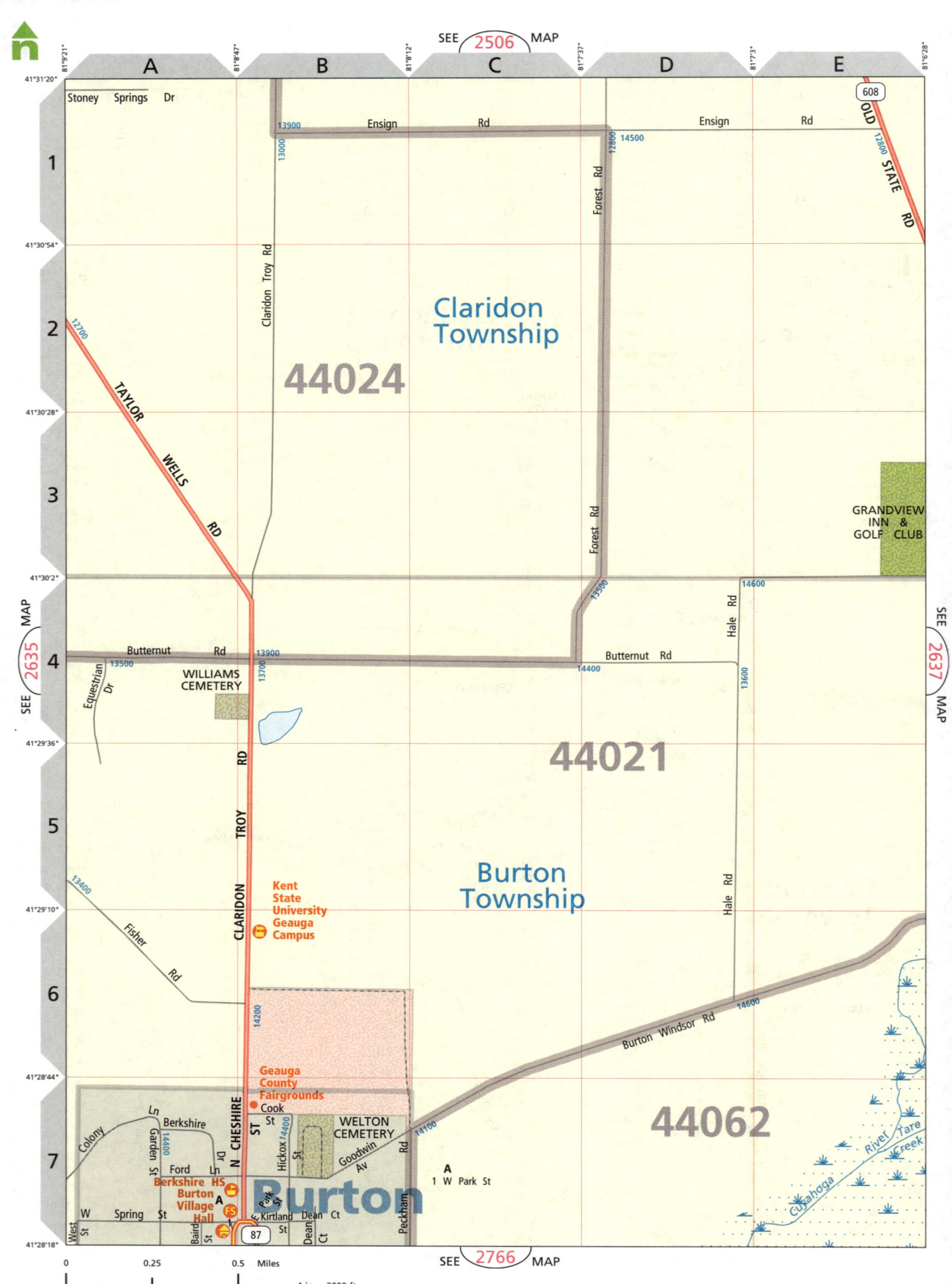

SEE 2506 MAP

A   B   C   D   E

Stoney Springs Dr

Ensign   Rd

13900

Ensign   Rd

OLD STATE RD

608

13000

12800 14500

12800

Claridon Troy Rd

Claridon
Township

44024

12700

TAYLOR

WELLS

RD

Forest Rd

Forest Rd

GRANDVIEW
INN &
GOLF CLUB

SEE 2635 MAP

13500

Butternut   Rd

13900

13700

Butternut   Rd

14400

13500

Hale Rd

14600

13600

SEE 2637 MAP

WILLIAMS
CEMETERY

44021

CLARIDON   TROY   RD

13400

Fisher

Rd

Kent
State
University
Geauga
Campus

Burton
Township

Hale Rd

14200

14600

Burton Windsor Rd

Geauga
County
Fairgrounds

44062

Cook

Colony   Ln
Berkshire

St

Garden St

14400

Ford   Dr   Ln

N CHESHIRE   ST

Hickox 14400

St

WELTON
CEMETERY

Goodwin
Av

Peckham Rd

14100

River Tare Creek

Cuyahoga

Berkshire HS
Burton
Village
Hall

A

A
1 W Park St

Burton

W   Spring St

West
St

E Park St

Kirtland
St

Baird St

87

Dean Ct

Dean Ct

SEE 2766 MAP

0   0.25   0.5   Miles

1 in. = 2000 ft.

MAP 2637

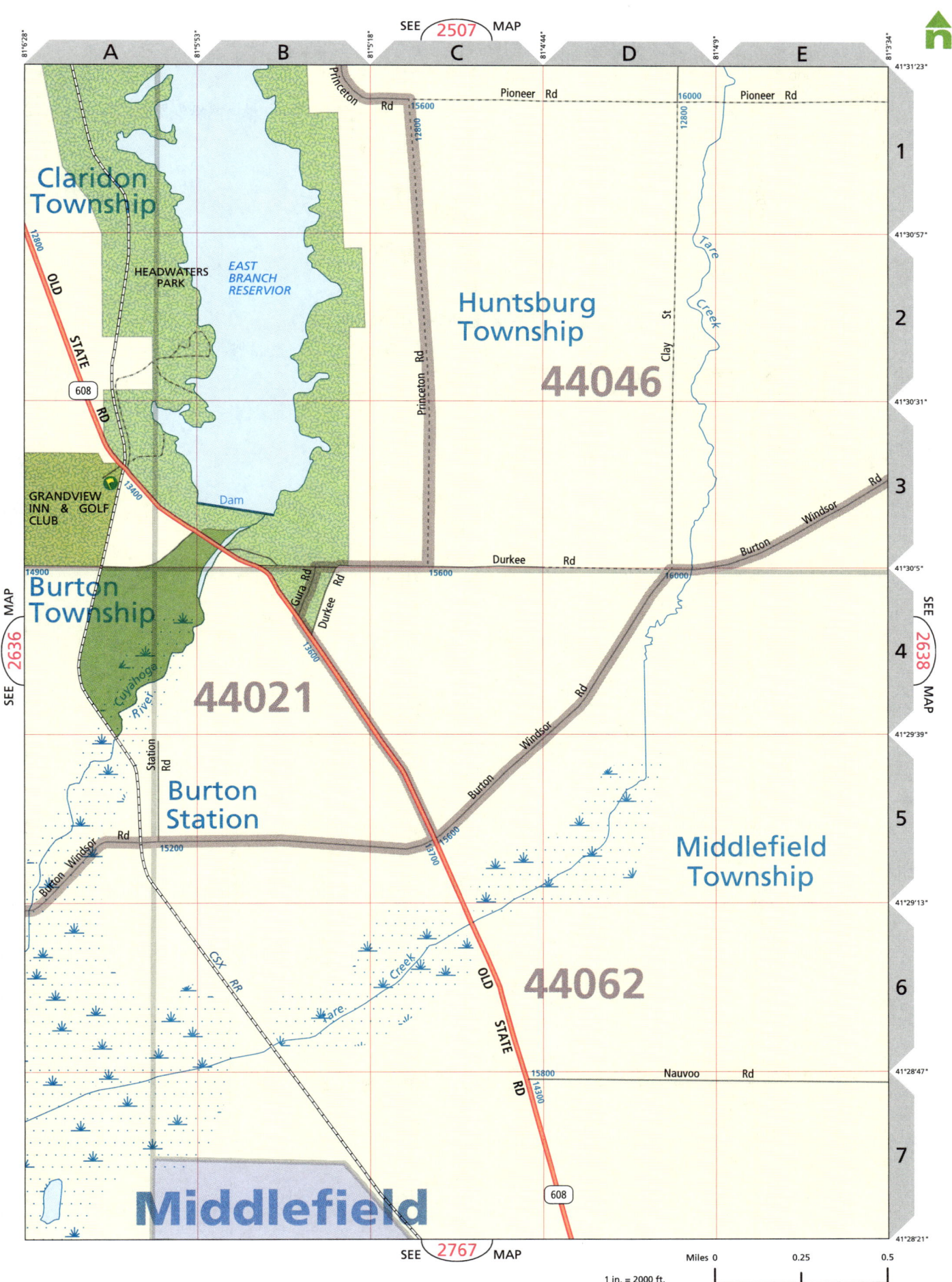

SEE 2507 MAP

A B C D E

81°16'28" 81°15'53" 81°15'18" 81°14'44" 81°14'9" 81°13'34"

Princeton Rd

Pioneer Rd 16000 Pioneer Rd

15600 12800

12800

41°31'23"

1

Claridon Township

41°30'57"

HEADWATERS PARK

EAST BRANCH RESERVOIR

Huntsburg Township

44046

Tare Creek

Clay St

2

41°30'31"

Princeton Rd

OLD STATE RD 608

13400

12800

Dam

GRANDVIEW INN & GOLF CLUB

Windsor Rd

Burton Windsor Rd

3

41°30'5"

14900

Durkee Rd

Gura Rd

Durkee Rd

15600

16000

SEE 2636 MAP

Burton Township

44021

Cuyahoga River

13600

Windsor Rd

4

41°29'39"

SEE 2638 MAP

Station Rd

Burton Station

Burton Windsor Rd

Burton Windsor Rd 15200

15600 15700

Middlefield Township

5

41°29'13"

CSX RR

Tare Creek

44062

6

41°28'47"

Nauvoo Rd

15800

OLD STATE RD 14300

Middlefield

15800

608

7

41°28'21"

SEE 2767 MAP

Miles 0 0.25 0.5

1 in. = 2000 ft.

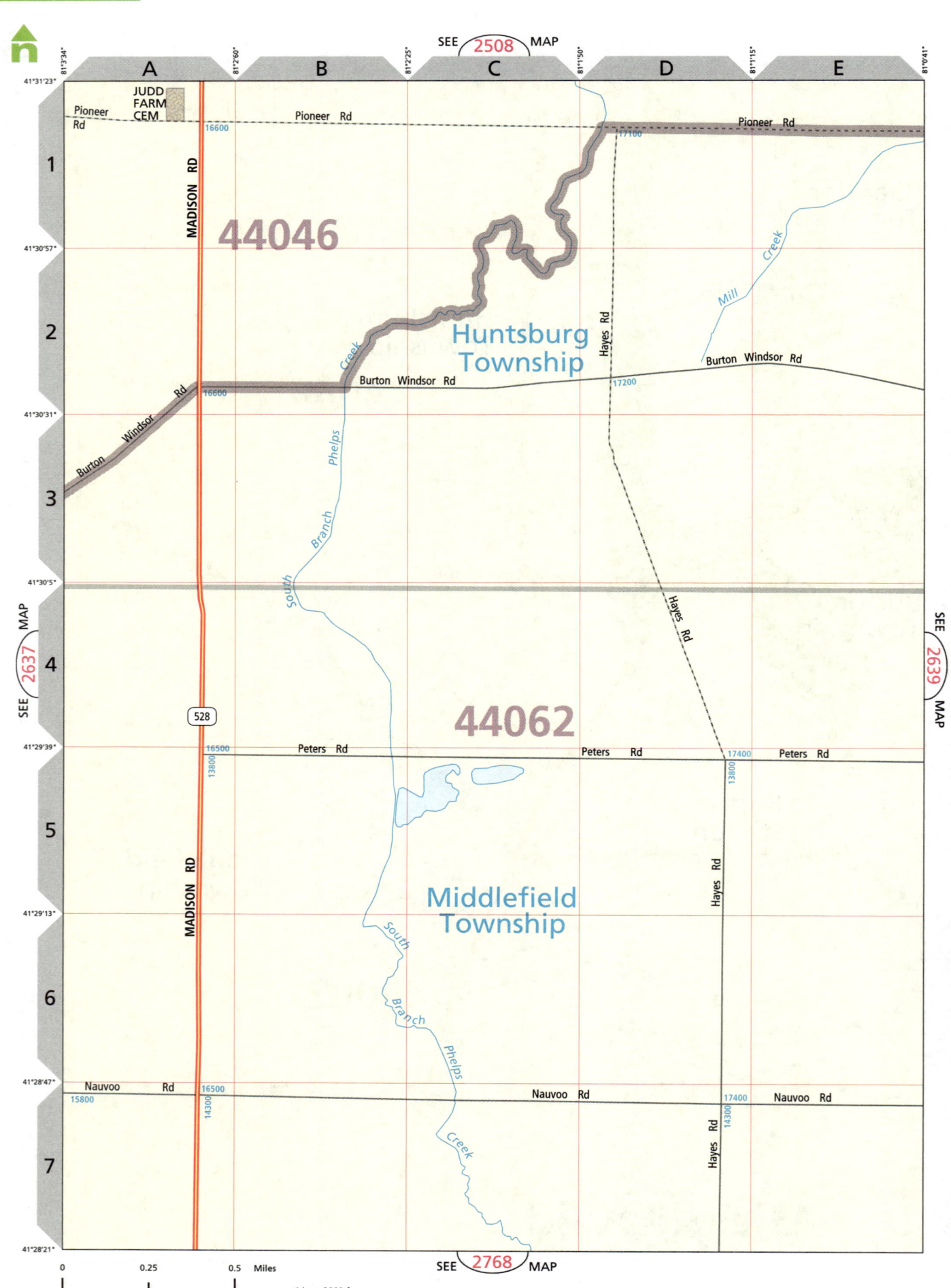

MAP 2638

SEE 2508 MAP

JUDD FARM CEM

Pioneer Rd

Pioneer Rd

Pioneer Rd

16600

17100

MADISON RD

44046

Mill Creek

Huntsburg Township

Hayes Rd

Burton Windsor Rd

Burton Windsor Rd

16600

17200

Phelps

South Branch

Burton Windsor Rd

16600

Hayes Rd

SEE 2637 MAP

SEE 2639 MAP

528

44062

Peters Rd

Peters Rd

Peters Rd

16500

13800

17400

13800

Hayes Rd

Middlefield Township

MADISON RD

South Branch Phelps

Hayes Rd

Nauvoo Rd

Nauvoo Rd

Nauvoo Rd

15800

16500

14300

17400

14300

Creek

Hayes Rd

SEE 2768 MAP

0   0.25   0.5   Miles

1 in. = 2000 ft.

MAP 2639-2739

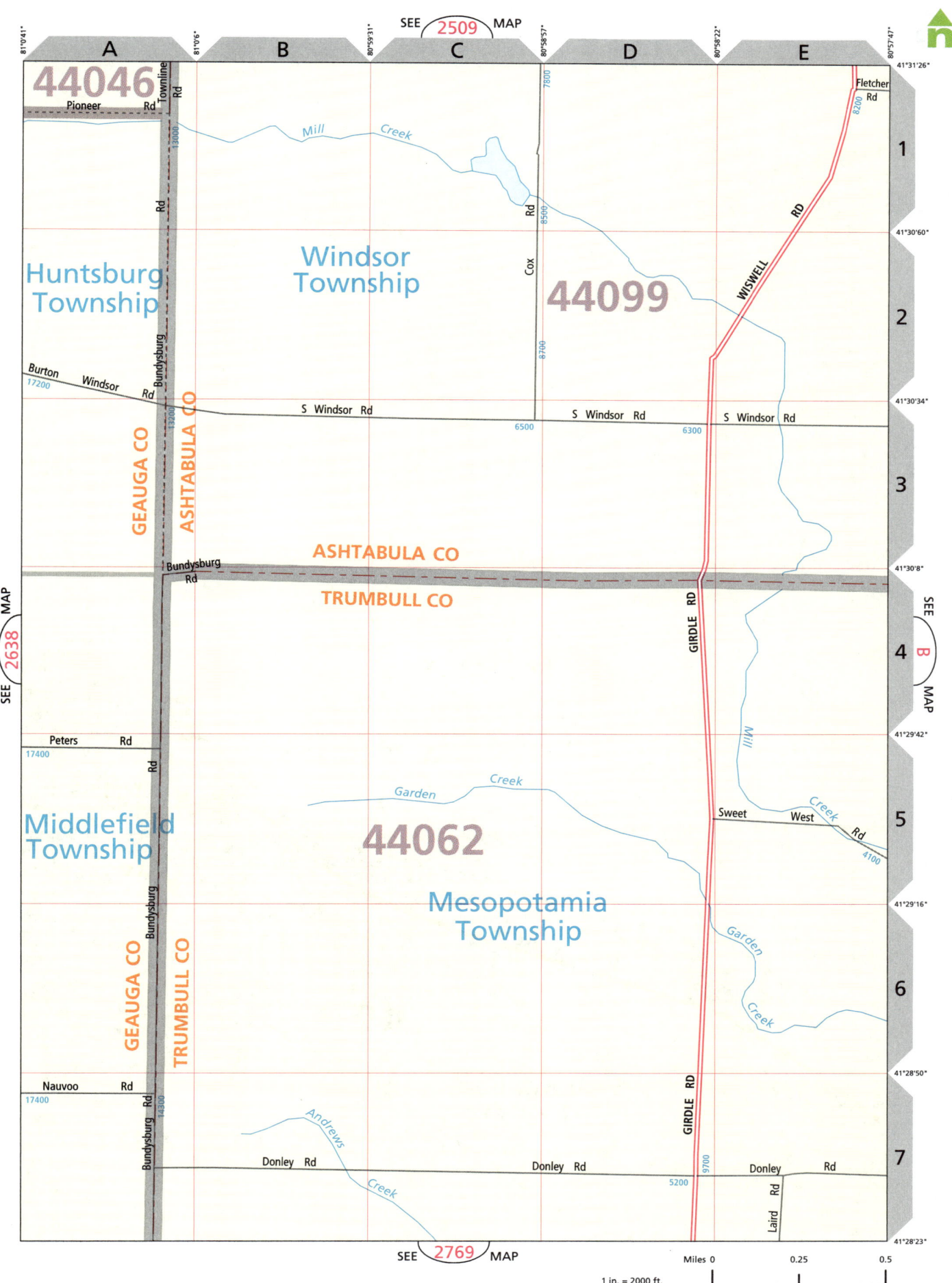

SEE 2509 MAP

N

A B C D E

81°0'41" 81°0'6" 80°59'31" 80°58'57" 80°58'22" 80°57'47"

44046

Pioneer   Rd   Townline Rd
Fletcher Rd
41°31'26"

Mill   Creek
1

Huntsburg
Township
Windsor
Township
41°30'60"

WISWELL RD
2

44099

Cox Rd

GEAUGA CO
ASHTABULA CO
Bundysburg Rd

Burton Windsor Rd
17200
S Windsor Rd   S Windsor Rd   S Windsor Rd
41°30'34"
6500   6300

3

ASHTABULA CO
41°30'8"
Bundysburg Rd
TRUMBULL CO

SEE 2638 MAP
GIRDLE RD
SEE B MAP
4

Peters Rd
17400
41°29'42"

Middlefield
Township
Garden   Creek
Mill   Creek

44062
Sweet   West   Creek Rd
5
4100

Bundysburg Rd
Mesopotamia
Township
41°29'16"

Garden
6

GEAUGA CO
TRUMBULL CO
41°28'50"

Nauvoo Rd
17400
Creek
7

Bundysburg Rd
14300
GIRDLE RD
9700
Andrews   Creek
Donley Rd   Donley Rd   Donley   Rd
5200
Laird Rd
41°28'23"

SEE 2769 MAP
Miles 0   0.25   0.5

1 in. = 2000 ft.

MAP 2740

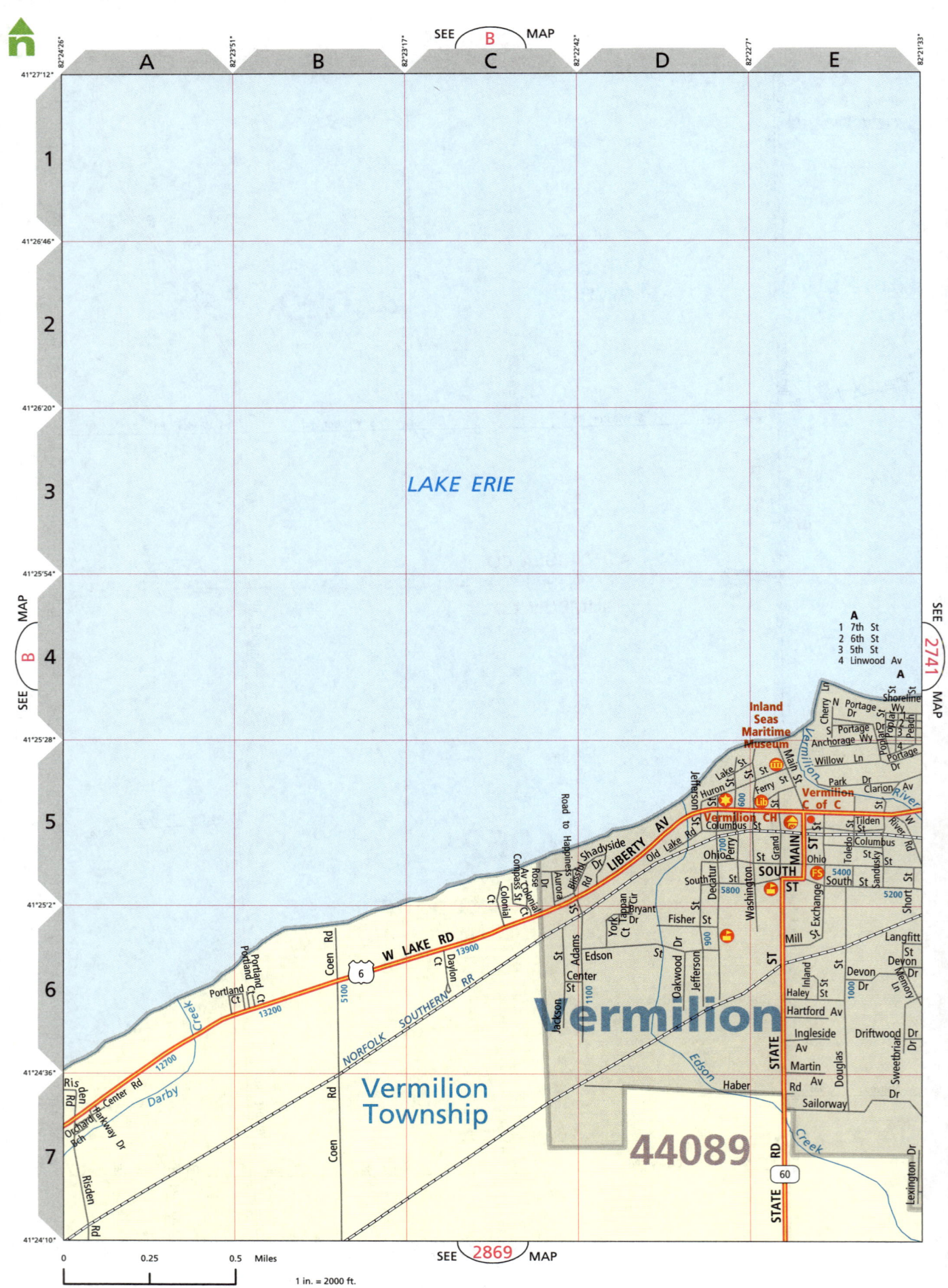

N

SEE B MAP

A B C D E

41°27'12"
41°26'46"
41°26'20"
41°25'54"
41°25'28"
41°25'2"
41°24'36"
41°24'10"

82°24'26" 82°23'51" 82°23'17" 82°22'42" 82°22'7" 82°21'33"

1
2
3
4
5
6
7

SEE B MAP

SEE 2741 MAP

LAKE ERIE

A
1 7th St
2 6th St
3 5th St
4 Linwood Av
A

Inland Seas Maritime Museum

Shoreline Wy
Cherry Ln
N Portage
Portola Dr
Peach
Anchorage Wy
Willow Ln
Park Dr
Clarion Av

Jefferson
Lake St
Huron St
Ferry St
Main St
Vermilion River W
River
Vermilion C of C

Road to Happiness
Shadyside
Rose Dr
Burns Rd
Old Lake Rd
LIBERTY AV
Columbus St
Vermilion CH
Tilden St
Columbus St

Compass Ct
Aurora
Ohio
Perry St
Grand St
MAIN ST
Ohio
Toledo St
Sandusky St

Colonial Ct
Colonial Ct
York Ct
Tappan Cir
Bryant
Southart
Decatur St
5800
SOUTH ST
Exchange
5400
South
5200
Short St

W LAKE RD
6
13900
Daylon
Rose Dr
Adams St
Edson St
Fisher St
900
Mill St
Langfitt St
Devon Dr

Portland Ct
Portland Ct
Coen Rd
5100
Center St
1100
Oakwood
Jefferson
Haley St
Inland St
1000
Devon Dr
Memory Ln

Portland Ct
NORFOLK SOUTHERN RR
Jackson St
Hartford Av
Ingleside Av
Driftwood Dr

Creek
13200
12700
Darby
Vermilion Township
Vermilion
Edson Creek
STATE ST
Martin Av
Sweetbriar Dr

Risden Rd
Orchard Rch
Parkway Dr
Coen Rd
Haber Rd
Sailorway
Douglas Dr

Risden Rd
44089
STATE RD
Creek
60
Lexington Dr

SEE 2869 MAP

0   0.25   0.5   Miles
1 in. = 2000 ft.

MAP 2741

SEE B MAP

A   B   C   D   E

1

LAKE ERIE

2

3

A
1 Cherry St
2 7th St
3 6th St
4 5th St
5 Wa Wa Taysee St
6 Hiawatha Dr

A

EDISON
VILLLAGE
PARK

Menlo Park Ln

Edgewater Dr

Edgewater

Blvd

Elyria Av

Lorain Av

Yorktown Pl

Edgewater Dr

Ford Dr

Cinelna Ln

Rowland Rd

Rowland Rd

Woodridge Rd

Delamere Rd

Guilford Rd

Berkshire Rd

Marlborough Rd

Kensington Rd

Lansing Rd

Claremont

SHOWSE
PARK

Shoreline

Shoreline

Morton Rd

Erie Rd

Elberta Rd

Niagara Rd

Firestone Ln

Thomas Alva Dr

Edison Dr

Aldrich Rd

Harcourt Rd

Fairfax Rd

Essex Rd

Parkland Rd

Roxboro Rd

Cummings Rd

Devonshire Rd

Altamont Rd

Overlook Rd

Mornington Rd

Berkley Rd

BMV

Newbury Dr

Salem Dr

Portland Dr

LIBERTY AV

Telegraph Ln

Berkley Ln

LIBERTY AV

Berkley Rd

6

Bridgeport Dr

Pin Oak Dr

NORFOLK SOUTHERN RR

Dr 3900

Essex 600 Dr

3400

Hazelwood Av

Woodside Av

Nantucket

S Shore Ct

Woodland Dr

Ridgeview Dr

Foxwood Dr

Dogwood Ln

Ann Dr

Morris Rd

Thornwood Rd

Elizabeth Dr

Claremont Rd

Hazelwood Av

Elmwood Dr

Virginia Rd

Woodside

Sunnyside

Frederick Dr

Gardiner Dr

Riverside Dr

Howard Dr

Lagoon Ln

Edgewood

Dorothy Av

Charles Av Dr

Midway Dr

Williams Dr

Frederick Av

Gardiner Rd

Edward Dr

Lewis Dr

Gilbert Dr

NORFOLK SOUTHERN RR

Hilltop Dr

Bridge 800 Rd

High Rd

Boynton Rd

Langfitt St

Devon Dr

Sweetbriar Dr

Nautical Dr

Anchor Point Dr

Larchmont Dr

River Rd

Howard Dr

Wayne Tr

Tomahawk Ln

Cherokee Pth

Arrowhead Dr

44089

Brownhelm Station Rd

3500

South W St

Driftwood Dr

1100

Northview Ct

1100

Holly View Dr

ERIE CO

LORAIN CO

Wildview

Vermilion

1300

4100

Brownhelm Station Rd

Vermilion

Vermilion HS

Southview Dr

Salloway St

Pine View Dr

Wood View Dr

Timber Dr

Birch Av

1400

Beech Dr

Rolling Meadows Dr

W River Rd

200

Marina Ln

Cliffside Dr

VERMILION RD

Hawthorne Ct

Sanford Dr

Maple View Dr

Oak View Dr

Holly Dr

Foreview Dr

View Dr

Idle View Dr

Concord Dr

Hartford Dr

4400

Candy Dr

Linda Dr

**Brownhelm
Township**

VERMILION
RIVER
RESERVATION

Vermilion River

Jerusalem Rd

SEE 2870 MAP

SEE 2740 MAP

SEE 2742 MAP

82°21'33"   82°20'58"   82°20'23"   82°19'49"   82°19'14"   82°18'39"

41°27'19"

41°26'53"

41°26'27"

41°26'1"

41°25'34"

41°25'8"

41°24'42"

41°24'16"

Miles 0   0.25   0.5

1 in. = 2000 ft.

MAP 2742

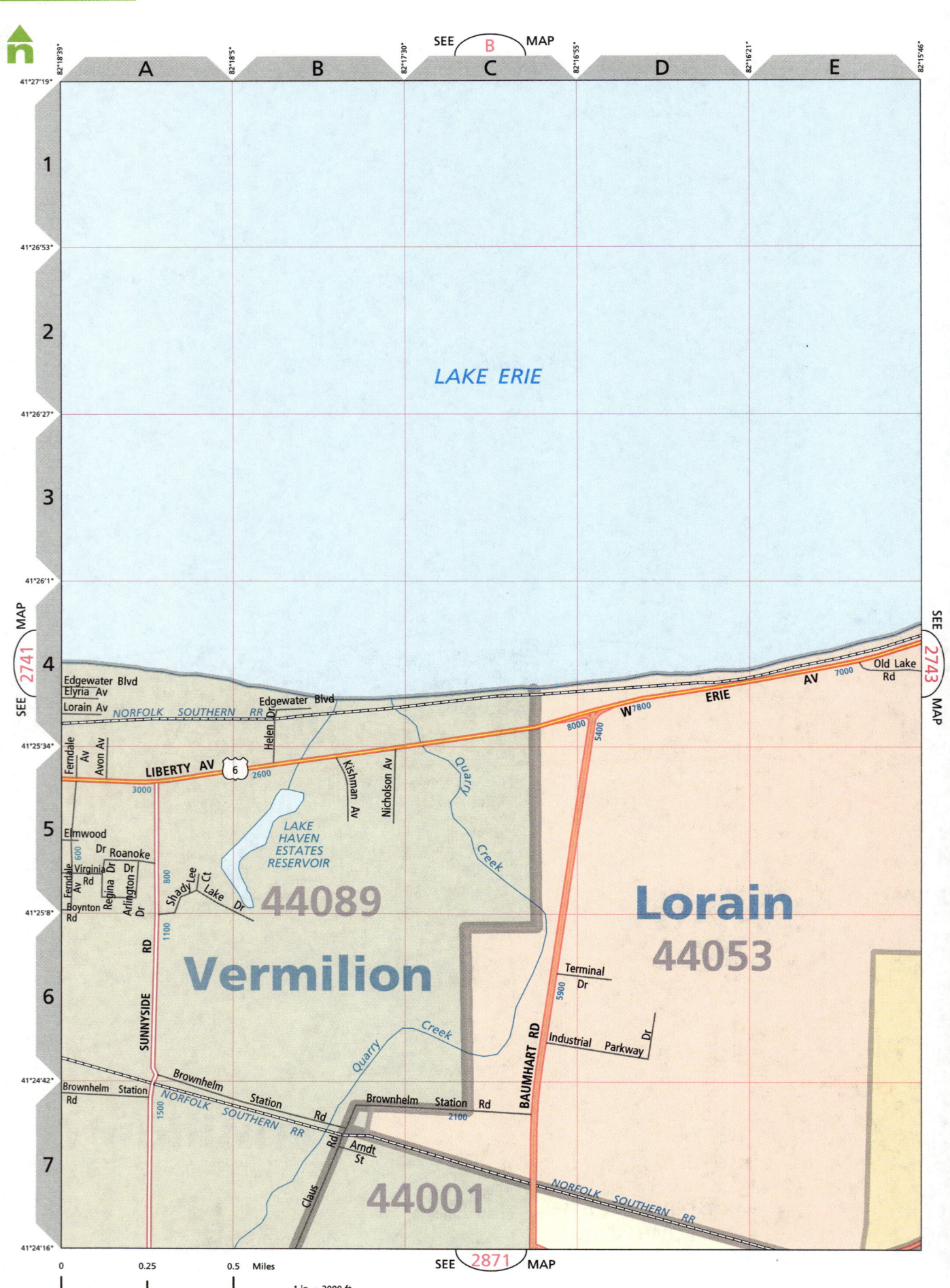

SEE B MAP

A   B   C   D   E

LAKE ERIE

SEE 2741 MAP

SEE 2743 MAP

Edgewater Blvd
Elyria Av
Lorain Av   *NORFOLK SOUTHERN RR*   Edgewater Blvd

Old Lake Rd

ERIE   AV   7000

W7800

8000   5400

Ferndale Av   Avon Av   Helen Dr

LIBERTY AV   6   2600

3000

Kishman Av   Nicholson Av   Quarry   Creek

Elmwood   Dr   Roanoke   Dr
600
Ferndale Av Rd   Virginia   Regina Dr
Arlington   Dr
Boynton Rd

Shady Lee Ct   Lake Dr

LAKE HAVEN ESTATES RESERVOIR

44089

Lorain
44053

Terminal Dr

5900

Industrial   Parkway   Dr

SUNNYSIDE   RD

800

1100

Vermilion

Creek

Quarry

BAUMHART RD

Brownhelm   Station
Brownhelm Station Rd

NORFOLK SOUTHERN RR

Brownhelm Station Rd   2100

1500

Arndt St

Claus

44001

NORFOLK SOUTHERN RR

SEE 2871 MAP

0   0.25   0.5   Miles

1 in. = 2000 ft.

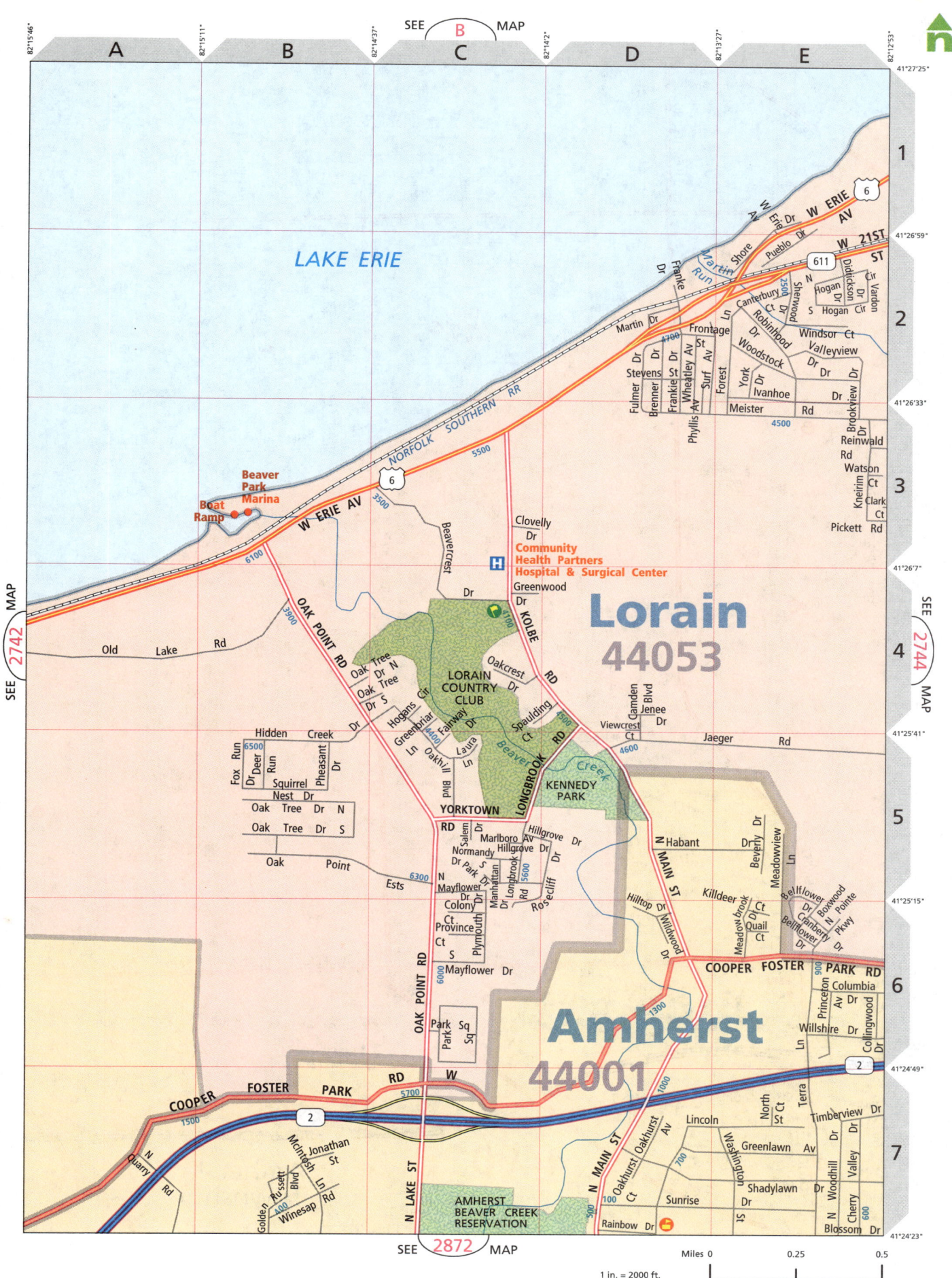

MAP 2743

A B C D E

SEE B MAP

1 2 3 4 5 6 7

LAKE ERIE

US 6
W ERIE AV
W ERIE Dr
W 21ST ST
611
W Erie Av
Martin Shore Dr
Franke Run
Pueblo Dr
Didickson Dr
Cir
Hogan Ln
N S
Hogan Cir
Vardon Dr
Canterbury Ct
2500
Sherwood Dr
Robinhood Dr
Windsor Ct
Valleyview Dr
Martin Dr
Frontage Dr
4700
Woodstock Dr
Stevens St
Wheatley Av
Surf Av
Forest
York
Ivanhoe
Dr
Brookview Dr
Fulmer
Brenner
Frankie St
Phyllis Av
Meister Rd
4500
Reinwald Rd
Watson Ct
Kneirim Ct
Clark Ct
Pickett Rd

Beaver Park Marina
Boat Ramp

NORFOLK SOUTHERN RR
6
5500
W ERIE AV
3500
6100
Beavercrest Dr

Clovelly Dr
Community Health Partners Hospital & Surgical Center
Greenwood Dr
H
4100

Lorain 44053

SEE 2742 MAP
Old Lake Rd
OAK POINT RD
3500
3900

Oakcrest Dr
LORAIN COUNTRY CLUB
Oak Tree Dr N
Oak Tree Dr S
Dr
Hogans Cir
Greenbriar Ln
Fairway Dr
Laura Ln
Oakhill Blvd
Spaulding
KOLBE RD
LONGBROOK RD
4500
Beaver Creek
Camden Blvd
Jenee Dr
Viewcrest Ct
4600
Jaeger Rd
SEE 2744 MAP

Hidden Creek Dr
Fox Run Dr
6500
Deer Run
Squirrel Nest Dr
Pheasant Dr
Oak Tree Dr N
Oak Tree Dr S
Oak Point Ests
6300
YORKTOWN RD

KENNEDY PARK

Salem Dr
Marlboro Av
Normandy Dr
Hillgrove Dr
Hillgrove Dr
Park Dr
Manhattan Dr
N Longbrook Rd
5600
Rosecliff
Mayflower Dr
Colony Ct
Plymouth Ct
Province Ct S
Mayflower Dr
N
N Habant
Dr
Beverly Dr
Drrly
Meadowview Ln
Hilltop Dr
Killdeer Dr
Meadowbrook Ct
Quail Ct
Bellflower Dr
Cranberry Dr
Boxwood Dr
N Pointe Pkwy
MAIN ST
Wildwood Dr
1300
COOPER FOSTER PARK RD
900
Columbia Dr
Princeton Av
Willshire Dr
Collingwood Dr
2

OAK POINT RD
6000
Park Sq

Amherst 44001

COOPER FOSTER PARK RD W
5700
2
1500
2
41°24'49"

Quarry Rd
N
McIntosh St
Jonathan St
Golden Russett Blvd
400
Winesap Rd
Ln
N LAKE ST
500
AMHERST BEAVER CREEK RESERVATION
N MAIN ST
Oakhurst Ct
700
Oakhurst Av
Lincoln Dr
North St
Ct
Terra Dr
Timberview Dr
Washington St
Greenlawn Av
Shadylawn Dr
Sunrise Dr
Rainbow Dr
100
Woodhill Dr
Valley Dr
N Cherry St
600
Blossom Dr

SEE 2872 MAP

Miles 0   0.25   0.5
1 in. = 2000 ft.

82°15'46" 82°15'11" 82°14'37" 82°14'2" 82°13'27" 82°12'53"
41°27'25" 41°26'59" 41°26'33" 41°26'7" 41°25'41" 41°25'15" 41°24'49" 41°24'23"

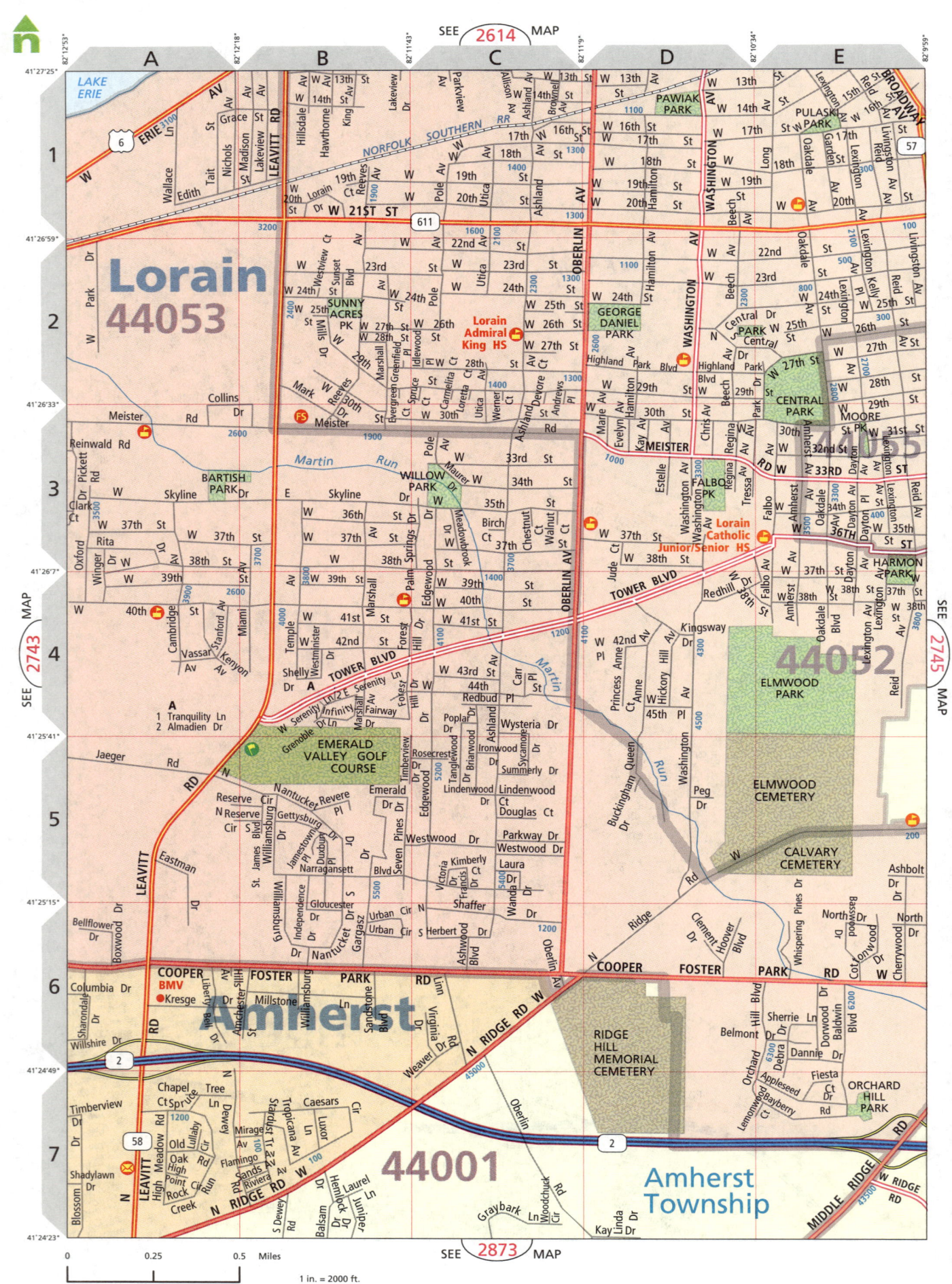

MAP 2744

SEE 2614 MAP

N

LAKE ERIE

Lorain 44053

Amherst

44001

44052

44055

Amherst Township

SEE 2743 MAP

SEE 2745 MAP

SEE 2873 MAP

0   0.25   0.5   Miles

1 in. = 2000 ft.

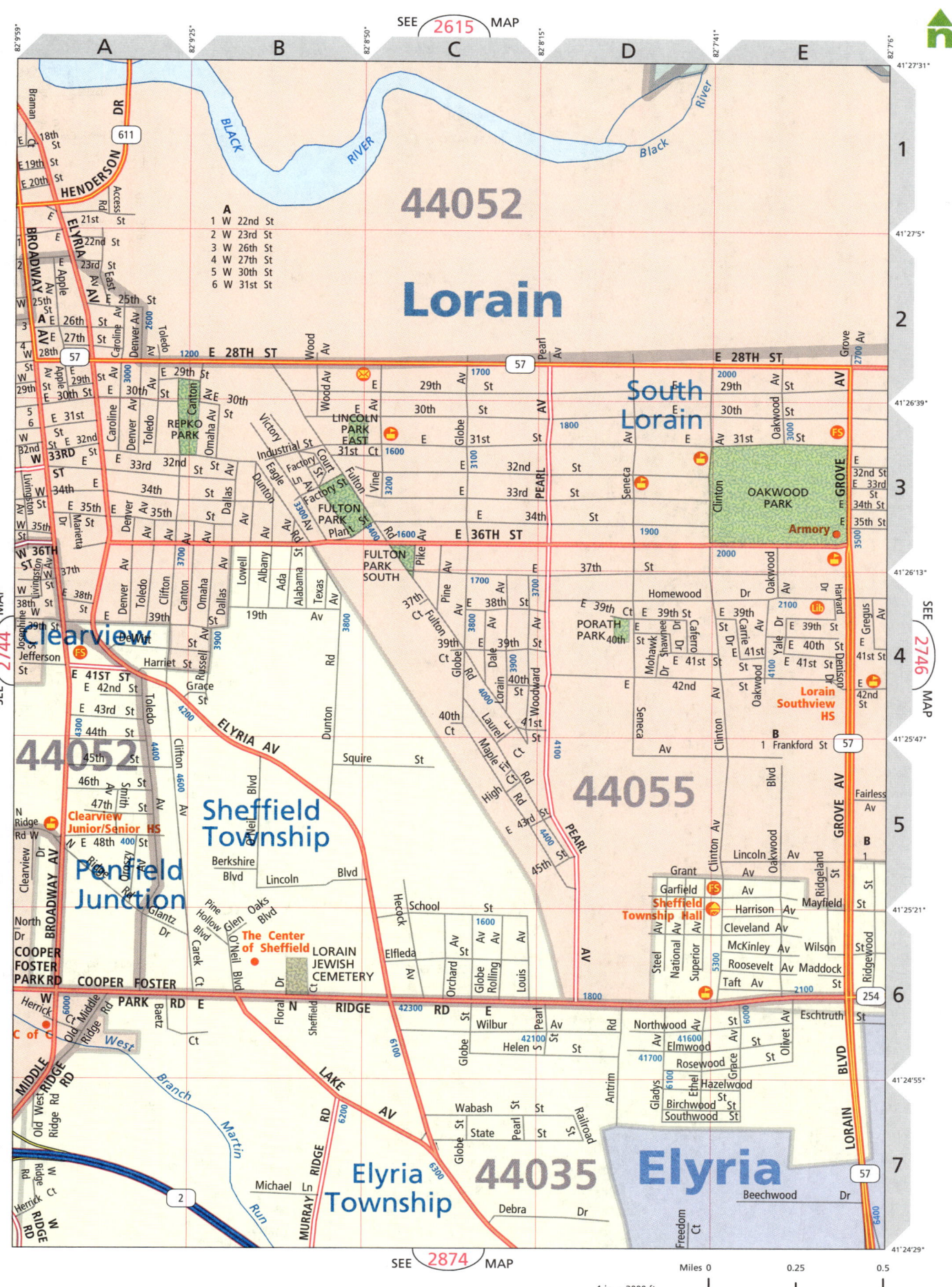

MAP 2745

SEE 2615 MAP

44052

Lorain

A
1 W 22nd St
2 W 23rd St
3 W 26th St
4 W 27th St
5 W 30th St
6 W 31st St

South Lorain

44055

OAKWOOD PARK

Armory

PORATH PARK

Lorain Southview HS

Clearview

Sheffield Township

44052

Clearview Junior/Senior HS

Penfield Junction

COOPER FOSTER PARK RD

The Center of Sheffield

LORAIN JEWISH CEMETERY

Sheffield Township Hall

Garfield

Grant

Elyria Township

44035

Elyria

SEE 2874 MAP

Miles 0   0.25   0.5

1 in. = 2000 ft.

SEE 2744 MAP

SEE 2746 MAP

MAP 2746

SEE 2616 MAP
SEE 2745 MAP
SEE 2747 MAP
SEE 2875 MAP

0   0.25   0.5   Miles

1 in. = 2000 ft.

MAP 2747

SEE 2617 MAP

SEE 2746 MAP

SEE 2748 MAP

SEE 2876 MAP

A   B   C   D   E

1   2   3   4   5   6   7

41°27'37"
41°27'11"
41°26'45"
41°26'19"
41°25'53"
41°25'27"
41°25'1"
41°24'35"

82°24'13"   82°23'38"   82°23'3"   82°22'29"   82°21'54"   82°21'19"

COLORADO   AV

French   Creek

Pin   Oak   Cir
Barkwood   Dr
Oakwood   Dr
Regent   Dr
Kaplan   Dr
Apple   Creek   Dr

Stonefield   Pl
Stonefield   Dr
Greenfield
Deerfield   Dr
Thornfield   Dr
Stonefield   Dr
Springfield   Dr
Deerfield   Dr
French   Creek   Rd

Sheffield
French   Creek   Rd

38500
3500

Eaton   Dr
Carleen
Doovys   St
Bridge   Point   Tr
Glenwood
Stonewood   St
Quail   Ln
Hllw
Yulia   Av
Miriam   Av
Candlewood
Applewood
Dr
Ct
Sandalwood   Dr
Oakwood   Ct
Harvest
Lib
Countryside

Clifton
Lake   Pointe   Wy
Ridgeland
Wisteria   Wy
Violet   Ct
Lilac   Ct
Lilac   Garden   Ln
Holly
Eagle   Creek   Dr
Eagle   Dr
Nest   Cir
Peregrine
Primrose
Periwinkle   Wy   Ln
Falcon   Crest   Av
Lakeland   Dr
Bauerdale   Av
Healthway   Dr
DETROIT   RD

1900
611
254
Hale   Av
Church   St
Julian   St
Orchard   St
37100

Avon   HS

Hatteras   Wy
Egg   Hbr
Silverton   St
Viking   Ct
Neptunis   Cir
Lakes   Ln
Fountain   Century
Briar   Cir
Century   Ln

Hayes   St
Centennial   Av

AVONDALE
GOLF
COURSE

Moon   Rd
Kline   Ditch

DETROIT   RD
254
39100
4000

Avon
44011

Deer   Run
Hunters   Tr
S   Ridge   Dr
Truxton   Pl
Pelham   Pl
Harriman   Tr
3600

Stoney   Ridge   Rd

French   Creek
Creekview   Ln   Mapleview   Ln
Oakview   Ln
Kinzel   Rd
36600

RESTHAVEN
MEMORY
GARDEN

Meadow   Ln

Long   Rd
Ridge   Rd
Arabian   Ct
Stoney   Ridge   4700

Haverford   Pl
Astoria   Wy
Cardonia   Cir
Park   S
Fernway   Dr   Cir

Case   Rd
Evergreen   Cir
Northfield   Dr
Stallion   Ct
Chase   Ct
Derby
Steeple   Dr
Belmont   Dr
Secretariat   Ct
Bridle   Wy
Churchill   Dr
Arabian   Ct
Camelot   Dr
Clover   Ln
Golden   Rod   Cir
4800

Mills   Rd   36600

North
Ridgeville   44039

Stoney   Ridge   Rd

Case   Rd

Miles   0   0.25   0.5
1 in. = 2000 ft.

MAP 2748

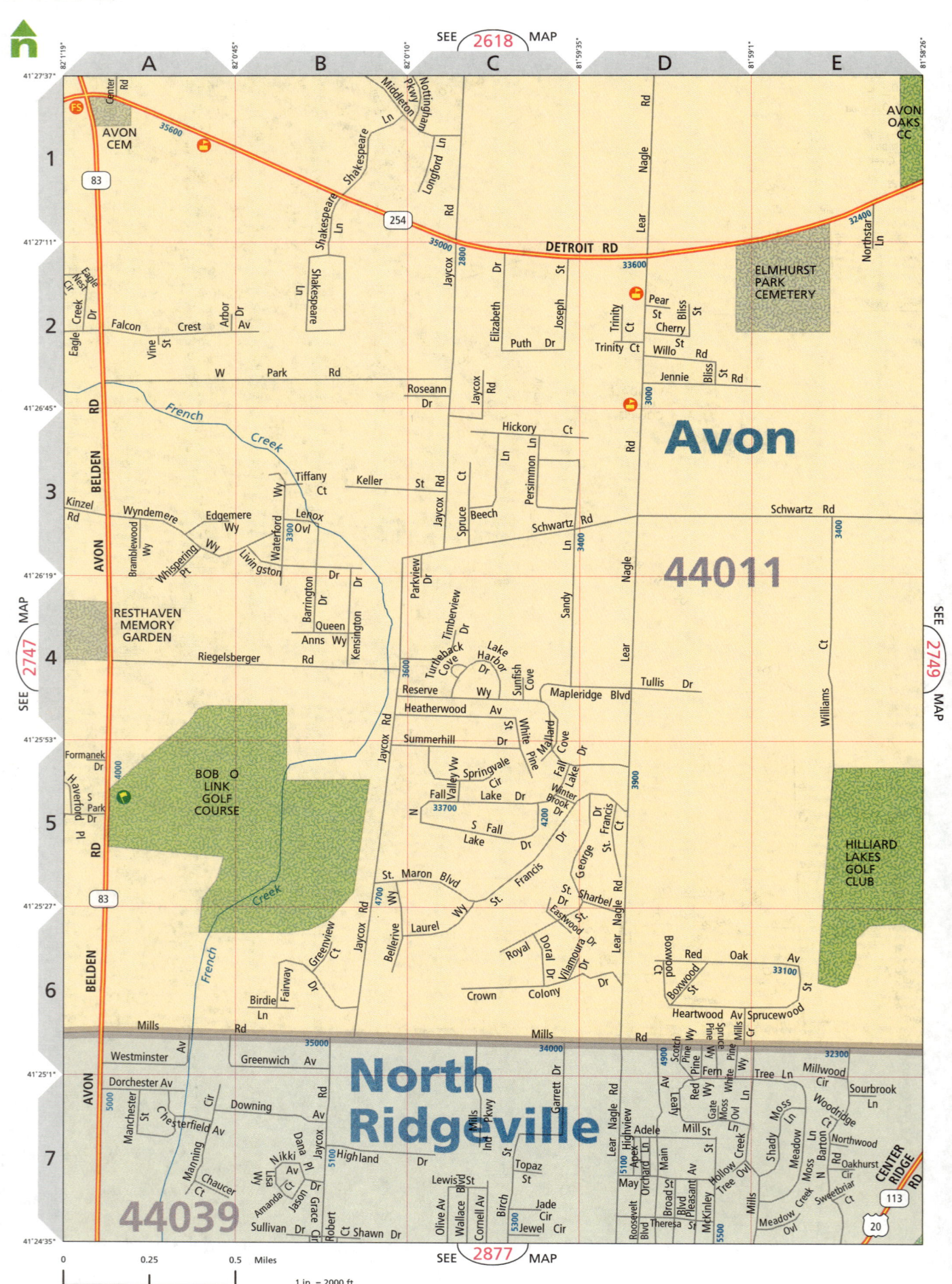

SEE 2618 MAP

A   B   C   D   E

Avon

44011

Avon Oaks CC

ELMHURST PARK CEMETERY

AVON CEM

RESTHAVEN MEMORY GARDEN

BOB O LINK GOLF COURSE

HILLIARD LAKES GOLF CLUB

North Ridgeville

44039

SEE 2747 MAP

SEE 2749 MAP

DETROIT RD

SEE 2877 MAP

0   0.25   0.5   Miles

1 in. = 2000 ft.

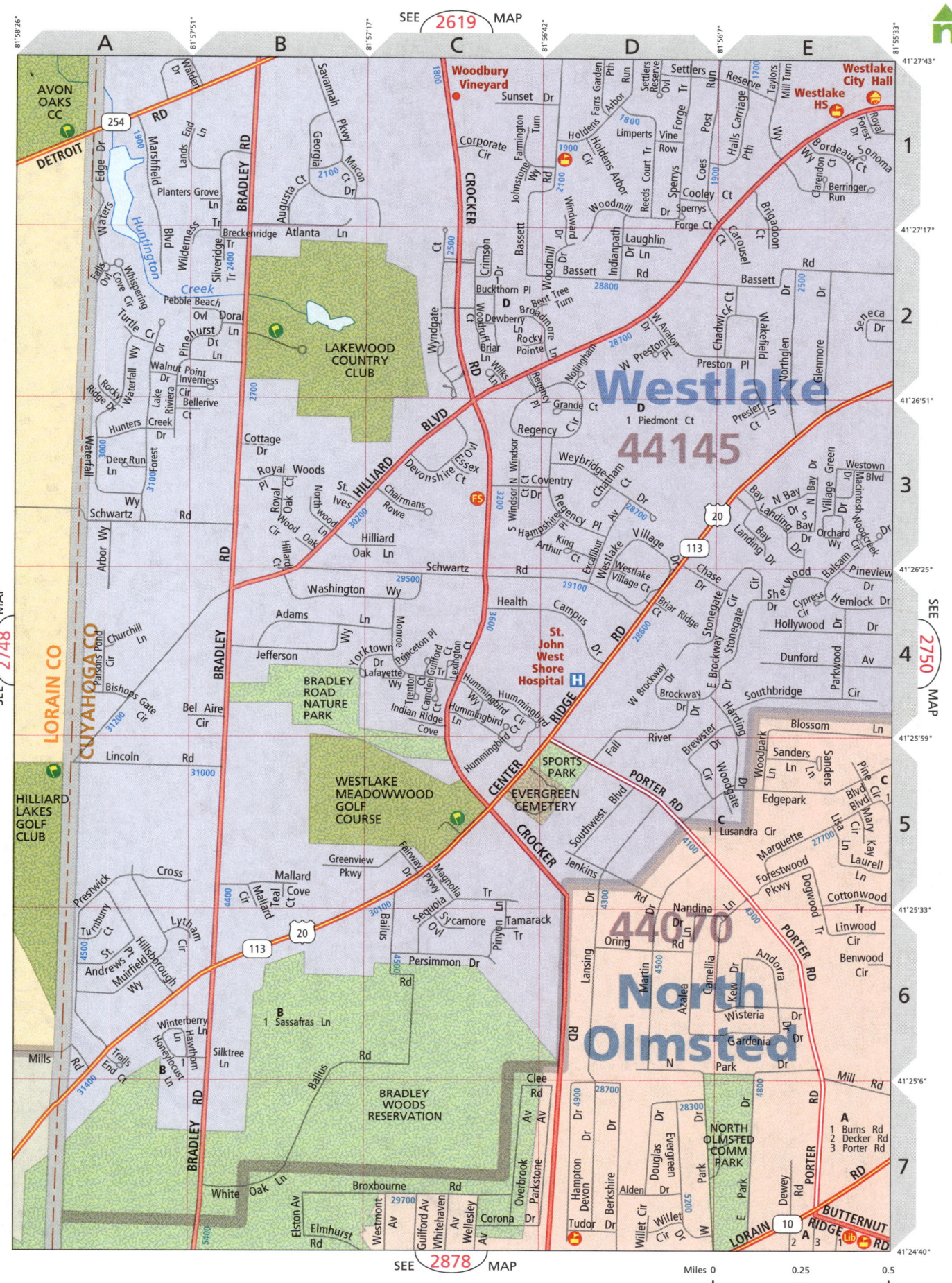

MAP 2749

SEE 2619 MAP

SEE 2748 MAP

SEE 2750 MAP

SEE 2878 MAP

Miles 0   0.25   0.5

1 in. = 2000 ft.

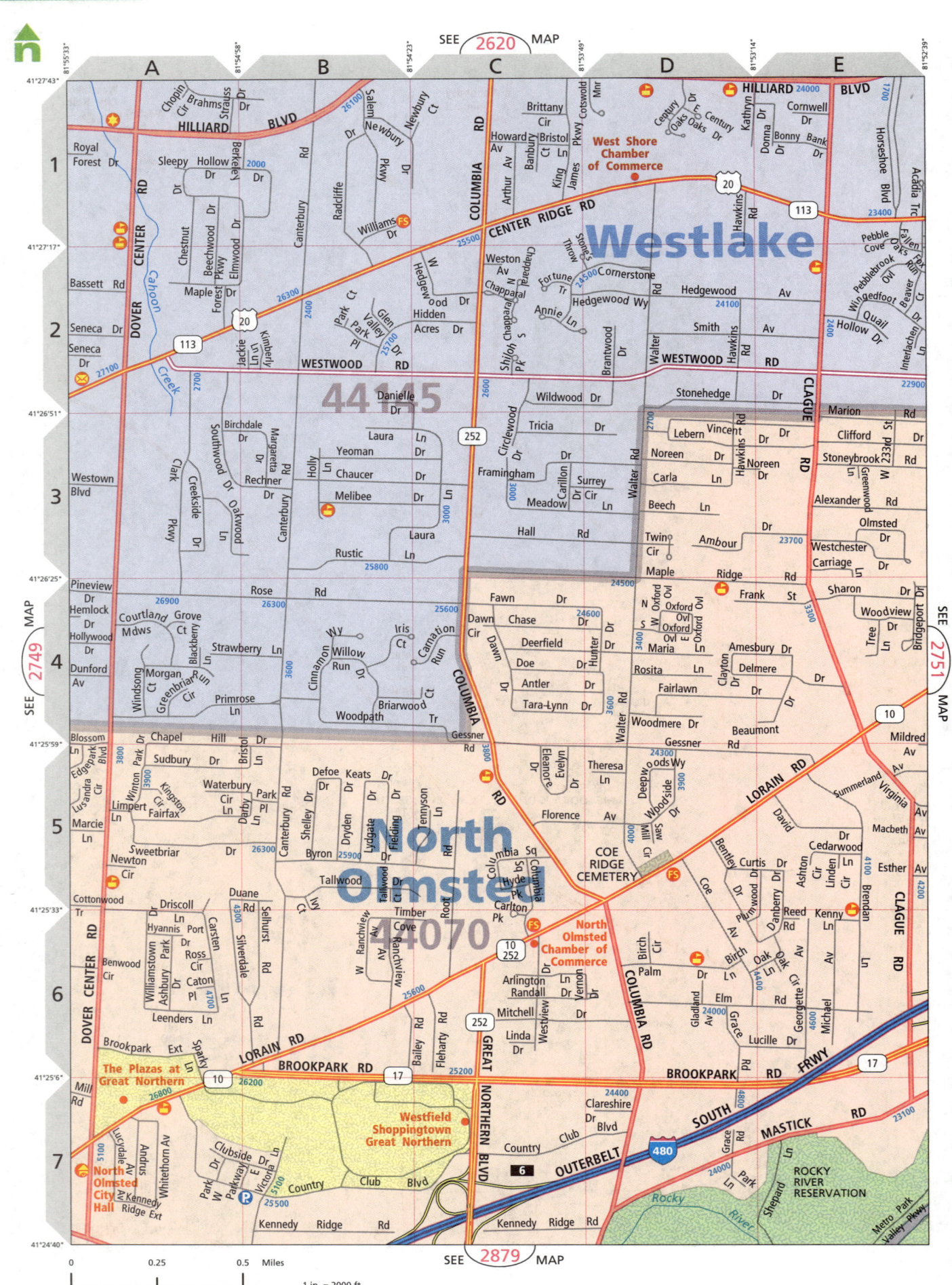

MAP 2750

SEE 2620 MAP

SEE 2749 MAP

SEE 2751 MAP

SEE 2879 MAP

Westlake

44145

North Olmsted 44070

West Shore Chamber of Commerce

North Olmsted Chamber of Commerce

North Olmsted City Hall

The Plazas at Great Northern

Westfield Shoppingtown Great Northern

ROCKY RIVER RESERVATION

Coe Ridge Cemetery

HILLIARD

0   0.25   0.5   Miles
1 in. = 2000 ft.

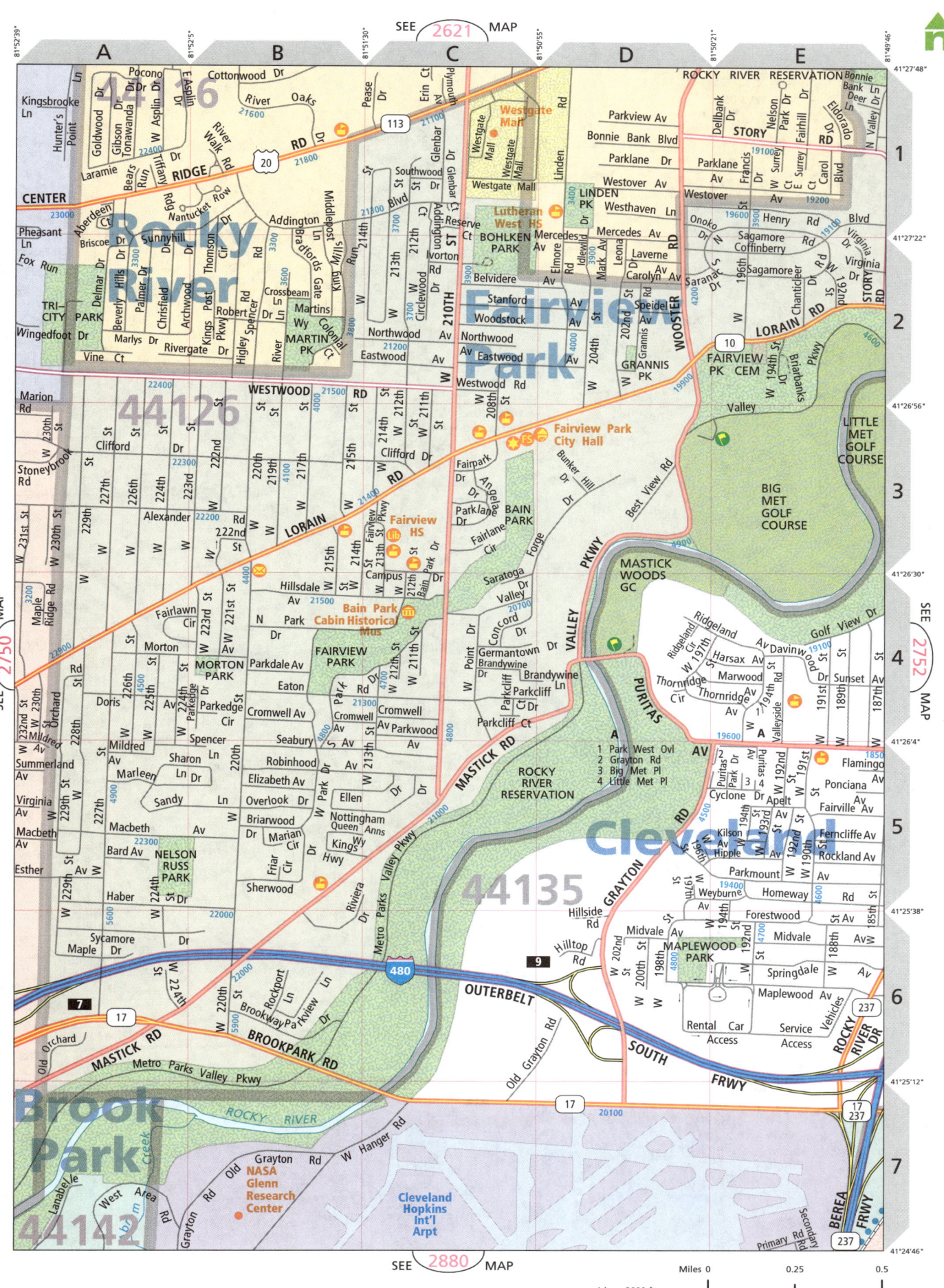

MAP 2751

SEE 2621 MAP

SEE 2750 MAP

SEE 2752 MAP

SEE 2880 MAP

Miles 0   0.25   0.5

1 in. = 2000 ft.

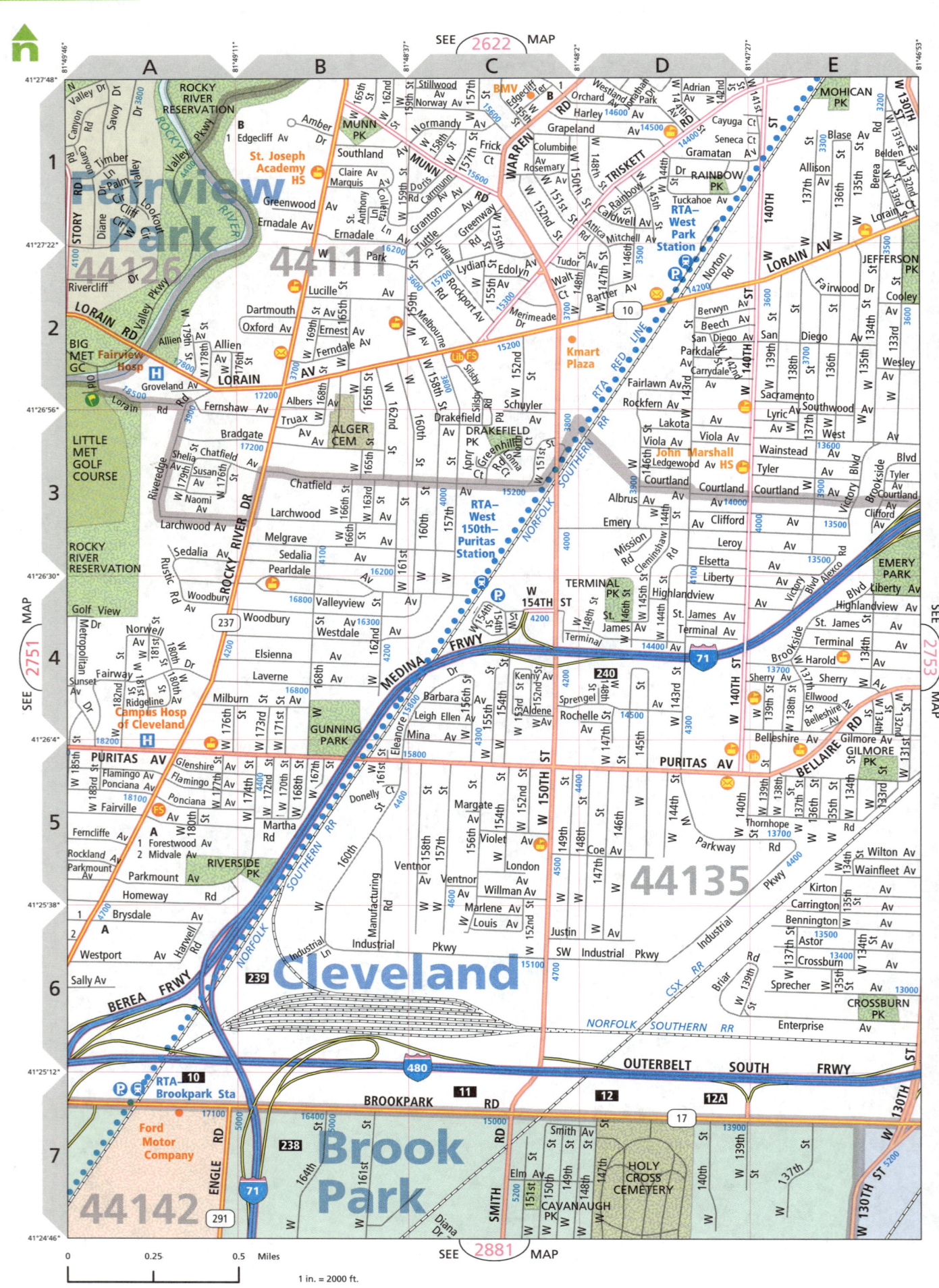

MAP 2752

SEE 2622 MAP

SEE 2751 MAP

SEE 2753 MAP

SEE 2881 MAP

N

Fairview Park 44126

44111

BIG MET GC

Fairview Hosp

LITTLE MET GOLF COURSE

ROCKY RIVER RESERVATION

ROCKY RIVER RESERVATION

St. Joseph Academy HS

ALGER CEM

Campus Hosp of Cleveland

GUNNING PARK

RIVERSIDE PK

Cleveland

44135

Ford Motor Company

44142

Brook Park

HOLY CROSS CEMETERY

EMERY PARK

JEFFERSON PK

MOHICAN PK

RAINBOW PK

RTA—West Park Station

John Marshall HS

RTA—West 150th—Puritas Station

TERMINAL PK

CROSSBURN PK

GILMORE PK

RTA—Brookpark Sta

0   0.25   0.5 Miles

1 in. = 2000 ft.

MAP 2753

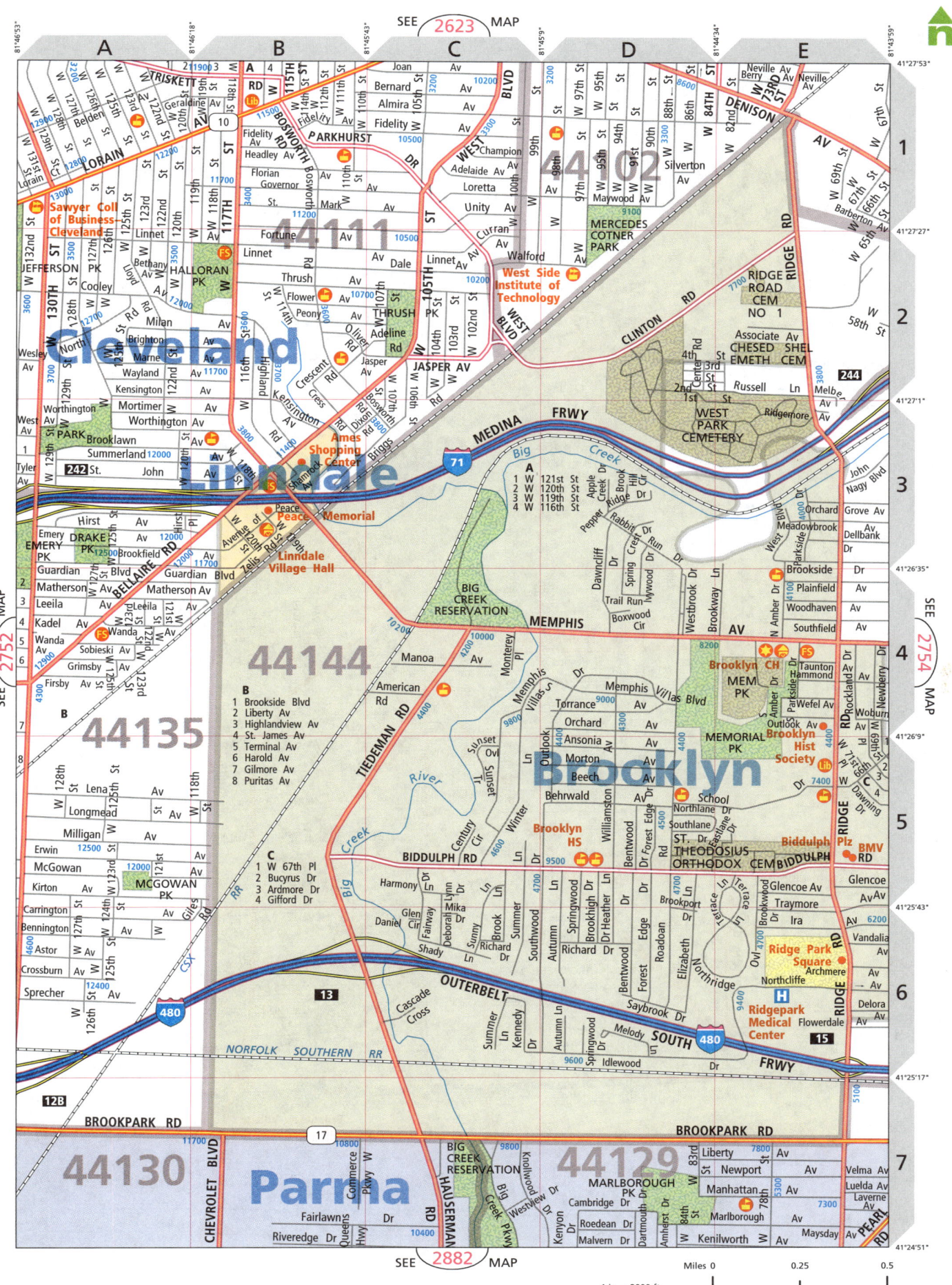

SEE 2623 MAP

44102

44111

Cleveland

Linndale

44135

44144

B
1 Brookside Blvd
2 Liberty Av
3 Highlandview Av
4 St. James Av
5 Terminal Av
6 Harold Av
7 Gilmore Av
8 Puritas Av

C
1 W 67th Pl
2 Bucyrus Dr
3 Ardmore Dr
4 Gifford Dr

A
1 W 121st St
2 W 120th St
3 W 119th St
4 W 116th St

Brooklyn

44130

Parma

44129

SEE 2752 MAP

SEE 2754 MAP

SEE 2882 MAP

Miles 0   0.25   0.5

1 in. = 2000 ft.

MAP 2754

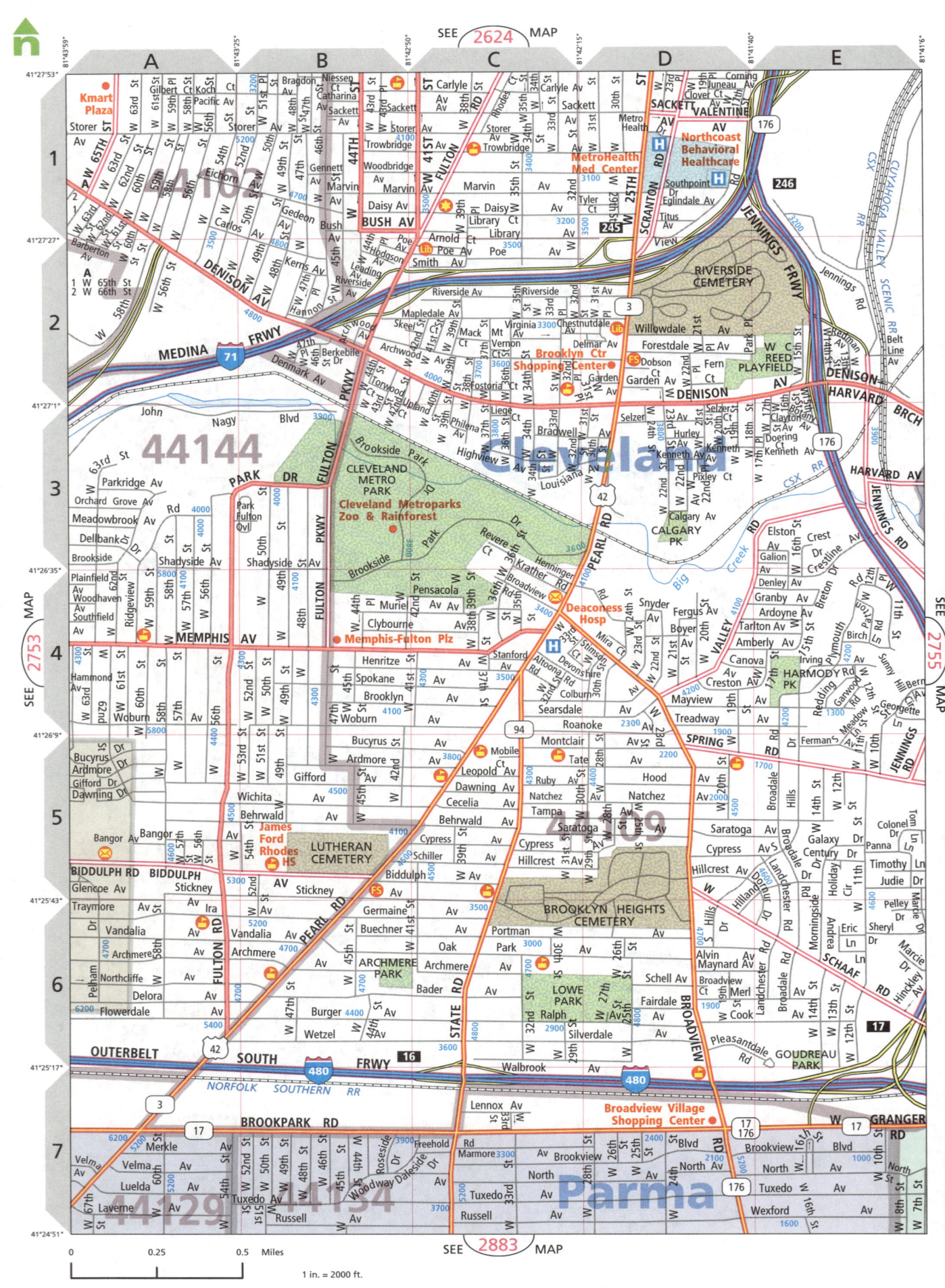

SEE 2624 MAP
SEE 2753 MAP
SEE 2755 MAP
SEE 2883 MAP

0   0.25   0.5   Miles

1 in. = 2000 ft.

MAP 2755

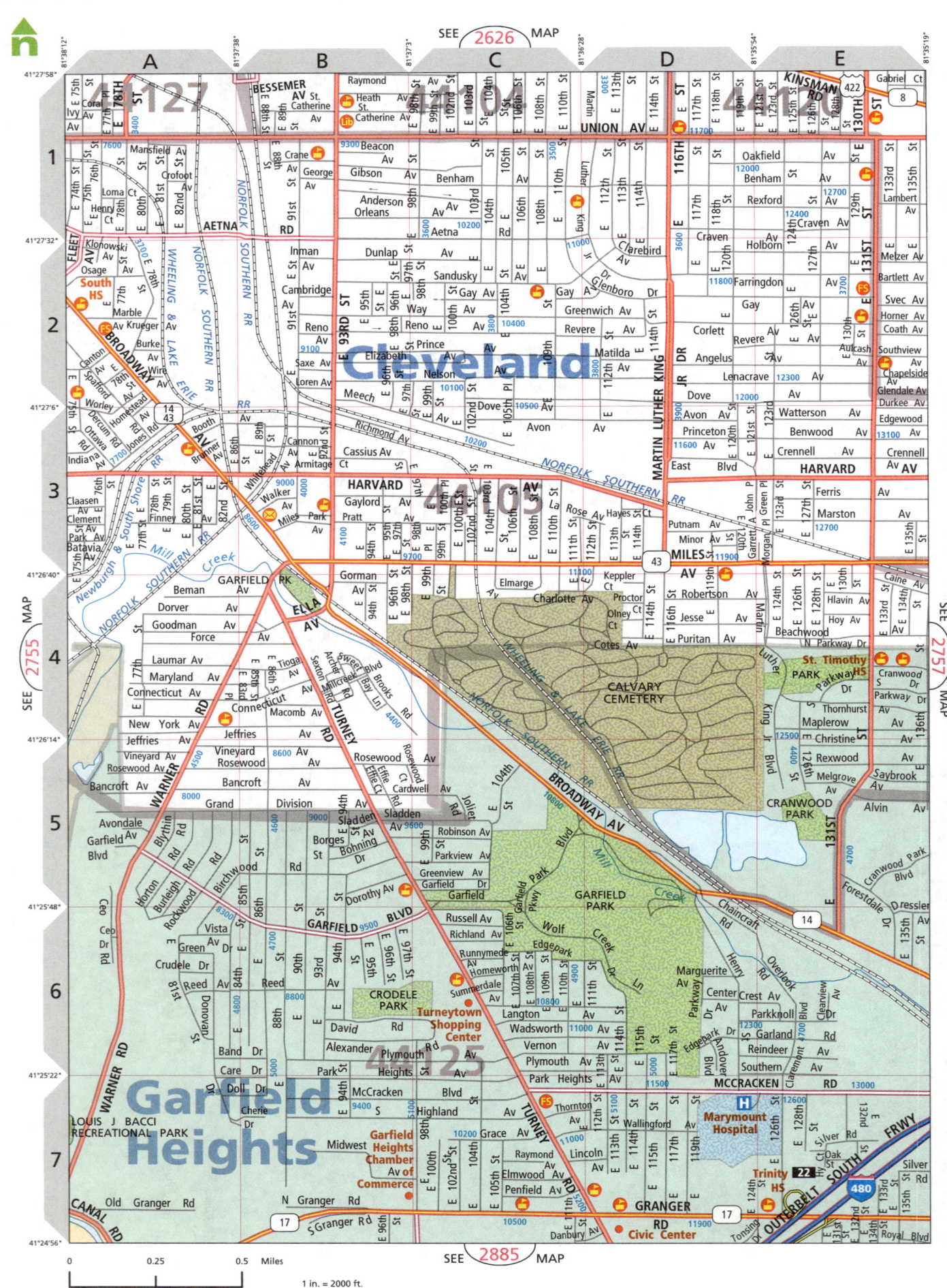

MAP 2756

SEE 2626 MAP

SEE 2755 MAP

SEE 2757 MAP

SEE 2885 MAP

Cleveland

Garfield Heights

1 in. = 2000 ft.

0   0.25   0.5 Miles

MAP 2757

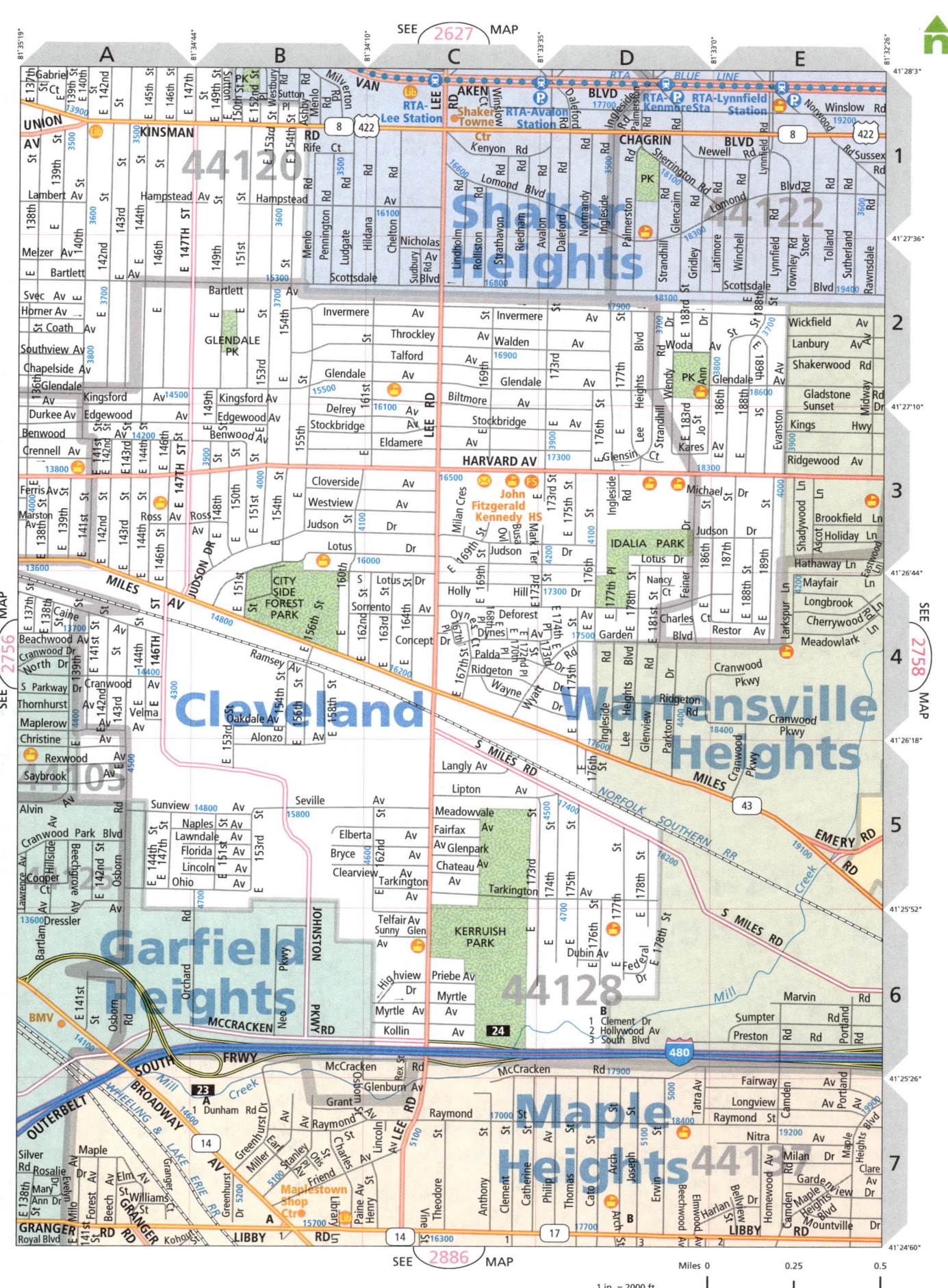

SEE 2627 MAP

SEE 2756 MAP

SEE 2758 MAP

SEE 2886 MAP

Miles 0   0.25   0.5

1 in. = 2000 ft.

MAP 2758

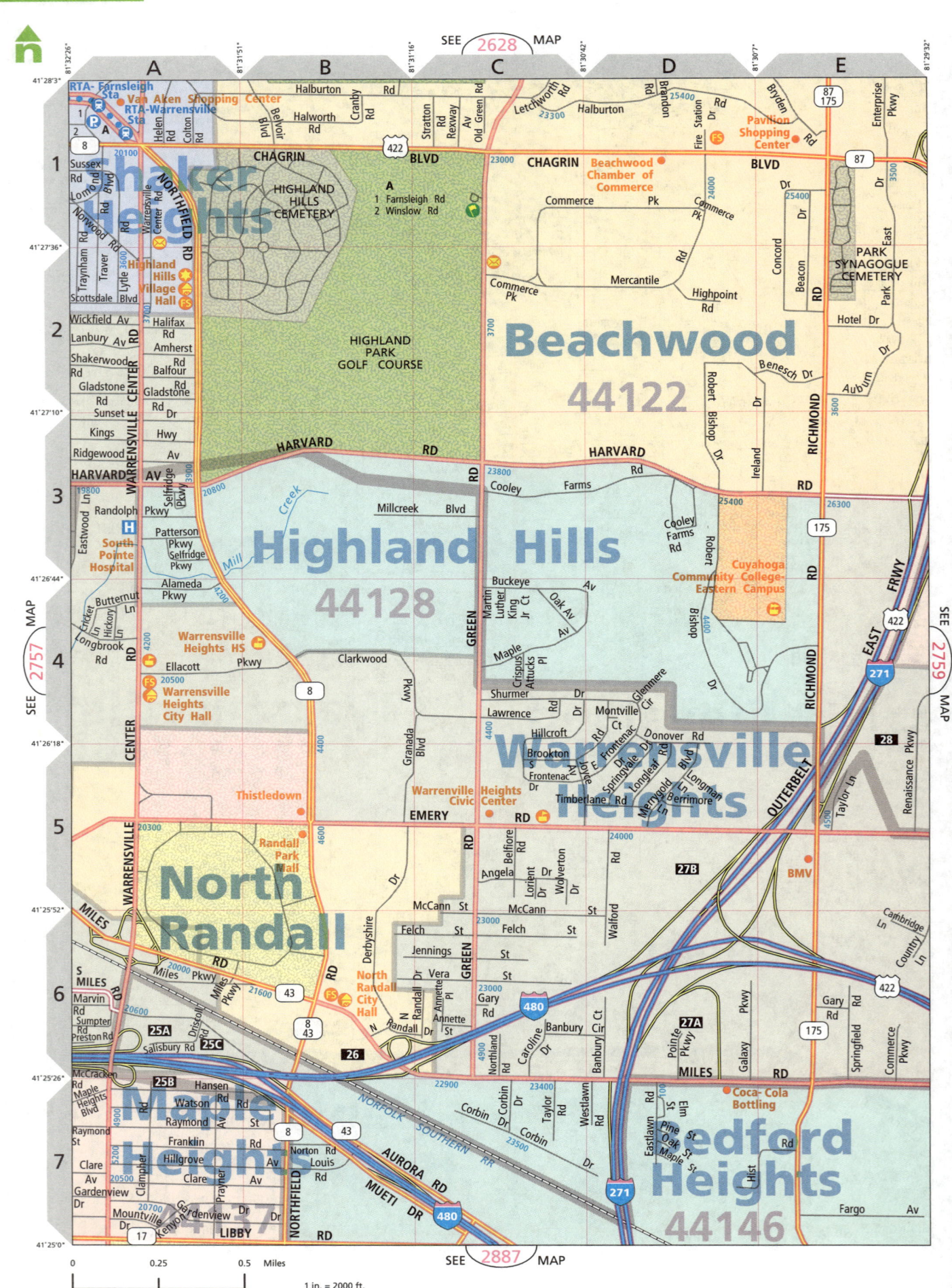

SEE 2628 MAP

SEE 2757 MAP

SEE 2759 MAP

SEE 2887 MAP

Shaker Heights

HIGHLAND HILLS CEMETERY

HIGHLAND PARK GOLF COURSE

A
1 Farnsleigh Rd
2 Winslow Rd

RTA- Farnsleigh Sta
Van Aken Shopping Center
RTA-Warrensville Sta

CHAGRIN BLVD

CHAGRIN

Beachwood 44122

Beachwood Chamber of Commerce

Pavilion Shopping Center

PARK SYNAGOGUE CEMETERY

Highland Hills Village Hall

HARVARD RD

HARVARD RD

Highland Hills 44128

Millcreek Blvd

Cooley Farms Rd

Cooley Farms Rd

South Pointe Hospital

Cuyahoga Community College- Eastern Campus

Warrensville Heights HS

Warrensville Heights City Hall

Clarkwood

Thistledown

Warrensville Heights

Randall Park Mall

Warrensville Heights Civic Center

EMERY RD

North Randall

McCann St

Felch St

Jennings St

North Randall City Hall

BMV

MILES RD

S MILES RD

MILES RD

Maple Heights 44137

Coca- Cola Bottling

Bedford Heights 44146

NORFOLK SOUTHERN RR

AURORA RD

MUETI DR

LIBBY

Fargo Av

0   0.25   0.5   Miles

1 in. = 2000 ft.

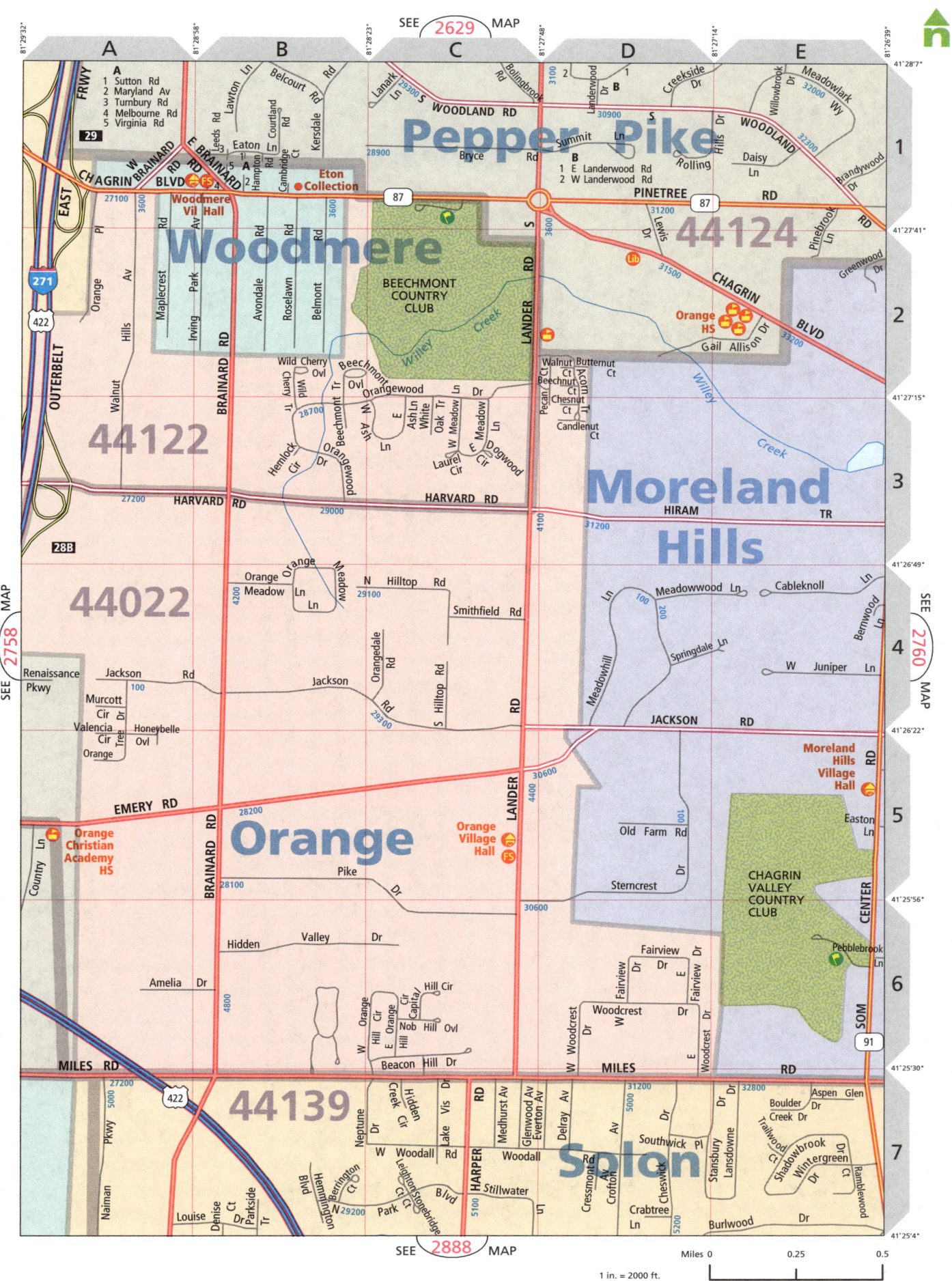

MAP 2759

SEE 2629 MAP

A   B   C   D   E

A
1 Sutton Rd
2 Maryland Av
3 Turnbury Rd
4 Melbourne Rd
5 Virginia Rd

FRWY
29
EAST
CHAGRIN
W BRAINARD RD
E BRAINARD RD
BLVD
Woodmere Vil Hall
Eton Collection

271
422
OUTERBELT

Lawton Ln
Belcourt Rd
Leeds Rd
Eaton Ln
Courtland Rd
Kersdale Rd
Hampton Ln
Cambridge Rd

S WOODLAND RD
Lanark Ln 29300
Bolingbrook Rd
3100
Landerwood 2
Creekside Dr
Willowbrook
Meadowlark
Wy 32000
30900
S
Bryce Rd
Summit Ln
Rolling Hills
WOODLAND
Daisy Ln
32300
Brandywood Dr

87   PINETREE   RD   87

Pepper Pike

B
1 E Landerwood Rd
2 W Landerwood Rd

Pinebrook Rd
Greenwood Dr

44124

Lewis Dr 31200
Lib 31500
CHAGRIN

Woodmere

Orange Av
Orange Hills Av
Walnut Av
Maplecrest Rd
Irving Park Rd
Avondale Rd
Roselawn Rd
Belmont Rd
BRAINARD RD

BEECHMONT COUNTRY CLUB
Willey Creek

LANDER RD S
3600

Orange HS
Gail Allison Dr 33200
BLVD

44122

Wild Cherry Ovl
Beechmont Tr
Cherry Tr
Wild Cherry Ovl
Beechmont Ovl
W Ash Ln
N Ash
Orangewood Dr
Ash Ln
White Ln
Oak Tr
W Meadow Ln
E Meadow Ln
Dr
Laurel Cir
E Cir
Dogwood
28700
Hemlock Cir
Orangewood Dr

Walnut Ct
Butternut Ct
Pecan Ct
Beechnut Ct
Chesnut Ct
Acorn Ct
Candlenut Ct

Willey Creek

Moreland

HARVARD   RD
27200
29000
HARVARD   RD
HIRAM   TR

Hills

31200

28B

44022

Orange Meadow Ln
Orange Meadow Ln
4200
Meadow Ln
N Hilltop Rd
29100
Smithfield Rd
Meadowwood Ln
100
Cableknoll Ln
200
Springdale Ln
Bernwood Ln
W Juniper Ln
Meadowhill Ln

Jackson Rd
100
Renaissance Pkwy
Murcott Cir Dr
Valencia Cir
Orange Tree Ovl
Honeybelle Ovl
Jackson Rd
Orangedale Rd
S Hilltop Rd
29300
LANDER RD
JACKSON   RD
4400
30600
Old Farm Rd
101

Moreland Hills Village Hall
Easton Ln

EMERY RD
28200
BRAINARD RD
Orange
Pike
28100
Dr
Lander
4400
Orange Village Hall
FS
Sterncrest
CHAGRIN VALLEY COUNTRY CLUB
Pebblebrook Ln

Orange Christian Academy HS
Country Ln

Hidden Valley Dr
Amelia Dr
4800
W Orange Hill Cir
E Orange Hill Cir
Orange Capital Cir
Nob Hill Ovl
Beacon Hill Dr
30600

Fairview Dr
W Fairview Dr
E Fairview Dr
Woodcrest Dr
W Woodcrest Dr
E Woodcrest Dr

CENTER RD
SOM 91

MILES   RD
27200
422
5000

44139

Neptune Dr
Hidden Creek Cir
Lake Vis Dr
Medhurst Av
Glenwood Av
Everton Av
Delray Av
Crofton Av
31200
Southwick Pl
32800
Aspen Glen Dr
Boulder Creek Dr
Trailwood Ct
Shadowbrook Dr
Wintergreen Dr
Ramblewood Dr

W Woodall Rd
Berrington Ln
Leighton Ct
Stonebridge Ct
Park Blvd
29200
Stillwater Dr
HARPER RD
5100
Woodall
Solon
Cressmont Av
Cheswick
Stansbury Dr
Lansdowne Dr
Crabtree Ln
Burlwood Dr

Naiman Pkwy
Louise Dr
Denise Ct
Parkside Tr
Hemmington Blvd
N
W MILES RD

SEE 2888 MAP

SEE 2758 MAP

SEE 2760 MAP

41°29'32"   81°28'58"   81°28'23"   81°27'48"   81°27'14"   81°26'39"

41°28'7"
41°27'41"
41°27'15"
41°26'49"
41°26'22"
41°25'56"
41°25'30"
41°25'4"

Miles 0   0.25   0.5
1 in. = 2000 ft.

MAP 2760

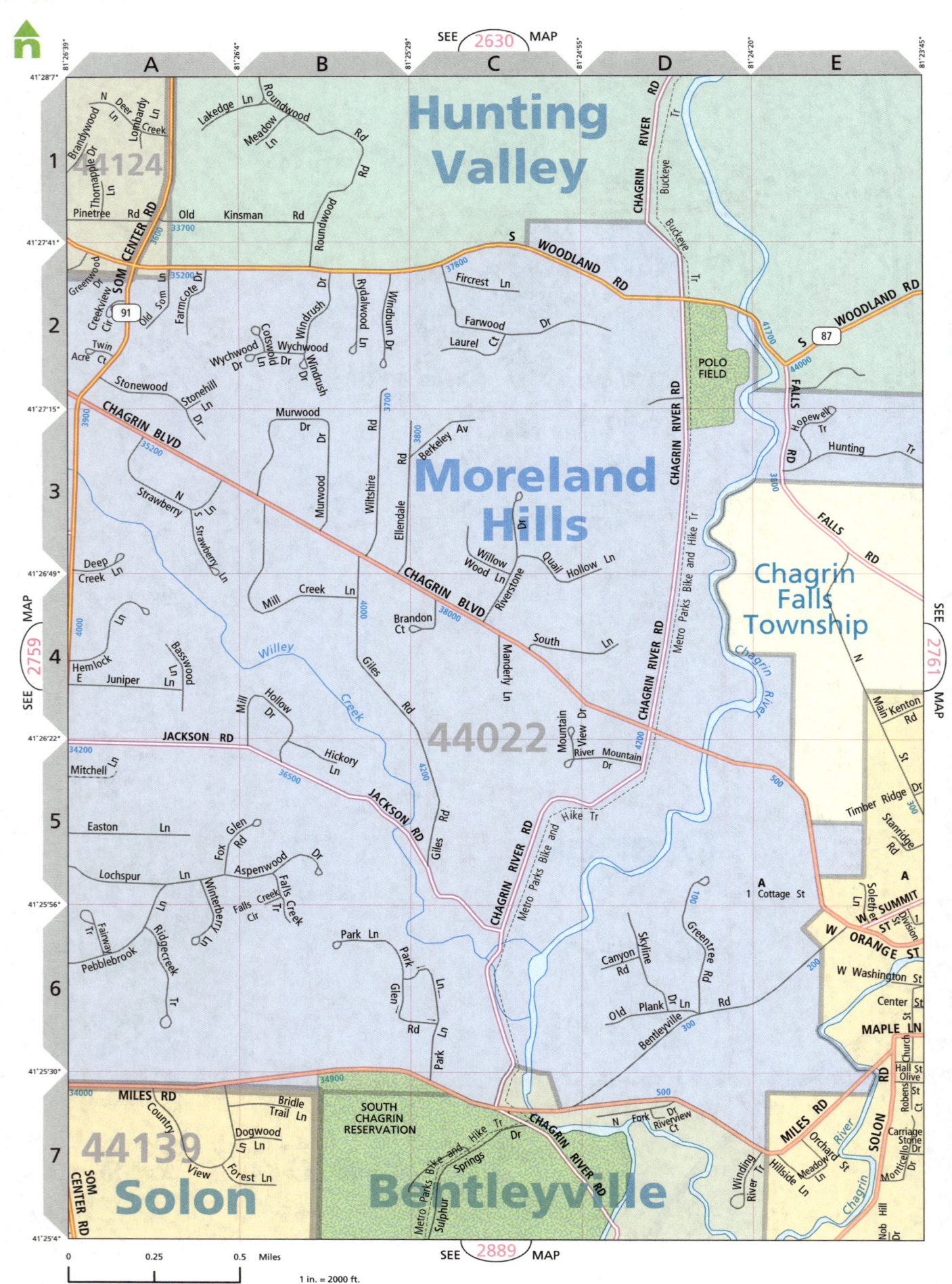

SEE 2630 MAP

N

Hunting Valley

44124

Moreland Hills

44022

Chagrin Falls Township

Bentleyville

Solon

44139

SEE 2759 MAP

SEE 2761 MAP

SEE 2889 MAP

0   0.25   0.5   Miles

1 in. = 2000 ft.

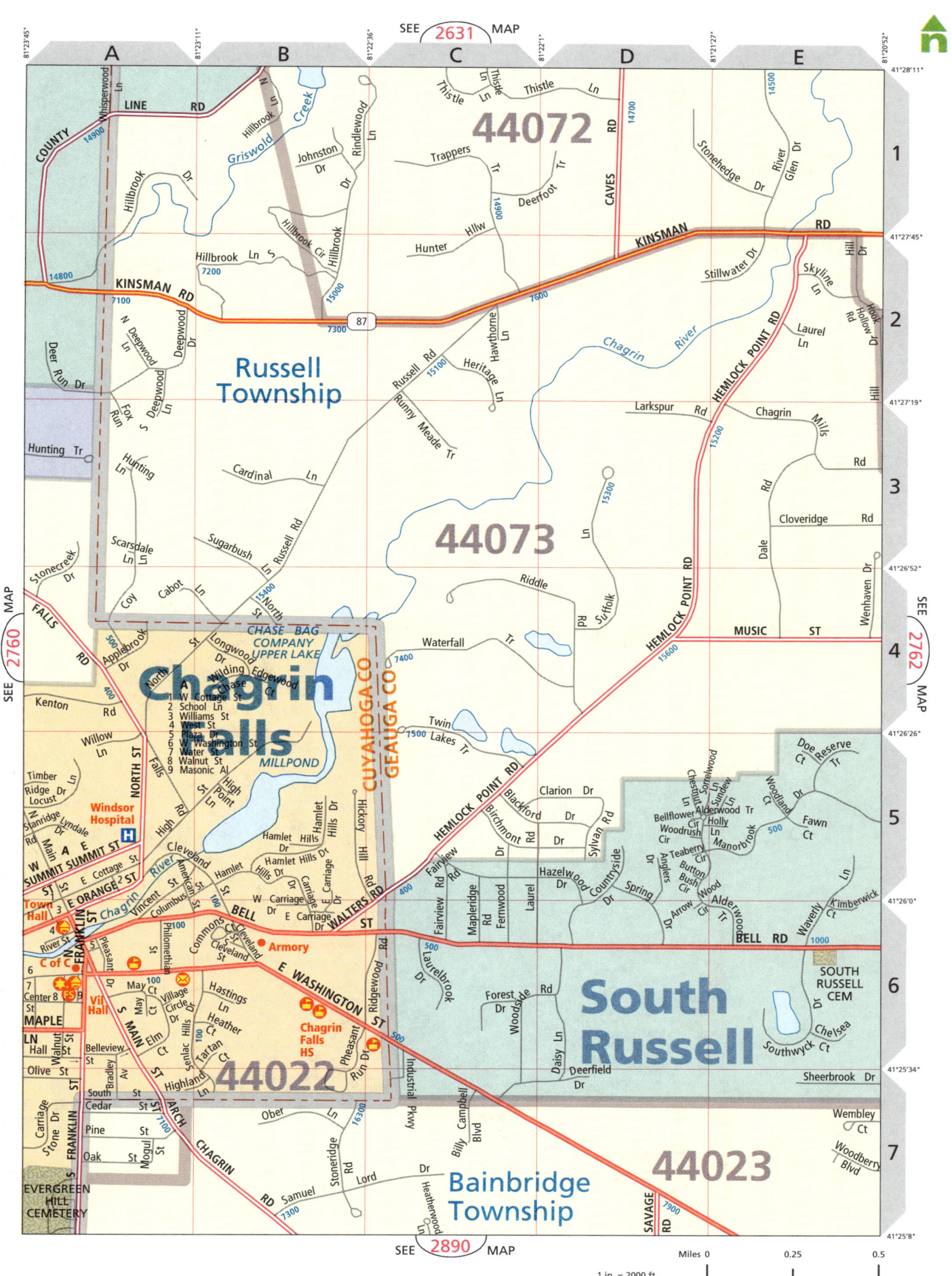

MAP 2761

MAP 2762

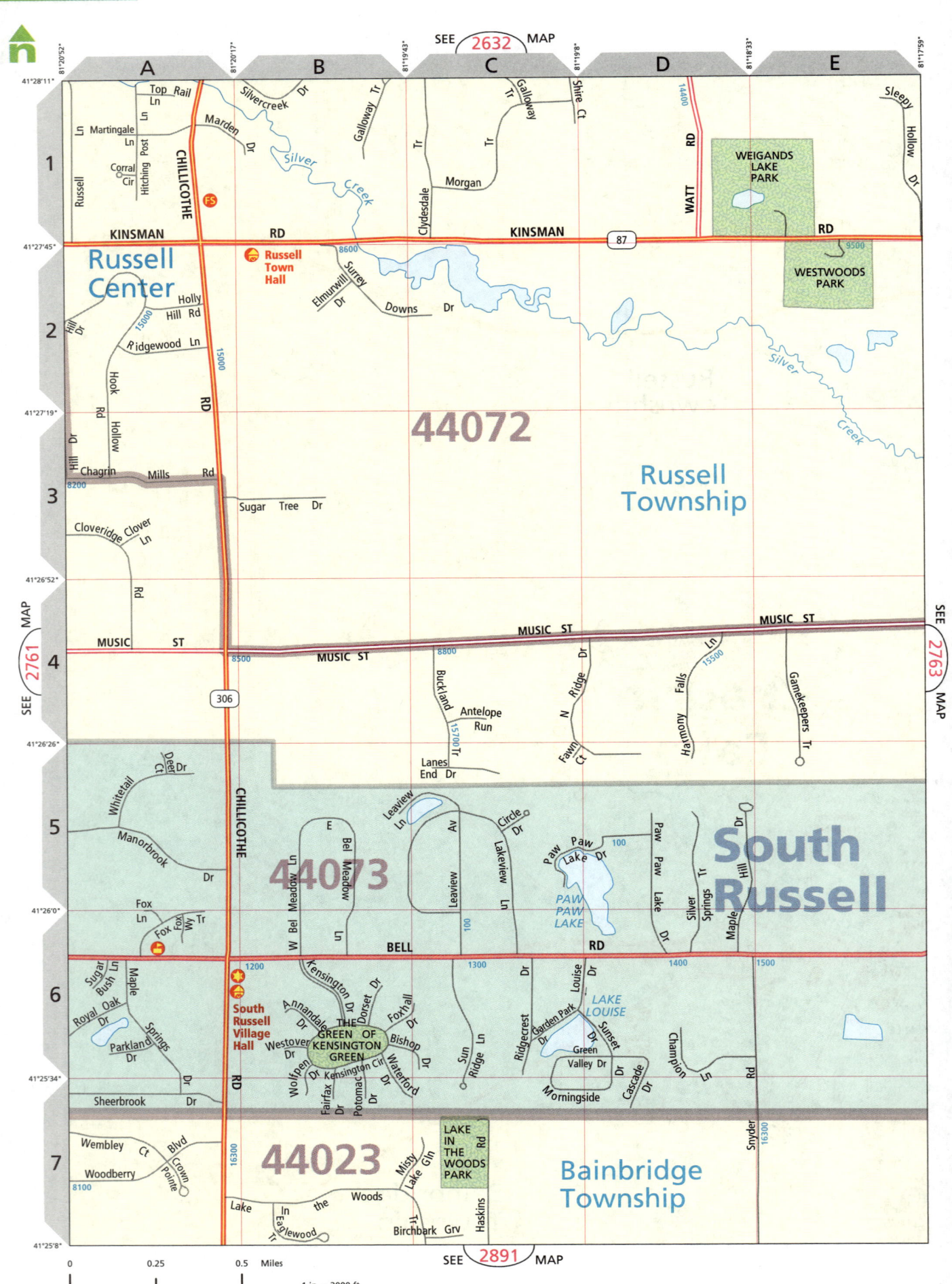

SEE 2632 MAP

A   B   C   D   E

Top Rail Ln
Silvercreek   Dr
Galloway   Tr
Galloway   Tr
Shire Ct
14400
Sleepy Hollow Dr

Martingale Ln
Ln
Marden   Dr
Silver   Creek
Clydesdale   Tr
Morgan
Tr

Russell Ln
Corral Cir
Hitching Post
CHILLICOTHE
FS

WEIGANDS LAKE PARK

1

KINSMAN   RD   KINSMAN   87   RD   9500

41°27'45"

Russell Center   Russell Town Hall   8600   Surrey
Holly Hill Rd   Elmurwill Dr   Downs   Dr
WESTWOODS PARK

2   Hill Dr   15000   Ridgewood Ln   15000

Hook Rd   Hollow   Silver   Creek

41°27'19"

Hill Dr   Chagrin   Mills   Rd   8200   RD   Sugar Tree Dr   **44072**   **Russell Township**

3

Cloveridge   Clover Ln   Rd

41°26'52"

MUSIC   ST   MUSIC ST   8800   MUSIC ST   MUSIC ST

4   8500   Music St   Buckland   N Ridge Dr   Ln   15500   Harmony Falls   Gamekeepers Tr
306   Antelope Run   15700 Tr   Fawn Ct

41°26'26"

Deer Dr   Dr   Lanes End Dr

Whitetail Ln   Leaview Ln   Circle Dr   100   Paw Paw   Silver Springs Tr   Dr   Hill Dr   **South Russell**

5   Manorbrook   Dr   E   Bel Meadow Ln   Leaview Av   Lakeview Dr   Paw Paw Lake Dr   Paw Paw Lake Dr

CHILLICOTHE   **44073**

41°26'0"

Fox Ln   Fox Tr   W Bel Meadow Ln   100   PAW PAW LAKE   Maple Dr

BELL   RD

6   Sugar Bush Ln   Maple   1200   Kensington Dr   Dorset Dr   1300   Dr   Louise   1400   1500
Royal Oak Dr   Annandale Dr   Foxhall Dr   Ridgecrest Dr   Garden Park Dr   LAKE LOUISE   Champion Ln
South Russell Village Hall   THE GREEN OF KENSINGTON GREEN   Bishop   Sun Ridge Ln   Sunset Dr
Parkland Dr   Springs   Westover Dr   Waterford Dr   Green Valley Dr   Cascade Dr   Snyder   Rd
Wolfpen Dr   Kensington Cir   Morningside   16300

41°25'34"

Sheerbrook   Dr   RD   Fairfax Dr   Potomac Dr   Dr   1630

7   Wembley Ct   Blvd   **44023**   Misty Ln   LAKE IN THE WOODS PARK   **Bainbridge Township**
Woodberry   Crown Pointe Dr   8100   Lake Gin Rd   Haskins Rd
Lake   In   the   Woods   Eaglewood   Birchbark Grv

41°25'8"

SEE 2891 MAP

SEE 2761 MAP   SEE 2763 MAP

0   0.25   0.5   Miles
1 in. = 2000 ft.

MAP 2763

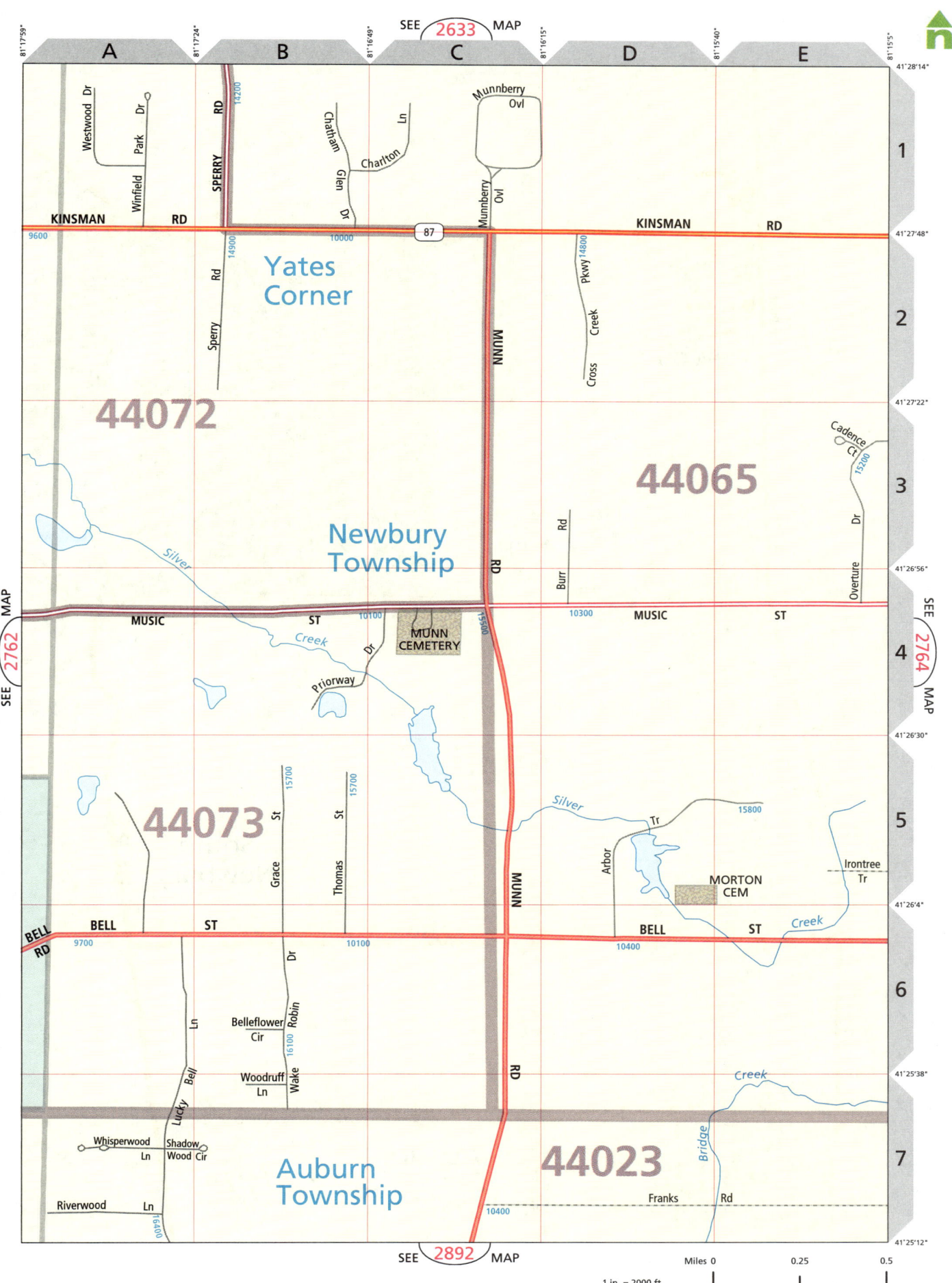

SEE 2633 MAP
SEE 2762 MAP
SEE 2764 MAP
SEE 2892 MAP

A   B   C   D   E

1   2   3   4   5   6   7

81°17'59"   81°17'24"   81°16'49"   81°16'15"   81°15'40"   81°15'5"
41°28'14"   41°27'48"   41°27'22"   41°26'56"   41°26'30"   41°26'4"   41°25'38"   41°25'12"

Westwood Dr
Park Dr
Winfield
KINSMAN RD
9600
SPERRY RD
14200

Chatham Glen Dr
Charlton
Charlton Ln
Munnberry Ovl
Munnberry Ovl

Yates Corner
44072
Sperry Rd
14900
10000
87
MUNN RD

Kinsman RD
14800
Cross Creek Pkwy
44065
Cadence Ct
15200
Overture Dr

Newbury Township
Silver Creek
MUSIC ST
10100
Dr
Priorway
MUNN CEMETERY
15500
Burr Rd
10300
MUSIC ST

44073
Grace St
15700
Thomas St
15700
Silver
Arbor Tr
15800
MORTON CEM
Irontree Tr

BELL RD
9700
BELL ST
10100
Belleflower Cir
16100
Robin Dr
Wake Dr
Woodruff Ln
Lucky Bell Ln
MUNN RD
BELL ST
10400
Creek

Whisperwood Ln
Shadow Wood Cir
Auburn Township
44023
Bridge Creek
Riverwood Ln
16400
10400
Franks Rd

Miles 0   0.25   0.5
1 in. = 2000 ft.

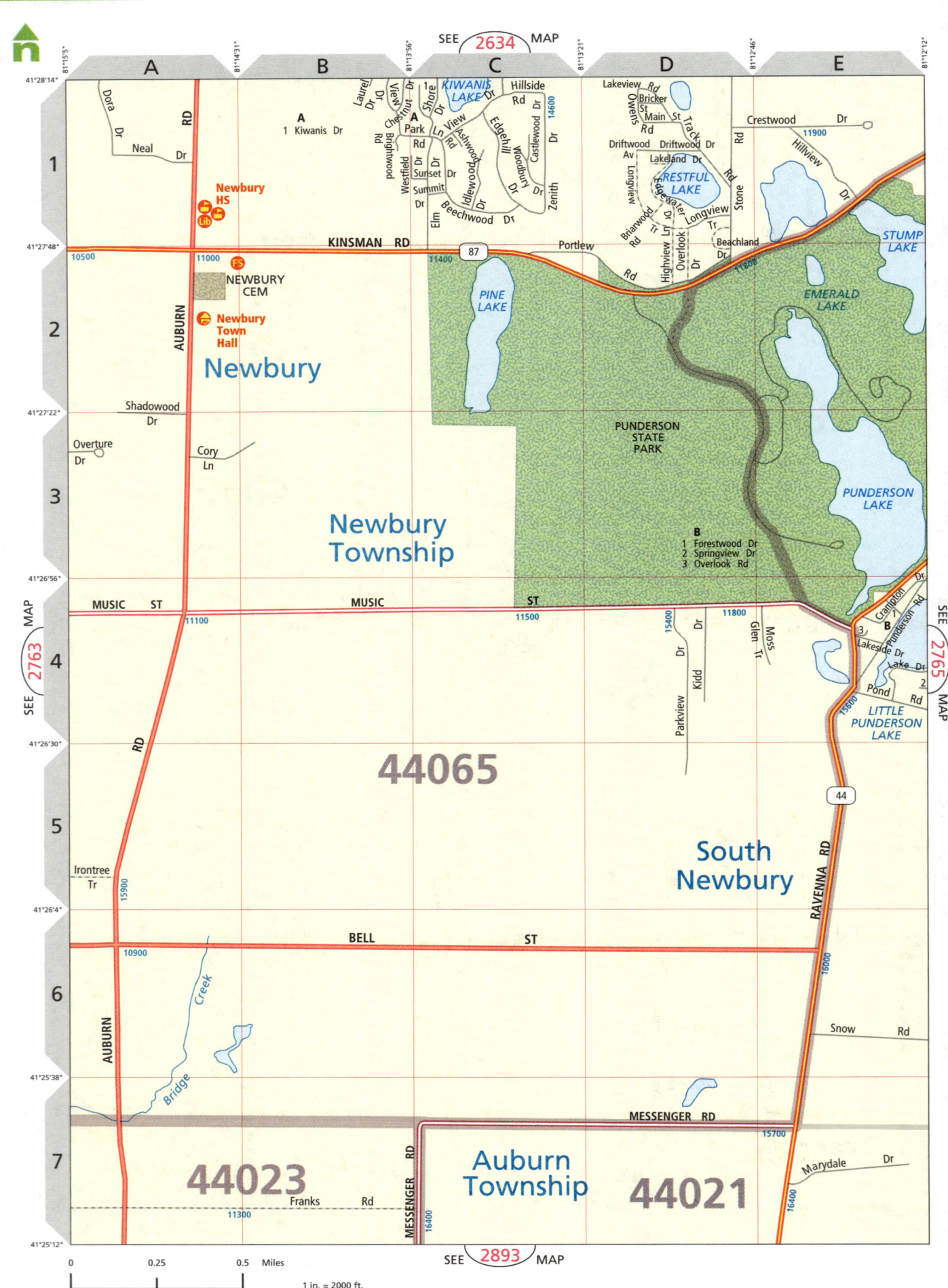

MAP 2764

SEE 2634 MAP

A   **B**   **C**   **D**   **E**

1

Dora Dr
Neal Dr

AUBURN RD

Newbury HS
Lib

1 Kiwanis Dr

Laurel Dr
Chestnut View
Brightwood Rd
Westfield Dr

Park Rd
Shore Ln
View Rd
Ashwood
Idlewood Dr
Sunset Dr
Summit Dr
Elm

Beechwood Dr

A
A

KIWANIS LAKE
Hillside Rd
Castlewood Dr
Edgehill Dr
Woodbury Dr
Zenith

14600

Lakeview Rd
Owens Rd
Bricker St
Main St
Track
Driftwood Av
Driftwood Dr
Lakeland Dr
Longview
Ridgewater
Stone Rd

Crestwood Dr
11900

Hillview Dr

RESTFUL LAKE

STUMP LAKE

KINSMAN   RD
87

Portlew

Brianwood Rd
Highview Ln
Overlook Tr
Beachland Dr

11800

EMERALD LAKE

41°27'48"
10500   11000   11400

FS
NEWBURY CEM

Newbury Town Hall

Newbury

PINE LAKE

PUNDERSON STATE PARK

2

41°27'22"
Shadowood Dr

Overture Dr

Cory Ln

Newbury Township

PUNDERSON LAKE

3

41°26'56"

MUSIC   ST   MUSIC   ST
11100   11500

15400

Parkview
Kidd
Dr
11800
Moss
Glen Tr

Crampton Dr
Punderson Rd
3
B
1
Lakeside Dr
Lake Dr
2
LITTLE PUNDERSON LAKE

SEE 2765 MAP

B
1 Forestwood Dr
2 Springview Dr
3 Overlook Rd

15600
Pond Rd

4

SEE 2763 MAP

41°26'30"

44065

5

Irontree Tr
15900

South Newbury

RAVENNA RD
44

41°26'4"

BELL   ST
10900

16000

6

AUBURN RD

Creek
Bridge

Snow Rd

41°25'38"

MESSENGER RD
15700

Marydale Dr

7

44023

Franks Rd
11300

MESSENGER RD
16400

Auburn Township

44021

16400

41°25'12"

SEE 2893 MAP

0   0.25   0.5   Miles

1 in. = 2000 ft.

MAP 2765

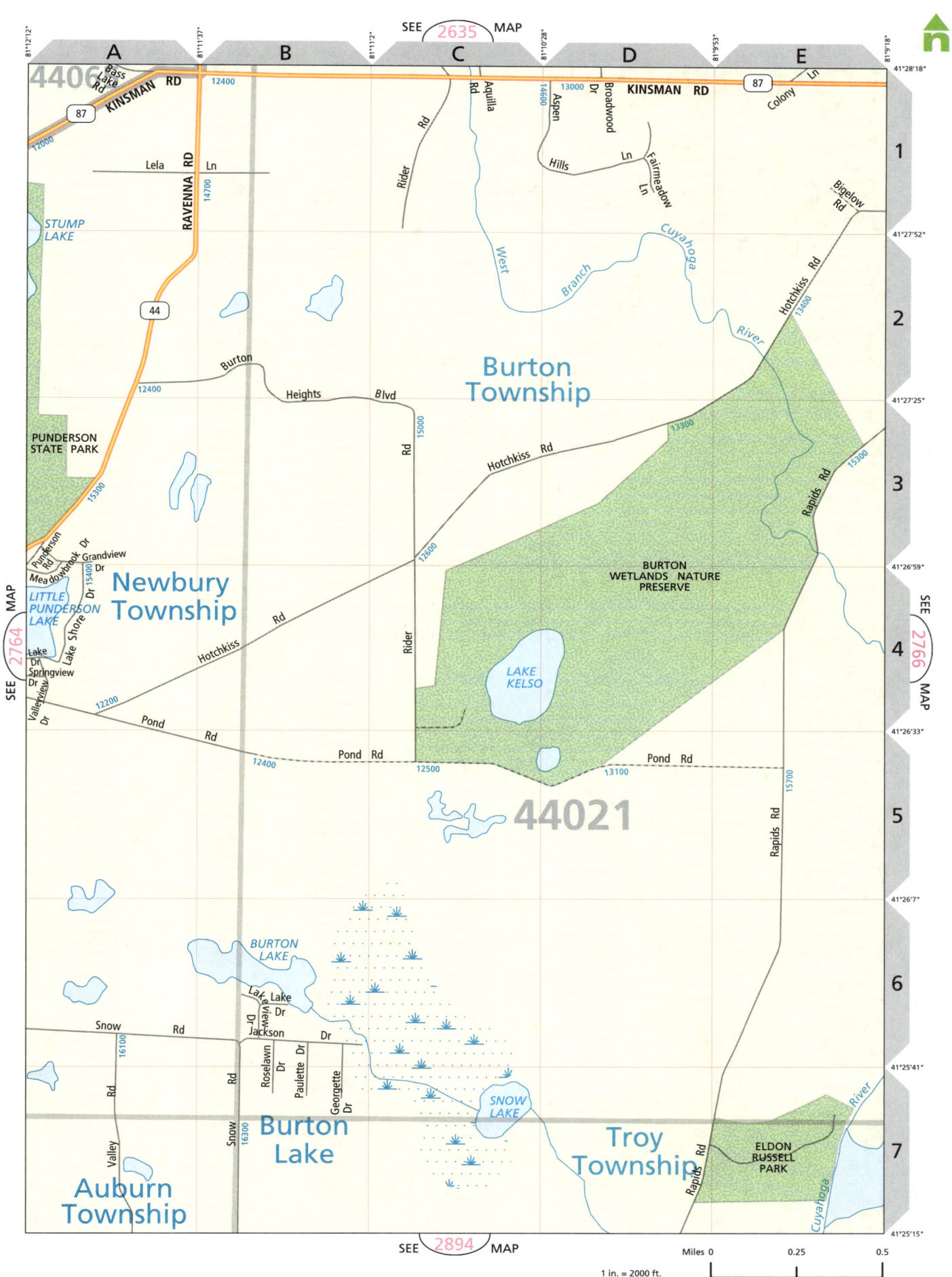

SEE 2635 MAP

4406

Bass Lake Rd
KINSMAN RD
87
12000

A

RAVENNA RD
Lela Ln
12400
14700

44

B

Rider Rd

Aquilla Rd

C

SEE 2635 MAP

Broadwood Dr
Aspen Dr
14600
13000
Hills
KINSMAN RD
Fairmeadow Ln
Ln

D

87
Colony Ln

E

41°28'18"

1

41°27'52"

STUMP LAKE

West Branch

Cuyahoga River

Hotchkiss Rd
13400

Bigelow Rd

2

41°27'25"

Burton Township

Burton Heights Blvd

Rd 15000

Hotchkiss Rd

13300

Rapids Rd
15300

3

41°26'59"

PUNDERSON STATE PARK

15300

Newbury Township

Meadowbrook Dr 15400
Grandview Dr
Punderson Rd
Lake Shore Dr

LITTLE PUNDERSON LAKE

Lake Dr
Springview Dr

Rd

Hotchkiss

Rd

12600

Rider Rd

BURTON WETLANDS NATURE PRESERVE

LAKE KELSO

4

41°26'33"

SEE 2764 MAP

SEE 2766 MAP

Valleyview Dr
12200
Pond Rd
12400

Pond Rd
12500

Pond Rd
13100

Pond Rd

Rapids Rd
15700

5

44021

41°26'7"

Snow Rd
16100

BURTON LAKE

Lakeview Dr
Lake Dr

Snow Rd
16300

Jackson Dr
Roselawn Dr
Paulette Dr
Georgette Dr

SNOW LAKE

Troy Township

Rapids Rd

ELDON RUSSELL PARK

Cuyahoga River

6

41°25'41"

Valley Rd

Burton Lake

7

41°25'15"

Auburn Township

SEE 2894 MAP

Miles 0   0.25   0.5

1 in. = 2000 ft.

MAP 2766

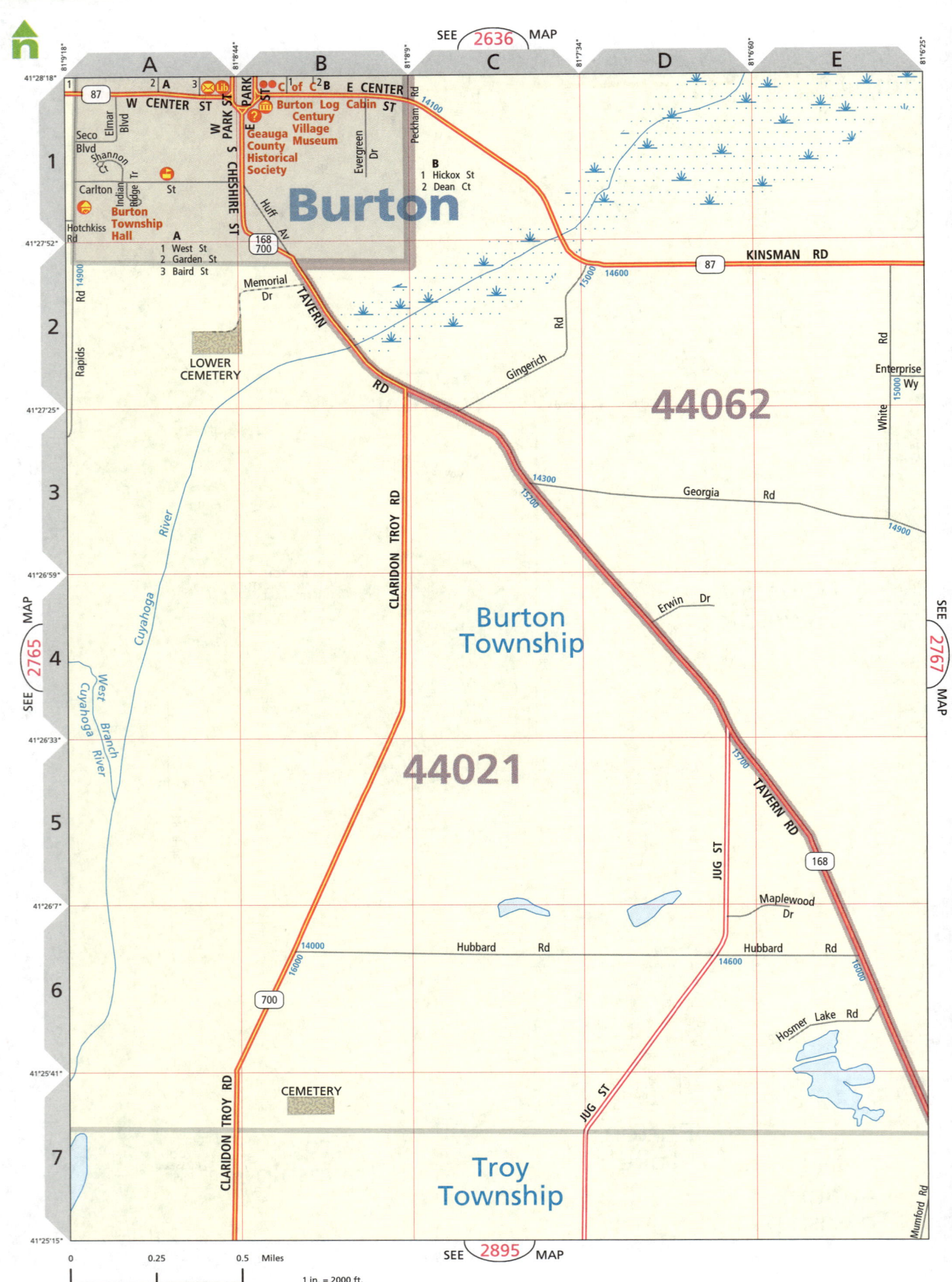

MAP 2767

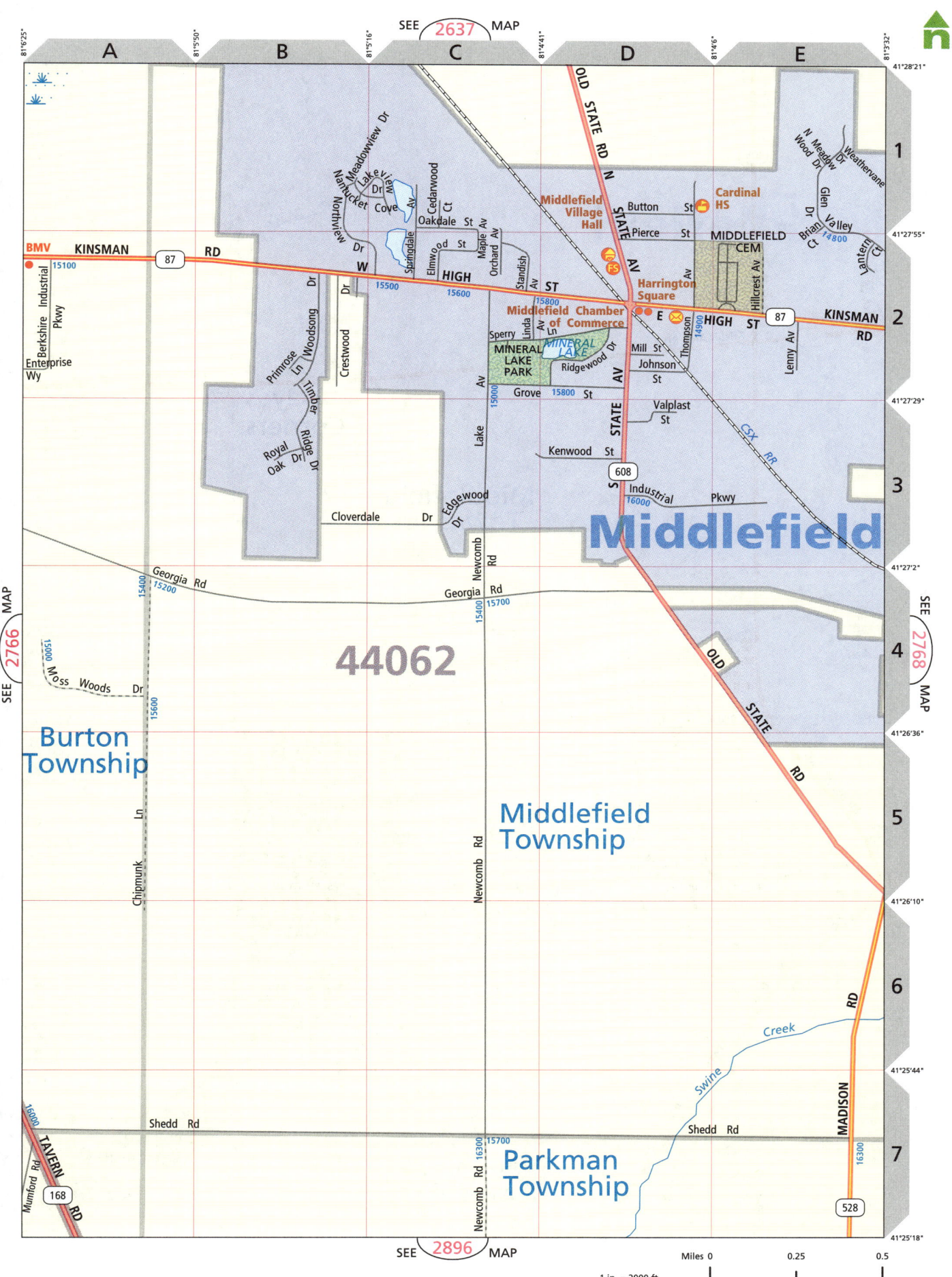

SEE 2637 MAP

A   B   C   D   E

SEE 2766 MAP

SEE 2768 MAP

BMV
KINSMAN 87 RD
15100
Berkshire Industrial Pkwy
Enterprise Wy

Meadowview Dr
Lakeview Dr
Nantucket
Northview Dr
Cove
Springdale Av
Cedarwood Ct
Oakdale St
Elmwood St
Maple Av
Orchard St
Standish St
HIGH ST
W
15500
15600

Middlefield Village Hall
Button St
Pierce St

Cardinal HS

MIDDLEFIELD CEM

N Meadow Wood Dr
Glen Valley Dr
Brian Ct
14800
Weathervane
Lantern Ct

OLD STATE RD N

STATE AV

Middlefield Chamber of Commerce
15800
FS
Harrington Square
E
14900
Thompson Av
High St
Hillcrest Av
Kinsman 87 RD

Sperry
Linda
Woodspong Dr
Primrose Ln
Timber Dr
Crestwood Dr
MINERAL LAKE PARK
MINERAL LAKE
Ridgewood Dr
Mill St
Johnson St
Lenny Av
Lake Av
15000
Grove St
15800
Valplast St
Royal Oak Dr
Ridge Dr
STATE AV
608
Kenwood St
CSX RR

Cloverdale Dr
Edgewood Dr
Newcomb Rd

Middlefield

Industrial Pkwy
16000

Georgia Rd
15400 15200
Georgia Rd
15400 15700

44062

Moss Woods Dr
00051
15600

Burton Township

Middlefield Township

Chipmunk Ln
Newcomb Rd

OLD STATE RD
MADISON RD

Creek
Swine

Shedd Rd
Newcomb Rd 16300
15700
Shedd Rd
16300

Parkman Township

Mumford Rd
168
TAVERN RD
00091
528

SEE 2896 MAP

Miles 0   0.25   0.5
1 in. = 2000 ft.

MAP 2768

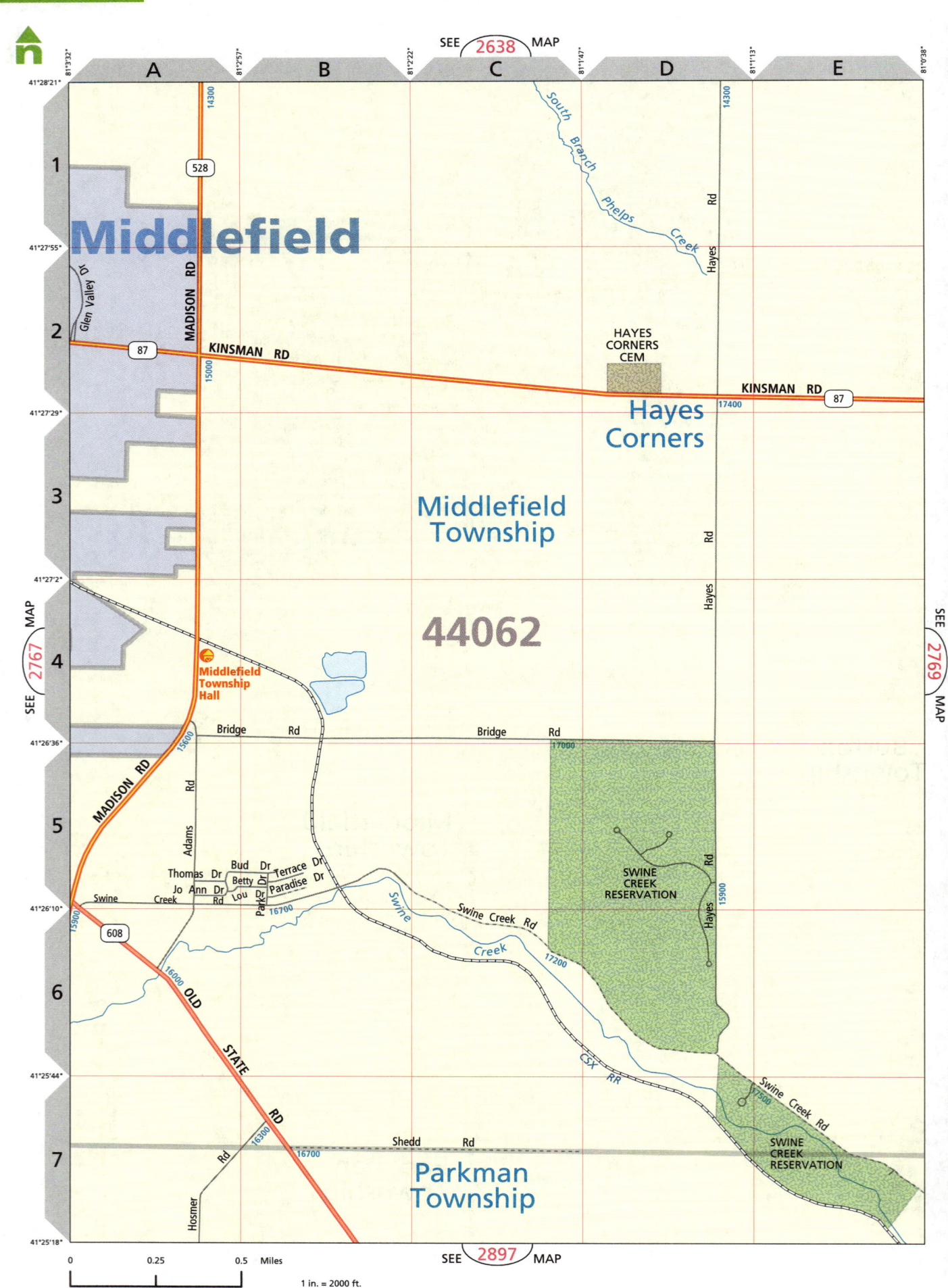

Middlefield

Middlefield
Township

44062

Middlefield
Township Hall

Hayes
Corners

HAYES
CORNERS
CEM

KINSMAN RD

SWINE
CREEK
RESERVATION

SWINE
CREEK
RESERVATION

Parkman
Township

SEE 2638 MAP
SEE 2767 MAP
SEE 2769 MAP
SEE 2897 MAP

Glen Valley Dr
MADISON RD
KINSMAN RD
Bridge Rd
Bridge Rd
MADISON RD
Rd
Adams Rd
Thomas Dr
Bud Dr
Betty Dr
Jo Ann Dr
Lou Dr
Park Dr
Terrace Dr
Paradise Dr
Swine Creek Rd
OLD STATE RD
Shedd Rd
Hosmer Rd
Swine Creek Rd
Swine Creek Rd
Swine Creek
Hayes Rd
Hayes Rd
Hayes Rd
South Branch Phelps Creek
CSX RR

528
87
608

0   0.25   0.5   Miles

1 in. = 2000 ft.

MAP 2769-2868

SEE 2639 MAP

A   B   C   D   E

Bundysburg Rd

Andrews

Creek

GIRDLE RD

Laird Rd

Rd

1

Wilcox 9000 Rd
4800

2

Coffee
Corners

KINSMAN RD

87

9300 KINSMAN RD

41°27'31"

Parkman Mesopotamia Rd

3

GIRDLE RD

Middlefield
Township

SEE 2768 MAP

44062

Gates East Rd
4

SEE B MAP

8400

GEAUGA CO   TRUMBULL CO

Andrews

Parks West Rd

Parks West Rd
4700

5

Mesopotamia
Township

Creek

6

Parkman Mesopotamia Rd
8000

COPPEDGE POND

GIRDLE RD

Clark Rd

7

Bundysburg Rd

10400

County Line Clark Rd

County Line
5000

Parkman
Township

Swine Creek
Rd

Farmington
Township

SEE 2898 MAP

Miles 0   0.25   0.5

1 in. = 2000 ft.

MAP 2869

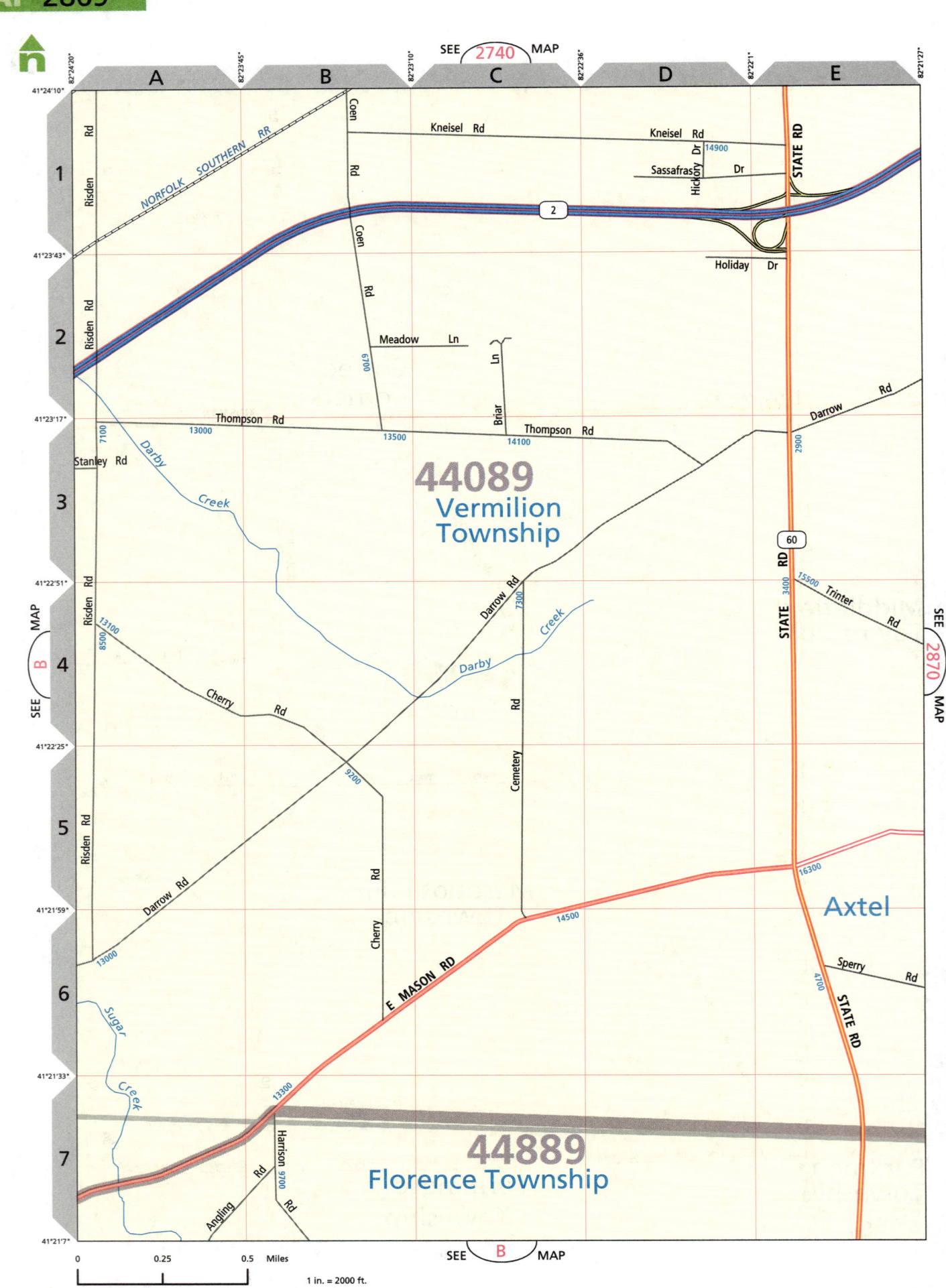

SEE 2740 MAP

A B C D E

41°24'20"
41°24'10"

Risden Rd

NORFOLK SOUTHERN RR

Coen Rd

Kneisel Rd

Kneisel Rd

Hickory Dr 14900

Sassafras Dr

STATE RD

1

2

41°23'43"

Risden Rd

Coen Rd

Meadow Ln

Ln

Briar Ln

Holiday Dr

Rd

Darrow Rd

2900

41°23'17"

Thompson Rd

13000

13500

Thompson Rd

14100

7100

Stanley Rd

Darby Creek

44089
Vermilion
Township

3

41°22'51"

Risden Rd

13100

8500

Darrow Rd

7300

Darby Creek

STATE RD 60

15500

Trinter Rd

3400

SEE 2870 MAP

B MAP SEE

4

41°22'25"

Cherry Rd

9200

Cemetery Rd

5

41°21'59"

Risden Rd

13000

Darrow Rd

Cherry Rd

14500

16300

Axtel

Sperry Rd

4700

STATE RD

6

E MASON RD

41°21'33"

Sugar Creek

13300

Harrison Rd 9700

44889
Florence Township

7

41°21'7"

Angling Rd

Rd

SEE B MAP

0   0.25   0.5   Miles

1 in. = 2000 ft.

MAP 2870

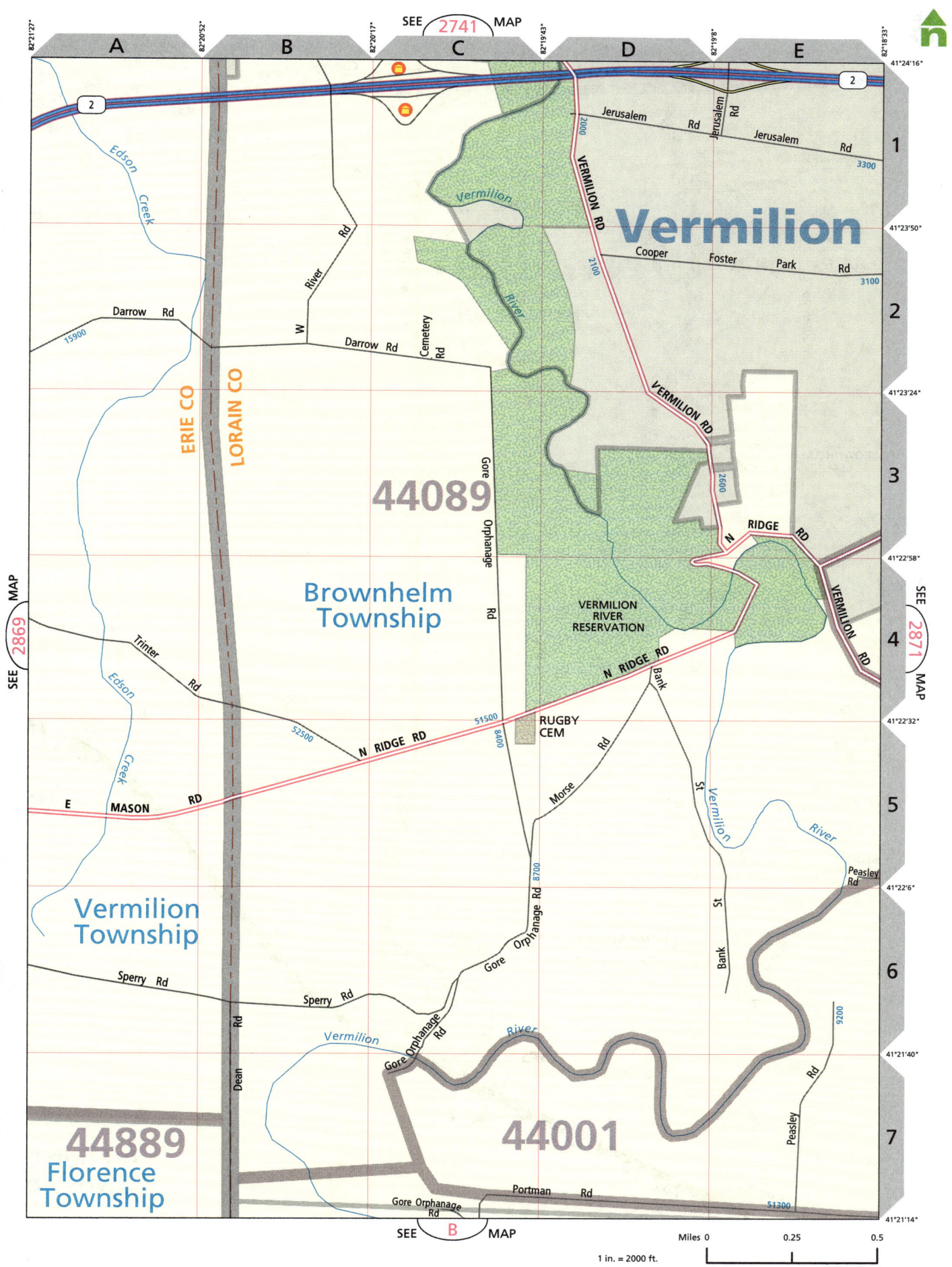

SEE 2741 MAP

A   B   C   D   E

82°21'27"   82°20'52"   82°20'17"   82°19'43"   82°19'8"   82°18'33"

2

Jerusalem   Rd
Jerusalem   Rd
3300

Vermilion

41°24'16"
1

41°23'50"

VERMILION RD
2000
2100

Cooper   Foster   Park   Rd
3100

41°23'24"
2

Edson   Creek

Darrow   Rd
15900

River   Rd

W   Darrow   Rd

Cemetery   Rd

ERIE CO   LORAIN CO

VERMILION RD
2600

41°22'58"
3

44089

Gore   Orphanage   Rd

Brownhelm Township

VERMILION RIVER RESERVATION

N   RIDGE   RD

RIDGE   RD

N   VERMILION   RD

SEE 2869 MAP

SEE 2871 MAP

4

Trinter   Rd

Edson   Creek

52500   N   RIDGE   RD
51500
8400
RUGBY CEM

N   RIDGE   RD

Bank

Morse   Rd

St   Vermilion   River

41°22'32"

E   MASON   RD

41°22'6"

Peasley   Rd

5

Vermilion Township

Gore   Orphanage   Rd
8700

St   Bank

Sperry   Rd

Sperry   Rd

Vermilion   River

Gore   Orphanage   Rd

41°21'40"
6

Dean   Rd

44889
Florence Township

44001

Peasley   Rd

Peasley   Rd
9200

41°21'14"
7

Gore Orphanage   Rd

Portman   Rd
51300

SEE B MAP

Miles   0   0.25   0.5

1 in. = 2000 ft.

MAP 2871

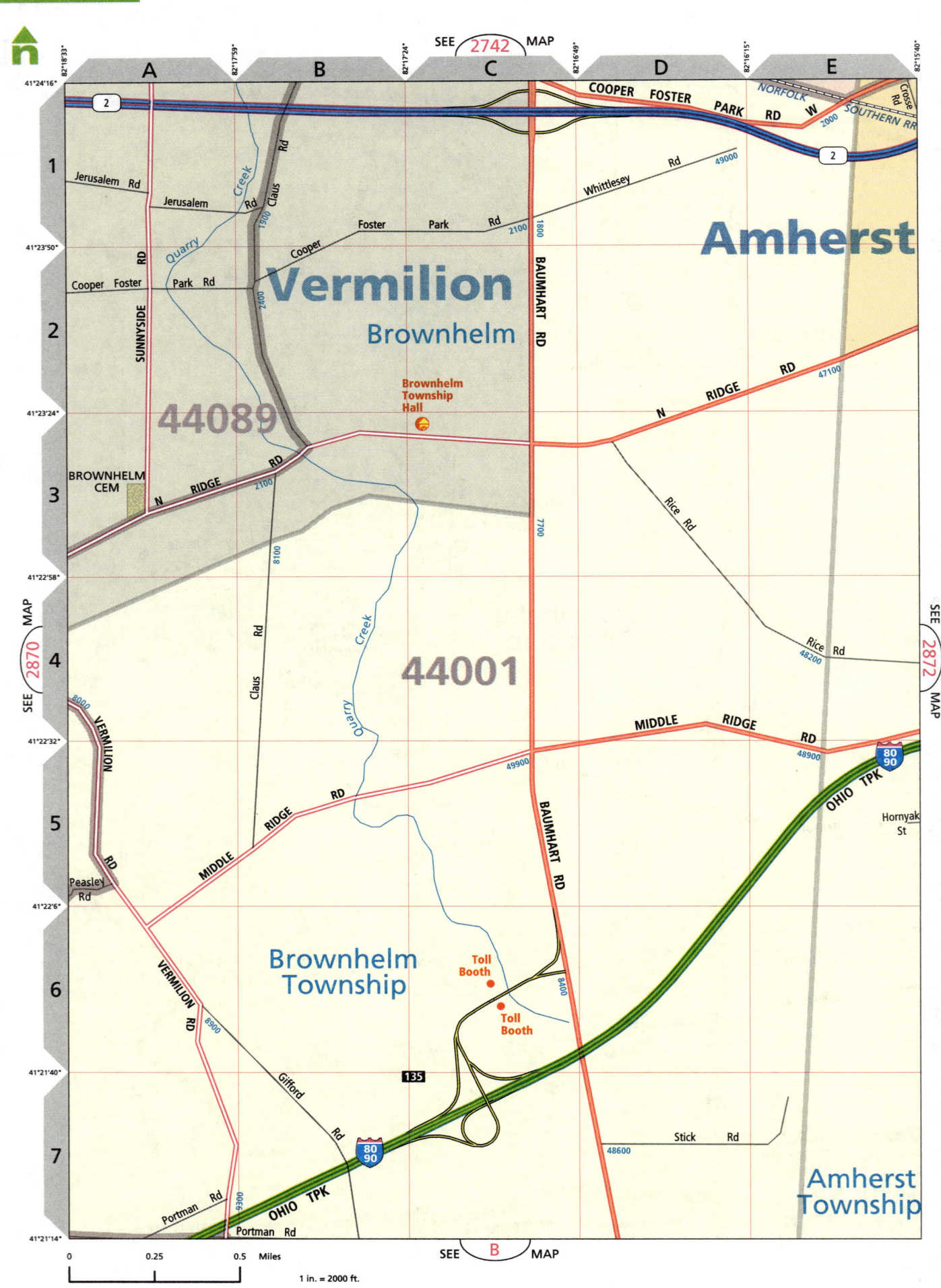

SEE 2742 MAP

COOPER FOSTER PARK RD W

NORFOLK SOUTHERN RR

Amherst

Jerusalem Rd

Jerusalem Rd

Claus Rd

Quarry Creek

Foster Park Rd

Cooper

Whittlesey Rd

49000

Vermilion

Brownhelm

BAUMHART RD

N RIDGE RD

47100

Cooper Foster Park Rd

SUNNYSIDE RD

44089

Brownhelm Township Hall

Rice Rd

BROWNHELM CEM

N RIDGE RD

Rice Rd
48200

Claus Rd

Quarry Creek

44001

SEE 2870 MAP

SEE 2872 MAP

VERMILION

MIDDLE RIDGE RD
48900

80 90

MIDDLE RIDGE RD
49900

BAUMHART RD

OHIO TPK

Hornyak St

Peasley Rd

Brownhelm Township

Toll Booth

VERMILION RD
8900

Toll Booth

8400

135

Gifford Rd

80 90

OHIO TPK

Stick Rd
48600

Amherst Township

Portman Rd

Portman Rd

SEE B MAP

0   0.25   0.5   Miles

1 in. = 2000 ft.

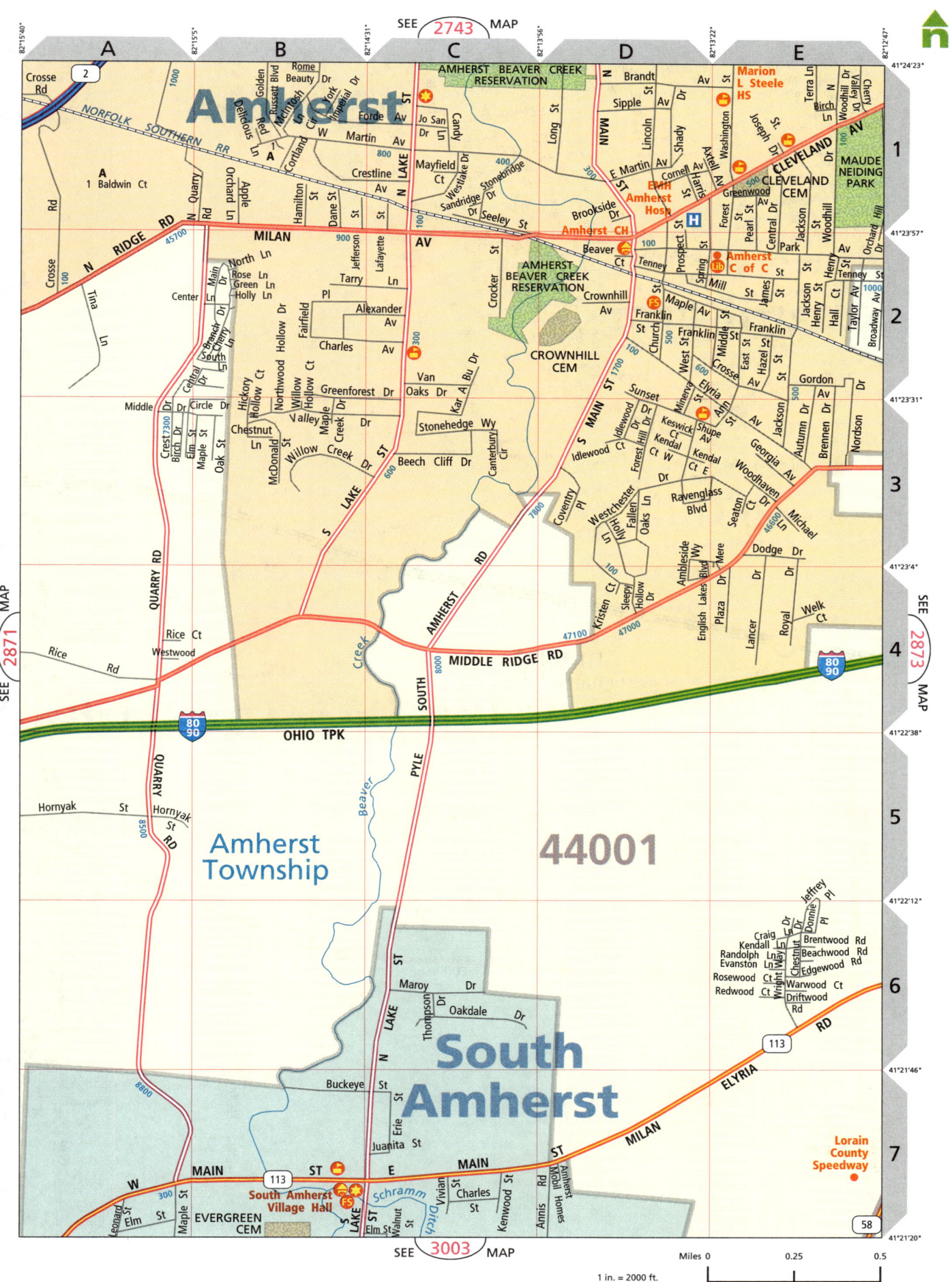

MAP 2872

MAP 2873

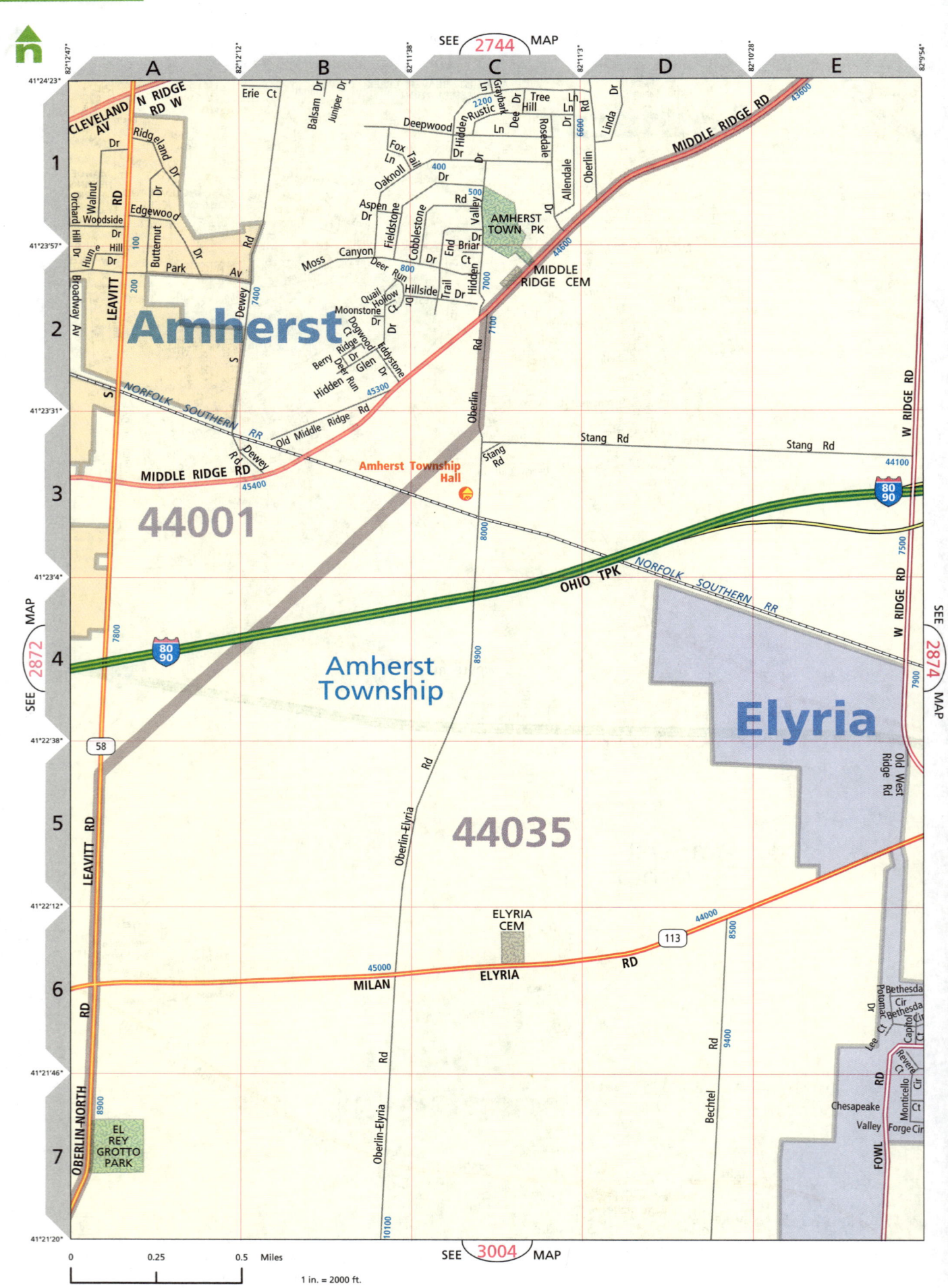

SEE 2744 MAP

Amherst

Amherst Township

44001

44035

Elyria

MIDDLE RIDGE RD

W RIDGE RD

OHIO TPK

NORFOLK SOUTHERN RR

MIDDLE RIDGE RD

MIDDLE RIDGE CEM

AMHERST TOWN PK

Amherst Township Hall

ELYRIA CEM

Stang Rd

Stang Rd

Stang Rd

EL REY GROTTO PARK

SEE 2872 MAP

SEE 2874 MAP

SEE 3004 MAP

0   0.25   0.5   Miles

1 in. = 2000 ft.

MAP 2874

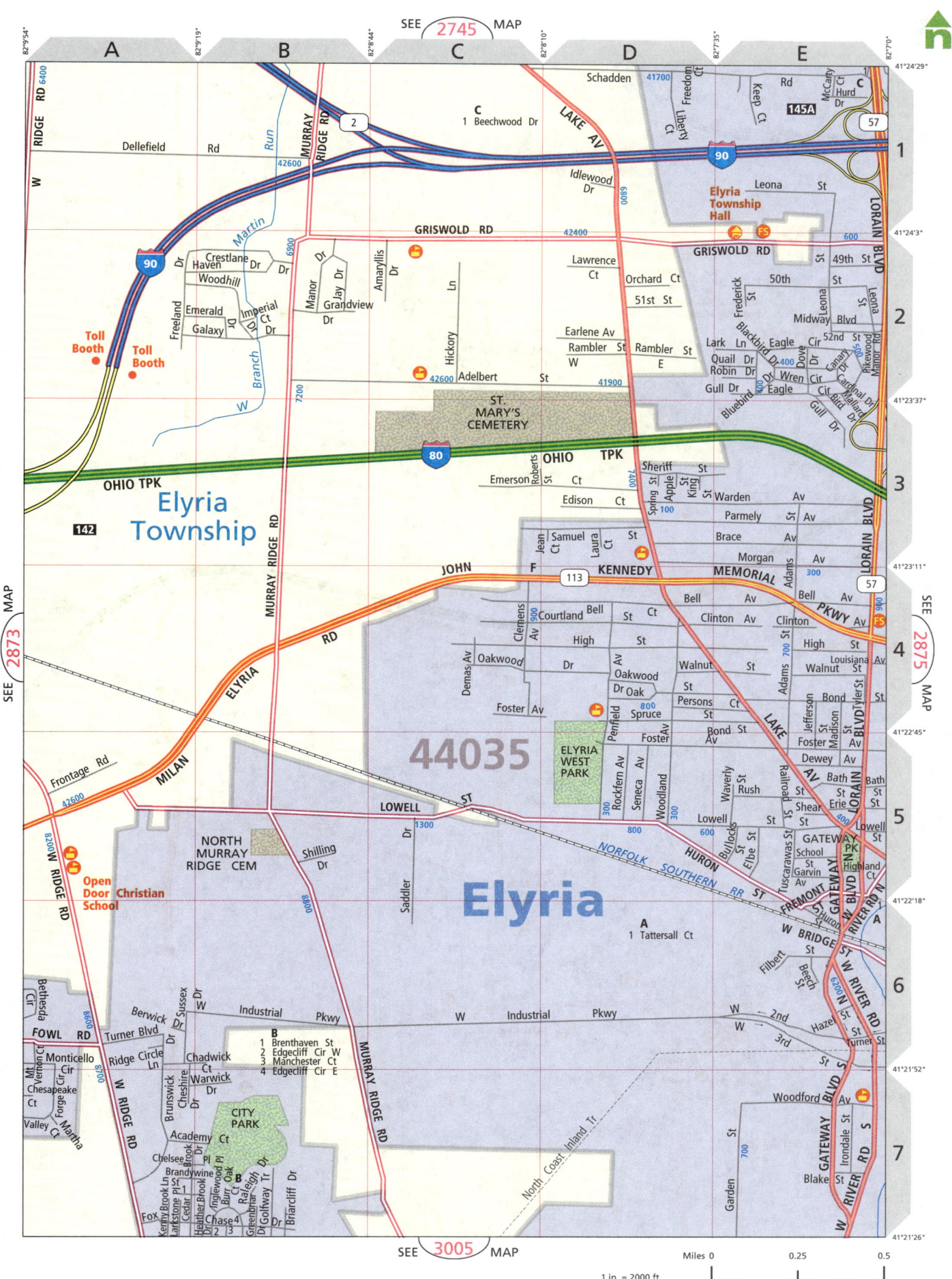

SEE 2745 MAP

SEE 2873 MAP

SEE 2875 MAP

SEE 3005 MAP

Elyria Township

Elyria

44035

Elyria

ST. MARY'S CEMETERY

OHIO TPK

Elyria Township Hall

ELYRIA WEST PARK

CITY PARK

NORTH MURRAY RIDGE CEM

Open Door Christian School

NORFOLK SOUTHERN RR

North Coast Inland Tr

Miles 0   0.25   0.5

1 in. = 2000 ft.

MAP 2875

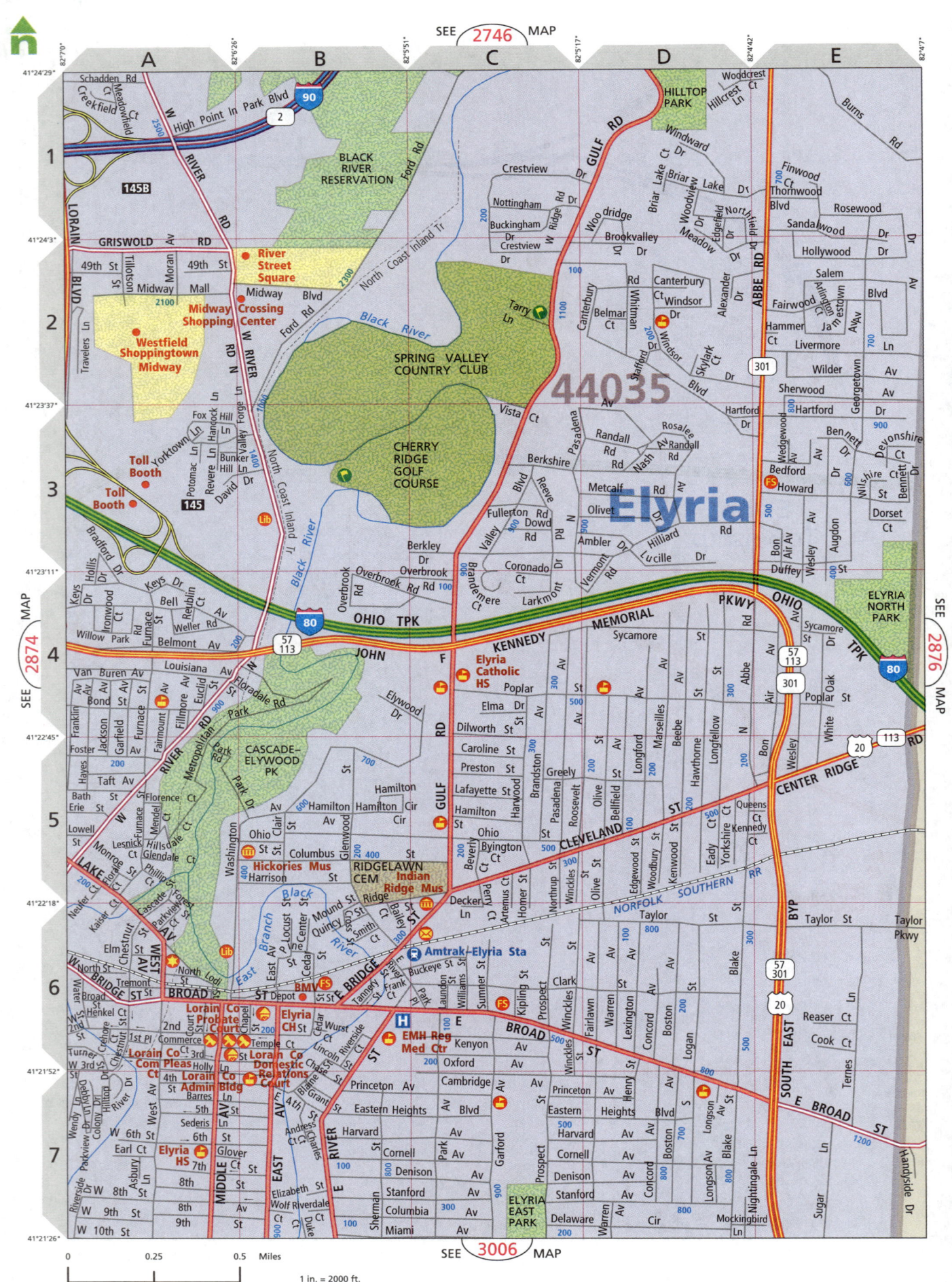

SEE 2746 MAP
SEE 2874 MAP
SEE 2876 MAP
SEE 3006 MAP

0   0.25   0.5 Miles

1 in. = 2000 ft.

MAP 2876

SEE 2747 MAP

A B C D E

82°47" 82°33" 82°2'58" 82°2'23" 82°1'49" 82°1'14"

Barres 38900 38400 Rd 38200 6500 Rd

Burns Rd 41°24'35"

6100

Case

Rd 7300 Otten Rd

Stoney

1

41°24'9"

Otten Rd 38300

Ridge

North Ridgeville

44039

2

41°23'43"

LORAIN COUNTY METROPARK NORTH RIDGEVILLE

Schaffer Dr 6900

Case Rd

RIDGEVIEW CEM

3

41°23'17"

Edwin Av

Alden Av

Watson Av

Center Ridge ▲

20

Dr 7200

Maple Dr Rd

Av

Dyke

CENTER RIDGE RD 113

Aurensen

Noll

Behm Dr

4

41°23'17"

39100 36900 7300

Lake Ridge Academy

Evergreen Dr

Maddock Rd

OHIO TPK

Westwood Dr

41°22'50"

Race Rd

80

Rd OHIO TPK

5

NORFOLK SOUTHERN RR

Maddock Rd

41°22'24"

Race Rd

SUGAR RIDGE RD

Taylor Pkwy

Sugar Ridge ▲

Taylor Pkwy

7900

Line Dr

Shady Rd

CITY BASEBALL COMPLEX

Westfield Dr 36300

Elda Wy 28800

6

41°21'58"

RIDGE RD 37900

8000

Lexington

SUGAR RIDGE CEM

38900 9500

Wy

Homecrest Dr

Shaw Dr Dr

Broadway Blvd

Euclid Dr

7

SUGAR

Bender Rd

Lakeside Dr

Shaker

Wayland Way Rd

CHESTNUT RIDGE RD

41°21'32"

SEE 3007 MAP

SEE 2875 MAP

SEE 2877 MAP

Miles 0 0.25 0.5

1 in. = 2000 ft.

MAP 2877

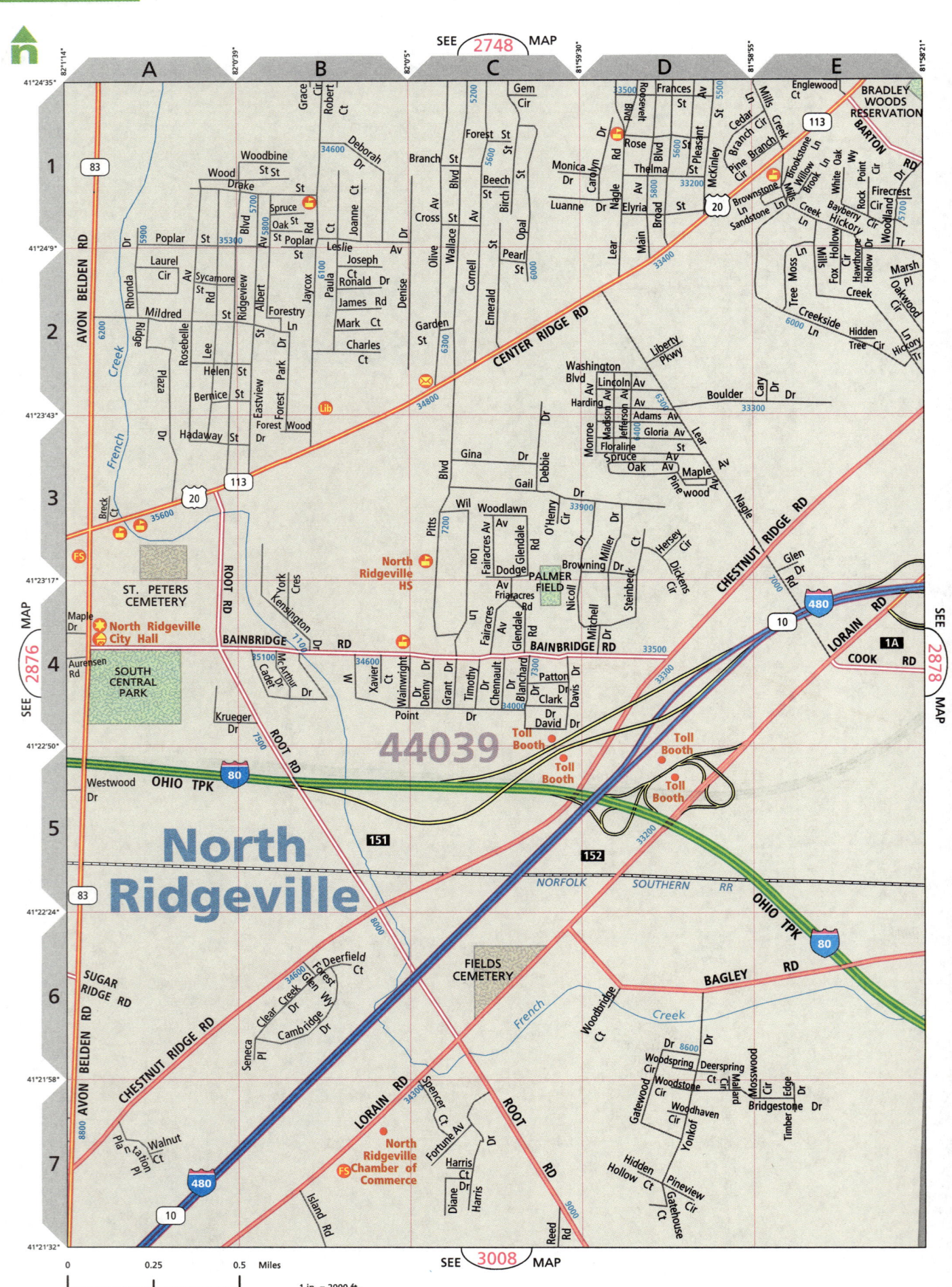

SEE 2748 MAP

SEE 2876 MAP

SEE 2878 MAP

SEE 3008 MAP

North Ridgeville

44039

0   0.25   0.5 Miles

1 in. = 2000 ft.

MAP 2878

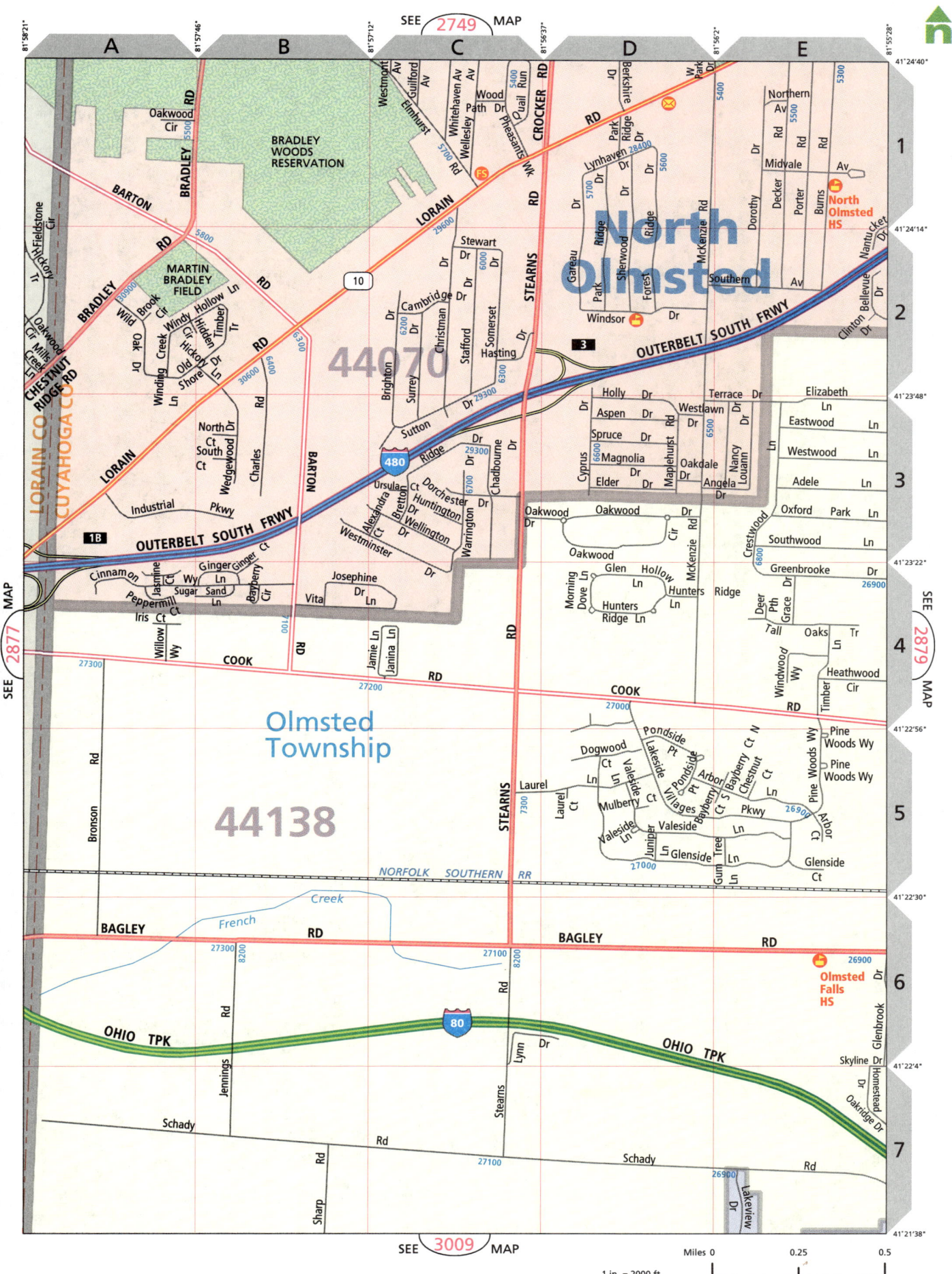

SEE 2749 MAP

A B C D E

81°58'21" 81°57'46" 81°57'12" 81°56'37" 81°56'2" 81°55'28"

41°24'40"

Oakwood Cir

BRADLEY WOODS RESERVATION

Westmont Av
Guilford Av
Elmhurst Av
Whitehaven Av
Wellesley
Wood Path Dr
Pheasants Wk
Quail Run

Berkshire Dr
W Park Dr

Northern Av

BARTON

BRADLEY RD

CROCKER RD

Park Ridge Dr

Decker Dr
Dorothy Dr
Porter
Burns

North Olmsted HS

41°24'14"

LORAIN

Lynhaven Dr

Gareau Dr
Ridge Dr
Sherwood Dr
Forest Dr

North Olmsted

Midvale Av

Nantucket Dr

FS

STEARNS RD

Stewart Dr

Cambridge Dr
Christman Dr

Park Ridge Dr
McKenzie Rd
Southern

Clinton
Bellevue Dr

10

MARTIN BRADLEY FIELD

Wild Oak Dr
Windy Hollow Ln
Hidden Cir
Timber Tr
Old Shore Ln

Brook Cir
Winding Creek Ln
Hickory Cir

Brighton Dr
Surrey Dr
Stafford Dr
Somerset Dr
Hasting Dr

Windsor Dr

41°23'48"

44070

Holly Dr
Aspen Dr
Spruce Dr
Magnolia Dr
Elder Dr

Terrace Dr

Elizabeth Ln

Eastwood Ln

BRADLEY RD

BARTON RD

Westlawn Dr
Maplehurst Rd
Oakdale Dr
Angela Dr

Cyprus
Nancy
Louann

Westwood Ln

Adele Ln

41°23'22"

North Dr
South Ct
Ct
Wedgewood Ln
Charles Rd

Sutton Dr

Ridge Dr

Chadbourne Dr

Oakwood Dr
Oakwood Dr
Oakwood Cir

Crestwood Dr

Oxford Park Ln

Southwood Ln

Greenbrooke Dr

LORAIN

Industrial Pkwy

480

Ursula Ct
Dorchester Dr
Alexandra Ct
Bretton
Huntington Dr
Wellington Dr
Warrington Dr

McKenzie Rd

Ridge

Deer Pth
Grace Dr
Tall Oaks Tr

SEE 2879 MAP

1B

OUTERBELT SOUTH FRWY

Westminster Dr

Morning Dove Ln
Glen Hollow Ln
Hunters Ridge Ln
Hunters Ln

Windwood Wy
Timber Ln
Heathwood Cir

Cinnamon
Ginger Ct
Ginger
Bayberry Cir
Jasmine Ct
Sugar Ln
Sand Ln

Josephine Dr
Vita Ln

COOK RD

Peppermill

Iris Ct

Willow Wy

Jamie Ln
Janina Ln

STEARNS RD

COOK RD

Pine Woods Wy
Pine Woods Wy

41°22'56"

SEE 2877 MAP

Olmsted Township

Dogwood Ct
Lakeside Ln
Valeside Ln
Pondside Pt
Pondside Pt
Arbor
Bayberry Ct N
Bayberry Ct S
Chestnut Ln

44138

Laurel Ct
Laurel
Mulberry Ln
Villages Pkwy

Pine Woods Wy
Arbor Ct

Bronson Rd

Valeside Ln
Juniper Ln
Glenside Ln
Gum Tree Ln

Glenside Ct

41°22'30"

NORFOLK SOUTHERN RR

BAGLEY RD

French Creek

BAGLEY RD

Olmsted Falls HS

80

OHIO TPK

OHIO TPK

Glenbrook Dr

Skyline Dr

41°22'4"

Jennings Rd

Lynn Dr

Stearns Rd

Homestead Dr
Oakridge Dr

Schady Rd

Schady Rd

Sharp Rd

Lakeview Dr

41°21'38"

1
2
3
4
5
6
7

SEE 3009 MAP

Miles 0   0.25   0.5

1 in. = 2000 ft.

MAP 2879

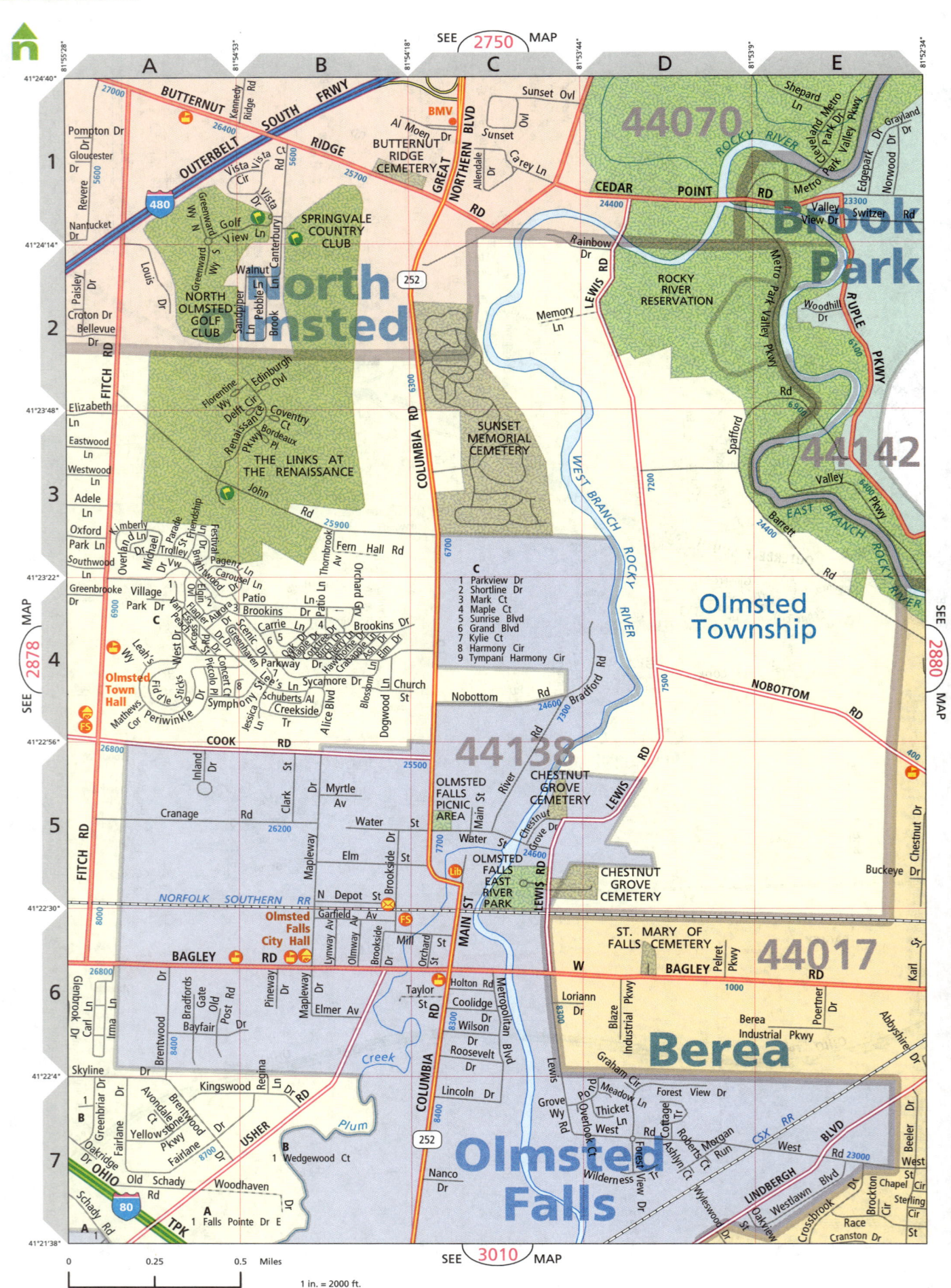

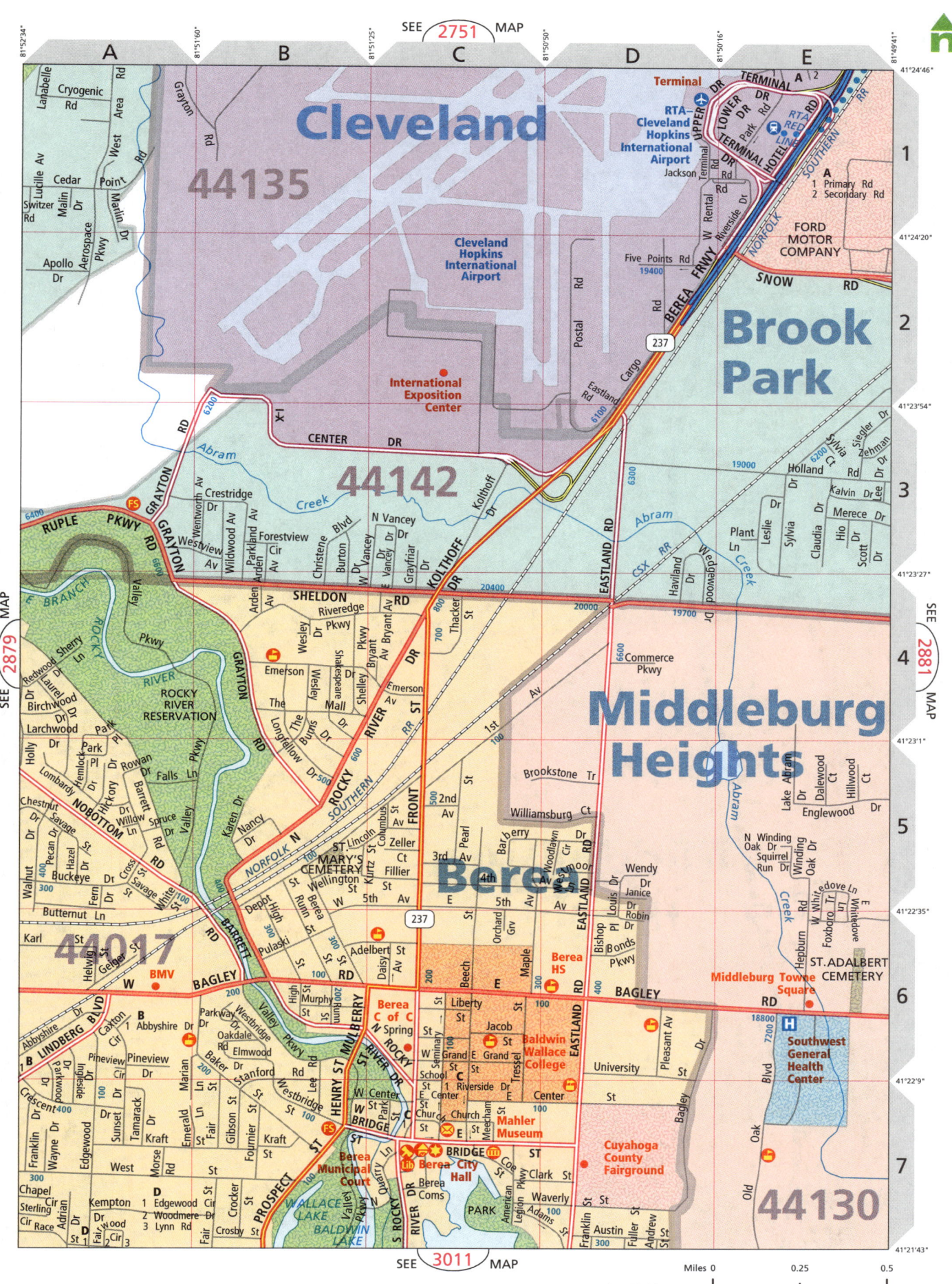

MAP 2881

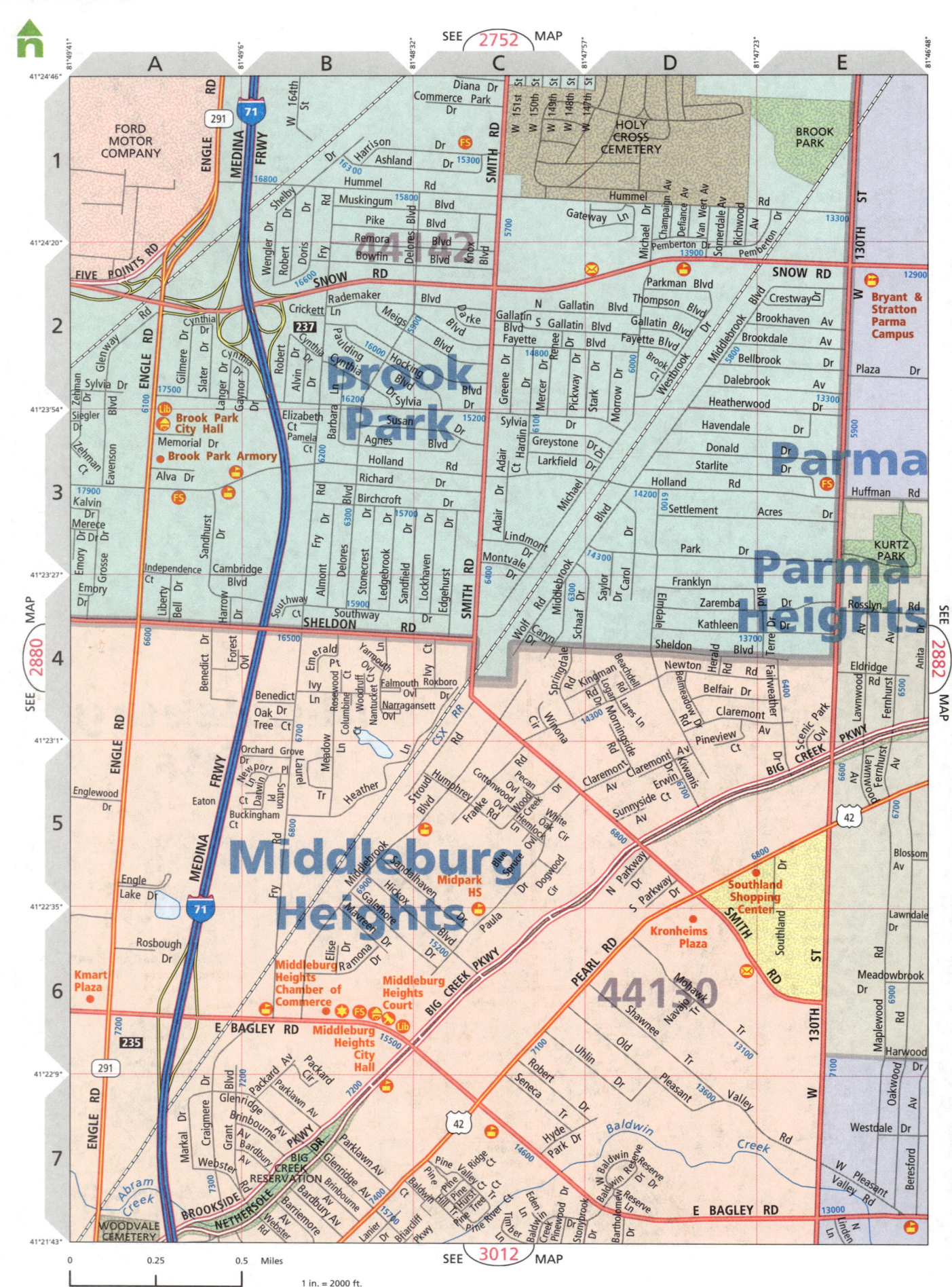

SEE 2752 MAP
SEE 2880 MAP
SEE 2882 MAP
SEE 3012 MAP

0   0.25   0.5 Miles

1 in. = 2000 ft.

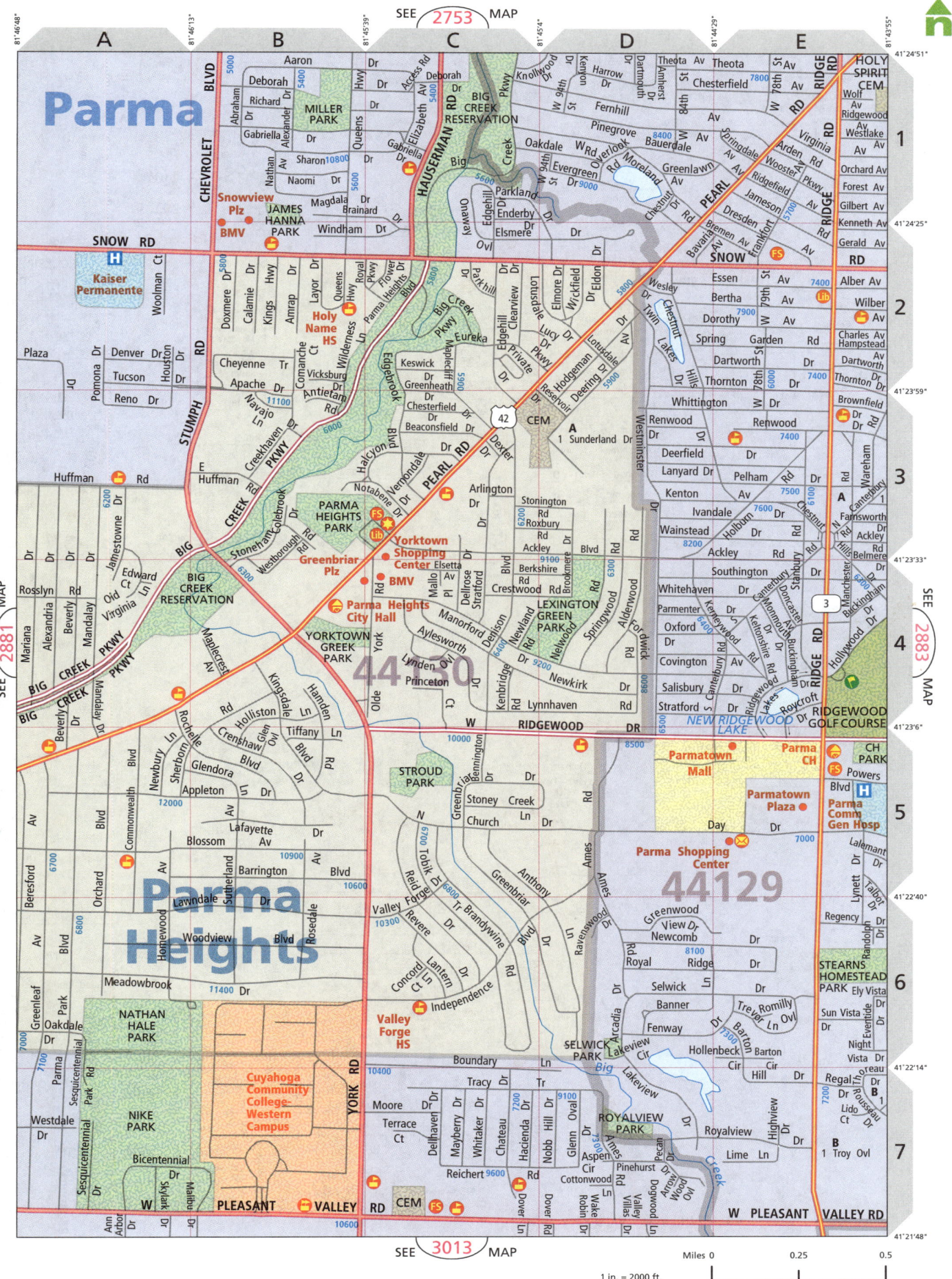

MAP 2882

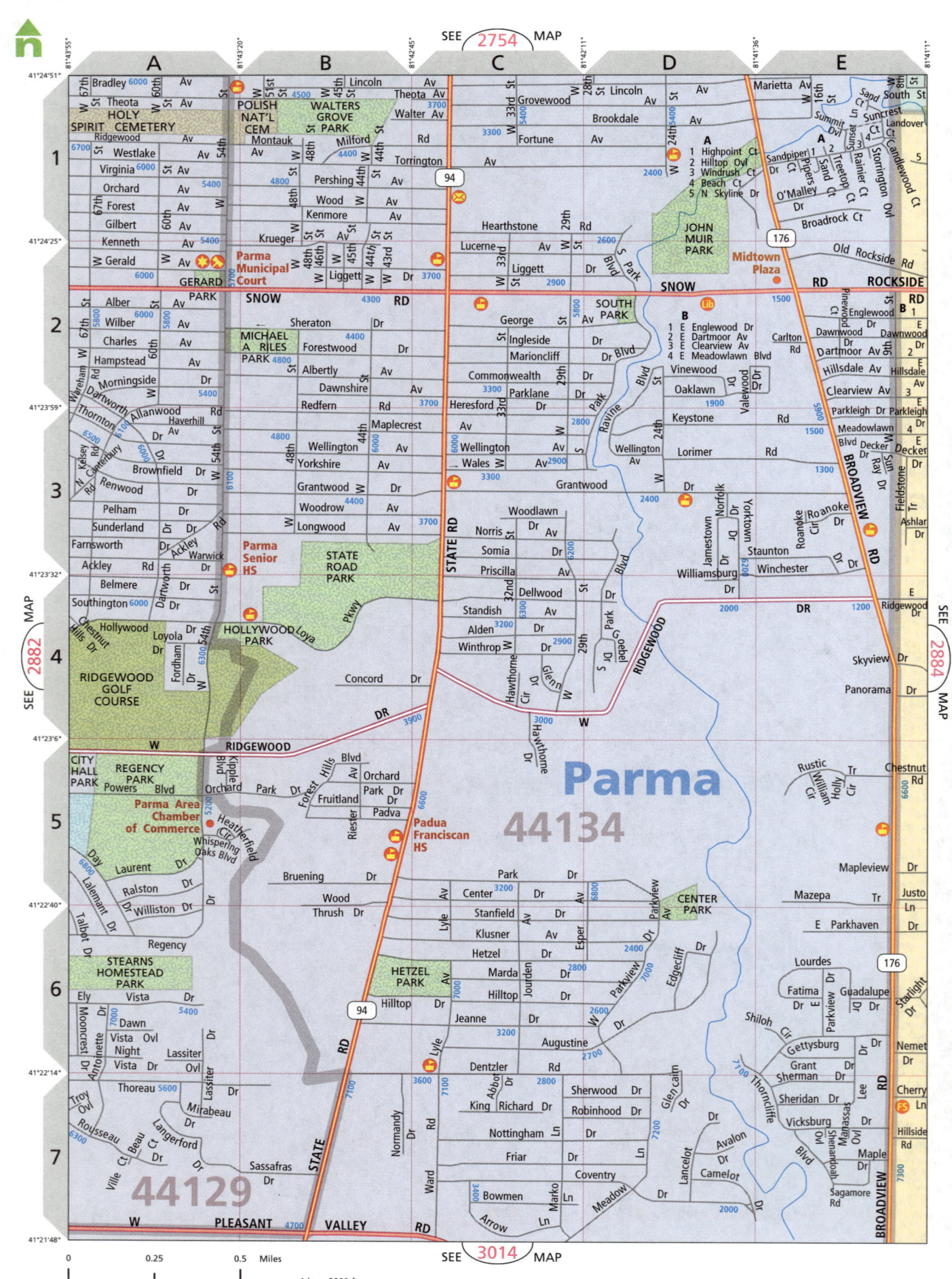

MAP 2883

SEE 2754 MAP

	A	B	C	D	E

Parma
44134

44129

SEE 2882 MAP

SEE 2884 MAP

SEE 3014 MAP

0   0.25   0.5 Miles

1 in. = 2000 ft.

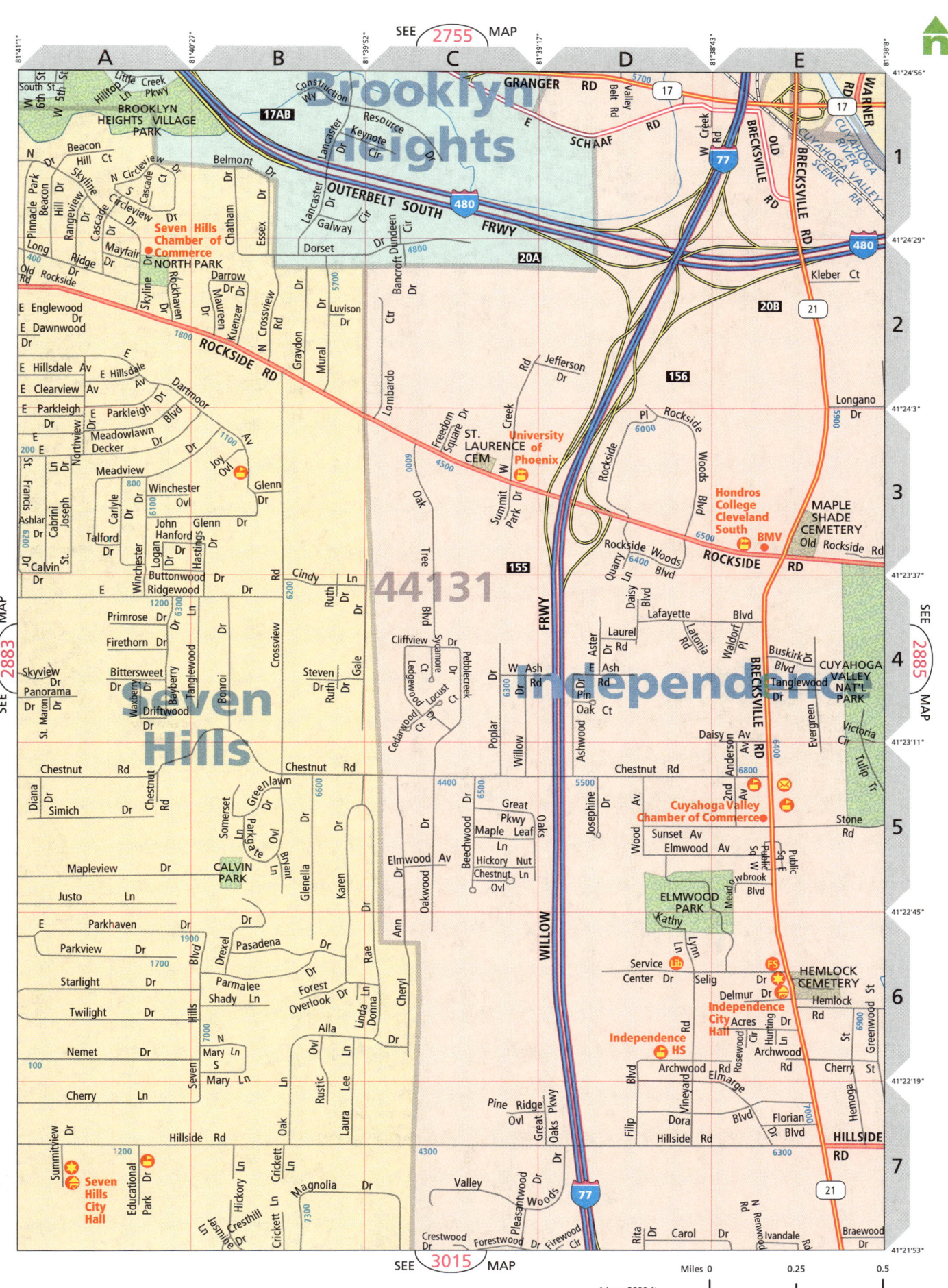

MAP 2884

SEE 2755 MAP

SEE 2883 MAP

SEE 2885 MAP

SEE 3015 MAP

Brooklyn Heights

Seven Hills

Independence

44131

Miles 0   0.25   0.5

1 in. = 2000 ft.

MAP 2885

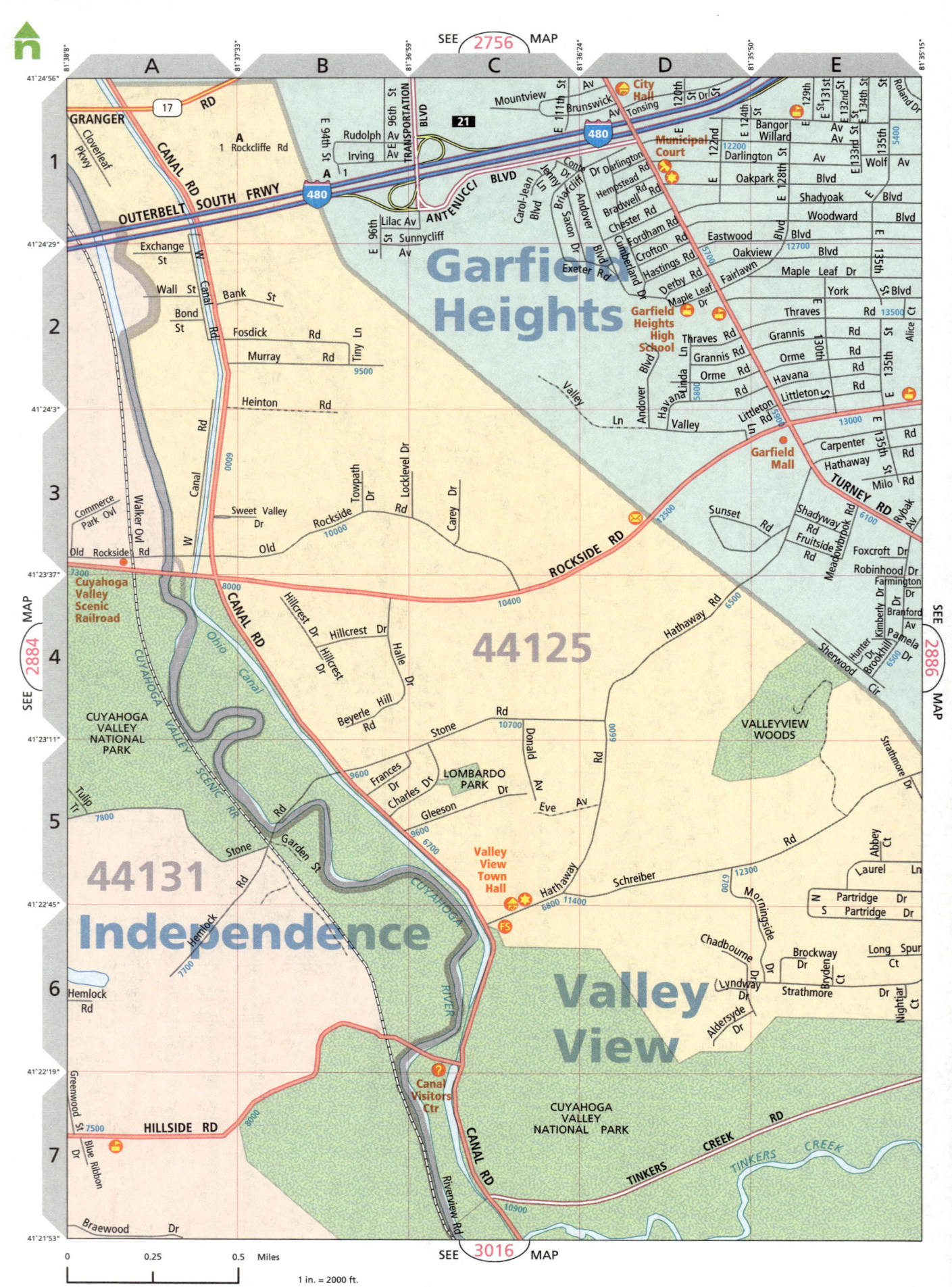

SEE 2756 MAP

A | B | C | D | E

1

2

3

4

5

6

7

Granger

GRANGER RD

CANAL RD SOUTH FRWY

OUTERBELT SOUTH FRWY

480

ANTENUCCI BLVD

TRANSPORTATION BLVD

21

Mountview

Brunswick

City Hall

Municipal Court

Bangor

Willard

Rockcliffe Rd

Rudolph

Irving

Lilac Av

Sunnycliff Av

Garfield Heights

Darlington

Oakpark Blvd

Shadyoak Blvd

Woodward Blvd

Eastwood Blvd

Oakview Blvd

Maple Leaf Dr

York Blvd

Exchange St

Wall St

Bank St

Bond St

Fosdick Rd

Murray Rd

Tiny Ln

Heinton Rd

Garfield Heights High School

Thraves Rd

Grannis Rd

Orme Rd

Havana

Littleton Rd

Thraves Rd

Grannis Rd

Orme Rd

Havana Rd

Littleton Rd

Alice

Garfield Mall

Carpenter Rd

Hathaway

Milo

TURNEY RD

Commerce Park Ovl

Sweet Valley Dr

Rockside Dr

Towpath Dr

Locklevel Dr

Carey Dr

Old Rockside Rd

Old

ROCKSIDE RD

Sunset Rd

Shadyway Rd

Fruitside Rd

Foxcroft Dr

Robinhood Dr

Cuyahoga Valley Scenic Railroad

CANAL RD

Hillcrest Dr

Hillcrest Dr

Hillcrest Dr

Halle Dr

Beyerle Hill Rd

44125

Hathaway Rd

Farmington Dr

Branford Av

Pamela

CUYAHOGA VALLEY NATIONAL PARK

Ohio Canal

CUYAHOGA VALLEY SCENIC RR

Stone Rd

Frances Dr

Charles Dr

LOMBARDO PARK

Gleeson

Stone Rd

Donald Av

Eve Av

VALLEYVIEW WOODS

Strathmore Dr

Sherwood Cir

44131

Independence

Tulip Tr

Hemlock Rd

Stone Rd

Garden St

CUYAHOGA RIVER

Valley View Town Hall

Hathaway

Schreiber Rd

Morningside

Abbey Ct

Laurel Ln

Partridge Dr

Partridge Dr

Chadbourne Dr

Brockway Dr

Bryden Ct

Long Spur Ct

Hemlock Rd

Lyndway Dr

Strathmore Dr

Aldersyde Dr

Nightjar Ct

Valley View

Canal Visitors Ctr

CUYAHOGA VALLEY NATIONAL PARK

Greenwood St

Blue Ribbon Dr

HILLSIDE RD

CANAL RD

Riverview Rd

TINKERS CREEK RD

TINKERS CREEK

Braewood Dr

SEE 2884 MAP

SEE 2886 MAP

SEE 3016 MAP

0   0.25   0.5   Miles

1 in. = 2000 ft.

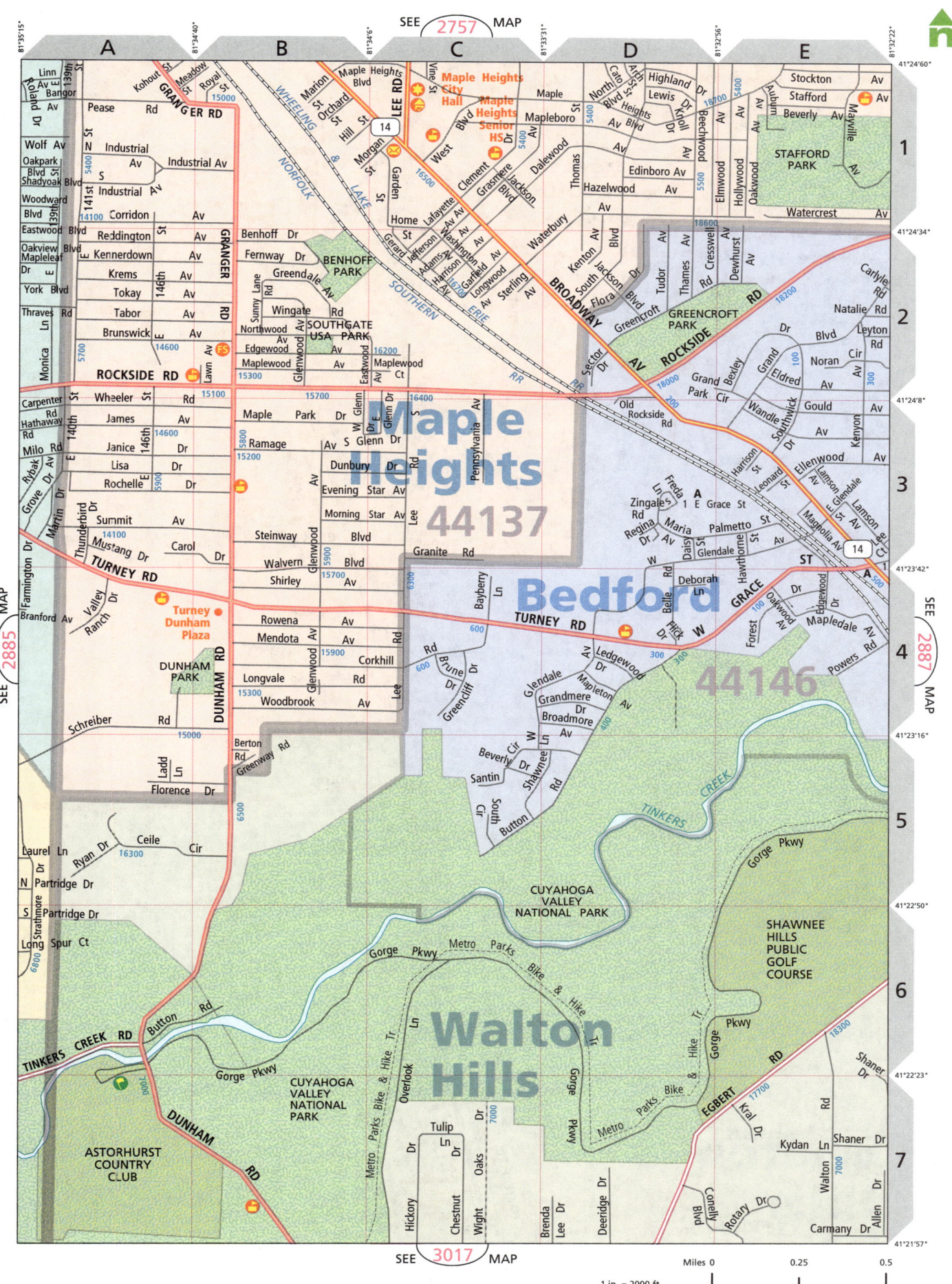

MAP 2886

MAP 2887

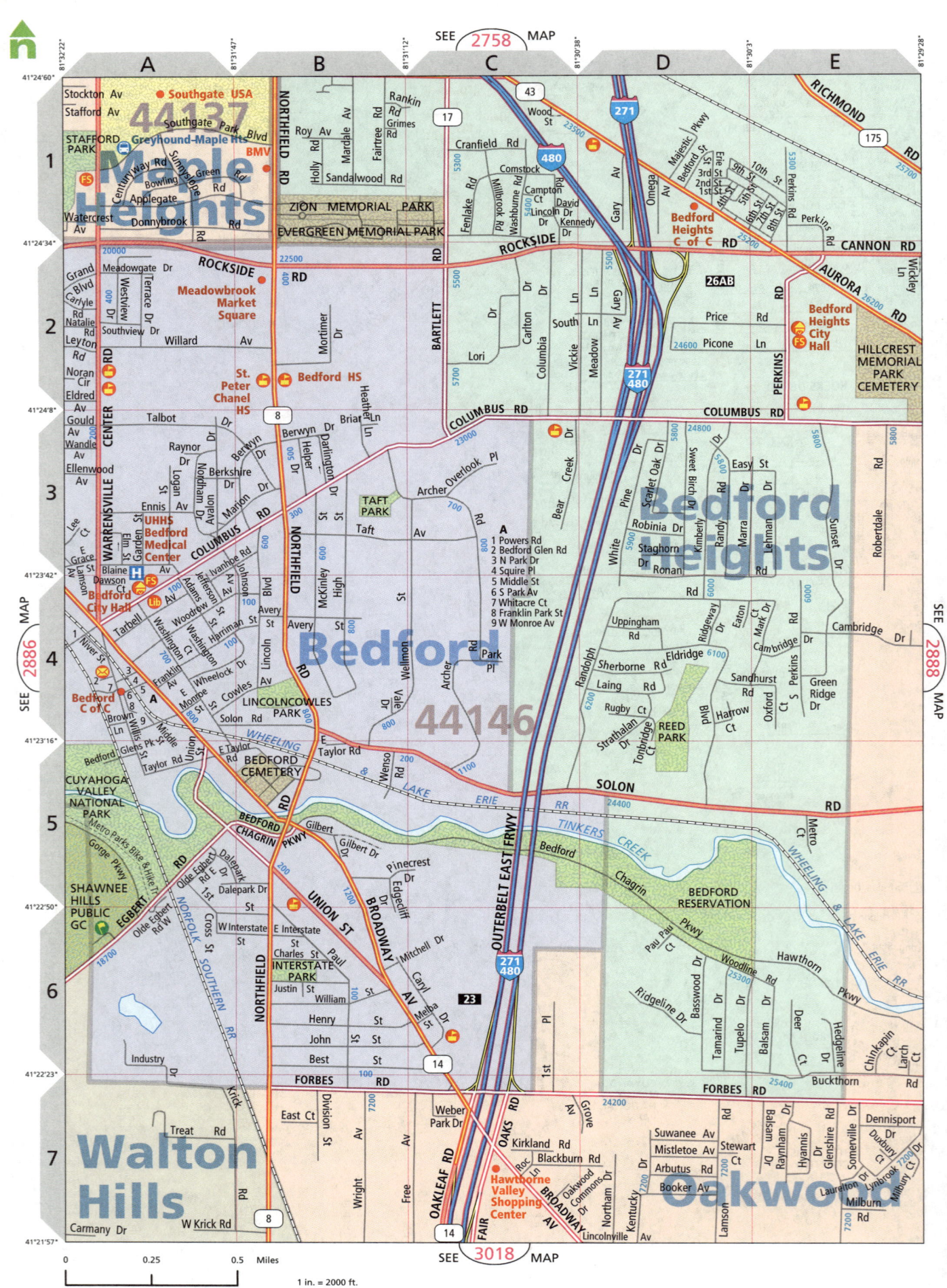

SEE 2758 MAP

RICHMOND RD

STOCKTON Av
Stafford Av
• Southgate USA
44137
STAFFORD PARK
Southgate Blvd
• Greyhound-Maple Hts
BMV
Maple Heights
Century Way Rd
Sunnydale Rd
Bowling Green Rd
Applegate
Watercrest Av
Donnybrook Rd

NORTHFIELD RD

Roy Av
Holly
Rd
Mardale Av
Sandalwood Rd
Fairtree Rd
Rankin Rd
Grimes Rd

43
17
Wood St 23500
271

ZION MEMORIAL PARK
EVERGREEN MEMORIAL PARK

Cranfield Rd
Comstock
Campton Lincoln Dr
David Kennedy
Majestic Pkwy
Bedford St
Erie St
3rd St
2nd St
1st St
9th St
10th St
Perkins Rd
5300

ROCKSIDE RD
ROCKSIDE
Gary Av
Omega Av
Bedford Heights C of C
RD
CANNON RD

ROCKSIDE 22500 RD
20000

Grand Blvd
Meadowgate Dr
Westview
Terrace Dr
Southview Dr
Willard Av
Meadowbrook Market Square
Mortimer Dr
BARTLETT RD
Dr
Carlton
South Ln
Vickie Ln
Meadow Ln
Columbia
Gary Av
271 480
Price Rd
24600 Picone Ln
26AB
PERKINS RD
AURORA 26200 RD
Wickley Ln
Bedford Heights City Hall
HILLCREST MEMORIAL PARK CEMETERY

Carlyle Rd
Natalie Rd
Leyton Rd
Noran Cir
Eldred Av
Gould Av
Wandle Av
Ellenwood Av
CENTER RD
Talbot
WARRENSVILLE
Raynor Dr
Berwyn Dr
Berkshire Dr
Logan Av
Nordham Av
Marion Av
Ennis St
Elm Garden
Lee Ct
E Grace Av
Lamson
Blaine Av
Dawson Av
Bedford City Hall
COLUMBUS RD
8
Helper Dr
Berwyn
Darlington Dr
Briar Ln
Heather Ln
NORTHFIELD
300
005
600
TAFT PARK
Archer
Overlook Pl
Taft Av
St
700
COLUMBUS RD
23000
Bear Creek Dr
Dr
White
Pine
Scarlet Oak
Robinia Dr
Staghorn Dr Ronan
Sweet Birch Rd
Kimberly
Randy
Marra
Easy St
Lehman
5900
6000
24800
5600
5800
COLUMBUS RD
5800
Bedford Heights
Sunset Dr
Robertdale
5800

UHHS Bedford Medical Center
Ivanhoe Rd
Jefferson Av
Jefferson Av
Johnson Av
McKinley St
High St
A
1 Powers Rd
2 Bedford Glen Rd
3 N Park Dr
4 Squire Pl
5 Middle St
6 S Park Av
7 Whitacre Ct
8 Franklin Park St
9 W Monroe Av
Uppingham Rd
Randolph Rd
Sherborne Rd
Laing Rd
Rugby Ct
Strathalan Dr
Tonbridge Dr
Ridgeway Dr
Eaton Ct
Eldridge 6100
Cambridge Dr
Sandhurst
Perkins S
Oxford Ct
Green Ridge Dr
Mark Dr
Cambridge Dr
6200
SEE 2888 MAP

Bedford
44146
Woodrew
Adams Av
Washington Av
Washington Ct
Tarbell
Franklin
E Monroe
Brown St
Willis Ln
Middle St
Harriman St
Wheelock Dr
Lincoln
Avery St
Avery St
St
LINCOLNCOWLES PARK
Cowles
Solon Rd
800
Wellmon Dr
Park Pl
Vale
Archer
800
800
1100
100
100
700
800
REED PARK
Harrow Ct
Blvd

SEE 2886 MAP

Bedford C of C
River Rd
1
7
3
4
5
6
A
Bedford Glens Pk Rd
Taylor Rd
Taylor Rd
BEDFORD
WHEELING
E Taylor Rd
E Taylor Rd
BEDFORD CEMETERY
Wenso Rd
200
LAKE ERIE RR
SOLON 24400 RD
Metro Ct
Metro Dr
WHEELING & LAKE ERIE RR

CUYAHOGA VALLEY NATIONAL PARK
Metro Parks Bike & Hike Tr
Gorge Pkwy
SHAWNEE HILLS PUBLIC GC
EGBERT RD
CHAGRIN PKWY
Gilbert
Gilbert Dr
Pinecrest Dr
Edgecliff Dr
OUTERBELT EAST FRWY
TINKERS CREEK
Bedford Chagrin
BEDFORD RESERVATION
Pau Pau Pkwy

Olde Egbert Rd E
Olde Egbert Rd W
Dalepark Dr
Dalepark St
W Interstate St
NORFOLK SOUTHERN RR
18700
1st St
Cross St
UNION ST
200
1200
BROADWAY
E Interstate St
Charles St
Paul St
Justin St
William St
INTERSTATE PARK
Mitchell Dr
Caryl St
Melba Dr
23
271 480
1 St Pl
Ridgeline Dr
Tamarind Dr
Tupelo Dr
Basswood
Woodline 25300
Balsam St
Hawthorn
Deer Ct
Ridgeline Dr
Hedgeline
Chinkapin Ct
Larch Rd

1 in. = 2000 ft.

Henry St
John St
Best St
FORBES RD
100
14
Industry Dr
Krick Rd
WALTON HILLS
Treat Rd
Carmany Dr
W Krick Rd
8
East Ct
Division St
Wright Av
Free Av
OAKLEAF RD
7200
Weber Park Dr
FAIR
14
OAKS RD
Roc Ln
Kirkland Rd
Blackburn Rd
BROADWAY AV
Hawthorne Valley Shopping Center
24200
Grove Av
Oakwood Commons Dr
Northam Dr
Lincolnville Av
Kentucky
Suwanee Av
Mistletoe Av
Arbutus Rd
Lamson Rd
Stewart Ct
Raynham
Hyannis Dr
Balsam Dr
Laurelton Dr
Glenshire Rd
Limbrook Dr
Milburn
Somerville Dr
Oakwood
Dennisport Dr
Duxbury Dr
Milbury Rd
7200
FORBES RD 25400
Buckthorn Rd

SEE 3018 MAP

0   0.25   0.5 Miles

41°24'60"
41°24'34"
41°24'8"
41°23'42"
41°23'16"
41°22'50"
41°22'23"
41°21'57"

81°32'22" 81°31'47" 81°31'12" 81°30'38" 81°30'3" 81°29'28"

A   B   C   D   E
1
2
3
4
5
6
7

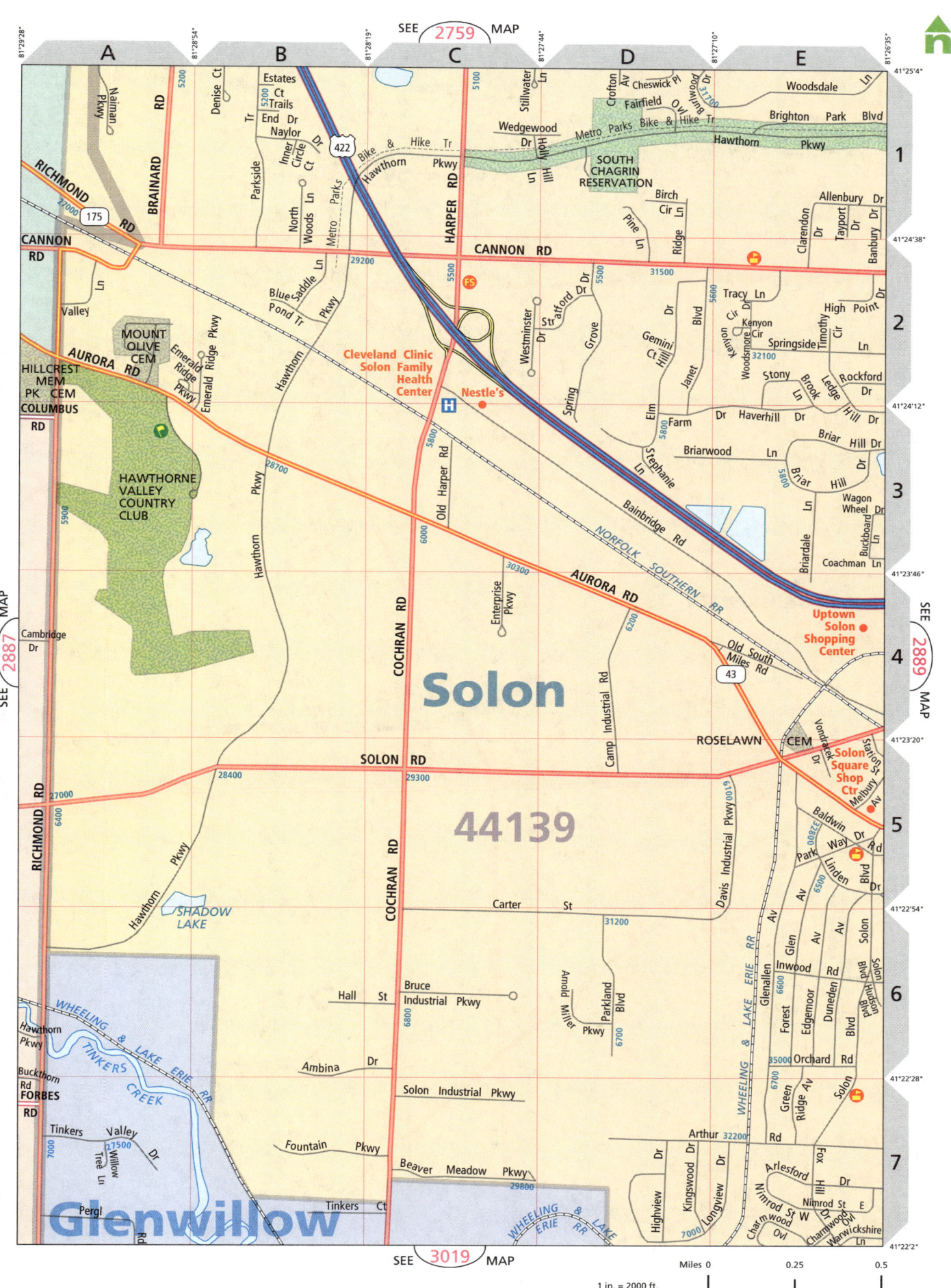

MAP 2888

A   B   C   D   E

SEE 2759 MAP

N

81°29'28"   81°28'54"   81°28'19"   81°27'44"   81°27'10"   81°26'35"

41°25'4"

Naiman Pkwy   5200   Denise Ct   Estates Ct Trails   Naylor   Stillwater Ln   Crofton Av   Cheswick Pl   Woodsdale Ln

BRAINARD   RD   End Dr   Inner Circle Ct Dr   Fairfield   Owl Burrow   37100   Brighton Park Blvd

RICHMOND   Parkside   422   Bike & Hike Tr   Wedgewood Dr   Holly Hill   Metro Parks Bike & Hike Tr   Hawthorn Pkwy   1

RD   175   North Woods Ln   Metro Parks   Hawthorn Pkwy   SOUTH CHAGRIN RESERVATION

27000   5100   HARPER   RD

CANNON RD   Valley Ln   CANNON RD   5100   CANNON RD   Birch Cir Ln   Allenbury Dr   41°24'38"

29200   5500   Pine Ln   Ridge Ln   Clarendon   Tayport Dr   Banbury Dr   2

AURORA   RD   Blue Saddle Ln   FS   Westminster   Stratford Dr Dr   Grove   Dr   Tracy Ln   5600   Kenyon Cir   Woodsmore Cir   High Point   Springside   Timothy Cir   Ln   31500

MOUNT OLIVE CEM   Emerald Ridge Pkwy   Pond Tr Pkwy   5500   Spring   Gemini Ct Hill   Janet   Kenyon Cir   32100   Stony Ln   Brook Ln   Ledge Hill   Rockford Dr

HILLCREST MEM PK CEM   Emerald Ridge Pkwy   Hawthorn   Cleveland Clinic Solon Family Health Center   Elm   Farm Dr   Haverhill Dr   41°24'12"

COLUMBUS RD   5900   Nestle's   H   5800   Stephanie   Briarwood   Ln   Briar Hill Dr   Briar   Hill   5800

HAWTHORNE VALLEY COUNTRY CLUB   28700   Old Harper Rd   6000   Bainbridge Rd   NORFOLK SOUTHERN RR   Briar   Ln   Wagon Wheel   Buckboard Ln   3

Hawthorn Pkwy   Briardale   Coachman Ln   41°23'46"

SEE 2887 MAP

Cambridge Dr   Enterprise Pkwy   30300   AURORA RD   6200   Old South Miles Rd   Uptown Solon Shopping Center   SEE 2889 MAP   4

RICHMOND   27000   COCHRAN RD   43   ROSELAWN   CEM   Vondracek Dr   Solon Square Shop Ctr   41°23'20"

RD   6400   SOLON RD   Camp Industrial Rd   Station St   Melbury Av   Baldwin Dr   5

28400   29300   Solon   44139   Davis Industrial Pkwy   33800   Park Way   Rd   41°22'54"

Carter   St   31200   Linden   Blvd Dr

Hawthorn Pkwy   SHADOW LAKE   Glen Av   6500   Solon Blvd

Arnold Miller Pkwy   6700   Glenallen   Inwood Rd   Solon Blvd   6

Hall St   Bruce Industrial Pkwy   6800   Parkland Blvd   6600   Forest   Edgemoor   Duneden Blvd   Solon Blvd Hudson

WHEELING & LAKE ERIE RR   35000   Orchard Rd   41°22'28"

Hawthorn Pkwy   Buckthorn Rd   Ambina   Dr   6700   Green Ridge Av   Solon Rd   E

FORBES RD   7000   Solon Industrial Pkwy   Arthur   32200   Rd   Fox Hill Dr   7

TINKERS CREEK   Tinkers Valley Dr   21500   Willow Tree Ln   Fountain   Pkwy   Beaver Meadow Pkwy   29800   Highview Dr   Kingswood Dr   Longview Dr   Arlesford Dr   Nimrod St W   Nimrod St E   Charnwood Ovl   Chamwood Ovl   Warwickshire Ln   41°22'2"

Pergl Rd   Tinkers Ct   WHEELING & LAKE ERIE RR

Glenwillow

SEE 3019 MAP

Miles 0   0.25   0.5

1 in. = 2000 ft.

MAP 2889

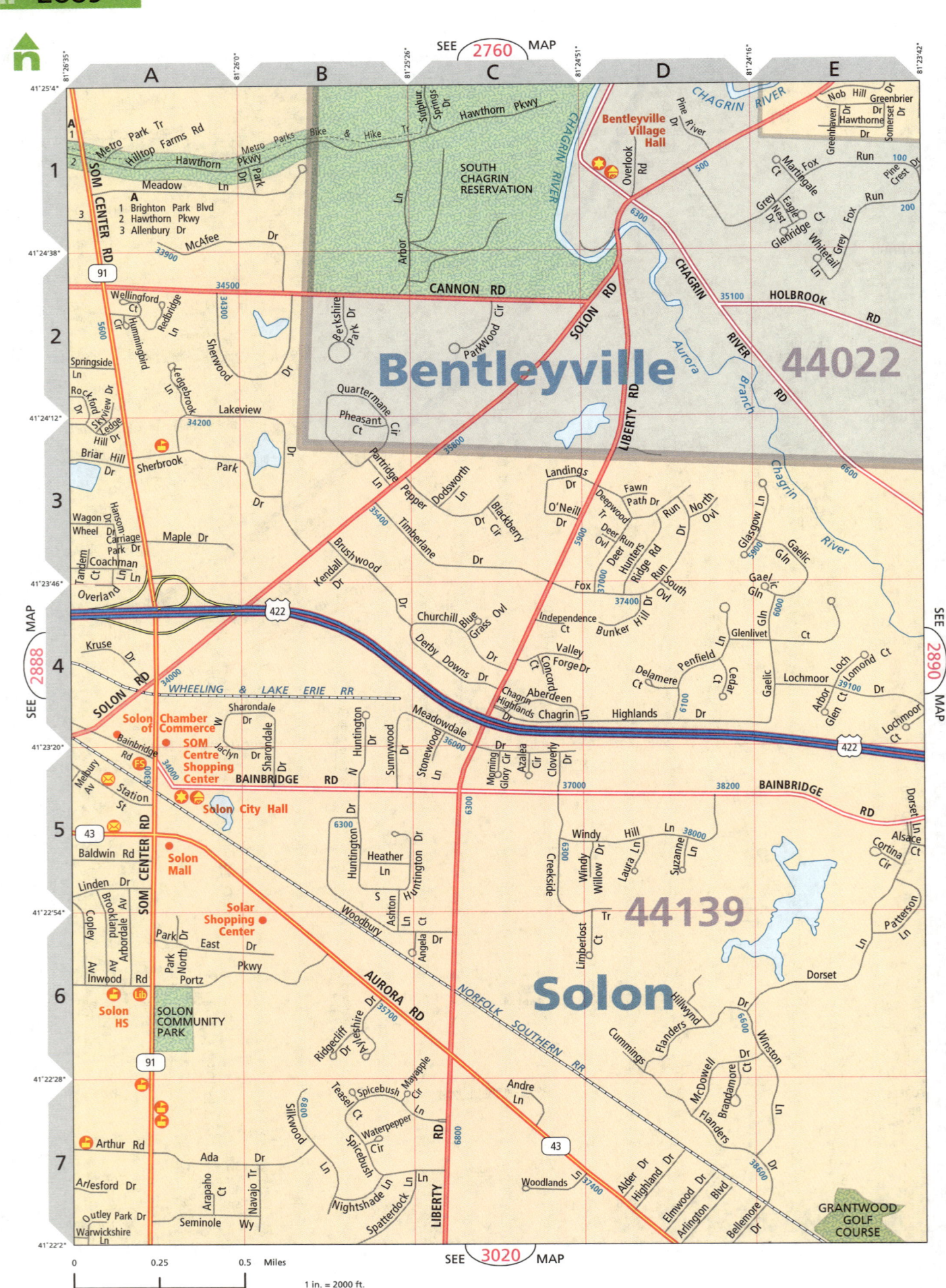

MAP 2890

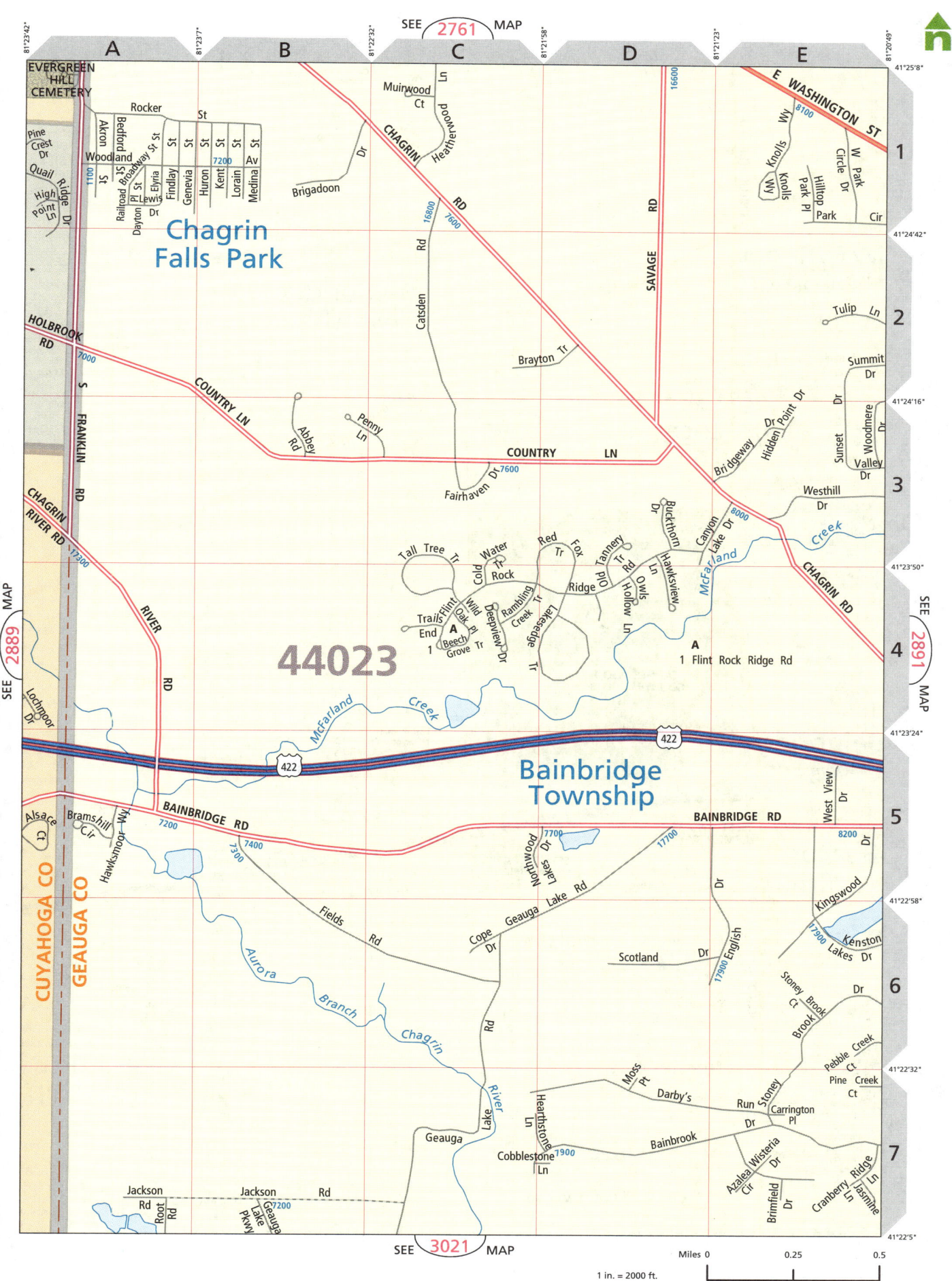

SEE 2761 MAP

EVERGREEN HILL CEMETERY

Pine Crest Dr
Quail
High Point Ln
Ridge Dr

Rocker St
Akron St
Bedford
Woodland St
Railroad
Broadway St
Dayton Pl
Elyria Dr
Lewis
Findlay St
Genevia St
Huron St
Kent St
Lorain St
Medina St
Av
7200

Chagrin Falls Park

Muirwood Ct
Heathewood Ln
CHAGRIN RD
16800
7600

Brigadoon

Dr

SAVAGE RD
16600

E WASHINGTON ST
8100
Wy Knolls
W Park
Circle Dr
Hilltop Park Pl
Park Cir

HOLBROOK RD
7000

S FRANKLIN RD

COUNTRY LN

Catsden Rd

Brayton Tr

Tulip Ln

Summit Dr
Woodmere Dr
Sunset Dr
Valley Dr

CHAGRIN RIVER RD
17300

RIVER RD

Abbey Rd
Penny Ln

COUNTRY LN
7600
Fairhaven Dr

Bridgeway
Hidden Point Dr
Dr

Westhill Dr

Creek

Lake Dr
8000
McFarland
CHAGRIN RD

44023

Tall Tree Tr
Water Tr
Rock
Colp
Flint
Wild
Oak
Beech Tr
Grove Tr
Deepview Dr
Rambling Creek Tr
Lakesedge Tr
Trails End 1
Ridge
Old
Red Tr
Fox Tr
Tannery Tr
Rd
Hawksview
Owls Hollow Ln
Buckthorn
Dr
Canyon

1 Flint Rock Ridge Rd
A

SEE 2889 MAP
Lochmoor Dr

McFarland Creek

422

422

Bainbridge Township

West View Dr

Alsace Ct
Bramshill Cir
Hawksmoor Wy

BAINBRIDGE RD
7200
7400
7300

Fields Rd

Aurora Branch Chagrin River

Cope Dr
Geauga Lake Rd
Northwood Dr
Lakes Dr
7700
17700

BAINBRIDGE RD
8200

Dr
Scotland Dr
English
17900

Kingswood Dr
Kenston Lakes Dr
17900

Stoney Brook Ct
Brook Dr
Pebble Creek Ct
Pine Creek Ct

Moss Pt
Darby's
Hearthstone Ln
Cobblestone Ln
1900

Stoney Run
Carrington Pl
Bainbrook Dr

Azalea Cir
Wisteria Dr
Brimfield Dr
Cranberry Ln
Ridge
Jasmine

Geauga Lake Pkwy

Jackson Rd
Root Rd
Jackson Rd
7200

SEE 3021 MAP

CUYAHOGA CO
GEAUGA CO

Miles 0   0.25   0.5
1 in. = 2000 ft.

MAP 2891

SEE 2762 MAP
SEE 2890 MAP
SEE 2892 MAP
SEE 3022 MAP

McFarlands Corners

Lake Lucerne

Bainbridge Township

Bainbridge

Beacon Hill

Bainbridge Township Town Hall

Tanglewood Country Club

Tanglewood Square Shopping Center

RESTLAND CEMETERY

SETTLERS PARK OF BAINBRIDGE

Kenston HS

Auburn Township

44023

A
1 Westhill Dr
2 Lakeshore Dr

B
1 East Brook Tr
2 N Hampton Ct
3 Concord Ct
4 Eastbrook Cir

C
1 Pebble Creek Ct

0   0.25   0.5 Miles
1 in. = 2000 ft.

MAP 2892

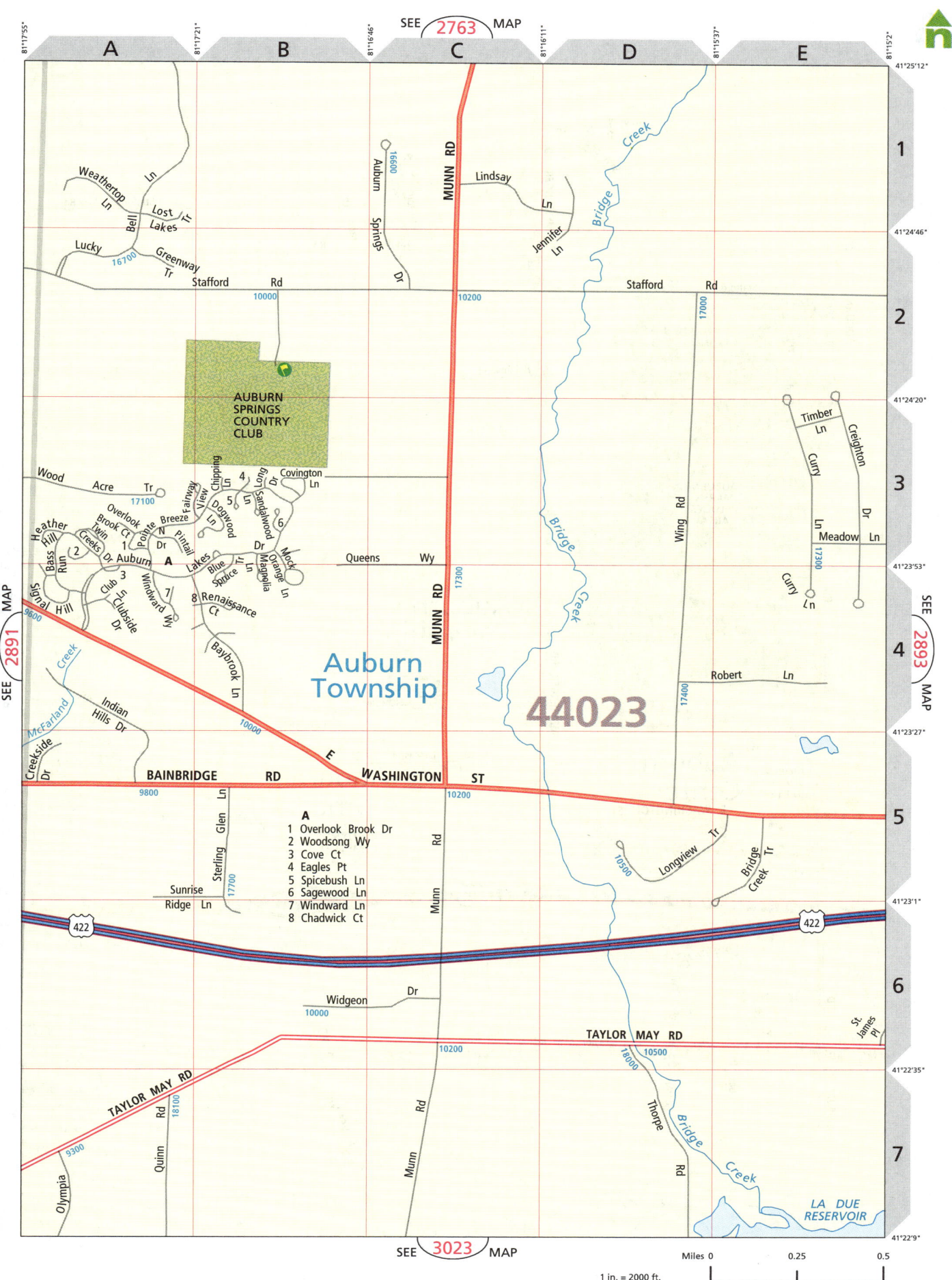

SEE 2763 MAP

A   B   C   D   E

Weathertop Ln
Bell Ln
Lost Lakes Tr
Lucky 16700
Greenway Tr
Stafford Rd
10000

16600
Auburn Springs Dr

MUNN RD

Lindsay Ln
Jennifer Ln
10200

Bridge Creek

Stafford Rd
17000

AUBURN SPRINGS COUNTRY CLUB

Wood Acre Tr
17100
Chipping View
Fairway
Dogwood Ln
Covington Ln
4
5
Sandalwood Ln
6

Bridge Creek

Timber Ln
Curry
Creighton Dr

Meadow Ln

Overlook Brook Ct
Pointe Breeze
Heather Hill
Bass Run
Twin Creeks Dr
2
N Dr
Pintail
Auburn
A
1
3
Club
Windward Wy
7
Clubside Dr
Lakes
Blue Spruce Tr
Orange Ln
Mock Magnolia Ln
8 Renaissance Ct
Baybrook Ln

Queens Wy

Wing Rd

MUNN RD
17300

Ln
17300
Curry Ln

Signal Hill
9600

Creek
McFarland

Indian Hills Dr

Auburn Township

44023

Robert Ln
17400

Creekside Dr
BAINBRIDGE RD
9800
WASHINGTON ST
10200

Longview Tr
10500

Bridge Creek Tr

SEE 2891 MAP

SEE 2893 MAP

Sterling Glen Ln
17700

A
1 Overlook Brook Dr
2 Woodsong Wy
3 Cove Ct
4 Eagles Pt
5 Spicebush Ln
6 Sagewood Ln
7 Windward Ln
8 Chadwick Ct

Munn Rd

422

422

Sunrise Ridge Ln

Widgeon Dr
10000

St. James Pl

TAYLOR MAY RD
10200

TAYLOR MAY RD
18000
10500

Bridge Creek

TAYLOR MAY RD
18100

Quinn Rd

Munn Rd

Thorpe Rd

Olympia
9300

LA DUE RESERVOIR

SEE 3023 MAP

Miles 0   0.25   0.5
1 in. = 2000 ft.

41°25'12"
41°24'46"
41°24'20"
41°23'53"
41°23'27"
41°23'1"
41°22'35"
41°22'9"

81°17'55" 81°17'21" 81°16'46" 81°16'11" 81°15'37" 81°15'2"

1
2
3
4
5
6
7

MAP 2893

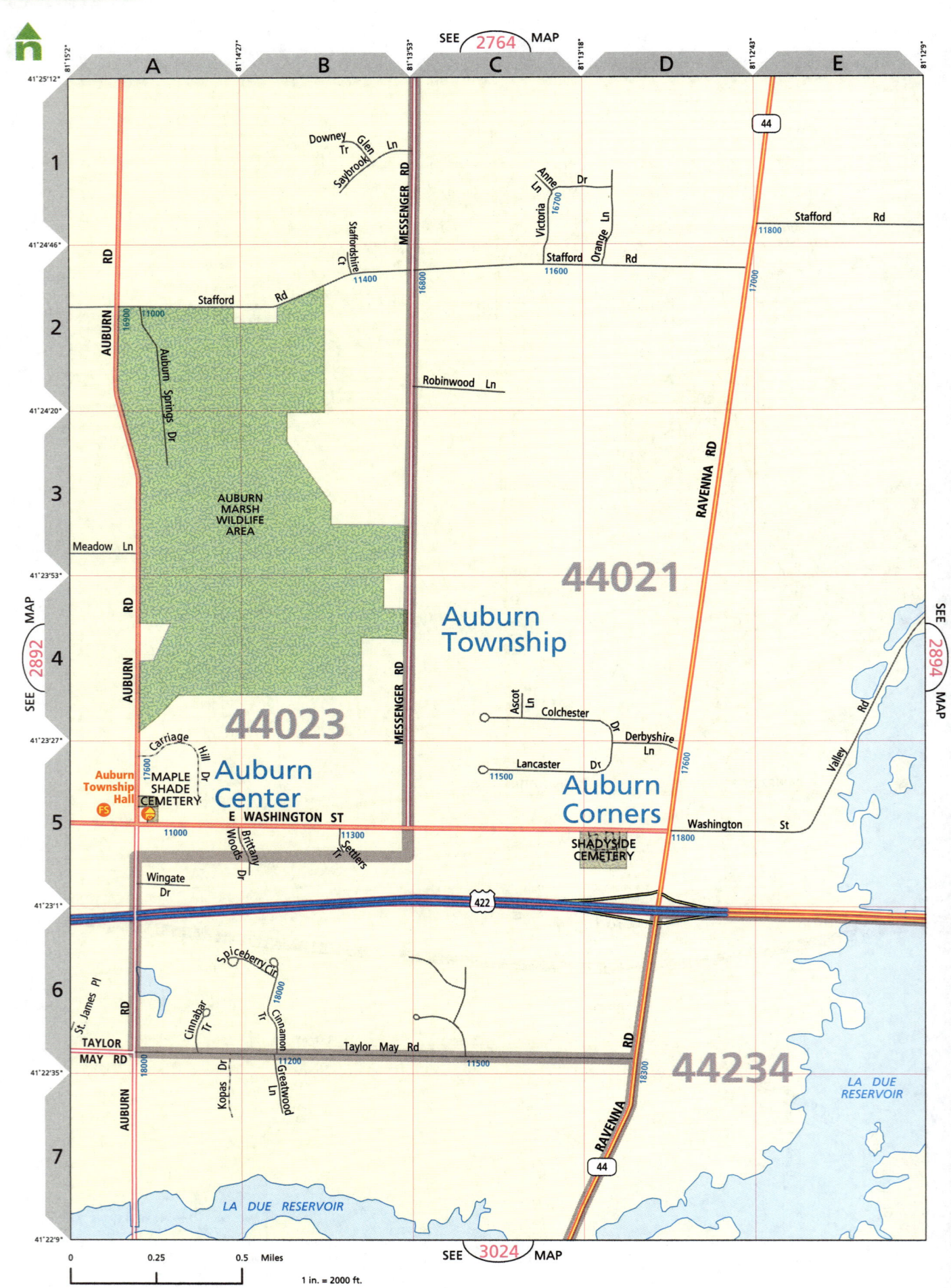

SEE 2764 MAP

A   B   C   D   E

44

Stafford   Rd

44021

Auburn
Township

44023

Auburn
Center

Auburn
Corners

Auburn
Township
Hall

MAPLE
SHADE
CEMETERY

E WASHINGTON ST

Washington   St

SHADYSIDE
CEMETERY

422

TAYLOR
MAY RD

Taylor May Rd

44234

LA DUE
RESERVOIR

LA DUE   RESERVOIR

SEE 3024 MAP

0   0.25   0.5   Miles

1 in. = 2000 ft.

MAP 2894

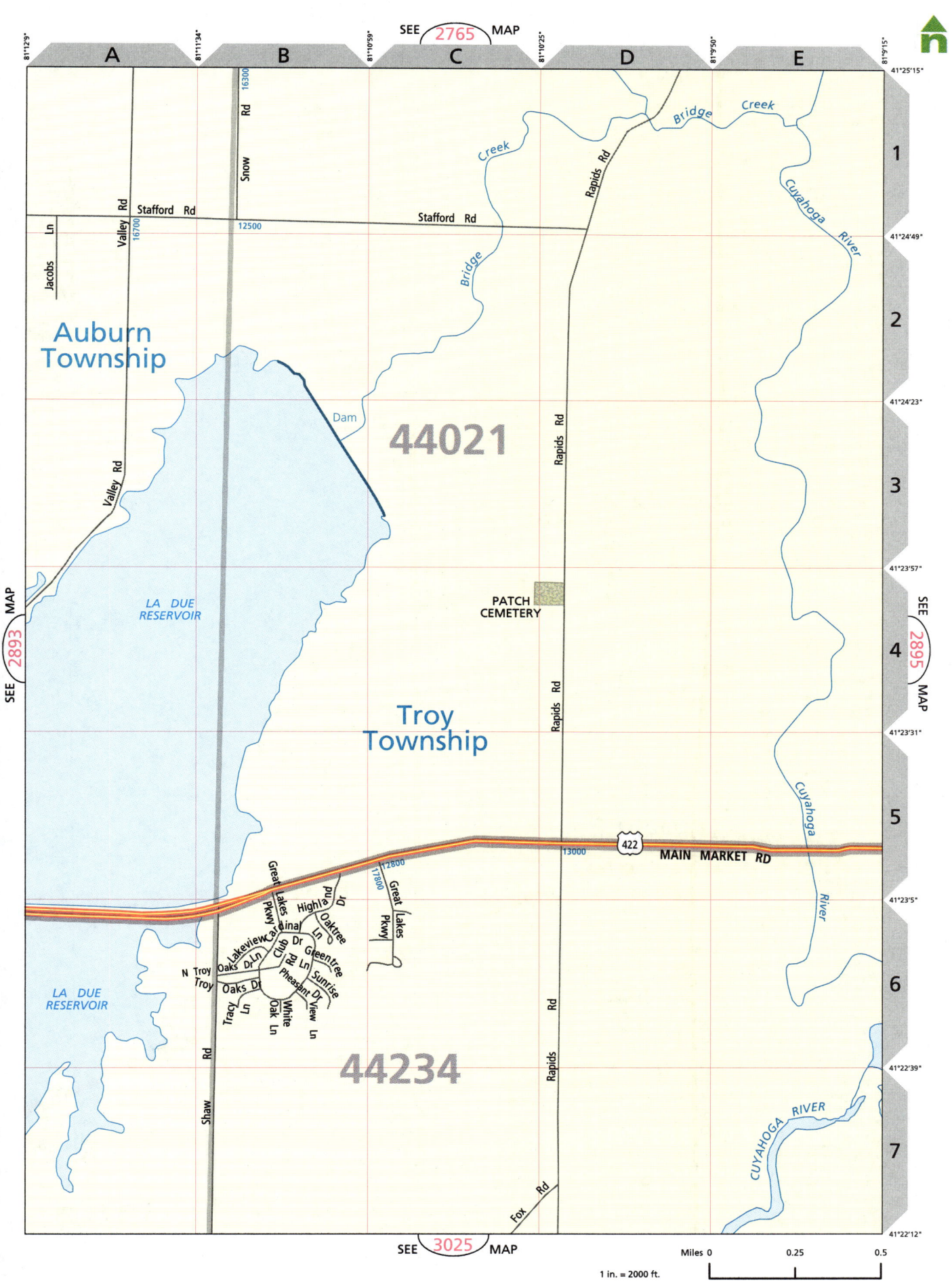

SEE 2765 MAP

A B C D E

41°12'9"
81°11'34"
81°10'59"
81°10'25"
81°9'50"
81°9'15"

1

41°25'15"

Snow Rd

16300

Creek

Bridge Creek

Cuyahoga River

Rapids Rd

Valley Rd

Stafford Rd

Stafford Rd

16700

12500

Ln

Jacobs

41°24'49"

Auburn
Township

2

41°24'23"

Dam

44021

Rapids Rd

3

LA DUE
RESERVOIR

Valley Rd

41°23'57"

PATCH
CEMETERY

SEE 2893 MAP

SEE 2895 MAP

4

Rapids Rd

Cuyahoga

Troy
Township

41°23'31"

5

422 MAIN MARKET RD

13000

12800

17800

Great Lakes Pkwy

Great Lakes Pkwy

Highla... Dr

Oaktree Ln

Cardinal Ln

Greentree Dr

Club Rd Ln

Lakeview Dr Ln

Sunrise

Oaks Dr

Pheasant Dr

White View Ln

Tracy Ln

Oak Ln

N Troy
Troy

Oaks Dr

Cuyahoga River

41°23'5"

LA DUE
RESERVOIR

6

44234

Rapids Rd

Shaw Rd

41°22'39"

CUYAHOGA RIVER

7

Fox Rd

41°22'12"

SEE 3025 MAP

Miles 0   0.25   0.5

1 in. = 2000 ft.

MAP 2895

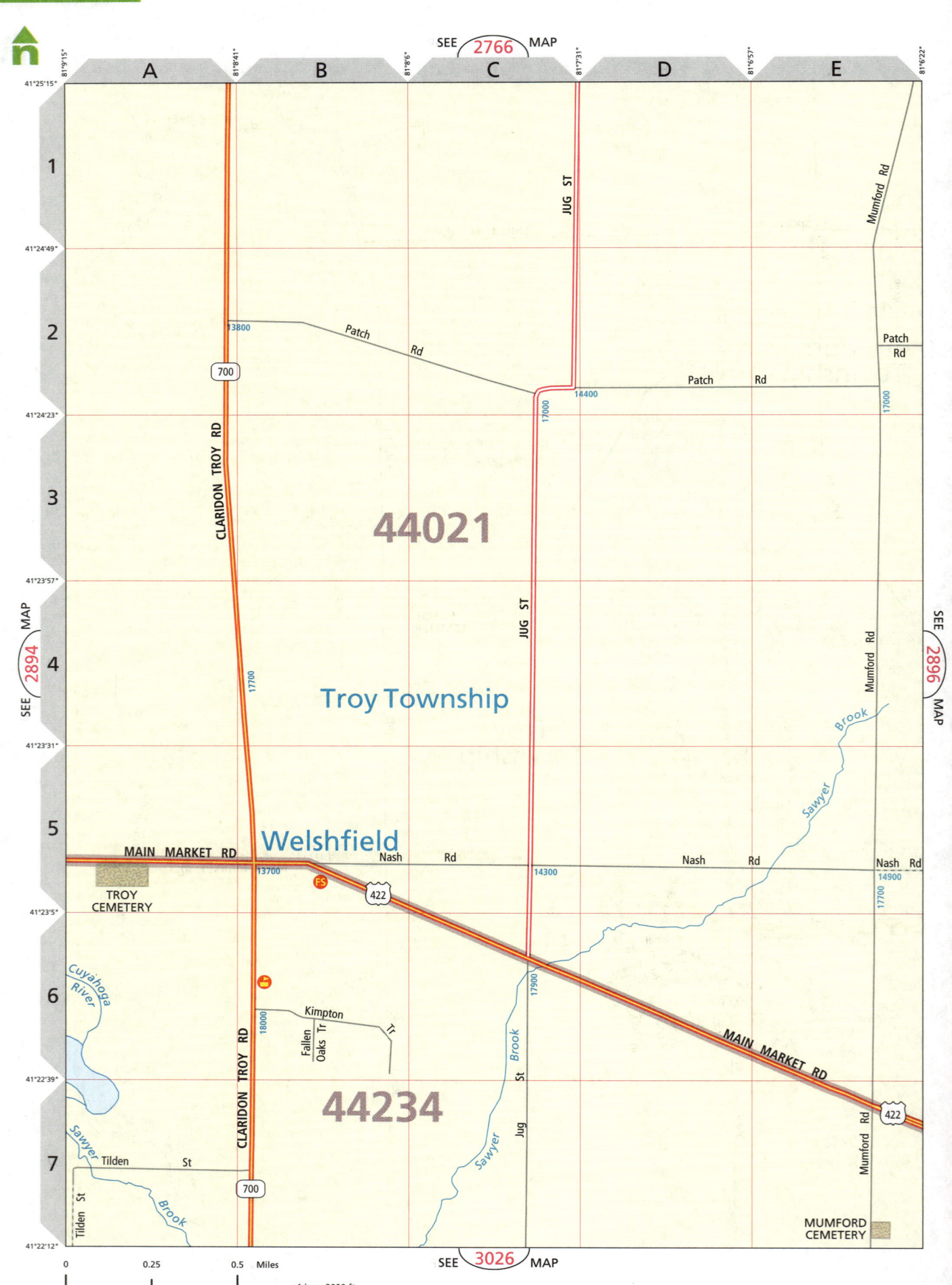

SEE 2766 MAP

A   B   C   D   E

41°25'15"

81°19'15"   81°18'41"   81°18'6"   81°17'31"   81°16'57"   81°16'22"

1

JUG ST

Mumford Rd

41°24'49"

2

13800   Patch   Rd   Patch   Rd
700   Patch   Rd
17000   14400   17000

41°24'23"

3

CLARIDON TROY RD   44021   JUG ST

41°23'57"

SEE 2894 MAP

4

17700   Troy Township   JUG ST   SEE 2896 MAP

Mumford Rd   Sawyer   Brook

41°23'31"

5

Welshfield
MAIN MARKET RD   Nash   Rd   Nash   Rd   Nash Rd
13700   14300   14900   17700
FS   422

TROY
CEMETERY

41°23'5"

6

Cuyahoga
River   18000   17900   Jug   St   Brook
Kimpton
Fallen   Oaks Tr   Tr   MAIN MARKET RD
44234   Mumford Rd   422

41°22'39"

7

Sawyer   Tilden   St   CLARIDON TROY RD   Sawyer   Jug   St   Brook   Brook
Tilden St
700   MUMFORD
CEMETERY

41°22'12"

SEE 3026 MAP

0   0.25   0.5   Miles

1 in. = 2000 ft.

MAP 2896

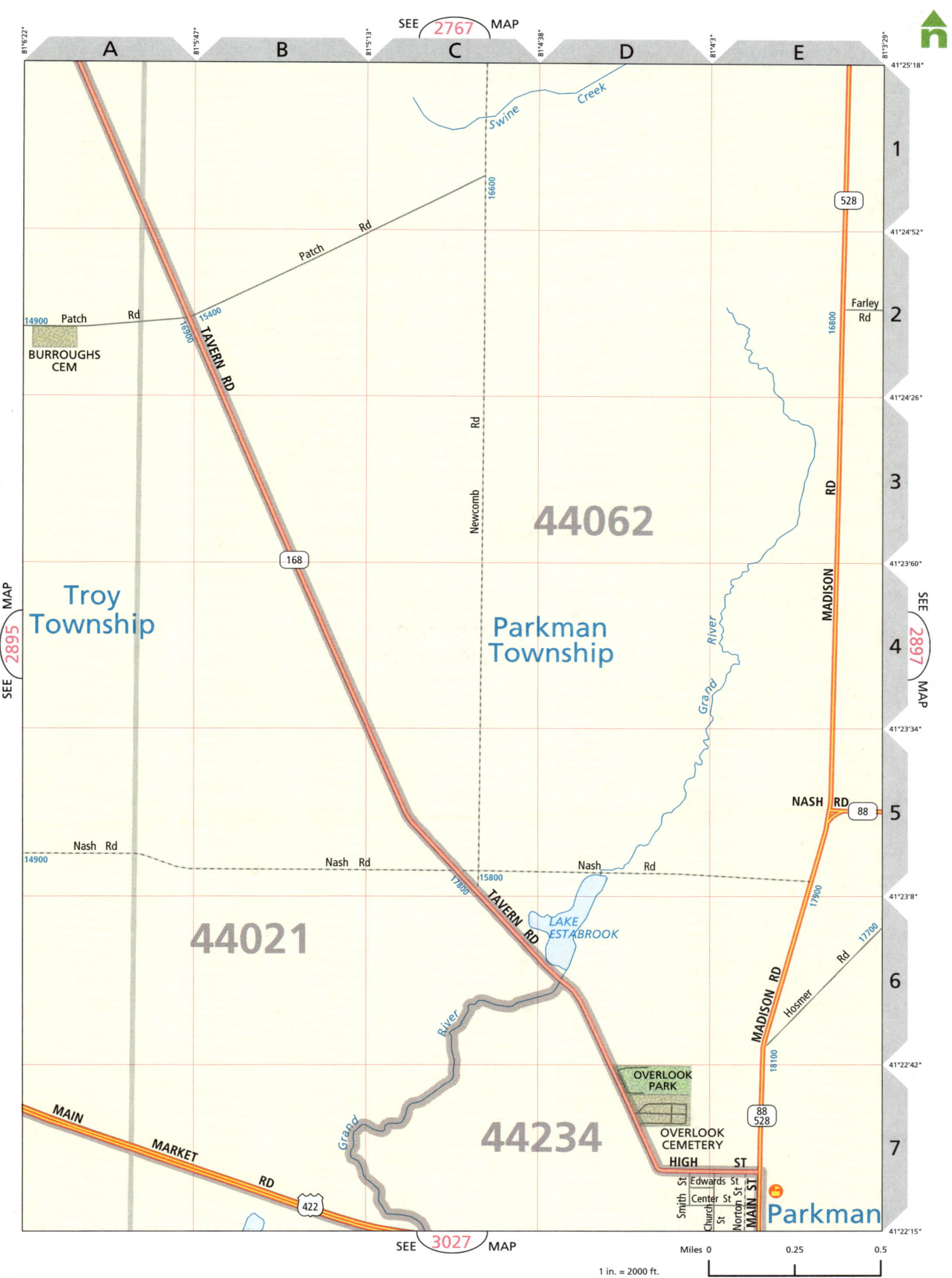

MAP 2897

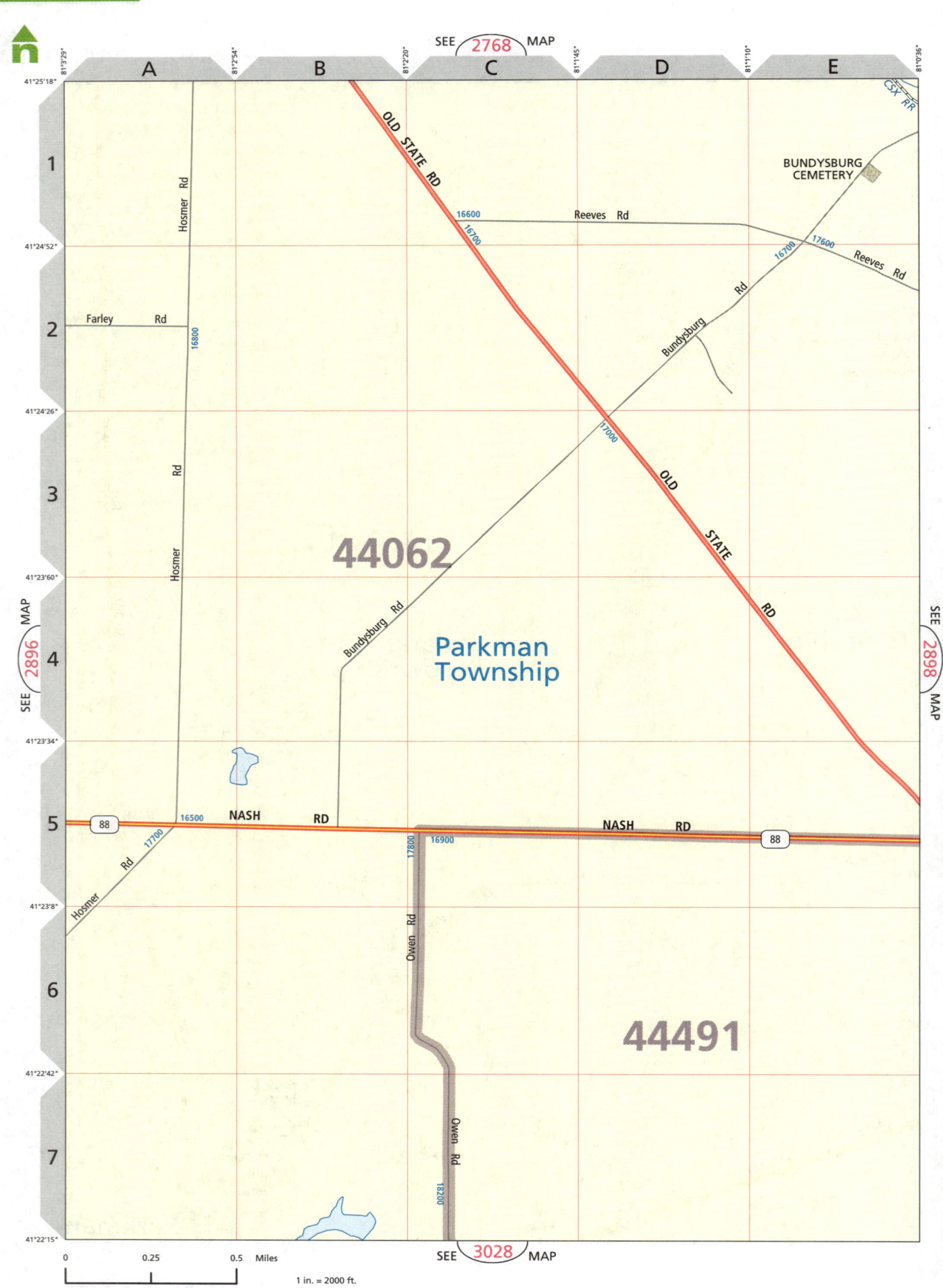

SEE 2768 MAP

A   B   C   D   E

81°3'29"   81°2'54"   81°2'20"   81°1'45"   81°1'10"   81°0'36"

CSX RR

1

41°25'18"

OLD STATE RD

BUNDYSBURG CEMETERY

Hosmer Rd

41°24'52"

16600   Reeves   Rd

16700   Bundysburg   Rd   16700   17600   Reeves   Rd

2

Farley   Rd   16800

Rd

Bundysburg

41°24'26"

17000

3

Hosmer   Rd

44062

OLD

Hosmer

41°23'60"

SEE 2896 MAP

Bundysburg   Rd

Parkman Township

STATE

4

SEE 2898 MAP

41°23'34"

RD

5

88   16500   NASH   RD   NASH   RD   88

17700   17800   16900

41°23'8"

Hosmer   Rd

Owen Rd

6

44491

41°22'42"

Owen   Rd

7

41°22'15"

18200

0   0.25   0.5   Miles

SEE 3028 MAP

1 in. = 2000 ft.

MAP 2898-3002

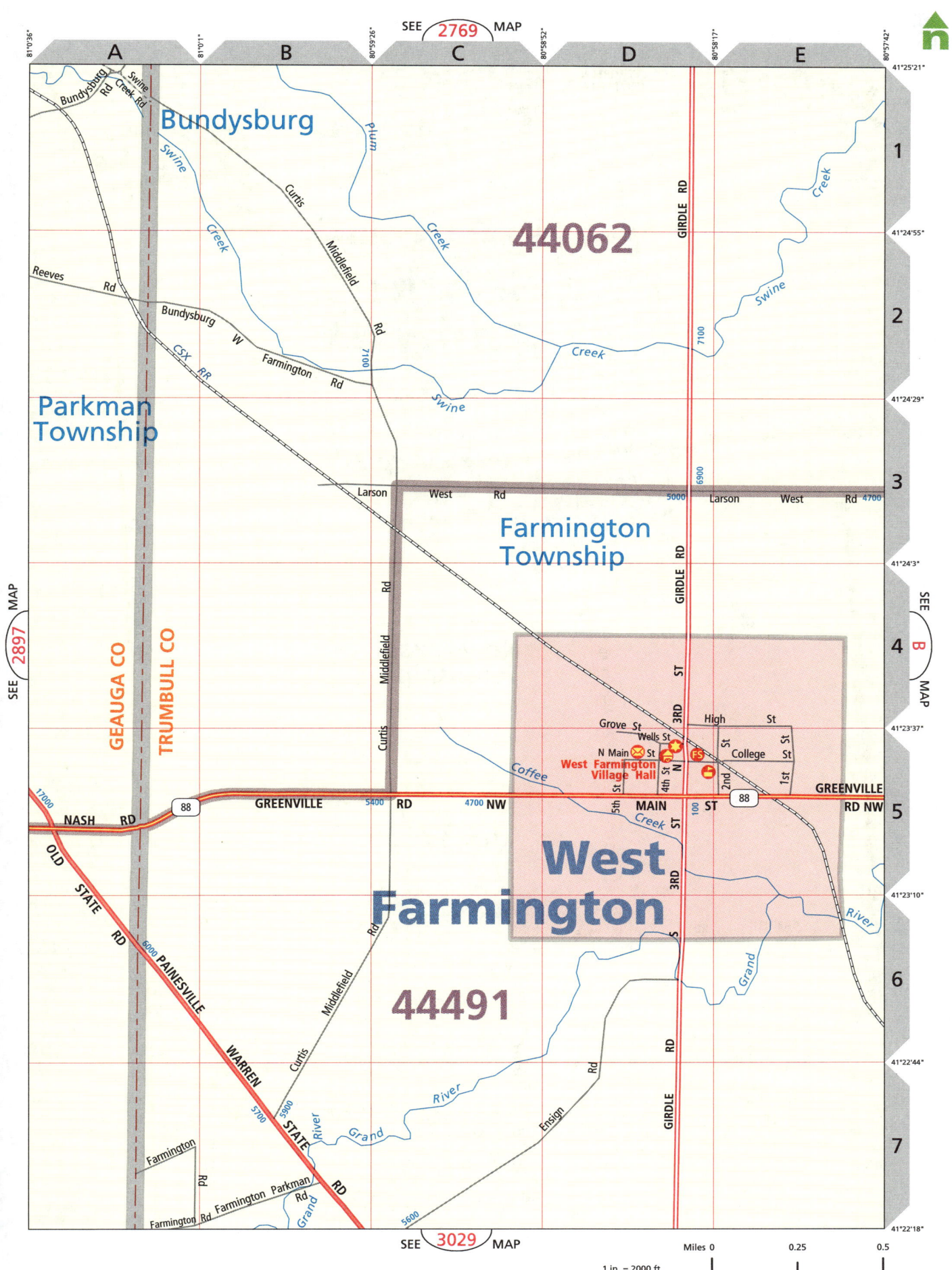

A   B   C   D   E

Bundysburg

44062

Parkman
Township

GEAUGA CO
TRUMBULL CO

SEE 2897 MAP

Larson   West   Rd   5000   Larson   West   Rd 4700

Farmington
Township

SEE B MAP

Grove St   Wells St   High   St

N Main   St   College   St

West Farmington
Village Hall

GREENVILLE   5400   RD   4700 NW   MAIN   ST   88   GREENVILLE   RD NW

NASH   RD   88

West
Farmington

44491

OLD STATE RD   PAINESVILLE

WARREN   STATE   RD

Farmington
Rd

Farmington   Parkman   Rd

Miles 0   0.25   0.5

1 in. = 2000 ft.

MAP 3003

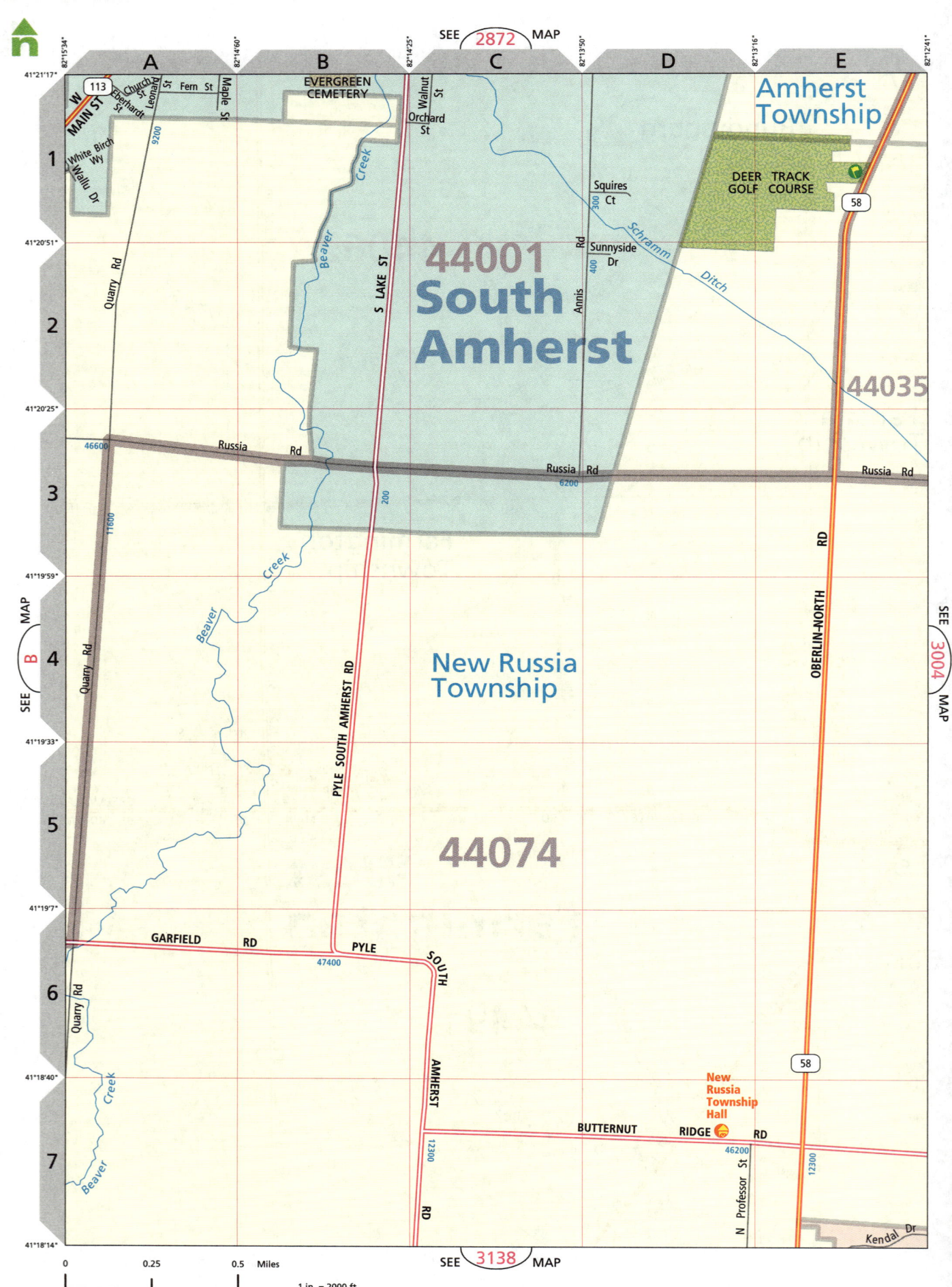

SEE 2872 MAP

A   B   C   D   E

41°21'17"

113 W MAIN ST

White Birch Wy
Wallu Dr
Church St
Eberhardt St
Avenue St
Fern St
Maple St

EVERGREEN CEMETERY

Walnut St
Orchard St

Amherst Township

DEER TRACK GOLF COURSE

58

Squires Ct

1

41°20'51"

Quarry Rd

9200

Beaver Creek

S LAKE ST

44001
South Amherst

Annis Rd
Sunnyside Dr
Schramm Ditch

44035

2

41°20'25"

46600
Russia   Rd

200

6200
Russia   Rd

Russia   Rd

3

11600

Beaver Creek

41°19'59"

SEE B MAP

Beaver Creek

Quarry Rd

New Russia Township

PYLE SOUTH AMHERST RD

OBERLIN-NORTH   RD

SEE 3004 MAP

4

41°19'33"

5

44074

41°19'7"

GARFIELD   RD   PYLE

47400

Quarry Rd

SOUTH

6

41°18'40"

58

New Russia Township Hall

AMHERST

BUTTERNUT   RIDGE   RD

12300

46200
N Professor St

12300

Beaver Creek

7

41°18'14"

RD

Kendal Dr

SEE 3138 MAP

0   0.25   0.5   Miles

1 in. = 2000 ft.

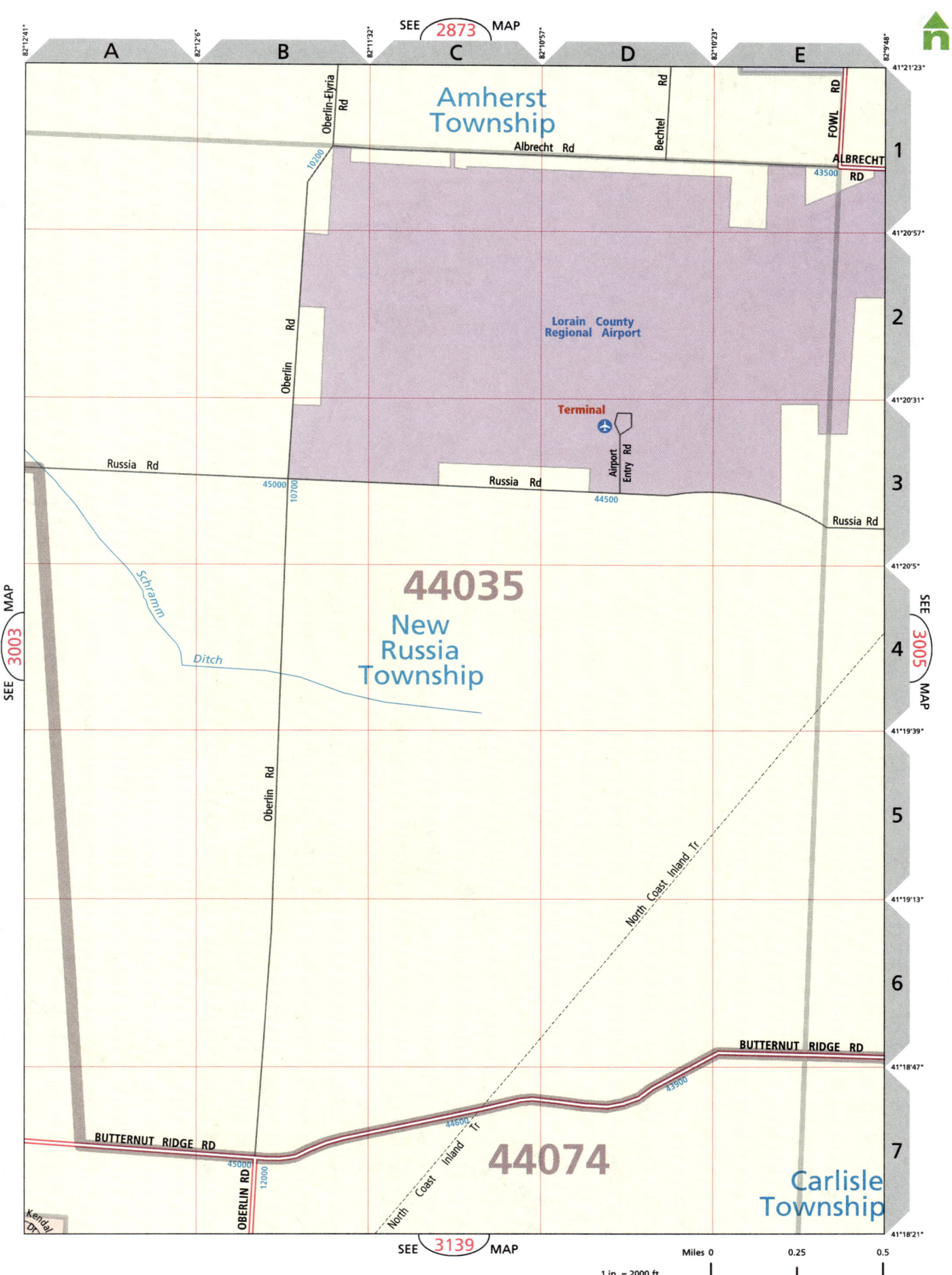

MAP 3004

SEE 2873 MAP

A 82°12'41"   B 82°12'6"   82°11'32"   C 82°10'57"   D 82°10'23"   E 82°9'48"

Amherst Township

Oberlin-Elyria Rd
10200

Rd
Bechtel

FOWL RD

Albrecht Rd

41°21'23"

1

ALBRECHT
43500 RD

41°20'57"

Oberlin Rd

Lorain County
Regional Airport

2

41°20'31"

Terminal

Airport Entry Rd

Russia Rd

45000
10700

Russia Rd

44500

Russia Rd

3

41°20'5"

Schramm

44035

New
Russia
Township

SEE 3003 MAP

Ditch

SEE 3005 MAP

4

41°19'39"

Oberlin Rd

North Coast Inland Tr

5

41°19'13"

6

BUTTERNUT RIDGE RD

41°18'47"

43900

BUTTERNUT RIDGE RD

45000

OBERLIN RD
12000

44600
North Coast Inland Tr

44074

7

Carlisle
Township

Kendal Dr

41°18'21"

SEE 3139 MAP

Miles 0   0.25   0.5

1 in. = 2000 ft.

MAP 3005

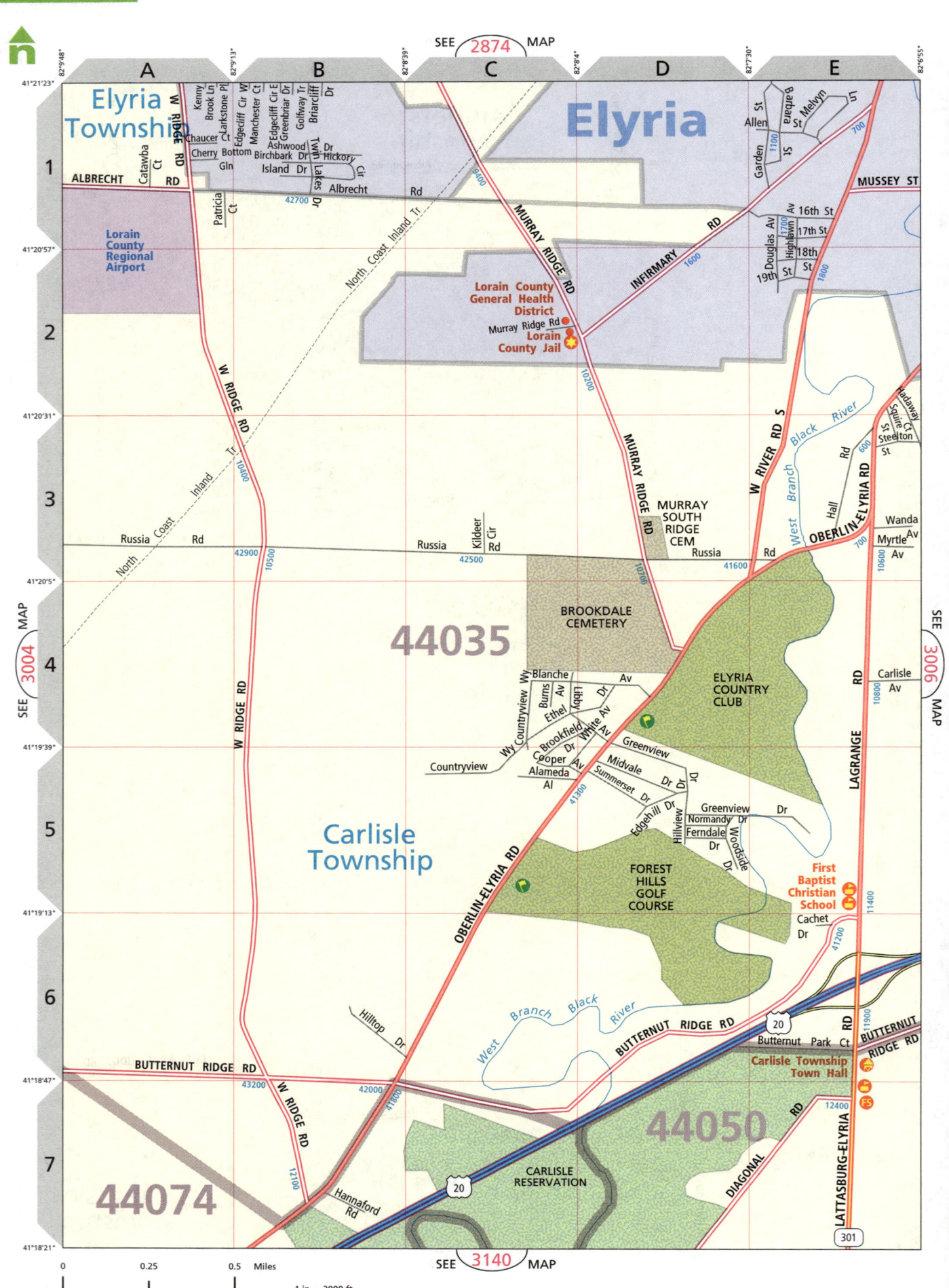

N

SEE 2874 MAP

A B C D E

Elyria Township

Elyria

W RIDGE RD

Kenny Brook Ln
Clarkstone Pl
Chaucer Ct
Edgecliff Cir W
Manchester Ct
Edgecliff Cir E
Greenbriar Dr
Golfway Tr
Briarcliff Dr

Catawba Ct

Cherry Bottom Gln
Ashwood Dr
Birchbark Dr
Island Dr
Twin Lakes Dr
Hickory Cir

Garden
Allen
1100
Barbara St
St
Melvyn Ln
700

1 ALBRECHT RD   Albrecht Rd

MUSSEY ST

42700

Patricia Ct

16th St Av
17th St
1700
18th St
1800
Douglas Av
Highland Av
19th St

Lorain County Regional Airport

MURRAY RIDGE RD

INFIRMARY 1600

2 Lorain County General Health District
Murray Ridge Rd
Lorain County Jail

10200

North Coast Inland Tr

W RIVER RD S

Black River

Radway
Squire Ct
Steelton St
600

3 Russia Rd

Russia Kildeer Rd
Cir

MURRAY RIDGE RD

MURRAY SOUTH RIDGE CEM

OBERLIN-ELYRIA RD
Hall Rd
700

Wanda
Myrtle Av

Russia Coast Inland Tr
10400

10500

42900

42500

Russia Rd
41600

10700

10600

SEE 3004 MAP   SEE 3006 MAP

4 44035

BROOKDALE CEMETERY

ELYRIA COUNTRY CLUB

LAGRANGE RD
10800

Carlisle Av

Blanche Av
Burns Av
Ethel Av
Libby Dr
White Av
Av

Countryview Wy
Brookfield Dr
Cooper Av
Alameda Al
Greenview

41300

Midvale Dr
Summerset Dr

Greenview Dr

5 Carlisle Township

Countryview

Edgehill Dr
Hillview Dr
Normandy Dr
Ferndale Dr
Greenview Dr
Woodside Dr

First Baptist Christian School

11400

FOREST HILLS GOLF COURSE

Cachet Dr
41200

OBERLIN-ELYRIA RD

6 Hilltop Dr

West Branch Black River

BUTTERNUT RIDGE RD
20

Butternut Park Ct

BUTTERNUT RIDGE RD
11900

W RIDGE RD
43200
42000

BUTTERNUT RIDGE RD

Carlisle Township Town Hall

LATTASBURG-ELYRIA RD
12400

7 44074

W RIDGE RD
12100

Hannaford Rd

20

CARLISLE RESERVATION

44050

DIAGONAL RD

301

SEE 3140 MAP

0   0.25   0.5 Miles

1 in. = 2000 ft.

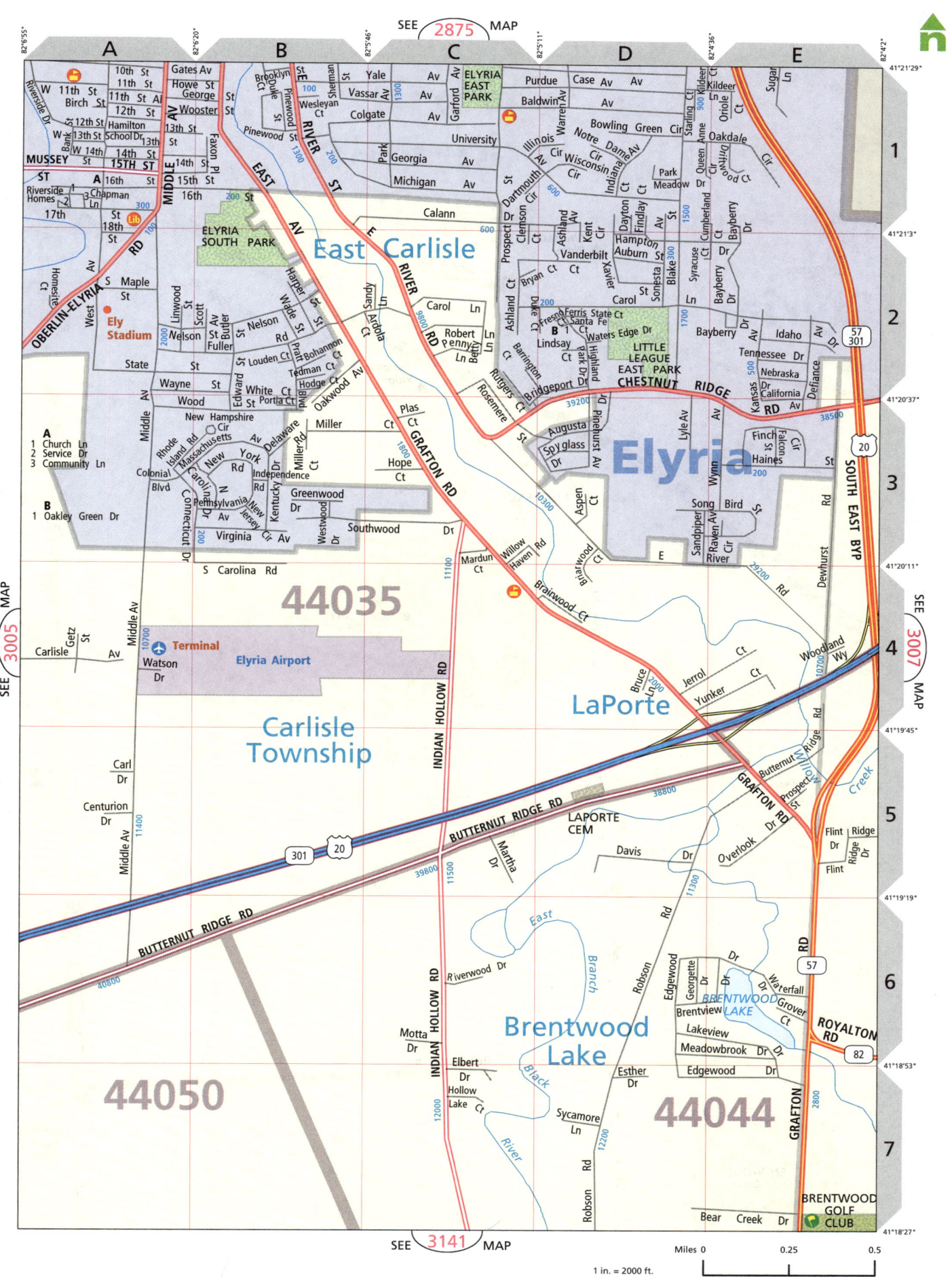

MAP 3006

SEE 2875 MAP

SEE 3005 MAP

SEE 3007 MAP

SEE 3141 MAP

A   B   C   D   E

East Carlisle

Elyria

44035

44050

44044

Carlisle Township

Elyria Airport

LaPorte

Brentwood Lake

ELYRIA EAST PARK

ELYRIA SOUTH PARK

Ely Stadium

LITTLE LEAGUE EAST PARK

CHESTNUT RIDGE

LAPORTE CEM

BRENTWOOD GOLF CLUB

Terminal

Watson Dr

BUTTERNUT RIDGE RD

GRAFTON RD

INDIAN HOLLOW RD

SOUTH EAST BYP

OBERLIN-ELYRIA RD

EAST RIVER RD

MIDDLE AV

Miles 0   0.25   0.5

1 in. = 2000 ft.

MAP 3007

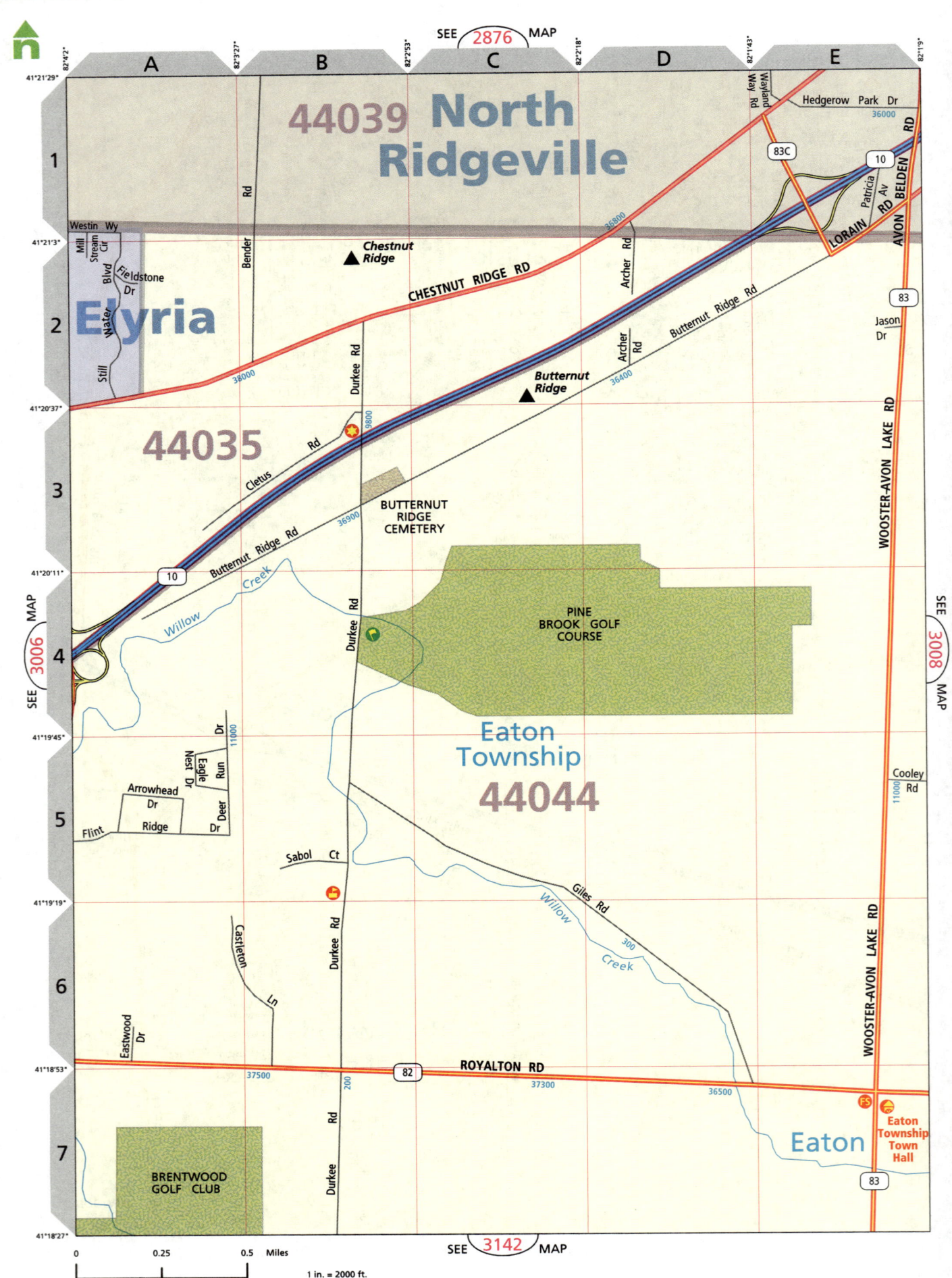

SEE 2876 MAP

N

A   B   C   D   E

41°21'29"

82°4'42"
82°3'27"
82°2'53"
82°2'18"
82°1'43"
82°1'28"

1

44039 North Ridgeville

Hedgerow Park Dr
36000

Wayland Way Rd

83C

10

Westin Wy

41°21'3"

Mill Stream Cir
Fieldstone Dr
Blvd
Water
Still

Elyria

Bender Rd

Chestnut Ridge

CHESTNUT RIDGE RD

36800

Archer Rd

Lorain

Patricia Av

Belden

Avon Rd

83

2

36000

Durkee Rd

Butternut Ridge Rd

Archer Rd

36400

Jason Dr

41°20'37"

44035

9800

Cletus Rd

Butternut Ridge

Wooster-Avon Lake Rd

3

Butternut Ridge Rd

36900

BUTTERNUT RIDGE CEMETERY

10

Willow Creek

41°20'11"

SEE 3006 MAP

4

Durkee Rd

PINE BROOK GOLF COURSE

SEE 3008 MAP

41°19'45"

Dr

11000

Nest Dr
Eagle Run
Deer Dr

Arrowhead Dr

Flint Ridge

Eaton Township

44044

Cooley Rd

11000

5

Sabol Ct

41°19'19"

Castleton Ln

Durkee Rd

Giles Rd

Willow Creek
300

Wooster-Avon Lake Rd

6

Eastwood Dr

41°18'53"

37500

200

82

ROYALTON RD

37300

36500

Eaton

F5

Eaton Township Town Hall

7

BRENTWOOD GOLF CLUB

Durkee Rd

83

41°18'27"

SEE 3142 MAP

0   0.25   0.5   Miles

1 in. = 2000 ft.

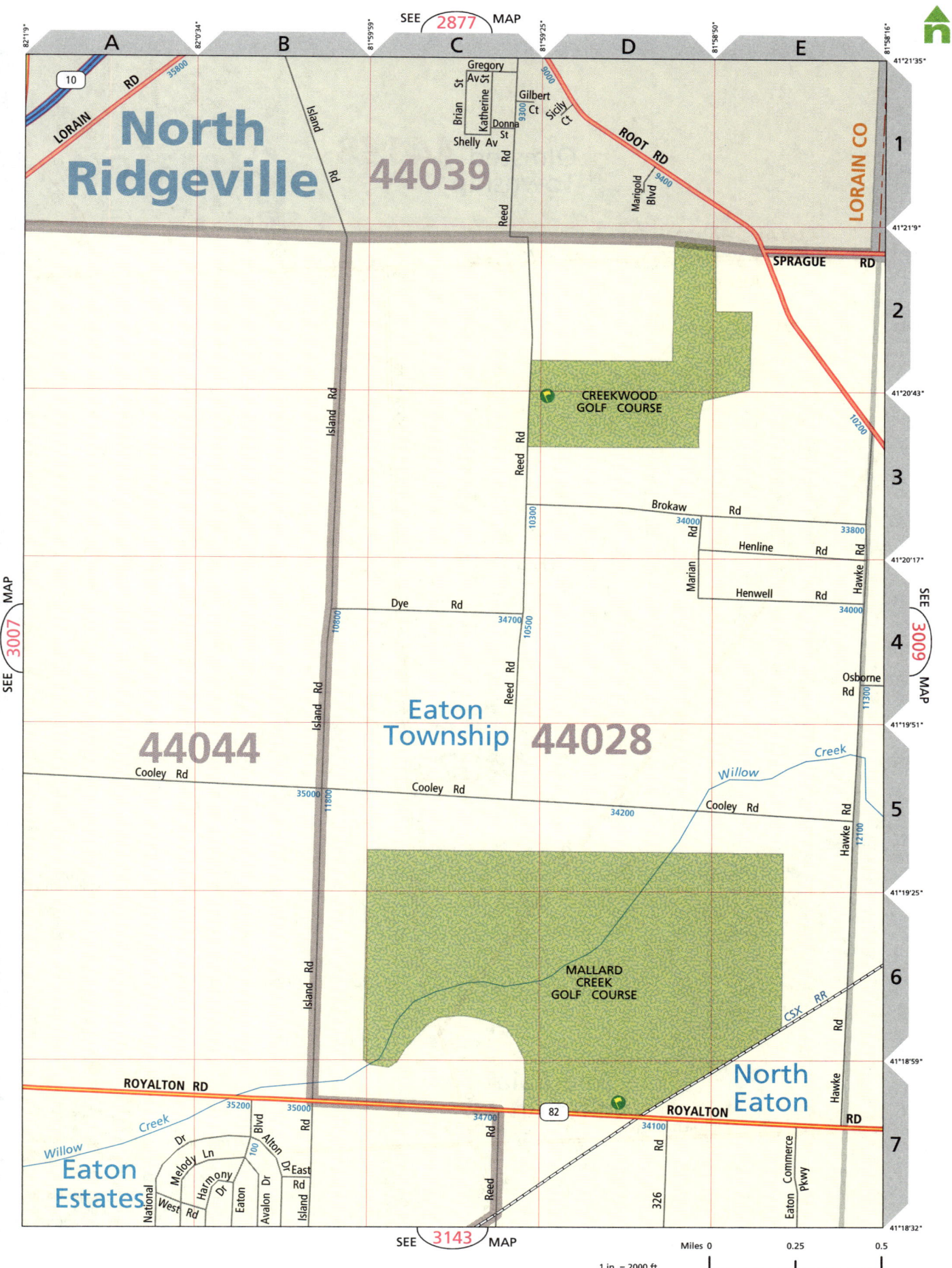

MAP 3008

SEE 2877 MAP

A · B · C · D · E

LORAIN RD
35800

10

North Ridgeville
44039

Gregory
Av St
Brian St
Katherine
Donna St
Shelly Av

Gilbert Ct
Sicily Ct
9300

9000

ROOT RD

Marigold Blvd
9400

LORAIN CO

SPRAGUE RD

Island Rd

Reed

1

2

CREEKWOOD
GOLF COURSE

Reed Rd
10200

41°20'43"

3

Brokaw Rd
34000 Rd
33800

Henline Rd
Marian
Hawke Rd
Henwell Rd
34000

10300

SEE 3007 MAP

Island Rd
10800

Dye Rd
34700
10500

Reed Rd

Eaton Township
44028

44044

Osborne Rd
11300

SEE 3009 MAP

Willow Creek

Cooley Rd
35000
11800
Cooley Rd
Cooley Rd
34200
Hawke Rd
12100

4

5

MALLARD
CREEK
GOLF COURSE

CSX RR

6

Island Rd

North Eaton

Hawke Rd

7

ROYALTON RD

82

ROYALTON RD

Willow Creek

Eaton Estates

National West Rd
Melody Ln
Harmony Dr
Eaton Dr
Alton Dr
100 Blvd
Avalon Dr
East Rd
Island Rd
35200
35000

Reed Rd
34700

34100 Rd

326

Eaton Commerce Pkwy

SEE 3143 MAP

Miles 0 · 0.25 · 0.5

1 in. = 2000 ft.

MAP 3009

MAP 3009

N

SEE 2878 MAP

A   B   C   D   E

Olmsted Township **44138**

Cascade   Springside Ln   Lakeview Falls

Waterside   Lakeview Cir   Millstream Cir   Fern Cole   Ashwood

Olmsted Falls

Rollingbrook Cir   Lakeview   W Windsor Dr   E Windsor Dr   St. James Ct

Brook Rd   10100   Plum Creek   USHER RD   9200

CUYAHOGA CO

SPRAGUE RD   27100   26700   26500

LORAIN CO

Sharp Rd   8800

Mitchell Rd   10200   10900

STATION RD

Jaquay Rd   10400

Quarry Ridge Rd

Columbia Township

JAQUAY LAKE PARK

Osborne Rd   25600   11100   24900

Joyce Dr   Ann Dr

ROOT RD   11100

Osborne Rd   Anderson Rd   26000

CSX RR

Osborne Rd   27600

44028

Jaquay Rd

Plum Creek

Nichols Rd   25000

Willow Creek

ROOT RD   12900

STATION RD   12600

COLUMBIA RESERVATION

Castlebar Ct   12600

Folley Rd

River Rd

Columbia Station Airport

Terminal

STATION RD   13400

Columbia Station

W   COLUMBIA PARK   CEM

ROYALTON RD   82   ROYALTON RD

FS   **Columbia Town Hall**

Lydia Rd   26900   Frederick Av

STATION RD

Michelle Ln   Eddie Ln   Plum Creek Dr

25600   W River Rd

Columbia Center   **Columbia HS**

COLUMBIA RESERVATION

SEE 3144 MAP

0   0.25   0.5   Miles

1 in. = 2000 ft.

SEE 3008 MAP

SEE 3010 MAP

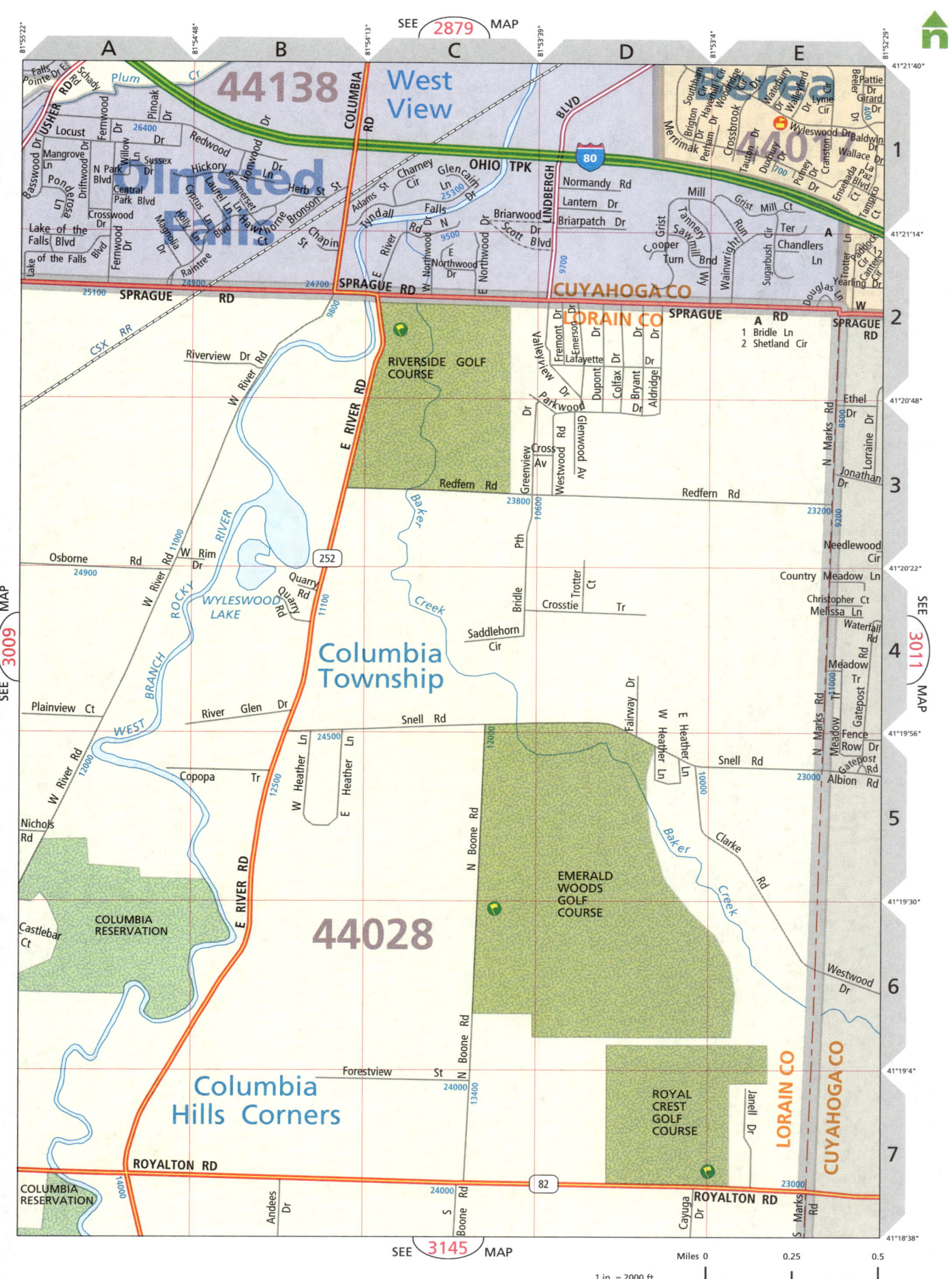

MAP 3010

MAP 3011

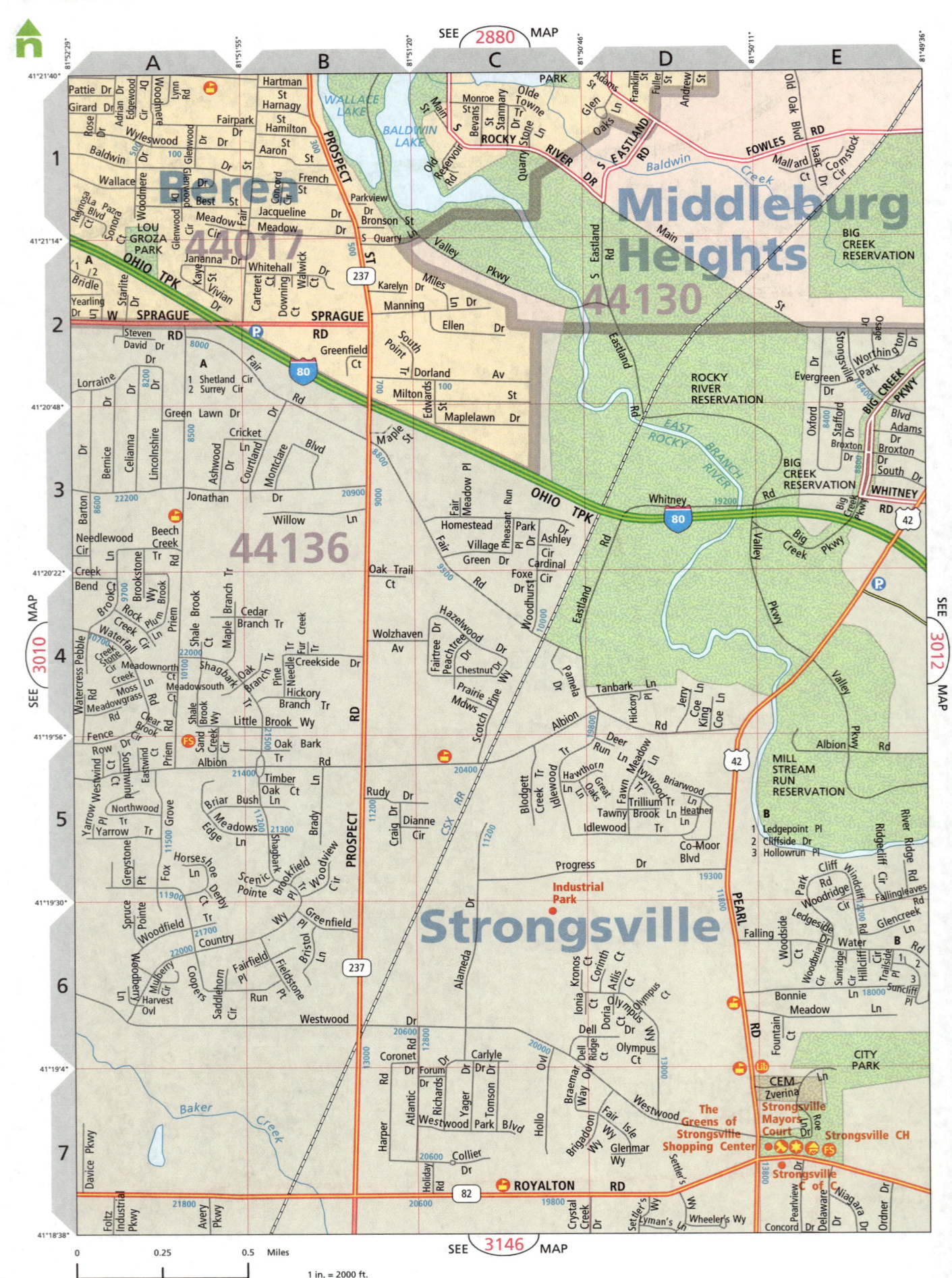

SEE 2880 MAP
SEE 3010 MAP
SEE 3012 MAP
SEE 3146 MAP

Berea 44017

Middleburg Heights 44130

44136

Strongsville

BIG CREEK RESERVATION

ROCKY RIVER RESERVATION

BIG CREEK RESERVATION

MILL STREAM RUN RESERVATION

LOU GROZA PARK

Industrial Park

CITY PARK

The Greens of Strongsville Shopping Center

Strongsville Mayors Court

Strongsville CH

0   0.25   0.5   Miles

1 in. = 2000 ft.

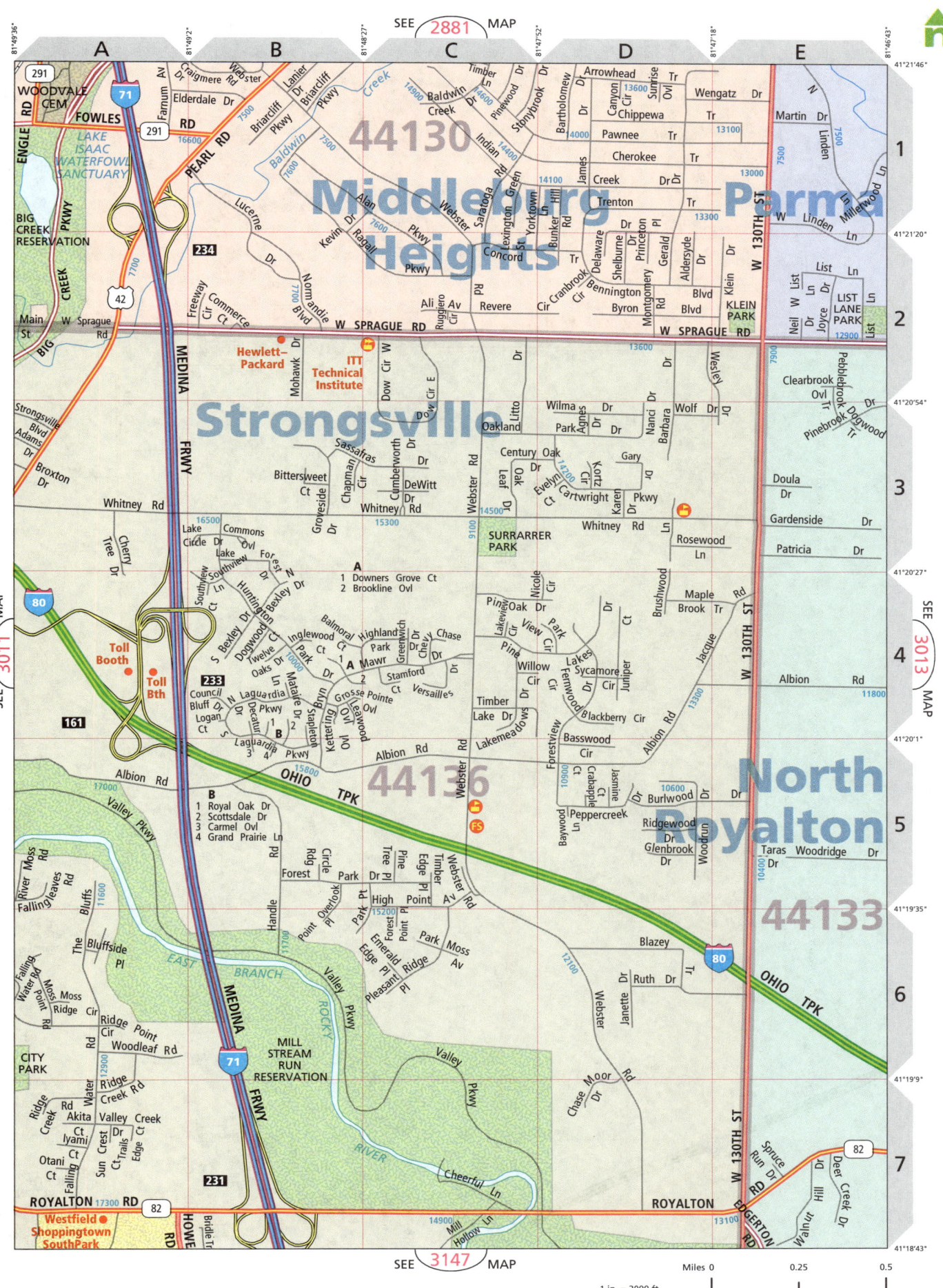

MAP 3012

SEE 2881 MAP

44130

Middleburg Heights

Parma

Strongsville

44136

North Royalton

44133

SEE 3011 MAP

SEE 3013 MAP

A   1
B
1 Royal Oak Dr
2 Scottsdale Dr
3 Carmel Ovl
4 Grand Prairie Ln

A
1 Downers Grove Ct
2 Brookline Ovl

SEE 3147 MAP

Miles 0   0.25   0.5

1 in. = 2000 ft.

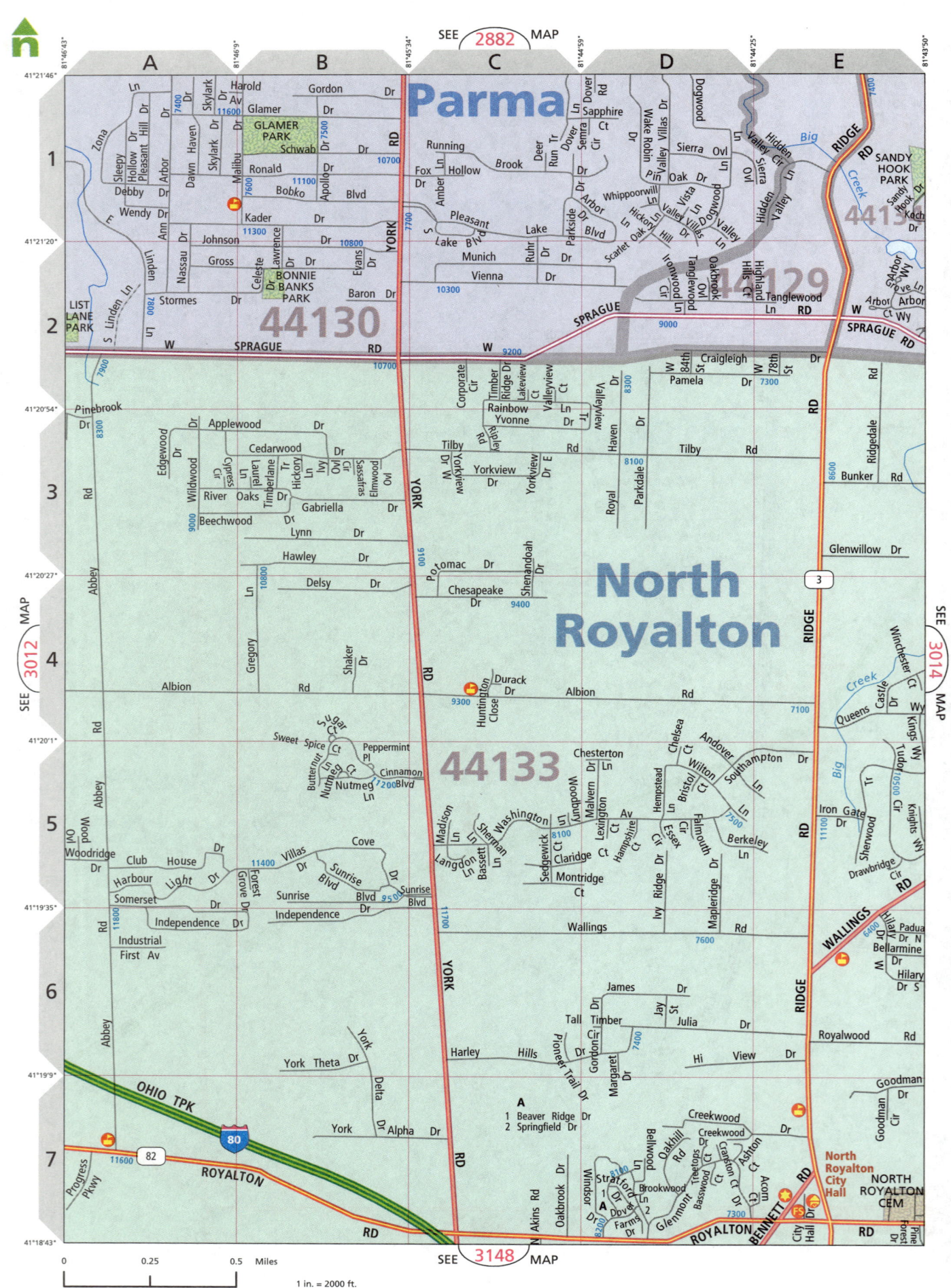

MAP 3013

SEE 2882 MAP

Parma

North Royalton

44130

44129

44136

44133

SANDY HOOK PARK

LIST LANE PARK

GLAMER PARK

BONNIE BANKS PARK

SEE 3012 MAP

SEE 3014 MAP

OHIO TPK

80

82

ROYALTON

North Royalton City Hall

NORTH ROYALTON CEM

A 1 Beaver Ridge Dr
2 Springfield Dr

SEE 3148 MAP

0   0.25   0.5 Miles

1 in. = 2000 ft.

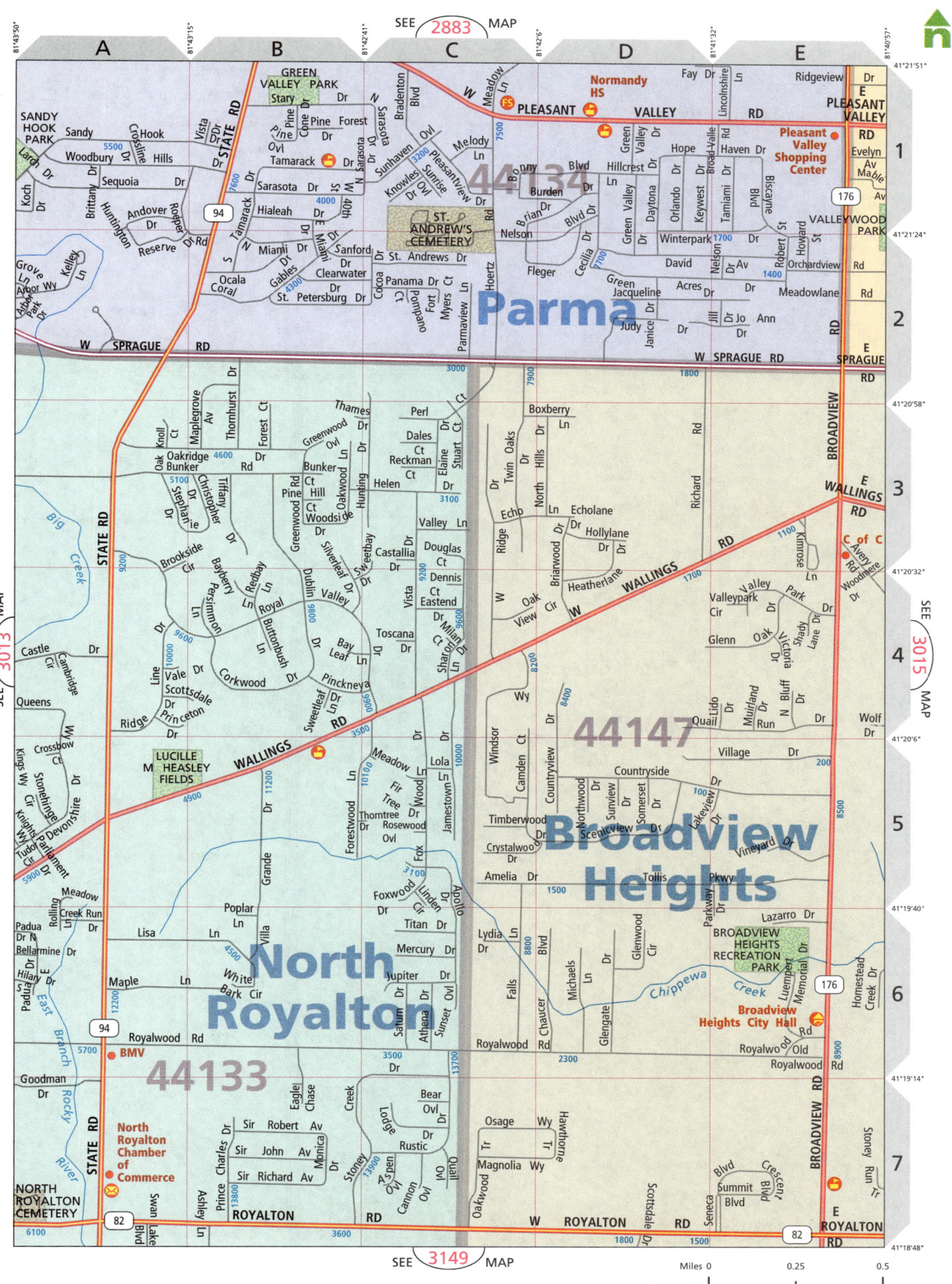

MAP 3014

SEE 2883 MAP

A   B   C   D   E

SANDY HOOK PARK

GREEN VALLEY PARK

Normandy HS

PLEASANT VALLEY RD

Pleasant Valley Shopping Center

44134

Parma

W SPRAGUE RD

E SPRAGUE RD

BROADVIEW RD

WALLINGS RD

44147

Broadview Heights

LUCILLE HEASLEY FIELDS

North Royalton

44133

North Royalton Chamber of Commerce

BMV

NORTH ROYALTON CEMETERY

BROADVIEW HEIGHTS RECREATION PARK

Broadview Heights City Hall

Chippewa Creek

W ROYALTON RD   E ROYALTON RD

SEE 3149 MAP

SEE 3013 MAP

SEE 3015 MAP

Miles 0   0.25   0.5

1 in. = 2000 ft.

MAP 3015

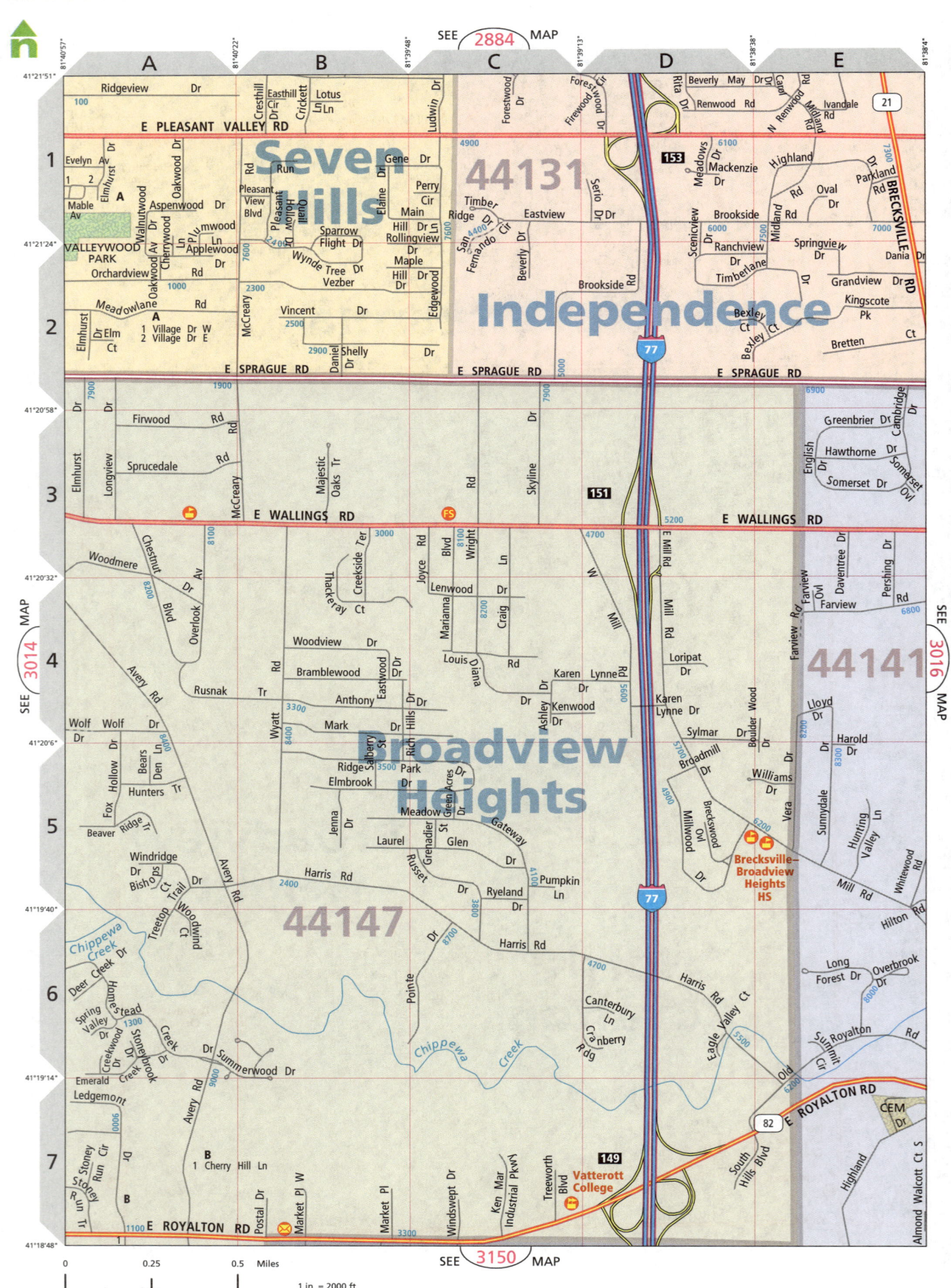

SEE 2884 MAP

Seven Hills

44131

Independence

Broadview Heights

44141

44147

Brecksville–Broadview Heights HS

Vatterott College

SEE 3014 MAP

SEE 3016 MAP

SEE 3150 MAP

0   0.25   0.5   Miles

1 in. = 2000 ft.

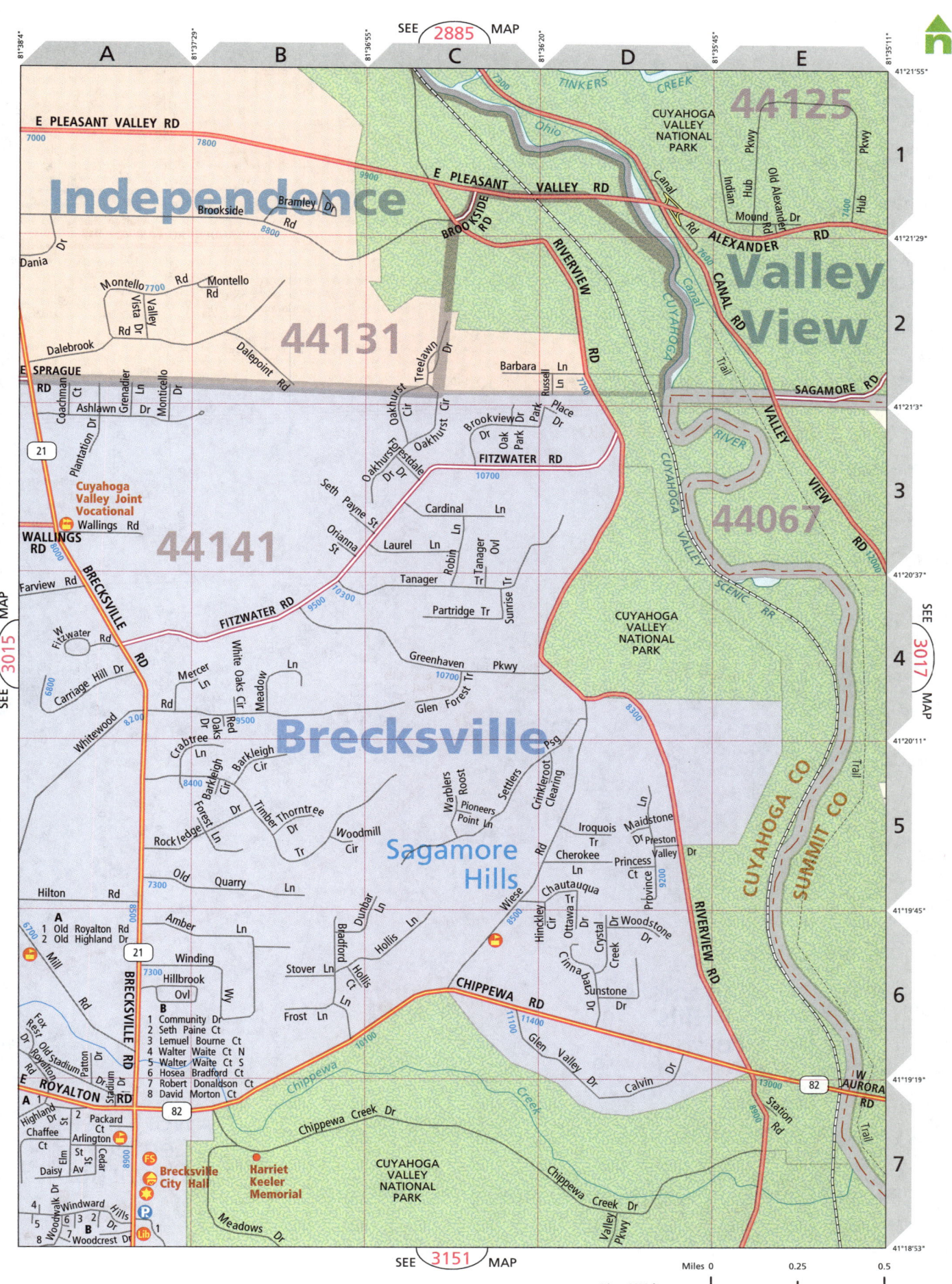

MAP 3016

A   B   C   D   E

SEE 2885 MAP

81°38'4"   81°37'29"   81°36'55"   81°36'20"   81°35'45"   81°35'11"

41°21'55"

E PLEASANT VALLEY RD
7000   7800

Independence

Brookside
Bramley Dr
Rd
8800

E PLEASANT VALLEY RD
9900

CUYAHOGA VALLEY NATIONAL PARK
44125

Pkwy   Pkwy
Hub
Indian
Old Alexander Dr
7400   Hub
Mound

41°21'29"

Valley View

Dania Dr

Montello 7700 Rd   Montello Rd
Vista Dr   Valley Rd

44131

Dalebrook
Dalepoint Rd

E SPRAGUE RD
Coachman Ct   Ashlawn   Grenadier Ln   Monticello Dr

Treelawn Dr
Oakhurst Cir

Barbara Ln
Russell Ln
7100

Brookview Dr   Oak Park Dr   Place Dr

RIVERVIEW RD

CANAL RD
ALEXANDER RD

CUYAHOGA

SAGAMORE RD

CANAL

RIVER

41°21'3"

21

Plantation Ln

Cuyahoga Valley Joint Vocational
Wallings Rd

WALLINGS RD
8000

44141

Farview Rd

Oakhurst Cir
Oakhurst Dr   Forestdale Dr

FITZWATER RD
10700

Seth Payne St
Orianna St

Cardinal Ln
Laurel Ln
Robin   Tanager Ovl

Tanager Tr   Sunrise Tr

CUYAHOGA VALLEY SCENIC RR

44067

VALLEY VIEW RD
13000

41°20'37"

BRECKSVILLE RD

W Fitzwater Rd
6800
Carriage Hill Dr

FITZWATER RD
9500   10300

Partridge Tr

CUYAHOGA VALLEY NATIONAL PARK

SEE 3015 MAP   SEE 3017 MAP

Mercer Rd
White Oaks Cir
Meadow Ln

Greenhaven Pkwy
10700

Whitewood
8200

Crabtree Ln
Oaks Dr
Red Dr
9500

Glen Forest Tr

Brecksville

41°20'11"

Barkleigh Cir
Barkleigh Cir
8400

Forest Ln
Rockledge Ln

Timber Dr   Thorntree Dr
Woodmill Cir

Warblers Roost   Pioneers Point Ln   Settlers   Crinkleroot Clearing
Wiese Rd
Iroquois Tr   Cherokee Ln   Princess Ct   Maidstone Dr   Preston Valley Dr
Chautauqua Tr   Ottawa Dr   Crystal Creek Dr   Woodstone Dr   Province Dr
Hinckley Cir   Cinnabar Dr   Sunstone Dr
9200

CUYAHOGA CO   SUMMIT CO

41°19'45"

Sagamore Hills

Hilton Rd
7300

Old Quarry Ln

A   1 Old Royalton Rd
     2 Old Highland Dr

Amber Ln

Mill Rd
6700

Fox Rest Dr   Old Royalton Rd
Old Stadium Dr

Patton Dr
Stadium Dr

21

7300

Winding Wy
Hillbrook Ovl

B   1 Community Dr
     2 Seth Paine Ct
     3 Lemuel Bourne Ct
     4 Walter Waite Ct N
     5 Walter Waite Ct S
     6 Hosea Bradford Ct
     7 Robert Donaldson Ct
     8 David Morton Ct

Stover Ln   Bradford   Hollis Ln   Dunbar Ln
Hollis Dr
Frost Ln
Hollis Ln

CHIPPEWA RD
11100   11400

Glen Valley Dr   Calvin Dr

RIVERVIEW RD

13000   82   W AURORA RD
Station Rd
8900

41°19'19"

E ROYALTON RD
Highland Dr
Chaffee Ct
Daisy
Woodwalk Dr   Windward Dr
Woodcrest Dr

BRECKSVILLE RD
82
8960

Packard Ct
Arlington
Cedar Av
Elm St
Hills Dr

Brecksville City Hall

Harriet Keeler Memorial

Chippewa Creek

CUYAHOGA VALLEY NATIONAL PARK

Chippewa Creek Dr

Meadows Dr

Chippewa Creek Dr

Valley Pkwy

41°18'53"

1   2   3   4   5   6   7

SEE 3151 MAP

Miles 0   0.25   0.5

1 in. = 2000 ft.

MAP 3017

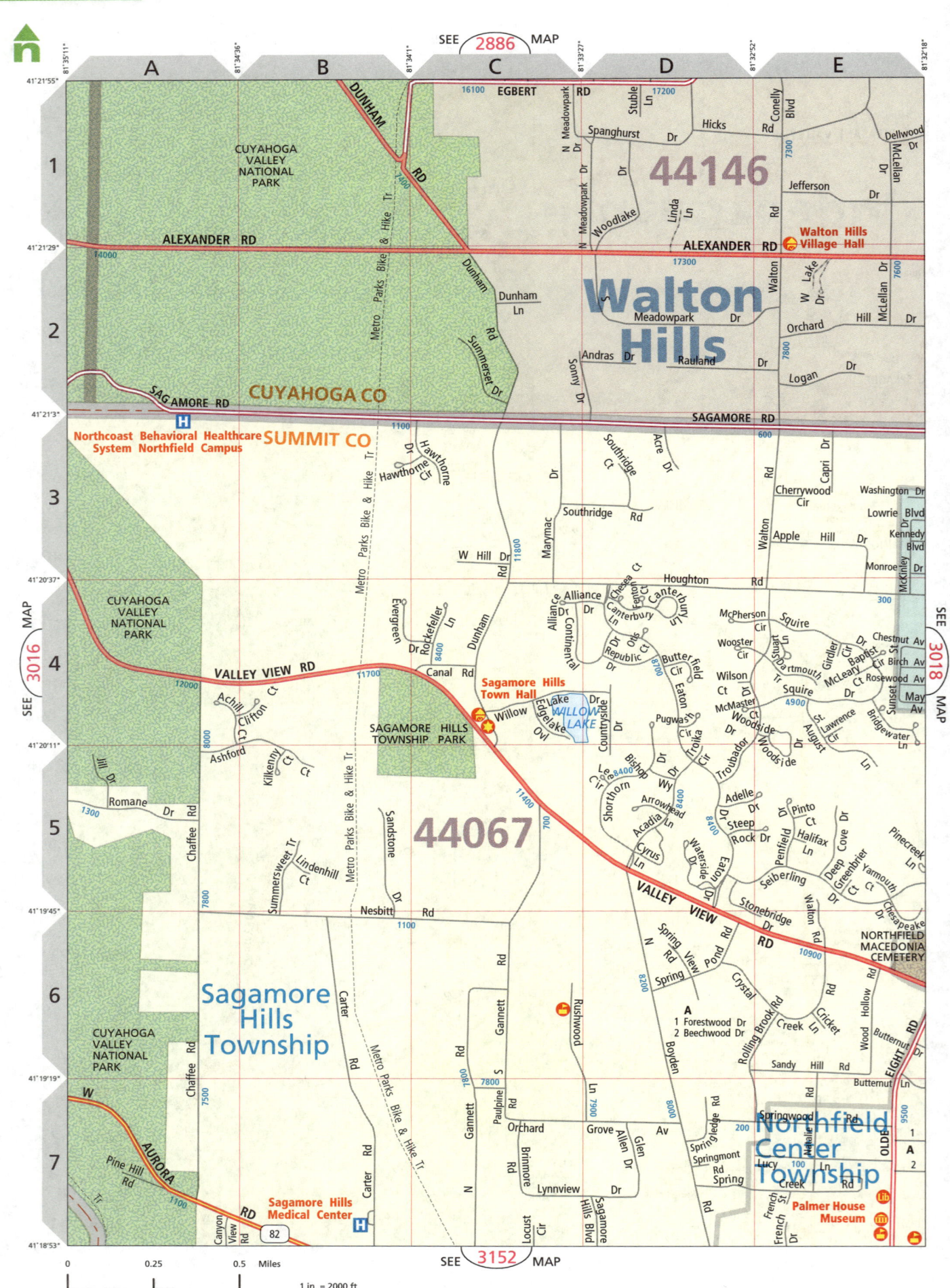

SEE 2886 MAP

A · B · C · D · E

1
2
3
4
5
6
7

81°35'11"
81°34'36"
81°34'11"
81°33'27"
81°33'52"

41°21'55"
41°21'29"
41°21'3"
41°20'37"
41°20'11"
41°19'45"
41°19'19"
41°18'53"

CUYAHOGA VALLEY NATIONAL PARK

ALEXANDER RD

14000

DUNHAM RD

Metro Parks Bike & Hike Tr

16100   EGBERT   RD   17200

Meadowpark Rd
Spanghurst   Dr
N Meadowpark Dr
Stuble Ln
Hicks
Conelly Blvd
Dellwood Dr
McLellan Dr

44146

Jefferson   Dr

Woodlake   Linda Ln

ALEXANDER   RD   17300

N Meadowpark Dr

Dunham Ln

Dunham Rd

Summerset Dr

Meadowpark Dr
Andras Dr
Sonny Dr
Rauland Dr
Logan

Walton Rd
W Lake Dr
Orchard
Hill
McLellan Dr
7600
7800

Walton Hills

Walton Hills Village Hall

SAGAMORE   RD

CUYAHOGA CO
SUMMIT CO

SAGAMORE   RD   1100

SAGAMORE   RD   600

Northcoast Behavioral Healthcare System Northfield Campus   H

Hawthorne Cir
Hawthorne Dr
Metro Parks Bike & Hike Tr

Southridge Ct
Acre Dr
Southridge Rd
Marymac Dr

Southridge Dr

Walton Rd
Capri
Cherrywood Cir
Washington Dr
Lowrie Blvd
Kennedy Blvd
Apple   Hill   Dr
Monroe Dr
McKinley Dr
300

W Hill Dr
11800

Houghton   Rd

CUYAHOGA VALLEY NATIONAL PARK

Evergreen Dr
Rockefeller Ln
8400
Dunham Rd

VALLEY VIEW RD   11700
12000

Canal Rd

Achill Ct
Clifton Ct
Ashford
Kilkenny Ct
8000

Sagamore Hills Town Hall

Willow
Lake Edgelake Ovl
Countryside Dr
WILLOW LAKE

Alliance Dr
Alliance
Continental Dr
Republic Dr
Canterbury Ln
Chelsea Ct
Fenton
Otis
Canterbury
Butterfield Cir
Eaton Cir
8700

McPherson Cir
Wooster Cir
Wilson Ct
McMaster Ct
Pugwash
Troika Cir
Squire
Stuart Dr
Dartmouth Cir
Girdler Cir
McLeary Ct
Squire
Woodside Dr
St. Lawrence Cir
August Cir
Bridgewater Ln
4900
Chestnut Av
Baptist St
Birch Av
Rosewood Av
May Av

SAGAMORE HILLS TOWNSHIP HILLS PARK

Romane Dr
Jill Dr
1300
Chaffee Rd
7800

Sandstone Dr
Lindenhill Ct
Summersweet Tr
Metro Parks Bike & Hike Tr

44067

11400   700

Le Cir
Shorthorn
Acadia Ln
Cyrus
Bishop Dr
Arrowhead Ln
Waterside Dr
8400
8400
Troika Cir
Adelle Dr
Steep Rock Dr
Eaton Dr
Penfield
Seiberling
8400
Woodside Dr
Troubador Dr
Pinto Ct
Halifax Ln
Deep Cove Dr
Greenbrier Ct
Stonebridge Dr
Walton Rd
Yarmouth Dr
Pinecreek Dr
Chesapeake Dr

NORTHFIELD MACEDONIA CEMETERY

Nesbitt   Rd   1100

Carter Rd

SAGAMORE HILLS TOWNSHIP

CUYAHOGA VALLEY NATIONAL PARK

Chaffee Rd
7500

Gannett Rd
S Gannett Rd
7800

Metro Parks Bike & Hike Tr

Rushwood
Boyden
Spring View Rd
N Spring Rd
8200
Pond Rd
Crystal
VALLEY VIEW   RD   10900

A
1 Forestwood Dr
2 Beechwood Dr

Rolling Brook Rd
Creek Ln
Cricket Ln
Wood Hollow Dr
Sandy Hill Rd
Butternut Ln

EIGHT RD
9500

Aurora RD
Pine Hill Rd
1100

Canyon View Rd
82

Sagamore Hills Medical Center   H

Carter Rd

Gannett Rd
N Gannett Rd
Paulpine Ln
7800
Orchard
Brinmore
Lynnview
Locust Cir

Grove Av
Allen Dr
Glen Dr
Sagamore Hills Blvd

Springledge Rd
Springmont Rd
Spring
Springwood Dr
Amhurst
Lucy
Creek
French St
French Dr
200
100
OLD Rd

Northfield Center Township

Palmer House Museum   Lib

A
2

0   0.25   0.5   Miles
1 in. = 2000 ft.

SEE 3016 MAP
SEE 3018 MAP
SEE 3152 MAP

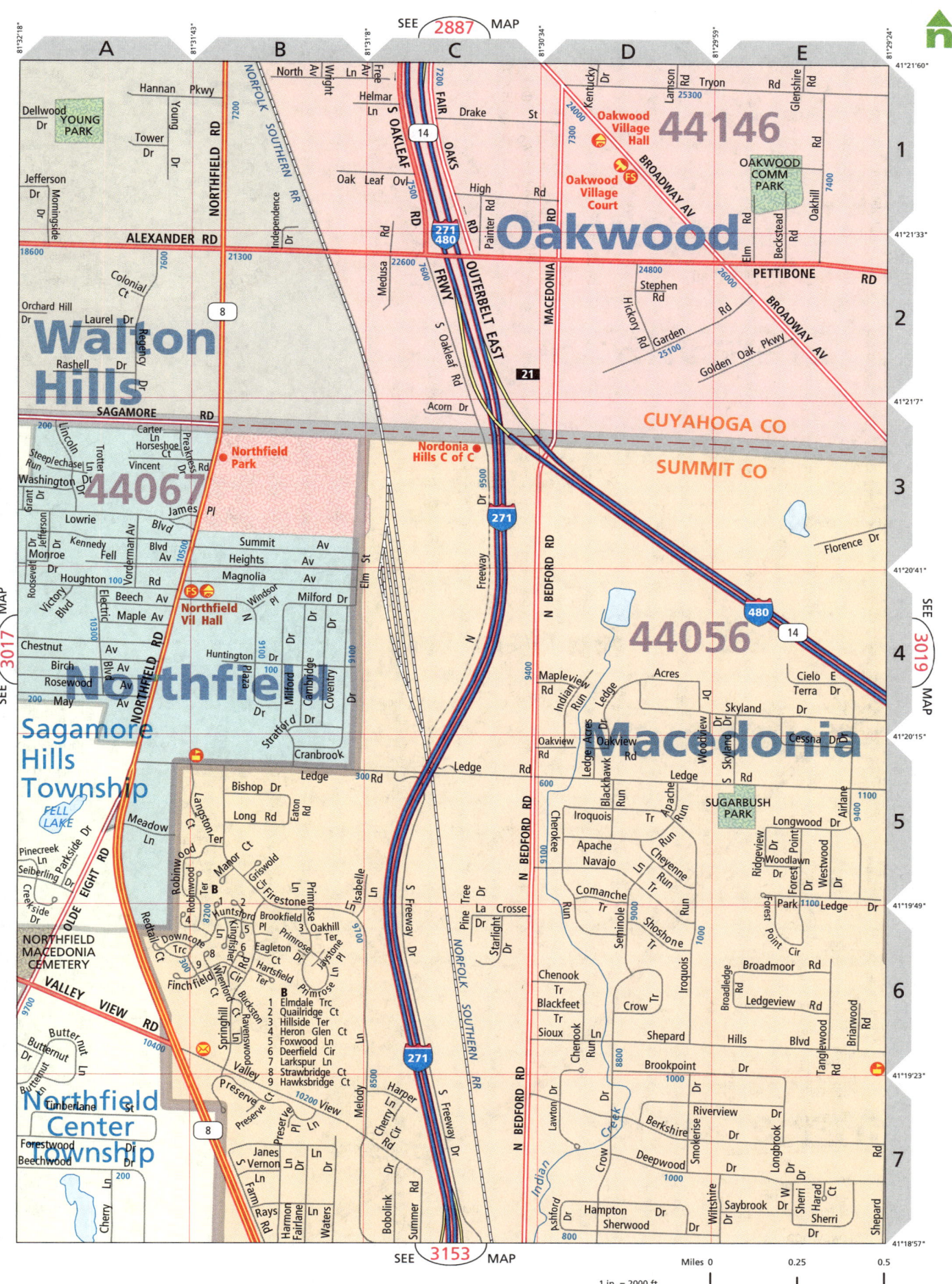

MAP 3018

SEE 2887 MAP

A | **B** | **C** | **D** | **E**

1

Dellwood Dr
YOUNG PARK
Hannan Pkwy
Young Dr
Tower Dr
Jefferson Dr
Morningside Dr
North Ln
Wright Ln
Free Av
Helmar Ln
S Oakleaf Rd
14
FAIR OAKS RD
Drake St
High Rd
Painter Rd
Kentucky Dr
Lamson Rd
Tryon Rd
Glenshire Rd
25300
Oakwood Village Hall
FS
Oakwood Village Court
44146
OAKWOOD COMM PARK
Oakhill Rd
Beckstead Rd
7400
Oak Leaf Ovl

ALEXANDER RD
18600
271 480
Medusa
22600
7600
Macedonia Rd
Oakwood
24800
26000
Elm Rd
Broadway Av
PETTIBONE RD
41°21'33"

2

Colonial Ct
Orchard Hill Dr
Laurel Dr
8
Regency Dr
Rashell Dr
7600
21300
Independence Dr
FRWY
S Oakleaf Rd
OUTERBELT EAST
21
Acorn Dr
Stephen Rd
Hickory Rd
Garden Rd
25100
Golden Oak Pkwy
Broadway Av
41°21'7"

Walton Hills

SAGAMORE RD

CUYAHOGA CO

3

200
Lincoln
Steeplechase Run
Trotter Dr
Washington Dr
Grant
Carter Ln
Horseshoe Ct
Preakness Rd
Vincent Ct
44067
James Pl
Northfield Park
Nordonia Hills C of C
Dr 9500
271
SUMMIT CO
Florence Dr
41°20'41"

Jefferson
Monroe
Fell
Kennedy
Lowrie
Vorderman Av
Blvd
Blvd
Summit Av
Heights Av
Magnolia Av
Elm St
N Bedford Rd
Freeway
44056

Rodsevelt
Victory Blvd
Houghton Rd
100
Beech Av
Electric
10300
Maple Av
FS
Northfield Vil Hall
Windsor N Pl
Milford Dr
Dr Dr Dr
Mapleview Rd
Indian Run
Acres
Cielo E Terra Dr
480
14
4

Northfield
Chestnut Av
Birch Av
Rosewood Av
May Av
200
NORTHFIELD RD
Huntington Plaza
100
Milford Dr
Cambridge Dr
Coventry Dr
9100
Stratford Dr
Cranbrook
9400
Oakview Rd
Ledge Acres Rd
Macedonia
Woodview Dr
Skyland Dr
Cessna Dr
S Skyland Rd
Airlane 1100
41°20'15"

Sagamore Hills Township
FELL LAKE

5

Pinecreek Ln
Seiberling
Creekside Dr
Parkside Dr
OLDE EIGHT RD
Meadow Ln
Redtail Ct
Langston Ter
Manor Ct
Robinwood Ter
B
8200
Griswold Cir
Firestone
Bishop Dr
Long Rd
Eaton Rd
Primrose Ln
Isabelle Ln
Ledge 300 Rd
Ledge Rd
Ledge Rd
600
Blackhawk Run
Iroquois Tr
Cherokee Run
Apache Run
Cheyenne Run
Ledge Rd
SUGARBUSH PARK
Ridgeview Dr
Woodlawn Dr
Longwood Dr
Westwood
9400
41°19'49"

NORTHFIELD MACEDONIA CEMETERY
9700
VALLEY VIEW RD
10400
Downcote Trc
300
Kingfisher
Huntsford Pl
Brookfield Pl
Oakhill Ter
Eagleton Dr
Hartsfield Ter
Primrose
Jaystone Ln
9100
S Freeway Dr
Pine Tree Dr
La Crosse Dr
Starlight Dr
Apache Navajo
Comanche Tr
Seminole Tr
Shoshone Tr
9000
Iroquois Run
Forest Point Cir
Forest Point Dr
Park 1100 Ledge Dr

6

8
Finchfield Ct
Redtail Ct
Springhill Ln
Ravenswood Dr
Buckston Dr
Wrenford Ct
Valley Dr
B
1 Elmdale Trc
2 Quailridge Ct
3 Hillside Ter
4 Heron Glen Dr
5 Foxwood Ln
6 Deerfield Cir
7 Larkspur Ln
8 Strawbridge Ct
9 Hawksbridge Ct
8500
Chenook Tr
Blackfeet Tr
Sioux Ln
Chenook Run Ln
Crow Tr
Shepard
Broadmoor Rd
Ledgeview Rd
Hills Blvd
Broadledge Rd
Briarwood Rd
Tanglewood Rd
41°19'23"

Butternut Dr
Butternut Ln
8
Preserve Ct
Preserve Pl
Preserve Ln
Janes Ln
Vernon Dr
10200 View
Melody Ln
Cherry Rd
Cir
Harper Dr
271
S Freeway Dr
Lawton Dr
Brookpoint Dr
1000
Berkshire Dr
Smokerise
Riverview Dr
Longbrook Dr
Briarwood Rd
7

Northfield Center Township
Timberlane Dr
Forestwood Dr
Beechwood Ln
200
Cherry
Harmon
Fairlane
Waters
Rays
Farm Rd
Bobolink
Summer Rd
Ashford Dr
800
Hampton Dr
Sherwood
Crow Creek
1000
Deepwood Dr
Wiltshire
Saybrook Dr
Sherri Dr
Harad Dr
Shepard Rd
41°18'57"

SEE 3153 MAP

Miles 0   0.25   0.5
1 in. = 2000 ft.

MAP 3019

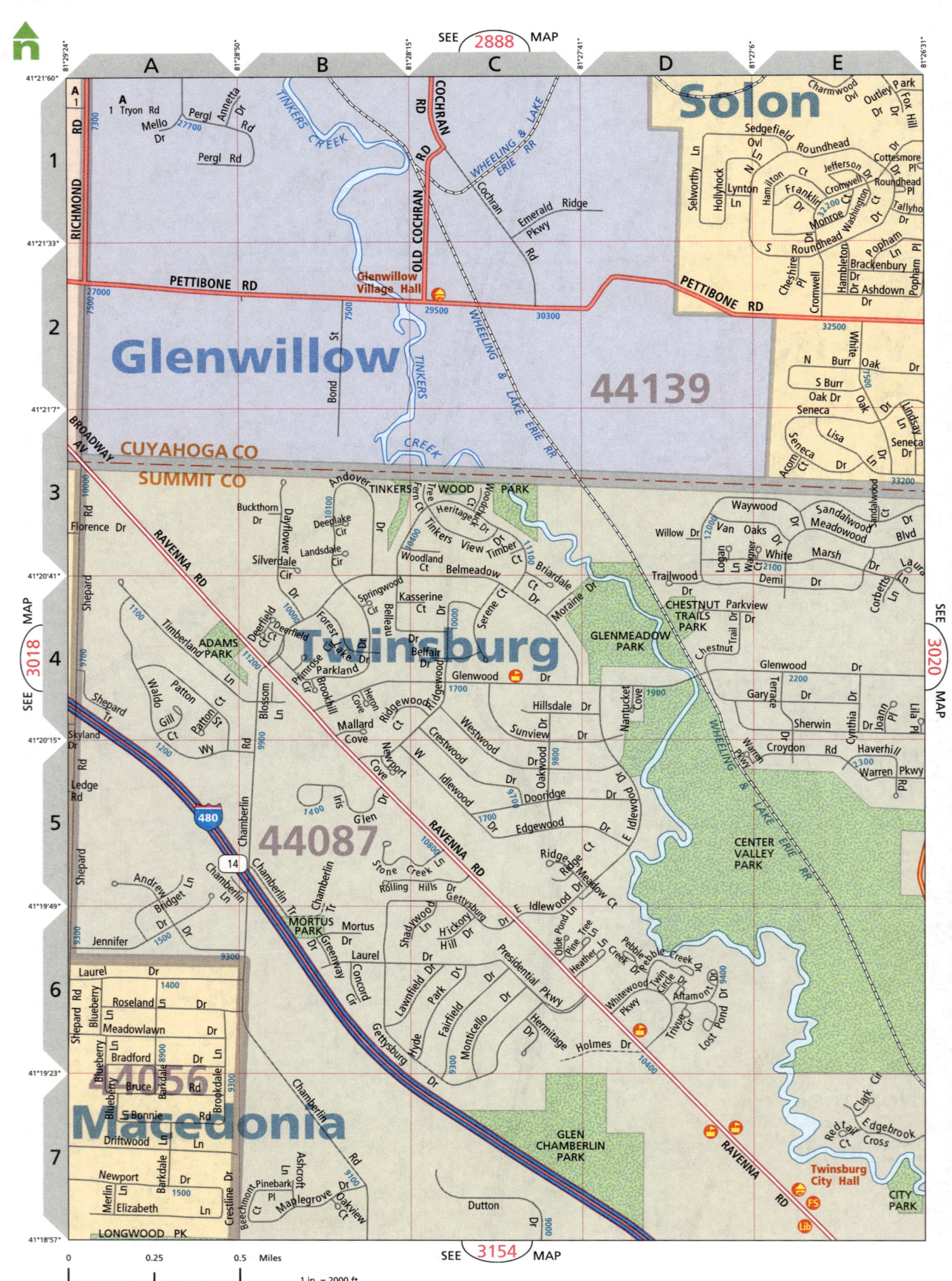

SEE 2888 MAP

SEE 3018 MAP

SEE 3020 MAP

SEE 3154 MAP

0   0.25   0.5 Miles

1 in. = 2000 ft.

MAP 3020

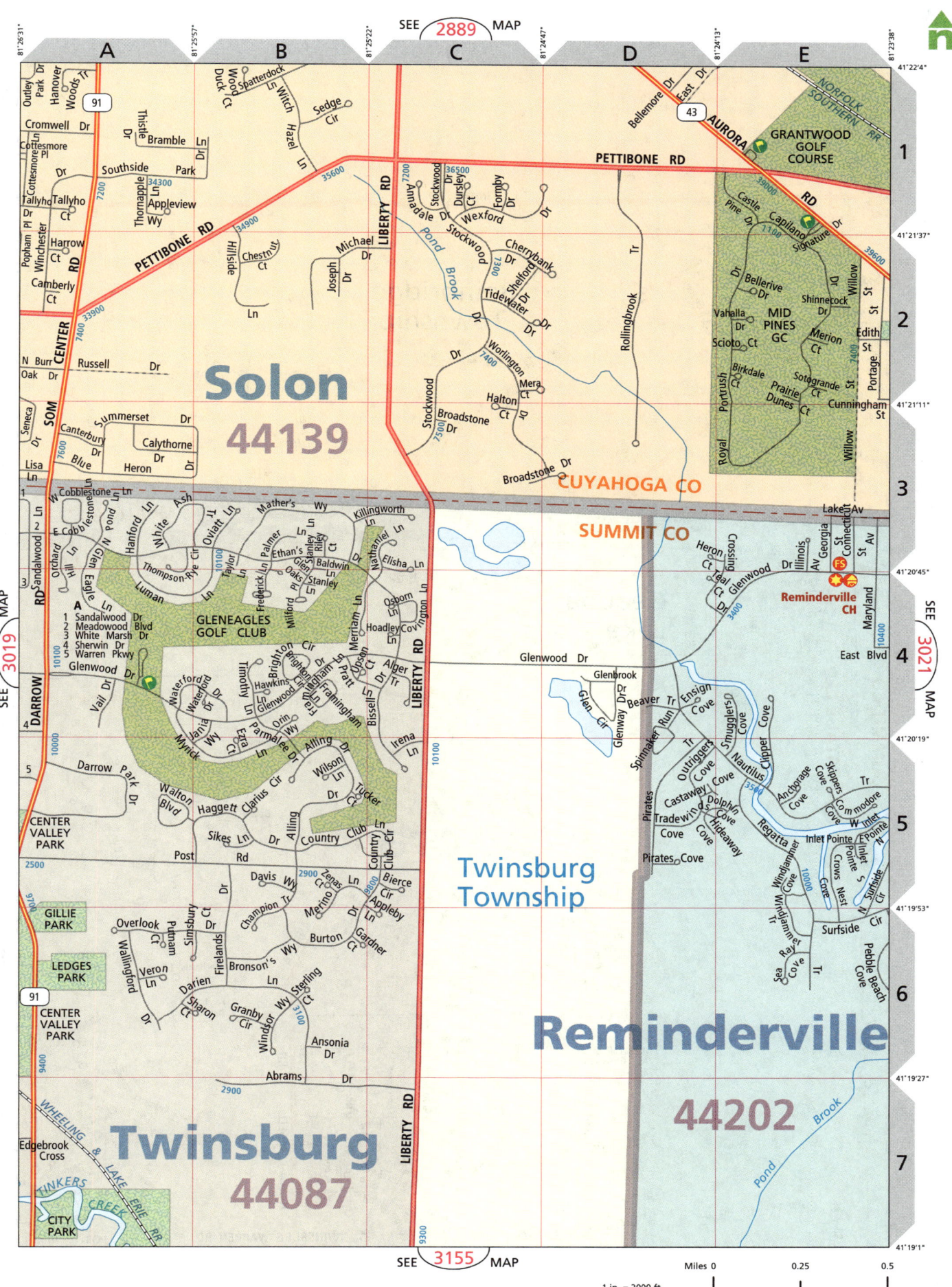

SEE 2889 MAP
SEE 3019 MAP
SEE 3021 MAP
SEE 3155 MAP

Solon
44139

Twinsburg
44087

Twinsburg
Township

Reminderville
44202

CUYAHOGA CO
SUMMIT CO

GRANTWOOD
GOLF COURSE

MID
PINES
GC

GLENEAGLES
GOLF CLUB

CENTER
VALLEY
PARK

GILLIE
PARK

LEDGES
PARK

CENTER
VALLEY
PARK

CITY
PARK

Reminderville
CH

Miles 0   0.25   0.5

1 in. = 2000 ft.

MAP 3021

SEE 2890 MAP

A B C D E

81°23'38" 81°23'4" 81°22'29" 81°21'54" 81°21'20" 81°20'45"
41°22'4"

GRANTWOOD GC

CUYAHOGA CO
GEAUGA CO

1

41°21'37"

Root Rd
18400

AURORA RD
Summit Rd

Lake Pkwy
7200

Geauga Lake Rd
18700

PETTIBONE RD

7900
18700

Aurora Branch

Sharon Dr
Rivers Edge Dr E
Highpoint Rd

PORTAGE PK

2

41°21'11"

Edith St
Geauga St
Cunningham St

N AURORA RD
7000

NORFOLK SOUTHERN RR

Geauga Lake Rd

Bainbridge Township 44023

Rivers Edge Dr W
Chagrin
Falling Water Rd

Timber Tr

3

Depot Rd
19000

Brewster Rd
18900

Lori Ln S
Elizabeth Ln

River

Cascade Dr
7900

GEAUGA CO

41°20'45"

1200
St
Glenwood Dr

Lake Av
Moneta Av
St

Six Flags Worlds of Adventure

Fairview Ln
Fairview Av
Brewster Rd

Riverside
19100

PORTAGE CO

4

Florida St
LIZ STRAHAN PK
Lloyd Pennsylvania Av
Bryce
East Blvd

Orchard Av
1000
Michigan St
500
Olin
900

Geauga Lake

Doralane Av

Bank St
McRoberts St
Squires
900 Av

Treat Rd
300

Dankorona Winery

41°20'19"

SUMMIT CO
PORTAGE CO

California Rd
Nautilus Tr

PICNIC LAKE PARK

Aurora Lake Rd

Cherry Park Ovl

43

Hardwick

Club Dr

Shinnecock Ln

5

Commodore Cove E
Collica Cove
N Surfside Cir

Oakmont Dr
Devonshire Ln
Glengarry Dr
Bradford Ln

Brighton Dr
Burgess Cir

SEE 3020 MAP
SEE 3022 MAP

41°19'53"

Surfside Cir
Surfside Cir

AURORA LAKE

44202 Aurora

Rock Dr
Valley View Cir
Creek Dr
Walnut
Sycamore Sycamore Tr
Cranberry Tr

Bristol Dr

B
1 Winchester Ct
2 Chisholm Ct
3 Raleigh Ct
4 Fareham Ct
5 Dunbar Ct

Berwick Cir
Bradmore Cir

6

Pebble Beach Cove

Sweetgrass Cir

Cimarron Ovl
Nancy
Stone Hill Ovl
Blair Cir

Walnut
Ridge Dr
Falling Leaves Cir
Ridge Tr

Stratford Camden Ln
Aberdeen

Robinhood Dr
Sussex Dr
Sherwood Dr
700
500

St Andrews Ln
Knightsbridge Ln
Wyndham Ln
Chelsea Ct
Southwick Blvd
Chillicothe

7

41°19'27"

A
1 Hedgecliff St
2 Ash Grove Cir
3 Beaumont Tr
4 Lakeview Cir

Colony Dr
Rd
Cambridge Dr
Oxford Dr

Sussex
Willowbrook Cove
Arborhurst Cir
Forestview Pl
Woodhaven Ct
Woodview

Holly Ln
Oak Grandview Ln
Vista Ln
Deerfield Ln
Devon Ln
Countrywood
Belcourt Ln
Ashland Ln
Crystal Tr
Pond Tr
Emerald Ln

BISSELL RD
N
100
200

Barrington Ln
4 3 2 1 B
5

Barrington Town Center

306

41°19'1"

Riley Rd
Aurora Hill Dr
Cochran
A
Fairfield Grand Ct
High Blf
Lake Tr

TWINSBURG WARREN RD

BREEZY POINT PARK
N

SEE 3156 MAP

0   0.25   0.5 Miles

1 in. = 2000 ft.

MAP 3022

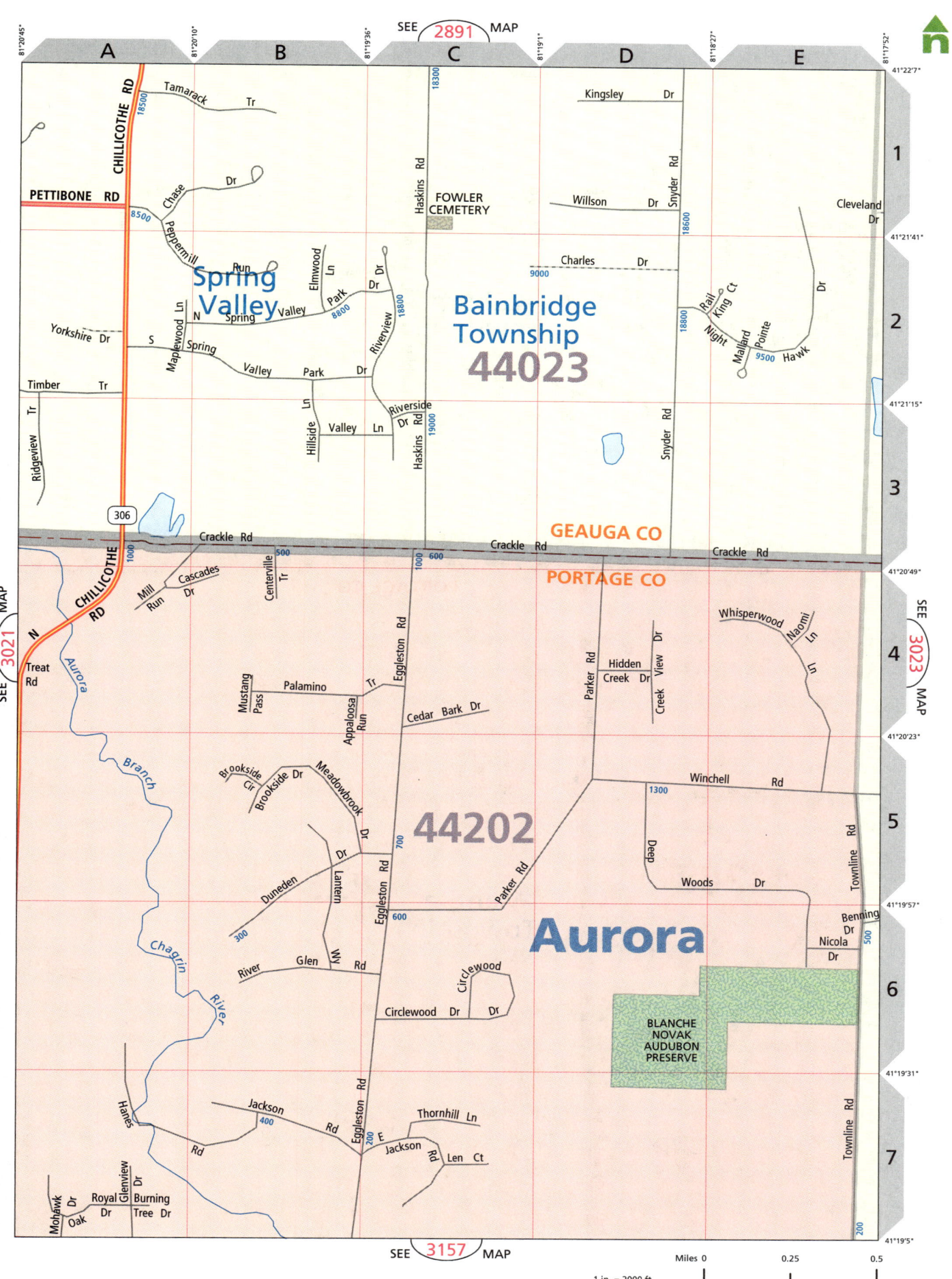

SEE 2891 MAP

A 81°20'45"   B 81°20'10"   C 81°19'36"   D 81°19'11"   E 81°18'27"   81°17'52"

CHILLICOTHE RD

Tamarack Tr

PETTIBONE RD

Kingsley Dr

41°22'7"

18500

18300

Haskins Rd

Chase Dr

8500

Peppermill

FOWLER CEMETERY

Willson Dr

Snyder Rd

Cleveland Dr

41°21'41"

Run

Elmwood Ln

Spring Valley

N Spring Valley Park Dr

Maplewood Ln

8800

Riverview Dr

18800

Charles Dr

9000

Bainbridge Township 44023

18600

18800

Rail

King Ct

Night

Mallard Pointe

9500

Hawk

Dr

2

Yorkshire Dr

S Spring

Park Dr

Valley

Timber Tr

Ridgeview Tr

Hillside Ln

Valley Ln

Riverside Dr

Haskins Rd

19000

Snyder Rd

41°21'15"

3

306

Crackle Rd

1000

Crackle Rd

GEAUGA CO

Crackle Rd

41°20'49"

CHILLICOTHE RD

Centerville Tr

500

Mill Run

Cascades Dr

1000 600

PORTAGE CO

SEE 3023 MAP

N

Eggleston Rd

Whisperwood

Naomi Ln

4

Aurora

Treat Rd

Mustang Pass

Palamino

Tr

Appaloosa Run

Cedar Bark Dr

Parker Rd

Hidden Creek Dr

Creek View Dr

Ln

41°20'23"

SEE 3021 MAP

Branch

Brookside Cir

Brookside Dr

Meadowbrook Dr

700

Winchell Rd

1300

Townline Rd

5

44202

Dr

Lantern

300

Egglest on Rd

600

Parker Rd

Deep Woods Dr

41°19'57"

Chagrin

Duneden

River Glen Wy Rd

Aurora

Benning Dr

Nicola Dr

500

6

River

Circlewood Dr

Circlewood Dr Dr

BLANCHE NOVAK AUDUBON PRESERVE

41°19'31"

Hanes

Jackson

400

Rd

Eggleston Rd

Thornhill Ln

7

Rd

200 E

Jackson Rd Len Ct

Townline Rd

Mohawk Dr

Royal Oak Dr

Glenview Dr

Burning Tree Dr

200

41°19'5"

SEE 3157 MAP

Miles 0   0.25   0.5

1 in. = 2000 ft.

MAP 3023

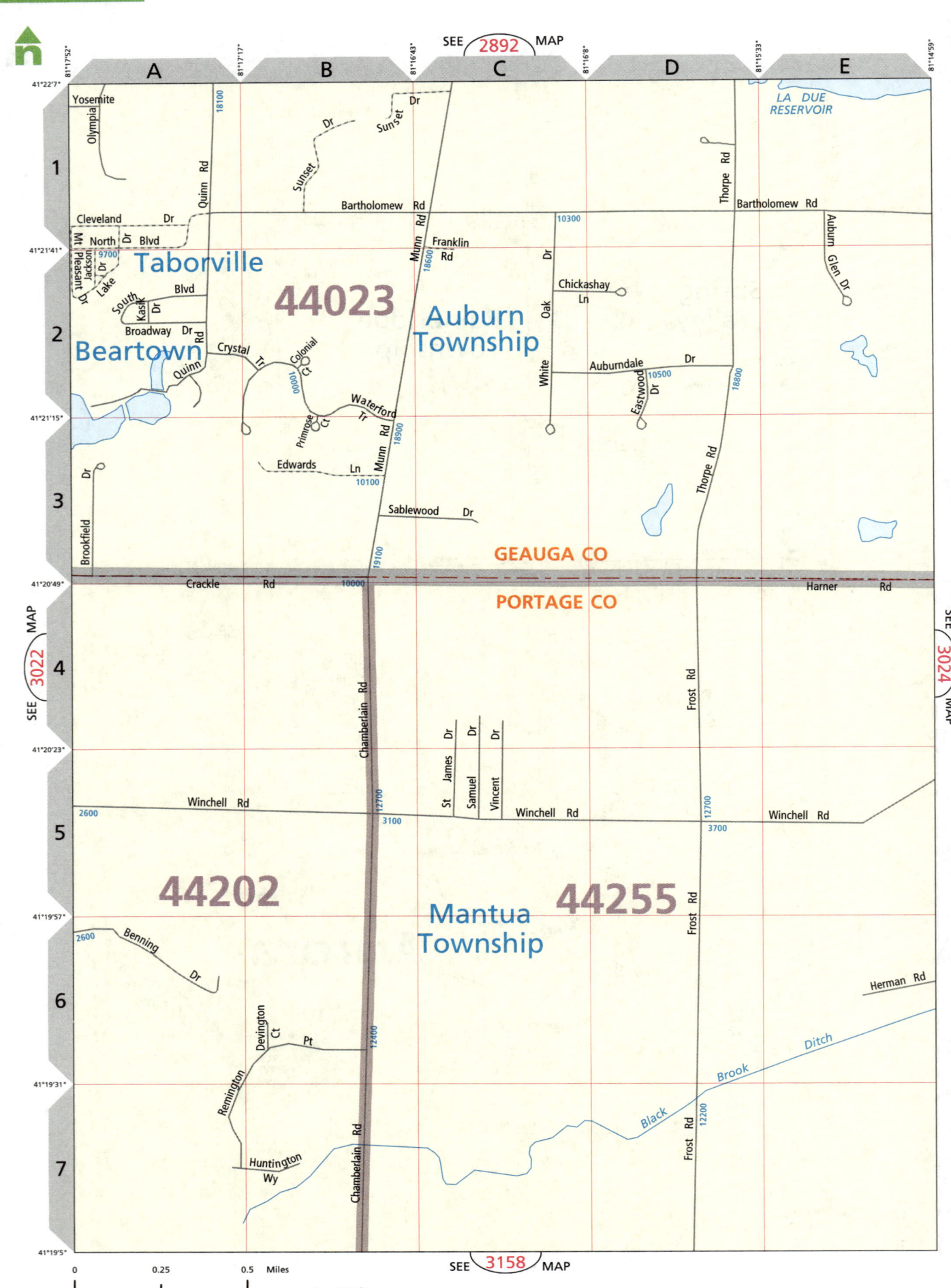

SEE 2892 MAP

A   B   C   D   E

Yosemite
Olympia Dr

Quinn Rd   18100

Sunset Dr   Sunset Dr

1

Cleveland   Dr   Bartholomew   Rd   10300   Bartholomew   Rd
Thorpe Rd

Mt Pleasant Dr   North   Dr   Blvd   Munn   Rd   Franklin   Rd   Auburn Glen Dr
Jackson Dr   9700   Lake

Taborville

Kask Dr   South   Blvd   44023   Chickashay   Ln

2   Broadway Dr   Auburn   Oak   Dr
Rd   Township   White
Crystal   Tr

Beartown   Colonial Ct   10000   Auburndale   Dr
Quinn Dr   Eastwood Dr   10500   18800
Waterford   Tr

Primrose Ct   Munn Rd   18900

41°21'15"

Edwards   Ln   10100

3   Brookfield   Dr   Sablewood   Dr   Thorpe Rd

GEAUGA CO   19100

41°20'49"   Crackle   Rd   10000   PORTAGE CO   Harner   Rd

SEE 3022 MAP   SEE 3024 MAP

4   Chamberlain Rd   Frost Rd

41°20'23"

St James Dr   Samuel Dr   Vincent Dr

Winchell   Rd   2600   12700   Winchell   Rd   12700   Winchell   Rd
5   3100   3700

44202   44255

6   Benning   Dr   2600   Mantua   Township
Herman   Rd

Devington Ct   Pt   12400   Black   Brook   Ditch

Remington   Frost Rd   12200
7   Huntington   Wy   Chamberlain   Rd

41°19'5"

SEE 3158 MAP

0   0.25   0.5   Miles

1 in. = 2000 ft.

MAP 3024

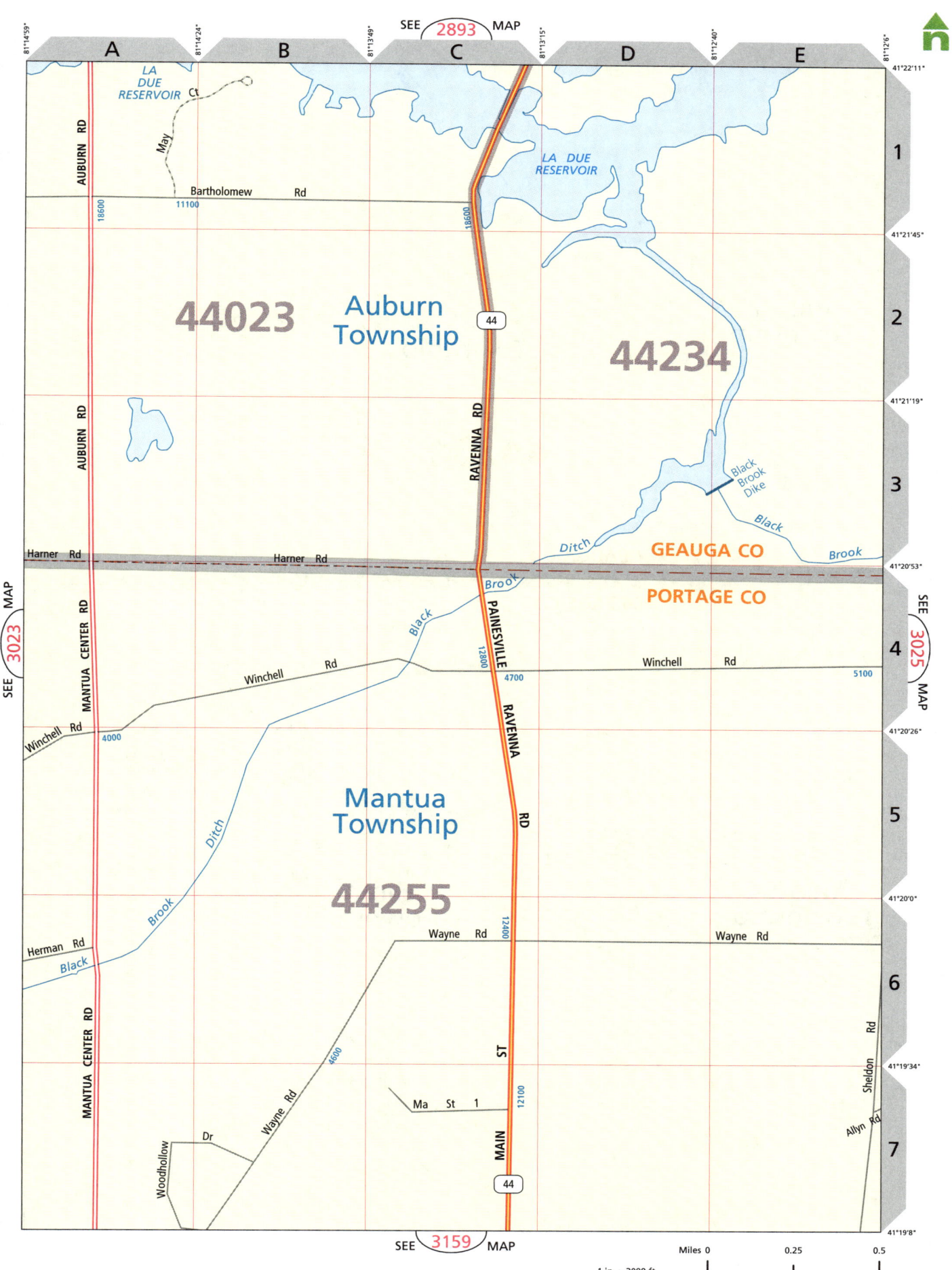

SEE 2893 MAP

A B C D E

81°14'59" 81°14'24" 81°13'49" 81°13'15" 81°12'40" 81°12'6"

41°22'11"

1

LA DUE RESERVOIR

May Ct

LA DUE RESERVOIR

41°21'45"

AUBURN RD

Bartholomew Rd
11100

18600

44023 Auburn Township

44234

44

RAVENNA RD

2

41°21'19"

18600

AUBURN RD

3

Black Brook Dike

Black Brook

41°20'53"

Harner Rd Harner Rd

Ditch

GEAUGA CO

PORTAGE CO

SEE 3023 MAP

SEE 3025 MAP

MANTUA CENTER RD

Black

Brook

PAINESVILLE

Winchell Rd

Winchell Rd
12800 4700

Winchell Rd
5100

4

41°20'26"

Winchell Rd
4000

RAVENNA

Ditch

Mantua Township

RD

5

41°20'0"

44255

Brook

Herman Rd
Black

Wayne Rd
12400

Wayne Rd

6

MANTUA CENTER RD

Sheldon Rd

41°19'34"

4600

Ma St 1

12100

Allyn Rd

Woodhollow Dr

Wayne Rd

ST

7

MAIN

44

41°19'8"

SEE 3159 MAP

Miles 0 0.25 0.5

1 in. = 2000 ft.

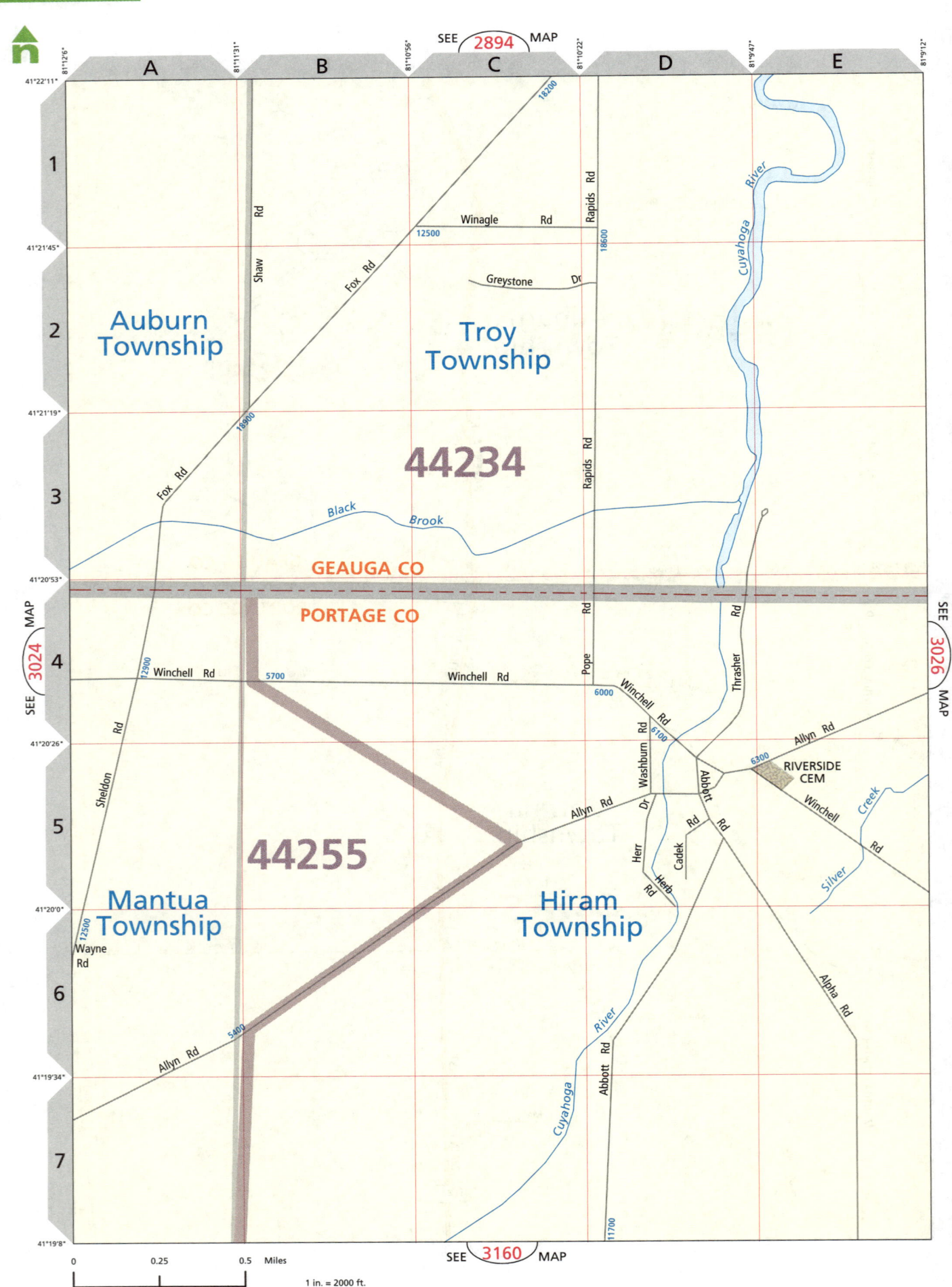

MAP 3025

SEE 2894 MAP

A   B   C   D   E

81°11'26"   81°11'18"   81°10'56"   81°10'22"   81°9'47"   81°6'18"

41°22'11"

1

41°21'45"

Auburn
Township

2

Troy
Township

41°21'19"

3

44234

41°20'53"

GEAUGA CO

PORTAGE CO

SEE 3024 MAP

4

SEE 3026 MAP

41°20'26"

5

44255

41°20'0"

Mantua
Township

Hiram
Township

RIVERSIDE
CEM

6

41°19'34"

7

41°19'8"

Shaw   Rd

Fox   Rd

Fox   Rd

18900

Winagle   Rd

12500

Greystone   Dr

18200

Rapids   Rd

18600

Rapids   Rd

Cuyahoga   River

Black   Brook

Winchell   Rd

12900

5700

Winchell   Rd

6000

Pope   Rd

Thrasher   Rd

Sheldon   Rd

Allyn   Rd

5400

12500

Wayne
Rd

Cuyahoga   River

Abbott   Rd

11700

Washburn   Rd

6100

Allyn   Rd

Herr
Dr

Herb
Rd

Cadek
Rd

Abbott
Rd

6300

Allyn   Rd

Winchell   Rd

Silver   Creek

Rd

Alpha   Rd

SEE 3160 MAP

0   0.25   0.5   Miles

1 in. = 2000 ft.

MAP 3026

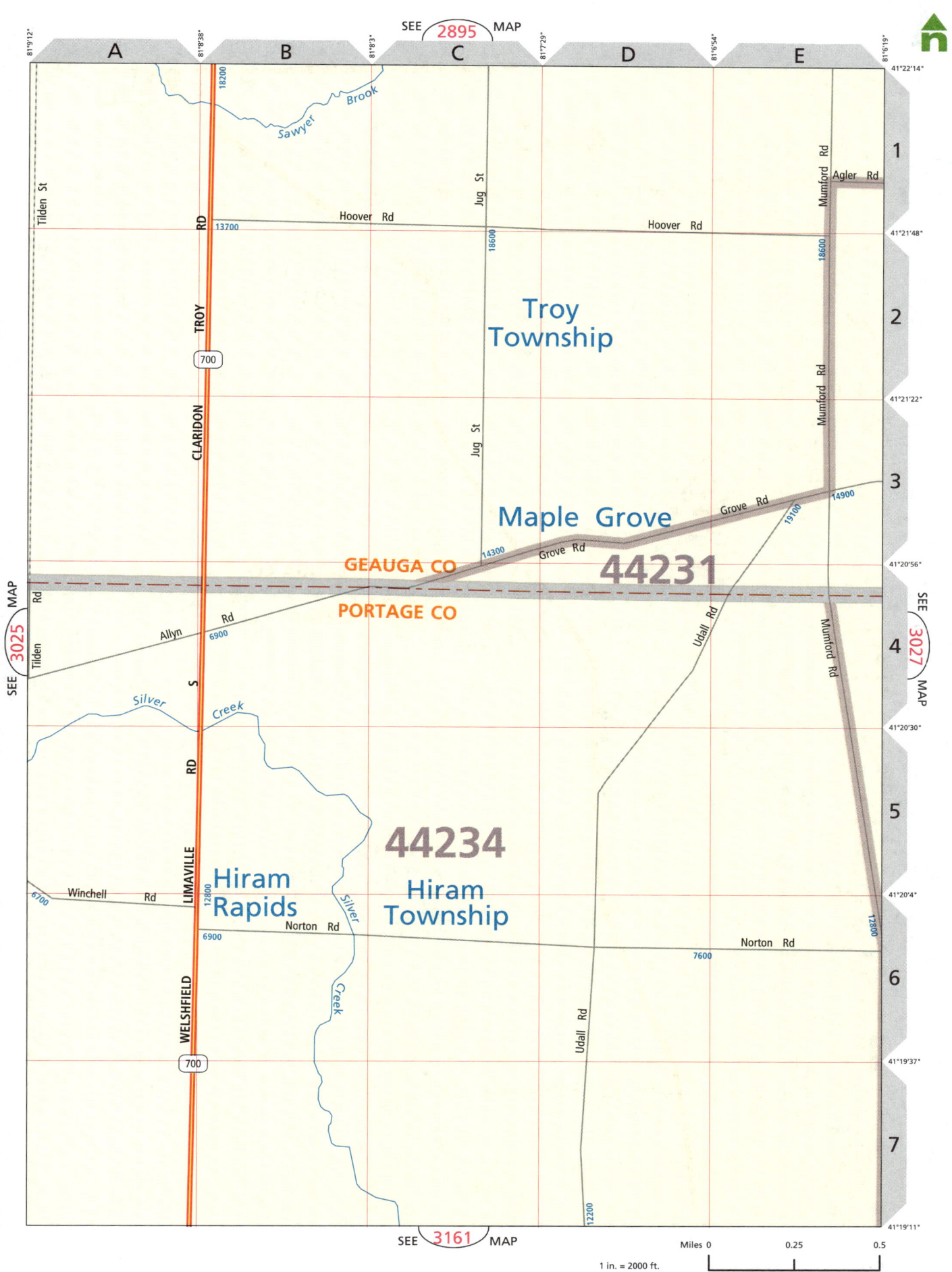

SEE 2895 MAP

A   B   C   D   E

81°9'12"   81°8'38"   81°8'3"   817°7'29"   81°6'54"   81°6'19"

41°22'14"

Sawyer Brook

18200

Tilden St

Jug St

Hoover Rd

RD   13700   Hoover Rd   41°21'48"

Mumford Rd

Agler Rd

1

TROY

Troy Township

18600

2

700

18600

41°21'22"

CLARIDON

Jug St

Mumford Rd

41°21'22"

Grove Rd

14900

3

Maple Grove

14300   Grove Rd   44231

19700

GEAUGA CO

41°20'56"

PORTAGE CO

Rd

Allyn   Rd   6900

SEE 3025 MAP

Tilden

Udall Rd

Mumford Rd

SEE 3027 MAP

4

41°20'30"

Silver   Creek

S

5

RD

44234

12800

Hiram Rapids

Silver

Hiram Township

41°20'4"

LIMAVILLE

6700   Winchell   Rd

Norton Rd

12800

6

6900

Norton Rd

7600

WELSHFIELD

Creek

Udall Rd

41°19'37"

700

7

12200

41°19'11"

SEE 3161 MAP

Miles 0   0.25   0.5

1 in. = 2000 ft.

MAP 3027

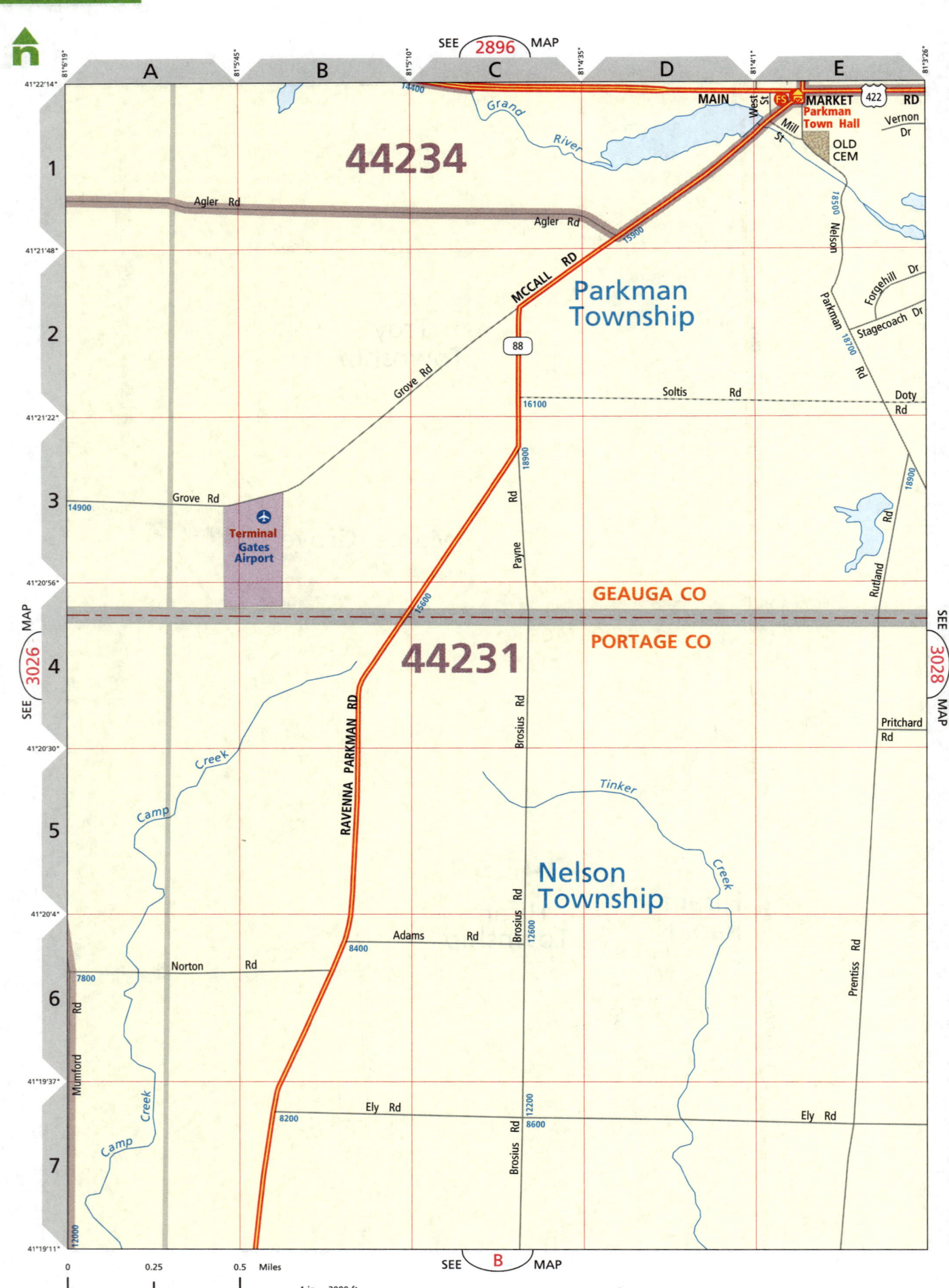

SEE 2896 MAP

A   B   C   D   E

44234

Parkman Township

MAIN West St MARKET RD
422
Parkman Town Hall Vernon Dr
OLD CEM

Agler Rd

Agler Rd

MCCALL RD

Nelson
Forgehill Dr
Parkman
Stagecoach Dr
Rd
Doty Rd

Grove Rd

88

Soltis Rd

16100

Grove Rd

Terminal Gates Airport

Payne Rd

Rutland Rd

GEAUGA CO

PORTANGE CO

44231

RAVENNA PARKMAN RD

Brosius Rd

Pritchard Rd

Creek

Camp

Tinker Creek

Nelson Township

Adams Rd

Brosius Rd

Norton Rd

Prentiss Rd

Mumford Rd

Ely Rd

Ely Rd

Brosius Rd

Camp Creek

SEE 3026 MAP

SEE 3028 MAP

SEE B MAP

0   0.25   0.5   Miles

1 in. = 2000 ft.

MAP 3028

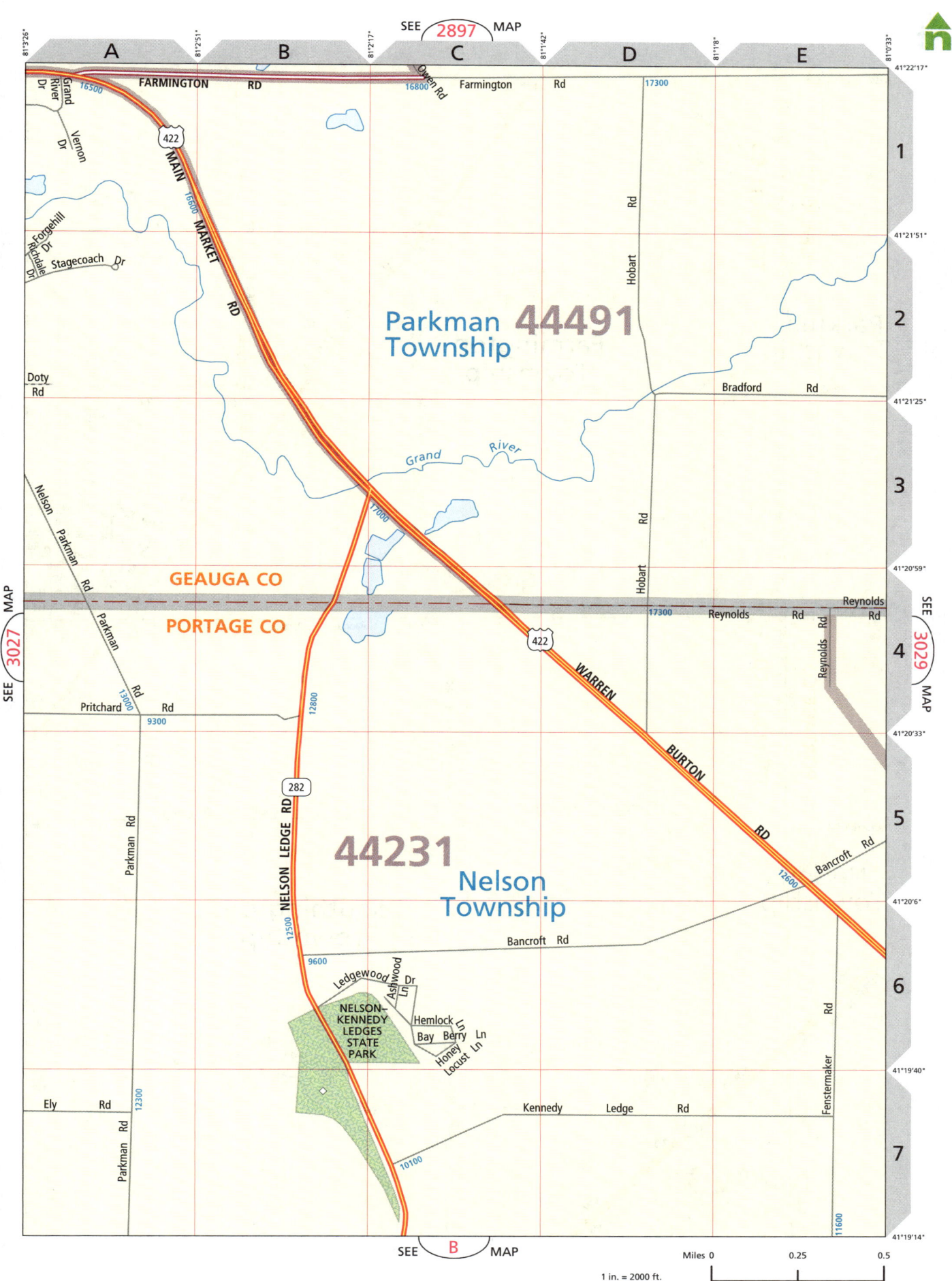

SEE 2897 MAP

FARMINGTON RD

Owen Rd   Farmington   Rd

Grand River Dr

Vernon Dr

16500

422 MAIN MARKET RD

16600

Forgehill Dr

Richdale Dr

Stagecoach Dr

Doty Rd

17300

Hobart Rd

Parkman Township **44491**

Bradford Rd

Grand River

17000

Hobart Rd

GEAUGA CO

PORTABLE CO

Nelson Parkman Rd

Parkman Rd

13000

Pritchard Rd

9300

12800

282 NELSON LEDGE RD

12500

Reynolds Rd

17300   Reynolds   Rd

Reynolds Rd

422 WARREN

BURTON RD

Bancroft Rd

12600

SEE 3029 MAP

SEE 3027 MAP

44231

Nelson Township

9600

Parkman Rd

Ledgewood Dr

Ashwood Ln

Bancroft   Rd

NELSON-KENNEDY LEDGES STATE PARK

Hemlock Ln

Bay Berry Ln

Honey Locust Ln

Fenstermaker Rd

Ely   Rd

12300

Parkman   Rd

Kennedy   Ledge   Rd

10100

11600

SEE B MAP

Miles 0   0.25   0.5

1 in. = 2000 ft.

MAP 3029-3137

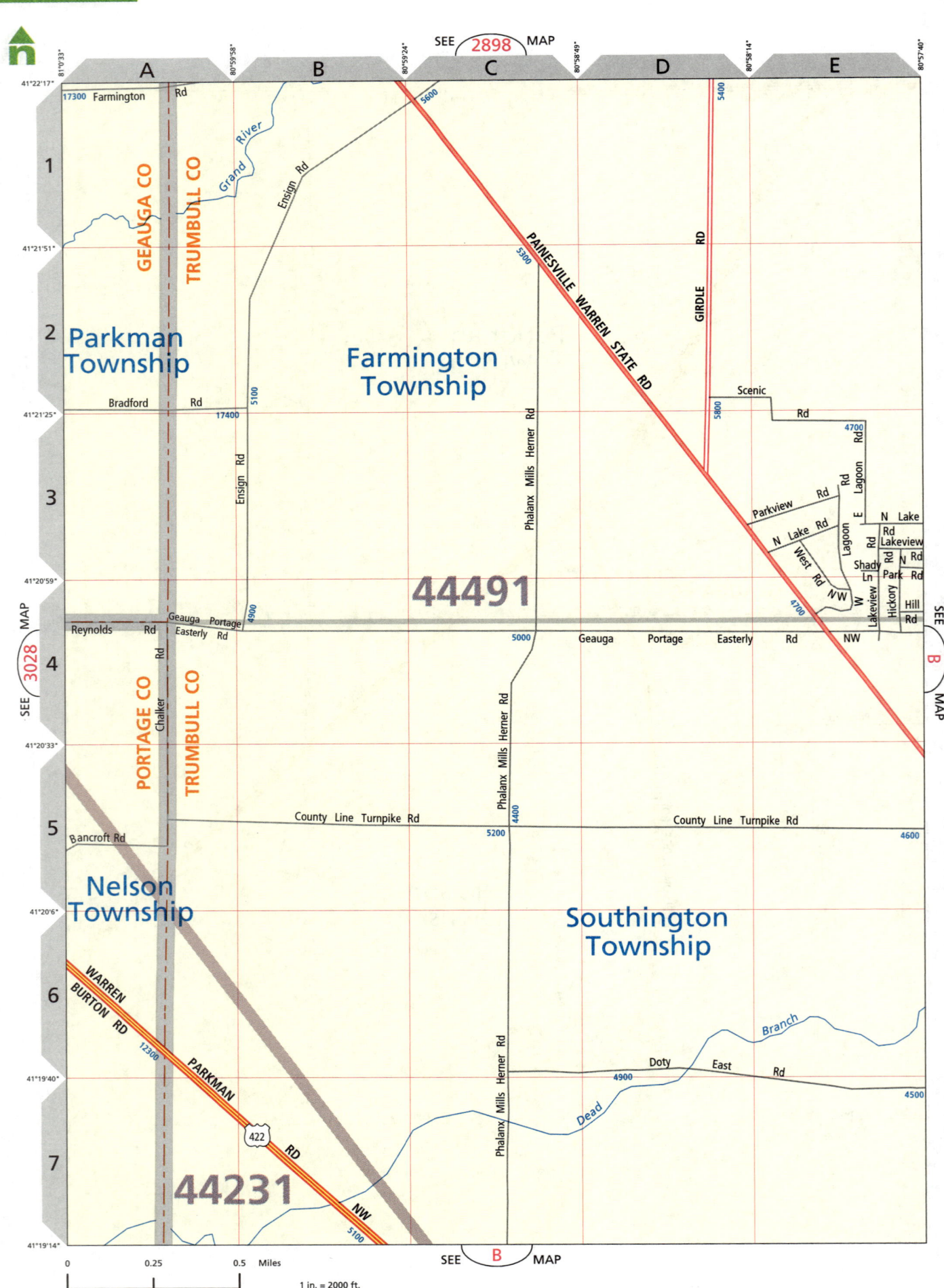

SEE 2898 MAP

N

A   B   C   D   E

41°22'17"
17300 Farmington Rd

Grand River
Ensign Rd

1

41°21'51"

GEAUGA CO
TRUMBULL CO

PAINESVILLE WARREN STATE RD

GIRDLE RD

5600

5400

2

Parkman
Township

Farmington
Township

5500

Bradford Rd
17400

Scenic Rd

5800

4700 Rd

3

Ensign Rd

5100

Phalanx Mills Herner Rd

Parkview Rd

Rd Lagoon

E Lagoon Rd

N Lake

N Lake Rd

Rd Lakeview

West Rd NW

Shady Ln

Park Rd

N Rd

Hickory Hill Rd

41°20'59"

44491

4900

4700

Lakeview

Geauga Portage
Easterly Rd

Reynolds Rd

5000

Geauga Portage Easterly Rd

NW

SEE 3028 MAP

SEE B MAP

4

PORTAGE CO
TRUMBULL CO

Chalker Rd

Phalanx Mills Herner Rd

41°20'33"

5

County Line Turnpike Rd

5200

4400

County Line Turnpike Rd

4600

Bancroft Rd

Nelson
Township

41°20'6"

Southington
Township

6

WARREN BURTON RD

12300

PARKMAN

Branch

41°19'40"

422 RD

Phalanx Mills Herner Rd

Doty East Rd

4900

Dead

4500

7

44231

NW

5100

41°19'14"

SEE B MAP

0   0.25   0.5   Miles

1 in. = 2000 ft.

81°0'33"   80°59'58"   80°59'24"   80°58'49"   80°58'14"   80°57'40"

MAP 3138

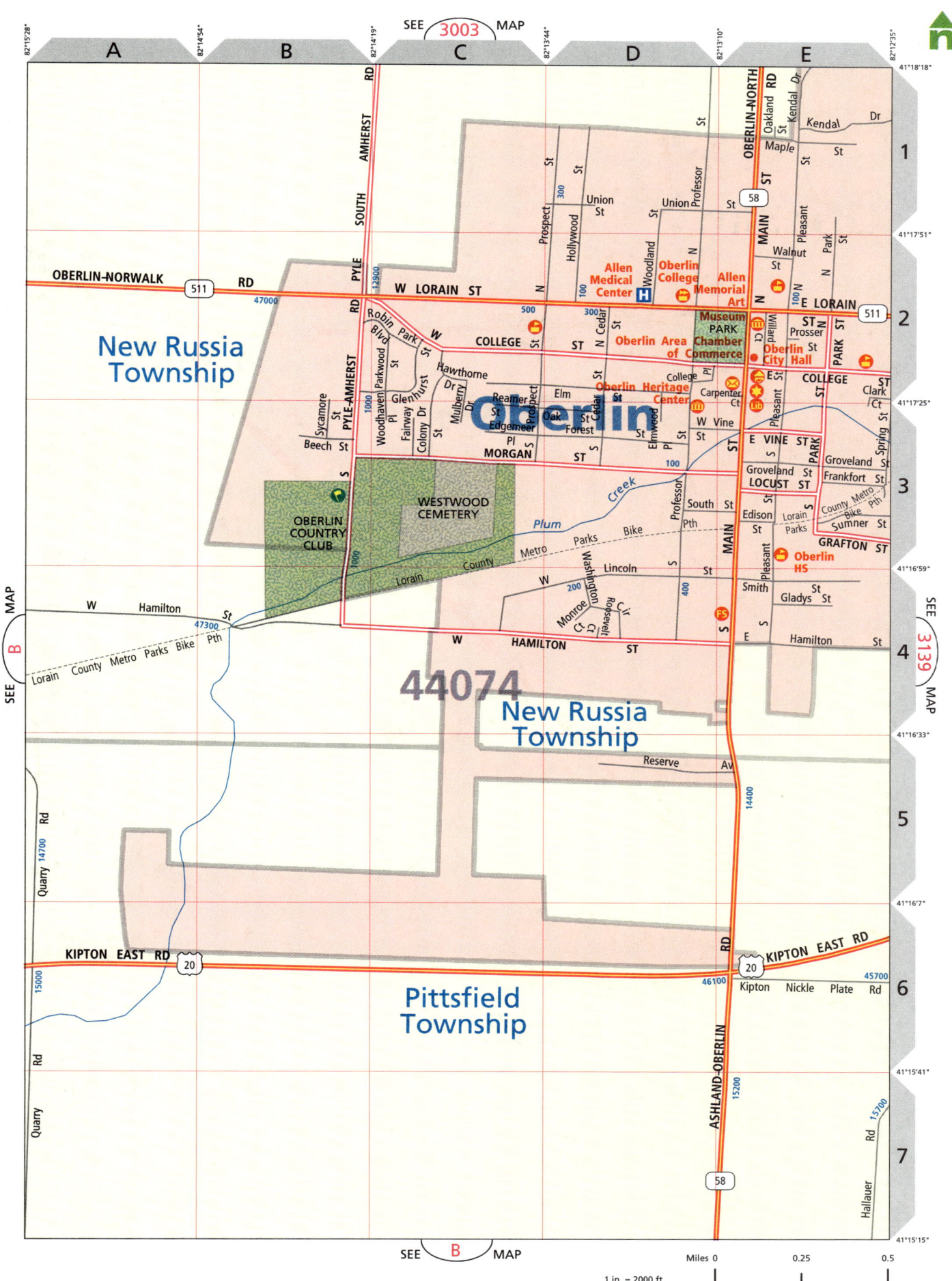

SEE 3003 MAP

A   B   C   D   E

82°15'28"   82°14'54"   82°14'19"   82°13'44"   82°13'10"   82°12'35"

41°18'18"

OBERLIN-NORTH RD

Oakland St   Kendal Dr

Kendal   Dr

Maple   St   1

41°17'51"

MAIN   ST   58   Pleasant

Prospect St   Union   Union   Professor   St   Walnut   Park

Hollywood St   St   St   N   St   N

OBERLIN-NORWALK   RD   511

Allen   Woodland   Oberlin   Allen   E Lorain   511

Medical   College   Memorial   2

Center   H   Art

New Russia   W LORAIN ST   N   Museum   Prosser

Township   RD   Robin Park   COLLEGE   ST   N Cedar   Oberlin Area   PARK   St

Pl   St   of Commerce   Chamber   Oberlin   ST

Blvd   W   Oberlin   City Hall

Parkwood   Hawthorne   College   Heritage   Carpenter   COLLEGE   Clark

Woodhaven   Dr   Pl   Oberlin   Center   Ct   Ct

Glenhurst   Mulberry   Reamer   Elm   Cedar   E St   3

Sycamore   Fairway   Dr   St   Oak   St   Lib   41°17'25"

St   Colony Dr   St   Edgemeer   Forest   Elmwood   W Vine   Pleasant

Beech St   PYLE-AMHERST   **Oberlin**   St   St   E VINE ST   Spring

MORGAN   ST   Groveland   St   Groveland St   Frankfort   St

PLUM   100   LOCUST ST   County Metro   St

Creek   Park

WESTWOOD   Professor   South   St   Edison   Lorain   Bike Pth

OBERLIN   CEMETERY   St   St   Parks   GRAFTON ST

COUNTRY   Plum   Bike   Sumner   Oberlin

CLUB   Metro   Pth   HS   41°16'59"

Lorain   County   Washington   Lincoln   St   Smith   Gladys St

W   Hamilton   St   W   Monroe   Roosevelt   400   FS   Hamilton   4

Lorain County Metro Parks Bike Pth   47300   200   Ct   St   E   St

SEE   B   MAP   Ct   W   HAMILTON   ST

44074   41°16'33"

New Russia

Township   Reserve   Av   MAIN   5

14400   41°16'7"

Quarry   Rd

Quarry 14700 Rd   RD   ASHLAND-OBERLIN   Kipton   Nickle   Plate   Rd

KIPTON EAST RD   20   KIPTON EAST RD   6

15000   20   46100   45700

Pittsfield   41°15'41"

Township   15200

58   Hallauer   Rd 15700   7

41°15'15"

SEE B MAP

Miles 0   0.25   0.5

1 in. = 2000 ft.

SEE 3139 MAP

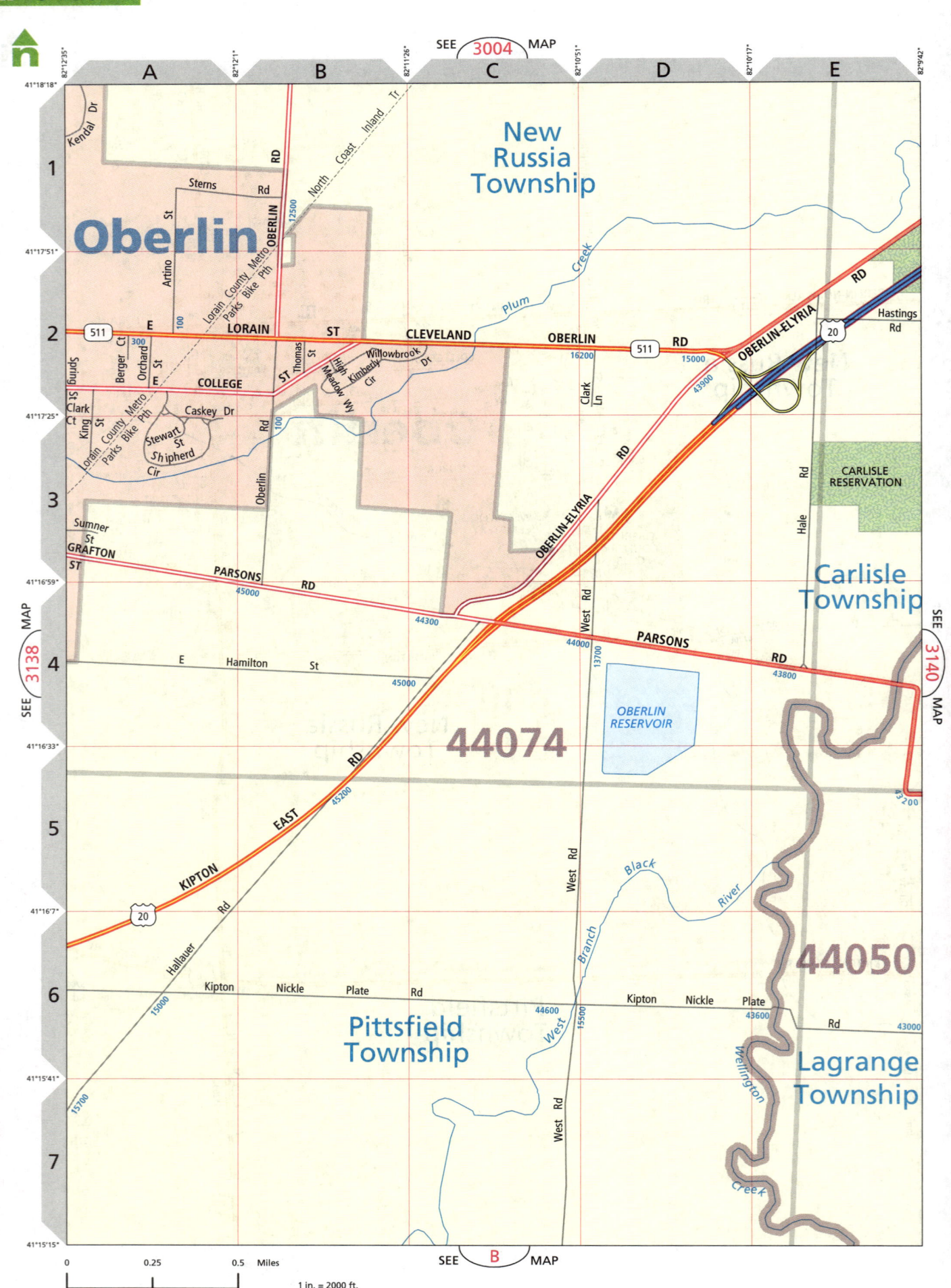

MAP 3139

SEE 3004 MAP

A B C D E

1

New
Russia
Township

Oberlin

Kendal Dr

Sterns Rd

RD

OBERLIN

North Coast Inland Tr

12500

Artino St

2

511

E

LORAIN

Spring St

Berger Ct

300

Orchard St

E

COLLEGE

Thomas St

High Meadow Wy

Willowbrook

Kimberly Cir

Dr

CLEVELAND

Plum

Creek

OBERLIN

511

RD

16200

15000

OBERLIN-ELYRIA

20

Hastings
Rd

RD

100

ST

ST

ST

Clark
Ct

King St

Clark
St

Lorain County Metro
Parks Bike Pth

Caskey Dr

Stewart
St

Shipherd
Cir

Oberlin

Rd

100

Clark
Ln

OBERLIN-ELYRIA

RD

43900

CARLISLE
RESERVATION

Hale Rd

Rd

3

Sumner
St

GRAFTON
ST

PARSONS

RD

45000

44300

West Rd

44000

13700

PARSONS

RD

43800

Carlisle
Township

SEE 3138 MAP

4

E Hamilton St

45000

OBERLIN
RESERVOIR

44074

SEE 3140 MAP

43200

5

EAST

RD

45200

KIPTON

20

Hallauer
Rd

West Rd

Black

River

44050

West
Branch

6

Kipton

Nickle

Plate

Rd

15000

44600

15500

West

Kipton

Nickle

Plate

43600

Rd

43000

Pittsfield
Township

West Rd

Wellington

Lagrange
Township

7

15700

Creek

SEE B MAP

41°18'18"
41°17'51"
41°17'25"
41°16'59"
41°16'33"
41°16'7"
41°15'41"
41°15'15"

82°12'35"
82°12'21"
82°11'26"
82°10'51"
82°10'17"
82°9'42"

0   0.25   0.5   Miles

1 in. = 2000 ft.

MAP 3140

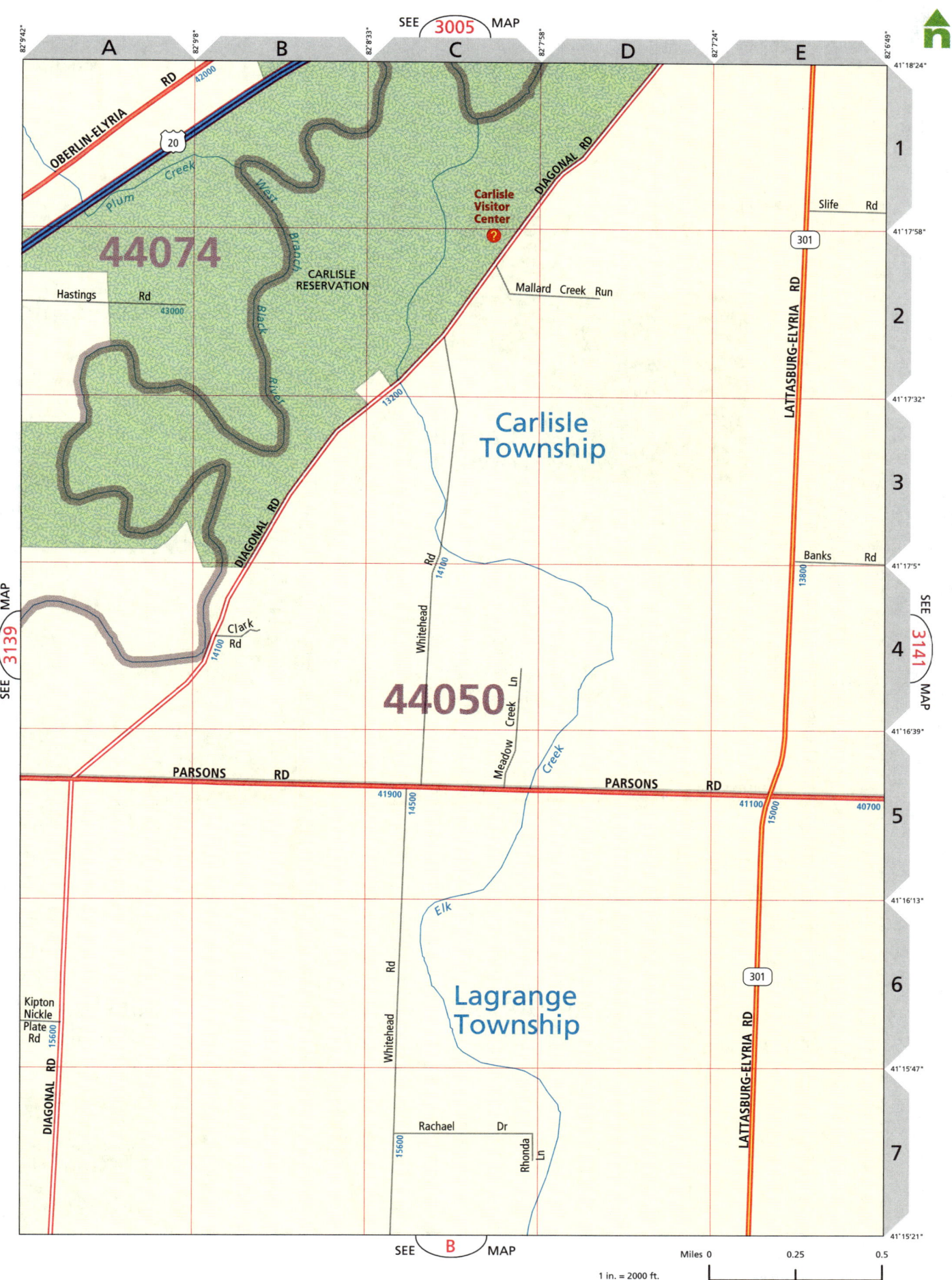

SEE 3005 MAP

82°9'42" 82°9'8" 82°8'33" 82°7'58" 82°7'24" 82°6'49"

A B C D E

OBERLIN-ELYRIA RD
42000
20
Plum Creek
41°18'24"
1

West Branch
Carlisle Visitor Center
?
41°17'58"
44074

CARLISLE RESERVATION
Hastings Rd
43000
Black River
Mallard Creek Run
2

13200
DIAGONAL RD
Carlisle Township
41°17'32"
3

SEE 3139 MAP

Rd 14100
Whitehead
Banks Rd
13800
41°17'5"

SEE 3141 MAP

Clark Rd
14100
44050
Ln
Meadow Creek
Creek
4

41°16'39"

PARSONS RD
41900 14500
Whitehead Rd
PARSONS RD
41100 15000 40700
301
41°16'13"
5

Elk
Lagrange Township
301
6

Kipton Nickle Plate Rd
15600
DIAGONAL RD
Whitehead Rd
15600
LATTASBURG-ELYRIA RD
41°15'47"
7

Rachael Dr
Rhonda Ln

41°15'21"

SEE B MAP

Miles 0   0.25   0.5
1 in. = 2000 ft.

MAP 3141

SEE 3006 MAP

A   B   C   D   E

BRENTWOOD GOLF CLUB

Robson Rd
Robson   Rd   38600
Robson Rd

57
Capel   Rd

Liberty   Ln

ST. MARY'S CEMETERY

Slife   Rd   40400
Slife   Rd

GRAFTON   RD

Eaton Township

River   Ridge   Ct   13000

CARLISLE GOLF CLUB

Carlisle Township

Rader   Ln
Fox   Rd
Oak   Rd
Arbor
Eaton Township   Rd   57
Ct   Rader   Ln   39000

INDIAN HOLLOW RD   13100

Grafton

Banks   Rd   40200   Banks   Rd   39600   13800

44044

Commerce Dr

East   Branch

Black   River

Novak Rd

Hidden   Ln

44050

Gondawood   Ln
Gondawood   Dr

INDIAN HOLLOW RESERVATION

PARSONS   RD   15700   39800   PARSONS   RD   39000   PARSONS   RD   38500

Wheeler   Rd

Lagrange Township

INDIAN   HOLLOW   RD   15200

Grafton Township

CSX   RR   Crook   St   38300

INDIAN HOLLOW RESERVATION

East   Branch   Black   River   Yarish   Rd

SEE B MAP

SEE 3140 MAP

SEE 3142 MAP

0   0.25   0.5   Miles
1 in. = 2000 ft.

82°6'49"   82°6'15"   82°5'40"   82°5'6"   82°4'31"   82°3'56"

41°18'24"
41°17'58"
41°17'32"
41°17'5"
41°16'39"
41°16'13"
41°15'47"
41°15'21"

MAP 3142

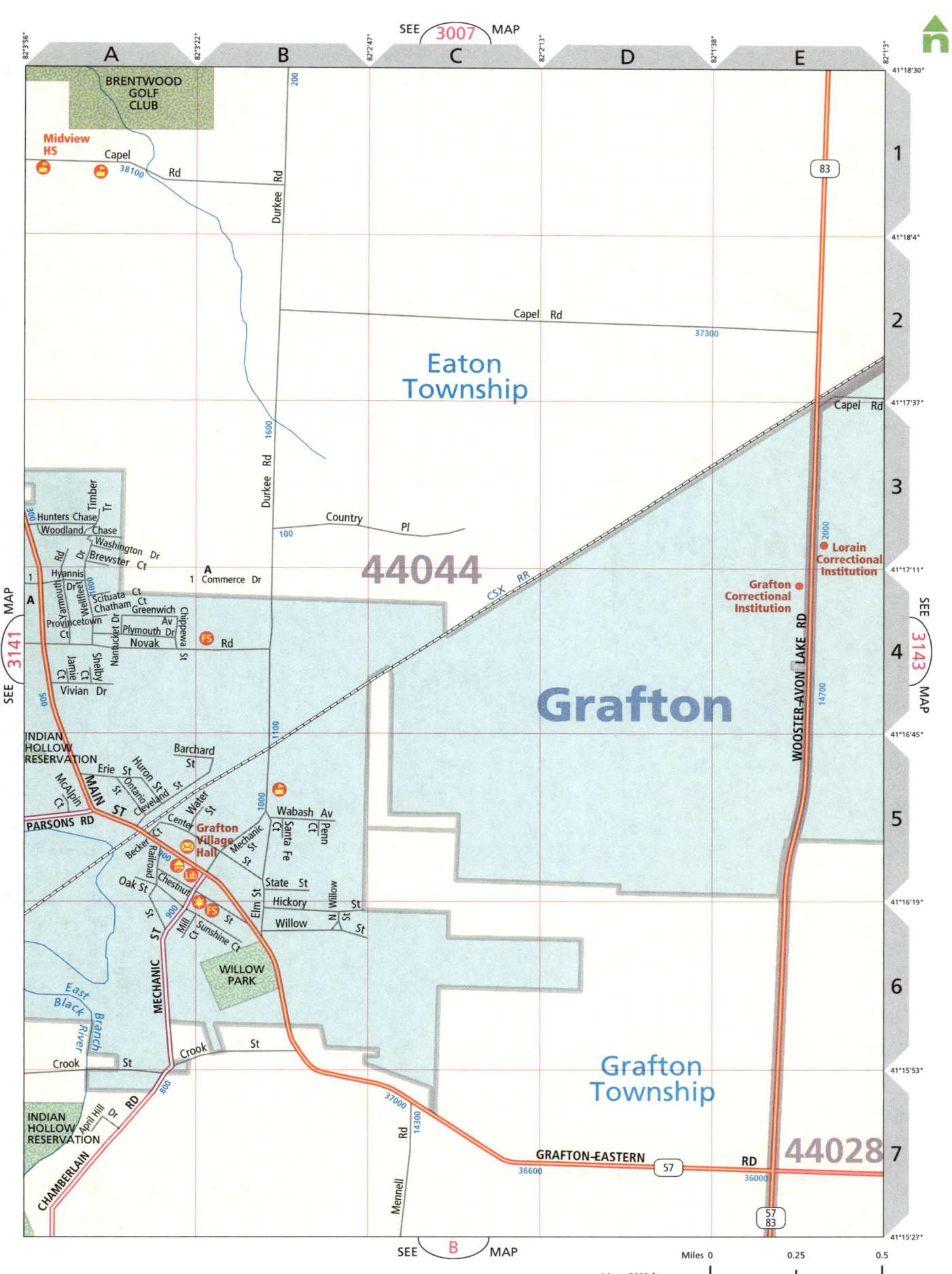

SEE 3007 MAP

A B C D E

82°3'56" 82°3'22" 82°2'47" 82°2'13" 82°1'38" 82°1'13"

41°18'30"

1

BRENTWOOD
GOLF
CLUB

Midview HS

Capel

38100 Rd

Durkee Rd

83

41°18'4"

200

Capel Rd

2

37300

Eaton
Township

Capel Rd

41°17'37"

Durkee Rd

1600

3

300

Country Pl

Hunters Chase

100

Timber Tr

Woodland Chase

Washington Dr

Brewster Ct

2000

Lorain
Correctional
Institution

41°17'11"

Hyannis Dr

A 1 Commerce Dr

44044

Grafton
Correctional
Institution

Scituata Ct

Chatham Ct

Greenwich Av

CSX RR

SEE 3141 MAP

A

1

Provincetown Ct

Yarmouth Rd

Wellfleet Dr

Chippewa St

Plymouth Dr

FS Rd

Nantucket Ct

Novak

4

500

Jamie Ct

Shelby Ct

Vivian Dr

Grafton

Wooster-Avon Lake RD

14700

SEE 3143 MAP

41°16'45"

INDIAN
HOLLOW
RESERVATION

Barchard St

Erie St

Huron St

McAlpin Ct

MAIN ST

Ontario St

Cleveland St

Water St

5

1100

1000

Wabash Av

Penn Ct

Center

Grafton
Village
Hall

Mechanic St

Santa Fe St

PARSONS RD

Becker

Railroad

900

Chestnut

Lib

Oak St

State St

Elm St

Hickory

Willow

N Willow St

St

41°16'19"

FS

St

Mill Ct

Sunshine Ct

MECHANIC ST

900

WILLOW
PARK

6

East Black Branch River

41°15'53"

Crook

Crook St

St

Grafton
Township

INDIAN
HOLLOW
RESERVATION

April Hill Dr

RD

800

37000

Mennell Rd

14300

GRAFTON-EASTERN

57

RD

36000

44028

7

CHAMBERLAIN

36600

57
83

41°15'27"

SEE B MAP

Miles 0   0.25   0.5

1 in. = 2000 ft.

MAP 3143

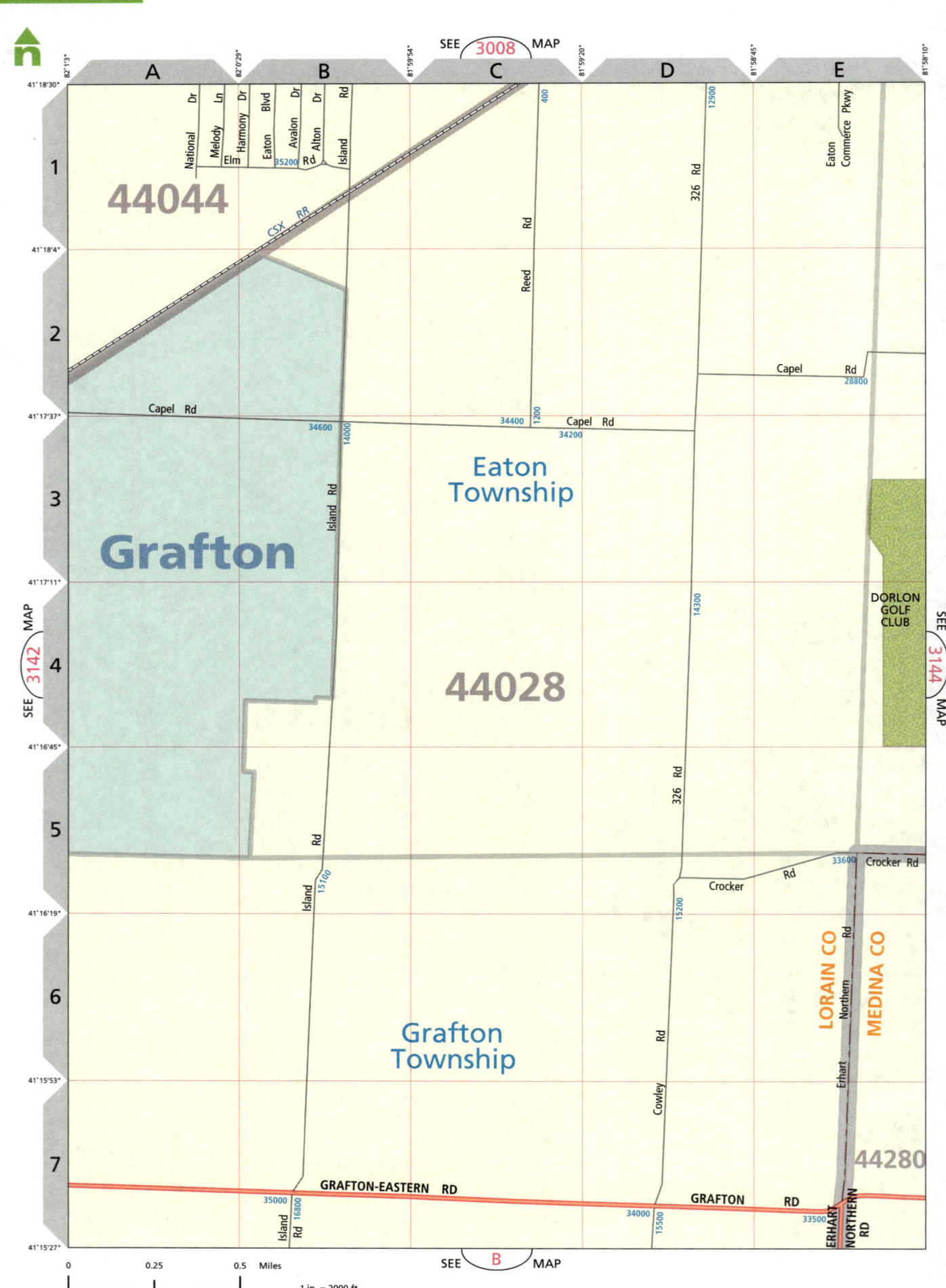

SEE 3008 MAP

A   B   C   D   E

44044

National Dr
Melody Ln
Elm
Harmony Dr
Eaton Blvd
Avalon Dr
Alton Dr
Island Rd

35200
Rd

CSX RR

Eaton Commerce Pkwy

400

12900

326 Rd

Reed Rd

Capel Rd
28800

SEE 3142 MAP

Capel Rd
34600
14000
Island Rd

Capel Rd
34400
1200
34200
Capel Rd

Eaton Township

Grafton

14300

DORLON GOLF CLUB

SEE 3144 MAP

44028

326 Rd

Rd
Island Rd
15100

326 Rd

Crocker Rd
33600
15200
Crocker Rd

Grafton Township

LORAIN CO
MEDINA CO
Northern Rd
Cowley Rd

Erhart

44280

GRAFTON-EASTERN RD
35000
Island Rd
16800

GRAFTON RD
34000
15500
33500
ERHART
NORTHERN RD

SEE B MAP

0   0.25   0.5   Miles

1 in. = 2000 ft.

MAP 3144

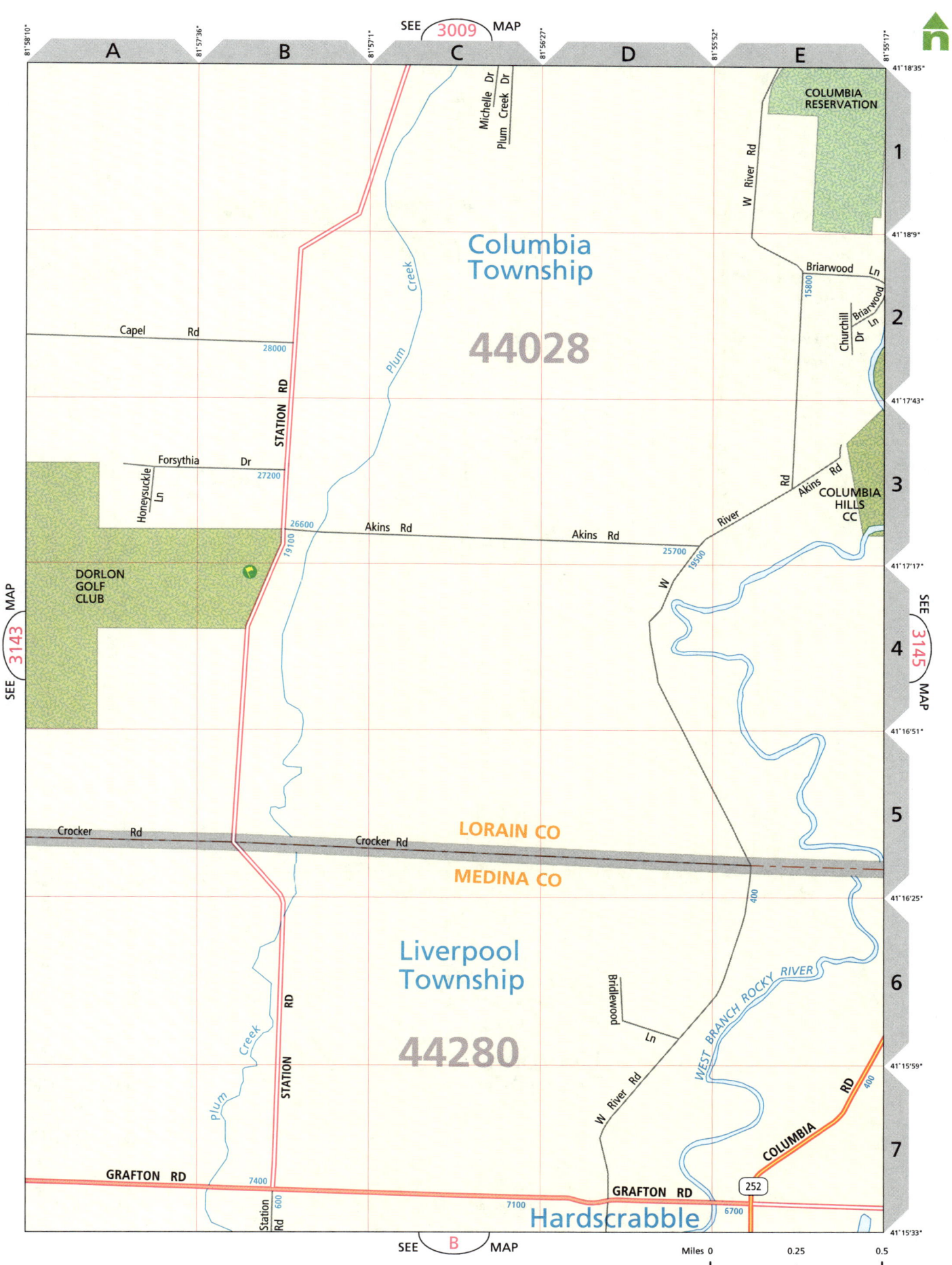

SEE 3009 MAP

A · B · C · D · E

81°58'10" 81°57'36" 81°57'1" 81°56'27" 81°55'52" 81°55'17"

41°18'35"

COLUMBIA
RESERVATION

W River Rd

1

41°18'9"

Columbia
Township

Briarwood Ln

15800

Churchill Dr Briarwood Ln

2

41°17'43"

Capel Rd
28000

44028

STATION RD

Plum Creek

Michelle Dr
Plum Creek Dr

Forsythia Dr
27200

Honeysuckle Ln

River Rd Akins Rd

COLUMBIA
HILLS
CC

3

41°17'17"

26600 Akins Rd Akins Rd
25700
19500

19100

DORLON
GOLF
CLUB

W River

SEE 3143 MAP

SEE 3145 MAP

4

41°16'51"

Crocker Rd

LORAIN CO

Crocker Rd

5

MEDINA CO

41°16'25"

Liverpool
Township

400

6

44280

STATION RD

Plum Creek

Bridlewood Ln

WEST BRANCH ROCKY RIVER

41°15'59"

W River Rd

COLUMBIA RD

400

7

GRAFTON RD
7400

Station Rd
600

GRAFTON RD

252

41°15'33"

7100 6700

Hardscrabble

SEE B MAP

Miles 0   0.25   0.5

1 in. = 2000 ft.

MAP 3145

SEE 3010 MAP

A   B   C   D   E

WEST BRANCH ROCKY RIVER

COLUMBIA RESERVATION

Briarwood Ln

252

Andees Dr

Squires Rd

S Boone Rd

Cayuga Dr

S Marks Rd

LORAIN CO

CUYAHOGA CO

Ascoa Ct

24400

17900

HICKORY NUT GOLF CLUB

44028

Columbia Township

COLUMBIA HILLS COUNTRY CLUB

E RIVER RD

S Boone Rd

Louise Ln

Lunn Dr

Strongsville

Industrial Park

Morgan Ct

18000

Emmons Rd

24000

16300

Emmons Rd

23000

18000

SEE 3144 MAP

Boone Rd

18800

SEE 3146 MAP

44136

S Marks Rd

18700

Marks Rd

CSX RR

LORAIN CO

Boston Rd

Boston Rd

MEDINA CO

S

252

COLUMBIA RD

300

Boston Rd

6200

6000

Boston Lake Dr

BOSTON RD

Boston

Reserve Ln

Roxanne Ln

MARKS RD

BEEBETOWN CEM

44212

44280

Liverpool Township

Cheyney Ln

Brunswick Hills Township

300

Mack Dr

Rita Dr

Pauline Dr

Liverpool Dr

Crane Dr

Bonneybrook Ln

GRAFTON RD

GRAFTON RD

6000

5900

5400

GRAFTON RD

600

41°18'35"
41°18'9"
41°17'43"
41°17'17"
41°16'51"
41°16'25"
41°15'59"
41°15'33"

81°55'17"
81°54'43"
81°54'8"
81°53'34"
81°52'59"
81°52'24"

1
2
3
4
5
6
7

SEE B MAP

0   0.25   0.5   Miles

1 in. = 2000 ft.

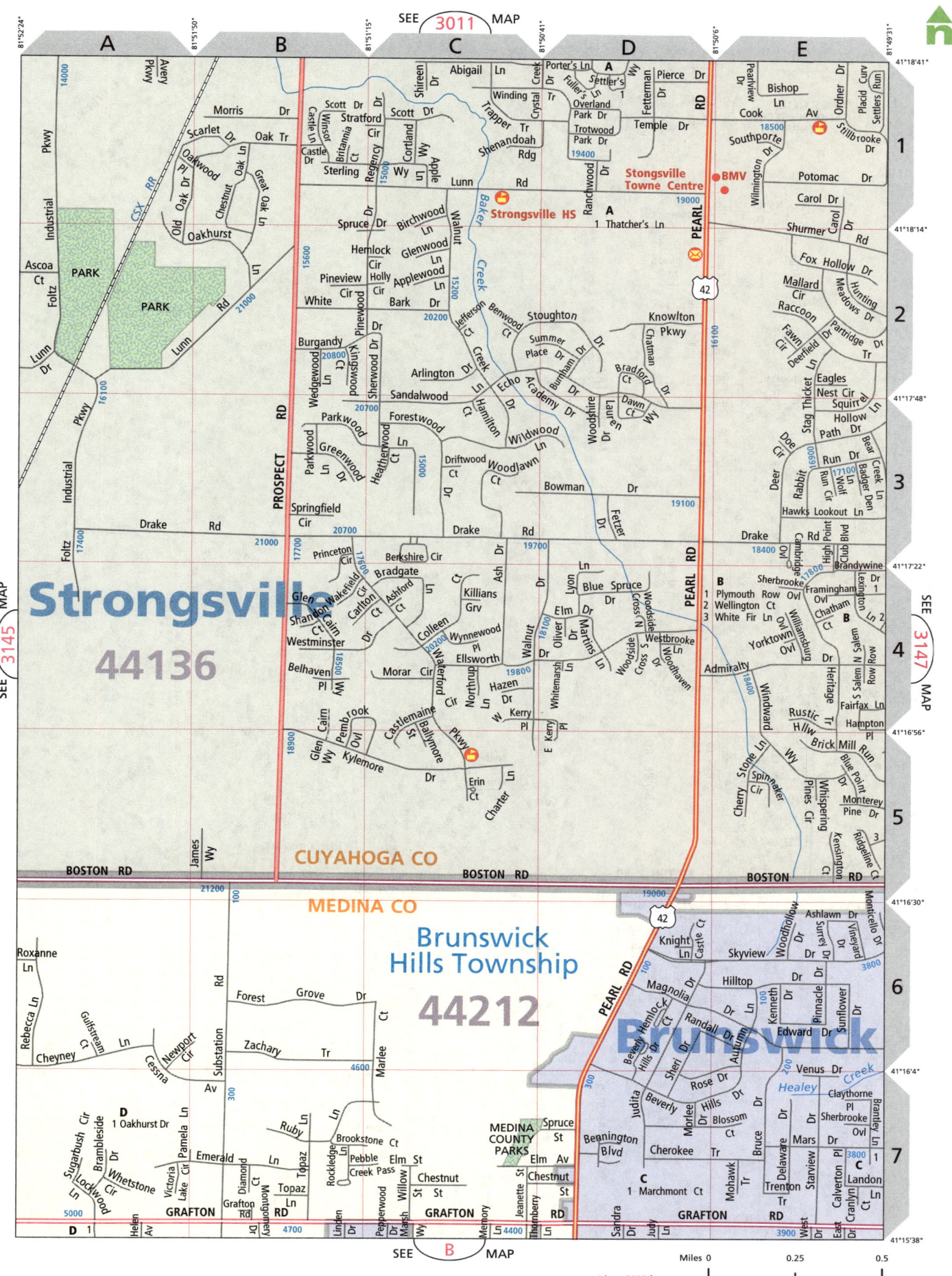

MAP 3146

SEE 3011 MAP

SEE 3145 MAP

SEE 3147 MAP

SEE B MAP

Strongsville
44136

CUYAHOGA CO

MEDINA CO

Brunswick Hills Township
44212

Brunswick

MEDINA COUNTY PARKS

Miles 0   0.25   0.5

1 in. = 2000 ft.

MAP 3147

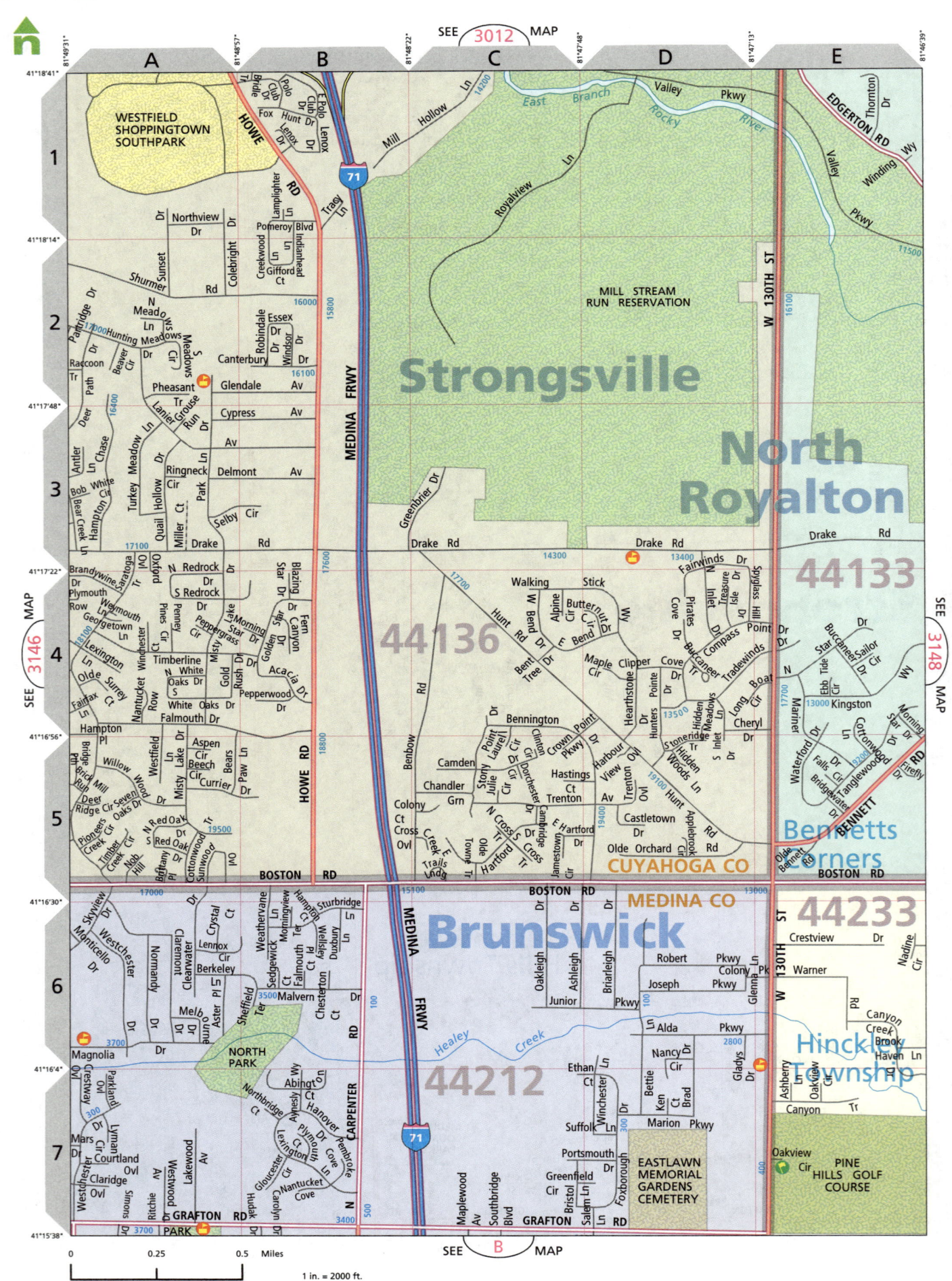

SEE 3012 MAP

WESTFIELD SHOPPINGTOWN SOUTHPARK

MILL STREAM RUN RESERVATION

Strongsville

North Royalton

44133

44136

CUYAHOGA CO

MEDINA CO

Brunswick

44233

44212

Hinckley Township

BENNETTS Corners

EASTLAWN MEMORIAL GARDENS CEMETERY

PINE HILLS GOLF COURSE

SEE 3146 MAP

SEE 3148 MAP

SEE B MAP

0   0.25   0.5 Miles
1 in. = 2000 ft.

MAP 3148

SEE 3013 MAP

A   B   C   D   E

81°46'38"   81°46'4"   81°45'29"   81°44'55"   81°44'20"   81°43'46"

41°18'46"

14100   King Arthur Ct   Lancelot Ln E   Merlin Ovl
Eagle Nest Dr   Quail Ridge Dr   Pheasant Run Cir   Lancelot Ln W

80

N Gateway Dr   8300   Center Dr   Hillside Dr
S Gateway Dr   Dan Dr

Cross Creek Ln

Royal Ridge Ln

North Royalton HS   NORTH ROYALTON MEMORIAL PARK

1

Akins   Rd   10000   9600   Akins   Rd   N Akins Rd

BENNETT RD

S Gateway Dr   8300

Akins   Rd   7200

YORK ROAD RECREATION FIELD

YORK RD

Martin Dr   Foldesy Ln

BRECKSVILLE RESERVATION

41°18'19"

OHIO TPK

Willow Lake Dr

80

Valley   Pkwy   Lindberg Dr   Louis Dr   9200   Valley   Pkwy   7200   15800

41°17'53"

2

EDGERTON RD   10600

ROYALTON CEM   16400   EDGERTON   RD

RIDGE RD

8000   EDGERTON   RD   5800

3

MILL STREAM RUN RESERVATION

RD

16700   Parkside Dr   BENNETT   A   A
1 W Ravine View Ct
2 E Ravine View Ct

North Royalton
44133

3

Drake   Rd   11000

River   Donmar Rd   Rock Ledge Wy   Rock Ln   Valley Blvd   River Run Ln   River   1 Marsh Harbor 2   Ct

East   Branch   Rocky   River

41°17'27"

SEE 3147 MAP

Kingston Wy   Kingston   Wy   Crystal Springs Dr   Hidden Valley Dr   Crystal Lakes Dr   Rock   Dr

Nottingham   Dr   Friar Post Pkwy   Buckingham Shire

Cady   Rd   5700

4

41°17'1"

SEE 3149 MAP

Founders Ct   Greyfriars Cir   Rye Gate   Cavendish Ct   Montague Ct
Spindlewood Ct   Harrow   Pl   Hardwood Tr   Tr
11900   Beckenham Ln   Rd   Fawnhaven Dr   20800   Sundown Tr   Tr
Lytle   Rd   Queensbridge   20900   Forest Glen Dr   Evergreen   20900

Wiltshire Rd

5

Whitestone Ct   20900

BOSTON   RD   11000   BOSTON   RD   9100   **CUYAHOGA CO**   6400   Boston   Rd   Wiltshire   Rd   Oakwood Ln

41°16'35"

MEDINA CO

Nadine Cir   Blvd   Dale Brook Cir   Brookside   Blvd   Blvd   100   Newbury Ovl   Dr   Providence Dr   Ct
Parkridge Dr   Lakecrest   Willow Brook Ln   Salem   Healey   Creek

Hinckley Township
44233

VALLEAIRE GOLF CLUB   Boston Rd

6

Brook   Brook Hollow Ovl   Concord Ln Cir   Somerset Ln   Plymouth Ovl   200
Brook   Haven Ln   Valley Brook Ovl   Oxford

Canyon Creek Dr   Babbling Ovl   Brook   Brookshire Ovl   Valley Brook Ovl

RIDGE RD   400

7

PINE HILLS GOLF COURSE

41°16'9"

41°15'43"

SEE B MAP

Miles 0   0.25   0.5

1 in. = 2000 ft.

MAP 3149

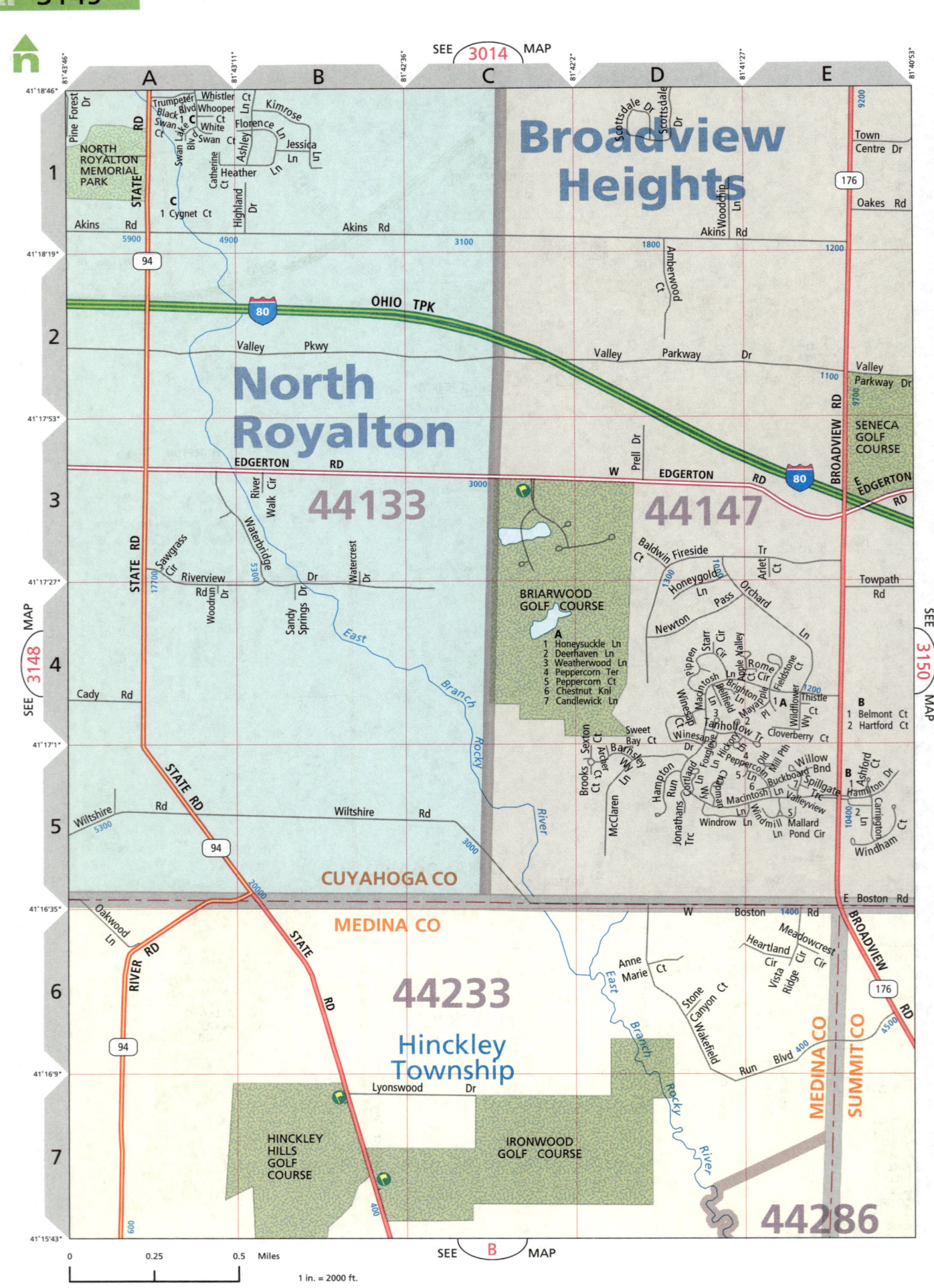

MAP 3149

SEE 3014 MAP

Broadview Heights

North Royalton

44133

44147

OHIO TPK

EDGERTON RD

CUYAHOGA CO

MEDINA CO

44233

Hinckley Township

BRIARWOOD GOLF COURSE

A
1 Honeysuckle Ln
2 Deerhaven Ln
3 Weatherwood Ln
4 Peppercorn Ter
5 Peppercorn Ct
6 Chestnut Knl
7 Candlewick Ln

B
1 Belmont Ct
2 Hartford Ct

B
1 Ashford Ct
2 Carrington Ct

SENECA GOLF COURSE

NORTH ROYALTON MEMORIAL PARK

HINCKLEY HILLS GOLF COURSE

IRONWOOD GOLF COURSE

44286

SEE 3148 MAP

SEE 3150 MAP

SEE B MAP

0   0.25   0.5 Miles

1 in. = 2000 ft.

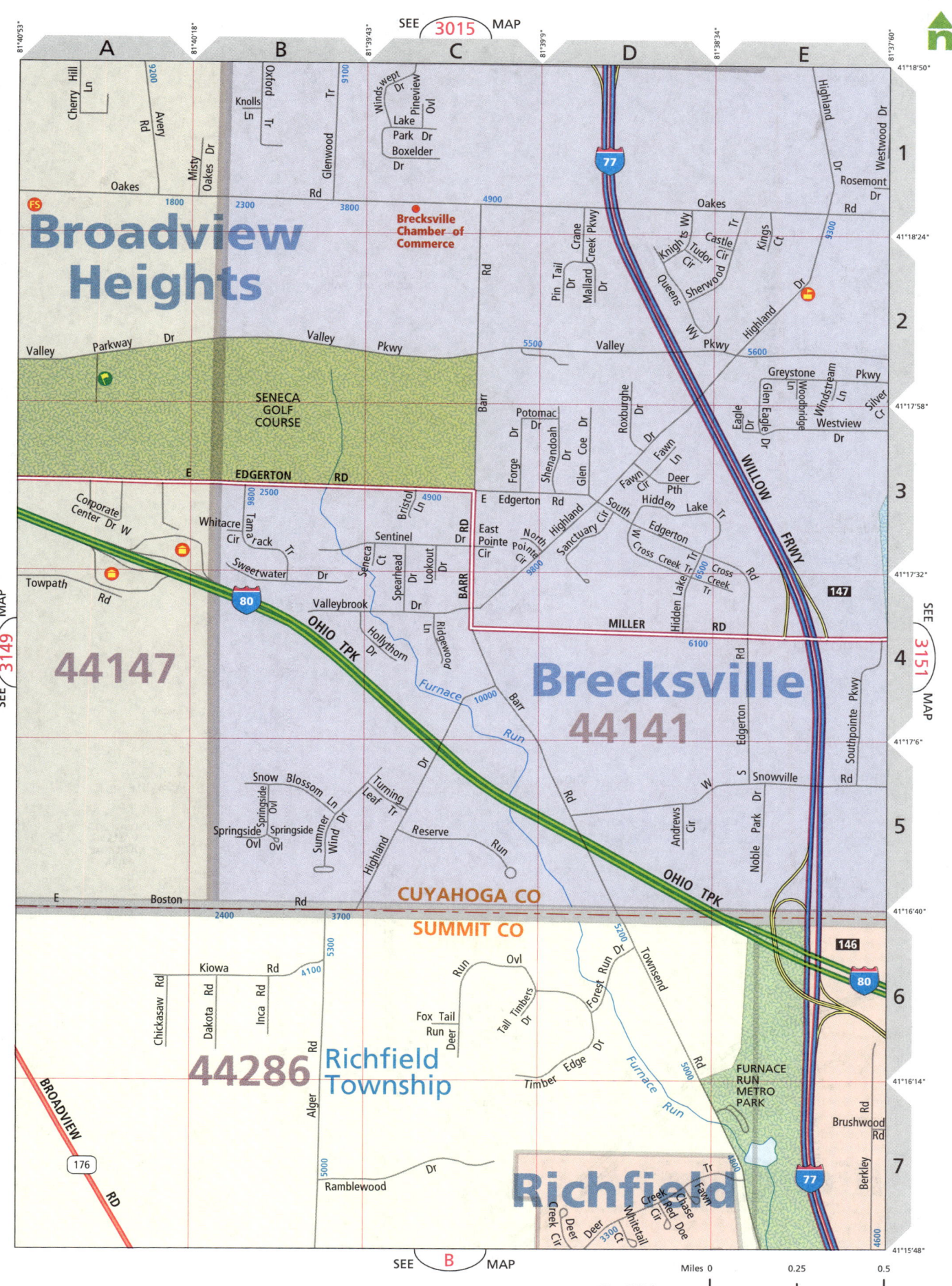

MAP 3150

SEE 3015 MAP

A B C D E

1
2
3
4
5
6
7

9200
Cherry Hill Ln
Avery Rd
Oakes
Misty Oaks Dr
1800

Knolls Ln
Oxford Tr
Glenwood Tr
9000
Rd
2300
3800

Windswept Dr
Pineview Ovl
Lake Park Dr
Boxelder Dr

Brecksville Chamber of Commerce
4900

Highland Dr
Westwood Dr
Rosemont Dr

FS
Broadview Heights

Rd

Crane Creek Pkwy
Pin Tail Dr
Mallard Dr
Queens Wy
Knights Wy
Tudor Cir
Castle Cir
Sherwood
Oakes Rd
Kings Tr
Kings Ct
Highland Dr
9300

Valley Parkway Dr
Valley Pkwy
Valley Pkwy
5500
Valley Pkwy
Highland Pkwy
5600

Greystone Pkwy
Glen Eagle Ln
Woodbridge Ln
Windstream Ln
Silver Cr
Westview Dr

SENECA GOLF COURSE

Barr Rd

Potomac Dr
Forge Dr
Shenandoah Dr
Glen Coe Dr
Roxburghe Dr
Fawn Ln
Fawn Cir
Fawn Dr
Deer Pth
Eagle Dr
Glen Eagle Dr

WILLOW FRWY

E EDGERTON RD

E Edgerton Rd
South Highland Dr
Hidden Lake Tr
Edgerton Rd

Corporate Center Dr W
Whitacre Cir
Tamarack Tr
2500
Bristol Ln
4900
Sentinel Ct
Seneca Ct
Spearhead Dr
Lookout Dr
Dr
BARR RD
East Pointe Cir
North Pointe Cir
Sanctuary Cir
South
Hidden Lake Tr
W Cross Creek Tr
6500
Cross Creek Tr
9600
Edgerton Rd
147

Towpath Rd
Sweetwater Dr
I-80
OHIO TPK
Valleybrook Dr
Hollythorn Dr
Ridgewood Ln
Furnace Run
Barr Run Dr

44147

Brecksville
44141

MILLER RD
6100

Snow Blossom Ln
Springside Ovl
Springside Ovl
Springside Ovl
Summer Wind Dr
Turning Leaf Tr
Reserve Run
Highland Run

Edgerton Rd
W Snowville Rd
S
Andrews Cir
Noble Park Dr
Southpointe Pkwy

E Boston Rd
2400 3700

CUYAHOGA CO
SUMMIT CO

146
I-80

Chickasaw Rd
Dakota Rd
Inca Rd
Kiowa Rd
4100
5300

Run Ovl
Fox Tail Run
Deer Run
Tall Timbers Dr
Timber Edge Dr
Forest Run Dr
Townsend Rd
5200

FURNACE RUN METRO PARK

Brushwood Rd

44286
Richfield Township

Alger Rd
5000
Ramblewood Dr

Furnace Run
5000

OHIO TPK

Berkley Dr
4800

BROADVIEW RD
176

Richfield
Deer Creek Cir
Whitetail Ct
3300
Fawn Creek Cir
Chase Cir
Red Doe Cir
4600
I-77

SEE B MAP

Miles 0   0.25   0.5
1 in. = 2000 ft.

81°40'53" 81°40'18" 81°39'43" 81°39'9" 81°38'34" 81°37'60"
41°18'50" 41°18'24" 41°17'58" 41°17'32" 41°17'6" 41°16'40" 41°16'14" 41°15'48"

SEE 3149 MAP
SEE 3151 MAP

MAP 3151

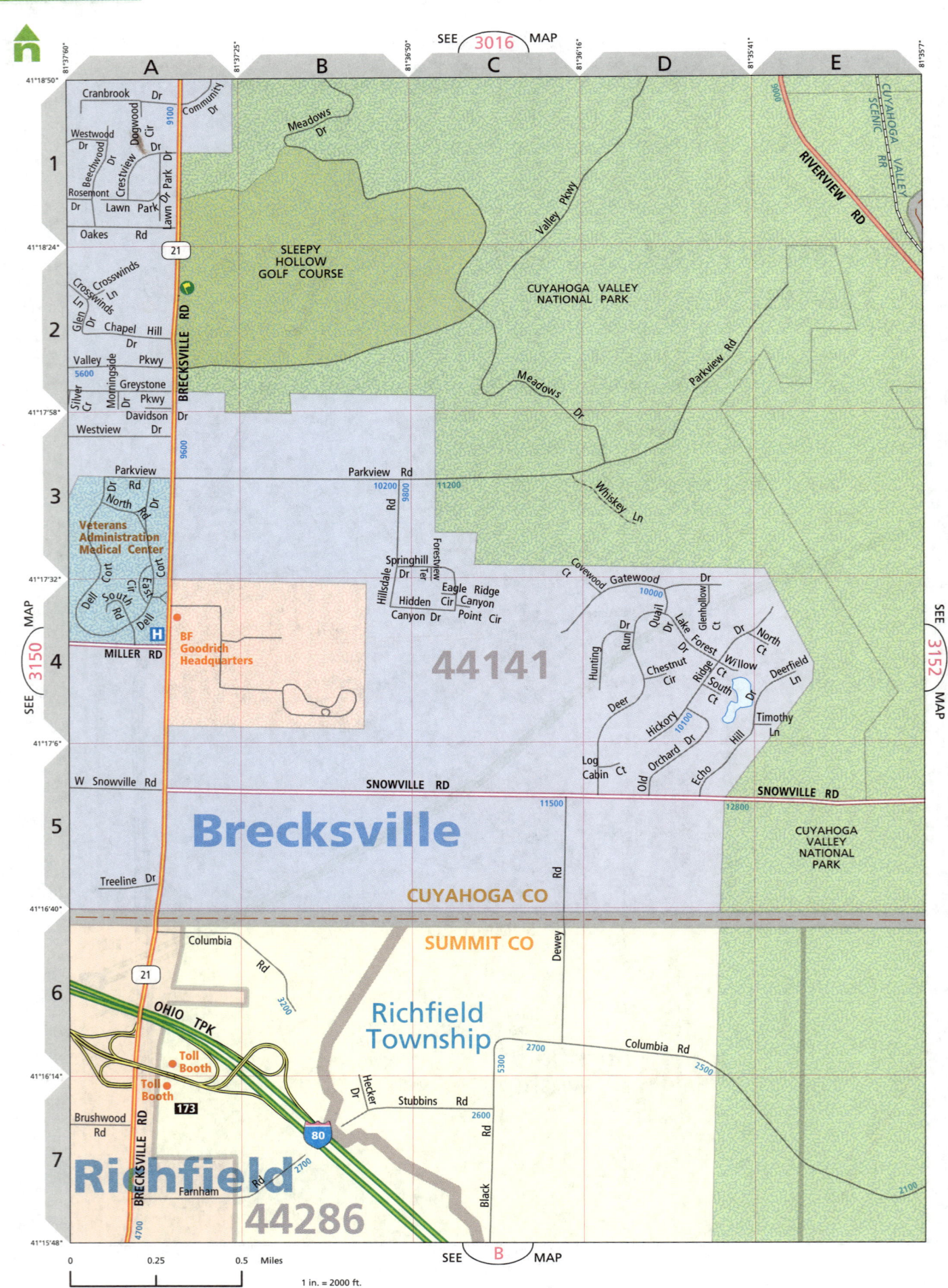

SEE 3016 MAP

SEE 3150 MAP

SEE 3152 MAP

Brecksville

44141

CUYAHOGA CO

SUMMIT CO

Richfield Township

SLEEPY HOLLOW GOLF COURSE

CUYAHOGA VALLEY NATIONAL PARK

CUYAHOGA VALLEY NATIONAL PARK

Veterans Administration Medical Center

BF Goodrich Headquarters

Richfield

44286

OHIO TPK

Toll Booth

Toll Booth

0   0.25   0.5   Miles

1 in. = 2000 ft.

SEE B MAP

MAP 3152

SEE 3017 MAP

SEE 3151 MAP

SEE 3153 MAP

SEE B MAP

A
1 Carter Rd
2 N Gannett Rd
3 Locust Cir
4 Sagamore Hills Blvd
5 N Boyden Rd
6 French Dr

82

W 6 AURORA RD
AURORA RD

Northfield Center Town Hall

Northfield Center

Smithfield Dr
Fleetwood Dr
Trailside Dr
Amherst Dr
Village Pkwy
Arboretum Cir
Spafford Ct
Village Club Dr
Tinkers Ln
Brittany Ct
Chandler Ct
Windsor Rd
Holzhauer
Canyon View Rd
Hampton Ct
Greengate
Greenwood
Geddes
Bluff Ln
Millrace
Pine Valley Ct
Stoney Brook Rd
Cranberry Tr
College Dr
Old North Dr
Brandywine Dr
Ballantrae Dr

Trimble Pl
Cedar Grove
Ironwood Tr
Hemlock Cir
Spiders Ln
Pinewood View Rd
Cone Ovl
Morning Sta Tr
Pine Tr
Timberline Tr
Fieldcrest
Meadow Creek Rd
Ravenhill Dr
Greenwood Ct
Rivendell Rd
Timbercreek Rd
Woodbridge Tr
Carriage Tr

Carlin Rd
Forsythe Blvd
Shearer Rd
Rehwinkle Rd

Sagamore Hills Township

Crestwood Ln
Surry Dr
Morningside Rd
Fairhaven Dr
Marwyck Dr

Meadowview Dr
Hrovat Dr

S Boyden Rd

McNeil Dr
Kingsview Dr
Ln
Kiltie Ln
Inverlane Rd

Lowell Ln
Beacon Hill
Skylane Dr
Blvd

Barton Rd
Glencrest Rd
S Boyden Rd
W Highland Rd

Metro Parks Bike & Hike Tr

44067

ALL SAINTS CEM

Dover Lake Waterpark
Brandywine Ski Resort

W Highland Rd

Vaughn Rd

Brandywine Creek

Brandywine Rd

CUYAHOGA CO
SUMMIT CO

RIVERVIEW RD

CUYAHOGA VALLEY NAT'L PARK

CUYAHOGA VALLEY NATIONAL PARK

Trail

Brecksville

SNOWVILLE RD

Latta Ln

Stanford Rd

44141

CUYAHOGA VALLEY SCENIC RR

CUYAHOGA RIVER

Stanford Rd

Trail

CUYAHOGA VALLEY NATIONAL PARK

271

Hill Rd
W Hines Rd

Boston Township

Columbia Rd

RIVERVIEW RD

Boston Mills Ski Resort

Main St
Center St
Boston Mills Rd

CUYAHOGA VALLEY NATIONAL PARK

Miles 0   0.25   0.5

1 in. = 2000 ft.

MAP 3153

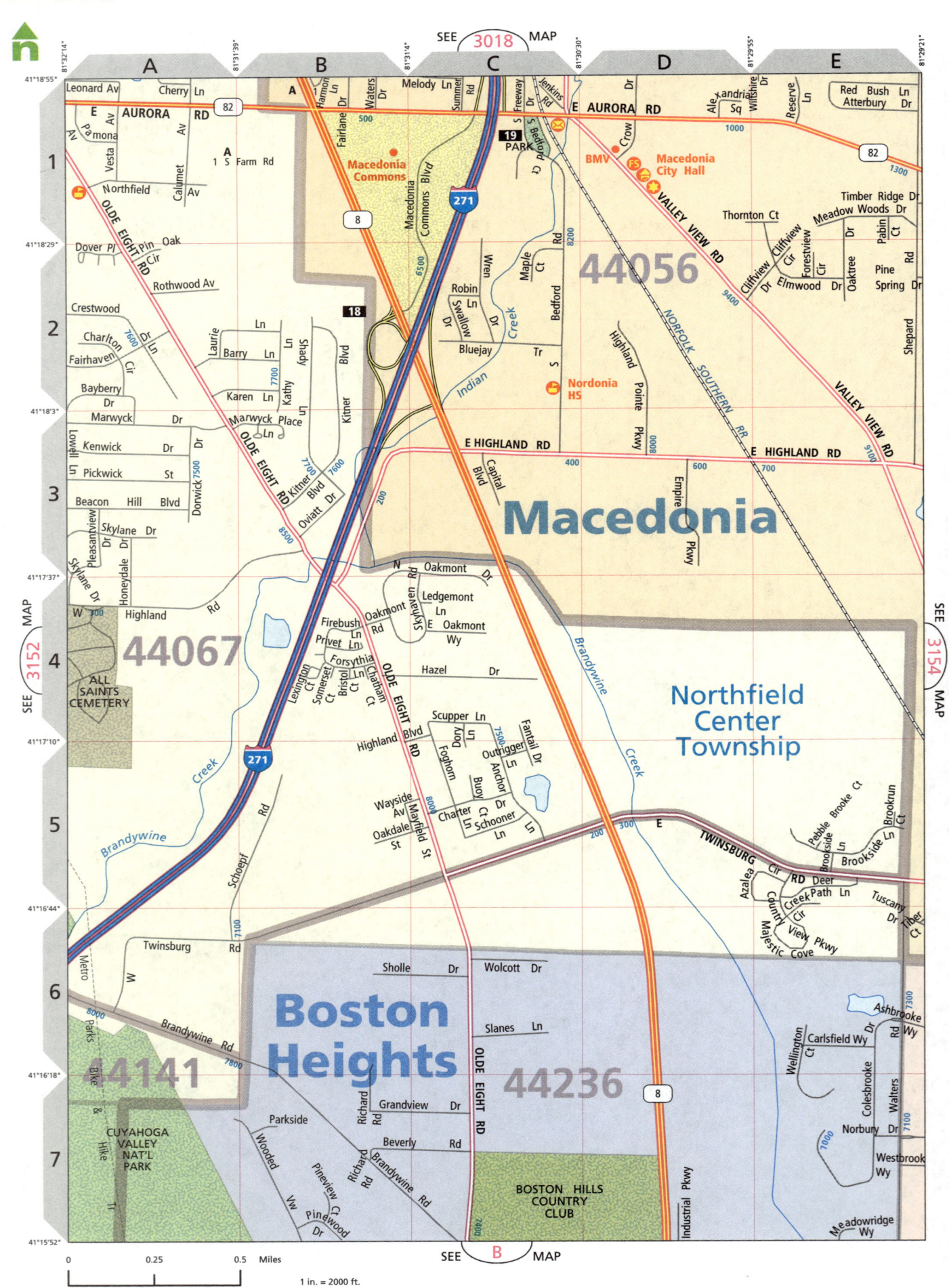

SEE 3018 MAP

A B C D E

81°32'14" 81°31'39" 81°31'4" 81°30'30" 81°29'55" 81°29'21"

41°18'55'

Leonard Av | Cherry Ln | 82 | Harmon Dr | Waters Dr | Melody Ln | Summer Rd | Jenkins Dr | E AURORA RD | Alexandria Sq | Wiltshire Dr | Reserve | Red Bush Ln | Atterbury Dr

E Av | AURORA RD | Pomona

1

Vesta Av | 1 S Farm Rd | A | Fairlane | 500 | Macedonia Commons | 19 PARK | Crow | BMV | FS | Macedonia City Hall | 82 | 1300

Northfield | Calumet Av | Macedonia Commons Blvd | 271 | 8 | Bedford | Valley View Rd | Thornton Ct | Cliffview Cir | Forestview Cir | Meadow Woods Dr | Pabin Ct | Timber Ridge Dr

Dover Pl | Pin Oak Cir | 8 | 6500 | Wren Dr | Maple Ct | Rd | 8200 | 44056 | Cliffview Dr | Elmwood Dr | Oaktree Dr | Pine Spring Dr | Rd

Rothwood Av | 18 | Robin Ln | Swallow Dr | Bedford | Creek | Highland Pointe Pkwy | Norfolk Southern RR | 9400 | Shepard

2

Crestwood | Laurie Ln | Shady Blvd | Bluejay | Tr S | 0008 | 9100

Charlton Dr Ln | 7600 | Barry Ln | Kathy | 7700 | Kitner | Indian | Nordonia HS | E HIGHLAND RD | 400 | E HIGHLAND RD | 600 | 700

Fairhaven Cir | Karen Ln | Marwyck Place | Kitner Blvd | 7600

Bayberry Dr | Marwyck Dr | Oviatt Dr | Olde Eight Rd | Donwick | 7500 | 200 | Capital Blvd | Macedonia | Empire Pkwy

3

Lowell | Kenwick Dr | 8500 | Skylane Dr

Pickwick St

Beacon Hill Blvd

Pleasantview Dr | Skylane Dr | Honeydale | Highland | Rd | N | Oakmont Dr | Ledgemont Ln | E Oakmont Wy | Brandywine | Northfield Center Township

41°17'37'

W 300 | 44067 | Firebush Ln | Oakmont Rd | Skyhaven Rd | Creek

4

ALL SAINTS CEMETERY | Privet Ln | Forsythia Ln | Hazel Dr

Lexington Ct | Somerset Ct | Bristol Ct | Chatham Ct | Olde Eight Rd

Creek | 271 | Scupper Ln | Fantail Dr | Pebble Brooke Ct | Brookrun Ct

Highland Blvd | Foghorn | Buoy | Outrigger Dr | Anchor Dr | 7500 | Brookside Ln | Brookside Ln

5

Brandywine | Wayside Av | Charter Ct | Buoy Ct | Schooner Dr | 800 | Azalea Cir | Deer Creek Path Ln | Tuscany Dr | Tiber Ct

Schoepf Rd | Oakdale St | Mayfield St | 200 300 | E TWINSBURG RD | County View Cir | Majestic Cove | Pkwy

41°16'44'

7100 | Twinsburg Rd | Sholle Dr | Wolcott Dr | Wellington Ct | Carlsfield Wy | Dr | Ashbrooke Rd | Wy | 7300

6

Metro | W | Brandywine Rd | Boston Heights | Slanes Ln | Olde Eight Rd | Colesbrooke Dr | Walters Dr | 7100

8000 | Parks | 7800 | Richard Rd | Grandview Dr | 44236 | 8 | 7060 | Norbury Dr

44141 | Bike & | Parkside | Beverly Rd | Westbrook Wy

7

CUYAHOGA VALLEY NAT'L PARK | Hike & Tr | Wooded Vw | Pineview Ct | Richard Rd | Brandywine Rd | Pinewood Dr | BOSTON HILLS COUNTRY CLUB | Industrial Pkwy | 7800 | Meadowridge Wy

41°15'52'

SEE B MAP

0 0.25 0.5 Miles

1 in. = 2000 ft.

SEE 3152 MAP

SEE 3154 MAP

MAP 3154

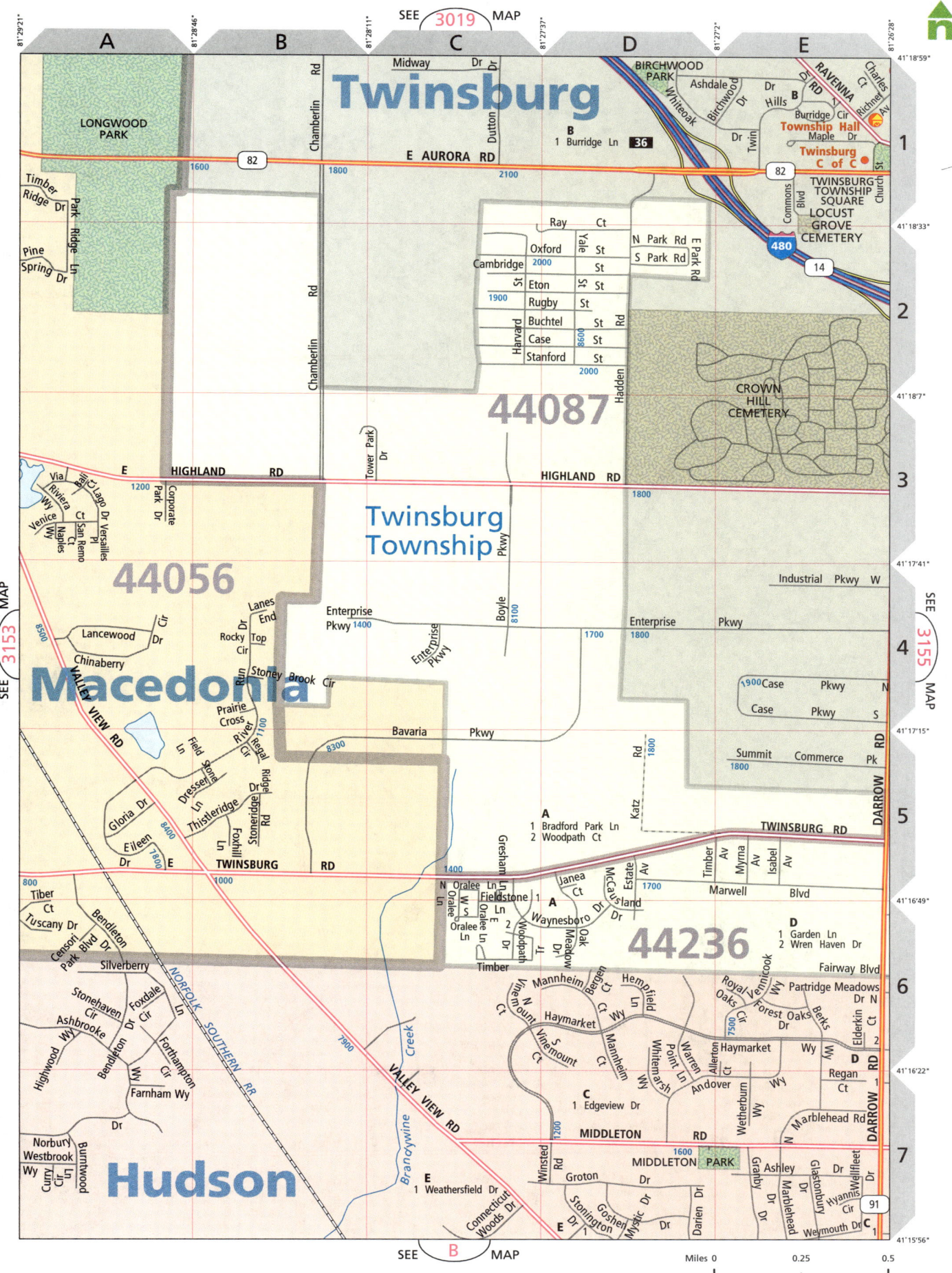

SEE 3019 MAP

Twinsburg

Longwood Park

Birchwood Park

Township Hall
Twinsburg C of C

TWINSBURG TOWNSHIP SQUARE
LOCUST GROVE CEMETERY

CROWN HILL CEMETERY

44087

44056

Macedonia

Twinsburg Township

44236

Hudson

SEE 3153 MAP

SEE 3155 MAP

SEE B MAP

E AURORA RD

HIGHLAND RD

HIGHLAND RD

Enterprise Pkwy

Bavaria Pkwy

TWINSBURG RD

TWINSBURG RD

MIDDLETON RD

MIDDLETON PARK

Miles 0   0.25   0.5

1 in. = 2000 ft.

A 1 Burridge Ln

A 1 Bradford Park Ln 2 Woodpath Ct

D 1 Garden Ln 2 Wren Haven Dr

C 1 Edgeview Dr

E 1 Weathersfield Dr

MAP 3155

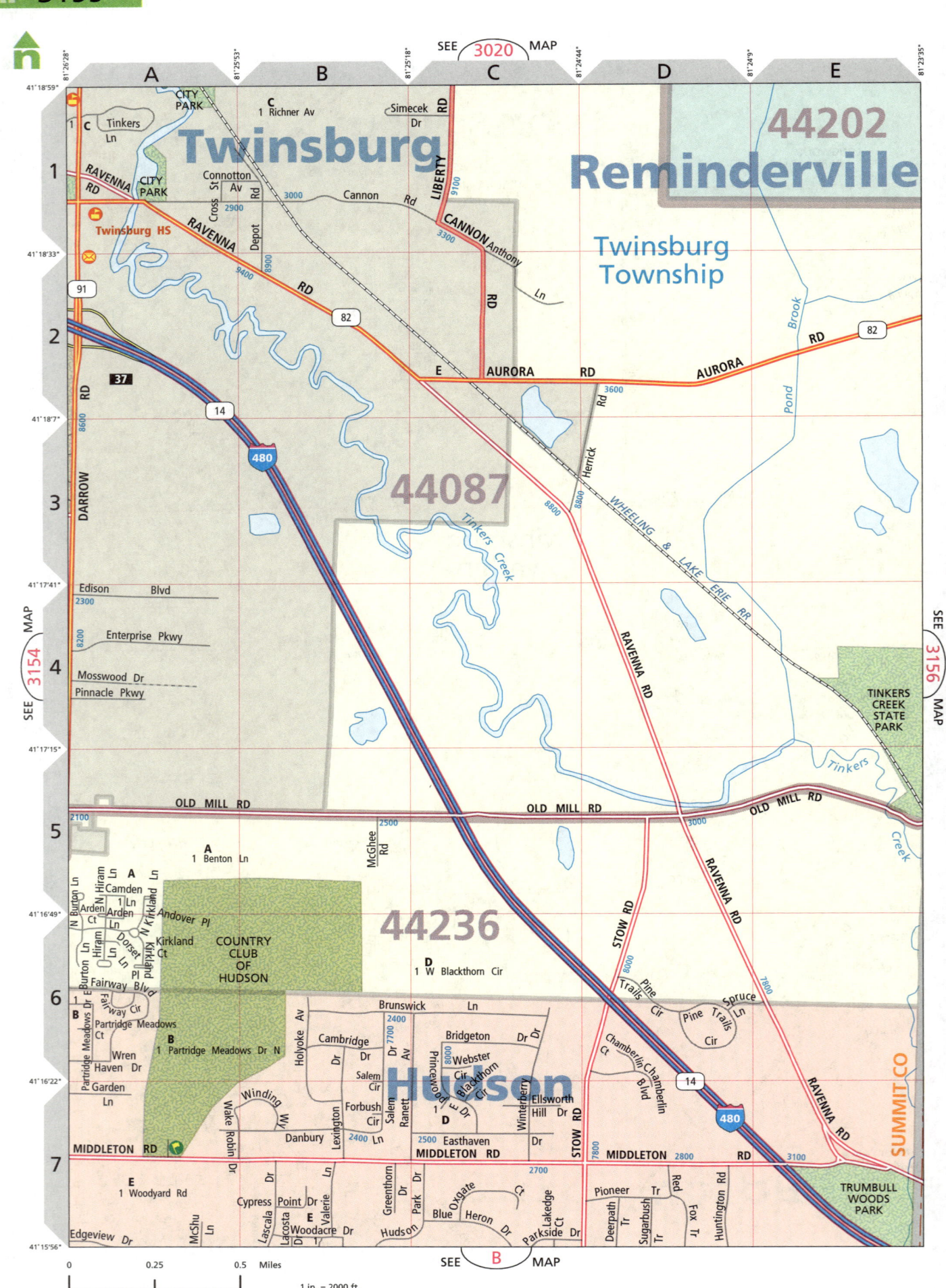

SEE 3020 MAP
SEE 3154 MAP
SEE 3156 MAP
SEE B MAP

44202
Reminderville

Twinsburg

Twinsburg Township

44087

44236

Hudson

COUNTRY CLUB OF HUDSON

SUMMIT CO

TINKERS CREEK STATE PARK

TRUMBULL WOODS PARK

CITY PARK

Twinsburg HS

Tinkers Creek

Wheeling & Lake Erie RR

Pond Brook

Tinkers Creek

0   0.25   0.5 Miles

1 in. = 2000 ft.

MAP 3156

SEE 3021 MAP

A | B | C | D | E

81°23'35" 81°22'60" 81°22'25" 81°21'51" 81°21'16" 81°20'42"

Riley Rd 1000 Dr

Hedgecliff St Rd Ash Grove Cir Beaumont Tr Parkway Countrywood Tr Blvd

82 TWINSBURG WARREN'S RD 306

Maple Ln 43 City Hall

W Parkway Cambridge Blvd Cochran Pinehurst Dr Linwood Ln Trc Clayton Woodland Clearbrook Ln Elmwood Treetop Ct Oaklawn Ct Shadowbrook Daleview Parkway Pt Dr

Aurora Commons Cir Aurora Commons Cir AURORA CITY CEMETERY

AURORA RD C of C S CHILLICOTHE RD 306

Chesterton Ln Chesterton Ct W Pioneer Tr W Pioneer Tr Poplar Ct 200 E Pioneer Tr

KIWANIS-MOORE PARK

TWINSBURG WARREN RD 1100 82

Inwood Tr Ravine Dr S Pine N Pine Ironwood White Aspen Oak

41°19'3"

41°18'37"

A
1 Arboretum Ct
2 Cherry Ridge Dr
3 Fountain View Tr
4 Glen Hollow Cir

Wood Ridge Rd Bent Creek Ovl Beech Ct Birchbark

WALDEN LAKE Red Fawn Pth White Tail Dr Windward Dr Honeysuckle Pth Laurel Cir Hawthorne Cedar Dogwood Tr Rd Heather

B
1 Chandler Pth
2 Concord Downs Cir
3 Concord Downs Ln
4 Concord Downs Pth
5 Meadowview Dr
6 Windward Cir

41°18'11"

Aurora Premium Outlets

Antler Pt Deer Pth Chandler Dr Dr Bramble Ln Willow Cir Ridgeway Chandler Ln B Pond

44202 Deer Run Buck Cross Walden Run Hill Dr Knollwood Dr

C
1 Chatham Dr
2 Chelmsford Dr

Deer Island Arbor Wy Fairington Dr Overlook Dr AURORA HUDSON RD Parkview N Briarcliff Dr Carriage Sq Kingston Dr Pine Villa Tr

D Cross Creek Ln Russett Woods Ln Creekside Dr Devorah Dr Timber Ln 700

WALDEN COUNTRY CLUB

D
1 Fairington Ln
2 Fairington Ovl
3 Russett Woods Ct

Cross Creek Ovl Glen Eden Ct Arcadia Point Claridge Ln Walden Brandon Cir SHELDON PARK Bent Tree Dr Greenbriar Dr 100 C

41°17'45"

COLEBROOK LAKE W Arcadia Point Dr E Arcadia Point Dr Summerhill Dr Ashton Ct N Park Dr S Parkview Dr 800

PLAINVIEW CEMETERY

Aurora Normandy Ct Brookfield Dr Hampton Cir W MENNONITE RD S Park Dr

SEE 3155 MAP

Oak Old Barn Dr Hollow Rd 1000 300 E MENNONITE RD

SEE 3157 MAP

Wheatfield Dr AURORA Equestra N Dr Tinkers Meadowlark Cir Aurora Industrial Pkwy

OLD MILL RD HUDSON Bonnie Ln Tinkers Creek Ln Rainbow End Goldenrod Dr

41°17'19"

OLD MILL RD 1100 1100 Equestra S RD Arrowhead Tr

PORTAGE CO

OLD MILL RD 1200 Equestra Ct

S CHILLICOTHE RD

41°16'52"

Kimberly Dr Lena Dr 43

TINKERS CREEK STATE PARK

WHEELING & LAKE ERIE RR

41°16'26"

Ethan Av Crane Centre Dr

44236 Streetsboro 44241

Philip Pkwy Holborn Rd Hazelton Rd Alden Dr Delmonte Blvd

WELLMAN RD Gloucester Rd Stratford Ct N

41°16'0"

SEE B MAP

Miles 0 0.25 0.5

1 in. = 2000 ft.

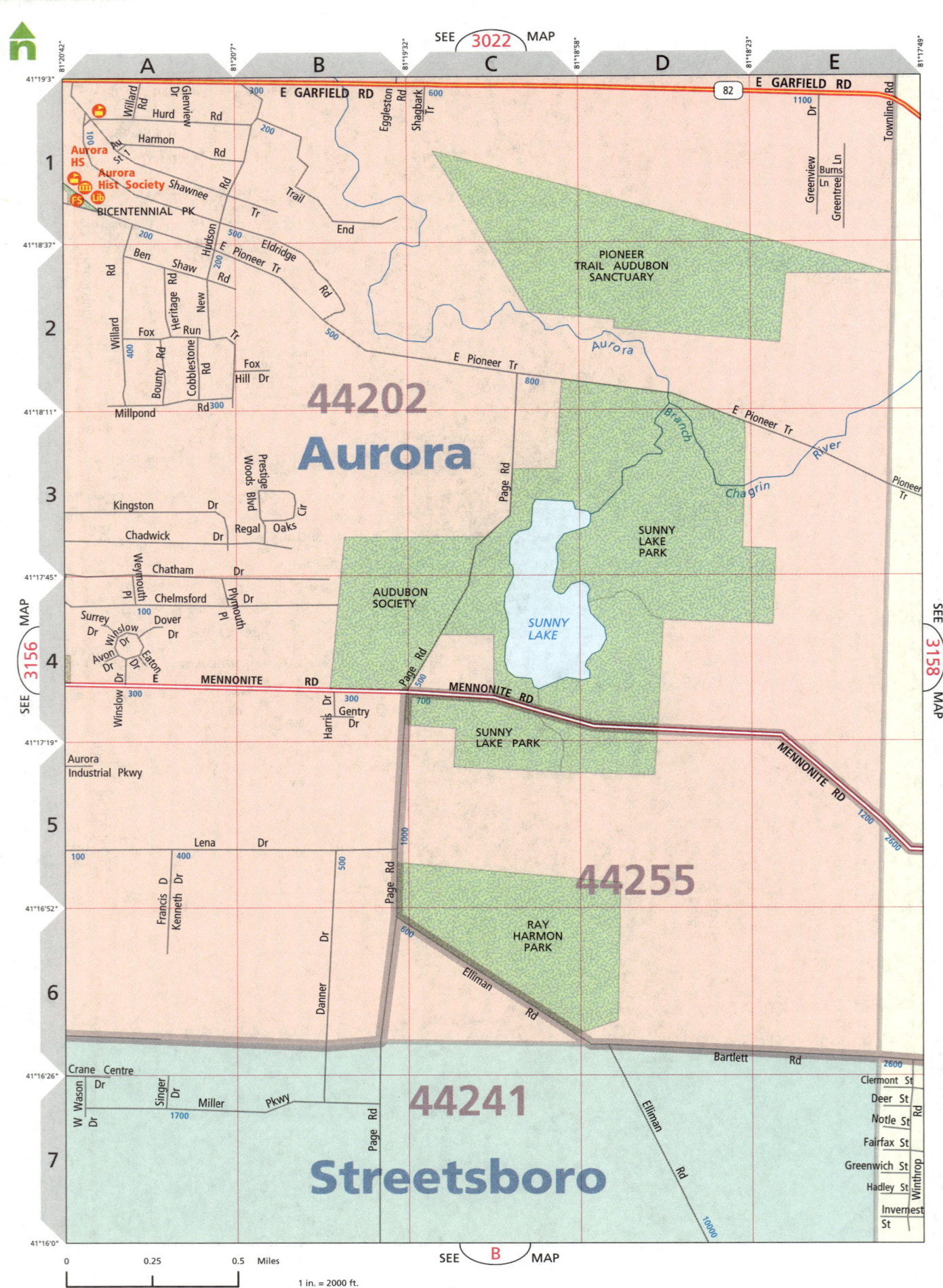

MAP 3157

SEE 3022 MAP

A   B   C   D   E

E GARFIELD RD   82   E GARFIELD RD

Willard Rd
Glenview Dr
Hurd Rd
Harmon Rd
Aurora HS
Aurora Hist Society
Lib
FS
Shawnee Rd
Bicentennial PK
Shawnee Tr
Trail End
Eggleston Rd
Shagbark Tr

1100
Greenview Dr
Burns Ln
Greentree Ln
Townline Rd

PIONEER TRAIL AUDUBON SANCTUARY

1

Hudson
Ben Rd
Shaw Rd
Heritage Rd
New Rd
Eldridge
E Pioneer Tr
E Pioneer Tr Rd
Aurora

E Pioneer Tr

2

Willard Rd
Fox Run
Bounty Rd
Cobblestone Rd
Fox Hill Dr
Millpond Rd

44202
Aurora

Chagrin Branch
River
Pioneer Tr

3

Kingston Dr
Chadwick Dr
Prestige Woods Blvd
Regal Oaks Cir

Page Rd

AUDUBON SOCIETY

SUNNY LAKE PARK

Weymouth Pl
Chatham Dr
Chelmsford Dr
Plymouth Pl
Surrey Dr
Winslow Dr
Dover Dr
Avon Dr
Eaton Dr

SUNNY LAKE

4

MENNONITE RD
Winslow Dr
Harris Dr
Gentry Dr

MENNONITE RD

SUNNY LAKE PARK

MENNONITE RD

Aurora Industrial Pkwy

5

Lena Dr
Francis D Dr
Kenneth Dr
Danner Dr
Page Rd

44255

RAY HARMON PARK

6

Elliman Rd
Page Rd

Bartlett Rd

Crane Centre Dr
W Wason Dr
Singer Dr
Miller Pkwy
Page Rd

44241
Streetsboro

Elliman Rd

Clermont St
Deer St
Notle St
Fairfax St
Greenwich St
Hadley St
Invernest St
Winthrop Rd

7

SEE 3156 MAP

SEE 3158 MAP

SEE B MAP

0   0.25   0.5   Miles

1 in. = 2000 ft.

MAP 3158

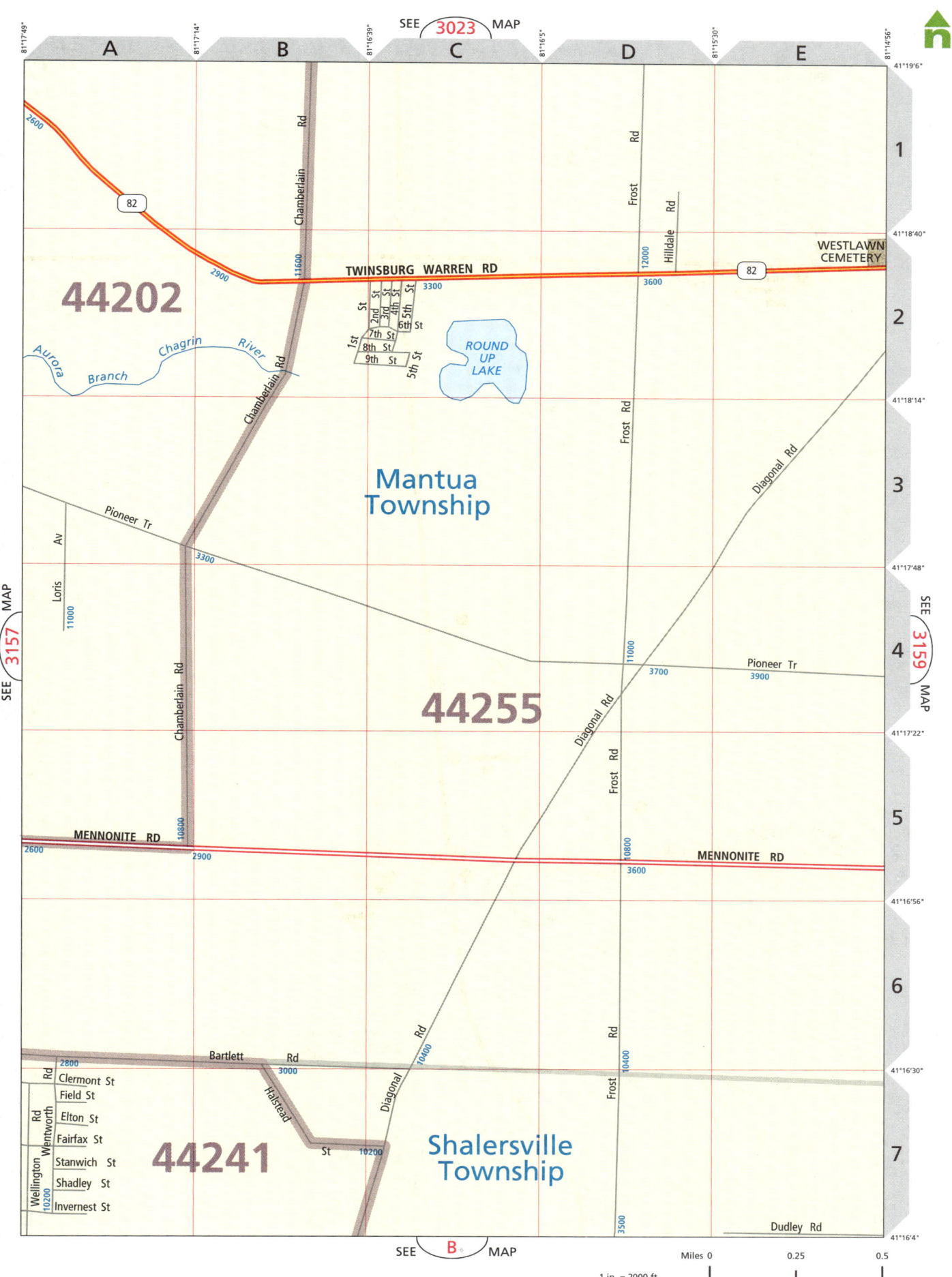

SEE 3023 MAP

A   B   C   D   E

82

44202

Chamberlain Rd

TWINSBURG WARREN RD

Frost Rd

Hilldale Rd

82

WESTLAWN CEMETERY

1st St 2nd St 3rd St 4th St 5th St 6th St
7th St
8th St
9th St
5th St

ROUND UP LAKE

Aurora Branch   Chagrin River

Chamberlain Rd

Mantua Township

Frost Rd

Diagonal Rd

Pioneer Tr

Av

Loris

11000

3300

Diagonal Rd

44255

11000

3700

Pioneer Tr
3900

Chamberlain Rd

Frost Rd

SEE 3157 MAP

SEE 3159 MAP

MENNONITE RD

10800

2600   2900

MENNONITE RD

10800

3600

Diagonal Rd

Frost Rd

Bartlett   Rd

Halstead

Clermont St
Field St
Elton St
Fairfax St
Stanwich St
Shadley St
Invernest St

Rd
Wentworth Rd
Wellington
10200

2800
3000

St   10200

44241

Diagonal Rd

10400

Frost Rd

10400

Shalersville Township

3500

Dudley Rd

SEE B MAP

Miles 0   0.25   0.5

1 in. = 2000 ft.

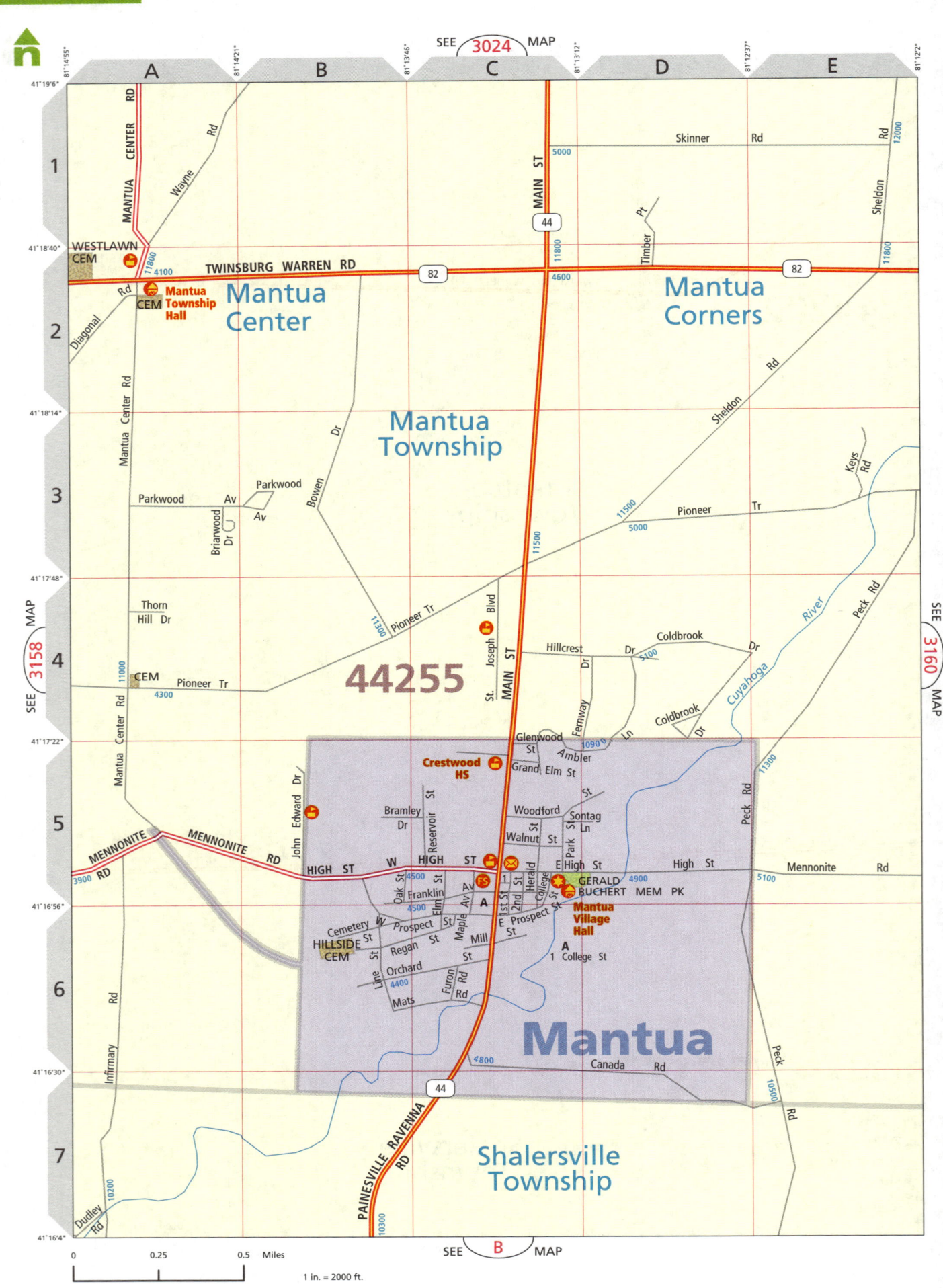

MAP 3159

N

SEE 3024 MAP

A B C D E

81°14'55"   81°14'21"   81°13'46"   81°13'12"   81°12'37"   81°12'22"

41°19'6"

1

MANTUA CENTER RD

Wayne Rd

Skinner Rd

Sheldon Rd

5000

MAIN ST

44

12000

41°18'40"

WESTLAWN CEM

TWINSBURG WARREN RD

82

82

Mantua Center

CEM

Mantua Township Hall

Diagonal Rd

4100

11800

4600

11800

11800

Mantua Corners

Timber Pt

2

41°18'14"

Mantua Center Rd

Mantua Township

Sheldon Rd

3

Parkwood Av Parkwood Av

Briarwood Dr

Bowen Dr

11500

Pioneer Tr

5000

Keys Rd

41°17'48"

SEE 3158 MAP

Thorn Hill Dr

Pioneer Tr

1300

11500

Pioneer Tr

Cuyahoga River

Peck Rd

SEE 3160 MAP

11000

CEM

4300

Pioneer Tr

44255

St. Joseph Blvd

MAIN ST

Hillcrest Dr

Coldbrook Dr

5100

Fenway Ln

Coldbrook Dr

4

41°17'22"

Mantua Center Rd

Glenwood St

Grand Elm St

Ambler Ln

1090

11300

5

MENNONITE RD

MENNONITE RD

3900

John Edward Dr

Crestwood HS

Bramley Dr

Reservoir St

W HIGH ST

HIGH ST

Woodford St

Walnut St

Park St

Sontag Ln

E High St

High St

High St

Mennonite Rd

4900

5100

41°16'56"

FS

Oak St

Franklin St

Elm St

Maple Av

2nd St

Herald St

College St

1

A

E Prospect St

GERALD BUCHERT MEM PK

Mantua Village Hall

6

Cemetery St

W Prospect St

HILLSIDE CEM

Regan St

Orchard St

Line St

Mill St

Furon Rd

Mats

4500

4400

4800

A

1 College St

Mantua

Canada Rd

Peck Rd

41°16'30"

Infirmary Rd

44

10500

Peck Rd

7

PAINESVILLE RAVENNA RD

Shalersville Township

Dudley Rd

10200

10300

41°16'4"

SEE B MAP

0   0.25   0.5   Miles

1 in. = 2000 ft.

MAP 3160

A B C D E

SEE 3025 MAP

81°11'22" 81°11'28" 81°10'53" 81°10'19" 81°9'44" 81°9'9"

41°19'10"

1

Abbott Rd

Alpha Rd

41°18'44"

Spencer Park Dr

TWINSBURG
WARREN RD

W WAKEFIELD RD

82

5700

11700

6000

12000

6500

2

44234

Beach Rd

River

Cuyahoga River

Vaughn Rd

11600

5600

41°18'18"

Pioneer Tr

CEMETERY

Pioneer Tr

5700

41°17'52"

Ryder Rd

Fairview
Airport
Terminal

11300

3

Mantua
Township

SEE 3159 MAP

Vaughn Rd

Limeridge Rd

Hiram
Township

Pioneer Tr

Asbury Rd

SEE 3161 MAP

4

41°17'25"

5

Mennonite Rd

5100

Eagle

10200

Creek

41°16'59"

10600

5500

Schustrich Rd

10700

5800

Schustrich Rd

6

44255

41°16'33"

Limeridge Rd

Asbury Rd

10300

44234

Hankee Rd

Rd

7

Vaughn Rd

Freedom
Township

Stamm Rd

10200

41°16'7"

SEE B MAP

Miles 0   0.25   0.5

1 in. = 2000 ft.

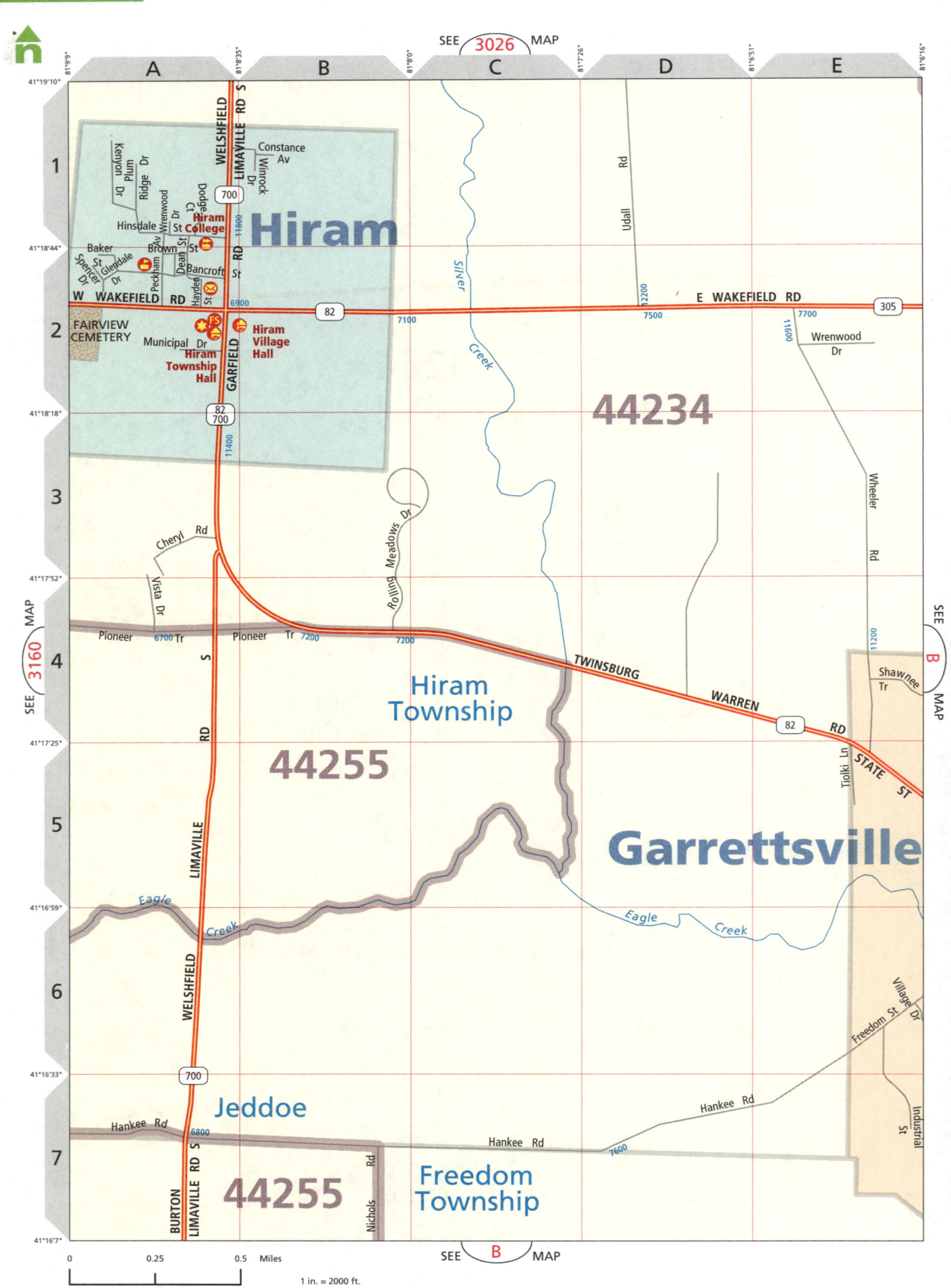

MAP 3161

SEE 3026 MAP

A   B   C   D   E

Hiram

1

Kenyon Dr
Kenyon Dr
Ridge Dr
Wrenwood Dr
Dodge St
Constance Av
Winrock Dr
WELSHFIELD
LIMAVILLE RD S
700
Hiram College
Hinsdale
Brown St
Dean St
St
Bancroft St
Baker St
Spencer Dr
Glendale Dr
Peckham
Hayden
St
W WAKEFIELD RD
6900

Udall Rd

E WAKEFIELD RD   305

2200

Silver

Creek

7500

7700
11600
Wrenwood Dr

82
7100

FAIRVIEW CEMETERY

Municipal Dr
Hiram Township Hall
FS
Hiram Village Hall

82
700

11400

44234

Wheeler Rd

3

Rolling Meadows Dr

Cheryl Rd

Vista Dr

41°17'52"

Pioneer   6700 Tr   Pioneer   Tr   7200   7200

SEE 3160 MAP

LIMAVILLE
RD
S

4

TWINSBURG

WARREN   82   RD

Shawnee Tr
11200

SEE B MAP

Hiram Township

44255

Tiolki Ln
STATE ST

5

Garrettsville

WELSHFIELD RD

Eagle

Creek

Eagle   Creek

6

Village Dr

Freedom St Dr

700

Industrial St

Jeddoe

Hankee Rd
6800

Hankee Rd

Hankee   Rd   7600

7

BURTON
LIMAVILLE RD S

44255

Nichols Rd

Freedom Township

SEE B MAP

0   0.25   0.5   Miles

1 in. = 2000 ft.

LIST OF ABBREVIATIONS

Admin	Administration	Curv	Curve	Lk	Lake	Rwy	Railway
Agri	Agricultural	Cto	Cut Off	Lndg	Landing	Rec	Recreation
Ag	Agriculture	Dept	Department	Ln	Lane	Reg	Regional
AFB	Air Force Base	Dev	Development	Lib	Library	Res	Reservoir
Arpt	Airport	Diag	Diagonal	Ldg	Lodge	Rst	Rest
Al	Alley	Div	Division	Lp	Loop	Rdg	Ridge
Amer	American	Dr	Drive	Mnr	Manor	Rd	Road
Anx	Annex	Drwy	Driveway	Mkt	Market	Rds	Roads
Arc	Arcade	E	East	Mdw	Meadow	St.	Saint
Arch	Archaeological	El	Elevation	Mdws	Meadows	Ste.	Sainte
Aud	Auditorium	Env	Environmental	Med	Medical	Sci	Science
Avd	Avenida	Est	Estate	Mem	Memorial	Sci	Sciences
Av	Avenue	Ests	Estates	Metro	Metropolitan	Sci	Scientific
Bfld	Battlefield	Exh	Exhibition	Mw	Mews	Shop Ctr	Shopping Center
Bch	Beach	Expm	Experimental	Mil	Military	Shr	Shore
Bnd	Bend	Expo	Exposition	Ml	Mill	Shrs	Shores
Bio	Biological	Expwy	Expressway	Mls	Mills	Skwy	Skyway
Blf	Bluff	Ext	Extension	Mon	Monument	S	South
Blvd	Boulevard	Frgds	Fairgrounds	Mtwy	Motorway	Spr	Spring
Brch	Branch	ft	Feet	Mnd	Mound	Sprs	Springs
Br	Bridge	Fy	Ferry	Mnds	Mounds	Sq	Square
Brk	Brook	Fld	Field	Mt	Mount	Stad	Stadium
Bldg	Building	Flds	Fields	Mtn	Mountain	St For	State Forest
Bur	Bureau	Flt	Flat	Mtns	Mountains	St Hist Site	State Historic Site
Byp	Bypass	Flts	Flats	Mun	Municipal	St Nat Area	State Natural Area
Bywy	Byway	For	Forest	Mus	Museum	St Pk	State Park
Cl	Calle	Fk	Fork	Nat'l	National	St Rec Area	State Recreation Area
Cap	Capitol	Ft	Fort	Nat'l For	National Forest	Sta	Station
Cath	Cathedral	Found	Foundation	Nat'l Hist Pk	National Historic Park	St	Street
Cswy	Causeway	Frwy	Freeway	Nat'l Hist Site	National Historic Site	Smt	Summit
Cem	Cemetery	Gdn	Garden	Nat'l Mon	National Monument	Sys	Systems
Ctr	Center	Gdns	Gardens	Nat'l Park	National Park	Tech	Technical
Ctr	Centre	Gen Hosp	General Hospital	Nat'l Rec Area	National Recreation Area	Tech	Technological
C of C	Chamber of Commerce	Gln	Glen	Nat'l Wld Ref	National Wildlife Refuge	Tech	Technology
Cir	Circle	GC	Golf Course	Nat	Natural	Ter	Terrace
CH	City Hall	Grn	Green	NAS	Naval Air Station	Terr	Territory
Clf	Cliff	Grds	Grounds	Nk	Nook	Theol	Theological
Clfs	Cliffs	Grv	Grove	N	North	Thwy	Throughway
Clb	Club	Hbr	Harbor/Harbour	Orch	Orchard	Toll Fy	Toll Ferry
Cltr	Cluster	Hvn	Haven	Ohwy	Outer Highway	TIC	Tourist Information Center
Col	Coliseum	HQs	Headquarters	Ovl	Oval	Trc	Trace
Coll	College	Ht	Height	Ovlk	Overlook	Trfwy	Trafficway
Com	Common	Hts	Heights	Ovps	Overpass	Tr	Trail
Coms	Commons	HS	High School	Pk	Park	Tun	Tunnel
Comm	Community	Hwy	Highway	Pkwy	Parkway	Tpk	Turnpike
Co.	Company	Hl	Hill	Psg	Passage	Unps	Underpass
Cons	Conservation	Hls	Hills	Pass	Passenger	Univ	University
Conv & Vis Bur	Convention and Visitors Bureau	Hist	Historical	Pth	Path	Vly	Valley
Cor	Corner	Hllw	Hollow	Pn	Pine	Vet	Veterans
Cors	Corners	Hosp	Hospital	Pns	Pines	Vw	View
Corp	Corporation	Hse	House	Pl	Place	Vil	Village
Corr	Corridor	Ind Res	Indian Reservation	Pln	Plain	Wk	Walk
Cte	Corte	Info	Information	Plns	Plains	Wall	Wall
CC	Country Club	Inst	Institute	Plgnd	Playground	Wy	Way
Co	County	Int'l	International	Plz	Plaza	W	West
Ct	Court	I	Island	Pt	Point	WMA	Wildlife Management Area
Ct Hse	Court House	Is	Islands	Pnd	Pond		
Cts	Courts	Isl	Isle	PO	Post Office		
Cr	Creek	Jct	Junction	Pres	Preserve		
Cres	Crescent	Knl	Knoll	Prov	Provincial		
Cross	Crossing	Knls	Knolls	RR	Railroad		

STREET Block City ZIP Map# Grid

HIGHWAYS

ALT - Alternate Route
BUS - Business Route
CO - County Highway/Road
HIST - Historic Highway
I - Interstate Highway
P - Provincial Highway
SR - State Route/Highway
US - United States Highway

I-71
- BKLN - 2753 C3
- BKPK - 2752 B7
- BKPK - 2881 A6
- BNWK - 3147 C7
- CLEV - 2624 E7
- CLEV - 2752 B7
- CLEV - 2753 C3
- CLEV - 2754 A2
- LNDL - 2753 C3
- MDBH - 2881 A6
- MDBH - 3012 A1
- SGVL - 3012 A1
- SGVL - 3147 C7

I-71 Innerbelt Frwy
- CLEV - 2624 E6

I-71 Medina Frwy
- BKLN - 2753 C3
- BKPK - 2752 B7
- BKPK - 2881 A6
- CLEV - 2624 E7
- CLEV - 2752 B7
- CLEV - 2753 C3
- CLEV - 2754 A2
- LNDL - 2753 C3
- MDBH - 2881 A6
- MDBH - 3012 A1
- SGVL - 3012 A1
- SGVL - 3147 B1

I-77
- BKVL - 3150 D1
- BWHT - 3015 D2
- CHHT - 2755 C1
- CLEV - 2625 C7
- CLEV - 2755 D6
- INDE - 2755 D6
- INDE - 2884 D7
- INDE - 3015 D2
- NBGH - 2755 C1
- RHFD - 3150 E7

I-77 Willow Frwy
- BKVL - 3150 D1
- BWHT - 3015 D2
- CHHT - 2755 C1
- CLEV - 2625 C7
- CLEV - 2755 D6
- INDE - 2755 D6
- INDE - 2884 D7
- INDE - 3015 D2
- NBGH - 2755 C1
- RHFD - 3150 E7

I-80
- AhtT - 2871 B7
- AhtT - 2872 E4
- AhtT - 2873 A4
- AMHT - 2872 E4
- BERA - 3010 D1
- BERA - 3011 D3
- BhmT - 2871 E5
- BKVL - 3150 B4
- BWHT - 3149 E3
- BWHT - 3150 B4
- ELYR - 2874 C3
- ELYR - 2875 E4
- EyrT - 2873 E3
- EyrT - 2874 C3
- NRDV - 2875 E4
- NRDV - 2876 D5
- NRDV - 2877 A5
- NRDV - 2878 C6
- NRDV - 3012 E6
- NRYN - 3013 A7
- NRYN - 3148 C1
- NRYN - 3149 E3
- ODFL - 3010 D1
- OmsT - 2878 C6
- OmsT - 2879 A7
- OmsT - 3010 D1
- RchT - 3150 E6
- RchT - 3151 B7
- RHFD - 3150 E6
- RHFD - 3151 B7
- SGVL - 3011 B2
- SGVL - 3012 E6

I-80 Ohio Tpk
- AhtT - 2871 B7
- AhtT - 2872 B4
- AhtT - 2873 E3
- AMHT - 2872 E4
- BERA - 3010 D1
- BERA - 3011 D3
- BhmT - 2871 B7
- BKVL - 3150 B4
- BWHT - 3149 E3
- BWHT - 3150 B4
- ELYR - 2874 C3
- ELYR - 2875 E4
- EyrT - 2873 E3
- EyrT - 2874 C3
- NRDV - 2875 E4
- NRDV - 2876 D5
- NRDV - 2877 A5
- NRDV - 2878 C6
- NRYN - 3012 E6
- NRYN - 3013 A7
- NRYN - 3148 C1
- NRYN - 3149 E3
- ODFL - 3010 D1
- OmsT - 2878 C6
- OmsT - 2879 A7
- OmsT - 3010 D1
- RchT - 3150 E6
- RchT - 3151 B7
- RHFD - 3150 E6
- RHFD - 3151 B7
- SGVL - 3011 B2
- SGVL - 3012 E6

I-90
- AhtT - 2871 B7
- AhtT - 2872 B5
- AhtT - 2873 A4
- AMHT - 2872 E4
- AVON - 2617 E7
- AVON - 2618 C7
- AVON - 2619 A6
- AVON - 2747 A1
- BhmT - 2871 E5
- BTNH - 2496 E2
- BTNH - 2497 A1
- CcdT - 2146 D6
- CcdT - 2147 B4
- CcdT - 2253 D3
- CcdT - 2254 B1
- CLEV - 2372 D7
- CLEV - 2373 B5
- CLEV - 2495 C6
- CLEV - 2496 B4
- CLEV - 2497 A1
- CLEV - 2622 A6
- CLEV - 2623 E7
- CLEV - 2624 A6
- CLEV - 2625 B2
- ELYR - 2746 C7
- ELYR - 2874 E1
- ELYR - 2875 B1
- EUCL - 2373 E3
- EUCL - 2374 C5
- EyrT - 2874 E1
- HpfT - 2045 B2
- KDHL - 2252 E4
- KDHL - 2253 D3
- LKWD - 2622 A6
- LryT - 2042 E7
- LryT - 2043 B6
- LryT - 2147 D2
- LryT - 2148 C1
- MadT - 2043 B6
- MadT - 2044 D3
- MadT - 2045 B2
- MDSN - 2043 B6
- MDSN - 2044 D3
- MNTR - 2251 B6
- MNTR - 2252 A4
- MNTR - 2253 D3
- PryT - 2043 B6
- RKRV - 2621 B6
- RKRV - 2622 A6
- SFLD - 2746 C7
- SFLD - 2747 A1
- WBHL - 2250 E7
- WBHL - 2374 C5
- WBHL - 2375 A4
- WKLF - 2374 C5
- WKLF - 2375 A4
- WLBY - 2250 E7
- WLBY - 2251 E4
- WLBY - 2375 D1
- WTHL - 2250 E7
- WTHL - 2251 B6
- WTLK - 2619 A6
- WTLK - 2620 D6
- WTLK - 2621 E6

I-90 Innerbelt Frwy
- CLEV - 2495 B7
- CLEV - 2624 E4
- CLEV - 2625 B2

I-90 Lakeland Frwy
- BTNH - 2496 E2
- BTNH - 2497 A1
- CLEV - 2372 D7
- CLEV - 2373 A6
- CLEV - 2495 C6
- CLEV - 2496 B4
- CLEV - 2497 A1
- EUCL - 2373 C4

I-90 Northwest Frwy
- CLEV - 2622 A6
- CLEV - 2623 E7
- CLEV - 2624 A6
- LKWD - 2622 A6
- RKRV - 2621 B6
- RKRV - 2622 A6
- WTLK - 2619 A6
- WTLK - 2620 D6
- WTLK - 2621 E6

I-90 Ohio Tpk
- AhtT - 2871 B7
- AhtT - 2872 E4
- AhtT - 2873 A4
- AMHT - 2872 E4
- BhmT - 2871 E5

I-271
- BDFD - 2887 C6
- BDHT - 2758 D7
- BDHT - 2887 D1
- BHWD - 2629 D2
- BHWD - 2758 E4
- BHWD - 2759 A2
- BosT - 3152 E7
- HDHT - 2499 E2
- LNHT - 2629 D2
- MAYF - 2499 E6
- MCDN - 3018 C3
- MCDN - 3153 C1
- MDHT - 2499 E6
- MDHT - 2500 A7
- MDHT - 2629 D2
- NCtT - 3152 E7
- NCtT - 3153 B5
- OKWD - 2887 C6
- OKWD - 3018 C2
- ORNG - 2758 E4
- ORNG - 2759 A2
- PRPK - 2629 D2
- PRPK - 2759 A2
- WBHL - 2374 E6
- WBHL - 2375 A4
- WVHT - 2758 E4

I-271 Outerbelt East Frwy
- BDFD - 2887 C6
- BDHT - 2758 D7
- BDHT - 2887 C6
- BHWD - 2629 D2
- BHWD - 2758 E4
- BHWD - 2759 A2
- HDHT - 2499 E2
- LNHT - 2629 D2
- MAYF - 2499 E6
- MDHT - 2499 E6
- MDHT - 2500 A7
- MDHT - 2629 D2
- OKWD - 2887 C6
- OKWD - 3018 C2
- ORNG - 2758 E4
- ORNG - 2759 A2
- PRPK - 2629 D2
- PRPK - 2759 A2
- WBHL - 2374 E7
- WVHT - 2758 E4

I-480
- BDFD - 2887 C6
- BDHT - 2758 C7
- BDHT - 2887 C1
- BKLN - 2753 D6
- BNHT - 2755 A7
- BNHT - 2884 C1
- CLEV - 2751 C6
- CLEV - 2752 C6
- CLEV - 2753 D6
- CLEV - 2754 D7
- CLEV - 2755 A7
- CLEV - 2757 D6
- FWPK - 2751 C6
- GDHT - 2756 E7
- GDHT - 2757 D6
- GDHT - 2885 B1
- HDSN - 3155 D7
- INDE - 2884 E2
- INDE - 2885 B1
- MCDN - 3018 C2
- MCDN - 3019 A5
- MPHT - 2757 D6
- MPHT - 2758 C7
- NOSD - 2750 D7
- NOSD - 2751 C6
- NOSD - 2878 C3
- NOSD - 2879 A1
- NRDL - 2758 C6
- NRDV - 2877 E4
- NRDV - 2878 C3
- OKWD - 2887 C6
- OKWD - 3018 E4
- OmsT - 2878 C3
- TNBG - 3019 A5
- TNBG - 3154 E2
- TNBG - 3155 D7
- TwbT - 3155 D7
- VLVW - 2885 B1
- WVHT - 2757 D6
- WVHT - 2758 C6

I-480 Outerbelt East Frwy
- BDFD - 2887 C6
- BDHT - 2887 C6
- OKWD - 2887 C6
- OKWD - 3018 C2

I-480 Outerbelt South Frwy
- BKLN - 2753 D6
- BNHT - 2755 A7
- BNHT - 2884 C1
- CLEV - 2751 C6
- CLEV - 2752 C6
- CLEV - 2753 A6
- CLEV - 2754 D7
- CLEV - 2755 A7
- FWPK - 2751 C6
- GDHT - 2756 E7
- GDHT - 2757 A7
- GDHT - 2885 B1
- INDE - 2884 E2
- INDE - 2885 B1
- MPHT - 2757 A7
- NOSD - 2750 D7
- NOSD - 2751 C6
- NOSD - 2878 C3
- NOSD - 2879 A1
- OmsT - 2878 C3
- VLVW - 2885 B1

I-490
- CLEV - 2624 E6
- CLEV - 2625 B6

SR-2
- AhtT - 2744 D7
- AhtT - 2745 A7
- AMHT - 2743 E7
- AMHT - 2744 D7
- AMHT - 2871 E1
- AMHT - 2872 A1
- AVON - 2617 C7
- AVON - 2618 B7
- AVON - 2619 A6
- AVON - 2747 A1
- BhmT - 2870 A1
- BhmT - 2871 E1
- BTNH - 2496 E2
- BTNH - 2497 B1
- CLEV - 2372 C7
- CLEV - 2373 B5
- CLEV - 2495 C7
- CLEV - 2496 A4
- CLEV - 2497 B1
- CLEV - 2624 E1
- CLEV 44102 2624 B4
- CLEV 44113 2624 B4
- CLEV - 2625 A1
- ELYR - 2746 B7
- ELYR - 2874 B1
- ELYR - 2875 B1
- ETLK - 2249 D7
- ETLK - 2250 A6
- EUCL - 2373 B5
- EUCL - 2374 B1
- EyrT - 2745 A7
- EyrT - 2874 B1
- LKWD 44107 2621 D5
- LORN - 2744 D7
- MNTR - 2143 E7
- MNTR - 2144 E2
- MNTR - 2145 A2
- MNTR - 2251 B2
- PNVL - 2039 E7
- PNVL - 2040 B5
- PNVL - 2145 B1
- PnvT - 2039 E7
- PnvT - 2040 B5
- PnvT - 2041 A3
- PnvT - 2145 B1
- RKRV - 2621 B6
- RKRV 44107 2621 D5
- SFLD - 2746 B7
- SFLD - 2747 A1
- VMLN - 2870 A1
- VMLN - 2871 E1
- VmnT - 2869 C1
- VmnT - 2870 A1
- WKLF - 2249 D7
- WKLF - 2374 B1
- WLBY - 2250 A6
- WLBY - 2251 B2
- WLWK - 2249 D7
- WTLK - 2619 A6
- WTLK - 2620 D6
- WTLK - 2621 B6
- 1100 LKWD 44107 2622 A4
- 9200 CLEV 44102 2623 C5
- 11700 LKWD 44102 2623 C5
- 11700 LKWD 44107 2623 C5
- 19000 RKRV 44116 2621 D5

SR-2 Cleveland Mem Shoreway
- CLEV - 2495 B7
- CLEV 44102 2623 E4
- CLEV - 2624 E1
- CLEV 44102 2624 B4
- CLEV 44113 2624 B4
- CLEV - 2625 A1

SR-2 Clifton Blvd
- 9200 CLEV 44102 2623 C5
- 11700 LKWD 44102 2623 C5
- 11700 LKWD 44107 2623 C5
- 13400 LKWD 44107 2622 B4

SR-2 W Clifton Blvd
- 1100 LKWD 44107 2622 A4

SR-2 Detroit Rd
- LKWD 44107 2621 D5
- RKRV 44107 2621 D5
- 19000 RKRV 44116 2621 D5

SR-2 Innerbelt Frwy
- CLEV - 2495 B7

SR-2 Lakeland Frwy
- BTNH - 2496 E2
- BTNH - 2497 B1
- CLEV - 2372 C7
- CLEV - 2373 B5
- CLEV - 2495 C7
- CLEV - 2496 A4
- CLEV - 2497 B1
- ETLK - 2249 D7
- ETLK - 2250 A6
- EUCL - 2373 B5
- EUCL - 2374 B1
- MNTR - 2143 E7
- MNTR - 2144 E2
- MNTR - 2145 A2
- MNTR - 2251 B2
- PNVL - 2145 B1
- PnvT - 2145 B1
- WKLF - 2249 D7
- WKLF - 2374 B1
- WLBY - 2250 A6
- WLBY - 2251 B2
- WLWK - 2249 D7

SR-2 Northwest Frwy
- RKRV - 2621 B6
- WTLK - 2619 A6
- WTLK - 2620 D6
- WTLK - 2621 B6

SR-2 Sloane Av
- 1300 LKWD 44107 2622 A4

SR-3
- 10 HkyT 44233 3148 D6
- 1400 CLEV 44113 2624 D7
- 3100 CLEV 44109 2624 D7
- 3200 CLEV 44109 2754 D2
- 4500 CLEV 44144 2754 A7
- 5000 CLEV 44129 2754 A7
- 5000 PRMA 44109 2754 A7
- 5000 PRMA 44129 2754 A7
- 5300 PRMA 44129 2753 E7
- 5300 PRMA 44129 2882 E4
- 7400 PRMA 44129 3013 E4
- 7400 PRMA 44134 3013 E4
- 7800 NRYN 44129 3013 E4
- 7800 NRYN 44133 3013 E4
- 14000 NRYN 44133 3148 D3

SR-3 W 25th St
- 1400 CLEV 44113 2624 D7
- 3100 CLEV 44109 2624 D7
- 3200 CLEV 44109 2754 D2

SR-3 Pearl Rd
- 3600 CLEV 44109 2754 D2
- 4500 CLEV 44144 2754 C5
- 5000 CLEV 44129 2754 A7
- 5000 PRMA 44109 2754 A7
- 5000 PRMA 44129 2754 A7
- 5300 PRMA 44129 2753 E7
- 5300 PRMA 44129 2882 E4

SR-3 Ridge Rd
- 10 HkyT 44233 3148 D6
- 5400 PRMA 44129 2882 E1
- 7400 PRMA 44129 3013 E4
- 7400 PRMA 44134 3013 E4
- 7800 NRYN 44129 3013 E4
- 7800 NRYN 44133 3013 E4
- 14000 NRYN 44133 3148 D3

SR-8
- BSHT 44236 3153 D7
- MCDN 44056 3018 B7
- MCDN 44056 3153 B1
- MCDN 44067 3018 B7
- MPHT 44146 2758 B7
- NCtT 44056 3018 B7
- NCtT 44067 3018 B7
- NCtT 44067 3153 B1
- NCtT 44236 3153 D7
- WVHT 44146 2758 B6
- 10 BDFD 44146 2887 B7
- 800 CLEV 44115 2625 A4
- 1900 CLEV 44114 2624 E3
- 2000 CLEV 44115 2624 E3
- 2100 CLEV 44113 2624 E3
- 3500 CLEV 44104 2625 D4
- 3500 HIHL 44122 2758 B4
- 3500 SRHT 44122 2758 A1
- 3700 WVHT 44122 2758 A1
- 3900 HIHL 44128 2758 B4
- 3900 WVHT 44128 2758 B4
- 4000 CLEV 44104 2625 E5
- 4300 NRDL 44128 2758 B4
- 5000 BDHT 44146 2758 B7
- 5000 MPHT 44137 2758 B7
- 5200 BDHT 44146 2887 B3
- 5200 MPHT 44137 2887 B3
- 6900 OKWD 44146 2887 B7
- 6900 WNHL 44146 2887 B7
- 7100 WNHL 44146 3018 B2
- 7200 CLEV 44104 2626 B6
- 10100 NHFD 44067 3018 B7
- 10100 SgHT 44067 3018 B7
- 11300 CLEV 44120 2626 B6
- 12500 CLEV 44120 2756 E1
- 13500 CLEV 44120 2757 B1
- 15400 SRHT 44120 2757 B1
- 17700 SRHT 44122 2757 E1

SR-8 Broadway Av
- 800 CLEV 44115 2625 A4

SR-8 Chagrin Blvd
- 15600 SRHT 44120 2757 B1
- 17700 SRHT 44122 2757 D1
- 19200 SRHT 44122 2758 A1

SR-8 Kinsman Rd
- 5500 CLEV 44104 2625 E5
- 7200 CLEV 44104 2626 B6
- 11300 CLEV 44120 2626 B6
- 12500 CLEV 44120 2756 E1
- 13500 CLEV 44120 2757 B1
- 15400 SRHT 44120 2757 B1

SR-8 Northfield Rd
- MPHT 44146 2758 B7
- WVHT 44146 2758 B6
- 10 BDFD 44146 2887 B7
- 3500 HIHL 44122 2758 B4
- 3500 SRHT 44122 2758 B4
- 3700 WVHT 44122 2758 B4
- 3900 HIHL 44128 2758 B4
- 3900 WVHT 44128 2758 B4
- 4300 NRDL 44128 2758 B4
- 5000 BDHT 44146 2758 B7
- 5000 MPHT 44137 2758 B7
- 5200 BDHT 44146 2887 B3
- 5200 MPHT 44137 2887 B3
- 6900 OKWD 44146 2887 B7
- 6900 WNHL 44146 2887 B7
- 7100 WNHL 44146 3018 B2
- 10100 NHFD 44067 3018 B2
- 10100 SgHT 44067 3018 B2

SR-8 Ontario St
- 1900 CLEV 44114 2624 E3
- 2000 CLEV 44115 2624 E3
- 2100 CLEV 44113 2624 E3

SR-8 Orange Av
- 1400 CLEV 44115 2625 A4

SR-8 Woodland Av
- 2500 CLEV 44115 2625 B4
- 4000 CLEV 44104 2625 C4

SR-10
- EatT - 3007 E1
- NRDV - 2877 E4
- NRDV - 3007 E1
- NRDV - 3008 A1
- 2000 CLEV 44113 2624 D5
- 4500 CLEV 44102 2624 B6
- 6800 CLEV 44102 2623 D7
- 10000 CLEV 44111 2623 D7
- 10600 CLEV 44111 2753 B1
- 13200 CLEV 44111 2752 D2
- 18800 FWPK 44126 2752 D2
- 18900 FWPK 44126 2751 E2
- 22900 NOSD 44070 2751 E2
- 22900 NOSD 44126 2751 E2
- 23200 NOSD 44070 2750 E4
- 27200 NOSD 44070 2749 E7
- 28000 NOSD 44070 2878 B2
- 31200 NRDV 44039 2878 B2
- 31200 NRDV 44070 2878 B2

SR-10 Carnegie Av
- CLEV 44113 2624 E4

SR-10 Lorain Av
- FWPK 44126 2752 D2
- 2000 CLEV 44113 2624 D5
- 4500 CLEV 44102 2624 B6
- 6800 CLEV 44102 2623 D7
- 10000 CLEV 44111 2623 D7
- 10600 CLEV 44111 2753 B1
- 13200 CLEV 44111 2752 D2

SR-10 Lorain Rd
- NRDV 44039 2877 E4
- 18800 FWPK 44126 2752 A2
- 18900 FWPK 44126 2751 E2
- 22900 NOSD 44070 2751 E2
- 22900 NOSD 44126 2751 E2
- 23200 NOSD 44070 2750 E4
- 27200 NOSD 44070 2749 E7
- 28000 NOSD 44070 2878 B2
- 31200 NRDV 44039 2878 B2
- 31200 NRDV 44070 2878 B2

SR-14
- HDSN - 3155 D7
- MCDN - 3018 E4
- MCDN - 3019 A5
- OKWD - 3018 C1
- TNBG - 3019 A5
- TNBG - 3154 E2
- TNBG - 3155 D7
- TwbT - 3155 D7
- CLEV 44115 2625 B4
- 10 BDFD 44146 2886 E3
- 10 MPHT 44137 2886 C1
- 10 MPHT 44146 2886 C1
- 500 BDFD 44146 2887 C6
- 1500 OKWD 44146 2887 C6
- 2100 CLEV 44113 2624 E3
- 2100 CLEV 44115 2624 E3
- 3900 CLEV 44127 2625 C6
- 5800 CLEV 44127 2755 E1
- 6300 CLEV 44105 2755 E1
- 7300 CLEV 44105 2756 A3
- 10100 CLEV 44125 2756 A3
- 10100 GDHT 44125 2756 A3
- 11900 GDHT 44105 2756 E6
- 13700 GDHT 44125 2757 B7
- 14100 MPHT 44125 2757 B7
- 14100 MPHT 44137 2757 B7
- 14300 GDHT 44128 2757 B7
- 14300 MPHT 44128 2757 B7

SR-14 E 34th St
- 2700 CLEV 44115 2625 C5

SR-14 Broadway Av
- CLEV 44115 2625 B4
- 10 BDFD 44146 2886 E3
- 10 MPHT 44137 2886 C1
- 10 MPHT 44146 2886 C1
- 500 BDFD 44146 2887 C6
- 1500 OKWD 44146 2887 C6
- 3900 CLEV 44115 2625 C6
- 3900 CLEV 44127 2625 C6
- 5800 CLEV 44127 2755 E1
- 6300 CLEV 44105 2755 E1
- 7300 CLEV 44105 2756 A3
- 10100 CLEV 44125 2756 A3
- 10100 GDHT 44125 2756 A3
- 11900 GDHT 44105 2756 E6
- 13700 GDHT 44125 2757 B7
- 14100 MPHT 44125 2757 B7
- 14100 MPHT 44137 2757 B7
- 14300 GDHT 44128 2757 B7
- 14300 MPHT 44128 2757 B7

SR-14 Lee Rd
- 5300 MPHT 44137 2757 C7
- 5300 MPHT 44137 2886 C1

SR-14 Oakleaf Rd
- OKWD 44146 2887 C7

SR-14 Ontario St
- 2100 CLEV 44113 2624 E3
- 2100 CLEV 44115 2624 E3

SR-14 Outerbelt East Frwy
- OKWD - 2887 C7
- OKWD - 3018 C1

SR-14 Pittsburgh Av
- 2200 CLEV 44115 2625 B4

SR-17
- INDE 44125 2884 E1
- VLVW 44131 2884 E1
- 10 BNHT 44131 2755 B7
- 700 BNHT 44109 2754 E7
- 700 BNHT 44131 2754 E7
- 700 CLEV 44109 2754 E7
- 1100 CLEV 44134 2754 D7
- 1100 PRMA 44109 2754 E7
- 1100 PRMA 44134 2754 D7
- 1200 BNHT 44131 2884 D1
- 1400 INDE 44131 2884 D1
- 5400 PRMA 44129 2754 A7
- 6000 CLEV 44129 2754 A7
- 6200 CLEV 44129 2753 B7
- 6200 PRMA 44129 2753 B7
- 7300 BKLN 44144 2753 B7
- 7300 PRMA 44144 2753 B7
- 7500 VLVW 44125 2884 E1
- 7500 VLVW 44125 2885 A1
- 7700 GDHT 44125 2885 A1
- 8900 GDHT 44125 2756 B7
- 10200 PRMA 44130 2753 B7
- 11700 CLEV 44135 2753 B7
- 11700 CLEV 44144 2753 B7
- 11700 PRMA 44135 2753 B7
- 13000 BKPK 44130 2752 D7
- 13000 BKPK 44135 2752 D7
- 13000 BKPK 44142 2752 D7
- 13000 CLEV 44135 2752 D7
- 13000 PRMA 44130 2752 D7
- 13000 PRMA 44135 2752 D7
- 13500 GDHT 44125 2757 D7
- 14000 MPHT 44137 2757 D7
- 18200 BKPK 44135 2751 E7
- 18200 BKPK 44142 2751 E7
- 18200 CLEV 44135 2751 E7
- 19800 MPHT 44137 2758 A7
- 21100 FWPK 44126 2751 D7
- 21800 BDHT 44146 2758 A7
- 22400 FWPK 44126 2751 A6
- 23000 NOSD 44070 2750 E6
- 23000 NOSD 44070 2751 A6
- 23000 NOSD 44126 2751 A6

SR-17 Brookpark Rd
- 700 BNHT 44109 2754 D7
- 700 BNHT 44131 2754 D7
- 700 CLEV 44109 2754 D7
- 1100 CLEV 44134 2754 D7
- 1100 PRMA 44109 2754 D7
- 1100 PRMA 44134 2754 D7
- 5400 PRMA 44129 2754 A7
- 6000 CLEV 44129 2754 A7
- 6200 CLEV 44129 2753 B7
- 6200 PRMA 44129 2753 B7
- 7300 BKLN 44144 2753 B7
- 7300 PRMA 44144 2753 B7
- 10200 PRMA 44130 2753 B7
- 11700 CLEV 44135 2753 B7
- 11700 CLEV 44144 2753 B7
- 11700 PRMA 44135 2753 B7
- 13000 BKPK 44130 2752 D7
- 13000 BKPK 44135 2752 D7
- 13000 BKPK 44142 2752 D7
- 13000 CLEV 44135 2752 D7
- 13000 PRMA 44130 2752 D7
- 13000 PRMA 44135 2752 D7
- 18200 BKPK 44135 2751 E7
- 18200 BKPK 44142 2751 E7
- 18200 CLEV 44135 2751 E7
- 21100 FWPK 44126 2751 D7
- 23000 NOSD 44070 2750 E6
- 23000 NOSD 44070 2751 A6
- 23000 NOSD 44126 2751 A6

SR-17 Granger Rd
- INDE 44125 2884 E1
- VLVW 44131 2884 E1
- 5500 INDE 44131 2884 D1
- 7500 VLVW 44125 2884 E1
- 7500 VLVW 44125 2885 A1
- 7700 GDHT 44125 2885 A1
- 8900 GDHT 44125 2756 B7
- 13500 GDHT 44125 2757 D7
- 14000 MPHT 44137 2757 D7

SR-17 E Granger Rd
- 10 BNHT 44131 2755 A7
- 1200 BNHT 44131 2884 D1
- 1400 INDE 44131 2884 D1

SR-17 W Granger Rd
- BNHT 44109 2754 E7
- BNHT 44131 2754 E7
- CLEV 44109 2754 E7
- 300 BNHT 44131 2755 B7

SR-17 Libby Rd
- 14400 MPHT 44137 2757 B7
- 19800 MPHT 44137 2758 A7
- 21800 BDHT 44146 2758 A7

SR-20
- EatT - 3006 B5

SR-21
- CHHT - 2755 D6
- CHHT 44131 2755 E7
- CLEV - 2625 C6
- CLEV - 2755 D6
- INDE 44125 2755 E7
- INDE 44131 2755 E7
- NBGH - 2755 C1
- VLVW 44125 2884 E2
- VLVW 44131 2884 E2
- 4700 RHFD 44286 3151 A6
- 5400 INDE 44131 2884 E2
- 7200 INDE 44131 3015 E1
- 7600 INDE 44131 3016 A3
- 7700 BKVL 44141 3016 A3
- 9000 BKVL 44141 3151 A2

SR-21 Brecksville Rd
- CHHT 44125 2755 E7
- CHHT 44131 2755 E7
- INDE 44125 2755 E7
- INDE 44131 2755 E7
- VLVW 44125 2884 E2
- VLVW 44131 2884 E2
- 4700 RHFD 44286 3151 A6
- 5400 INDE 44131 2884 E2
- 7200 INDE 44131 3015 E1
- 7600 INDE 44131 3016 A3
- 7700 BKVL 44141 3016 A3
- 9000 BKVL 44141 3151 A2

SR-21 Willow Frwy
- CHHT - 2755 C1
- CLEV - 2625 C6
- CLEV - 2755 D6
- NBGH - 2755 C1

SR-43
- CLEV 44115 2625 B4
- MPHT 44137 2758 B7
- WVHT 44146 2758 B6
- 10 AURA 44202 3021 C5
- 10 AURA 44202 3156 E1
- 10 BbgT 44023 3021 C5
- 10 BbgT 44139 3021 C5
- 10 SLN 44139 3021 C5
- 1000 AURA 44023 3021 C5
- 3900 CLEV 44127 2625 C6
- 4900 NRDL 44128 2758 B6
- 5800 CLEV 44127 2755 E1
- 6300 CLEV 44105 2755 E1
- 7300 CLEV 44105 2756 A3
- 10100 STBR 44241 3156 E7
- 13100 CLEV 44128 2756 D3
- 13600 CLEV 44105 2757 E5
- 13600 CLEV 44128 2757 E5
- 17600 WVHT 44128 2757 E5
- 19400 NRDL 44128 2757 E5
- 19600 WVHT 44128 2758 B6
- 21700 BDHT 44146 2758 B7
- 21700 MPHT 44146 2758 B7
- 23100 BDHT 44146 2887 C1
- 26200 BDHT 44146 2888 E4
- 27000 SLN 44139 2888 E4
- 33200 SLN 44139 2889 A5
- 37900 SLN 44139 3020 D1

SR-43 E 34th St
- 2700 CLEV 44115 2625 C5

SR-43 Aurora Rd
- 21700 BDHT 44146 2758 B7
- 21700 MPHT 44146 2758 B7
- 23100 BDHT 44146 2887 C1
- 26200 BDHT 44146 2888 E4
- 27000 SLN 44139 2888 E4
- 33200 SLN 44139 2889 A5
- 37900 SLN 44139 3020 D1
- 39700 SLN 44139 3021 C5
- 40000 BbgT 44023 3021 C5
- 40000 BbgT 44139 3021 C5

SR-43 N Aurora Rd
- 10 AURA 44202 3021 E7
- 10 BbgT 44023 3021 A3
- 10 BbgT 44139 3021 A2
- 10 SLN 44139 3021 A2
- 1000 AURA 44023 3021 B3

SR-43 S Aurora Rd
- 10 AURA 44202 3156 E1

SR-43 Bartlett Rd
- BDHT 44146 2758 C7

SR-43 Broadway Av
- CLEV 44115 2625 B4
- 3900 CLEV 44127 2625 C6
- 5800 CLEV 44127 2755 E1
- 6300 CLEV 44105 2755 E1
- 7300 CLEV 44105 2756 A3

SR-43 S Chillicothe Rd
- 100 AURA 44202 3156 E1
- 10100 STBR 44241 3156 E7

SR-43 Miles Av
- 9100 CLEV 44105 2756 B3
- 13100 CLEV 44128 2756 E3
- 13600 CLEV 44105 2757 A3
- 13600 CLEV 44128 2757 A3
- 17600 WVHT 44128 2757 D5

SR-43 Miles Rd
- 17700 WVHT 44128 2757 E5
- 19400 NRDL 44128 2757 E5
- 19600 WVHT 44128 2758 B6
- 20000 NRDL 44128 2758 B6

SR-43 Mueti Dr
- BDHT 44146 2758 B7
- MPHT 44137 2758 B7

SR-43 Northfield Rd
- BDHT 44146 2758 B6
- MPHT 44137 2758 B6
- MPHT 44146 2758 B6
- WVHT 44146 2758 B6
- 4900 NRDL 44128 2758 B6

SR-43 Pittsburgh Av
- 2200 CLEV 44115 2625 B4

SR-44
- CcdT - 2145 E4
- CcdT - 2146 A6
- CcdT 44024 2254 B7
- CcdT 44077 2254 B3
- CdnT 44024 2254 B7
- CdnT 44024 2379 B1
- GDRV 44045 2039 B5
- GDRV 44077 2039 B5
- MNTR 44060 2039 B7
- MNTR 44060 2145 A1
- PNVL - 2145 D2
- PnvT 44045 2039 B5
- PnvT 44060 2039 B7
- PnvT 44077 2039 B7
- PnvT - 2145 E4
- 100 CRDN 44024 2379 D5
- 100 CRDN 44024 2380 A6
- 300 CRDN 44024 2505 A1
- 800 MsnT 44024 2505 A1
- 10300 MNTU 44255 3159 C7
- 10300 ShvT 44255 3159 C7
- 10900 ManT 44255 3159 C7
- 11900 ManT 44255 3024 C7
- 12500 MsnT 44024 2635 B1
- 12800 AbnT 44255 3024 C2
- 13400 NbyT 44024 2635 B1
- 13700 NbyT 44021 2635 B7
- 13700 NbyT 44065 2635 B7
- 14200 NbyT 44021 2765 A2
- 14200 NbyT 44065 2765 A2
- 15400 NbyT 44021 2764 E5
- 15500 NbyT 44065 2764 E5
- 16300 AbnT 44021 2764 E5
- 16400 AbnT 44021 2893 E1
- 17900 AbnT 44234 2893 D7
- 18300 AbnT 44023 2893 D7

INDEX 3

SR-44 | SR-168 Tavern Rd

Cleveland Street Index

STREET Block City ZIP Map# Grid

SR-44
18300 AbnT 44023 3024 C2
18300 AbnT 44234 3024 C2
SR-44 Center St
100 CRDN 44024 2379 E6
100 CRDN 44024 2380 A7
SR-44 N Hambden St
100 CRDN 44024 2380 A6
SR-44 Heisley Rd
- GDRV 44045 2039 B5
- GDRV 44077 2039 B5
- MNTR 44060 2039 B7
- MNTR 44060 2145 A1
- PnvT 44045 2039 B5
- PnvT 44060 2039 B7
- PnvT 44077 2039 B7
SR-44 Lakeland Frwy
- MNTR - 2145 B1
- PNVL - 2145 B1
- PnvT - 2145 B1
SR-44 Main St
100 CRDN 44024 2380 A6
10400 MNTU 44255 3159 C7
10900 ManT 44255 3159 C7
11900 ManT 44255 3024 C7
SR-44 Painesville Ravenna Rd
10300 MNTU 44255 3159 C7
10300 ShvT 44255 3159 B7
12400 ManT 44255 3024 C5
12800 AbnT 44255 3024 C4
SR-44 E Park St
100 CRDN 44024 2380 A6
SR-44 Ravenna Rd
11100 MsnT 44024 2505 A3
12500 MsnT 44024 2635 B1
13400 NbyT 44024 2635 B1
13700 NbyT 44021 2635 B7
13700 NbyT 44065 2635 B7
14200 NbyT 44021 2765 A2
14200 NbyT 44065 2765 A2
15400 NbyT 44021 2764 E5
15500 NbyT 44065 2764 E5
16300 AbnT 44021 2764 E5
16400 AbnT 44021 2893 E1
17900 AbnT 44234 2893 D7
18300 AbnT 44023 2893 D7
18300 AbnT 44023 3024 C2
18300 AbnT 44234 3024 C2
SR-44 South St
100 CRDN 44024 2380 A6
300 CRDN 44024 2505 A1
800 MsnT 44024 2505 A1
SR-44 Water St
100 CRDN 44024 2380 A6
SR-57
- EatT 44035 3006 E2
- EatT 44044 3006 E6
- EatT 44044 3007 A4
- ELYR 44035 2875 E4
- ELYR 44035 3006 E2
100 LORN 44055 2745 A2
300 EatT 44044 3141 E3
300 GFTN 44044 3141 E3
300 GFTN 44044 3142 D7
300 LORN 44052 2614 E7
500 LORN 44052 2745 A2
1100 ELYR 44035 2874 E4
1100 GftT 44044 3142 E7
1500 LORN 44052 2744 E1
1800 ELYR 44035 2875 B4
2100 ELYR 44035 2874 E1
2300 CrlT 44044 3006 E6
3700 LORN 44055 2745 E5
4800 ShfT 44055 2745 E5
6000 EyrT 44035 2745 E7
6000 ShfT 44035 2745 E7
6200 ELYR 44035 2745 E7
15500 GftT 44028 3142 E7
SR-57 E 28th St
100 LORN 44055 2745 A2
500 LORN 44052 2745 A2
SR-57 Broadway Av
300 LORN 44052 2614 E7
1500 LORN 44052 2744 E1
1900 LORN 44052 2745 A2
2300 LORN 44055 2745 A2
SR-57 Grafton Rd
2300 CrlT 44044 3006 E5
2300 EatT 44044 3006 E5
3000 EatT 44044 3141 E1
SR-57 Grafton-Eastern Rd
36000 GftT 44044 3142 D7
36700 GFTN 44044 3142 C7
SR-57 Grove Av
3700 LORN 44055 2745 E5
4800 ShfT 44055 2745 E5
SR-57 John F Kennedy Mem Pkwy
- ELYR 44035 2875 E4
SR-57 Lorain Blvd
1100 ELYR 44035 2874 E4
1800 ELYR 44035 2875 A2
2100 ELYR 44035 2874 E1
6000 EyrT 44035 2745 E7
6000 ShfT 44035 2745 E7
6000 ShfT 44055 2745 E7
6200 ELYR 44035 2745 E7
SR-57 Main St
300 EatT 44044 3141 E3
300 GFTN 44044 3141 E3
300 GFTN 44044 3142 D7
1100 GftT 44044 3142 D7
SR-57 South East Byp
- CrlT 44044 3006 E6
- EatT 44035 3006 E2
- EatT 44044 3006 E6
- EatT 44044 3007 A4
- ELYR 44035 2875 E6
- ELYR 44035 3006 E2
SR-57 Wooster-Avon Lake Rd
15500 GftT 44028 3142 E7
15500 GftT 44044 3142 E7
SR-58
10 OBLN 44074 3138 E1
100 AhtT 44001 2873 A5
100 AMHT 44001 2744 A7
100 AMHT 44001 2873 A5
500 NRsT 44074 3138 E1
800 AMHT 44053 2744 A7
1200 LORN 44052 2614 B7
1200 LORN 44053 2614 B7
1300 LORN 44052 2744 A7
1300 LORN 44053 2744 A7
8000 AhtT 44035 2873 A5
9000 AhtT 44001 2872 E7
9000 AhtT 44035 2872 E7
9200 AhtT 44001 3003 E1
9200 AhtT 44035 3003 E1
9200 NRsT 44001 3003 E1
9200 NRsT 44035 3003 E1
10700 NRsT 44074 3003 E6
12400 OBLN 44074 3003 E6
14200 PtfT 44074 3138 E7
SR-58 Ashland-Oberlin Rd
500 NRsT 44074 3138 E4
500 OBLN 44074 3138 E4
14200 PtfT 44074 3138 E5
SR-58 Leavitt Rd
1200 LORN 44052 2614 B7
1200 LORN 44053 2614 B7
1300 LORN 44052 2744 A7
1300 LORN 44053 2744 A7
7400 AhtT 44001 2873 A3
7400 AMHT 44001 2873 A3
8000 AhtT 44035 2873 A5
SR-58 N Leavitt Rd
100 AMHT 44001 2744 A7
100 AMHT 44001 2873 A5
800 AMHT 44053 2744 A6
SR-58 S Leavitt Rd
100 AhtT 44001 2873 A1
100 AMHT 44001 2873 A1
SR-58 N Main St
10 OBLN 44074 3138 E2
SR-58 S Main St
10 OBLN 44074 3138 E2
SR-58 Oberlin-North Rd
8700 AhtT 44001 2873 A6
8700 AhtT 44035 2873 A6
9000 AhtT 44001 2872 E7
9000 AhtT 44035 2872 E7
9200 AhtT 44001 3003 E1
9200 AhtT 44035 3003 E1
9200 NRsT 44001 3003 E1
9200 NRsT 44035 3003 E1
10700 NRsT 44074 3003 E6
12400 OBLN 44074 3003 E6
12500 NRsT 44074 3138 E1
SR-60
600 VMLN 44089 2740 E7
1200 VmnT 44089 2740 E7
1400 VmnT 44089 2869 E3
4700 FrnT 44889 2869 E3
4700 VmnT 44889 2869 E3
SR-60 Main St
600 VMLN 44089 2740 E7
SR-60 South St
5500 VMLN 44089 2740 E5
SR-60 State Rd
1400 VmnT 44089 2740 E7
1400 VmnT 44089 2869 E3
4700 FrnT 44889 2869 E3
4700 VmnT 44889 2869 E3
SR-60 State St
800 VMLN 44089 2740 E6
1200 VmnT 44089 2740 E7
SR-82
- BWHT 44141 3015 E7
10 AURA 44202 3157 D1
10 NCtT 44067 3152 C1
10 NCtT 44067 3153 A1
100 BWHT 44147 3014 E7
100 SgHT 44067 3152 C1
300 MCDN 44056 3153 A1
500 AURA 44202 3021 D7
500 AURA 44202 3156 C1
500 BWHT 44147 3015 E7
500 EatT 44044 3007 B7
900 SgHT 44067 3017 B7
1100 SgHT 44067 3016 E7
1200 ManT 44202 3157 D1
1400 MCDN 44056 3154 B1
1600 TNBG 44087 3154 B1
2400 BKVL 44141 3015 E7
2400 BKVL 44147 3015 E7
2600 EatT 44044 3006 E6
2600 ManT 44202 3158 A1
2800 TNBG 44087 3155 B2
3000 ManT 44255 3158 A1
3500 TwbT 44087 3155 B2
3600 NRYN 44133 3014 C7
3600 TwbT 44087 3156 A2
3700 ManT 44255 3159 C2
5300 ManT 44255 3160 C2
5500 HrmT 44255 3160 C2
5700 HrmT 44234 3160 C2
6200 NRYN 44133 3013 A7
6500 HRM 44234 3160 C2
6600 HRM 44234 3161 A3
6900 BKVL 44141 3016 A7
7200 HrmT 44234 3161 E4
7200 HrmT 44255 3161 E4
7800 GTVL 44234 3161 E4
11700 NRYN 44133 3012 E7
12800 SGVL 44133 3012 E7
12800 SGVL 44136 3012 E7
17800 SGVL 44136 3011 C7
22200 SGVL 44136 3010 D7
23000 ClbT 44028 3010 D7
23000 ClbT 44136 3010 D7
25000 ClbT 44028 3009 C7
26900 ClbT 44028 3008 D7
26900 EatT 44028 3008 D7
34700 EatT 44044 3008 D7
SR-82 Aurora Rd
3600 TwbT 44087 3155 E2
3600 TwbT 44087 3156 A2
SR-82 E Aurora Rd
10 NCtT 44067 3152 E1
10 NCtT 44067 3153 A1
300 MCDN 44056 3153 A1
1400 MCDN 44056 3154 B1
1600 TNBG 44087 3154 B1
2800 TNBG 44087 3155 B2
3500 TwbT 44087 3155 B2
SR-82 W Aurora Rd
10 NCtT 44067 3152 C1
100 SgHT 44067 3152 C1
900 SgHT 44067 3017 B7
1100 SgHT 44067 3016 E7
SR-82 Chippewa Rd
7300 BKVL 44141 3016 A7
SR-82 Garfield Rd
11400 HRM 44234 3161 A2
SR-82 E Garfield Rd
10 AURA 44202 3157 A1
1200 ManT 44202 3157 E1
SR-82 Ravenna Rd
9100 TNBG 44087 3155 C2
SR-82 Royalton Rd
500 EatT 44044 3007 B7
2600 EatT 44044 3006 E6
2900 BWHT 44147 3014 C7
3600 NRYN 44133 3014 C7
6200 NRYN 44133 3013 A7
11700 NRYN 44133 3012 E7
12800 SGVL 44133 3012 E7
12800 SGVL 44136 3012 E7
17800 SGVL 44136 3011 C7
22200 SGVL 44136 3010 D7
23000 ClbT 44028 3010 D7
23000 ClbT 44136 3010 D7
25000 ClbT 44028 3009 C7
26900 ClbT 44028 3008 D7
26900 EatT 44028 3008 D7
34700 EatT 44044 3008 D7
SR-82 E Royalton Rd
- BWHT 44141 3015 E7
100 BWHT 44147 3014 E7
500 BWHT 44147 3015 E7
2400 BKVL 44141 3015 E7
2400 BKVL 44147 3015 E7
6900 BKVL 44141 3016 A7
SR-82 W Royalton Rd
1000 BWHT 44147 3014 E7
SR-82 State St
7800 GTVL 44234 3161 E5
7800 HrmT 44234 3161 E5
SR-82 Twinsburg Warren Rd
10 AURA 44202 3156 E1
500 AURA 44202 3021 D7
500 AURA 44202 3156 C1
2600 AURA 44202 3157 D1
2600 ManT 44202 3157 D1
2600 ManT 44202 3158 A1
3000 ManT 44255 3158 A1
3700 ManT 44255 3159 C2
5300 ManT 44255 3160 C2
5500 HrmT 44255 3160 C2
7200 HrmT 44234 3161 E4
7200 HrmT 44255 3161 C4
SR-82 W Wakefield Rd
5700 HrmT 44234 3160 B2
5700 HrmT 44255 3160 A2
6500 HRM 44234 3160 E2
6600 HRM 44234 3161 B2
SR-82 Welshfield Limavle Rd S
11300 HRM 44234 3161 A3
11300 HrmT 44234 3161 A3
SR-83
100 AVLK 44012 2488 A7
100 AVLK 44012 2618 A6
800 AVON 44011 2618 A3
800 AVON 44012 2618 A6
1600 EatT 44028 3142 E1
1600 EatT 44044 3142 E1
1600 GFTN 44028 3142 E1
1600 GFTN 44044 3142 E1
2200 AVON 44011 2748 A1
4900 NRDV 44011 2748 A5
4900 NRDV 44039 2748 A5
5000 NRDV 44039 2877 A1
8900 NRDV 44039 3007 E2
8900 NRDV 44039 3008 A1
9700 EatT 44044 3007 E2
14700 GftT 44028 3142 E7
14700 GftT 44044 3142 E7
SR-83 Avon Belden Rd
800 AVON 44011 2618 A3
800 AVON 44012 2618 A3
2200 AVON 44011 2748 A1
4900 NRDV 44011 2748 A5
4900 NRDV 44039 2748 A5
5000 NRDV 44039 2877 A1
8900 NRDV 44039 3007 E2
8900 NRDV 44039 3008 A1
SR-83 Avon-Belden Center Rd
100 AVLK 44012 2488 A7
100 AVLK 44012 2618 A6
SR-83 Chester Rd
36500 AVON 44011 2618 A7
SR-83 Wooster-Avon Lake Rd
1600 EatT 44028 3142 E1
1600 EatT 44044 3142 E1
1600 GFTN 44028 3142 E1
1600 GFTN 44044 3142 E1
9700 EatT 44044 3007 E2
14700 GftT 44028 3142 E7
14700 GftT 44044 3142 E7
SR-83C
- EatT 44039 3007 E1
- EatT 44044 3007 E2
- NRDV 44039 3007 E1
10800 EatT 44039 3007 E2
10800 EatT 44044 3007 E2
10800 NRDV 44039 3007 E2
SR-83C Lorain Rd
10800 EatT 44039 3007 E2
10800 EatT 44039 3007 E2
10800 EatT 44044 3007 E2
10800 EatT 44044 3007 E2
10800 NRDV 44039 3007 E2
10800 NRDV 44039 3007 E2
SR-84
- MNTR 44094 2251 D3
10 GNVA 44041 1944 B6
10 MDSN 44057 2044 A1
10 PnvT 44077 2146 A4
200 PNVL 44077 2146 C1
500 GnvT 44041 1944 E5
700 MDSN 44057 2043 E2
800 PnvT 44077 2147 B1
1400 PryT 44077 2147 B1
2400 WKLF 44092 2374 B5
2500 PryT 44077 2041 D6
2600 PryT 44081 2041 D6
2700 WBHL 44092 2374 B5
2800 PryT 44081 2042 A5
4400 PRRY 44081 2042 E3
4500 PryT 44057 2042 E3
5000 MadT 44057 2043 B3
5000 MadT 44081 2043 B3
5000 PryT 44057 2043 B3
5000 PryT 44081 2043 B3
5500 HpfT 44041 1944 B6
5800 HpfT 44041 1943 C7
6800 HpfT 44057 1943 C7
7100 MadT 44057 1942 E7
7100 MadT 44057 1943 C7
7100 MadT 44057 2044 D1
7300 MNTR 44060 2251 D3
7800 HpfT 44057 1943 C7
8000 MNTR 44060 2252 B2
8400 KDHL 44060 2252 B2
9300 MNTR 44060 2253 A2
9600 CcdT 44060 2253 A2
9800 CcdT 44060 2145 C7
9800 CcdT 44077 2145 C7
10600 CcdT 44077 2146 A4
21000 EUCL 44117 2498 B1
23800 RDHT 44143 2498 B1
24400 RDHT 44143 2373 D7
26500 RDHT 44143 2374 B6
33300 WLBY 44094 2375 A3
36800 WLBY 44094 2250 D7
38500 WLBY 44094 2251 D3
SR-84 Bank St
800 PNVL 44077 2146 A4
800 PnvT 44077 2146 A4
SR-84 Bishop Rd
2400 WKLF 44092 2374 B4
2700 WBHL 44092 2374 B5
SR-84 Chardon Rd
21000 EUCL 44117 2498 B1
23800 RDHT 44143 2498 B1
24400 RDHT 44143 2373 D7
26500 RDHT 44143 2374 A6
27200 WBHL 44092 2374 A6
SR-84 Johnnycake Ridge Rd
- MNTR 44094 2251 D3
10 PnvT 44077 2146 B3
7300 MNTR 44060 2251 D3
8000 MNTR 44060 2252 B2
8400 KDHL 44060 2252 B2
9300 MNTR 44060 2253 A2
9600 CcdT 44060 2253 A2
9800 CcdT 44060 2145 C7
9800 CcdT 44077 2145 C7
10600 CcdT 44077 2146 A4
38200 WLBY 44094 2250 E6
38500 WLBY 44094 2251 D3
SR-84 E Main St
10 MDSN 44057 2044 B1
SR-84 W Main St
10 MDSN 44057 2044 A1
700 MDSN 44057 2043 E2
SR-84 Ridge Rd
28700 WKLF 44092 2374 B5
33300 WLBY 44094 2375 A3
36800 WLBY 44094 2250 D7
SR-84 S Ridge Rd
2600 PryT 44077 2041 D6
2600 PryT 44081 2041 D6
2800 PryT 44081 2042 A5
4400 PRRY 44081 2042 E3
4500 PryT 44057 2042 E3
5000 MadT 44057 2043 A3
5000 MadT 44081 2043 A3
5000 PryT 44057 2043 A3
5000 PryT 44081 2043 A3
7100 MadT 44057 1942 E7
7100 MadT 44057 1943 A7
7100 MadT 44057 2044 D1
7800 HpfT 44057 1943 B7
SR-84 S Ridge Rd E
10 GNVA 44041 1944 B6
500 GnvT 44041 1944 E5
SR-84 S Ridge Rd W
10 GNVA 44041 1944 B6
5500 HpfT 44041 1944 B6
5800 HpfT 44041 1943 C7
6800 HpfT 44057 1943 C7
SR-84 Riverside Dr
400 PnvT 44077 2146 D2
800 PnvT 44077 2147 B1
1400 PryT 44077 2147 B1
2500 PryT 44077 2041 C7
SR-84 S State St
400 PNVL 44077 2146 C2
700 PnvT 44077 2146 C2
SR-84 E Walnut Av
200 PNVL 44077 2146 C1
600 PnvT 44077 2146 C1
SR-86
- WndT 44064 2509 A2
- WndT 44099 2509 A2
10 PNVL 44077 2040 B7
10 PNVL 44077 2146 C1
700 PnvT 44077 2146 C3
6100 CcdT 44077 2146 C3
7800 TpnT 44064 2257 B3
7800 TpnT 44086 2257 B3
8300 MtlT 44064 2257 E7
8400 MtlT 44086 2257 E7
8700 MtlT 44064 2382 E1
9000 MtlT 44064 2383 A4
10600 HtbT 44064 2508 E1
10600 HtbT 44064 2509 A2
10600 MtlT 44064 2508 E1
11100 WndT 44064 2509 A2
11900 CcdT 44077 2147 B5
12200 LryT 44077 2147 B5
13000 LryT 44077 2255 E1
13000 LryT 44077 2256 D3
14100 LryT 44086 2256 D3
14500 LryT 44086 2257 B3
SR-86 Painesville Warren Rd
- PnvT 44077 2146 C3
6100 CcdT 44077 2146 C4
11900 CcdT 44077 2147 B5
12200 LryT 44077 2147 B5
13000 LryT 44077 2255 E1
13000 LryT 44077 2256 D3
14100 LryT 44086 2256 D3
14500 LryT 44086 2257 B3
14500 TpnT 44086 2257 B3
SR-86 Plank Rd
7800 TpnT 44064 2257 B4
7800 TpnT 44086 2257 B4
8300 MtlT 44064 2257 D5
8400 MtlT 44086 2257 D6
8700 MtlT 44064 2382 E1
9000 MtlT 44064 2383 A4
10600 HtbT 44064 2508 E1
10600 HtbT 44064 2509 A2
10600 MtlT 44064 2508 E1
11100 WndT 44064 2509 A2
SR-86 N State St
10 PNVL 44077 2040 B7
SR-86 S State St
10 PNVL 44077 2040 B7
10 PNVL 44077 2146 C1
700 PnvT 44077 2146 C3
SR-87
800 CLEV 44115 2625 A4
1900 CLEV 44114 2624 E3
2000 CLEV 44115 2624 E3
2100 CLEV 44113 2624 E3
2900 BHWD 44122 2628 D6
3000 BHWD 44122 2758 E1
3500 CLEV 44115 2625 D4
4000 CLEV 44104 2625 E4
4400 MstT 44062 2769 C2
7000 HGVL 44022 2761 B2
7100 RslT 44073 2761 B2
7300 RslT 44072 2761 B2
7500 CLEV 44104 2626 D5
8200 RslT 44072 2762 D2
9600 NbyT 44072 2763 C2
9600 RslT 44072 2763 C2
9900 NbyT 44065 2763 C2
10500 NbyT 44065 2764 C2
11600 CLEV 44120 2626 D5
11700 NbyT 44021 2764 C2
12000 NbyT 44021 2765 A1
12000 NbyT 44065 2765 A1
12400 BtnT 44021 2765 A1
13300 BtnT 44021 2766 A1
13300 CLEV 44120 2627 B5
13600 BURT 44021 2766 A1
13800 BURT 44021 2636 B7
13800 BURT 44021 2766 D2
14000 SRHT 44120 2627 B5
14100 BtnT 44062 2766 D2
15000 BtnT 44062 2767 A2
15100 MDFD 44062 2767 A2
15100 MdfT 44062 2767 A2
16300 MDFD 44062 2768 A2
16400 MdfT 44062 2768 A2
17400 MdfT 44062 2769 C2
17400 MstT 44062 2769 C2
17400 SRHT 44122 2627 E6
19500 SRHT 44122 2628 D6
26900 BHWD 44122 2759 C1
27000 ORNG 44122 2759 C1
27000 WDMR 44122 2759 C1
29000 ORNG 44124 2759 C1
29000 PRPK 44124 2759 C1
32900 PRPK 44124 2760 E2
33700 PRPK 44022 2760 E2
35200 HGVL 44022 2760 E2
35200 MDHL 44022 2760 E2
SR-87 Broadway Av
800 CLEV 44115 2625 A4
SR-87 Buckeye Rd
8400 CLEV 44104 2626 A5
SR-87 E Center St
13800 BURT 44021 2766 D2
SR-87 W Center St
13700 BURT 44021 2766 A1
SR-87 Chagrin Blvd
25600 BHWD 44122 2758 E1
26900 BHWD 44122 2759 C1
27000 ORNG 44122 2759 C1
27000 WDMR 44122 2759 C1
29000 ORNG 44124 2759 C1
29000 PRPK 44124 2759 C1
SR-87 E High St
15800 MDFD 44062 2767 D2
SR-87 W High St
15300 MDFD 44062 2767 B2
15400 MdfT 44062 2767 B2
SR-87 Kinsman Rd
4400 MstT 44062 2769 C2
7000 HGVL 44022 2761 B2
7100 RslT 44073 2761 B2
7300 RslT 44072 2761 B2
8200 RslT 44072 2762 D2
9600 NbyT 44072 2763 C2
9600 RslT 44072 2763 C2
9900 NbyT 44065 2763 C2
10500 NbyT 44065 2764 C2
11700 NbyT 44021 2764 C2
12000 NbyT 44021 2765 A1
12000 NbyT 44065 2765 A1
12400 BtnT 44021 2765 A1
13300 BtnT 44021 2766 A1
13600 BURT 44021 2766 A1
14100 BtnT 44062 2766 A1
15000 BtnT 44062 2767 A2
15100 MDFD 44062 2767 A2
15100 MdfT 44062 2767 A2
16200 MDFD 44062 2767 E2
16300 MDFD 44062 2768 A2
16400 MdfT 44062 2768 A2
17400 MdfT 44062 2769 C2
17400 MstT 44062 2769 C2
SR-87 Kirtland St
13800 BURT 44021 2636 B7
SR-87 Ontario St
1900 CLEV 44114 2624 E3
2000 CLEV 44115 2624 E3
2100 CLEV 44113 2624 E3
SR-87 Orange Av
1400 CLEV 44115 2625 A4
SR-87 E Park St
- BURT 44021 2636 B7
14600 BURT 44021 2766 B1
SR-87 W Park St
- BURT 44021 2636 A7
- BURT 44021 2766 A1
SR-87 Pinetree Rd
30400 PRPK 44124 2759 D1
SR-87 Richmond Rd
2900 BHWD 44122 2628 E7
3000 BHWD 44122 2758 E1
SR-87 Shaker Blvd
10000 CLEV 44104 2626 D5
11600 CLEV 44120 2626 D5
13300 CLEV 44120 2627 B5
14000 SRHT 44120 2627 B5
17400 SRHT 44122 2627 E6
19500 SRHT 44122 2628 D6
24300 BHWD 44122 2628 D6
SR-87 W Spring St
13800 BURT 44021 2636 B7
SR-87 Woodland Av
2500 CLEV 44115 2625 E4
4000 CLEV 44104 2625 E4
7500 CLEV 44104 2626 A4
SR-87 S Woodland Rd
32900 PRPK 44124 2759 D1
32900 PRPK 44124 2760 E2
33700 PRPK 44022 2760 E2
35200 HGVL 44022 2760 E2
35200 MDHL 44022 2760 E2
44000 HGVL 44022 2761 A2
SR-88
100 WFAR 44491 2898 E5
4400 FnTp 44491 2898 E5
4700 FnTp 44062 2898 A5
11900 NsnT 44231 3027 C2
15600 PkmT 44231 3027 C2
15900 PkmT 44234 3027 C2
16300 PkmT 44062 2896 E5
16300 PkmT 44062 2897 A5
16900 PkmT 44062 2898 A5
16900 PkmT 44491 2897 E5
16900 PkmT 44491 2898 A5
17800 FnTp 44062 2898 A5
17800 FnTp 44491 2898 A5
18200 PkmT 44234 2896 E7
SR-88 Greenville Rd NW
4400 FnTp 44491 2898 E5
4700 FnTp 44062 2898 C5
SR-88 Madison Rd
17700 PkmT 44062 2896 E7
SR-88 Main St
100 WFAR 44491 2898 E5
18200 PkmT 44062 2896 E7
18200 PkmT 44234 2896 E7
SR-88 McCall Rd
15600 NsnT 44231 3027 C2
15600 PkmT 44231 3027 C2
15900 PkmT 44234 3027 C2
SR-88 Nash Rd
16300 PkmT 44062 2896 E5
16300 PkmT 44062 2897 A5
16900 PkmT 44062 2898 A5
16900 PkmT 44491 2897 E5
16900 PkmT 44491 2898 A5
17800 FnTp 44062 2898 A5
17800 FnTp 44491 2898 A5
SR-88 Nelson Parkman Rd
- PkmT 44231 3027 E1
- PkmT 44234 3027 E1
SR-88 Ravenna Parkman Rd
11900 NsnT 44231 3027 B7
SR-91
- MDHT 44040 2630 A1
- WLBY 44094 2250 B4
- WLBY 44095 2250 B4
200 MAYF 44143 2500 A2
400 ETLK 44095 2250 B4
700 MAYF 44040 2500 A6
1000 MDHT 44124 2500 A6
1500 MDHT 44124 2630 A1
1700 GSML 44040 2630 A1
2400 HGVL 44022 2630 A1
2400 PRPK 44124 2630 A1
2500 WBHL 44094 2375 A5
2900 WBHL 44092 2375 A5
3000 WBHL 44092 2500 A2
3000 WBHL 44094 2500 A2
3300 HGVL 44022 2760 A2
3300 PRPK 44124 2760 A2
3500 PRPK 44022 2760 A2
3600 MDHL 44022 2760 A2
3600 MDHL 44124 2760 A2
4000 MDHL 44022 2759 E6
5000 SLN 44139 2759 E6
5100 SLN 44139 2760 A2
5200 SLN 44139 2889 A2
5200 WLBY 44094 2375 A1
7000 SLN 44139 3020 A1
7300 HDSN 44236 3154 E7
7700 TwbT 44236 3154 E7
7900 TNBG 44087 3154 E7
7900 TNBG 44236 3154 E7
7900 TwbT 44087 3154 E7
8700 TNBG 44087 3155 A2
9700 TNBG 44087 3019 E5
9800 TNBG 44087 3020 A6
SR-91 Darrow Rd
7300 HDSN 44236 3154 E7
7700 TwbT 44236 3154 E7
7900 TNBG 44087 3154 E7
7900 TNBG 44236 3154 E7
7900 TwbT 44087 3154 E7
8700 TNBG 44087 3155 A2
9700 TNBG 44087 3019 E5
9800 TNBG 44087 3020 A6
SR-91 Som Center Rd
- MDHT 44040 2630 A1
- WLBY 44094 2250 B4
- WLBY 44095 2250 B4
200 MAYF 44143 2500 A2
400 ETLK 44095 2250 B4
700 MAYF 44040 2500 A6
1000 MDHT 44124 2500 A6
1500 MDHT 44124 2630 A1
1700 GSML 44040 2630 A1
2400 HGVL 44022 2630 A1
2400 PRPK 44124 2630 A1
2500 WBHL 44094 2375 A5
2900 WBHL 44092 2375 A5
3000 WBHL 44092 2500 A2
3000 WBHL 44094 2500 A2
3300 HGVL 44022 2760 A2
3300 PRPK 44124 2760 A2
3500 PRPK 44022 2760 A2
3600 MDHL 44022 2760 A2
3600 MDHL 44124 2760 A2
4000 MDHL 44022 2759 E6
5000 SLN 44139 2759 E6
5100 SLN 44139 2760 A2
5200 SLN 44139 2889 A2
5200 WLBY 44094 2375 A1
7000 SLN 44139 3020 A1
SR-94
10 HkyT 44133 3149 A5
10 HkyT 44233 3149 A5
10 NRYN 44133 3149 A5
4200 CLEV 44109 2754 C4
4900 CLEV 44134 2754 C4
5200 PRMA 44134 2754 C4
5300 PRMA 44134 2883 C1
7100 PRMA 44129 2883 B6
7400 PRMA 44134 3014 B1
7800 NRYN 44134 3014 B1
7900 NRYN 44133 3014 B1
SR-94 River Rd
10 HkyT 44133 3149 A5
10 HkyT 44233 3149 A6
10 NRYN 44133 3149 A5
SR-94 State Rd
4200 CLEV 44109 2754 C4
4900 CLEV 44134 2754 C4
5200 PRMA 44134 2754 C4
5300 PRMA 44134 2883 C1
7100 PRMA 44129 2883 B6
7400 PRMA 44134 3014 B1
7800 NRYN 44134 3014 B1
7900 NRYN 44133 3014 B1
14000 NRYN 44133 3149 A2
20000 HkyT 44133 3149 A6
20000 HkyT 44233 3149 A6
SR-113
- ELYR 44035 2874 D4
- ELYR 44035 2875 B4
- EyrT 44035 2874 D4
100 SAHT 44001 2872 B7
300 AhtT 44001 2872 E6
400 SAHT 44001 3003 A1
700 ELYR 44035 2875 E4
900 ELYR 44039 2875 E5
1500 RKRV 44116 2621 E6
2500 LKWD 44126 2621 E6
2500 RKRV 44126 2621 E6
20500 RKRV 44116 2751 C1
20600 FWPK 44116 2751 C1
20600 FWPK 44126 2751 C1
21600 RKRV 44126 2751 C1
23000 WTLK 44116 2751 C1
23000 WTLK 44145 2751 C1
23200 WTLK 44145 2750 E1
27100 WTLK 44145 2749 D3
31400 NRDV 44039 2749 B6
31400 NRDV 44145 2749 B6
31700 NRDV 44039 2748 E7
31700 NRDV 44039 2877 E1
36000 NRDV 44039 2876 D4
39100 NRDV 44039 2875 E5
42900 ELYR 44035 2873 D6
42900 EyrT 44035 2873 D6
43000 AhtT 44035 2873 D6
46000 AhtT 44001 2873 D6
SR-113 Center Ridge Rd
19400 RKRV 44116 2621 E7
20500 RKRV 44116 2751 C1
20600 FWPK 44116 2751 C1
20600 FWPK 44126 2751 C1
21600 RKRV 44126 2751 C1
23000 WTLK 44116 2751 C1
23000 WTLK 44145 2751 C1
23200 WTLK 44145 2750 E1
27100 WTLK 44145 2749 D3
31400 NRDV 44039 2749 B6
31400 NRDV 44145 2749 B6
31700 NRDV 44039 2748 E7
31700 NRDV 44039 2877 E1
36000 NRDV 44039 2876 D4
39100 NRDV 44039 2875 E5
SR-113 Cleveland St
700 ELYR 44035 2875 E5
900 ELYR 44039 2875 E4
SR-113 John F Kennedy Mem Pkwy
- ELYR 44035 2874 D4
- ELYR 44035 2875 B4
- EyrT 44035 2874 D4
SR-113 E Main St
100 SAHT 44001 2872 C7
300 AhtT 44001 2872 D7
SR-113 W Main St
100 SAHT 44001 2872 B7
400 SAHT 44001 3003 A1
SR-113 Milan Elyria Rd
42900 ELYR 44035 2873 D6
42900 EyrT 44035 2873 D6
42900 EyrT 44035 2874 A5
43000 AhtT 44035 2873 D6
46000 AhtT 44001 2873 D6
46100 AhtT 44001 2872 E6
SR-113 Wooster Rd
1500 RKRV 44116 2621 E6
2500 LKWD 44126 2621 E6
2500 RKRV 44126 2621 E6
SR-166
- TmbT 44084 2259 C2
- TmbT 44086 2259 C2
13900 HmbT 44024 2381 C2
14300 HmbT 44024 2256 E7
14800 HmbT 44024 2257 C4
14800 MtlT 44024 2257 C4
14800 MtlT 44064 2257 C4
14800 TpnT 44064 2257 C4
15600 TpnT 44086 2257 C4
16100 TpnT 44086 2258 D2
17500 TpnT 44086 2259 C2
17700 TmbT 44086 2259 C2
SR-166 Rock Creek Rd
13900 HmbT 44024 2381 C2
14300 HmbT 44024 2256 E7
14800 HmbT 44024 2257 C4
14800 MtlT 44024 2257 C4
14800 MtlT 44064 2257 C4
14800 TpnT 44064 2257 C4
15600 TpnT 44086 2257 C4
16100 TpnT 44086 2258 D2
17500 TpnT 44086 2259 C2
17700 TmbT 44086 2259 C2
SR-168
- BURT 44021 2766 B2
14800 BtnT 44021 2766 E5
14800 BtnT 44062 2766 E5
16000 PkmT 44062 2896 B4
16000 PkmT 44234 2896 B4
16300 BtnT 44021 2767 A7
16300 BtnT 44062 2767 A7
16300 PkmT 44021 2896 B4
16300 TroT 44021 2767 A7
16300 TroT 44062 2767 A7
16300 TroT 44021 2896 B4
16300 TroT 44062 2896 B4
SR-168 S Cheshire Rd
- BtnT 44021 2766 B2
14700 BURT 44021 2766 B1
SR-168 S Cheshire St
- BURT 44021 2766 B2
SR-168 High St
16000 PkmT 44062 2896 D7
16000 PkmT 44234 2896 D7
SR-168 Tavern Rd
14800 BtnT 44021 2766 E5
14800 BtnT 44062 2766 E5
14800 BURT 44021 2766 E5
16300 BtnT 44021 2767 A7

INDEX 4

SR-168 Tavern Rd

Cleveland Street Index

US-6 Lake Rd

STREET Block	City	ZIP	Map#	Grid
SR-168 Tavern Rd				
16300	BtnT	44062	2767	A7
16300	PkmT	44021	2896	B4
16300	PkmT	44062	2896	B4
16300	TroT	44021	2767	A7
16300	TroT	44062	2767	A7
16300	TroT	44021	2896	B4
16300	TroT	44062	2896	B4
17800	PkmT	44234	2896	B4
SR-174				
400	GSML	44040	2500	D2
1400	GSML	44040	2630	E1
2100	WBHL	44094	2375	D2
2900	GSML	44094	2500	D2
2900	WBHL	44094	2500	D2
4100	WLBY	44094	2250	E6
SR-174 Chagrin River Rd				
-	GSML	44094	2500	C1
-	WBHL	44094	2500	C1
400	GSML	44040	2500	D2
1400	GSML	44040	2630	E1
SR-174 Ridge Rd				
37700	WLBY	44094	2250	E7
SR-174 River Rd				
-	WLBY	44094	2250	D7
2100	WBHL	44094	2375	D2
2900	GSML	44040	2500	D2
2900	GSML	44094	2500	D2
2900	WBHL	44094	2500	D2
SR-174 River St				
4100	WLBY	44094	2250	E6
SR-175				
100	EUCL	44117	2373	E7
100	EUCL	44143	2373	E7
100	RDHT	44143	2373	E7
200	EUCL	44132	2373	E1
300	RDHT	44143	2498	E2
800	LNHT	44124	2498	E6
1500	LNHT	44124	2628	E5
2100	BHWD	44122	2628	E7
3000	BHWD	44122	2758	E1
4100	HIHL	44122	2758	E3
4100	WVHT	44122	2758	E3
4500	WVHT	44022	2758	E6
4500	WVHT	44128	2758	E3
5000	BDHT	44146	2758	E6
5500	BDHT	44146	2888	A1
5500	SLN	44139	2888	A1
25700	BDHT	44146	2887	E1
25700	SLN	44146	2888	A1
SR-175 E 260th St				
200	EUCL	44132	2373	E1
SR-175 Cannon Rd				
27200	SLN	44139	2888	A2
27300	SLN	44146	2888	A2
SR-175 Richmond Rd				
100	EUCL	44117	2373	E7
100	EUCL	44143	2373	E7
100	RDHT	44143	2373	E7
300	RDHT	44143	2498	E2
800	LNHT	44124	2498	E6
1500	LNHT	44124	2628	E5
2100	BHWD	44122	2628	E7
3000	BHWD	44122	2758	E1
4100	HIHL	44122	2758	E3
4100	WVHT	44122	2758	E3
4500	WVHT	44022	2758	E6
4500	WVHT	44128	2758	E3
5000	BDHT	44146	2758	E6
25700	BDHT	44146	2887	E1
25700	BDHT	44146	2888	A1
25700	SLN	44146	2888	A1
27000	SLN	44139	2888	A1
SR-176				
-	CLEV	-	2754	E1
-	CLEV	-	2755	A5
1500	CLEV	44134	2754	D7
1500	PRMA	44134	2754	D7
4800	RchT	44286	3149	E6
4800	RchT	44286	3150	A7
5300	PRMA	44134	2883	E2
5300	RchT	44147	3149	E6
5300	RchT	44233	3149	E6
5300	RchT	44286	3149	E6
6300	PRMA	44131	2883	E6
6300	SVHL	44131	2883	E6
7300	PRMA	44131	3014	E1
7300	PRMA	44134	3014	E1
7300	SVHL	44131	3014	E1
7900	BWHT	44147	3014	E1
9200	BWHT	44147	3149	E1
SR-176 Broadview Rd				
4800	RchT	44286	3149	E6
4800	RchT	44286	3150	A7
5200	PRMA	44134	2754	D7
5300	PRMA	44134	2883	E2
5300	RchT	44147	3149	E6
5300	RchT	44233	3149	E6
5300	RchT	44286	3149	E6
6300	PRMA	44131	2883	E6
6300	SVHL	44131	2883	E6
7300	PRMA	44131	3014	E1
7300	PRMA	44134	3014	E1
7300	SVHL	44131	3014	E1
7900	BWHT	44147	3014	E1
9200	BWHT	44147	3149	E1
SR-176 Brookpark Rd				
1500	CLEV	44134	2754	D7
1500	PRMA	44134	2754	D7
SR-176 Jennings Frwy				
-	CLEV	-	2754	E1
-	CLEV	-	2755	A5
SR-237				
-	BKPK	-	2751	E7
-	BKPK	-	2880	D2
-	CLEV	-	2880	C6
-	CLEV	44142	2880	C6
10	BERA	44017	2880	C6
200	BERA	44017	3011	B2
700	SGVL	44017	3011	B2
800	BERA	44142	2880	C6
800	BKPK	44142	2880	C6
1100	LKWD	44107	2622	A4
2300	CLEV	44111	2622	A5
2300	LKWD	44111	2622	A5
3200	CLEV	44111	2752	A4
3900	CLEV	44135	2752	A4
4800	CLEV	44135	2751	E6
8500	SGVL	44136	3011	B2
18200	BKPK	44135	2751	E7
18200	BKPK	44135	2752	A4
18200	BKPK	44142	2752	A4
SR-237 W Bagley Rd				
10	BERA	44017	2880	C6
SR-237 Berea Frwy				
-	BKPK	-	2751	E7
-	BKPK	-	2880	D2
-	CLEV	-	2880	C6
-	CLEV	44142	2880	C6
SR-237 Brookpark Rd				
18200	BKPK	44135	2751	E7
18200	BKPK	44142	2751	E7
18200	BKPK	44135	2752	A7
18200	BKPK	44142	2752	A7
18200	CLEV	44135	2751	E7
18200	CLEV	44135	2752	A7
SR-237 W Clifton Blvd				
1100	LKWD	44107	2622	A4
SR-237 Front St				
200	BERA	44017	2880	C6
SR-237 Henry St				
10	BERA	44017	2880	B7
SR-237 Kolthoff Dr				
6500	BERA	44142	2880	C4
6500	BKPK	44142	2880	C4
SR-237 Mulberry St				
200	BERA	44017	2880	B6
SR-237 Prospect Rd				
8500	SGVL	44017	3011	B2
8500	SGVL	44136	3011	B3
SR-237 Prospect St				
10	BERA	44017	2880	B7
200	BERA	44017	3011	B2
700	SGVL	44017	3011	B2
SR-237 Riverside Dr				
1500	LKWD	44107	2622	A5
2300	CLEV	44111	2622	A7
2300	LKWD	44111	2622	A7
SR-237 Rocky River Dr				
3100	CLEV	44111	2622	B7
3200	CLEV	44111	2752	A4
3900	CLEV	44135	2752	A4
4800	CLEV	44135	2751	E6
SR-237 N Rocky River Dr				
800	BERA	44017	2880	C4
800	BERA	44142	2880	C4
800	BKPK	44142	2880	C4
SR-252				
10	LvpT	44028	3145	A5
10	LvpT	44280	3145	A5
300	BYVL	44140	2620	C6
300	LvpT	44280	3144	E7
600	WTLK	44145	2620	C6
1700	WTLK	44145	2750	C3
3200	WTLK	44070	2750	C3
4800	NOSD	44070	2750	C6
5200	NOSD	44070	2879	C2
6200	OmsT	44070	2879	C2
6200	OmsT	44138	2879	C2
6700	ODFL	44138	2879	C2
8400	ODFL	44138	3010	B3
9800	ClbT	44028	3010	B3
14000	ClbT	44028	3145	A2
18000	LvpT	44028	3145	A5
24400	ClbT	44138	3010	B3
SR-252 Columbia Rd				
10	LvpT	44028	3145	A5
10	LvpT	44280	3145	A5
300	BYVL	44140	2620	C6
300	LvpT	44280	3144	E7
600	WTLK	44145	2620	C6
1700	WTLK	44145	2750	C3
3200	NOSD	44070	2750	C3
3200	WTLK	44070	2750	C3
5900	NOSD	44070	2879	C1
6200	OmsT	44070	2879	C2
6200	OmsT	44138	2879	C2
6700	ODFL	44138	2879	C4
8400	ODFL	44138	3010	B3
SR-252 Great Northern Blvd				
4500	NOSD	44070	2750	C6
5200	NOSD	44070	2879	C2
SR-252 Lorain Rd				
24700	NOSD	44070	2750	C6
SR-252 Main St				
7900	ODFL	44138	2879	C5
SR-252 E River Rd				
9800	ClbT	44028	3010	C2
14000	ClbT	44028	3145	A2
18000	LvpT	44028	3145	A5
SR-252 Sprague Rd				
24400	ClbT	44028	3010	B2
24400	ClbT	44138	3010	B2
24400	ODFL	44138	3010	B2
SR-254				
-	LKWD	44107	2621	D5
-	RKRV	44107	2621	D5
-	WTLK	44116	2621	B6
1300	LKWD	44107	2622	A5
2100	ShfT	44035	2745	E6
2100	ShfT	44055	2745	E6
2300	ShfT	44055	2746	A6
3200	SFLD	44035	2746	A6
3200	SFLD	44054	2746	A6
3200	ShfT	44035	2746	A6
3200	ShfT	44054	2746	A6
5300	AVON	44011	2747	A4
5300	SFLD	44011	2747	A4
5300	SFLD	44035	2747	A4
5300	SFLD	44054	2747	A4
19000	RKRV	44116	2621	D5
22900	WTLK	44145	2621	B6
23300	WTLK	44145	2620	B7
27300	WTLK	44145	2619	C7
30600	WTLK	44145	2749	A1
31400	AVON	44145	2749	A1
32200	AVON	44011	2748	B1
32200	AVON	44011	2749	A1
SR-254 Detroit Rd				
-	LKWD	44107	2621	D5
-	RKRV	44107	2621	D5
-	WTLK	44116	2621	B6
4700	SFLD	44035	2746	E5
4700	SFLD	44054	2746	E5
5300	AVON	44011	2747	A4
5300	SFLD	44011	2747	A4
5300	SFLD	44035	2747	A4
5300	SFLD	44054	2747	A4
19000	RKRV	44116	2621	D5
22900	WTLK	44145	2621	B6
23300	WTLK	44145	2620	B7
27300	WTLK	44145	2619	C7
30600	WTLK	44145	2749	A1
31400	AVON	44145	2749	A1
32200	AVON	44011	2748	B1
32200	AVON	44011	2749	A1
SR-254 N Ridge Rd				
2100	ShfT	44035	2745	E6
2100	ShfT	44055	2745	E6
2300	ShfT	44055	2746	A6
3200	SFLD	44035	2746	C6
3200	SFLD	44054	2746	C6
3200	ShfT	44035	2746	C6
3200	ShfT	44054	2746	C6
SR-254 Sloane Av				
1300	LKWD	44107	2622	A5
SR-282				
-	PkmT	44491	3028	B5
11500	NsnT	44231	3028	B5
12800	PkmT	44231	3028	B5
SR-282 Nelson Ledge Rd				
-	PkmT	44491	3028	B5
11500	NsnT	44231	3028	B5
12800	PkmT	44231	3028	B5
SR-283				
10	PNVL	44077	2040	A7
100	GDRV	44045	2039	C6
400	PnvT	44077	2039	E7
600	PNVL	44077	2039	E7
600	PnvT	44060	2039	A7
700	PnvT	44045	2039	C6
5500	MONT	44060	2143	E1
7000	MNTR	44060	2143	B4
8000	MONT	44060	2144	B1
8100	MNTR	44060	2144	B1
9100	MNTR	44060	2038	E7
9300	MNTR	44060	2039	A7
13600	BTNH	44108	2497	A1
13600	BTNH	44110	2497	A1
13800	CLEV	44110	2372	C6
16900	CLEV	44119	2372	C6
18400	EUCL	44119	2372	C6
19500	EUCL	44119	2373	D1
19800	EUCL	44123	2373	D1
24800	EUCL	44132	2373	D1
25700	EUCL	44132	2248	E7
27200	EUCL	44132	2249	B6
28100	WLWK	44095	2249	B6
33000	ETLK	44095	2249	D4
33500	LKLN	44095	2249	D4
34400	TMLK	44095	2249	D4
34700	ETLK	44095	2250	B1
34700	TMLK	44095	2250	B1
35900	ETLK	44095	2142	C7
37900	WLBY	44094	2142	D5
37900	WLBY	44095	2142	D5
38400	WLBY	44094	2143	B4
38800	MNTR	44094	2143	B4
SR-283 Andrews Rd				
5500	MONT	44060	2143	E1
SR-283 Lake Shore Blvd				
500	PnvT	44077	2039	C6
600	PnvT	44060	2039	B7
7000	MNTR	44060	2143	B4
SR-283 Lake shore Blvd				
7200	MNTR	44060	2143	B4
SR-283 Lake Shore Blvd				
7700	MONT	44060	2143	E1
8000	MONT	44060	2144	B1
8100	MNTR	44060	2144	B1
9100	MNTR	44060	2038	E7
9300	MNTR	44060	2039	A7
13600	BTNH	44108	2497	A1
13600	BTNH	44110	2497	A1
13800	CLEV	44110	2372	C6
16900	CLEV	44119	2372	C6
18400	EUCL	44119	2372	C6
19500	EUCL	44119	2373	D1
19800	EUCL	44123	2373	D1
24800	EUCL	44132	2373	D1
25700	EUCL	44132	2248	E7
27200	EUCL	44132	2249	B6
28100	WLWK	44095	2249	B6
33000	ETLK	44095	2249	D4
33500	LKLN	44095	2249	D4
34400	TMLK	44095	2249	D4
34700	ETLK	44095	2250	B1
34700	TMLK	44095	2250	B1
35900	ETLK	44095	2142	C7
37900	WLBY	44094	2142	D5
37900	WLBY	44095	2142	D5
38400	WLBY	44094	2143	B4
38800	MNTR	44094	2143	B4
SR-283 Richmond Rd				
800	PnvT	44077	2039	E7
1000	GDRV	44045	2039	C6
1000	PnvT	44045	2039	C6
SR-283 Richmond St				
10	PNVL	44077	2040	A7
600	PNVL	44077	2039	E7
600	PnvT	44077	2039	E7
SR-283 River St				
600	GDRV	44045	2039	C6
700	PnvT	44045	2039	C6
SR-283 Singer Av				
100	GDRV	44045	2039	C6
400	PnvT	44077	2039	C6
SR-291				
5000	BKPK	44142	2752	A7
5000	BKPK	44142	2881	A1
6600	MDBH	44130	2881	A6
7400	MDBH	44130	3012	A1
SR-291 Engle Rd				
5000	BKPK	44142	2752	A7
5000	BKPK	44142	2881	A1
6600	MDBH	44130	2881	A6
7400	MDBH	44130	3012	A1
SR-291 Fowles Rd				
16600	MDBH	44130	3012	B1
SR-301				
-	CrlT	-	3006	B5
-	EatT	-	3006	B5
-	EatT	44035	3006	E2
-	EatT	44044	3006	E2
-	ELYR	44035	2875	E6
-	ELYR	44035	3006	E2
100	SDLK	44054	2616	E6
400	ELYR	44035	2875	E4
600	SFLD	44054	2616	E6
800	ELYR	44035	2746	E6
2400	SFLD	44054	2746	E1
4900	SFLD	44035	2746	E6
11900	CrlT	44035	3005	E7
12000	CrlT	44050	3005	E7
12200	CrlT	44050	3140	E2
13800	LrgT	44050	3140	E6
SR-301 Abbe Rd				
100	SDLK	44054	2616	E6
400	ELYR	44035	2875	E2
600	SFLD	44054	2616	E6
800	ELYR	44035	2746	E6
2400	SFLD	44054	2746	E1
4900	SFLD	44035	2746	E6
SR-301 John F Kennedy Mem Pkwy				
-	ELYR	44035	2875	E4
SR-301 Lattasburg-Elyria Rd				
11900	CrlT	44035	3005	E7
12000	CrlT	44050	3005	E7
12200	CrlT	44050	3140	E2
13800	LrgT	44050	3140	E6
SR-301 South East Byp				
-	EatT	44035	3006	E2
-	EatT	44044	3006	E2
-	ELYR	44035	2875	E6
-	ELYR	44035	3006	E2
SR-305				
6900	HRM	44234	3161	E2
7100	HrmT	44234	3161	E2
SR-305 E Wakefield Rd				
6900	HRM	44234	3161	E2
7100	HrmT	44234	3161	E2
SR-306				
-	WLBY	44060	2251	C3
-	WLBY	44094	2251	C3
10	AURA	44202	3021	E7
10	AURA	44202	3156	E1
200	AURA	44202	3022	A3
5000	SRSL	44073	2762	A4
6200	MNTR	44060	2143	C5
7300	MNTR	44060	2251	C3
8700	KTLD	44094	2251	D7
9100	KTLD	44094	2376	E2
9500	KTLD	44094	2377	A3
11000	KTLD	44094	2502	B5
11100	CsTp	44026	2502	B5
11100	CsTp	44094	2502	B5
12700	CsTp	44026	2632	A5
13400	CsTp	44072	2632	A5
13400	RslT	44072	2632	A5
14600	RslT	44072	2762	A4
15200	RslT	44073	2762	A4
15800	BbgT	44023	2762	A4
16400	BbgT	44023	2891	A1
18400	BbgT	44023	3022	A3
SR-306 Broadmoor Rd				
-	WLBY	44060	2251	C5
-	WLBY	44094	2251	C5
8000	MNTR	44060	2251	C3
SR-306 Chillicothe Rd				
5000	SRSL	44073	2762	A4
8700	KTLD	44094	2251	D6
9100	KTLD	44094	2376	E2
9500	KTLD	44094	2377	A3
11000	KTLD	44094	2502	B5
11100	CsTp	44026	2502	B5
11100	CsTp	44094	2502	B5
12700	CsTp	44026	2632	A5
13400	CsTp	44072	2632	A5
13400	RslT	44072	2632	A5
14600	RslT	44072	2762	A4
15200	RslT	44073	2762	A4
15800	BbgT	44023	2762	A4
16400	BbgT	44023	2891	A1
18400	BbgT	44023	3022	A3
SR-306 N Chillicothe Rd				
10	AURA	44202	3021	E7
200	AURA	44202	3022	A5
SR-306 S Chillicothe Rd				
10	AURA	44202	3156	E1
SR-306 Reynolds Rd				
6200	MNTR	44060	2143	C5
7300	MNTR	44060	2251	C3
SR-307				
5800	HpfT	44041	2045	D3
6700	HpfT	44057	2045	D3
6700	MadT	44057	2044	C3
6700	MDSN	44057	2044	C3
7200	HpfT	44057	2045	D3
7200	MadT	44057	2045	D3
SR-307 N River Rd W				
5800	HpfT	44041	2045	D3
6700	HpfT	44057	2045	D3
SR-307 Warner Rd				
6700	MadT	44057	2044	C3
6700	MDSN	44057	2044	C3
7200	HpfT	44057	2045	B3
7200	MadT	44057	2045	A3
SR-511				
10	OBLN	44074	3138	E2
100	OBLN	44074	3139	A2
600	NRsT	44074	3138	A2
700	NRsT	44074	3139	D2
SR-511 Cleveland Oberlin Rd				
700	NRsT	44074	3139	B2
700	OBLN	44074	3139	B2
SR-511 E Lorain St				
10	OBLN	44074	3138	E2
100	OBLN	44074	3139	A2
SR-511 W Lorain St				
10	OBLN	44074	3138	E2
600	NRsT	44074	3138	B2
SR-511 Oberlin-Norwalk Rd				
47000	NRsT	44074	3138	A2
SR-528				
10	MDSN	44057	2044	B1
200	MDSN	44057	1942	B6
2700	MadT	44057	1942	B6
4300	MadT	44057	2044	B3
5200	MadT	44057	2150	B3
5500	TpnT	44057	2150	B3
5900	TpnT	44086	2150	B6
6700	TpnT	44086	2258	B2
8400	MtlT	44086	2258	B5
8600	MtlT	44064	2258	B5
8600	MtlT	44064	2383	B2
11000	HtbT	44064	2508	A4
11000	MtlT	44064	2508	A4
11400	HtbT	44046	2508	A4
12400	HtbT	44046	2638	A4
13200	HtbT	44062	2638	A4
13200	MdfT	44062	2638	A4
14300	MDFD	44062	2768	A1
14300	MdfT	44062	2768	A1
15900	MdfT	44062	2767	E7
16300	PkmT	44062	2767	E7
16300	PkmT	44062	2896	E1
18200	PkmT	44234	2896	E7
SR-528 Chardon-Madison Rd				
4400	MadT	44057	2044	B4
4400	MDSN	44057	2044	B4
5200	MadT	44057	2150	B3
5500	TpnT	44057	2150	B3
SR-528 Hubbard Rd				
2700	MadT	44057	1942	B6
2700	MDSN	44057	1942	B6
SR-528 N Lake St				
-	MadT	44057	1942	B6
10	MDSN	44057	2044	B1
200	MDSN	44057	1942	B7
SR-528 Madison Rd				
4300	MadT	44057	2044	B3
4300	MDSN	44057	2044	B3
5900	TpnT	44086	2150	B6
6700	TpnT	44086	2258	B2
8400	MtlT	44086	2258	B5
8600	MtlT	44064	2258	B5
8600	MtlT	44064	2383	B2
11000	HtbT	44064	2508	A4
11000	MtlT	44064	2508	A4
11400	HtbT	44046	2508	A4
12400	HtbT	44046	2638	A4
13200	HtbT	44062	2638	A4
13200	MdfT	44062	2638	A4
14300	MDFD	44062	2768	A1
14300	MdfT	44062	2768	A1
15900	MdfT	44062	2767	E7
16300	PkmT	44062	2767	E7
16300	PkmT	44062	2896	E1
SR-528 Main St				
18200	PkmT	44062	2896	E7
18200	PkmT	44234	2896	E7
SR-528 W Main St				
10	MDSN	44057	2044	B1
SR-528 River St				
10	MDSN	44057	2044	B3
SR-528 Thompson Rd				
-	TpnT	44086	2150	B5
SR-534				
10	GNVA	44041	1944	C2
700	GnvT	44041	1944	C2
2100	HpfT	44041	1944	C7
SR-534 N Broadway				
10	GNVA	44041	1944	C4
SR-534 S Broadway				
10	GNVA	44041	1944	B4
SR-534 N Broadway St				
700	GNVA	44041	1944	C2
700	GnvT	44041	1944	C2
SR-534 S Broadway St				
1200	GNVA	44041	1944	C6
SR-535				
10	PnvT	44077	2040	C4
500	FTHR	44077	2039	D5
500	PnvT	44077	2039	D5
600	PNVL	44077	2039	E6
SR-535 East St				
600	FTHR	44077	2039	D4
SR-535 Fairport Nursery Rd				
10	PnvT	44077	2040	C4
500	FTHR	44077	2039	D5
500	PnvT	44077	2039	D5
SR-535 Richmond St				
600	PNVL	44077	2039	E6
600	PnvT	44077	2039	E6
900	FTHR	44077	2039	E6
SR-608				
8400	HmbT	44024	2255	D6
8400	HmbT	44077	2255	D6
8800	HmbT	44024	2380	E1
8800	HmbT	44024	2381	A2
10900	ClrT	44024	2506	C2
10900	HmbT	44024	2506	C2
11500	CcdT	44077	2146	D7
11500	CcdT	44077	2254	E1
11900	CcdT	44077	2255	B4
12400	ClrT	44021	2506	C2
12400	ClrT	44021	2636	E1
12700	CcdT	44024	2255	D6
12700	CcdT	44077	2255	D6
12700	HmbT	44077	2255	D6
12800	ClrT	44021	2637	A2
13400	HtbT	44021	2637	A2
13500	MdfT	44021	2637	A2
13600	MdfT	44046	2637	A2
13700	MdfT	44062	2637	D7
14300	MDFD	44062	2767	D3
14300	MdfT	44062	2767	D3
SR-608 Concord-Hambden Rd				
11500	CcdT	44077	2146	D7
11500	CcdT	44077	2254	E1
11900	CcdT	44077	2255	B4
12700	CcdT	44024	2255	D6
12700	CcdT	44077	2255	D6
12700	HmbT	44024	2255	D6
12700	HmbT	44077	2255	D6
SR-608 Old State Rd				
8400	HmbT	44024	2255	D6
8400	HmbT	44077	2255	C5
8800	HmbT	44024	2380	E1
8800	HmbT	44024	2381	A2
10900	ClrT	44024	2506	C2
10900	HmbT	44024	2506	C2
12400	ClrT	44021	2506	C2
12400	ClrT	44021	2636	E1
12800	ClrT	44021	2637	A2
13400	HtbT	44021	2637	A2
13500	MdfT	44021	2637	A2
13600	MdfT	44046	2637	A2
13700	MdfT	44062	2637	D7
14300	MDFD	44062	2767	D3
14300	MdfT	44062	2767	D3
SR-608 N State Av				
14700	MDFD	44062	2767	D1
SR-608 S State Av				
14900	MDFD	44062	2767	D2
15300	MdfT	44062	2767	D4
SR-611				
100	LORN	44052	2744	C1
100	LORN	44052	2745	A1
1400	LORN	44052	2615	A7
3200	LORN	44053	2744	C1
3300	LORN	44053	2743	E2
3500	LORN	44054	2615	C7
3500	SFLD	44054	2615	C7
3600	SFLD	44054	2616	D7
5400	SFLD	44011	2617	A6
5400	SFLD	44054	2617	A6
37100	AVON	44011	2747	D1
38300	AVON	44011	2617	C7
SR-611 W 21st St				
100	LORN	44052	2744	C1
3200	LORN	44053	2744	C1
3300	LORN	44053	2743	E2
SR-611 Colorado Av				
1400	LORN	44052	2615	A7
3500	LORN	44054	2615	C7
3500	SFLD	44054	2615	C7
3600	SFLD	44054	2616	D7
5400	SFLD	44011	2617	A6
5400	SFLD	44054	2617	A6
37100	AVON	44011	2747	D1
38300	AVON	44011	2617	C7
SR-611 Henderson Dr				
100	LORN	44052	2745	A1
1700	LORN	44052	2615	B7
SR-615				
-	KDHL	44060	2251	E6
-	KTLD	44060	2251	E6
-	KTLD	44060	2252	B3
-	KTLD	44094	2252	B3
6300	MNTR	44060	2144	A3
7200	MNTR	44060	2252	B3
7700	MNTR	44060	2143	E3
7700	MONT	44060	2143	E3
8300	KDHL	44060	2252	B3
8800	KTLD	44094	2251	E6
SR-615 Center St				
6300	MNTR	44060	2144	B4
7200	MNTR	44060	2252	B3
8300	KDHL	44060	2252	B3
SR-615 Chillicothe Rd				
-	KDHL	44060	2251	E6
-	KTLD	44060	2251	E6
-	KTLD	44060	2252	A6
-	KTLD	44094	2252	A6
8400	KDHL	44060	2252	A6
8800	KTLD	44094	2251	E6
SR-615 Munson Rd				
7700	MNTR	44060	2143	E3
7700	MONT	44060	2143	E3
8000	MNTR	44060	2144	A3
SR-631				
11500	SgHT	44067	3017	C5
SR-631 Valley View Rd				
11500	SgHT	44067	3017	C5
SR-633				
200	EUCL	44132	2249	A7
400	EUCL	44132	2374	B2
400	WKLF	44092	2374	B2
SR-633 Lloyd Rd				
200	EUCL	44132	2249	A7
400	EUCL	44132	2374	B2
400	WKLF	44092	2374	B2
SR-640				
31000	WLWK	44095	2249	E5
32700	ETLK	44095	2249	E5
33700	ETLK	44095	2250	A5
36300	ETLK	44094	2250	D5
36300	WLBY	44094	2250	D5
SR-640 Vine St				
31000	WLWK	44095	2249	E5
32700	ETLK	44095	2249	E5
33700	ETLK	44095	2250	A5
36300	ETLK	44094	2250	D5
36300	WLBY	44094	2250	D5
SR-700				
-	BURT	44021	2766	B2
10000	FdmT	44255	3161	A7
10000	HrmT	44255	3161	A7
10300	HrmT	44234	3161	A7
11300	HRM	44234	3161	A3
11900	HrmT	44234	3026	A7
13000	TroT	44234	3026	B2
14400	BtnT	44021	2766	B6
14400	BtnT	44062	2766	B6
16000	TroT	44021	2766	B6
16000	TroT	44021	2895	A2
17700	TroT	44234	2895	B7
18200	TroT	44234	3026	B2
SR-700 Burton Limaville Rd S				
10000	FdmT	44255	3161	A7
10000	HrmT	44255	3161	A7
SR-700 S Cheshire Rd				
-	BtnT	44021	2766	B2
14700	BURT	44021	2766	B1
SR-700 S Cheshire St				
-	BURT	44021	2766	B2
SR-700 Claridon Troy Rd				
14400	BtnT	44021	2766	B6
14400	BtnT	44062	2766	B6
16000	TroT	44021	2766	B6
16000	TroT	44021	2895	A2
17700	TroT	44234	2895	B7
18200	TroT	44234	3026	B2
SR-700 Garfield Rd				
11400	HRM	44234	3161	A2
SR-700 Tavern Rd				
14800	BtnT	44021	2766	B2
14800	BtnT	44062	2766	B2
14800	BURT	44021	2766	B2
SR-700 Welshfield Limavle Rd S				
10300	HrmT	44234	3161	A7
10300	HrmT	44255	3161	A7
11300	HRM	44234	3161	A3
11900	HrmT	44234	3026	A7
11900	HrmT	44234	3161	A1
13000	TroT	44234	3026	A7
US-6				
-	CLEV	44102	2624	A4
-	KTLD	44094	2378	A7
-	RKRV	44107	2621	C5
10	CLEV	44114	2624	E2
100	CRDN	44024	2379	D6
100	CRDN	44024	2380	B6
200	CLEV	44113	2624	A4
200	CLEV	44115	2624	E2
200	LORN	44052	2614	E6
600	CdnT	44024	2379	D6
800	LORN	44052	2615	B5
1200	CLEV	44114	2625	B2
1800	VMLN	44053	2742	B5
1800	VMLN	44089	2742	B5
2400	LORN	44053	2614	C7
2700	LORN	44053	2744	A1
3100	LORN	44053	2743	E1
3300	VMLN	44089	2741	E5
3500	LORN	44054	2615	E4
3500	SDLK	44054	2615	E4
3800	CLEV	44103	2625	D1
3900	SDLK	44054	2616	A3
4600	VMLN	44089	2741	E5
5000	VMLN	44089	2740	B6
5100	CLEV	44103	2495	D7
5400	SDLK	44054	2617	B2
5500	SDLK	44012	2617	B2
5600	HgvT	44041	2384	D3
5600	HgvT	44099	2384	D3
6100	LORN	44053	2742	B5
6600	HgvT	44064	2384	D3
6600	MtlT	44064	2384	D3
6700	HgvT	44064	2384	D3
7000	KTLD	44094	2376	A5
7000	WBHL	44094	2376	A5
7400	CLEV	44103	2496	A7
7900	KTLD	44094	2377	A6
8400	CLEV	44106	2496	A7
8400	CLEV	44108	2496	A7
9200	CLEV	44102	2623	C5
9600	CdnT	44024	2378	A7
9600	CdnT	44094	2378	A7
11700	LKWD	44102	2623	C5
11700	LKWD	44107	2623	C5
12500	ECLE	44112	2496	E7
12500	HmbT	44024	2380	B6
12500	VmnT	44089	2740	B6
13200	ECLE	44112	2497	A7
13400	LKWD	44107	2622	B4
13500	HmbT	44024	2381	A3
14900	HmbT	44024	2382	A3
14900	MtlT	44024	2382	A3
15200	MtlT	44064	2382	E3
16000	MtlT	44064	2383	A3
16300	CLEV	44112	2497	E2
18000	LKWD	44107	2621	C5
18100	CLEV	44121	2497	E2
18900	EUCL	44117	2497	E2
19200	RKRV	44116	2621	C5
19700	EUCL	44117	2498	A1
22900	BYVL	44116	2621	C5
22900	BYVL	44140	2621	C5
23400	BYVL	44140	2620	A4
23800	RDHT	44143	2498	C1
24400	RDHT	44143	2373	D7
26500	RDHT	44143	2374	A6
27200	WBHL	44092	2374	A6
27500	BYVL	44140	2619	D3
29600	WBHL	44094	2374	E6
31500	AVLK	44140	2619	D3
31700	AVLK	44012	2618	D1
31700	AVLK	44012	2619	D3
32100	AVLK	44012	2488	B7
32800	AVLK	44012	2487	E7
32900	AVLK	44012	2617	B2
33700	WBHL	44094	2375	A5
US-6 W 25th St				
-	CLEV	44113	2624	A4
US-6 Buckley Blvd				
-	CLEV	44113	2624	C4
US-6 Chardon Rd				
-	KTLD	44094	2378	A7
7000	KTLD	44094	2376	A5
7000	WBHL	44094	2376	A5
7900	KTLD	44094	2377	A6
9600	CdnT	44024	2378	A7
9600	CdnT	44094	2378	A7
10700	CdnT	44024	2379	A6
11100	CRDN	44024	2379	A6
21000	EUCL	44117	2498	C1
23800	RDHT	44143	2498	C1
24400	RDHT	44143	2373	D7
26500	RDHT	44143	2374	A6
27200	WBHL	44092	2374	A6
29600	WBHL	44094	2374	E6
33700	WBHL	44094	2375	A5
US-6 Cleveland Mem Shoreway				
-	CLEV	44102	2623	E4
-	CLEV	44102	2624	A4
-	CLEV	44113	2624	B4
US-6 Clifton Blvd				
-	RKRV	44107	2621	C5
-	RKRV	44116	2621	C5
9200	CLEV	44102	2623	C5
11700	LKWD	44102	2623	C5
11700	LKWD	44107	2623	C5
13400	LKWD	44107	2622	B4
18000	LKWD	44107	2621	C5
US-6 Detroit Av				
2400	CLEV	44113	2624	C4
US-6 E Erie Av				
200	LORN	44052	2614	E6
800	LORN	44052	2615	A5
3500	LORN	44054	2615	D4
3500	SDLK	44054	2615	D4
US-6 W Erie Av				
300	LORN	44052	2614	D6
2400	LORN	44053	2614	B7
2700	LORN	44053	2744	A1
3100	LORN	44053	2743	E1
6100	LORN	44053	2742	B5
US-6 E Erie Br				
-	LORN	44052	2614	D6
US-6 Euclid Av				
13500	ECLE	44112	2497	E2
16300	CLEV	44112	2497	E2
18100	CLEV	44121	2497	E2
18900	EUCL	44117	2497	E2
19700	EUCL	44117	2498	A1
US-6 GAR Hwy				
6600	HgvT	44064	2384	D3
6600	MtlT	44064	2384	D3
6700	HgvT	44064	2384	D3
6700	HgvT	44099	2384	D3
12500	HmbT	44024	2380	B6
13500	HmbT	44024	2381	A3
14900	HmbT	44024	2382	A3
14900	MtlT	44024	2382	A3
15200	MtlT	44064	2382	E3
16000	MtlT	44064	2383	A3
US-6 N Hambden St				
100	CRDN	44024	2380	A6
US-6 Lake Rd				
3500	SDLK	44054	2615	E4
3900	SDLK	44054	2616	A3
5400	SDLK	44054	2617	B2
5500	SDLK	44012	2617	B2
19200	RKRV	44116	2621	E5
22900	BYVL	44116	2621	A5
22900	BYVL	44140	2621	A5
23400	BYVL	44140	2620	A4
27500	BYVL	44140	2619	D3
31500	AVLK	44140	2619	D3
31700	AVLK	44012	2618	D1
31700	AVLK	44012	2619	D3
32100	AVLK	44012	2488	B7

INDEX 6

Aletha Av

Cleveland Street Index

Ashford Ct

STREET Block City ZIP Map# Grid

Aletha Av
500 GNVA 44041 1944 B5
Alexander Av
100 AMHT 44001 2872 B2
300 LORN 44052 2615 B5
Alexander Ct
12200 CLEV 44106 2626 E1
16300 HtbT 44046 2508 A5
Alexander Dr
100 ELYR 44035 2875 D2
5400 PRMA 44130 2882 B1
13900 RslT 44072 2632 A5
Alexander Rd
7000 CcdT 44077 2146 E7
7000 CcdT 44077 2254 D3
9300 GDHT 44125 2756 B6
12000 VLVW 44125 3016 E2
13600 VLVW 44125 3017 A1
14000 WNHL 44146 3017 A1
18600 WNHL 44146 3018 A2
21500 OKWD 44146 3018 A2
22000 FWPK 44126 2751 A3
22900 NOSD 44070 2751 A3
22900 NOSD 44126 2751 A3
23100 NOSD 44070 2750 E3
Alexandra Ct
- NOSD 44070 2878 C3
Alexandria Dr
6200 PMHT 44130 2882 A4
Alexandria Sq
8600 MCDN 44056 3153 D1
Alexco Rd
4100 CLEV 44135 2752 E4
Alfred Dr
5200 MNTR 44060 2038 E7
Alger Rd
2100 LKWD 44107 2622 D6
4700 RchT 44286 3150 B7
14400 CLEV 44111 2622 D7
Alger Tr
10100 TNBG 44087 3020 C4
Algiers Dr
1500 MDHT 44124 2499 D3
1500 MDHT 44124 2629 D1
Algonac Rd
1700 CLEV 44112 2497 C3
Algonquin Rd
2100 EUCL 44117 2498 A3
Alhambra Rd
700 CLEV 44110 2497 C2
Ali Av
- MDBH 44130 3012 C2
Alice Av
7100 CLEV 44105 2755 E4
Alice Blvd
10 OmsT 44138 2879 B4
Alice Ct
- GDHT 44125 2885 E2
Alla Dr
3100 SVHL 44131 2884 B6
Allandale Av
1700 ECLE 44112 2497 B4
Allanwood Rd
5400 PRMA 44129 2883 A3
Allegheny Av
1400 ECLE 44112 2497 A5
Allegheny Cir
1600 ECLE 44112 2497 A5
Allegheny Rd
7500 CcdT 44060 2253 B2
Allen Av
- SDLK 44054 2616 B4
10 PnvT 44077 2039 D6
Allen Blvd
2300 BHWD 44122 2629 A5
Allen Ct
- SDLK 44054 2616 C3
1200 RKRV 44116 2621 D5
Allen Dr
1400 WTLK 44145 2620 D7
7100 WNHL 44146 2886 E7
10600 MsnT 44024 2503 E6
Allen St
800 ELYR 44035 3005 E1
Allen Bradley Dr
10 MDHT 44124 2629 D2
Allenbury Dr
32500 SLN 44139 2888 E1
33100 SLN 44139 2889 A1
Allendale Dr
4800 RDHT 44143 2498 E1
5600 NOSD 44070 2879 C1
6500 AhtT 44001 2873 C1
7100 MNTR 44060 2251 B1
Allen Troy Ct
8700 MNTR 44060 2252 C1
Allerton Ct
7500 HDSN 44236 3154 E6
Alliance Dr
400 SgHT 44067 3017 C4
Allien Av
17500 CLEV 44111 2752 A2
Alling Dr
2800 TNBG 44087 3020 B5
Allison Av
500 LORN 44052 2614 C7
1200 LORN 44052 2744 C1
13600 CLEV 44111 2752 E1
Allison Dr
600 RDHT 44143 2498 D4
Allison Rd
2200 UNHT 44118 2627 D4
Allman Ct
1600 CLEV 44113 2624 E6
Allston Rd
1000 CVHT 44121 2498 A6
Allyn Rd
5300 ManT 44255 3024 E7
5300 ManT 44255 3025 A6
5400 HrmT 44234 3025 C5
5400 HrmT 44255 3025 C5
6600 HrmT 44234 3026 A4
6900 TroT 44234 3026 A4
Allynd Blvd
10 CRDN 44024 2380 A5
Almadien Dr
4300 LORN 44053 2744 A4
Almar Dr
20400 BHWD 44122 2628 A7
20400 SRHT 44122 2628 A7
Almira Av
8000 CLEV 44102 2753 C1
10000 CLEV 44111 2753 C1
Al Moen Dr
25300 NOSD 44070 2879 B1
Almond Walcott Ct S
6700 BKVL 44141 3015 E7
Almont Dr
6300 BKPK 44142 2881 B4
Alonzo Av
15300 CLEV 44128 2757 B5
Alpha Av
4200 NBGH 44105 2755 C3
Alpha Dr
600 HDHT 44143 2499 E4
Alpha Pk
10 HDHT 44143 2499 E4
Alpha Rd
12000 HrmT 44234 3025 E6
12000 HrmT 44234 3160 E1
Alpine Av
2800 CLEV 44104 2626 B6
Alpine Cir
17900 SGVL 44136 3147 C4
Alpine Dr
8200 KTLD 44094 2377 A3
W Alpine Dr
8200 KTLD 44094 2377 A3
Alpine Rd
1100 CVHT 44121 2497 E6
Alsace Ct
- SLN 44139 2889 E5
26700 BHWD 44122 2629 A4
39700 SLN 44139 2890 A5
Altamont Dr
9400 TNBG 44087 3019 D6
Altamont Rd
200 VMLN 44089 2741 D4
3200 CVHT 44118 2627 C1
Althea Dr
6100 CcdT 44077 2145 E4
6100 CcdT 44077 2146 A3
Althen Av
2100 CLEV 44109 2624 D7
Alton Dr
200 EatT 44044 3008 B7
200 EatT 44044 3143 B1
Alton Rd
2000 CLEV 44112 2497 D4
2000 ECLE 44112 2497 D4
28700 WKLF 44092 2374 B3
Altoona Rd
3100 CLEV 44109 2754 C4
Alva Dr
- BKPK 44142 2881 A3
Alva St
32800 ETLK 44095 2249 E5
Alvason Rd
1800 ECLE 44112 2496 E7
1800 ECLE 44112 2497 A7
Alvey Rd
1100 LNHT 44124 2499 A6
Alvin Av
1700 CLEV 44109 2754 D6
13100 GDHT 44105 2756 E5
13100 GDHT 44125 2756 E5
13600 GDHT 44105 2757 A5
13600 GDHT 44125 2757 A5
Alvin Dr
6000 BKPK 44142 2881 B2
Alvord Pl
2800 PRPK 44124 2629 C6
Amanda Ct
5200 NRDV 44039 2748 B7
Amanda Pl
7300 CcdT 44077 2253 C1
Amaryllis Dr
6900 EyrT 44035 2874 C2
Amber Ct
5700 WLBY 44094 2375 A2
Amber Dr
17000 CLEV 44111 2752 B1
N Amber Dr
4100 BKLN 44144 2753 E4
S Amber Dr
4300 BKLN 44144 2753 E4
Amber Ln
7300 BKVL 44141 3016 A6
7500 PRMA 44130 3013 C1
Amberly Av
1500 CLEV 44109 2754 D4
Amberwood Ct
- BWHT 44147 3149 D2
Amber Wood Dr
9300 KTLD 44094 2377 C1
Amberwood Ln
1400 PnvT 44077 2041 A7
Ambina Dr
28600 SLN 44139 2888 B6
Ambler Av
2700 CLEV 44104 2626 B6
Ambler Dr
400 ELYR 44035 2875 D3
Ambler Ln
10800 ManT 44255 3159 C5
10800 MNTU 44255 3159 C5
Ambleside Dr
- AVLK 44012 2617 D3
2100 CLEV 44106 2626 D3
9000 MNTR 44060 2252 D1
Ambleside Wy
100 AMHT 44001 2872 D4
Ambour Dr
23700 NOSD 44070 2750 D3
Ambrose Dr
6300 MNTR 44060 2143 B4
Amchester St
900 AMHT 44001 2744 B6
900 AMHT 44053 2744 B6
Amelia Av
4100 WLBY 44094 2251 B5
Amelia Dr
- ORNG 44022 2759 A6
2500 BWHT 44147 3014 C5
American Rd
10 BKLN 44144 2753 C4
American St
10 CNFL 44022 2761 A5
American Legion Pkwy
10 BERA 44017 2880 C7
Amerwood Ct
1500 PnvT 44077 2041 A7
Ames Rd
6600 PMHT 44129 2882 D5
6600 PMHT 44130 2882 D5
6600 PRMA 44129 2882 D5
6700 PRMA 44130 2882 D5
7200 PRMA 44129 2882 D7
7200 PRMA 44130 2882 D7
Amesbury Av
9300 CLEV 44106 2626 B2
Amesbury Dr
23700 NOSD 44070 2750 D4
Amhearst Cir
- BHWD 44122 2629 A4
Amherst Av
3100 LORN 44052 2744 E3
3100 LORN 44055 2744 E3
Amherst Dr
5200 PRMA 44129 2753 D7
5300 PRMA 44129 2882 D1
6800 SgHT 44067 3152 B1
Amherst Rd
20400 WVHT 44122 2758 A2
Amherst St
1700 ECLE 44112 2497 A6
Amherst Mobil Homes
200 SAHT 44001 2872 D7
Amity Dr
7000 MadT 44057 1843 D6
Ammon Rd
- RDHT 44143 2498 D4
4300 SELD 44143 2498 C4
Amor Av
10500 CLEV 44108 2496 C6
Amos Av
7900 CLEV 44104 2626 A4
Amrap Dr
5800 PMHT 44130 2882 B2
Amsterdam Rd
1200 CLEV 44110 2372 E7
Amy Ct
34800 ETLK 44095 2250 A3
Anaconda Av
5500 MNTR 44060 2144 A1
Anchor Dr
200 SDLK 44054 2615 D4
7500 MNTR 44060 2143 D4
Anchor Ln
7300 NCtT 44067 3153 C5
Anchorage Wy
5300 VMLN 44089 2740 E5
Anchorage Cove
10100 RMDV 44202 3020 E5
Anchor Point Dr
- VMLN 44089 2741 A6
Anchors Away
- AVLK 44012 2619 A3
Andees Dr
- ClbT 44028 3010 B7
Anderson Av
6500 INDE 44131 2884 E5
9300 CLEV 44105 2756 B1
Anderson Rd
4400 SELD 44121 2498 C5
4700 LNHT 44124 2498 C5
4700 SELD 44143 2498 C5
26400 ClbT 44028 3009 C4
28900 WKLF 44092 2374 B3
W Anderson Rd
4200 SELD 44121 2498 B6
Andorra Dr
4500 NOSD 44070 2749 E6
Andover Av
4300 LORN 44055 2746 A4
Andover Blvd
5400 GDHT 44125 2885 C1
11900 GDHT 44125 2756 D6
Andover Dr
5100 PRMA 44134 3014 A1
7000 MNTR 44060 2143 B7
10000 TNBG 44087 3019 B3
Andover Ln
7500 NRYN 44133 3013 D4
Andover Pl
2100 TwbT 44236 3155 A6
Andover Rd
3000 SRHT 44120 2627 C6
Andover Wy
7400 HDSN 44236 3154 D7
Andras Dr
17000 WNHL 44146 3017 D2
Andre Ln
6600 SLN 44139 2889 C7
Andrea Dr
7400 CcdT 44060 2253 B2
Andrea Ln
4700 CLEV 44109 2754 E6
Andress Ct
10 LORN 44052 2615 A5
100 ELYR 44035 2875 B7
Andrew Dr
9500 TNBG 44087 3019 A5
Andrew St
10 BERA 44017 2880 D7
10 BERA 44017 3011 D1
Andrews Av
1100 LKWD 44107 2622 C4
Andrews Cir
10 BKVL 44141 3150 D5
Andrews Ln
800 GSML 44040 2500 C5
15300 LKWD 44107 2622 C4
Andrews Pl
2900 LORN 44052 2744 C3
38800 WLBY 44094 2251 A5
Andrews Rd
1700 CVHT 44118 2627 E2
1700 CVHT 44121 2627 E2
5500 MONT 44060 2143 E2
Andrews Rd SR-283
5500 MONT 44060 2143 E2
Andrus Av
5000 NOSD 44070 2750 A7
Angela Cir
10 PnvT 44077 2145 D3
Angela Ct
6600 SLN 44139 2889 C6
Angela Dr
4300 SELD 44121 2498 B6
4400 FWPK 44126 2751 C3
10700 KTLD 44094 2376 E6
23000 WVHT 44128 2758 C5
27900 NOSD 44070 2878 D3
Angela Ln
- MadT 44057 1844 A5
Angelina Cir
9200 MNTR 44060 2144 E1
Angelus Av
11600 CLEV 44105 2756 D2
Anglers Dr
100 SRSL 44073 2761 D5
Angling Rd
9600 FrnT 44889 2869 A7
Anita Dr
6200 PMHT 44130 2881 E4
6200 PMHT 44130 2882 A3
Ann Ct
8900 CLEV 44108 2496 B7
Ann Dr
3600 VMLN 44089 2741 E5
27600 ClbT 44028 3009 A3
Ann St
100 AMHT 44001 2872 E3
Anna Ct
5600 MONT 44060 2143 D1
Anna Ln
31500 BYVL 44140 2619 A2
Annadale Dr
7200 SLN 44139 3020 C1
Annandale Dr
10 SRSL 44073 2762 B6
Annandale Rd
6500 MDHT 44124 2630 A2
Ann Arbor Dr
7400 PRMA 44130 2882 A7
7400 PRMA 44130 3013 A1
Anne Dr
300 BERA 44017 3010 E1
300 BERA 44017 3011 A1
Anne Ln
16600 AbnT 44021 2893 C1
Anne Marie Ct
- HkyT 44233 3149 D6
Annesley Rd
25700 BHWD 44122 2628 E6
26200 BHWD 44122 2629 A5
Annetta Dr
27800 GNWL 44139 3019 A1
Annette Pl
4800 WVHT 44128 2758 C6
Annette St
22900 WVHT 44128 2758 C6
Annie Ln
24400 WTLK 44145 2750 C2
Annis Rd
200 SAHT 44001 2872 D7
200 SAHT 44001 3003 C2
Ansel Rd
100 GNVA 44041 1944 D3
800 CLEV 44103 2496 B7
900 CLEV 44108 2496 B7
1200 CLEV 44106 2496 B7
1400 CLEV 44106 2626 B1
Anson Av
4900 CLEV 44127 2625 C7
Ansonia Av
1400 MadT 44057 1843 C7
8500 BKLN 44144 2753 D5
Ansonia Dr
3000 TNBG 44087 3020 B6
Antelope Run
8800 RslT 44073 2762 C4
Antenucci Blvd
- GDHT 44125 2885 C1
Anthony Ct
7100 MadT 44057 1843 D6
Anthony Dr
3300 BWHT 44147 3015 B4
Anthony Ln
3300 TNBG 44087 3155 C1
3300 TwbT 44087 3155 C1
6700 PMHT 44130 2882 C5
Anthony St
600 RDHT 44143 2498 D4
5000 MPHT 44137 2757 C7
Antietam Rd
10700 PMHT 44130 2882 B3
Antioch Dr
100 ELYR 44035 2746 D6
Antioch Rd
2300 NPRY 44081 1940 E4
Antisdale Av
3400 CVHT 44118 2627 D2
E Antisdale Rd
3700 CVHT 44118 2627 E2
3700 SELD 44118 2627 E2
3800 SELD 44118 2628 A2
Antler Dr
24600 NOSD 44070 2750 C4
Antler Ln
16900 SGVL 44136 3147 A3
Antler Pt
400 AURA 44202 3156 B2
Antoinette Dr
6300 MNTR 44060 2143 B4
7000 PRMA 44129 2883 A7
Antoinette St
100 ELYR 44035 2746 D7
Antrim Rd
6000 EyrT 44035 2745 D7
6000 EyrT 44055 2745 D7
Apache Dr
- PMHT 44130 2882 B2
Apache Run
600 MCDN 44056 3018 D5
Apelt Av
19100 CLEV 44135 2751 E5
Apex
- NRDV 44039 2748 D7
Apollo Dr
500 ETLK 44095 2250 A2
1000 BKPK 44142 2880 A2
3100 NRYN 44133 3014 C5
7500 PRMA 44130 3013 B1
Apollo Pkwy
38000 WLBY 44094 2250 E3
Appaloosa Run
800 AURA 44202 3022 B5
Appaloosa Tr
10 MDSN 44057 2043 E2
8400 KTLD 44094 2377 B7
Apple Av
2400 LORN 44052 2745 A2
2400 LORN 44055 2745 A2
4200 CLEV 44113 2624 B6
Apple Ct
21600 RKRV 44116 2621 C4
Apple Dr
2000 EUCL 44143 2498 C1
Apple Ln
15000 SGVL 44136 3146 C1
Apple St
10 ELYR 44035 2874 D3
Appleblossom Ln
300 BYVL 44140 2619 B4
7500 CsTp 44026 2501 C4
Applebrook Cir
19500 SGVL 44136 3147 D5
Applebrook Dr
200 CNFL 44022 2761 A4
Appleby Ln
3000 TNBG 44087 3020 C5
Apple Creek Dr
4000 BKLN 44144 2753 D3
5400 SFLD 44054 2746 E1
5500 SFLD 44054 2747 A1
N Applecross Rd
400 HDHT 44143 2499 E2
S Applecross Rd
500 HDHT 44143 2499 E3
Applegate Rd
20600 MPHT 44137 2887 A1
Apple Hill Dr
200 SgHT 44067 3017 E3
8500 BbgT 44023 2891 B6
Apple Orchard Ln
1000 AMHT 44001 2872 B1
Appleseed Dr
500 LORN 44053 2744 E7
Appleton Ct
6900 MNTR 44060 2143 E6
Appleton Dr
10600 PMHT 44130 2882 A5
Appletree Ct
400 PnvT 44077 2146 E2
Appletree Dr
300 PnvT 44077 2146 E1
Apple Valley Ct
1300 BWHT 44147 3149 D4
Appleview Wy
34500 SLN 44139 3020 A1
Applewood Ct
1900 AVON 44011 2747 D1
Applewood Ct E
8700 MNTR 44060 2144 C4
Applewood Ct W
8700 MNTR 44060 2144 C3
Applewood Dr
600 SVHL 44131 3015 A2
9500 NRYN 44133 3013 A3
9800 KTLD 44094 2377 A3
30000 BYVL 44140 2619 C4
Applewood Ln
20200 SGVL 44136 3146 C2
April Hill Dr
10 GftT 44044 3142 A7
Aquarius Pkwy
38100 WLBY 44094 2142 E6
38100 WLBY 44094 2143 A6
Aquilla Blvd
- AQLA 44024 2505 D4
Aquilla Rd
11100 ClrT 44024 2505 B1
11100 CRDN 44024 2505 B1
11800 AQLA 44024 2505 C3
12400 ClrT 44024 2635 C1
13200 BtnT 44024 2635 C3
13600 BtnT 44021 2635 C5
14000 BtnT 44021 2765 C1
Arabella Rd
1600 CLEV 44112 2497 C3
Arabian Ct
- AVON 44011 2747 A6
Arapaho Ct
6900 SLN 44139 2889 A7
Arbor Av
4700 SFLD 44054 2746 C4
20100 EUCL 44119 2373 A4
20100 EUCL 44123 2373 A4
Arbor Ct
6700 PRMA 44134 3013 E2
7300 OmsT 44138 2878 E5
39000 CrlT 44044 3141 D3
39000 EatT 44044 3141 D3
Arbor Dr
- AVON 44011 2748 A2
7700 PRMA 44130 3013 D1
Arbor Ln
- BTVL 44022 2889 B2
1900 PnvT 44077 2041 A5
26900 OmsT 44138 2878 D5
Arbor Rd
300 CLEV 44108 2496 E3
Arbor St
1500 WKLF 44092 2374 D1
2100 MadT 44057 1942 C2
Arbor Tr
15800 NbyT 44065 2763 D5
Arbor Wy
600 AURA 44202 3156 C3
3300 WTLK 44145 2749 A3
6600 PRMA 44134 3013 E2
6600 PRMA 44134 3014 A2
Arbor Cliff Ln
22200 RKRV 44116 2621 B5
Arbordale Av
6500 SLN 44139 2889 A6
Arbordale Ln
10 PnvT 44077 2145 B5
Arboretum Cir
700 SgHT 44067 3152 B1
Arboretum Ct
300 AURA 44202 3156 C1
Arbor Glen Ct
6100 SLN 44139 2889 E4
Arbor Glen Dr
11700 CdnT 44024 2254 D6
Arbor Glenn Pl
7300 CcdT 44060 2253 C1
Arborhurst Cir
- AURA 44202 3021 C7
Arborhurst Ln
8700 KTLD 44094 2377 C2
Arbor Park Dr
7800 PRMA 44134 3013 E2
7800 PRMA 44134 3014 A2
Arborside Ln
600 AVLK 44012 2618 E4
Arborvine Ln
300 MDSN 44057 1942 B7
Arbutus Rd
24800 OKWD 44146 2887 D7
Arcade Av
15600 CLEV 44110 2372 C7
Arcadia Dr
7000 PRMA 44129 2882 D6
Arcadia Point Dr
700 AURA 44202 3156 C4
E Arcadia Point Dr
500 AURA 44202 3156 C4
W Arcadia Point Dr
600 AURA 44202 3156 C4
Arch St
5000 MPHT 44137 2757 D7
5300 MPHT 44137 2886 D1
16300 BbgT 44022 2761 A7
Archdale Av
17300 LKWD 44107 2622 B5
Archer Ct
2600 BWHT 44147 3149 D5
Archer Rd
600 BDFD 44146 2887 C3
4300 CLEV 44105 2756 B4
6800 EatT 44044 3007 D2
9700 EatT 44035 3007 D2
9800 NRDV 44039 3007 D2
Archmere Av
4300 CLEV 44109 2754 C6
4500 CLEV 44144 2754 A6
6000 BKLN 44144 2754 A6
6200 BKLN 44144 2753 E6
Archwood Av
900 LORN 44052 2614 B7
2500 CLEV 44109 2754 B2
Archwood Dr
3300 RKRV 44116 2751 A2
Archwood Rd
6000 INDE 44131 2884 D6
Arcola Rd
2800 MadT 44057 1942 E5
Arctic Ct
6700 CLEV 44103 2495 E6
Arden Av
800 BERA 44017 2880 B4
800 PnvT 44077 2040 C2
6500 BKPK 44142 2880 B4
11700 CLEV 44111 2623 A7
14900 LKWD 44107 2622 C6
Arden Ct
2000 TwbT 44236 3155 A5
Arden Dr
8900 MNTR 44060 2144 D3
N Arden Dr
- MNTR 44060 2144 D3
Arden Ln
2000 TwbT 44236 3155 A6
Arden Rd
7400 PRMA 44129 2882 E1
Ardenall Av
13800 ECLE 44112 2497 A5
Ardendale Rd
4400 SELD 44121 2628 C1
Ardleigh Dr
- CVHT 44106 2626 E4
Ardmore Av
100 PNVL 44077 2146 A2
3900 CLEV 44109 2754 B5
4500 CLEV 44144 2754 B5
Ardmore Dr
5800 CLEV 44144 2754 A5
6000 BKLN 44144 2754 A5
6300 BKLN 44144 2753 B5
Ardmore Rd
3200 SRHT 44120 2627 D7
3900 CVHT 44121 2498 A7
4000 SELD 44121 2498 A7
Ardola Ct
10 CrlT 44035 3006 C2
Ardoon Av
13400 CLEV 44120 2627 A5
Ardoon St
1300 CVHT 44121 2498 A7
Ardoye Av
800 PnvT 44077 2040 D2
Ardoyne Av
1400 CLEV 44109 2754 E4
Ardwell Dr
20000 EUCL 44123 2373 A3
Arey Rd
2100 CLEV 44106 2626 D2
Argee Dr
7200 MNTR 44060 2144 B7
Argonne Dr
500 PnvT 44077 2040 A5
Argonne Rd
900 CVHT 44121 2498 B6
900 SELD 44121 2498 B6
Argus Av
13300 CLEV 44110 2496 E1
13300 CLEV 44110 2497 A1
Argyle Dr
1200 MadT 44057 1843 D6
24700 EUCL 44117 2373 D7
24700 RDHT 44117 2373 D7
24700 RDHT 44143 2373 D7
Argyle Ovl
19400 RKRV 44116 2621 E4
Argyle Rd
200 RKRV 44116 2621 D5
Arizona Av
10 LORN 44052 2614 E5
Arkansas Av
100 LORN 44052 2614 E5
5600 CLEV 44102 2624 A7
Arlesford Dr
32300 SLN 44139 2888 E7
33200 SLN 44139 2889 A7
Arlet Ct
1200 BWHT 44147 3149 E3
Arline Av
700 ETLK 44095 2250 B2
Arlington Av
100 PnvT 44077 2146 D1
3800 NBGH 44105 2755 B3
12000 CLEV 44108 2496 D5
Arlington Blvd
6900 SLN 44139 2889 D7
Arlington Cir
10 WKLF 44092 2374 C3
28400 WLWK 44095 2249 A7
30900 BYVL 44140 2619 B3
Arlington Ct
800 ELYR 44035 2875 E2
Arlington Dr
600 VMLN 44089 2742 A5
2300 LNHT 44124 2629 C3
9600 PMHT 44130 2882 C3
20100 SGVL 44136 3146 C2
37200 WLBY 44094 2250 D7
Arlington Ln
24600 NOSD 44070 2750 C6
Arlington Rd
1200 LKWD 44107 2622 A4
2400 CVHT 44118 2627 B4
Arlington St
6900 BKVL 44141 3016 A7
Arlis Av
13800 CLEV 44111 2622 E7
Arliss Dr
12500 LKWD 44107 2623 A4
Armadale Av
29200 WKLF 44092 2374 C4
Armi Cir
400 PnvT 44077 2147 A2
Armin Av
14600 LKWD 44107 2622 D6
Armitage Av
10 PnvT 44077 2040 D2
Armitage Ct
9200 CLEV 44105 2756 B3
Armour Rd
100 AVLK 44012 2488 B7
100 AVLK 44012 2618 B2
Arms Av
- EUCL 44117 2373 B4
22200 EUCL 44123 2373 B4
Arndt St
2200 VMLN 44001 2742 B7
Arnold Ct
3800 CLEV 44109 2754 C2
Arnold Dr
30200 WLWK 44095 2249 C6
Arnold Miller Pkwy
6000 SLN 44139 2888 D6
Arrow Ln
2800 PRMA 44134 2883 C7
10600 CdnT 44024 2378 C6
Arrowhead Av
18500 CLEV 44119 2372 E5
19300 CLEV 44119 2373 A5
Arrowhead Dr
100 EatT 44044 3007 A5
1000 VMLN 44089 2741 C6
Arrowhead Ln
500 SgHT 44067 3017 D5
Arrowhead Tr
1000 AURA 44202 3156 E5
13500 MDBH 44130 3012 D1
Arrowood Ct
8800 MNTR 44060 2144 C3
Arrowood Dr
8700 MNTR 44060 2144 C3
Arrow Wood Cir
100 SRSL 44073 2761 D6
Arrow Wood Ovl
7300 PRMA 44130 2882 D7
Artemus Ct
10 ELYR 44035 2875 C6
Arthur Av
1300 LKWD 44107 2622 C4
1900 WTLK 44145 2750 C1
2000 LKWD 44107 2622 C6
10500 CLEV 44106 2626 C3
29400 WKLF 44092 2249 B7
Arthur Ct
1200 MadT 44057 1843 D6
Arthur Rd
31200 SLN 44139 2888 D7
32800 SLN 44139 2889 A7
Arthur St
37300 WLBY 44094 2250 C7
Artino St
100 OBLN 44074 3139 A2
Artmar Dr
6000 CcdT 44077 2145 E4
Artsdale Dr
100 AVLK 44012 2617 D2
Arundel Rd
200 RKRV 44116 2621 E4
Asbury Ln
100 ELYR 44035 2875 A7
Asbury Rd
10100 FdmT 44255 3160 D7
10100 HrmT 44255 3160 D7
10700 HrmT 44234 3160 E4
Ascoa Ct
22300 SGVL 44136 3145 E2
22300 SGVL 44136 3146 A2
Ascot Ln
4000 WVHT 44122 2757 E3
11700 AbnT 44021 2893 C4
Ascot Pl
8700 KTLD 44094 2377 C6
Ascot Rd
6000 MDHT 44124 2629 C1
Ash Av
- EUCL 44132 2374 A2
Ash Dr
10 OmsT 44138 2879 B4
17600 SGVL 44136 3146 C4
E Ash Ln
3900 ORNG 44122 2759 C3
W Ash Ln
3900 ORNG 44122 2759 B3
Ash Rd
2500 WLBY 44094 2250 E1
E Ash Rd
5600 INDE 44131 2884 D4
W Ash Rd
4900 INDE 44131 2884 C4
Ash St
400 VMLN 44089 2741 E5
Ashberry Ln
300 HkyT 44233 3147 E7
Ashbolt Dr
- LORN 44053 2744 E5
Ashbrooke Wy
- HDSN 44236 3153 E6
600 HDSN 44236 3154 A6
Ashburton Av
13400 CLEV 44110 2497 A3
Ashbury Av
10200 CLEV 44106 2496 C7
10700 CLEV 44106 2626 C1
Ashbury Park Dr
4400 NOSD 44070 2750 A6
Ashby Rd
3300 SRHT 44120 2627 B7
3400 SRHT 44120 2757 B1
Ashcroft Dr
5800 MDHT 44124 2629 C2
Ashcroft Ln
9100 TNBG 44087 3019 B7
Ashdale Dr
2300 TNBG 44087 3154 D1
Ashdale Rd
6300 MDHT 44124 2629 E2
Ashdown Dr
32500 SLN 44139 3019 E2
Ashford Ct
300 BWHT 44147 3149 E5

STREET Block	City	ZIP	Map#	Grid
Ashford Ct				
1300	SgHT	44067	3017	A5
20400	SGVL	44136	3146	C4
Ashford Dr				
8500	MCDN	44056	3018	D7
Ashford Rd				
3000	SRHT	44120	2627	B6
Ashford St				
8200	CcdT	44077	2254	E5
Ash Grove Cir				
200	AURA	44202	3021	B6
200	AURA	44202	3156	B1
Ashland Av				
100	ELYR	44035	3006	D2
100	LORN	44052	2614	C6
1300	LORN	44052	2744	C1
3200	LORN	44053	2744	C4
Ashland Ct				
-	ELYR	44035	3006	C2
Ashland Dr				
15300	BKPK	44142	2881	B1
Ashland Ln				
10	AURA	44202	3021	D7
Ashland Rd				
2100	CLEV	44103	2625	D3
Ashland-Oberlin Rd				
500	NRsT	44074	3138	E7
500	OBLN	44074	3138	E7
14200	PtfT	44074	3138	E7
Ashland-Oberlin Rd SR-58				
500	NRsT	44074	3138	E7
500	OBLN	44074	3138	E7
14200	PtfT	44074	3138	E7
Ashlar Dr				
100	SVHL	44131	2883	E3
Ashlawn Dr				
3800	BNWK	44212	3146	E6
7100	BKVL	44141	3016	A3
Ashleigh Dr				
10	BNWK	44212	3147	C6
Ashley Cir				
500	AVLK	44012	2618	D3
5600	HDHT	44143	2499	B3
20200	SGVL	44136	3011	C3
Ashley Ct				
10	RKRV	44116	2621	C4
Ashley Dr				
1700	HDSN	44236	3154	E7
8400	BWHT	44147	3015	C4
Ashley Ln				
9800	CcdT	44060	2253	B1
14000	NRYN	44133	3014	B7
14000	NRYN	44133	3149	B1
Ashley Rd				
2600	SRHT	44122	2628	B5
Ashlyn Ct				
8800	ODFL	44138	2879	D7
Ashton Cir				
4100	NOSD	44070	2750	E5
Ashton Ct				
800	AURA	44202	3156	D4
7500	NRYN	44133	3013	D7
8400	MNTR	44060	2251	C5
Ashton Ln				
6500	SLN	44139	2889	B6
30000	BYVL	44140	2619	B5
Ashton Rd				
2500	CVHT	44118	2627	D5
Ashton Tr				
12500	MsnT	44024	2504	C7
Ashurst Rd				
2200	UNHT	44118	2627	E4
2600	SRHT	44118	2627	E5
Ashview Dr				
900	MadT	44057	1844	A5
Ashwood				
-	MNTR	44060	2144	E7
Ashwood Blvd				
-	LORN	44053	2744	C6
Ashwood Ct				
8900	ODFL	44138	3009	E1
Ashwood Dr				
100	AVLK	44012	2617	D2
100	ELYR	44035	3005	B1
5100	LNHT	44124	2499	A6
6400	INDE	44131	2884	D5
8600	SGVL	44136	3011	A3
29200	WKLF	44092	2374	C4
Ashwood Ln				
12400	NsnT	44231	3028	C6
Ashwood Rd				
3000	CLEV	44120	2626	D7
3000	CLEV	44120	2627	A6
3100	SRHT	44120	2627	A6
14100	NbyT	44065	2764	C1
Ashwood Tr				
9800	CcdT	44060	2253	B3
Aspen Cir				
8800	PRMA	44130	2882	D7
16600	SGVL	44136	3147	A5
Aspen Ct				
300	AURA	44202	3156	E1
6000	CLEV	44102	2624	A6
9900	CcdT	44060	2253	C2
10200	CrlT	44035	3006	D3
Aspen Dr				
10	AhtT	44001	2873	B1
28300	NOSD	44070	2878	D3
Aspen Ovl				
13900	NRYN	44133	3014	C7
Aspen Glen Dr				
32700	SLN	44139	2759	E7
Aspen Hills Ln				
14600	BtnT	44021	2765	D1
Aspenwood Ct				
8800	MNTR	44060	2144	D3
Aspenwood Dr				
100	MDHL	44022	2760	B5
600	SVHL	44131	3015	A1
Aspenwood Ln				
34800	WLBY	44094	2375	A1
Asper St				
100	PNVL	44077	2040	A7
Aspinwall Av				
14000	CLEV	44110	2497	A2
E Asplin Dr				
2600	RKRV	44116	2751	A1
W Asplin Dr				
-	RKRV	44116	2621	A7
2600	RKRV	44116	2751	A1
Associate Av				
7300	BKLN	44144	2753	E2
Aster Dr				
5900	INDE	44131	2884	D4
7600	MNTR	44060	2143	D5
Aster Pl				
100	BNWK	44212	3147	A6
Astor Av				
12400	CLEV	44135	2753	A6
13000	CLEV	44135	2752	E6
Astoria Wy				
-	AVON	44011	2747	E5
Athena Dr				
12300	NRYN	44133	3014	C6
Athens Av				
10	PnvT	44077	2041	B5
13000	LKWD	44107	2623	A6
13300	LKWD	44107	2622	E6
Atherstone Rd				
3500	CVHT	44121	2497	D4
Atkins Av				
2000	LKWD	44107	2622	B6
Atkins Rd				
300	HpfT	44041	2045	C7
700	HpfT	44041	2151	C1
900	TmbT	44041	2151	C4
Atlanta Ln				
30500	WTLK	44145	2749	B2
Atlantic Rd				
12800	SGVL	44136	3011	B7
Atlas Dr				
300	LORN	44052	2615	C5
Atlis Ct				
12200	SGVL	44136	3011	D6
Atterbury Dr				
1100	MCDN	44056	3153	E1
Attica Rd				
3500	CLEV	44111	2752	D1
Attleboro Rd				
3100	SRHT	44120	2627	C7
Atwater Dr				
1100	MadT	44057	1843	E6
Atwood Dr				
1100	CLEV	44108	2496	D6
Atwood Pl				
5800	WLBY	44094	2375	A2
Auburn Av				
1600	CLEV	44113	2624	D6
5300	MPHT	44137	2886	E1
Auburn Dr				
-	BHWD	44122	2758	E2
Auburn Rdg				
6900	CcdT	44077	2146	A7
Auburn Rd				
-	CRDN	44024	2379	B4
-	MsnT	44024	2504	B2
6200	CcdT	44077	2146	B5
7200	CcdT	44077	2254	B1
8400	CcdT	44024	2254	B6
8400	CdnT	44024	2254	B6
9000	CdnT	44024	2379	B1
10700	CdnT	44024	2504	B2
11100	MsnT	44024	2504	A6
12500	MsnT	44024	2634	A3
13400	MsnT	44026	2634	A5
13400	MsnT	44065	2634	A5
13400	NbyT	44026	2634	A3
13400	NbyT	44065	2634	A3
14600	NbyT	44065	2764	A2
16000	NbyT	44023	2764	A6
16300	AbnT	44023	2764	A6
16400	AbnT	44023	2893	A2
17700	AbnT	44021	2893	A7
18000	AbnT	44023	3024	A1
Auburn St				
400	ELYR	44035	3006	D2
400	PNVL	44077	2040	A7
Auburndale Av				
1600	CLEV	44112	2496	E7
1600	ECLE	44112	2496	E7
12300	CLEV	44106	2496	E7
Auburndale Dr				
10400	AbnT	44023	3023	D2
Auburn Glen Dr				
18600	AbnT	44023	3023	E1
Auburn Lakes Dr				
10	AbnT	44023	2892	A3
Auburn Springs Dr				
-	AbnT	44023	2893	A2
16600	AbnT	44023	2892	C1
Audrey Dr				
300	RDHT	44143	2498	D2
800	ETLK	44095	2250	B3
Audubon Blvd				
3000	CLEV	44104	2626	C7
Augdon Dr				
400	ELYR	44035	2875	E3
August Ln				
8000	SgHT	44067	3017	E4
Augusta Av				
200	LORN	44052	2615	A5
Augusta Ct				
2100	WTLK	44145	2749	B1
Augusta Dr				
-	ELYR	44035	3006	D3
32100	AVLK	44012	2618	D5
Augusta Ln				
-	CcdT	44077	2253	E3
Augustine Dr				
2200	PRMA	44134	2883	C6
Augustus Dr				
-	HDHT	44143	2499	C2
Aulcash Av				
-	CLEV	44105	2756	E2
Aurensen Rd				
36000	NRDV	44039	2876	E4
36000	NRDV	44039	2877	A4
Aurora Dr				
10	OmsT	44138	2879	A4
700	VMLN	44089	2740	C5
Aurora Rd				
3600	TwbT	44087	3155	D2
20600	WVHT	44146	2758	B7
21700	BDHT	44146	2758	B7
21700	MPHT	44146	2758	B7
23100	BDHT	44146	2887	E2
26200	BDHT	44146	2888	A2
27000	SLN	44139	2888	A2
33200	SLN	44139	2889	B6
37900	SLN	44139	3020	D1
39700	SLN	44139	3021	A2
40000	BbgT	44023	3021	A2
40000	BbgT	44139	3021	A2
Aurora Rd SR-43				
21700	BDHT	44146	2758	B7
21700	MPHT	44146	2758	B7
23100	BDHT	44146	2887	E2
26200	BDHT	44146	2888	A2
27000	SLN	44139	2888	A2
33200	SLN	44139	2889	B6
37900	SLN	44139	3020	D1
39700	SLN	44139	3021	A2
40000	BbgT	44023	3021	A2
40000	BbgT	44139	3021	A2
Aurora Rd SR-82				
3600	TwbT	44087	3155	D2
E Aurora Rd				
10	NCtT	44067	3152	E1
10	NCtT	44067	3153	A1
300	MCDN	44056	3153	A1
1400	MCDN	44056	3154	C1
1600	TNBG	44087	3154	C1
2800	TNBG	44087	3155	C2
3500	TwbT	44087	3155	C2
E Aurora Rd SR-82				
10	NCtT	44067	3152	E1
10	NCtT	44067	3153	A1
300	MCDN	44056	3153	A1
1400	MCDN	44056	3154	C1
1600	TNBG	44087	3154	C1
2800	TNBG	44087	3155	C2
3500	TwbT	44087	3155	C2
N Aurora Rd				
10	AURA	44202	3021	D6
10	BbgT	44023	3021	A2
10	BbgT	44139	3021	A2
10	SLN	44139	3021	A2
1000	AURA	44023	3021	A2
N Aurora Rd SR-43				
10	AURA	44202	3021	D6
10	BbgT	44023	3021	A2
10	BbgT	44139	3021	A2
10	SLN	44139	3021	A2
1000	AURA	44023	3021	A2
S Aurora Rd				
10	AURA	44202	3156	E1
S Aurora Rd SR-43				
10	AURA	44202	3156	E1
W Aurora Rd				
10	NCtT	44067	3152	E1
100	SgHT	44067	3152	E1
900	SgHT	44067	3017	A7
1100	SgHT	44067	3016	E7
W Aurora Rd SR-82				
10	NCtT	44067	3152	E1
100	SgHT	44067	3152	E1
900	SgHT	44067	3017	A7
1100	SgHT	44067	3016	E7
Aurora Commons Cir				
-	AURA	44202	3156	D1
Aurora Hill Dr				
1100	AURA	44202	3021	A7
Aurora Hudson Rd				
200	AURA	44202	3156	D3
10400	STBR	44236	3156	C5
10400	STBR	44241	3156	C5
Aurora Industrial Pkwy				
-	AURA	44202	3156	E5
-	AURA	44202	3157	A5
Aurora Lake Rd				
700	AURA	44202	3021	B5
Au St 1				
-	AURA	44202	3157	A1
Austen Ln				
5100	RDHT	44143	2498	E4
5100	RDHT	44143	2499	A4
Austin Av				
12800	CLEV	44108	2496	E5
Austin Rd				
100	GNVA	44041	1944	D3
200	GnvT	44041	1944	D3
Austin St				
200	BERA	44017	2880	D7
Austin Point Dr				
7000	CcdT	44077	2146	C7
Austrian Ct				
7900	CLEV	44104	2626	A4
Autumn Dr				
600	AMHT	44001	2872	E3
8000	LryT	44077	2256	B4
Autumn Ln				
100	BNWK	44212	3146	E6
4700	BKLN	44144	2753	D6
Autumn Ridge Dr				
6300	MadT	44057	1942	A4
Avalon Dr				
10	AVLK	44012	2617	C1
10	BDFD	44146	2887	A3
100	EatT	44044	3008	B7
100	EatT	44044	3143	B1
1300	MadT	44057	1843	C6
2000	PRMA	44134	2883	D7
20600	RKRV	44116	2621	B5
Avalon Rd				
1600	CLEV	44112	2497	D2
3100	SRHT	44120	2627	D7
3400	SRHT	44120	2757	D2
Avenue Sq				
2500	PryT	44077	2041	B7
Avenue of Peace				
-	LNDL	44111	2753	B3
11900	LNDL	44135	2753	B3
Avery Av				
4600	CLEV	44127	2625	C6
Avery Pkwy				
-	SGVL	44136	3011	A7
-	SGVL	44136	3146	A1
Avery Rd				
8100	BWHT	44147	3014	E3
8200	BWHT	44147	3015	A4
9200	BWHT	44147	3150	A1
Avery St				
300	BDFD	44146	2887	B4
Avery Ter				
200	PNVL	44077	2040	B7
Avion Park Dr				
5300	HDHT	44143	2499	A2
Avon Av				
300	VMLN	44089	2742	A5
10200	CLEV	44105	2756	C3
Avon Dr				
-	AURA	44202	3157	A4
7300	MNTR	44060	2251	C1
Avon Ln				
7400	CsTp	44026	2631	C1
Avon Rd				
31200	WTLK	44145	2619	A7
31600	AVON	44011	2618	E7
31600	AVON	44011	2619	A7
31600	AVON	44145	2619	A7
Avon Belden Rd				
800	AVON	44011	2618	A6
800	AVON	44012	2618	A6
2200	AVON	44011	2748	A3
4900	NRDV	44011	2748	A7
4900	NRDV	44039	2748	A7
5000	NRDV	44039	2877	A2
8900	NRDV	44039	3007	E2
8900	NRDV	44039	3008	A1
Avon Belden Rd SR-83				
800	AVON	44011	2618	A6
800	AVON	44012	2618	A6
2200	AVON	44011	2748	A3
4900	NRDV	44011	2748	A7
4900	NRDV	44039	2748	A7
5000	NRDV	44039	2877	A2
8900	NRDV	44039	3007	E2
8900	NRDV	44039	3008	A1
Avon-Belden Center Rd				
100	AVLK	44012	2488	A7
100	AVLK	44012	2618	A2
Avon-Belden Center Rd SR-83				
100	AVLK	44012	2488	A7
100	AVLK	44012	2618	A2
Avondale Av				
100	AVLK	44012	2617	B2
2700	CVHT	44118	2627	A1
7600	GDHT	44125	2756	A5
Avondale Ct				
8500	OmsT	44138	2879	A7
Avondale Rd				
-	WLBY	44094	2250	C6
1000	CVHT	44121	2498	B7
1000	SELD	44121	2498	B7
3600	WDMR	44122	2759	B2
Avon Point Av				
100	AVLK	44012	2488	B7
100	AVLK	44012	2618	B2
Avrina Av				
7900	CLEV	44104	2626	A7
Axtell Av				
10	PNVL	44077	2040	A7
100	AMHT	44001	2872	D1
Ayleshire Dr				
6600	SLN	44139	2889	B6
Aylesworth Dr				
6300	PMHT	44130	2882	C4
Aynesly Wy				
200	BNWK	44212	3147	B7
Azalea				
-	MNTR	44060	2144	E6
Azalea Cir				
-	NCtT	44236	3153	D5
6200	SLN	44139	2889	C5
8000	BbgT	44023	2890	E7
Azalea Dr				
600	SELD	44143	2498	C4
Azalea Ln				
4400	NOSD	44070	2749	D6
B				
B & O Bike Tr				
-	CcdT	44077	2146	B2
-	CcdT	44077	2254	D1
-	PNVL	44077	2146	B2
-	PnvT	44077	2146	B2
Babbitt Rd				
200	EUCL	44123	2373	C3
1000	EUCL	44117	2373	D4
1000	EUCL	44132	2373	D4
Babbling Brook Ovl				
200	HkyT	44233	3148	A7
Bacon Rd				
400	PnvT	44077	2041	A2
Bader Av				
3200	CLEV	44109	2754	C6
4600	CLEV	44144	2754	C6
Badger Den Ln				
16700	SGVL	44136	3146	E3
Bading Av				
3400	CLEV	44105	2755	C1
Baetz Ct				
6000	EyrT	44035	2745	A6
6000	EyrT	44055	2745	A6
Bagley Dr				
-	BERA	44017	2880	D7
-	BERA	44130	2880	D7
-	MDBH	44017	2880	D7
-	MDBH	44130	2880	D7
Bagley Rd				
24600	ODFL	44017	2879	A6
24600	ODFL	44138	2879	A6
26800	OmsT	44138	2879	A6
26900	OmsT	44138	2878	D6
31000	NRDV	44039	2877	D6
E Bagley Rd				
10	BERA	44017	2880	D6
200	BERA	44130	2880	D6
12800	PRMA	44130	2881	D7
13100	MDBH	44130	2881	D7
17800	MDBH	44130	2880	D6
19200	MDBH	44017	2880	D6
W Bagley Rd				
10	BERA	44017	2880	B6
600	BERA	44017	2879	D6
W Bagley Rd SR-237				
10	BERA	44017	2880	C6
Bailey Av				
3500	CLEV	44113	2624	B6
Bailey Ct				
-	CLEV	44113	2624	C6
100	ELYR	44035	2875	B6
Bailey Dr				
1200	WKLF	44092	2374	C1
Bailey Rd				
4600	NOSD	44070	2750	C6
4800	MadT	44057	2044	B5
Bailus Rd				
4400	WTLK	44145	2749	C6
Bainbridge Rd				
3400	CVHT	44118	2627	D2
7100	BbgT	44023	2890	A5
8500	BbgT	44023	2891	D5
9600	AbnT	44023	2892	A5
29800	SLN	44139	2888	D3
33400	SLN	44139	2889	A4
33500	NRDV	44039	2877	C4
39700	SLN	44139	2890	A5
Bainbrook Dr				
7800	BbgT	44023	2890	D7
8300	BbgT	44023	2891	A7
Bain Farm Ct				
11100	CcdT	44077	2146	B4
Bain Park Dr				
4500	FWPK	44126	2751	C4
Baintree Rd				
4300	UNHT	44118	2628	B3
4300	UNHT	44121	2628	B3
E Baintree Rd				
23200	BHWD	44122	2628	D3
Baird St				
14500	BURT	44021	2636	A7
14500	BURT	44021	2766	A2
Baker Av				
8000	CLEV	44102	2623	E5
8600	MNTR	44060	2144	C7
Baker Rd				
4900	LryT	44057	2043	A6
14100	LryT	44057	2148	D1
Baker St				
10	BERA	44017	2880	B6
6600	HRM	44234	3161	A2
Balboa Ct				
900	PnvT	44077	2146	D2
Balch Rd				
14400	LryT	44057	2148	E2
14400	LryT	44057	2149	A2
14400	TpnT	44057	2149	A2
Baldwin Av				
500	ELYR	44035	3006	C1
13800	ECLE	44112	2497	A4
Baldwin Blvd				
6200	LORN	44053	2744	E6
Baldwin Ct				
10	AMHT	44001	2872	A1
1300	BWHT	44147	3149	D3
15300	MDBH	44130	2881	B7
Baldwin Dr				
-	RKRV	44116	2621	B6
100	BERA	44017	3011	A1
300	BERA	44017	3010	E1
Baldwin Ln				
10	RKRV	44116	2621	A6
11200	TNBG	44087	3020	B3
Baldwin Pl				
17800	LKWD	44107	2622	A4
Baldwin Rd				
2300	CLEV	44104	2626	C4
2300	CLEV	44106	2626	C4
4300	PryT	44057	2042	D4
4300	PryT	44081	2042	D4
8300	KDHL	44060	2252	B5
9300	KDHL	44060	2253	A6
32700	SLN	44139	2888	E5
33300	SLN	44139	2889	A5
Baldwin Creek Dr				
7300	MDBH	44130	2881	C7
7400	MDBH	44130	3012	C1
Baldwin Reserve Dr				
7200	MDBH	44130	2881	D7
W Baldwin Reserve Dr				
7200	MDBH	44130	2881	D7
Balfour Rd				
20400	WVHT	44122	2758	A2
Bali Ct				
-	MCDN	44056	3154	A3
Ball Av				
20100	EUCL	44123	2373	A4
Ballantrae Dr				
100	NCtT	44067	3152	E1
100	SgHT	44067	3152	E1
Ballymore St				
18800	SGVL	44136	3146	C4
Balmoral Ct				
15600	SGVL	44136	3012	B4
Balmoral Dr				
300	EUCL	44143	2498	C1
300	RDHT	44143	2498	C1
Balmoral Wy				
1500	WTLK	44145	2620	B7
Balsam Dr				
3200	WTLK	44145	2749	E4
6300	AhtT	44001	2744	B7
6300	AhtT	44001	2873	B1
6600	BDHT	44146	2887	E6
7200	OKWD	44146	2887	E7
Baltic Rd				
9500	CLEV	44102	2623	C5
Baltusrol Cir				
-	CcdT	44077	2253	E3
Banbury Cir				
23600	WVHT	44128	2758	C6
Banbury Ct				
1800	WTLK	44145	2750	C1
4800	WVHT	44128	2758	D6
Banbury Dr				
5400	SLN	44139	2888	E2
Banbury Ovl				
5600	MadT	44057	1941	C3
Bancroft Av				
7400	GDHT	44105	2756	A5
7600	CLEV	44105	2756	A5
Bancroft Dr				
5700	BNHT	44131	2884	C2
Bancroft Rd				
9600	NsnT	44231	3028	C6
10500	NsnT	44231	3029	A5
10500	NsnT	44491	3029	A5
10500	StnT	44491	3029	A5
Bancroft St				
6700	HRM	44234	3161	A2
Band Dr				
8300	GDHT	44125	2756	A6
Bangor Av				
5800	CLEV	44144	2754	A5
13500	GDHT	44125	2885	E1
13700	GDHT	44125	2886	A1
14000	MPHT	44137	2886	A1
Bank Rd				
7300	MadT	44057	1843	E5
Bank St				
800	AURA	44202	3021	B4
800	PNVL	44077	2146	B3
800	PnvT	44077	2146	B3
1200	ELYR	44035	3006	A1
8200	BhmT	44089	2870	E6
9000	VLVW	44125	2885	A2
Bank St SR-84				
800	PNVL	44077	2146	B3
800	PnvT	44077	2146	B3
Banks Rd				
-	CrlT	44044	3141	C3
39600	CrlT	44050	3141	C3
40500	CrlT	44050	3140	E3
Banner Ln				
6900	PRMA	44129	2882	D6
Bannerstone Dr				
10	PnvT	44077	2041	A7
Baptist Cir				
200	SgHT	44067	3017	E4
Bar Hbr				
37600	WLBY	44094	2250	D3
Barbara Av				
15600	CLEV	44135	2752	C4
Barbara Dr				
7900	SGVL	44136	3012	D3
8400	MNTR	44060	2144	B2
Barbara Ln				
-	INDE	44141	3016	C2
6000	BKPK	44142	2881	B3
Barbara St				
1000	ELYR	44035	3005	E1
32800	ETLK	44095	2249	E5
Barber Av				
1700	CLEV	44113	2624	D6
37000	WLBY	44094	2250	D6
Barberry Dr				
10	BERA	44017	2880	C5
100	BERA	44130	2880	C5
Barberry Hill Dr				
8000	MNTR	44060	2251	E1
8000	MNTR	44060	2252	A1
Barberton Av				
6100	CLEV	44102	2754	A2
6500	CLEV	44102	2753	E1
Barchard St				
700	GFTN	44044	3142	A5
Barchester Dr				
10000	CcdT	44077	2145	C7
10100	CcdT	44077	2253	E1
Barclay Blvd				
1400	WTLK	44145	2619	B7
Barclay St				
10	GDRV	44045	2039	C6
Bard Av				
22400	FWPK	44126	2751	A5
Bardbury Av				
16000	MDBH	44130	2881	B7
Bardwell Av				
14000	ECLE	44112	2497	A5
Bardwell Dr				
12000	CsTp	44026	2502	B5
Barfield Dr				
12500	CsTp	44026	2502	C7
Bar Harbor Dr				
300	BYVL	44140	2619	B4
Bar Harbour Ln				
7500	MNTR	44060	2251	B2
Barjode Rd				
28900	WLWK	44095	2249	C7
Barkdale Ln				
8900	MCDN	44056	3019	A7
Barkleigh Cir				
6700	BKVL	44141	3016	B5
Barkston Dr				
800	HDHT	44143	2499	C6
Barkwill Av				
4800	CLEV	44127	2625	C7
Barkwood Ct				
5800	MNTR	44060	2144	C3
Barkwood Dr				
2500	SFLD	44054	2747	A1
5300	SFLD	44054	2616	E7
5500	SFLD	44054	2617	A7
Barley Dr				
10	PnvT	44077	2040	E7
10	PnvT	44077	2146	E1
Barnaby Ln				
7700	MNTR	44060	2143	D6
Barnes Av				
100	PNVL	44077	2040	A7
Barnes Ct				
37900	WLBY	44094	2250	D6
Barnsley Wy				
2300	BWHT	44147	3149	D5
Barnum Rd				
1900	HpfT	44041	1944	E7
2500	GnvT	44041	1944	E5
Baron Dr				
10700	PRMA	44130	3013	B2
Barr Rd				
9300	BKVL	44141	3150	C3
10300	RchT	44141	3150	C4
Barres Ln				
200	ELYR	44035	2875	A7
Barres Rd				
38200	NRDV	44039	2876	B1
Barrett Av				
10300	CLEV	44108	2496	C4
Barrett Rd				
200	BERA	44017	2880	A5
600	BERA	44017	2879	E3
600	OmsT	44017	2879	E3
6000	TmbT	44041	2151	E6
6700	TmbT	44086	2151	B6
24400	OmsT	44138	2879	E3
Barriemore Av				
16200	MDBH	44130	2881	B7
Barrington Av				
12600	CLEV	44108	2496	E5
Barrington Blvd				
-	AURA	44202	3021	E7
10000	PMHT	44130	2882	B5
Barrington Ct				
-	ELYR	44035	3006	C2
Barrington Dr				
3300	AVON	44011	2748	B4
12600	CsTp	44026	2501	C7
E Barrington Dr				
400	CRDN	44024	2505	B2
W Barrington Dr				
300	CRDN	44024	2505	B2
Barrington Rdg				
200	PnvT	44077	2145	C6
Barrington Rd				
2100	UNHT	44118	2627	E3
Barrington Ridge Rd				
200	PnvT	44077	2145	C4
Barry Ct				
6100	MNTR	44060	2144	A3
Barry Ln				
10	NCtT	44067	3153	A2
Bartfield Av				
12700	CLEV	44108	2496	E4
Bartholomew Dr				
7300	MDBH	44130	2881	D7
7300	MDBH	44130	3012	D1
Bartholomew Rd				
9900	AbnT	44023	3023	B1
10800	AbnT	44023	3024	B1
Bartlam Av				
4700	GDHT	44125	2757	A6
Bartlett Av				
13100	CLEV	44120	2756	E2
13800	CLEV	44120	2757	A2
14300	CLEV	44128	2757	A2
Bartlett Dr				
22200	RKRV	44116	2621	A6
Bartlett Rd				
-	BDHT	44146	2758	C7
600	AURA	44255	3157	D6
600	STBR	44241	3157	D6
2600	ManT	44255	3157	D6
2600	ShvT	44241	3157	D6
2600	ShvT	44255	3157	D6
2700	ManT	44255	3158	B6
2700	ShvT	44241	3158	B6
2700	ShvT	44255	3158	B6
5200	BDHT	44146	2887	C2
5500	BDFD	44146	2887	C2
Bartlett Rd SR-43				
-	BDHT	44146	2758	C7
Bartley Ln				
8400	MNTR	44060	2144	B3
Barton Cir				
7200	PRMA	44129	2882	E6
Barton Dr				
7000	MNTR	44060	2144	D7
8300	SGVL	44136	3011	A3
Barton Rd				
-	LNHT	44124	2498	E5
700	SgHT	44067	3152	D3
5300	NRDV	44039	2877	E1
5400	NOSD	44070	2878	A1
5400	NRDV	44039	2878	A1
5400	NRDV	44070	2878	A1
7100	OmsT	44138	2878	B3
N Barton Rd				
4800	NRDV	44039	2748	E7
4900	LNHT	44124	2498	E5
5200	NRDV	44039	2877	E1
S Barton Rd				
-	LNHT	44124	2498	E5
Barton Hill Dr				
7200	PRMA	44129	2882	E6
Bartow Ln				
500	RDHT	44143	2498	C3
Bartter Av				
14500	CLEV	44111	2752	D2
Bartwood Dr				
2500	PnvT	44077	2041	B5
2500	PryT	44077	2041	B5
Barwick Ct				
800	PnvT	44077	2040	E2
Bascom Rd				
9000	HmbT	44024	2256	D7
9000	HmbT	44024	2381	D2
Base Dr				
10	PnvT	44077	2041	A4
Basquin Dr				
200	CRDN	44024	2380	A5
Bass Run				
10	AbnT	44023	2892	A4
Bassett Ln				
9300	NRYN	44133	3013	C5
Bassett Rd				
-	WTLK	44140	2619	C5
200	BYVL	44140	2619	C5
700	WTLK	44145	2619	C5
1600	WTLK	44145	2749	C2
27200	WTLK	44145	2750	A2
Bass Lake Rd				
-	CRDN	44024	2505	A2
11400	MsnT	44024	2505	A2
11500	MsnT	44024	2504	D6
12500	MsnT	44024	2634	D2
13500	NbyT	44024	2634	D2
13700	NbyT	44065	2634	D6
14400	NbyT	44065	2635	A7
14400	NbyT	44021	2765	A1
14400	NbyT	44065	2765	A1
Basswood Cir				
13800	SGVL	44136	3012	D5
Basswood Ct				
7500	NRYN	44133	3013	D7
Basswood Dr				
5800	LORN	44053	2744	E5
6500	BDHT	44146	2887	D6
9200	ODFL	44138	3010	A1
Basswood Ln				
10	MDHL	44022	2760	A4
7500	MNTR	44060	2251	D4
Basswood Rd				
11500	MsnT	44024	2504	B3
Batavia Av				
7500	CLEV	44105	2756	A3
Bates Dr				
300	BYVL	44140	2619	A4
Bates Ln				
2500	WBHL	44094	2375	B4
Bates Rd				
200	MadT	44057	2044	D2
200	MDSN	44057	2044	D2
700	RKRV	44116	2621	B6
3100	MadT	44057	1942	D7
3300	MDSN	44057	1942	D7
Bath St				
100	ELYR	44035	2874	E5
100	ELYR	44035	2875	A5
Bathgate Dr				
1600	MadT	44057	1842	E7
1800	MadT	44057	1941	E1
Battersea Blvd				
19200	RKRV	44116	2621	D5
Battles Ct				
10	CRDN	44024	2380	A6
Battles Rd				
400	GSML	44040	2500	E3
7700	GSML	44040	2501	A2
Bauer Ln				
7200	MNTR	44060	2143	C4
Bauerdale Av				
8100	PRMA	44129	2882	D1
36900	AVON	44011	2747	E2
Baumhart Rd				
-	BhmT	44001	2871	C2
-	VMLN	44001	2871	C2
1400	BhmT	44001	2742	C7
1400	BhmT	44053	2742	C7
1400	VMLN	44001	2742	C7
1400	VMLN	44053	2742	C7
5400	LORN	44053	2742	C7
Bavaria Av				
5700	PRMA	44129	2882	D2
Bavaria Pkwy				
7800	TwbT	44087	3154	C5
8000	MCDN	44087	3154	C5

INDEX 9

Billy Campbell Blvd

Cleveland Street Index

Briarwood Dr

STREET
Block City ZIP Map# Grid
Billy Campbell Blvd
7600 BbgT 44023 2761 C7
Biltamy Blvd
1700 SELD 44121 2628 C1
Biltmore Av
15500 CLEV 44128 2757 C2
Biltmore Pl
36400 WLBY 44094 2250 C6
Biltmore Rd
1400 LNHT 44124 2499 C4
1400 LNHT 44124 2629 A1
7500 MNTR 44060 2252 C2
Birch Av
10 NHFD 44067 3018 A4
100 NHFD 44067 3017 E4
500 EUCL 44132 2374 A1
Birch Cir
4300 NOSD 44070 2750 D6
31200 SLN 44139 2888 D1
Birch Ct
1400 LORN 44053 2744 C3
Birch Dr
100 PnvT 44077 2041 B4
200 AhtT 44001 2872 A3
Birch Ln
10 OmsT 44138 2879 B4
800 AMHT 44001 2872 E1
1000 CLEV 44109 2754 E4
5800 MONT 44060 2143 E2
23900 NOSD 44070 2750 D6
Birch St
- ELYR 44035 3006 A1
5100 NRDV 44039 2748 C7
5300 NRDV 44039 2877 C1
Birchbark Dr
100 ELYR 44035 3005 B1
Birchbark Grv
8800 BbgT 44023 2762 B7
Birchbark Tr
200 AURA 44202 3156 D2
Birchcroft Dr
15200 BKPK 44142 2881 B3
Birchdale Av
8600 CLEV 44106 2626 B1
Birchdale Dr
26400 WTLK 44145 2750 A3
Birch Hill Rd
17900 BbgT 44023 2891 B6
Birchmont Dr
7600 RslT 44073 2761 C5
Birchtree Pth
3500 CVHT 44121 2497 D7
Birch View Dr
1200 VMLN 44089 2741 A7
Birchwold Rd
4400 SELD 44121 2628 C2
Birchwood Av
14000 CLEV 44111 2622 D7
Birchwood Dr
400 BERA 44017 2880 A4
600 WLBY 44094 2143 A4
5600 MNTR 44060 2143 E2
8000 CsTp 44026 2631 D2
8900 TNBG 44087 3154 E1
Birchwood Ln
20200 SGVL 44136 3146 C2
32400 AVLK 44012 2618 C2
Birchwood Rd
4600 GDHT 44125 2756 A5
Birchwood St
41500 EyrT 44035 2745 D7
Bird
10 ELYR 44035 2874 E3
Birdie Ln
- AVON 44011 2748 B6
1500 PnvT 44077 2040 E4
Birdland Tr
13100 CsTp 44026 2631 B2
Birkdale Ct
7400 SLN 44139 3020 E2
Birmingham Av
10800 CcdT 44077 2146 A7
Biscayne Blvd
2500 BHWD 44122 2628 E5
7500 PRMA 44134 3014 E1
Bishop Ct
7500 MNTR 44060 2252 B2
Bishop Dr
10 SRSL 44073 2762 B6
200 MCDN 44056 3018 B5
Bishop Ln
18200 SGVL 44136 3146 E1
Bishop Pl
500 BERA 44017 2880 D6
Bishop Rd
200 HDHT 44143 2499 B1
1500 WKLF 44092 2374 B3
2700 WBHL 44092 2374 B7
5800 HpfT 44041 2045 E2
Bishop Rd SR-84
2400 WKLF 44092 2374 B4
2700 WBHL 44092 2374 B4
Bishop Wy
300 SgHT 44067 3017 D5
Bishop Park Dr
27000 WBHL 44092 2374 B5
Bishops Ct
8100 BWHT 44147 3015 A5
Bishops Gate Cir
31200 WTLK 44145 2749 A4
Bissell Dr
10000 TNBG 44087 3020 C4
N Bissell Rd
10 AURA 44202 3021 D7
S Bissell Rd
10 AURA 44202 3156 D1
Bittern Av
7400 CLEV 44103 2496 A5
Bittersweet Ct
15600 SGVL 44136 3012 B3
Bittersweet Dr
800 SVHL 44131 2884 A4
Bittersweet Tr
17100 BbgT 44023 2891 D3
Black Rd
4900 RchT 44141 3151 C7
Blackberry Cir
13700 SGVL 44136 3012 D4
36600 SLN 44139 2889 C3
Blackberry Ln
3500 WTLK 44145 2750 A4
7700 GSML 44040 2500 E2
7700 GSML 44040 2501 A2
11400 CsTp 44026 2502 D3

STREET
Block City ZIP Map# Grid
Blackbird Dr
200 ELYR 44035 2874 E2
Blackbrook Rd
10 PnvT 44077 2039 C7
10 PnvT 44077 2145 B1
600 PnvT 44060 2145 B1
9600 MNTR 44060 2039 B7
9600 MNTR 44060 2145 B1
Blackburn Rd
23000 OKWD 44146 2887 C7
Blackfeet Tr
800 MCDN 44056 3018 D6
Blackfoot Av
20200 EUCL 44117 2498 A3
Blackford Dr
7600 RslT 44073 2761 C5
Blackhawk Run
9100 MCDN 44056 3018 D5
Blackmore Rd
1300 CVHT 44118 2497 C7
3300 PryT 44081 1939 D7
3300 PryT 44081 2041 D1
Black River Cir
4100 LORN 44055 2746 B4
Blackstone Av
23100 EUCL 44123 2373 C3
Blackstone Ct
- CLEV 44113 2624 D3
Black Swan Ct
5300 NRYN 44133 3149 A1
E Blackthorn Cir
2600 HDSN 44236 3155 C7
W Blackthorn Cir
2500 HDSN 44236 3155 C6
Blackwell Ct
9500 CLEV 44106 2626 B1
Blaine Av
10 BDFD 44146 2887 A3
8600 CLEV 44106 2626 B1
Blaine St
100 ELYR 44035 2875 B7
400 GNVA 44041 1944 C4
Blair Cir
- AURA 44202 3021 B6
Blair Dr
5600 HDHT 44143 2499 C4
Blair Ln
10100 KTLD 44094 2377 E5
10100 KTLD 44094 2378 A4
Blair Pl
500 PNVL 44077 2040 C6
Blair Rd
5100 PryT 44081 2042 B7
5200 PryT 44057 2042 B7
5200 PryT 44077 2042 B7
5300 LryT 44057 2042 B7
5300 LryT 44077 2042 B7
5300 LryT 44057 2148 C1
5300 LryT 44077 2148 C1
Blake St
- ELYR 44035 2874 E7
100 ELYR 44035 2875 D6
800 ELYR 44035 3006 D2
Blakely Dr
5800 HDHT 44143 2499 C4
Blanch Av
35400 ETLK 44095 2250 B4
Blanchard Dr
7300 NRDV 44039 2877 C4
Blanche Av
5200 CLEV 44127 2755 D1
41600 CrlT 44035 3005 C4
Blanche Rd
3300 CVHT 44118 2627 D2
Blanchester Rd
1000 LNHT 44124 2499 A6
Blandford Rd
18000 CLEV 44121 2497 E3
Blase Av
13500 CLEV 44111 2752 E1
Blase Nemeth Rd
1500 PnvT 44077 2040 E4
1800 PnvT 44077 2041 A3
Blatt Ct
2500 CLEV 44109 2624 D7
Blaze Industrial Pkwy
100 BERA 44017 2879 D6
Blazey Tr
12100 SGVL 44136 3012 D6
Blazing Star Dr
17700 SGVL 44136 3147 B3
Blenheim Rd
13400 CLEV 44110 2497 A3
Bletch Ct
7100 CHHT 44125 2755 E6
Blish Av
10 PnvT 44077 2145 B4
Bliss Av
6600 CLEV 44103 2495 E7
Bliss Ovl
500 MDSN 44057 2044 A3
Bliss St
2800 AVON 44011 2748 D2
Blissfield Dr
300 WLWK 44095 2249 B7
Blissful Rd
700 VMLN 44089 2740 C5
Blodgett Creek Tr
10800 SGVL 44136 3011 C5
Blossom Av
10600 PMHT 44130 2882 B5
12600 PMHT 44130 2881 E5
Blossom Ct
4000 BNWK 44212 3146 E7
Blossom Dr
- AMHT 44001 2744 A7
600 AMHT 44001 2743 E7
700 LORN 44052 2615 D5
8600 MNTR 44060 2252 C1
22200 RKRV 44116 2621 A6
Blossom Ln
10 OmsT 44138 2879 B4
2400 BHWD 44122 2628 D4
9900 TNBG 44087 3019 B4
27200 NOSD 44070 2750 A4
27300 NOSD 44070 2749 E4
Blossom Park Av
1400 LKWD 44107 2622 D5
Blue Bell Ct
9400 MNTR 44060 2145 A6
Bluebell Dr
5300 LNHT 44124 2629 A1
Blueberry Cir
400 MAYF 44143 2500 A2

STREET
Block City ZIP Map# Grid
Blueberry Hl
10700 KTLD 44094 2376 D6
Blueberry Ln
9300 MCDN 44056 3019 A6
Bluebird Dr
100 ELYR 44035 2874 E3
Blue Grass Ovl
36300 SLN 44139 2889 C4
Blue Heron Dr
2600 HDSN 44236 3155 C7
33700 SLN 44139 3020 A3
Blue Heron Tr
11600 MsnT 44024 2504 C5
Bluejay Ln
8900 MNTR 44060 2144 D2
Bluejay Tr
400 MCDN 44056 3153 C2
Blue Point Dr
19100 SGVL 44136 3146 E5
Blue Pond Tr
28400 SLN 44139 2888 B2
Blue Ribbon Dr
7100 INDE 44131 2885 A7
Blue Ridge Dr
7400 CcdT 44060 2253 B1
Blue Spruce Dr
18900 SGVL 44136 3146 D4
Blue Spruce Ovl
6800 MDBH 44130 2881 C5
Blue Spruce St
2900 PryT 44081 2041 D3
Blue Spruce Tr
600 AbnT 44023 2892 B4
Bluestone Rd
3900 CVHT 44121 2498 A6
4000 SELD 44121 2498 A6
N Bluff Dr
8400 BWHT 44147 3014 E4
Bluff St
8900 KTLD 44094 2251 D7
Bluffside Pl
11900 SGVL 44136 3012 A6
Blythin Rd
4600 GDHT 44105 2756 A5
4600 GDHT 44125 2756 A5
Bobby Ln
1300 WTLK 44145 2619 C7
Bobko Blvd
10700 PRMA 44130 3013 B1
Bobolink Dr
8300 MCDN 44056 3018 C7
Bob White Cir
16900 SGVL 44136 3147 A3
Bogie Ln
1500 PnvT 44077 2040 E4
Bohannon Ct
100 ELYR 44035 3006 B2
Bohning Dr
9300 GDHT 44125 2756 B5
Bolingbrook Rd
28500 PRPK 44124 2629 C6
29800 PRPK 44124 2759 C1
Bolivar Rd
700 CLEV 44115 2624 E3
Bolton Rd
2500 CVHT 44118 2497 C7
2500 CVHT 44118 2627 C1
Bon Air Av
200 ELYR 44035 2875 E5
Bond Av
5000 ShfT 44055 2746 A6
Bond St
- VLVW 44125 2885 A2
100 ELYR 44035 2875 A4
400 ELYR 44035 2874 E4
7500 GNWL 44139 3019 B2
Bonds Pkwy
200 BERA 44017 2880 D6
Bonna Av
5600 CLEV 44103 2495 D7
Bonneybrook Ln
600 BHIT 44212 3145 E7
Bonnie Ct
30500 WKLF 44092 2374 E1
Bonnie Ln
200 AURA 44202 3156 D4
1100 MDHT 44124 2499 E7
18000 SGVL 44136 3011 E6
Bonnie Pl
1100 MDHT 44124 2499 E6
Bonnie Rd
1400 MCDN 44056 3019 A7
Bonnie Bank Blvd
19900 RKRV 44116 2751 D1
Bonnie Bank Ln
18900 FWPK 44126 2751 E1
Bonnieview Av
1200 LKWD 44107 2622 B4
Bonnieview Dr
30100 WKLF 44092 2374 D3
33200 AVLK 44012 2617 C1
Bonnieview Rd
6600 MAYF 44143 2500 A5
Bonniewood Dr
200 CLEV 44110 2372 B7
Bonny Blvd
2400 PRMA 44134 3014 C1
Bonny Bank Dr
23800 WTLK 44145 2750 E1
Bonroi Dr
6300 SVHL 44131 2884 B4
Booker Av
24500 OKWD 44146 2887 D7
Boone Rd
16300 ClbT 44028 3145 C5
N Boone Rd
12000 ClbT 44028 3010 C5
S Boone Rd
14000 ClbT 44028 3010 C7
14000 ClbT 44028 3145 C1
Booth Av
8100 CLEV 44105 2756 A3
Booth Rd
8700 KDHL 44060 2252 D6
9100 KDHL 44060 2377 C2
9100 KTLD 44060 2377 C2
9100 KTLD 44094 2377 C2
Bordeaux Ln
10 BHWD 44122 2628 E3
Bordeaux Pl
10 OmsT 44138 2879 B3
Bordeaux Wy
1800 WTLK 44145 2749 E1
Borges St
9200 GDHT 44125 2756 B5

STREET
Block City ZIP Map# Grid
Born Av
10100 CLEV 44108 2496 C5
Bosley Cove
6600 MNTR 44060 2145 A5
Boston Av
100 ELYR 44035 2875 D6
6600 CLEV 44127 2625 E7
Boston Rd
1500 HkyT 44133 3148 D5
1500 HkyT 44233 3148 D5
1500 NRYN 44133 3148 D5
2400 HkyT 44133 3147 E5
2400 HkyT 44233 3147 E5
2400 NRYN 44133 3147 E5
2700 BNWK 44136 3147 E5
2700 BNWK 44212 3147 E5
2700 SGVL 44136 3147 E5
3700 BHIT 44136 3146 E5
3700 BHIT 44212 3146 E5
3700 BNWK 44212 3146 E5
3700 SGVL 44136 3146 E5
3900 BNWK 44136 3146 C5
4900 BHIT 44136 3145 E5
4900 BHIT 44212 3145 E5
4900 SGVL 44136 3145 E5
5300 ClbT 44028 3145 D5
5300 ClbT 44136 3145 D5
5300 ClbT 44280 3145 D5
5300 LvpT 44028 3145 D5
5300 LvpT 44136 3145 D5
5300 LvpT 44212 3145 D5
5300 LvpT 44280 3145 D5
E Boston Rd
10 BWHT 44147 3149 E5
10 BWHT 44147 3150 A5
10 RchT 44147 3149 E5
10 RchT 44286 3149 E5
10 RchT 44147 3150 A5
10 RchT 44286 3150 A5
2400 BKVL 44141 3150 A5
2400 RchT 44141 3150 A5
W Boston Rd
10 BWHT 44147 3149 D6
10 HkyT 44147 3149 D6
10 HkyT 44233 3149 D6
10 RchT 44147 3149 D6
10 RchT 44233 3149 D6
Boston Lake Dr
200 LvpT 44280 3145 C6
Boston Mills Rd
1400 BosT 44141 3152 C7
Boston Reserve Ln
- BHIT 44212 3145 E6
Bosworth Rd
3300 CLEV 44111 2753 B1
Botany Av
1400 CLEV 44109 2754 E3
Boulder Dr
32700 NRDV 44039 2877 D2
Boulder Creek Dr
5000 SLN 44139 2759 E7
Boulder Glen Dr
13100 MsnT 44026 2633 E2
Boulder Ridge Pl
10 PnvT 44077 2041 A7
10 PnvT 44077 2147 A1
Boulder Wood Dr
7200 BWHT 44147 3015 E4
Boundary Ln
9100 PRMA 44130 2882 C6
Bounty Rd
400 AURA 44202 3157 A2
Bounty Wy
300 AVLK 44012 2618 E2
Bowdoin Dr
1200 PnvT 44077 2147 A1
Bowen Dr
11300 ManT 44255 3159 B3
Bower Av
5300 CLEV 44127 2625 D6
Bowfin Blvd
15300 BKPK 44142 2881 B2
Bowhall Rd
10 PnvT 44077 2041 A6
Bowling Green Cir
600 ELYR 44035 3006 D1
Bowling Green Rd
20600 MPHT 44137 2887 A1
Bowman Dr
19100 SGVL 44136 3146 D3
Bowmen Ln
2700 PRMA 44134 2883 C7
Boxberry Ln
2400 BWHT 44147 3014 C3
Boxelder Dr
3500 BKVL 44141 3150 C1
Boxwood
5500 LORN 44053 2743 E6
Boxwood Cir
- MsnT 44024 2504 C2
8900 BKLN 44144 2753 D4
Boxwood Ct
- AVON 44011 2748 D6
Boxwood Dr
5700 LORN 44053 2744 A6
Boxwood St
4800 AVON 44011 2748 D6
Boxwood Tr
1900 PnvT 44077 2145 B5
Boyce Rd
2900 SRHT 44122 2628 A6
Boyd Ct
35600 WLBY 44094 2375 B2
N Boyden Rd
7800 NCtT 44067 3152 D1
7800 SgHT 44067 3017 D6
7800 SgHT 44067 3152 D1
S Boyden Rd
7100 SgHT 44067 3152 D3
7800 NCtT 44067 3152 D2
Boyer Av
2100 CLEV 44109 2754 D4
Boyer Ln
9000 KDHL 44060 2252 D4
Boyle Pkwy
8300 TwbT 44087 3154 C4
Boynton Rd
- VMLN 44089 2742 A5
3200 VMLN 44089 2741 E6
3400 CVHT 44121 2497 D6
Brace Av
100 ELYR 44035 2874 E3
Bracken Wy
400 BYVL 44140 2619 D5

STREET
Block City ZIP Map# Grid
Brackenbury Dr
32700 SLN 44139 3019 E2
Brackland Av
12300 CLEV 44108 2496 E5
Brad Dr
200 BNWK 44212 3147 D7
Braddock Av
16400 CLEV 44110 2497 C2
Bradenton Blvd
7400 PRMA 44134 3014 C1
Bradford Av
1600 CLEV 44113 2624 D5
Bradford Ct
19200 SGVL 44136 3146 D2
Bradford Dr
900 ELYR 44035 2875 A3
1400 MCDN 44056 3019 A6
4600 SELD 44121 2498 C6
12000 MsnT 44024 2634 E2
12100 MsnT 44024 2635 A2
Bradford Ln
- AURA 44202 3021 D5
8600 BKVL 44141 3016 B6
Bradford Rd
3200 CVHT 44118 2627 C4
3600 UNHT 44118 2627 D4
5600 PkmT 44491 3028 E2
7100 ODFL 44138 2879 C4
7100 OmsT 44138 2879 C4
17400 FnTp 44491 3029 A2
17400 PkmT 44491 3029 A2
Bradford Park Ln
7700 TwbT 44236 3154 D5
Bradfords Gate
3300 RKRV 44116 2751 B2
8200 ODFL 44138 2879 A6
Bradgate Av
16300 CLEV 44111 2752 A3
Bradgate Ln
20000 SGVL 44136 3146 C4
Bradley Av
100 CNFL 44022 2761 A7
5400 PRMA 44129 2883 A1
6700 PRMA 44129 2882 E1
Bradley Ct
10800 CcdT 44077 2146 A4
Bradley Rd
100 BYVL 44140 2619 B4
600 WTLK 44140 2619 B4
600 WTLK 44145 2619 B7
1900 WTLK 44145 2749 B1
4100 CLEV 44109 2755 A4
5400 NOSD 44070 2749 B7
5400 NOSD 44070 2878 A1
30900 NRDV 44039 2878 A2
30900 NRDV 44070 2878 A2
Bradmore Cir
- AURA 44202 3021 E6
Bradwell Av
2900 CLEV 44109 2754 C3
Bradwell Rd
11400 GDHT 44125 2885 D1
Brady Ln
11100 SGVL 44136 3011 B5
Braeburn Ln
13500 RslT 44072 2631 E3
Braeburn Park Dr
1700 EUCL 44117 2373 D6
Braemar Rd
3200 SRHT 44120 2627 C7
Braemar Way Ovl
19700 SGVL 44136 3011 C7
Braewood Dr
7200 INDE 44131 2884 E7
7200 INDE 44131 2885 A7
Bragdon Av
4600 CLEV 44102 2754 B1
Bragg Rd
5300 CLEV 44127 2625 D6
Brahms Dr
26600 WTLK 44145 2750 A1
Brainard Av
1600 CLEV 44109 2624 D7
Brainard Ct
7500 MNTR 44060 2143 D6
Brainard Dr
10400 PRMA 44130 2882 B1
Brainard Rd
800 HDHT 44143 2499 B6
1100 LNHT 44124 2499 B6
1400 LNHT 44124 2629 B1
2400 PRPK 44124 2629 B1
3200 PRPK 44124 2759 B3
3600 WDMR 44122 2759 B3
3900 ORNG 44122 2759 B3
4000 ORNG 44022 2759 B3
5000 SLN 44022 2759 B5
5000 SLN 44139 2759 B5
5200 SLN 44139 2888 A1
E Brainard Rd
3400 PRPK 44124 2759 B1
3400 WDMR 44122 2759 B1
3400 WDMR 44124 2759 B1
W Brainard Rd
3400 ORNG 44122 2759 A1
3400 PRPK 44124 2759 A1
3400 WDMR 44122 2759 A1
3400 WDMR 44124 2759 A1
Brainard Hills Dr
2700 PRPK 44124 2629 B5
Braintree Ln
10 CcdT 44060 2145 B2
Brairwood Ct
- CrlT 44035 3006 D4
Brakeman Rd
6700 LryT 44077 2148 B7
6700 LryT 44077 2256 B2
8400 HmbT 44024 2256 B6
8400 HmbT 44024 2381 B2
Braman Ct
1500 LORN 44052 2745 A1
Bramble Ct
5500 WLBY 44094 2375 A1
Bramble Ln
400 AURA 44202 3156 C2
34200 SLN 44139 3020 A1
Brambleside Dr
400 BHIT 44212 3146 A7
Brambleside Ln
6100 MNTR 44060 2143 C3
Bramblewood Dr
2500 BWHT 44147 3015 B4
Bramblewood Ln
6600 MAYF 44143 2500 B3

STREET
Block City ZIP Map# Grid
Bramblewood Pl
6100 MNTR 44060 2143 D3
Bramblewood Wy
3200 AVON 44011 2748 A3
Bramley Av
- LKWD 44107 2622 E7
Bramley Dr
4400 MNTU 44255 3159 B5
8700 INDE 44131 3016 B1
Bramshill Cir
7000 BbgT 44023 2890 A5
Branch Av
10 PnvT 44077 2040 C7
1600 CLEV 44113 2624 D6
Branch Dr
10 AhtT 44001 2872 B2
Branch St
34300 NRDV 44039 2877 C1
Brandamore Ct
6600 SLN 44139 2889 D7
Brandemere Ct
100 ELYR 44035 2875 C3
Brandon Cir
800 AURA 44202 3156 C4
Brandon Ct
10 MDHL 44022 2760 B4
500 CRDN 44024 2505 A1
Brandon Pl
10 RKRV 44116 2621 A5
32200 AVLK 44012 2618 C3
Brandon Rd
1000 CVHT 44112 2497 C6
3300 BHWD 44122 2628 D7
3300 BHWD 44122 2758 D1
Brandston Av
10 ELYR 44035 2875 C5
Brandt Av
100 AMHT 44001 2872 D1
Brandt Rd
700 HpfT 44041 2045 E4
Brandywine Dr
2000 EUCL 44143 2498 D2
2000 RDHT 44143 2498 D2
7000 CcdT 44060 2145 A7
7000 MNTR 44060 2145 A7
17400 SGVL 44136 3146 E4
17400 SGVL 44136 3147 A4
20700 FWPK 44126 2751 C4
Brandywine Ln
- BHWD 44122 2628 E3
20700 FWPK 44126 2751 C4
Brandywine Rd
6700 PMHT 44130 2882 C6
7300 BSHT 44236 3153 B7
7800 NCtT 44067 3153 A6
7800 NCtT 44141 3153 A6
8000 NCtT 44067 3152 E5
8000 NCtT 44141 3152 E5
8200 SgHT 44067 3152 E5
Brandywine Sq
10 EUCL 44143 2498 A2
Brandywine St
100 ELYR 44035 2874 A7
Brandywood Dr
10 PRPK 44124 2759 E1
10 PRPK 44124 2760 A1
Branford Av
13600 GDHT 44125 2885 E4
13600 GDHT 44125 2886 A4
Branford Ln
300 RDHT 44143 2498 E1
Brantley Ln
300 BNWK 44212 3146 E7
Brantley Rd
20600 SRHT 44122 2628 A6
Brantwood Dr
2400 WTLK 44145 2750 D2
Bratenahl Pl
10 BTNH 44108 2496 D3
Bratenahl Rd
100 BTNH 44108 2496 C3
Brayes Manor Dr
9500 MNTR 44060 2253 A3
Brayton Av
700 CLEV 44113 2625 A6
Brayton Tr
7700 BbgT 44023 2890 C2
Brazil Rd
17600 CLEV 44119 2372 D5
Breakwater Av
5900 CLEV 44102 2624 A4
Breck Ct
3200 CLEV 44114 2625 B1
6800 NRDV 44039 2877 A3
Breckenridge Dr
9700 CdnT 44024 2379 B3
25500 EUCL 44117 2373 D6
Breckenridge Tr
30800 WTLK 44145 2749 B2
Brecksville Rd
- CHHT 44125 2755 E7
- CHHT 44131 2755 E7
- INDE 44125 2755 E7
- INDE 44131 2755 E7
- VLVW 44125 2884 E1
- VLVW 44131 2884 E1
4700 RHFD 44286 3151 A7
5400 INDE 44131 2884 E1
7200 INDE 44131 3015 E1
7600 INDE 44131 3016 A4
7700 BKVL 44141 3016 A4
9000 BKVL 44141 3151 A2
Brecksville Rd SR-21
- CHHT 44125 2755 E7
- CHHT 44131 2755 E7
- INDE 44125 2755 E7
- INDE 44131 2755 E7
- VLVW 44125 2884 E1
- VLVW 44131 2884 E1
4700 RHFD 44286 3151 A7
5400 INDE 44131 2884 E1
7200 INDE 44131 3015 E1
7600 INDE 44131 3016 A4
7700 BKVL 44141 3016 A4
9000 BKVL 44141 3151 A2
Breckswood Ovl
5500 BWHT 44147 3015 D5
Breezevale Cole
22600 RKRV 44116 2621 A5
Breezewood Dr
200 BYVL 44140 2619 C4
6500 CcdT 44077 2146 E5
6500 CcdT 44077 2147 A5
Breezy Acres Dr
- ClrT 44024 2505 D7

STREET
Block City ZIP Map# Grid
Bremen Av
7900 PRMA 44129 2882 D2
Bremerton Rd
1800 LNHT 44124 2629 B2
3000 PRPK 44124 2629 B7
Brenda Lee Dr
7000 WNHL 44146 2886 D7
Brendan Ln
3800 NOSD 44070 2750 E5
Brenel Dr
7300 CcdT 44060 2253 C1
Brennans Ct
- AVLK 44012 2618 E4
Brennen Dr
700 AMHT 44001 2872 E3
Brenner Dr
2800 LORN 44053 2743 D3
Brenthaven St
100 ELYR 44035 2874 B6
Brentview Dr
100 CrlT 44044 3006 D6
Brentwood Ct
5300 HDHT 44143 2499 A3
Brentwood Dr
200 PNVL 44077 2145 E3
8200 ODFL 44138 2879 A6
8500 OmsT 44138 2879 A7
Brentwood Ln
11100 CdnT 44024 2379 B4
Brentwood Rd
- AhtT 44001 2872 E6
1100 CVHT 44121 2497 E6
2400 BHWD 44122 2628 C5
7800 MNTR 44060 2251 D3
Breton Dr
4100 CLEV 44109 2754 E4
Brett Dr
30100 WBHL 44092 2374 D5
Bretten Ct
6400 INDE 44131 3015 E2
Bretton Ct
5500 WLBY 44094 2375 A1
Bretton Ridge Dr
6600 NOSD 44070 2878 C3
Brevier Av
1700 CLEV 44113 2624 D6
Brewer Ct
6300 MNTR 44060 2144 A4
Brewster Ct
1000 GFTN 44044 3142 A3
Brewster Dr
4000 WTLK 44145 2749 D5
N Brewster Pl
7100 CcdT 44077 2146 A6
S Brewster Pl
7200 CcdT 44077 2146 B7
Brewster Rd
2800 PRPK 44124 2629 E6
15300 ECLE 44112 2497 B6
16200 CVHT 44112 2497 B6
18600 BbgT 44023 3021 D3
19100 AURA 44202 3021 C4
19100 BbgT 44202 3021 D3
Brian Av
17800 CLEV 44119 2372 D6
Brian Ct
16000 MDFD 44062 2767 E2
Brian Dr
2300 BHWD 44122 2628 E4
2400 PRMA 44134 3014 C1
10200 CcdT 44077 2145 D6
Brian St
9000 NRDV 44039 3008 C1
Briar Ct
10 AhtT 44001 2873 C2
30400 WKLF 44092 2374 E2
Briar Ln
- VmnT 44089 2869 C3
500 BDFD 44146 2887 B3
29300 WTLK 44145 2749 C2
Briar Rd
4700 CLEV 44135 2752 D6
Briarbanks Dr
4400 FWPK 44126 2751 E2
Briar Bush Ln
21300 SGVL 44136 3011 A5
Briarcliff Ct
7100 MNTR 44060 2145 A7
Briarcliff Dr
100 ELYR 44035 3005 B1
200 ELYR 44035 2874 B7
600 AURA 44202 3156 D3
5500 GDHT 44125 2885 C1
Briarcliff Pkwy
7400 MDBH 44130 2881 B7
7500 MDBH 44130 3012 B1
Briardale Av
23100 EUCL 44123 2373 C3
25100 EUCL 44132 2373 D2
Briardale Ct
1100 TNBG 44087 3019 C3
Briardale Ln
5800 SLN 44139 2888 E3
Briargate Ct
200 AVLK 44012 2618 C2
Briar Hill Dr
5800 SLN 44139 2888 E3
5800 SLN 44139 2889 A3
10400 KTLD 44094 2376 B5
Briar Hill Rd
100 PnvT 44077 2147 A2
Briar Lake Ct
100 ELYR 44035 2875 D1
Briar Lake Dr
100 ELYR 44035 2875 D1
Briar Lakes
- AVON 44011 2747 C3
Briarleigh Dr
10 BNWK 44212 3147 D6
Briarpatch Dr
24000 ODFL 44138 3010 D1
Briar Ridge Ct
3400 WTLK 44145 2749 D4
Briarwood Ct
10500 CrlT 44035 3006 D4
25700 WTLK 44145 2750 B4
Briarwood Dr
- ManT 44255 3159 A3
4500 LORN 44053 2744 C5
7300 MNTR 44060 2252 E1
8100 BWHT 44147 3014 D2
11700 CsTp 44026 2502 A3
21700 FWPK 44126 2751 B5
24400 ODFL 44138 3010 C1

STREET Block	City	ZIP	Map#	Grid
Briarwood Ln				
5800	SLN	44139	2888	D3
19200	SGVL	44136	3011	D5
24400	ClbT	44028	3144	E2
24400	ClbT	44028	3145	A2
Briarwood Rd				
2100	CVHT	44118	2627	B3
9100	MCDN	44056	3018	E6
14700	NbyT	44065	2764	D1
Briarwood St				
32700	AVLK	44012	2618	A2
Briarwyck Woods Av				
11700	CcdT	44077	2254	D5
Brichford Rd				
7900	MNTR	44060	2251	E3
Bricker Ct				
8500	MNTR	44060	2144	B3
Bricker St				
-	NbyT	44065	2764	D1
Brick Mill Run				
600	RKRV	44116	2621	A6
600	WTLK	44116	2621	A6
600	WTLK	44145	2621	A6
17600	SGVL	44136	3146	E5
17600	SGVL	44136	3147	A5
Bridge Av				
2500	CLEV	44113	2624	C5
4500	CLEV	44102	2624	A5
Bridge Ct				
4500	CLEV	44102	2624	B5
Bridge Dr				
1000	LORN	44052	2615	A7
Bridge Pth				
18900	SGVL	44136	3147	A5
Bridge Rd				
15500	MdfT	44062	2768	A4
E Bridge St				
10	BERA	44017	2880	C7
100	ELYR	44035	2875	B6
W Bridge St				
10	BERA	44017	2880	B7
100	ELYR	44035	2875	A6
200	ELYR	44035	2874	E6
Bridge Creek Tr				
17800	AbnT	44023	2892	E5
Bridge Point Tr				
-	AVON	44011	2747	C1
Bridgeport Dr				
100	ELYR	44035	3006	C2
3200	NOSD	44070	2750	E4
4600	VMLN	44089	2741	A5
Bridgeport Ln				
8400	MNTR	44060	2144	B5
Bridgeport Tr				
300	RDHT	44143	2498	E1
Bridgeside Dr				
500	AVLK	44012	2618	E4
Bridgestone Dr				
-	NRDV	44039	2877	E7
Bridget Ln				
1200	TNBG	44087	3019	A6
Bridgeton Dr				
2500	HDSN	44236	3155	C6
25000	BHWD	44122	2628	E5
Bridgeview Av				
3900	NBGH	44105	2755	C2
Bridgeview Dr				
3700	CLEV	44121	2497	E4
3700	SELD	44121	2497	E4
Bridgewater Dr				
4500	PryT	44081	2042	C5
11100	NRYN	44133	3147	E5
Bridgewater Ln				
100	CRDN	44024	2379	E5
200	SgHT	44067	3017	E4
Bridgewater Rd				
5100	LNHT	44124	2628	E1
5100	LNHT	44124	2629	A1
Bridgeway Dr				
17100	BbgT	44023	2890	E3
Bridgeway Tr				
-	ELYR	44035	2746	B7
-	LORN	44055	2746	B7
-	SFLD	44055	2746	B7
-	SFLD	44035	2746	B7
-	SFLD	44054	2746	B7
-	ShfT	44054	2746	B7
-	ShfT	44055	2746	B7
Bridle Ct				
-	AVON	44011	2747	B6
8300	MNTR	44060	2251	C5
Bridle Ln				
-	MNTR	44060	2144	D2
-	NbyT	44065	2634	B6
400	BERA	44017	3010	E2
400	BERA	44017	3011	A2
Bridle Pth				
1500	PnvT	44077	2041	B7
1600	PryT	44077	2041	B7
10600	ClbT	44028	3010	C4
Bridle Tr				
10800	MsnT	44024	2634	A2
14100	SGVL	44136	3012	B7
14100	SGVL	44136	3147	B1
N Bridle Tr				
13100	MsnT	44024	2634	A2
Bridlehurst Tr				
8200	KTLD	44094	2377	A7
Bridle Path Tr				
30300	WKLF	44092	2374	E3
Bridle Trail Ln				
34400	SLN	44139	2760	B7
Bridlewood Dr				
6900	CcdT	44077	2146	E7
7200	CcdT	44077	2254	D3
Bridlewood Ln				
-	LvpT	44280	3144	D6
N Brier Patch Ln				
500	MDSN	44057	1942	B7
S Brier Patch Ln				
400	MDSN	44057	1942	B7
Brigadoon Ct				
2200	WTLK	44145	2749	E1
Brigadoon Dr				
16600	BbgT	44023	2890	B1
Brigadoon Wy				
13600	SGVL	44136	3011	C7
Briggs Rd				
10200	CLEV	44111	2753	C3
Brigham Rd				
7200	GSML	44040	2500	D4
7700	GSML	44040	2501	A4
Brighton Av				
11700	CLEV	44111	2753	A2
Brighton Cir				
10100	TNBG	44087	3020	B4
Brighton Dr				
-	AURA	44202	3021	E5
6100	NOSD	44070	2878	C2
Brighton Ln				
1500	BWHT	44147	3149	D4
Brighton Pl				
2200	MadT	44057	1942	C3
Brighton Pth				
38200	WLBY	44094	2250	E2
Brighton Rd				
2800	SRHT	44120	2627	D6
4400	MNTR	44060	2039	A4
10300	BTNH	44108	2496	B3
Brighton Park Blvd				
32300	SLN	44139	2888	E1
32500	SLN	44139	2889	A1
Brightwood Av				
1800	ECLE	44112	2626	E1
Brightwood Dr				
10	OmsT	44138	2879	A3
7000	CcdT	44077	2145	C7
Brightwood Rd				
14600	NbyT	44065	2764	B1
Brigton Dr				
500	BERA	44017	3010	D1
Brimfield Dr				
-	BbgT	44023	2890	E7
9400	MNTR	44060	2145	A7
Brinbourne Av				
16500	MDBH	44130	2881	A7
Brinkmore Rd				
3500	CVHT	44121	2497	D4
Brinmore Rd				
7500	SgHT	44067	3017	C7
Brinsmade Av				
7100	CLEV	44102	2623	E7
Briscoe Dr				
22600	RKRV	44116	2751	A2
Bristlewood Dr				
7000	CcdT	44077	2146	C7
Bristol Av				
10	PnvT	44077	2041	B6
2500	PryT	44077	2041	B6
7900	CLEV	44104	2626	A6
Bristol Ct				
7200	NCtT	44067	3153	B4
11100	NRYN	44133	3013	D5
Bristol Dr				
-	AURA	44202	3021	D5
Bristol Ln				
400	BNWK	44212	3147	C7
3800	NOSD	44070	2750	B5
7500	BKVL	44141	3150	C3
12200	SGVL	44136	3011	B6
25000	WTLK	44145	2750	C1
Bristol Rd				
10	CLEV	44110	2372	C6
Britannia Ct				
14800	SGVL	44136	3146	B1
Brittania Pkwy				
300	AVLK	44012	2618	C3
Brittany Cir				
25300	WTLK	44145	2750	C1
Brittany Ct				
600	SgHT	44067	3152	C1
9800	CcdT	44060	2145	B7
Brittany Dr				
7600	PRMA	44134	3014	A1
Brittany Pl				
16900	SGVL	44136	3147	A5
Brittany Woods Dr				
17700	AbnT	44021	2893	B5
17700	AbnT	44023	2893	B5
Brittney Ct				
800	WLWK	44095	2249	D7
Britton Dr				
300	GNVA	44041	1944	A5
12400	CLEV	44120	2626	E4
Britton Ln				
-	MsnT	44024	2504	E3
Broad Av				
-	CLEV	44103	2496	A5
Broad Blvd				
5200	NRDV	44039	2748	D7
5400	NRDV	44039	2877	D1
Broad St				
10	ELYR	44035	2875	A6
E Broad St				
10	ELYR	44035	2875	C6
1200	ELYR	44039	2875	E7
Broadale Rd				
4200	CLEV	44109	2754	E5
Broadledge Rd				
9000	MCDN	44056	3018	E6
Broadmill Dr				
5500	BWHT	44147	3015	D5
Broadmoor Cir				
7400	MNTR	44060	2251	C3
Broadmoor Rd				
-	WLBY	44060	2251	C4
-	WLBY	44094	2251	C4
1000	MCDN	44056	3018	E6
8000	MNTR	44060	2251	C4
Broadmoor Rd SR-306				
-	WLBY	44060	2251	C4
-	WLBY	44094	2251	C4
8000	MNTR	44060	2251	C4
Broadmore Av				
10	BDFD	44146	2886	D4
Broadmore Ln				
2600	WTLK	44145	2749	C2
Broadrock Ct				
1000	PRMA	44134	2883	E1
Broadstone Dr				
37200	SLN	44139	3020	C3
Broad-Valle Rd				
7500	PRMA	44134	3014	E1
Broadview Ct				
1900	CLEV	44109	2754	D6
Broadview Rd				
2000	CLEV	44109	2754	C4
4800	RchT	44286	3149	E6
4800	RchT	44286	3150	A7
5000	CLEV	44134	2754	D6
5200	PRMA	44134	2754	D6
5300	PRMA	44134	2883	E3
5300	RchT	44233	3149	E6
5300	RchT	44286	3149	E6
5300	RchT	44147	3149	E6
6300	PRMA	44131	2883	E3
6300	SVHL	44131	2883	E3
7300	PRMA	44131	3014	E3
7300	PRMA	44134	3014	E3
7300	SVHL	44131	3014	E3
7900	BWHT	44147	3014	E7
9200	BWHT	44147	3149	E3
Broadview Rd SR-176				
4800	RchT	44286	3149	E6
4800	RchT	44286	3150	A7
5200	PRMA	44134	2754	D6
5300	PRMA	44134	2883	E3
5300	RchT	44233	3149	E6
5300	RchT	44286	3149	E6
5300	RchT	44147	3149	E6
6300	PRMA	44131	2883	E3
6300	SVHL	44131	2883	E3
7300	PRMA	44131	3014	E3
7300	PRMA	44134	3014	E3
7300	SVHL	44131	3014	E3
7900	BWHT	44147	3014	E7
9200	BWHT	44147	3149	E3
Broadway				
100	LORN	44052	2614	D6
N Broadway				
10	GNVA	44041	1944	C3
N Broadway SR-534				
10	GNVA	44041	1944	C3
S Broadway				
10	GNVA	44041	1944	B4
S Broadway SR-534				
10	GNVA	44041	1944	B4
Broadway Av				
10	BDFD	44146	2886	D2
10	MPHT	44146	2886	D2
10	MPHT	44137	2886	D2
200	AhtT	44001	2872	E2
200	AhtT	44001	2873	A2
200	AMHT	44001	2873	A2
300	LORN	44052	2614	E7
500	BDFD	44146	2887	B5
800	CLEV	44115	2625	A4
1500	LORN	44052	2744	E1
1500	OKWD	44146	2887	C7
1900	LORN	44052	2745	A2
2300	LORN	44055	2745	A6
3900	CLEV	44115	2625	C6
3900	ShfT	44052	2745	A6
3900	ShfT	44055	2745	A6
4700	ShfT	44053	2745	A6
5000	LORN	44053	2745	A6
5800	CLEV	44127	2755	D1
6100	EyrT	44035	2745	A6
6100	LORN	44035	2745	A6
6300	CLEV	44105	2755	D1
7300	CLEV	44105	2756	A2
10100	CLEV	44125	2756	C5
10100	GDHT	44125	2756	C5
11900	GDHT	44105	2756	C5
13700	GDHT	44125	2757	A7
14100	MPHT	44125	2757	A7
14100	MPHT	44137	2757	A7
14300	GDHT	44128	2757	A7
14300	MPHT	44128	2757	A7
23900	OKWD	44146	3018	D1
26100	GNWL	44139	3019	A3
26100	MCDN	44146	3019	A3
26100	MCDN	44056	3019	A3
26100	OKWD	44146	3019	A3
Broadway Av SR-8				
800	CLEV	44115	2625	A4
Broadway Av SR-14				
-	CLEV	44115	2625	A4
10	BDFD	44146	2886	D2
10	MPHT	44146	2886	D2
10	MPHT	44137	2886	D2
500	BDFD	44146	2887	B5
1500	OKWD	44146	2887	B5
3900	CLEV	44115	2625	C6
3900	CLEV	44127	2625	C6
5800	CLEV	44127	2755	D1
6300	CLEV	44105	2755	D1
7300	CLEV	44105	2756	A2
10100	CLEV	44125	2756	C5
10100	GDHT	44125	2756	C5
11900	GDHT	44105	2756	C5
13700	GDHT	44125	2757	A7
14100	MPHT	44125	2757	A7
14100	MPHT	44137	2757	A7
14300	GDHT	44128	2757	A7
14300	MPHT	44128	2757	A7
Broadway Av SR-43				
-	CLEV	44115	2625	A4
3900	CLEV	44127	2625	C6
5800	CLEV	44127	2755	D1
6300	CLEV	44105	2755	D1
7300	CLEV	44105	2756	A2
Broadway Av SR-57				
300	LORN	44052	2614	E7
1500	LORN	44052	2744	E1
1900	LORN	44052	2745	A2
2300	LORN	44055	2745	A2
Broadway Av SR-87				
800	CLEV	44115	2625	A4
Broadway Av US-422				
800	CLEV	44115	2625	A4
Broadway Blvd				
36100	NRDV	44039	2876	E7
Broadway Dr				
9700	AbnT	44023	3023	A2
Broadway St				
16700	BbgT	44023	2890	A1
N Broadway St				
700	GNVA	44041	1944	C1
700	GnvT	44041	1944	C1
N Broadway St SR-534				
700	GNVA	44041	1944	C1
700	GnvT	44041	1944	C1
S Broadway St				
1200	GNVA	44041	1944	C6
S Broadway St SR-534				
1200	GNVA	44041	1944	C6
Broadwood Dr				
14300	BtnT	44021	2635	D7
14500	BtnT	44021	2765	D1
Brock Ct				
-	EUCL	44123	2373	B2
Brockley Av				
1100	LKWD	44107	2622	C4
4100	SDLK	44054	2616	A4
Brockton Cir				
300	BERA	44017	2879	E7
Brockway Dr				
12600	VLVW	44125	2885	E6
28500	WTLK	44145	2749	D4
E Brockway Dr				
28500	WTLK	44145	2749	E4
W Brockway Dr				
29000	WTLK	44145	2749	D4
Brockway Rd				
2100	UNHT	44118	2627	E3
6200	LryT	44057	2148	E5
6200	LryT	44086	2148	E5
Brokaw Rd				
33800	EatT	44028	3008	D3
Bromley Rd				
2300	UNHT	44118	2628	B4
Bromton Dr				
1800	LNHT	44124	2629	A2
Bronson Rd				
7400	OmsT	44138	2878	A5
Bronson St				
10	BERA	44017	3011	B1
25500	ODFL	44138	3010	B1
Bronson's Wy				
2600	TNBG	44087	3020	B6
Brook Cir				
6000	NOSD	44070	2878	A2
Brook Ct				
6000	BKPK	44142	2881	D2
Brook Dr				
400	ETLK	44095	2142	D7
400	ETLK	44095	2250	D1
Brook Ln				
1000	RKRV	44116	2621	B6
4700	BKLN	44144	2753	C6
Brook Rd				
-	CVHT	44118	2627	A4
-	SRHT	44118	2627	A4
-	SRHT	44120	2627	A4
9300	ODFL	44138	3009	D2
Brookcrest Ct				
-	AVLK	44012	2617	C3
Brookdale Av				
1600	PRMA	44134	2883	D1
13300	BKPK	44130	2881	D2
13300	BKPK	44142	2881	D2
Brookdale Ct				
-	CLEV	44106	2496	B7
Brookdale Dr				
400	ETLK	44095	2142	D7
Brookdale Ln				
9200	MCDN	44056	3019	A7
25600	EUCL	44117	2373	D6
Brookdale Rd				
1900	RDHT	44143	2373	E7
Brooke Ln				
500	BYVL	44140	2619	B5
Brookfield Av				
10	CLEV	44110	2372	B6
11700	CLEV	44135	2753	A3
11700	LNDL	44135	2753	A3
Brookfield Dr				
700	AURA	44202	3156	D4
10000	CcdT	44077	2253	C1
11000	CrlT	44035	3005	C5
19000	AbnT	44023	3023	A3
19000	ManT	44023	3023	A3
Brookfield Ln				
19300	WVHT	44122	2757	E3
19300	WVHT	44128	2757	E3
Brookfield Pl				
200	MCDN	44056	3018	B6
21400	SGVL	44136	3011	B5
Brookfield Rd				
100	AVLK	44012	2488	A7
100	AVLK	44012	2618	A1
200	AVLK	44012	2617	E2
Brookhaven Av				
13300	BKPK	44130	2881	E2
13300	BKPK	44142	2881	E2
Brookhaven Dr				
6700	MNTR	44060	2144	A6
Brook Haven Ln				
2200	HkyT	44233	3148	A6
2400	HkyT	44233	3147	E6
Brookhigh Dr				
4700	BKLN	44144	2753	D6
Brook Hill Cir				
4000	BKLN	44144	2753	D3
Brookhill Cir				
9900	TNBG	44087	3019	B4
Brookhill Dr				
6300	GDHT	44125	2885	E4
Brook Hollow Ovl				
2200	HkyT	44233	3148	A6
Brookins Dr				
10	OmsT	44138	2879	B4
Brookland Av				
6500	SLN	44139	2889	A5
Brook Lane Rd				
7000	CsTp	44026	2501	A2
Brooklawn Av				
11800	CLEV	44111	2753	A3
Brookline Av				
8200	CLEV	44103	2626	A2
8200	CLEV	44106	2626	A2
Brookline Ovl				
9600	SGVL	44136	3012	B4
Brookline Pl				
1100	WLBY	44094	2142	E5
Brookline Rd				
1300	SELD	44121	2498	A7
Brooklyn Av				
3600	CLEV	44109	2754	B4
Brooklyn St				
100	ELYR	44035	3006	B1
Brookmere Dr				
6200	PMHT	44130	2882	D4
Brookpark Ext				
26600	NOSD	44070	2750	A6
Brookpark Rd				
700	BNHT	44109	2754	B7
700	BNHT	44131	2754	B7
700	CLEV	44109	2754	B7
1100	CLEV	44134	2754	B7
1100	PRMA	44134	2754	B7
1100	PRMA	44109	2754	B7
5400	PRMA	44129	2754	B7
6000	CLEV	44129	2754	B7
6200	CLEV	44129	2753	D7
6200	PRMA	44129	2753	D7
7300	BKLN	44144	2753	D7
7300	PRMA	44144	2753	D7
10200	PRMA	44130	2753	D7
11700	CLEV	44135	2753	A7
11700	CLEV	44144	2753	A7
11700	PRMA	44135	2753	A7
13000	BKPK	44130	2752	B7
13000	BKPK	44135	2752	B7
13000	BKPK	44142	2752	B7
13000	CLEV	44135	2752	B7
13000	PRMA	44130	2752	B7
13000	PRMA	44135	2752	B7
18200	BKPK	44135	2751	B6
18200	BKPK	44142	2751	B6
18200	CLEV	44135	2751	B6
22400	FWPK	44126	2751	B6
23000	NOSD	44070	2750	D7
23000	NOSD	44126	2751	B6
23000	NOSD	44070	2751	B6
Brookpark Rd SR-17				
700	BNHT	44131	2754	B7
700	BNHT	44109	2754	B7
700	CLEV	44109	2754	B7
1100	CLEV	44134	2754	B7
1100	PRMA	44134	2754	B7
1100	PRMA	44109	2754	B7
5400	PRMA	44129	2754	B7
6000	CLEV	44129	2754	B7
6200	CLEV	44129	2753	D7
6200	PRMA	44129	2753	D7
7300	BKLN	44144	2753	D7
7300	PRMA	44144	2753	D7
10200	PRMA	44130	2753	D7
11700	CLEV	44135	2753	A7
11700	CLEV	44144	2753	A7
11700	PRMA	44135	2753	A7
13000	BKPK	44130	2752	B7
13000	BKPK	44135	2752	B7
13000	BKPK	44142	2752	B7
13000	CLEV	44135	2752	B7
13000	PRMA	44135	2752	B7
13000	PRMA	44130	2752	B7
18200	BKPK	44135	2751	B6
18200	BKPK	44142	2751	B6
18200	CLEV	44135	2751	B6
22400	FWPK	44126	2751	B6
23000	NOSD	44070	2750	D7
23000	NOSD	44126	2751	B6
23000	NOSD	44070	2751	B6
Brookpark Rd SR-176				
1500	CLEV	44134	2754	E7
1500	PRMA	44134	2754	E7
Brookpark Rd SR-237				
18200	BKPK	44135	2751	E7
18200	BKPK	44142	2751	E7
18200	BKPK	44135	2752	B7
18200	BKPK	44142	2752	B7
18200	CLEV	44135	2751	E7
18200	CLEV	44135	2752	B7
Brookpoint Dr				
900	MCDN	44056	3018	D6
Brookport Dr				
8400	BKLN	44144	2753	D5
Brookrun Ct				
7600	NCtT	44067	3153	E5
Brooks Blvd				
6100	MNTR	44060	2143	D4
Brooks Ct				
2800	BWHT	44147	3149	D5
Brooks Rd				
4300	CLEV	44105	2756	B4
Brooksdale Rd				
4600	MNTR	44060	2038	D6
Brookshire Ovl				
200	HkyT	44233	3148	A7
Brookside Blvd				
10	HkyT	44233	3148	A6
400	SDLK	44054	2616	B4
3800	CLEV	44111	2752	E3
3800	CLEV	44111	2753	B4
3900	CLEV	44135	2752	E3
Brookside Cir				
-	AURA	44202	3022	B5
8900	MNTR	44060	2144	D7
10000	NRYN	44133	3014	A3
Brookside Dr				
-	AURA	44202	3022	B5
100	AMHT	44001	2872	D1
5800	CLEV	44144	2754	A3
6300	CLEV	44144	2753	E4
7300	BKLN	44144	2753	E4
7700	ODFL	44138	2879	B5
Brookside Ln				
-	NCtT	44067	3153	E5
Brookside Pkwy				
7300	MDBH	44130	2881	A7
Brookside Rd				
-	INDE	44141	3016	C2
700	SDLK	44054	2616	B5
5000	INDE	44131	3015	D2
7200	INDE	44131	3016	B1
11200	MsnT	44024	2504	B3
Brookside Park Dr				
3600	CLEV	44109	2754	B4
Brookstone Ct				
-	BHIT	44212	3146	B7
Brookstone Ln				
32700	NRDV	44039	2877	E1
Brookstone Tr				
20300	MDBH	44130	2880	C5
Brookstone Wy				
9500	SGVL	44136	3011	A4
Brookton Rd				
4400	WVHT	44128	2758	C5
Brookvalley Dr				
100	ELYR	44035	2875	D2
Brookview Blvd				
2100	PRMA	44134	2754	C7
Brookview Dr				
2800	LORN	44053	2743	E3
10900	BKVL	44141	3016	C3
12100	HtbT	44046	2508	E5
Brookway Dr				
21600	FWPK	44126	2751	B6
Brookway Ln				
4100	BKLN	44144	2753	E4
Brookwood Dr				
-	CLEV	44108	2496	D4
4600	BKLN	44144	2753	E6
4700	LNHT	44124	2628	D1
30400	PRPK	44124	2629	D7
Brookwood Ln				
7900	NRYN	44133	3013	D7
Brosius Rd				
11900	NsnT	44231	3027	C7
Brow Av				
5200	NBGH	44105	2755	D2
Brown Av				
37800	WLBY	44094	2250	D6
Brown Ln				
10	BDFD	44146	2887	A4
Brown Rd				
2000	LKWD	44107	2622	D6
N Brown Rd				
8700	HmbT	44024	2255	C7
8700	HmbT	44024	2380	C1
S Brown Rd				
9200	HmbT	44024	2380	C2
Brown St				
10	CLEV	44110	2372	B6
6700	HRM	44234	3161	A2
Brownell Av				
100	LORN	44052	2614	C6
1200	LORN	44052	2744	C1
Brownell Ct				
1200	CLEV	44115	2625	A3
Brownell Dr				
7000	MNTR	44060	2251	B1
Brownfield Dr				
5400	PRMA	44129	2883	A3
6800	PRMA	44129	2882	E3
Brownhelm Station Rd				
-	VMLN	44001	2742	B7
2100	LORN	44053	2742	B7
2100	LORN	44089	2742	B7
2100	VMLN	44053	2742	B7
2400	VMLN	44089	2742	A6
3400	VMLN	44089	2741	D6
Browning Av				
11700	CLEV	44120	2626	D5
Browning Dr				
33500	NRDV	44039	2877	C3
Brownstone Cir				
-	AVLK	44012	2619	A4
Brownstone Ln				
32800	NRDV	44039	2877	D1
Broxbourne Rd				
29400	NOSD	44070	2749	B7
Broxton Av				
14400	CLEV	44111	2622	D7
Broxton Dr				
18000	SGVL	44136	3011	E3
18000	SGVL	44136	3012	A3
Broxton Rd				
2800	SRHT	44120	2627	C6
Bruce Av				
21500	EUCL	44123	2373	B3
Bruce Dr				
200	BNWK	44212	3146	E7
29500	WLWK	44095	2249	B6
Bruce Ln				
-	WLWK	44095	2249	B6
100	CrlT	44035	3006	D4
Bruce Rd				
1400	MCDN	44056	3019	A7
23700	BYVL	44140	2620	D5
Brucefield Rd				
25200	BHWD	44122	2628	E7
Bruce Industrial Pkwy				
30100	SLN	44139	2888	C6
Bruening Dr				
4300	PRMA	44134	2883	B5
Brune Dr				
10	BDFD	44146	2886	C4
Brunner Av				
8100	CLEV	44105	2756	A3
Brunswick Av				
10800	GDHT	44125	2885	C1
14100	MPHT	44137	2886	A2
Brunswick Dr				
100	AVLK	44012	2619	A2
100	ELYR	44035	2874	A7
Brunswick Ln				
2300	HDSN	44236	3155	B6
Brunswick Rd				
900	CVHT	44112	2497	C5
2000	ECLE	44112	2497	C5
Brush Av				
26000	EUCL	44132	2373	E5
26400	EUCL	44132	2374	A4
Brush Rd				
100	EUCL	44143	2373	E6
100	RDHT	44143	2373	E5
100	RDHT	44143	2374	A6
Brushview Dr				
1800	RDHT	44143	2374	A6
Brushwood Dr				
35600	SLN	44139	2889	B3
Brushwood Ln				
9400	SGVL	44136	3012	D4
Brushwood Rd				
3200	RHFD	44286	3151	A7
4800	RHFD	44286	3150	E7
Brussels Rd				
1200	CLEV	44110	2372	E7
Bryan Ct				
100	ELYR	44035	3006	C2
Bryan Dr				
900	SELD	44121	2498	D5
900	SELD	44143	2498	D5
Bryandale Dr				
27600	WTLK	44145	2619	E6
27600	WTLK	44145	2620	A6
Bryant Av				
-	BERA	44017	2880	C4
10500	CLEV	44108	2496	C5
Bryant Dr				
800	VMLN	44089	2740	D6
9900	ClbT	44028	3010	D2
Bryant Ln				
6700	SVHL	44131	2884	B5
Bryce Av				
900	AURA	44202	3021	A4
15900	CLEV	44128	2757	B5
Bryce Rd				
28900	PRPK	44124	2759	C1
Bryden Ct				
6800	VLVW	44125	2885	E6
Bryden Rd				
-	SELD	44121	2498	D6
23200	BHWD	44122	2628	D7
23200	SRHT	44122	2628	D7
25400	BHWD	44122	2758	E1
Bryn Mawr Av				
600	WKLF	44092	2249	A7
600	WKLF	44092	2374	A1
Bryn Mawr Dr				
-	SGVL	44136	3012	B4
10	PnvT	44077	2146	D3
Bryn Mawr Rd				
1700	ECLE	44112	2497	A6
Bryon Rd				
22600	SRHT	44122	2628	C6
E Bryon Rd				
21800	SRHT	44122	2628	B6
Brysdale Av				
-	CLEV	44135	2752	A6
Bryson Dr				
6100	MNTR	44060	2143	E4
Bryson Ln				
300	BYVL	44140	2620	A4
Buccaneer Dr				
18200	NRYN	44133	3147	E4
Buccaneer Tr				
18600	SGVL	44136	3147	D4
Buchanan Ct				
7100	MNTR	44060	2143	D7
Buchanan Dr				
28900	BYVL	44140	2619	D5
Buchtel St				
1800	TwbT	44087	3154	C2
Buck Av				
7900	CLEV	44103	2496	A5
Buck Cross				
400	AURA	44202	3156	C3
Buck Ct				
-	CLEV	44114	2625	B1
Buckboard Ln				
1300	BWHT	44147	3149	E5
5900	SLN	44139	2888	E3
8100	CcdT	44060	2253	B4
Buckeye Av				
-	HIHL	44122	2758	C4
4200	WLBY	44094	2250	D5
Buckeye Ct				
2500	CLEV	44109	2624	D7
Buckeye Dr				
-	BERA	44017	2879	E5
100	SDLK	44054	2616	D3
200	BERA	44017	2880	A5
12500	CsTp	44026	2502	A7
Buckeye Ln				
5800	MONT	44060	2143	E2
Buckeye Rd				
10	PnvT	44077	2145	D4
8400	CLEV	44104	2626	B5
11600	CLEV	44120	2626	D6
Buckeye Rd SR-87				
8400	CLEV	44104	2626	B5
Buckeye St				
100	ELYR	44035	2875	C6
100	SAHT	44001	2872	B7
Buckeye Tr				
-	CcdT	44060	2145	C7
-	CcdT	44077	2145	D7
-	CcdT	44077	2146	A7
-	CcdT	44077	2147	A7
-	CcdT	44024	2253	E6
-	CcdT	44077	2253	E6
-	CcdT	44077	2254	E1
-	CcdT	44077	2255	C2
-	CdnT	44060	2378	C1
-	CdnT	44024	2380	A2
-	CsTp	44026	2501	C2
-	CsTp	44094	2501	A1
-	GSML	44040	2500	E5
-	GSML	44143	2500	C2
-	GSML	44094	2500	C2
-	GSML	44040	2501	A7
-	GSML	44040	2631	A1
-	HGVL	44022	2630	E6
-	HGVL	44040	2631	B4
-	HGVL	44073	2631	A5
-	HGVL	44022	2631	A5
-	HGVL	44073	2631	B4
-	HGVL	44022	2760	D1
-	HmbT	44024	2380	B3
-	HmbT	44024	2381	B4
-	KDHL	44060	2378	A3
-	KTLD	44094	2376	A7
-	KTLD	44094	2377	C3
-	KTLD	44060	2378	A3
-	KTLD	44094	2378	A3
-	KTLD	44094	2501	A1
-	MAYF	44143	2500	B3
-	MAYF	44040	2500	B3
-	MDHL	44022	2760	D1
-	MNTR	44060	2038	D6
-	MNTR	44060	2039	B4
-	MNTR	44060	2144	E4
-	MNTR	44060	2145	A6
-	PnvT	44060	2039	B4
-	PnvT	44077	2039	B4
-	WBHL	44094	2375	D7
-	WBHL	44094	2376	A7
-	WBHL	44094	2500	C2
Buckhill Ct				
9700	CcdT	44060	2253	B3
Buckhurst Dr				
2400	BHWD	44122	2628	D5
Buckhurst Pl				
7000	CcdT	44060	2145	B1
Buckingham Av				
11600	CLEV	44120	2626	D5
Buckingham Ct				
16800	MDBH	44130	2881	A5
Buckingham Dr				
100	ELYR	44035	2875	C1
200	GNVA	44041	1944	A5
4700	LORN	44052	2744	D5
4700	LORN	44053	2744	D5
6400	PRMA	44129	2882	E4
Buckingham Pl				
-	CcdT	44077	2253	E4
-	CcdT	44077	2254	A4
Buckingham Rd				
10	RKRV	44116	2621	E4
Buckingham Shire				
19400	NRYN	44133	3148	B4
Buckland Tr				
15500	RslT	44073	2762	C4
Buckley Av				
-	CLEV	44113	2624	B6
Buckley Blvd				
-	CLEV	44113	2624	C4
Buckley Blvd US-6				
-	CLEV	44113	2624	C4
Buckley Blvd US-20				
-	CLEV	44113	2624	C4
Buckner Dr				
200	EUCL	44123	2373	C1
Buckston Ct				
8500	MCDN	44056	3018	B6
Buckthorn Dr				
-	TNBG	44087	3019	B3
7800	MNTR	44060	2253	A3
17200	BbgT	44023	2890	D3
Buckthorn Pl				
29300	WTLK	44145	2749	C2
Buckthorn Rd				
24900	BDHT	44146	2887	E7
26000	OKWD	44146	2887	E7

INDEX 11
Buckthorn Rd — Cleveland Street Index — Carriage Pl

Cleveland Street Index

STREET Block City ZIP Map# Grid

Buckthorn Rd
26300 OKWD 44146 2888 A6
Bucyrus Av
3800 CLEV 44109 2754 B5
Bucyrus Dr
5800 CLEV 44144 2754 A5
6000 BKLN 44144 2754 A5
6300 BKLN 44144 2753 B5
Bud Dr
10 MdfT 44062 2768 A5
Buechner Av
3600 CLEV 44109 2754 B6
Buena Vista Dr
1700 EUCL 44117 2498 A2
2100 WKLF 44092 2374 C3
9300 MNTR 44060 2252 E1
Buffalo Ct
18000 CLEV 44119 2372 D7
Bugby Dr
6300 MadT 44057 1942 A3
Buhrer Av
1600 CLEV 44109 2624 D7
Bullocks St
100 ELYR 44035 2874 E5
Bunbury Ln
6900 CcdT 44077 2146 C6
Bundy Dr
2500 CLEV 44104 2625 E4
Bundysburg Rd
- WndT 44062 2639 A4
- WndT 44099 2639 A4
- WndT 44062 2639 A4
8300 FnTp 44062 2769 A7
8300 MdfT 44062 2769 A3
8300 MstT 44062 2769 A7
8300 PkmT 44062 2769 A7
8700 MdfT 44062 2639 A7
8700 MstT 44062 2639 A7
10200 WndT 44062 2639 A2
10200 WndT 44099 2639 A2
10300 HtbT 44062 2639 A2
16500 PkmT 44062 2898 A1
16600 PkmT 44062 2897 D2
Bundysburg W Farmington Rd
- FnTp 44062 2898 A2
Bunker Ct
4000 NRYN 44133 3014 B3
Bunker Ln
2400 WLBY 44094 2251 A1
Bunker Rd
300 WLWK 44095 2249 C6
4500 NRYN 44133 3014 A3
5500 NRYN 44133 3013 E3
Bunker Cove
7100 MNTR 44060 2251 B2
Bunker Hill Dr
20400 FWPK 44126 2751 D3
37300 SLN 44139 2889 D4
Bunker Hill Ln
10 ELYR 44035 2875 A3
Bunker Hill Rd
7500 MDBH 44130 3012 D2
Bunts Rd
1200 LKWD 44107 2622 E4
Buoy Ct
- NCtT 44067 3153 C5
Burbank Ct
16000 CLEV 44110 2372 C7
Burbridge Rd
3600 CVHT 44121 2497 E5
Burden Dr
2600 PRMA 44134 3014 C1
Burgandy Dr
20700 SGVL 44136 3146 B2
Burger Av
3500 CLEV 44109 2754 B6
4700 CLEV 44144 2754 B6
Burger Dr
10 EUCL 44123 2373 C1
Burger Rd
4700 SELD 44121 2498 D6
Burgess Cir
- AURA 44202 3021 E5
Burgess Rd
1600 CLEV 44112 2497 D2
Burke Av
7800 CLEV 44105 2756 A2
Burleigh Rd
4600 GDHT 44105 2756 A6
4600 GDHT 44125 2756 A6
Burlington Rd
1200 CVHT 44118 2497 C7
Burlington Rdg
10900 MsnT 44024 2504 A4
Burlington Glen Dr
11900 MsnT 44024 2504 A5
Burlington Oval Dr
10 CRDN 44024 2505 A1
Burlwood Dr
13300 SGVL 44136 3012 D5
31700 SLN 44139 2759 E7
31700 SLN 44139 2888 D1
Burnette Av
1800 ECLE 44112 2497 C4
Burnham Dr
16200 SGVL 44136 3146 D2
Burning Tree Dr
100 AURA 44202 3022 A7
Burns Av
10900 CrlT 44035 3005 C4
Burns Ln
- AURA 44202 3157 E1
Burns Rd
100 ELYR 44035 2746 D7
200 ELYR 44035 2875 E1
200 ELYR 44035 2876 A1
200 ELYR 44039 2876 A1
2600 MadT 44057 1941 E5
3000 MDSN 44057 1941 E5
5300 NOSD 44070 2749 E7
5300 NOSD 44070 2878 E1
39100 NRDV 44039 2876 A1
Burnside Av
16500 CLEV 44110 2497 C2
Burntwood Ln
7300 HDSN 44236 3154 A7
Burr Rd
- NbyT 44065 2763 D4
Burr St
- GNVA 44041 1944 C4
Burridge Av
7000 MNTR 44060 2144 C7
7200 MNTR 44060 2252 C1
Burridge Cir
2500 TNBG 44087 3154 E1
Burridge Ln
9000 TNBG 44087 3154 D1
Burr Oak Ct
100 ELYR 44035 2874 B7
N Burr Oak Dr
32200 SLN 44139 3019 E2
32800 SLN 44139 3020 A2
S Burr Oak Dr
32200 SLN 44139 3019 E2
Burrows Rd
15800 MtlT 44064 2257 D5
15800 MtlT 44086 2257 D5
15800 TpnT 44086 2257 D5
16100 MtlT 44086 2258 A5
16100 TpnT 44086 2258 A5
17500 HgvT 44086 2259 A5
17500 MtlT 44086 2259 A5
17500 TmbT 44086 2259 A5
17500 TpnT 44086 2259 A5
Burrows St
100 GNVA 44041 1944 B4
Burten Ct
3700 CLEV 44115 2625 C4
Burton Av
9900 BTNH 44108 2496 B4
Burton Ct
4000 CLEV 44113 2624 C6
Burton Dr
6500 BKPK 44142 2880 B3
9700 TNBG 44087 3020 B6
Burton Ln
7900 TwbT 44236 3155 A6
N Burton Ln
7800 TwbT 44236 3155 A6
Burton St
10 PNVL 44077 2040 A7
100 AVLK 44012 2617 C2
200 FTHR 44077 2039 D5
Burton Heights Blvd
12400 BtnT 44021 2765 B2
12400 NbyT 44021 2765 B2
Burton Limaville Rd S
10000 FdmT 44255 3161 A7
10000 HrmT 44255 3161 A7
Burton Limaville Rd S SR-700
10000 FdmT 44255 3161 A7
10000 HrmT 44255 3161 A7
Burton Windsor Rd
14100 BtnT 44021 2636 D6
14100 BtnT 44062 2636 D6
14100 BURT 44021 2636 D6
14600 BtnT 44021 2637 A5
14600 BtnT 44062 2637 A5
15100 MdfT 44021 2637 A5
15100 MdfT 44062 2637 C5
15600 HtbT 44046 2637 C5
15600 HtbT 44062 2637 C5
15600 MdfT 44046 2637 C5
16000 HtbT 44046 2637 E3
16000 HtbT 44062 2637 E3
16000 HtbT 44046 2638 A3
16000 HtbT 44062 2638 A3
16000 MdfT 44062 2637 E3
17200 HtbT 44062 2639 A2
17200 WndT 44062 2639 A2
Burwell Av
3500 CLEV 44115 2625 C4
Burwick Rd
- HDHT 44143 2499 D2
Busa Ovl
4100 CLEV 44128 2757 C3
Bush Av
3900 CLEV 44109 2754 B1
Bushnell Ct
6600 CLEV 44104 2625 E5
8400 MNTR 44060 2144 B3
Bushnell Rd
3700 UNHT 44118 2627 E3
3800 UNHT 44118 2628 A3
4000 UNHT 44121 2628 A3
Buskirk Blvd
7100 INDE 44131 2884 E4
Butler Av
6000 CLEV 44127 2625 D6
Butler St
- ELYR 44035 3006 B2
Butterfield Cir
300 SgHT 44067 3017 D4
Buttermilk Falls Pkwy
- WBHL 44094 2375 B6
Butternut Cir
18200 SGVL 44136 3147 C4
Butternut Ct
3700 ORNG 44022 2759 D2
Butternut Dr
10 NCtT 44067 3017 E6
10 NCtT 44067 3018 A6
100 AMHT 44001 2873 A2
700 MAYF 44040 2500 A5
Butternut Ln
10 NCtT 44067 3017 E7
10 NCtT 44067 3018 A7
200 BERA 44017 2880 A6
2500 PRPK 44124 2630 A4
7100 MNTR 44060 2143 B5
11100 NRYN 44133 3013 B5
20000 WVHT 44128 2758 A4
20100 HIHL 44128 2758 A4
Butternut Rd
10300 MsnT 44024 2503 D7
10300 MsnT 44024 2633 D1
10300 MsnT 44026 2503 D7
10300 MsnT 44026 2633 D1
10600 MsnT 44024 2634 A3
10600 MsnT 44026 2634 A3
11100 MsnT 44026 2634 A3
11100 NbyT 44065 2634 C4
11100 NbyT 44024 2634 C4
11800 NbyT 44024 2635 A4
11800 NbyT 44065 2635 A4
12400 BtnT 44021 2635 C4
12400 BtnT 44024 2635 C4
12400 NbyT 44021 2635 A4
13200 BtnT 44021 2636 A4
13200 BtnT 44024 2636 A4
Butternut Park Ct
40900 CrlT 44035 3005 E6
40900 CrlT 44050 3005 E6
Butternut Ridge Rd
10800 EatT 44044 3007 D2
22500 NOSD 44070 2879 A1
27100 NOSD 44070 2750 A7
Butternut Ridge Rd
27200 NOSD 44070 2749 E7
37200 CrlT 44044 3006 E5
37200 EatT 44044 3006 E5
38100 CrlT 44035 3006 C5
38100 CrlT 44044 3006 C5
40200 CrlT 44050 3006 A6
40800 CrlT 44050 3005 E6
41200 CrlT 44035 3005 D6
42000 CrlT 44074 3005 A6
43200 CrlT 44035 3004 E6
43200 CrlT 44074 3004 E6
43200 NRsT 44035 3004 E6
43200 NRsT 44074 3004 E6
45700 NRsT 44074 3003 D7
Butterwing Rd
2500 PRPK 44124 2629 B4
Button Av
200 PNVL 44077 2039 D7
Button Rd
500 BDFD 44146 2886 C5
7200 CcdT 44060 2253 C1
7200 CcdT 44077 2253 C1
14500 WNHL 44146 2886 A6
Button St
15900 MDFD 44062 2767 D1
Button Bush
- AVLK 44012 2618 D4
Button Bush Cir
100 SRSL 44073 2761 D5
Buttonbush Ln
5000 NRYN 44133 3014 B4
Buttonwood Dr
1600 SVHL 44131 2884 A4
Buxton Cir
1600 PnvT 44077 2040 E2
Buxton Rd
4000 SELD 44121 2628 A1
Byington Ct
100 ELYR 44035 2875 C5
Byron Av
13200 CLEV 44120 2626 E7
13700 CLEV 44120 2627 A7
Byron Blvd
13300 MDBH 44130 3012 D2
Byron Dr
1600 MDHT 44124 2629 C1
25500 NOSD 44070 2750 B5
Byron Rd
6800 MadT 44057 1942 C2
20400 SRHT 44122 2628 A7
W Byron Rd
20800 SRHT 44122 2628 A6

C

C St
500 LORN 44052 2614 E6
700 LORN 44052 2615 A6
Cabin Dr
2600 WKLF 44092 2374 B4
Cable Av
5800 CLEV 44127 2625 D7
Cableknoll Ln
10 MDHL 44022 2759 E4
Cabot Ct
6000 MNTR 44060 2144 B3
Cabot Ln
7100 CNFL 44022 2761 A4
7100 CNFL 44073 2761 A4
7100 RslT 44073 2761 A4
Cabrini Ln
6000 SVHL 44131 2884 A3
Cabriolet Av
9000 CcdT 44060 2253 B4
Cachet Dr
- CrlT 44035 3005 E6
Caddie Ln
- CcdT 44077 2254 B1
Caddy Ln
1500 PnvT 44077 2040 E4
Cadek Rd
12500 HrmT 44234 3025 D5
Cadence Ct
10800 NbyT 44065 2763 E3
Cadet Dr
10 NRDV 44039 2877 B4
Cadle Av
7200 MNTR 44060 2252 A1
Cadwell Av
1700 CVHT 44118 2627 B2
Cady Rd
5600 NRYN 44133 3148 D4
5600 NRYN 44133 3149 A4
Caesars Cir
10 AMHT 44001 2744 B7
Caferro Dr
4000 LORN 44055 2745 D4
Cahoon Rd
400 BYVL 44140 2619 E7
400 BYVL 44140 2620 A4
600 WTLK 44140 2620 A6
600 WTLK 44145 2620 A6
900 WTLK 44145 2619 E7
Caine Av
13100 CLEV 44105 2756 E4
13600 CLEV 44105 2757 A4
14000 CLEV 44128 2757 A4
Cairn Ln
7500 GSML 44040 2500 E3
Calamie Dr
5800 PMHT 44130 2882 B2
Calann Dr
600 CrlT 44035 3006 C1
39500 ELYR 44035 3006 C1
Calcutta Av
15400 CLEV 44110 2372 B7
Caldwell Av
- AVLK 44012 2617 B2
14500 CLEV 44111 2752 D1
Caleb Ct
5400 CLEV 44127 2625 D7
Caledonia Av
800 CVHT 44112 2497 C6
800 ECLE 44112 2497 C6
Calgary Av
2200 CLEV 44109 2754 D3
Cali Ct
11600 CcdT 44077 2254 D1
Cali Dr
11700 CcdT 44077 2254 E1
Calico Ln
10500 CdnT 44024 2378 E6
California Av
10 LORN 44052 2614 E5
California Av
100 ELYR 44035 3006 E2
California St
1200 AURA 44202 3021 A4
1200 RMDV 44202 3021 A4
Call Rd
3200 PryT 44081 1940 D7
3500 PryT 44081 2042 D2
3700 PRRY 44081 2042 D2
Callahan Rd
- TmbT 44086 2259 B5
- TmbT 44099 2259 B5
6100 HgvT 44084 2259 B5
6300 HgvT 44099 2259 B5
6600 HgvT 44084 2259 B5
6600 TmbT 44084 2259 B5
Callendar Blvd
800 PnvT 44077 2039 C7
800 PnvT 44077 2145 C1
Calley Ln
7300 RslT 44072 2631 B5
Callow Rd
6900 LryT 44077 2147 D7
6900 LryT 44077 2255 D1
Calumet Av
- NCtT 44067 3153 A1
Calverton Pl
400 BNWK 44212 3146 E7
Calverton Rd
21900 SRHT 44118 2628 B5
21900 SRHT 44122 2628 B5
Calvin Dr
200 SVHL 44131 2884 A3
12100 BKVL 44141 3016 D7
Calythorne Dr
34200 SLN 44139 3020 A3
Camberly Ct
33800 SLN 44139 3020 A2
Camberly Dr
1800 LNHT 44124 2629 A2
Cambrian Wy
2200 MadT 44057 1941 D3
Cambridge Av
200 ELYR 44035 2875 C7
3500 LORN 44053 2744 A4
9100 CLEV 44105 2756 B2
Cambridge Blvd
16900 BKPK 44142 2881 A3
Cambridge Cir
10500 NRYN 44133 3014 A4
30600 BYVL 44140 2619 B6
32100 AVLK 44012 2618 C4
Cambridge Ct
4100 WDMR 44122 2759 B1
Cambridge Ct E
30600 BYVL 44140 2619 B6
Cambridge Ct W
30600 BYVL 44140 2619 B6
Cambridge Dr
- NRDV 44039 2877 B6
100 AURA 44202 3156 B1
200 AURA 44202 3021 B7
2300 HDSN 44236 3155 B6
7700 BKVL 44141 3015 E3
8500 PRMA 44129 2753 D7
8900 NHFD 44067 3018 B4
11600 CsTp 44026 2501 E3
19400 SGVL 44136 3147 C5
25400 BDHT 44146 2887 E4
25700 OKWD 44146 2887 E4
26200 OKWD 44146 2888 A4
29800 NOSD 44070 2878 C2
30600 BYVL 44140 2619 B5
Cambridge Ln
400 WLBY 44094 2250 A7
26000 WVHT 44128 2758 E6
27900 PRPK 44124 2629 B6
Cambridge Ovl
17700 SGVL 44136 3146 E3
Cambridge Rd
- SELD 44121 2498 A5
800 CVHT 44121 2498 A5
9100 CdnT 44024 2378 E1
Cambridge St
1900 TwbT 44087 3154 C2
Cambridge Park Dr
6100 MNTR 44060 2144 A4
Camden Av
3200 LORN 44055 2746 A3
6800 CLEV 44102 2624 A7
6900 CLEV 44102 2623 E7
Camden Blvd
- LORN 44053 2743 D4
Camden Ct
3700 WTLK 44145 2749 C4
8400 BWHT 44147 3014 C5
Camden Dr
14400 SGVL 44136 3147 C5
Camden Ln
- AURA 44202 3021 E6
2000 TwbT 44236 3155 A5
Camden Rd
4900 WVHT 44128 2757 E7
5100 MPHT 44137 2757 E7
Camellia Ln
4400 NOSD 44070 2749 D6
Camelot Ct
2800 WBHL 44092 2374 C6
6700 MNTR 44060 2143 E5
Camelot Dr
2000 PRMA 44134 2883 D7
6800 MNTR 44060 2143 E6
8400 CsTp 44026 2632 B2
Camelot Ln
2000 RKRV 44116 2621 C7
Camelot Wy
39100 AVON 44011 2747 B6
Cameron Av
27000 EUCL 44132 2373 E1
27100 EUCL 44132 2374 A1
Cameron Ct
5300 SFLD 44054 2746 E4
Camino Dr
700 ETLK 44095 2250 C2
Campagna St
100 ELYR 44035 2746 D7
Campbell Dr
- CLEV 44105 2755 B1
6100 MadT 44057 1941 E1
Campbell Rd
4900 WLBY 44094 2250 A7
5900 MONT 44060 2143 C3
6100 MNTR 44060 2143 C3
Campers Dr
100 LKLN 44095 2249 E2
Campers Dr
400 ETLK 44095 2249 E2
Camp Industrial Rd
6200 SLN 44139 2888 D5
Campton Ct
5400 BDHT 44146 2887 C1
Campton Rdg
9900 CdnT 44024 2379 C3
Campus Ct
300 ETLK 44095 2142 C7
Campus Dr
1900 SELD 44121 2628 C3
21000 FWPK 44126 2751 C4
N Campus Dr
- KTLD 44094 2251 E7
- KTLD 44094 2376 D1
S Campus Dr
- KTLD 44094 2376 D1
Campus Rd
2100 BHWD 44122 2628 C3
2100 UNHT 44121 2628 C3
Canada Rd
4800 MNTU 44255 3159 D6
5000 ManT 44255 3159 D6
5000 ShvT 44255 3159 D6
Canal Rd
600 CLEV 44113 2624 E4
900 SgHT 44067 3017 C4
4900 CHHT 44125 2755 D6
5100 GDHT 44125 2756 A7
5100 VLVW 44125 2756 A7
5400 GDHT 44125 2885 A1
5400 VLVW 44125 2885 A1
7300 VLVW 44125 3016 D1
W Canal Rd
5600 VLVW 44125 2885 A2
Canary Dr
200 ELYR 44035 2874 E2
Candlenut Ct
3900 ORNG 44022 2759 D3
Candlestick Ln
10000 CcdT 44077 2145 C7
Candlewick Ct
25700 WTLK 44145 2620 B6
Candlewick Ln
1200 BWHT 44147 3149 C4
Candlewood
- AVON 44011 2617 D7
Candlewood Ct
5500 PRMA 44134 2883 E1
6300 MNTR 44060 2144 C4
Candlewood Dr
3300 AVON 44011 2747 D1
Candy Ln
300 AMHT 44001 2872 C1
6700 BhmT 44089 2741 B7
Canfield Ct
1300 CLEV 44114 2624 E2
1300 CLEV 44114 2625 A2
Canfield Dr
200 PNVL 44077 2040 A7
Canfield Rd
100 CRDN 44024 2379 E5
100 CRDN 44024 2380 A5
Cannon Av
8600 CLEV 44105 2756 B3
17400 LKWD 44107 2622 A4
Cannon Ovl
13900 NRYN 44133 3014 C7
Cannon Rd
2800 TNBG 44087 3155 B1
23000 BDHT 44146 2887 E2
26400 BDHT 44146 2888 A2
27200 SLN 44139 2888 C2
27300 SLN 44146 2888 A2
33100 SLN 44139 2889 C2
35000 BTVL 44022 2889 C2
Cannon Rd SR-175
27200 SLN 44139 2888 A2
27300 SLN 44146 2888 A2
Cannon Ridge Dr
7700 MNTR 44060 2253 A3
Canova Av
1700 CLEV 44109 2754 D4
Canter Cir
700 BERA 44017 3010 E2
Canter Ct
- GnvT 44041 1944 C2
Canterbury Cir
- AMHT 44001 2872 C3
Canterbury Ct
300 ELYR 44035 2875 D2
2900 WBHL 44092 2374 C6
4000 LORN 44053 2743 E2
8300 BbgT 44023 2891 A6
Canterbury Dr
6700 MadT 44057 1942 B2
16100 SGVL 44136 3147 A2
33700 SLN 44139 3020 A3
Canterbury Ln
400 SgHT 44067 3017 D4
4700 BWHT 44147 3015 D6
5500 HDHT 44143 2499 B3
9200 MNTR 44060 2252 E1
9300 MNTR 44060 2253 A1
22300 SRHT 44122 2628 B7
Canterbury Rd
- AVLK 44012 2618 A2
100 ELYR 44035 2875 D2
200 BYVL 44140 2620 B4
600 WTLK 44145 2620 B6
1000 WTLK 44145 2750 B1
2200 UNHT 44118 2627 E5
2400 CVHT 44118 2627 E5
3800 NOSD 44070 2750 B5
5600 NOSD 44070 2879 B2
17800 CLEV 44119 2372 D4
32900 AVLK 44012 2617 D2
N Canterbury Rd
6100 PRMA 44129 2883 A3
6200 PRMA 44129 2882 E3
S Canterbury Rd
6400 PRMA 44129 2882 E4
Canterwood Tr
7500 CcdT 44060 2253 C2
Canton Av
2800 LORN 44052 2745 B3
3500 LORN 44055 2745 A4
7100 CLEV 44105 2755 E2
7500 CLEV 44105 2756 A2
Cantor Av
- CLEV 44102 2624 B7
Cantwell Dr
5800 MDHT 44124 2629 C2
Canyon Cir
7400 MDBH 44130 3012 D1
Canyon Ct
5400 WLBY 44094 2375 A1
Canyon Rd
100 MDHL 44022 2760 D6
18800 FWPK 44126 2752 A1
Canyon Tr
2600 HkyT 44233 3147 E7
Canyon Creek Dr
2400 HkyT 44233 3147 E6
2400 HkyT 44233 3148 A7
Canyon Lake Dr
8000 BbgT 44023 2890 D3
Canyon Point Cir
- BKVL 44141 3151 C4
Canyon Ridge Dr
5400 PryT 44077 2147 B1
Canyon View Dr
5600 PryT 44077 2147 B2
Canyon View Rd
900 SgHT 44067 3152 B1
1000 SgHT 44067 3017 A7
Capel Rd
900 EatT 44044 3142 E3
900 GFTN 44028 3142 E3
900 GFTN 44044 3142 E3
28000 ClbT 44028 3143 E2
28000 ClbT 44028 3144 A2
28000 EatT 44028 3143 E2
34500 GFTN 44028 3143 A2
36000 EatT 44044 3142 C2
38100 EatT 44044 3141 E1
Capilano Dr
7100 SLN 44139 3020 E1
Capital Blvd
7700 MCDN 44056 3153 C3
Capital Pkwy
10900 CcdT 44077 2254 A3
Capital Hill Cir
200 ORNG 44022 2759 C6
Capitol Av
8600 CLEV 44104 2626 B4
Capitol Ct
100 ELYR 44035 2873 E6
Capri Dr
10 SgHT 44067 3017 E3
Captain's Ct
7500 MNTR 44060 2143 D4
Captains Wk
13200 MsnT 44024 2635 A3
Captains Cove
17800 LKWD 44107 2621 E4
Captains Galley
32500 AVLK 44012 2618 B3
Carabell Av
2000 LKWD 44107 2622 C6
Carbon Rd
2100 CLEV 44111 2623 B6
Cardinal Av
14900 CLEV 44110 2497 B2
Cardinal Cir
20200 SGVL 44136 3011 C3
Cardinal Ct
600 ETLK 44095 2250 D1
Cardinal Dr
- KDHL 44060 2252 B7
10 TroT 44234 2894 B6
100 ELYR 44035 2874 E2
5500 MNTR 44060 2144 E1
8400 KTLD 44094 2252 B7
8500 KTLD 44060 2252 B7
Cardinal Ln
1400 GSML 44040 2500 C7
7100 RslT 44073 2761 B3
10600 BKVL 44141 3016 C3
Cardington Dr
25000 BHWD 44122 2628 E4
Cardwell Av
9400 CLEV 44105 2756 B5
9400 CLEV 44125 2756 B5
9900 GDHT 44125 2756 B5
Care Dr
8300 GDHT 44125 2756 A6
Carek Ct
5400 EyrT 44055 2745 B6
5400 ShfT 44055 2745 B6
Carey Dr
6000 VLVW 44125 2885 C3
Carey Ln
24700 NOSD 44070 2879 C1
Cargo Rd
5800 CLEV 44135 2880 D2
Carillon Dr
2900 WTLK 44145 2750 C3
Carl Av
6200 CLEV 44103 2495 E7
Carl Ct
4200 WLBY 44094 2251 B5
Carl Dr
40600 CrlT 44035 3006 A5
Carl Ln
10 OmsT 44138 2879 A6
Carla Ln
24000 NOSD 44070 2750 D3
Carleen Av
37100 AVON 44011 2747 D1
Carlenroy Dr
10 ETLK 44095 2142 B6
Carlin Rd
400 SgHT 44067 3152 C1
Carlisle Av
40500 CrlT 44035 3006 A4
40700 CrlT 44035 3005 E4
Carlone Pl
900 SELD 44121 2498 C5
Carlos Av
4600 CLEV 44102 2754 A1
Carlsfield Wy
400 BSHT 44236 3153 E6
Carlton Ct
8600 MNTR 44060 2144 B7
20500 SGVL 44136 3146 B4
Carlton Dr
300 ETLK 44095 2250 B2
5500 BDHT 44146 2887 C2
31200 BYVL 44140 2619 A4
Carlton Pk
25100 NOSD 44070 2750 C5
Carlton Rd
1600 PRMA 44134 2883 E2
2800 SRHT 44122 2627 E6
11800 CLEV 44106 2626 D3
11800 CVHT 44106 2626 D3
Carlton St
13500 BURT 44021 2766 A1
Carlyle Av
3700 CLEV 44109 2754 C1
Carlyle Dr
900 SVHL 44131 2884 A3
20200 SGVL 44136 3011 C6
Carlyle Rd
10 BDFD 44146 2887 A2
Carlyon Pl
1000 CLEV 44108 2496 D6
1000 ECLE 44108 2496 D6
1000 ECLE 44112 2496 D6
Carlyon Rd
1000 ECLE 44108 2496 E6
1000 ECLE 44112 2496 E6
Carmany Dr
18500 WNHL 44146 2886 E7
18700 WNHL 44146 2887 A7
Carmel Ln
11200 ClrT 44024 2505 C2
Carmel Ovl
10600 SGVL 44136 3012 B5
Carmelita Ct
2900 LORN 44052 2744 C2
Carmen Dr
2600 RKRV 44116 2621 C7
Carmen Pl
7200 MNTR 44060 2144 E7
7200 MNTR 44060 2252 E1
Carmichael Dr
8500 CsTp 44026 2632 B3
Carmody Dr
100 PNVL 44077 2040 A7
100 PNVL 44077 2146 A1
Carnation Ct
12400 CLEV 44108 2496 E4
Carnation Run
- WTLK 44145 2750 C4
Carnegie Av
- CLEV 44113 2624 E4
10 CLEV 44115 2624 E4
500 CLEV 44115 2625 C3
4000 CLEV 44103 2625 C3
7100 CLEV 44103 2626 C3
8300 CLEV 44106 2626 C3
Carnegie Av SR-10
- CLEV 44113 2624 E4
10 CLEV 44115 2624 E4
Carnegie St
6300 MNTR 44060 2145 A4
Carnes Dr
8700 BbgT 44023 2891 B7
Carol Av
21000 EUCL 44119 2373 A4
Carol Blvd
3700 RKRV 44116 2751 E1
Carol Dr
6100 BKPK 44142 2881 D4
6600 INDE 44131 2884 D7
6600 INDE 44131 3015 E1
14900 MPHT 44137 2886 A3
15200 SGVL 44136 3146 E1
Carol Ln
200 ELYR 44035 3006 D2
39700 CrlT 44035 3006 C2
Carole Dr
7300 MNTR 44060 2252 A1
N Carolina Dr
200 ELYR 44035 3006 A3
Carolina Rd
11400 CLEV 44108 2496 D6
S Carolina Rd
- CrlT 44035 3006 B4
Caroline Av
2300 LORN 44052 2745 A2
2300 LORN 44055 2745 A2
Caroline Cir
27600 WTLK 44145 2619 E5
Caroline Dr
4900 WVHT 44128 2758 C6
37500 AVON 44011 2617 C7
Caroline St
100 ELYR 44035 2875 C5
Carol-Jean Blvd
5500 GDHT 44125 2885 C1
Carolyn Av
19900 FWPK 44116 2751 D2
19900 FWPK 44126 2751 D2
19900 RKRV 44126 2751 D2
19900 RKRV 44116 2751 D2
Carolyn Dr
500 BNWK 44212 3147 B7
5600 NRDV 44039 2877 D1
6100 MNTR 44060 2143 E4
Caronia Cir
- AVON 44011 2747 E5
Caronia Dr
1800 LNHT 44124 2629 C2
Carousel Ct
2300 WTLK 44145 2749 E2
Carousel Ln
10 OmsT 44138 2879 A3
Carpenter Av
6100 CLEV 44127 2625 D6
Carpenter Ct
10 OBLN 44074 3138 D2
Carpenter Rd
1200 GSML 44040 2500 D7
12800 GDHT 44125 2885 E3
13500 GDHT 44125 2886 A3
N Carpenter Rd
10 BNWK 44212 3147 B7
Carr Av
9100 CLEV 44103 2496 B4
9100 CLEV 44108 2496 B4
Carr Pl
4300 LORN 44053 2744 C4
Carrbridge Dr
23700 EUCL 44143 2498 C1
Carriage Cir
7900 MNTR 44060 2143 E6
Carriage Dr
10 CNFL 44022 2761 B5
E Carriage Dr
10 CNFL 44022 2761 B5
W Carriage Dr
100 CNFL 44022 2761 B6
Carriage Ln
23400 NOSD 44070 2750 E3
32500 AVLK 44012 2618 A1
36400 WLBY 44094 2375 C1
Carriage Pl
1700 GSML 44040 2630 C2

INDEX 12

Carriage Sq — Cleveland Street Index — Chatham Ct

STREET
Block City ZIP Map# Grid

Carriage Sq
10 AURA 44202 3156 E3
Carriage Tr
700 SgHT 44067 3152 C2
Carriage Hill Dr
6800 BKVL 44141 3016 A4
11000 AbnT 44023 2893 A5
Carriage Hills Dr
8000 CcdT 44060 2253 C4
Carriage Park Dr
33600 SLN 44139 2889 A3
Carriage Park Ovl
700 WTLK 44145 2620 A6
Carriage Stone Dr
10 CNFL 44022 2760 E7
10 CNFL 44022 2761 A7
Carrie Ct
9000 CLEV 44106 2626 B2
Carrie Dr
4000 LORN 44055 2745 E4
Carrie Ln
10 OmsT 44138 2879 B4
Carrington Av
11800 CLEV 44135 2753 A6
13000 CLEV 44135 2752 E6
Carrington Ct
600 WLWK 44095 2249 B6
Carrington Dr
7400 MNTR 44060 2253 A1
Carrington Ln
400 BWHT 44147 3149 E5
Carrington Pl
- BbgT 44023 2890 E7
Carrmunn Av
3400 CLEV 44111 2752 C1
Carroll Av
10 PNVL 44077 2146 A2
2500 CLEV 44113 2624 C5
Carroll Blvd
4000 UNHT 44118 2628 A5
E Carroll Blvd
14300 UNHT 44118 2628 C4
Carroll Dr
12200 MsnT 44024 2503 E6
Carry Av
5500 CLEV 44103 2495 D6
Carrydale Av
14000 CLEV 44111 2752 D2
Carson Av
300 GDRV 44045 2039 C6
400 PnvT 44045 2039 C6
400 PnvT 44077 2039 C6
6900 CLEV 44104 2625 E6
6900 CLEV 44127 2625 E6
7400 CLEV 44104 2626 A6
Carson Dr
100 CRDN 44024 2380 A7
Carsten Ln
4400 NOSD 44070 2750 A6
Carter Blvd
6300 MNTR 44060 2143 C4
Carter Ln
10 NHFD 44067 3018 A3
Carter Rd
1800 CLEV 44113 2624 D4
7500 SgHT 44067 3017 B7
7500 SgHT 44067 3152 D1
12100 CcdT 44077 2147 B5
12100 LryT 44077 2147 C4
13100 LryT 44077 2148 A3
Carter St
30000 SLN 44139 2888 C6
Carteret Ct
700 BERA 44017 3011 B2
Carton Av
9300 CLEV 44104 2626 B7
Cartwright Pkwy
13600 SGVL 44136 3012 D3
Carver Rd
1000 CVHT 44112 2497 C6
Cary Dr
6300 NRDV 44039 2877 E2
Cary Jay Blvd
300 RDHT 44143 2498 E3
Caryl Dr
1200 BDFD 44146 2887 C6
Caryn Dr
14700 BKPK 44142 2881 C4
14700 MDBH 44130 2881 C4
14700 MDBH 44142 2881 C4
Casa Bella Dr
4200 PryT 44081 1940 C7
Cascade Cross
- BKLN 44144 2753 C6
Cascade Ct
- AVLK 44012 2617 D3
5400 WLBY 44094 2375 A1
5600 SVHL 44131 2884 A1
19100 BbgT 44023 3021 D3
19100 BbgT 44202 3021 D3
27000 ODFL 44138 3009 D1
Cascade Dr
10 SRSL 44073 2762 D7
5500 SVHL 44131 2884 A1
Cascade Rd
6500 CcdT 44077 2147 B7
6500 CcdT 44077 2255 C1
Cascade St
100 ELYR 44035 2875 A6
Cascades Dr
- AURA 44202 3022 A4
- AURA 44023 3022 A4
- BbgT 44023 3022 A4
Case Av
500 ELYR 44035 3006 D1
5000 LNHT 44124 2498 E5
5000 LNHT 44124 2499 A5
7300 MNTR 44060 2252 A1
Case Ct
4000 CLEV 44104 2625 C4
Case Pkwy N
1900 TNBG 44087 3154 E4
Case Pkwy S
1900 TNBG 44087 3154 E4
Case Rd
4000 AVON 44011 2747 A5
4800 NRDV 44011 2747 A7
4800 NRDV 44039 2747 A7
4800 NRDV 44039 2876 A1
Case St
1800 TwbT 44087 3154 C2
Casement Av
10 PNVL 44077 2040 C7
100 PnvT 44077 2040 C7
Casement Av US-20
400 PnvT 44077 2040 C6
Caskey Dr
300 OBLN 44074 3139 A2
Casper Rd
13300 CLEV 44110 2497 A3
Cass Av
5500 CLEV 44102 2624 A4
Cassie Ln
12700 CsTp 44026 2502 E7
12700 CsTp 44026 2632 E1
Cassius Av
9300 CLEV 44105 2756 B3
Castalia Av
13800 CLEV 44110 2497 A3
Castallia Dr
- NRYN 44133 3014 C3
Castaway Cove
3500 RMDV 44202 3020 D5
Castle Av
1600 CLEV 44113 2624 D7
Castle Cir
6400 BKVL 44141 3150 D2
Castle Ct
10 BNWK 44212 3146 D6
Castle Dr
6100 NRYN 44133 3013 E4
6100 NRYN 44133 3014 A4
20900 SGVL 44136 3146 B1
Castlehill Dr
5900 HDHT 44143 2499 D2
Castlemaine Cir
20300 SGVL 44136 3146 C5
Castleman Ct
1100 PnvT 44077 2146 E2
Castle Pine Dr
7200 SLN 44139 3020 E1
Castleton Ln
10 EatT 44044 3007 A6
Castleton Rd
1000 CVHT 44121 2497 D6
Castletown Dr
19400 SGVL 44136 3147 D5
Castlewood Av
11500 CLEV 44108 2496 D6
Castlewood Ct
4000 PRRY 44081 2042 B1
Castlewood Dr
14600 NbyT 44065 2764 C1
Caswell Ct
1400 EUCL 44132 2373 D5
Catalano Dr
6000 MDHT 44124 2629 D2
Catalpa Cir
9400 MNTR 44060 2253 A3
Catalpa Dr
12100 CdnT 44024 2380 A3
Catalpa Rd
1600 CLEV 44112 2497 D2
Catawba Ct
100 EyrT 44035 3005 A1
Catawba St
29500 WKLF 44092 2374 C2
Catharina Av
4400 CLEV 44109 2754 B1
Catherine Ct
14100 NRYN 44133 3149 A1
Catherine St
5000 MPHT 44137 2757 C7
Catlin Dr
400 RDHT 44143 2498 D4
Cato St
5000 MPHT 44137 2757 D7
5300 MPHT 44137 2886 D1
Caton Pl
26600 NOSD 44070 2750 A6
Catsden Rd
16800 BbgT 44023 2890 C2
Cattail Run
- SFLD 44035 2746 E6
Cavendish Ct
19400 NRYN 44133 3148 A5
Caves Rd
11100 CsTp 44026 2501 D2
12800 CsTp 44026 2631 D1
13400 CsTp 44072 2631 D3
13400 RsIT 44072 2631 D3
14600 RsIT 44072 2761 D1
Caxton Cir
300 BERA 44017 2880 A6
Cayuga Ct
14000 CLEV 44111 2752 D1
Cayuga Dr
14000 ClbT 44028 3010 D7
14000 ClbT 44028 3145 D1
Cecelia Av
3500 CLEV 44109 2754 C5
Cecelia Ct
34200 ETLK 44095 2250 A4
Cecil Pl
12400 CVHT 44106 2626 E3
Cecilia Dr
7500 PRMA 44134 3014 D2
Cedar
- SDLK 44054 2616 E2
Cedar Av
2200 CLEV 44115 2625 C3
4000 CLEV 44103 2625 D3
7200 CLEV 44103 2626 A3
8300 CLEV 44106 2626 C3
Cedar Ct
1700 EUCL 44117 2498 A2
6100 SLN 44139 2889 D4
Cedar Dr
1500 LORN 44052 2615 D6
Cedar Gln
100 CRDN 44024 2505 B1
Cedar Rd
400 AURA 44202 3156 D2
7000 CsTp 44026 2631 B2
8100 CsTp 44026 2632 A2
9700 MsnT 44026 2633 A3
9700 MsnT 44072 2633 A3
9700 NbyT 44072 2633 A3
10100 MsnT 44026 2633 D3
10100 NbyT 44026 2633 D3
10100 NbyT 44072 2633 D3
10300 MsnT 44026 2634 A4
10300 NbyT 44065 2633 E3
10300 NbyT 44026 2634 A4
10300 NbyT 44065 2634 A4
12300 CLEV 44106 2626 E3
12300 CVHT 44106 2626 E3
12500 CVHT 44106 2627 A3
12800 CVHT 44118 2627 A3
13400 UNHT 44118 2627 D3
13700 SELD 44118 2627 D3
13800 SELD 44118 2628 A3
13800 UNHT 44118 2628 A3
14000 SELD 44121 2628 A3
14000 UNHT 44121 2628 A3
14500 BHWD 44121 2628 D3
14500 BHWD 44122 2628 D3
23300 LNHT 44122 2628 D3
24300 BHWD 44124 2628 D3
24300 LNHT 44124 2628 D3
26800 BHWD 44122 2629 C3
26800 BHWD 44124 2629 C3
26800 LNHT 44124 2629 C3
27900 PRPK 44122 2629 C3
27900 PRPK 44124 2629 C3
29200 MDHT 44124 2629 C3
32400 MDHT 44124 2630 A3
32400 PRPK 44124 2630 A3
33900 GSML 44040 2630 B3
33900 HGVL 44040 2630 B3
33900 HGVL 44022 2630 B3
Cedar St
10 ELYR 44035 2875 B6
10 GNVA 44041 1944 C3
7000 BbgT 44022 2761 A7
8900 BKVL 44141 3016 A7
N Cedar St
10 OBLN 44074 3138 D2
100 GNVA 44041 1944 C3
S Cedar St
10 GNVA 44041 1944 C4
10 OBLN 44074 3138 D3
Cedar Acres Dr
13200 CsTp 44026 2632 A3
Cedar Bark Dr
600 AURA 44202 3022 C4
Cedar Branch Cir
33000 NRDV 44039 2877 D1
Cedar Branch Tr
21500 SGVL 44136 3011 B4
Cedar Brook Dr
100 ELYR 44035 2874 A7
Cedarbrook Dr
300 PNVL 44077 2146 A3
700 PNVL 44077 2145 E3
Cedarbrook Rd
3200 CVHT 44118 2627 C3
3400 UNHT 44118 2627 C3
Cedar Creek Ct
1300 PnvT 44077 2041 A7
Cedarcrest Tr
7200 CsTp 44026 2631 B1
Cedar Glen Dr
10 PnvT 44077 2041 A7
Cedar Glen Pkwy
11300 CLEV 44106 2626 D3
11400 CVHT 44106 2626 D3
Cedar Grove Cir
800 SgHT 44067 3152 C1
Cedarhurst Dr
1800 WKLF 44092 2374 E2
Cedar Point Rd
- BKPK 44135 2880 A1
- CLEV 44135 2880 A1
- CLEV 44142 2880 A1
22500 BKPK 44142 2880 A1
23000 BKPK 44142 2879 E1
24000 NOSD 44070 2879 E1
24000 NOSD 44142 2879 E1
Cedarview Dr
2100 BHWD 44122 2628 C3
Cedarville Av
- SFLD 44054 2746 D4
Cedarwood Av
14100 LKWD 44107 2622 D5
Cedarwood Ct
4100 INDE 44131 2884 C5
14700 MDFD 44062 2767 C1
Cedarwood Dr
1300 WTLK 44145 2619 B7
9500 NRYN 44133 3013 B3
Cedarwood Ln
23400 NOSD 44070 2750 E5
Cedarwood Rd
2400 PRPK 44124 2629 E3
2400 PRPK 44124 2630 A4
5900 MONT 44060 2143 B3
6100 MNTR 44060 2143 B3
S Cedarwood Rd
6300 MNTR 44060 2143 B4
Ceile Cir
16200 WNHL 44146 2886 A5
Celeste Dr
- PRMA 44130 3013 B2
Celestia Rd
400 RDHT 44143 2498 D3
Celianna Dr
8200 SGVL 44136 3011 A3
Celizic Ln
- LryT 44077 2147 D6
Cemetery Rd
7300 VmnT 44089 2869 C5
Cemetery St
- MNTU 44255 3159 B6
Censori Park Blvd
- MCDN 44056 3154 A6
Centennial Av
37000 AVON 44011 2747 D2
Centennial St
100 GNVA 44041 1944 D4
600 GnvT 44041 1944 D4
Center Av
12000 GDHT 44125 2756 D6
Center Ct
10 CLEV 44113 2624 C2
10 CLEV 44115 2624 C2
Center Dr
2400 PRMA 44134 2883 C5
8600 NRYN 44133 3148 D1
Center Ln
- AhtT 44001 2872 A2
- AMHT 44001 2872 A2
Center Rd
- CLEV 44144 2753 D2
10 VmnT 44089 2740 A7
900 ETLK 44095 2250 B3
900 PnvT 44077 2041 B3
2400 AVON 44011 2618 A7
2400 AVON 44011 2748 A1
3100 NPRY 44081 1940 B5
3100 PryT 44081 1940 B5
3500 PryT 44081 2042 B2
3700 PRRY 44081 2042 B2
Center St
10 CLEV 44110 2372 C5
10 CNFL 44022 2760 E6
10 CNFL 44022 2761 A6
10 PnvT 44077 2041 B4
100 CRDN 44024 2379 E6
100 CRDN 44024 2380 A6
200 ELYR 44035 2875 B6
900 GFTN 44044 3142 A5
1000 CLEV 44113 2624 D4
1000 VMLN 44089 2740 C6
4200 WLBY 44094 2250 E6
5800 BosT 44141 3152 C7
5900 MNTR 44060 2144 B3
7200 MNTR 44060 2252 B1
8300 KDHL 44060 2252 B4
16000 PkmT 44234 2896 D7
Center St SR-44
100 CRDN 44024 2379 E6
100 CRDN 44024 2380 A6
Center St SR-615
6300 MNTR 44060 2144 B5
7200 MNTR 44060 2252 B1
8300 KDHL 44060 2252 B4
E Center St
10 BERA 44017 2880 C7
13800 BURT 44021 2766 B1
E Center St SR-87
13800 BURT 44021 2766 B1
W Center St
10 BERA 44017 2880 C7
13700 BURT 44021 2766 A1
W Center St SR-87
13700 BURT 44021 2766 A1
Center Wy N
14600 LKWD 44107 2622 D4
Center Ridge Rd
19400 RKRV 44116 2621 E7
20500 RKRV 44116 2751 A1
20600 FWPK 44116 2751 A1
20600 FWPK 44126 2751 A1
21600 RKRV 44126 2751 A1
23000 WTLK 44145 2751 A1
23000 WTLK 44116 2751 A1
23200 WTLK 44145 2750 C1
27100 WTLK 44145 2749 C5
31400 NRDV 44039 2749 C5
31400 NRDV 44145 2749 C5
31700 NRDV 44039 2748 E7
31700 NRDV 44039 2877 C2
36000 NRDV 44039 2876 B4
39100 NRDV 44039 2875 E5
Center Ridge Rd SR-113
19400 RKRV 44116 2621 E7
20500 RKRV 44116 2751 A1
20600 FWPK 44116 2751 A1
20600 FWPK 44126 2751 A1
21600 RKRV 44126 2751 A1
23000 WTLK 44116 2751 A1
23000 WTLK 44145 2751 A1
23200 WTLK 44145 2750 C1
27100 WTLK 44145 2749 C5
31400 NRDV 44039 2749 C5
31400 NRDV 44145 2749 C5
31700 NRDV 44039 2748 E7
31700 NRDV 44039 2877 C2
36000 NRDV 44039 2876 B4
39100 NRDV 44039 2875 E5
Center Ridge Rd US-20
19400 RKRV 44116 2621 E7
20500 RKRV 44116 2751 A1
20600 FWPK 44116 2751 A1
20600 FWPK 44126 2751 A1
21600 RKRV 44126 2751 A1
23000 WTLK 44145 2751 A1
23000 WTLK 44116 2751 A1
23200 WTLK 44145 2750 C1
27100 WTLK 44145 2749 C5
31400 NRDV 44039 2749 C5
31400 NRDV 44145 2749 C5
31700 NRDV 44039 2748 E7
31700 NRDV 44039 2877 C2
36000 NRDV 44039 2876 B4
39100 NRDV 44039 2875 E5
Centerville Tr
- AURA 44202 3022 B4
Central Av
1800 CLEV 44115 2625 A3
3900 CLEV 44103 2625 D3
4000 CLEV 44104 2625 D3
7400 CLEV 44103 2626 A3
7400 CLEV 44104 2626 A3
8400 CLEV 44106 2626 A3
Central Dr
100 AMHT 44001 2872 E2
400 AhtT 44001 2872 A2
N Central Dr
800 LORN 44052 2744 D2
S Central Dr
800 LORN 44052 2744 D2
Central Furnace Dr
2000 CLEV 44115 2625 A5
Central Park Blvd
9400 ODFL 44138 3010 A1
Central Viaduct
300 CLEV 44113 2624 C2
300 CLEV 44115 2624 C2
Centurion Dr
100 CrlT 44035 3006 A5
Century Cir
4600 BKLN 44144 2753 C5
Century Dr
1100 CLEV 44109 2754 E5
Century Ln
8500 RsIT 44072 2632 B5
37800 AVON 44011 2747 C3
Century Oak Dr
14400 SGVL 44136 3012 C3
Century Oaks Dr
1700 WTLK 44145 2750 D1
E Century Oaks Dr
1700 WTLK 44145 2750 D1
Centuryway Rd
20600 MPHT 44137 2887 A1
Ceo Dr
- GDHT 44125 2756 A6
Ceo Rd
4700 GDHT 44125 2756 A5
Cesko Av
3500 CLEV 44109 2624 C7
Cessna Av
- BHIT 44212 3146 A6
Cessna Dr
900 MCDN 44056 3018 E5
Chablis Ct
6800 MNTR 44060 2143 E6
Chadbourne Dr
6600 NOSD 44070 2878 C3
6800 VLVW 44125 2885 D6
Chadbourne Rd
2700 CLEV 44120 2627 A6
2800 SRHT 44120 2627 A6
Chadwick Ct
100 AbnT 44023 2892 B6
100 ELYR 44035 2874 A6
2600 WTLK 44145 2749 E2
Chadwick Dr
- AURA 44202 3156 E3
- AURA 44202 3157 A3
Chadwick Rd
5100 LryT 44057 2042 E7
5100 LryT 44057 2148 E1
Chaffee Ct
6500 BKVL 44141 3016 A7
Chaffee Rd
7400 SgHT 44067 3017 A7
Chagrin Blvd
- PRPK 44124 2759 E2
200 CNFL 44022 2760 B4
200 MDHL 44022 2760 B4
400 CFIT 44022 2760 B4
15600 SRHT 44120 2757 D1
17700 SRHT 44122 2757 D1
19200 SRHT 44122 2758 B1
21100 BHWD 44122 2758 B1
21100 HIHL 44122 2758 B1
26900 BHWD 44122 2759 A1
27000 ORNG 44122 2759 A1
27000 WDMR 44122 2759 A1
29000 ORNG 44124 2759 A1
29000 PRPK 44124 2759 A1
33000 MDHL 44022 2759 E2
Chagrin Blvd SR-8
15600 SRHT 44120 2757 D1
17700 SRHT 44122 2757 D1
19200 SRHT 44122 2758 B1
Chagrin Blvd SR-87
25600 BHWD 44122 2758 E1
26900 BHWD 44122 2759 A1
27000 ORNG 44122 2759 A1
27000 WDMR 44122 2759 A1
29000 ORNG 44124 2759 A1
29000 PRPK 44124 2759 A1
Chagrin Blvd US-422
- BHWD 44122 2759 A1
15600 SRHT 44120 2757 D1
17700 SRHT 44122 2757 D1
19200 SRHT 44122 2758 B1
21100 BHWD 44122 2758 B1
21100 HIHL 44122 2758 B1
Chagrin Dr
2500 WBHL 44094 2375 E3
2500 WTHL 44094 2375 E3
5500 MONT 44060 2143 D2
35800 ETLK 44095 2250 C1
Chagrin Rd
7100 BbgT 44022 2761 B7
7100 BbgT 44023 2761 B7
7300 BbgT 44023 2890 C1
8300 BbgT 44023 2891 A4
Chagrin Highlands Dr
6000 SLN 44139 2889 C4
Chagrin Mills Rd
8000 RsIT 44073 2761 E3
8200 RsIT 44072 2762 A3
8200 RsIT 44073 2762 A3
Chagrin River Rd
- GSML 44094 2500 D1
- WBHL 44094 2500 D1
400 GSML 44040 2500 D3
1400 GSML 44040 2630 E1
2100 HGVL 44022 2630 E3
3200 HGVL 44022 2760 D1
3500 MDHL 44022 2760 D1
4500 BTVL 44022 2760 C7
6100 BTVL 44022 2889 D2
6600 BbgT 44023 2890 A3
6600 BbgT 44139 2890 A3
6600 SLN 44022 2889 D2
6600 SLN 44139 2889 D2
6600 SLN 44139 2890 A3
Chagrin River Rd SR-174
- GSML 44094 2500 D1
- WBHL 44094 2500 D1
400 GSML 44040 2500 D3
1400 GSML 44040 2630 E1
Chagrin Woods Dr
14200 NbyT 44065 2634 B7
Chaincraft Rd
4600 GDHT 44125 2756 D6
Chairmans Ct
6900 CcdT 44077 2145 B6
Chairmans Rowe
29800 WTLK 44145 2749 C3
Chalet Dr
7800 CsTp 44026 2501 D1
Chalfant Rd
3200 SRHT 44120 2627 C7
Chalker Rd
- FnTp 44491 3029 A4
- NsnT 44491 3029 A4
- StnT 44491 3029 A4
Chalmers Ct
200 LORN 44052 2614 B7
Chamberlain Av
7100 CLEV 44104 2625 E3
7100 CLEV 44104 2626 A3
Chamberlain Rd
800 GFTN 44044 3142 A7
800 GftT 44044 3142 A7
10800 ManT 44202 3158 A5
10800 ManT 44255 3158 A5
11600 ManT 44202 3023 B7
11600 ManT 44255 3023 B7
12700 AbnT 44255 3023 B5
12700 AbnT 44202 3023 B5
Chamberlin Blvd
2800 HDSN 44236 3155 D6
Chamberlin Ct
7900 HDSN 44236 3155 D6
Chamberlin Ln
1300 TNBG 44087 3019 A5
Chamberlin Rd
1300 TwbT 44087 3154 B2
8600 TNBG 44087 3154 B1
8900 TNBG 44087 3019 B7
9100 MCDN 44056 3019 B7
Chamberlin Tr
9600 TNBG 44087 3019 B5
Chambers Av
6500 CLEV 44105 2755 E2
Chambers Ct
6500 MNTR 44060 2144 B5
Champ Dr
19900 EUCL 44117 2498 A2
Champaign Av
5700 BKPK 44142 2881 D1
Champaign Dr
7700 MNTR 44060 2143 D6
Champion Av
10100 CLEV 44111 2753 C1
Champion Ln
100 SRSL 44073 2762 D6
Champion Tr
2200 TNBG 44087 3020 B6
Champions Ct
- AVLK 44012 2618 C4
Chancellor Ct
500 AVLK 44012 2618 C3
Chandler Ct
7500 SgHT 44067 3152 C1
Chandler Dr
400 AURA 44202 3156 C2
Chandler Grn
14900 SGVL 44136 3147 C5
Chandler Ln
800 AURA 44202 3156 C2
Chandler Pth
400 AURA 44202 3156 D2
Chandlers Ln
23200 ODFL 44138 3010 E2
Channing Ln
7200 CcdT 44060 2145 B7
Channing Rd
2300 UNHT 44118 2628 A4
Chanticleer Dr
4200 FWPK 44126 2751 E2
Chapek Pkwy
6600 CHHT 44125 2755 E5
Chapel Cir
300 BERA 44017 2879 E7
300 BERA 44017 2880 A7
Chapel Ct
1200 AMHT 44001 2744 A7
Chapel Ln
10 PnvT 44077 2041 A4
Chapel Rd
5400 MadT 44057 1941 C2
6200 MadT 44057 1942 B2
Chapel St
100 ELYR 44035 2875 B6
Chapel Hill Dr
6700 BKVL 44141 3151 A2
26300 NOSD 44070 2750 A4
Chapel Road Ext
5200 MadT 44057 1941 B2
Chapelside Av
13100 CLEV 44120 2756 E2
13100 CLEV 44120 2757 A2
Chapelway Dr
7800 MNTR 44060 2252 D3
Chapin Rd
5400 MadT 44057 2150 E2
Chapin St
11400 CsTp 44026 2501 C2
25500 ODFL 44138 3010 B2
Chapin Falls Ln
7600 KTLD 44094 2376 C5
Chapman Av
1400 MadT 44057 1843 C7
1800 ECLE 44112 2497 B5
Chapman Cir
8700 SGVL 44136 3012 B3
Chapman Ln
400 ELYR 44035 3006 A1
Chapman Wy
1500 BWHT 44147 3149 D5
Chapparal
- WTLK 44145 2750 C2
Chapparal N
2300 WTLK 44145 2750 C2
Chapparal S
2300 WTLK 44145 2750 C2
Chappel Ln
- AVLK 44012 2617 E4
- AVLK 44012 2618 A4
Character Cir
- PryT 44081 2042 B1
Chard Av
- CLEV 44105 2755 C1
Chardon Av
100 CRDN 44024 2380 A5
Chardon Rd
- CLEV 44117 2372 E6
- CLEV 44117 2373 A7
- CLEV 44119 2372 E6
- KTLD 44094 2377 A6
1200 EUCL 44117 2373 A7
7000 KTLD 44094 2376 A5
7000 WBHL 44094 2376 A5
7900 KTLD 44094 2377 A6
9600 CdnT 44024 2378 C6
9600 CdnT 44094 2378 C6
10700 CdnT 44024 2379 A6
11100 CRDN 44024 2379 A6
21000 EUCL 44117 2498 B1
23800 RDHT 44143 2498 B1
24400 RDHT 44143 2373 E7
26500 RDHT 44143 2374 A6
27200 WBHL 44092 2374 A6
29600 WBHL 44094 2374 C6
33700 WBHL 44094 2375 A5
Chardon Rd SR-84
21000 EUCL 44117 2498 B1
23800 RDHT 44143 2498 B1
24400 RDHT 44143 2373 E7
26500 RDHT 44143 2374 B6
27200 WBHL 44092 2374 B6
Chardon Rd US-6
- KTLD 44094 2378 C6
7000 KTLD 44094 2376 A5
7000 WBHL 44094 2376 A5
7900 KTLD 44094 2377 A6
9600 CdnT 44024 2378 C6
9600 CdnT 44094 2378 C6
10700 CdnT 44024 2379 A6
11100 CRDN 44024 2379 A6
21000 EUCL 44117 2498 B1
23800 RDHT 44143 2498 B1
24400 RDHT 44143 2373 E7
26500 RDHT 44143 2374 A6
27200 WBHL 44092 2374 A6
Chardon Rd US-6
29600 WBHL 44094 2374 C6
33700 WBHL 44094 2375 A5
Chardon St
400 PNVL 44077 2040 A7
Chardon-Madison Rd
4400 MadT 44057 2044 B5
4400 MDSN 44057 2044 B5
5200 MadT 44057 2150 B2
5500 TpnT 44057 2150 B2
Chardon-Madison Rd SR-528
4400 MadT 44057 2044 B5
4400 MDSN 44057 2044 B5
5200 MadT 44057 2150 B2
5500 TpnT 44057 2150 B2
Chardonview Dr
26200 RDHT 44143 2373 E7
26200 RDHT 44143 2374 A7
Chardon Windsor Rd
7000 WndT 44099 2509 A2
7000 WndT 44064 2509 A2
12400 HmbT 44024 2380 C6
13500 HmbT 44024 2506 B1
14000 ClrT 44024 2506 D2
14700 ClrT 44024 2507 A2
14700 HtbT 44024 2507 A2
15200 HtbT 44064 2507 A2
15500 HtbT 44046 2507 D2
16000 HtbT 44046 2508 A2
16000 HtbT 44064 2508 A2
17100 HtbT 44064 2509 A2
17100 HtbT 44046 2509 A2
17100 WndT 44046 2509 A2
Chardonwood Dr
8000 KDHL 44060 2252 C4
N Chariot St
8000 CcdT 44060 2253 B4
S Chariot St
8100 CcdT 44060 2253 B4
Charlane Ct
5100 NPRY 44081 1941 A2
Charles Av
200 AMHT 44001 2872 B2
5400 PRMA 44129 2883 A2
6700 PRMA 44129 2882 E2
Charles Ct
100 ELYR 44035 2875 B7
4800 NRDV 44039 2877 B2
9000 TNBG 44087 3154 E1
18200 CLEV 44122 2757 D4
Charles Dr
- VMLN 44089 2741 B6
9000 BbgT 44023 3022 D2
9700 VLVW 44125 2885 B5
Charles Pl
500 HDHT 44143 2499 A3
Charles Rd
1800 ECLE 44112 2497 B5
6400 NOSD 44070 2878 B3
Charles St
10 BDFD 44146 2887 B6
10 GDRV 44045 2039 C5
200 SAHT 44001 2872 C7
700 WLWK 44095 2249 E6
5100 MPHT 44137 2757 B7
Charlesderry Rd
8000 KTLD 44094 2376 E1
Charleston Av
2800 LORN 44055 2746 A3
33300 AVLK 44012 2617 C2
Charleston Sq
10 EUCL 44143 2498 A2
Charles V Carr Pl
3000 CLEV 44104 2626 A6
Charlotte Av
11000 CLEV 44105 2756 C4
Charlotte St
10 PNVL 44077 2146 B2
Charlton Cir
7500 NCtT 44067 3153 A2
Charlton Ln
10100 NbyT 44065 2763 B1
Charlton Rd
4000 SELD 44121 2628 A1
Charmar Dr
- MNTR 44060 2144 C2
Charmwood Ovl
32700 SLN 44139 3019 E1
32800 SLN 44139 2888 E7
Charney Cir
9500 ODFL 44138 3010 C1
Charney Rd
2300 UNHT 44118 2627 E4
Charter Av
6600 CLEV 44127 2755 E1
Charter Dr
10 NCtT 44067 3153 C5
Charter Ln
19100 SGVL 44136 3146 C5
Charter Oak Ln
1100 WTLK 44145 2620 D6
Chartley Ct
10300 MsnT 44024 2503 C6
Chartley Rd
1700 GSML 44040 2630 B1
Chase Av
1200 LKWD 44107 2622 E4
Chase Dr
6200 MNTR 44060 2143 D4
6400 MAYF 44143 2499 E5
6400 MAYF 44143 2500 A5
8600 BbgT 44023 3022 A1
24700 NOSD 44070 2750 C4
28400 WTLK 44145 2749 D4
Chase Ln
10 LKWD 44107 2622 E4
Chase St
100 ELYR 44035 2875 B6
Chase Moor Dr
12900 SGVL 44136 3012 D7
Chateau Av
16500 CLEV 44128 2757 C5
Chateau Dr
7200 PRMA 44130 2882 C7
Chatfield Av
17500 CLEV 44111 2752 A3
17500 CLEV 44135 2752 A3
Chatfield Dr
10 PNVL 44077 2145 E2
2100 CVHT 44106 2627 A3
Chatham Av
2500 CLEV 44113 2624 C5
Chatham Ct
1000 GFTN 44044 3142 A4

Cleveland Street Index

STREET Block City ZIP Map# Grid

Chatham Ct
3000 WTLK 44145 2749 D3
7200 NCtT 44067 3153 B4
17900 SGVL 44136 3146 E4
Chatham Dr
10 AURA 44202 3156 E3
10 AURA 44202 3157 A3
10 PnvT 44077 2145 B5
5500 SVHL 44131 2884 B1
33400 AVLK 44012 2617 C2
Chatham Pl
900 RKRV 44116 2621 B6
Chatham Rd
2800 PRPK 44124 2629 E6
Chatham Wy
100 MDHT 44124 2500 A6
Chatham Glen Dr
14600 NbyT 44065 2763 B1
Chatham Point Dr
30200 BYVL 44140 2619 C5
Chatman Dr
16100 SGVL 44136 3146 D2
Chatworth Dr
25500 EUCL 44117 2373 D6
Chaucer Blvd
8700 BWHT 44147 3014 D6
Chaucer Ct
100 ELYR 44035 3005 A1
35300 NRDV 44039 2748 A7
Chaucer Dr
25500 WTLK 44145 2750 B3
Chaucer Wy
2200 MadT 44057 1942 B2
Chaumont Rd
- WLWK 44095 2249 C5
Chautauqua Tr
11400 BKVL 44141 3016 D5
Checquers Ct
9800 CcdT 44060 2253 B4
Cheerful Ln
11600 SGVL 44136 3012 C7
Chelford Rd
1900 RDHT 44117 2373 D7
1900 RDHT 44143 2373 D7
Chelmsford Dr
10 AURA 44202 3156 E3
10 AURA 44202 3157 A4
5600 LNHT 44124 2629 C3
Chelmsford Rd
1500 MDHT 44124 2499 D7
1500 MDHT 44124 2629 D1
Chelsea Av
33300 AVLK 44012 2617 C2
Chelsea Ct
- AURA 44202 3021 E7
10 SRSL 44073 2761 E6
11000 NRYN 44133 3013 D5
Chelsea Dr
200 WLBY 44094 2250 A7
200 WLBY 44094 2375 A1
3000 CVHT 44118 2497 C7
4700 LORN 44055 2746 B5
29500 BYVL 44140 2619 D3
Chelsea Ln
10 BHWD 44122 2628 E4
7500 GSML 44040 2630 D2
Chelsee Pl
100 ELYR 44035 2874 A7
Chelston Av
900 SELD 44121 2498 B5
Cheltenham Blvd
5000 LNHT 44124 2628 E1
5100 LNHT 44124 2629 A1
Cheltenham Dr
38200 WLBY 44094 2250 E2
Chelton Rd
3500 SRHT 44120 2757 C2
Chennault Dr
7300 NRDV 44039 2877 C4
Chenook Run
8800 MCDN 44056 3018 D6
Chenook Tr
700 MCDN 44056 3018 D6
Cheppards Pt
- BYVL 44140 2621 A5
Cherie Dr
8400 GDHT 44125 2756 B7
Cheriton Dr
700 HDHT 44143 2499 A4
Cherokee Av
- EUCL 44119 2373 A5
18500 CLEV 44119 2372 E5
19300 CLEV 44119 2373 A5
Cherokee Dr
5600 LNHT 44124 2629 B1
Cherokee Ln
11500 BKVL 44141 3016 D5
Cherokee Pth
- VMLN 44089 2741 C6
Cherokee Run
8900 MCDN 44056 3018 D5
Cherokee Tr
500 WLBY 44094 2143 B4
4000 BNWK 44212 3146 D7
13000 MDBH 44130 3012 D1
Cherokee Strip Tr
10 ClrT 44024 2505 D6
Cherry Av
100 CRDN 44024 2379 E6
Cherry Cir
8500 MCDN 44056 3018 C7
Cherry Ln
- AhtT 44001 2872 B2
- VMLN 44089 2740 E4
10 OmsT 44138 2879 B4
100 AVLK 44012 2618 C1
100 SVHL 44131 2883 E7
100 SVHL 44131 2884 A7
8000 NCtT 44067 3018 A7
8000 NCtT 44067 3153 A1
12800 CsTp 44026 2631 D1
Cherry Rd
9200 VmnT 44089 2869 B6
Cherry St
- MONT 44060 2144 A1
- VMLN 44089 2741 A4
7200 INDE 44131 2884 E6
33500 AVON 44011 2748 D2
Cherry Wy
21400 RKRV 44116 2621 C6
Cherrybank Dr
37000 SLN 44139 3020 C2
Cherry Blossom Dr
6800 MNTR 44060 2143 C6

Cherry Bottom Gln
100 ELYR 44035 3005 A1
Cherry Hill Dr
10200 CcdT 44077 2145 D5
Cherry Hill Ln
1200 BWHT 44147 3150 A1
8300 BWHT 44147 3015 A7
Cherry Hollow Dr
11400 CdnT 44024 2254 C6
Cherry Park Ovl
600 AURA 44202 3021 C4
Cherry Ridge Dr
300 AURA 44202 3156 C1
Cherrystone Dr
9200 MNTR 44060 2144 E7
9200 MNTR 44060 2252 E1
Cherry Stone Ln
19000 SGVL 44136 3146 E5
Cherry Tree Dr
9200 SGVL 44136 3012 A3
Cherry Valley Dr
300 AMHT 44001 2872 E1
600 AMHT 44001 2743 E7
Cherrywood Cir
- MNTR 44060 2145 A7
10 GNVA 44041 1944 C7
400 SgHT 44067 3017 E3
Cherrywood Dr
5600 LORN 44053 2744 E6
Cherrywood Ln
7600 SVHL 44131 3015 A2
19100 WVHT 44128 2757 E4
Cheryl Dr
6100 CcdT 44077 2146 B4
13100 SGVL 44136 3147 D4
Cheryl Rd
6700 HrmT 44234 3161 A3
Cheryl Ann Dr
6500 INDE 44131 2884 C6
6800 SVHL 44131 2884 C6
Chesapeake Ct
100 ELYR 44035 2873 E7
100 ELYR 44035 2874 A7
Chesapeake Dr
8400 SgHT 44067 3017 E5
9300 NRYN 44133 3013 C4
Chesapeake Pl
100 PnvT 44077 2145 B5
Chesapeake Cove
300 PnvT 44077 2145 B6
Chesea Ct
8700 SgHT 44067 3017 D4
Cheshire Ct
7700 MNTR 44060 2253 A2
Cheshire Dr
100 ELYR 44035 2874 A7
Cheshire Pl
7300 SLN 44139 3019 E2
Cheshire Rd
2500 SRHT 44120 2626 E5
S Cheshire Rd
- BtnT 44021 2766 B2
14700 BURT 44021 2766 B1
S Cheshire Rd SR-168
- BtnT 44021 2766 B2
14700 BURT 44021 2766 B1
S Cheshire Rd SR-700
- BtnT 44021 2766 B2
14700 BURT 44021 2766 B1
N Cheshire St
14300 BURT 44021 2636 B7
S Cheshire St
- BURT 44021 2766 A1
S Cheshire St SR-168
- BURT 44021 2766 A1
S Cheshire St SR-700
- BURT 44021 2766 A1
Chesnut Ct
3800 ORNG 44022 2759 D3
Chester Av
900 CLEV 44114 2624 E3
1200 CLEV 44114 2625 B2
4000 CLEV 44103 2625 B2
7300 CLEV 44103 2626 A2
8400 CLEV 44106 2626 A2
Chester Av US-322
1300 CLEV 44114 2625 B2
4000 CLEV 44103 2625 B2
7300 CLEV 44103 2626 B2
8400 CLEV 44106 2626 B2
Chester Pkwy
8100 CLEV 44103 2626 A2
Chester Rd
11300 GDHT 44125 2885 D1
33800 AVON 44011 2618 C7
36600 AVON 44011 2617 E7
Chester Rd SR-83
36500 AVON 44011 2618 A7
Chester St
10 PNVL 44077 2039 D7
10 PNVL 44077 2040 A6
Chesterbrook Rd
7600 CsTp 44026 2631 C3
Chesterfield Av
7500 PRMA 44129 2882 D1
11500 CLEV 44108 2496 D6
35400 NRDV 44039 2748 A7
Chesterfield Dr
10000 PMHT 44130 2882 C3
Chesterfield Ln
12500 CsTp 44026 2502 D7
Chester Industrial Pkwy
1200 AVON 44011 2617 B6
Chesterland Av
2000 LKWD 44107 2622 E6
Chesterton Ct
- AURA 44202 3156 B1
100 BNWK 44212 3147 B6
Chesterton Ln
- AURA 44202 3156 A1
8100 NRYN 44133 3013 C5
Chesterton Rd
2600 SRHT 44118 2628 A6
2600 SRHT 44122 2628 A6
Chestnut Av
10 NHFD 44067 3018 A4
100 NHFD 44067 3017 E4
Chestnut Blvd
8100 BWHT 44147 3015 A3
Chestnut Cir
12200 BKVL 44141 3151 D4
Chestnut Ct
200 AVLK 44012 2618 C2
3500 LORN 44053 2744 C3

Chestnut Ct
7200 OmsT 44138 2878 E5
35100 SLN 44139 3020 B2
Chestnut Dr
- AhtT 44001 2872 E6
- BtnT 44021 2635 E6
300 BERA 44017 2879 E5
400 BERA 44017 2880 A5
2000 WTLK 44145 2750 A2
5700 PRMA 44129 2882 D1
7000 WNHL 44146 2886 C7
14500 NbyT 44065 2634 B7
14500 NbyT 44065 2764 B1
20600 SGVL 44136 3011 C4
Chestnut Knl
1300 BWHT 44147 3149 C4
Chestnut Ln
- WBHL 44092 2374 A6
100 RDHT 44143 2374 A6
100 SRSL 44073 2761 D5
800 AMHT 44001 2872 B3
31800 PRPK 44124 2629 E4
Chestnut Ovl
4700 INDE 44131 2884 C5
Chestnut Pl
- CLEV 44104 2625 C4
- CLEV 44115 2625 C4
Chestnut Rd
10 SVHL 44131 2883 E5
600 WLBY 44094 2143 A4
1500 SVHL 44131 2884 A5
4000 INDE 44131 2884 B5
Chestnut Run
900 GSML 44040 2500 E5
Chestnut St
10 ELYR 44035 2875 A6
10 GNVA 44041 1944 B5
10 PNVL 44077 2145 E3
300 CcdT 44077 2145 E3
300 FTHR 44077 2039 D3
400 VMLN 44089 2741 A4
900 GFTN 44044 3142 A5
1200 WLBY 44094 2142 E5
2300 HpfT 44041 1944 B5
4300 BNWK 44212 3146 C7
4500 BHIT 44212 3146 C7
5400 MONT 44060 2143 E1
N Chestnut Commons Dr
7300 MNTR 44060 2143 C4
S Chestnut Commons Dr
7300 MNTR 44060 2143 C4
Chestnutdale Av
3100 CLEV 44109 2754 C2
Chestnutdale Rd
11600 MsnT 44024 2504 C3
Chestnut Grove Dr
7700 ODFL 44138 2879 C5
Chestnut Hills Dr
1800 CVHT 44106 2626 D3
2200 CLEV 44106 2626 D3
5000 WLBY 44094 2250 B7
5000 WLBY 44094 2375 B1
5800 PRMA 44129 2882 D2
6300 PRMA 44129 2883 A4
Chestnut Oak Ln
- SGVL 44136 3146 B1
Chestnut Ridge Rd
31600 NOSD 44070 2878 A3
31600 NRDV 44070 2878 A3
31600 NRDV 44039 2878 A3
32300 NRDV 44039 2877 D4
36000 NRDV 44039 2876 E7
36000 NRDV 44039 3007 C2
36800 EatT 44039 3007 C2
36800 EatT 44035 3007 C2
38000 EatT 44035 3006 D2
38000 ELYR 44035 3006 D2
38000 ELYR 44035 3007 C2
38500 CrlT 44035 3006 D2
Chestnut Trail Dr
1600 TNBG 44087 3019 D4
Cheswick Dr
5000 SLN 44139 2759 D7
Cheswick Pl
31400 SLN 44139 2888 D1
Chevrolet Blvd
5000 PRMA 44130 2753 B7
5000 PRMA 44130 2882 B1
Chevy Chase
9900 SGVL 44136 3012 C4
Cheyenne Run
9100 MCDN 44056 3018 D5
Cheyenne Tr
10 ClrT 44024 2505 C6
10000 PMHT 44130 2882 B2
Cheyenne Falls
300 AVLK 44012 2618 C2
Cheyney Ln
- BHIT 44212 3145 E6
- BHIT 44212 3146 A6
- LvpT 44212 3145 E6
Chicago St
500 PNVL 44077 2145 E1
Chickadee Ln
5000 LNHT 44124 2628 E1
5000 LNHT 44124 2629 A1
Chickasaw Av
18500 CLEV 44119 2372 E5
19300 CLEV 44119 2373 A5
20000 EUCL 44119 2373 A5
Chickasaw Rd
5200 RchT 44286 3150 A6
Chickashay Ln
10400 AbnT 44023 3023 C2
Chillicothe Rd
- KDHL 44060 2251 E6
- KTLD 44060 2251 E6
- KTLD 44060 2252 A6
- KTLD 44094 2252 A6
5000 SRSL 44073 2762 A5
7000 MNTR 44060 2145 A7
7100 MNTR 44060 2253 A1
7200 MNTR 44060 2252 C4
7900 KDHL 44060 2252 C4
8700 KTLD 44060 2251 E6
9100 KTLD 44094 2376 E2
9500 KTLD 44094 2377 A4
11000 KTLD 44094 2502 A3
11100 CsTp 44026 2502 A3
11100 CsTp 44094 2502 A3
12700 CsTp 44026 2632 A2
13400 CsTp 44072 2632 A2
13400 RslT 44072 2632 A2
14600 RslT 44072 2762 A1
15200 RslT 44073 2762 A1

Chillicothe Rd
15800 BbgT 44023 2762 A5
16400 BbgT 44023 2891 A1
18400 BbgT 44023 3022 A1
Chillicothe Rd SR-306
5000 SRSL 44073 2762 A5
8700 KTLD 44094 2251 D7
9100 KTLD 44094 2376 E2
9500 KTLD 44094 2377 A4
11000 KTLD 44094 2502 A3
11100 CsTp 44026 2502 A3
11100 CsTp 44094 2502 A3
12700 CsTp 44026 2632 A2
13400 CsTp 44072 2632 A2
13400 RslT 44072 2632 A2
14600 RslT 44072 2762 A1
15200 RslT 44073 2762 A1
15800 BbgT 44023 2762 A5
16400 BbgT 44023 2891 A1
18400 BbgT 44023 3022 A1
Chillicothe Rd SR-615
- KDHL 44060 2251 E6
- KTLD 44060 2251 E6
- KTLD 44060 2252 A6
- KTLD 44094 2252 A6
8400 KDHL 44060 2252 A6
8800 KTLD 44094 2251 E6
N Chillicothe Rd
10 AURA 44202 3021 E7
200 AURA 44202 3022 A4
N Chillicothe Rd SR-306
10 AURA 44202 3021 E7
200 AURA 44202 3022 A4
S Chillicothe Rd
10 AURA 44202 3156 E2
10100 STBR 44241 3156 E5
S Chillicothe Rd SR-43
100 AURA 44202 3156 E2
10100 STBR 44241 3156 E2
S Chillicothe Rd SR-306
10 AURA 44202 3156 E2
Chimney Rdg
100 CRDN 44024 2379 E5
Chimney Ridge Dr
2000 MadT 44057 1942 A2
Chimney Ridge Tr
38300 WBHL 44094 2376 A6
Chinaberry Cir
- MCDN 44056 3154 A4
Chinkapin Ct
6700 OKWD 44146 2887 E6
Chipeewa Dr
19600 EUCL 44117 2497 D2
19600 EUCL 44117 2498 A2
Chipendale Ln
11400 MsnT 44024 2503 E2
11400 MsnT 44024 2504 A2
Chipmunk Ln
15400 BtnT 44062 2767 A5
15400 MdfT 44062 2767 A5
Chipmunk Ridge Dr
10000 CcdT 44077 2253 C1
Chippenham Ct
10 RKRV 44116 2621 C4
Chippewa Rd
7300 BKVL 44141 3016 C6
Chippewa Rd SR-82
7300 BKVL 44141 3016 C6
Chippewa St
1000 GFTN 44044 3142 A4
Chippewa Tr
7400 MDBH 44130 3012 D1
Chippewa Creek Dr
- BKVL 44141 3016 B7
Chipping Ln
400 AbnT 44023 2892 B3
Chisholm Ct
- AURA 44202 3021 D6
Chisholm Tr
10 ClrT 44024 2505 C6
Chopin Cir
27000 WTLK 44145 2750 A1
Chris Av
3100 LORN 44052 2744 D3
Chrisfield Dr
3300 RKRV 44116 2751 A2
Christene Blvd
6400 BKPK 44142 2880 B4
Christian Av
11700 CcdT 44077 2254 D1
Christina Ct
1000 GDRV 44045 2039 C6
1000 PnvT 44045 2039 C6
1000 PnvT 44077 2039 C6
Christina Dr
10200 KTLD 44094 2377 C5
Christine Av
12600 GDHT 44105 2756 E5
13600 GDHT 44105 2757 A5
14000 CLEV 44105 2757 A5
21800 EUCL 44119 2373 B5
Christine Ct
100 ETLK 44095 2142 D5
Christine Dr
2800 WBHL 44092 2374 C5
Christman Dr
6000 NOSD 44070 2878 C2
Christopher Ct
5900 MNTR 44060 2144 C2
22400 SGVL 44136 3010 E4
Christopher Dr
8600 NRYN 44133 3014 B3
Church Av
2500 CLEV 44113 2624 C4
N Church Dr
9000 PMHT 44130 2882 C5
9000 PRMA 44130 2882 C5
9000 PRMA 44129 2882 C5
Church Ln
10 ELYR 44035 3006 A3
Church St
- SAHT 44001 3003 A1
10 BERA 44017 2880 C7
10 CNFL 44022 2760 E6
10 OmsT 44138 2879 B4
100 AMHT 44001 2872 D2
2500 AVON 44011 2747 D2
3800 WLBY 44094 2250 D4
9000 TNBG 44087 3154 E1
18100 PkmT 44234 2896 E7
Churchill Av
10500 CLEV 44106 2496 C7

Churchill Blvd
4200 UNHT 44118 2628 C4
Churchill Ct
10200 CLEV 44106 2496 C7
Churchill Dr
- AVON 44011 2747 B6
15900 ClbT 44028 3144 E2
35900 SLN 44139 2889 C4
Churchill Ln
- WTLK 44145 2749 A4
N Churchill Pl
7100 CcdT 44077 2146 A6
S Churchill Pl
7200 CcdT 44077 2146 B6
Churchill Rd
1000 LNHT 44124 2499 A7
Churchill Sq
7300 MNTR 44060 2143 C7
Cielo E Terra Dr
900 MCDN 44056 3018 E4
Cimarron Ovl
- AURA 44202 3021 B6
Cimarron Tr
100 ClrT 44024 2505 C6
Cindy Ln
3500 SVHL 44131 2884 B4
Cinema Ct
200 VMLN 44089 2741 C4
Cinnabar Dr
8900 BKVL 44141 3016 D6
Cinnabar Tr
18000 AbnT 44021 2893 A6
Cinnamon Blvd
11100 NRYN 44133 3013 B5
Cinnamon Tr
17900 AbnT 44021 2893 B6
Cinnamon Wy
3600 WTLK 44145 2750 B4
30000 NOSD 44070 2878 A4
Circle Dr
10 SRSL 44073 2762 C5
300 AhtT 44001 2872 B3
2200 CLEV 44106 2626 D2
2500 PryT 44077 2041 B7
5800 MDHT 44124 2629 C1
6700 MadT 44057 1843 B6
Circle Rdg
11500 SGVL 44136 3012 B5
N Circleview Dr
1100 BNHT 44131 2884 A1
1100 SVHL 44131 2884 A1
S Circleview Dr
1100 SVHL 44131 2884 A1
Circlewood Dr
500 AURA 44202 3022 C6
2600 WTLK 44145 2750 C3
3800 FWPK 44126 2751 C2
City Hall Dr
13900 NRYN 44133 3013 E7
City Hall Pl
200 LORN 44052 2614 D6
Civic Center Blvd
8400 MNTR 44060 2144 B4
CJ Ct
9200 MNTR 44060 2144 E6
Claasen Av
7100 CLEV 44105 2755 E3
7400 CLEV 44105 2756 A3
Clague Pkwy
500 BYVL 44140 2620 E5
Clague Rd
300 BYVL 44140 2620 E4
600 WTLK 44145 2620 E7
1700 WTLK 44145 2750 E2
2700 NOSD 44070 2750 E5
2700 WTLK 44070 2750 E2
Claiborne Rd
13300 ECLE 44112 2497 A5
Claiborne Hartford Connector
- ECLE 44112 2497 A5
Clairdoan Av
10500 CLEV 44108 2496 C4
Claire Av
16200 CLEV 44111 2752 B1
W Claire Dr
4300 SELD 44121 2628 B2
Clairidge Dr
5500 WLBY 44094 2375 B2
Clairmont Dr
10 PnvT 44077 2145 C4
Clairview Av
14000 CLEV 44111 2622 D7
Clampher Rd
4900 MPHT 44137 2758 A7
Clare Av
19700 MPHT 44137 2757 E7
20500 MPHT 44137 2758 A7
Clarebird Av
11200 CLEV 44105 2756 D2
Claremont Av
13100 MDBH 44130 2881 D4
Claremont Blvd
4700 GDHT 44125 2756 E7
Claremont Dr
10 BNWK 44212 3147 A6
Claremont Rd
200 VMLN 44089 2741 E4
2800 SRHT 44122 2627 E7
Clarence Av
1300 LKWD 44107 2623 A5
2000 LKWD 44107 2622 E6
Clarence Rd
800 CVHT 44121 2497 E5
Clarendon Ct
1900 WTLK 44145 2749 E1
Clarendon Dr
5400 SLN 44139 2888 E2
Clarendon Rd
3200 CVHT 44118 2627 C4
Clareshire Dr
24400 NOSD 44070 2750 D7
Clarewood Dr
30900 BYVL 44140 2619 B4
Claridge Ct
8100 NRYN 44133 3013 C5
Claridge Ln
600 AURA 44202 3156 C3
Claridge Ovl
3700 BNWK 44212 3147 A7
3700 SRHT 44118 2627 E5
3700 UNHT 44118 2627 E5
Claridon Rd
100 CRDN 44024 2380 A7
300 CRDN 44024 2505 B1

Claridon-Park Dr
13900 ClrT 44024 2506 B3
Claridon Troy Rd
10700 HmbT 44024 2381 B7
10700 HmbT 44024 2506 B1
11100 ClrT 44024 2506 B2
12400 ClrT 44021 2506 B7
12400 ClrT 44021 2636 B2
12400 ClrT 44024 2636 B2
13000 BtnT 44024 2636 B6
13700 BtnT 44021 2636 B6
14200 BURT 44021 2636 B6
14400 BtnT 44021 2766 B4
14400 BtnT 44062 2766 B4
16000 TroT 44021 2766 A7
16000 TroT 44021 2895 A3
17700 TroT 44234 2895 B7
18200 TroT 44234 3026 B3
Claridon Troy Rd SR-700
14400 BtnT 44021 2766 B4
14400 BtnT 44062 2766 B4
16000 TroT 44021 2766 A7
16000 TroT 44021 2895 A3
17700 TroT 44234 2895 B7
18200 TroT 44234 3026 B3
Clarion Av
- VMLN 44089 2740 E5
Clarion Dr
7600 RslT 44073 2761 D5
35800 ETLK 44095 2250 C1
Clarius Cir
9800 TNBG 44087 3020 B5
Clark Av
- CLEV 44113 2625 A7
- CLEV 44105 2625 B7
- CLEV 44115 2625 B7
300 CLEV 44109 2625 B7
900 CLEV 44109 2624 D7
900 CLEV 44113 2624 D7
4000 WLBY 44094 2250 E5
4500 CLEV 44102 2624 A7
7000 CLEV 44102 2623 E7
Clark Cir
- TNBG 44087 3019 E7
Clark Ct
10 OBLN 44074 3138 E2
3500 LORN 44053 2743 E3
3500 LORN 44053 2744 A3
37900 WLBY 44094 2250 D5
Clark Dr
28700 WKLF 44092 2374 B4
33900 NRDV 44039 2877 C4
Clark Ln
13000 NRsT 44074 3139 D2
Clark Pkwy
2700 WTLK 44145 2750 A3
Clark Rd
- CrlT 44050 3140 B4
2900 PryT 44081 1939 D6
3400 PryT 44081 1940 A6
10600 CdnT 44024 2253 E7
10700 CdnT 44024 2254 A7
12000 CcdT 44024 2255 A6
12000 CcdT 44077 2255 A6
12000 CdnT 44024 2255 A6
Clark St
100 BERA 44017 2880 C7
100 ELYR 44035 2875 C6
7500 ODFL 44138 2879 B5
Clarke Rd
10000 ClbT 44028 3010 E5
10000 ClbT 44136 3010 E5
10000 SGVL 44136 3010 E5
Clarkson Rd
2600 CVHT 44106 2627 A3
2700 CVHT 44118 2627 B3
Clarkstone Rd
1700 CLEV 44112 2497 C3
Clarkwood Dr
11700 CdnT 44024 2379 D4
Clarkwood Pkwy
4300 HIHL 44128 2758 B4
4300 WVHT 44128 2758 B4
Clarkwood Rd
2100 CLEV 44103 2625 E3
Clarmont Rd
300 WLWK 44095 2249 C7
Claudia Dr
6300 BKPK 44142 2880 E3
Claus Rd
- VMLN 44053 2742 B7
1200 VMLN 44089 2742 B7
1200 VMLN 44001 2742 B7
1300 VMLN 44001 2871 B1
1300 VMLN 44089 2871 B1
7800 VMLN 44001 2871 B4
7800 VMLN 44089 2871 B4
8100 BhmT 44001 2871 B4
Claver Rd
2400 UNHT 44118 2628 B4
Clay St
4400 HpfT 44041 1944 E7
4800 GNVA 44041 1944 E7
5800 MadT 44086 2149 C5
5800 TpnT 44086 2149 C5
6700 TpnT 44086 2257 C1
8000 TpnT 44064 2257 D5
8400 MtlT 44064 2257 D5
8700 MtlT 44064 2382 D1
10900 HtbT 44064 2507 D1
10900 MtlT 44064 2507 D1
11400 HtbT 44046 2507 D3
12400 HtbT 44046 2637 D2
Claymoor Av
6800 MadT 44057 1843 C6
Claymore Blvd
300 RDHT 44143 2498 D1
Claythorne Pl
3800 BNWK 44212 3146 E7
Claythorne Rd
- SRHT 44118 2628 A6
2600 SRHT 44122 2628 A6
Clayton Av
1600 CLEV 44109 2754 E3
29200 WKLF 44092 2374 B2
Clayton Blvd
3300 SRHT 44120 2627 C7
3300 SRHT 44120 2757 C1
Clayton Dr
- AURA 44202 3156 B1
3400 NOSD 44070 2750 D4
Clearair Dr
6200 MNTR 44060 2143 C4

Clearaire Rd
1200 CLEV 44110 2372 E7
1200 CLEV 44110 2497 E1
Clear Brook Cir
10800 SGVL 44136 3011 A4
Clearbrook Dr
- AVLK 44012 2617 D3
Clearbrook Ln
100 AURA 44202 3156 C1
Clearbrook Ovl
12600 NRYN 44133 3012 E2
Clear Creek Dr
- NRDV 44039 2877 B6
Clearfield Ln
11300 MsnT 44024 2504 D2
Clearlake Dr
10500 CcdT 44077 2145 E5
Clearmont Dr
7200 MNTR 44060 2143 C4
Clearview Av
900 PRMA 44134 2883 E2
4900 GDHT 44125 2756 E6
15900 CLEV 44128 2757 B5
E Clearview Av
10 SVHL 44131 2883 D2
10 SVHL 44131 2884 A2
Clearview Dr
400 EUCL 44123 2373 B3
4900 LORN 44053 2745 A5
4900 ShfT 44053 2745 A5
4900 ShfT 44052 2745 A5
5800 PMHT 44130 2882 C2
Clearview Rd
1000 LNHT 44124 2498 E7
11800 CsTp 44026 2502 A4
Clearwater Dr
10 BNWK 44212 3147 A6
3700 PRMA 44134 3014 B2
Clearwater Ln
2500 PryT 44077 2041 B7
Clearway Dr
36900 ETLK 44095 2142 D7
Clee Rd
- NOSD 44070 2749 C7
Clemens Av
500 ELYR 44035 2874 C4
Clemens Rd
27900 WTLK 44145 2619 D6
Clement Av
7100 CLEV 44105 2755 E3
7400 CLEV 44105 2756 A3
Clement Dr
5300 MPHT 44137 2757 D6
5300 MPHT 44137 2886 C1
5800 LORN 44053 2744 D6
Clement St
5000 MPHT 44137 2757 C7
Cleminshaw Rd
14400 CLEV 44135 2752 D3
Clemson Ct
100 ELYR 44035 3006 C2
Clermont Rd
1400 CLEV 44110 2497 D1
Clermont St
2600 ShvT 44241 3157 E7
2600 ShvT 44241 3158 A7
Cletus Rd
- EatT 44035 3007 B3
Cleveland Av
- LORN 44055 2745 E6
100 AMHT 44001 2872 E1
1100 AMHT 44001 2873 A1
1200 MadT 44057 1843 D6
2000 ShfT 44055 2745 E6
Cleveland Blvd
1700 LORN 44052 2615 B5
Cleveland Dr
9600 AbnT 44023 3022 E1
9700 AbnT 44023 3023 A1
Cleveland Rd
300 CLEV 44108 2496 E3
Cleveland St
10 CNFL 44022 2761 B6
100 ELYR 44035 2875 C5
900 ELYR 44039 2875 C5
1000 GFTN 44044 3142 A5
Cleveland St SR-113
700 ELYR 44035 2875 E5
900 ELYR 44039 2875 E4
Cleveland St US-20
700 ELYR 44035 2875 E5
900 ELYR 44039 2875 E4
S Cleveland St
10 CNFL 44022 2761 B6
Cleveland Heights Blvd
1100 CVHT 44121 2497 E7
Cleveland Memorial Shoreway
- CLEV - 2495 B7
- CLEV 44102 2623 D4
- CLEV - 2624 C4
- CLEV - 2625 A1
5800 CLEV 44102 2624 A4
5800 CLEV 44113 2624 A4
Cleveland Mem Shoreway SR-2
- CLEV - 2495 B7
- CLEV 44102 2623 E4
- CLEV - 2624 C4
- CLEV 44102 2624 A4
- CLEV 44113 2624 A4
- CLEV - 2625 A1
Cleveland Mem Shoreway US-6
- CLEV 44102 2623 E4
- CLEV 44102 2624 A4
- CLEV 44113 2624 A4
Cleveland Mem Shoreway US-20
- CLEV 44102 2623 E4
- CLEV 44102 2624 A4
- CLEV 44113 2624 A4
Cleveland Metro Park Dr
- GSML 44040 2500 B2
- MAYF 44040 2500 B2
- MAYF 44143 2500 B2
- NOSD 44070 2879 E1
Cleveland Oberlin Rd
700 NRsT 44074 3139 C2
700 OBLN 44074 3139 C2
Cleveland Oberlin Rd SR-511
700 NRsT 44074 3139 C2
700 OBLN 44074 3139 C2

INDEX 14
Cleviden Rd — Cleveland Street Index — Cortland Cir

Cleveland Street Index

STREET Block City ZIP Map# Grid

Cleviden Rd
15600 ECLE 44112 2497 C6
Cliff Cir
18800 FWPK 44126 2752 A1
Cliff Ct
5600 WLBY 44094 2375 A2
Cliff Dr
1100 CLEV 44102 2623 C4
5000 SDLK 44054 2616 D2
13400 LKWD 44107 2622 E3
23700 BYVL 44140 2620 E5
Cliffdale Av
1000 LKWD 44107 2622 C4
Clifford Av
13500 CLEV 44135 2752 D3
Clifford Dr
21500 FWPK 44126 2751 C3
22900 NOSD 44126 2751 A3
22900 NOSD 44070 2751 A3
23000 NOSD 44070 2750 E3
Clifford Rd
1100 CVHT 44121 2498 A6
1100 SELD 44121 2498 A6
Cliffside Coms
100 RKRV 44116 2621 C6
Cliffside Dr
6600 VMLN 44089 2741 B7
6800 BhmT 44089 2741 B7
17800 SGVL 44136 3011 E5
Cliffview Cir
- MCDN 44056 3153 E2
Cliffview Dr
1000 ETLK 44095 2250 B4
4100 INDE 44131 2884 C4
8400 MCDN 44056 3153 D2
Cliff View Ln
11300 CsTp 44026 2502 C2
Cliffview Rd
1600 CLEV 44112 2497 D2
1800 CLEV 44121 2497 D2
Cliffwood Ct E
8700 MNTR 44060 2144 C4
Cliffwood Ct W
8600 MNTR 44060 2144 C4
Clifton Av
2900 LORN 44055 2745 A4
3900 ShfT 44055 2745 A5
Clifton Blvd
- RKRV 44107 2621 D5
- RKRV 44116 2621 D5
9200 CLEV 44102 2623 C5
11700 LKWD 44102 2623 C5
11700 LKWD 44107 2623 C5
13400 LKWD 44107 2622 D4
18000 LKWD 44107 2621 D5
Clifton Blvd SR-2
9200 CLEV 44102 2623 C5
11700 LKWD 44102 2623 C5
11700 LKWD 44107 2623 C5
13400 LKWD 44107 2622 D4
Clifton Blvd US-6
- RKRV 44107 2621 D5
- RKRV 44116 2621 D5
9200 CLEV 44102 2623 C5
11700 LKWD 44102 2623 C5
11700 LKWD 44107 2623 C5
13400 LKWD 44107 2622 D4
18000 LKWD 44107 2621 D5
Clifton Blvd US-20
9200 CLEV 44102 2623 C5
11700 LKWD 44102 2623 C5
11700 LKWD 44107 2623 C5
13400 LKWD 44107 2622 D4
W Clifton Blvd
1100 LKWD 44107 2622 A5
W Clifton Blvd SR-2
1100 LKWD 44107 2622 A5
W Clifton Blvd SR-237
1100 LKWD 44107 2622 A5
W Clifton Blvd US-20
1100 LKWD 44107 2622 A5
Clifton Ct
1200 SgHT 44067 3017 B4
8100 MNTR 44060 2144 A4
N Clifton Dr
17800 LKWD 44107 2622 A4
Clifton Pl
1400 LKWD 44107 2622 A5
Clifton Rd
18000 LKWD 44107 2622 A4
W Clifton Rd
18100 LKWD 44107 2622 A4
Clifton Wy
- AVON 44011 2617 E7
2100 AVON 44011 2747 E1
Clifton Park Ln
17800 LKWD 44107 2621 E4
Clifton Prado
1200 LKWD 44107 2623 A4
Clinic Dr
- CLEV 44106 2626 B3
Clinton Av
- AVLK 44012 2617 B2
100 ELYR 44035 2874 D4
900 SELD 44121 2498 B5
2800 CLEV 44113 2624 B5
2800 LORN 44055 2745 E3
4500 CLEV 44102 2624 B5
5100 ShfT 44055 2745 E5
W Clinton Av
5800 CLEV 44102 2624 A5
6500 CLEV 44102 2623 E5
Clinton Cir
19000 SGVL 44136 3147 C5
Clinton Dr
27300 NOSD 44070 2878 E2
30800 BYVL 44140 2619 B5
Clinton Ln
500 HDHT 44143 2499 B3
Clinton Rd
7300 BKLN 44144 2753 D2
7300 CLEV 44144 2753 D2
10000 CLEV 44102 2753 D2
Clipper Cove
10300 RMDV 44202 3020 E5
Clipper Cove Dr
13500 SGVL 44136 3147 D4
Clocktower Dr
- KTLD 44060 2251 E5
- MNTR 44060 2251 E5
7700 KTLD 44094 2251 D5
N Clocktower Dr
- KTLD 44060 2251 D5
- KTLD 44094 2251 D5
- MNTR 44060 2251 D5

S Clocktower Dr
- KTLD 44094 2251 D6
Clopton Ct
9300 MNTR 44060 2145 A1
Cloud Av
4100 CLEV 44113 2624 B7
Clovelly Dr
5300 LORN 44053 2743 C3
Clover Av
1700 CLEV 44109 2754 D1
7400 MNTR 44060 2251 C2
Clover Cir
5600 WLBY 44094 2375 A1
Clover Ln
- SFLD 44035 2746 E6
- SFLD 44035 2747 A6
8300 RslT 44073 2762 A3
Cloverberry Ct
1200 BWHT 44147 3149 E4
Cloverdale Av
11900 CLEV 44111 2623 A7
Cloverdale Dr
15400 MDFD 44062 2767 B3
15400 MdfT 44062 2767 B3
Cloveridge Rd
8000 RslT 44073 2761 E3
8000 RslT 44073 2762 A3
Clover Lake Dr
13500 NbyT 44065 2634 C5
Cloverleaf Pkwy
5400 VLVW 44125 2885 A1
Cloverleigh Dr
1000 MadT 44057 1843 E6
Cloverly Dr
6200 SLN 44139 2889 C5
Cloverside Av
15500 CLEV 44128 2757 B3
Club Ct
6000 MNTR 44060 2144 D3
30400 WKLF 44092 2374 E2
Club Dr
- AURA 44202 3021 E5
- SELD 44121 2628 C1
10 HDHT 44143 2499 C2
Club Ln
10 AbnT 44023 2892 A4
Club Rd
- TroT 44234 2894 B6
Clubhouse
400 RDHT 44143 2498 C3
Club House Dr
11600 NRYN 44133 3013 A5
Clubside Cir
1000 WTLK 44145 2621 A6
Clubside Ct
100 CRDN 44024 2505 B2
Clubside Dr
10 AbnT 44023 2892 A4
25300 NOSD 44070 2750 A7
Clubside Rd
1500 LNHT 44124 2498 D7
1500 LNHT 44124 2628 D1
Clybourne Av
3800 CLEV 44109 2754 B4
Clyde Rd
1700 MadT 44057 1941 D1
Clyde Hill Rd
- HpfT 44041 2045 B4
- HpfT 44057 2045 B4
Clydesdale Tr
14600 RslT 44072 2762 C1
Coachman Ct
7700 BKVL 44141 3016 A3
Coachman Dr
13000 MsnT 44024 2634 C2
Coachman Ln
33000 SLN 44139 2888 E3
33000 SLN 44139 2889 A3
Coast Guard Rd
10 PnvT 44077 2039 B3
Coath Av
13100 CLEV 44120 2756 E2
13100 CLEV 44120 2757 A2
Cobalt Av
13900 CLEV 44110 2497 A2
Cobb Ct
- CLEV 44108 2496 B5
Cobble Ct
- GSML 44040 2630 D1
Cobblestone Ln
- BbgT 44023 2890 C7
7000 CcdT 44060 2145 B7
7000 CcdT 44077 2145 B7
E Cobblestone Ln
10400 TNBG 44087 3020 A3
W Cobblestone Ln
10300 TNBG 44087 3020 A3
Cobblestone Rd
400 AURA 44202 3157 A2
600 AhtT 44001 2873 C2
Cobblestone Wy
1300 WTLK 44145 2620 B7
Cobblestone Chase
1200 WTLK 44145 2620 B7
Cobden Ct
- ECLE 44112 2496 E7
Cobleigh Ct
5500 CLEV 44104 2625 D5
Cochran Av
18500 CLEV 44110 2372 E7
18800 CLEV 44110 2497 E1
Cochran Rd
10 AURA 44202 3156 B1
200 AURA 44202 3021 B7
6000 SLN 44139 2888 C4
6900 GNWL 44139 2888 C6
7000 GNWL 44139 3019 C1
Cockle Cove
- PnvT 44077 2145 B5
Cocoa Dr
7700 PRMA 44134 3014 C2
Code Av
37000 WLBY 44094 2250 C4
Coe Av
4100 NOSD 44070 2750 D5
14400 CLEV 44135 2752 D5
Coe St
100 BERA 44017 2880 C7
Coen Rd
4800 VmnT 44089 2740 B6
5800 VmnT 44089 2869 B1
Coes Post Run
1700 WTLK 44145 2619 E7
1700 WTLK 44145 2749 D1

Coffinberry Blvd
18900 FWPK 44126 2751 E2
Cohassett Av
1400 LKWD 44107 2623 A6
Cohassett Pl
1300 LKWD 44107 2623 A5
Coit Av
1200 ECLE 44110 2497 B4
1200 ECLE 44112 2497 B4
Coit Rd
- CLEV 44110 2496 E3
12100 BTNH 44108 2496 D2
12700 CLEV 44108 2496 E2
13300 CLEV 44110 2497 A3
Colahan Dr
18900 RKRV 44116 2621 E6
Colbourne Rd
23400 EUCL 44123 2373 C3
Colburn Av
2300 CLEV 44109 2754 C4
Colburn Rd
11100 CcdT 44024 2254 B5
11100 CcdT 44077 2254 B5
11100 CdnT 44024 2254 B5
Colby Ct
10 BHWD 44122 2628 E4
Colby Rd
20700 SRHT 44122 2628 A5
Colchester Dr
11500 AbnT 44021 2893 C4
Colchester Rd
- CVHT 44106 2627 A4
2600 CVHT 44118 2627 A4
Coldbrook Dr
5100 ManT 44255 3159 D4
Coldstream Rd
6100 HDHT 44143 2499 E1
Cold Water Tr
17300 BbgT 44023 2890 C4
Cole Dr
7300 MNTR 44060 2143 C4
Cole Plz
400 WLWK 44095 2249 C6
Colebright Dr
15100 SGVL 44136 3147 A2
Colebrook Dr
6200 PMHT 44130 2882 B3
Coleridge Rd
2700 CVHT 44118 2627 B4
6200 CcdT 44077 2145 D5
6200 PnvT 44077 2145 D5
Colesbrooke Dr
- BSHT 44236 3153 E7
Colfax Dr
9900 ClbT 44028 3010 D2
Colfax Rd
6800 CLEV 44104 2625 E5
7100 CLEV 44104 2626 A6
Colgate Av
200 ELYR 44035 3006 B1
6500 CLEV 44102 2624 A6
7000 CLEV 44102 2623 E6
Colgate Ct
6500 CLEV 44102 2624 A6
7000 CLEV 44102 2623 E6
Collamer Av
1600 ECLE 44110 2497 B4
1600 ECLE 44112 2497 B4
Colleen Ct
19900 SGVL 44136 3146 C4
Colleen Dr
6100 CcdT 44077 2146 B4
College Av
700 CLEV 44113 2625 A5
800 CLEV 44113 2624 E5
College Ct
- WLBY 44094 2142 E4
- WLBY 44094 2143 C5
College Pl
- OBLN 44074 3138 D2
College Rd
4400 SELD 44121 2628 C2
College St
100 WFAR 44491 2898 E5
4700 MNTU 44255 3159 C5
E College St
10 OBLN 44074 3138 E2
200 OBLN 44074 3139 A2
W College St
10 OBLN 44074 3138 C2
500 NRsT 44074 3138 C2
College Heights Blvd
5200 SFLD 44054 2746 E4
College Park Dr
100 ELYR 44035 2746 D7
10000 CcdT 44060 2253 B3
Colletta Ln
3400 CLEV 44111 2752 B1
Collica Cove
800 AURA 44202 3021 A5
800 RMDV 44202 3021 A5
Collier Av
6400 CLEV 44105 2755 E3
Collier Dr
20200 SGVL 44136 3011 C7
Collingwood Dr
900 AMHT 44001 2743 E6
Collins Dr
2600 LORN 44053 2744 A2
Collins Rd
5900 MNTR 44060 2144 A3
Collver Rd
10 RKRV 44116 2621 D4
Colonel Dr
600 CLEV 44109 2754 E5
600 CLEV 44109 2755 A5
Colonial Av
9900 CLEV 44108 2496 B4
Colonial Blvd
100 ELYR 44035 3006 A3
5700 WLBY 44094 2375 A2
Colonial Ct
800 VmnT 44089 2740 C5
3900 RKRV 44116 2751 B2
10800 CLEV 44106 2626 C3
18800 AbnT 44023 3023 B2
19500 WNHL 44146 3018 A2
Colonial Dr
1600 CVHT 44118 2627 C1
6800 MNTR 44060 2143 E6
Colonial St
10 CLEV 44110 2372 C6
Colonial Heights Dr
17700 CLEV 44112 2497 D3

Colonnade Dr
6600 MadT 44057 1942 B4
Colonnade Rd
1800 CLEV 44112 2497 C4
Colony Ct
400 GNVA 44041 1944 A5
500 WLBY 44094 2250 A7
5900 LORN 44053 2743 C6
9400 MNTR 44060 2253 A2
15000 SGVL 44136 3147 B5
Colony Dr
10 ELYR 44035 2875 A7
800 AURA 44202 3021 B7
800 HDHT 44143 2499 A5
33200 AVLK 44012 2617 C1
Colony Ln
10 BTNH 44108 2496 D2
13400 BtnT 44021 2635 E7
13400 BtnT 44021 2765 E1
13600 BtnT 44021 2636 A7
13600 BURT 44021 2636 A7
Colony Pk
100 BNWK 44212 3147 D6
Colony Rd
3700 SELD 44118 2627 E3
3800 SELD 44118 2628 A3
4000 SELD 44121 2628 A3
Colony St
10 OBLN 44074 3138 C3
Colorado Av
100 LORN 44052 2614 E5
300 LORN 44052 2615 C7
3500 LORN 44054 2615 C7
3500 SFLD 44054 2615 C7
3600 SFLD 44054 2616 A7
5400 SFLD 44011 2617 A6
5400 SFLD 44054 2617 A6
37100 AVON 44011 2747 C1
38300 AVON 44011 2617 A6
Colorado Av SR-611
1400 LORN 44052 2615 C7
3500 LORN 44054 2615 C7
3500 SFLD 44054 2615 C7
3600 SFLD 44054 2616 A7
5400 SFLD 44011 2617 A6
5400 SFLD 44054 2617 A6
37100 AVON 44011 2747 C1
38300 AVON 44011 2617 A6
Colt Dr
7200 MNTR 44060 2253 A1
Coltman Rd
1800 CLEV 44106 2626 D1
Colton Rd
3400 SRHT 44122 2758 A1
Columbia Av
100 ELYR 44035 2875 B7
8900 CLEV 44108 2496 B5
Columbia Ct
25400 BYVL 44140 2620 C5
Columbia Dr
800 AMHT 44001 2743 E6
1000 AMHT 44001 2744 A6
5500 BDHT 44146 2887 C2
Columbia Rd
- RHFD 44286 3151 A6
10 LvpT 44028 3145 A6
10 LvpT 44280 3145 A6
300 BYVL 44140 2620 C7
300 LvpT 44280 3144 E7
600 WTLK 44145 2620 C7
1500 BosT 44141 3152 A7
1700 WTLK 44145 2750 C1
1900 BosT 44141 3151 D6
1900 RchT 44141 3151 D6
3200 NOSD 44070 2750 C4
3200 RchT 44286 3151 A6
3200 WTLK 44070 2750 C4
5300 NOSD 44070 2879 C3
5800 NOSD 44138 2879 C3
5800 OmsT 44138 2879 C3
5800 OmsT 44070 2879 C3
6700 ODFL 44138 2879 C3
8400 ODFL 44138 3010 B1
Columbia Rd SR-252
10 LvpT 44028 3145 A6
10 LvpT 44280 3145 A6
300 BYVL 44140 2620 C7
300 LvpT 44280 3144 E7
600 WTLK 44145 2620 C7
1700 WTLK 44145 2750 C1
3200 NOSD 44070 2750 C4
3200 WTLK 44070 2750 C4
5900 NOSD 44070 2879 C3
6200 OmsT 44070 2879 C3
6200 OmsT 44138 2879 C3
6700 ODFL 44138 2879 C3
8400 ODFL 44138 3010 B1
Columbia Sq
4100 NOSD 44070 2750 C5
Columbine Av
15000 CLEV 44111 2752 C1
Columbine Ct
- MDBH 44130 2881 B4
Columbo Ln
4300 LORN 44055 2746 B4
Columbus Rd
10 BDFD 44146 2887 A3
600 BDHT 44146 2887 C3
1600 CLEV 44113 2624 D5
26000 OKWD 44146 2887 D3
26300 BDHT 44146 2888 A3
26300 OKWD 44146 2888 A3
Columbus St
- VMLN 44089 2740 D5
10 BERA 44017 2880 C5
100 CNFL 44022 2761 A6
100 ELYR 44035 2875 B5
Colvin Rd
7600 GSML 44040 2500 E7
Colwyn Rd
3300 SRHT 44120 2627 B7
Comanche Ct
6000 PMHT 44130 2882 B2
Comanche Tr
700 MCDN 44056 3018 D5
7000 MNTR 44060 2143 B5
38700 WLBY 44094 2143 A5
Comet Ct
8200 MNTR 44060 2144 A3
Commerce Av
4000 CLEV 44103 2625 D2
Commerce Ct
300 ELYR 44035 2875 A6
16500 MDBH 44130 3012 B2
16500 SGVL 44130 3012 B2

Commerce Ct
16500 SGVL 44136 3012 B2
Commerce Dr
900 GFTN 44044 3141 E4
900 GFTN 44044 3142 B4
7100 MNTR 44060 2251 B3
Commerce Pk
23100 BHWD 44122 2758 C2
Commerce Pkwy
- MDBH 44130 2880 D4
4800 WVHT 44128 2758 E6
Commerce Pkwy W
5200 PRMA 44130 2753 B7
Commerce Pl
100 GNVA 44041 1944 C5
Commerce Park Dr
15400 BKPK 44142 2881 C1
Commerce Park Ovl
7600 INDE 44131 2885 A3
Commercial Rd
2600 CLEV 44113 2624 C2
Commodore Cir
- ELYR 44035 2746 D7
Commodore Rd
1500 LNHT 44124 2499 C4
1500 LNHT 44124 2629 A1
Commodore Cove
31700 AVLK 44012 2619 A2
Commodore Cove E
3800 RMDV 44202 3021 A5
Commodore Cove W
3700 RMDV 44202 3020 E5
Commons Blvd
8800 TNBG 44087 3154 E1
N Commons Blvd
300 MAYF 44143 2500 A1
Commons Ct
10 CNFL 44022 2761 B6
Commons Ovl
16200 SGVL 44136 3012 B3
Commonwealth Av
1100 MDHT 44124 2499 D7
Commonwealth Blvd
6600 PMHT 44130 2882 A5
Commonwealth Dr
2700 PRMA 44134 2883 C2
Community Dr
- HGVL 44022 2630 C5
- LNHT 44124 2628 D3
10 BKVL 44141 3016 A6
10 BKVL 44141 3151 A1
5100 WLBY 44094 2250 B7
24200 BHWD 44122 2628 D3
24200 LNHT 44122 2628 D3
Community Ln
10 ELYR 44035 3006 A3
Community Rd
700 SDLK 44054 2616 A4
Community College Av
2200 CLEV 44115 2625 B4
Co-Moor Blvd
11200 SGVL 44136 3011 D5
Compass St
4600 VmnT 44089 2740 C5
Compass Cove
31600 AVLK 44012 2619 A2
Compass Point Dr
13000 SGVL 44136 3147 D4
Compton Rd
1400 CVHT 44118 2497 D7
1400 CVHT 44118 2627 D1
S Compton Rd
1800 CVHT 44118 2627 D2
Compton St
2100 MadT 44057 1942 B2
Comstock Cir
18600 MDBH 44130 3011 E1
Comstock Rd
5400 BDHT 44146 2887 C1
Concept Dr
16600 CLEV 44128 2757 C4
Concert Ct
10 OmsT 44138 2879 A4
Concord Av
200 ELYR 44035 2875 D6
Concord Cir
500 BERA 44017 3011 B1
9400 TNBG 44087 3019 B6
Concord Ct
6100 SLN 44139 2889 C4
8700 BbgT 44023 2891 C5
10000 PMHT 44130 2882 C6
Concord Dr
- AVLK 44012 2618 A2
- PRMA 44134 2883 B4
300 LORN 44052 2615 D5
1100 WTLK 44145 2620 E7
2000 LKWD 44107 2622 B6
3500 BHWD 44122 2758 E2
4500 FWPK 44126 2751 C4
5100 VMLN 44089 2741 A7
8100 MNTR 44060 2144 A3
18300 SGVL 44136 3146 E1
18500 SGVL 44136 3011 E7
Concord Ln
100 HkyT 44233 3148 B6
Concord Rd
2800 PRPK 44124 2629 D6
Concord St
- WKLF 44092 2374 C2
Concord Tr
14100 MDBH 44130 3012 C2
Concord Downs Cir
400 AURA 44202 3156 D2
Concord Downs Ln
400 AURA 44202 3156 D2
Concord Downs Pth
400 AURA 44202 3156 D2
Concord-Hambden Rd
11200 CcdT 44077 2146 B7
11500 CcdT 44077 2254 E1
11900 CcdT 44077 2255 B3
12700 CcdT 44024 2255 B3
12700 CcdT 44077 2255 B3
12700 HmbT 44077 2255 B3
12700 HmbT 44024 2255 B3
12700 HmbT 44077 2255 B3
Concord-Hambden Rd SR-608
11500 CcdT 44077 2146 D7
11500 CcdT 44077 2254 E1
11900 CcdT 44077 2255 B3
12700 CcdT 44024 2255 B3
12700 CcdT 44077 2255 B3
12700 HmbT 44024 2255 B3

Concord-Hambden Rd SR-608
12700 HmbT 44077 2255 B3
Concordia Dr
20000 EUCL 44117 2498 A1
Concord Point Ct
9900 CcdT 44060 2253 C1
Condon Ct
300 PNVL 44077 2040 B7
Conelly Blvd
7100 WNHL 44146 2886 D7
7100 WNHL 44146 3017 E1
Conestoga Tr
8000 CcdT 44060 2253 C3
Conley Rd
6100 CcdT 44077 2146 E4
6100 CcdT 44077 2147 A4
8900 KTLD 44094 2251 D7
Connecticut Av
200 LORN 44052 2614 E6
7600 CLEV 44105 2756 A4
Connecticut Dr
200 CrlT 44035 3006 A3
200 ELYR 44035 3006 A3
Connecticut St
10500 RMDV 44202 3020 E3
Connecticut Wy
- SgHT 44067 3152 E1
Connecticut Colony Cir
6600 MNTR 44060 2144 D6
Connecticut Woods Dr
1200 HDSN 44236 3154 C7
Connie Ct
300 ETLK 44095 2142 D7
Connie Dr
7000 MNTR 44060 2143 B7
7200 MNTR 44060 2251 B1
Connor Dr
900 ETLK 44095 2250 B3
Connotton Av
2900 TNBG 44087 3155 A1
Conover Ct
8100 MNTR 44060 2144 A4
8300 CLEV 44102 2623 D6
Conover Dr
25300 BYVL 44140 2620 C5
Conover Rd
4000 UNHT 44118 2628 A4
Constance Av
- HRM 44234 3161 B1
Constance Ct
7100 CLEV 44103 2495 E5
Constantine Ct
7000 MNTR 44060 2143 A7
Construction Wy
- BNHT 44131 2884 B1
Consul Av
6600 CLEV 44127 2755 E1
Conte Dr
5400 GDHT 44125 2885 C1
Continental Av
11100 CLEV 44104 2626 D6
11600 CLEV 44120 2626 D6
Continental Dr
400 SgHT 44067 3017 C4
Cook Av
1100 LKWD 44107 2622 D4
1200 CLEV 44109 2754 D6
18000 SGVL 44136 3146 E1
Cook Ct
100 ELYR 44035 2875 E6
Cook Ln
- CLEV 44106 2626 C1
Cook Rd
25500 ODFL 44138 2879 A5
26100 OmsT 44138 2879 A5
26900 OmsT 44138 2878 D4
31600 NRDV 44039 2877 E4
31600 NRDV 44039 2878 B4
31600 NRDV 44138 2878 B4
Cook St
13800 BURT 44021 2636 B7
Cooley Av
11700 CLEV 44111 2753 A2
13300 CLEV 44111 2752 E2
Cooley Ct
28100 WTLK 44145 2749 D1
Cooley Rd
33500 EatT 44028 3008 E5
35000 EatT 44044 3008 A5
35800 EatT 44044 3007 E5
Cooley Farms Rd
4000 HIHL 44122 2758 D3
Coolidge Ct
7600 MNTR 44060 2143 D6
Coolidge Dr
- ODFL 44138 2879 C6
27500 EUCL 44132 2374 A4
Cooper Av
4000 CLEV 44103 2625 C1
11100 CrlT 44035 3005 C5
Cooper Ct
13600 GDHT 44125 2757 A5
Cooper Ln
8400 MNTR 44060 2144 B3
Cooper Foster Park Rd
- ELYR 44035 2746 A6
- ShfT 44035 2746 A6
300 LORN 44053 2744 A6
1300 AMHT 44001 2744 A6
1300 AMHT 44053 2744 A6
1800 VMLN 44001 2871 B2
2600 VMLN 44089 2871 A2
3000 VMLN 44089 2870 D2
3700 AMHT 44001 2743 E6
3700 AMHT 44053 2743 E6
3700 LORN 44053 2743 E6
Cooper Foster Park Rd E
300 EyrT 44035 2745 A6
300 EyrT 44052 2745 A6
300 EyrT 44055 2745 A6
300 EyrT 44053 2745 A6
300 LORN 44052 2745 A6
300 LORN 44053 2745 A6
300 ShfT 44052 2745 A6
Cooper Foster Park Rd W
200 LORN 44053 2744 D6
200 LORN 44052 2745 A6
200 LORN 44053 2745 A6
200 ShfT 44053 2745 A6
900 AhtT 44001 2744 D6
900 AhtT 44053 2744 D6
1200 AMHT 44001 2743 A7

Cooper Foster Park Rd W
1300 AMHT 44053 2743 A7
1300 LORN 44053 2743 A7
1300 LORN 44001 2743 A7
1900 AMHT 44001 2871 D1
1900 AMHT 44053 2871 D1
1900 LORN 44053 2871 D1
2000 BhmT 44053 2871 D1
2000 BhmT 44001 2871 D1
Coopers Run
11700 SGVL 44136 3011 A6
Cooper Turn
23800 ODFL 44138 3010 D2
Cope Dr
7600 BbgT 44023 2890 C6
Copley Av
6500 SLN 44139 2889 A6
Copopa Tr
24800 ClbT 44028 3010 A5
Copperfield Ct
200 PnvT 44077 2040 E6
Coral Av
- CLEV 44127 2756 A1
Coral Pl
- CVHT 44118 2497 D7
Coral Gables Dr
3800 PRMA 44134 3014 B2
Corbetts Ln
10200 TNBG 44087 3019 E5
Corbin Dr
23500 BDHT 44128 2758 C7
Corbus Rd
11200 CLEV 44108 2496 D3
Corby Rd
13500 CLEV 44120 2627 A6
Cordova Av
1400 LKWD 44107 2622 B5
Cordova Rd
1100 MDHT 44124 2500 A6
Corduroy Rd
4600 MNTR 44060 2038 E5
Corinth Ct
12200 SGVL 44136 3011 D6
Cork Cold Springs Rd
5500 HpfT 44041 2045 D7
6600 HpfT 44041 2151 B1
6600 HpfT 44057 2151 B1
Corkhill Rd
500 BDFD 44146 2886 B4
600 MPHT 44137 2886 B4
Corktree Dr
10 OmsT 44138 2879 B4
Corkwood Dr
4900 NRYN 44133 3014 B4
Corlett Av
11400 CLEV 44105 2756 D2
Corliss Rd
4800 LNHT 44124 2498 D5
Cormere Av
13500 CLEV 44120 2627 A5
Cornado Av
12500 CLEV 44108 2496 E4
Cornelia Av
1700 CLEV 44103 2496 A7
Cornelia Dr
10 AQLA 44024 2505 C4
Cornell Av
100 ELYR 44035 2875 B7
200 AMHT 44001 2872 D1
5200 NRDV 44039 2748 C7
5400 NRDV 44039 2877 C2
Cornell Ct
900 PNVL 44077 2145 E3
Cornell Ln
7000 MNTR 44060 2251 B2
Cornell Pl
500 LORN 44052 2614 D6
Cornell Rd
2000 CLEV 44106 2626 D2
Cornerstone
2400 WTLK 44145 2750 D2
Corning Av
1700 CLEV 44109 2754 D1
Corning Dr
200 BTNH 44108 2496 C3
Cornwall Av
5300 LNHT 44124 2629 A2
Cornwall Ct
8500 MNTR 44060 2144 B2
Cornwall Rd
200 RKRV 44116 2621 D5
18000 CLEV 44119 2372 E4
Cornwell Dr
23700 WTLK 44145 2750 E1
Corona Dr
- NOSD 44070 2749 C7
Coronada Dr
- MONT 44060 2037 E7
- MONT 44060 2143 D1
5400 MNTR 44060 2144 A1
5400 MONT 44060 2144 A1
Coronado Ct
100 ELYR 44035 2875 C3
Coronet Dr
20700 SGVL 44136 3011 B6
Corporate Blvd
7300 MNTR 44060 2143 D7
7300 MNTR 44060 2251 D1
Corporate Cir
- WTLK 44145 2749 C1
8000 NRYN 44133 3013 C2
Corporate Pl
100 CRDN 44024 2379 D5
Corporate Wy
800 WTLK 44145 2620 D6
Corporate Center Dr W
10 BWHT 44147 3150 A3
Corporate Park Dr
- MCDN 44056 3154 A3
Corral Cir
8300 RslT 44072 2762 A1
Corralberry Ln
700 MDSN 44057 1942 A7
Corridon Av
14100 MPHT 44137 2886 A1
Corrigan Rd
7300 HgvT 44099 2259 B6
Corsica Av
15600 CLEV 44110 2372 C6
Cortina Cir
39300 SLN 44139 2889 E5
Cortland Cir
10 AMHT 44001 2872 B1
10 GNVA 44041 1944 C7

INDEX 15
Cortland Ln — Cleveland Street Index — Danbury Av

STREET Block City ZIP Map# Grid

Cortland Ln
1600 BWHT 44147 3149 D5
Cortland Wy
14700 SGVL 44136 3146 C1
Corwin Dr
10 PNVL 44077 2145 D3
Corwin Rd
4000 SELD 44121 2628 A1
Cory Av
7900 CLEV 44103 2626 A1
Cory Ln
11000 NbyT 44065 2764 A3
Corydon Rd
2700 CVHT 44118 2627 B3
Cotes Av
11300 CLEV 44105 2756 D4
Cotswold Ln
10 MDHL 44022 2760 B2
Cotswold Mnr
- WTLK 44145 2750 D1
Cottage Ct
10 PnvT 44077 2040 C2
Cottage Dr
30500 WTLK 44145 2749 B3
E Cottage St
10 CNFL 44022 2761 A5
W Cottage St
10 CNFL 44022 2760 E5
10 CNFL 44022 2761 B4
Cottage Tr
23600 ODFL 44138 2879 D7
Cottage Grove Dr
1900 CVHT 44118 2627 B3
Cottesmore Ln
7100 SLN 44139 3020 A1
Cottesmore Pl
33200 SLN 44139 3019 E1
33200 SLN 44139 3020 A1
Cottesworth Ln
1800 GSML 44040 2630 B2
Cottingham Dr
- LNHT 44124 2629 B3
Cottonwood Ct
300 AVLK 44012 2618 C3
800 ETLK 44095 2250 B3
9900 CcdT 44060 2253 B3
Cottonwood Dr
5600 LORN 44053 2744 E6
21600 RKRV 44116 2621 B7
21600 RKRV 44116 2751 B1
Cottonwood Ln
8800 PRMA 44130 2882 D7
12700 NRYN 44133 3147 E4
Cottonwood Ovl
15500 MDBH 44130 2881 C5
Cottonwood Tr
19500 SGVL 44136 3147 A5
27200 NOSD 44070 2749 E5
27200 NOSD 44070 2750 A5
Cottrell Rd
8500 CsTp 44026 2632 B1
Coudry St
9000 KTLD 44094 2251 D7
Coulby Ct
28800 WKLF 44092 2374 B4
Coulter Av
22300 EUCL 44117 2373 B7
Council Bluff Dr
10100 SGVL 44136 3012 B4
Country Ct
7800 MNTR 44060 2252 E3
Country Ln
10 PnvT 44077 2040 D7
10 PnvT 44077 2146 D1
10 PRPK 44124 2629 C5
4600 WVHT 44128 2758 E6
4600 WVHT 44128 2759 A5
7000 BbgT 44022 2890 B2
7000 BbgT 44023 2890 B2
Country Pl
100 EatT 44044 3142 B3
Country Wy
21600 SGVL 44136 3011 A6
Country Club Blvd
2600 RKRV 44116 2621 B7
24400 NOSD 44070 2750 C7
Country Club Cir
9800 TNBG 44087 3020 C5
Country Club Dr
2000 WKLF 44092 2374 E3
32100 AVLK 44012 2618 C5
Country Club Ln
2900 TNBG 44087 3020 B5
Country Meadow Ln
22200 SGVL 44136 3010 E4
Country Oaks Tr
12000 MsnT 44024 2634 E3
12000 MsnT 44024 2635 A3
Country River Ln
14000 NbyT 44065 2633 D6
14000 NbyT 44072 2633 D6
Country Scene Ln
9600 CcdT 44060 2145 B7
Countryside
- AVON 44011 2747 D1
Countryside Dr
10 BWHT 44147 3014 D5
10 SRSL 44073 2761 D5
8500 SgHT 44067 3017 D5
Countryside Rd
4800 LNHT 44124 2498 D7
4800 LNHT 44124 2628 E1
Countryview Dr
8400 BWHT 44147 3014 D5
Country View Ln
33700 SLN 44139 2760 A7
34300 MDHL 44022 2760 A7
34300 SLN 44022 2760 A7
Country View Pkwy
- NCtT 44236 3153 E5
Countryview Wy
11000 CrlT 44035 3005 C4
Countrywood Tr
- AURA 44202 3021 C7
600 AURA 44202 3156 C1
County Line Rd
- CsTp 44026 2501 A6
- GSML 44040 2501 A6
200 CsTp 44026 2501 A2
200 CsTp 44040 2501 A2
200 GSML 44040 2501 A2
800 HpfT 44041 2045 B4
800 HpfT 44057 2045 B4
800 MadT 44057 2045 B4
1000 GnvT 44041 1844 B6

County Line Rd
1000 GnvT 44057 1844 B6
1000 MadT 44057 1844 B6
1200 GnvT 44041 1943 B2
1200 GnvT 44057 1943 B2
1200 MadT 44057 1943 B2
1400 CsTp 44026 2631 A2
1400 GSML 44040 2631 A2
2900 HpfT 44057 1943 B6
2900 HpfT 44041 1943 B6
2900 HpfT 44057 1943 B6
13400 HGVL 44022 2631 B4
13400 HGVL 44073 2631 B4
13400 RsIT 44073 2631 B6
13500 RsIT 44073 2631 B6
14600 HGVL 44073 2761 A1
14600 RsIT 44073 2761 A1
14600 RsIT 44072 2761 A1
14900 HGVL 44073 2761 A1
14900 HGVL 44022 2761 A1
S County Line Rd
700 HpfT 44041 2045 B5
County Line Clark Rd
4500 FnTp 44062 2769 E7
4500 MsT 44062 2769 E7
County Line Turnpike Rd
4600 StnT 44491 3029 D5
Court St
- LORN 44055 2745 B3
100 CRDN 44024 2379 E6
100 CRDN 44024 2380 A6
100 ELYR 44035 2875 A6
Courtland Av
14300 CLEV 44111 2752 D3
14300 CLEV 44135 2752 D3
Courtland Blvd
100 ETLK 44095 2142 D6
2600 SRHT 44118 2627 E5
2700 SRHT 44122 2627 E5
Courtland Ct
5400 CLEV 44102 2624 A5
Courtland Dr
8600 SGVL 44136 3011 B3
38400 WLBY 44094 2250 D1
38400 WLBY 44094 2251 A1
Courtland Mdws
26900 WTLK 44145 2750 A4
Courtland Ovl
2600 SRHT 44118 2627 E5
3700 BNWK 44212 3147 A7
Courtland Rd
3400 PRPK 44124 2759 B1
Courtland St
10 ELYR 44035 2874 D4
200 FTHR 44077 2039 C4
200 PNVL 44077 2040 A7
Coutant Av
1400 LKWD 44107 2623 B6
Cove Av
100 AVLK 44012 2618 E2
1000 LKWD 44107 2623 A4
Cove Ct
10 AbnT 44023 2892 B5
800 ETLK 44095 2250 C3
Cove Dr
9500 NRYN 44133 3013 B5
Cove Beach Av
100 SDLK 44054 2616 E3
Coveland Dr
10 AVLK 44012 2488 C7
Coventry Ct
10 OmsT 44138 2879 B3
32700 AVLK 44012 2618 A2
Coventry Dr
10 PnvT 44077 2145 D4
2000 PRMA 44134 2883 C7
9000 NHFD 44067 3018 B4
29300 WTLK 44145 2749 C3
Coventry Ln
300 WLBY 44094 2250 A7
Coventry Pl
- AMHT 44001 2872 D3
Coventry Rd
- CVHT 44106 2627 A5
- SRHT 44106 2627 A5
1500 CVHT 44106 2627 A3
1500 ECLE 44112 2497 A7
1500 ECLE 44118 2497 A7
1500 ECLE 44106 2627 A3
1500 ECLE 44112 2627 A3
1500 ECLE 44118 2627 A3
1600 CVHT 44118 2627 A3
2500 SRHT 44120 2627 A5
2500 SRHT 44118 2627 A5
Coverley Rd
800 WTLK 44145 2621 A6
Covert Av
7100 CLEV 44105 2755 E3
Covewood Ct
9900 BKVL 44141 3151 C3
Covington Av
8100 PRMA 44129 2882 D4
Covington Ln
500 AbnT 44023 2892 B3
10300 TNBG 44087 3020 C4
Covington Rd
3700 SELD 44121 2497 E5
3800 SELD 44121 2498 A5
Cowan Av
5100 CLEV 44127 2625 D7
Cowles Av
10 BDFD 44146 2887 A4
Cowles Dr
29100 BYVL 44140 2619 D4
Cowley Rd
15200 GftT 44028 3143 D7
Cox Dr
- GNVA 44041 1944 B5
Cox Rd
7800 WndT 44099 2509 C7
7800 WndT 44099 2639 C2
Coy Ln
500 CNFL 44022 2761 A4
500 CNFL 44073 2761 A4
500 RsIT 44073 2761 A4
Crabapple Ct
10900 SGVL 44136 3012 D5
Crabapple Ln
10 OmsT 44138 2879 B4
Crabtree Ln
3100 HGVL 44022 2630 B7
6400 BKVL 44141 3016 A5
31400 SLN 44139 2759 D7

Crackle Rd
500 AURA 44023 3022 B3
500 AURA 44202 3022 B3
500 BbgT 44023 3022 B3
800 AbnT 44023 3023 A4
800 ManT 44023 3023 A4
800 ManT 44202 3023 A4
900 AbnT 44202 3023 A4
900 AbnT 44023 3023 A4
Crafton Rd
3000 BHWD 44122 2628 E6
Craig Dr
11300 SGVL 44136 3011 B5
E Craig Dr
8500 BbgT 44023 2891 B1
W Craig Dr
8300 BbgT 44023 2891 A1
Craig Ln
- AhtT 44001 2872 E6
8100 BWHT 44147 3015 C4
Craigleigh Dr
7500 NRYN 44133 3013 D2
7500 NRYN 44129 3013 D2
7500 PRMA 44129 3013 D2
Craigmere Dr
7200 MDBH 44130 2881 A7
16200 MDBH 44130 3012 A1
Crampton Dr
12000 NbyT 44021 2764 E4
Cranage Rd
26100 ODFL 44138 2879 A5
26800 OmsT 44138 2879 A5
Cranberry Dr
- LORN 44053 2743 E6
Cranberry Ln
7700 MNTR 44060 2143 D6
Cranberry Rdg
8700 BWHT 44147 3015 D6
Cranberry Tr
- AURA 44202 3021 D6
100 SgHT 44067 3152 D1
Cranberry Ridge Ln
18200 BbgT 44023 2890 E7
Cranbrook Cir
7700 MDBH 44130 3012 D2
Cranbrook Dr
800 HDHT 44143 2499 C6
6800 BKVL 44141 3151 A1
8900 NHFD 44067 3018 B5
Cranby Rd
3400 BHWD 44122 2758 B1
Crane Av
8800 CLEV 44105 2756 B1
Crane Dr
- LvpT 44280 3145 D7
Crane Centre Dr
3600 STBR 44241 3156 E6
3600 STBR 44241 3157 A6
Crane Creek Pkwy
2500 BKVL 44141 3150 D2
Craneing Rd
1300 WKLF 44092 2374 A3
Cranfield Rd
22900 BDHT 44146 2887 C1
Cranford Av
1100 LKWD 44107 2622 C4
Cranleigh Ct
400 RDHT 44143 2499 A3
Cranlyn Ct
400 BNWK 44212 3146 E7
Cranlyn Rd
2600 SRHT 44118 2628 C6
2600 SRHT 44122 2628 C6
Cranover Rd
1300 LNHT 44124 2498 E7
Cranston Cir
500 BERA 44017 3010 E1
Cranston Ct
7500 NRYN 44133 3013 D7
Cranston Dr
300 BERA 44017 2879 E7
300 BERA 44017 3010 E1
Cranston Rd
2100 UNHT 44118 2627 E3
Cranwood Av
14000 CLEV 44128 2757 A4
14000 GDHT 44105 2757 A4
Cranwood Dr
8300 CsTp 44026 2502 A2
13100 GDHT 44105 2756 E4
13600 GDHT 44105 2757 A4
Cranwood Pkwy
4300 WVHT 44128 2757 E4
Cranwood Park Blvd
13100 GDHT 44125 2756 E5
13700 GDHT 44125 2757 A5
Crary Ln
10400 KTLD 44094 2377 C6
Craven Av
11600 CLEV 44105 2756 D2
Crawford Ct
700 CLEV 44113 2624 E5
8900 CLEV 44106 2626 B1
Crawford Rd
1700 CLEV 44103 2626 A2
1700 CLEV 44106 2626 A2
Crayton Av
4500 CLEV 44104 2625 C5
4500 CLEV 44115 2625 C5
Creawood Dr
7900 CcdT 44077 2254 A3
Creek Cir
- NCtT 44236 3153 E6
Creek Ln
1000 RKRV 44116 2621 B6
W Creek Rd
- INDE 44131 2884 D1
Creek Bend Ct
22400 SGVL 44136 3011 A4
Creekfield Ct
100 ELYR 44035 2875 A1
Creekhaven Dr
6100 PMHT 44130 2882 B3
Creek Moss Ln
10700 SGVL 44136 3011 A4
Creek Run Dr
5500 NRYN 44133 3014 A6
Creekside Dr
300 AVLK 44012 2618 D3
600 AURA 44202 3156 C3
2900 WTLK 44145 2750 A3
6700 MadT 44057 1942 B2
8500 SgHT 44067 3018 A5
17600 AbnT 44023 2892 A5
21100 SGVL 44136 3011 B4

Creekside Dr
31400 PRPK 44124 2629 E7
31400 PRPK 44124 2630 A7
31400 PRPK 44124 2759 D1
Creekside Ln
5600 NRDV 44039 2877 E2
Creekside Ter
8100 BWHT 44147 3015 B4
Creekside Tr
10 OmsT 44138 2879 B4
6300 SLN 44139 2889 C5
Creek Stone Cir
10700 SGVL 44136 3011 A4
Creekview Cir
10 MDHL 44022 2760 A2
Creek View Dr
- AURA 44202 3022 D4
Creekview Dr
600 ETLK 44095 2250 D1
1000 CLEV 44119 2372 D6
4000 MDSN 44057 1941 E6
Creekview Ln
3000 AVON 44011 2747 E3
Creekwood Dr
7400 NRYN 44133 3013 D7
8900 BWHT 44147 3015 A6
9000 MNTR 44060 2252 D1
Creekwood Ln
1100 WTLK 44145 2619 E6
6800 MAYF 44143 2500 B3
15600 SGVL 44136 3147 B2
Crehore Ct
10 ELYR 44035 2875 A6
Crehore St
1400 LORN 44052 2615 B6
Creighton Dr
17000 AbnT 44023 2892 E3
Crennell Av
12300 CLEV 44105 2756 E3
13600 CLEV 44105 2757 A3
Crenshaw Dr
6600 PMHT 44130 2882 B5
Crescent Av
4500 CLEV 44102 2624 B4
Crescent Blvd
9100 BWHT 44147 3014 E7
Crescent Dr
300 BERA 44017 2880 A7
500 WLWK 44095 2249 D6
1100 PNVL 44077 2145 D3
2100 EUCL 44117 2498 A2
Crescent Rd
11000 CLEV 44111 2753 B2
Cress Rd
3700 CLEV 44111 2753 B2
Cressmont Av
5000 SLN 44139 2759 D7
Cresswell Av
10 BDFD 44146 2886 D2
Crest Av
12300 GDHT 44125 2756 D6
Crest Dr
200 AhtT 44001 2872 A3
4000 CLEV 44109 2754 E3
Crest Ln
17700 LKWD 44107 2622 A5
Crest Rd
1400 CVHT 44118 2497 E7
1400 CVHT 44121 2497 E7
1400 CVHT 44118 2627 E1
1400 CVHT 44121 2627 E1
Cresthaven Dr
28300 WLWK 44095 2249 B6
Cresthill Dr
7800 SVHL 44131 2884 B7
7800 SVHL 44131 3015 B1
Crestland Rd
17400 CLEV 44119 2372 D4
Crestlane Dr
42600 EyrT 44035 2874 B2
Crestline Av
800 AMHT 44001 2872 B1
1300 CLEV 44109 2754 E4
Crestline Dr
9100 MCDN 44056 3019 A7
Creston Av
1700 CLEV 44109 2754 D4
Crest Pointe
9800 HmbT 44024 2381 E3
Crestridge Dr
10000 CdnT 44024 2379 E4
21800 BKPK 44142 2880 B3
Crestview Dr
100 ELYR 44035 2875 C2
500 BYVL 44140 2619 B5
2500 HkyT 44233 3147 E6
6900 BKVL 44141 3151 A1
14300 RsIT 44072 2632 B7
Crestway Dr
13300 BKPK 44142 2881 E2
Crestway Ovl
200 BNWK 44212 3147 A7
Crestwood Av
4800 WLBY 44094 2250 E7
10300 CLEV 44104 2626 C5
Crestwood Dr
10 PnvT 44077 2041 B5
100 AVLK 44012 2617 E2
2500 PryT 44077 2041 B5
4600 INDE 44131 2884 C7
4600 INDE 44131 3015 C1
9700 TNBG 44087 3019 C4
10700 KTLD 44094 2376 E7
11800 NbyT 44065 2764 E1
14900 MdfT 44062 2767 B2
Crestwood Ln
6500 OmsT 44138 2878 E3
7500 NCtT 44067 3153 A2
7600 NCtT 44067 3152 E2
Crestwood Rd
1500 MDHT 44124 2499 D3
1500 MDHT 44124 2629 D1
9100 PMHT 44130 2882 C4
Crete Av
3700 CLEV 44105 2755 C2
Cricket Ln
2800 WBHL 44092 2374 C6
4200 WVHT 44128 2758 A4
8200 SgHT 44067 3017 E6
21900 SGVL 44136 3011 A3
Crickett Ln
7400 SVHL 44131 2884 B7
7400 SVHL 44131 3015 B1
16600 BKPK 44142 2881 B2

Crickett Rd
400 CRDN 44024 2380 B7
Crile Rd
7600 CcdT 44077 2254 B2
Crimson Ct
7600 MNTR 44060 2252 E2
Crimson Dr
2400 WTLK 44145 2749 C2
Crinkleroot Clearing
8300 BKVL 44141 3016 D5
Crispus Attucks Pl
- HIHL 44122 2758 C4
Crocker Blvd
400 CRDN 44024 2380 B7
Crocker Rd
- NOSD 44070 2749 C1
- NOSD 44145 2749 C1
- NOSD 44070 2878 C1
- WTLK 44070 2749 C1
600 WTLK 44145 2619 C5
1800 WTLK 44145 2749 C1
27000 ClbT 44028 3144 B5
27000 ClbT 44280 3144 B5
30000 ClbT 44028 3143 E5
30000 ClbT 44280 3143 E5
30000 EatT 44028 3143 E5
30000 GftT 44028 3143 D5
Crocker St
10 BERA 44017 2880 B7
200 AMHT 44001 2872 C2
Crofoot Av
8100 CLEV 44105 2756 A1
Crofton Av
5000 SLN 44139 2759 D7
5100 SLN 44139 2888 D1
Crofton Rd
11600 GDHT 44125 2885 D2
Cromwell Av
100 WLBY 44094 2250 A7
11600 CLEV 44120 2626 D5
21300 FWPK 44126 2751 B4
Cromwell Dr
100 GNVA 44041 1944 A4
2800 LORN 44052 2615 C7
7300 SLN 44139 3019 E2
33100 SLN 44139 3020 A1
Crook St
1000 GFTN 44044 3142 A6
1000 GftT 44044 3142 A6
38000 GftT 44044 3141 E6
38200 LrgT 44044 3141 E6
Crooked Stick Dr
7800 CcdT 44077 2253 E4
Crosby St
10 BERA 44017 2880 B7
Cross Av
- ClbT 44028 3010 D3
Cross St
- BDFD 44146 2887 A6
- ELYR 44035 2875 B6
200 BERA 44017 2880 A5
7400 MNTR 44060 2252 D1
9000 TNBG 44087 3155 A1
34300 NRDV 44039 2877 C1
N Cross Tr
19500 SGVL 44136 3147 C5
S Cross Tr
19700 SGVL 44136 3147 C5
Crossbeam Ln
21800 RKRV 44116 2751 B2
Crossbow Ct
6600 NRYN 44133 3014 A5
Crossbrook Av
38300 WLBY 44094 2142 E5
38400 WLBY 44094 2143 A5
Crossbrook Dr
300 BERA 44017 2879 E7
300 ODFL 44138 2879 E7
400 BERA 44017 3010 E1
Crossburn Av
12400 CLEV 44135 2753 A6
13000 CLEV 44135 2752 E6
Cross Creek Dr
7000 CcdT 44060 2145 B3
Cross Creek Ln
700 AURA 44202 3156 B3
14500 NRYN 44133 3148 E1
Cross Creek Ovl
700 AURA 44202 3156 C3
19500 SGVL 44136 3147 B5
Cross Creek Pkwy
14800 NbyT 44065 2763 D2
Cross Creek Tr
6500 BKVL 44141 3150 E3
W Cross Creek Tr
7000 BKVL 44141 3150 D3
Crosse Av
600 AMHT 44001 2872 E2
Crosse Rd
- AMHT 44001 2871 E1
100 AhtT 44001 2872 A2
100 AMHT 44001 2872 A2
Crossfield Av
7300 MNTR 44060 2251 C4
Crossing Dr
10500 RMDV 44202 3020 D4
Crossings Pkwy
1300 WTLK 44145 2619 B7
Crossings Wy
- AVLK 44012 2617 D3
Crossline Dr
7600 PRMA 44134 3014 A1
Crossover Rd
- RDHT 44143 2498 E1
Crosstie Tr
25100 ClbT 44028 3010 D4
Crossview Rd
5900 SVHL 44131 2884 B4
N Crossview Rd
5700 BNHT 44131 2884 B2
5700 SVHL 44131 2884 B2
Crosswinds Ln
7300 BKVL 44141 3151 A2
Crosswood Dr
26600 ODFL 44138 3010 A1
Croton Av
3400 CLEV 44115 2625 C4
Croton Dr
6100 NOSD 44070 2879 A2
Crow Dr
8400 MCDN 44056 3153 D1
8500 MCDN 44056 3018 D7
Crow Tr
900 MCDN 44056 3018 D6

Crowell Av
7500 CLEV 44104 2626 A5
N Crowell Av
100 GNVA 44041 1944 D3
S Crowell Av
100 GNVA 44041 1944 D4
Crown Av
1400 CLEV 44113 2624 E5
Crown Ct
5600 WLBY 44094 2375 C2
7400 MNTR 44060 2251 C1
Crown Colony Dr
- AVON 44011 2748 C6
Crownhill Av
100 AMHT 44001 2872 D2
Crown Point Dr
10 GNVA 44041 1944 C7
Crown Point Pkwy
14100 SGVL 44136 3147 C5
Crown Pointe
16400 BbgT 44023 2762 A7
Crows Hollow Dr
13000 MsnT 44024 2634 E2
Crows Nest Cove
9900 RMDV 44202 3020 E5
Croyden Av
- CLEV 44110 2372 C5
- CLEV 44119 2372 C5
Croyden Rd
10 CLEV 44110 2372 C6
1000 LNHT 44124 2499 B7
Croydon Rd
2200 TNBG 44087 3019 E5
Crudele Dr
8100 GDHT 44125 2756 A6
Crumb Av
7900 CLEV 44103 2496 A6
8400 CLEV 44108 2496 A6
Cryogenic Rd
- BKPK 44142 2880 A1
Crystal Av
20100 EUCL 44123 2373 A3
Crystal Ct
10 BNWK 44212 3147 A6
Crystal Ln
10 AURA 44202 3021 D7
Crystal Tr
9900 AbnT 44023 3023 A2
Crystal Creek Dr
6900 BKVL 44141 3016 D6
14000 SGVL 44136 3011 C7
14000 SGVL 44136 3146 C1
Crystal Creek Rd
8100 SgHT 44067 3017 D6
Crystal Lakes Dr
18200 NRYN 44133 3148 B4
Crystal Springs Dr
10200 NRYN 44133 3148 B4
Crystalwood Dr
2500 BWHT 44147 3014 C5
Cudell Av
9800 CLEV 44102 2623 C6
Cullen Dr
3800 CLEV 44105 2755 C2
Culver Blvd
7000 MNTR 44060 2143 B7
Cumberland Av
10 CLEV 44110 2372 C5
8900 CLEV 44104 2626 B5
Cumberland Ct
100 ELYR 44035 3006 D2
6100 MNTR 44060 2144 A3
9400 CLEV 44104 2626 B5
Cumberland Dr
5500 GDHT 44125 2885 D1
6200 MNTR 44060 2144 A4
Cumberland Rd
1600 CVHT 44118 2627 C1
Cumberworth Dr
- SGVL 44136 3012 C3
Cumings Blvd
1300 MadT 44057 1843 C6
Cumings Rd
100 PNVL 44077 2146 C2
Cummings
- SLN 44139 2889 C5
Cummings Av
10 GNVA 44041 1944 C4
Cummings Rd
- VMLN 44089 2741 D4
3400 CVHT 44118 2627 D2
Cunningham Rd
7500 GnvT 44057 1943 A1
7500 MadT 44057 1942 E1
7500 MadT 44057 1943 A1
Cunningham St
- SLN 44139 3021 A2
Curberry Dr
7700 MNTR 44060 2253 A3
Curran Av
10100 CLEV 44102 2753 C2
10100 CLEV 44111 2753 C2
Currier Dr
16300 SGVL 44136 3147 A5
Curry Cir
7200 HDSN 44236 3154 A7
Curry Dr
1500 LNHT 44124 2629 A1
Curry Ln
17000 AbnT 44023 2892 E3
Curtis Blvd
32900 ETLK 44095 2249 E6
32900 WLWK 44095 2249 E6
33600 ETLK 44095 2250 A5
Curtis Dr
100 AVLK 44012 2617 D2
23700 NOSD 44070 2750 D5
Curtis Middlefield Rd
5900 FnTp 44491 2898 B7
6800 FnTp 44062 2898 B1
Curtiss Ct
5700 CLEV 44103 2625 D2
6400 MNTR 44060 2144 A4
Curtiss Wright Pkwy
- RDHT 44143 2498 E1
26000 RDHT 44143 2499 A1
26300 HDHT 44143 2499 A1
26500 HDHT 44092 2374 A7
26500 HDHT 44143 2374 A7
26500 WBHL 44092 2374 A7
Cushing Ln
- BTNH 44108 2496 B4
4400 RDHT 44143 2498 C3
Cutts Rd
9700 HmbT 44024 2380 D4

Cutty Sark Dr
9800 CdnT 44024 2378 B6
Cuyahoga Tr
13500 RsIT 44072 2632 D4
Cyclone Dr
19300 CLEV 44135 2751 E5
Cygnet Ct
14000 NRYN 44133 3149 A1
Cynthia Ct
500 RDHT 44143 2498 E4
Cynthia Dr
- BKPK 44142 2881 A2
300 CRDN 44024 2380 B7
9900 TNBG 44087 3019 E4
Cypress Av
2800 CLEV 44109 2754 C5
16000 SGVL 44136 3147 A3
Cypress Blvd
10 MadT 44057 1941 B6
Cypress Cir
3400 WTLK 44145 2749 E4
8900 NRYN 44133 3013 A3
9800 CcdT 44060 2253 B3
Cypress Point Dr
2300 HDSN 44236 3155 B7
Cyprus Dr
6400 NOSD 44070 2878 D3
Cyprus Ln
9500 ODFL 44138 3010 A1
Cyrano Ct
4100 CLEV 44113 2624 B5
Cyril Av
4100 CLEV 44109 2624 B7
Cyrus Ln
8100 SgHT 44067 3017 D5
Czar Av
4500 CLEV 44127 2625 C7

D

D St
1300 LORN 44052 2615 A5
Dade Ln
500 RDHT 44143 2498 C4
Dahlia Dr
1300 MONT 44060 2143 C3
Daisy Av
200 BERA 44017 2880 C6
2500 CLEV 44109 2754 C1
6600 INDE 44131 2884 D4
6800 BKVL 44141 3016 A7
Daisy Blvd
6000 INDE 44131 2884 D4
Daisy Ct
9500 MNTR 44060 2145 A5
Daisy Ln
10 BbgT 44023 2761 D6
10 BbgT 44073 2761 D6
10 PRPK 44124 2759 E1
10 SRSL 44073 2761 D6
5700 WLBY 44094 2375 A2
Daisy St
400 BDFD 44146 2886 D3
Daisy's Wood Ln
7300 GSML 44040 2630 C2
Dakota Av
700 LORN 44052 2615 D5
4800 CLEV 44127 2625 C7
Dakota Rd
5200 RchT 44286 3150 B6
Dakota Run
32100 AVLK 44012 2618 C2
Dale Av
2400 RKRV 44116 2621 C7
3800 LORN 44055 2745 C4
10200 CLEV 44111 2753 C2
Dale Rd
15200 RsIT 44073 2761 E3
Dalebrook Av
13300 BKPK 44130 2881 D2
13300 BKPK 44142 2881 D2
Dale Brook Cir
2300 HkyT 44233 3148 A6
Dalebrook Rd
7400 INDE 44131 3016 A2
Daleford Dr
7700 MNTR 44060 2143 D6
Daleford Rd
3200 SRHT 44120 2627 C7
3400 SRHT 44120 2757 D1
Dalepark Dr
200 BDFD 44146 2887 A5
Dalepoint Rd
8100 INDE 44131 3016 B2
Dales Ct
3200 NRYN 44133 3014 C3
Daleside Dr
5200 PRMA 44134 2754 B7
Daleview Dr
- AURA 44202 3156 C1
17300 LKWD 44107 2622 B6
Dalewood Av
5400 MPHT 44137 2886 C1
Dalewood Ct
- MDBH 44130 2880 E5
Dalewood Rd
900 LNHT 44124 2498 E6
Dallas Av
3200 LORN 44055 2745 B3
3700 ShfT 44055 2745 B4
Dallas Dr
8200 MNTR 44060 2144 A4
Dallas Rd
1100 CLEV 44108 2496 B6
Dalton Av
4900 CLEV 44127 2755 C1
Dalton Ct
8100 MNTR 44060 2144 A4
Dalton Dr
1100 PnvT 44077 2040 E6
1100 PnvT 44077 2041 A6
Dalwood Dr
300 CLEV 44110 2372 A7
Damon Av
15600 CLEV 44110 2372 C6
Dan Dr
8500 NRYN 44133 3148 D1
Dana Av
14900 CLEV 44111 2622 C7
Dana Pl
5300 NRDV 44039 2748 B7
Danberry Dr
4100 NOSD 44070 2750 E6
Danbury Av
11100 GDHT 44125 2756 C7

INDEX 16
Danbury Ct — Cleveland Street Index — Dogwood Cir

Cleveland Street Index

STREET Block City ZIP Map# Grid

Danbury Ct
- CLEV 44103 2626 A1
8100 MNTR 44060 2144 A4
Danbury Dr
8000 MNTR 44060 2144 A4
Danbury Ln
300 RDHT 44143 2498 E1
500 AVLK 44012 2618 B3
2200 HDSN 44236 3155 B7
Dane St
100 AMHT 44001 2872 B1
Danford Ct
3000 CLEV 44114 2625 B1
Dania Dr
7200 INDE 44131 3015 E2
7200 INDE 44131 3016 A2
Daniel Av
15300 CLEV 44110 2372 B7
Daniel Dr
7800 SVHL 44131 3015 B2
31400 WLWK 44095 2249 D6
Daniel Ln
10 HmbT 44024 2381 A3
Danielle Dr
2700 WTLK 44145 2750 B2
Daniels Dr
10 CRDN 44024 2379 E7
N Danley Sq
1300 LORN 44052 2615 A5
S Danley Sq
1300 LORN 44052 2615 A6
Danner Dr
500 AURA 44202 3157 B6
10400 STBR 44241 3157 B6
Dannie Dr
500 LORN 44053 2744 E6
Dansy Dr
1800 EUCL 44117 2373 B7
1800 EUCL 44117 2498 B1
Danvers Dr
10100 CcdT 44077 2145 D6
Danville Ct
11000 CLEV 44104 2626 C4
Darby Ct
10 CcdT 44060 2145 B1
Darby Ln
3900 NOSD 44070 2750 B5
Darby's Run
- BbgT 44023 2890 D7
Darbys Run
300 BYVL 44140 2620 E5
300 BYVL 44140 2621 A5
Darien Dr
7200 HDSN 44236 3154 D7
Darien Ln
2900 TNBG 44087 3020 A6
Darke Blvd
15200 BKPK 44142 2881 C2
Darlene Cir
6100 CcdT 44077 2146 B4
Darley Av
13300 BTNH 44108 2496 E1
13300 BTNH 44110 2496 E1
13300 CLEV 44110 2496 E1
13300 CLEV 44110 2497 A1
Darlington Av
11700 GDHT 44125 2885 D1
Darlington Dr
500 BDFD 44146 2887 B3
Darlington Rd
11400 GDHT 44125 2885 D1
Darrow Dr
5700 SVHL 44131 2884 B2
Darrow Rd
7300 HDSN 44236 3154 E7
7700 TwbT 44236 3154 E7
7900 TNBG 44236 3154 E5
7900 TNBG 44087 3154 E5
7900 TwbT 44087 3154 E5
8700 TNBG 44087 3155 A3
9700 TNBG 44087 3019 E5
9800 TNBG 44087 3020 A4
11000 BhmT 44089 2870 B2
13000 VmnT 44089 2869 A6
15400 VmnT 44089 2870 A2
Darrow Rd SR-91
7300 HDSN 44236 3154 E7
7700 TwbT 44236 3154 E7
7900 TNBG 44236 3154 E5
7900 TNBG 44087 3154 E5
7900 TwbT 44087 3154 E5
8700 TNBG 44087 3155 A3
9700 TNBG 44087 3019 E5
9800 TNBG 44087 3020 A4
Darrow Park Dr
9900 TNBG 44087 3020 A5
Dartford Rd
4000 SELD 44121 2498 A4
Dartmoor Av
900 PRMA 44134 2883 E2
E Dartmoor Av
10 SVHL 44131 2883 D2
10 SVHL 44131 2884 A2
Dartmoor Rd
2500 CVHT 44118 2627 C5
7900 MNTR 44060 2251 C4
Dartmouth Av
16500 CLEV 44111 2752 B2
Dartmouth Cir
100 ELYR 44035 3006 C1
Dartmouth Dr
1000 PnvT 44077 2146 E1
1100 PnvT 44077 2147 A1
5300 PRMA 44129 2753 D7
5400 PRMA 44129 2882 D1
Dartmouth Tr
300 SgHT 44067 3017 E4
Dartworth Dr
5800 PRMA 44129 2883 A4
6700 PRMA 44129 2882 E2
Darwin Av
14100 CLEV 44110 2497 A1
Darwin Pl
16600 MDBH 44130 2881 B5
Daryl Dr
900 SELD 44143 2498 D5
Dave Dr
6600 MadT 44057 1843 B7
Davenport Av
1400 CLEV 44114 2625 A1
Daventree Dr
8100 BKVL 44141 3015 E4
Davice Pkwy
- SGVL 44136 3011 A7
David Av
1400 PRMA 44134 3014 D2
David Dr
100 ELYR 44035 2875 A3
7400 NRDV 44039 2877 C4
10200 CcdT 44077 2145 D6
18000 CLEV 44121 2497 E2
23400 NOSD 44070 2750 E5
23800 BDHT 44146 2887 C1
David Rd
9300 GDHT 44125 2756 B6
David Morton Ct
6800 BKVL 44141 3016 A7
David Myers Pkwy
10 BHWD 44122 2629 A3
Davidson Dr
600 HDHT 44143 2499 D3
9600 BKVL 44141 3151 A3
Davie Ct
900 MDSN 44057 2043 E2
Davinwood Dr
19100 CLEV 44135 2751 E4
Davis Ct
11800 LKWD 44107 2623 B5
Davis Dr
5500 MONT 44060 2143 D1
7000 NRDV 44039 2877 C4
39000 CrlT 44044 3006 D5
Davis Rd
3000 PryT 44081 2042 E3
Davis Wy
9100 TNBG 44087 3020 B5
Davis Industrial Pkwy
6100 SLN 44139 2888 E5
Davista Av
1300 MadT 44057 1843 C7
Dawn Cir
3400 NOSD 44070 2750 C4
Dawn Ct
7300 CcdT 44060 2253 C1
19200 SGVL 44136 3146 D3
Dawn Dr
500 MDSN 44057 2044 A2
700 MDSN 44057 2043 E2
3400 NOSD 44070 2750 C4
22700 EUCL 44117 2373 C7
Dawncliff Dr
4100 BKLN 44144 2753 D4
Dawn Haven Dr
7400 PRMA 44130 3013 A1
Dawning Av
3500 CLEV 44109 2754 C5
Dawning Dr
5800 CLEV 44144 2754 A5
6000 BKLN 44144 2754 A5
6300 BKLN 44144 2753 E5
Dawnshire Av
3700 PRMA 44134 2883 B2
Dawn Vista Ovl
5800 PRMA 44129 2883 A6
Dawnwood Dr
900 PRMA 44134 2883 E2
E Dawnwood Dr
10 SVHL 44131 2883 E2
10 SVHL 44131 2884 A2
Dawsey Rd
5700 TmbT 44084 2259 E4
Dawson Blvd
6100 MNTR 44060 2143 D4
Dawson Ct
10 BDFD 44146 2887 A4
Day Dr
200 LORN 44052 2615 D4
6800 PRMA 44129 2882 E5
6800 PRMA 44129 2883 A5
Day St
4500 SFLD 44054 2746 B2
Dayflower Dr
10300 TNBG 44087 3019 B3
Daylon Ct
4800 VmnT 44089 2740 C6
Dayton Av
3000 LORN 44055 2744 E3
3600 LORN 44052 2744 E4
Dayton Ct
- CLEV 44114 2625 C2
100 ELYR 44035 3006 D1
S Dayton Ext
4600 MadT 44057 2043 D5
Dayton Pl
3500 LORN 44055 2744 E3
Dayton Rd
10 MadT 44057 2043 E1
10 MDSN 44057 2043 E1
3100 MadT 44057 1941 E7
Dayton St
16600 BbgT 44023 2890 A2
Daytona Dr
7500 PRMA 44134 3014 D1
Daytona Rd
1400 LNHT 44124 2498 D7
Dean Ct
14500 BURT 44021 2636 B7
14500 BURT 44021 2766 C1
Dean Dr
1400 SELD 44121 2498 C7
Dean Rd
8800 BhmT 44089 2870 B7
8900 BhmT 44889 2870 B7
8900 HetT 44889 2870 B7
Dean St
11700 HRM 44234 3161 A2
Deanna Ct
24400 EUCL 44123 2373 D3
Deanwood St
2000 ECLE 44112 2497 D5
Dearborn Av
7100 CLEV 44102 2623 E7
Dearfield Dr
- AVLK 44012 2618 D5
Deb Ann Ct
11900 CcdT 44077 2254 E1
Debbie Dr
6400 NRDV 44039 2877 C3
Debbie Pl
2700 MadT 44057 1941 B4
Debbington Dr
500 BYVL 44140 2619 D5
Debby Dr
12100 PRMA 44130 3013 A1
Debby Ln
500 ELYR 44035 2875 A7
Debonair Dr
7500 MNTR 44060 2251 B2
Deborah Ct
7900 MNTR 44060 2252 D3
Deborah Dr
800 WLWK 44095 2249 D6
2400 BHWD 44122 2628 D4
6000 NRDV 44039 2877 B1
11200 PRMA 44130 2882 B1
Deborah Ln
200 BDFD 44146 2886 D4
Deborah Lynn Dr
4700 BKLN 44144 2753 C6
Debra Dr
6100 LORN 44053 2744 E6
42100 EyrT 44035 2745 C7
Decatur Dr
10400 SGVL 44136 3012 B4
Decatur St
600 VMLN 44089 2740 D5
Decker Av
7400 CLEV 44103 2495 E7
7400 CLEV 44103 2496 A7
8400 CLEV 44106 2496 A7
Decker Dr
900 PRMA 44134 2883 E3
E Decker Dr
10 SVHL 44131 2883 E3
200 SVHL 44131 2884 A3
Decker Ln
- ELYR 44035 2875 C6
Decker Rd
5300 NOSD 44070 2749 E7
5300 NOSD 44070 2878 E1
Dee Dr
6500 AhtT 44001 2873 C1
Deep Cove Dr
8500 SgHT 44067 3017 E5
Deep Creek Ln
10 MDHL 44022 2760 A3
Deeplake Cir
1500 TNBG 44087 3019 B3
Deepview Dr
17400 BbgT 44023 2890 C4
Deepwood Blvd
8200 MNTR 44060 2251 D4
Deepwood Ct
100 CRDN 44024 2505 B1
Deepwood Dr
900 MCDN 44056 3018 D7
6000 RslT 44073 2761 A2
Deepwood Ln
200 AhtT 44001 2873 C1
6800 MAYF 44143 2500 B4
N Deepwood Ln
15000 RslT 44073 2761 A2
S Deepwood Ln
15100 RslT 44073 2761 A3
Deepwood Tr
5800 SLN 44139 2889 D3
Deep Woods Dr
400 AURA 44202 3022 D5
Deepwoods Wy
3900 NOSD 44070 2750 D5
Deer Ct
400 SRSL 44073 2762 A5
6600 BDHT 44146 2887 E6
Deer Dr
200 CdnT 44024 2379 A6
Deer Hllw
9400 MNTR 44060 2039 A7
Deer Ln
18900 FWPK 44126 2751 E1
Deer Pth
400 AURA 44202 3156 C2
6900 OmsT 44138 2878 E4
7500 BKVL 44141 3150 D3
Deer Rdg
5100 MNTR 44060 2039 A7
Deer Run
- AVON 44011 2747 D3
- LORN 44053 2743 B5
500 AURA 44202 3156 B3
900 AhtT 44001 2873 B2
2600 WBHL 44094 2375 B4
10000 BKVL 44141 3151 D4
37000 SLN 44139 2889 D3
Deer St
2600 ShvT 44241 3157 E7
Deerborn Av
5500 MNTR 44060 2144 A1
Deerbrook Dr
7800 RslT 44072 2631 D7
Deer Creek Cir
4700 RHFD 44286 3150 D7
Deercreek Ct
- SFLD 44054 2746 E4
Deer Creek Dr
8600 BWHT 44147 3015 A6
12400 NRYN 44133 3012 E7
Deercreek Dr
5600 WBHL 44094 2375 B2
N Deer Creek Ln
33200 PRPK 44124 2760 A1
Deer Creek Tr
3200 RchT 44286 3150 D7
3200 RHFD 44286 3150 D7
Deerfield Cir
8600 MCDN 44056 3018 B6
Deerfield Ct
- NRDV 44039 2877 B6
100 ELYR 44035 2746 C7
10000 TNBG 44087 3019 B4
Deerfield Dr
- AVON 44011 2747 A2
10 MDSN 44057 1942 B6
10 PnvT 44077 2040 E7
10 PnvT 44077 2146 E1
10 SRSL 44073 2761 D7
7500 PRMA 44129 2882 D3
9700 KTLD 44094 2377 C3
16900 SGVL 44136 3146 E2
24500 NOSD 44070 2750 C4
Deerfield Ln
10 BHWD 44122 2628 E4
100 AURA 44202 3021 C7
10000 BKVL 44141 3151 E4
Deerfield Rd
7600 GSML 44040 2630 E1
Deerfoot Tr
7600 RslT 44072 2761 C1
Deer Haven Dr
6600 CcdT 44077 2146 A6
8300 CsTp 44026 2502 A2
Deerhaven Ln
1900 BWHT 44147 3149 C4
Deeridge Dr
7100 WNHL 44146 2886 D7
Deering Av
5800 PMHT 44130 2882 D3
10700 CLEV 44106 2626 C3
Deer Island Dr
300 AURA 44202 3156 C3
Deermont Av
1300 MadT 44057 1843 C7
Deer Path Dr
16900 SGVL 44136 3146 E3
16900 SGVL 44136 3147 A3
Deer Path Ln
- NCtT 44236 3153 E5
Deerpath Tr
7500 HDSN 44236 3155 D7
Deer Ridge Cir
17400 SGVL 44136 3147 A5
Deer Run Dr
- HGVL 44022 2761 A2
- MDHL 44022 2761 A2
900 AhtT 44001 2873 B2
10600 EatT 44044 3007 A5
Deer Run Ln
500 AVLK 44012 2617 E4
19600 SGVL 44136 3011 D5
31500 WTLK 44145 2749 A3
Deer Run Ovl
3700 RchT 44286 3150 C6
5800 SLN 44139 2889 D3
Deer Run Tr
7500 PRMA 44130 3013 C1
12000 CcdT 44077 2254 E4
Deerspring Ct
- NRDV 44039 2877 D6
Deer Wood Ct
9300 MNTR 44060 2039 A7
Defiance Av
200 ELYR 44035 3006 E2
5700 BKPK 44142 2881 D1
Defoe Dr
26000 NOSD 44070 2750 B5
Deforest Av
16500 CLEV 44128 2757 C4
18100 CLEV 44122 2757 C4
De Forest Rd
- CLEV 44106 2626 D3
Deise Av
13600 CLEV 44110 2497 A2
Delamere Ct
37500 SLN 44139 2889 D4
Delamere Dr
2200 CVHT 44106 2626 E3
Delamere Rd
200 VMLN 44089 2741 D4
Delavan Av
17700 CLEV 44119 2372 D6
Delaware Av
100 LORN 44052 2614 E5
300 LORN 44052 2615 A6
14200 LKWD 44107 2622 D7
Delaware Cir
200 ELYR 44035 2875 C7
Delaware Ct
19400 EUCL 44117 2497 D2
Delaware Dr
300 BNWK 44212 3146 E7
2100 CVHT 44106 2626 E3
7600 MDBH 44130 3012 D2
13800 SGVL 44136 3011 E7
Delaware Rd
100 CrlT 44035 3006 B3
100 ELYR 44035 3006 B3
19500 EUCL 44117 2497 E2
19700 EUCL 44117 2498 A2
Delaware St
2400 WKLF 44092 2374 D4
Delevan Dr
4800 LNHT 44124 2498 D5
Delft Cir
- OmsT 44138 2879 A3
Dell Av
7100 CLEV 44104 2625 E5
7300 CLEV 44104 2626 A5
Dell Dr
19600 SGVL 44136 3011 C6
Dellbank Dr
3400 RKRV 44116 2751 E1
6000 CLEV 44144 2754 A3
6300 CLEV 44144 2753 E3
7400 BKLN 44144 2753 E3
Dell Cort Dr
- BKVL 44141 3151 A4
Dellefield Rd
42600 EyrT 44035 2874 A1
Dellenbaugh Av
7100 CLEV 44103 2625 E1
7100 CLEV 44103 2626 A1
Dellhaven Av
6400 MNTR 44060 2145 A5
Dellhaven Dr
7200 PRMA 44130 2882 C7
Dell Ridge Ct
12800 SGVL 44136 3011 C6
Dellrose Dr
6200 PMHT 44130 2882 C4
Dellwood Dr
1100 WTLK 44145 2619 E7
2600 PRMA 44134 2883 C4
18500 WNHL 44146 3017 E1
18500 WNHL 44146 3018 A1
27300 WTLK 44145 2620 A6
Dellwood Rd
200 AVLK 44012 2617 E2
3200 CVHT 44118 2627 C3
Delmar Av
2600 CLEV 44109 2754 C2
Delmar Dr
3300 RKRV 44116 2751 A2
Delmere Dr
23500 NOSD 44070 2750 D4
Delmont Av
1600 CLEV 44106 2496 E7
1600 CLEV 44112 2496 E7
1600 ECLE 44112 2496 E7
16000 SGVL 44136 3147 A3
N Delmonte Blvd
10000 STBR 44241 3156 D7
Delmore Rd
3700 CVHT 44121 2497 E6
3900 CVHT 44121 2498 A6
Delmur Dr
6700 INDE 44131 2884 E6
Delora Av
5300 CLEV 44144 2754 A6
5300 CLEV 44109 2754 A6
5900 BKLN 44144 2754 A6
6200 BKLN 44144 2753 E6
Delores Blvd
5700 BKPK 44142 2881 C2
Delray Av
5000 SLN 44139 2759 D7
Delrey Av
15500 CLEV 44128 2757 B3
Delroy Rd
4100 SELD 44121 2498 B7
Delsy Dr
9900 NRYN 44133 3013 B4
Delta Cir
5600 WLBY 44094 2375 A2
Demas Av
700 ELYR 44035 2874 C4
Demi Dr
2000 TNBG 44087 3019 E4
Demington Dr
2100 CVHT 44106 2627 A3
Demshar Dr
7300 MNTR 44060 2253 A1
Denise Ct
5200 SLN 44139 2759 B7
5200 SLN 44139 2888 B1
Denise Dr
5900 NRDV 44039 2877 B2
Denison Av
- BKLN 44102 2753 E1
- BKLN 44144 2753 E1
100 ELYR 44035 2875 B7
1300 CLEV 44109 2754 D2
4400 CLEV 44102 2754 A2
6700 CLEV 44102 2753 E1
9200 CLEV 44102 2623 D7
10000 CLEV 44111 2623 D7
Denison Blvd
6000 PMHT 44130 2882 C4
Denison Dr
4100 LORN 44055 2745 E4
Denison-Harvard Brch
- CHHT 44105 2755 A3
- CHHT 44109 2755 A3
- CHHT 44125 2755 A3
800 CLEV 44109 2754 E2
800 CLEV 44109 2755 A3
Denley Av
1400 CLEV 44109 2754 E4
Denmark Av
4600 CLEV 44102 2754 B2
4600 CLEV 44144 2754 B2
Dennis Cir
1100 SELD 44121 2498 B6
Dennis Ct
10 GnvT 44041 1944 C2
9400 NRYN 44133 3014 C4
Dennis Dr
1500 WKLF 44092 2374 E1
Dennison Ct
8400 MNTR 44060 2144 B3
Dennisport Dr
26200 OKWD 44146 2887 E7
Denny Dr
7300 NRDV 44039 2877 C4
Densmore Rd
31600 WLWK 44095 2249 D5
Denton Dr
1900 CVHT 44106 2626 D3
Dentzler Rd
2200 PRMA 44134 2883 C6
Denver Av
2500 LORN 44052 2745 A2
2500 LORN 44055 2745 A2
Denver Dr
11900 PRMA 44130 2882 A2
Depot Rd
8900 TNBG 44087 3155 B1
19000 BbgT 44023 3021 B3
19000 BbgT 44202 3021 B3
Depot St
10 BERA 44017 2880 B6
10 GNVA 44041 1944 B4
100 ELYR 44035 2875 B6
4100 PRRY 44081 2042 C3
19000 RKRV 44116 2621 E5
37800 WLBY 44094 2250 D4
N Depot St
25700 ODFL 44138 2879 B5
Deptford Dr
2500 BHWD 44122 2628 D5
Derby Ct
12000 SGVL 44136 3011 A5
Derby Dr
700 PNVL 44077 2039 E6
700 PNVL 44077 2040 A6
4500 AVON 44011 2747 A6
6400 MAYF 44143 2499 E5
6400 MAYF 44143 2500 A5
Derby Rd
11700 GDHT 44125 2885 D2
Derby Run
300 WBHL 44092 2374 B5
Derby Downs Dr
36000 SLN 44139 2889 C4
Derbyshire Dr
4600 NRDL 44128 2758 B6
Derbyshire Ln
11700 AbnT 44021 2893 D4
Derbyshire Rd
2400 CVHT 44106 2626 E2
2500 CVHT 44106 2627 A3
E Derbyshire Rd
2800 CVHT 44118 2627 B3
Dercum Rd
7600 CLEV 44105 2756 A3
Derubertis Dr
1500 MadT 44057 1942 A4
Desmond Av
8700 CLEV 44102 2623 D5
Desota Av
3200 CVHT 44118 2627 C1
Detour Av
700 RKRV 44116 2621 C5
7300 CLEV 44103 2496 A5
Detroit Av
2400 CLEV 44113 2624 B5
4500 CLEV 44102 2624 B5
7000 CLEV 44102 2623 E5
11700 LKWD 44102 2623 A5
11700 LKWD 44107 2623 A5
13400 LKWD 44107 2622 C5
Detroit Av US-6
2400 CLEV 44113 2624 C4
Detroit Av US-20
2400 CLEV 44113 2624 C4
Detroit Av US-322
2400 CLEV 44113 2624 C4
Detroit Ext
18600 LKWD 44107 2622 A5
Detroit Rd
- LKWD 44107 2621 C6
- RKRV 44107 2621 C6
- WTLK 44116 2621 A6
4700 SFLD 44035 2746 E5
4700 SFLD 44054 2746 E5
5300 AVON 44011 2747 B4
5300 SFLD 44011 2747 B4
5300 SFLD 44035 2747 B4
5300 SFLD 44054 2747 B4
18600 LKWD 44107 2622 A5
19000 RKRV 44116 2621 C6
22900 WTLK 44145 2621 A6
24100 WTLK 44145 2620 C7
27300 WTLK 44145 2619 D7
30600 WTLK 44145 2749 A1
31400 AVON 44145 2749 A1
32200 AVON 44011 2748 C2
32200 AVON 44011 2749 A1
Detroit Rd SR-2
- LKWD 44107 2621 C6
- RKRV 44107 2621 C6
19000 RKRV 44116 2621 C6
Detroit Rd SR-254
- LKWD 44107 2621 C6
- RKRV 44107 2621 C6
- WTLK 44116 2621 A6
4700 SFLD 44035 2746 E5
4700 SFLD 44054 2746 E5
5300 AVON 44011 2747 B4
5300 SFLD 44011 2747 B4
5300 SFLD 44035 2747 B4
5300 SFLD 44054 2747 B4
19000 RKRV 44116 2621 C6
22900 WTLK 44145 2621 A6
23300 WTLK 44145 2620 C7
27300 WTLK 44145 2619 D7
30600 WTLK 44145 2749 A1
31400 AVON 44145 2749 A1
32200 AVON 44011 2748 C2
32200 AVON 44011 2749 A1
Detroit Rd US-20
- LKWD 44107 2621 E5
- RKRV 44107 2621 E5
- RKRV 44116 2621 E5
Deveny Av
7100 CLEV 44105 2755 E4
Devington Ct
- ManT 44202 3023 B6
Devoe Av
23700 EUCL 44123 2373 C3
24900 EUCL 44132 2373 C3
Devon Dr
4900 NOSD 44070 2749 D7
5100 VMLN 44089 2741 A6
5200 VMLN 44089 2740 E6
Devon Ln
7400 CsTp 44026 2501 C7
Devon Rd
17500 CLEV 44119 2372 D5
Devon St
6200 MadT 44057 1843 A7
Devon Hill Rd
2600 RKRV 44116 2621 B7
Devon Pond
300 AURA 44202 3021 C7
Devonshire Av
700 SDLK 44054 2615 E4
Devonshire Ct
100 ELYR 44035 2875 E3
400 BYVL 44140 2620 B5
6500 MNTR 44060 2144 A5
Devonshire Dr
- CVHT 44106 2626 D3
6500 NRYN 44133 3014 A5
Devonshire Ln
- AURA 44202 3021 D5
Devonshire Ovl
29500 WTLK 44145 2749 C3
Devonshire Rd
200 VMLN 44089 2741 D4
3000 CLEV 44109 2754 C4
Devorah Dr
100 AURA 44202 3156 E3
Devore Ct
2900 LORN 44052 2744 C2
Dewberry Ln
29300 WTLK 44145 2749 C2
Dewey Av
500 ELYR 44035 2874 E5
Dewey Dr
35400 ETLK 44095 2142 B7
Dewey Rd
- CsTp 44026 2502 E1
- CsTp 44094 2502 E1
- KTLD 44094 2502 E1
5100 NOSD 44070 2749 E7
5300 RchT 44141 3151 A7
5600 MadT 44057 2150 A3
5900 TpnT 44086 2149 E5
5900 TpnT 44086 2150 A3
6700 TpnT 44086 2257 E2
7400 AhtT 44001 2873 B3
8400 MtlT 44086 2257 E5
8600 MtlT 44064 2257 E5
10300 BKVL 44141 3151 C6
N Dewey Rd
100 AMHT 44001 2744 A7
S Dewey Rd
1200 AhtT 44001 2744 B7
1200 AhtT 44001 2873 B2
1200 AMHT 44001 2744 B7
6900 AMHT 44001 2873 B2
Dewhurst Av
10 BDFD 44146 2886 E2
Dewhurst Rd
10100 EatT 44035 3006 E4
10100 ELYR 44035 3006 E4
10500 CrlT 44035 3006 E4
DeWitt Dr
500 HDHT 44143 2499 B3
15000 SGVL 44136 3012 C3
DeWitt St
300 ShfT 44055 2745 A4
900 LORN 44055 2745 A4
Dexter Dr
6100 PMHT 44130 2882 C3
Dexter Pl
1500 CLEV 44113 2624 C4
Diagonal Rd
10000 ShvT 44241 3158 C7
10000 ShvT 44255 3158 C7
10400 ManT 44255 3158 C7
11100 ManT 44255 3159 A2
12400 CrlT 44050 3005 D7
12400 CrlT 44050 3140 D1
14100 LrgT 44050 3140 B3
Diamond Av
5500 CLEV 44104 2625 D5
Diamond Ct
400 BHIT 44212 3146 B7
Diamond Centre Dr
9500 MNTR 44060 2145 A2
Diana Av
13600 CLEV 44110 2497 A1
Diana Ct
400 HDHT 44143 2499 D2
Diana Dr
- BKPK 44142 2752 C7
- BKPK 44142 2881 C1
3800 BWHT 44147 3015 C4
6600 SVHL 44131 2884 A5
Diane Ct
30800 WBHL 44092 2374 D4
Diane Dr
4000 FWPK 44126 2752 A1
8800 NRDV 44039 2877 C7
Dianne Cir
20600 SGVL 44136 3011 B5
Dianne Dr
10800 NbyT 44065 2634 A7
24500 BHWD 44122 2628 D5
Dibble Av
5500 CLEV 44103 2495 D7
Dickens Av
8900 CLEV 44104 2626 B6
Dickens Cir
33400 NRDV 44039 2877 D3
Dickens Dr
5100 RDHT 44143 2498 E3
5100 RDHT 44143 2499 A3
Dickerson Rd
500 WLWK 44095 2249 D5
Didrickson Dr
2300 LORN 44053 2743 E2
Diemer Ct
6400 CLEV 44103 2495 E6
Difranco Ln
- BNHT 44131 2755 A7
Dill Rd
1200 SELD 44121 2498 C7
Dille Rd
1400 EUCL 44117 2373 A7
1400 EUCL 44117 2498 A1
3900 CLEV 44115 2625 C6
3900 CLEV 44127 2625 C6
Dillewood Av
800 SDLK 44054 2615 E4
Dillewood Rd
1000 CLEV 44119 2372 D6
Dilworth St
100 ELYR 44035 2875 C4
Dines Rd
7300 RslT 44072 2631 C6
7800 RslT 44072 2632 A6
Discovery Ln
7500 CcdT 44077 2253 E2
7500 CcdT 44077 2254 A2
Division Av
2500 CLEV 44113 2624 C4
4500 CLEV 44102 2624 B4
Division Dr
1100 MadT 44057 1843 E5
7700 MNTR 44060 2251 D1
Division Rd
- AVLK 44012 2618 B1
4500 SELD 44121 2628 C2
Division St
100 CNFL 44022 2760 E6
7200 OKWD 44146 2887 B7
Divot Dr
300 WLWK 44095 2249 C6
Dixon Rd
10800 CLEV 44111 2753 B3
34900 WBHL 44094 2375 A6
Doan Av
1500 ECLE 44112 2497 A6
N Doan Av
10 PnvT 44077 2145 B4
S Doan Av
10 PnvT 44077 2145 C5
Dobson Ct
2400 CLEV 44109 2754 D2
Dock Rd
800 MadT 44057 1844 A5
1200 MadT 44057 1843 E7
1200 MadT 44057 1942 E1
2000 MadT 44057 1943 A2
Dr Martin Luther King Blvd
- CLEV 44104 2496 A4
Dr Martin Luther King Dr
- CLEV 44103 2496 A6
- CLEV 44108 2496 A6
Dodd Rd
2400 WBHL 44094 2375 E3
2400 WBHL 44094 2376 A4
2600 WBHL 44094 2375 E5
Dodd's Lndg
38400 WBHL 44094 2376 A4
Dodd's Hill Rd
38000 WBHL 44094 2375 E4
38100 WBHL 44094 2376 A4
Dodge Av
33900 NRDV 44039 2877 C3
Dodge Ct
- HRM 44234 3161 A1
Dodge Dr
800 AMHT 44001 2872 E3
Dodsworth Ln
5800 SLN 44139 2889 C3
Doe Cir
16600 SGVL 44136 3146 E3
Doe Ct
600 SRSL 44073 2761 E5
Doe Dr
24700 NOSD 44070 2750 C4
Doering Ct
1700 CLEV 44109 2754 E3
Dogwood Cir
4000 ORNG 44122 2759 C3
6800 MDBH 44130 2881 C5
9100 BKVL 44141 3151 A1

Column headers throughout: **STREET / Block City ZIP Map# Grid**

Dogwood Ct
- OmsT 44138 2878 D5
- 300 AhT 44001 2873 B2
- 9800 SGVL 44136 3012 B4

Dogwood Ln
- 10 OmsT 44138 2879 B4
- 500 AbnT 44023 2892 B3
- 500 VMLN 44089 2741 C5
- 7000 MNTR 44060 2144 C7
- 7400 PRMA 44130 2882 D7
- 7400 PRMA 44130 3013 D1
- 34500 SLN 44139 2760 B7

Dogwood Tr
- 100 AURA 44202 3156 D2
- 4200 NOSD 44070 2749 E5
- 5000 LNHT 44124 2628 E1
- 5100 LNHT 44124 2629 A1
- 12600 NRYN 44133 3012 E3

Doll Dr
- 8300 CLEV 44125 2756 A7

Dolloff Rd
- 4900 CLEV 44127 2628 E7
- 5400 CLEV 44127 2755 D1

Dolores Dr
- 38100 ETLK 44095 2250 E1

Dolphin Rd
- 5600 MONT 44060 2143 E1

Dolphin Cove
- 3500 RMDV 44202 3020 D5

Dominion Dr
- 900 WTLK 44145 2620 A6

Donald Av
- 1200 LKWD 44107 2623 A4
- 4700 RDHT 44143 2498 E5
- 6600 VLVW 44125 2885 C4
- 7100 CLEV 44103 2495 E7
- 7200 CLEV 44103 2496 A7
- 27200 BYVL 44140 2619 A6

Donald Dr
- 8200 MNTR 44060 2144 A4
- 13300 BKPK 44130 2881 D3
- 16300 PkmT 44231 3027 E2
- 16300 PkmT 44231 3028 A2

Donald Ross Dr
- WBHL 44094 2375 B4

Doncaster Av
- 6300 PRMA 44129 2882 E4

Doncaster Ct
- 10 CcdT 44060 2145 B2

Donelly Rd
- 16000 CLEV 44135 2752 B5

Donley Rd
- 4200 MstT 44062 2639 E7

Donmar Rd
- 10700 NRYN 44133 3148 A4

Donna Dr
- 1700 WTLK 44145 2750 E1
- 4400 RDHT 44143 2498 C3

Donna St
- 33900 NRDV 44039 3008 C1

Donna Rae Dr
- 6500 SVHL 44131 2884 C6

Donner Pass
- ClrT 44024 2505 C6

Donnie Pl
- AhT 44001 2872 E6

Donnybrook Rd
- 20500 MPHT 44137 2887 A1

Donovan Dr
- 4800 GDHT 44125 2756 A6

Donover Rd
- 24200 WVHT 44128 2758 D4

Donwell Dr
- 1600 SELD 44121 2628 B1

Dooridge Dr
- 1700 TNBG 44087 3019 C5

Doovys St
- 1800 AVON 44011 2617 C7
- 2000 AVON 44011 2747 C1

Dora Blvd
- 6000 INDE 44131 2884 D7

Dora Dr
- 14500 NbyT 44065 2634 A7
- 14500 NbyT 44065 2764 A1

Dorado St
- 1300 LORN 44052 2615 B6

Doral Dr
- 800 AURA 44202 3021 B4
- 8800 MNTR 44060 2144 D3

Doral Ln
- 30800 WTLK 44145 2749 B2

Doralane Dr
- 800 AURA 44202 3021 B4

Dorchester Av
- 35400 NRDV 44039 2748 A7

Dorchester Cir
- 19100 SGVL 44136 3147 C5

Dorchester Dr
- 1200 MadT 44057 1843 C6
- 17000 CLEV 44128 2372 D5
- 29100 NOSD 44070 2878 C3
- 32000 AVLK 44012 2618 D4

Dorchester Ln
- 10 CcdT 44060 2145 B2

Dorchester Rd
- 10 PnvT 44077 2041 B6
- 100 PryT 44077 2041 B6
- 3200 SRHT 44120 2627 D7
- 33900 GSML 44040 2630 B2

Doria Ct
- 12500 SGVL 44136 3011 D6

Doris Av
- 22300 FWPK 44126 2751 A4

Doris Cir
- 700 PNVL 44077 2040 A5

Doris Dr
- 5700 BKPK 44142 2881 B2

Doris Rd
- 3200 CLEV 44111 2752 C1

Dorland Av
- 10 BERA 44017 3011 A1

Dormae Ct
- 10600 CcdT 44077 2146 A4

Dornach Ln
- HDHT 44143 2499 C2

Dornback Pkwy
- ETLK 44095 2250 E6

Dornur Dr
- 4600 CLEV 44109 2754 E5

Dorothea Dr
- 1200 PnvT 44077 2040 E6
- 1200 PnvT 44077 2041 A6

Dorothy Dr
- VMLN 44089 2741 B5
- 9800 PRMA 44129 2882 D2
- 9400 GDHT 44125 2756 B5

Dorothy Av
- 19100 RKRV 44116 2621 E5

Dorothy Ct
- 5500 CLEV 44103 2625 D1

Dorothy Dr
- 5400 NOSD 44070 2878 E1
- 30000 WKLF 44092 2374 D2

Dorothy Rd
- 12900 CsTp 44026 2632 A2

Dorrwood Dr
- 5700 MNTR 44060 2144 C2

Dorset Ct
- 10 BHWD 44122 2628 E3
- 100 ELYR 44035 2875 E3

Dorset Dr
- 10 SRSL 44073 2762 B6
- 2400 SVHL 44131 2884 B2
- 2900 BNHT 44131 2884 B2

Dorset Ln
- 2100 TwbT 44236 3155 A6
- 6400 SLN 44139 2889 E5

Dorset Rd
- 5500 LNHT 44124 2499 B7

Dorsh Rd
- 1000 SELD 44121 2498 D7

Dorshwood Dr
- 4700 SELD 44121 2498 D6

Dorver Av
- 7700 CLEV 44105 2756 A4

Dorwick Dr
- 7300 NCtT 44067 3153 A3

Dorwood Dr
- 6000 LORN 44053 2744 D4

Dory Ln
- 7400 NCtT 44067 3153 C5

Doty Rd
- 7100 HpfT 44057 2045 A6
- 7100 MadT 44057 2044 E6
- 7100 MadT 44057 2045 A6

Doty East Rd
- 4500 StnT 44491 3029 D6

Douglas Av
- 1600 ELYR 44035 3005 E2

Douglas Blvd
- 300 RDHT 44143 2498 D2

Douglas Ct
- 1300 LORN 44053 2744 C5
- 9100 NRYN 44133 3014 C5

Douglas Dr
- 200 BYVL 44140 2620 A5
- 4900 NOSD 44070 2749 D7
- 5900 MadT 44057 1941 D1
- 31400 WLWK 44095 2249 D6

Douglas Ln
- 9700 ODFL 44138 3010 E2

Douglas Rd
- 1500 WKLF 44092 2249 B4
- 1500 WKLF 44092 2374 E1
- 22000 SRHT 44122 2628 B5

Doula Dr
- 900 NRYN 44133 3012 E3

Douse Av
- 4400 CLEV 44127 2625 C6

Dove
- MNTR 44060 2144 D2

Dove Av
- 10200 CLEV 44105 2756 C3

Dove Dr
- ELYR 44035 2874 E2

Dover Av
- 14300 ECLE 44112 2497 A4

Dover Ct
- 1200 ECLE 44112 2497 B4

Dover Dr
- AURA 44202 3157 A4

Dover Ln
- 7300 PRMA 44130 2882 C4
- 7300 PRMA 44130 3013 C1

Dover Pl
- 10 NCtT 44067 3153 A2

Dover Rd
- PRMA 44130 2882 D7
- PRMA 44130 3013 D1

Dover Center Rd
- 200 BYVL 44140 2620 A6
- 600 WTLK 44140 2620 A6
- 600 WTLK 44140 2620 A6
- 1400 WTLK 44145 2750 A2
- 3800 NOSD 44070 2750 A6

Dover Farms Dr
- 8000 NRYN 44133 3013 D7

Dow Cir E
- 7900 SGVL 44136 3012 C3

Dow Cir W
- 7900 SGVL 44136 3012 C2

Dowd Av
- 2000 LKWD 44107 2623 A6

Dowd Rd
- 200 ELYR 44035 2875 D3

Downcote Trc
- 200 MCDN 44056 3018 A6

Downers Grove Ct
- 9400 SGVL 44136 3012 B4

Downey Glen Tr
- 16600 AbnT 44023 2893 B1

Downing Av
- 35200 NRDV 44039 2748 B7

Downing Ct
- 700 BERA 44017 3011 B2

Downing Dr
- 700 CRDN 44024 2380 A5

N Downing Pl
- 7100 CcdT 44077 2146 A6

S Downing Pl
- 7200 CcdT 44077 2146 B6

Doxmere Dr
- 5800 PMHT 44130 2882 B2

Drake Av
- 5500 CLEV 44127 2625 D7

Drake Dr
- 31300 BYVL 44140 2619 A4

Drake Rd
- 11000 NRYN 44133 3147 E3
- 11000 NRYN 44133 3148 A3
- 11000 SGVL 44136 3147 D3
- 17500 SGVL 44136 3146 E3

Drakefield Av
- 15600 CLEV 44111 2752 C3

Drakefield Av
- 24700 EUCL 44123 2373 D2
- 26800 EUCL 44132 2373 D2
- 26800 EUCL 44132 2374 C2

Drawbridge Cir
- 6600 NRYN 44133 3013 E5

Drayton Dr
- 1800 MDHT 44124 2629 C2

Drenik Dr
- 1600 WKLF 44092 2374 D1

Dresden Dr
- 7400 PRMA 44129 2882 E1

Dresden Rd
- 800 CVHT 44112 2497 C5

Dresser Ln
- 1000 MCDN 44056 3154 A5

Dressler Av
- 13400 GDHT 44125 2756 E6

Dressler Ct
- 7100 CHHT 44125 2755 E6

Drexel Dr
- 6700 SVHL 44131 2884 B6

Drexmore Rd
- 2600 CLEV 44120 2626 E5
- 12400 CLEV 44120 2627 A5
- 12400 SRHT 44120 2627 A5

Driftwood Ct
- AVLK 44012 2619 A2
- 100 ELYR 44035 3006 E1

Driftwood Dr
- 1100 SVHL 44131 2884 A4
- 5200 VMLN 44089 2740 E6
- 5200 VMLN 44089 2741 A6
- 7700 MONT 44060 2143 E2
- 9200 ODFL 44138 3010 A1
- 11700 NbyT 44065 2764 D1

Driftwood Ln
- 1300 MCDN 44056 3019 A7

Driftwood Rd
- AhT 44001 2872 E6

Driscoll Ln
- 26700 NOSD 44070 2750 A5

Driscoll Rd
- 4900 WVHT 44146 2758 A6

Drummond Rd
- 13400 CLEV 44120 2627 B6

Drummond St
- 100 AVLK 44012 2488 B7
- 100 AVLK 44012 2618 B1

Drury Ct
- 1200 MDHT 44124 2500 A6

Drury Ln
- WTHL 44094 2375 E1
- 10 MDHT 44124 2500 A6
- 7500 CsTp 44026 2631 C2
- 8800 WLBY 44094 2250 E5

Dryden Av
- 3900 NOSD 44070 2750 B5

Dryden Dr
- 3900 NOSD 44070 2750 B5

Dryden Rd
- 2200 SRHT 44122 2628 B5

Drydock St
- CLEV 44113 2625 A4

D Termination Rd
- GNVA 44041 1944 A4

Duane Rd
- 26200 NOSD 44070 2750 A5

Dubay Ct
- 600 PNVL 44077 2146 B2

Dubin Av
- 17500 CLEV 44128 2757 D6

Dublin Dr
- 4700 NRYN 44133 3014 B4

Dublin Ln
- 9500 MNTR 44060 2145 A6

Duckworth Ln
- 7700 MNTR 44060 2143 D5

Dudley Av
- 7300 CLEV 44103 2623 E6

Dudley Rd
- 3700 ShvT 44255 3158 E7
- 3700 ShvT 44255 3159 A7

Duff Dr
- 10 AVLK 44012 2617 C2

Duffey St
- 700 ELYR 44035 2875 E4

Duffield Rd
- 22300 SRHT 44122 2628 C6
- 24400 BHWD 44122 2628 C6

Duffton Ct
- 10 PnvT 44077 2040 E2
- 1700 PnvT 44077 2041 A2

Dugan Farms
- 3800 PRRY 44081 2042 B7

Dugans Lndg
- 3900 PRRY 44081 2042 B7

Duke Av
- 5000 CLEV 44102 2624 B6

Duke Ct
- 900 ELYR 44035 2875 B7

Duluth Av
- 7100 CLEV 44103 2495 E7

Dumbarton Blvd
- 300 RDHT 44143 2498 D3

Dunbar Ct
- AURA 44202 3021 D6
- 10 PnvT 44077 2146 D1

Dunbar Dr
- 6100 MNTR 44060 2143 E4

Dunbar Ln
- 8600 BKVL 44141 3016 B6

Dunbar Rd
- 1600 MadT 44057 1842 E7
- 1700 MadT 44057 1941 E1

Dunbury Dr
- 15600 MPHT 44137 2886 B3

Dundee Dr
- 3500 CLEV 44108 2496 D3
- 24700 RDHT 44143 2498 D1

Dundee St
- CLEV 44115 2625 B3

Dundeen Cir
- 34200 AVON 44011 2877 A1

Duneden Av
- 6500 SLN 44139 2888 E6
- 300 AURA 44202 3022 B5

Dunedin Av
- 1300 MadT 44057 1843 C6

Dunellon Dr
- 1800 LNHT 44124 2629 C2

Dunfield Dr
- 6200 MDHT 44124 2499 E6

Dunford Av
- 27200 WTLK 44145 2749 E4
- 27200 WTLK 44145 2750 A4

Dunham Av
- 6600 CLEV 44105 2625 E2

Dunham Ln
- 16400 WNHL 44146 3017 C4

Dunham Rd
- MPHT 44137 2757 B7
- 5300 MPHT 44137 2886 B4
- 7100 WNHL 44146 3017 B1
- 11500 SgHT 44067 3017 C4
- 11800 SgHT 44067 3017 C4

Dunlap Av
- 9300 CLEV 44105 2756 B2

Dunny Av
- 600 SDLK 44054 2616 B4

Dunton Rd
- 3600 LORN 44055 2745 B3
- 3600 ShfT 44055 2745 B3
- 6100 MNTR 44060 2144 C3

Dupont Av
- 10500 CLEV 44108 2496 C4

Dupont Dr
- 9800 ClbT 44028 3010 D2

Durack Dr
- 9100 NRYN 44133 3013 C4

Durant Av
- 11300 CLEV 44106 2496 D6

Durham Ct
- 6500 MNTR 44060 2143 E5

Durham Dr
- WTLK 44145 2619 A4

Durkee Av
- 13100 CLEV 44105 2756 C3
- 13600 CLEV 44105 2757 A3

Durkee Rd
- 10 EatT 44044 3007 B7
- 10 EatT 44044 3142 B1
- 1800 EatT 44044 3142 B3
- 9700 EatT 44044 3007 B2
- 15400 HtbT 44046 2637 B4
- 15400 HtbT 44021 2637 B4
- 15400 MdfT 44046 2637 B4
- 15400 MdfT 44046 2637 B4

Durrell Av
- AVLK 44012 2617 D2
- AVLK 44012 2618 A2

Dursley Ct
- 7200 SLN 44139 3020 C1

Dusty Ln
- 8700 CcdT 44077 2254 A6

Dute Av
- ELYR 44035 2746 A5
- ShfT 44035 2746 A6
- ShfT 44035 2746 A6

Dutton Dr
- TNBG 44087 3154 C1
- 9000 TNBG 44087 3019 C7

Duval Rd
- 6400 MDHT 44124 2630 A3

Duxbury Ct
- 7200 OKWD 44146 2887 E7
- 21100 OKWD 44146 2887 B7

Duxbury Dr
- 600 BERA 44017 3010 E1

Duxbury Ln
- 10 BNWK 44212 3147 B6

Duxbury Pl
- 5500 LORN 44053 2744 B5

Dwayne Ct
- 9900 CcdT 44060 2253 B1

Dwight Dr
- 500 BYVL 44140 2619 D5

Dye Rd
- 34700 EatT 44028 2872 E4

Dyke Av
- 7100 NRDV 44039 2876 A4

Dynes Av
- 16700 CLEV 44128 2757 C4

Dysart Rd
- 2300 UNHT 44118 2627 E5

E

E St
- 500 LORN 44052 2614 E6
- 700 LORN 44052 2615 A6

Eady Ct
- 100 ELYR 44035 2875 D5

Eagle Av
- 3100 LORN 44055 2745 B3

W Eagle Av
- 300 CLEV 44113 2624 E4
- 300 CLEV 44115 2624 E4
- 300 CLEV 44115 2625 A4

Eagle Cir
- 100 ELYR 44035 2874 E2

Eagle Dr
- BKVL 44141 3150 E3

Eagle St
- 7700 KTLD 44094 2376 D3
- 7800 WBHL 44094 2377 A3
- 36600 WBHL 44094 2375 D4
- WLWK 44095 2249 C5
- 10 MDSN 44057 2044 M1
- 10 FTHR 44077 2039 D3

N Eagle St
- 200 GNVA 44041 1944 B3

S Eagle St
- 200 GNVA 44041 1944 B4

W Eagle St
- 100 PNVL 44077 2145 E1

Eagle Trc
- 500 NbyT 44065 3011 D1
- 7600 MDBH 44130 3011 D1
- 7700 MDBH 44130 3011 D1

Eagle Chase
- 13000 NRYN 44133 3014 B7

Eagle Cliff Dr
- 24700 RDHT 44143 2498 D1

Eagle Creek Dr
- 34200 ETLK 44095 2250 A4
- 36200 AVON 44011 2748 A2

Eagle Mills Rd
- WBHL 44094 2375 B3
- 6700 WTHL 44094 2376 A3
- 6800 WTHL 44094 2376 A3
- 19100 RKRV 44116 2621 D5

Eagle Nest Cir
- 2200 AVON 44011 2747 E2
- 2200 AVON 44011 2748 A2

Eagle Nest Dr
- 10 BTVL 44022 2889 E1
- 12200 NRYN 44133 3148 A1
- 37500 EatT 44044 3007 A5

Eagle Nest Ln
- 8700 KTLD 44094 2252 C7
- 38300 WBHL 44094 2376 A4

Eagle Point Dr
- 2600 MadT 44057 1941 E4
- 2600 MadT 44057 1942 A3

Eagle Ridge Cir
- BKVL 44141 3151 C4

Eagle Ridge Dr
- 8200 CcdT 44077 2253 D5

Eagles Pt
- 400 AbnT 44023 2892 B5

Eaglesmere Av
- 13300 CLEV 44110 2496 E1
- 13300 CLEV 44110 2497 A2

Eagles Nest Cir
- 17000 SGVL 44136 3146 E2

Eagles Nest Rd
- 200 BNHT 44131 2755 B6
- 4400 INDE 44131 3015 C1

Eagleton Ct
- 4600 NOSD 44056 3018 B6

Eagle Valley Ct
- 9800 ClbT 44028 3010 D2

Eaglewood Dr
- 10 BWHT 44147 3015 D6

Eaglewood Tr
- 8500 BbgT 44023 2762 B7

Eardley Rd
- 2300 UNHT 44118 2627 E4

Earl Av
- 6500 MadT 44057 1843 B7
- 15600 MPHT 44137 2757 B7

Earl Ct
- 400 ELYR 44035 2875 A7

Earle Av
- 10500 CLEV 44108 2496 C5

Earlene Av
- 41900 EyrT 44035 2874 D2

Earlwood Rd
- 13400 CLEV 44110 2497 A3

East Av
- 200 AVON 44011 2748 C6
- 1300 LORN 44052 2745 A2
- 1300 CrlT 44035 3006 B1
- 2100 LORN 44052 2745 A2
- 4400 LORN 44055 2745 A2
- 8500 MNTR 44060 2144 C6

East Blvd
- CLEV 44103 2496 A5
- 700 CLEV 44108 2496 A4
- 700 AURA 44202 3021 A4
- 1200 CLEV 44106 2496 C7
- 10600 CLEV 44106 2626 C1
- 11600 CLEV 44120 2756 D3

East Cir
- BKVL 44141 3151 A4

East Ct
- 300 PNVL 44077 2145 E3

East Dr
- 600 BNWK 44212 3147 A6
- 600 SDLK 44054 2616 A4
- 6700 SLN 44139 3020 D1

East Pk
- 8700 TwbT 44087 3154 D2

East Rd
- 35000 EatT 44044 3008 B7

East St
- 100 FTHR 44077 2039 D3

East St SR-535
- 100 FTHR 44077 2039 D4

Eastbrook Cir
- 16700 CLEV 44128 2757 C4

Eastbrook Dr
- 8700 BbgT 44023 2891 C5

Eastbrook Tr
- 17600 BbgT 44023 2891 C4

Eastend Dr
- 9000 NRYN 44133 3014 C4

Eastern Heights Blvd
- ELYR 44035 2875 B7

Eastgate Dr
- 6600 MDHT 44124 2500 A7
- 6700 MAYF 44143 2500 B4

Eastham Av
- 1700 ECLE 44112 2497 A4

Easthaven Dr
- 700 HDSN 44236 3155 C4

Easthill Cir
- 2600 SVHL 44131 3015 B1

Easthill Dr
- 11500 CsTp 44026 2501 C4

Easthill Wy
- 11900 CsTp 44026 2501 C4

Eastlake Dr
- 11900 CsTp 44026 2254 E2

Eastland Rd
- SGVL 44136 3011 D2
- 10 BERA 44017 2880 D6
- 500 BERA 44017 2880 D6
- 6200 BKPK 44142 2880 D4
- 8200 SGVL 44136 3011 D2
- 8300 SGVL 44136 3011 D2

S Eastland Rd
- 7600 MDBH 44130 3011 D1
- 7700 MDBH 44130 3011 D1

Eastlane Dr
- 13000 BKLN 44144 2753 C5

Eastlawn Av
- 1500 ECLE 44112 2627 B1
- 1600 CVHT 44118 2627 B1

Eastlawn Dr
- 300 GNVA 44041 1944 C4
- 1600 ECLE 44112 2497 A4

Eastlawn St
- 6700 WTHL 44094 2376 A3
- 6800 WTHL 44094 2376 A3

Eastlook Dr
- 19100 RKRV 44116 2621 D5

Eastman Dr
- 5000 LORN 44053 2744 A5

Eastmoor Rd
- 8200 MNTR 44060 2251 C4

Easton Av
- 1400 MadT 44057 1843 B7
- 8800 CLEV 44104 2626 B7

Easton Ln
- 10 MDHT 44022 2759 E5
- 10 MDHT 44022 2760 A5

Eastondale Rd
- 6200 MDHT 44124 2629 E3

Eastover Rd
- 5000 LNHT 44124 2498 E7
- 5000 LNHT 44124 2499 A7

Eastpoint Dr
- 5000 LNHT 44124 2498 D6

East Pointe Cir
- 9800 BKVL 44141 3150 C3

Eastridge Dr
- 11400 MsnT 44024 2634 C3

Eastview Ct
- 7800 LryT 44077 2256 A3

Eastview Dr
- 5700 NRDV 44039 2877 B2

Eastway Dr
- 8000 MNTR 44060 2143 E4
- 8000 MNTR 44060 2144 A4

Eastway Rd
- 3700 SELD 44118 2627 E2
- 3800 SELD 44118 2628 A2
- 4000 SELD 44121 2628 A2

Eastwick Dr
- 3000 UNHT 44118 2497 C7

Eastwind Ct
- 11000 SGVL 44136 3011 A5

Eastwood Av
- 1100 MDHT 44124 2499 C7
- 5600 MPHT 44137 2886 C2
- 21000 FWPK 44126 2751 C2

Eastwood Blvd
- 12300 GDHT 44125 2885 D1
- 13500 GDHT 44125 2886 A2

Eastwood Dr
- AVON 44011 2748 C6
- 700 PNVL 44077 2146 C2
- 4000 WVHT 44128 2758 A3
- 4000 WVHT 44128 2758 A3
- 4100 WVHT 44128 2757 E3
- 26900 OmsT 44138 2878 A3
- 26900 OmsT 44138 2879 A3

Eastwood St
- 10 GNVA 44041 1944 C4

Easy St
- 25100 BDHT 44146 2887 D3

Eaton Blvd
- 100 EatT 44044 3008 B7
- 200 EatT 44044 3143 B1

Eaton Cir
- 5400 MNTR 44060 2145 B1

Eaton Ct
- 300 PNVL 44077 2145 E3
- 6000 BDHT 44146 2887 D4
- 16700 MDBH 44130 2881 A5

Eaton Dr
- AURA 44202 3157 A4
- 100 SgHT 44067 3017 D4
- 2100 AVON 44011 2617 D7
- 2100 AVON 44011 2747 D1
- 8300 BbgT 44023 2891 A4

Eaton Ln
- PRPK 44124 2759 B4
- WDMR 44122 2759 B1
- WDMR 44122 2759 B1

Eaton Rd
- 2400 UNHT 44118 2627 E4
- 2600 SRHT 44122 2627 E5
- 2600 SRHT 44122 2628 A5
- 8800 MCDN 44056 3018 A6

Eaton Wy
- 25500 BYVL 44140 2620 C5

Eaton Commerce Pkwy
- EatT 44028 3008 D7
- EatT 44028 3143 E1

Eaton Township Rd
- EatT 44044 3141 E2

Eavenson Dr
- 6600 BKPK 44142 2881 A3

Ebb Tide Dr
- 13100 NRYN 44133 3147 A4

Eberhardt St
- 50 SAHT 44001 3003 A1

Echo Dr
- 600 MAYF 44040 2500 C4
- 8800 MNTR 44060 2144 C6

E Echo Dr
- 2000 HDSN 44236 2254 E2

Echo Gln
- 1300 GSML 44040 2500 E7
- 1400 GSML 44040 2501 A7

Echo Hill Dr
- 10000 BKVL 44141 3151 D5

Echolane Dr
- 2400 BWHT 44147 3014 A3

Eckstein Ct
- 10400 CLEV 44111 2623 C4

Edanola Dr
- 1200 LKWD 44107 2622 A4

Eddie Ln
- ClbT 44028 3009 D7

Eddie Rd
- 10 MadT 44057 1844 A6

Eddy Rd
- 100 BTNH 44108 2496 E3
- 200 ECLE 44108 2496 D4
- 300 CLEV 44108 2496 D4
- 1600 ECLE 44112 2497 A4
- 28700 WBHL 44094 2374 C5
- 30800 WBHL 44094 2375 A5

Eddystone Dr
- 1100 AhT 44001 2873 B4

Eddywood Ln
- 8000 CsTp 44026 2501 E4

Eden Ln
- 14700 MDBH 44130 2881 C7

Edendale St
- 1300 CVHT 44121 2497 E7

Edenhall Dr
- 1700 LNHT 44124 2629 B1

Edenhurst Rd
- 5000 LNHT 44124 2498 E6
- 5100 LNHT 44124 2499 A6

Edenwood Rd
- 4700 SELD 44121 2498 D6

Edgebrook Blvd
- 5900 PMHT 44130 2882 C2

Edgebrook Cross
- 2500 TNBG 44087 3019 E7
- 2600 TNBG 44087 3020 E1

Edgebrook Ct
- 7800 LryT 44077 2256 A3

Edgecliff Av
- 15200 CLEV 44111 2752 B1
- 15300 CLEV 44111 2622 B7

Edgecliff Cir E
- 100 ELYR 44035 2874 B7
- 100 ELYR 44035 3005 B1

Edgecliff Cir W
- 100 ELYR 44035 2874 B6

Edgecliff Dr
- 1100 BDFD 44146 2887 B5
- 6900 PRMA 44134 2883 D6
- 19500 EUCL 44119 2372 E3
- 20000 EUCL 44123 2373 A3
- 22500 EUCL 44123 2373 D1
- 25500 EUCL 44132 2248 D7
- 25500 EUCL 44132 2373 D1

Edgecliff Ter
- 21000 FWPK 44126 2751 C2
- CLEV 44111 2752 C1

Edgedale Dr
- 28400 PRPK 44124 2629 B6

Edgefield Dr
- 10 ELYR 44035 3005 D1

Edgefield Rd
- 1400 LNHT 44124 2499 C4
- 1400 LNHT 44124 2629 B1

Edgehill Dr
- 5600 PMHT 44130 2882 C2
- 5700 PMHT 44130 2882 C2
- 14600 NbyT 44065 2764 C1
- 23800 BHWD 44122 2628 D3
- 41500 CrlT 44035 3005 D5

Edgehill Rd
- 2100 CLEV 44106 2626 C1
- 2200 CLEV 44106 2626 C1
- 2300 CLEV 44106 2627 A1
- 2500 CVHT 44106 2627 A2
- 25100 BHWD 44122 2627 A2
- 8700 MNTR 44060 2252 C1

Edgehurst Dr
- 6300 BKPK 44142 2881 C4

Edgelake Ovl
- 8400 SgHT 44067 3017 C4

Edgemeer Pl
- 300 OBLN 44074 3138 C3

Edgemere Wy
- 35800 AVON 44011 2748 A3

Edgemont Rd
- 25000 BHWD 44122 2373 D7

Edgemoor Av
- 300 CLEV 2888 E6

Edgepark Blvd
- 3800 NOSD 44070 2749 E5
- 27300 NOSD 44070 2749 E5
- 28100 WTLK 44145 2749 E5
- 28100 WTLK 44145 2749 E5

Edgepark Dr
- 5200 GDHT 44125 2885 E1
- 5700 BKPK 44142 2879 E1

Edgerly Rd
- 600 CVHT 44121 2497 E4

Edgerton Rd
- 2100 UNHT 44118 2627 E4
- 3000 NRYN 44133 3149 B3
- 11800 NRYN 44133 3148 E1
- 11900 NRYN 44133 3147 E1
- 12200 SGVL 44136 3147 E1
- 12200 SGVL 44136 3012 E7

N Edgerton Rd
- 900 BWHT 44147 3150 B3
- 900 BWHT 44147 3150 B3
- 10 BKVL 44141 3150 B2

S Edgerton Rd
- BKVL 44141 3150 E4

W Edgerton Rd
- BWHT 44147 3149 D3

Edgeview Dr
- 1900 HDSN 44236 3155 A7
- 2000 HDSN 44236 3155 A7

Edgewater Blvd
- 3100 VMLN 44089 2742 A4
- 3300 VMLN 44089 2741 D4

Edgewater Dr
- 4500 SDLK 44054 2616 B3
- 4500 VMLN 44054 2741 B4
- 5100 SDLK 44054 2616 B3
- 9900 CLEV 44102 2623 C6
- 11700 LKWD 44107 2623 C4
- 14200 LKWD 44107 2623 C4
- 14700 NbyT 44065 2764 D1
- 15300 MPHT 44137 2886 B2

Edgewater Ln
- 1000 MadT 44057 1844 A5
- 13600 CLEV 44110 2756 A3
- 15600 CLEV 44110 2757 A3
- 15300 MPHT 44137 2886 B2

Edgewood Ct
- 400 BERA 44017 3011 A1

Edgewood Dr
- 10 CNFL 44022 2761 B4
- 10 AVLK 44012 2617 D1
- 10 BDFD 44146 2887 C4
- 10 BERA 44017 2880 A7

INDEX 18

Edgewood Dr

Cleveland Street Index

Evening Star Av

STREET
Block City ZIP Map# Grid

Edgewood Dr
10 CrlT 44044 3006 D7
10 EatT 44044 3006 D7
100 AhtT 44001 2873 A1
100 AMHT 44001 2873 A1
1000 VMLN 44089 2741 B6
1800 TNBG 44087 3019 C5
3600 LORN 44053 2744 C4
8800 NRYN 44133 3013 A3
15600 MDFD 44062 2767 C3
18300 RKRV 44116 2622 A6
28900 WLWK 44095 2249 B7
Edgewood Ln
5800 WLBY 44094 2375 A2
7500 SVHL 44131 3015 C2
Edgewood Rd
- AhtT 44001 2872 E6
600 RDHT 44143 2499 A4
2100 CVHT 44118 2627 C3
2500 BHWD 44122 2628 D5
2900 PRPK 44124 2629 D7
5900 MDHT 44124 2499 C6
8000 MNTR 44060 2143 E5
8000 MNTR 44060 2144 A5
11500 MsnT 44024 2504 C3
28900 BYVL 44140 2619 D4
Edgewood St
100 ELYR 44035 2875 D5
Edinboro Av
17800 MPHT 44137 2886 D1
Edinboro Pl
6700 CcdT 44077 2146 C6
Edinborough Dr
400 BYVL 44140 2621 A5
500 BYVL 44140 2620 E5
E Edinburgh Dr
- HDHT 44143 2499 C1
W Edinburgh Dr
300 HDHT 44143 2499 C1
Edinburgh Ovl
10 OmsT 44138 2879 B2
Edison Blvd
2300 TNBG 44087 3155 A4
Edison Ct
41700 EyrT 44035 2874 D3
Edison Dr
10 ETLK 44095 2250 B1
100 VMLN 44089 2741 C4
Edison Rd
3400 CVHT 44121 2497 D7
Edison St
10 OBLN 44074 3138 E3
Edith Ct
11500 CLEV 44106 2496 D7
Edith St
2400 LORN 44052 2744 A1
2400 LORN 44053 2744 A1
39600 SLN 44139 3020 E2
39900 SLN 44139 3021 A2
Edmond Dr
4400 SELD 44121 2498 C7
Edmonton Av
12300 CLEV 44108 2496 E5
Edmund Cir
9300 MNTR 44060 2039 A7
Edmunds Av
9000 CLEV 44106 2626 B1
Edna Av
6100 CLEV 44103 2495 D7
Ednil Dr
29900 BYVL 44140 2619 C4
Edolyn Av
15300 CLEV 44111 2752 C2
Edsal Dr
4700 LNHT 44124 2498 D6
Edson St
5800 VMLN 44089 2740 D6
8600 MNTR 44060 2038 C7
Educational Park Dr
10 SVHL 44131 2884 A7
Edward Av
32800 ETLK 44095 2249 E5
Edward Ct
6300 PMHT 44130 2882 A4
Edward Dr
- VMLN 44089 2741 B6
3900 BNWK 44212 3146 E6
Edward St
100 ELYR 44035 3006 B3
6500 MNTR 44060 2144 A5
Edwards Av
1100 LKWD 44107 2622 B4
Edwards Ln
9900 AbnT 44023 3023 B3
Edwards Rd
2300 CVHT 44106 2626 E3
Edwards St
10 MDSN 44057 1942 B7
10 MDSN 44057 2044 B1
700 BERA 44017 3011 C3
16100 PkmT 44234 2896 D7
Edwin Av
38900 NRDV 44039 2876 A3
Edwin Ct
12300 CLEV 44106 2496 E7
12300 CLEV 44112 2496 E7
Effie Ct
- CLEV 44105 2756 B5
Effie Rd
- GDHT 44105 2756 B5
- GDHT 44125 2756 B5
4500 CLEV 44105 2756 B5
Effingham Blvd
23400 EUCL 44117 2373 C7
Egbert Rd
10 BDFD 44146 2887 A6
15500 WNHL 44146 3017 C1
17500 WNHL 44146 2886 D7
18300 WNHL 44146 2887 A6
Egg Hbr
- AVON 44011 2747 C2
Eggers Av
2900 CLEV 44105 2755 B1
Eggleston Rd
10 AURA 44202 3022 B7
10 AURA 44202 3157 B1
Eglindale Av
1800 CLEV 44109 2754 D1
Eichorn Av
4500 CLEV 44109 2754 A1
4600 CLEV 44102 2754 A1
Eileen Dr
700 MCDN 44056 3154 A5
Eisenhower Dr
- KTLD 44094 2251 D6

Elaine Dr
7500 SVHL 44131 3015 B1
8100 NRYN 44133 3014 C3
Elaine St
700 RDHT 44143 2498 D5
Elandon Dr
2100 CVHT 44106 2626 D3
Elbe St
100 ELYR 44035 2874 E5
Elberon Av
1600 CLEV 44106 2496 E7
1600 CLEV 44112 2496 E7
1600 ECLE 44112 2496 E7
Elbert Dr
100 CrlT 44044 3006 C7
Elberta Av
15900 CLEV 44128 2757 B5
Elberta Rd
10 PNVL 44077 2145 D2
10 PnvT 44077 2145 D2
400 VMLN 44089 2741 B4
4400 PryT 44081 2042 D4
Elbertson Av
- AVLK 44012 2617 B2
Elbon Rd
800 CVHT 44121 2497 D6
Elbur Av
1100 LKWD 44107 2622 E4
Elbur Ln
13500 LKWD 44107 2622 E5
Elda Wy
- NRDV 44039 2876 E6
Eldamere Av
15500 CLEV 44128 2757 C3
Elder Dr
28300 NOSD 44070 2878 D3
Elderdale Dr
16400 MDBH 44130 3012 A1
Elderkin Ct
7500 HDSN 44236 3154 E6
Elderwood Av
14400 ECLE 44112 2497 A6
Eldo St
4700 WLBY 44094 2250 D7
Eldon Ct
8200 MNTR 44060 2144 A5
Eldon Dr
1600 WKLF 44092 2374 D1
5700 PRMA 44130 2882 D2
5800 PMHT 44130 2882 D2
Eldora Rd
19800 RKRV 44116 2621 D5
Eldorado Dr
3500 RKRV 44116 2751 E1
Eldred Av
10 BDFD 44146 2886 E2
10 BDFD 44146 2887 A2
2100 LKWD 44107 2622 B6
Eldridge Blvd
6100 BDHT 44146 2887 D4
Eldridge Rd
10 AURA 44202 3157 B2
12500 PMHT 44130 2881 E4
Eleanor Ct
7900 MNTR 44060 2251 E4
Eleanore Dr
3800 NOSD 44070 2750 C5
15600 CLEV 44135 2752 B5
Electric Blvd
10200 NHFD 44067 3018 A4
31600 AVLK 44012 2619 A2
31600 AVLK 44140 2619 A2
31600 BYVL 44140 2619 A2
31900 AVLK 44012 2618 D1
32800 AVLK 44012 2617 D1
Electric Dr
24300 BYVL 44140 2620 D5
29600 BYVL 44140 2619 C4
Elevator Av
10 PNVL 44077 2146 B2
Elfleda St
1600 ShfT 44055 2745 C6
Elgin Av
10500 CLEV 44108 2496 C5
Elgin Ovl
10 OmsT 44138 2879 A4
Elgin Rd
29900 WKLF 44092 2249 C7
Elinore Av
26100 EUCL 44132 2373 E2
26900 EUCL 44132 2374 A2
Eliot Av
10200 CLEV 44104 2626 C7
Elise Dr
7000 MDBH 44130 2881 B6
Elisha Ln
3100 TNBG 44087 3020 C3
Eliza Av
5300 CLEV 44105 2755 D1
Elizabeth Av
5400 PRMA 44130 2882 C1
9300 CLEV 44105 2756 B2
21700 FWPK 44126 2751 B5
Elizabeth Ct
6100 BKPK 44142 2881 B3
7000 MNTR 44060 2251 B1
Elizabeth Dr
10 GNVA 44041 1944 C6
2700 AVON 44011 2748 C2
3500 VMLN 44089 2741 E5
Elizabeth Ln
1300 MCDN 44056 3019 A7
4700 BKLN 44144 2753 D6
19000 BbgT 44023 3021 D3
26900 OmsT 44138 2878 E2
26900 OmsT 44138 2879 A3
Elizabeth St
100 ELYR 44035 2875 B7
Elk Av
9900 CLEV 44108 2496 B4
Elk Run
11100 MsnT 44024 2634 B3
Ella Av
8300 CLEV 44105 2756 B4
Ellacott Pkwy
20500 WVHT 44128 2758 A4
Ellen Av
5800 CLEV 44102 2624 A5
Ellen Dr
10 BERA 44017 3011 C2
21200 FWPK 44126 2751 B5
Ellendale Rd
3800 MDHL 44022 2760 B3
Ellenwood Av
10 BDFD 44146 2886 E3

Ellenwood Av
10 BDFD 44146 2887 A3
Elleroy Ct
13900 CLEV 44111 2622 E7
Ellie Pl
7600 MNTR 44060 2253 A2
Elliman Rd
600 AURA 44202 3157 C6
600 AURA 44241 3157 C6
600 AURA 44255 3157 C6
600 STBR 44241 3157 C6
Ellington Pl
7600 MNTR 44060 2251 B2
Ellington Rd
27200 WTLK 44145 2620 A6
Elliot Dr
17900 BbgT 44023 2891 B6
Ellison Rd
4000 SELD 44121 2628 B1
Ellison Creek Dr
10700 CcdT 44077 2146 A6
Ellsworth Av
24600 EUCL 44123 2373 D1
24800 EUCL 44132 2373 D1
Ellsworth Dr
19300 SGVL 44136 3146 C4
Ellsworth Hill Dr
2600 HDSN 44236 3155 C7
Ellwood Av
13500 CLEV 44135 2752 E4
Elm Av
- EUCL 44132 2374 A2
1000 MadT 44057 1844 A5
4300 BHIT 44212 3146 D7
4300 BNWK 44212 3146 D7
13800 ECLE 44112 2497 B4
14700 BKPK 44142 2752 C7
29000 WKLF 44092 2374 C3
Elm Ct
10 CNFL 44022 2761 A6
300 SVHL 44131 3015 A2
1300 CLEV 44102 2623 E5
Elm Dr
10 OmsT 44138 2879 B4
14600 NbyT 44065 2764 C1
19400 SGVL 44136 3146 D4
Elm Rd
- OKWD 44146 3018 E2
500 EatT 44044 3143 A1
23300 NOSD 44070 2750 D6
Elm St
- AhtT 44001 2872 B3
- BHIT 44212 3146 C7
- SFLD 44054 2746 C5
10 BDFD 44146 2887 A3
10 GNVA 44041 1944 B3
10 OBLN 44074 3138 D2
10 SAHT 44001 2872 C7
200 BDHT 44146 2758 D7
300 SAHT 44001 2872 A7
400 ELYR 44035 2875 A6
400 PNVL 44077 2040 B6
900 PNVL 44077 2039 E5
1000 GFTN 44044 3142 B6
2000 CLEV 44113 2624 C3
5000 VMLN 44089 2741 A5
8900 BKVL 44141 3016 A7
8900 KTLD 44094 2251 D7
8900 MNTR 44060 2252 D1
8900 WTHL 44094 2251 D7
10400 MCDN 44056 3018 C4
10400 NHFD 44067 3018 C4
10500 NHFD 44056 3018 C4
10600 MNTU 44255 3159 C6
14400 MPHT 44137 2757 A7
25500 ODFL 44138 2879 B5
37800 WLBY 44094 2250 D4
Elma Dr
100 ELYR 44035 2875 C4
Elmar Blvd
14600 BURT 44021 2766 A1
Elmarge Av
10400 CLEV 44105 2756 C4
Elmarge Dr
6000 INDE 44131 2884 E6
Elmbrook Dr
3300 BWHT 44147 3015 B5
Elmdale Rd
2400 UNHT 44118 2628 B4
6100 BKPK 44142 2881 D4
6400 MDBH 44130 2881 D4
Elmdale Trc
8700 MCDN 44056 3018 B6
Elmer Av
25800 ODFL 44138 2879 B6
Elm Hill Dr
5500 SLN 44139 2888 D3
Elmhurst Av
14500 CLEV 44110 2497 B3
Elmhurst Dr
2500 BHWD 44122 2628 C5
7500 SVHL 44131 3015 A1
7900 BWHT 44147 3015 A3
Elmhurst Rd
5700 NOSD 44070 2749 B7
5700 NOSD 44070 2878 C1
Elmore Dr
5800 PMHT 44130 2882 D2
Elmore Rd
3900 FWPK 44126 2751 D2
3900 RKRV 44116 2751 D2
Elmurwill Dr
- RslT 44072 2762 B2
Elmwood Av
- INDE 44131 2884 C5
800 WKLF 44092 2374 B1
1400 LKWD 44107 2622 C5
5300 MPHT 44137 2757 D7
5300 MPHT 44137 2886 E1
10600 GDHT 44125 2756 C7
11800 CLEV 44111 2623 A7
N Elmwood Av
600 WKLF 44092 2249 A7
600 WKLF 44092 2374 B1
Elmwood Dr
200 BERA 44017 2880 B6
800 MCDN 44056 3153 E2
900 WLBY 44094 2142 E4
2100 WTLK 44145 2750 A2
3100 VMLN 44089 2742 A5
3200 VMLN 44089 2741 E5
4900 SDLK 44054 2616 D4
6800 SLN 44139 2889 D7
8100 KTLD 44094 2376 E6
23800 EUCL 44123 2373 C1

Elmwood Ln
18700 BbgT 44023 3022 B2
Elmwood Ovl
8900 NRYN 44133 3013 B3
Elmwood Pl
10 OBLN 44074 3138 D3
Elmwood Pt
- AURA 44202 3156 C1
Elmwood Rd
200 RKRV 44116 2621 C5
300 BYVL 44140 2620 B5
1100 MDHT 44124 2499 C7
3900 CVHT 44121 2498 A6
4000 SELD 44121 2498 B6
6400 MNTR 44060 2143 E5
Elmwood St
15500 MDFD 44062 2767 C2
41400 EyrT 44035 2745 D6
Eloise Dr
800 CVHT 44112 2497 C5
Elsa Ct
8000 CLEV 44102 2623 E5
Elsetta Av
10000 PMHT 44130 2882 C4
14000 CLEV 44135 2752 D3
Elsienna Av
16200 CLEV 44135 2752 B4
Elsinore Av
1600 ECLE 44112 2497 A6
Elsmere Dr
8700 PRMA 44130 2882 C2
24300 EUCL 44117 2373 C6
Elsmere Rd
3200 SRHT 44120 2627 C7
Elston Av
- NOSD 44070 2749 B7
1600 CLEV 44109 2754 E3
Elton Av
6900 CLEV 44102 2623 E6
Elton Ct
6800 CLEV 44102 2623 E6
6800 CLEV 44102 2624 A3
Elton St
2700 ShvT 44241 3158 A7
Elwell Av
9600 CLEV 44104 2626 C6
Elwood Rd
1300 ECLE 44112 2497 A4
Ely Av
11600 CLEV 44120 2626 D7
Ely Rd
8200 NsnT 44231 3027 B7
9100 NsnT 44231 3028 A7
Elyria Av
100 AMHT 44001 2872 D2
1600 LORN 44052 2745 A2
2200 LORN 44055 2745 B4
3100 VMLN 44089 2742 A4
3200 VMLN 44089 2741 E4
3900 ShfT 44055 2745 B4
3900 ShfT 44052 2745 B4
5500 EyrT 44055 2745 B4
5500 EyrT 44035 2745 B4
Elyria St
16600 BbgT 44023 2890 A1
33300 NRDV 44039 2877 D1
Ely Vista Dr
5400 PRMA 44129 2883 A6
6500 PRMA 44129 2882 E6
Elywood Dr
900 ELYR 44035 2875 B4
Emerald Ct
600 AURA 44202 3021 C7
1400 CLEV 44114 2625 A2
5600 MNTR 44060 2145 A2
Emerald Dr
1700 LORN 44053 2744 B5
42900 EyrT 44035 2874 A2
Emerald Ln
100 BERA 44017 2880 A7
4700 BHIT 44212 3146 B7
Emerald Pt
16100 MDBH 44130 2881 B4
Emerald St
5800 NRDV 44039 2877 C2
Emerald Creek Dr
1200 BWHT 44147 3015 A7
Emerald Edge Pl
11600 SGVL 44136 3012 C6
Emerald Glen Dr
8200 KTLD 44094 2377 A4
Emerald Lakes Blvd
2800 WBHL 44092 2374 B6
Emerald Ridge Pkwy
5500 GNWL 44139 3019 C1
5600 SLN 44139 2888 A2
Emerson Av
10 BERA 44017 2880 C4
12900 LKWD 44107 2623 A4
13400 LKWD 44107 2622 E4
Emerson Ct
41800 EyrT 44035 2874 C3
Emerson Dr
10 BERA 44017 2880 B4
2700 PRPK 44124 2629 D4
9900 ClbT 44028 3010 D2
Emerson Rd
4400 SELD 44121 2498 C6
4800 MadT 44057 2044 D5
Emery Av
11900 CLEV 44135 2753 A3
13500 CLEV 44135 2752 D3
Emery Cir
6100 MNTR 44060 2143 E3
Emery Rd
19500 NRDL 44128 2757 E5
19500 WVHT 44128 2757 E5
20100 NRDL 44128 2758 C5
21200 WVHT 44128 2758 C5
25500 WVHT 44022 2758 C5
26500 WVHT 44022 2759 A5
26500 WVHT 44128 2759 A5
28100 ORNG 44022 2759 A5
30700 MDHL 44022 2759 A5
Emily Av
2200 LKWD 44107 2622 D6
Emily Ct
8200 CLEV 44102 2623 D7
Emily Ext
13700 ECLE 44112 2497 A6
Emily St
13300 ECLE 44112 2496 E7
13300 ECLE 44112 2497 A6
30900 WKLF 44092 2374 E1

Emmet Rd
4900 LNHT 44124 2498 E6
Emmons Rd
23000 ClbT 44028 3145 D3
23000 ClbT 44136 3145 D3
Emory Dr
6400 BKPK 44142 2881 A3
Empire Av
8800 CLEV 44108 2496 B5
Empire Pkwy
7800 MCDN 44056 3153 D3
Empire Rd
1500 WKLF 44092 2374 E2
Emsley Ct
38100 WLBY 44094 2250 E1
Enderby Dr
9500 PRMA 44130 2882 C1
Enderby Rd
3200 SRHT 44120 2627 B7
Endicott Rd
2600 SRHT 44120 2627 A5
Endora Rd
16500 CLEV 44112 2497 C4
16500 ECLE 44112 2497 C4
Endsley Av
20800 RKRV 44116 2621 C6
Enfield Dr
6700 MDHT 44124 2630 A1
7000 MNTR 44060 2251 B1
Engel Av
5900 CLEV 44127 2625 D7
5900 CLEV 44127 2755 D1
Engle Rd
5000 BKPK 44142 2752 A7
5000 BKPK 44142 2881 A1
6600 MDBH 44130 2881 A5
7400 MDBH 44130 3012 A1
Engle Rd SR-291
5000 BKPK 44142 2752 A7
5000 BKPK 44142 2881 A1
6600 MDBH 44130 2881 A5
7400 MDBH 44130 3012 A1
Engle Lake Dr
17500 MDBH 44130 2881 A5
Englewood Av
10500 CLEV 44108 2496 C5
Englewood Ct
32600 NRDV 44039 2877 E1
Englewood Dr
100 AVLK 44012 2488 A7
100 AVLK 44012 2618 A1
900 PRMA 44134 2883 E2
17700 MDBH 44130 2880 E5
17700 MDBH 44130 2881 A5
E Englewood Dr
10 SVHL 44131 2883 D2
Englewood Rd
800 CVHT 44121 2498 A5
English Dr
7800 BKVL 44141 3015 E3
17800 BbgT 44023 2890 E6
English Lakes Blvd
200 AMHT 44001 2872 D4
Enid Rd
29900 WKLF 44092 2249 C7
Ennis Av
10 BDFD 44146 2887 A3
Ensenada Ct
600 BERA 44017 3010 E1
Ensign Av
5500 CLEV 44104 2625 D5
Ensign Rd
4900 FnTp 44491 3029 B3
4900 StnT 44491 3029 B3
5600 FnTp 44491 2898 D7
13900 ClrT 44021 2636 B1
13900 ClrT 44024 2636 B1
Ensign Cove
3400 RMDV 44202 3020 D4
Enterprise Av
13000 CLEV 44135 2752 E6
Enterprise Dr
7800 MNTR 44060 2251 B2
Enterprise Pkwy
1400 TwbT 44087 3154 B4
1800 TNBG 44087 3154 D4
3200 BHWD 44122 2628 E7
3200 BHWD 44122 2758 E1
6000 SLN 44139 2888 C4
Enterprise Wy
14900 BtnT 44062 2766 E2
14900 BtnT 44062 2767 A2
Entrence Rd
- EUCL 44117 2373 B7
- EUCL 44117 2498 B1
Epping Rd
1600 GSML 44040 2630 E2
Epping Tr
11900 MsnT 44024 2504 B4
Equestra N
- AURA 44202 3156 D4
Equestra S
- AURA 44202 3156 D5
Equestra Ct
- AURA 44202 3156 D5
Equestrian Ct
8000 CcdT 44060 2253 B4
Equestrian Dr
13600 BtnT 44021 2636 A4
Erhart Northern Rd
- ClbT 44280 3143 E6
- ClbT 44028 3143 E6
- EatT 44028 3143 E6
15500 GftT 44028 3143 E7
15500 LvpT 44028 3143 E7
15500 LvpT 44280 3143 E7
Eric Dr
7200 MNTR 44060 2143 C3
Eric Ln
1100 CLEV 44109 2754 E6
Erich Dr
2800 WBHL 44092 2374 D7
Ericson Ln
5500 WLBY 44094 2375 B2
Ericston Ct
600 PNVL 44077 2040 A5
Erie Av
6700 MadT 44057 1843 B6
E Erie Av
100 LORN 44052 2614 E6
800 LORN 44052 2615 C5
3500 LORN 44054 2615 C5
3500 SDLK 44054 2615 C5
E Erie Av US-6
200 LORN 44052 2614 E6

E Erie Av US-6
800 LORN 44052 2615 C5
3500 LORN 44054 2615 C5
3500 SDLK 44054 2615 C5
W Erie Av
300 LORN 44052 2614 C6
2400 LORN 44053 2614 C6
2700 LORN 44053 2744 A1
4200 LORN 44053 2743 E1
6100 LORN 44053 2742 D4
W Erie Av US-6
300 LORN 44052 2614 C6
2400 LORN 44053 2614 C6
2700 LORN 44053 2744 A1
3100 LORN 44053 2743 E1
6100 LORN 44053 2742 D4
E Erie Br
- LORN 44052 2614 E6
E Erie Br US-6
- LORN 44052 2614 E6
Erie Ct
200 AhtT 44001 2873 B1
1000 CLEV 44115 2625 A3
Erie Dr
7000 MNTR 44060 2251 B1
Erie Rd
- WLBY 44095 2250 C3
10 ETLK 44095 2142 A7
10 ETLK 44095 2250 B1
400 VMLN 44089 2741 B4
900 ETLK 44094 2250 C3
900 WLBY 44094 2250 C3
20500 RKRV 44116 2621 C6
Erie St
10 GNVA 44041 1944 C4
100 ELYR 44035 2874 E5
100 ELYR 44035 2875 A5
100 SAHT 44001 2872 C7
600 GFTN 44044 3142 A5
3700 WLBY 44094 2250 E4
5300 BDHT 44146 2887 D1
Erie St US-20
4000 WLBY 44094 2250 E5
E Erie St
10 PNVL 44077 2040 C6
800 PnvT 44077 2040 C6
E Erie St US-20
10 PNVL 44077 2040 C6
800 PnvT 44077 2040 C6
W Erie St
10 PNVL 44077 2146 A1
W Erie St US-20
10 PNVL 44077 2146 A1
Erie Cliff Dr
1000 LKWD 44107 2622 C3
Erieside Av
10 CLEV 44114 2624 D2
Erie Street Ext
900 PnvT 44077 2040 D6
Erieview Blvd
100 SDLK 44054 2617 A3
Erieview Dr
100 ETLK 44095 2142 C6
1200 MadT 44057 1843 E6
Erieview Rd
1100 CVHT 44121 2498 A6
Eriewood Dr
1100 RKRV 44116 2621 C6
Erin Av
2600 CLEV 44113 2624 C7
Erin Ct
10 RKRV 44116 2621 C7
10 RKRV 44116 2751 C1
19100 SGVL 44136 3146 C5
Ernadale Av
16200 CLEV 44111 2752 B1
Ernest Av
16500 CLEV 44111 2752 B2
Erwin Av
11700 CLEV 44135 2753 A5
Erwin Ct
13900 MDBH 44130 2881 D5
Erwin Dr
14500 BtnT 44062 2766 D4
Erwin St
5000 MPHT 44137 2757 D7
Eschtruth St
- EyrT 44035 2745 E6
2200 ELYR 44035 2745 E6
2300 ELYR 44035 2746 A6
2300 ShfT 44035 2746 A6
Esma Ln
8400 MNTR 44060 2144 B3
Esmeralda Av
14400 CLEV 44110 2372 A7
Esper Av
6800 PRMA 44134 2883 D6
Essen Av
7400 PRMA 44129 2882 E2
Essex Cir
11200 NRYN 44133 3013 D5
Essex Ct
14400 ClrT 44024 2506 D2
29700 WTLK 44145 2749 C3
Essex Dr
5500 SVHL 44131 2884 B2
7300 MNTR 44060 2251 C1
16100 SGVL 44136 3147 B2
Essex Rd
400 VMLN 44089 2741 D4
2900 CVHT 44118 2627 B3
Estate Av
7600 TwbT 44236 3154 D5
Estates Ct
28600 SLN 44139 2888 B1
Estelle Av
3100 LORN 44052 2744 D3
Esterbrook Av
- CLEV 44103 2496 B5
8800 CLEV 44108 2496 B5
Esther Av
14900 LKWD 44107 2622 C6
22700 FWPK 44126 2751 A5
22900 NOSD 44070 2750 E5
22900 NOSD 44126 2751 A5
22900 NOSD 44070 2751 A5
Esther Dr
38900 CrlT 44044 3006 D7
Esther Rd
700 HDHT 44143 2499 B4
Esther St
8400 MNTR 44060 2252 B2
Estill Dr
1000 LKWD 44107 2622 D3

Ethan Av
1200 STBR 44241 3156 E6
Ethan Ct
3000 BNWK 44212 3147 C7
Ethan's Dr
2500 TNBG 44087 3020 B3
Ethel Av
1100 LKWD 44107 2622 B4
6000 EyrT 44035 2745 D7
6000 ShfT 44035 2745 D7
6000 ShfT 44055 2745 D7
Ethel Ct
8900 CLEV 44106 2496 B7
Ethel Dr
24400 SGVL 44136 3010 E3
41700 CrlT 44035 3005 C4
Eton St
1900 TwbT 44087 3154 C2
Euclid Av
100 CLEV 44114 2624 E3
100 CLEV 44115 2624 E3
200 LORN 44052 2615 C4
900 CLEV 44114 2625 B2
900 CLEV 44115 2625 B2
4000 CLEV 44103 2625 B2
7300 CLEV 44103 2626 A2
8500 CLEV 44106 2626 A2
12200 CLEV 44112 2626 E1
12200 ECLE 44106 2626 E1
12400 ECLE 44112 2626 E1
12600 ECLE 44112 2496 E7
13500 ECLE 44112 2497 B5
16300 CLEV 44112 2497 D3
18100 CLEV 44121 2497 D3
19500 EUCL 44117 2497 E2
19700 EUCL 44117 2498 A1
20700 EUCL 44117 2373 C6
25600 EUCL 44132 2373 C6
26000 EUCL 44143 2373 C6
27100 EUCL 44132 2374 B3
28600 WKLF 44092 2374 B3
30400 WLWK 44092 2374 D1
30700 WKLF 44092 2249 E7
30700 WKLF 44094 2249 E7
30700 WLBY 44094 2249 E7
30700 WLWK 44092 2249 E7
34000 WLBY 44094 2250 B7
Euclid Av US-6
13500 ECLE 44112 2497 B5
16300 CLEV 44112 2497 D3
18100 CLEV 44121 2497 D3
18900 EUCL 44117 2497 D3
19700 EUCL 44117 2498 A1
Euclid Av US-20
100 CLEV 44114 2624 E3
100 CLEV 44115 2624 E3
900 CLEV 44114 2625 B2
900 CLEV 44115 2625 B2
4000 CLEV 44103 2625 B2
7300 CLEV 44103 2626 A2
8500 CLEV 44106 2626 A2
12200 CLEV 44112 2626 E1
12200 ECLE 44106 2626 E1
12400 ECLE 44112 2626 E1
12600 ECLE 44112 2496 E7
13500 ECLE 44112 2497 B5
16300 CLEV 44112 2497 D3
18100 CLEV 44121 2497 D3
18900 EUCL 44117 2497 D3
19700 EUCL 44117 2498 A1
20700 EUCL 44117 2373 C6
25600 EUCL 44132 2373 C6
26000 EUCL 44143 2373 C6
27100 EUCL 44132 2374 B3
28300 WKLF 44092 2374 B3
30400 WLWK 44092 2374 D1
30700 WKLF 44092 2249 E7
30700 WKLF 44094 2249 E7
30700 WLBY 44094 2249 E7
30700 WLWK 44092 2249 E7
34000 WLBY 44094 2250 B7
Euclid Av US-322
10900 CLEV 44106 2626 D2
Euclid Dr
36000 NRDV 44039 2876 E7
Euclid St
100 ELYR 44035 2875 A4
Euclid Beach Blvd
10 CLEV 44110 2372 C6
Euclid Chagrin Pkwy
25800 RDHT 44143 2498 D2
Euclid Creek Pkwy
6600 EUCL 44117 2498 A2
6600 EUCL 44143 2498 A2
Euclid Heights Blvd
2300 CVHT 44106 2626 E3
2500 CVHT 44106 2627 A2
2700 CVHT 44118 2627 C2
Euclid Square Mall
- EUCL 44132 2373 D4
Euclid Vets Dr
1300 EUCL 44132 2373 E4
Eureka Pkwy
9400 PMHT 44130 2882 C2
Euston Dr
1800 MDHT 44124 2629 C2
Evangeline Rd
800 CLEV 44110 2497 B2
Evans Dr
7700 PRMA 44130 3013 B2
Evanston Av
3800 CLEV 44122 2757 E3
3800 WVHT 44122 2757 E3
Evanston Ln
- AhtT 44001 2872 E6
Evanston Rd
1400 LNHT 44124 2498 D7
Evarts Rd
8800 CLEV 44104 2626 B5
Eve Av
6700 VLVW 44125 2885 C5
7600 CLEV 44102 2623 E6
Eve Ct
- CLEV 44102 2623 E6
Evelyn Av
100 SVHL 44131 3014 E1
100 SVHL 44131 3015 A1
3100 LORN 44052 2744 D3
Evelyn Ct
14000 SGVL 44136 3012 D3
Evelyn Dr
3800 NOSD 44070 2750 C5
5200 GDHT 44125 2757 A7
Evening Star Av
15700 MPHT 44137 2886 B3

INDEX 19
Eventide Dr
Cleveland Street Index
Fordham Rd

STREET Block City ZIP Map# Grid

Eventide Dr
6900 PRMA 44129 2882 E6
Everett Av
10 PnvT 44077 2145 B5
7500 CLEV 44103 2626 A1
Everett Rd
100 PnvT 44077 2145 B5
Everett St
100 GDRV 44045 2039 B6
400 PnvT 44045 2039 B6
400 PnvT 44077 2039 B6
Evergreen Cir
39300 AVON 44011 2747 A5
Evergreen Ct
300 AVLK 44012 2618 C2
2900 LORN 44052 2744 B3
Evergreen Dr
- TpnT 44086 2259 A2
5000 NOSD 44070 2749 D7
6300 INDE 44131 2884 E4
7200 CsTp 44026 2501 B1
7400 NRDV 44039 2876 C4
8200 PRMA 44129 2882 D1
8500 SgHT 44067 3017 B4
8700 MNTR 44060 2252 C1
14600 BURT 44021 2766 B1
18500 SGVL 44136 3011 E2
28300 WBHL 44092 2374 B6
Evergreen Pkwy
5300 SFLD 44054 2746 E1
Evergreen Pl
10 CLEV 44110 2372 B6
Evergreen Rd
2000 NPRY 44081 1941 A2
Evergreen Tr
20800 NRYN 44133 3148 B5
Everton Av
5000 SLN 44139 2759 D7
10500 CLEV 44108 2496 C5
Evins Av
8600 CLEV 44104 2626 A5
Ewa Yea St
400 VMLN 44089 2741 A4
Excaliber Dr
7200 CcdT 44077 2146 A7
Excalibur Av
3000 WTLK 44145 2749 D4
Excalibur Dr
7100 CcdT 44077 2146 A7
Exchange St
600 VMLN 44089 2740 E6
7300 VLVW 44125 2885 A2
Exeter Rd
2500 CVHT 44118 2627 C5
11100 GDHT 44125 2885 C2
Exmoor Dr
11300 CcdT 44077 2146 C6
Ezmor Ln
500 WKLF 44092 2249 A7
Ezra Ct
10000 TNBG 44087 3020 B4

F

F St
600 LORN 44052 2615 A6
Fackler Av
2700 ELYR 44035 2746 A6
Factory Ln
- LORN 44055 2745 B3
Factory St
1200 LORN 44055 2745 B3
Fair Rd
8000 SGVL 44136 3011 B2
Fair St
300 BERA 44017 2880 B7
300 BERA 44017 3011 B1
Fairacres Av
6900 NRDV 44039 2877 C3
Fairchild Av
11400 CLEV 44106 2626 D3
Fairdale Av
2100 CLEV 44109 2754 D6
Fairdale Rd
10 PnvT 44077 2145 D4
Fairfax Av
16500 CLEV 44128 2757 C5
Fairfax Dr
10 SRSL 44073 2762 B7
6400 MNTR 44060 2144 A5
Fairfax Ln
17400 SGVL 44136 3146 E4
17400 SGVL 44136 3147 A4
26400 NOSD 44070 2750 A5
Fairfax Rd
400 VMLN 44089 2741 D5
2700 CVHT 44118 2627 A4
E Fairfax Rd
3200 CVHT 44118 2627 C4
Fairfax St
2600 ShvT 44241 3157 E7
2600 ShvT 44241 3158 A7
Fairfield Av
1000 CLEV 44113 2624 E5
Fairfield Dr
9300 TNBG 44087 3019 C6
Fairfield Ln
600 AURA 44202 3021 C7
Fairfield Ovl
5200 SLN 44139 2888 D1
Fairfield Pl
400 AMHT 44001 2872 B2
21600 SGVL 44136 3011 A6
Fairfield Rd
10 PnvT 44077 2145 C5
100 AVLK 44012 2617 E2
6800 CcdT 44077 2145 C5
Fairfield Tr
12900 CsTp 44026 2631 C2
Fairgate Blvd
13800 NbyT 44065 2634 A6
Fairgrounds Rd
10 PnvT 44077 2145 D4
200 CcdT 44077 2145 D4
Fairhaven Ct
7700 MNTR 44060 2252 D2
Fairhaven Dr
- BbgT 44023 2890 C3
10 NCtT 44067 3153 A2
100 NCtT 44067 3152 E2
Fairhaven Rd
6200 MDHT 44124 2629 E3
6200 MDHT 44124 2630 A2
Fairhill Dr
3200 RKRV 44116 2751 E1
Fairhill Rd
- CVHT 44106 2627 A4
- CVHT 44118 2627 A4
- SRHT 44118 2627 A4
- SRHT 44106 2627 A4
11600 CLEV 44120 2626 D4
12300 CLEV 44106 2626 D4
12300 CVHT 44106 2626 D4
12600 SRHT 44120 2626 D4
13700 SRHT 44120 2627 A4
Fairidge Rd
7700 KTLD 44094 2251 D7
Fairington Dr
600 AURA 44202 3156 C3
Fairington Ln
600 AURA 44202 3156 B3
Fairington Ovl
600 AURA 44202 3156 B3
Fair Isle Wy
19500 SGVL 44136 3011 D7
Fairlane Cir
20900 FWPK 44126 2751 C3
Fairlane Dr
8200 MCDN 44056 3018 B7
8200 MCDN 44056 3153 B1
8500 OmsT 44138 2879 A7
Fairlawn Av
100 ELYR 44035 2875 D6
400 PNVL 44077 2039 E7
7700 MNTR 44060 2252 E2
14300 CLEV 44111 2752 D2
Fairlawn Blvd
12400 GDHT 44125 2885 D2
Fairlawn Cir
22300 FWPK 44126 2751 A4
Fairlawn Dr
300 RDHT 44143 2498 E1
3600 NOSD 44070 2750 D4
10400 PRMA 44130 2753 B7
17500 BbgT 44023 2891 B4
22700 EUCL 44117 2373 C7
Fairlawn Rd
4700 LNHT 44124 2498 D6
Fairless Av
2200 LORN 44055 2745 E5
2200 LORN 44055 2746 A5
Fairlie Av
- CLEV 44103 2495 D6
- CLEV 44114 2495 D6
Fairmeadow Ln
14700 BtnT 44021 2765 D1
Fair Meadow Pl
9100 SGVL 44136 3011 C3
Fairmount Av
500 ELYR 44035 2875 A5
Fairmount Blvd
2400 CVHT 44106 2626 E3
2500 CVHT 44106 2627 C5
2700 CVHT 44118 2627 C5
18700 SRHT 44118 2627 D5
20600 SRHT 44118 2628 A5
20600 SRHT 44122 2628 A5
23000 BHWD 44122 2628 C5
24200 SRHT 44122 2628 C5
26000 BHWD 44122 2629 A5
28500 PRPK 44124 2629 A5
32900 PRPK 44124 2630 A4
33800 HGVL 44022 2630 D4
39000 HGVL 44022 2631 A5
39000 HGVL 44073 2631 A5
Fairmount Cir
- SRHT 44118 2628 A5
- SRHT 44122 2628 A5
- UNHT 44118 2628 A5
Fairmount Rd
7300 RsIT 44072 2631 D5
8200 RsIT 44072 2632 B5
9200 NbyT 44072 2633 A5
9200 RsIT 44072 2633 A5
10200 NbyT 44065 2633 A5
10800 NbyT 44065 2634 A5
Fair Oaks Dr
3700 SELD 44121 2497 E4
Fair Oaks Rd
7000 OKWD 44146 2887 C7
7200 OKWD 44146 3018 C1
Fairpark Dr
100 BERA 44017 3011 A1
20800 FWPK 44126 2751 C3
Fairport Av
11300 CLEV 44108 2496 D6
Fairport Nursery Rd
10 PnvT 44077 2040 D4
500 FTHR 44077 2039 D4
500 PnvT 44077 2039 D4
Fairport Nursery Rd SR-535
10 PnvT 44077 2040 D4
500 FTHR 44077 2039 D4
500 PnvT 44077 2039 D4
Fairtree Dr
9800 SGVL 44136 3011 C4
Fairtree Rd
5200 BDHT 44146 2887 B1
Fairview Av
600 AURA 44202 3021 C4
2000 CLEV 44106 2626 E2
2000 CVHT 44106 2626 E2
7500 MNTR 44060 2252 A2
Fairview Ct
12200 CLEV 44106 2626 E2
Fairview Dr
7700 KTLD 44094 2251 D7
31100 ORNG 44022 2759 D6
E Fairview Dr
4800 ORNG 44022 2759 D6
W Fairview Dr
4800 ORNG 44022 2759 D6
Fairview Ln
1000 AURA 44202 3021 C3
Fairview Pkwy
4400 FWPK 44126 2751 C3
Fairview Rd
10 GNVA 44041 1944 B6
2800 WBHL 44092 2374 C5
31100 RsIT 44073 2761 C5
31100 SRSL 44073 2761 C5
Fairville Av
17400 CLEV 44135 2752 A5
18500 CLEV 44135 2751 E5
Fairway Av
18700 MPHT 44137 2757 E7
Fairway Blvd
300 WLWK 44095 2249 B6
500 WKLF 44092 2249 B6
1900 HDSN 44236 3154 E6
1900 HDSN 44236 3155 A6
1900 TwbT 44236 3154 E6
1900 TwbT 44236 3155 A6
Fairway Cir
2000 HDSN 44236 3155 A6
Fairway Dr
- LORN 44053 2743 C4
10 OBLN 44074 3138 C3
1700 LORN 44053 2744 B4
1900 WKLF 44092 2374 E2
4300 CLEV 44135 2752 A4
4400 WTLK 44145 2749 C5
4700 BKLN 44144 2753 C6
11000 ClbT 44028 3010 D4
34900 AVON 44011 2748 B6
Fairway Tr
10 MDHL 44022 2760 A6
Fairway Vw
400 AbnT 44023 2892 A3
Fairweather Dr
6400 MDBH 44130 2881 E4
Fairwin Dr
31200 BYVL 44140 2619 A4
Fairwinds Dr
13100 SGVL 44136 3147 D4
Fairwood Blvd
700 ELYR 44035 2875 E2
Fairwood Cir
300 BERA 44017 2880 A7
Fairwood Dr
2500 PRPK 44124 2629 B4
13500 CLEV 44111 2752 E2
Falbo Av
3000 LORN 44052 2744 E3
Falcon St
100 ELYR 44035 3006 E3
Falcon Crest Av
35000 AVON 44011 2748 A2
36100 AVON 44011 2747 E2
Falcon Ridge Rd
- CsTp 44026 2502 C6
Falkirk Dr
- WTLK 44145 2619 B7
Falkirk Rd
1600 MadT 44057 1843 A7
1600 MadT 44057 1942 A1
5600 LNHT 44124 2629 B2
Fall St
1600 CLEV 44113 2624 D4
Fallen Oaks
2200 WTLK 44145 2750 E1
Fallen Oaks Ln
10 AMHT 44001 2872 D3
Fallen Oaks Tr
18000 TroT 44234 2895 B6
Falling Leaves Cir
400 AURA 44202 3021 C6
Fallingleaves Rd
17600 SGVL 44136 3012 A6
17800 SGVL 44136 3011 E6
Falling Rock Ln
1200 PnvT 44077 2147 A1
Falling Water Rd
17700 SGVL 44136 3012 A6
18900 BbgT 44023 3021 E2
Fall Lake Dr
4200 AVON 44011 2748 C5
N Fall Lake Dr
33700 AVON 44011 2748 C5
S Fall Lake Dr
4200 AVON 44011 2748 C5
Fall River Dr
28700 WTLK 44145 2749 D5
Falls Cir
15000 NRYN 44133 3147 E5
Falls Ln
- BERA 44017 2880 A5
8700 BWHT 44147 3014 C6
Falls Ovl
2100 WTLK 44145 2749 A2
Falls Rd
- MsnT 44024 2504 B5
200 CNFL 44022 2761 A5
500 CFIT 44022 2761 A4
600 CFIT 44022 2760 E3
3800 HGVL 44022 2760 E2
3800 MDHL 44022 2760 E2
Falls Creek Cir
10 MDHL 44022 2760 B6
Falls Creek Tr
10 MDHL 44022 2760 B5
Falls Pointe Dr E
- ODFL 44138 2879 A7
- ODFL 44138 3010 A1
26900 ODFL 44138 3009 E1
Falmouth Cir
11200 NRYN 44133 3013 D5
Falmouth Ct
100 BNWK 44212 3147 B6
Falmouth Dr
200 RKRV 44116 2621 D5
16000 SGVL 44136 3147 A4
S Falmouth Dr
500 RKRV 44116 2621 D5
Falmouth Ovl
- MDBH 44130 2881 B4
Falmouth Rd
2800 SRHT 44122 2628 A7
Fancher Av
8200 CLEV 44103 2496 A7
Fanta Ct
4800 CLEV 44102 2624 B7
Fantail Dr
7300 NCtT 44067 3153 C4
Fanwood Ct
1200 PnvT 44077 2146 E1
Fanwood Dr
300 PnvT 44077 2146 E1
Faraday Rd
5600 LNHT 44124 2629 B1
Farbar Rd
8700 KTLD 44094 2377 C6
Fareham Ct
- AURA 44202 3021 D6
Fargo Av
25900 BDHT 44146 2758 E7
Far Hills Dr
7200 CcdT 44077 2254 D1
Farland Rd
3500 UNHT 44118 2627 D3
Farley Dr
4500 MNTR 44060 2038 E5
Farley Rd
16300 PkmT 44062 2896 E2
16300 PkmT 44062 2897 A2
Farm Dr
31500 SLN 44139 2888 D3
S Farm Rd
8200 MCDN 44056 3018 B7
8200 MCDN 44056 3153 B1
Farmcote Dr
10 MDHL 44022 2760 A2
Farmingdale Ln
6700 MNTR 44060 2143 B6
Farmington Ct
9800 CcdT 44060 2145 B2
Farmington Dr
6400 GDHT 44125 2885 E4
6400 GDHT 44125 2886 A4
Farmington Rd
1800 ECLE 44112 2496 E7
5500 PkmT 44062 3028 A1
5500 PkmT 44231 3028 A1
5500 PkmT 44491 3028 A1
17300 FnTp 44491 2898 A7
17300 PkmT 44491 3029 A1
Farmington Parkman Rd
5500 FnTp 44491 2898 B7
Farmington Turn
1900 WTLK 44145 2749 C1
Farnham Dr
7000 MNTR 44060 2143 B7
Farnham Rd
2700 RchT 44286 3151 A7
3000 RHFD 44286 3151 A7
Farnham Wy
- HDSN 44236 3154 A7
Farnhurst Rd
4700 LNHT 44124 2498 D7
E Farnhurst Rd
5000 LNHT 44124 2498 E7
5000 LNHT 44124 2499 A7
W Farnhurst Rd
4600 SELD 44121 2498 D7
Farnsleigh Rd
3400 SRHT 44122 2758 B1
20100 SRHT 44122 2628 A7
20700 BHWD 44122 2628 A7
Farnsworth Dr
5700 PRMA 44129 2883 A3
6600 PRMA 44129 2882 E3
Farnum Av
7400 MDBH 44130 3012 A1
Farr Av
5000 ShfT 44055 2746 A6
Farragut Dr
35000 ETLK 44095 2142 B7
Farringdon Av
11600 CLEV 44105 2756 D2
23200 EUCL 44123 2373 C2
24700 EUCL 44123 2373 D2
26800 EUCL 44132 2374 C2
Farrs Garden Pth
1700 WTLK 44145 2619 D7
1700 WTLK 44145 2749 D1
Farview Ovl
8000 BKVL 44141 3015 E4
Farview Rd
6300 BKVL 44141 3015 E4
6300 BWHT 44141 3015 E4
6300 BWHT 44147 3015 E4
6800 BKVL 44141 3016 A4
Farwood Dr
10 MDHL 44022 2760 C2
Father Caruso Dr
- CLEV 44102 2623 E4
- CLEV 44102 2624 A4
Fatima Dr
1400 PRMA 44134 2883 E6
Faversham Rd
3800 UNHT 44118 2627 E4
3800 UNHT 44118 2628 A4
Fawn Cir
5800 BKVL 44141 3150 D3
18100 SGVL 44136 3146 E2
Fawn Ct
500 SRSL 44073 2761 E5
9000 RsIT 44073 2762 C5
9700 CcdT 44060 2253 B3
Fawn Dr
24600 NOSD 44070 2750 C4
Fawn Ln
5800 BKVL 44141 3150 D3
Fawn Chase
2400 RHFD 44286 3150 D7
Fawnhaven Dr
20800 NRYN 44133 3148 B5
Fawnhaven Wy
- AVLK 44012 2617 D3
Fawn Hill Pl
36100 WLBY 44094 2375 B2
Fawn Meadow Ln
10800 SGVL 44136 3011 D5
Fawn Path Dr
37400 SLN 44139 2889 D3
Faxon Pl
1400 ELYR 44035 3006 B1
Fay Av
100 AVLK 44012 2488 B7
100 AVLK 44012 2618 B2
Fay Dr
1800 PRMA 44134 3014 D1
4700 SELD 44121 2498 D5
Fay Rd
6300 CcdT 44077 2146 C4
Fay St
1700 ECLE 44112 2497 A6
Faye Ln
7300 MNTR 44060 2143 C5
Fayette Blvd
14400 BKPK 44142 2881 C2
Fayette Rd
20600 SRHT 44122 2628 A6
Federal Dr
17700 CLEV 44128 2757 D6
Feiner Dr
4000 CLEV 44122 2757 D4
4000 CLEV 44128 2757 D4
Felch St
22400 WVHT 44128 2758 B6
Fell Av
10 NHFD 44067 3018 A3
Felton Rd
1400 SELD 44121 2498 B7
1400 SELD 44121 2628 B1
Fence Row Dr
10800 SGVL 44136 3010 E5
10800 SGVL 44136 3011 A5
Fenemore Rd
15600 ECLE 44112 2497 B6
Fenlake Rd
5400 BDHT 44146 2887 C1
Fenley Rd
3500 CVHT 44121 2497 D4
Fenstermaker Rd
11600 NsnT 44231 3028 E7
Fenton Ct
8800 SgHT 44067 3017 D4
Fenway Dr
2100 BHWD 44122 2628 C3
2100 UNHT 44121 2628 C3
7900 PRMA 44129 2882 D6
Fenwick Av
4200 CLEV 44113 2624 B6
4800 CLEV 44102 2624 B6
Fenwick Dr
28900 WKLF 44092 2374 C4
Fenwick Rd
1900 SELD 44118 2628 A3
2100 UNHT 44118 2628 A3
2200 UNHT 44118 2627 E3
2400 UNHT 44118 2628 A5
Fenwood Ct
5700 MONT 44060 2143 C2
Fenwood Rd
2300 UNHT 44118 2628 A4
Fergus Av
2000 CLEV 44109 2754 D4
Ferman Av
1100 CLEV 44109 2754 E5
Fern Ct
2000 CLEV 44109 2754 D2
Fern Dr
10 PNVL 44077 2145 D3
300 BERA 44017 2880 A5
7300 MONT 44060 2143 D2
30000 WLWK 44095 2249 C6
Fern St
300 SAHT 44001 3003 A1
Fern Canyon Dr
18000 SGVL 44136 3147 B4
Ferncliffe Av
18200 CLEV 44135 2752 A5
18500 CLEV 44135 2751 E5
Fern Cove E
9000 ODFL 44138 3009 E1
Fern Cove W
9000 ODFL 44138 3009 E1
Ferndale Av
400 VMLN 44089 2742 A5
2000 LKWD 44107 2622 D6
3700 SDLK 44054 2615 E4
3800 SDLK 44054 2616 A4
16500 CLEV 44111 2752 B2
Ferndale Dr
- CrlT 44035 3005 D5
Fern Hall Rd
25800 OmsT 44138 2879 B3
Fernhill Av
7700 PRMA 44129 2882 D1
Fernhurst Av
6300 PMHT 44130 2881 E4
Fernshaw Av
17100 CLEV 44111 2752 A3
Fern Tree Ln
32800 NRDV 44039 2748 D6
Fernway Av
14700 CLEV 44111 2622 C7
Fernway Cir
- AVON 44011 2747 E5
Fernway Dr
- MsnT 44024 2504 C3
10900 ManT 44255 3159 C4
10900 MNTU 44255 3159 C4
15300 MPHT 44137 2886 B2
Fernway Rd
15600 SRHT 44120 2627 C7
17700 SRHT 44122 2627 C7
Fernwood Av
- AVLK 44012 2617 D2
13700 ECLE 44112 2497 A7
Fernwood Cir
14100 SGVL 44136 3012 D4
Fernwood Dr
10 SRSL 44073 2761 C6
1000 WTLK 44145 2620 E7
9000 ODFL 44138 3010 A1
15900 RsIT 44073 2761 C6
23100 BHWD 44122 2628 C5
Ferrell Av
7900 CLEV 44102 2623 E6
Ferris Av
100 CRDN 44024 2379 E7
12300 CLEV 44105 2756 E3
13100 CLEV 44105 2757 A3
Ferris State Ct
100 ELYR 44035 3006 D2
Ferro Av
5600 CLEV 44105 2755 D3
Ferry Rd
11400 CsTp 44026 2501 B2
Ferry St
5500 VMLN 44089 2740 E5
Festival Dr
10 OmsT 44138 2879 A3
Fetterman Dr
14200 SGVL 44136 3146 D1
Fetzer Dr
17300 SGVL 44136 3146 D3
Fiddlers Wy
100 PnvT 44077 2145 B1
Fiddle Sticks
10 OmsT 44138 2879 A4
Fidelity Av
10100 CLEV 44102 2753 C1
11400 CLEV 44111 2753 B1
Field Av
4800 CLEV 44102 2624 B7
Field St
2700 ShvT 44241 3158 A7
Fieldcrest Ct
700 SgHT 44067 3152 C1
Fielding Dr
3900 NOSD 44070 2750 B5
Fields Rd
7300 BbgT 44023 2890 B6
Fieldstone Cir
5900 NRDV 44039 2878 A2
Fieldstone Ct
1300 BWHT 44147 3149 E4
7900 CcdT 44060 2253 C3
Fieldstone Dr
- ELYR 44035 3007 A2
500 AhtT 44001 2873 B1
Field Stone Ln
7900 MCDN 44056 3154 A5
Fieldstone Ln
1400 TwbT 44236 3154 C6
Fieldstone Pt
12300 SGVL 44136 3011 B6
Fieldstone Tr
6000 SVHL 44131 2883 E3
Fiesta Ct
6300 LORN 44053 2744 E7
Figgie Dr
4600 WLBY 44094 2251 B7
Figgie Rd
300 PNVL 44077 2039 E7
Filbert St
100 ELYR 44035 2874 E6
Filip Blvd
6900 INDE 44131 2884 D7
Fillier St
10 BERA 44017 2880 C5
Fillmore Av
500 ELYR 44035 2875 A4
1600 LORN 44052 2615 B6
Fillmore Cir
1200 LORN 44052 2615 B6
Fillmore Ct
7100 MNTR 44060 2143 D7
Filo Av
5300 CLEV 44105 2755 D2
Finch Cir
100 ELYR 44035 3006 E3
Fincherie Dr
10500 CdnT 44024 2378 E7
Finchfield Cir
200 MCDN 44056 3018 A6
Findlay Ct
100 ELYR 44035 3006 D1
Findlay St
16600 BbgT 44023 2890 A1
Findley Dr
8200 MNTR 44060 2144 A4
Finn Av
4800 CLEV 44127 2625 C6
Finney Av
7600 CLEV 44105 2756 A3
Finwood Ct
700 ELYR 44035 2875 E1
Fir Av
5800 CLEV 44102 2624 A5
Fir Ct
1700 LORN 44055 2745 C5
Fircrest Ln
10 MDHL 44022 2760 C2
Firebush Ln
10 NCtT 44067 3153 B4
Firecrest Ct
5700 NRDV 44039 2877 E1
Firefly Dr
11900 NRYN 44133 3147 E5
Firelands Dr
9600 TNBG 44087 3020 B6
Fireside Ct
6800 MNTR 44060 2143 B6
Fireside Tr
1000 BWHT 44147 3149 D3
Fire Station Dr
- BHWD 44122 2758 D1
Firestone Dr
700 AVLK 44012 2618 C5
Firestone Ln
4100 VMLN 44089 2741 C4
9700 MCDN 44056 3018 B5
Firethorn Dr
800 SVHL 44131 2884 A4
Firewood Cir
7300 INDE 44131 2884 D7
7300 INDE 44131 3015 D1
Firsby Av
12500 CLEV 44135 2753 A4
Fir Tree Dr
3100 NRYN 44133 3014 C5
Firwood Rd
1000 BWHT 44147 3015 A3
6000 MONT 44060 2143 B3
6100 MNTR 44060 2143 B3
19000 CLEV 44110 2372 E7
Fischer Rd
- LKWD 44111 2622 B7
16500 CLEV 44107 2622 B7
16500 CLEV 44111 2622 B7
16500 LKWD 44107 2622 B7
Fisher Rd
5800 MadT 44057 2149 C2
13400 BtnT 44021 2635 E5
13400 BtnT 44024 2635 E5
13400 BtnT 44021 2636 A6
24800 EUCL 44117 2373 D5
Fisher St
5800 VMLN 44089 2740 D6
Fishermans Tr
1800 MadT 44057 1941 D1
Fitch Rd
5400 NOSD 44070 2879 A2
6200 OmsT 44138 2879 A2
Fitzroy St
1300 WTLK 44145 2620 B7
Fitzwater Rd
7000 BKVL 44141 3016 B4
W Fitzwater Rd
6800 BKVL 44141 3016 A4
Five Points Rd
- BKPK 44135 2880 D2
- BKPK 44142 2880 D2
17800 BKPK 44142 2881 A2
19400 CLEV 44135 2880 D2
Flagler Dr
10 OmsT 44138 2879 A4
Flamingo Av
- AMHT 44001 2744 A7
17400 CLEV 44135 2752 A5
18500 CLEV 44135 2751 E5
Flanders Dr
37700 SLN 44139 2889 D6
Flat Rock Dr
10400 MsnT 44024 2503 C2
Fleet Av
- NBGH 44105 2755 D2
4900 CLEV 44105 2755 D2
7300 CLEV 44105 2756 A2
Fleetwood Dr
1000 SgHT 44067 3152 A1
Fleger Dr
2600 PRMA 44134 3014 C2
Fleharty Rd
4600 NOSD 44070 2750 C6
Fleming Av
5000 ShfT 44055 2746 A6
Fletcher Rd
8300 WndT 44099 2639 E1
Flick Dr
400 BDFD 44146 2886 D4
Flint Ridge Dr
10 EatT 44044 3006 E5
37500 EatT 44044 3007 A5
Flint Rock Ridge Rd
7800 BbgT 44023 2890 D4
Flora Av
10000 CLEV 44108 2496 C5
Flora Dr
10 BDFD 44137 2886 D2
10 BDFD 44146 2886 D2
10 MPHT 44137 2886 D2
Floradale St
100 ELYR 44035 2875 B4
Floral Ct
100 ELYR 44035 2875 A5
Floral Dr
1100 ShfT 44055 2745 B6
Floraline St
33700 NRDV 44039 2877 D3
Florence Av
10 PnvT 44077 2039 D7
24500 NOSD 44070 2750 C5
Florence Ct
100 ELYR 44035 2875 A5
Florence Dr
900 MCDN 44056 3018 E3
900 MCDN 44056 3019 A3
14900 MPHT 44137 2886 A5
38400 WBHL 44094 2376 A5
Florence Ln
14100 NRYN 44133 3149 B1
Florence Rd
9100 KTLD 44094 2251 E7
9100 KTLD 44094 2376 E1
Florence St
300 BYVL 44140 2619 C3
Florentine Wy
10 OmsT 44138 2879 A2
Florian Av
10600 CLEV 44111 2753 B1
Florian Blvd
- INDE 44131 2884 E7
Florida Av
200 LORN 44052 2615 A6
14800 CLEV 44128 2757 A5
Florida St
4100 PryT 44081 2041 D4
10400 RMDV 44202 3021 A4
Flower Av
10700 CLEV 44111 2753 B2
Flower Dr
5800 PMHT 44130 2882 C2
Flowerdale Av
5400 CLEV 44109 2754 A6
5400 CLEV 44144 2754 A6
5700 CLEV 44144 2753 E6
Flowerside Rd
12200 HtbT 44046 2509 A6
Fobes St
500 PNVL 44077 2040 C6
Foghorn Ln
7300 NCtT 44067 3153 C5
Foldesy Ln
- NRYN 44133 3148 B2
Folk Av
10000 CLEV 44108 2496 C5
Folkstone Dr
10900 CcdT 44077 2146 A7
Follett Ct
- CLEV 44113 2624 D5
Folley Rd
25800 ClbT 44028 3009 D6
Folsom Av
8600 CLEV 44104 2626 B4
Foltz Industrial Pkwy
14000 SGVL 44136 3011 A7
14000 SGVL 44136 3146 A2
Fontenay Rd
2800 SRHT 44120 2627 D6
Foote Rd
29600 BYVL 44140 2619 C4
Foothill Blvd
3600 WLBY 44094 2250 D4
Foothill Rd
8700 MNTR 44060 2252 C1
Foraker Ct
8400 MNTR 44060 2144 B3
Forbes Ct
6500 MNTR 44060 2144 B5
Forbes Dr
- CLEV 44108 2496 E6
Forbes Rd
200 BDFD 44146 2887 B7
200 OKWD 44146 2887 B7
24200 BDFD 44146 2887 D7
26400 OKWD 44146 2888 A7
Forbush Cir
7600 HDSN 44236 3155 B7
Force Av
7700 CLEV 44105 2756 A4
Ford Dr
1900 CLEV 44106 2626 D2
Ford Ln
4000 VMLN 44089 2741 C4
13700 BURT 44021 2636 A7
Ford Rd
- LryT 44057 2148 C1
- LryT 44077 2148 C1
800 HDHT 44143 2499 B5
1000 ELYR 44035 2875 B2
1000 LNHT 44124 2499 B7
2200 ELYR 44035 2746 C7
5200 MadT 44057 2149 D1
5400 SFLD 44035 2746 B6
5900 MadT 44057 2150 A1
7300 MNTR 44060 2143 C4
14600 LryT 44057 2149 A1
Forde Av
700 AMHT 44001 2872 B1
Fordham Dr
6300 PRMA 44129 2883 A4
Fordham Pkwy
300 BYVL 44140 2620 E5
Fordham Rd
11500 GDHT 44125 2885 D1

INDEX 20
Fordwick Rd
Cleveland Street Index
Gate Post Ln

STREET Block City ZIP Map# Grid

Fordwick Rd
6400 PMHT 44130 2882 D4
Forest Av
5100 MPHT 44137 2757 A7
5400 PRMA 44129 2883 A1
6700 PRMA 44129 2882 E1
11000 CLEV 44104 2626 C6
11600 CLEV 44120 2626 E6
Forest Blvd
100 AVLK 44012 2618 E2
Forest Ct
8000 NRYN 44133 3014 B3
Forest Dr
10 BDFD 44146 2886 E4
10 ETLK 44095 2142 B6
10 PNVL 44077 2145 E2
10 SRSL 44073 2761 C6
500 BYVL 44140 2619 E5
2900 PRPK 44124 2629 D6
5600 WLBY 44094 2375 A2
Forest Ln
2600 LORN 44053 2743 E2
2800 WBHL 44094 2375 B6
5500 BKVL 44141 3016 B5
8100 MNTR 44060 2251 D4
8900 CsTp 44026 2632 D2
34000 SLN 44139 2760 A7
Forest Ovl
16800 MDBH 44130 2881 A4
Forest Pkwy
- HDHT 44143 2499 C4
2400 WTLK 44145 2750 A2
Forest Rd
1100 LKWD 44107 2622 A4
1700 EUCL 44117 2498 A1
4600 MNTR 44060 2038 D6
7500 MadT 44057 1844 A5
11500 MsnT 44024 2504 C3
12400 ClrT 44021 2506 D7
12400 ClrT 44021 2636 D1
12800 ClrT 44024 2636 D1
13500 BtnT 44024 2636 D3
13500 BtnT 44021 2636 D3
28300 WLWK 44095 2249 B7
W Forest Rd
1000 LKWD 44107 2621 E4
1000 LKWD 44107 2622 A4
Forest St
- GNVA 44041 1944 C4
10 ELYR 44035 2875 A5
100 AMHT 44001 2872 E1
100 OBLN 44074 3138 D3
34100 NRDV 44039 2877 C1
N Forest St
10 GNVA 44041 1944 C4
S Forest St
10 GNVA 44041 1944 C4
Forest Cliff Dr
1000 LKWD 44107 2622 C3
Forestdale Av
1800 CLEV 44109 2754 D2
Forestdale Dr
4800 GDHT 44125 2756 E5
7800 BKVL 44141 3016 C3
8000 KTLD 44094 2251 E7
8000 KTLD 44094 2252 A7
Forest Edge Dr
4500 BKLN 44144 2753 D5
8800 KTLD 44094 2377 C1
Forest Glen Av
6500 SLN 44139 2888 E6
Forest Glen Dr
10000 NRYN 44133 3148 B5
Forest Glen Rd
2300 MadT 44057 1941 B3
Forest Glen Wy
- NRDV 44039 2877 B6
Forest Grove Av
12300 CLEV 44108 2496 D6
Forest Grove Dr
- BHIT 44212 3146 B6
- NRYN 44133 3013 B5
Forestgrove Rd
28900 WLWK 44095 2249 C7
30200 WLWK 44092 2249 C7
Forest Hill Av
12500 CLEV 44106 2626 E1
12600 CLEV 44112 2626 E1
12600 CVHT 44106 2626 E1
12600 ECLE 44112 2626 E1
13100 ECLE 44112 2497 A7
Forest Hill Dr
100 AMHT 44001 2872 D3
100 AVLK 44012 2488 B7
100 AVLK 44012 2618 B1
4000 LORN 44053 2744 B4
Forest Hills Blvd
1200 CVHT 44112 2497 C7
1200 CVHT 44118 2497 C7
1800 ECLE 44112 2497 A7
4200 PRMA 44134 2883 B5
Forest Lake Dr
2700 WTLK 44145 2749 A3
9900 TNBG 44087 3019 B4
Forestlawn Av
- SFLD 44054 2616 B4
3700 SDLK 44054 2615 E4
3800 SDLK 44054 2616 B4
Forest Oaks Dr
1700 HDSN 44236 3154 E6
10800 CdnT 44024 2378 D7
10900 CdnT 44024 2503 D1
10900 MsnT 44024 2503 D1
Forest Overlook Dr
3200 SVHL 44131 2884 B6
Forest Park Dr
6200 NRDV 44039 2877 B2
15200 SGVL 44136 3012 B5
Forest Point Cir
9200 MCDN 44056 3018 E5
Forest Point Dr
9200 MCDN 44056 3018 E5
Forest Point Pl
11600 SGVL 44136 3012 C6
Forest Ridge Dr
5600 NOSD 44070 2878 D2
Forest Run Dr
3600 RchT 44286 3150 D6
Forestry Ln
- NRDV 44039 2877 B2
Forestview Av
2600 RKRV 44116 2621 C7
8400 MNTR 44060 2252 B2
25500 EUCL 44132 2373 E1
27100 EUCL 44132 2374 A1
Forestview Cir
- MCDN 44056 3153 E2
21600 BKPK 44142 2880 B3
Forestview Ct
24900 BYVL 44140 2620 D5
Forest View Dr
1800 CVHT 44118 2627 C2
8700 ODFL 44138 2879 D7
11500 MsnT 44024 2504 A3
Forestview Dr
1400 VMLN 44089 2741 A7
9700 SGVL 44136 3012 D5
Forestview Pl
100 AURA 44202 3021 C7
Forestview Rd
300 BYVL 44140 2620 D4
Forestview St
24000 ClbT 44028 3010 B7
Forestview Ter
- BKVL 44141 3151 C3
Forestwood Av
18400 CLEV 44135 2752 A5
18500 CLEV 44135 2751 E6
Forest Wood Dr
- NRDV 44039 2877 B3
Forestwood Dr
10 NCtT 44067 3017 D6
10 NCtT 44067 3018 A7
3700 PRMA 44134 2883 B2
7200 INDE 44131 2884 C7
7300 INDE 44131 3015 C1
12000 NbyT 44021 2764 D3
15000 SGVL 44136 3146 C3
Forestwood Ln
10100 NRYN 44133 3014 C5
Forestwood Pkwy
27800 NOSD 44070 2749 E5
Forge Dr
9600 BKVL 44141 3150 C3
Forgehill Dr
16200 PkmT 44231 3027 E2
16400 PkmT 44231 3028 A2
N Fork Dr
10 BTVL 44022 2760 D7
10 MDHL 44022 2760 D7
Forman Av
6500 CLEV 44105 2755 E2
Formanek Dr
36000 AVON 44011 2748 A5
Formby Dr
7200 SLN 44139 3020 C1
Forsythe Blvd
400 SgHT 44067 3152 D1
Forsythe Ln
9200 MNTR 44060 2144 E7
9200 MNTR 44060 2145 A7
Forsythia Dr
27200 ClbT 44028 3144 A3
Forsythia Ln
400 RDHT 44143 2498 C3
7300 NCtT 44067 3153 B4
Fort Av
8200 CLEV 44104 2626 A6
Forthampton Cir
- HDSN 44236 3154 A6
Fort Myers Ct
7700 PRMA 44134 3014 C2
Fortuna Dr
5600 MNTR 44060 2144 E2
Fortune Av
2400 PRMA 44134 2883 C1
10400 CLEV 44111 2753 B2
34400 NRDV 44039 2877 C7
Fortune Tr
24500 WTLK 44145 2750 C2
Forum Dr
20600 SGVL 44136 3011 C7
Fosdick Rd
8300 VLVW 44125 2885 B2
Foster Av
100 ELYR 44035 2875 A5
400 ELYR 44035 2874 E5
9900 BTNH 44108 2496 B4
Fostoria Ct
- CLEV 44109 2754 C2
Founders Cir
- AVLK 44012 2618 C3
Founders Ct
19400 NRYN 44133 3148 A5
Fountain Av
100 PNVL 44077 2145 E1
Fountain Cir
- AVON 44011 2747 C2
Fountain Ct
12800 SGVL 44136 3011 E6
Fountain Pkwy
28600 SLN 44139 2888 B7
Fountain View Tr
- AURA 44202 3156 C2
Fournier St
100 BERA 44017 2880 B7
Fowl Rd
1900 ELYR 44035 2873 E7
1900 ELYR 44035 2874 A6
1900 ELYR 44035 3004 E1
1900 EyrT 44035 2873 E7
1900 EyrT 44035 2874 A6
1900 EyrT 44035 3004 E1
9300 AhtT 44035 3004 E1
Fowler Av
5000 CLEV 44127 2625 D7
Fowler Dr
2700 WBHL 44094 2375 A6
Fowlers Mill Rd
11100 MsnT 44024 2504 A1
Fowles Rd
200 BERA 44017 3011 E1
200 BERA 44130 3011 E1
200 MDBH 44130 3011 E1
16600 MDBH 44130 3012 A1
Fowles Rd SR-291
16600 MDBH 44130 3012 A1
Fox Av
22600 EUCL 44123 2373 B3
Fox Grv
11200 SGVL 44136 3011 A5
Fox Ln
10 CdnT 44024 2379 A6
200 SRSL 44073 2762 A5
Fox Rd
- CrlT 44044 3141 D3
18200 TroT 44234 2894 C7
18200 TroT 44234 3025 B2
18900 AbnT 44234 3025 A3
Fox Run
- CsTp 44026 2501 D5
2300 WTLK 44145 2750 E2
2300 WTLK 44145 2751 A2
15200 RslT 44073 2761 A3
Fox Tr
100 SRSL 44073 2762 A6
Fox Wy
300 SRSL 44073 2762 A6
Foxboro Dr
6400 MAYF 44143 2499 E5
6400 MAYF 44143 2500 A6
Foxboro Rd
7400 GSML 44040 2630 D1
Foxboro St
28800 WLWK 44095 2249 B6
Foxboro Tr
6900 MDBH 44130 2880 E6
Foxborough Dr
300 BNWK 44212 3147 D7
Fox Chappell Ln
32700 AVLK 44012 2618 A4
Fox Chase Dr
100 ELYR 44035 2874 A7
Foxcroft Dr
13500 GDHT 44125 2885 E3
Foxcroft Pl
7000 CcdT 44077 2145 C7
Foxdale Cir
- HDSN 44236 3154 A6
Fox Den E
13500 RslT 44072 2632 A4
Fox Den Ln
1300 WLBY 44094 2143 A5
Foxe Dr
20200 SGVL 44136 3011 C4
Foxfire Dr
1100 PnvT 44077 2040 E7
1200 PnvT 44077 2041 A7
Fox Glen Rd
10 MDHL 44022 2760 A5
Foxglove Ln
2000 BWHT 44147 3149 D5
Foxhall Dr
10 SRSL 44073 2762 B6
Fox Haven Dr
11400 CsTp 44026 2501 E2
11400 CsTp 44026 2502 A2
Fox Hill Dr
400 AURA 44202 3157 B2
1200 GSML 44040 2500 E7
6900 SLN 44139 2888 E7
7000 SLN 44139 3019 E1
7800 GSML 44040 2501 A6
13500 RslT 44072 2631 E4
13500 RslT 44072 2632 A4
Foxhill Dr
8800 KTLD 44094 2377 C3
Fox Hill Dr E
1100 GSML 44040 2500 E6
Fox Hill Ln
10 ELYR 44035 2875 A3
Foxhill Ln
7800 MCDN 44056 3154 B5
Fox Hill Tr
9600 CcdT 44060 2253 B3
Fox Hollow Cir
6000 NRDV 44039 2877 E2
Fox Hollow Ct
100 MDHT 44124 2629 E2
Fox Hollow Dr
- MDHT 44124 2629 E2
3100 PRPK 44124 2629 D7
8400 BWHT 44147 3015 A5
10000 PRMA 44130 3013 C1
13800 RslT 44072 2631 C5
17800 SGVL 44136 3146 E2
Fox Hollow Ln
8700 KDHL 44060 2252 B6
Fox Hunt Dr
16000 SGVL 44136 3147 B1
Foxlair Tr
4800 RDHT 44143 2498 E3
Fox Ledges Ln
7100 CsTp 44026 2631 A3
Fox Meadow Ln
9500 CdnT 44024 2379 C2
Fox Mill Rd
7200 MNTR 44060 2144 D7
7200 MNTR 44060 2252 D1
Foxmoor Tr
13200 CsTp 44026 2631 B2
Fox Rest Dr
8600 BKVL 44141 3016 A6
Fox Run Dr
- LORN 44053 2743 B5
1300 WLBY 44094 2143 A5
37000 SLN 44139 2889 C4
Fox Run Ln
1300 WLBY 44094 2143 A5
Fox Run Tr
100 AURA 44202 3157 A2
12200 CsTp 44026 2501 D5
Fox Tail Ln
6500 AhtT 44001 2873 B1
Fox Tail Run
3900 RchT 44286 3150 C6
Foxwood Ct
6200 MNTR 44060 2144 D4
Fox Wood Dr
9500 CdnT 44024 2379 D2
10000 NRYN 44133 3014 C5
Foxwood Dr
700 VMLN 44089 2741 C5
3200 NRYN 44133 3014 C5
Foxwood Ln
10 PRPK 44124 2630 A7
8600 MCDN 44056 3018 B6
Foxwynde Tr
4800 RDHT 44143 2498 D3
Fracci Ct
7000 MNTR 44060 2144 B6
Framingham Dr
24500 WTLK 44070 2750 C3
24500 WTLK 44145 2750 C3
Framingham Ln
2900 TNBG 44087 3020 B4
Framingham Ovl
17800 SGVL 44136 3146 E4
Frances Dr
1900 WKLF 44092 2374 E2
9600 VLVW 44125 2885 B5
Frances St
33200 NRDV 44039 2877 D1
Francis Av
5500 CLEV 44127 2625 D6
Francis Ct
1300 SELD 44121 2498 B7
Francis Dr
3700 RKRV 44116 2751 E1
5400 LORN 44053 2744 C5
Francis St
5500 MNTR 44060 2144 C1
Francis D Kenneth Dr
300 AURA 44202 3157 A6
Frank Av
10500 CLEV 44106 2626 C3
Frank Ct
10 ELYR 44035 2875 B6
Frank Dr
30000 WKLF 44092 2374 D2
Frank St
23700 NOSD 44070 2750 D4
Franke Dr
2000 LORN 44053 2743 D2
Franke Rd
6700 MDBH 44130 2881 C5
Frankford St
- LORN 44055 2745 E5
- LORN 44055 2746 A5
- ShfT 44055 2745 E5
2300 ShfT 44055 2746 A5
Frankfort Av
200 CLEV 44113 2624 D3
5600 PRMA 44129 2882 E2
Frankfort St
- OBLN 44074 3138 E3
Frankie Dr
- LORN 44053 2743 D3
Franklin Av
10 BDFD 44146 2887 A4
100 ELYR 44035 2875 A4
4400 MNTU 44255 3159 C5
17300 LKWD 44107 2622 B5
29600 WKLF 44092 2249 B7
29600 WKLF 44092 2374 B1
Franklin Blvd
600 HDHT 44143 2499 A5
2500 CLEV 44113 2624 D4
4600 CLEV 44102 2624 A5
6900 CLEV 44102 2623 D6
11700 LKWD 44102 2623 B5
11700 LKWD 44107 2623 B5
13300 LKWD 44107 2622 D5
Franklin Dr
100 BERA 44017 2880 A7
32200 SLN 44139 3019 E1
Franklin Rd
6100 MDHT 44124 2499 D6
10200 AbnT 44023 3023 C1
20500 MPHT 44137 2758 A7
S Franklin Rd
1100 BbgT 44022 2890 A3
1100 BbgT 44023 2890 A3
1100 BTVL 44022 2890 A3
6600 BbgT 44139 2890 A3
6600 SLN 44139 2890 A3
16600 CNFL 44022 2890 A3
Franklin St
100 BERA 44017 2880 D7
100 BERA 44017 3011 D1
300 AMHT 44001 2872 D2
500 PNVL 44077 2146 B2
N Franklin St
10 CNFL 44022 2761 A6
S Franklin St
10 CNFL 44022 2761 A7
200 BbgT 44022 2761 A7
16500 BbgT 44023 2761 A7
16500 BbgT 44022 2890 A1
16500 BbgT 44023 2890 A1
16500 CNFL 44022 2890 A1
Franklin Park St
- BDFD 44146 2887 C4
Franklyn Blvd
5000 WLBY 44094 2250 A7
5100 WLBY 44094 2375 A1
6300 BKPK 44142 2881 D4
Frank Morgan Pl
- CLEV 44106 2496 E7
Franks Rd
10400 AbnT 44023 2763 D7
10400 AbnT 44023 2764 B7
Frantz Pastorius Blvd
- CLEV 44114 2624 E2
Fraser Ln
9100 CsTp 44026 2632 D3
Frazee Av
4900 CLEV 44127 2625 C7
Frazier Dr
13000 MsnT 44024 2635 A2
19200 RKRV 44116 2621 D4
Freas Av
3800 CLEV 44113 2624 C6
Freda Ln
300 BDFD 44146 2886 D3
Frederick Av
- VMLN 44089 2741 B6
8600 CLEV 44104 2626 B4
26700 ClbT 44028 3009 B7
Frederick Dr
4600 VMLN 44089 2741 A5
5600 MNTR 44060 2144 B1
Frederick Ln
11200 TNBG 44087 3020 B3
Frederick St
- ELYR 44035 2874 E2
10 PNVL 44077 2146 B2
Fredericksburg Dr
100 AVLK 44012 2618 D1
Fredle Dr
- CcdT 44077 2254 B2
Free Av
7200 OKWD 44146 2887 C7
7200 OKWD 44146 3018 C1
Freed Ct
35900 ETLK 44095 2250 B3
Freed Dr
35400 ETLK 44095 2250 B3
Freedom Ct
10 ELYR 44035 2745 D7
10 ELYR 44035 2874 D1
Freedom Rd
100 PnvT 44077 2145 C1
Freedom St
10400 GTVL 44234 3161 E6
10400 HrmT 44234 3161 E6
Freedom Square Dr
5700 INDE 44131 2884 C3
Freehold Rd
3700 PRMA 44134 2754 C7
Freeland Dr
6900 EyrT 44035 2874 A2
Freeman Av
1900 CLEV 44113 2624 D5
Freemon Pl
- AVON 44011 2617 C5
Freemont Rd
3700 SELD 44121 2497 E4
3700 SELD 44121 2498 A4
Freeport Ln
9400 MNTR 44060 2145 A5
Freeway Cir
7800 MDBH 44130 3012 B2
N Freeway Dr
- OKWD 44146 3018 C4
9400 MCDN 44056 3018 C4
9500 MCDN 44146 3018 C4
S Freeway Dr
9000 MCDN 44056 3018 C6
9000 MCDN 44056 3153 C1
Fremont Av
800 PnvT 44077 2040 D2
Fremont Dr
9800 ClbT 44028 3010 D2
Fremont St
100 ELYR 44035 2874 E6
French Av
1100 LKWD 44107 2622 C4
French Blvd
5600 MNTR 44060 2144 C1
French Dr
7800 NCtT 44067 3017 E7
7800 NCtT 44067 3152 D1
French St
- NCtT 44067 3017 E7
10 BERA 44017 3011 B1
1000 CLEV 44113 2624 D4
French Creek Rd
4500 SFLD 44054 2746 E2
4500 SFLD 44011 2747 A2
4500 SFLD 44054 2747 A2
Fresno Ct
100 ELYR 44035 3006 D2
Fresno Dr
1000 WTLK 44145 2620 E7
Friar Cir
5400 FWPK 44126 2751 B5
Friar Dr
2400 PRMA 44134 2883 C7
Friaracres Rd
- NRDV 44039 2877 C4
Friar Post
11700 NRYN 44133 3148 A4
Frick Ct
15500 CLEV 44111 2752 C1
Friend Av
15200 MPHT 44137 2757 B7
Friendship Ln
10 OmsT 44138 2879 A3
Fries Av
17300 LKWD 44107 2622 B5
Front Av
900 CLEV 44113 2624 C3
Front St
10 BERA 44017 2880 C5
4800 VMLN 44089 2741 A4
Front St SR-237
200 BERA 44017 2880 C5
Frontage Rd
- EyrT 44035 2874 A5
Frontage St
4400 LORN 44053 2743 D2
E Frontenac Dr
4400 WVHT 44128 2758 D5
S Frontenac Dr
4500 WVHT 44128 2758 C5
Frontier Av
5800 CLEV 44102 2624 A7
Frontier Dr
7800 MNTR 44060 2253 A3
Frost Ln
8800 BKVL 44141 3016 B6
Frost Rd
3400 ShvT 44255 3158 D7
10400 ManT 44255 3158 D7
11900 ManT 44255 3023 D7
12700 AbnT 44255 3023 D4
Fruit Av
900 CLEV 44113 2624 E6
Fruitland Av
10 PnvT 44077 2041 A5
1500 MDHT 44124 2499 D3
1500 MDHT 44124 2629 E1
Fruitland Ct
11500 CLEV 44102 2623 B5
Fruitland Dr
4000 PRMA 44134 2883 B5
Fruitside Rd
12800 GDHT 44125 2885 E3
Fry Av
1200 LKWD 44107 2623 B5
Fry Rd
5700 BKPK 44142 2881 B2
6600 MDBH 44130 2881 B5
Fulham Dr
1800 MDHT 44124 2629 C2
Fuller Av
8900 CLEV 44104 2626 B7
20100 EUCL 44123 2373 A3
28900 WKLF 44092 2374 A1
Fuller Rd
100 CrlT 44035 3006 B2
200 ELYR 44035 3006 B2
Fuller St
10 BERA 44017 2880 D7
10 BERA 44017 3011 D1
Fuller's Ln
14300 SGVL 44136 3146 D1
Fullerton Av
5700 CLEV 44105 2755 D2
Fullerton Rd
100 ELYR 44035 2875 C3
Fullerwood Dr
27000 EUCL 44132 2373 E1
27100 EUCL 44132 2374 A1
27600 EUCL 44132 2249 A7
Fulmer Dr
2800 LORN 44053 2743 D3
Fulton Ct
3800 CLEV 44113 2624 B5
Fulton Pkwy
- CLEV 44102 2754 B3
4000 CLEV 44109 2754 B3
Fulton Pkwy
4000 CLEV 44144 2754 B3
Fulton Rd
2000 CLEV 44113 2624 C5
2800 LORN 44052 2745 B3
2800 LORN 44055 2745 B3
3100 CLEV 44109 2624 C7
3200 CLEV 44109 2754 C1
4000 CLEV 44144 2754 A6
4900 CLEV 44109 2754 A6
Fur Creek Tr
- SGVL 44136 3011 B4
Furnace St
100 ELYR 44035 2875 A5
Furon Rd
- MNTU 44255 3159 C6

G

G St
900 LORN 44052 2615 A6
Gable Ln
32200 AVLK 44012 2618 C2
Gabriel
- WLBY 44094 2250 E3
Gabriel Ct
6800 MNTR 44060 2144 E6
13200 CLEV 44120 2756 E1
13500 CLEV 44120 2757 A1
Gabriella Dr
9900 NRYN 44133 3013 B3
10500 PRMA 44130 2882 C1
Gabriels Lndg
7200 CcdT 44077 2146 D6
Gaelic Gln
38500 SLN 44139 2889 E3
Gail Dr
33700 NRDV 44039 2877 C3
Gail Allison Dr
- MDHL 44022 2759 D2
- MDHL 44124 2759 D2
- PRPK 44124 2759 D2
Gainsboro Av
13300 ECLE 44112 2497 A4
Gaitside Tr
- KTLD 44094 2377 C6
N Galahad Pl
7100 CcdT 44077 2146 A7
S Galahad Pl
7200 CcdT 44077 2146 B6
Galalina Blvd
35600 ETLK 44095 2142 B7
Galaxie Dr
5900 MNTR 44060 2144 A3
Galaxy Dr
1100 CLEV 44109 2754 E5
42700 EyrT 44035 2874 B2
Galaxy Pkwy
4800 WVHT 44128 2758 D6
Gale Dr
6200 SVHL 44131 2884 B4
Gale Rd
2900 WLBY 44094 2250 E2
Galemore Dr
15300 MDBH 44130 2881 B5
Galewood Dr
1000 CLEV 44110 2497 A3
Galion Av
1600 CLEV 44109 2754 E3
Gallant Wy
7300 CcdT 44077 2254 D1
Gallatin Blvd
15000 BKPK 44142 2881 C2
N Gallatin Blvd
14400 BKPK 44142 2881 C2
S Gallatin Blvd
14400 BKPK 44142 2881 C2
Gallowae Ct
7800 MNTR 44060 2143 E5
Galloway Tr
8700 RslT 44072 2632 B7
8700 RslT 44072 2762 B1
Gallup Av
4600 CLEV 44127 2625 C6
Galway Cir
3600 BNHT 44131 2884 B1
Gambier Av
9800 CLEV 44102 2623 C7
Gamekeeper Ct
9700 CcdT 44060 2145 B7
Gamekeepers Tr
15500 RslT 44073 2762 E4
Gamma Av
4300 NBGH 44105 2755 C3
N Gannett Rd
7500 SgHT 44067 3017 C7
7500 SgHT 44067 3152 D1
S Gannett Rd
7800 SgHT 44067 3017 C6
GAR Hwy
6600 HgvT 44064 2384 A3
6600 MtlT 44064 2384 A3
6700 HgvT 44064 2384 A3
6700 HgvT 44099 2384 A3
12500 HmbT 44024 2380 D5
13500 HmbT 44024 2381 A4
14900 HmbT 44024 2382 C3
14900 MtlT 44024 2382 C3
15200 MtlT 44064 2382 C3
16000 MtlT 44064 2383 C3
GAR Hwy US-6
6600 HgvT 44064 2384 A3
6600 MtlT 44064 2384 A3
6700 HgvT 44099 2384 A3
6700 HgvT 44064 2384 A3
12500 HmbT 44024 2380 D5
13500 HmbT 44024 2381 A4
14900 HmbT 44024 2382 C3
14900 MtlT 44024 2382 C3
15200 MtlT 44064 2382 C3
16000 MtlT 44064 2383 C3
Garden Av
1700 LORN 44052 2744 E1
2300 CLEV 44109 2754 D2
Garden Blvd
17500 CLEV 44128 2757 D4
17600 WVHT 44128 2757 D4
18100 CLEV 44122 2757 D4
18100 WVHT 44122 2757 D4
Garden Ct
10 PnvT 44077 2040 D1
Garden Dr
1400 SELD 44121 2498 C7
1900 WKLF 44092 2374 E2
2200 AVON 44011 2747 E2
Garden Dr
24400 EUCL 44123 2373 D3
Garden Ln
2000 HDSN 44236 3154 E6
2000 HDSN 44236 3155 A7
2800 MNTR 44060 2038 D6
Garden Rd
- MadT 44057 1942 B4
900 WLBY 44094 2143 A4
13300 ECLE 44112 2497 A5
24500 OKWD 44146 3018 D2
Garden St
100 BDFD 44146 2887 A3
500 ELYR 44035 2874 E7
1000 ELYR 44035 3005 E1
5500 MPHT 44137 2886 C1
6600 INDE 44131 2885 B5
14400 BURT 44021 2636 A7
14500 BURT 44021 2766 A2
34400 NRDV 44039 2877 C2
Gardenia Dr
27800 NOSD 44070 2749 E6
Garden Park Dr
10 SRSL 44073 2762 C6
Gardenside Dr
- AVLK 44012 2618 E4
9800 WTHL 44094 2376 B3
12600 NRYN 44133 3012 E3
38800 WLBY 44094 2251 A5
Garden Valley Av
6900 CLEV 44104 2625 E6
6900 CLEV 44104 2626 A7
6900 CLEV 44127 2625 E6
6900 CLEV 44127 2626 A7
Gardenview Dr
19300 MPHT 44137 2757 E7
20500 MPHT 44137 2758 A7
Gardiner Ln
17700 BbgT 44023 2891 A5
Gardiner Rd
700 VMLN 44089 2741 A5
Gardner Ct
2400 TNBG 44087 3020 B6
Gareau Dr
5700 NOSD 44070 2878 D2
Garfield Av
- LORN 44055 2745 D5
500 ELYR 44035 2875 A5
2000 ShfT 44055 2745 D5
5600 MPHT 44137 2886 C2
9600 CLEV 44108 2496 B5
14200 LKWD 44107 2622 D6
25700 ODFL 44138 2879 B6
Garfield Blvd
2100 LORN 44052 2615 B5
7500 GDHT 44125 2756 A5
Garfield Dr
10 PnvT 44077 2145 B4
9800 GDHT 44125 2756 C5
Garfield Ln
10 BTNH 44108 2496 B4
Garfield Pkwy
- GDHT 44125 2756 C6
Garfield Rd
1800 ECLE 44112 2496 E7
1800 ECLE 44112 2497 A7
7600 MNTR 44060 2251 E2
7800 KDHL 44094 2251 E5
7800 KDHL 44060 2251 E5
7800 KTLD 44094 2251 E5
8400 KTLD 44060 2251 E5
11400 HRM 44234 3161 A2
47400 NRsT 44074 3003 A6
48000 NRsT 44001 3003 A6
Garfield Rd SR-82
11400 HRM 44234 3161 A3
Garfield Rd SR-700
11400 HRM 44234 3161 A2
E Garfield Rd
10 AURA 44202 3157 B1
1200 ManT 44202 3157 E1
E Garfield Rd SR-82
10 AURA 44202 3157 B1
1200 ManT 44202 3157 E1
Garfield St
300 GNVA 44041 1944 C4
Garfield Park Blvd
- GDHT 44125 2756 C5
Garford Av
100 ELYR 44035 2875 C7
1200 ELYR 44035 3006 C1
Gargasz Dr
5200 LORN 44053 2744 B6
Garland Rd
12300 GDHT 44125 2756 E6
Garrett Dr
3300 NRDV 44011 2748 C7
3300 NRDV 44039 2748 C7
Garrett Sq
- CLEV 44108 2496 D7
Garrett A Morgan Pl
4100 CLEV 44105 2756 D3
Garretts Cove Dr
36500 ETLK 44095 2250 C3
Garvin Av
100 ELYR 44035 2874 E5
Garwood Dr
1100 PnvT 44077 2146 E1
1200 PnvT 44077 2147 A1
Garwood Rd
4300 CLEV 44109 2754 E4
Gary Av
2700 LORN 44055 2746 A2
5400 BDHT 44146 2887 D1
26800 EUCL 44132 2373 E2
26800 EUCL 44132 2374 C2
Gary Ct
1000 WKLF 44092 2374 B1
Gary Dr
2000 TNBG 44087 3019 E4
13300 SGVL 44136 3012 D3
Gary Rd
- WVHT 44128 2758 E6
Gaslight Ln
100 MDHT 44124 2500 B6
Gasser Blvd
2400 RKRV 44116 2621 D7
Gatehouse Ct
- NRDV 44039 2877 D7
Gate House Ln
21700 RKRV 44116 2621 B6
Gate Moss Ovl
4900 NRDV 44039 2748 D7
Gate Post Ln
- MsnT 44024 2504 C2

STREET Block	City	ZIP	Map#	Grid
Gatepost Rd				
10700	SGVL	44136	3010	E4
Gates Av				
200	ELYR	44035	3006	A1
Gates Rd				
6900	GSML	44040	2500	B7
Gates East Rd				
4800	MstT	44062	2769	E4
Gates Mills Blvd				
6800	GSML	44040	2500	C7
6800	GSML	44040	2630	B1
Gates Mills Blvd E				
6300	MDHT	44124	2629	E3
6300	PRPK	44124	2629	E3
6500	MDHT	44124	2630	A2
6600	GSML	44040	2630	A2
Gates Mills Blvd NE				
30600	PRPK	44124	2629	B6
31300	MDHT	44124	2629	B6
Gates Mills Blvd SW				
30600	PRPK	44124	2629	B6
31200	MDHT	44124	2629	B6
Gates Mills Blvd W				
6300	MDHT	44124	2629	E3
6300	PRPK	44124	2629	E3
6500	MDHT	44124	2630	A2
6700	GSML	44040	2630	A2
Gates Mills Estates Dr				
7700	GSML	44040	2501	A2
Gates Mills Tower				
6800	GSML	44040	2500	B7
6800	MDHT	44124	2500	B7
Gateway				
10	EUCL	44119	2373	A5
Gateway Blvd N				
100	ELYR	44035	2874	E6
Gateway Blvd S				
6100	ELYR	44035	2874	E7
N Gateway Dr				
8600	NRYN	44133	3148	C1
S Gateway Dr				
-	NRYN	44133	3148	C1
Gateway Ln				
5700	BKPK	44142	2881	C1
N Gateway St				
-	NRYN	44133	3148	D2
Gatewood Dr				
6100	MNTR	44060	2144	D4
8600	NRDV	44039	2877	D7
9900	BKVL	44141	3151	D4
Gatewood Ovl				
7800	GSML	44040	2501	A1
Gatsby Ln				
2900	WBHL	44092	2374	D7
Gay Av				
9900	CLEV	44105	2756	C2
Gay St				
23100	EUCL	44123	2373	C2
Gayle Dr				
200	SDLK	44054	2617	A3
Gaylord Av				
9300	CLEV	44105	2756	B3
Gaynor Dr				
6000	BKPK	44142	2881	B2
Geauga St				
7300	SLN	44139	3021	A2
W Geauga Tr				
12800	CsTp	44026	2631	B2
Geauga Lake Pkwy				
-	BbgT	44023	2890	B7
-	BbgT	44023	3021	B2
Geauga Lake Rd				
17700	BbgT	44023	2890	C6
18400	BbgT	44023	3021	C1
18900	BbgT	44202	3021	C2
Geauga Portage Easterly Rd				
-	FnTp	44491	3029	A4
-	StnT	44491	3029	A4
Geauga Portage Easterly Rd NW				
4000	StnT	44491	3029	D4
Gebhart Pl				
30100	WLWK	44095	2249	D6
Geddes Bluff Ln				
700	SgHT	44067	3152	C1
Gedeohn				
31900	AVLK	44012	2618	D1
Gedeon Av				
4800	CLEV	44102	2754	B1
Gehring St				
2000	CLEV	44113	2624	D5
Geiger St				
400	BERA	44017	2880	A6
Gem Cir				
34100	NRDV	44039	2877	C1
Gemini Ct				
5600	SLN	44139	2888	D2
Gene Dr				
4200	SVHL	44131	3015	B1
Genesee Av				
1100	MDHT	44124	2499	D7
Genesee Rd				
1400	SELD	44121	2498	A7
1400	SELD	44121	2628	A1
18900	EUCL	44117	2497	D1
Genevia St				
16600	BbgT	44023	2890	A1
Gennett Av				
-	CLEV	44102	2754	B1
-	CLEV	44109	2754	B1
Gentry Cir				
7600	CcdT	44077	2254	C2
Gentry Dr				
-	AURA	44202	3157	B4
Genung St				
3100	MadT	44057	1942	B6
3100	MDSN	44057	1942	B6
Geon Ct				
10	AVLK	44012	2617	C3
George Av				
2500	PRMA	44134	2883	C2
9100	CLEV	44105	2756	B1
George St				
200	ELYR	44035	3006	A1
Georgeanne Ct				
5100	MNTR	44060	2039	A6
Georgetown Av				
500	ELYR	44035	2875	E3
Georgetown Dr				
6700	MNTR	44060	2143	D6
27200	WTLK	44145	2620	A6
Georgetown Ln				
16400	SGVL	44136	3147	A4
Georgetown Rd				
-	RDHT	44143	2498	B2
22100	EUCL	44143	2498	B2
Georgetown Sq				
10	EUCL	44143	2498	B2
Georgette Av				
4300	NOSD	44070	2750	E6
Georgette Dr				
100	CrlT	44044	3006	D6
16200	BtnT	44021	2765	B7
Georgette Ln				
900	CLEV	44109	2754	E4
George Zakany Dr				
-	HmbT	44024	2381	B3
George Zeiger Dr				
26000	BHWD	44122	2628	E4
26100	BHWD	44122	2629	A4
Georgia Av				
200	ELYR	44035	3006	C1
300	LORN	44052	2615	A5
800	AMHT	44001	2872	E3
Georgia Ct				
-	LORN	44052	2615	A5
Georgia Dr				
2000	WTLK	44145	2749	B1
Georgia Rd				
14300	BtnT	44021	2766	D3
14300	BtnT	44062	2766	D3
14900	BtnT	44062	2767	A4
14900	MdfT	44062	2767	A4
Georgia St				
10500	RMDV	44202	3020	E3
Georgie Ct				
8700	MNTR	44060	2144	C7
Gerald Av				
5400	PRMA	44129	2883	A2
6700	PRMA	44129	2882	E2
Gerald Dr				
7400	MDBH	44130	3012	D2
Geraldine Av				
11700	CLEV	44111	2753	A1
Geraldine Rd				
4700	RDHT	44143	2498	D4
Gerard Av				
16700	MPHT	44137	2886	C2
Germaine Av				
3500	CLEV	44109	2754	B6
4500	CLEV	44144	2754	B6
Germantown Dr				
20700	FWPK	44126	2751	C4
Gershwin Dr				
26600	WTLK	44145	2620	A7
Gertrude Av				
5700	CLEV	44105	2755	D2
Gessner Rd				
23600	NOSD	44070	2750	D5
25300	NOSD	44145	2750	C4
25300	WTLK	44145	2750	C4
Gettysburg Dr				
1000	PRMA	44134	2883	E6
2000	LORN	44053	2744	B5
8600	TNBG	44087	3019	C5
Getz St				
10800	CrlT	44035	3006	A4
Gibson Av				
9300	CLEV	44105	2756	B1
Gibson Dr				
2600	RKRV	44116	2751	A1
Gibson St				
100	BERA	44017	2880	B7
Giddings Rd				
1300	CLEV	44103	2495	E7
1300	CLEV	44103	2625	E1
Giel Av				
1200	LKWD	44107	2622	E4
Giesse Dr				
1000	MDHT	44124	2499	E6
Gifford Av				
4000	CLEV	44109	2754	B5
4500	CLEV	44144	2754	B5
Gifford Ct				
15600	SGVL	44136	3147	B2
Gifford Dr				
5800	CLEV	44144	2754	A5
6000	BKLN	44144	2754	A5
6300	BKLN	44144	2753	B5
Gifford Rd				
8800	BhmT	44001	2871	B7
Gilbert Av				
5400	PRMA	44129	2883	A1
6700	PRMA	44129	2882	E1
Gilbert Ct				
-	NRDV	44039	3008	C1
5800	CLEV	44102	2754	A1
Gilbert Dr				
-	VMLN	44089	2741	B6
10	BDFD	44146	2887	B5
1600	MDHT	44124	2629	C1
Gilbert Rd				
-	ETLK	44095	2250	B1
Gilchrist Dr				
27700	EUCL	44132	2249	A6
28300	WLWK	44095	2249	A6
Gildersleeve Cir				
7800	KTLD	44094	2376	D5
Gildersleeve Dr				
-	KTLD	44094	2377	A5
7700	KTLD	44094	2376	E5
Giles Rd				
10	EatT	44044	3007	C5
4000	MDHL	44022	2760	B4
4600	CLEV	44135	2753	B6
Gill Av				
8200	CLEV	44104	2626	A6
Gill Ct				
1300	TNBG	44087	3019	A4
Gillett St				
10	PNVL	44077	2146	A2
Gilmer Ln				
4400	RDHT	44143	2498	C3
Gilmere Dr				
6000	BKPK	44142	2881	A2
Gilmore Av				
13000	CLEV	44135	2753	B5
13100	CLEV	44135	2752	E5
25500	EUCL	44132	2373	D1
Gina Dr				
34000	NRDV	44039	2877	C3
Ginger Ct				
30000	NOSD	44070	2878	B4
Ginger Ln				
30100	NOSD	44070	2878	B4
Gingerich Rd				
15000	BtnT	44021	2766	C2
15000	BtnT	44062	2766	C2
Ginger Wren Rd				
2400	PRPK	44124	2629	A4
Gino Ln				
700	CLEV	44109	2755	A4
Girard Dr				
300	BERA	44017	3010	E1
300	BERA	44017	3011	A1
Girdle Rd				
-	WFAR	44491	2898	D4
5000	FnTp	44491	2898	D7
5400	FnTp	44491	3029	D2
6100	FnTp	44491	2898	D4
6900	FnTp	44062	2898	D4
7100	FnTp	44062	2769	D7
7500	MstT	44062	2769	D7
9000	WndT	44099	2639	D4
9600	MstT	44062	2639	D7
10100	WndT	44062	2639	D4
Girdled Rd				
10500	CcdT	44024	2253	E5
10500	CcdT	44077	2253	E5
10500	CdnT	44024	2253	E5
10600	CcdT	44077	2254	A5
12000	CcdT	44077	2255	B2
12800	LryT	44077	2255	B2
13000	LryT	44077	2256	A1
Girdler Cir				
200	SgHT	44067	3017	E4
Givens Ct				
3000	PryT	44081	2041	D3
Glade Av				
8200	CLEV	44104	2626	A6
Gladland Av				
4500	NOSD	44070	2750	D6
Gladstone Rd				
19000	WVHT	44122	2757	E2
20400	WVHT	44122	2758	A2
Gladwin Dr				
1700	MDHT	44124	2629	C2
Gladys Av				
1100	LKWD	44107	2622	C4
6000	EyrT	44035	2745	D7
6000	EyrT	44055	2745	D7
Gladys Dr				
200	BNWK	44212	3147	D7
Gladys St				
10	OBLN	44074	3138	E4
Glamer Dr				
10700	PRMA	44130	3013	B1
Glantz Dr				
700	ShfT	44055	2745	A6
Glasgow Dr				
-	HDHT	44143	2499	C1
Glasgow Ln				
5800	SLN	44139	2889	D3
Glasgow St				
6000	MadT	44057	1941	D1
Glass Av				
6000	CLEV	44103	2495	D7
Glastonbury Cir				
4700	RDHT	44143	2498	D1
Glastonbury Dr				
7200	HDSN	44236	3154	E7
Glazier Av				
5000	CLEV	44127	2625	D6
Gleeson Dr				
9600	VLVW	44125	2885	C5
Gleeten Rd				
4800	RDHT	44143	2498	E4
Glen Av				
18300	CLEV	44110	2497	D1
Glen Cir				
10300	TwbT	44087	3020	D4
Glen Ct				
7700	MONT	44060	2143	D1
Glen Dr				
9500	BKVL	44141	3151	A2
32700	NRDV	44039	2877	E3
33800	ETLK	44095	2250	A3
33900	ETLK	44095	2249	E3
Glen Ovl				
1800	RDHT	44143	2373	E7
6900	CcdT	44077	2145	C7
11200	PMHT	44130	2882	B5
Glen Rd				
10	MDHL	44022	2760	B6
Glenallen Av				
6300	SLN	44139	2888	E6
Glen Allen Dr				
3400	CVHT	44121	2497	D7
7800	SgHT	44067	3017	D7
Glen Arbor Ct				
7900	MNTR	44060	2252	D3
Glen Arden Dr				
32200	WLWK	44095	2249	D4
Glenbar Ct				
3700	FWPK	44126	2751	C1
Glenbar Dr				
3200	FWPK	44126	2751	C1
Glenboro Dr				
11100	CLEV	44105	2756	D2
Glenbrook Blvd				
23500	EUCL	44117	2373	C7
Glenbrook Ct				
1300	WTLK	44145	2620	E7
Glenbrook Dr				
3200	TwbT	44087	3020	D4
8400	OmsT	44138	2878	E6
8400	OmsT	44138	2879	A6
13300	SGVL	44136	3012	D5
Glenbrook Ln				
1300	WTLK	44145	2620	E7
Glenbrook Rd				
4300	WLBY	44094	2250	C6
Glenburn Av				
16000	MPHT	44128	2757	C7
Glenbury Av				
2100	LKWD	44107	2622	B6
Glenbury Ln				
2600	WLBY	44094	2250	E1
Glencairn Ct				
6800	MNTR	44060	2143	D6
Glencairn Dr				
7100	PRMA	44134	2883	D7
Glencairn Ln				
9500	ODFL	44138	3010	C1
Glencairn Rd				
3200	SRHT	44120	2627	D7
3200	SRHT	44122	2627	D7
3400	SRHT	44122	2757	D1
Glen Cairn Wy				
18000	SGVL	44136	3146	B4
Glencliffe Rd				
14400	CLEV	44111	2752	D1
14600	CLEV	44111	2622	D7
Glencoe Av				
6200	BKLN	44144	2754	A5
7300	BKLN	44144	2753	E5
15300	CLEV	44110	2372	B6
Glen Coe Dr				
6500	BKVL	44141	3150	D3
Glencoe Ln				
400	HDHT	44143	2499	C2
Glencreek Ln				
18200	SGVL	44136	3011	E6
Glencrest Rd				
800	SgHT	44067	3152	D3
Glendale Av				
13100	CLEV	44105	2756	E2
13100	CLEV	44120	2756	E2
13100	CLEV	44105	2757	A2
14000	CLEV	44120	2757	A2
14000	CLEV	44128	2757	B2
16000	SGVL	44136	3147	A2
18100	CLEV	44122	2757	C2
W Glendale Av				
10	BDFD	44146	2886	D3
Glendale Ct				
200	ELYR	44035	2875	A5
Glendale Dr				
1100	HRM	44234	3161	A2
20200	RKRV	44116	2621	D7
Glendale Rd				
3800	NRDV	44039	2877	C3
E Glendale St				
10	BDFD	44146	2886	E3
Glen Daniel Cir				
10400	BKLN	44144	2753	C6
Glendenning Dr				
400	BYVL	44140	2619	E5
Glendon Rd				
2200	UNHT	44118	2628	A4
Glendora Ln				
10400	PMHT	44130	2882	B5
Glen Eagle Dr				
4500	BKVL	44141	3150	E2
E Glen Eagle Dr				
300	HDHT	44143	2499	D2
W Glen Eagle Dr				
300	HDHT	44143	2499	D2
Glen Eagle Ln				
10000	TNBG	44087	3020	A3
Glen Eagles Ct				
11200	CcdT	44077	2146	D6
Glen Echo Dr				
7600	GSML	44040	2500	E7
Glen Eden Ct				
600	AURA	44202	3156	C3
Glenella Dr				
6600	SVHL	44131	2884	B5
Glenfield Rd				
18500	CLEV	44119	2372	E6
Glenforest Rd				
24200	EUCL	44123	2373	D3
Glen Forest Tr				
10600	BKVL	44141	3016	C4
Glengarry Dr				
-	AURA	44202	3021	D5
E Glengary Cir				
300	HDHT	44143	2499	C2
W Glengary Cir				
300	HDHT	44143	2499	C2
Glengary Rd				
2800	SRHT	44120	2627	D6
Glengate Dr				
7700	BWHT	44147	3014	D6
Glengate Rd				
2300	WBHL	44094	2375	D2
Glenhill Dr				
13300	CsTp	44026	2631	D3
23700	BHWD	44122	2628	D3
Glen Hollow Cir				
-	AURA	44202	3156	C2
Glenhollow Ct				
10000	BKVL	44141	3151	D4
Glenhollow Dr				
11400	CsTp	44026	2501	A2
Glen Hollow Ln				
7000	OmsT	44138	2878	D4
Glenhurst Rd				
600	WLWK	44095	2249	D6
Glenhurst St				
10	OBLN	44074	3138	C3
Glen Kyle Ln				
34900	WBHL	44094	2375	A4
Glenlivet Ct				
39200	SLN	44139	2889	D4
Glen Lodge Rd				
4700	MNTR	44060	2038	D6
Glenlyn Rd				
4800	LNHT	44124	2498	D7
Glen Lyon Dr				
1400	WTLK	44145	2619	B7
Glenmar Wy				
19500	SGVL	44136	3011	D7
Glenmere Cir				
4300	WVHT	44128	2758	D4
Glenmont Dr				
7400	NRYN	44133	3013	D7
Glenmont Rd				
1500	ECLE	44118	2497	B7
1500	ECLE	44118	2627	B1
1600	CVHT	44118	2627	B1
Glenmora Dr				
11300	CdnT	44024	2379	C2
Glenmore Dr				
2500	WTLK	44145	2749	E2
Glenmore Rd				
2800	SRHT	44122	2628	C6
Glenn Av				
38200	WLBY	44094	2250	E5
Glenn Dr				
1200	SVHL	44131	2884	B3
6400	PRMA	44134	2883	C4
E Glenn Dr				
5800	MPHT	44137	2886	C3
S Glenn Dr				
16100	MPHT	44137	2886	B3
W Glenn Dr				
5800	MPHT	44137	2886	B3
Glenna Ln				
100	BNWK	44212	3147	E6
Glenn Oak Dr				
8200	BWHT	44147	3014	E4
Glenn Oval Dr				
7200	PRMA	44130	2882	D7
Glen Oak Dr				
-	GSML	44040	2630	B3
Glen Oaks				
11200	TNBG	44087	3020	B3
Glen Oaks Blvd				
700	ShfT	44055	2745	B6
Glen Oaks Ln				
10	BERA	44017	3011	D1
10	BERA	44130	3011	D1
10	MDBH	44017	3011	D1
10	MDBH	44130	3011	D1
Glenpark Av				
16500	CLEV	44128	2757	C5
Glen Park Dr				
200	BYVL	44140	2620	B4
W Glen Park Dr				
300	BYVL	44140	2620	B4
Glenpark Rd				
8000	KTLD	44094	2376	E2
Glenridge Av				
15600	MDBH	44130	2881	B7
Glenridge Ct				
10	BTVL	44022	2889	E1
Glenridge Rd				
1700	EUCL	44117	2498	A1
2200	SELD	44117	2498	B3
4100	SELD	44121	2498	B3
Glen Russ Ln				
20200	EUCL	44117	2498	A3
Glenshire Av				
17400	CLEV	44135	2752	A5
Glenshire Rd				
7200	OKWD	44146	2887	E7
7200	OKWD	44146	3018	E1
Glenside Ct				
26900	OmsT	44138	2878	E5
Glenside Ln				
7300	OmsT	44138	2878	D5
Glenside Rd				
900	SELD	44121	2498	B5
13400	CLEV	44110	2497	A4
Glensin Ct				
-	CLEV	44128	2757	D3
Glenstone Dr				
9600	KTLD	44094	2377	B3
Glen Valley Dr				
2300	WTLK	44145	2750	B2
11100	BKVL	44141	3016	C6
14700	MDFD	44062	2767	E1
14800	MDFD	44062	2768	A2
Glenview Av				
1500	MadT	44057	1843	A7
10800	CLEV	44108	2496	C4
Glenview Dr				
10	AURA	44202	3022	A7
10	AURA	44202	3157	A1
100	AVLK	44012	2618	A1
Glenview Rd				
4300	WVHT	44128	2757	D5
6600	MAYF	44143	2500	A5
Glenville Av				
10500	CLEV	44108	2496	C4
Glenway Dr				
10200	TwbT	44087	3020	D5
Glenway Rd				
5900	BKPK	44142	2881	A2
Glenwillow Dr				
6300	NRYN	44133	3013	E3
Glenwood Av				
-	ClbT	44028	3010	D3
4600	WLBY	44094	2250	D6
5000	SLN	44139	2759	C7
6300	MPHT	44137	2886	B4
11400	CLEV	44106	2626	D3
15300	MPHT	44137	2886	B2
Glenwood Cir				
600	BERA	44017	3011	A2
7700	BWHT	44147	3014	D6
Glenwood Dr				
-	BERA	44017	3011	A1
-	TwbT	44087	3020	C4
400	PNVL	44077	2146	A3
1600	TNBG	44087	3019	C4
2500	TNBG	44087	3020	A4
3200	RMDV	44202	3020	C4
3700	RMDV	44202	3021	A4
6100	MNTR	44060	2144	A4
10800	MsnT	44024	2634	A3
Glenwood Ln				
-	AVON	44011	2747	C1
20200	SGVL	44136	3146	C2
Glenwood Rd				
3700	CVHT	44121	2497	E7
3800	CVHT	44121	2498	A7
7500	GSML	44040	2500	D7
Glenwood St				
100	ELYR	44035	2875	B5
4700	MNTU	44255	3159	C5
Glenwood Tr				
9100	BKVL	44141	3150	B1
Globe Av				
2700	LORN	44052	2745	C3
2700	LORN	44055	2745	C3
5200	ShfT	44055	2745	C6
Globe St				
6000	EyrT	44035	2745	C6
6000	EyrT	44055	2745	C6
Gloria Av				
33700	NRDV	44039	2877	D3
Gloria Dr				
800	MCDN	44056	3154	A5
Gloucester Cir				
400	BNWK	44212	3147	B7
Gloucester Dr				
500	HDHT	44143	2499	C3
1800	LORN	44053	2744	B6
27100	NOSD	44070	2879	A1
Gloucester Rd				
10000	STBR	44241	3156	D7
Glouchester Dr				
2100	LNHT	44124	2629	B3
Glover Ct				
10	ELYR	44035	2875	A7
Glynn Rd				
15300	ECLE	44112	2497	B6
16200	CVHT	44112	2497	B6
Goble Dr				
2300	LORN	44055	2746	A5
Goebel Dr				
6300	PRMA	44134	2883	D4
Gold Coast Ln				
-	LKWD	44107	2623	A3
Golden Av				
7900	CLEV	44103	2626	A3
Goldengate Av				
3100	RKRV	44116	2621	D7
Golden Gate Blvd				
1100	MDHT	44124	2499	E7
Golden Oak Pkwy				
300	OKWD	44146	3018	D2
Golden Rod Cir				
-	SFLD	44011	2747	A6
-	SFLD	44035	2747	A6
Goldenrod Dr				
200	AURA	44202	3156	E5
7300	MONT	44060	2143	C3
Goldenrod Rd				
7400	MONT	44060	2143	C3
Golden Russett Blvd				
300	AMHT	44001	2743	B7
500	AMHT	44001	2872	B1
Golden Star Dr				
17100	SGVL	44136	3147	B4
Gold Finch Ct				
9000	MNTR	44060	2144	D1
Gold Rush Dr				
17100	SGVL	44136	3147	A4
Goldwood Dr				
2600	RKRV	44116	2751	A1
Golf Dr				
10	PnvT	44077	2146	D3
Golf View Dr				
18400	CLEV	44135	2752	A4
18500	CLEV	44135	2751	E4
Golf View Ln				
10	NOSD	44070	2879	A1
Golfway Dr				
300	PnvT	44077	2040	E4
Golfway Ln				
5200	LNHT	44124	2629	A2
Golfway Rd				
4400	SELD	44121	2628	C2
Golfway Tr				
100	ELYR	44035	2874	B7
100	ELYR	44035	3005	B1
Goller Av				
20100	EUCL	44119	2373	A5
Gondawood Dr				
49600	CrlT	44050	3141	B5
49600	LrgT	44050	3141	B5
Gondawood Ln				
400	CrlT	44050	3141	A4
400	LrgT	44050	3141	A4
Goodell Ct				
9300	MNTR	44060	2252	E3
Gooding Av				
10500	CLEV	44108	2496	C5
Goodman Av				
7700	CLEV	44105	2756	A4
Goodman Cir				
5700	NRYN	44133	3013	E7
Goodman Dr				
5500	NRYN	44133	3013	E7
5500	NRYN	44133	3014	A7
Goodnor Rd				
1900	CVHT	44118	2627	C3
Goodrich Ct				
100	CRDN	44024	2380	A6
Goodwalt Av				
7400	CLEV	44102	2623	E5
Goodwin Av				
-	BtnT	44021	2636	B7
13800	BURT	44021	2636	B7
Gordon Av				
500	AMHT	44001	2872	E2
Gordon Dr				
10700	PRMA	44130	3013	B1
12600	NRYN	44133	3013	D6
Gordon Rd				
1000	LNHT	44124	2499	A6
Goredon Dr				
10	AQLA	44024	2505	C4
Gore Orphanage Rd				
-	BhmT	44001	2870	C7
7400	BhmT	44089	2870	C3
9600	BhmT	44889	2870	C7
9600	HetT	44889	2870	C7
Gorge Pkwy				
-	BDFD	44146	2887	A5
-	WNHL	44146	2886	C6
-	WNHL	44146	2887	A5
Gorman Av				
9300	CLEV	44105	2756	B4
Goshen Dr				
1500	HDSN	44236	3154	D7
Gosling Wy				
8300	MNTR	44060	2144	B2
Gould Av				
10	BDFD	44146	2886	E3
10	BDFD	44146	2887	A3
Gould Ct				
-	CLEV	44113	2624	C5
Goulders Grn				
29300	BYVL	44140	2619	D4
Governor Av				
6000	CLEV	44111	2753	B1
Governors Pl				
6100	MNTR	44060	2144	B3
Graber Dr				
1400	LKWD	44107	2622	A5
Grace Av				
1400	LKWD	44107	2623	A5
6000	EyrT	44035	2745	E6
6000	ShfT	44035	2745	E6
6000	ShfT	44055	2745	E6
7300	CLEV	44102	2623	E7
9000	GDHT	44125	2756	C7
Grace Cir				
5400	NRDV	44039	2748	B7
5400	NRDV	44039	2877	B1
Grace Ct				
8700	MNTR	44060	2038	C7
Grace Dr				
5400	MNTR	44060	2038	D7
5400	MNTR	44060	2144	D1
6900	OmsT	44138	2878	E4
Grace Rd				
4600	NOSD	44070	2750	D6
Grace St				
900	ShfT	44055	2745	B4
2400	LORN	44052	2744	A1
2400	LORN	44053	2744	A1
15700	NbyT	44073	2763	B5
E Grace St				
10	BDFD	44146	2886	D3
10	BDFD	44146	2887	A3
W Grace St				
10	BDFD	44146	2886	E4
Grafton Rd				
-	BHIT	44212	3146	B7
1500	CrlT	44035	3006	C3
2000	CrlT	44044	3006	E5
2300	EatT	44044	3006	E5
Grafton Rd				
2700	CrlT	44044	3006	E7
2700	EatT	44044	3006	E7
2800	BNWK	44212	3147	C7
3000	EatT	44044	3141	E2
3800	BNWK	44212	3146	D7
5000	BHIT	44212	3145	E7
5100	LvpT	44212	3145	E7
5300	LvpT	44280	3145	C7
6000	LvpT	44280	3144	D7
7400	LvpT	44280	3143	D7
7800	LvpT	44028	3143	D7
7800	LvpT	44280	3143	D7
33500	GftT	44028	3143	D7
Grafton Rd SR-57				
2300	CrlT	44044	3006	E7
2300	EatT	44044	3006	E7
3000	EatT	44044	3141	E2
Grafton St				
200	OBLN	44074	3138	E3
200	OBLN	44074	3139	A3
Grafton-Eastern Rd				
34000	GftT	44028	3143	B7
35000	GftT	44028	3142	D7
36000	GftT	44044	3142	D7
36700	GFTN	44044	3142	D7
Grafton-Eastern Rd SR-57				
36000	GftT	44044	3142	D7
36700	GFTN	44044	3142	D7
Graham Cir				
8600	ODFL	44138	2879	D6
Graham Dr				
5100	LNHT	44124	2498	E5
5100	LNHT	44124	2499	A5
Graham Rd				
3200	TmbT	44084	2259	D3
3500	HgvT	44084	2259	D5
13300	ECLE	44112	2497	A5
Gramatan Av				
14000	CLEV	44111	2752	D1
Granada Blvd				
4400	WVHT	44128	2758	B5
Granada Dr				
5400	MONT	44060	2144	A1
Granby Av				
1400	CLEV	44109	2754	E4
Granby Cir				
2900	TNBG	44087	3020	B6
Granby Dr				
7200	HDSN	44236	3154	E7
Grand Av				
1000	MadT	44057	1843	E5
5600	CLEV	44104	2625	D5
7300	CLEV	44104	2626	A5
Grand Blvd				
10	BDFD	44146	2886	E2
10	OmsT	44138	2879	C4
300	BDFD	44146	2887	A2
1700	EUCL	44117	2498	A1
29100	EUCL	44132	2374	A1
29100	WKLF	44092	2374	A1
29600	WKLF	44092	2249	B7
29800	WKLF	44095	2249	B7
29800	WLWK	44095	2249	B7
Grand Ct				
600	AURA	44202	3021	C7
Grand Pl				
5500	WLBY	44094	2375	A2
Grand St				
500	VMLN	44089	2740	E5
E Grand St				
10	BERA	44017	2880	C6
W Grand St				
10	BERA	44017	2880	C6
Grand Division Av				
7400	GDHT	44105	2756	A5
7400	GDHT	44125	2756	A5
7600	CLEV	44105	2756	A5
Grande Ct				
29200	WTLK	44145	2749	D3
Grand Elm St				
4700	MNTU	44255	3159	C5
Grand Key Dr				
10	GDRV	44045	2039	C6
Grandmere Dr				
10	BDFD	44146	2886	D4
Grand Park Cir				
200	BDFD	44146	2886	D2
Grand Prairie Ln				
10600	SGVL	44136	3012	B5
Grandridge Pt				
6100	CcdT	44077	2146	D4
Grand River Av				
100	PNVL	44077	2146	C1
Grand River Dr				
18300	PkmT	44231	3028	A1
Grandview Av				
2100	CVHT	44106	2626	C5
10300	CLEV	44104	2626	C5
Grandview Dr				
10	BSHT	44236	3153	B7
6700	INDE	44131	3015	E2
10400	KTLD	44094	2376	B5
12200	NbyT	44021	2765	A3
42500	EyrT	44035	2874	B2
Grand View Ln				
600	AURA	44202	3021	C7
Grandview Ln				
-	AURA	44202	3021	C7
Grandview Ter				
14900	ECLE	44112	2497	B5
Granger Av				
-	PnvT	44077	2039	C7
1200	LKWD	44107	2622	B4
Granger Ct				
5200	MPHT	44137	2757	A7
Granger Rd				
-	INDE	44125	2884	C1
-	VLVW	44131	2884	C1
5500	INDE	44131	2884	C1
7500	VLVW	44125	2884	C1
7500	VLVW	44131	2884	C1
7500	GDHT	44125	2885	A1
7700	GDHT	44125	2885	A1
8900	GDHT	44125	2756	D7
13500	GDHT	44125	2757	A7
14000	MPHT	44137	2757	A7
14500	MPHT	44137	2886	A1
Granger Rd SR-17				
-	INDE	44125	2884	C1
-	VLVW	44131	2884	C1
5500	INDE	44131	2884	C1
7500	VLVW	44125	2884	C1
7500	VLVW	44131	2884	C1
7700	GDHT	44125	2885	A1

INDEX 22

Granger Rd SR-17 — Cleveland Street Index — Hardwick Dr

STREET
Block City ZIP Map# Grid

Granger Rd SR-17
8900 GDHT 44125 2756 D7
13500 GDHT 44125 2757 A7
14000 MPHT 44137 2757 A7
E Granger Rd
10 BNHT 44131 2755 A7
1200 BNHT 44131 2884 C1
1400 INDE 44131 2884 D1
E Granger Rd SR-17
10 BNHT 44131 2755 A7
1200 BNHT 44131 2884 C1
1400 INDE 44131 2884 D1
N Granger Rd
9000 GDHT 44125 2756 B7
S Granger Rd
9200 GDHT 44125 2756 B7
W Granger Rd
- BNHT 44131 2754 E7
- BNHT 44109 2754 E7
- CLEV 44109 2754 E7
300 BNHT 44131 2755 A7
W Granger Rd SR-17
- BNHT 44109 2754 E7
- BNHT 44131 2754 E7
- CLEV 44109 2754 E7
300 BNHT 44131 2755 A7
Granite Rd
16600 BDFD 44137 2886 C3
16600 BDFD 44146 2886 C3
16600 MPHT 44137 2886 C3
Grannis Rd
4200 FWPK 44126 2751 D2
12100 GDHT 44125 2885 D2
Grant Av
2000 LORN 44055 2745 D5
2000 ShfT 44055 2745 D5
4900 CHHT 44125 2755 D4
5700 CHHT 44105 2755 D4
6800 CLEV 44105 2755 D4
15800 MPHT 44137 2757 B7
Grant Blvd
7200 MDBH 44130 2881 A7
Grant Dr
1200 PRMA 44134 2883 E6
7300 NRDV 44039 2877 C4
9200 NHFD 44067 3018 A3
Grant Rd
30400 WKLF 44092 2374 E1
Grant St
10 PNVL 44077 2145 E2
100 CRDN 44024 2380 B6
100 ELYR 44035 2875 B7
100 GNVA 44041 1944 C4
100 HmbT 44024 2380 B6
2800 LORN 44052 2615 C5
7100 MNTR 44060 2143 C7
Grantham Ln
9500 HmbT 44024 2381 C2
Grantham Rd
1800 CLEV 44112 2497 D3
Grantleigh Rd
1300 SELD 44121 2498 A7
Granton Av
3400 CLEV 44111 2752 C1
Grantwood Av
200 SDLK 44054 2616 B4
10500 CLEV 44108 2496 C6
Grantwood Dr
1400 PRMA 44134 2883 C3
Grapeland Av
14500 CLEV 44111 2752 C1
Grasmere Av
1800 ECLE 44112 2497 B5
5400 MPHT 44137 2886 C1
Gray Av
11300 CLEV 44108 2496 D5
Gray Rd
6300 CcdT 44077 2146 D4
Graybark Ln
100 AhtT 44001 2744 C7
100 AhtT 44001 2873 C1
Graydon Dr
5700 SVHL 44131 2884 B2
Gray Eagle Chase
7800 GSML 44040 2631 A3
Grayfriar Dr
6400 BKPK 44142 2880 C4
Gray Friar Wy
- MsnT 44024 2504 C7
11300 MsnT 44024 2634 C1
Gray Gull Dr
10 AVLK 44012 2488 B7
Grayland Dr
5600 BKPK 44142 2879 E1
Graylock Dr
2600 KTLD 44094 2376 A5
2600 WBHL 44094 2376 A5
Graystone Ln
9400 MNTR 44060 2145 A5
Grayton Rd
- CLEV 44135 2751 B7
- CLEV 44135 2880 A1
500 BERA 44017 2880 B4
800 BERA 44142 2880 B4
800 BKPK 44142 2880 A3
4400 CLEV 44135 2751 D5
6200 CLEV 44135 2880 A3
6200 CLEV 44142 2880 A3
Grayview Ct
11500 CcdT 44077 2146 D4
Grdina Av
6100 CLEV 44103 2495 D6
Great Lakes Pkwy
- TroT 44021 2894 B5
- TroT 44234 2894 B5
Great Northern Blvd
4500 NOSD 44070 2750 C6
5200 NOSD 44070 2879 C1
Great Northern Blvd SR-252
4500 NOSD 44070 2750 C6
5200 NOSD 44070 2879 C1
Great Oaks Ln
20000 SGVL 44136 3011 D5
Great Oaks Pkwy
4800 INDE 44131 2884 C5
Greatwood Ln
18100 AbnT 44023 2893 B6
Greely St
- ELYR 44035 2875 C5
Green Cir
5700 WLBY 44094 2375 A2
Green Ct
300 PNVL 44077 2145 E1
Green Dr
8100 GDHT 44125 2756 A6
29200 WLWK 44095 2249 C6
37100 ETLK 44095 2142 D6
Green Rd
- MadT 44057 1842 D7
1700 MadT 44057 1941 E1
1800 CLEV 44121 2497 E2
2100 CLEV 44121 2498 A3
2100 SELD 44121 2498 A3
2600 SRHT 44122 2628 C6
3200 BHWD 44122 2628 C7
3200 BHWD 44122 2758 C4
3400 HIHL 44122 2758 C4
4200 HIHL 44128 2758 C4
4300 WVHT 44128 2758 C4
13200 CsTp 44026 2631 E3
E Green Rd
800 SELD 44121 2498 C5
N Green Rd
1900 CLEV 44112 2497 E3
1900 CLEV 44121 2497 E3
S Green Rd
- CLEV 44121 2498 B4
100 SELD 44121 2498 B4
1500 SELD 44121 2628 C2
2100 UNHT 44118 2628 C2
2100 UNHT 44121 2628 C2
2200 BHWD 44122 2628 C4
2600 SRHT 44118 2628 C4
Green St
3800 PRRY 44081 2042 C2
Green Acres Dr
1400 PRMA 44134 3014 D2
8500 BWHT 44147 3015 C5
Greenbriar Cir
3700 WTLK 44145 2750 A4
Greenbriar Ct
100 EUCL 44143 2498 B2
Greenbriar Dr
10 AURA 44202 3156 E3
100 ELYR 44035 3005 B1
200 ELYR 44035 2874 B7
300 AVLK 44012 2618 C2
6600 PMHT 44130 2882 C5
8500 OmsT 44138 2879 A7
12700 MsnT 44024 2634 E1
Greenbriar Ln
4700 LORN 44053 2743 C5
Greenbrier Ct
8500 SgHT 44067 3017 E5
Greenbrier Dr
100 CNFL 44022 2889 E1
6600 BKVL 44141 3015 E3
17000 SGVL 44136 3147 B3
Greenbrook Dr
2600 MadT 44057 1942 A4
Greenbrooke Dr
26900 OmsT 44138 2878 E4
26900 OmsT 44138 2879 A4
Greencliff Dr
10 BDFD 44146 2886 C4
Greencroft Rd
10 BDFD 44146 2886 D2
Greendale Av
15300 MPHT 44137 2886 B2
Greene Dr
6000 BKPK 44142 2881 C2
Greenfield
- AVON 44011 2747 A1
Greenfield Cir
3000 BNWK 44212 3147 C7
Greenfield Ct
10 BERA 44017 3011 B2
Greenfield Dr
300 PnvT 44077 2041 A6
Greenfield Ln
- BHWD 44122 2628 E3
Greenfield Pl
2700 LORN 44052 2744 B2
21100 SGVL 44136 3011 B6
Greenfield Tr
7200 CsTp 44026 2631 B1
Greenforest Dr
800 AMHT 44001 2872 B2
Greengate Ovl
800 SgHT 44067 3152 B1
Greenhaven Dr
10 OmsT 44138 2879 A4
400 CNFL 44022 2889 E1
Greenhaven Pkwy
9500 BKVL 44141 3016 C4
Greenheath Dr
10000 PMHT 44130 2882 C2
Greenhill Rd
15100 CLEV 44111 2752 C3
Greenhurst Dr
5000 MPHT 44137 2757 B7
Greening Av
4500 PryT 44081 2042 D4
Green Jacket Ct
- AVLK 44012 2618 C4
Greenlawn Av
300 AMHT 44001 2743 E7
8200 PRMA 44129 2882 D1
10500 CLEV 44108 2496 C6
23000 BHWD 44122 2628 C4
Green Lawn Dr
22100 SGVL 44136 3011 A3
Greenlawn Dr
2500 SVHL 44131 2884 B5
Greenleaf Av
6600 PMHT 44130 2882 A6
7100 PRMA 44130 2882 A6
Greenleaf Cir
1500 WTLK 44145 2620 D7
Green Oak Av
5500 MNTR 44060 2144 A1
Green Oak Dr
19900 EUCL 44117 2498 A1
Green Ridge Av
6700 SLN 44139 2888 E7
Green Ridge Ct
7900 MNTR 44060 2251 E3
Green Ridge Dr
2100 WKLF 44092 2374 C3
6200 BDHT 44146 2887 E4
Greenridge Dr
10 GNVA 44041 1944 C7
Greenside Dr
500 PnvT 44077 2040 E3
Greenthorn Dr
7500 HDSN 44236 3155 B7
Greentree Ln
10 TroT 44234 2894 B6
Greentree Ln
100 AURA 44202 3157 E1
Greentree Rd
100 MDHL 44022 2760 D6
Greenvale Dr
100 SELD 44121 2498 A4
Greenvale Rd
2300 CLEV 44121 2497 E3
2400 CLEV 44121 2498 A3
Green Valley Dr
- PRMA 44134 3014 D1
10 SRSL 44073 2762 C6
Greenvalley Dr
7100 MNTR 44060 2145 A7
Greenview Av
9800 GDHT 44125 2756 C5
11100 CLEV 44108 2496 C5
Greenview Ct
4600 AVON 44011 2748 B6
Greenview Dr
- CrlT 44035 3005 D4
100 AURA 44202 3157 E1
10000 ClbT 44028 3010 C3
Greenview Pkwy
29900 WTLK 44145 2749 B5
Greenville Rd NW
4400 FnTp 44491 2898 E5
4700 FnTp 44062 2898 B5
Greenville Rd NW SR-88
4400 FnTp 44491 2898 E5
4700 FnTp 44062 2898 B5
Greenward Wy N
10 NOSD 44070 2879 A1
Greenward Wy S
100 NOSD 44070 2879 A2
N Greenway Ct
5500 HDHT 44143 2499 B3
S Greenway Ct
5600 HDHT 44143 2499 B3
Greenway Dr
100 CRDN 44024 2505 B2
100 ELYR 44035 2746 D7
300 CRDN 44024 2379 E7
9500 TNBG 44087 3019 B6
Greenway Rd
- MPHT 44137 2886 B5
- WNHL 44137 2886 B5
- WNHL 44146 2886 B5
4300 SELD 44121 2628 B2
15400 CLEV 44111 2752 C1
Greenway Tr
300 CRDN 44024 2379 E7
9700 AbnT 44023 2892 A2
Greenwich Av
1000 GFTN 44044 3142 A4
10900 CLEV 44105 2756 C2
35200 NRDV 44011 2748 B6
35200 NRDV 44039 2748 B6
Greenwich Ct
1500 PnvT 44077 2041 B6
Greenwich Dr
9800 SGVL 44136 3012 C4
Greenwich Ln
24400 BHWD 44122 2628 D4
Greenwich St
2600 ShvT 44241 3157 E7
Greenwold Rd
4400 SELD 44121 2628 C3
Greenwood Av
500 AMHT 44001 2872 E1
3600 CLEV 44115 2625 C3
17000 CLEV 44111 2752 B1
Greenwood Ct
600 SgHT 44067 3152 C2
32700 AVLK 44012 2618 A2
Greenwood Dr
- LORN 44053 2743 C4
300 ELYR 44035 3006 B3
3600 MDHL 44022 2759 E2
3600 MDHL 44124 2759 E2
3600 PRPK 44124 2759 E2
3600 PRPK 44124 2760 A2
4900 SDLK 44054 2616 D4
7100 MNTR 44060 2143 B3
16900 SGVL 44136 3146 B3
32500 AVLK 44012 2618 A2
Greenwood Ln
23400 NOSD 44070 2750 E3
Greenwood Ovl
4000 NRYN 44133 3014 B3
Greenwood Pkwy
800 SgHT 44067 3152 B1
Greenwood Rd
8500 NRYN 44133 3014 B3
23600 EUCL 44117 2373 C7
Greenwood St
6900 INDE 44131 2884 E6
6900 INDE 44131 2885 A7
Greenwood View Dr
7900 PRMA 44129 2882 D6
Gregory Av
33000 NRDV 44039 3008 C1
Gregory Ct
9000 MNTR 44060 2144 D6
Gregory Ln
10800 NRYN 44133 3013 B4
Gregus Av
3900 LORN 44055 2745 E4
Grenadier Ln
7700 BKVL 44141 3016 A3
Grenadier St
8600 BWHT 44147 3015 C5
Grenleigh Rd
1400 LNHT 44124 2498 D7
Grenney Ln
100 PNVL 44077 2146 C3
Grenoble Dr
2100 LORN 44053 2744 B5
Grenville Rd
3800 UNHT 44118 2627 E4
3800 UNHT 44118 2628 A4
Grenway Dr
8400 MNTR 44060 2252 B2
Grenway Rd
3200 SRHT 44122 2627 D7
Gresham Ln
7700 TwbT 44236 3154 C5
Gretna Green Dr
- HDHT 44143 2499 D1
Grey Fox Run
10 BTVL 44022 2889 E1
Greyfriars Cir
11800 NRYN 44133 3148 A5
Greystone Dr
- TroT 44234 3025 C2
Greystone Dr
14500 BKPK 44142 2881 C3
Greystone Pkwy
9400 BKVL 44141 3150 E2
9500 BKVL 44141 3151 A2
Greystone Pt
11600 SGVL 44136 3011 A5
Greyton Rd
800 CVHT 44112 2497 D6
800 ECLE 44112 2497 D4
Gridley Av
1400 LKWD 44107 2622 A5
Gridley Rd
3500 SRHT 44122 2757 D2
Griffing Av
11600 CLEV 44120 2626 D6
Grimes Rd
- BDHT 44146 2887 B1
Grimsby Av
12300 CLEV 44135 2753 A4
Grist Mill Ct
23100 ODFL 44138 3010 E1
Gristmill Dr
10 PNVL 44077 2040 C7
Grist Mill Run
9500 ODFL 44138 3010 D1
Griswold Av
5700 CLEV 44104 2625 D5
Griswold Cir
8900 MCDN 44056 3018 B5
Griswold Rd
300 ELYR 44035 2875 A2
600 ELYR 44035 2874 D2
6800 MadT 44057 2044 C6
10100 CdnT 44024 2253 C7
41200 EyrT 44035 2874 D2
Gross Dr
10800 PRMA 44130 3013 A2
Grosse Dr
6300 BKPK 44142 2881 A4
Grosse Pointe Ovl
15500 SGVL 44136 3012 B4
Grosvenor Rd
3500 CVHT 44118 2627 D2
3700 SELD 44118 2627 D2
3800 SELD 44118 2628 A2
Groton Dr
1400 HDSN 44236 3154 D7
Groton Rd
18100 CLEV 44121 2497 E3
18100 CLEV 44121 2498 A3
Grouse Run
16600 SGVL 44136 3147 A3
Grouse Ridge Dr
8500 CdnT 44024 2254 E5
Grove Av
10 PnvT 44077 2040 E7
1500 MadT 44057 1843 A7
2700 LORN 44055 2745 E2
4200 WLBY 44094 2250 D5
4800 ShfT 44055 2745 E5
5500 MNTR 44060 2144 A1
7200 OKWD 44146 2887 D7
Grove Av SR-57
2800 LORN 44055 2745 E3
4800 ShfT 44055 2745 E5
Grove Ct
27000 WTLK 44145 2750 A4
Grove Dr
13600 GDHT 44125 2886 A3
13800 GDHT 44137 2886 A3
13800 MPHT 44137 2886 A3
Grove Ln
6500 PRMA 44134 3013 E2
6500 PRMA 44134 3014 A2
Grove Rd
14200 HrmT 44234 3026 D3
14200 TroT 44231 3026 D3
14200 TroT 44234 3026 D3
14200 TroT 44234 3026 D3
14900 PkmT 44231 3027 B2
14900 TroT 44231 3027 A3
Grove St
- WFAR 44491 2898 D4
15700 MDFD 44062 2767 C2
31900 AVLK 44012 2618 D2
38500 WLBY 44094 2143 A4
Groveland Av
17900 CLEV 44111 2752 A2
Groveland Dr
32500 AVLK 44012 2618 A1
Groveland Rd
4200 UNHT 44118 2628 B3
E Groveland Rd
23000 BHWD 44122 2628 D3
Groveland St
10 OBLN 44074 3138 E3
Groveland Club Dr
300 CLEV 44110 2372 B7
Grove Pond Wy
24400 ODFL 44138 2879 C7
Grover Ct
10 CrlT 44044 3006 E6
10 EatT 44044 3006 E6
Grover Rd
35100 ETLK 44095 2250 B2
Groveside Dr
8300 SGVL 44136 3012 B3
Grovewood Av
1600 PRMA 44134 2883 C1
15200 CLEV 44110 2372 B6
17200 CLEV 44119 2372 B6
35300 ETLK 44095 2250 B3
Grovewood Dr
5600 MNTR 44060 2144 A2
8000 MNTR 44060 2143 E1
Gruss Av
12400 CLEV 44108 2496 E4
Guadalupe Dr
1000 PRMA 44134 2883 E6
Guardian Blvd
11600 LNDL 44135 2753 A4
11700 CLEV 44135 2753 A4
Guilbert Rd
33500 ETLK 44095 2249 E3
Guildford Rd
500 VMLN 44089 2741 D5
Guilford Av
- NOSD 44070 2749 C7
- NOSD 44070 2878 C1
Guilford Ct
3600 WTLK 44145 2749 C4
Guilford Rd
200 VMLN 44089 2741 D4
2400 CVHT 44118 2627 C5
Guinevere Dr
11200 NbyT 44065 2634 B5
Gulf Rd
100 ELYR 44035 2875 C5
1300 ELYR 44035 2746 C7
5000 SFLD 44035 2746 C7
5000 SFLD 44054 2746 C7
Gulfstream Ct
- BHIT 44212 3146 A6
Gull Dr
200 ELYR 44035 2874 D2
Gulls Cove
200 PnvT 44077 2145 B6
Gum Tree Ln
- OmsT 44138 2878 E5
Gura Rd
13500 HtbT 44021 2637 B4
13500 HtbT 44046 2637 B4
13500 MdfT 44046 2637 B4
13500 MdfT 44021 2637 B4
Gurss Rd
32400 AVLK 44012 2618 A2
Guthrie Av
6500 CLEV 44102 2623 E6
6500 CLEV 44102 2624 A6
Guy Av
4900 CLEV 44127 2755 C1
Gwendolyn Farms Dr
12500 MsnT 44024 2504 D7

H

H St
900 LORN 44052 2615 A7
Habant Dr
200 AMHT 44001 2743 D5
Haber Dr
22000 FWPK 44126 2751 A5
Haber Rd
5700 VMLN 44089 2740 D7
5700 VmnT 44089 2740 D7
Habersham Ln N
4400 RDHT 44143 2498 C3
Habersham Ln S
4400 RDHT 44143 2498 B3
Hacienda Dr
7200 PRMA 44130 2882 C7
Hackberry Dr
7900 MNTR 44060 2253 A4
Hackney Ct
- KTLD 44094 2377 C6
8000 MNTR 44060 2143 E6
8000 MNTR 44060 2144 A6
Hackney Rd
33900 HGVL 44022 2630 A7
33900 PRPK 44124 2630 A7
Hadaway Ct
100 CrlT 44035 3005 E2
Hadaway St
35300 NRDV 44039 2877 A3
Haddam Dr
300 LORN 44052 2615 D5
Haddam Rd
2600 CLEV 44120 2627 A5
2600 SRHT 44120 2627 A5
Hadden Rd
2000 EUCL 44117 2498 B1
8400 TNBG 44087 3154 D3
8400 TwbT 44087 3154 D3
Hadleigh Rd
- SRHT 44122 2628 A5
4100 SRHT 44118 2628 A5
4100 UNHT 44118 2628 A5
Hadley Rd
31800 WLWK 44095 2249 E5
Hadley St
2600 ShvT 44241 3157 E7
Hafely Dr
300 LORN 44052 2615 B5
Haggett Dr
2700 TNBG 44087 3020 B5
Hague Av
6700 CLEV 44102 2624 A6
6900 CLEV 44102 2623 E6
Haines Rd
1800 MadT 44057 1941 C1
Haines St
100 ELYR 44035 3006 E3
Halburton Rd
20800 SRHT 44122 2758 B1
21000 BHWD 44122 2758 B1
Halcyon Dr
10000 PMHT 44130 2882 C3
Halcyon Rd
2100 BHWD 44122 2628 D3
Haldane Rd
1800 CLEV 44112 2497 D3
Hale Av
2500 AVON 44011 2747 D2
14000 CLEV 44110 2497 A1
Hale Rd
10 PnvT 44077 2041 B4
2500 PryT 44077 2041 B4
13000 NRsT 44074 3139 E3
13300 BtnT 44021 2636 D4
13300 ClrT 44021 2636 D4
Haley St
5400 VMLN 44089 2740 E6
Halifax Ln
300 SgHT 44067 3017 E5
Halifax Rd
20400 WVHT 44122 2758 A2
Halifax St
29900 WKLF 44092 2249 C7
Hall Av
1100 LKWD 44107 2622 B4
6500 MadT 44057 1843 B7
Hall Ct
300 AMHT 44001 2872 E2
1400 EUCL 44132 2373 D5
Hall Rd
- ClrT 44024 2505 D3
600 CrlT 44035 3005 E3
13500 ClrT 44024 2506 A4
24500 WTLK 44070 2750 C3
24500 WTLK 44145 2750 C3
Hall St
10 CNFL 44022 2761 A6
100 CNFL 44022 2760 E6
29100 SLN 44139 2888 B6
Hallauer Rd
14500 PtfT 44074 3139 A6
15700 PtfT 44074 3138 E7
Halle Av
7400 CLEV 44102 2623 E7
Halle Dr
200 EUCL 44132 2373 D1
6000 VLVW 44125 2885 B4
34000 WLBY 44094 2375 A2
Halle Farm Dr
5900 WLBY 44094 2375 A2
Hallford Cir
5300 LNHT 44124 2629 A2
Halliday Av
15600 CLEV 44110 2497 C3
Hallnorth Dr
8400 MNTR 44060 2252 B2
Hallock Ct
900 CLEV 44110 2497 A3
Halls Carriage Pth
1700 WTLK 44145 2619 E7
1700 WTLK 44145 2749 E1
Halsey Dr
35000 ETLK 44095 2142 B7
Halsey Rd
2000 CVHT 44118 2627 E2
2000 SELD 44118 2627 E2
Halstead Av
2000 LKWD 44107 2623 A6
Halstead St
10200 ShvT 44241 3158 B7
10200 ShvT 44255 3158 B7
Haltnorth Ct
5500 CLEV 44104 2625 D4
Halton Ct
36800 SLN 44139 3020 C2
Halworth Rd
20600 SRHT 44122 2628 A7
20600 SRHT 44122 2758 B1
20900 BHWD 44122 2758 B1
Hamann Pkwy
4200 WLBY 44094 2250 C6
N Hambden St
100 CRDN 44024 2380 A6
N Hambden St SR-44
100 CRDN 44024 2380 A6
N Hambden St US-6
100 CRDN 44024 2380 A6
S Hambden St
100 CRDN 44024 2380 A6
Hambleton Dr
7300 SLN 44139 3019 E2
Hamden Rd
6400 PMHT 44130 2882 B4
Hamden St
2100 MadT 44057 1942 C2
Hamilton Av
100 LORN 44052 2614 D6
200 ELYR 44035 2875 B5
1200 CLEV 44114 2624 E2
1200 LORN 44052 2744 D1
1300 CLEV 44114 2625 A1
2700 LORN 44052 2744 D3
3800 CLEV 44114 2495 C7
Hamilton Cir
300 ELYR 44035 2875 B5
Hamilton Ct
16700 SGVL 44136 3146 C3
32000 SLN 44139 3019 E1
Hamilton Dr
900 BWHT 44147 3149 E5
9300 MNTR 44060 2144 E5
9300 MNTR 44060 2145 A4
Hamilton St
10 BERA 44017 3011 B1
100 AMHT 44001 2872 B1
100 ELYR 44035 2875 C5
E Hamilton St
10 NRsT 44074 3138 E4
10 OBLN 44074 3138 E4
200 NRsT 44074 3139 A4
200 OBLN 44074 3139 A4
W Hamilton St
100 OBLN 44074 3138 C4
46700 NRsT 44074 3138 C4
Hamilton School Dr
- ELYR 44035 3006 A1
Hamlen Av
11600 CLEV 44120 2626 D5
Hamlet Av
5600 CLEV 44127 2625 D7
Hamlet Ct
10 BTNH 44108 2496 D2
Hamlet Ln
800 WTLK 44145 2621 A6
Hamlet Hills Dr
100 CNFL 44022 2761 B5
Hamm Av
4900 CLEV 44127 2625 C7
Hammer Ct
700 ELYR 44035 2875 E2
Hammock Lake Dr
- HtbT 44046 2508 E6
Hammond Av
6600 CLEV 44144 2754 A4
6700 BKLN 44144 2753 E4
Hampden Av
9900 CLEV 44108 2496 B7
Hampshire Ct
10 BHWD 44122 2629 A4
11200 NRYN 44133 3013 D5
Hampshire Ln
1700 CVHT 44106 2627 A2
Hampshire Pl
27200 WTLK 44145 2749 C3
Hampshire Rd
2500 CVHT 44106 2627 A2
2700 CVHT 44118 2627 A2
Hampshire Cove
100 PnvT 44077 2145 B6
Hampstead Av
5400 PRMA 44129 2883 A2
6700 PRMA 44129 2882 E2
14600 CLEV 44120 2757 A1
15400 SRHT 44120 2757 B1
Hampstead Rd
2000 CVHT 44118 2627 D3
Hampton Cir
600 AURA 44202 3156 D4
Hampton Ct
10 BHWD 44122 2628 E4
10 BNWK 44212 3147 B5
100 BTNH 44108 2496 E2
700 SgHT 44067 3152 B1
1500 PnvT 44077 2041 B5
5400 WLBY 44094 2375 C2
32100 AVLK 44012 2618 C4
N Hampton Ct
17600 BbgT 44023 2891 C5
S Hampton Ct
10 RKRV 44116 2621 C4
10100 CcdT 44060 2253 C3
Hampton Dr
400 ELYR 44035 3006 D2
800 MCDN 44056 3018 D7
4900 NOSD 44070 2749 D7
W Hampton Dr
1400 RKRV 44116 2621 B7
S Hampton Pkwy
10 RKRV 44116 2621 B7
Hampton Pl
17400 SGVL 44136 3146 E4
17400 SGVL 44136 3147 A4
Hampton Rd
1300 ECLE 44112 2497 B4
1500 RKRV 44116 2621 D6
2800 CLEV 44120 2626 D7
2900 CLEV 44120 2627 A6
3500 PRPK 44124 2759 B1
Hampton Run
1800 BWHT 44147 3149 D5
Hampton Bay Ln
11200 CcdT 44077 2146 B7
Hampton Chase
16400 SGVL 44136 3147 A3
Hampton Ridge Dr
11200 CdnT 44024 2379 B3
Hancock Av
2900 CLEV 44113 2624 C6
Hancock Ln
10 ELYR 44035 2875 A3
Hancock St
1800 LORN 44052 2615 B6
Hand Av
7100 CLEV 44127 2755 E1
Handle Rd
11100 SGVL 44136 3012 B6
Handover Ln
10 BHWD 44122 2628 E3
Handyside Dr
9100 NRDV 44039 2875 E7
Hanes Rd
100 AURA 44202 3022 A7
Hanford Dr
500 HDHT 44143 2499 C3
1600 SVHL 44131 2884 A3
Hanford Ln
10300 TNBG 44087 3020 A3
W Hanger Rd
5300 CLEV 44135 2751 C7
Hankee Rd
6400 FdmT 44255 3160 E7
6400 HrmT 44255 3160 E7
6400 HrmT 44234 3160 E7
6500 FdmT 44255 3161 A7
6500 HrmT 44234 3161 A7
6500 HrmT 44255 3161 A7
6800 FdmT 44234 3161 C7
7600 GTVL 44234 3161 D7
Hanks Av
10500 CLEV 44108 2496 C5
Hanley Rd
900 LNHT 44124 2498 D6
Hanna Ct
10 BTNH 44108 2496 D2
E Hanna Ln
10 BTNH 44108 2496 D2
W Hanna Ln
10 BTNH 44108 2496 D2
Hanna Rd
2500 WBHL 44094 2375 B3
Hannaford Rd
- CrlT 44074 3005 B7
Hannan Pkwy
20200 WNHL 44146 3018 A1
Hannon St
- CLEV 44102 2754 B2
Hanover Dr
1900 CVHT 44112 2497 C5
1900 ECLE 44112 2497 C5
3400 BNWK 44212 3147 B7
Hanover Rd
700 MAYF 44040 2500 B5
700 MAYF 44143 2500 B5
Hanover Woods Tr
33300 SLN 44139 3020 A1
Hansen Rd
20500 MPHT 44137 2758 A7
20700 MPHT 44146 2758 A7
Hansford Rd
1000 LNHT 44124 2499 B6
2000 MDHT 44124 2630 A2
Hansom Dr
5900 SLN 44139 2889 A3
Hansom Pl
7900 CcdT 44060 2253 B3
Harad Ct
8800 MCDN 44056 3018 E7
Harbor Dr
- MNTR 44060 2038 B7
8300 MNTR 44060 2144 B1
Harbor Creek Dr
100 MONT 44060 2144 A1
Harbor Ridge Ln
200 FTHR 44077 2039 D5
Harborside Lndg
6600 MNTR 44060 2145 A5
Harborview Blvd
2100 LORN 44052 2614 B7
2300 LORN 44053 2614 B7
Harbor View Dr
11200 CLEV 44102 2623 B4
Harbour Light Dr
11400 NRYN 44133 3013 A5
Harbour View Ovl
14000 SGVL 44136 3147 D5
Harcourt Dr
2100 CLEV 44106 2626 E3
2100 CVHT 44106 2626 E3
Harcourt Rd
100 VMLN 44089 2741 D4
Hardin Dr
6000 BKPK 44142 2881 C3
Harding Av
33800 NRDV 44039 2877 C2
Harding Dr
1500 WKLF 44092 2249 E7
1500 WKLF 44092 2374 E1
4000 WTLK 44145 2749 E4
Harding St
7400 MNTR 44060 2143 C7
Hardwick Dr
- AURA 44202 3021 D5

INDEX 23
Hardwick Rd
Cleveland Street Index
Hidden Point Dr

STREET Block City ZIP Map# Grid

Hardwick Rd
23100 SRHT 44122 2628 C6
Hardwood Ct
800 MAYF 44143 2500 B5
Hardwood Tr
10000 NRYN 44133 3148 B5
Hardy Rd
600 PnvT 44077 2040 C3
Harkness Rd
8600 CLEV 44106 2626 B1
Harlan Dr
18600 MPHT 44137 2757 E7
Harland Av
17300 CLEV 44119 2372 D5
Harlem Av
4900 CLEV 44103 2625 D1
Harlem Ct
4900 CLEV 44103 2625 D1
Harleston Dr
5300 LNHT 44124 2629 A2
Harley Av
14500 CLEV 44111 2752 D1
Harley Ln
8800 MNTR 44060 2144 C1
Harley Hills Dr
7400 NRYN 44133 3013 C6
Harlon Av
12900 LKWD 44107 2623 A4
13400 LKWD 44107 2622 E4
Harlow Dr
37200 WLBY 44094 2250 D7
Harlowe St
- RDHT 44143 2373 D7
Harmon Av
- PNVL 44077 2145 D2
Harmon Ln
8200 MCDN 44056 3018 B7
8200 MCDN 44056 3153 B1
Harmon Rd
10 AURA 44202 3157 A1
Harmondale Dr
38800 WLBY 44094 2251 B5
Harmony Cir
10 OmsT 44138 2879 C4
Harmony Dr
300 EatT 44044 3143 B1
12200 EatT 44044 3008 B7
Harmony Ln
5000 WLBY 44094 2250 B7
5000 WLBY 44094 2375 B1
10200 BKLN 44144 2753 C5
Harmony Falls Ln
15500 RslT 44073 2762 D5
Harms Rd
22100 EUCL 44143 2498 C2
22100 RDHT 44143 2498 C2
Harnagy St
10 BERA 44017 3011 B1
Harner Rd
3700 AbnT 44023 3023 E4
3700 AbnT 44023 3024 A3
3700 AbnT 44255 3023 E4
3700 AbnT 44255 3024 A3
3700 ManT 44255 3023 E4
3700 ManT 44255 3024 A3
Harold Av
11600 PRMA 44130 3013 B1
13000 CLEV 44135 2752 E4
13000 CLEV 44135 2753 B5
Harold Dr
6600 BKVL 44141 3015 E5
12300 CsTp 44026 2501 E7
Harold St
- WKLF 44092 2375 A2
- WLBY 44094 2375 A2
Harper Dr
6800 CcdT 44077 2145 E6
Harper Ln
600 MCDN 44056 3018 C7
Harper Rd
5000 SLN 44139 2759 C7
5100 SLN 44139 2888 C1
13100 SGVL 44136 3011 B7
Harper St
1300 ELYR 44035 3006 B2
4000 PRRY 44081 2042 C3
Harriet St
700 ShfT 44055 2745 A4
900 LORN 44055 2745 A4
Harriman St
10 BDFD 44146 2887 A4
Harriman Tr
- AVON 44011 2747 D3
Harris Av
8800 CLEV 44104 2626 B7
Harris Ct
- NRDV 44039 2877 C7
9000 CLEV 44104 2626 B7
Harris Dr
- AURA 44202 3157 B4
8600 NRDV 44039 2877 C7
Harris Rd
100 SDLK 44054 2616 C3
300 BWHT 44147 3015 B5
400 RDHT 44143 2498 C3
900 SFLD 44054 2616 C5
Harris St
100 AMHT 44001 2872 D1
Harrison Av
2000 ShfT 44055 2745 E6
5600 MPHT 44137 2886 C2
Harrison Dr
15300 BKPK 44142 2881 B1
Harrison Rd
9500 FrnT 44889 2869 B7
9500 VmnT 44089 2869 B7
9500 VmnT 44889 2869 B7
30800 WKLF 44092 2374 E1
30800 WKLF 44092 2375 A1
Harrison St
10 BDFD 44146 2886 E3
100 ELYR 44035 2875 B5
600 CLEV 44113 2624 E4
5900 MNTR 44060 2144 A3
30000 WLWK 44095 2249 C6
Harrow Ct
6200 BDHT 44146 2887 D4
33700 SLN 44139 3020 A2
Harrow Dr
6500 BKPK 44142 2881 A4
8600 PRMA 44129 2882 D1
Harrow Pl
11600 NRYN 44133 3148 A5
Harsax Av
19400 CLEV 44135 2751 E4

Hart Av
- CLEV 44108 2496 E6
Hart Rd
7900 KDHL 44060 2252 D4
7900 MNTR 44060 2252 D4
15200 MtlT 44064 2382 C1
16300 MtlT 44064 2383 A1
Hart St
7100 MNTR 44060 2144 B7
7200 MNTR 44060 2252 B1
Hartford Av
- VMLN 44089 2741 B7
5400 VMLN 44089 2740 E6
Hartford Ct
100 BWHT 44147 3149 E4
Hartford Dr
500 ELYR 44035 2875 D3
E Hartford Dr
14100 SGVL 44136 3147 C5
Hartford Rd
300 ETLK 44095 2250 C1
13300 ECLE 44112 2497 A5
Hartland Dr
23400 EUCL 44123 2373 C3
Hartley Dr
4800 LNHT 44124 2498 E5
Hartley Rd
1000 CLEV 44110 2497 B3
Hartman St
10 BERA 44017 3011 B1
Hartsfield Ter
200 MCDN 44056 3018 B6
Hartshire Dr
5600 WLBY 44094 2375 A2
Hartshorn Dr
10 PNVL 44077 2145 E2
Hartshorn Rd
1700 ECLE 44112 2497 A6
Hartwell Tr
14300 RslT 44072 2631 C7
Hartwood Rd
3300 CVHT 44112 2497 D5
3400 CVHT 44121 2497 D5
Harvard Av
100 ELYR 44035 2875 B7
500 CLEV 44109 2754 E3
600 CHHT 44105 2755 A3
600 CHHT 44125 2755 A3
1700 NBGH 44105 2755 A3
5500 CLEV 44105 2755 E3
7400 CLEV 44105 2756 B3
13600 CLEV 44105 2757 C3
14000 CLEV 44128 2757 C3
18200 CLEV 44122 2757 C3
19100 WVHT 44122 2757 C3
19800 HIHL 44128 2758 A3
19800 WVHT 44122 2758 A3
19800 WVHT 44128 2758 A3
Harvard Dr
3700 WLBY 44094 2250 C4
3800 LORN 44055 2745 E4
12200 MsnT 44024 2505 A4
Harvard Rd
- ORNG 44122 2758 D3
20800 HIHL 44122 2758 D3
20800 HIHL 44128 2758 B3
23800 BHWD 44122 2758 D3
26300 WVHT 44122 2758 D3
26800 ORNG 44022 2759 A3
26800 ORNG 44122 2759 A3
Harvard St
8600 TwbT 44087 3154 C2
Harvest Dr
17900 BbgT 44023 2891 D6
37300 AVON 44011 2747 D1
Harvest Ovl
22200 SGVL 44136 3011 A6
Harvest Home Dr
8500 MNTR 44060 2144 B3
Harvey Av
11000 CLEV 44104 2626 C6
Harvey Pkwy
100 AVLK 44012 2488 C7
100 AVLK 44012 2618 C1
Harvey Rd
3500 CVHT 44118 2627 D2
Harwell Rd
- CLEV 44135 2752 A6
Harwich Ct
1000 RKRV 44116 2621 B6
Harwich Rd
1600 LNHT 44124 2628 E1
Harwood Dr
- PMHT 44130 2881 E6
- PRMA 44130 2881 E6
Harwood Ln
8200 CcdT 44077 2253 C4
Harwood Rd
4000 SELD 44121 2628 A1
Harwood St
100 ELYR 44035 2875 C5
Haselton Rd
1100 CVHT 44121 2497 E6
Haskell Dr
10 BTNH 44108 2496 D3
Haskins Rd
16300 BbgT 44023 2762 C7
16400 BbgT 44023 2891 C2
18300 BbgT 44023 3022 C1
Hasting Dr
6200 NOSD 44070 2878 C2
Hastings Av
1800 ECLE 44112 2497 B4
7300 CLEV 44105 2755 E4
Hastings Ct
14100 SGVL 44136 3147 C5
Hastings Dr
6200 SVHL 44131 2884 B3
Hastings Ln
10 CNFL 44022 2761 B6
Hastings Rd
11600 GDHT 44125 2885 D2
13700 NRsT 44074 3139 E2
43000 CrlT 44074 3139 E2
43000 CrlT 44074 3140 A2
Hastings St
37900 WLBY 44094 2250 D7
Hathaway Av
1200 LKWD 44107 2622 E4
10500 CLEV 44108 2496 C7
Hathaway Dr
9400 MNTR 44060 2039 A7
Hathaway Ln
19000 WVHT 44122 2757 E3
19000 WVHT 44128 2757 E3

Hathaway Rd
6100 GDHT 44125 2885 E3
6500 VLVW 44125 2885 D4
13500 GDHT 44125 2886 A3
Hatteras Wy
- AVON 44011 2747 C2
Hauserman Rd
5200 PRMA 44130 2753 C7
5400 PRMA 44130 2882 C1
Hautala Rd
16000 MtlT 44064 2382 E7
16000 MtlT 44064 2383 A7
Havana Rd
12000 GDHT 44125 2885 D3
Havel Av
11600 CLEV 44120 2626 D7
Havel Dr
3200 BHWD 44122 2628 C7
Haven Ct
5400 WLBY 44094 2375 A1
Haven Dr
43100 EyrT 44035 2874 B2
Havendale Dr
5900 BKPK 44142 2881 D3
Havenhurst Ct
6700 MNTR 44060 2144 A5
Haverford Blvd
7100 MNTR 44060 2143 B7
7100 MNTR 44060 2251 A1
Haverford Dr
5000 LNHT 44124 2628 E1
5000 LNHT 44124 2629 A1
Haverford Pl
- AVON 44011 2747 E4
- AVON 44011 2748 A5
Haverhill Av
5400 PRMA 44129 2883 A3
Haverhill Cir
400 BERA 44017 3010 D1
Haverhill Ct
10 BHWD 44122 2629 A4
Haverhill Dr
31900 SLN 44139 2888 E3
Haverhill Rd
1900 CLEV 44112 2497 D3
2300 TNBG 44087 3019 E5
Haverston Rd
1000 LNHT 44124 2499 B6
Haviland Dr
6400 BKPK 44142 2880 D4
Hawaiian Dr
10 MadT 44057 1941 B6
Hawk Av
7300 MNTR 44060 2143 C6
Hawke Rd
10000 ClbT 44028 3008 E4
10000 EatT 44028 3008 E4
Hawkins Dr
400 PNVL 44077 2146 A3
Hawkins Ln
2800 TNBG 44087 3020 B4
Hawkins Rd
2000 WTLK 44145 2750 D1
2900 NOSD 44070 2750 D3
Hawk Ridge Dr
200 PnvT 44077 2040 E6
200 PnvT 44077 2041 A6
Hawksbridge Ct
8500 MCDN 44056 3018 B7
Hawks Lookout Ln
17000 SGVL 44136 3146 E3
Hawksmoor Wy
17800 BbgT 44023 2890 A5
Hawksview Ln
17300 BbgT 44023 2890 D3
Hawley Dr
9800 NRYN 44133 3013 B3
Hawthorn Ln
4800 WTLK 44145 2749 A6
19900 SGVL 44136 3011 C5
Hawthorn Pkwy
- BDHT 44146 2887 E6
- BTVL 44022 2889 C1
- OKWD 44146 2887 E6
- OKWD 44146 2888 A6
- SLN 44139 2888 E1
- SLN 44139 2889 A1
Hawthorne Av
1000 LORN 44052 2614 B7
1200 LORN 44052 2744 B1
3800 SDLK 44054 2615 E4
3900 SDLK 44054 2616 A4
5400 SDLK 44054 2617 A2
5500 CLEV 44103 2625 D3
Hawthorne Cir
1000 SgHT 44067 3017 B3
6400 PRMA 44134 2883 C4
Hawthorne Ct
- AVLK 44012 2618 D2
1400 VMLN 44089 2741 A7
26100 ODFL 44138 3010 B1
Hawthorne Dr
10 OBLN 44074 3138 C2
10 OmsT 44138 2879 B4
10 PnvT 44077 2145 D3
100 AURA 44202 3156 C2
100 CNFL 44022 2889 E1
1500 MDHT 44124 2629 C1
1700 LNHT 44124 2629 C1
5500 HDHT 44143 2499 B4
6500 PRMA 44134 2883 C4
6600 BKVL 44141 3015 E3
7100 MNTR 44060 2143 B7
9000 CdnT 44024 2380 A4
11900 SgHT 44067 3017 C3
24300 EUCL 44117 2373 D6
24400 BHWD 44122 2628 D5
Hawthorne Ln
15000 RslT 44073 2761 C2
Hawthorne St
10 ELYR 44035 2875 D5
400 BDFD 44146 2886 E4
Hawthorne Tr
3500 BWHT 44147 3014 D7
Hawthorne Farm Dr
400 GSML 44040 2500 E2
Hawthorne Hollow Dr
5900 NRDV 44039 2877 E2
Hayden Av
- ECLE 44108 2496 E6
1100 CLEV 44110 2497 A4
1200 ECLE 44112 2497 A4
1900 ECLE 44112 2496 E6
Hayden St
11600 HRM 44234 3161 A2

Hayer Dr
100 PNVL 44077 2145 E1
Hayes Av
100 ELYR 44035 2875 A5
800 WLBY 44094 2143 A4
Hayes Blvd
7000 MNTR 44060 2143 C7
7300 MNTR 44060 2251 C1
Hayes Ct
- CLEV 44105 2756 D3
Hayes Dr
100 BNHT 44131 2755 A6
2800 WBHL 44094 2375 D6
Hayes Rd
12700 HtbT 44062 2638 D2
13800 MdfT 44062 2638 D5
14300 MdfT 44062 2768 D2
Hayes St
10 PNVL 44077 2145 E1
10 PNVL 44077 2146 A2
2900 AVON 44011 2747 D2
Haymarket Wy
1200 HDSN 44236 3154 D6
Haywood Av
6400 MadT 44057 1843 B7
Haywood Rd
800 SELD 44121 2498 C5
Hazel Av
1400 MadT 44057 1843 B7
28700 WKLF 44092 2374 B3
Hazel Dr
10 NCtT 44067 3153 C4
400 BERA 44017 2880 A5
1500 CLEV 44106 2626 C1
11400 CcdT 44077 2146 C4
Hazel Rd
15600 ECLE 44112 2497 C6
Hazel St
100 ELYR 44035 2874 E6
600 AMHT 44001 2872 E2
Hazeldell Dr
11800 CLEV 44108 2496 D3
Hazelmere Av
13700 CLEV 44111 2622 D7
Hazelmere Rd
23300 SRHT 44122 2628 C7
24300 BHWD 44122 2628 D7
Hazelton Rd
10000 STBR 44241 3156 D7
Hazelwood Av
400 VMLN 44089 2741 E5
13000 LKWD 44107 2623 A4
13300 LKWD 44107 2622 E4
17800 MPHT 44137 2886 D1
Hazelwood Cir
10 GNVA 44041 1944 C7
Hazelwood Dr
- RslT 44073 2761 D5
100 SRSL 44073 2761 D5
9600 SGVL 44136 3011 C4
Hazelwood Ln
31800 AVLK 44012 2618 E4
Hazelwood St
41500 EyrT 44035 2745 D7
Hazen Dr
19800 SGVL 44136 3146 C4
Headlands Rd
- PnvT 44060 2039 A4
- PnvT 44077 2039 A4
8800 MNTR 44060 2038 D5
9300 MNTR 44060 2039 A4
Headley Av
11300 CLEV 44111 2753 B1
Health Campus Dr
29000 WTLK 44145 2749 C4
Healthway Dr
- AVON 44011 2617 E7
- AVON 44011 2747 E1
Hearn Dr
1100 MadT 44057 1843 D6
Hearthstone Dr
18400 SGVL 44136 3147 D4
Hearthstone Ln
18200 BbgT 44023 2890 C7
Hearthstone Rd
2600 PRMA 44134 2883 C1
Heartland Cir
- HkyT 44233 3149 E6
Heartwood Av
32800 AVON 44011 2748 D6
Heath Av
9300 CLEV 44104 2756 B1
Heath Rd
10800 KTLD 44094 2377 E7
10800 KTLD 44094 2502 E1
11000 CsTp 44024 2502 E1
11000 CsTp 44026 2502 E1
11000 CsTp 44094 2502 E1
11700 CsTp 44024 2503 A4
11700 CsTp 44026 2503 A4
11900 MsnT 44024 2503 A5
12300 MsnT 44026 2503 A5
12700 CsTp 44026 2633 A1
12700 MsnT 44026 2633 A1
13500 CsTp 44072 2633 A4
13500 MsnT 44072 2633 A4
13500 NbyT 44072 2633 A4
13500 RslT 44072 2633 A4
Heather Ct
10 CNFL 44022 2761 B6
200 MDHT 44124 2629 E1
Heather Hl
200 AbnT 44023 2892 A3
Heather Ln
200 ETLK 44095 2142 C7
400 AURA 44202 3156 D2
500 BDFD 44146 2887 B6
2200 TNBG 44087 3019 C6
4600 NRYN 44133 3149 A1
4700 BKLN 44144 2753 D6
16200 MDBH 44130 2881 B5
19200 SGVL 44136 3011 D5
25000 RDHT 44143 2498 D1
35600 SLN 44139 2889 B5
E Heather Ln
13000 ClbT 44028 3010 D4
W Heather Ln
14000 ClbT 44028 3010 D5
Heather Rd
1600 MadT 44057 1842 E7
1700 MadT 44057 1941 E1
Heather Brook Dr
100 ELYR 44035 2874 B7
Heatherfield Cir
5200 PRMA 44129 2883 A5

Heathergreen Ct
5500 WLBY 44094 2375 A1
Heather Hill Dr
5400 MNTR 44060 2144 E1
Heatherlane Dr
2000 BWHT 44147 3014 D4
Heatherstone Dr
1000 PnvT 44077 2146 E2
1100 PnvT 44077 2147 A2
Heatherwood Av
34300 AVON 44011 2748 C4
Heatherwood Ct
15000 SGVL 44136 3146 C3
Heatherwood Dr
13300 BKPK 44130 2881 D2
13300 BKPK 44142 2881 D2
Heatherwood Ln
16500 BbgT 44023 2761 C7
16500 BbgT 44023 2890 C1
Heathwood Cir
26900 OmsT 44138 2878 E4
Heckathorne Dr
10 PnvT 44077 2041 A4
Hecker Av
6900 CLEV 44103 2495 E7
7100 CLEV 44103 2496 A7
Hecker Dr
5100 RchT 44141 3151 B7
Hecock Av
5000 ShfT 44055 2745 C5
Hector Av
5100 CLEV 44127 2625 D7
Hedgecliff St
100 AURA 44202 3021 B6
100 AURA 44202 3156 B1
Hedgeline Dr
6600 BDHT 44146 2887 E6
Hedgerow Park Dr
36000 NRDV 44039 3007 E1
Hedgewood Av
23700 WTLK 44145 2750 D2
W Hedgewood Dr
2300 WTLK 44145 2750 C2
Hedgewood Wy
24400 WTLK 44145 2750 C2
Hege Av
5600 CLEV 44105 2755 D3
Heidi Ct
7400 CcdT 44060 2253 C2
Heights Av
10 NHFD 44067 3018 B3
Heinton Rd
5600 VLVW 44125 2885 B2
Heisley Av
6100 CLEV 44105 2755 E1
Heisley Cr
5900 MNTR 44060 2144 E2
Heisley Rd
- GDRV 44045 2039 B6
- GDRV 44077 2039 B6
- MNTR 44060 2039 B6
- MNTR 44060 2145 A2
- PnvT 44060 2039 B6
- PnvT 44077 2039 B6
- PnvT 44045 2039 B6
5800 MNTR 44060 2144 E3
6900 MNTR 44060 2145 A6
Heisley Rd SR-44
- GDRV 44045 2039 B6
- GDRV 44077 2039 B6
- MNTR 44060 2039 B6
- MNTR 44060 2145 A1
- PnvT 44045 2039 B6
- PnvT 44060 2039 B6
- PnvT 44077 2039 B6
E Heisley Rd
5200 MNTR 44060 2039 B7
5400 MNTR 44060 2145 A1
W Heisley Rd
5300 MNTR 44060 2039 A7
5300 MNTR 44060 2145 A1
Helen Av
500 BHIT 44212 3146 A7
25600 EUCL 44132 2373 E2
Helen Dr
300 VMLN 44089 2742 B4
3100 NRYN 44133 3014 C3
Helen Rd
3400 SRHT 44122 2628 A7
3400 SRHT 44122 2758 A1
Helen St
35300 NRDV 44039 2877 A2
41100 EyrT 44035 2745 C6
Helena Av
10500 CLEV 44108 2496 C5
Helene Dr
- PnvT 44077 2040 E7
10 PnvT 44077 2146 E1
Helmar Ln
- OKWD 44146 3018 B1
Helmsdale Dr
2000 EUCL 44143 2498 C1
Helmsdale Rd
800 CVHT 44112 2497 D5
16100 ECLE 44112 2497 D5
Helmut Dr
10900 CdnT 44024 2379 A7
10900 CdnT 44024 2504 A1
Helper Dr
500 BDFD 44146 2887 B3
Helwig Dr
10 GNVA 44041 1944 D7
Helwig St
400 BERA 44017 2880 A6
Hemingway Rd
6100 MAYF 44143 2499 D5
Hemlock Av
1200 CLEV 44113 2624 C3
Hemlock Cir
4000 ORNG 44122 2759 B3
20500 SGVL 44136 3146 B2
Hemlock Ct
100 PnvT 44077 2040 E7
100 PnvT 44077 2041 A7
200 BNWK 44212 3146 D6
Hemlock Dr
- TpnT 44086 2259 A2
100 ELYR 44035 2746 C7
300 BERA 44017 2880 A5
500 EUCL 44132 2374 A1
2300 NPRY 44081 1940 D3
2800 WBHL 44094 2375 E7
6200 AhtT 44001 2744 B7
27300 WTLK 44145 2749 E4
27300 WTLK 44145 2750 A4

Hemlock Ln
10 MDHL 44022 2760 A4
800 SgHT 44067 3152 B2
9700 NsnT 44231 3028 C6
15200 MDBH 44130 2881 C5
Hemlock Rd
7200 INDE 44131 2884 E6
7600 INDE 44131 2885 A6
Hemlock Point Rd
400 CNFL 44022 2761 C5
400 RslT 44022 2761 C5
400 RslT 44073 2761 C5
400 SRSL 44073 2761 C5
Hemlock Ridge Dr
8400 KTLD 44094 2252 B7
8400 KTLD 44094 2377 B1
10300 MsnT 44024 2503 D3
Hemmington Blvd
5100 SLN 44139 2759 B7
Hemoga St
6900 INDE 44131 2884 E7
Hempfield Ln
7500 HDSN 44236 3154 D6
Hempstead Ln
11100 NRYN 44133 3013 D5
Hempstead Rd
11400 GDHT 44125 2885 D1
Henderson Dr
100 LORN 44052 2745 A1
1700 LORN 44052 2615 A7
Henderson Dr SR-611
100 LORN 44052 2745 A1
1700 LORN 44052 2615 A7
Henderson Rd
3300 CVHT 44112 2497 D6
Hendon Rd
25700 BHWD 44122 2628 E5
26200 BHWD 44122 2629 A5
Hendricks Rd
8300 MNTR 44060 2144 B3
Henkel Ct
10 ELYR 44035 2875 A6
Henley Ct
9500 CLEV 44102 2623 D7
Henley Rd
15500 ECLE 44112 2497 C6
Henline Rd
- ClbT 44028 3008 E3
- EatT 44028 3008 E3
Henning Dr
1300 LNHT 44124 2499 A7
10700 CdnT 44024 2379 A7
10900 CdnT 44024 2504 A1
Henninger Rd
2300 CLEV 44109 2754 C3
Henritze Av
3500 CLEV 44109 2754 B4
Henry Ct
3600 CLEV 44105 2756 A1
Henry Rd
19100 FWPK 44126 2751 E1
26500 BYVL 44140 2620 B5
Henry St
10 BERA 44017 2880 B7
10 BDFD 44146 2887 B6
100 GDRV 44045 2039 C5
300 AMHT 44001 2872 E2
300 ELYR 44035 2875 D7
400 PNVL 44077 2040 B6
4700 GDHT 44125 2756 D6
7500 MPHT 44137 2757 C7
Henry St SR-237
10 BERA 44017 2880 B7
Henwell Rd
34000 EatT 44028 3008 E4
Hepburn Dr
6900 MDBH 44130 2880 E5
Hepburn Rd
- MDBH 44130 2880 E6
Herald Rd
- MDBH 44130 2881 D4
Herald St
10600 MNTU 44255 3159 C5
Herb Rd
12500 HrmT 44234 3025 D5
Herb St
25600 ODFL 44138 3010 B1
Herbert Dr
1400 LORN 44053 2744 C6
Hereford Rd
1000 CVHT 44112 2497 C6
1200 CVHT 44118 2497 C6
Heresford Dr
2700 PRMA 44134 2883 C3
Heritage
- EUCL 44117 2373 C6
Heritage Av
5700 MadT 44057 1941 C2
Heritage Dr
11000 TNBG 44087 3019 C3
Heritage Ln
15000 RslT 44073 2761 C2
Heritage Rd
300 AURA 44202 3157 A2
Heritage Tr
17800 SGVL 44136 3146 E4
Herman Av
6500 CLEV 44102 2624 A5
7300 CLEV 44102 2623 E5
Herman Rd
3900 ManT 44255 3023 E6
3900 ManT 44255 3024 A6
Hermann Dr
10 AVLK 44012 2488 B7
10 AVLK 44012 2618 B2
Hermit Av
2700 NBGH 44105 2755 B3
Hermitage Dr
2000 TNBG 44087 3019 C6
Hermitage Rd
7100 CcdT 44077 2145 E7
7200 CcdT 44077 2253 E2
8400 CcdT 44024 2253 E4
8400 CdnT 44024 2253 E6
9000 CdnT 44024 2378 E1
23600 BHWD 44122 2628 C7
23600 SRHT 44122 2628 C7
Herold Rd
4000 SELD 44121 2628 A1
Heron Ct
3300 RMDV 44202 3020 D3
Heron Dr
- HmbT 44024 2381 E2
Heron Cove
1900 TNBG 44087 3019 B4

Heron Glen Ct
1900 MCDN 44056 3018 B6
Herr Dr
12700 HrmT 44234 3025 D5
Herrick Ct
- AhtT 44035 2745 A7
- EyrT 44035 2745 A7
- LORN 44053 2745 A6
Herrick Dr
8500 CsTp 44026 2502 B7
Herrick Mw
10 CLEV 44106 2626 E2
10 CVHT 44106 2626 E2
Herrick Pl
800 CLEV 44108 2496 B6
Herrick Rd
10 TwbT 44087 3155 D3
800 CLEV 44108 2496 B5
8800 TNBG 44087 3155 D3
Herschel Ct
500 CLEV 44113 2625 A5
Hersey Cir
6500 NRDV 44039 2877 D3
Hervie Dr
11700 CsTp 44026 2502 E4
Hessler Ct
1900 CLEV 44106 2626 D1
Hessler Rd
11200 CLEV 44106 2626 D2
Hetzel Dr
2400 PRMA 44134 2883 C6
Hialeah Dr
3900 PRMA 44134 3014 B1
Hiawatha Blvd
10 ETLK 44095 2142 B7
Hiawatha Dr
4800 VMLN 44089 2741 A4
Hickory Cir
100 ELYR 44035 3005 B1
Hickory Ct
- AVON 44011 2748 C3
27300 EUCL 44132 2374 A2
Hickory Dr
200 BERA 44017 2880 A5
2000 VmnT 44089 2869 D1
5000 LNHT 44124 2498 E5
5100 LNHT 44124 2499 A5
7000 WNHL 44146 2886 C7
Hickory Ln
100 MDHL 44022 2760 B5
200 PNVL 44077 2146 A2
1800 BWHT 44147 3149 D5
2500 PRPK 44124 2629 E4
4200 WVHT 44128 2758 A4
5200 WLBY 44094 2374 E1
6200 NOSD 44070 2878 A2
6800 GSML 44040 2500 B6
7200 SVHL 44131 2884 B7
8900 NRYN 44133 3013 B3
26000 ODFL 44138 3010 B1
32100 AVLK 44012 2618 C3
42000 EyrT 44035 2874 C2
Hickory Pl
10500 SGVL 44136 3011 D4
Hickory Rd
4500 FnTp 44491 3029 E4
4500 StnT 44491 3029 E4
7500 OKWD 44146 3018 D2
Hickory St
1100 GFTN 44044 3142 B6
5500 MONT 44060 2143 E1
Hickory St S
8000 CsTp 44026 2631 E3
Hickory Tr
5600 NRDV 44039 2877 E1
5900 NRDV 44039 2878 A2
Hickory Branch Tr
21300 SGVL 44136 3011 B4
Hickory Hill Av
4400 LORN 44052 2744 D4
Hickory Hill Ct
10500 KTLD 44094 2376 B6
Hickory Hill Dr
400 MAYF 44143 2500 A2
9500 TNBG 44087 3019 C6
Hickory Hill Ln
7800 PRMA 44130 3013 D1
Hickory Hill Rd
10 PnvT 44077 2147 B1
300 CNFL 44022 2761 B5
Hickory Hollow Ct
10 AMHT 44001 2872 B3
Hickory Hollow Dr
8500 CdnT 44024 2254 D6
Hickory Nut Ln
4800 INDE 44131 2884 C5
Hickory Ridge Dr
10000 BKVL 44141 3151 D4
Hickox Blvd
15200 MDBH 44130 2881 B5
Hickox St
14400 BURT 44021 2636 B7
14500 BURT 44021 2766 C1
Hicks Rd
17500 WNHL 44146 3017 D1
Hidden Cir
30800 NOSD 44070 2878 B2
Hidden Ln
13900 CrlT 44050 3141 B4
Hidden Acres Dr
25500 WTLK 44145 2750 C2
Hidden Canyon Dr
9900 BKVL 44141 3151 B4
Hidden Creek Cir
5000 SLN 44139 2759 C7
Hidden Creek Dr
- AURA 44202 3022 D4
6300 LORN 44053 2743 B5
Hidden Glen Dr
7100 AhtT 44001 2873 B2
Hidden Glenn Dr
9000 MNTR 44060 2252 E3
Hidden Hollow Ct
- NRDV 44039 2877 D7
Hidden Hollow Dr
7700 MNTR 44060 2252 E3
Hidden Lake Tr
6400 BKVL 44141 3150 D4
Hidden Meadows Ln
18800 SGVL 44136 3147 D4
Hidden Oaks Dr
13100 MsnT 44026 2633 A3
Hidden Point Dr
17100 BbgT 44023 2890 E3

INDEX 24

Hidden Springs Dr   Cleveland Street Index   Hunters Chase Dr

STREET
Block City ZIP Map# Grid

Hidden Springs Dr
11200 MsnT 44024 2503 C1
Hidden Tree Cir
32600 NRDV 44039 2877 E2
Hidden Tree Ln
100 AhtT 44001 2873 C1
Hidden Valley Cir
7600 PRMA 44129 3013 E1
7600 PRMA 44130 3013 E1
Hidden Valley Ct
9200 MNTR 44060 2252 E3
Hidden Valley Dr
10 RKRV 44116 2621 B5
6600 AhtT 44001 2873 C2
7600 KTLD 44094 2376 C7
7600 KTLD 44094 2501 D1
10200 NRYN 44133 3148 B4
28100 ORNG 44022 2759 B6
Hidden Valley Ln
7500 PRMA 44129 3013 E1
7600 PRMA 44130 3013 E1
Hidden Woods Ln
19200 SGVL 44136 3147 D5
Hideaway Cove
10000 RMDV 44202 3020 D5
Higbee Av
8200 CLEV 44104 2626 A6
High Blf
300 AURA 44202 3021 C7
High Ct
1700 LORN 44055 2745 C5
High Pkwy
18400 RKRV 44116 2621 E6
18400 RKRV 44116 2622 A6
High Rd
22000 OKWD 44146 3018 C1
High St
10 CLEV 44115 2624 E3
100 CNFL 44022 2761 A5
100 ELYR 44035 2874 D4
200 BERA 44017 2880 B6
200 FTHR 44077 2039 C4
200 WFAR 44491 2898 D4
600 BDFD 44146 2887 B4
4400 MNTU 44255 3159 B5
16000 PkmT 44062 2896 D7
16000 PkmT 44234 2896 D7
High St SR-168
16000 PkmT 44062 2896 D7
16000 PkmT 44234 2896 D7
E High St
10 PNVL 44077 2146 B1
4600 MNTU 44255 3159 C5
15800 MDFD 44062 2767 D2
E High St SR-87
15800 MDFD 44062 2767 D2
W High St
200 PNVL 44077 2146 A1
4400 MNTU 44255 3159 C5
15300 MDFD 44062 2767 C2
15400 MdfT 44062 2767 C2
W High St SR-87
15300 MDFD 44062 2767 C2
15400 MdfT 44062 2767 C2
Highbridge Ct
9400 MNTR 44060 2145 A7
High Bridge Rd
500 VMLN 44089 2741 D6
High Country Dr
9700 HmbT 44024 2381 C3
Highgate Ct
9800 CcdT 44060 2145 B7
Highland Av
10 AVLK 44012 2618 E1
S Highland Av
8800 GDHT 44125 2756 C7
Highland Blvd
- NCtT 44067 3153 B5
Highland Ct
100 ELYR 44035 2874 E5
8500 KTLD 44094 2377 B4
9000 MNTR 44060 2252 D1
Highland Dr
100 TroT 44021 2894 B6
100 TroT 44234 2894 B6
4600 WLBY 44094 2250 D6
6500 INDE 44131 3015 E1
6800 SLN 44139 2889 D7
8900 BKVL 44141 3015 E7
8900 BKVL 44141 3016 A7
9000 BKVL 44141 3150 E1
10300 RchT 44141 3150 C5
14900 NRYN 44133 3149 B1
18200 MPHT 44137 2886 D1
34600 NRDV 44039 2748 B7
35800 ETLK 44095 2250 C2
Highland Ln
10 CNFL 44022 2761 A7
Highland Rd
1300 TwbT 44087 3154 D3
1800 TNBG 44087 3154 D3
3600 CLEV 44111 2753 B2
5300 HDHT 44143 2499 A3
6400 MAYF 44143 2499 D3
6400 MAYF 44143 2500 A3
22100 EUCL 44117 2498 B2
22100 EUCL 44143 2498 B2
22100 RDHT 44143 2498 E3
27000 RDHT 44143 2499 A3
E Highland Rd
10 MCDN 44056 3153 C3
10 NCtT 44067 3153 C3
1000 MCDN 44056 3154 A3
1200 TwbT 44087 3154 A3
W Highland Rd
10 NCtT 44067 3153 A4
400 NCtT 44067 3152 E4
400 SgHT 44067 3152 E4
Highland Hills Ct
7900 PRMA 44129 3013 E2
Highland Park Blvd
800 LORN 44052 2744 D2
Highland Park Dr
200 ELYR 44035 3006 D2
15200 SGVL 44136 3012 C4
Highland Pointe Pkwy
8000 MCDN 44056 3153 D2
Highlandview Av
- CLEV 44135 2752 D4
13000 CLEV 44135 2753 B4
Highland View Dr
6900 CcdT 44077 2145 D7
11200 MsnT 44024 2503 D1
Highlawn Av
1600 ELYR 44035 3005 E2

High Meadow Rd
400 AMHT 44001 2744 A7
High Meadow Wy
- OBLN 44074 3139 B2
High Point Av
15200 SGVL 44136 3012 C5
High Point Cir
1200 AMHT 44001 2744 A7
Highpoint Ct
5500 PRMA 44134 2883 D1
High Point Dr
5500 SLN 44139 2888 E2
High Point Ln
10 BTVL 44022 2890 A1
10 CNFL 44022 2761 B5
Highpoint Rd
18700 BbgT 44023 3021 E2
24400 BHWD 44122 2758 D2
High Point Club Blvd
17800 SGVL 44136 3146 E3
High Point In Park Blvd
2400 ELYR 44035 2875 A1
High Tech Av
10 PNVL 44077 2146 C2
High Tee St
300 WLWK 44095 2249 C6
Highview
- NRDV 44039 2748 D7
Highview Av
3300 CLEV 44109 2754 C3
Highview Dr
6900 SLN 44139 2888 D7
7200 PRMA 44129 2882 E7
16200 CLEV 44128 2757 C6
Highview Ln
14700 NbyT 44065 2764 D2
Highwood Wy
- HDSN 44236 3154 A7
Higley Rd
3200 RKRV 44116 2751 B2
4100 FWPK 44126 2751 B2
Hilary Dr S
6100 NRYN 44133 3013 E6
6100 NRYN 44133 3014 A6
Hilary Dr W
11900 NRYN 44133 3013 E6
Hilda Av
2200 LKWD 44107 2622 D7
Hildana Rd
3500 SRHT 44120 2757 C2
Hilgert Dr
9400 CLEV 44104 2626 B7
Hill Dr
400 AURA 44202 3156 D3
15000 RslT 44072 2761 E2
15000 RslT 44072 2762 A2
15000 RslT 44073 2761 E2
15000 RslT 44073 2762 A3
W Hill Dr
700 GSML 44040 2500 C5
900 SgHT 44067 3017 C3
Hill Rd
4400 FnTp 44491 3029 E4
Hill St
5400 MPHT 44137 2886 B1
Hilland Dr
4500 CLEV 44109 2754 D6
Hillandale Dr
1600 EUCL 44132 2374 A4
Hillard Ct
30400 WTLK 44145 2749 B3
Hillard Bell
- WTLK 44145 2619 C6
Hillary Ln
600 RDHT 44143 2498 E4
4700 SELD 44143 2498 D4
N Hillary Ovl
4700 RDHT 44143 2498 D4
Hillbrook Cir
14000 RslT 44072 2761 B1
14000 RslT 44073 2761 B1
Hillbrook Dr
14700 RslT 44072 2761 B2
14800 HGVL 44022 2761 A1
14800 RslT 44022 2761 A1
14800 RslT 44073 2761 A1
Hillbrook Ln N
14600 RslT 44072 2761 B1
14600 RslT 44073 2761 B1
Hillbrook Ln S
7100 RslT 44073 2761 B2
7200 RslT 44072 2761 B2
Hillbrook Ovl
7500 BKVL 44141 3016 A6
Hillbrook Rd
3700 UNHT 44118 2627 E4
3800 UNHT 44118 2628 A4
Hillcliff Cir
12300 SGVL 44136 3011 E6
Hillcreek Ln
900 GSML 44040 2500 B6
Hillcrest Av
2900 CLEV 44109 2754 C5
5500 MNTR 44060 2144 B1
14700 MDFD 44062 2767 E2
Hillcrest Dr
400 RDHT 44143 2498 C3
4700 ManT 44255 3159 C4
6200 VLVW 44125 2885 B4
12200 MsnT 44026 2503 A6
12300 CsTp 44026 2503 A6
19900 EUCL 44117 2498 A1
35900 ETLK 44095 2250 C1
36000 ETLK 44095 2142 C7
Hillcrest Ln
100 ELYR 44035 2746 D7
100 ELYR 44035 2875 D1
2100 PRMA 44134 3014 D1
7000 CsTp 44026 2631 A1
Hillcrest Rd
1500 CVHT 44118 2627 B1
1500 ECLE 44112 2627 B1
1500 ECLE 44118 2627 B1
10000 KTLD 44094 2377 B4
Hillcroft Dr
4400 WVHT 44128 2758 C4
Hilldale Rd
11600 ManT 44255 3158 D2
Hillendale Rd
7200 CsTp 44026 2501 B2
Hiller Av
18000 CLEV 44119 2372 D5
Hillgrove Av
17800 CLEV 44119 2372 D5

Hillgrove Av
20500 MPHT 44137 2758 A7
Hillgrove Dr
- LORN 44053 2743 C5
Hilliard Blvd
- LKWD 44107 2622 A6
- RKRV 44107 2622 A6
- WTLK 44116 2621 A7
18500 RKRV 44116 2621 E6
18500 RKRV 44116 2622 A6
20500 RKRV 44116 2621 A7
22900 WTLK 44145 2620 E7
22900 WTLK 44145 2621 A7
23200 WTLK 44145 2750 D1
24300 WTLK 44145 2620 C7
25900 WTLK 44145 2750 A1
27200 WTLK 44145 2749 B3
Hilliard Rd
100 ELYR 44035 2875 D3
14800 LKWD 44107 2622 C5
Hilliard Oak Ln
29600 WTLK 44145 2749 C3
Hillman Av
6000 CLEV 44127 2625 E7
6000 CLEV 44127 2755 D1
Hillock Av
9100 CLEV 44108 2496 B4
Hillrock Dr
1000 SELD 44121 2498 D6
Hills Av
1800 AMHT 44001 2744 A6
1800 AMHT 44053 2744 A6
S Hills Dr
2700 CLEV 44109 2754 D6
Hillsboro Av
- CcdT 44077 2146 A7
Hillsboro Rd
1700 CLEV 44112 2497 C4
1700 ECLE 44112 2497 C4
Hillsborough Pt
4800 WTLK 44145 2749 A6
Hillsdale Av
900 PRMA 44134 2883 E2
1000 LORN 44052 2614 B7
1300 LORN 44052 2744 B1
21200 FWPK 44126 2751 B4
E Hillsdale Av
10 SVHL 44131 2883 E2
800 SVHL 44131 2884 A2
Hillsdale Ct
100 ELYR 44035 2875 A5
Hillsdale Dr
1800 TNBG 44087 3019 C4
Hillsdale Rd
9800 BKVL 44141 3151 B4
Hillside Av
1800 ECLE 44112 2497 C4
2800 CLEV 44104 2626 A6
4600 GDHT 44125 2757 A5
Hillside Cir
10 GNVA 44041 1944 C6
Hillside Dr
10 ETLK 44095 2142 B7
10 PNVL 44077 2040 D7
900 AhtT 44001 2873 C2
14200 NRYN 44133 3148 D1
Hillside Ln
200 CNFL 44022 2760 E7
400 GSML 44040 2500 D3
7200 SLN 44139 3020 B2
18900 BbgT 44023 3022 B3
Hillside Rd
- VLVW 44131 2885 A7
10 SVHL 44131 2883 E7
10 SVHL 44131 2884 A7
4300 INDE 44131 2884 D7
7500 INDE 44131 2885 A7
11000 VLVW 44125 2885 A7
11400 NbyT 44065 2764 C1
20300 CLEV 44135 2751 D6
Hillside Ter
300 MCDN 44056 3018 B6
Hillsover Dr
10300 KTLD 44094 2376 A5
Hillstone Rd
1000 CVHT 44121 2498 A6
Hilltop Cir
100 ELYR 44035 2746 D7
Hilltop Dr
- VMLN 44089 2741 D6
10 ELYR 44035 2875 A7
100 AMHT 44001 2743 D6
100 CRDN 44024 2380 A6
100 CrlT 44035 3005 B6
3500 PRMA 44134 2883 B6
3900 BNWK 44212 3146 E6
8400 MNTR 44060 2144 B2
24200 BHWD 44122 2628 D3
Hilltop Ln
5100 BNHT 44131 2884 A1
Hilltop Ovl
5500 PRMA 44134 2883 D1
Hilltop Rd
2200 EUCL 44143 2498 B3
2200 RDHT 44143 2498 B3
20400 CLEV 44135 2751 D6
N Hilltop Rd
4200 ORNG 44022 2759 C4
S Hilltop Rd
4300 ORNG 44022 2759 C4
Hilltop Farms Rd
12200 SLN 44139 2889 A1
Hilltop Park Pl
16600 BbgT 44023 2890 E1
Hillview Dr
- CrlT 44035 3005 D5
11900 NbyT 44065 2764 E1
Hillview Rd
1600 CLEV 44112 2497 D2
Hillward St
3500 WLBY 44094 2250 D4
Hillwood Ct
- MDBH 44130 2880 E5
Hillwynd
- SLN 44139 2889 D6
Hilo Farm Dr
9000 KDHL 44060 2252 D4
Hilton Rd
1900 CLEV 44112 2497 D3
6800 BKVL 44141 3015 E6
6800 BKVL 44141 3016 A5
Hinckley Av
4300 CLEV 44109 2754 E6
Hinckley Cir
8500 BKVL 44141 3016 D6

Hinckley Industrial Pkwy
4500 CLEV 44109 2755 A6
Hinde Av
6200 CLEV 44127 2755 D1
Hine Av
700 PNVL 44077 2039 E6
900 PNVL 44077 2040 A5
Hine Dr
- MNTR 44060 2038 A7
W Hines Hill Rd
600 BosT 44141 3152 D7
1100 NCtT 44141 3152 D7
Hinsdale Rd
4000 SELD 44121 2628 A2
Hinsdale St
6700 HRM 44234 3161 A1
Hio Dr
6400 BKPK 44142 2880 E3
Hipple Av
19200 CLEV 44135 2751 E5
Hiram Ln
2100 TwbT 44236 3155 A6
N Hiram Ln
7700 TwbT 44236 3155 A5
Hiram Tr
31200 MDHL 44022 2759 D3
Hiram College Dr
10 NCtT 44067 3152 E1
10 SgHT 44067 3152 E1
Hird Av
1100 LKWD 44107 2623 B4
Hirst Av
11900 CLEV 44135 2753 A3
Hirst Pl
- CLEV 44135 2753 A3
Hist Rd
5000 BDHT 44146 2758 D7
Hitching Post Ln
14400 RslT 44072 2762 A1
Hi View Dr
7200 NRYN 44133 3013 D6
Hlavin Av
12800 CLEV 44105 2756 E4
Hoadley Ln
2900 TNBG 44087 3020 C4
Hoag Dr
5300 SFLD 44035 2746 E6
Hobart Rd
9300 WTHL 44094 2376 B2
9800 KTLD 44094 2376 B3
12800 NsnT 44231 3028 D4
12800 PkmT 44231 3028 D4
17400 PkmT 44491 3028 D2
Hobbie Dr
35400 ETLK 44095 2250 B3
Hobbit Ct
10800 CcdT 44077 2146 A7
Hobby Horse Ln
7500 CcdT 44060 2253 C2
Hocking Blvd
15200 BKPK 44142 2881 B2
Hodge Ct
100 CrlT 44035 3006 B2
100 ELYR 44035 3006 B2
Hodgeman Dr
5800 PMHT 44129 2882 D2
5800 PMHT 44130 2882 D2
5800 PRMA 44129 2882 D2
Hodgson Av
4200 CLEV 44109 2754 B2
Hodgson Rd
7000 MNTR 44060 2143 A7
38300 WLBY 44094 2143 A7
38500 MNTR 44094 2143 A7
Hoertz Rd
7500 PRMA 44134 3014 C2
N Hogan Cir
3700 LORN 44053 2743 E2
S Hogan Cir
3700 LORN 44053 2743 E2
Hogans Cir
- LORN 44053 2743 C4
Hogsback Rd
- CLEV 44111 2622 A7
Holborn Av
11800 CLEV 44105 2756 D2
Holborn Rd
900 STBR 44241 3156 D7
Holbrook Rd
16700 SRHT 44120 2627 C7
35100 BTVL 44022 2889 E2
35100 BTVL 44022 2890 A2
Holburn Rd
6000 PRMA 44129 2882 E3
Holden Ct
- KDHL 44060 2253 A4
300 GNVA 44041 1944 B4
Holden Ln
- BTNH 44108 2496 B4
Holden Rdg
- CcdT 44060 2253 B5
Holdens Arbor Cir
1900 WTLK 44145 2749 D1
Holdens Arbor Run
1600 WTLK 44145 2619 D7
1800 WTLK 44145 2749 D1
Holdens Arbor Run Run
1700 WTLK 44145 2619 D7
1700 WTLK 44145 2749 D1
Holi-Dale Dr
10600 HmbT 44024 2380 E7
10600 HmbT 44024 2381 A6
Holiday Cir
4500 CLEV 44109 2754 E5
Holiday Dr
15000 VmnT 44089 2869 D2
Holiday Ln
19300 WVHT 44122 2757 E3
19300 WVHT 44128 2757 E3
Holiday Rd
13900 SGVL 44136 3011 C7
Holl Av
4100 SDLK 44054 2616 A5
Holland Rd
13300 BKPK 44130 2881 D3
13300 BKPK 44142 2881 D3
18200 BKPK 44142 2880 E3
Holland St
- GDRV 44045 2039 C5
Hollenbeck Cir
7900 PRMA 44129 2882 D6
Hollis Ct
8600 BKVL 44141 3016 B6

Hollis Dr
900 ELYR 44035 2875 A4
Hollis Ln
8600 BKVL 44141 3016 C6
Hollister Rd
3300 CVHT 44118 2497 D7
3400 CVHT 44121 2497 D7
Holliston Ln
10700 PMHT 44130 2882 B4
Hollo Ovl
13100 SGVL 44136 3011 C7
Hollow Lake Ct
22000 CrlT 44044 3006 C7
Hollowrun Pl
17800 SGVL 44136 3011 E5
Hollow Tree Ovl
33000 NRDV 44039 2748 D7
Hollow Wood Ln
- AVON 44011 2617 E6
Holly Cir
1200 PRMA 44134 2883 E5
20500 SGVL 44136 3146 C2
Holly Dr
300 BERA 44017 2880 A5
7500 MONT 44060 2143 D2
28300 NOSD 44070 2878 D3
Holly Ln
- AhtT 44001 2872 B2
- AMHT 44001 2872 D3
100 SRSL 44073 2761 E5
200 ELYR 44035 2875 A6
2200 AVON 44011 2747 E1
2900 WTLK 44145 2750 B3
8800 ODFL 44138 3010 A1
Holly Rd
5300 BDHT 44146 2887 B1
Hollycroft Ln
7400 MNTR 44060 2251 E2
7400 MNTR 44060 2252 A1
Holly Hill Dr
16500 CLEV 44128 2757 C4
Holly Hill Ln
5300 SLN 44139 2888 C1
Holly Hill Rd
8300 RslT 44072 2762 A2
Hollyhock Ln
7100 SLN 44139 3019 D1
Hollylane Dr
2100 BWHT 44147 3014 D3
Holly Oak Ln
800 AURA 44202 3021 C7
Holly Park Dr
7200 CcdT 44060 2253 B1
Holly Springs Tr
8700 BbgT 44023 2891 B4
Hollythorn Dr
5500 BKVL 44141 3150 C4
Holly View Dr
1100 VMLN 44089 2741 A6
Hollyview Dr
700 SDLK 44054 2616 C4
Hollywood Av
600 SDLK 44054 2616 B4
5300 MPHT 44137 2757 D6
5300 MPHT 44137 2886 E1
14400 CLEV 44111 2622 D7
Hollywood Dr
800 ELYR 44035 2875 E2
5400 PRMA 44129 2883 A4
6600 PRMA 44129 2882 E4
27200 WTLK 44145 2749 E4
27200 WTLK 44145 2750 A4
Hollywood St
100 OBLN 44074 3138 D2
Holmden Av
1000 CLEV 44109 2625 A7
1000 CLEV 44113 2625 A7
1600 CLEV 44109 2624 D7
Holmden Ct
1000 CLEV 44109 2624 D7
Holmden Rd
1400 SELD 44121 2498 A7
1400 SELD 44121 2628 A1
Holmes Av
15200 CLEV 44110 2497 C2
Holmes Dr
2000 TNBG 44087 3019 D6
N Holmes Pl
7100 CcdT 44077 2146 A6
S Holmes Pl
7200 CcdT 44077 2146 B6
Holmwood Rd
22600 SRHT 44122 2628 C6
Holton Av
7500 CLEV 44104 2626 A5
Holton Ct
7900 CLEV 44104 2626 A5
Holton Rd
25300 ODFL 44138 2879 C6
Holyoke Av
1500 ECLE 44112 2497 A6
4700 CLEV 44104 2625 C5
7600 HDSN 44236 3155 B6
Holyrood Rd
1600 CLEV 44106 2626 B1
Holzhauer Rd
7100 SgHT 44067 3152 C1
Home Ct
7600 CLEV 44103 2626 A2
Home St
16300 MPHT 44137 2886 C1
Homecrest Dr
36000 NRDV 44039 2876 E7
Homeland Dr
1000 RKRV 44116 2621 C6
Homer Av
5300 CLEV 44103 2495 D7
Homer St
100 ELYR 44035 2875 C6
Homesite Ct
100 ELYR 44035 3006 A2
Homestead Av
7800 CLEV 44105 2756 A3
Homestead Dr
8500 OmsT 44138 2878 E7
Homestead Rd
1000 SELD 44121 2498 B6
5700 MadT 44057 1941 D1
Homestead Creek Dr
1200 BWHT 44147 3014 E6
1200 BWHT 44147 3015 A6
Homestead Park Dr
20100 SGVL 44136 3011 C3
Homeway Rd
18300 CLEV 44135 2752 A5

Homeway Rd
18500 CLEV 44135 2751 E5
Homewood Av
5100 MPHT 44137 2757 E7
6700 PMHT 44130 2882 A6
Homewood Dr
800 PNVL 44077 2146 C2
1000 LKWD 44107 2622 E4
1800 LORN 44055 2745 D4
2200 LORN 44055 2746 A4
4600 MNTR 44060 2038 E5
28900 WKLF 44092 2374 A2
Homeworth Av
500 PNVL 44077 2040 A6
10300 GDHT 44125 2756 C6
Honeybelle Ovl
100 ORNG 44022 2759 A5
Honeydale Av
11600 CLEV 44120 2626 D6
Honeydale Dr
7200 NCtT 44067 3153 A4
Honeygold Ln
1400 BWHT 44147 3149 D4
Honey Locust Ct
100 PnvT 44077 2041 B7
Honey Locust Ln
12300 NsnT 44231 3028 C6
Honeylocust Ln
4800 WTLK 44145 2749 A6
Honeysuckle Ln
10200 BWHT 44147 3149 C4
17300 ClbT 44028 3144 A3
Honeysuckle Pth
400 AURA 44202 3156 D2
Hood Av
2000 CLEV 44109 2754 D5
Hook Hollow Rd
14800 RslT 44072 2761 E2
14800 RslT 44072 2762 A2
14800 RslT 44073 2761 E2
Hoose Rd
9400 KDHL 44060 2252 E4
9400 MNTR 44060 2252 E4
9400 MNTR 44060 2253 A3
9600 CcdT 44060 2253 B2
10000 CcdT 44077 2253 C1
10200 CcdT 44060 2253 D1
Hoover Av
700 CLEV 44119 2372 D5
Hoover Blvd
5900 LORN 44053 2744 D6
Hoover Ct
7700 MNTR 44060 2143 D6
Hoover Dr
7000 MNTR 44060 2143 D7
Hoover Rd
13700 TroT 44234 3026 B1
Hope Av
6700 CLEV 44102 2623 E7
6700 CLEV 44102 2624 A7
Hope Ct
100 CrlT 44035 3006 C3
Hope Haven Dr
1600 PRMA 44134 3014 D1
Hopewell Tr
10 MDHL 44022 2760 E3
Hopkins Av
1400 LKWD 44107 2623 A5
11200 CLEV 44108 2496 D5
Hopkins Rd
5500 MNTR 44060 2144 B2
7200 MNTR 44060 2252 D2
Hoppensack Av
6500 CLEV 44127 2625 E7
Horace Ct
3300 CLEV 44113 2624 C6
Horizon Dr
4900 RDHT 44143 2373 E7
Horizons Dr
12800 LryT 44077 2147 C7
Horner Av
13100 CLEV 44120 2756 E2
13100 CLEV 44120 2757 A2
Hornyak St
10 AhtT 44001 2872 A5
100 AhtT 44001 2871 E5
Horseshoe Blvd
1700 WTLK 44145 2750 E1
23200 WTLK 44145 2620 E7
Horseshoe Ct
10 NHFD 44067 3018 A3
Horseshoe Ln
22100 SGVL 44136 3011 A5
Horton Rd
4600 GDHT 44105 2756 A5
4600 GDHT 44125 2756 A5
Hosea Bradford Ct
6900 BKVL 44141 3016 A6
Hosford Rd
11100 CdnT 44024 2379 C2
Hosmer Av
5700 CLEV 44105 2755 D2
Hosmer Rd
16300 MdfT 44062 2768 A7
16300 PkmT 44062 2768 A7
16300 PkmT 44062 2897 A1
17700 PkmT 44062 2896 E6
Hosmer Lake Rd
- BtnT 44021 2766 E6
- BtnT 44062 2766 E6
Hospital Dr
- BtnT 44024 2635 B4
- NbyT 44024 2635 B4
12400 MsnT 44024 2635 B2
Hotchkiss Rd
12200 BtnT 44021 2765 B4
12200 NbyT 44021 2765 B4
13500 BtnT 44021 2766 A1
Hotel Dr
- BHWD 44122 2758 E2
Hotel Rd
- BKPK 44135 2880 E1
- CLEV 44135 2880 E1
Hough Av
5500 CLEV 44103 2625 D2
7300 CLEV 44103 2626 A2
8400 CLEV 44106 2626 A2
Houghton Ct
10 FTHR 44077 2039 D3
Houghton Rd
10 NHFD 44067 3018 A4
300 NHFD 44067 3017 D4
300 SgHT 44067 3017 D4
House Av
5000 CLEV 44127 2625 D6

House Ct
200 FTHR 44077 2039 D3
Houston Av
300 CLEV 44113 2625 A6
Houston Dr
5900 PRMA 44130 2882 A2
Hovey Dr
12500 CsTp 44026 2502 B7
Howard Av
1400 CLEV 44113 2624 D6
25300 WTLK 44145 2750 C1
Howard Dr
800 VMLN 44089 2741 A5
10700 CdnT 44024 2378 E7
10800 CdnT 44024 2379 A7
Howard St
700 ELYR 44035 2875 E3
7600 PRMA 44134 3014 E2
Howe Rd
14000 SGVL 44136 3012 A7
14000 SGVL 44136 3147 A1
Howe St
200 ELYR 44035 3006 A1
Howell Dr
8000 MNTR 44060 2143 E4
Howell St
700 SDLK 44054 2616 A4
Howells Ct
500 ETLK 44094 2142 E7
500 ETLK 44095 2142 E7
Hower Av
1400 CLEV 44112 2496 E7
1400 ECLE 44112 2496 E7
Howlett Av
4100 CLEV 44113 2624 B7
Hoy Av
12800 CLEV 44105 2756 E4
Hoyt Ct
8500 MNTR 44060 2252 B1
Hoyt St
500 PNVL 44077 2146 B2
Hrovat Dr
- SgHT 44067 3152 E2
Hub Pkwy
7400 VLVW 44125 3016 E1
Hubbard Av
6500 CLEV 44127 2625 E7
Hubbard Rd
1300 MadT 44057 1843 B6
1600 MadT 44057 1942 B3
2700 MDSN 44057 1942 B5
14000 BtnT 44021 2766 C6
Hubbard Rd SR-528
2700 MadT 44057 1942 B5
2700 MDSN 44057 1942 B5
Huckleberry Dr
26700 RDHT 44143 2374 A5
Hudak Dr
500 BNWK 44212 3147 B7
Hudson Av
6400 MNTR 44060 2145 A5
10500 CLEV 44106 2626 C3
Hudson Blvd
- SLN 44139 2888 E6
Hudson Park Dr
7500 HDSN 44236 3155 B7
Huff Av
14800 BURT 44021 2766 B1
Huffman Rd
11700 PMHT 44130 2882 A3
11700 PRMA 44130 2882 A3
12900 PMHT 44130 2881 E3
12900 PRMA 44130 2881 E3
E Huffman Rd
11300 PMHT 44130 2882 B3
Hughes St
4200 WLBY 44094 2250 D5
Hugo Av
3400 CLEV 44105 2755 C1
Hulda Av
9900 CLEV 44104 2626 C5
Hulett Av
1200 ETLK 44095 2250 A4
Hull Av
10700 CLEV 44106 2496 C7
Hulls Cove
7100 MNTR 44060 2251 B2
Hume Hill Dr
10 AMHT 44001 2873 A2
Humiston Dr
400 BYVL 44140 2621 A5
Hummel Rd
13300 BKPK 44130 2881 D1
13300 BKPK 44142 2881 D1
Hummingbird Cir
5500 SLN 44139 2889 A2
29400 WTLK 44145 2749 C4
Hummingbird Ct
- WTLK 44145 2749 C5
Hummingbird Ln
- WTLK 44145 2749 C4
Hummingbird Wy
29400 WTLK 44145 2749 C4
Humphrey Ct
16700 CLEV 44110 2372 C6
Humphrey Rd
15100 MDBH 44130 2881 C5
Hunt Cir
6500 MAYF 44143 2500 A5
Hunt Rd
11400 HtbT 44046 2508 C3
17600 SGVL 44136 3147 C4
Hunter Av
- RKRV 44116 2621 D7
Hunter Dr
3300 NOSD 44070 2750 D4
6400 GDHT 44125 2885 E4
Hunter Hllw
7400 RslT 44072 2761 C2
Hunter Rd
32700 AVLK 44012 2618 A2
Hunter Tr
7200 CcdT 44077 2254 C1
Hunters Ln
12500 NRYN 44133 3013 A3
Hunters Tr
900 BWHT 44147 3015 A5
7200 CcdT 44077 2146 D7
7200 CcdT 44077 2254 D2
37000 AVON 44011 2747 D3
Hunters Chase
1000 GFTN 44044 3142 A3
Hunters Chase Dr
1400 WTLK 44145 2619 D7

INDEX 25

Hunters Creek Dr — Jasmine Ln

Cleveland Street Index

STREET Block City ZIP Map# Grid

Hunters Creek Dr
31500 WTLK 44145 2749 A3
Hunter's Point Ln
1700 WTLK 44145 2621 A7
Hunters Pointe Dr
18500 SGVL 44136 3147 D4
Hunters Ridge Ln
28500 OmsT 44138 2878 D4
Hunters Ridge Rd
37400 SLN 44139 2889 D3
Hunters Woods Ln
2900 WBHL 44094 2375 D7
Hunting Dr
8200 NRYN 44133 3014 C3
10000 BKVL 44141 3151 D4
Hunting Ln
6800 INDE 44131 2884 E6
7000 RslT 44073 2761 A3
Hunting Tr
10 MDHL 44022 2760 E3
10 MDHL 44022 2761 A3
Hunting Hills Dr
8500 KDHL 44060 2251 E6
8500 KDHL 44060 2252 A6
14300 RslT 44072 2631 C7
Huntinghollow Dr
10 PRPK 44124 2629 E7
Hunting Lake Dr
7200 CcdT 44077 2254 D1
Hunting Meadows Dr
16900 SGVL 44136 3147 A2
17000 SGVL 44136 3146 E2
Huntington Blvd
28000 BYVL 44140 2619 D4
Huntington Cir
100 ELYR 44035 2746 D7
Huntington Dr
100 NHFD 44067 3018 B4
6300 SLN 44139 2889 B5
29500 NOSD 44070 2878 C3
N Huntington Dr
6200 SLN 44139 2889 B5
S Huntington Dr
35600 SLN 44139 2889 B5
Huntington Ln
1500 CVHT 44118 2497 D7
Huntington Rd
10 PnvT 44077 2040 C5
2800 SRHT 44120 2627 B6
7500 HDSN 44236 3155 D7
Huntington St
100 CRDN 44024 2380 A6
Huntington Wy
- ManT 44202 3023 B7
Huntington Beach Dr
200 FTHR 44077 2039 C3
Huntington Close
10900 NRYN 44133 3013 C4
Huntington Park Dr
9200 SGVL 44136 3012 B4
Huntington Reserve Dr
5000 PRMA 44134 3014 A1
Huntington Woods Pkwy
10 BYVL 44140 2619 A2
Hunting Valley Ln
4500 BKVL 44141 3015 E5
Huntley Ct
500 BYVL 44140 2621 A5
Huntley Rd
6000 WndT 44099 2509 E5
6500 WndT 44046 2509 A4
15300 HtbT 44024 2507 C4
15300 HtbT 44046 2507 C4
15900 HtbT 44046 2508 A4
17100 HtbT 44046 2509 A4
Huntmere Av
15200 CLEV 44110 2372 B7
Huntmere Dr
300 BYVL 44140 2620 C5
Huntoon Rd
12000 CcdT 44077 2146 E6
12000 CcdT 44077 2147 A6
12200 LryT 44077 2147 C6
Huntsford
200 MCDN 44056 3018 B6
Hurd Dr
41100 ELYR 44035 2874 E1
Hurd Rd
10 AURA 44202 3157 A1
Hurley Av
2100 CLEV 44109 2754 D3
Hurlingham Rd
25700 BHWD 44122 2628 E6
26300 BHWD 44122 2629 A6
Huron Av
6700 MadT 44057 1843 B6
Huron Rd
5300 LNHT 44124 2629 A1
E Huron Rd
100 CLEV 44115 2624 E3
900 CLEV 44115 2625 A3
W Huron Rd
- CLEV 44115 2624 D3
100 CLEV 44113 2624 D3
Huron St
100 ELYR 44035 2874 E6
800 GFTN 44044 3142 A5
5500 VMLN 44089 2740 D5
16600 BbgT 44023 2890 B1
Hurricane Dr
38100 WLBY 44094 2250 E2
Hurst Dr
10 PnvT 44077 2145 C4
300 BYVL 44140 2619 A4
Huss Av
5600 CLEV 44105 2755 D1
Hy Ct
5200 GDHT 44125 2756 E7
Hyannis Cir
1900 HDSN 44236 3154 E7
Hyannis Dr
- GFTN 44044 3142 A4
7200 OKWD 44146 2887 E7
Hyannis Port Dr
26700 NOSD 44070 2750 A6
Hyde Av
4400 CLEV 44109 2624 B7
Hyde Pk
10 BHWD 44122 2629 A4
4300 NOSD 44070 2750 C5
Hyde Rd
4700 HgvT 44041 2384 E2
4700 HgvT 44099 2384 E2
6200 HgvT 44099 2509 E2
6200 WndT 44099 2509 E2
Hyde St
6000 MNTR 44060 2143 E3
Hyde Park Av
3200 CVHT 44118 2627 C2
Hyde Park Dr
7200 MDBH 44130 2881 C7
9300 TNBG 44087 3019 C6
Hyder Dr
10 MDSN 44057 2044 C2

I

I-71
- BNWK - 3147 B6
- CLEV - 2624 E7
- CLEV - 2752 A6
I-71 Innerbelt Frwy
- CLEV - 2624 E6
I-71 Medina Frwy
- BKLN - 2753 C3
- BKPK - 2752 B7
- BKPK - 2881 A6
- CLEV - 2624 E7
- CLEV - 2752 B7
- CLEV - 2753 C3
- CLEV - 2754 A2
- LNDL - 2753 C3
- MDBH - 2881 A6
- MDBH - 3012 B6
- SGVL - 3012 A1
- SGVL - 3147 B1
I-77
- RHFD - 3150 E7
I-77 Willow Frwy
- BKVL - 3150 D1
- BWHT - 3015 D2
- CHHT - 2755 C1
- CLEV - 2625 C7
- CLEV - 2755 D6
- INDE - 2755 D6
- INDE - 2884 D7
- INDE - 3015 D2
- NBGH - 2755 C1
- RHFD - 3150 E7
I-80 Ohio Tpk
- AhtT - 2871 B7
- AhtT - 2872 E4
- AhtT - 2873 E3
- AMHT - 2872 E4
- BERA - 3010 D1
- BERA - 3011 B2
- BhmT - 2871 E5
- BKVL - 3150 B4
- BWHT - 3149 E3
- BWHT - 3150 B4
- ELYR - 2874 C3
- ELYR - 2875 B4
- EyrT - 2873 E3
- EyrT - 2874 C3
- NRDV - 2875 E4
- NRDV - 2876 D5
- NRDV - 2877 A5
- NRDV - 2878 C6
- NRYN - 3012 E6
- NRYN - 3013 A7
- NRYN - 3148 C1
- NRYN - 3149 E3
- ODFL - 3010 D1
- OmsT - 2878 C6
- OmsT - 2879 A7
- OmsT - 3010 D1
- RchT - 3150 E6
- RchT - 3151 B7
- RHFD - 3150 E6
- RHFD - 3151 B7
- SGVL - 3011 B2
- SGVL - 3012 E6
I-90
- AVON - 2617 E7
- AVON - 2618 C7
- AVON - 2619 A6
- AVON - 2747 A1
- CcdT - 2146 D6
- CcdT - 2147 B4
- CcdT - 2253 D3
- CcdT - 2254 B1
- CLEV - 2624 E6
- ELYR - 2746 C7
- ELYR - 2874 E1
- ELYR - 2875 B1
- EUCL - 2373 B5
- EUCL - 2374 C5
- EyrT - 2874 E1
- HpfT - 2045 B2
- KDHL - 2252 E4
- KDHL - 2253 D3
- LryT - 2042 E7
- LryT - 2043 B6
- LryT - 2147 D2
- LryT - 2148 C1
- MadT - 2043 B6
- MadT - 2044 D3
- MadT - 2045 B2
- MDSN - 2043 B6
- MDSN - 2044 D3
- MNTR - 2251 B6
- MNTR - 2252 A4
- MNTR - 2253 D3
- PryT - 2043 B6
- SFLD - 2746 C7
- SFLD - 2747 A1
- WBHL - 2250 E7
- WBHL - 2374 C5
- WBHL - 2375 A4
- WKLF - 2374 C5
- WKLF - 2375 A4
- WLBY - 2250 E7
- WLBY - 2251 E4
- WLBY - 2375 D1
- WTHL - 2250 E7
- WTHL - 2251 B6
I-90 Innerbelt Frwy
- CLEV - 2495 B7
- CLEV - 2624 E4
- CLEV - 2625 B2
I-90 Lakeland Frwy
- BTNH - 2496 E2
- BTNH - 2497 A1
- CLEV - 2372 D7
- CLEV - 2373 A6
- CLEV - 2495 C6
- CLEV - 2496 B4
- CLEV - 2497 A1
- EUCL - 2373 B5
I-90 Northwest Frwy
- CLEV - 2622 A6
- CLEV - 2623 E7
- CLEV - 2624 A6
- LKWD - 2622 A6
- RKRV - 2621 B6
- RKRV - 2622 A6
- WTLK - 2619 A6
- WTLK - 2620 D6
- WTLK - 2621 E6
I-90 Ohio Tpk
- AhtT - 2871 B7
- AhtT - 2872 E4
- AhtT - 2873 A4
- AMHT - 2872 E4
- BhmT - 2871 E5
I-271
- BosT - 3152 E7
- MCDN - 3018 C3
- MCDN - 3153 B5
- NCtT - 3152 E7
- NCtT - 3153 B5
- WBHL - 2374 E6
- WBHL - 2375 A4
I-271 Outerbelt East Frwy
- BDFD - 2887 C6
- BDHT - 2758 D7
- BDHT - 2887 D1
- BHWD - 2629 D2
- BHWD - 2758 E4
- BHWD - 2759 A2
- HDHT - 2499 E2
- LNHT - 2629 D2
- MAYF - 2499 E6
- MDHT - 2499 E6
- MDHT - 2500 A7
- MDHT - 2629 D2
- OKWD - 2887 C6
- OKWD - 3018 C2
- ORNG - 2758 E4
- ORNG - 2759 A2
- PRPK - 2629 D2
- PRPK - 2759 A2
- WBHL - 2374 E7
- WVHT - 2758 E4
I-480
- BDHT - 2758 C7
- BDHT - 2887 C1
- CLEV - 2757 D6
- FWPK - 2751 A6
- GDHT - 2757 D6
- HDSN - 3155 D7
- MCDN - 3018 E4
- MCDN - 3019 A5
- MPHT - 2757 D6
- MPHT - 2758 C7
- NRDL - 2758 C6
- NRDV - 2877 E4
- NRDV - 2878 A4
- OKWD - 3018 E4
- TNBG - 3019 A5
- TNBG - 3154 E2
- TNBG - 3155 B3
- TwbT - 3155 B3
- WVHT - 2757 D6
- WVHT - 2758 C6
I-480 Outerbelt East Frwy
- BDFD - 2887 C6
- BDHT - 2887 C6
- OKWD - 2887 C6
- OKWD - 3018 C2
I-480 Outerbelt South Frwy
- BKLN - 2753 A6
- BNHT - 2755 A7
- BNHT - 2884 C1
- CLEV - 2751 C6
- CLEV - 2752 C6
- CLEV - 2753 D6
- CLEV - 2754 D7
- CLEV - 2755 A7
- FWPK - 2751 C6
- GDHT - 2756 E7
- GDHT - 2757 A7
- GDHT - 2885 B1
- INDE - 2884 E2
- INDE - 2885 B1
- MPHT - 2757 A7
- NOSD - 2750 D7
- NOSD - 2751 C6
- NOSD - 2878 C3
- NOSD - 2879 A1
- OmsT - 2878 C3
- VLVW - 2885 B1
I-490
- CLEV - 2624 E6
- CLEV - 2625 B6
Ida Av
800 CLEV 44103 2496 A6
Idaho Av
300 LORN 44052 2615 A5
Idaho Dr
100 ELYR 44035 3006 E2
Idarose Av
13800 CLEV 44110 2497 A3
Idlehurst Dr
1700 EUCL 44117 2373 D7
2000 RDHT 44143 2373 D7
Idle View Dr
4600 VMLN 44089 2741 A7
Idlewild Dr
3800 RKRV 44116 2751 D2
3900 FWPK 44116 2751 D2
4000 FWPK 44126 2751 D2
Idlewood Av
500 SDLK 44054 2616 B4
800 SFLD 44054 2616 B4
1200 LKWD 44107 2623 B4
1800 ECLE 44112 2496 E7
1800 ECLE 44112 2497 A7
Idlewood Ct
100 AMHT 44001 2872 D3
Idlewood Dr
100 AMHT 44001 2872 D3
9000 MNTR 44060 2252 D1
9400 BKLN 44144 2753 D6
14600 NbyT 44065 2764 C1
41800 EyrT 44035 2874 D1
E Idlewood Dr
9500 TNBG 44087 3019 C6
W Idlewood Dr
1600 TNBG 44087 3019 C5
Idlewood Ln
100 AURA 44202 3156 B1
Idlewood Pl
2700 LORN 44052 2744 C2
Idlewood Rd
2500 CVHT 44118 2627 D5
Idlewood Tr
19100 SGVL 44136 3011 D5
Ignatius Av
10200 CLEV 44111 2623 C7
Ike Thompson
12300 CLEV 44106 2496 D7
Illinois Av
300 LORN 44052 2615 A5
10600 RMDV 44202 3020 E3
Illinois Cir
100 ELYR 44035 3006 C1
Ilsley Sq
10200 CcdT 44060 2253 D1
Imperial Av
11600 CLEV 44120 2626 D7
Imperial Ct
7000 EyrT 44035 2874 B2
Inca Rd
5200 RchT 44286 3150 B6
Independence Blvd
9200 PMHT 44129 2882 C6
9200 PMHT 44130 2882 C6
9200 PRMA 44129 2882 C6
Independence Ct
17300 BKPK 44142 2881 A3
36800 SLN 44139 2889 C4
Independence Dr
5500 LORN 44053 2744 B6
7500 WNHL 44146 3018 B2
7900 MNTR 44060 2143 E6
8000 MNTR 44060 2144 A6
11100 NRYN 44133 3013 A6
Independence Rd
100 ELYR 44035 3006 B3
2900 CLEV 44115 2625 B6
3100 CLEV 44105 2625 B6
3100 CLEV 44105 2755 B1
3100 CLEV 44127 2625 B6
Independence St
400 FTHR 44077 2039 D4
Indian Run
9300 MCDN 44056 3018 D4
Indiana Av
100 ELYR 44035 3006 D1
300 LORN 44052 2615 A5
6500 MDHT 44124 2500 A7
6800 CLEV 44105 2755 E3
7400 CLEV 44105 2756 A3
Indiana St
3600 PryT 44081 2041 E1
Indian Creek Dr
13300 MDBH 44130 3012 C1
Indianhead Ln
15600 SGVL 44136 3147 B2
Indian Hills Dr
17400 AbnT 44023 2892 A4
Indian Hollow Rd
200 CrlT 44035 3006 C5
11100 CrlT 44044 3006 C5
12000 CrlT 44044 3141 C2
13100 CrlT 44050 3141 C2
14500 LrgT 44044 3141 D7
14500 LrgT 44050 3141 D7
Indian Mound Dr
7400 VLVW 44125 3016 E1
Indianola Av
10 PnvT 44077 2040 C2
17600 LKWD 44107 2622 A6
Indianola Dr
6500 MadT 44057 1843 A7
Indianpath Dr
2200 WTLK 44145 2749 D2
Indian Point Rd
6100 LryT 44077 2147 E5
Indian Pointe Dr
1300 WLBY 44094 2142 E5
1300 WLBY 44094 2143 A5
Indian Ridge Tr
14700 BURT 44021 2766 A1
Indian Ridge Cove
29500 WTLK 44145 2749 C4
Industrial Av
14700 MPHT 44137 2886 A1
N Industrial Av
14100 MPHT 44137 2886 A1
S Industrial Av
14200 MPHT 44137 2886 A1
Industrial Ln
16000 CLEV 44135 2752 B6
Industrial Pkwy
100 CRDN 44024 2379 D5
100 SRSL 44073 2761 C6
4400 CLEV 44135 2752 D6
6700 BSHT 44236 3153 D7
6700 NOSD 44070 2878 A3
15100 CLEV 44135 2752 B6
16000 MDFD 44062 2767 D3
N Industrial Pkwy
37400 WLBY 44094 2250 D5
SW Industrial Pkwy
- CLEV 44135 2752 D6
W Industrial Pkwy
- ELYR 44035 2874 C6
- EyrT 44035 2874 B6
Industrial Pkwy W
- TNBG 44087 3154 E4
Industrial St
- GTVL 44234 3161 E7
1100 LORN 44055 2745 B3
Industrial First Av
10700 NRYN 44133 3013 A6
Industrial Park Blvd
7100 MNTR 44060 2251 B3
Industrial Parkway Dr
7400 LORN 44053 2742 C6
Industry Dr
10 BDFD 44146 2887 A6
Infinity Ln
4300 LORN 44053 2744 B4
Infirmary Rd
700 ELYR 44035 3005 D2
1100 CrlT 44035 3005 D2
10100 ShvT 44255 3159 A7
10200 ManT 44255 3159 A7
Ingalton Av
14500 CLEV 44110 2497 B3
Ingersoll Dr
19800 RKRV 44116 2621 D5
Ingleside Av
5500 VMLN 44089 2740 E6
Ingleside Dr
100 BERA 44017 2880 A6
2400 PRMA 44134 2883 C2
Ingleside Rd
- SRHT 44120 2627 D7
3200 SRHT 44122 2627 D7
3400 SRHT 44120 2757 D1
3400 SRHT 44122 2757 D1
4000 CLEV 44128 2757 D3
4300 WVHT 44128 2757 D4
17600 CLEV 44119 2372 D4
Inglewood Av
18600 RKRV 44116 2621 E6
18600 RKRV 44116 2622 A6
Inglewood Ct
15800 SGVL 44136 3012 B4
Inglewood Dr
1200 CVHT 44121 2497 E7
Inglewood Pl
100 ELYR 44035 2874 B7
Ingomar Av
11900 CLEV 44108 2496 D6
12400 CLEV 44106 2496 D6
12500 ECLE 44112 2496 D6
Inland Dr
7500 ODFL 44138 2879 A5
Inland St
1000 VMLN 44089 2740 E6
Inland Shores Dr
6200 MNTR 44060 2143 D5
N Inlet Dr
17600 SGVL 44136 3147 D4
S Inlet Dr
18700 SGVL 44136 3147 D5
Inlet Pointe E
10100 RMDV 44202 3020 E5
Inlet Pointe N
10100 RMDV 44202 3020 E5
Inlet Pointe S
10100 RMDV 44202 3020 E5
Inman Av
9100 CLEV 44105 2756 B2
Innerbelt Frwy I-71
- CLEV - 2624 E6
Innerbelt Frwy I-90
- CLEV - 2495 B7
- CLEV - 2624 E5
- CLEV - 2625 B3
Innerbelt Frwy SR-2
- CLEV - 2495 B7
Inner Circle Ct
28700 SLN 44139 2888 B1
Interlachen Ln
2400 WTLK 44145 2750 E2
E Interstate St
10 BDFD 44146 2887 B6
W Interstate St
10 BDFD 44146 2887 A6
Inverlane Rd
500 NCtT 44067 3152 E3
500 SgHT 44067 3152 E3
Invermere Av
15400 CLEV 44128 2757 B2
18100 CLEV 44122 2757 C2
Inverness Cir
30800 WTLK 44145 2749 A2
Inverness Ct
9800 CcdT 44060 2145 B2
Inverness Dr
6100 MadT 44057 1941 E1
29100 BYVL 44140 2619 D4
E Inverness Dr
400 HDHT 44143 2499 B2
W Inverness Dr
- HDHT 44143 2499 B2
Inverness Rd
2600 SRHT 44122 2628 B6
Invernest St
2600 ShvT 44241 3157 E7
2600 ShvT 44241 3158 A7
Inwood Blvd
100 AVLK 44012 2487 E7
100 AVLK 44012 2617 E2
Inwood Rd
32800 SLN 44139 2888 E6
33600 SLN 44139 2889 A6
Inwood Tr
300 AURA 44202 3156 C1
Ionia Ct
12500 SGVL 44136 3011 C6
Iowa Av
200 LORN 44052 2615 A5
11600 CLEV 44108 2496 D3
Iowa Ct
4300 PryT 44081 2041 D3
Ira Av
4600 CLEV 44109 2754 A6
4600 CLEV 44144 2754 A6
6000 BKLN 44144 2754 A6
6200 BKLN 44144 2753 E6
Ireland Dr
- BHWD 44122 2758 E3
Ireland Rd
4000 HgvT 44084 2259 C7
4000 HgvT 44099 2259 C7
4500 HgvT 44099 2384 C2
6400 HgvT 44099 2509 C1
6400 WndT 44099 2509 C1
Irena Ln
3000 TNBG 44087 3020 C5
Irene Rd
1000 LNHT 44124 2499 A6
Iris Ct
- WTLK 44145 2750 B4
30500 OmsT 44138 2878 A4
Iris Ln
33900 ETLK 44095 2250 A3
34300 ETLK 44095 2249 E3
Iris Glen Dr
1400 TNBG 44087 3019 B5
Irma Av
7100 CLEV 44105 2755 E3
Irma Dr
200 CRDN 44024 2380 B7
Irma Ln
10 OmsT 44138 2879 A6
Iron Ct
3800 CLEV 44115 2625 C5
3800 CLEV 44127 2625 C5
Irondale St
100 ELYR 44035 2874 E7
Iron Gate Dr
6800 NRYN 44133 3013 E5
Irontree Tr
15800 NbyT 44065 2763 E5
15800 NbyT 44065 2764 A5
Ironwood Av
18700 CLEV 44110 2372 E7
Ironwood Cir
200 AURA 44202 3156 D1
7900 PRMA 44129 3013 D2
Ironwood Ct
500 ELYR 44035 2875 A4
Ironwood Dr
1400 LORN 44053 2744 C5
9200 ODFL 44138 3010 B1
Ironwood Tr
900 SgHT 44067 3152 B2
Iroquois Av
10 PnvT 44077 2040 C2
1100 MDHT 44124 2499 C7
12800 CLEV 44108 2496 E5
Iroquois Run
800 MCDN 44056 3018 D6
Iroquois Tr
400 MONT 44060 2143 B4
400 MONT 44094 2143 B4
400 WLBY 44094 2143 B4
500 MNTR 44060 2143 B4
500 MNTR 44094 2143 B4
600 MCDN 44056 3018 D5
11500 BKVL 44141 3016 D5
Irving Av
1000 CLEV 44109 2754 E4
9700 GDHT 44125 2885 B1
Irving Park Av
3600 WDMR 44122 2759 B2
Irving Park Blvd
200 SDLK 44054 2616 D4
Irvington Av
12600 CLEV 44108 2496 E5
Isaac Dr
7600 MDBH 44130 3011 E1
Isabel Av
7700 TwbT 44236 3154 E5
Isabelle Ln
8800 MCDN 44056 3018 B5
Island Dr
100 ELYR 44035 3005 B1
E Island Dr
- ETLK 44095 2142 B7
W Island Dr
35400 ETLK 44095 2142 B7
35400 ETLK 44095 2250 B1
Island Rd
10 EatT 44044 3008 B7
200 EatT 44044 3143 B1
700 EatT 44028 3143 B3
700 GFTN 44028 3143 B3
9300 NRDV 44039 2877 B7
9500 NRDV 44039 3008 B1
9600 EatT 44028 3008 B3
14500 GftT 44028 3143 B7
Island View Cir
17900 BbgT 44023 2891 E6
Istra Ln
2800 WBHL 44092 2374 D6
Itasca Av
11200 CLEV 44106 2496 D7
Ithaca Ct
5400 CLEV 44102 2624 A6
Ivan Av
21500 EUCL 44119 2373 B4
21500 EUCL 44123 2373 B4
23200 EUCL 44117 2373 B4
Ivan Ct
9300 MNTR 44060 2145 A1
Ivana Ct
6500 MNTR 44060 2143 E5
Ivandale Dr
7500 PRMA 44129 2882 D3
Ivandale Rd
6700 INDE 44131 3015 E1
6900 INDE 44131 2884 E7
Ivanhoe Av
4000 SDLK 44054 2616 A4
Ivanhoe Dr
- SDLK 44054 2616 D4
3900 LORN 44053 2743 E2
Ivanhoe Rd
100 BDFD 44146 2887 A3
900 CLEV 44110 2497 C3
1700 CLEV 44112 2497 C3
1700 ECLE 44112 2497 C3
Ivorton Rd
- FWPK 44126 2751 C2
Ivy Av
7000 CLEV 44127 2755 E1
7200 CLEV 44127 2756 A1
Ivy Ct
- NOSD 44070 2750 B5
5500 WLBY 44094 2375 A1
6600 MDBH 44130 2881 C4
7000 MNTR 44060 2143 B3
Ivy Dr
5500 MONT 44060 2143 D1
Ivy Ln
- MDBH 44130 2881 B4
200 PNVL 44077 2145 E3
18300 BbgT 44023 2891 A7
Ivy Ovl
8900 NRYN 44133 3013 B3
Ivydale Rd
1500 CVHT 44118 2627 C1
Ivy Ridge Dr
11700 NRYN 44133 3013 D6
Ivywood Dr
4100 BKLN 44144 2753 D4
Ivywood Tr
19300 SGVL 44136 3011 D5
I-X Center Dr
- BKPK 44142 2880 B3
- CLEV 44142 2880 B3
- CLEV 44135 2880 B3
Iyami Ct
17200 SGVL 44136 3012 A7

J

Jackie Ct
9100 MNTR 44060 2144 D6
Jackie Ln
1100 MDHT 44124 2499 E7
2500 WTLK 44145 2750 B2
Jackson Av
200 ELYR 44035 2875 A5
1200 LKWD 44107 2622 E4
30000 WKLF 44092 2374 D4
Jackson Blvd
10 BDFD 44146 2886 D2
2100 UNHT 44118 2627 D3
16700 MPHT 44137 2886 C1
Jackson Dr
12400 BtnT 44021 2765 B6
18600 AbnT 44023 3023 A2
Jackson Rd
- CLEV 44135 2880 D1
100 ORNG 44022 2759 A4
200 AURA 44202 3022 B7
7000 BbgT 44023 2890 A7
30600 MDHL 44022 2759 D4
34200 MDHL 44022 2760 A5
E Jackson Rd
500 AURA 44202 3022 C7
Jackson St
200 AMHT 44001 2872 E2
900 VMLN 44089 2740 C6
2100 LORN 44052 2615 B6
7000 MNTR 44060 2144 C6
7200 MNTR 44060 2252 C1
9300 MNTR 44060 2145 A5
9500 PnvT 44060 2145 A5
E Jackson St
10 PNVL 44077 2040 A7
W Jackson St
10 PNVL 44077 2040 A7
10 PNVL 44077 2146 A1
200 PNVL 44077 2145 D2
1200 PnvT 44077 2145 C3
1900 MNTR 44060 2145 C3
1900 PnvT 44060 2145 C3
Jaclyn Dr
34300 SLN 44139 2889 A5
Jacob St
100 BERA 44017 2880 C6
Jacobs Ln
- AbnT 44021 2894 A2
Jacque Rd
13000 NRYN 44133 3012 D4
13000 SGVL 44133 3012 D4
13000 SGVL 44136 3012 D4
Jacqueline Dr
10 BERA 44017 3011 B1
1600 PRMA 44134 3014 D2
Jade Cir
34100 NRDV 44039 2748 C7
Jaeger Dr
1400 LNHT 44124 2499 A7
1400 LNHT 44124 2629 A1
Jaeger Rd
2400 LORN 44053 2744 A5
4600 LORN 44053 2743 D5
Jakse Dr
1200 ETLK 44095 2249 E4
James Av
14000 MPHT 44137 2886 A3
James Cir
200 AVLK 44012 2618 A1
James Dr
7300 NRYN 44133 3013 D6
7400 MDBH 44130 3012 D1
13800 RslT 44072 2631 D5
James Pl
10 NHFD 44067 3018 A3
James Rd
4700 NRDV 44039 2877 B2
James St
300 AMHT 44001 2872 E2
31600 WLWK 44095 2249 E6
James Wy
19600 SGVL 44136 3146 B5
Jameson Rd
7400 PRMA 44129 2882 E1
Jamestown Av
800 ELYR 44035 2875 E2
Jamestown Cir
19600 SGVL 44136 3147 C5
Jamestown Dr
2400 RKRV 44116 2621 D7
6100 PRMA 44134 2883 D3
9900 NRYN 44133 3014 C5
Jamestown Pkwy
200 AVLK 44012 2618 D1
Jamestown Pl
5200 LORN 44053 2744 B5
Jamestowne Dr
6200 PMHT 44130 2882 A4
Jamesway Ct
8700 MNTR 44060 2144 C4
Jamie Ct
1000 GFTN 44044 3142 A4
Jamie Ln
10 OmsT 44138 2878 C4
Jananna Dr
100 BERA 44017 3011 A2
Janda Pl
- CRDN 44024 2380 A5
Jane Dr
5900 MNTR 44060 2144 D3
Janea Ct
1500 TwbT 44236 3154 D5
Janell Dr
13500 ClbT 44028 3010 E7
Janes Ln
300 MCDN 44056 3018 B7
Janet Blvd
5500 SLN 44139 2888 D2
Janette Av
1700 CVHT 44118 2627 D2
Janette Dr
12200 SGVL 44136 3012 D6
Jania Wy
9900 TNBG 44087 3020 B4
Janice Dr
- PRMA 44134 3014 D2
300 BERA 44017 2880 D5
300 BERA 44130 2880 D5
300 MDBH 44130 2880 D5
14000 MPHT 44137 2886 A3
Janina Ln
100 OmsT 44138 2878 C4
Jaquay Rd
9800 ClbT 44028 3009 D3
Jasani Ct
7300 MNTR 44060 2251 C1
Jasmine Ct
10900 SGVL 44136 3012 D5
30500 NOSD 44070 2878 A4
Jasmine Ln
2900 SVHL 44131 2884 B7
2900 SVHL 44131 3015 B1
18300 BbgT 44023 2890 E7

INDEX 26

Jason Av

Cleveland Street Index

Kingsbrooke Ln

STREET Block	City	ZIP	Map#	Grid
Jason Av				
11700	CcdT	44077	2254	D1
Jason Dr				
35000	NRDV	44039	2748	B7
36000	EatT	44044	3007	E2
Jasper Av				
10100	CLEV	44111	2753	C2
Jay Av				
2500	CLEV	44113	2624	C5
Jay Dr				
7000	EyrT	44035	2874	B2
Jay St				
12400	NRYN	44133	3013	D6
Jaycox Rd				
-	AVON	44011	2748	C2
100	AVLK	44012	2488	C7
100	AVLK	44012	2618	C2
900	AVON	44011	2618	C7
900	AVON	44012	2618	C7
4900	NRDV	44011	2748	B7
4900	NRDV	44039	2748	B7
5300	NRDV	44039	2877	B2
Jaystone Pl				
600	MCDN	44056	3018	B6
Jean Av				
14400	CLEV	44110	2372	B7
Jean Ct				
100	ELYR	44035	2874	D3
Jean Dr				
800	ETLK	44095	2250	B3
Jeanette Dr				
400	RDHT	44143	2498	C4
Jeanette St				
400	BHIT	44212	3146	C7
Jeanne Dr				
2800	PRMA	44134	2883	C6
Jefferson Av				
100	CLEV	44113	2625	A5
800	CLEV	44113	2624	E6
5600	MPHT	44137	2886	C2
6300	NRDV	44039	2877	D3
N Jefferson Blvd				
2300	LORN	44052	2615	C5
S Jefferson Blvd				
2300	LORN	44052	2615	C5
Jefferson Ct				
20100	SGVL	44136	3146	C2
26600	BYVL	44140	2620	B4
Jefferson Dr				
500	HDHT	44143	2499	D3
6000	INDE	44131	2884	D2
9000	NHFD	44067	3018	A3
18000	WNHL	44146	3017	E1
18500	WNHL	44146	3018	A1
32400	SLN	44139	3019	E1
E Jefferson Dr				
7000	MNTR	44060	2143	D7
W Jefferson Dr				
7000	MNTR	44060	2143	D7
Jefferson St				
10	PNVL	44077	2146	A1
100	AMHT	44001	2872	B2
100	LORN	44052	2745	A4
100	ShfT	44052	2745	A4
200	PNVL	44077	2040	A7
400	ELYR	44035	2874	E4
600	BDFD	44146	2887	A4
600	VMLN	44089	2740	D5
Jefferson Wy				
30000	WTLK	44145	2749	B4
Jeffrey Pl				
-	AhtT	44001	2872	E5
Jeffries Av				
8200	CLEV	44105	2756	A4
Jenee Dr				
-	LORN	44053	2743	D4
Jenkins Rd				
8500	MCDN	44056	3153	C1
28600	NOSD	44070	2749	D5
28600	NOSD	44145	2749	D5
28600	WTLK	44145	2749	D5
28600	WTLK	44070	2749	D5
Jenna Dr				
8600	BWHT	44147	3015	B5
Jenne Av				
14000	CLEV	44110	2497	A1
Jennie Ln				
35800	WBHL	44094	2375	C2
Jennie Rd				
33400	AVON	44011	2748	D2
Jennifer Ct				
11700	CcdT	44077	2254	D1
Jennifer Dr				
1600	TNBG	44087	3019	A6
Jennifer Ln				
16600	AbnT	44023	2892	C2
Jennings Dr				
7500	LryT	44077	2256	A3
Jennings Frwy SR-176				
-	CLEV	-	2754	D1
-	CLEV	-	2755	A4
Jennings Rd				
3200	CLEV	44109	2754	E2
4000	CLEV	44109	2755	A4
4300	CLEV	44109	2754	E5
8200	OmsT	44138	2878	B7
Jennings St				
22400	WVHT	44128	2758	C6
Jennings Ridge Dr				
4200	CLEV	44109	2755	A4
Jennison St				
33900	ETLK	44095	2250	A4
Jenny Ln				
10800	GDHT	44125	2885	C1
Jens Wy				
3300	PryT	44081	1940	D7
Jenther Dr				
7500	MNTR	44060	2251	D1
Jeptha Dr				
-	CLEV	44105	2626	C1
Jeremy Av				
7300	MNTR	44060	2143	C5
Jerome				
-	MNTR	44060	2251	B2
Jerrol Ct				
100	CrlT	44035	3006	D4
Jerry Coe Ln				
10300	SGVL	44136	3011	D4
Jerusalem Rd				
-	VMLN	44089	2741	E7
2600	VMLN	44001	2871	A1
2600	VMLN	44089	2871	A1
3300	VMLN	44089	2870	E1
Jesse Av				
11600	CLEV	44105	2756	D4
Jesse L Jackson Pl				
500	CLEV	44108	2496	C4
Jessica Ln				
10	OmsT	44138	2879	B4
4500	NRYN	44133	3149	B1
Jessica Cove				
2300	WLBY	44094	2251	A1
N Jester Pl				
7100	CcdT	44077	2146	A6
S Jester Pl				
7200	CcdT	44077	2146	B6
Jet Center Dr				
38300	WLBY	44094	2143	A6
Jewel Cir				
34100	NRDV	44039	2748	C7
Jewett Av				
4400	CLEV	44127	2625	C7
Jill Dr				
7700	PRMA	44134	3014	E2
7900	SgHT	44067	3017	A5
Jim Batey				
-	WTLK	44145	2619	C6
Joan Av				
10200	CLEV	44111	2753	C1
Jo Ann Dr				
10	MdfT	44062	2768	A5
1600	PRMA	44134	3014	E2
3700	CLEV	44122	2757	D3
Joann Dr				
7600	CcdT	44077	2254	E2
16300	MtlT	44064	2383	A2
Joann Pl				
9900	TNBG	44087	3019	E4
Joanne Ct				
5600	NRDV	44039	2877	B1
Jodi Dr				
12900	LryT	44077	2147	D7
Jody Lynn Dr				
4700	MNTR	44060	2038	D6
John Av				
3800	CLEV	44113	2624	B5
John Ct				
3800	CLEV	44113	2624	B5
John Rd				
25600	OmsT	44138	2879	B3
John St				
10	BDFD	44146	2887	B6
John Bailey Dr				
-	PnvT	44077	2040	C2
John Edward Dr				
10700	ManT	44255	3159	B5
10700	MNTU	44255	3159	B5
John F Kennedy Memorial Pkwy				
-	ELYR	44035	2874	C4
-	ELYR	44035	2875	B4
-	EyrT	44035	2874	C4
John F Kennedy Mem Pkwy SR-57				
-	ELYR	44035	2875	B4
John F Kennedy Mem Pkwy SR-113				
-	ELYR	44035	2874	C4
-	ELYR	44035	2875	B4
-	EyrT	44035	2874	C4
John F Kennedy Mem Pkwy SR-301				
-	ELYR	44035	2875	B4
John Glenn Dr				
900	SVHL	44131	2884	A3
John Nagy Blvd				
3900	BKLN	44144	2753	E3
3900	CLEV	44144	2753	E3
3900	CLEV	44144	2754	A3
Johnnycake Ridge Rd				
-	MNTR	44094	2251	A6
10	PnvT	44077	2146	A4
7300	MNTR	44060	2251	A6
8000	MNTR	44060	2252	C3
8400	KDHL	44060	2252	C3
9300	MNTR	44060	2253	A2
9600	CcdT	44060	2253	A2
9800	CcdT	44060	2145	C6
9800	CcdT	44077	2145	C6
10600	CcdT	44077	2146	A4
38200	WLBY	44094	2250	E7
38500	WLBY	44094	2251	A6
Johnnycake Ridge Rd SR-84				
-	MNTR	44094	2251	A6
10	PnvT	44077	2146	A4
7300	MNTR	44060	2251	A6
8000	MNTR	44060	2252	C3
8400	KDHL	44060	2252	C3
9300	MNTR	44060	2253	A2
9600	CcdT	44060	2253	A2
9800	CcdT	44060	2145	C6
9800	CcdT	44077	2145	C6
10600	CcdT	44077	2146	A4
38200	WLBY	44094	2250	E7
38500	WLBY	44094	2251	A6
John P Green Pl				
4000	CLEV	44105	2756	D3
Johnson Av				
600	BDFD	44146	2887	B3
Johnson Ct				
600	CLEV	44113	2624	D3
Johnson Dr				
10700	PRMA	44130	3013	A2
28700	WKLF	44092	2374	B5
Johnson St				
15900	MDFD	44062	2767	D2
Johnston Dr				
7300	RslT	44072	2761	B1
Johnston Pkwy				
4400	CLEV	44128	2757	B6
4700	GDHT	44128	2757	B6
Johnstone Wy				
2100	WTLK	44145	2749	C1
Joliet Rd				
4500	GDHT	44105	2756	C5
4500	GDHT	44125	2756	C5
Jonathan Cir				
10	GNVA	44041	1944	C7
Jonathan Dr				
3200	CLEV	44111	2622	D7
3200	CLEV	44111	2752	D1
20900	SGVL	44136	3011	A3
22300	SGVL	44136	3010	E3
Jonathan Ln				
31000	BYVL	44140	2619	B5
Jonathan St				
800	AMHT	44001	2743	B7
Jonathans Trc				
1700	BWHT	44147	3149	D5
Jones Rd				
7600	CLEV	44105	2756	A3
Jonquil Ln				
500	MDSN	44057	1942	A7
Jordan Dr				
9100	MNTR	44060	2038	E5
9200	MNTR	44060	2039	A4
37400	WLBY	44094	2250	D6
Jo San Dr				
600	AMHT	44001	2872	C1
Joseph Ct				
4700	NRDV	44039	2877	B2
34200	ETLK	44095	2250	A4
Joseph Dr				
7300	SLN	44139	3020	B2
Joseph Pkwy				
2800	BNWK	44212	3147	D6
Joseph St				
2700	AVON	44011	2748	C2
5000	MPHT	44137	2757	D7
7600	KTLD	44094	2251	D7
Josephine Dr				
6500	INDE	44131	2884	D5
7000	NOSD	44070	2878	B4
Josephine St				
3900	LORN	44052	2745	A4
Joseph Lloyd Pkwy				
1700	WLBY	44094	2142	E7
Joslyn Rd				
3000	CLEV	44111	2622	E7
Joughin Al				
200	PNVL	44077	2040	D7
Joughin St				
600	FTHR	44077	2039	D4
600	PnvT	44077	2039	D4
Jourden Av				
6800	PRMA	44134	2883	C6
Jovanna Ct				
9300	MNTR	44060	2144	E1
Joy Ovl				
900	SVHL	44131	2884	B3
Joyacre Ln				
11700	CdnT	44024	2379	D4
Joyce Av				
4500	WVHT	44128	2758	C5
Joyce Dr				
7800	PRMA	44130	3012	E2
27600	ClbT	44028	3009	A3
Joyce Rd				
800	MAYF	44143	2499	E5
8100	BWHT	44147	3015	C3
Juanita St				
100	SAHT	44001	2872	C7
Jubilee Dr				
10200	CdnT	44024	2378	C6
Jude Ct				
3700	LORN	44052	2744	D4
Judie Dr				
600	CLEV	44109	2754	E5
600	CLEV	44109	2755	A5
Judita Dr				
100	BNWK	44212	3146	D7
Judson Dr				
14700	CLEV	44128	2757	B4
18300	CLEV	44122	2757	D3
Judy Ct				
15500	CLEV	44111	2752	C3
Judy Dr				
2000	PRMA	44134	3014	D2
Judy Ln				
500	BNWK	44212	3146	D7
Jug St				
14400	BtnT	44021	2766	D5
14400	BtnT	44062	2766	D5
16000	TroT	44021	2766	D7
16000	TroT	44021	2895	C1
17900	TroT	44234	2895	C7
17900	TroT	44234	3026	C1
Julia Av				
1800	AVON	44011	2617	D7
2100	AVON	44011	2747	D1
5400	CLEV	44104	2625	D5
Julia Dr				
7200	NRYN	44133	3013	D6
Julia St				
10	GDRV	44045	2039	C6
Julian Ct				
7400	MNTR	44060	2253	A1
Julian St				
36900	AVON	44011	2747	D2
Julie Cir				
19200	SGVL	44136	3147	C5
Julius Weil Dr				
1200	MDHT	44124	2500	A7
Juna St				
30900	WKLF	44092	2374	E1
Junction Rd				
2100	CLEV	44102	2624	B6
June Av				
-	SDLK	44054	2616	B5
June St				
33400	AVLK	44012	2617	C2
Juneau Ct				
1700	CLEV	44109	2754	D1
Juneway Dr				
400	BYVL	44140	2620	C5
Juniata Av				
6500	CLEV	44103	2495	E6
Junior Pkwy				
2900	BNWK	44212	3147	C6
Juniper Ct				
9500	SGVL	44136	3012	D4
9800	CcdT	44060	2253	B2
Juniper Dr				
-	TpnT	44086	2259	A2
1600	WTLK	44145	2619	B7
6300	AhtT	44001	2744	B7
6300	AhtT	44001	2873	B1
9400	HmbT	44024	2380	E2
Juniper Ln				
-	OmsT	44138	2878	D5
E Juniper Ln				
10	MDHL	44022	2760	A4
W Juniper Ln				
10	MDHL	44022	2759	E4
Juniper Rd				
11200	CLEV	44106	2626	D1
Jupiter Dr				
3100	NRYN	44133	3014	C6
Just Imagine Dr				
-	AVON	44011	2619	A6
-	AVON	44145	2619	A6
32200	AVON	44011	2618	D7
Justin Av				
14500	CLEV	44135	2752	C6
Justin St				
10	BDFD	44146	2887	B6
Justin Wy				
7100	MNTR	44060	2143	E7
Justo Ln				
10	SVHL	44131	2883	E5
10	SVHL	44131	2884	A5
K				
Kadel Av				
12600	CLEV	44135	2753	A4
Kader Dr				
10700	PRMA	44130	3013	B1
Kaiser Ct				
100	ELYR	44035	2875	A6
35000	WLBY	44094	2250	A7
Kalene Ct				
500	ETLK	44095	2142	E7
Kalvin Dr				
17900	BKPK	44142	2881	A3
18200	BKPK	44142	2880	E3
Kansas Av				
200	LORN	44052	2615	B6
300	ELYR	44035	3006	E3
Kapel Dr				
1700	EUCL	44117	2373	E7
Kaplan Dr				
5300	SFLD	44054	2747	A1
Kar A Bu Dr				
400	AMHT	44001	2872	C3
Karelyn Dr				
10	BERA	44017	3011	B2
Karen Ct				
8600	CLEV	44106	2626	B1
Karen Dr				
-	SGVL	44136	3012	D3
300	CRDN	44024	2380	A7
400	BERA	44017	2880	B5
1700	EUCL	44117	2498	A2
6600	SVHL	44131	2884	B5
9500	CsTp	44026	2633	A1
33300	AVLK	44012	2617	C2
Karen Ln				
10	NCtT	44067	3153	A2
Karen Isle Dr				
4800	RDHT	44143	2498	E1
5000	WLBY	44094	2250	B7
5000	WLBY	44094	2375	B1
Karen Lynne Dr				
3800	BWHT	44147	3015	C4
Kares Av				
18100	CLEV	44122	2757	D3
18100	CLEV	44128	2757	D3
Karl Dr				
400	RDHT	44143	2498	C3
Karl St				
10	BERA	44017	2879	E6
10	BERA	44017	2880	A6
Kasik Dr				
100	AbnT	44023	3023	A2
Kasserine Ct				
1600	TNBG	44087	3019	B4
Katey Rose Ln				
300	EUCL	44143	2498	B2
Katherine Ct				
9100	MNTR	44060	2038	E7
Katherine St				
9100	NRDV	44039	3008	C1
Kathleen Dr				
6900	MNTR	44060	2144	E6
13300	BKPK	44142	2881	D4
Kathryn Dr				
1700	WTLK	44145	2750	D1
Kathy Dr				
20200	EUCL	44117	2498	A2
Kathy Ln				
7600	NCtT	44067	3153	B2
Kathy Lynn Ln				
6700	INDE	44131	2884	D6
Katz Rd				
1800	TwbT	44087	3154	D5
1800	TwbT	44236	3154	D5
Kay Av				
3100	LORN	44052	2744	D3
Kay Dr				
1100	AhtT	44001	2744	D7
Kaye St				
700	BERA	44017	3011	A2
Kayne Dr				
8000	MNTR	44060	2143	E4
Kazimier Av				
6600	CLEV	44105	2755	E4
Keats Dr				
25800	NOSD	44070	2750	B5
Keemar Ct				
10000	CLEV	44106	2626	C2
Keene Ct				
-	CLEV	44113	2624	C5
Keener Rd				
-	PryT	44081	2041	D5
Keep Ct				
100	ELYR	44035	2874	E1
Keewaydin Dr				
10	TMLK	44095	2250	A1
Keith Dr				
5900	MadT	44057	1941	D2
Keller St				
35400	AVON	44011	2748	B3
Kelley Av				
3700	CLEV	44114	2625	C2
Kelley Ln				
5800	PRMA	44134	3014	A2
Kellogg Ct				
5400	WLBY	44094	2374	E1
Kellogg Rd				
7300	CcdT	44060	2253	D2
7300	CcdT	44077	2253	D2
Kellogg Creek Dr				
7800	MNTR	44060	2253	A3
9300	MNTR	44060	2252	E3
Kelly Dr				
8200	MNTR	44060	2144	B6
Kelly Pl				
2400	LORN	44052	2744	E2
Kelsey Ct				
7000	KTLD	44094	2376	A7
Kelsey Rd				
6100	PRMA	44129	2883	A3
Kelso Av				
13400	CLEV	44110	2497	A1
Kelso St				
6000	MadT	44057	1941	E1
Kelton Av				
11500	CLEV	44106	2496	D7
Keltonshire Rd				
6400	PRMA	44129	2882	E4
Kemper Rd				
2500	SRHT	44120	2626	E4
2600	CLEV	44120	2626	E5
2600	CLEV	44120	2627	A5
Kempton Av				
8900	CLEV	44108	2496	B6
Kempton Dr				
100	BERA	44017	2880	A7
Ken Ct				
300	BNWK	44212	3147	D7
Kenarden Dr				
300	HDHT	44143	2499	E1
Kenbridge Dr				
600	HDHT	44143	2499	A4
600	RDHT	44143	2499	A4
Kenbridge Rd				
6500	PMHT	44130	2882	C4
Kendal Ct E				
300	AMHT	44001	2872	D3
Kendal Ct W				
200	AMHT	44001	2872	D3
Kendal Dr				
10	OBLN	44074	3138	E1
400	NRsT	44074	3138	E1
600	OBLN	44074	3003	E7
600	OBLN	44074	3004	A7
600	OBLN	44074	3139	A1
Kendall Dr				
-	SLN	44139	2889	B3
Kendall Ln				
-	AhtT	44001	2872	E6
Kendall Rd				
2500	SRHT	44120	2626	E5
Kenilworth Av				
10	PnvT	44077	2040	D2
100	SDLK	44054	2616	B4
1000	CLEV	44113	2624	E6
1300	LKWD	44107	2622	A5
7300	PRMA	44129	2753	D7
Kenilworth Ln				
2300	CVHT	44106	2626	E2
Kenilworth Rd				
300	BYVL	44140	2620	B5
2200	CVHT	44106	2626	E2
33500	ETLK	44095	2249	E3
Kenison Av				
21400	EUCL	44123	2373	B3
Kenley Ct				
26800	WTLK	44145	2620	A6
Ken Mar Industrial Pkwy				
10	BWHT	44147	3015	C7
Kenmore Av				
3700	PRMA	44134	2883	B1
8600	CLEV	44106	2626	B1
Kenmore Dr				
300	BYVL	44140	2620	D5
Kenmore Rd				
3200	SRHT	44122	2627	D7
Kennedy Av				
8900	CLEV	44104	2626	B5
Kennedy Blvd				
10	NHFD	44067	3018	A3
200	NHFD	44067	3017	E3
Kennedy Ct				
10	ELYR	44035	2875	D5
7500	MNTR	44060	2143	D7
9300	CLEV	44104	2626	B5
Kennedy Dr				
1800	WKLF	44092	2374	D2
4800	BKLN	44144	2753	C6
23800	BDHT	44146	2887	C1
Kennedy Pkwy				
38600	WLBY	44094	2143	A5
Kennedy Ledge Rd				
10100	NsnT	44231	3028	C7
Kennedy Ridge Ext				
26900	NOSD	44070	2750	A7
Kennedy Ridge Rd				
5300	NOSD	44070	2879	B1
25600	NOSD	44070	2750	B7
Kennelly Dr				
2500	WBHL	44094	2375	E3
Kennelwood Dr				
700	HDHT	44143	2499	C5
Kennerdown Av				
14100	MPHT	44137	2886	A2
Kenneth Av				
2100	CLEV	44109	2754	D3
5400	PRMA	44129	2883	A2
6700	PRMA	44129	2882	E2
Kenneth Dr				
100	BNWK	44212	3146	E6
1000	LKWD	44107	2622	B3
Kenneth Ln				
16500	LKWD	44107	2622	B3
Kenny Av				
-	CLEV	44135	2752	C4
Kenny Dr				
10800	HmbT	44024	2380	D7
11000	ClrT	44024	2505	D1
11000	HmbT	44024	2505	D1
Kenny Ln				
23400	NOSD	44070	2750	E6
Kenny Brook Ln				
100	ELYR	44035	3005	A1
200	ELYR	44035	2874	A7
Kensington Av				
10	PNVL	44077	2146	B2
11200	CLEV	44111	2753	B2
Kensington Cir				
-	SRSL	44073	2762	B7
100	BYVL	44140	2619	A2
Kensington Ct				
-	AURA	44202	3156	B1
19400	SGVL	44136	3146	E5
Kensington Dr				
10	SRSL	44073	2762	B6
3300	AVON	44011	2748	B4
7100	NRDV	44039	2877	B4
25700	WTLK	44145	2620	B6
Kensington Ovl				
10	RKRV	44116	2621	D4
Kensington Rd				
100	VMLN	44089	2741	E4
200	RKRV	44116	2621	D4
2900	CVHT	44118	2627	C3
S Kensington Rd				
500	RKRV	44116	2621	D5
Kenston Lakes Dr				
17700	BbgT	44023	2890	E6
17900	BbgT	44023	2891	A6
Kent Cir				
700	ELYR	44035	3006	D2
Kent Rd				
2000	CVHT	44106	2627	A2
Kent St				
8500	RslT	44072	2632	A5
16600	BbgT	44023	2890	B1
Kenton Av				
5500	MPHT	44137	2886	D2
7500	PRMA	44129	2882	D3
Kenton Cir				
1700	LNHT	44124	2629	B2
Kenton Rd				
10	CNFL	44022	2760	E4
10	CNFL	44022	2761	A4
Kentucky Av				
300	LORN	44052	2615	A5
Kentucky Dr				
-	OKWD	44146	3018	D1
100	ELYR	44035	3006	B3
7200	OKWD	44146	2887	D7
Kenwick Dr				
10	NCtT	44067	3153	A3
Kenwood Av				
21000	RKRV	44116	2621	B5
Kenwood Ct				
10	BHWD	44122	2628	E4
Kenwood Dr				
400	EUCL	44123	2373	B3
700	MAYF	44040	2500	B5
4300	BWHT	44147	3015	C4
Kenwood St				
100	ELYR	44035	2875	D5
100	SAHT	44001	2872	C7
15700	MDFD	44062	2767	D3
Kenwyn Pl				
36000	GSML	44040	2630	C2
Kenyon Av				
200	BDFD	44146	2886	E3
200	ELYR	44035	2875	C6
4100	LORN	44053	2744	A4
5900	CLEV	44105	2755	D1
Kenyon Cir				
31900	SLN	44139	2888	E2
Kenyon Ct				
6200	MNTR	44060	2144	A4
Kenyon Dr				
5200	PRMA	44129	2753	D7
5400	PRMA	44129	2882	D1
11700	HRM	44234	3161	A1
12700	CsTp	44026	2503	A7
12700	CsTp	44026	2633	A1
12900	CsTp	44026	2632	E2
20600	MPHT	44137	2758	A7
Kenyon Rd				
100	ETLK	44095	2142	D5
16600	SRHT	44120	2757	C1
Kephart Dr				
9000	MNTR	44060	2252	D2
Keppler Ct				
11300	CLEV	44105	2756	D4
Kerneywood Rd				
6200	PRMA	44129	2882	D4
Kerns Av				
4600	CLEV	44102	2754	B2
Kerr Av				
-	WKLF	44092	2374	B3
10	PNVL	44077	2040	A7
100	PNVL	44077	2146	A1
Kerrwood Rd				
2100	CVHT	44118	2627	B3
Kerry Ln				
30500	WKLF	44092	2374	E1
E Kerry Pl				
19500	SGVL	44136	3146	D5
W Kerry Pl				
19800	SGVL	44136	3146	C4
Kersdale Rd				
2700	PRPK	44124	2629	B4
3300	PRPK	44124	2759	B1
Kerwick Rd				
2500	UNHT	44118	2628	B5
Kerwin Rd				
2100	UNHT	44118	2628	C3
Keswick Ct				
100	AMHT	44001	2872	D3
Keswick Dr				
10100	PMHT	44130	2882	C2
Keswick Rd				
2900	CLEV	44120	2627	A6
2900	SRHT	44120	2627	A6
Kettering Ovl				
10300	SGVL	44136	3012	B5
Kevin Dr				
-	MDBH	44130	3012	B2
Kevin Ln				
12900	HmbT	44024	2380	D7
13000	HmbT	44024	2505	D1
Kevin St				
5200	SFLD	44054	2746	E4
Kew Dr				
4500	NOSD	44070	2749	E6
Kew Rd				
1500	CVHT	44118	2497	C7
Kewanee Av				
18500	CLEV	44119	2372	E5
19300	CLEV	44119	2373	A5
Key St				
-	MNTR	44060	2144	C5
Keyes Av				
7900	CLEV	44104	2626	A4
Keynote Cir				
900	BNHT	44131	2884	B1
Keys Dr				
500	ELYR	44035	2875	A4
Keys Rd				
11400	ManT	44255	3159	E3
Keystone Dr				
800	CVHT	44121	2498	A5
7600	CcdT	44077	2254	E2
Keystone Ln				
-	MsnT	44024	2634	C1
Keystone Rd				
1500	PRMA	44134	2883	D3
Keywest Dr				
7500	PRMA	44134	3014	D1
Khristopher Ct				
7200	CcdT	44077	2253	D1
Kidd Dr				
15400	NbyT	44065	2764	D4
Kidder Av				
5400	CLEV	44102	2624	A7
Kilarney Rd				
35400	WLBY	44094	2250	B7
Kilbourne Dr				
5300	LNHT	44124	2629	A3
E Kilbridge Dr				
300	HDHT	44143	2499	D1
W Kilbridge Dr				
300	HDHT	44143	2499	D2
Kildare Rd				
3200	CVHT	44118	2627	C3
Kildeer Av				
18500	CLEV	44119	2372	E5
19300	CLEV	44119	2373	A5
Kildeer Cir				
-	CrlT	44035	3005	C3
Kildeer Ct				
10	ELYR	44035	3006	D1
Kildeer Ln				
10	ELYR	44035	3006	E1
Kile Rd				
9100	MtlT	44024	2382	A2
9100	MtlT	44064	2382	A2
10900	HtbT	44024	2507	A1
10900	HtbT	44064	2507	A1
10900	MtlT	44064	2507	A1
10900	MtlT	44024	2507	A1
11400	ClrT	44024	2507	A4
Kilgour Dr				
-	WTLK	44145	2619	B7
Kilkenny Ct				
7900	SgHT	44067	3017	B5
Killdeer Ct				
300	AMHT	44001	2743	D5
Killdeer Dr				
10400	KTLD	44094	2376	C6
Killians Grv				
20000	SGVL	44136	3146	C4
Killingworth Ln				
3000	TNBG	44087	3020	B3
Kilson Av				
19300	CLEV	44135	2751	E5
Kiltie Ln				
7200	SgHT	44067	3152	E3
Kim Dr				
300	MDSN	44057	2044	C1
9500	CsTp	44026	2633	A2
Kimberly				
-	MNTR	44060	2144	E7
Kimberly Av				
10500	CLEV	44108	2496	C5
Kimberly Cir				
600	OBLN	44074	3139	B2
Kimberly Ct				
500	BYVL	44140	2619	A4
1500	LORN	44053	2744	C5
E Kimberly Ct				
32800	ETLK	44095	2249	E5
Kimberly Dr				
500	AURA	44202	3156	C6
2100	WKLF	44092	2374	D3
5800	BDHT	44146	2887	D3
6400	GDHT	44125	2885	E4
10200	KTLD	44094	2376	E5
31100	BYVL	44140	2619	A5
Kimberly Ln				
10	OmsT	44138	2879	A3
2500	WTLK	44145	2750	B2
7500	CsTp	44026	2501	D1
Kimberwick Ct				
10	SRSL	44073	2761	E6
Kimmel Rd				
3400	CLEV	44105	2755	C1
Kimmeridge Tr				
11000	NbyT	44065	2634	A5
Kimpton Tr				
13900	TroT	44234	2895	B6
Kimrose Ln				
-	BWHT	44147	3014	E3
4500	NRYN	44133	3149	B1
King Av				
1000	LORN	44052	2614	B7
1200	LORN	44052	2744	B1
3300	CLEV	44114	2495	B7
King Dr				
35400	ETLK	44095	2250	B1
King St				
10	ELYR	44035	2874	D3
10	OBLN	44074	3139	A3
10	PNVL	44077	2146	B1
200	FTHR	44077	2039	C4
E King St				
200	CRDN	44024	2380	A7
King Arthur Ct				
13800	NbyT	44065	2634	B5
14700	NRYN	44133	3148	A1
29100	WTLK	44145	2749	D3
King Coe Ln				
10300	SGVL	44136	3011	D4
King Edward Ct				
39200	MNTR	44060	2251	B5
39200	WLBY	44060	2251	B5
39200	WLBY	44094	2251	B5
Kingfisher Ln				
8600	MCDN	44056	3018	B6
King George Blvd				
800	SELD	44121	2498	C5
King James Pkwy				
1700	WTLK	44145	2750	C1
Kingman Rd				
14300	MDBH	44130	2881	D4
King Memorial Rd				
7400	MNTR	44060	2252	E2
8000	KDHL	44060	2252	E2
8000	KDHL	44060	2253	A4
8400	CdnT	44024	2253	A5
8400	CdnT	44060	2253	A5
King Mills Run				
3400	FWPK	44126	2751	B2
3400	RKRV	44126	2751	B2
3400	RKRV	44116	2751	B2
King Richard Dr				
2900	PRMA	44134	2883	C7
Kings Ct				
9300	BKVL	44141	3150	E2
Kings Hwy				
5200	FWPK	44126	2751	B5
5800	PMHT	44130	2882	B2
19000	WVHT	44122	2757	E3
19700	WVHT	44122	2758	A3
Kings Wy				
10500	NRYN	44133	3013	E4
10500	NRYN	44133	3014	A5
Kingsborough Dr				
2000	PnvT	44077	2145	B6
Kingsbrooke Ln				
23100	WTLK	44145	2751	A1

INDEX 27
Kingsbury Blvd
Cleveland Street Index
Landerbrook Cir

STREET
Block City ZIP Map# Grid
Kingsbury Blvd
9700 CLEV 44104 2626 C7
Kingsbury Dr
2700 RKRV 44116 2621 C7
Kingscote Pk
6600 INDE 44131 3015 E2
Kingsdale Blvd
6300 PMHT 44130 2882 B4
Kingsford Av
14000 CLEV 44128 2757 A2
Kings Hollow Ct
9300 KDHL 44060 2252 E4
9300 MNTR 44060 2252 E4
Kingsley Dr
9100 BbgT 44023 3022 D1
Kingsley Rd
2800 SRHT 44122 2627 E7
Kings Orchard Tr
8800 BbgT 44023 2891 C3
Kings Post Pkwy
3500 RKRV 44116 2751 B2
Kingston Cir
26800 NOSD 44070 2750 A5
Kingston Ct
5300 SFLD 44054 2746 E4
7300 MNTR 44060 2251 C1
Kingston Dr
- AURA 44202 3156 E3
- AURA 44202 3157 A3
Kingston Rd
2400 CVHT 44118 2627 D5
Kingston Wy
12700 NRYN 44133 3148 A4
12800 NRYN 44133 3147 E4
Kingsview Dr
7100 SgHT 44067 3152 E3
Kingsway
1300 WTLK 44145 2620 D7
Kingsway Dr
900 LORN 44052 2744 D4
12700 CsTp 44026 2501 C7
12700 CsTp 44026 2631 C1
Kingswood Ct
15800 SGVL 44136 3146 B2
Kingswood Dr
6500 MDHT 44124 2629 D3
6500 MDHT 44124 2630 A3
6900 SLN 44139 2888 D7
17700 BbgT 44023 2890 E6
26200 OmsT 44138 2879 A7
Kingwood Dr
8200 KDHL 44060 2252 A5
Kinkel Av
2100 CLEV 44109 2624 D7
Kinkshire Ct
300 HDHT 44143 2499 C2
Kinsman Rd
- BURT 44021 2766 E2
4400 MstT 44062 2769 D2
5500 CLEV 44104 2625 D5
7000 HGVL 44022 2761 A2
7100 RsIT 44073 2761 A2
7200 CLEV 44104 2626 B7
7300 RsIT 44072 2761 D2
8200 RsIT 44072 2762 A1
9600 NbyT 44072 2763 A1
9600 RsIT 44072 2763 A1
9900 NbyT 44065 2763 A1
10500 NbyT 44065 2764 B2
11700 NbyT 44021 2764 B2
12000 NbyT 44021 2765 A1
12000 NbyT 44065 2765 A1
12400 BtnT 44021 2765 A1
12500 CLEV 44120 2756 E1
13500 CLEV 44120 2757 A1
14100 BtnT 44021 2766 E2
14100 BtnT 44062 2766 E2
15000 BtnT 44062 2767 A2
15100 MDFD 44062 2767 A2
15100 MdfT 44062 2767 A2
15400 SRHT 44120 2757 A1
16200 MDFD 44062 2767 E2
16300 MDFD 44062 2768 A2
16400 MdfT 44062 2768 A2
17400 MdfT 44062 2769 A2
17400 MstT 44062 2769 A2
Kinsman Rd SR-8
5500 CLEV 44104 2625 D5
7200 CLEV 44104 2626 B7
12500 CLEV 44120 2756 E1
13500 CLEV 44120 2757 A1
15400 SRHT 44120 2757 A1
Kinsman Rd SR-87
- BURT 44021 2766 E2
4400 MstT 44062 2769 D2
7000 HGVL 44022 2761 A2
7100 RsIT 44073 2761 A2
7300 RsIT 44072 2761 D2
8200 RsIT 44072 2762 A1
9600 NbyT 44072 2763 A1
9600 RsIT 44072 2763 A1
9900 NbyT 44065 2763 A1
10500 NbyT 44065 2764 B2
11700 NbyT 44021 2764 B2
12000 NbyT 44021 2765 A1
12000 NbyT 44065 2765 A1
12400 BtnT 44021 2765 A1
14100 BtnT 44021 2766 E2
14100 BtnT 44062 2766 E2
15000 BtnT 44062 2767 A2
15100 MDFD 44062 2767 A2
15100 MdfT 44062 2767 A2
16200 MDFD 44062 2767 E2
16300 MDFD 44062 2768 A2
16400 MdfT 44062 2768 A2
17400 MdfT 44062 2769 A2
17400 MstT 44062 2769 A2
Kinsman Rd US-422
5500 CLEV 44104 2625 D5
7200 CLEV 44104 2626 B7
12500 CLEV 44120 2756 E1
13500 CLEV 44120 2757 A1
15400 SRHT 44120 2757 A1
Kinzel Rd
36200 AVON 44011 2747 E3
36200 AVON 44011 2748 A3
Kiowa Rd
4100 RchT 44286 3150 B6
Kipling Av
15400 CLEV 44110 2497 C2
Kipling Ct
500 RDHT 44143 2498 E4
N Kipling Pl
7100 CcdT 44077 2146 A7
S Kipling Pl
7200 CcdT 44077 2146 B6
Kipling St
100 ELYR 44035 2875 C6
Kipple Blvd
- PRMA 44134 2883 A5
Kipton East Rd
44900 NRsT 44074 3139 A5
45000 PtfT 44074 3139 A5
45200 PtfT 44074 3138 E6
Kipton East Rd US-20
- NRsT 44074 3139 A5
45200 PtfT 44074 3138 E6
45200 PtfT 44074 3139 A5
Kipton Nickle Plate Rd
43000 LrgT 44050 3139 D6
43000 LrgT 44050 3140 A6
43000 PtfT 44050 3139 D6
43600 PtfT 44074 3139 D6
45700 PtfT 44074 3138 E6
Kirby Av
12300 CLEV 44108 2496 E3
Kirkham Av
5000 CLEV 44105 2755 D1
Kirkland
7700 TwbT 44236 3155 A6
Kirkland Ct
2100 TwbT 44236 3155 A6
N Kirkland Ln
7800 TwbT 44236 3155 A6
Kirkland Pl
2000 TwbT 44236 3155 A6
Kirkland Rd
22900 OKWD 44146 2887 C7
Kirkwall St
6100 MadT 44057 1941 E1
6200 MadT 44057 1942 A1
Kirkwood Av
9500 CLEV 44102 2623 D6
Kirkwood Dr
6700 MNTR 44060 2144 A6
8300 CsTp 44026 2502 B1
Kirkwood Rd
3700 CVHT 44121 2497 E6
3700 CVHT 44121 2498 A6
Kirtland Ln
1000 LKWD 44107 2622 E3
Kirtland Rd
3800 WLBY 44094 2251 B6
39400 KTLD 44094 2251 B6
Kirtland St
13800 BURT 44021 2636 B7
Kirtland St SR-87
13800 BURT 44021 2636 B7
Kirtland Chardon Rd
7800 KTLD 44094 2251 E7
8100 KTLD 44094 2252 A7
8100 KTLD 44094 2377 B1
9500 KTLD 44094 2378 A4
9700 CdnT 44024 2378 B4
Kirtland-Chardon Rd
7800 KTLD 44094 2251 E6
Kirton Av
11700 CLEV 44135 2753 A5
13100 CLEV 44135 2752 E5
Kirtstone Ter
1700 PnvT 44077 2041 A2
Kishman Av
- VMLN 44089 2742 B5
Kitner Blvd
7500 NCtT 44067 3153 B3
Kittery Ln
7500 MNTR 44060 2251 B2
Kiwanis Dr
6700 MDBH 44130 2881 D5
14500 NbyT 44065 2764 B1
Kiwanis Park Dr
400 GNVA 44041 1944 C5
400 GnvT 44041 1944 C5
Klann St
5000 PryT 44077 2041 C6
Klasen Rd
4900 MadT 44057 2044 B6
Klatka Dr
12500 MsnT 44024 2504 A7
Kleber Ct
7100 INDE 44131 2884 E2
Klein Dr
7600 MDBH 44130 3012 E2
Klonowski Av
7400 CLEV 44105 2756 A2
Klusner Av
2400 PRMA 44134 2883 C6
Kneale Dr
5000 LNHT 44124 2498 E6
5000 LNHT 44124 2499 A6
Kneirim Dr
3200 LORN 44053 2743 E3
Kneisel Rd
13700 VmnT 44089 2869 C1
Knickerbocker Rd
4100 SDLK 44054 2616 A5
23700 BYVL 44140 2620 D5
27800 BYVL 44140 2619 E5
Kniffen Rd
6700 LryT 44077 2148 C7
6700 LryT 44086 2148 C7
6700 LryT 44077 2256 C2
6700 LryT 44086 2256 C2
Knight Ln
4100 BNWK 44212 3146 D6
Knights Wy
9300 BKVL 44141 3150 D2
10600 NRYN 44133 3013 E5
10600 NRYN 44133 3014 A5
Knightsbridge Ln
- AURA 44202 3021 E7
8100 CcdT 44060 2253 B4
Knobel Dr
32100 WLWK 44095 2249 D5
Knoll Dr
18200 MPHT 44137 2886 D1
Knolls Ln
2600 BKVL 44141 3150 B1
Knolls Wy
8100 BbgT 44023 2890 E1
Knollwood Dr
300 AURA 44202 3156 D3
5200 PRMA 44129 2753 C7
5300 PRMA 44129 2882 C1
Knollwood Rdg
9900 CcdT 44077 2145 C6
Knollwood Tr
200 RDHT 44143 2498 D1
Knowles Dr
3300 PRMA 44134 3014 C1
Knowles St
1800 ECLE 44112 2497 B6
Knowlton Av
11200 CLEV 44106 2496 D7
Knowlton Pkwy
19200 SGVL 44136 3146 D2
Knox Blvd
5700 BKPK 44142 2881 C2
Knuth Av
1400 EUCL 44117 2373 E5
1400 EUCL 44132 2373 E5
Koch Ct
4800 CLEV 44102 2754 A1
Koch Dr
7600 PRMA 44134 3013 E1
7600 PRMA 44134 3014 A1
Kohout St
5200 MPHT 44137 2757 A7
5200 MPHT 44137 2886 A1
Kolar Av
9500 CLEV 44104 2626 B5
Kolbe Rd
3100 LORN 44053 2743 C4
Kollin Av
16200 CLEV 44128 2757 C6
Kolthoff Dr
6300 BKPK 44142 2880 C3
6500 BERA 44142 2880 C4
Kolthoff Dr SR-237
6500 BERA 44142 2880 C4
6500 BKPK 44142 2880 C4
Kopas Dr
11100 AbnT 44023 2893 A7
Korman Av
7400 CLEV 44103 2496 A6
7900 CLEV 44108 2496 A6
Kortz Cir
8600 SGVL 44136 3012 D3
Kory Ct
7100 CcdT 44077 2145 D7
Kosciuszko Av
7900 CLEV 44103 2496 A7
8500 CLEV 44108 2496 A7
Kouba Av
5400 CLEV 44102 2624 A7
Kourtney Ct
30400 WBHL 44092 2374 E7
Kraft St
100 BERA 44017 2880 A7
Krakow Av
6800 CLEV 44105 2755 E4
Kral Dr
7000 WNHL 44146 2886 E7
Kramer Dr
20100 RKRV 44116 2621 D6
Krather Rd
3400 CLEV 44109 2754 C3
Krebs Rd
31700 AVLK 44012 2618 E5
31700 AVLK 44012 2619 A5
31700 AVON 44012 2618 E5
31700 AVON 44011 2618 E5
Krems Av
14100 MPHT 44137 2886 A2
Kresge Dr
1900 AMHT 44001 2744 A6
Krick Rd
7000 BDFD 44146 2887 A7
7000 WNHL 44146 2887 A7
W Krick Rd
20000 WNHL 44146 2887 A7
Kristen Ct
100 AMHT 44001 2872 D4
Kristin Ct
30100 WBHL 44092 2374 D6
Kristine Dr
11300 CsTp 44026 2502 B2
Kronos Ct
12200 SGVL 44136 3011 C6
Krueger Av
4300 PRMA 44134 2883 B2
8000 CLEV 44105 2756 A2
Krueger Dr
- NRDV 44039 2877 A4
Kruse Dr
6000 SLN 44139 2889 A4
Kuenzer Dr
5700 SVHL 44131 2884 B2
Kuhlman Av
13300 CLEV 44110 2496 E1
13300 CLEV 44110 2497 A2
Kulow Ln
- MadT 44057 2150 A1
Kurtz St
400 BERA 44017 2880 C5
Kurzemes Dr
16800 BbgT 44023 2891 B2
Kydan Ln
18100 WNHL 44146 2886 E7
Kylemore Dr
20000 SGVL 44136 3146 B5
Kylie Ct
10 OmsT 44138 2879 C4

L

Labrador Ln
11300 CcdT 44077 2254 C1
Laburnum Dr
4300 PryT 44077 2041 C4
Laburnum St
4300 PryT 44077 2041 C3
Laclede Rd
1400 SELD 44121 2498 B7
1400 SELD 44121 2628 B1
Lacosta Dr
7300 HDSN 44236 3155 B7
La Crosse Dr
500 MCDN 44056 3018 C6
Ladd Ln
6900 MPHT 44137 2886 A5
Lafayette Av
5500 MPHT 44137 2886 C1
Lafayette Blvd
200 SDLK 44054 2616 C4
6100 INDE 44131 2884 D4
Lafayette Dr
- ClbT 44028 3010 D2
2500 UNHT 44118 2628 C4
6400 MNTR 44060 2144 B5
10600 PMHT 44130 2882 B5
Lafayette St
- AMHT 44001 2872 C2
100 ELYR 44035 2875 C5
Lafayette Wy
29700 WTLK 44145 2749 C4
Lafevre Rd
2200 HpfT 44041 1944 A7
Lagoon Dr
35800 ETLK 44095 2250 C1
Lagoon Ln
- VMLN 44089 2741 A6
E Lagoon Rd
4600 FnTp 44491 3029 E3
W Lagoon Rd
4600 FnTp 44491 3029 E3
La Grange Av
7500 CLEV 44103 2626 A2
Lagrange Rd
10400 CrlT 44035 3005 E5
N Laguardia Pkwy
15800 SGVL 44136 3012 B4
S Laguardia Pkwy
15800 SGVL 44136 3012 B5
Laing Rd
24000 BDHT 44146 2887 D4
Laird Av
9500 CLEV 44102 2623 D6
Laird Rd
9000 MstT 44062 2639 E7
9000 MstT 44062 2769 E1
Laisy Av
8800 CLEV 44104 2626 B7
Lake Av
10 ELYR 44035 2875 A5
300 ELYR 44035 2874 E4
900 AURA 44023 3021 B3
900 AURA 44202 3021 B3
900 BbgT 44023 3021 B3
1700 EyrT 44035 2874 D1
3600 RMDV 44202 3020 E3
3600 RMDV 44139 3020 E3
3600 SLN 44139 3020 E3
3700 RMDV 44139 3021 B3
3700 RMDV 44202 3021 B3
3700 SLN 44139 3021 B3
6100 EyrT 44035 2745 B6
6100 EyrT 44055 2745 B6
6100 ShfT 44055 2745 B6
7500 CLEV 44102 2623 E5
11700 LKWD 44102 2623 B4
11700 LKWD 44107 2623 B4
13400 LKWD 44107 2622 E4
14900 MDFD 44062 2767 C3
S Lake Blvd
10000 PRMA 44130 3013 C2
Lake Ct
5400 CLEV 44103 2495 D6
5400 CLEV 44114 2495 D6
Lake Dr
12100 NbyT 44021 2764 E4
12100 NbyT 44021 2765 A4
12400 BtnT 44021 2765 B6
18600 AbnT 44023 3023 A2
37400 AVON 44011 2617 C7
W Lake Dr
7600 WNHL 44146 3017 E2
Lake Pl
200 LORN 44052 2614 D6
Lake Rd
- LKWD 44107 2621 E4
10 PnvT 44077 2040 C2
1800 PnvT 44077 2041 A1
3500 SDLK 44054 2615 E4
3900 SDLK 44054 2616 B3
5400 SDLK 44054 2617 A2
5500 SDLK 44012 2617 A2
6300 GnvT 44041 1844 E4
6300 GOTL 44041 1844 E4
7800 GnvT 44057 1844 B4
7800 MadT 44057 1844 B4
11600 MsnT 44024 2504 C4
17800 LKWD 44107 2622 A4
18500 RKRV 44116 2621 E5
22900 BYVL 44116 2621 C5
22900 BYVL 44140 2621 C5
23400 BYVL 44140 2620 D5
27500 BYVL 44140 2619 E4
31500 AVLK 44140 2619 B2
31700 AVLK 44012 2618 D1
31700 AVLK 44012 2619 B2
32100 AVLK 44012 2488 B7
32900 AVLK 44012 2487 E7
32900 AVLK 44012 2617 D1
Lake Rd US-6
3500 SDLK 44054 2615 E4
3900 SDLK 44054 2616 B3
5400 SDLK 44054 2617 A2
5500 SDLK 44012 2617 A2
19200 RKRV 44116 2621 C5
22900 BYVL 44116 2621 C5
22900 BYVL 44140 2621 C5
23400 BYVL 44140 2620 D5
27500 BYVL 44140 2619 E4
31500 AVLK 44140 2619 B2
31700 AVLK 44012 2618 D1
31700 AVLK 44012 2619 B2
32100 AVLK 44012 2488 B7
32900 AVLK 44012 2487 E7
32900 AVLK 44012 2617 D1
N Lake Rd
4600 FnTp 44491 3029 E3
W Lake Rd
12500 VmnT 44089 2740 C6
14200 VMLN 44089 2740 C6
W Lake Rd US-6
12500 VmnT 44089 2740 C6
14200 VMLN 44089 2740 C6
Lake Rd E
6700 MadT 44057 1843 C6
7500 MadT 44057 1844 A6
Lake Rd W
6200 GnvT 44041 1844 D5
6400 MadT 44057 1843 A7
6500 GnvT 44057 1844 B4
Lake St
- MadT 44057 1941 D1
5700 MONT 44060 2143 C2
5700 VMLN 44089 2740 D5
6100 MNTR 44060 2143 C2
N Lake St
- AhtT 44001 2872 C6
- MadT 44057 1942 B7
10 MDSN 44057 2044 B1
100 AMHT 44001 2872 C6
200 MDSN 44057 1942 B7
900 AMHT 44001 2743 C7
1700 SAHT 44001 2872 C6
N Lake St SR-528
- MadT 44057 1942 B7
10 MDSN 44057 2044 B1
200 MDSN 44057 1942 B7
S Lake St
- SAHT 44001 3003 B2
10 MDSN 44057 2044 B1
10 SAHT 44074 3003 B2
100 SAHT 44001 2872 B7
200 AMHT 44001 2872 C1
Lake Tr
600 AURA 44202 3156 C1
700 AURA 44202 3021 B7
Lake Abram Dr
6800 MDBH 44130 2880 E5
Lake Breeze Dr
2600 MadT 44057 1942 A4
Lake Breeze Rd
100 SDLK 44054 2616 A3
1200 SFLD 44054 2616 A6
Lakebrook Dr
10800 KTLD 44094 2378 A7
10800 KTLD 44094 2503 A1
Lake Circle Dr
16500 SGVL 44136 3012 B3
Lake County Ln
- KTLD 44094 2377 C7
Lakecrest Blvd
10 HkyT 44233 3148 A6
Lakedge Ct
7500 HDSN 44236 3155 C7
Lakedge Ln
- HGVL 44022 2760 A1
Lake Edge Dr
10 EUCL 44123 2373 C1
Lake Forest Ct
8600 BbgT 44023 2891 B4
Lake Forest Dr
300 BYVL 44140 2620 C5
11200 CsTp 44026 2501 E1
12200 BKVL 44141 3151 D4
16000 SGVL 44136 3012 B3
Lake Forest Tr
8600 BbgT 44023 2891 B4
Lakefront Av
1200 ECLE 44108 2496 E6
1400 ECLE 44112 2496 E6
1500 ECLE 44112 2497 A6
Lake Harbor Dr
- AVON 44011 2748 C4
Lakehurst Dr
100 ETLK 44095 2142 C6
2300 NPRY 44081 1940 D3
N Lakehurst Dr
10 ETLK 44095 2142 C6
Lake In The Woods Tr
8500 BbgT 44023 2762 A7
8700 BbgT 44023 2891 C1
Lakeland Av
100 AVLK 44012 2618 E2
1000 LKWD 44107 2622 C4
Lakeland Blvd
20000 EUCL 44119 2373 A6
22200 EUCL 44117 2373 A6
24300 EUCL 44132 2373 D3
26400 EUCL 44132 2374 A2
27700 WKLF 44092 2374 A2
29900 WKLF 44092 2249 D7
30500 WLWK 44092 2249 D7
32800 ETLK 44095 2249 D7
33700 ETLK 44095 2250 A6
36600 WLBY 44094 2250 B5
N Lakeland Blvd
20000 CLEV 44119 2373 A5
22000 EUCL 44117 2373 A5
20000 EUCL 44119 2373 A5
22000 EUCL 44123 2373 A5
24300 EUCL 44132 2373 D4
Lakeland Dr
11700 NbyT 44065 2764 D1
36600 AVON 44011 2747 E2
Lakeland Frwy I-90
- BTNH - 2496 B4
- BTNH - 2497 A1
- CLEV - 2372 C7
- CLEV - 2373 A6
- CLEV - 2495 E5
- CLEV - 2496 B4
- CLEV - 2497 B1
- EUCL - 2373 B5
Lakeland Frwy SR-2
- BTNH - 2496 B4
- BTNH - 2497 A1
- CLEV - 2372 C7
- CLEV - 2373 E3
- CLEV - 2495 E5
- CLEV - 2496 B4
- CLEV - 2497 B1
- ETLK - 2249 D7
- ETLK - 2250 C4
- EUCL - 2373 E3
- EUCL - 2374 A2
- MNTR - 2143 D7
- MNTR - 2144 E3
- MNTR - 2145 A1
- MNTR - 2251 B3
- PNVL - 2145 A1
- PnvT - 2145 A1
- WKLF - 2249 D7
- WKLF - 2374 A2
- WLBY - 2250 C4
- WLBY - 2251 B3
- WLWK - 2249 D7
Lakeland Frwy SR-44
- MNTR - 2145 B1
- PNVL - 2145 B1
- PnvT - 2145 B1
Lakemeadows Dr
10000 SGVL 44136 3012 C5
Lakemont Av
22200 EUCL 44123 2373 B3
Lake of the Falls Blvd
26600 ODFL 44138 3010 A2
Lake Overlook Dr
1900 MadT 44057 1941 B1
8900 MNTR 44060 2038 D5
Lake Park Dr
300 BYVL 44140 2620 E5
3400 BKVL 44141 3150 C1
Lake Point Dr
1000 LKWD 44107 2621 E4
Lake Pointe Dr
2100 AVON 44011 2617 E7
2100 AVON 44011 2747 E1
Lakeport Av
17400 CLEV 44119 2372 D5
Lakesedge Tr
17400 BbgT 44023 2890 D4
Lake Shore Blvd
500 PnvT 44077 2039 A7
600 PnvT 44060 2039 A7
7000 MNTR 44060 2143 B4
7200 MNTR 44060 2143 B4
7400 MadT 44057 1843 E5
7500 MadT 44057 1844 A5
7700 MONT 44060 2143 B4
8000 MONT 44060 2144 C1
8100 MNTR 44060 2144 C1
8700 BTNH 44108 2496 B4
8700 CLEV 44103 2496 B4
8700 CLEV 44108 2496 B4
9100 MNTR 44060 2038 E7
9300 MNTR 44060 2039 A7
13200 BTNH 44108 2497 A1
13200 BTNH 44110 2497 A1
13800 CLEV 44110 2372 C6
16900 CLEV 44119 2372 C6
18400 EUCL 44119 2372 D4
19500 EUCL 44119 2373 B2
19800 EUCL 44123 2373 B2
24800 EUCL 44132 2373 B2
25700 EUCL 44132 2248 E7
27100 EUCL 44132 2249 A7
28100 WLWK 44095 2249 A7
33000 ETLK 44095 2249 E2
33500 LKLN 44095 2249 E2
34400 TMLK 44095 2249 E2
34700 ETLK 44095 2250 A2
34700 TMLK 44095 2250 A2
35900 ETLK 44095 2142 C6
37900 ETLK 44095 2142 C6
37900 WLBY 44095 2142 C6
38400 WLBY 44094 2143 A4
38800 MNTR 44094 2143 A4
Lake Shore Blvd SR-283
500 PnvT 44077 2039 A7
600 PnvT 44060 2039 A7
7000 MNTR 44060 2143 B4
7200 MNTR 44060 2143 B4
7700 MONT 44060 2143 B4
8000 MONT 44060 2144 C1
8100 MNTR 44060 2144 C1
9100 MNTR 44060 2038 E7
9300 MNTR 44060 2039 A7
13600 BTNH 44108 2497 A1
13600 BTNH 44110 2497 A1
13800 CLEV 44110 2372 C6
16900 CLEV 44119 2372 C6
18400 EUCL 44119 2372 D4
19500 EUCL 44119 2373 B2
19800 EUCL 44123 2373 B2
24800 EUCL 44132 2373 B2
25700 EUCL 44132 2248 E7
27100 EUCL 44132 2249 A7
28100 WLWK 44095 2249 A7
33000 ETLK 44095 2249 E2
33500 LKLN 44095 2249 E2
34400 TMLK 44095 2249 E2
34700 ETLK 44095 2250 A2
34700 TMLK 44095 2250 A2
35900 ETLK 44095 2142 C6
37900 WLBY 44095 2142 C6
37900 WLBY 44094 2142 C6
38400 WLBY 44094 2143 A4
38800 MNTR 44094 2143 A4
Lakeshore Blvd
19000 EUCL 44119 2372 E4
19400 EUCL 44119 2373 A3
21500 EUCL 44123 2373 A3
S Lakeshore Blvd
36400 ETLK 44095 2142 D6
Lake Shore Dr
15400 NbyT 44021 2765 A4
Lakeshore Dr
8400 BbgT 44023 2891 A3
13700 BTNH 44110 2497 A1
13700 CLEV 44110 2497 A1
Lakeside Av
100 LORN 44052 2614 D6
E Lakeside Av
200 CLEV 44114 2624 D2
W Lakeside Av
10 CLEV 44114 2624 D2
600 CLEV 44113 2624 D2
Lakeside Av E
900 CLEV 44114 2624 E2
1200 CLEV 44114 2625 A1
3300 CLEV 44114 2495 B7
Lakeside Dr
8700 NRDV 44039 2876 E7
12000 NbyT 44021 2764 E4
12000 NbyT 44065 2764 E4
Lakeside Pl
10 CLEV 44110 2372 B6
Lakeside St
- CLEV 44110 2372 B6
Lakeside Villages Pkwy
- OmsT 44138 2878 D5
Lakeview Av
300 SDLK 44054 2616 E3
1300 LORN 44053 2614 A7
1300 LORN 44053 2744 B1
1400 MadT 44057 1843 B7
1400 RKRV 44116 2621 D6
Lakeview Blvd
10 PnvT 44077 2040 C2
N Lakeview Blvd
1400 LORN 44052 2614 C7
S Lakeview Blvd
1300 LORN 44052 2614 C7
Lakeview Cir
300 AURA 44202 3021 B7
8800 PRMA 44129 2882 D6
9000 ODFL 44138 3009 E1
9700 SGVL 44136 3012 C4
Lakeview Ct
8000 NRYN 44133 3013 C2
20100 RKRV 44116 2621 D6
Lakeview Dr
10 CrlT 44044 3006 D6
100 AVLK 44012 2618 D1
800 LORN 44052 2614 B7
1200 LORN 44052 2744 B1
4700 MNTR 44060 2038 D6
7100 PRMA 44129 2882 D7
8500 BWHT 44147 3014 D5
8800 ODFL 44138 2878 E7
8800 ODFL 44138 3009 D1
14700 MDFD 44062 2767 B1
16100 BtnT 44021 2765 B6
24800 BYVL 44140 2620 C4
33800 ETLK 44095 2249 E2
34100 SLN 44139 2889 A2
Lakeview Ln
10 SRSL 44073 2762 C5
100 TroT 44234 2894 B6
Lakeview Rd
600 CLEV 44108 2496 D6
1300 CLEV 44106 2496 D6
1500 CLEV 44112 2496 D6
1500 ECLE 44112 2496 D6
1600 ECLE 44112 2626 E1
1800 CLEV 44106 2626 E1
1800 CLEV 44112 2626 E1
4400 StnT 44491 3029 E4
4800 FnTp 44491 3029 E3
11400 MsnT 44024 2504 C3
11700 NbyT 44065 2764 D1
Lake Vista Dr
5000 SLN 44139 2759 C7
Lakeway Blvd
6000 MONT 44060 2143 E3
Lakewood Av
300 BNWK 44212 3147 A7
1300 LKWD 44107 2623 A5
Lakewood Ct
6200 MNTR 44060 2144 D4
Lakewood Dr
100 AVLK 44012 2618 D2
13300 CsTp 44026 2632 C3
Lakewood Beach Dr
600 SDLK 44054 2615 E5
Lakewood Heights Blvd
- CLEV 44111 2622 D7
- CLEV 44107 2622 D7
13000 CLEV 44107 2623 A7
13000 CLEV 44111 2623 A7
13000 LKWD 44107 2623 A7
14900 LKWD 44107 2622 C7
Lakomis Dr
35900 ETLK 44095 2142 B7
Lakota Av
14000 CLEV 44111 2752 D3
Lalemant Dr
6800 PRMA 44129 2882 E5
6800 PRMA 44129 2883 A5
Lalemant Rd
2200 UNHT 44118 2628 B4
Lamar Ct
4400 RDHT 44143 2498 C4
Lambert Av
13200 CLEV 44120 2756 E1
13800 CLEV 44120 2757 A1
Lambert Rd
4000 SELD 44121 2628 B1
Lambert St
13400 ECLE 44112 2497 A7
Lamberton Rd
2100 CVHT 44118 2627 B3
Lambton Ct
7500 CcdT 44060 2253 B2
Lamoille Ct
1700 CLEV 44113 2624 D6
Lamont Av
9300 CLEV 44106 2626 B2
Lamontier Av
9400 CLEV 44104 2626 C6
Lamplight Ln
2800 WBHL 44092 2374 E6
2800 WBHL 44094 2374 E6
Lamplighter Ln
15100 SGVL 44136 3147 B1
Lampson Rd
1800 CLEV 44112 2497 C3
Lamson Av
400 BDFD 44146 2886 E3
500 BDFD 44146 2887 A3
Lamson Rd
7200 OKWD 44146 2887 D7
7200 OKWD 44146 3018 D1
Lanabelle
- BKPK 44142 2751 A7
- BKPK 44142 2880 A1
Lanark Ln
600 PnvT 44077 2040 E2
3400 PRPK 44124 2759 C1
Lanbury Av
19000 WVHT 44122 2757 E2
19700 WVHT 44122 2758 A2
Lancashire Rd
2700 CVHT 44106 2627 A2
2700 CVHT 44118 2627 A2
Lancaster Ct
7100 CcdT 44077 2145 D7
7200 CcdT 44077 2253 D1
Lancaster Dr
5300 BNHT 44131 2755 B7
5300 BNHT 44131 2884 B1
8200 MNTR 44060 2144 A6
11500 AbnT 44021 2893 C5
Lancaster Rd
3900 SELD 44121 2498 A4
Lancelot Av
12400 CLEV 44108 2496 E4
Lancelot Dr
7200 PRMA 44134 2883 D7
Lancelot Ln E
14700 NRYN 44133 3148 A1
Lancelot Ln W
14700 NRYN 44133 3148 A1
Lancer Dr
1100 AMHT 44001 2872 E4
Lancewood Dr
- MCDN 44056 3154 A4
Landchester Rd
4600 CLEV 44109 2754 E5
Lander Rd
500 HDHT 44143 2499 D4
800 MAYF 44143 2499 D6
1100 MDHT 44124 2499 D6
1500 MDHT 44124 2629 D3
3700 ORNG 44022 2759 C5
3700 ORNG 44122 2759 C5
Lander Rd N
2400 PRPK 44124 2629 D4
Lander Rd S
2700 PRPK 44124 2629 C7
3100 PRPK 44124 2759 C2
3700 ORNG 44122 2759 C2
Landerbrook Cir
2000 MDHT 44124 2629 C2

INDEX 29

W Linden Ln

Cleveland Street Index

Magnolia Pkwy

STREET Block City ZIP Map# Grid

W Linden Ln
12800 PRMA 44130 3012 E1
Linden Rd
3000 RKRV 44116 2621 D7
3000 RKRV 44116 2751 D1
Linden St
400 VMLN 44089 2741 A5
7800 MONT 44060 2143 E1
8000 MONT 44060 2144 A1
Lindenhill Ct
1000 SgHT 44067 3017 B5
Linden Way Dr
11400 MsnT 44024 2504 C2
Lindenwood Ct
1300 LORN 44053 2744 C5
Lindenwood Dr
1400 LORN 44053 2744 C5
Lindford Dr
500 BYVL 44140 2619 C5
Lindholm Rd
3500 SRHT 44120 2757 C2
Lindmar Dr
10500 CcdT 44077 2145 E4
10600 CcdT 44077 2146 A4
Lindmont Dr
14900 BKPK 44142 2881 C3
Lindsay Ct
100 ELYR 44035 3006 D2
Lindsay Dr
6900 MNTR 44060 2144 B7
Lindsay Ln
7600 SLN 44139 3019 E3
10300 AbnT 44023 2892 C1
Lindsey Ln
4700 RDHT 44143 2498 D4
Lindsey Ovl
4800 RDHT 44143 2498 D4
Line Dr
- NRDV 44039 2876 D6
Line St
10500 MNTU 44255 3159 B6
Links Rd
5300 MNTR 44060 2038 D7
5300 MNTR 44060 2144 D1
Linn Av
13600 GDHT 44125 2886 A1
Linn Dr
700 CLEV 44108 2496 C5
Linn Rd
5500 AhtT 44001 2744 C6
5500 AMHT 44001 2744 C6
5500 AMHT 44053 2744 C6
Linnell Rd
4000 SELD 44121 2628 A1
Linnet Av
10300 CLEV 44111 2753 C2
Linton Av
5400 CLEV 44105 2755 D1
Linwood Av
- VMLN 44089 2740 E4
5100 VMLN 44089 2741 A5
5500 CLEV 44103 2625 D1
8200 CLEV 44103 2626 A1
8400 CLEV 44106 2626 A1
Linwood Cir
27300 NOSD 44070 2749 E6
Linwood Ln
200 AURA 44202 3156 C1
Linwood St
1300 ELYR 44035 3006 A2
Lione Dr
9700 CcdT 44060 2253 B2
Lipton Av
16500 CLEV 44128 2757 C5
Lisa Dr
14000 MPHT 44137 2886 A3
Lisa Ln
- ClrT 44024 2506 D1
4100 NOSD 44070 2749 E5
4500 NRYN 44133 3014 A6
32500 SLN 44139 3019 E3
33400 SLN 44139 3020 A3
Lisa Wy
5200 NRDV 44039 2748 B7
Lisaview Dr
29500 BYVL 44140 2619 C5
Lisbon Rd
2600 CLEV 44104 2626 A5
Lisle Ct
35000 WLBY 44094 2375 A2
Lismore Ln
9400 MNTR 44060 2145 A5
List Ct
4000 CLEV 44113 2624 C7
List Ln
12800 PRMA 44130 3012 E2
W List Ln
7800 PRMA 44130 3012 E2
Litchfield Dr
7700 MNTR 44060 2252 A2
Litchfield Rd
2800 SRHT 44120 2627 D6
Literary Rd
300 CLEV 44113 2625 A5
700 CLEV 44113 2624 E5
Little Brook Wy
21200 SGVL 44136 3011 A4
Little Creek Pkwy
200 BNHT 44131 2884 A1
300 BNHT 44131 2755 A7
Little Green Ln
6100 MadT 44057 1941 E1
Little Met Pl
4500 CLEV 44135 2751 D5
Little Mountain Rd
7300 MNTR 44060 2252 C1
7900 KDHL 44060 2252 C3
9300 KDHL 44060 2253 A5
9700 CcdT 44024 2253 B5
9700 CcdT 44060 2253 B5
9700 CdnT 44024 2253 B5
9800 CcdT 44077 2253 B5
Littleton Rd
12500 GDHT 44125 2885 D3
Litto Dr
7900 SGVL 44136 3012 C3
Live Oaks
5800 MONT 44060 2143 D2
Livermore Ln
700 ELYR 44035 2875 E2
Liverpool Dr
600 LvpT 44280 3145 C7
Livingston Av
- LORN 44052 2745 A4
1700 LORN 44052 2744 E1
3200 LORN 44055 2745 A3
Livingston Dr
35000 AVON 44011 2748 B3
Livingston Rd
3000 CLEV 44120 2626 D7
3000 CLEV 44120 2627 A7
Ljubljana Dr
700 EUCL 44119 2373 A5
Lloyd Av
800 AURA 44202 3021 A4
Lloyd Dr
6500 BKVL 44141 3015 E4
6500 BWHT 44141 3015 E4
6500 BWHT 44147 3015 E4
Lloyd Rd
10 EUCL 44132 2249 A7
400 EUCL 44132 2374 A1
400 WKLF 44092 2374 A1
3500 CLEV 44111 2753 A2
Lloyd Rd SR-633
200 EUCL 44132 2249 A7
400 EUCL 44132 2374 A1
400 WKLF 44092 2374 A1
Locherie Av
18500 EUCL 44119 2372 E4
19300 EUCL 44119 2373 A4
Loch Lomond Ct
6100 SLN 44139 2889 E4
Lochmoor Ct
6200 SLN 44139 2889 E4
Lochmoor Dr
38700 SLN 44139 2889 E4
39100 SLN 44139 2890 A4
Lochness Dr
7100 CcdT 44077 2146 A7
Lochspur Ln
10 MDHL 44022 2760 A5
Locke Av
12200 CLEV 44108 2496 E4
Lockhaven Dr
6300 BKPK 44142 2881 C4
Locklevel Dr
- VLVW 44125 2885 B3
Locklie Dr
400 HDHT 44143 2499 D2
Lockridge
- CcdT 44077 2146 A7
Lockwood Av
1600 ECLE 44112 2496 E7
N Lockwood Av
1100 ECLE 44112 2496 E6
Lockwood Dr
6400 MNTR 44060 2144 A4
Lockwood Ln
400 BHIT 44212 3146 A7
Lockwood Rd
4300 NPRY 44081 1940 C3
4700 NPRY 44081 1941 A3
5200 MadT 44057 1941 C3
5200 MadT 44081 1941 A3
Lockwood St
10 GNVA 44041 1944 B5
Lockyear Av
7100 CLEV 44103 2495 E7
7200 CLEV 44103 2496 A7
Locust Cir
7600 SgHT 44067 3017 C7
7600 SgHT 44067 3152 D1
Locust Ct
4400 INDE 44131 2884 C4
Locust Dr
9100 ODFL 44138 3010 A1
N Locust Dr
8200 KTLD 44094 2377 A5
S Locust Dr
8200 KTLD 44094 2377 A5
Locust Ln
10 CNFL 44022 2761 A5
22500 RKRV 44116 2621 A6
Locust St
10 OBLN 44074 3138 E3
100 ELYR 44035 2875 B6
Locust Grove Dr
10000 HmbT 44024 2381 A5
Lodge Dr
3000 NRYN 44133 3014 C7
Lodi St
10 ELYR 44035 2875 A6
Logan Ct
9700 CLEV 44106 2626 B2
16300 SGVL 44136 3012 B4
31000 WTLK 44145 2619 A7
Logan Dr
6200 SVHL 44131 2884 A3
6500 MDBH 44130 2881 D4
18000 WNHL 44146 3017 E2
Logan Ln
10200 TNBG 44087 3019 D3
Logan St
100 BDFD 44146 2887 A3
S Logan St
100 ELYR 44035 2875 D6
Loganberry Dr
26600 RDHT 44143 2373 E6
26600 RDHT 44143 2374 A6
Loganberry Ovl
800 MDSN 44057 1942 B7
Logans Wy
- PRRY 44081 2042 B2
Log Cabin Ct
10200 BKVL 44141 3151 D5
Lois Ln
10 HmbT 44024 2380 E3
10 HmbT 44024 2381 A3
Lola Ct
10200 CcdT 44077 2253 D1
Lola Ln
- NRYN 44133 3014 C5
Loma Ct
- CLEV 44105 2756 A1
Lombardo Ctr
5700 INDE 44131 2884 C3
Lombardy Dr
200 BERA 44017 2880 A5
Lombardy Ln
33600 PRPK 44124 2760 A1
Lomond Blvd
16600 SRHT 44120 2757 C1
17600 SRHT 44122 2757 E1
20000 SRHT 44122 2758 A1
London Av
15300 CLEV 44135 2752 C5
London Rd
700 CLEV 44110 2497 C2
1700 CLEV 44112 2497 D3
Long Av
900 LORN 44052 2614 D7
1200 LORN 44052 2744 E1
Long Dr
400 AbnT 44023 2892 B3
Long Rd
200 MCDN 44056 3018 B5
3800 AVON 44011 2747 C4
Long St
400 AMHT 44001 2872 D1
Longano Dr
7300 INDE 44131 2884 E2
Longbeach Pkwy
300 BYVL 44140 2619 D4
Long Boat Cir
13000 SGVL 44136 3147 D4
Longbrook Dr
8900 MCDN 44056 3018 E7
Longbrook Rd
4600 LORN 44053 2743 C5
19100 WVHT 44128 2757 E4
19800 WVHT 44128 2758 A4
Longfellow Av
5500 CLEV 44103 2625 D3
Longfellow Dr
500 BERA 44017 2880 B4
Longfellow Pkwy
300 LORN 44052 2615 B5
Longfellow St
200 ELYR 44035 2875 D5
Longford Av
100 ELYR 44035 2875 D5
Longford Ln
- AVON 44011 2748 C1
Long Forest Dr
8000 BKVL 44141 3015 E6
Longhorn Rd
7500 MNTR 44060 2143 D6
Longleaf Rd
4400 WVHT 44128 2758 D5
Longman Ln
24500 WVHT 44128 2758 D5
Longmead Av
11700 BKLN 44144 2753 A5
11700 CLEV 44135 2753 A5
11700 CLEV 44144 2753 A5
Longmeadow Ln
10 BHWD 44122 2628 E4
10 BHWD 44122 2629 A4
Long Meadow Tr
17200 BbgT 44023 2891 C4
Long Pointe Dr
300 AVLK 44012 2618 E2
Long Ridge Dr
200 SVHL 44131 2884 A2
Longridge Rd
6300 MDHT 44124 2629 E2
6400 MDHT 44124 2630 A2
Longson Av
800 ELYR 44035 2875 D7
Long Spur Ct
13300 VLVW 44125 2885 E6
13300 VLVW 44125 2886 A6
Longspur Rd
200 HDHT 44143 2499 E2
Longton Rd
5100 LNHT 44124 2628 E1
5100 LNHT 44124 2629 A1
Longvale Rd
15300 MPHT 44137 2886 B4
Longview Av
7200 MNTR 44060 2144 D7
7200 MNTR 44060 2252 D1
18700 MPHT 44137 2757 E7
Longview Dr
6900 SLN 44139 2888 E7
7900 BWHT 44147 3015 A3
10200 KTLD 44094 2376 A5
10300 WBHL 44094 2376 A5
Longview Tr
10500 AbnT 44023 2892 D5
14700 NbyT 44065 2764 D1
Longwood Av
3500 CLEV 44115 2625 C4
3700 PRMA 44134 2883 B3
5600 MPHT 44137 2886 C2
13000 BtnT 44021 2635 D7
Longwood Ct
- CVHT 44118 2497 D7
Longwood Dr
10 CNFL 44022 2761 B4
900 MCDN 44056 3018 E5
1500 MDHT 44124 2499 C4
1500 MDHT 44124 2629 C1
Lonna Ct
3900 CLEV 44111 2752 C3
Lookout Cir
18700 FWPK 44126 2752 A1
Lookout Ct
300 AVLK 44012 2618 E3
Lookout Dr
9800 BKVL 44141 3150 C4
Loop Rd
2500 CLEV 44113 2624 C4
Lorain Av
- FWPK 44126 2752 A2
1600 CLEV 44113 2624 C5
3100 VMLN 44089 2742 A4
3200 VMLN 44089 2741 E4
3700 LORN 44055 2745 C4
4500 CLEV 44102 2624 B6
7100 CLEV 44102 2623 E7
10000 CLEV 44111 2623 C7
10600 CLEV 44111 2753 A1
13200 CLEV 44111 2752 E1
Lorain Av SR-10
- FWPK 44126 2752 A2
2000 CLEV 44113 2624 C5
4500 CLEV 44102 2624 B6
7100 CLEV 44102 2623 C7
10000 CLEV 44111 2623 C7
10600 CLEV 44111 2753 A1
13200 CLEV 44111 2752 E1
Lorain Blvd
200 ELYR 44035 2874 E5
1800 ELYR 44035 2875 A1
2100 ELYR 44035 2874 E1
6000 EyrT 44035 2745 E7
6000 ShfT 44035 2745 E7
6000 ShfT 44055 2745 E7
6200 ELYR 44035 2745 E7
Lorain Blvd SR-57
1100 ELYR 44035 2874 E3
1800 ELYR 44035 2875 A1
2100 ELYR 44035 2874 E1
6000 EyrT 44035 2745 E7
6000 ShfT 44035 2745 E7
6000 ShfT 44055 2745 E7
6200 ELYR 44035 2745 E7
Lorain Ct
- CLEV 44102 2624 B6
- CLEV 44113 2624 B6
12800 CLEV 44111 2753 A1
13100 CLEV 44111 2752 E1
Lorain Dr
2100 LORN 44052 2744 B1
Lorain Rd
10800 EatT 44039 3007 E2
10800 EatT 44044 3007 E2
10800 NRDV 44039 3007 E2
18800 FWPK 44126 2752 A2
18900 FWPK 44126 2751 E2
22900 NOSD 44126 2751 B3
22900 NOSD 44070 2751 B3
23200 NOSD 44070 2750 E5
27200 NOSD 44070 2749 E7
28000 NOSD 44070 2878 C1
31200 NRDV 44070 2878 A3
31200 NRDV 44039 2878 A3
33000 NRDV 44039 2877 E4
35800 NRDV 44039 3008 A1
Lorain Rd SR-10
- NRDV 44039 2877 E1
18800 FWPK 44126 2752 A2
18900 FWPK 44126 2751 E2
22900 NOSD 44070 2751 B3
22900 NOSD 44126 2751 B3
23200 NOSD 44070 2750 E5
27200 NOSD 44070 2749 E7
28000 NOSD 44070 2878 C1
31200 NRDV 44039 2878 A3
31200 NRDV 44070 2878 A3
Lorain Rd SR-83C
10800 EatT 44044 3007 E2
10800 EatT 44039 3007 E2
10800 NRDV 44039 3007 E2
Lorain Rd SR-252
24700 NOSD 44070 2750 C6
Lorain St
16600 BbgT 44023 2890 B1
E Lorain St
10 OBLN 44074 3138 E2
100 OBLN 44074 3139 A2
E Lorain St SR-511
10 OBLN 44074 3138 E2
100 OBLN 44074 3139 A2
W Lorain St
10 OBLN 44074 3138 C2
600 NRsT 44074 3138 C2
W Lorain St SR-511
10 OBLN 44074 3138 C2
600 NRsT 44074 3138 C2
Lorain Co Metro Parks Bike Pth
- NRsT 44074 3138 A4
- NRsT 44074 3139 A2
- OBLN 44074 3138 C4
- OBLN 44074 3139 A2
Loren Av
9100 CLEV 44105 2756 B2
Lorenzo Av
13000 CLEV 44120 2626 E7
Loreto Dr
2700 WBHL 44094 2376 A6
2800 WBHL 44094 2375 E6
Loreto Ridge Dr
10200 KTLD 44094 2377 C5
Loretta Av
9700 CLEV 44102 2753 C1
10000 CLEV 44111 2753 C1
Loretta Ct
2900 LORN 44052 2744 C3
Lori Dr
5500 BDHT 44146 2887 C2
Lori Ln
7700 BbgT 44023 3021 D3
33000 ETLK 44095 2249 E6
Lori Ann Dr
33400 ETLK 44095 2249 E5
Loriann Dr
1400 BERA 44017 2879 C6
Lorie Blvd
37500 AVON 44011 2617 C7
Lorient Dr
4600 WVHT 44128 2758 C5
Lori Jean Dr
9200 MNTR 44060 2144 E6
Lorimer Rd
1300 PRMA 44134 2883 D3
Loring Dr
10 AQLA 44024 2505 D4
Loripat Dr
5600 BWHT 44147 3015 D4
Loris Av
11000 ManT 44202 3158 A4
Lorraine Dr
8300 SGVL 44136 3010 E3
22200 SGVL 44136 3011 A2
Lorrey Pl
5300 MNTR 44060 2038 E7
5400 MNTR 44060 2144 D1
Lorrich Dr
9100 MNTR 44060 2144 E1
Lost Rd
- HmbT 44024 2380 D7
Lost Tr
17700 BbgT 44023 2891 B5
Lost Lakes Tr
9800 AbnT 44023 2892 A1
Lost Nation Rd
- WLBY 44094 2250 E2
1000 WLBY 44094 2143 A5
2100 WLBY 44094 2142 E7
2300 ETLK 44095 2250 E2
2300 WLBY 44095 2250 E2
3400 WLBY 44094 2250 E4
Lost Pond Dr
9400 TNBG 44087 3019 D6
Lost Pond Pkwy
300 CRDN 44024 2505 A2
Lotus Dr
14800 CLEV 44128 2757 B3
S Lotus Dr
16000 CLEV 44128 2757 C4
Lotus Ln
3200 SVHL 44131 3015 B1
7400 MNTR 44060 2143 C3
Lotusdale Dr
5800 PMHT 44130 2882 C2
Louann Dr
6500 NOSD 44070 2878 E3
Louden Ct
100 ELYR 44035 3006 B2
Louis Av
5400 ShfT 44055 2745 C6
15200 CLEV 44135 2752 C6
Louis Dr
10 PRPK 44124 2629 D3
500 BERA 44017 2880 D5
500 MDBH 44130 2880 D5
5800 NOSD 44070 2879 A2
15800 NRYN 44133 3148 B2
Louis Rd
3600 BWHT 44147 3015 C4
21800 BDHT 44146 2758 B7
Louis St
33200 ETLK 44095 2249 E5
Louisa Ct
5000 CLEV 44127 2625 D6
Louise Dr
10 SRSL 44073 2762 C6
5600 MNTR 44060 2144 B2
27700 SLN 44139 2759 A7
Louise Ln
23100 ClbT 44028 3145 D2
Louisiana Av
100 ELYR 44035 2875 A4
200 LORN 44052 2615 B5
400 ELYR 44035 2874 E4
3000 CLEV 44109 2754 C3
Lourdes Dr
1100 PRMA 44134 2883 E6
Loveland Ct
10 GNVA 44041 1944 B3
E Loveland Rd
- MadT 44057 2044 A7
- MadT 44057 2150 A1
W Loveland Rd
5300 MadT 44057 2043 D7
5300 MadT 44057 2149 D1
Lovett Pl
800 LORN 44052 2614 D7
Lowden Rd
4000 SELD 44121 2498 A4
Lowell Av
3300 LORN 44055 2745 B4
3700 ShfT 44055 2745 B4
9300 CLEV 44108 2496 B5
Lowell Dr
300 HDHT 44143 2499 D2
Lowell Ln
8900 NCtT 44067 3152 E3
8900 NCtT 44067 3153 A3
Lowell Rd
3700 CVHT 44121 2497 E5
Lowell St
100 ELYR 44035 2875 A5
300 ELYR 44035 2874 D5
42000 EyrT 44035 2874 C5
Lower Dr
- CLEV 44135 2880 E1
Lower Ter
20000 EUCL 44117 2498 A1
Lower Chelsea Dr
11500 MsnT 44024 2504 B3
Lownesdale Rd
3300 CVHT 44112 2497 D6
Low Ridge Ln
7700 MNTR 44060 2252 C3
Lowrie Blvd
10 NHFD 44067 3018 A3
200 NHFD 44067 3017 E3
Loya Pkwy
5200 PRMA 44134 2883 B4
Loyola Dr
100 ELYR 44035 2746 D7
5400 PRMA 44129 2883 A4
Loyola Rd
2200 UNHT 44118 2628 B4
Luanna Dr
1500 ETLK 44095 2249 E5
Luanne Dr
33900 NRDV 44039 2877 C1
Luary Dr
200 PNVL 44077 2146 A2
Lucas Ct
4600 ELYR 44035 2746 B7
Lucerne Av
2700 PRMA 44134 2883 C2
6600 CLEV 44103 2625 E2
Lucerne Dr
7500 MDBH 44130 3012 B1
8200 BbgT 44023 2891 A3
Lucia Av
7900 CLEV 44104 2626 A3
Lucille Av
300 PNVL 44077 2145 E3
300 PNVL 44077 2146 A3
4100 SELD 44121 2498 B6
5800 BKPK 44142 2880 A1
15900 CLEV 44111 2752 B2
Lucille Dr
700 ELYR 44035 2875 D3
23700 NOSD 44070 2750 D6
Lucknow Av
14900 CLEV 44110 2372 B7
Lucky Bell Ln
16000 AbnT 44023 2763 A7
16000 AbnT 44073 2763 A7
16000 NbyT 44073 2763 A7
16400 AbnT 44023 2892 A2
Lucretia Ct
7600 MNTR 44060 2251 E2
Lucy Dr
9400 PMHT 44130 2882 D2
Lucy Ln
10 NCtT 44067 3017 E7
Lucydale Av
5000 NOSD 44070 2750 A7
Ludgate Rd
3500 SRHT 44120 2757 B2
Ludlow Rd
2800 CLEV 44120 2626 D7
2800 CLEV 44120 2627 A6
2900 SRHT 44120 2627 A6
Ludwin Dr
7400 SVHL 44131 3015 C1
Luelda Av
5400 PRMA 44129 2754 A7
6700 PRMA 44129 2753 E7
Luempert Memorial Dr
900 BWHT 44147 3014 E6
Lufkin Av
5500 CLEV 44127 2625 D7
Luikart Dr
10 EUCL 44123 2373 C1
Luke Av
11600 CLEV 44120 2626 D7
Lullaby Cir
400 AMHT 44001 2744 A7
Luman Ln
10100 TNBG 44087 3020 A4
Lunn Dr
- SGVL 44136 3145 E2
- SGVL 44136 3146 A2
Lunn Rd
19000 SGVL 44136 3146 C1
Luoem Tr
9100 MNTR 44060 2144 E2
Lupine Dr
7700 MNTR 44060 2143 D5
Lusandra Cir
27300 NOSD 44070 2749 E5
27300 NOSD 44070 2750 A5
Lusard St
10 PNVL 44077 2146 B1
Luther Av
4900 CLEV 44103 2625 D1
Luvison Dr
- SVHL 44131 2884 B2
Luxona Av
29300 WKLF 44092 2374 D4
Luxor Ln
100 AMHT 44001 2744 B7
Luxor Rd
1500 ECLE 44118 2497 A7
1500 ECLE 44118 2627 A1
Lydgate Dr
3900 NOSD 44070 2750 B5
Lydia Dr
2700 BWHT 44147 3014 C6
Lydia Rd
14000 ClbT 44028 3009 B7
Lydian Av
15100 CLEV 44111 2752 C2
Lydian Ct
3500 CLEV 44111 2752 C2
Lyle Av
- ELYR 44035 3006 D3
7000 PRMA 44134 2883 C6
Lyman Blvd
23100 BHWD 44122 2628 C5
23100 SRHT 44122 2628 C5
Lyman Cir
10 SRHT 44122 2628 C5
300 BNWK 44212 3147 A7
Lyman Rd
11600 CsTp 44026 2502 A3
Lyman's Ln
19300 SGVL 44136 3011 D7
Lyme Cir
400 BERA 44017 3010 E1
S Lyn Cir
1300 SELD 44121 2498 D7
Lynbrook Dr
7200 OKWD 44146 2887 E7
Lynch Av
10 PNVL 44077 2040 A6
Lynd Av
5000 LNHT 44124 2498 E5
5000 LNHT 44124 2499 A5
Lyndale Dr
10 CNFL 44022 2761 A5
Lyndale Rd
10 PnvT 44077 2041 B4
Lynden Dr
400 HDHT 44143 2499 D2
Lynden Ovl
10000 PMHT 44130 2882 C4
Lyndhurst Rd
1400 LNHT 44124 2499 C4
1400 LNHT 44124 2629 B1
Lyndway Dr
12100 VLVW 44125 2885 D6
Lyndway Rd
2100 BHWD 44122 2628 C3
Lynett Dr
6600 PRMA 44129 2882 E5
Lynford Cir
5800 HDHT 44143 2499 C5
Lynhaven Dr
28400 NOSD 44070 2878 D1
Lynn Dr
2900 WBHL 44092 2374 C7
9900 NRYN 44133 3013 B3
12700 CsTp 44026 2502 A7
12700 CsTp 44026 2632 A1
27100 OmsT 44138 2878 C6
Lynn Rd
400 BERA 44017 3011 A1
Lynne Dr
100 SDLK 44054 2617 A3
Lynnfield Rd
3400 SRHT 44122 2757 E1
Lynnhaven Rd
8600 PMHT 44130 2882 C4
Lynn Park Dr
1300 CVHT 44121 2497 E7
Lynnview Dr
300 SgHT 44067 3017 C7
Lynton Ln
31800 SLN 44139 3019 D1
Lynton Rd
18200 SRHT 44122 2627 D7
Lynway Av
8000 ODFL 44138 2879 B6
Lyon Ln
17700 SGVL 44136 3146 D4
Lyons Av
4100 WLBY 44094 2250 D5
Lyonswood Dr
400 HkyT 44233 3149 B7
Lyric Av
13800 CLEV 44111 2752 E3
Lytham Cir
30800 WTLK 44145 2749 A6
Lytle Rd
3500 SRHT 44122 2758 A2
19400 NRYN 44133 3148 A5
Lytton Av
14700 CLEV 44110 2372 B7

M

Ma St 1
- ManT 44255 3024 C7
Mable Av
100 SVHL 44131 3014 E1
100 SVHL 44131 3015 A1
Macauley Av
15200 CLEV 44110 2372 B7
Macbeth Av
22900 FWPK 44126 2751 A5
22900 NOSD 44070 2750 E5
22900 NOSD 44070 2751 A5
22900 NOSD 44126 2751 A5
Macbeth Dr
2900 RKRV 44116 2621 E7
Mace Ct
1100 CLEV 44109 2624 E7
Macedonia Rd
7300 OKWD 44146 3018 D2
Macedonia Commons Blvd
6400 MCDN 44056 3153 C1
Machinery Av
6700 CLEV 44103 2495 E6
Macintosh Dr
3000 WTLK 44145 2749 E3
Macintosh Ln
1100 BWHT 44147 3149 D4
Mack Ct
3700 CLEV 44109 2754 C2
Mack Dr
5600 LvpT 44280 3145 D7
Mackall Rd
4400 SELD 44121 2628 C3
Mackenzie Dr
5900 INDE 44131 3015 D1
Macomb Av
8600 CLEV 44105 2756 B4
Macon Av
9800 CLEV 44102 2623 C6
Macon Ct
2100 WTLK 44145 2749 B1
Maddock Rd
7300 NRDV 44039 2876 D4
Maddock St
2100 ShfT 44055 2745 E6
Madison Av
600 PnvT 44077 2040 D7
1200 PnvT 44077 2041 B7
1300 LORN 44053 2614 A7
1300 LORN 44053 2744 B1
1500 PryT 44077 2041 B7
4100 WLBY 44094 2250 D5
4900 SDLK 44054 2616 D3
5800 CLEV 44102 2624 A6
6400 NRDV 44039 2877 D3
6700 MadT 44057 1843 C7
6800 CLEV 44102 2623 D6
11700 LKWD 44102 2623 A6
11700 LKWD 44107 2623 A6
13300 LKWD 44107 2622 D6
Madison Ct
10 BHWD 44122 2629 A4
7800 CLEV 44103 2626 A3
Madison Ln
9400 NRYN 44133 3013 C5
Madison Rd
4300 MadT 44057 2044 B3
4300 MDSN 44057 2044 B3
5900 TpnT 44086 2150 B3
6700 TpnT 44086 2258 B3
8400 MtlT 44086 2258 B7
8600 MtlT 44064 2258 B7
8600 MtlT 44064 2383 B1
11000 HtbT 44064 2508 A1
11000 MtlT 44064 2508 A1
11400 HtbT 44046 2508 A4
12400 HtbT 44046 2638 A1
13200 HtbT 44062 2638 A1
13200 MdfT 44062 2638 A6
14300 MDFD 44062 2768 A2
14300 MdfT 44062 2768 A2
15900 MdfT 44062 2767 E7
16300 PkmT 44062 2767 E7
16300 PkmT 44062 2896 E4
Madison Rd SR-88
17700 PkmT 44062 2896 E6
Madison Rd SR-528
4300 MadT 44057 2044 B3
4300 MDSN 44057 2044 B3
5900 TpnT 44086 2150 B3
6700 TpnT 44086 2258 B3
8400 MtlT 44086 2258 B7
8600 MtlT 44064 2258 B7
8600 MtlT 44064 2383 B1
11000 HtbT 44064 2508 A1
11000 MtlT 44064 2508 A1
11400 HtbT 44046 2508 A4
12400 HtbT 44046 2638 A1
13200 HtbT 44062 2638 A1
13200 MdfT 44062 2638 A6
14300 MDFD 44062 2768 A2
14300 MdfT 44062 2768 A2
15900 MdfT 44062 2767 E7
16300 PkmT 44062 2767 E7
16300 PkmT 44062 2896 E4
Madison St
100 ELYR 44035 2874 E5
Magdala Dr
10800 PRMA 44130 2882 B1
Magee Av
2000 LKWD 44107 2623 A6
Maggie Ln
13700 LryT 44077 2148 B3
Magnet Av
5300 CLEV 44127 2625 D7
Magnolia Av
10 BDFD 44146 2886 E3
10 NHFD 44067 3018 B4
Magnolia Dr
- EUCL 44132 2373 E5
- EUCL 44143 2373 E5
10 CLEV 44110 2372 C6
500 PNVL 44077 2146 E2
1600 CLEV 44106 2626 C1
2000 RKRV 44116 2621 D6
3300 SVHL 44131 2884 B7
3600 BNWK 44212 3147 A6
3700 BNWK 44212 3146 D6
4300 PryT 44081 1940 C7
6000 MONT 44060 2143 C3
6100 MNTR 44060 2143 C3
6500 MadT 44057 1843 B7
9900 ODFL 44138 3010 A1
28300 NOSD 44070 2878 D3
Magnolia Ln
600 AbnT 44023 2892 B3
Magnolia Pkwy
4200 WTLK 44145 2749 C5

INDEX 30

Magnolia Wy

Cleveland Street Index

Mastick Rd

STREET Block City ZIP Map# Grid

Magnolia Wy
3300 BWHT 44147 3014 C7
Mahoning Av
100 CLEV 44113 2625 A5
Maiden Ln
8700 MNTR 44060 2038 D5
Maidstone Dr
4700 BKVL 44141 3016 D5
9700 CcdT 44060 2145 B2
Maidstone Ln
24300 BHWD 44122 2628 D4
Maile Av
1400 LKWD 44107 2622 A5
Maile Ct
10 MadT 44057 1941 B5
Main Av
1100 CLEV 44113 2624 C4
4900 NRDV 44039 2748 D7
5400 NRDV 44039 2877 D2
W Main Ct
1000 GNVA 44041 1944 A5
1000 GnvT 44041 1944 A5
Main Dr
10 AhtT 44001 2872 B2
Main St
- MNTR 44060 2144 E7
100 CRDN 44024 2380 A6
100 PNVL 44077 2040 D7
100 WFAR 44491 2898 D5
200 BERA 44017 3011 C1
300 EatT 44044 3141 E3
300 GFTN 44044 3141 E3
300 GFTN 44044 3142 A5
400 VMLN 44089 2740 E5
1100 GftT 44044 3142 A5
3300 PRRY 44081 2041 E2
3300 PRRY 44081 2042 B2
3300 PryT 44081 2041 E2
5800 BosT 44141 3152 C7
7400 GSML 44040 2630 D1
7600 ODFL 44138 2879 C5
10400 MNTU 44255 3159 C4
10900 ManT 44255 3159 C4
11700 NbyT 44065 2764 D1
11900 ManT 44255 3024 C7
17400 MDBH 44130 3012 A2
17400 SGVL 44130 3012 A2
17400 SGVL 44136 3012 A2
18000 MDBH 44130 3011 D1
18000 SGVL 44130 3011 D1
18000 SGVL 44136 3011 D1
18200 PkmT 44062 2896 E7
18200 PkmT 44234 2896 E7
Main St SR-44
100 CRDN 44024 2380 A6
10400 MNTU 44255 3159 C4
10900 ManT 44255 3159 C4
11900 ManT 44255 3024 C7
Main St SR-57
300 EatT 44044 3141 E3
300 GFTN 44044 3141 E3
300 GFTN 44044 3142 A5
1100 GftT 44044 3142 A5
Main St SR-60
600 VMLN 44089 2740 E5
Main St SR-88
100 WFAR 44491 2898 D5
18200 PkmT 44062 2896 E7
18200 PkmT 44234 2896 E7
Main St SR-252
7900 ODFL 44138 2879 C6
Main St SR-528
18200 PkmT 44062 2896 E7
18200 PkmT 44234 2896 E7
Main St US-6
100 CRDN 44024 2380 A6
E Main St
10 GNVA 44041 1944 C3
10 MDSN 44057 2044 C1
100 SAHT 44001 2872 C7
200 PNVL 44077 2040 B7
300 AhtT 44001 2872 C7
300 PNVL 44077 2146 C1
E Main St SR-84
10 MDSN 44057 2044 C1
E Main St SR-113
100 SAHT 44001 2872 C7
300 AhtT 44001 2872 C7
E Main St US-20
10 GNVA 44041 1944 C3
N Main St
10 CNFL 44022 2761 A5
10 OBLN 44074 3138 E2
100 AMHT 44001 2872 D1
200 WFAR 44491 2898 D5
300 CFIT 44022 2760 E4
300 CNFL 44022 2760 E4
500 AMHT 44001 2743 D7
1300 AMHT 44053 2743 D5
1300 LORN 44053 2743 D5
1300 LORN 44001 2743 D5
N Main St SR-58
10 OBLN 44074 3138 E2
S Main St
10 CNFL 44022 2761 A6
10 OBLN 44074 3138 E3
100 AMHT 44001 2872 D3
100 BbgT 44022 2761 A6
1700 AhtT 44001 2872 D3
S Main St SR-58
10 OBLN 44074 3138 E3
W Main St
10 GNVA 44041 1944 A4
10 MDSN 44057 2044 A1
100 SAHT 44001 2872 B7
400 SAHT 44001 3003 A1
700 MDSN 44057 2043 E2
1000 GnvT 44041 1944 A4
5900 GnvT 44041 1943 E4
W Main St SR-84
10 MDSN 44057 2044 A1
700 MDSN 44057 2043 E2
W Main St SR-113
100 SAHT 44001 2872 B7
400 SAHT 44001 3003 A1
W Main St SR-528
10 MDSN 44057 2044 B1
W Main St US-20
10 GNVA 44041 1944 A4
1000 GnvT 44041 1944 A4
5900 GnvT 44041 1943 E4
Maine Av
200 LORN 44052 2615 B5
2800 PryT 44077 2041 D4
2800 PryT 44081 2041 D4
Main Hill Dr
4600 SVHL 44131 3015 B1
Main Market Rd
12500 TroT 44021 2894 D5
12500 TroT 44234 2894 D5
13400 TroT 44021 2895 A5
13400 TroT 44234 2895 A5
14400 PkmT 44021 2896 A7
14400 PkmT 44021 3027 D1
14400 PkmT 44234 2896 A7
14400 PkmT 44234 3027 D1
14400 TroT 44021 2895 D6
14400 TroT 44021 2896 A7
14400 TroT 44234 2895 D6
14400 TroT 44234 2896 A7
16300 PkmT 44062 3027 D1
16300 PkmT 44231 3027 D1
16300 PkmT 44062 3028 A1
16300 PkmT 44231 3028 A1
16500 PkmT 44491 3028 A1
17000 PkmT 44231 3028 A1
Main Market Rd US-422
12500 TroT 44021 2894 D5
12500 TroT 44234 2894 D5
13400 TroT 44021 2895 A5
13400 TroT 44234 2895 A5
14400 PkmT 44021 2896 A7
14400 PkmT 44234 2896 A7
14400 PkmT 44234 3027 D1
14400 PkmT 44021 3027 D1
14400 TroT 44021 2895 D6
14400 TroT 44234 2895 D6
14400 TroT 44021 2896 A7
14400 TroT 44234 2896 A7
16300 PkmT 44062 3027 D1
16300 PkmT 44062 3028 A1
16300 PkmT 44231 3027 D1
16300 PkmT 44231 3028 A1
16500 PkmT 44491 3028 A1
17000 PkmT 44231 3028 A1
Majestic Pkwy
5300 BDHT 44146 2887 D1
Majestic Cove
- NCtT 44236 3153 E6
Majestic Oaks Tr
- BWHT 44147 3015 B3
Majesty Ln
10500 CcdT 44077 2253 E5
Major Dr
20200 EUCL 44117 2498 A2
Malabar Ct
7200 MNTR 44060 2143 B4
Malden Rd
2300 CLEV 44121 2497 E3
2400 CLEV 44121 2498 A3
Malibu Dr
7400 PRMA 44130 2882 A7
7400 PRMA 44130 3013 B1
Malin Dr
5800 BKPK 44142 2880 A1
W Mall Dr
1300 CLEV 44114 2624 E3
Mallard Av
26100 EUCL 44132 2373 E1
26800 EUCL 44132 2374 C1
Mallard Cir
- NRDV 44039 2877 D7
4400 WTLK 44145 2749 B5
18100 SGVL 44136 3146 E2
Mallard Ct
5800 MNTR 44060 2144 E2
18700 MDBH 44130 3011 E1
Mallard Dr
600 ELYR 44035 2874 E2
1500 MDHT 44124 2629 C1
6700 BKVL 44141 3150 D2
Mallard Bay
3900 PRRY 44081 2042 B1
Mallard Cove
1400 TNBG 44087 3019 B4
4200 AVON 44011 2748 C5
30500 WTLK 44145 2749 B5
Mallard Creek Run
- CrlT 44050 3140 C2
Mallard Pointe
9200 BbgT 44023 3022 E2
S Mallard Pond Cir
1300 BWHT 44147 3149 E5
Mallo Pl
6300 PMHT 44130 2882 C4
Malone Av
5200 SFLD 44054 2746 D4
Malvern Av
19200 RKRV 44116 2621 E6
Malvern Dr
400 PNVL 44077 2146 A3
3400 BNWK 44212 3147 B6
9000 PRMA 44129 2753 D7
9000 PRMA 44129 2882 D1
11100 NRYN 44133 3013 D5
Malvern Rd
19700 SRHT 44122 2627 E7
19700 SRHT 44122 2628 A6
Manassas Ovl
1100 PRMA 44134 2883 E7
Manatee Av
1300 MadT 44057 1843 C6
Manchester Av
3900 PRRY 44081 2042 C1
Manchester Ct
200 ELYR 44035 2874 B6
200 ELYR 44035 3005 B1
300 RDHT 44143 2498 E1
Manchester Dr
12700 CsTp 44026 2501 C7
12800 CsTp 44026 2631 C1
Manchester Ln
31000 BYVL 44140 2619 A3
Manchester Rd
2800 SRHT 44122 2627 E6
6000 PRMA 44129 2882 E4
Manchester St
5100 NRDV 44039 2748 A7
Mandalay Av
15700 CLEV 44110 2497 C3
Mandalay Dr
6200 PMHT 44130 2882 A4
Manderly Ln
10 MDHL 44022 2760 C4
Mangrove Ln
26700 ODFL 44138 3010 A1
Manhasset Dr
30300 BYVL 44140 2619 B3
Manhattan Av
1400 ECLE 44112 2497 A5
Manhattan Av
7300 PRMA 44129 2753 D7
Manhattan Dr
5500 LORN 44053 2743 C6
Manhattan Pkwy
300 PnvT 44077 2041 B6
Mann Av
13300 ECLE 44112 2497 A4
Mannering Dr
600 ETLK 44095 2249 E3
Mannering Rd
1800 CLEV 44112 2497 C3
Mannheim Ct
7500 HDSN 44236 3154 C6
Manning Cir
5300 NRDV 44039 2748 A7
Manning Dr
10 BERA 44017 3011 B2
Manoa Av
10000 BKLN 44144 2753 C4
Manor Av
9000 CLEV 44104 2626 B6
Manor Ct
8900 MCDN 44056 3018 B5
Manor Dr
6900 EyrT 44035 2874 B2
7400 MONT 44060 2143 D3
13000 MsnT 44024 2635 A2
Manorbrook Dr
100 SRSL 44073 2762 A5
500 SRSL 44073 2761 E5
Manorford Dr
7800 PRMA 44129 2882 C4
8700 PMHT 44130 2882 C4
Manor Park Av
1200 LKWD 44107 2622 D4
Manry Ct
7500 MNTR 44060 2143 D5
Mansfield Av
8000 CLEV 44105 2756 A1
Mansfield Ct
10 CcdT 44060 2145 B2
Mansfield St
800 SDLK 44054 2616 A4
Mansion Blvd
8400 MNTR 44060 2144 B5
Mantle Rd
10 PnvT 44077 2040 C5
Mantle Road Ext
10 PnvT 44077 2040 C6
Mantua Center Rd
10800 ManT 44255 3159 A5
10800 MNTU 44255 3159 A5
11700 ManT 44255 3159 A1
11800 ManT 44255 3024 A7
12800 AbnT 44255 3024 A4
Manufacturing Rd
4500 CLEV 44135 2752 B6
Maple Av
- EUCL 44132 2374 A2
- HIHL 44122 2758 C4
- NRDV 44039 2877 D3
10 NHFD 44067 3018 A4
100 CRDN 44024 2380 A5
300 AMHT 44001 2872 D2
300 BERA 44017 2880 C6
300 SDLK 44054 2616 D3
1000 MadT 44057 1843 E5
10600 MNTU 44255 3159 C6
12400 CLEV 44108 2496 E3
14000 MPHT 44137 2757 A7
14800 MDFD 44062 2767 C2
E Maple Av
4600 GnvT 44041 1944 E1
W Maple Av
5300 GnvT 44041 1943 E1
5300 GnvT 44041 1944 A1
6300 GnvT 44041 1943 C1
6300 GnvT 44057 1943 C1
Maple Cir
13800 SGVL 44136 3147 D4
Maple Ct
10 OmsT 44138 2879 C4
500 MCDN 44056 3153 C2
Maple Dr
- BtnT 44021 2635 E6
10 OmsT 44138 2879 B4
1000 PRMA 44134 2883 E7
1300 LORN 44052 2615 D6
2500 TNBG 44087 3154 E1
8200 CsTp 44026 2502 A6
11100 NbyT 44065 2634 C7
17000 BbgT 44023 2891 A3
22500 FWPK 44126 2751 A6
26600 WTLK 44145 2750 A2
30400 BYVL 44140 2619 B4
33900 SLN 44139 2889 A3
36200 NRDV 44039 2876 E4
36200 NRDV 44039 2877 A4
Maple Ln
10 AURA 44202 3156 E1
10 CNFL 44022 2760 E6
10 CNFL 44022 2761 A6
4600 NRYN 44133 3014 A6
Maple Rd
1400 CVHT 44121 2497 E7
1500 CVHT 44121 2627 E1
1600 CVHT 44118 2627 E1
4100 LORN 44055 2745 C5
Maple St
- AhtT 44001 2872 B3
10 CLEV 44110 2372 C5
10 OBLN 44074 3138 E1
100 SAHT 44001 2872 A7
200 NRsT 44074 3138 E1
300 SAHT 44001 3003 A1
400 VMLN 44089 2741 A4
500 BDHT 44146 2758 D7
1500 WKLF 44092 2374 B3
4100 PRRY 44081 2042 B3
4400 PryT 44081 2042 C4
4600 WLBY 44094 2250 D7
7000 MNTR 44060 2144 B7
7200 MNTR 44060 2252 B1
7600 KTLD 44094 2251 D7
20900 SGVL 44136 3011 B3
S Maple St
300 ELYR 44035 3006 A2
Mapleboro Av
16800 MPHT 44137 2886 C1
Maple Branch Tr
10000 SGVL 44136 3011 A4
Maplebrook Dr
10 PnvT 44077 2041 A7
Maple Brook Tr
13100 SGVL 44136 3012 D4
Maple Cliff Dr
1000 LKWD 44107 2622 B3
Maplecliff Dr
10 AVLK 44012 2488 B7
5900 PMHT 44130 2882 C2
Maplecliff Rd
17900 CLEV 44119 2372 D4
Maple Creek Dr
500 AMHT 44001 2872 B3
Maplecrest Av
2800 PRMA 44134 2883 B3
6400 PMHT 44130 2882 B4
Maplecrest Rd
3600 WDMR 44122 2759 A2
Mapledale Av
10 BDFD 44146 2886 E4
2600 CLEV 44109 2754 B2
Mapledale Rd
1500 WKLF 44092 2249 B4
1500 WKLF 44092 2374 E1
1500 WKLF 44094 2249 B4
7900 MNTR 44060 2143 E4
Maple Glen Dr
8600 CdnT 44024 2254 E6
Maplegrove
- MNTR 44060 2144 E6
Maplegrove Av
4500 NRYN 44133 3014 B3
Maple Grove Dr
400 SDLK 44054 2615 E3
400 SDLK 44054 2616 A3
7500 CsTp 44026 2631 D3
Maplegrove Dr
1600 TNBG 44087 3019 B7
Maplegrove Rd
1400 SELD 44121 2498 B7
1400 SELD 44121 2628 B1
34600 WLBY 44094 2375 B3
35400 WBHL 44094 2375 B3
Maple Heights Blvd
15900 MPHT 44137 2886 B1
19200 MPHT 44137 2757 E7
20000 MPHT 44137 2758 A7
Maple Hill Dr
100 SRSL 44073 2762 D6
4000 SVHL 44131 3015 B2
Maplehurst Rd
6500 NOSD 44070 2878 D3
Maplelane Dr
10 GNVA 44041 1944 C6
Maplelawn Dr
100 BERA 44017 3011 C3
Maple Leaf Dr
12000 GDHT 44125 2885 D2
13500 GDHT 44125 2886 A2
Maple Leaf Ln
4800 INDE 44131 2884 C5
Maple Leap Ter
12000 CsTp 44026 2503 A5
Maple Park Dr
15200 MPHT 44137 2886 B3
Mapleridge Blvd
33700 AVON 44011 2748 C4
Mapleridge Dr
11500 NRYN 44133 3013 D6
Maple Ridge Rd
22900 NOSD 44070 2751 A4
23700 NOSD 44070 2750 D3
24500 NOSD 44145 2750 D3
24500 WTLK 44070 2750 D3
24500 WTLK 44145 2750 D3
Mapleridge Rd
10 SRSL 44073 2761 C6
Maplerow Av
12500 GDHT 44105 2756 E4
13600 GDHT 44105 2757 A4
14000 CLEV 44105 2757 A4
14000 CLEV 44128 2757 A4
Mapleside Rd
2300 CLEV 44104 2626 C4
Maple Springs Dr
5200 SRSL 44073 2762 A6
Mapleton Av
10 BDFD 44146 2886 D4
Mapleview Av
300 SDLK 44054 2616 E3
Maple View Dr
4400 BhmT 44089 2741 A7
4400 VMLN 44089 2741 A7
Mapleview Dr
10 SVHL 44131 2883 E5
10 SVHL 44131 2884 A5
Mapleview Ln
2400 WBHL 44094 2375 C3
3100 AVON 44011 2747 E3
Mapleview Rd
400 MCDN 44056 3018 D4
Mapleway Dr
7500 ODFL 44138 2879 B5
Maplewood Av
400 SDLK 44054 2616 C4
500 BNWK 44212 3147 C7
800 PnvT 44077 2040 C3
15300 MPHT 44137 2886 B2
18500 CLEV 44135 2751 E6
21000 RKRV 44116 2621 C5
24100 EUCL 44123 2373 D2
Maplewood Cir
- AVLK 44012 2617 E3
5300 SFLD 44054 2746 E1
Maplewood Ct
200 PNVL 44077 2146 A2
16200 MPHT 44137 2886 C2
Maplewood Dr
400 WLWK 44095 2249 B7
14600 BtnT 44021 2766 E5
Maplewood Ln
18800 BbgT 44023 3022 A2
Maplewood Rd
2100 CVHT 44118 2627 B3
5900 MDHT 44124 2499 C7
5900 MONT 44060 2143 B3
6100 MNTR 44060 2143 B3
6500 MDHT 44124 2500 A7
6700 PMHT 44130 2881 E6
7100 PRMA 44130 2881 E6
11600 MsnT 44024 2504 C3
Marah Av
9300 CLEV 44104 2626 B7
Marble Av
7600 CLEV 44105 2756 A2
Marble Ln
5600 WLBY 44094 2375 C2
Marblehead Dr
7200 HDSN 44236 3154 E7
N Marblehead Rd
7400 HDSN 44236 3154 E7
Marbrook Ln
500 AVLK 44012 2618 D4
Marcella Rd
17800 CLEV 44119 2372 D6
Marcelline Ct
7100 CHHT 44125 2755 E6
Marchmont Ct
400 BNWK 44212 3146 D7
Marchmont Rd
19600 SRHT 44122 2627 E7
19800 SRHT 44122 2628 A7
Marcie Dr
4600 CLEV 44109 2754 E5
4700 CLEV 44109 2755 A6
Marcie Ln
27200 NOSD 44070 2750 A5
Marcum Blvd
2900 WBHL 44092 2375 A7
33800 WBHL 44094 2375 A7
Marcus Dr
4300 SFLD 44054 2616 B7
Marda Dr
2500 PRMA 44134 2883 C6
Mardale Av
5200 BDHT 44146 2887 B1
Marden Dr
8400 RslT 44072 2762 A1
Mardon Ct
10400 CcdT 44077 2145 E5
Mardon Dr
6200 CcdT 44077 2145 E4
6200 PnvT 44077 2145 E4
Mardun Ct
100 CrlT 44035 3006 C3
Marengo Dr
700 BNHT 44131 2755 B7
Margaret Av
15900 LKWD 44107 2622 B6
Margaret Dr
- NRYN 44133 3013 D7
Margaretta Dr
2800 WTLK 44145 2750 B3
Margate Av
15600 CLEV 44135 2752 C5
N Marginal Dr
- CLEV 44102 2623 D7
- LKWD 44107 2622 B6
30500 WLWK 44092 2249 D7
30500 WLWK 44095 2249 D7
31900 ETLK 44095 2249 D7
S Marginal Dr
- CLEV 44111 2622 B7
- CLEV 44102 2623 D7
- CLEV 44111 2623 D7
- LKWD 44111 2622 B7
- LKWD 44107 2622 D7
N Marginal Rd
900 CLEV 44114 2624 E1
1300 CLEV 44114 2495 D6
1300 CLEV 44114 2625 A1
5500 CLEV 44103 2495 D6
7300 CLEV 44103 2496 A4
S Marginal Rd
900 CLEV 44114 2624 E2
1100 CLEV 44114 2625 A1
2400 CLEV 44114 2495 C6
5400 CLEV 44103 2495 C6
Marguerite Av
12000 GDHT 44125 2756 D6
Maria Av
100 BDFD 44146 2886 D3
Maria Ln
24100 NOSD 44070 2750 D4
Marian Cir
21800 FWPK 44126 2751 B5
Marian Dr
5200 LNHT 44124 2499 A6
Marian Ln
100 BERA 44017 2880 A7
20200 RKRV 44116 2621 D7
Marian Rd
- EatT 44028 3008 D4
Mariana Dr
6200 PMHT 44130 2882 A4
Marianna Blvd
8100 BWHT 44147 3015 C4
Marie Av
3100 LORN 44052 2744 D3
Marietta Av
1600 PRMA 44134 2883 E1
9800 CLEV 44102 2623 C6
Marietta Dr
900 FTHR 44077 2039 D5
900 PNVL 44077 2145 E3
3500 LORN 44055 2745 A3
Marigold Blvd
9400 NRDV 44039 3008 D1
Marigold Rd
4600 MNTR 44060 2038 E6
Marilyn Av
10 MadT 44057 1844 A6
Marilyn Ln
100 ETLK 44095 2142 C7
Marilyn Rd
12900 CsTp 44026 2632 A2
Marina Dr
4300 VMLN 44089 2741 B7
Marine Pkwy
5500 MONT 44060 2143 E2
6000 MNTR 44060 2143 E2
Marine St
600 FTHR 44077 2039 C4
Mariner Dr
13000 NRYN 44133 3147 E4
Mariners Ct
32600 AVLK 44012 2618 A3
Mariners Wy
200 SDLK 44054 2615 D4
Marion Av
200 PNVL 44077 2146 B2
Marion Ct
500 RKRV 44116 2621 E5
Marion Dr
200 BDFD 44146 2887 A3
7200 MNTR 44060 2144 C7
7200 MNTR 44060 2252 C1
Marion Pkwy
2800 BNWK 44212 3147 D7
Marion Rd
23000 NOSD 44070 2750 E3
23000 NOSD 44070 2751 A2
Marion St
800 SDLK 44054 2616 A4
5300 MPHT 44137 2886 B1
Marioncliff Dr
2600 PRMA 44134 2883 C2
Maritime Ct
31700 AVLK 44012 2619 A2
Marjory Dr
8600 MNTR 44060 2144 C2
Mark Av
3900 RKRV 44116 2751 D2
Mark Ct
10 OmsT 44138 2879 C4
4700 NRDV 44039 2877 B2
30400 WKLF 44092 2374 E1
Mark Dr
1900 LORN 44052 2744 B2
3400 BWHT 44147 3015 B4
6000 BDHT 44146 2887 E4
Mark Ter
4100 CLEV 44128 2757 C3
Markal Dr
7200 MDBH 44130 2881 A7
Markbarry Av
27200 EUCL 44132 2374 A1
Markell Rd
7200 WTHL 44094 2251 C7
7200 WTHL 44094 2376 B1
7400 WLBY 44094 2251 C7
7500 KTLD 44094 2251 C7
Market Av
- CLEV 44113 2624 D5
Market Pl
9100 BWHT 44147 3015 B7
Market Pl W
9100 BWHT 44147 3015 B7
Market St
8400 MNTR 44060 2144 B5
Marko Ln
- BNHT 44131 2755 A7
7100 PRMA 44134 2883 C7
Marks Rd
10 BHIT 44212 3145 E6
10 LvpT 44212 3145 E6
10 LvpT 44280 3145 E6
N Marks Rd
8000 BERA 44017 3010 E3
8000 ClbT 44017 3010 E3
8000 ClbT 44028 3010 E3
8100 ClbT 44136 3010 E3
8100 SGVL 44136 3010 E3
S Marks Rd
14100 ClbT 44028 3010 E7
14100 ClbT 44028 3145 E1
14100 ClbT 44136 3010 E7
14100 ClbT 44136 3145 E1
14100 SGVL 44136 3010 E7
14100 SGVL 44136 3145 E1
Markwood Dr
8300 MNTR 44060 2144 B2
Marlboro Av
5300 LORN 44053 2743 C5
Marlboro Ct
- MAYF 44143 2500 A5
Marlboro Rd
2400 CVHT 44118 2627 B4
Marlborough
- VMLN 44089 2741 E5
Marlborough Av
7300 PRMA 44129 2753 E7
Marlborough Rd
100 VMLN 44089 2741 E4
Marlee Ct
200 BHIT 44212 3146 C7
Marleen Dr
22100 FWPK 44126 2751 A5
Marlene Av
15200 CLEV 44135 2752 C6
Marlin Dr
- BKPK 44142 2880 A1
13700 HmbT 44024 2381 A1
Marlindale Rd
1900 CVHT 44118 2627 D3
Marlo Dr
6100 CcdT 44077 2146 A3
Marloes Av
1800 ECLE 44112 2497 B6
Marlowe Av
1100 LKWD 44107 2622 D4
10300 CLEV 44108 2496 C4
Marlys Dr
22400 RKRV 44116 2751 A2
Marmore Av
2800 PRMA 44134 2754 C7
Marne Av
11700 CLEV 44111 2753 A2
Marnell Av
5700 MDHT 44124 2629 C1
Marnell Dr
- GnvT 44041 1943 E1
Maroy Dr
100 SAHT 44001 2872 C6
Marquardt Av
500 CLEV 44113 2625 A6
Marquette Blvd
4200 NOSD 44070 2749 E5
Marquette Rd
1000 CLEV 44114 2495 D6
1300 CLEV 44103 2495 D6
Marquis Av
16200 CLEV 44111 2752 B1
Marra Dr
5800 BDHT 44146 2887 D3
Mars Av
1400 LKWD 44107 2622 C5
Mars Dr
3800 BNWK 44212 3146 E7
3800 BNWK 44212 3147 A7
Marsdon Dr
25100 EUCL 44132 2373 D2
Marseilles Av
100 ELYR 44035 2875 D5
Marsh Ln
1800 PnvT 44077 2041 A3
Marsh Pl
6000 NRDV 44039 2877 E2
Marsh Wy
- BHIT 44212 3146 C7
- BNWK 44212 3146 C7
Marshall Av
2300 LORN 44052 2744 B2
3500 LORN 44053 2744 B4
8800 CLEV 44104 2626 B7
Marshall Dr
800 PNVL 44077 2146 C3
Marshfield Blvd
1900 WTLK 44145 2749 A1
Marshfield Rd
1900 MDHT 44124 2629 E3
Marsh Harbor Ct
17600 NRYN 44133 3148 B3
Marsh Hawk Run
9400 CsTp 44026 2632 E3
9400 CsTp 44026 2633 A3
Marsol Rd
6100 MDHT 44124 2629 D1
6500 MDHT 44124 2630 A1
Marston Av
12300 CLEV 44105 2756 E3
13400 CLEV 44105 2757 A3
Martha Av
10 GnvT 44041 1944 E3
10 MadT 44057 1844 A6
Martha Ct
100 ELYR 44035 2874 A7
Martha Dr
11400 CrlT 44044 3006 C5
Martha Rd
16900 CLEV 44135 2752 B5
Martin Av
4300 CLEV 44127 2625 C6
5500 VMLN 44089 2740 E6
E Martin Av
100 AMHT 44001 2872 D1
W Martin Av
100 AMHT 44001 2872 B1
Martin Dr
- LORN 44053 2743 D2
4200 NOSD 44070 2749 D6
12900 PRMA 44130 3012 E1
13600 GDHT 44125 2886 A3
15300 NRYN 44133 3148 B2
Martin Rd
8800 KTLD 44094 2377 D1
34900 WBHL 44094 2375 A6
Martingale Ct
10 BTVL 44022 2889 E1
Martingale Dr
- CsTp 44026 2501 B5
Martingale Ln
8300 RslT 44072 2762 A1
Martinique Dr
9600 CcdT 44060 2253 B1
Martin Luther King Jr Blvd
- CLEV 44105 2756 D4
4400 GDHT 44105 2756 D4
Martin Luther King Jr Ct
- HIHL 44122 2758 C4
Martin Luther King Jr Dr
- CLEV 44104 2626 C5
- CLEV 44106 2496 B6
- CLEV 44106 2626 B1
- CLEV 44108 2496 B6
- CVHT 44106 2626 D3
2400 CLEV 44104 2626 D3
2400 CLEV 44120 2626 D3
3300 CLEV 44104 2756 D1
3500 CLEV 44105 2756 D1
10900 CLEV 44106 2626 D3
Martins Ln
18100 SGVL 44136 3146 D4
Martins Wy
21600 RKRV 44116 2751 B2
Marview Dr
1300 WTLK 44145 2620 B7
Marvin Av
- GNVA 44041 1944 B5
2500 CLEV 44109 2754 C1
Marvin Rd
19100 WVHT 44128 2757 E6
19800 WVHT 44128 2758 A6
Marvis Dr
500 BYVL 44140 2619 A5
Marwell Blvd
1700 TwbT 44236 3154 E5
Marwood Av
19400 CLEV 44135 2751 E4
Marwyck Dr
10 NCtT 44067 3153 A3
200 NCtT 44067 3152 E3
Marwyck Place Ln
100 NCtT 44067 3153 B3
Mary Ct
- CLEV 44113 2625 A6
Mary Ln
7600 MNTR 44060 2252 A2
N Mary Ln
2100 SVHL 44131 2884 B6
S Mary Ln
2100 SVHL 44131 2884 B7
Mary Ann Dr
13800 GDHT 44125 2757 A7
Marydale Dr
11900 AbnT 44021 2764 E7
Mary Dale St
35600 WLBY 44094 2375 B1
Marygate Dr
500 BYVL 44140 2619 C5
Mary Kay Cir
4100 NOSD 44070 2749 E5
Maryland Av
1300 LORN 44052 2615 B6
3400 WDMR 44122 2759 A1
7600 CLEV 44105 2756 A4
10400 RMDV 44202 3020 E4
Marymac Dr
11800 SgHT 44067 3017 C3
E Mason Rd
11300 FrnT 44089 2869 B6
11300 FrnT 44889 2869 B6
12600 VmnT 44089 2869 B6
12600 VmnT 44889 2869 B6
16300 BhmT 44089 2870 A5
16300 VmnT 44089 2870 A5
Masonic Al
10 CNFL 44022 2761 A5
Massachusetts Av
200 ELYR 44035 3006 A3
1400 LORN 44052 2615 B5
Massie Av
10500 CLEV 44108 2496 C6
Masters Ln
- AVLK 44012 2618 C3
Mastick Rd
20000 FWPK 44126 2751 C5
22900 NOSD 44126 2751 A6
23000 NOSD 44070 2750 E7

INDEX 31

Mastick Rd

Cleveland Street Index

Middlepost Ln

STREET
Block City ZIP Map# Grid

Mastick Rd
23000 NOSD 44070 2751 A6
Mataire Ln
10100 SGVL 44136 3012 B4
Mather Ln
100 BTNH 44108 2496 E2
45000 HGVL 44073 2631 A7
W Mather Ln
10 BTNH 44108 2496 D2
Mather's Wy
2700 TNBG 44087 3020 B3
Matherson Av
11700 CLEV 44135 2753 A4
Mathews Av
1200 LKWD 44107 2622 A5
Mathews Cor
10 OmsT 44138 2879 A4
Mathews St
100 PNVL 44077 2146 A1
Matilda Av
11200 CLEV 44105 2756 D2
Matoma Blvd
35700 ETLK 44095 2142 B7
Mats Rd
- MNTU 44255 3159 B6
Matson Rd
6100 HpfT 44041 2151 D2
6100 TmbT 44041 2151 D2
Matthew Ct
9100 MNTR 44060 2144 E6
Maud St
800 CLEV 44103 2496 A6
Maureen Dr
5700 SVHL 44131 2884 B2
Maurer Dr
3300 LORN 44053 2744 C3
Maurice Av
5500 CLEV 44127 2625 D6
Maury Av
8700 CLEV 44108 2496 B5
Mavec Av
24300 EUCL 44123 2373 D4
Mavreen Dr
15700 MDBH 44130 2881 B6
Maxim Ct
8300 CLEV 44102 2623 E6
Maxwell Av
13600 CLEV 44110 2497 A2
Maxwell Dr
6100 MadT 44057 1941 E1
6200 MadT 44057 1942 A1
May Av
10 NHFD 44067 3017 E4
10 NHFD 44067 3018 A4
3700 CLEV 44105 2755 C1
May Ct
100 CNFL 44022 2761 A6
18400 AbnT 44023 3024 A1
May St
33200 NRDV 44039 2748 D7
Mayapple Cir
6800 SLN 44139 2889 B7
Mayapple Dr
2000 PnvT 44077 2041 A3
Mayapple Pl
10200 BWHT 44147 3149 E4
Maybelle Dr
23100 WTLK 44145 2620 E7
23100 WTLK 44145 2621 A7
Mayberry Av
5900 MDHT 44124 2629 C1
Mayberry Dr
7200 PRMA 44130 2882 C7
Maydale Av
21500 EUCL 44123 2373 B3
Maydor Ln
1300 SELD 44121 2498 D7
Mayfair Av
13800 ECLE 44112 2497 A5
Mayfair Blvd
1500 MDHT 44124 2499 C4
1600 MDHT 44124 2629 C1
Mayfair Dr
1000 SVHL 44131 2884 A2
Mayfair Ln
19100 WVHT 44128 2757 E4
Mayfield Ct
600 AMHT 44001 2872 C1
Mayfield Rd
- MDHT 44124 2629 E1
1500 MDHT 44124 2499 D7
2400 CVHT 44106 2626 D2
2400 CVHT 44106 2627 A2
2700 CVHT 44118 2627 A2
3200 CVHT 44118 2497 D7
3400 CVHT 44121 2497 D7
3800 CVHT 44121 2498 A7
3900 SELD 44121 2498 A7
4600 LNHT 44121 2498 E7
4600 LNHT 44124 2498 E7
5000 LNHT 44124 2499 A7
5700 MDHT 44124 2499 A7
6500 GSML 44040 2500 A7
6500 MDHT 44124 2500 A7
6800 GSML 44040 2500 E6
7000 CsTp 44026 2501 D7
7700 GSML 44040 2501 A7
8200 CsTp 44026 2502 A7
9500 CsTp 44026 2503 B7
9700 MsnT 44026 2503 B7
10100 MsnT 44024 2503 B7
10800 MsnT 44024 2504 C6
11400 CLEV 44106 2626 D2
11800 MsnT 44024 2505 C6
12400 ClrT 44024 2505 C6
13400 ClrT 44024 2506 A6
13900 ClrT 44021 2506 A6
14900 ClrT 44021 2507 C6
14900 ClrT 44024 2507 C6
15100 HtbT 44021 2507 C6
15100 HtbT 44024 2507 C6
15500 HtbT 44046 2507 C6
16000 HtbT 44046 2508 B6
17600 HtbT 44046 2509 A6
17700 WndT 44046 2509 A6
Mayfield Rd US-322
2400 CVHT 44106 2626 D2
2400 CVHT 44106 2627 A2
2700 CVHT 44118 2627 A2
3200 CVHT 44118 2497 D7
3400 CVHT 44121 2497 D7
3800 CVHT 44121 2498 A7
3900 SELD 44121 2498 A7
4600 LNHT 44121 2498 E7
4600 LNHT 44124 2498 E7

Mayfield Rd US-322
5000 LNHT 44124 2499 A7
5700 MDHT 44124 2499 A7
6500 GSML 44040 2500 A7
6500 MDHT 44124 2500 A7
6800 GSML 44040 2500 E6
7000 CsTp 44026 2501 D7
7700 GSML 44040 2501 A7
8200 CsTp 44026 2502 A7
9500 CsTp 44026 2503 B7
9700 MsnT 44026 2503 B7
10100 MsnT 44024 2503 B7
10800 MsnT 44024 2504 C6
11400 CLEV 44106 2626 D2
11800 MsnT 44024 2505 C6
12400 ClrT 44024 2505 C6
13400 ClrT 44024 2506 A6
13900 ClrT 44021 2506 A6
14900 ClrT 44021 2507 C6
14900 ClrT 44024 2507 C6
15100 HtbT 44021 2507 C6
15100 HtbT 44024 2507 C6
15500 HtbT 44046 2507 C6
16000 HtbT 44046 2508 B6
17600 HtbT 44046 2509 A6
17700 WndT 44046 2509 A6
Mayfield St
- NCtT 44067 3153 C5
2100 ShfT 44055 2745 E5
2200 ShfT 44055 2746 A5
Mayfield Park Blvd
- MDHT 44124 2499 D3
Mayfield Ridge Rd
1100 MDHT 44124 2499 C7
Mayflower Av
5900 MDHT 44124 2629 C1
N Mayflower Dr
5700 LORN 44053 2743 C5
S Mayflower Dr
6100 LORN 44053 2743 C6
Mayflower Ln
3700 SELD 44118 2627 E3
Mayfriars Dr
37200 WBHL 44094 2375 D3
Mayland Av
5900 MDHT 44124 2629 C1
Maynard Av
1700 CLEV 44109 2754 D6
Maynard Rd
3200 SRHT 44122 2627 E7
Maysday Av
7100 PRMA 44129 2753 E7
Mayview Av
1200 CLEV 44109 2754 D4
Mayview Ln
7200 CsTp 44026 2501 B7
Mayview Rd
5000 LNHT 44124 2498 E7
5000 LNHT 44124 2499 A7
Mayville Av
5100 MPHT 44137 2757 E7
5300 MPHT 44137 2886 E1
Maywood Av
8800 CLEV 44102 2753 D1
Maywood Rd
1400 SELD 44121 2498 D7
1500 SELD 44121 2628 C1
Mazepa Tr
100 PRMA 44134 2883 E5
McAfee Dr
33900 SLN 44139 2889 A1
McAlpin Ct
1000 GFTN 44044 3142 A5
McArthur Dr
7300 NRDV 44039 2877 B4
McBride Av
4900 CLEV 44127 2625 C7
McCall Rd
15600 NsnT 44231 3027 C2
15600 PkmT 44231 3027 C2
15900 PkmT 44234 3027 C2
McCall Rd SR-88
15600 NsnT 44231 3027 C2
15600 PkmT 44231 3027 C2
15900 PkmT 44234 3027 C2
McCann St
22700 WVHT 44128 2758 C5
McCarty Ct
6500 ELYR 44035 2874 E1
McCauley Rd
21900 SRHT 44122 2628 B6
McCausland Dr
1500 TwbT 44236 3154 D5
McClaren Ln
2000 BWHT 44147 3149 D5
McCracken Blvd
8800 GDHT 44125 2756 B7
McCracken Rd
- GDHT 44137 2757 B6
- MPHT 44125 2757 B6
10800 GDHT 44125 2756 D7
13000 GDHT 44125 2757 B6
15400 GDHT 44128 2757 B6
15400 MPHT 44128 2757 B6
16300 CLEV 44128 2757 B6
16400 MPHT 44137 2757 B6
17400 WVHT 44128 2757 C6
19800 MPHT 44128 2758 A6
19800 MPHT 44137 2758 A6
19800 WVHT 44128 2758 A6
McCreary Rd
7500 SVHL 44131 3015 B2
7900 BWHT 44147 3015 B2
McCurdy St
2700 CLEV 44104 2626 B5
McDonald St
- AMHT 44001 2872 B3
McDowell Dr
37900 SLN 44139 2889 D7
McElhatten Av
13600 BTNH 44110 2497 A1
13600 CLEV 44110 2497 A1
McFarland Rd
4400 SELD 44121 2498 C5
McGhee Rd
- TwbT 44236 3155 B5
McGowan Av
12300 CLEV 44135 2753 A5
McGregor Av
4200 NBGH 44105 2755 C3
McIntosh Ln
300 AMHT 44001 2743 B7
400 AMHT 44001 2872 B1
McKenzie Rd
5400 NOSD 44070 2878 D2

McKenzie Rd
6700 OmsT 44138 2878 D4
McKinley Av
2000 LKWD 44107 2622 B6
2000 ShfT 44055 2745 E6
2200 LKWD 44111 2622 B7
McKinley Dr
9000 NHFD 44067 3017 E4
McKinley St
600 BDFD 44146 2887 B4
2700 LORN 44052 2615 C5
5500 NRDV 44039 2748 D7
5500 NRDV 44039 2877 D1
7400 MNTR 44060 2143 C7
McKinney Av
4100 WLBY 44094 2250 D5
McLean Ct
2500 CLEV 44113 2624 C5
McLeary Ct
100 SgHT 44067 3017 E4
McLellan Dr
7300 WNHL 44146 3017 E1
McMackin Rd
2000 MadT 44057 1941 B3
McMaster Ct
400 SgHT 44067 3017 D4
McNeil Dr
400 SgHT 44067 3152 D3
McPherson Cir
500 SgHT 44067 3017 D4
McRoberts Av
700 AURA 44202 3021 C4
McShu Ln
7300 HDSN 44236 3155 A7
Mead Av
4900 CLEV 44127 2625 D7
Mead Ct
- CLEV 44127 2625 D6
Meade Hollow Rd
5700 HgvT 44099 2384 E7
Meadow Cir
100 BERA 44017 3011 A1
Meadow Dr
10 BERA 44017 3011 B1
100 ELYR 44035 2875 D1
10000 CdnT 44024 2379 D4
N Meadow Dr
6900 CcdT 44077 2145 C7
S Meadow Dr
7000 CcdT 44077 2145 D7
7200 CcdT 44077 2253 D1
Meadow Ln
- SgHT 44067 3018 A5
10 NHFD 44067 3018 A5
100 SLN 44139 2889 A1
300 CNFL 44022 2760 E7
400 PNVL 44077 2146 B1
2900 WTLK 44145 2750 C3
3200 NRYN 44133 3014 C5
4300 LORN 44055 2746 A4
5500 BDHT 44146 2887 D2
6700 MDBH 44130 2881 B5
7100 PRMA 44134 2883 D7
7400 PRMA 44134 3014 C1
9100 BKVL 44141 3016 B4
10800 AbnT 44023 2892 E3
10900 AbnT 44023 2893 A3
13200 VmnT 44089 2869 B2
18000 SGVL 44136 3011 E6
24400 ODFL 44138 2879 D7
24500 WTLK 44070 2750 C3
33900 HGVL 44022 2760 B1
37000 AVON 44011 2747 D4
E Meadow Ln
3900 ORNG 44122 2759 C3
S Meadow Ln
4400 CLEV 44109 2754 E4
W Meadow Ln
3900 ORNG 44122 2759 C3
Meadow St
5300 MPHT 44137 2886 A1
29500 WKLF 44092 2374 C2
Meadow Tr
10700 SGVL 44136 3010 E4
Meadoway Dr
2600 BHWD 44122 2628 E5
Meadowbrook Av
6000 CLEV 44144 2754 A3
6300 CLEV 44144 2753 E3
7400 BKLN 44144 2753 E3
Meadowbrook Blvd
2800 CVHT 44118 2627 B3
3600 UNHT 44118 2627 D4
3800 UNHT 44118 2628 A4
6700 INDE 44131 2884 E5
Meadowbrook Dr
10 CrlT 44044 3006 D6
600 AURA 44202 3022 B5
1100 AMHT 44001 2743 E6
3600 LORN 44053 2744 C3
6100 MNTR 44060 2143 D4
10600 PMHT 44130 2882 A6
12100 NbyT 44021 2765 A4
12500 PMHT 44130 2881 E6
30000 WKLF 44092 2374 D4
30200 WBHL 44092 2374 D4
Meadowbrook Rd
6300 GDHT 44125 2885 E3
Meadow Creek Ln
14300 CrlT 44050 3140 C5
14300 LrgT 44050 3140 C5
Meadow Creek Ovl
32900 NRDV 44039 2748 E7
Meadow Creek Rd
7300 SgHT 44067 3152 C2
Meadowcrest Cir
- HkyT 44233 3149 E6
Meadowdale Dr
8000 MNTR 44060 2143 E4
8000 MNTR 44060 2144 A4
35600 SLN 44139 2889 C4
Meadowfield Ct
10 ELYR 44035 2875 A1
Meadowgate Dr
10 BDFD 44146 2887 A2
Meadow Gateway
3000 BWHT 44147 3015 B5
Meadowgrass Rd
10700 SGVL 44136 3011 A4
Meadowhill Ln
10 MDHL 44022 2759 D4
22500 RKRV 44116 2621 A6
Meadowhurst Ln
10300 MsnT 44024 2503 D1

Meadowlake Ct
10000 CcdT 44060 2253 C2
Meadowlands Dr
100 CRDN 44024 2379 D6
Meadow Lane Ct
5300 SFLD 44035 2746 E6
Meadowlane Dr
500 RDHT 44143 2499 A4
30100 BYVL 44140 2619 C4
Meadowlane Rd
10 SVHL 44131 3014 E2
10 SVHL 44131 3015 A2
Meadowlark Cir
900 AURA 44202 3156 E4
Meadowlark Ln
13900 NbyT 44065 2634 B5
19100 WVHT 44128 2757 E4
Meadowlark Rd
600 PnvT 44077 2039 C6
Meadowlark Wy
31600 PRPK 44124 2759 E1
Meadowlawn Blvd
900 PRMA 44134 2883 E3
E Meadowlawn Blvd
10 SVHL 44131 2883 D2
800 SVHL 44131 2884 A3
Meadowlawn Dr
10 MNTR 44060 2252 C1
1300 MCDN 44056 3019 A6
7200 MNTR 44060 2144 D7
Meadow Moss Ln
4800 NRDV 44039 2748 E7
Meadownorth Ct
22100 SGVL 44136 3011 A4
Meadowood Blvd
- TNBG 44087 3020 A4
800 MDSN 44057 1942 A6
1700 TNBG 44087 3019 E3
Meadowood Dr
600 MAYF 44040 2500 B4
600 MAYF 44143 2500 B4
N Meadowpark Dr
7200 WNHL 44146 3017 C1
S Meadowpark Dr
16800 WNHL 44146 3017 D2
Meadowridge Dr
10 GNVA 44041 1944 C7
11600 CsTp 44026 2501 E4
Meadowridge Wy
500 BSHT 44236 3153 E7
S Meadows Cir
16900 SGVL 44136 3147 A2
Meadows Dr
- BKVL 44141 3016 B7
- BKVL 44141 3151 B1
10 PnvT 44077 2040 E7
10 PnvT 44077 2146 E1
7200 INDE 44131 3015 D1
N Meadows Ln
16900 SGVL 44136 3147 A2
Meadows Rd
1600 MadT 44057 1842 E7
1700 MadT 44057 1941 E1
Meadows Edge Ln
21300 SGVL 44136 3011 A5
Meadowsouth Ct
22100 SGVL 44136 3011 A4
Meadowvale Av
16500 CLEV 44128 2757 C5
Meadowview Dr
200 NCtT 44067 3152 D2
200 SgHT 44067 3152 D2
400 AURA 44202 3156 D2
15400 MDFD 44062 2767 B1
30200 WKLF 44092 2374 D3
Meadowview Ln
700 MAYF 44143 2500 C5
800 GSML 44040 2500 C5
1100 AMHT 44001 2743 E5
Meadow Wood Blvd
5000 LNHT 44124 2628 E1
5100 LNHT 44124 2629 A1
Meadow Wood Dr
6000 MadT 44057 1941 E2
Meadowwood Dr
- ClrT 44024 2505 C2
N Meadow Wood Dr
- MDFD 44062 2767 E1
Meadowwood Ln
200 MDHL 44022 2759 D4
Meadow Woods Dr
- MCDN 44056 3153 E1
Meadview Dr
800 SVHL 44131 2884 A3
Meanderingwood Av
6300 MadT 44057 1942 A2
Mechanic St
800 GFTN 44044 3142 A6
800 GftT 44044 3142 A6
Medfield Dr
1000 RKRV 44116 2621 B6
Medfield Rd
2800 PRPK 44124 2629 A5
Medford Rd
800 CVHT 44121 2497 D5
Medhurst Av
5000 SLN 44139 2759 C7
Medina Av
7900 CLEV 44103 2496 A6
8200 CLEV 44108 2496 A6
Medina Frwy I-71
- BKLN - 2753 C3
- BKPK - 2752 B4
- BKPK - 2881 A1
- CLEV - 2624 E7
- CLEV - 2752 B4
- CLEV - 2753 C3
- CLEV - 2754 A2
- LNDL - 2753 C3
- MDBH - 2881 A5
- MDBH - 3012 A2
- SGVL - 3012 A2
- SGVL - 3147 B3
Medina St
16600 BbgT 44023 2890 B1
Medusa Rd
7500 OKWD 44146 3018 C2
Medway Rd
300 HDHT 44143 2499 E2
Meech Av
9300 CLEV 44105 2756 B2
Meecham St
10 BERA 44017 2880 C7
Megan Ct
9300 MNTR 44060 2145 A1

Mehling Ct
4600 CLEV 44102 2624 B7
Meigs Av
300 GDRV 44045 2039 C6
700 PnvT 44045 2039 C6
700 PnvT 44077 2039 C6
Meigs Blvd
15200 BKPK 44142 2881 B2
Meister Rd
700 LORN 44052 2744 D3
1300 LORN 44053 2744 B3
3600 LORN 44053 2743 E3
5500 MNTR 44060 2144 E2
Melba Av
11100 CLEV 44104 2626 D6
Melba St
- BDFD 44146 2887 C6
Melber Av
7100 CLEV 44144 2753 E2
Melbourne Av
3600 CLEV 44111 2752 C2
Melbourne Dr
100 BNWK 44212 3147 A6
Melbourne Rd
1100 ECLE 44112 2496 E7
3400 WDMR 44122 2759 A1
Melbury Av
6300 SLN 44139 2888 E5
6300 SLN 44139 2889 A5
Meldon Blvd
2700 BHWD 44122 2628 D6
Meldon Dr
6100 MNTR 44060 2143 E4
Melgrave Av
15700 CLEV 44135 2752 B3
Melgrove Av
12600 GDHT 44105 2756 E5
Melibee Dr
25600 WTLK 44145 2750 B3
Melissa Ln
22500 SGVL 44136 3010 E4
Mello Dr
27600 GNWL 44139 3019 A1
Melody Ln
100 EatT 44044 3008 A7
300 EatT 44044 3143 A1
3100 PRMA 44134 3014 C1
5000 WLBY 44094 2250 B7
5000 WLBY 44094 2375 B1
5800 MONT 44060 2143 C2
8200 MCDN 44056 3153 C1
9600 BKLN 44144 2753 D6
Meloria Dr
7900 MNTR 44060 2251 E3
Melridge Dr
6600 CcdT 44077 2145 E5
Melrose Av
7100 CLEV 44103 2625 E1
7100 CLEV 44103 2626 A1
Melrose Cir
1500 WTLK 44145 2620 E7
Melrose Dr
10 PnvT 44077 2145 C4
1000 WTLK 44145 2621 A6
E Melrose Dr
1200 WTLK 44145 2621 A7
S Melrose Dr
23100 WTLK 44145 2621 A7
23200 WTLK 44145 2620 E7
W Melrose Dr
1200 WTLK 44145 2620 E7
Melshore Dr
6100 MNTR 44060 2144 A5
Melville Rd
18300 CLEV 44110 2372 E7
Melvyn Ln
1100 ELYR 44035 3005 E1
Melzer Av
13100 CLEV 44120 2756 E2
13800 CLEV 44120 2757 A2
Memorial Dr
- BKPK 44142 2881 A3
- BtnT 44021 2766 B2
300 CRDN 44024 2380 A5
Memory Ln
500 BHIT 44212 3146 C7
900 VMLN 44089 2740 E6
6500 MNTR 44060 2144 A5
9200 RslT 44072 2632 D7
24500 OmsT 44138 2879 C2
Memphis Av
3400 CLEV 44109 2754 A4
3900 LNDL 44111 2753 C4
3900 LNDL 44135 2753 C4
4700 CLEV 44144 2754 A4
6600 CLEV 44144 2753 C4
9500 BKLN 44144 2753 C4
Memphis Villas S
4500 BKLN 44144 2753 C4
Memphis Villas Blvd
8600 BKLN 44144 2753 D4
Mendel Ct
100 ELYR 44035 2875 A5
Mendelssohn Dr
1300 WTLK 44145 2620 A7
Mendota Av
15500 MPHT 44137 2886 B4
Menlo Rd
3400 SRHT 44120 2757 B1
Menlo Park Ln
4100 VMLN 44089 2741 C4
Mennell Rd
14300 GftT 44044 3142 C7
Mennonite Rd
700 AURA 44202 3157 C4
700 AURA 44255 3157 C4
800 ManT 44202 3157 E5
2600 ManT 44202 3158 A5
2600 ManT 44255 3157 E5
2600 ManT 44255 3158 A5
3900 ManT 44255 3159 A5
4000 MNTU 44255 3159 A5
5100 ManT 44255 3159 E5
5100 ManT 44255 3160 A5
E Mennonite Rd
300 AURA 44202 3156 E4
300 AURA 44202 3157 A4
W Mennonite Rd
10 AURA 44202 3156 E4
Mentor Av
10 PNVL 44077 2146 A1
500 PNVL 44077 2145 D3
1100 PnvT 44077 2145 D3
1600 CLEV 44113 2624 D6
2100 MNTR 44060 2145 B5

Mentor Av
2100 PnvT 44060 2145 B5
7000 MNTR 44060 2251 A4
7000 WLBY 44060 2251 A4
7000 WLBY 44094 2251 A4
8000 MNTR 44060 2252 A2
8700 MNTR 44060 2144 D7
38100 WLBY 44094 2250 E5
38800 MNTR 44094 2251 A4
Mentor Av US-20
100 PNVL 44077 2146 A1
500 PNVL 44077 2145 D3
1100 PnvT 44077 2145 D3
2100 MNTR 44060 2145 B5
2100 PnvT 44060 2145 B5
7000 MNTR 44060 2251 A4
7000 WLBY 44060 2251 A4
7000 WLBY 44094 2251 A4
8000 MNTR 44060 2252 A2
8700 MNTR 44060 2144 D7
38100 WLBY 44094 2250 E5
38800 MNTR 44094 2251 A4
Mentor Rd
8700 CdnT 44024 2253 B6
8900 CdnT 44024 2378 E1
9300 CdnT 44024 2379 A2
10200 CRDN 44024 2379 B4
Mentor Harbor Blvd
8100 MNTR 44060 2144 A1
8700 MNTR 44060 2038 C6
Mentor Hills Dr
- KDHL 44060 2252 A4
- MNTR 44060 2252 A4
Mentor Marina
- MNTR 44060 2038 A7
- MNTR 44060 2144 A1
- MONT 44060 2038 A7
Mentor Park Blvd
6100 MNTR 44060 2143 E4
Mentorwood Dr
8200 MNTR 44060 2144 A5
Mera Ct
37300 SLN 44139 3020 C2
Mercantile Dr
9200 MNTR 44060 2144 E4
9200 MNTR 44060 2145 A4
Mercantile Rd
23000 BHWD 44122 2758 D2
Mercedes Av
20000 RKRV 44116 2751 D1
Mercer Dr
6000 BKPK 44142 2881 C2
Mercer Ln
9000 BKVL 44141 3016 A4
Mercury Dr
3100 NRYN 44133 3014 C6
Mere
- AMHT 44001 2872 E3
Merece Dr
18000 BKPK 44142 2881 A3
18200 BKPK 44142 2880 E3
Meredith Av
18500 EUCL 44119 2372 E4
19300 EUCL 44119 2373 A4
Meredith Ln
12200 CcdT 44077 2255 A4
Meridan Ct
400 AVLK 44012 2618 E3
Meriden Rd
100 PNVL 44077 2146 C2
Meridian Av
8600 CLEV 44106 2626 B1
Merimeade Dr
15000 CLEV 44111 2752 C2
Merino Ln
3000 TNBG 44087 3020 B6
Merion Ct
- SLN 44139 3020 E2
Merit Dr
10 RDHT 44143 2373 E7
10 RDHT 44143 2374 A7
Merkle Av
5400 PRMA 44129 2754 A7
Merl Av
1500 CLEV 44109 2754 D6
13200 LKWD 44107 2623 A4
13400 LKWD 44107 2622 E4
Merlin Ln
8900 MCDN 44056 3019 A7
Merlin Ovl
14800 NRYN 44133 3148 A1
N Merlyn Pl
7100 CcdT 44077 2146 A6
S Merlyn Pl
7200 CcdT 44077 2146 B6
Merriam Ln
10200 TNBG 44087 3020 B4
Merrie Ln
8200 CsTp 44026 2502 A4
Merrill Av
5900 CLEV 44102 2624 A7
Merrimak Dr
400 BERA 44017 3010 D1
Merritt Dr
- BtnT 44021 2635 B5
- NbyT 44021 2635 B5
- NbyT 44065 2635 B5
Merritt Rd
12500 ClrT 44024 2635 B3
12500 MsnT 44024 2635 B3
Merrygold Blvd
4400 WVHT 44128 2758 D5
Merrymound Rd
3700 SELD 44121 2497 E4
3700 SELD 44121 2498 A4
Merry Oaks Tr
17400 BbgT 44023 2891 B4
Mersey Ct
10 CcdT 44060 2145 B7
Merwin Av
1700 CLEV 44113 2624 D4
Messenger Rd
15700 AbnT 44021 2764 D7
15700 AbnT 44023 2764 D7
15700 NbyT 44023 2764 B7
15700 NbyT 44021 2764 D7
15700 NbyT 44065 2764 D7
16400 AbnT 44021 2893 B1
16400 AbnT 44023 2893 B1
Metcalf Av
12800 CLEV 44120 2626 E7
Metcalf Rd
500 ELYR 44035 2875 D3
9000 WTHL 44094 2251 C7
9000 WTHL 44094 2376 C2

Methyl Av
11200 CLEV 44104 2626 D5
Metric Dr
7700 MNTR 44060 2251 D1
Metro Ct
6400 BDHT 44146 2887 E5
Metro Dr
1700 EUCL 44132 2373 E5
1700 EUCL 44143 2373 E5
1700 EUCL 44132 2374 A5
Metro Health Dr
2500 CLEV 44109 2754 D1
Metro Park Dr
6600 MAYF 44143 2500 A3
Metro Park Tr
- SLN 44139 2889 A1
Metro Parks Bike & Hike Tr
- BDFD 44146 2887 A5
- BosT 44141 3153 A6
- BSHT 44236 3153 A6
- BTVL 44022 2760 C7
- BTVL 44022 2889 B1
- HGVL 44022 2760 C6
- MDHL 44022 2760 C6
- NCtT 44067 3152 E4
- NCtT 44141 3153 A6
- NCtT 44067 3153 A6
- SgHT 44146 3017 B2
- SgHT 44067 3017 B5
- SgHT 44067 3152 E4
- SLN 44139 2888 B2
- SLN 44139 2889 B1
- WNHL 44146 2886 C6
- WNHL 44146 2887 A5
- WNHL 44146 3017 B2
Metro Pks Buttermilk Flls Pkwy
- MAYF 44143 2500 B1
Metro Parks Ox Ln
- GSML 44094 2500 C1
- GSML 44040 2500 C1
- GSML 44143 2500 C1
- MAYF 44143 2500 B1
- WBHL 44094 2500 C1
Metro Parks Valley Pkwy
- BKPK 44142 2751 A6
- BKPK 44126 2751 A6
- FWPK 44126 2751 C6
- NOSD 44142 2751 A6
- NOSD 44070 2751 A6
Metro Park Valley Pkwy
- BKPK 44142 2751 A7
- BKPK 44070 2879 E1
- BKPK 44138 2879 E2
- BKPK 44142 2879 E1
- NOSD 44070 2750 E7
- NOSD 44142 2751 A7
- NOSD 44070 2751 A7
- NOSD 44142 2879 E2
- NOSD 44070 2879 E1
- OmsT 44138 2879 E2
- OmsT 44142 2879 E2
Metropolitan Blvd
8200 ODFL 44138 2879 C6
Metropolitan Dr
4200 CLEV 44135 2752 A4
Metropolitan Park Rd
- ELYR 44035 2875 A5
Metta Av
6500 CLEV 44103 2495 E6
Meyer Av
2100 CLEV 44109 2624 C7
35700 ETLK 44095 2250 B4
Miami Av
100 ELYR 44035 2875 B7
3700 LORN 44053 2744 B4
E Miami Dr
7700 PRMA 44134 3014 B2
N Miami Dr
4200 PRMA 44134 3014 B2
Miami Rd
2000 EUCL 44117 2497 E3
2000 EUCL 44117 2498 A3
7500 MONT 44060 2143 D2
Michael Av
4300 NOSD 44070 2750 E6
Michael Dr
10 OmsT 44138 2879 A3
5700 BKPK 44142 2881 D2
6800 MNTR 44060 2144 E6
18300 CLEV 44122 2757 D3
35400 SLN 44139 3020 B2
Michael Ln
900 AMHT 44001 2872 E3
42700 EyrT 44035 2745 B7
Michaels Ln
8800 BWHT 44147 3014 D6
Michelle Dr
- ClbT 44028 3009 C7
- ClbT 44028 3144 C1
Michelle Ln
200 MDSN 44057 2043 E2
37800 ETLK 44095 2142 D5
Michigan Av
200 ELYR 44035 3006 C1
200 LORN 44052 2615 B5
3200 PryT 44081 2041 E1
Michigan St
500 AURA 44202 3021 B4
Middle Av
100 ELYR 44035 2875 A7
900 ELYR 44035 3006 A3
10500 CrlT 44035 3006 A4
Middle Dr
300 AhtT 44001 2872 A3
Middle St
400 AMHT 44001 2872 E2
600 BDFD 44146 2887 C4
Middlebrook Blvd
5700 BKPK 44142 2881 D2
6600 MDBH 44130 2881 B5
6600 MDBH 44142 2881 C4
13300 BKPK 44130 2881 D2
Middledale Rd
4800 LNHT 44124 2628 D1
Middlefield Ct
300 PnvT 44077 2146 E2
Middlefield Rd
2100 CVHT 44106 2627 A3
Middlehurst Rd
1700 CVHT 44118 2627 B1
Middlepost Ln
2900 RKRV 44116 2751 B1

INDEX 32

Middle Post Pt

Mussey St

Cleveland Street Index

STREET Block City ZIP Map# Grid

Middle Post Pt
100 CRDN 44024 2505 A2
Middle Ridge Rd
- AhtT 44053 2744 E7
- LORN 44035 2744 E7
1900 AhtT 44001 2873 A3
3800 PryT 44081 1940 B7
4500 MadT 44081 1941 A7
4500 PryT 44081 1941 A7
5200 MadT 44057 1941 A7
6200 EyrT 44035 2745 A7
6200 LORN 44035 2745 A7
6200 LORN 44053 2745 A7
6200 MDSN 44057 1941 D6
6300 MDSN 44057 1942 A6
6400 AhtT 44035 2744 E7
6400 AhtT 44035 2745 A7
6400 LORN 44053 2744 E7
6700 MadT 44057 1942 D6
7400 GrvT 44057 1943 A6
7400 HpfT 44057 1943 A6
7400 MadT 44057 1943 A6
43500 AhtT 44001 2744 E7
43600 AhtT 44035 2873 D1
45900 AMHT 44001 2873 A3
46000 AhtT 44001 2872 C4
46100 AMHT 44001 2872 C4
48000 AhtT 44001 2871 D4
48900 BhmT 44001 2871 A5
Middlesex Rd
7800 MNTR 44060 2251 D4
Middleton
- AVON 44011 2618 B7
- AVON 44011 2748 B1
Middleton Dr
100 CcdT 44077 2145 D5
100 PnvT 44077 2145 D5
Middleton Rd
- HDSN 44236 3155 D7
1300 HDSN 44236 3154 D7
1400 CVHT 44121 2498 A7
2100 HDSN 44236 3155 A7
Midland Av
15900 CLEV 44110 2497 C1
Midland Rd
7300 INDE 44131 3015 E1
8000 MNTR 44060 2251 C4
26500 BYVL 44140 2620 A5
Midvale Av
- NOSD 44070 2878 E1
18300 CLEV 44135 2752 A5
19900 CLEV 44135 2751 D6
Midvale Dr
11100 CrlT 44035 3005 D5
Midway Av
3800 WVHT 44122 2757 E3
32400 AVLK 44012 2618 B1
Midway Blvd
- ELYR 44035 2875 B2
- PnvT 44077 2040 D2
100 ELYR 44035 2874 E2
Midway Dr
- VMLN 44089 2741 B6
1900 TNBG 44087 3154 C1
Midway Mall
1700 ELYR 44035 2875 A2
Midwest Av
9000 GDHT 44125 2756 B7
Mika Dr
10200 BKLN 44144 2753 C6
Milan Av
100 AMHT 44001 2872 B2
1100 AhtT 44001 2872 B2
11700 CLEV 44111 2753 A2
13300 ECLE 44112 2497 A5
Milan Cres
4100 CLEV 44128 2757 C3
Milan Ct
9700 NRYN 44133 3014 C4
Milan Dr
19300 MPHT 44137 2757 E7
21000 EUCL 44119 2373 A5
Milan Elyria Rd
- ELYR 44035 2874 A5
- EyrT 44035 2874 A5
42900 ELYR 44035 2873 B6
42900 EyrT 44035 2873 B6
43000 AhtT 44035 2873 B6
46000 AhtT 44001 2873 B6
46100 AhtT 44001 2872 D7
Milan Elyria Rd SR-113
- EyrT 44035 2874 A5
42900 ELYR 44035 2873 B6
42900 EyrT 44035 2873 B6
43000 AhtT 44035 2873 B6
46000 AhtT 44001 2873 B6
46100 AhtT 44001 2872 D7
Milann Dr
37500 WBHL 44094 2375 E4
Milburn Av
16800 CLEV 44135 2752 A4
Milburn Rd
26200 OKWD 44146 2887 E7
Milbury Ct
7200 OKWD 44146 2887 E7
Mildon Dr
6800 LryT 44077 2147 D7
7100 LryT 44077 2255 D1
Mildred Av
800 LORN 44052 2614 C7
1200 WTLK 44145 2619 C6
22500 FWPK 44126 2751 A5
22900 NOSD 44070 2751 A4
23200 NOSD 44070 2750 E4
Mildred Dr
30000 WLWK 44095 2249 C6
Mildred St
300 PNVL 44077 2146 B2
35100 NRDV 44039 2877 A2
Miles Av
9100 CLEV 44105 2756 D3
13100 CLEV 44128 2756 D3
13600 CLEV 44105 2757 A4
13600 CLEV 44128 2757 A4
17600 WVHT 44128 2757 A4
Miles Av SR-43
9100 CLEV 44105 2756 D3
13100 CLEV 44128 2756 D3
13600 CLEV 44105 2757 A4
13600 CLEV 44128 2757 A4
17600 WVHT 44128 2757 A4
Miles Ln
500 BERA 44017 3011 C2
Miles Pkwy
20500 NRDL 44128 2758 A6

Miles Pkwy
20500 WVHT 44128 2758 A6
Miles Rd
100 CNFL 44022 2760 E7
100 MDHL 44022 2760 E7
300 BTVL 44022 2760 E7
17700 WVHT 44128 2757 D5
19400 NRDL 44128 2757 D5
19600 WVHT 44128 2758 A6
20000 NRDL 44128 2758 D6
22400 BDHT 44128 2758 D6
24100 BDHT 44146 2758 D6
26300 BDHT 44022 2759 A7
26300 BDHT 44128 2759 A7
26300 BDHT 44146 2759 A7
26300 WVHT 44022 2759 A7
26300 WVHT 44128 2759 A7
27000 ORNG 44022 2759 A7
27000 SLN 44022 2759 A7
27000 SLN 44139 2759 A7
27000 SLN 44146 2759 A7
32200 MDHL 44022 2759 D7
33100 SLN 44022 2760 A7
33100 SLN 44139 2760 A7
Miles Rd SR-43
17700 WVHT 44128 2757 D5
19400 NRDL 44128 2757 D5
19600 WVHT 44128 2758 A6
20000 NRDL 44128 2758 A6
S Miles Rd
16600 CLEV 44128 2757 C5
17800 WVHT 44128 2757 E6
18200 WVHT 44128 2758 A6
Miles Park Av
9100 CLEV 44105 2756 B3
Milford Dr
4600 PryT 44081 2042 B5
9000 NHFD 44067 3018 B4
Milford Ln
9300 MNTR 44060 2144 E7
9300 MNTR 44060 2145 A7
Milford Pl
11200 TNBG 44087 3020 B4
Milford Rd
2500 UNHT 44118 2628 A4
3700 PRMA 44134 2883 B1
Mill Ct
- CLEV 44113 2624 C6
- GFTN 44044 3142 A6
W Mill Dr
900 HDHT 44143 2499 A5
Mill Rd
4700 BWHT 44147 3015 D4
6200 BWHT 44141 3015 E5
6500 BKVL 44141 3015 E5
6700 BKVL 44141 3016 A6
27200 NOSD 44070 2749 E6
27200 NOSD 44070 2750 A7
E Mill Rd
- BWHT 44147 3015 D3
W Mill Rd
4700 BWHT 44147 3015 D4
Mill Run
- AURA 44202 3022 A4
Mill St
10 PNVL 44077 2040 B7
300 AMHT 44001 2872 E2
4500 MNTU 44255 3159 C6
5500 VMLN 44089 2740 E6
15900 MDFD 44062 2767 D2
18300 PkmT 44231 3027 E1
18300 PkmT 44234 3027 E1
25500 ODFL 44138 2879 B6
Millard Dr
600 BYVL 44140 2619 D5
Millbrook Dr
17500 BbgT 44023 2891 A4
Millbrook Rd
5400 BDHT 44146 2887 C1
Millcreek Blvd
- CLEV 44105 2756 B4
22900 HIHL 44128 2758 B3
Mill Creek Ln
10 MDHL 44022 2760 B4
Miller Av
5000 MPHT 44137 2757 B7
20000 EUCL 44119 2373 A5
22200 EUCL 44123 2373 A5
22300 EUCL 44117 2373 A5
30000 WKLF 44092 2374 D5
30500 WBHL 44092 2374 D5
W Miller Av
- WKLF 44092 2374 C5
29000 WBHL 44092 2374 C5
Miller Ct
200 CrlT 44035 3006 B3
300 PNVL 44077 2145 E3
400 CLEV 44113 2625 A5
16800 SGVL 44136 3147 A3
Miller Dr
6500 NRDV 44039 2877 D3
Miller Pkwy
1500 STBR 44241 3157 A7
Miller Rd
100 AVLK 44012 2617 A3
1100 AVON 44012 2617 A6
1100 AVON 44011 2617 A6
5000 BKVL 44141 3150 D4
6800 BKVL 44141 3151 A4
Millerwood Ln
7600 PRMA 44130 3012 E1
Mill Gate Dr
2800 WBHL 44094 2375 E6
2900 WBHL 44094 2376 A7
Mill Hollow Dr
10 MDHL 44022 2760 B4
Mill Hollow Ln
13900 SGVL 44136 3012 C7
14200 SGVL 44136 3147 B1
Milligan Av
11700 CLEV 44135 2753 A5
Millikin Ct
1500 CVHT 44118 2497 D7
Mill Morr Rd
10 PnvT 44077 2145 B4
Mill Pond Cir
4300 PryT 44081 2041 D3
Millpond Rd
100 AURA 44202 3157 A3
Millrace Ln
7400 SgHT 44067 3152 C1
Millridge Rd
800 HDHT 44143 2499 B5
Mills Av
27500 EUCL 44132 2374 A3

Mills Cr
- AVON 44011 2748 D6
Mills Dr
2700 LORN 44052 2744 B2
Mills Rd
- WTLK 44145 2749 A6
31600 AVON 44011 2748 C6
31600 AVON 44011 2749 A6
31600 AVON 44145 2749 A6
31600 NRDV 44011 2748 C6
31600 NRDV 44011 2749 A6
31600 NRDV 44039 2748 C6
31600 NRDV 44039 2749 A6
31600 NRDV 44145 2749 A6
36200 AVON 44011 2747 D6
36200 NRDV 44011 2747 D6
36200 NRDV 44039 2747 D6
Mills Creek Ln
4700 NRDV 44039 2748 E7
5300 NRDV 44039 2877 E1
6400 NRDV 44039 2878 A2
Millside Ln
- AVLK 44012 2618 E4
Mills Ind Pkwy
5200 NRDV 44011 2748 C7
5200 NRDV 44039 2748 C7
Millstone Dr
10 PNVL 44077 2040 C7
13000 MsnT 44024 2634 C1
17900 BbgT 44023 2891 C6
Millstone Ln
- AMHT 44001 2744 B6
Mill Stream Cir
- ELYR 44035 3007 A2
Millstream Cir
9000 ODFL 44138 3009 E1
Millview Ln
12600 MsnT 44024 2503 E7
Millwood Cir
32600 NRDV 44039 2748 E6
Millwood Dr
4900 BWHT 44147 3015 D5
Millwood Ln
5400 WLBY 44094 2375 A1
Milo Av
5100 MPHT 44137 2757 A7
Milo Rd
12800 GDHT 44125 2885 E3
13500 GDHT 44125 2886 A3
Milton Dr
7100 MNTR 44060 2143 B7
7100 MNTR 44060 2251 B1
22300 EUCL 44123 2373 B3
Milton Rd
- SRHT 44118 2628 B5
- SRHT 44122 2628 B5
2100 UNHT 44118 2628 B3
Milton St
10 BERA 44017 3011 B2
Milverton Rd
3200 CLEV 44120 2627 A7
3300 SRHT 44120 2757 B1
Mina Av
15600 CLEV 44135 2752 C4
Miner Rd
200 HDHT 44143 2499 D1
E Miner Rd
1100 MDHT 44124 2499 D7
W Miner Rd
1100 MDHT 44124 2499 D7
Minerva St
700 AMHT 44001 2872 D3
Minkon Av
800 CLEV 44113 2625 A4
Minnewawa Rd
10 TMLK 44095 2250 A1
Minnie Av
2800 CLEV 44104 2626 A6
Minnie Wawa St
400 VMLN 44089 2741 A4
Minor Av
11900 CLEV 44105 2756 D3
Minor Park Rd
1800 CVHT 44118 2627 D2
Mira Ct
2400 CLEV 44109 2754 D4
Mirabeau Dr
5300 PRMA 44129 2883 A7
Mirage Av
10 AMHT 44001 2744 B7
Miramar Blvd
1500 SELD 44121 2628 A1
2100 UNHT 44121 2628 A4
2200 UNHT 44118 2628 A4
Miriam Av
1800 AVON 44011 2617 D7
1800 AVON 44011 2747 D1
Mirlo Ct
- CLEV 44102 2623 E7
Mission Rd
14500 CLEV 44135 2752 D3
Mississippi Av
200 LORN 44052 2615 B5
Missouri Av
200 LORN 44052 2615 C5
Mistletoe Av
24900 OKWD 44146 2887 D7
Mistletoe Dr
1500 CLEV 44106 2626 D1
Misty Hllw
10400 KTLD 44094 2376 C6
Misty Ln
300 PnvT 44077 2039 D7
Misty Rdg
10300 CcdT 44077 2253 D2
Misty Lake Dr
17100 SGVL 44136 3147 A4
Misty Lake Gln
16300 BbgT 44023 2762 B7
Misty Oakes Dr
9300 BWHT 44147 3150 B1
Mitchell Av
14600 CLEV 44111 2752 D1
18900 RKRV 44116 2621 E6
Mitchell Dr
10 BDFD 44146 2887 B6
6800 NRDV 44039 2877 D4
24500 NOSD 44070 2750 C6
Mitchell Ln
10 MDHL 44022 2760 A5
Mitchell Rd
9800 ClbT 44028 3009 B3
Mitchells Mill Rd
9600 KDHL 44060 2378 A2
9600 KTLD 44060 2378 A2

Mitchells Mill Rd
9600 KTLD 44094 2378 A2
9700 CdnT 44024 2378 A2
10000 CdnT 44024 2379 A3
Mobile Ct
3500 CLEV 44109 2754 C5
Moccasin Run
9100 BbgT 44023 2891 D1
Mockingbird Ln
10 ELYR 44035 2875 D7
Mock Orange Ln
500 AbnT 44023 2892 B3
Moffet Av
100 CRDN 44024 2380 A7
Mogul St
16300 BbgT 44022 2761 A7
Mohawk Av
18500 CLEV 44119 2372 E5
19300 CLEV 44119 2373 A5
Mohawk Dr
- AURA 44202 3022 A7
1400 MadT 44057 1843 B7
4100 LORN 44055 2745 D4
8100 SGVL 44136 3012 B2
Mohawk Rd
7000 MNTR 44060 2143 A3
38800 WLBY 44094 2143 A3
Mohawk Tr
400 BNWK 44212 3146 E7
13100 MDBH 44130 2881 D6
Mohegan Tr
900 WLBY 44094 2143 A5
Mohican Av
19200 CLEV 44119 2372 E6
19700 CLEV 44119 2373 A6
Mohican Tr
16500 BbgT 44023 2891 C1
Moltke Ct
1900 CLEV 44113 2624 D6
Monarch Rd
1000 SELD 44121 2498 B6
Mondamin Dr
35300 ETLK 44095 2250 B1
Moneta Av
800 AURA 44202 3021 A3
Monica Dr
13600 NRYN 44133 3014 B7
34000 NRDV 44039 2877 C1
Monica Ln
5800 GDHT 44125 2886 A2
Monmouth Ct
100 CcdT 44060 2145 B2
Monmouth Dr
6300 PRMA 44129 2882 E4
Monmouth Rd
2900 CVHT 44118 2627 B4
E Monmouth Rd
3200 CVHT 44118 2627 C4
Monroe Av
- LORN 44052 2615 C6
2500 CLEV 44113 2624 D5
6400 NRDV 44039 2877 D3
W Monroe Av
10 BDFD 44146 2887 C4
Monroe Blvd
400 PNVL 44077 2146 A3
Monroe Ct
- SDLK 44054 2616 B5
10 OBLN 44074 3138 D4
7800 MNTR 44060 2143 D7
32200 SLN 44139 3019 E1
Monroe Dr
200 NHFD 44067 3017 E3
200 NHFD 44067 3018 A3
Monroe St
10 BERA 44017 3011 C1
100 ELYR 44035 2875 A5
E Monroe St
10 BDFD 44146 2887 A4
Monroe Tr
3500 WTLK 44145 2749 C4
Mont Av
13900 ECLE 44118 2627 A1
Montagano Blvd
4300 SELD 44121 2498 B6
Montague Ct
19400 NRYN 44133 3148 B5
Montana Av
200 LORN 44052 2615 C5
5800 CLEV 44102 2624 A7
Montauk Av
4800 PRMA 44134 2883 B1
Montclair Av
2200 CLEV 44109 2754 C5
Montclair Cir
900 WTLK 44145 2620 A6
Montclair Dr
- HmbT 44024 2381 A6
Montclare Blvd
20900 SGVL 44136 3011 B3
Monte Dr
6400 LryT 44077 2147 B5
Montello Rd
7600 INDE 44131 3016 A2
Monterey Av
18600 EUCL 44119 2372 E4
19300 EUCL 44119 2373 A4
Monterey Dr
6500 MDHT 44124 2500 A6
8000 KTLD 44094 2376 E7
8000 KTLD 44094 2377 A7
Monterey Pl
- BKLN 44144 2753 C4
Monterey Bay Dr
7500 MONT 44060 2143 D2
Monterey Pine Dr
17700 SGVL 44136 3146 E5
Montevista Rd
3700 CVHT 44121 2497 E7
3800 CVHT 44121 2498 A7
Montford Rd
800 CVHT 44121 2498 A5
Montgomery Av
7100 CLEV 44104 2625 E4
7100 CLEV 44104 2626 A4
Montgomery Dr
500 BHIT 44212 3146 B7
Montgomery Rd
2800 SRHT 44122 2627 E7
2900 SRHT 44122 2628 A7
7800 MDBH 44130 3012 D2
Monticello Blvd
10 CVHT 44118 2627 B1
3100 CVHT 44112 2497 D6
3300 CVHT 44121 2497 D6

Monticello Blvd
3800 CVHT 44121 2498 A6
4000 SELD 44121 2498 A6
4300 SELD 44143 2498 D5
4800 RDHT 44143 2498 D5
Monticello Cir
100 ELYR 44035 2873 E7
100 ELYR 44035 2874 A6
Monticello Dr
- AVLK 44012 2618 D4
10 BNWK 44212 3146 E5
10 BNWK 44212 3147 A6
200 CNFL 44022 2760 E7
7700 BKVL 44141 3016 A3
9300 TNBG 44087 3019 C6
Montridge Ct
8100 NRYN 44133 3013 C5
Montrose Av
14200 CLEV 44111 2622 D7
Montrose Dr
6100 MadT 44057 1941 E1
Montvale Dr
15000 BKPK 44142 2881 C3
Montville Ct
4400 WVHT 44128 2758 D4
Moon Rd
3500 AVON 44011 2747 B3
Mooncrest Dr
7000 PRMA 44129 2883 A6
Moonglow Ln
4300 CLEV 44109 2755 A5
Moonstone Dr
900 AhtT 44001 2873 B2
Moore Ct
1900 CLEV 44113 2624 D5
Moore Dr
10100 PRMA 44130 2882 C7
Moore Rd
10 AVLK 44012 2617 C1
800 AVON 44012 2617 C6
1700 AVON 44011 2617 C7
Mooreland Av
4000 WLBY 44094 2250 C5
Mooreland Rd
5400 MONT 44060 2037 E7
5400 MONT 44060 2143 E1
Moorewood Av
100 AVLK 44012 2617 E2
Moraine Dr
11000 TNBG 44087 3019 C4
Moran Av
- ELYR 44035 2875 A2
Morar Cir
20300 SGVL 44136 3146 C4
N Moreland Blvd
- SRHT 44120 2626 E5
2500 SRHT 44120 2627 A5
2600 CLEV 44120 2626 E5
S Moreland Blvd
2700 CLEV 44120 2626 E5
Moreland Dr
100 AVLK 44012 2617 D2
W Moreland Rd
8300 PRMA 44129 2882 D1
Morewood Pkwy
200 RKRV 44116 2621 D4
Morgan Av
100 ELYR 44035 2874 E3
6500 CLEV 44127 2625 E7
7300 CLEV 44127 2626 A7
Morgan Ct
- SGVL 44136 3145 E3
Morgan Dr
100 PnvT 44077 2041 B6
Morgan Rd
8600 MtlT 44064 2259 A6
8600 MtlT 44064 2384 A1
9300 MtlT 44064 2383 E3
Morgan Run
8700 ODFL 44138 2879 D7
26800 WTLK 44145 2750 A4
Morgan St
10 OBLN 44074 3138 C3
5400 MPHT 44137 2886 B1
Morgan Tr
14600 RslT 44072 2762 C1
Morison Av
10500 CLEV 44108 2496 C6
Morlee Dr
300 BNWK 44212 3146 D7
Morley Av
19500 RKRV 44116 2621 D7
Morley Rd
2800 SRHT 44122 2628 A7
6400 CcdT 44077 2145 E6
7200 CcdT 44077 2253 D2
7300 CcdT 44060 2253 D2
8300 CcdT 44024 2253 B5
8300 CcdT 44077 2253 B5
Morning Dove Ln
6900 OmsT 44138 2878 D4
Morning Glory Cir
6200 SLN 44139 2889 C5
Morning Glory Tr
12700 CsTp 44026 2501 B7
12700 CsTp 44026 2631 B1
Morningside Dr
10 SRSL 44073 2762 C7
4500 CLEV 44109 2754 E6
5400 PRMA 44129 2883 A2
6600 BKVL 44141 3151 A2
6700 VLVW 44125 2885 D5
7400 WNHL 44146 3018 A1
7500 NCtT 44067 3152 E2
Morningside Rd
6700 MDBH 44130 2881 D4
Morning Star Av
15700 MPHT 44137 2886 B3
Morningstar Ct
2700 WBHL 44094 2375 A5
11200 NbyT 44065 2634 B5
Morning Star Dr
13000 NRYN 44133 3147 E4
16400 SGVL 44136 3147 A4
Morningstar Dr
2600 MadT 44057 1942 A4
Morning Star Tr
7000 SgHT 44067 3152 C2
Mornington Ln
1800 CVHT 44106 2627 A2
Mornington Rd
100 VMLN 44089 2741 E4
Morningview Ter
10 BNWK 44212 3147 B6

Morrell Av
300 PnvT 44077 2039 C6
Morris Av
20100 EUCL 44123 2373 A4
33100 ETLK 44095 2249 E5
Morris Ct
8900 CLEV 44106 2496 B7
Morris Dr
21000 SGVL 44136 3146 B1
Morris Rd
600 VMLN 44089 2741 E5
Morris Black Pl
2400 CLEV 44104 2626 C4
Morrison Av
2000 LKWD 44107 2622 C6
Morrison St
300 GNVA 44041 1944 C4
Morrow Dr
6000 BKPK 44142 2881 D3
Morse Av
10 PNVL 44077 2146 A1
Morse Rd
200 BERA 44017 2880 A7
8300 BhmT 44089 2870 D5
Mortimer Av
11700 CLEV 44111 2753 A3
Mortimer Dr
300 BDFD 44146 2887 B2
Morton Av
6100 CLEV 44127 2755 E1
8500 BKLN 44144 2753 D5
22000 FWPK 44126 2751 A4
Morton Rd
400 VMLN 44089 2741 B4
Mortus Dr
1600 TNBG 44087 3019 B6
Moseley Rd
- TmbT 44086 2151 A4
15100 TpnT 44057 2149 B3
15100 TpnT 44086 2149 B3
16400 TpnT 44086 2150 A3
17500 TpnT 44086 2151 A4
Moss Pt
- BbgT 44023 2890 D7
Moss Canyon Dr
800 AhtT 44001 2873 B2
Moss Glen Tr
15400 NbyT 44065 2764 E4
Moss Point Rd
12200 SGVL 44136 3012 A6
Moss Ridge Cir
12200 SGVL 44136 3012 A6
Mosswood Cir
- NRDV 44039 2877 E7
Mosswood Dr
2300 TNBG 44087 3155 A4
Moss Woods Dr
15000 BtnT 44062 2767 A4
15000 MdfT 44062 2767 A4
Motta Dr
39700 CrlT 44044 3006 C6
Moulton Av
12000 CLEV 44106 2496 D7
Mound Av
5300 CLEV 44105 2755 D1
Mound St
100 ELYR 44035 2875 B6
Mountain Ash Dr
7600 CcdT 44060 2253 B3
Mountain Park Dr
7300 CcdT 44060 2253 B1
Mountain Quail Pl
7200 CcdT 44077 2254 C1
Mountainside Dr
200 PnvT 44077 2147 A1
Mountain View Dr
10 MDHL 44022 2760 C5
8800 MNTR 44060 2252 D3
9700 WTHL 44094 2376 A3
E Mountain View Dr
9000 CdnT 44024 2253 E7
W Mountain View Dr
9000 CdnT 44024 2253 E7
Mount Auburn Av
9300 CLEV 44104 2626 C6
Mount Carmel Dr
1500 WKLF 44092 2374 C2
Mount Carmel Rd
10500 CLEV 44104 2626 C4
Mount Laurel Rd
3600 CVHT 44121 2497 E4
Mount Overlook Av
10800 CLEV 44104 2626 D4
10800 CLEV 44106 2626 D4
11700 CLEV 44120 2626 D4
Mount Pleasant Dr
18600 AbnT 44023 3023 A1
Mount Royal Dr
8100 CcdT 44077 2253 E4
Mount Sinai Dr
10 CLEV 44106 2626 C1
Mount Union Av
1800 ECLE 44112 2497 A7
Mount Vernon Blvd
1100 CVHT 44112 2497 C6
1100 CVHT 44118 2497 C6
2000 ECLE 44112 2497 C6
Mount Vernon Ct
- CLEV 44109 2754 C2
10 CcdT 44060 2145 B2
100 ELYR 44035 2874 A7
Mountview Av
5400 GDHT 44125 2885 C1
10500 CLEV 44104 2626 C7
Mountville Dr
19600 MPHT 44137 2757 E7
19800 MPHT 44137 2758 A7
Mourning Dove Ln
11300 CcdT 44077 2254 C1
Moving Wy
- MNTR 44060 2144 A7
Mozart Dr
1300 WTLK 44145 2620 A7
Mozina Dr
1000 CLEV 44119 2372 E6
Mueti Dr
- BDHT 44146 2758 B7
- MPHT 44137 2758 B7
Mueti Dr SR-43
- BDHT 44146 2758 B7
- MPHT 44137 2758 B7
Muirfield Dr
300 HDHT 44143 2499 C2
Muirfield Wy
4300 WTLK 44145 2749 A6

Muirland Dr
8400 BWHT 44147 3014 E4
Muirwood Ct
7500 BbgT 44023 2890 C1
Mulberry Av
2300 CLEV 44113 2624 C3
Mulberry Cir
12300 SGVL 44136 3011 A6
26600 RDHT 44143 2373 E5
26600 RDHT 44143 2374 A5
Mulberry Ct
7300 OmsT 44138 2878 D5
Mulberry Dr
10 OBLN 44074 3138 C3
Mulberry Ln
- SFLD 44035 2746 E6
300 AVLK 44012 2618 C3
Mulberry Rd
7000 CsTp 44026 2501 B2
8100 CsTp 44026 2502 A3
9400 CsTp 44024 2502 C2
9400 CsTp 44024 2503 A2
9400 MsnT 44024 2503 A2
Mulberry St
200 BERA 44017 2880 B6
Mulberry St SR-237
200 BERA 44017 2880 B6
Mulberry Woods
8000 CsTp 44026 2501 E2
Mull Av
100 AVLK 44012 2618 D1
Mulwal Dr
10 PNVL 44077 2145 E2
Mumford Av
5400 CLEV 44127 2625 D7
Mumford Rd
12000 HrmT 44231 3027 A7
12000 HrmT 44234 3027 A7
12800 HrmT 44231 3026 E4
12800 HrmT 44234 3026 E4
16300 TroT 44021 2766 E7
16300 TroT 44021 2767 A7
16300 TroT 44021 2895 E1
16300 TroT 44062 2767 A7
18100 TroT 44234 2895 E7
18100 TroT 44234 3026 E1
18500 TroT 44231 3026 E1
Munich Dr
9000 PRMA 44130 3013 C2
Municipal Dr
- HRM 44234 3161 A2
Munn Rd
14800 NbyT 44065 2763 C2
14800 NbyT 44072 2763 C2
15500 CLEV 44111 2752 C1
15500 NbyT 44073 2763 C2
16300 AbnT 44023 2763 C5
16300 NbyT 44023 2763 C5
16400 AbnT 44023 2892 C1
18000 AbnT 44023 3023 C2
Munnberry Ovl
14700 NbyT 44065 2763 C1
Munson Rd
7700 MNTR 44060 2143 E3
7700 MONT 44060 2143 E3
8000 MNTR 44060 2144 A3
Munson Rd SR-615
7700 MNTR 44060 2143 E3
7700 MONT 44060 2143 E3
8000 MNTR 44060 2144 A3
Munson St
400 PNVL 44077 2040 A7
Mural Dr
5700 BNHT 44131 2884 B2
5700 SVHL 44131 2884 B2
Murcott Cir
100 ORNG 44022 2759 A4
Muriel Av
3500 CLEV 44109 2754 B4
Murphy Rd
4000 HgvT 44086 2259 B6
4000 HgvT 44099 2259 B6
4000 HgvT 44086 2259 B6
4000 MtlT 44086 2259 B6
4000 TmbT 44086 2259 B6
4000 TmbT 44099 2259 B6
4000 TmbT 44086 2259 B6
8600 HgvT 44064 2259 B6
8600 MtlT 44064 2259 B6
8700 HgvT 44064 2259 B6
Murphy St
10 BERA 44017 2880 B6
100 GDRV 44045 2039 C6
400 PnvT 44077 2039 C6
Murray Av
4200 WLBY 44094 2250 D5
7400 MNTR 44060 2252 C1
Murray Rd
900 SELD 44121 2498 B5
8400 VLVW 44125 2885 B2
Murray St
5200 PryT 44077 2041 B7
Murray Hill Rd
2000 CLEV 44106 2626 D2
2300 CVHT 44106 2626 D2
Murray Ridge Rd
1000 ELYR 44035 3005 C2
6200 EyrT 44035 2745 B7
6400 EyrT 44035 2874 B1
8100 ELYR 44035 2874 B4
9100 EyrT 44035 3005 C1
9500 CrlT 44035 3005 C1
Murwood Dr
10 MDHL 44022 2760 B3
Music St
7900 RslT 44073 2761 E4
8200 RslT 44073 2762 A4
8500 RslT 44072 2762 B4
9300 NbyT 44072 2763 A4
9300 NbyT 44073 2763 A4
9300 RslT 44073 2763 A4
9300 RslT 44072 2763 A4
10300 NbyT 44065 2763 D4
10800 NbyT 44065 2764 A4
11900 NbyT 44021 2764 B4
Musket Dr
9500 MNTR 44060 2253 A1
Muskingum Blvd
15200 BKPK 44142 2881 B1
Muskoka Av
18500 CLEV 44119 2372 E5
19300 CLEV 44119 2373 A5
Mussey St
400 ELYR 44035 3005 E1
400 ELYR 44035 3006 A1

Cleveland Street Index

INDEX 34

Oakfield Av

Outerbelt East Frwy

Cleveland Street Index

STREET Block City ZIP Map# Grid

Oakfield Av
11800 CLEV 44105 2756 D1
Oak Glen Dr
8800 CdnT 44024 2254 E6
Oakham Rd
1600 EUCL 44117 2373 C7
Oakhill Blvd
4400 LORN 44053 2743 C5
Oak Hill Cir
38300 WLBY 44094 2251 A3
Oak Hill Dr
400 RDHT 44143 2498 C3
7500 CsTp 44026 2501 C4
Oakhill Dr
24200 EUCL 44117 2373 D6
Oak Hill Ln
38300 WLBY 44094 2250 E3
38400 WLBY 44094 2251 A2
Oakhill Rd
7300 OKWD 44146 3018 E1
7700 NRYN 44133 3013 D7
15400 ECLE 44112 2497 C5
16200 CVHT 44112 2497 C5
Oakhill Ter
300 MCDN 44056 3018 B6
Oak Hollow Dr
400 MDSN 44057 2044 A2
11400 CdnT 44024 2254 C6
Oak Hollow Rd
500 AURA 44202 3156 C4
Oakhurst Av
700 AMHT 44001 2743 D7
11700 CcdT 44077 2254 E5
Oakhurst Cir
7600 BKVL 44131 3016 C3
7600 BKVL 44141 3016 C3
7600 INDE 44141 3016 C3
7600 INDE 44131 3016 C3
32500 NRDV 44039 2748 E7
Oakhurst Ct
600 AMHT 44001 2743 D7
Oakhurst Dr
- BHIT 44212 3146 A7
7800 BKVL 44141 3016 C3
Oakhurst Ln
- SGVL 44136 3146 B2
Oak Knoll Ct
8300 NRYN 44133 3014 A3
Oak Knoll Dr
3200 PRPK 44124 2629 D7
Oak Knoll St
34000 ETLK 44095 2249 E2
34000 ETLK 44095 2250 A2
Oakland Av
12000 CLEV 44106 2496 D7
Oakland Dr
4800 LNHT 44124 2498 E7
E Oakland Rd
23700 BYVL 44140 2620 D5
W Oakland Rd
27800 BYVL 44140 2619 E5
27800 BYVL 44140 2620 A5
29400 BYVL 44140 2619 C4
Oakland St
10 NRsT 44074 3138 E1
Oakland Park Dr
14000 SGVL 44136 3012 C3
Oaklawn Ct
- AURA 44202 3156 D1
Oaklawn Dr
1700 PRMA 44134 2883 D2
Oak Leaf Dr
8600 SGVL 44136 3012 C3
Oak Leaf Ovl
100 OKWD 44146 3018 B1
Oakleaf Rd
7300 OKWD 44146 2887 C7
7300 OKWD 44146 3018 C1
Oakleaf Rd SR-14
- OKWD 44146 2887 C7
S Oakleaf Rd
7400 OKWD 44146 3018 C1
Oakleigh Dr
10 BNWK 44212 3147 C6
Oakley Av
4600 CLEV 44102 2624 B7
Oakley Green Dr
100 ELYR 44035 3006 A3
Oak Meadow Dr
7600 TwbT 44236 3154 D6
Oakmont Dr
700 AVLK 44012 2618 D5
5000 LNHT 44124 2628 E1
5000 LNHT 44124 2629 A1
N Oakmont Dr
10 NCtT 44067 3153 C3
Oakmont Ln
- AURA 44202 3021 D5
Oakmont Rd
10 NCtT 44067 3153 B4
Oakmont Wy
7900 CcdT 44077 2253 E3
E Oakmont Wy
10 NCtT 44067 3153 C4
Oakmoor Rd
300 BYVL 44140 2620 C5
Oakmount Rd
1400 SELD 44121 2498 D7
1400 SELD 44121 2628 C1
Oaknoll Dr
400 AhtT 44001 2873 B1
Oak Park Av
2100 CLEV 44109 2754 C6
Oakpark Blvd
12000 GDHT 44125 2885 D1
13500 GDHT 44125 2886 A1
Oak Park Dr
9500 BKVL 44141 3016 C3
Oak Point Ests
6300 LORN 44053 2743 B5
Oak Point Rd
- AMHT 44001 2743 C6
- AMHT 44053 2743 C6
- LORN 44001 2743 C6
3700 LORN 44053 2743 B4
Oak Ridge Dr
5400 WLBY 44094 2374 E1
5400 WLBY 44094 2375 A1
Oakridge Dr
10 GNVA 44041 1944 D6
1200 CVHT 44121 2497 E6
4100 NRYN 44133 3014 A3
5100 WLBY 44094 2249 B4
5100 WLBY 44094 2374 E1
7600 CcdT 44060 2253 C2
Oakridge Dr
8500 OmsT 44138 2878 E7
8500 OmsT 44138 2879 A7
Oak Shore Grn
10 BTNH 44108 2496 E2
Oakstone Tr
8000 CdnT 44024 2254 C7
9100 CdnT 44024 2379 C1
Oakton Cir
400 MAYF 44143 2500 B2
Oak Trail Ct
20700 SGVL 44136 3011 B4
Oak Tree Blvd
6000 INDE 44131 2884 C3
Oak Tree Ct
- MDBH 44130 2881 B4
Oaktree Dr
- MCDN 44056 3153 E2
34600 WLBY 44094 2375 A1
Oak Tree Dr N
6200 LORN 44053 2743 B4
Oak Tree Dr S
6300 LORN 44053 2743 B4
Oaktree Ln
100 TroT 44234 2894 B6
Oak Tree Tr
13600 NbyT 44065 2634 C5
Oakview Av
11700 CLEV 44108 2496 D4
Oakview Blvd
12300 GDHT 44125 2885 D2
13500 GDHT 44125 2886 A2
Oak View Cir
2600 BWHT 44147 3014 C4
Oakview Cir
- HkyT 44233 3147 E7
Oakview Ct
9100 TNBG 44087 3019 B7
Oak View Dr
4900 VMLN 44089 2741 A7
Oakview Dr
900 HDHT 44143 2499 A6
3000 WBHL 44092 2374 B7
Oakview Ln
36200 AVON 44011 2747 E3
Oakview Rd
500 MCDN 44056 3018 D5
Oakview St
23200 ODFL 44138 2879 D7
Oakville Rd
5700 MDHT 44124 2499 C7
Oakwood Av
- SVHL 44131 3015 A2
10 BDFD 44146 2886 E4
200 CrlT 44035 3006 B3
500 SDLK 44054 2616 C4
2700 LORN 44055 2745 E3
5300 MPHT 44137 2886 E1
Oakwood Blvd
10 PnvT 44077 2040 D2
5000 LORN 44055 2745 E5
5000 ShfT 44055 2745 E5
Oakwood Cir
6000 NRDV 44039 2877 E2
6000 NRDV 44039 2878 A2
27000 OmsT 44138 2878 D3
30300 NOSD 44070 2878 A1
Oakwood Ct
2000 AVON 44011 2747 D1
Oakwood Dr
- OmsT 44138 2878 C3
100 AVLK 44012 2618 E2
700 MAYF 44040 2500 B5
900 ELYR 44035 2874 C4
1100 VMLN 44089 2740 D6
2800 WBHL 44094 2374 E6
5300 SFLD 44054 2746 E1
5400 SFLD 44054 2747 A1
6500 INDE 44131 2884 C5
6500 SVHL 44131 3015 A1
8000 KTLD 44094 2376 E7
9600 TNBG 44087 3019 C5
29400 WKLF 44092 2374 A1
Oakwood Ln
1100 HkyT 44133 3149 A6
1100 HkyT 44233 3149 A6
1100 NRYN 44133 3149 A6
1200 HkyT 44133 3148 E5
1200 HkyT 44233 3148 E5
1200 NRYN 44133 3148 E5
3000 WTLK 44145 2750 A3
8500 NRYN 44133 3014 B3
11900 CsTp 44026 2502 B4
Oakwood Pl
- SGVL 44136 3146 A1
Oakwood Rd
- CVHT 44121 2498 A7
6700 PMHT 44130 2881 E7
7100 PRMA 44130 2881 E7
Oakwood Tr
3100 BWHT 44147 3014 C7
Oakwood Commons Dr
21200 OKWD 44146 2887 C7
Oasis Blvd
10 MadT 44057 1941 A6
Ober Ln
7100 BbgT 44023 2761 B7
Oberlin Av
- AhtT 44001 2744 C6
- AhtT 44053 2744 C6
100 LORN 44052 2614 D6
1200 LORN 44052 2744 C2
3200 LORN 44053 2744 C4
Oberlin Rd
10 NRsT 44074 3139 B3
10 OBLN 44074 3139 B3
5500 AhtT 44001 2744 C7
6300 AhtT 44001 2873 D1
6500 AhtT 44035 2873 D1
7100 AhtT 44001 2873 C3
7100 AhtT 44035 2873 C3
10200 AhtT 44035 3004 B2
10200 NRsT 44035 3004 B2
12000 NRsT 44074 3004 B7
Oberlin-Elyria Rd
100 ELYR 44035 3006 A2
400 CrlT 44035 3005 E3
400 ELYR 44035 3005 E3
8500 AhtT 44035 2873 B5
9400 AhtT 44035 3004 B1
41800 CrlT 44074 3005 C6
42000 CrlT 44074 3139 D2
42000 CrlT 44074 3140 A1
42000 NRsT 44074 3139 D2
45100 OBLN 44074 3139 C3
Oberlin-North Rd
8700 AhtT 44001 2873 A7
8700 AhtT 44035 2873 A7
9200 AhtT 44001 2872 E7
9200 AhtT 44035 2872 E7
9200 AhtT 44001 3003 E4
9200 AhtT 44035 3003 E4
9200 NRsT 44035 3003 E4
9200 NRsT 44001 3003 E4
10700 NRsT 44074 3003 E4
12400 OBLN 44074 3003 E4
12500 NRsT 44074 3138 E1
Oberlin-North Rd SR-58
8700 AhtT 44001 2873 A7
8700 AhtT 44035 2873 A7
9200 AhtT 44001 2872 E7
9200 AhtT 44035 2872 E7
9200 AhtT 44001 3003 E4
9200 AhtT 44035 3003 E4
9200 NRsT 44035 3003 E4
9200 NRsT 44001 3003 E4
10700 NRsT 44074 3003 E4
12400 OBLN 44074 3003 E4
12500 NRsT 44074 3138 E1
Oberlin-Norwalk Rd
47000 NRsT 44074 3138 A2
Oberlin-Norwalk Rd SR-511
47000 NRsT 44074 3138 A2
Ocala Dr
4400 PRMA 44134 3014 B2
Ocean Pt
6600 MNTR 44060 2145 A5
Ocean Reef
37300 WLBY 44094 2250 D3
Octavia Rd
1600 CLEV 44112 2497 C3
October Ln
5800 MadT 44057 1941 D1
Ogontz Av
2200 LKWD 44107 2622 B7
2300 CLEV 44111 2622 B7
2300 LKWD 44111 2622 B7
O'Henry Cir
6500 NRDV 44039 2877 C3
Ohio Av
1600 LORN 44052 2615 D6
14200 GDHT 44128 2757 A5
14400 CLEV 44128 2757 A5
Ohio St
100 ELYR 44035 2875 B5
800 AURA 44202 3021 B4
3200 PryT 44081 2041 E2
5200 VMLN 44089 2740 E5
6900 MNTR 44060 2143 C7
Ohio Tpk I-80
- AhtT - 2871 E5
- AhtT - 2872 B5
- AhtT - 2873 C4
- AMHT - 2872 B5
- BERA - 3010 C1
- BERA - 3011 A2
- BhmT - 2871 B7
- BKVL - 3150 B4
- BWHT - 3149 B2
- BWHT - 3150 B4
- ELYR - 2874 D3
- ELYR - 2875 B4
- EyrT - 2873 C4
- EyrT - 2874 D3
- NRDV - 2875 E4
- NRDV - 2876 B5
- NRDV - 2877 A5
- NRDV - 2878 D6
- NRYN - 3012 E6
- NRYN - 3013 A7
- NRYN - 3148 D2
- NRYN - 3149 B2
- ODFL - 3010 C1
- OmsT - 2878 A6
- OmsT - 2879 A7
- OmsT - 3010 C1
- RchT - 3150 D5
- RchT - 3151 A6
- RHFD - 3150 D5
- RHFD - 3151 A6
- SGVL - 3011 A2
- SGVL - 3012 E6
Ohio Tpk I-90
- AhtT - 2871 B7
- AhtT - 2872 B5
- AhtT - 2873 A4
- AMHT - 2872 B5
- BhmT - 2871 E5
Ohlman Av
11300 CLEV 44108 2496 D5
Okalona Rd
4000 SELD 44121 2628 A3
Old Abbe Rd
3600 SFLD 44054 2746 E3
Old Alexander Rd
- VLVW 44125 3016 E1
Old Barn Dr
900 AURA 44202 3156 C4
Old Brecksville Rd
5400 INDE 44131 2884 E1
Old Brookpark Rd
- CLEV 44131 2755 A7
500 BNHT 44131 2755 A7
500 BNHT 44109 2755 A7
500 CLEV 44109 2755 A7
Old Cochran Rd
7200 GNWL 44139 3019 C2
Old Colorado Av
- SFLD 44054 2615 E7
- SFLD 44054 2616 C7
Old Cord Ln
- GSML 44040 2500 E7
Old Detroit Rd
19000 RKRV 44116 2621 E5
Olde Bennett Rd
19400 NRYN 44133 3147 E5
Olde Egbert Rd E
10 BDFD 44146 2887 A5
Olde Egbert Rd W
100 BDFD 44146 2887 A6
Olde Eight Rd
7400 BSHT 44236 3153 C6
7800 NCtT 44236 3153 C6
7900 NCtT 44067 3153 C6
9100 NCtT 44067 3152 E1
9300 NCtT 44067 3017 E7
9500 SgHT 44067 3017 E7
9700 NCtT 44067 3018 A6
9700 SgHT 44067 3018 A6
Olde Eight Rd
10000 NHFD 44067 3018 A6
Olde Farm Ln
7200 MNTR 44060 2143 C5
Olde Field Ct
6600 MNTR 44060 2143 C5
Olde Meadows Ct
6800 MNTR 44060 2143 C6
Olde Orchard Rd
13200 SGVL 44136 3147 D5
Olde Pond Ln
9500 TNBG 44087 3019 C6
Olde Stone Ct
11500 CcdT 44077 2254 D2
Olde Surrey Ct
17300 SGVL 44136 3147 A4
Olde Towne Tr
100 BERA 44017 3011 C1
19800 SGVL 44136 3147 C5
Olde Village Ln
8600 MNTR 44060 2144 C7
Olde York Rd
6300 PMHT 44130 2882 C4
Old Farm Rd
10 MDHL 44022 2759 D5
Old Granger Rd
7800 GDHT 44125 2756 A7
Old Grayton Rd
- CLEV 44135 2751 B7
Old Green Rd
3400 BHWD 44122 2758 C1
Old Harper Rd
5800 SLN 44139 2888 C3
Old Heisley Rd
6900 MNTR 44060 2145 A6
Old Highland Dr
8900 BKVL 44141 3016 A6
Old Hogsback Rd
- CLEV 44111 2622 A7
- LKWD 44111 2622 A7
Old Johnnycake Rd
9600 CcdT 44060 2145 A6
9600 CcdT 44077 2145 A6
9600 MNTR 44060 2145 A6
Old Kinsman Rd
33600 PRPK 44022 2760 A1
33700 HGVL 44022 2760 A1
Old Lake Rd
- LORN 44053 2742 E4
- VMLN 44089 2740 D5
6300 LORN 44053 2743 A4
Old Lorain Rd
- FWPK 44126 2752 A2
17800 CLEV 44135 2752 A2
17800 CLEV 44111 2752 A2
Old Meadow Dr
8900 BbgT 44023 2891 C5
Old Middle Ridge Rd
- EyrT 44035 2745 A6
- EyrT 44052 2745 A6
- EyrT 44053 2745 A6
- LORN 44035 2745 A6
- LORN 44053 2745 A6
45200 AhtT 44001 2873 B3
Old Mill Pth
1300 BWHT 44147 3149 E5
Old Mill Rd
700 AURA 44202 3156 C4
1200 AURA 44087 3156 A5
2000 MadT 44057 1941 C2
2100 TNBG 44087 3155 A5
2100 TNBG 44236 3155 A5
2100 TwbT 44236 3155 A5
2100 TwbT 44087 3155 A5
7000 CsTp 44026 2501 A7
7000 GSML 44040 2500 C7
7200 GSML 44040 2630 D1
7600 GSML 44040 2500 E7
Old Munson Rd
8400 MNTR 44060 2144 B4
Old North Dr
10 NCtT 44067 3152 E1
10 SgHT 44067 3152 E1
Old Oak Blvd
7200 MDBH 44130 2880 E7
7200 MDBH 44130 3011 E1
Old Oak Dr
- SGVL 44136 3146 A2
Old Oak Rd
1200 AMHT 44001 2744 A7
Old Orchard
22900 FWPK 44126 2751 A6
Old Orchard Dr
10100 BKVL 44141 3151 D5
Old Plank Ln
10 MDHL 44022 2760 D6
Old Pleasant Valley Rd
13000 MDBH 44130 2881 D6
Old Post Rd
8200 ODFL 44138 2879 A6
Old Quarry Ln
7300 BKVL 44141 3016 A5
Old Reservoir Rd
400 BERA 44017 3011 C1
Old River Rd
1000 CLEV 44113 2624 C3
Old Rockside Rd
100 SVHL 44131 2883 E2
100 SVHL 44131 2884 A2
800 PRMA 44134 2883 E2
7400 INDE 44131 2884 E3
7400 INDE 44131 2885 A3
8000 INDE 44125 2885 B3
8000 VLVW 44125 2885 B3
18000 BDFD 44146 2886 D3
Old Royalton Rd
6200 BKVL 44141 3015 E6
6200 BWHT 44141 3015 E6
6200 BWHT 44147 3015 E6
6600 BKVL 44141 3016 A6
Old Royalwood Rd
900 BWHT 44147 3014 E6
Old Schady Rd
26800 OmsT 44138 2879 A7
Old Shore Dr
30700 NOSD 44070 2878 A2
Oldsmar Av
1300 MadT 44057 1843 C7
Old Som Ln
- PRPK 44022 2760 A2
10 MDHL 44022 2760 A2
Old South Miles Rd
32100 SLN 44139 2888 E4
Old State Rd
8400 HmbT 44024 2255 D5
Old State Rd
8400 HmbT 44077 2255 D5
8800 HmbT 44024 2380 E1
8800 HmbT 44024 2381 A2
10900 ClrT 44024 2506 C1
10900 HmbT 44024 2506 C1
12400 ClrT 44021 2506 E6
12400 ClrT 44021 2636 E1
12800 ClrT 44021 2637 A2
13400 HtbT 44021 2637 A2
13500 MdfT 44021 2637 C6
13600 MdfT 44046 2637 C6
13700 MdfT 44062 2637 C6
14300 MDFD 44062 2767 D1
14300 MdfT 44062 2767 D1
15000 MDFD 44062 2767 D4
15000 MdfT 44062 2767 D4
15900 MdfT 44062 2768 A6
16300 PkmT 44062 2768 A6
16300 PkmT 44062 2897 B1
17000 PkmT 44062 2898 A5
17600 FnTp 44491 2898 A5
17600 PkmT 44491 2898 A5
Old State Rd SR-608
8400 HmbT 44024 2255 D5
8400 HmbT 44077 2255 D5
8800 HmbT 44024 2380 E1
8800 HmbT 44024 2381 A2
10900 ClrT 44024 2506 C1
10900 HmbT 44024 2506 C1
12400 ClrT 44021 2506 E6
12400 ClrT 44021 2636 E1
12800 ClrT 44021 2637 A2
13400 HtbT 44021 2637 A2
13500 MdfT 44021 2637 C6
13600 MdfT 44046 2637 C6
13700 MdfT 44062 2637 C6
14300 MDFD 44062 2767 D1
14300 MdfT 44062 2767 D1
15000 MDFD 44062 2767 D4
15000 MdfT 44062 2767 D4
Old Tannery Tr
17300 BbgT 44023 2890 D4
Old Virginia Ln
6200 PMHT 44130 2882 A4
Old West Ridge Rd
- ELYR 44035 2873 E5
- EyrT 44035 2745 A7
- EyrT 44035 2873 E5
- LORN 44035 2745 A7
- LORN 44053 2745 A7
Oleander Ovl
400 MDSN 44057 1942 B7
Olive Av
2000 LKWD 44107 2622 C6
5100 NRDV 44039 2748 C7
5100 NRDV 44039 2877 C2
Olive Ct
5500 CLEV 44103 2625 D2
Olive St
10 CNFL 44022 2761 A7
100 CNFL 44022 2760 E7
100 ELYR 44035 2875 D5
100 GDRV 44045 2039 B5
Oliver Dr
18100 SGVL 44136 3146 D4
Oliver Rd
10800 CLEV 44111 2753 B2
Oliver St
400 SDLK 44054 2616 A4
Olivet Av
- EyrT 44035 2745 E6
- ShfT 44035 2745 E6
- ShfT 44055 2745 E6
9900 CLEV 44108 2496 B7
Olivet Ct
- CLEV 44108 2496 C7
Olivet Dr
400 ELYR 44035 2875 D3
Olivewood Av
1400 LKWD 44107 2622 D5
Olmar Dr
10900 CdnT 44024 2378 E7
10900 CdnT 44024 2503 E1
10900 MsnT 44024 2503 E1
Olmsted Dr
3100 NOSD 44070 2750 E3
Olmway Av
8000 ODFL 44138 2879 B6
Olney Ct
11300 CLEV 44105 2756 D4
Olympia
- AbnT 44023 2892 A7
- AbnT 44023 3023 A1
Olympia Rd
17100 CLEV 44112 2497 C3
Olympus Ct
- SGVL 44136 3011 D6
Olympus Wy
12400 SGVL 44136 3011 D6
Omaha Av
3100 LORN 44055 2745 B3
O'Malley Dr
100 PRMA 44134 2883 E1
Omega Av
5400 BDHT 44146 2887 D1
Omega Ct
9500 MNTR 44060 2145 A5
Omega Pkwy
- HDHT 44143 2499 B2
Onaway Ovl
5600 PRMA 44130 2882 C1
Onaway Rd
3100 SRHT 44120 2627 B7
O'Neil Blvd
5100 ShfT 44055 2745 B5
O'Neill Dr
37100 SLN 44139 2889 C3
Onoko Dr
19800 FWPK 44126 2751 D1
Onondaga Av
1500 LKWD 44107 2622 D6
Ontario St
700 GFTN 44044 3142 A5
1200 CLEV 44113 2624 C2
1200 CLEV 44114 2624 D2
2000 CLEV 44115 2624 C2
Ontario St SR-8
1900 CLEV 44114 2624 D2
2000 CLEV 44115 2624 D2
2100 CLEV 44113 2624 D2
Ontario St SR-14
2100 CLEV 44113 2624 E3
2100 CLEV 44115 2624 E3
Ontario St SR-87
1900 CLEV 44114 2624 D2
2000 CLEV 44115 2624 D2
2100 CLEV 44113 2624 D2
Ontario St US-422
1900 CLEV 44114 2624 D2
2000 CLEV 44115 2624 D2
2100 CLEV 44113 2624 D2
Opal St
5800 NRDV 44039 2877 C1
Opalocka Dr
12600 CsTp 44026 2502 B7
Opportunity Av
3700 PRRY 44081 2042 C1
E Oralee Ln
7400 TwbT 44236 3154 C6
N Oralee Ln
1300 TwbT 44236 3154 C5
S Oralee Ln
1300 TwbT 44236 3154 C6
W Oralee Ln
7400 TwbT 44236 3154 C5
Orange Av
1400 CLEV 44115 2625 B4
Orange Av SR-8
1400 CLEV 44115 2625 B4
Orange Av SR-87
1400 CLEV 44115 2625 B4
Orange Av US-422
1400 CLEV 44115 2625 B4
Orange Ln
16600 AbnT 44021 2893 D2
Orange Pl
3600 BHWD 44122 2759 A2
3600 ORNG 44122 2759 A2
E Orange St
10 CNFL 44022 2761 A6
W Orange St
10 CNFL 44022 2760 E6
10 CNFL 44022 2761 A6
Orangedale Rd
4200 ORNG 44022 2759 C4
E Orange Hill Cir
100 ORNG 44022 2759 C6
W Orange Hill Cir
10 ORNG 44022 2759 C6
Orange Meadow Ln
4100 ORNG 44022 2759 B4
Orange Tree Dr
100 ORNG 44022 2759 A5
Orangewood Dr
- ORNG 44022 2759 C2
3900 ORNG 44122 2759 B3
Orchard Av
800 AURA 44202 3021 A4
4100 CLEV 44113 2624 B6
4200 WLBY 44094 2250 D5
5200 ShfT 44055 2745 C6
5400 PRMA 44129 2883 A1
6700 PRMA 44129 2882 E1
8500 BKLN 44144 2753 D4
14800 MDFD 44062 2767 C2
Orchard Bch
- VmnT 44089 2740 A7
Orchard Blvd
6600 PMHT 44130 2882 A6
Orchard Ct
2000 SFLD 44054 2616 C7
41600 EyrT 44035 2874 D2
Orchard Dr
- CcdT 44077 2254 C4
- MNTR 44060 2251 B4
2800 WBHL 44092 2374 C5
31500 WLWK 44095 2249 C4
Orchard Ext
2000 WBHL 44092 2374 C5
Orchard Grv
10 OmsT 44138 2879 B3
10 PNVL 44077 2145 E2
300 BERA 44017 2880 C6
Orchard Ln
1000 BWHT 44147 3149 D4
5200 NRDV 44039 2748 D7
Orchard Rd
500 WLBY 44094 2143 A4
3900 CVHT 44121 2498 A6
4500 FWPK 44126 2751 A4
4600 MNTR 44060 2038 D5
4700 CLEV 44128 2757 A6
4800 GDHT 44128 2757 A6
8100 CcdT 44077 2254 C4
11400 MsnT 44024 2504 C2
35000 SLN 44139 2888 E6
Orchard St
- SAHT 44001 3003 C1
10 OBLN 44074 3139 A2
100 GNVA 44041 1944 C4
200 CNFL 44022 2760 E7
200 FTHR 44077 2039 C4
4400 MNTU 44255 3159 B6
5400 MPHT 44137 2886 B1
8100 ODFL 44138 2879 C6
36900 AVON 44011 2747 D2
Orchard Wy
3100 WTLK 44145 2749 E3
Orchard Grove Av
300 SgHT 44067 3017 C7
1400 LKWD 44107 2622 C6
6000 CLEV 44144 2754 A3
6300 CLEV 44144 2753 E3
7400 BKLN 44144 2753 E3
20200 RKRV 44116 2621 D7
Orchard Grove Dr
700 RDHT 44143 2498 E5
16600 MDBH 44130 2881 B5
Orchard Heights Dr
1100 MDHT 44124 2499 E7
Orchard Hill Blvd
6100 LORN 44053 2744 D7
Orchard Hill Dr
100 AMHT 44001 2872 E2
100 AMHT 44001 2873 A1
18000 WNHL 44146 3017 E2
18500 WNHL 44146 3018 A2
Orchard Hill Ln
10200 TNBG 44087 3020 A4
Orchard Park Av
14400 CLEV 44111 2752 C1
Orchard Park Dr
700 RKRV 44116 2621 A6
4800 PRMA 44129 2883 A5
4800 PRMA 44134 2883 A5
32200 AVLK 44012 2618 C2
Orchardview Rd
100 SVHL 44131 3014 E2
Orchardview Rd
100 SVHL 44131 3015 A2
1100 PRMA 44134 3014 E2
Orchid Av
5500 MNTR 44060 2144 B1
Ordner Dr
13900 SGVL 44136 3011 E7
13900 SGVL 44136 3146 E1
Oregon Av
4200 PryT 44081 2041 D4
Oregon Tr
10 ClrT 44024 2505 C6
Orey Av
5400 CLEV 44105 2755 D2
Orianna St
7900 BKVL 44141 3016 B3
Orin Wy
2800 TNBG 44087 3020 B4
Oring Rd
28600 NOSD 44070 2749 D6
Orinoco Av
13800 ECLE 44112 2497 A5
Oriole Av
26000 EUCL 44132 2373 E1
26800 EUCL 44132 2374 C1
Oriole Ct
10 ELYR 44035 3006 E1
5700 MNTR 44060 2144 E2
Oriole Dr
600 ETLK 44095 2250 D1
Oriole Pl
11500 MsnT 44024 2504 B3
Orkney Rd
1600 MadT 44057 1842 E7
1700 MadT 44057 1941 E1
Orlando Dr
7500 PRMA 44134 3014 D1
Orleans Av
9300 CLEV 44105 2756 B1
Orme Rd
12000 GDHT 44125 2885 D2
Ormiston Av
19300 EUCL 44119 2372 E5
19300 EUCL 44119 2373 A5
Ormond Av
1300 MadT 44057 1843 C6
Ormond Rd
3200 CVHT 44118 2627 C4
Ornelda Av
- MadT 44057 1843 C7
Oroszy Av
5000 ShfT 44052 2745 A5
Orton Ct
6300 CLEV 44103 2495 E7
Orton Rd
10 PnvT 44077 2147 B2
Orville Av
10500 CLEV 44106 2496 C7
Orvos Ct
9100 MNTR 44060 2144 E1
Osage Av
7400 CLEV 44105 2756 A2
Osage Dr
7900 SGVL 44136 3011 E2
Osage Wy
3000 BWHT 44147 3014 C7
Osborn Ln
2900 TNBG 44087 3020 C4
Osborn Rd
4600 GDHT 44125 2757 A5
4600 GDHT 44128 2757 A5
25500 BYVL 44140 2620 C5
27800 BYVL 44140 2619 D5
27800 BYVL 44140 2620 A5
Osborn St
5000 MPHT 44128 2757 B7
Osborne Av
800 LORN 44052 2614 C7
Osborne Dr
8900 MNTR 44060 2144 D6
Osborne Rd
24900 ClbT 44028 3009 D3
24900 ClbT 44028 3010 A3
27600 ClbT 44028 3008 E4
27600 ClbT 44028 3009 A4
27600 EatT 44028 3008 E4
Osceola Av
11700 CLEV 44108 2496 D6
Osmond Ct
6500 CLEV 44105 2755 E1
Osmond Rd
13400 BtnT 44024 2635 E4
13400 ClrT 44024 2635 E4
13600 BtnT 44021 2635 D5
Ostend Av
9900 CLEV 44108 2496 B6
Oster Rd
4700 SDLK 44054 2616 D4
4700 SFLD 44054 2616 D4
Otani Ct
17200 SGVL 44136 3012 A7
Othello Av
13500 CLEV 44110 2497 A1
Otis Ct
400 SgHT 44067 3017 D4
7100 CLEV 44104 2625 E5
7300 CLEV 44104 2626 A5
Otis Pl
15700 MPHT 44137 2757 B7
Otokar Av
3000 CLEV 44127 2625 D6
Ottawa Av
6700 MadT 44057 1843 B7
Ottawa Dr
8500 BKVL 44141 3016 D6
Ottawa Rd
6700 CLEV 44105 2755 E3
7400 CLEV 44105 2756 A3
Otten Rd
6200 NRDV 44039 2876 B2
Otter Av
8100 CLEV 44104 2626 A
Otto Ct
5600 CLEV 44102 2624 A
Outerbelt East Frwy I-271
- BDFD - 2887 C
- BDHT - 2758 E
- BDHT - 2887 C
- BHWD - 2629 C
- BHWD - 2758 E
- BHWD - 2759 A
- HDHT - 2499 E
- LNHT - 2629 C
- MAYF - 2499 E

INDEX 35
Outerbelt East Frwy
Cleveland Street Index
Patio Ln

STREET Block City ZIP Map# Grid

Outerbelt East Frwy I-271
- MDHT - 2499 E4
- MDHT - 2500 A7
- MDHT - 2629 C2
- OKWD - 2887 C6
- OKWD - 3018 C2
- ORNG - 2758 E5
- ORNG - 2759 A3
- PRPK - 2629 C2
- PRPK - 2759 A3
- WBHL - 2374 E7
- WVHT - 2758 E5
Outerbelt East Frwy I-480
- BDFD - 2887 C6
- BDHT - 2887 C6
- OKWD - 2887 C6
- OKWD - 3018 C2
Outerbelt East Frwy SR-14
- OKWD - 2887 C7
- OKWD - 3018 C2
Outerbelt East Frwy US-422
- BHWD - 2758 E5
- BHWD - 2759 A2
- ORNG - 2758 E5
- ORNG - 2759 A2
- WVHT - 2758 E5
Outerbelt South Frwy I-480
- BKLN - 2753 C6
- BNHT - 2755 A7
- BNHT - 2884 B1
- CLEV - 2751 C6
- CLEV - 2752 D6
- CLEV - 2753 C6
- CLEV - 2754 A6
- CLEV - 2755 A7
- FWPK - 2751 C6
- GDHT - 2756 E7
- GDHT - 2757 A7
- GDHT - 2885 A1
- INDE - 2884 B1
- INDE - 2885 A1
- MPHT - 2757 A7
- NOSD - 2750 C7
- NOSD - 2751 C6
- NOSD - 2878 D2
- NOSD - 2879 A1
- OmsT - 2878 D2
- VLVW - 2885 A1
Outhwaite Av
4000 CLEV 44104 2625 D4
Outley Park Dr
33100 SLN 44139 3019 E1
33100 SLN 44139 3020 A1
33600 SLN 44139 2889 A7
Outlook Av
7400 BKLN 44144 2753 E4
Outlook Dr
4400 BKLN 44144 2753 D5
Outrigger Ln
100 NCtT 44067 3153 C5
Outriggers Cove
10100 RMDV 44202 3020 D5
Oval Dr
- SRHT 44120 2627 B6
7400 INDE 44131 3015 E1
Overbrook Av
- NOSD 44070 2749 C7
2100 LKWD 44107 2622 A6
Overbrook Dr
4100 BKVL 44141 3015 E6
Overbrook Rd
300 ELYR 44035 2875 B4
1500 LNHT 44124 2629 A1
Overland Dr
10 OmsT 44138 2879 A3
Overland Ln
33300 SLN 44139 2889 A4
Overland Park Dr
19400 SGVL 44136 3146 D1
Overlook Av
8100 BWHT 44147 3015 A4
Overlook Ct
400 PNVL 44077 2146 A3
24800 ODFL 44138 2879 C7
Overlook Dr
400 AURA 44202 3156 C3
2600 TNBG 44087 3020 A6
8700 KTLD 44094 2251 D6
11400 NbyT 44065 2764 D2
17000 BbgT 44023 2891 A3
21700 FWPK 44126 2751 B5
22700 EUCL 44117 2373 B7
30100 WKLF 44092 2374 E2
38600 CrlT 44044 3006 E5
E Overlook Dr
100 ETLK 44095 2142 D6
W Overlook Dr
100 ETLK 44095 2142 C6
Overlook Ln
- WNHL 44146 2886 C7
2000 CVHT 44106 2627 A3
Overlook Pl
10 BDFD 44146 2887 C3
Overlook Rd
10 BTVL 44022 2889 D1
10 PnvT 44077 2146 D1
300 VMLN 44089 2741 D4
400 GSML 44040 2500 D2
1100 LKWD 44107 2622 A4
2100 CLEV 44106 2626 E2
2100 CVHT 44106 2626 E2
2500 CVHT 44106 2627 A2
4900 GDHT 44125 2756 E6
5500 PRMA 44129 2882 D1
11600 MsnT 44024 2504 C3
12000 NbyT 44021 2764 D3
12000 NbyT 44065 2764 D3
31900 AVLK 44012 2618 E2
E Overlook Rd
2600 CVHT 44106 2627 B2
2800 CVHT 44118 2627 B2
S Overlook Rd
2100 CVHT 44106 2626 E3
Overlook Brook Ct
300 AbnT 44023 2892 A3
Overlook Brook Dr
200 AbnT 44023 2892 B5
Overlook Park Dr
200 CLEV 44110 2372 B7

Overlook Ridge Dr
800 CLEV 44109 2755 A4
Overture Dr
15100 NbyT 44065 2763 E4
15100 NbyT 44065 2764 A3
Oviatt Dr
10 NCtT 44067 3153 B3
Oviatt Ln
10400 TNBG 44087 3020 B3
E Oviatt Rd
26100 BYVL 44140 2620 B5
W Oviatt Rd
27200 BYVL 44140 2620 A5
27900 BYVL 44140 2619 E5
Ovington Av
6500 CLEV 44127 2755 E1
Owaissa Dr
10 TMLK 44095 2250 A2
Owego Av
1400 LKWD 44107 2622 A5
Owego St
400 PNVL 44077 2040 A6
900 PNVL 44077 2039 E5
Owen Rd
17800 PkmT 44062 2897 C6
17800 PkmT 44491 2897 C6
18200 PkmT 44062 3028 C1
18200 PkmT 44491 3028 C1
Owens Rd
14600 NbyT 44065 2764 D1
Owls Hollow Ln
17300 BbgT 44023 2890 D4
Owosso Av
6700 CLEV 44105 2755 E3
Oxford Av
200 ELYR 44035 2875 C6
17200 CLEV 44111 2752 B2
Oxford Cir
2000 HkyT 44233 3148 B6
Oxford Ct
6200 BDHT 44146 2887 E4
Oxford Dr
200 AURA 44202 3021 B7
1200 MadT 44057 1843 D6
3400 LORN 44053 2744 A3
7900 SGVL 44136 3011 E3
8100 PRMA 44129 2882 D4
Oxford Ln
7900 CsTp 44026 2501 E3
Oxford Ovl
17600 SGVL 44136 3147 A3
E Oxford Ovl
3300 NOSD 44070 2750 D4
N Oxford Ovl
24200 NOSD 44070 2750 D4
S Oxford Ovl
24200 NOSD 44070 2750 D4
W Oxford Ovl
3300 NOSD 44070 2750 D4
Oxford Rd
- CVHT 44121 2497 E5
18800 SRHT 44122 2627 E6
37200 ETLK 44095 2142 D6
Oxford St
100 TwbT 44087 3154 C2
Oxford Tr
9200 BKVL 44141 3150 B1
Oxford Glen Dr
9600 MNTR 44060 2145 A1
Oxford Park Ln
26900 OmsT 44138 2878 E3
26900 OmsT 44138 2879 A3
Oxgate Ct
7500 HDSN 44236 3155 C7
Oxgate Ln
32000 HGVL 44022 2630 A7
N Oxshire Pl
7100 CcdT 44077 2146 A7
Oynes Ct
4200 CLEV 44128 2757 C4
Ozark Av
16700 CLEV 44110 2372 C6
16900 CLEV 44119 2372 C6

P

Pabin Ct
- MCDN 44056 3153 E1
Pacific Av
5600 CLEV 44102 2754 A1
Packard Av
7200 MDBH 44130 2881 B7
Packard Cir
7100 MDBH 44130 2881 B6
Packard Ct
6500 MNTR 44060 2144 B5
7000 BKVL 44141 3016 A7
Packard Dr
2300 LORN 44055 2746 A5
2300 ShfT 44055 2746 A5
Padanarum Rd
2800 GnvT 44041 1943 E3
4000 GnvT 44041 1844 E7
4600 GOTL 44041 1844 E5
Paddock Cir
600 BERA 44017 3010 E2
Paddock Ct
8300 MNTR 44060 2251 C5
Paddock Dr
7400 CsTp 44026 2501 C6
13100 MsnT 44024 2634 A2
Padua Dr E
12000 NRYN 44133 3014 A6
Padua Dr N
6000 NRYN 44133 3013 E6
6000 NRYN 44133 3014 A6
Padva
- PRMA 44134 2883 B5
Page Av
1800 ECLE 44112 2497 B5
Page Ct
- SDLK 44054 2616 B5
5900 CLEV 44103 2625 D1
Page Dr
10100 CcdT 44077 2253 D3
Page Rd
500 AURA 44202 3157 C3
500 AURA 44255 3157 C4
1300 AURA 44241 3157 B5
10100 STBR 44241 3157 B7
Pagent Ln
10 OmsT 44138 2879 A3
Paige Pl
10 PNVL 44077 2146 A1

Paine Av
5200 MPHT 44137 2757 C7
Paine Rd
5400 LryT 44057 2148 B2
5400 LryT 44077 2148 B2
Paine St
1500 LORN 44052 2615 C6
Painesville Ravenna Rd
10300 MNTU 44255 3159 B7
10300 ShvT 44255 3159 B7
12400 ManT 44255 3024 C4
12800 AbnT 44255 3024 C4
Painesville Ravenna Rd SR-44
10300 MNTU 44255 3159 B7
10300 ShvT 44255 3159 B7
12400 ManT 44255 3024 C4
12800 AbnT 44255 3024 C4
Painesville Warren Rd
- PnvT 44077 2146 C3
6100 CcdT 44077 2146 C3
11900 CcdT 44077 2147 C5
12200 LryT 44077 2147 C5
13000 LryT 44077 2255 E1
13000 LryT 44077 2256 A1
14100 LryT 44086 2256 B2
14500 LryT 44086 2257 A3
14500 TpnT 44086 2257 A3
Painesville Warren Rd SR-86
- PnvT 44077 2146 C3
6100 CcdT 44077 2146 C3
11900 CcdT 44077 2147 C5
12200 LryT 44077 2147 C5
13000 LryT 44077 2255 E1
13000 LryT 44077 2256 A1
14100 LryT 44086 2256 B2
14500 LryT 44086 2257 A3
14500 TpnT 44086 2257 A3
Painesville Warren State Rd
4400 StnT 44491 3029 C1
4700 FnTp 44491 3029 C1
5600 FnTp 44491 2898 A6
Painter Rd
7400 OKWD 44146 3018 C2
Paisley Dr
5900 NOSD 44070 2879 A2
Paisley Rd
1800 MadT 44057 1941 E2
Palamino Tr
300 AURA 44202 3022 B4
Palda Dr
16700 CLEV 44128 2757 C4
Palisades Dr
4700 MadT 44057 2044 A5
Palisades Pkwy
7300 MNTR 44060 2251 B2
30300 WKLF 44092 2374 D1
Pallister Dr
4000 CLEV 44105 2755 C2
Palm Av
2800 LORN 44055 2746 A3
Palm Blvd
10 MadT 44057 1941 B6
Palm Cir
18800 FWPK 44126 2752 A1
Palm Dr
24000 NOSD 44070 2750 D6
Palmer Av
10 PnvT 44077 2145 C4
Palmer Dr
2400 WBHL 44094 2375 B3
3300 RKRV 44116 2751 A2
Palmer Ln
11200 TNBG 44087 3020 B3
Palmer Rd
11200 CcdT 44077 2146 C4
N Palmerston Dr
6600 MNTR 44060 2143 D5
Palmerston Rd
3400 SRHT 44122 2757 D1
Palmerstone Dr
6700 MNTR 44060 2143 D6
Palmetto St
10 BDFD 44146 2886 E3
Palm Springs Dr
3500 LORN 44053 2744 C4
Palomino Tr
8500 KTLD 44094 2377 B7
Palo Verde Ct
800 ETLK 44095 2250 B3
Pam Ct
23300 EUCL 44123 2373 C2
Pamela Ct
6100 BKPK 44142 2881 B3
Pamela Dr
7200 NRYN 44133 3013 D2
10100 SGVL 44136 3011 C4
13500 GDHT 44125 2885 E4
Pamela Ln
- BHIT 44212 3146 A7
Pamona Av
7900 NCtT 44067 3153 A1
Panama Dr
3300 PRMA 44134 3014 C2
Panna Ln
900 CLEV 44109 2754 E5
Panorama Dr
10 SVHL 44131 2883 E4
10 SVHL 44131 2884 A4
Par Ln
2200 WLBY 44094 2375 A3
Parade St
10 OmsT 44138 2879 A3
Paradise Al
400 FTHR 44077 2039 D4
Paradise Blvd
10 MadT 44057 1941 B6
Paradise Ct
10 FTHR 44077 2039 D4
Paradise Dr
100 MdfT 44062 2768 B5
Paradise Ln
24300 EUCL 44123 2373 D1
Paradise Rd
10 PnvT 44077 2147 A2
300 PryT 44077 2147 A2
Parafine Av
- CLEV 44113 2624 D5
Paris Av
3100 CLEV 44109 2624 C7
Park Av
- AVLK 44012 2618 B2
- RDHT 44143 2499 A3

Park Av
100 AMHT 44001 2872 E2
100 CRDN 44024 2379 E7
100 CRDN 44024 2380 A7
100 ELYR 44035 2875 C7
1100 AMHT 44001 2873 A2
1200 AhtT 44001 2873 A2
1200 ELYR 44035 3006 C1
1300 MadT 44057 1843 B6
7100 CLEV 44105 2755 E3
7500 CLEV 44105 2756 A3
37200 WLBY 44094 2250 D5
S Park Av
10 BDFD 44146 2887 C4
Park Blvd
100 PNVL 44077 2146 A2
800 SELD 44117 2498 B5
800 SELD 44121 2498 B5
N Park Blvd
1600 CVHT 44106 2626 E4
2500 CVHT 44106 2627 A4
2600 CVHT 44118 2627 D5
18200 CVHT 44120 2627 D5
18200 SRHT 44120 2627 D5
18700 SRHT 44122 2627 D5
18700 SRHT 44118 2627 D5
19800 SRHT 44118 2628 A5
19800 SRHT 44122 2628 A5
20600 UNHT 44118 2628 A5
26500 ODFL 44138 3010 A1
28900 SLN 44139 2759 C7
S Park Blvd
2600 CVHT 44118 2627 B5
2600 SRHT 44118 2627 B5
5600 PRMA 44134 2883 D2
13800 SRHT 44120 2627 A4
17500 SRHT 44122 2627 E6
19400 SRHT 44122 2628 A6
W Park Blvd
2600 SRHT 44120 2627 B5
Park Cir
16600 BbgT 44023 2890 E1
16600 BbgT 44023 2891 A1
Park Ct
1700 EUCL 44117 2498 A2
2400 WTLK 44145 2750 B2
Park Dr
- ELYR 44035 2875 A5
- MDHT 44124 2500 A7
- SLN 44139 2889 B1
10 MdfT 44062 2768 B6
100 SDLK 44054 2616 C3
200 BNHT 44131 2755 A7
200 CRDN 44024 2379 D5
400 BYVL 44140 2620 E5
2400 PRMA 44134 2883 C5
2700 CVHT 44118 2627 D6
2700 LORN 44052 2744 E3
2700 SRHT 44118 2627 D6
2700 SRHT 44120 2627 D5
4700 CLEV 44144 2754 A3
5000 VMLN 44089 2740 E5
5000 VMLN 44089 2741 A5
13300 BKPK 44130 2881 D3
13300 BKPK 44142 2881 D3
17000 BbgT 44023 2891 A3
E Park Dr
4800 NOSD 44070 2749 E7
16800 CLEV 44119 2372 D5
N Park Dr
10 BDFD 44146 2887 C3
200 AURA 44202 3156 E4
21000 FWPK 44126 2751 B4
27800 NOSD 44070 2749 E6
S Park Dr
- AVON 44011 2747 E5
- AVON 44011 2748 A5
200 AURA 44202 3156 E4
4800 FWPK 44126 2751 B4
5200 LORN 44053 2743 C5
W Park Dr
2300 LORN 44053 2744 A2
4600 FWPK 44126 2751 B5
4800 NOSD 44070 2749 D7
5400 NOSD 44070 2878 D1
Park Dr W
- NOSD 44070 2750 A7
Park Ln
- BYVL 44140 2619 D4
10 CLEV 44110 2372 C6
100 MDHL 44022 2760 B6
3800 NBGH 44105 2755 C2
5100 NOSD 44070 2750 D7
10500 CLEV 44106 2626 C2
30800 PRPK 44124 2629 D6
Park Ovl
600 MDSN 44057 2044 A2
Park Pl
10 BDFD 44146 2887 C4
400 BERA 44017 2880 A5
500 ELYR 44035 2875 C6
2400 WTLK 44145 2750 B2
3700 CLEV 44109 2754 D2
15800 LKWD 44107 2622 C6
26300 NOSD 44070 2750 B5
N Park Pl
10 PNVL 44077 2040 D7
S Park Pl
10 PNVL 44077 2040 D7
10 PNVL 44077 2146 B1
Park Pt
11700 SGVL 44136 3012 B6
Park Rd
- CLEV 44119 2372 C5
- ELYR 44035 2875 A5
- PnvT 44077 2147 B1
10 PnvT 44077 2041 B7
5300 CLEV 44135 2880 E1
N Park Rd
2100 TwbT 44087 3154 D2
4500 FnTp 44491 3029 E4
W Park Rd
- AVON 44011 2748 B2
3600 CLEV 44111 2752 B2
Park Sq
- LORN 44053 2743 C6
Park St
10 BERA 44017 2880 C7
10 GNVA 44041 1944 B4
10 MDSN 44057 2044 B1
5500 MONT 44060 2143 E1
10700 MNTU 44255 3159 C5
29300 WKLF 44092 2374 C3
E Park St
- BURT 44021 2636 B7

E Park St
100 CRDN 44024 2380 A6
14500 BURT 44021 2766 B1
E Park St SR-44
100 CRDN 44024 2380 A6
E Park St SR-87
- BURT 44021 2636 B7
14500 BURT 44021 2766 B1
E Park St US-6
100 CRDN 44024 2380 A6
N Park St
10 OBLN 44074 3138 E2
S Park St
10 OBLN 44074 3138 E3
W Park St
- BURT 44021 2636 C7
14500 BURT 44021 2766 A1
W Park St SR-87
- BURT 44021 2636 A7
14500 BURT 44021 2766 A1
W Park Circle Dr
16600 BbgT 44023 2890 E1
Parkcliff Ct
20700 FWPK 44126 2751 C4
Parkcliff Dr
20600 FWPK 44126 2751 C4
Park Cliff Rd
12100 SGVL 44136 3011 E5
Parkdale Av
14000 CLEV 44111 2752 D2
21700 FWPK 44126 2751 B4
Parkdale Dr
8300 NRYN 44133 3013 D3
Parkdale Rd
3700 CVHT 44121 2497 E7
3800 CVHT 44121 2498 A7
Park East Dr
3500 BHWD 44122 2758 E2
34300 SLN 44139 2889 A6
Parkedge Cir
22300 FWPK 44126 2751 B4
Parkedge Dr
4500 FWPK 44126 2751 B4
10900 CLEV 44104 2626 C7
Parker Ct
100 CRDN 44024 2379 C6
Parker Dr
1500 MDHT 44124 2500 B7
1500 MDHT 44124 2630 A1
7300 MNTR 44060 2252 C1
12000 CsTp 44026 2502 C5
Parker Rd
600 AURA 44202 3022 C5
Park Fulton Ovl
4000 CLEV 44144 2754 B3
Parkgate Av
9000 CLEV 44108 2496 B6
Parkgate Dr
- WLBY 44094 2250 C7
Parkgate Ovl
6600 SVHL 44131 2884 B5
Parkgrove Av
15200 CLEV 44110 2372 B7
Parkhall Dr
10 PnvT 44077 2041 A6
E Parkhaven Dr
100 SVHL 44131 2883 E6
500 SVHL 44131 2884 A6
1000 PRMA 44134 2883 E6
Parkhaven Row
1400 LKWD 44107 2622 E5
Park Heights Av
8800 GDHT 44125 2756 B6
Park Heights Rd
10200 CLEV 44104 2626 C7
Parkhill Av
11600 CLEV 44120 2626 D6
Parkhill Dr
5800 PMHT 44130 2882 C2
Parkhill Rd
1400 CVHT 44121 2497 E7
Parkhurst Dr
5200 SFLD 44054 2746 D5
10500 CLEV 44111 2753 B1
Parkknoll Dr
12300 GDHT 44125 2756 D6
Parkland Av
6400 BKPK 44142 2880 B3
Parkland Blvd
200 VMLN 44089 2741 D4
6000 MDHT 44124 2629 D2
6500 SLN 44139 2888 D6
Parkland Dr
- ETLK 44095 2249 E3
10 AVLK 44012 2617 D1
5700 PRMA 44130 2882 C1
6000 SRSL 44073 2762 A6
9700 TNBG 44087 3019 B4
15600 SRHT 44120 2627 B6
18600 SRHT 44122 2627 E7
Parkland Ovl
200 BNWK 44212 3147 A7
Parkland Rd
- VMLN 44089 2741 D5
7000 INDE 44131 3015 E1
32200 WLWK 44095 2249 D4
33000 ETLK 44095 2249 D4
Parklane Av
19600 RKRV 44116 2751 D1
Parklane Dr
2800 PRMA 44134 2883 C2
19900 RKRV 44116 2751 D1
20900 FWPK 44126 2751 C3
26200 EUCL 44132 2373 E2
Parklawn Av
15700 MDBH 44130 2881 B7
Parklawn Dr
300 RKRV 44116 2621 B5
4200 WLBY 44094 2251 A6
11200 CLEV 44108 2496 D5
Park Ledge Dr
1000 MCDN 44056 3018 E6
Parkleigh Dr
900 PRMA 44134 2883 E3
E Parkleigh Dr
10 SVHL 44131 2883 E3
10 SVHL 44131 2884 A3
Park Ln Dr
16400 SGVL 44136 3147 A3
Park Ln Rd
11300 NbyT 44065 2764 C1
Parkman Blvd
14100 BKPK 44142 2881 D2
Parkman Rd
12000 NsnT 44231 3028 A7

Parkman Rd NW
5100 StnT 44231 3029 A6
Parkman Rd NW US-422
5100 StnT 44231 3029 A6
Parkman Mesopotamia Rd
- FnTp 44062 2769 B7
- MstT 44062 2769 B7
- PkmT 44062 2769 B7
7300 MstT 44062 2769 B7
Park Meadow Dr
100 ELYR 44035 3006 D1
Park Moss Av
11500 SGVL 44136 3012 C6
Parkmount Av
18200 CLEV 44135 2752 A5
18500 CLEV 44135 2751 E5
Park North Dr
6500 SLN 44139 2889 A6
Park Place Dr
9500 BKVL 44141 3016 C3
Parkridge Av
5900 CLEV 44144 2754 A3
Park Ridge Dr
5600 NOSD 44070 2878 D1
Parkridge Dr
2400 HkyT 44233 3148 A6
Park Ridge Ln
- MCDN 44056 3154 A1
Park Row Av
1300 LKWD 44107 2622 A5
Parkside
200 BSHT 44236 3153 B7
Parkside Blvd
500 SELD 44143 2498 B4
Parkside Cir
1500 LNHT 44124 2498 D7
Parkside Dr
- AVLK 44012 2618 E4
200 BYVL 44140 2620 B4
1000 LKWD 44107 2622 D3
2600 HDSN 44236 3155 C7
4000 BKLN 44144 2753 E3
7500 PRMA 44130 3013 C1
8500 CsTp 44026 2502 B7
8600 SgHT 44067 3018 A5
17300 NRYN 44133 3148 A3
20100 RKRV 44116 2621 D4
S Parkside Dr
4300 BKLN 44144 2753 E4
Parkside Pl
1000 CLEV 44108 2496 B6
Parkside Rd
1000 CLEV 44108 2496 B6
11300 MsnT 44024 2504 C3
Parkside Tr
5000 SLN 44139 2759 B7
5100 SLN 44139 2888 B1
Parkstone Av
- NOSD 44070 2749 C7
Parks West Rd
4700 MstT 44062 2769 E5
Parkton Dr
4300 WVHT 44128 2757 D5
Parkview Av
700 LORN 44052 2614 C7
1200 LORN 44052 2744 C1
1400 MadT 44057 1843 B6
6800 PRMA 44134 2883 D6
9400 CLEV 44104 2626 C6
9700 GDHT 44125 2756 C5
11600 CLEV 44120 2626 D6
19900 RKRV 44116 2751 D1
Park View Cir
9700 SGVL 44136 3012 D4
Parkview Ct
100 ELYR 44035 2875 A6
Parkview Dr
- MAYF 44143 2500 A1
10 BERA 44017 3011 B1
10 OmsT 44138 2879 C4
10 PNVL 44077 2040 B6
100 ELYR 44035 2875 A7
200 AVLK 44012 2618 A2
300 SDLK 44054 2616 D4
300 SVHL 44131 2884 A6
1300 LNHT 44124 2499 A7
2000 TNBG 44087 3019 D4
3400 AVON 44011 2748 C4
12500 CsTp 44026 2502 B7
15400 NbyT 44065 2634 D4
27700 EUCL 44132 2249 A7
E Parkview Dr
6900 PRMA 44134 2883 E6
N Parkview Dr
100 AURA 44202 3156 D3
S Parkview Dr
600 AURA 44202 3156 E4
W Parkview Dr
6900 PRMA 44134 2883 D6
Parkview Ln
5800 FWPK 44126 2751 B6
34500 WLBY 44094 2375 A2
Parkview Rd
4600 FnTp 44491 3029 E3
7300 BKVL 44141 3151 B3
33800 WBHL 44092 2375 A7
Parkway E
- NOSD 44070 2750 A7
Parkway Blvd
10 MDSN 44057 2044 A2
600 AURA 44202 3156 C1
38000 WLBY 44094 2250 E1
E Parkway Blvd
- AURA 44202 3156 C1
W Parkway Blvd
- AURA 44202 3156 A1
Parkway Ct
38700 WLBY 44094 2143 A3
Park Way Dr
32700 SLN 44139 2888 E5
Parkway Dr
- BtnT 44021 2635 E7
- BWHT 44147 3014 E6
- VmnT 44089 2740 A7
10 OmsT 44138 2879 B4
100 ETLK 44095 2142 C7
200 BERA 44017 2880 B6
1300 LORN 44053 2744 C3
1400 LKWD 44107 2622 E5
1800 CVHT 44118 2627 C2
4800 GDHT 44125 2756 D6
11400 MsnT 44024 2504 C3
E Parkway Dr
100 MDSN 44057 2044 A2

N Parkway Dr
10 ETLK 44095 2142 C6
6800 MDBH 44130 2881 D5
12500 CLEV 44105 2756 E4
12600 GDHT 44105 2756 E4
S Parkway Dr
6800 MDBH 44130 2881 D5
13100 GDHT 44105 2756 E4
13600 GDHT 44105 2757 A4
W Parkway Dr
100 MDSN 44057 2043 E2
100 MDSN 44057 2044 A3
Parkway Rd
800 CLEV 44108 2496 D5
W Parkway Rd
13700 CLEV 44135 2752 D5
Park West Ovl
4300 CLEV 44135 2751 D5
Parkwood Av
- ManT 44255 3159 B3
100 AVLK 44012 2617 E2
21000 FWPK 44126 2751 C4
Park Wood Cir
5600 BTVL 44022 2889 C2
Parkwood Dr
100 BERA 44017 2880 A6
600 CLEV 44108 2496 D6
3500 WTLK 44145 2749 E4
8100 KTLD 44094 2376 E6
8100 KTLD 44094 2377 A6
11700 CdnT 44024 2379 D1
23500 ClbT 44028 3010 D3
27100 EUCL 44132 2248 E7
28300 EUCL 44132 2249 A6
28300 WLWK 44132 2249 A6
28300 WLWK 44095 2249 A6
29300 WKLF 44092 2249 A7
Parkwood Ln
10500 CdnT 44024 2379 A6
20800 SGVL 44136 3146 B3
Parkwood Rd
1400 LKWD 44107 2622 E5
6100 MNTR 44060 2143 E3
Parkwood St
10 OBLN 44074 3138 C2
Parliament Dr
10700 NRYN 44133 3014 A5
Parma Heights Blvd
5800 PMHT 44130 2882 C2
Parmalee Dr
2100 SVHL 44131 2884 B6
6900 MNTR 44060 2144 C6
10000 TNBG 44087 3020 B4
Parma Park Blvd
6600 PMHT 44130 2882 A7
7100 PRMA 44130 2882 A7
Parmaview Ln
7700 PRMA 44134 3014 C2
Parmelee Av
8900 CLEV 44108 2496 B5
Parmely Av
100 ELYR 44035 2874 E3
Parmenter Dr
7900 PRMA 44129 2882 D4
Parmly Pl
200 PNVL 44077 2040 B7
Parmly Rd
3100 NPRY 44081 1940 B6
3400 PryT 44081 1939 E5
3700 PryT 44081 1940 A5
Parnell Rd
21700 SRHT 44122 2628 B5
Parsons Ct
1200 RKRV 44116 2621 E5
Parsons Dr
100 AVLK 44012 2618 C1
2400 WBHL 44094 2375 B3
Parsons Rd
1000 GFTN 44044 3141 D5
1000 GFTN 44044 3142 A5
38500 CrlT 44044 3141 D5
38500 LrgT 44044 3141 D5
38900 CrlT 44050 3141 C5
38900 LrgT 44050 3141 C5
40700 CrlT 44050 3140 D5
40700 LrgT 44050 3140 D5
43200 CrlT 44050 3139 D4
43200 CrlT 44074 3139 D4
43200 LrgT 44050 3139 D4
43500 NRsT 44074 3139 D4
44200 OBLN 44074 3139 A3
Parsons Pond Cir
3600 WTLK 44145 2749 A4
Partridge Ct
7800 MNTR 44060 2143 E5
Partridge Dr
17000 SGVL 44136 3146 E2
17000 SGVL 44136 3147 A2
N Partridge Dr
12700 VLVW 44125 2885 E5
13100 VLVW 44125 2886 A5
S Partridge Dr
12700 VLVW 44125 2885 E6
12700 VLVW 44125 2886 A6
Partridge Ln
100 HGVL 44073 2631 A5
100 SLN 44139 2889 B3
Partridge Tr
9800 KTLD 44094 2377 B3
10500 BKVL 44141 3016 C4
Partridge Meadows Ct
2000 HDSN 44236 3155 A6
Partridge Meadows Dr E
7500 HDSN 44236 3155 A7
Partridge Meadows Dr N
2000 HDSN 44236 3154 E6
2000 HDSN 44236 3155 A6
Pasadena Av
100 ELYR 44035 2875 C5
500 SDLK 44054 2616 B4
10500 CLEV 44108 2496 C6
N Pasadena Av
900 ELYR 44035 2875 C3
Pasadena Dr
2400 SVHL 44131 2884 B6
Pasnow Av
18600 EUCL 44119 2372 E4
18600 EUCL 44119 2373 A4
Patch Rd
13800 TroT 44021 2895 B2
14900 PkmT 44021 2896 A2
14900 TroT 44021 2896 A2
15400 PkmT 44062 2896 B2
Patio Ln
- OmsT 44138 2879 B4

STREET Block City ZIP Map# Grid

Patricia Av
- NRDV 44039 3007 E1
Patricia Ct
9600 CrlT 44035 3005 A1
Patricia Dr
12600 NRYN 44133 3012 E3
Patriot Dr
13900 BtnT 44021 2635 C5
Patt Ct
- WLBY 44094 2250 D4
Patterson Dr
6800 MNTR 44060 2144 C6
Patterson Ln
39400 SLN 44139 2889 E6
Patterson Pkwy
20400 HIHL 44128 2758 A3
Patti Pk
1300 WTLK 44145 2619 C7
Pattie Dr
300 BERA 44017 3010 E1
300 BERA 44017 3011 A1
Patton Ct
1200 TNBG 44087 3019 A4
Patton Dr
- BKVL 44141 3016 A6
33800 NRDV 44039 2877 C4
Patton Rd
4100 CLEV 44109 2754 E4
Patton St
9800 TNBG 44087 3019 A4
Paul Av
12000 CLEV 44106 2626 E2
Paul St
10 BDFD 44146 2887 B6
Paula Ct
5800 NRDV 44039 2877 B2
Paula Dr
6700 MDBH 44130 2881 C6
Paulding Blvd
15500 BKPK 44142 2881 B2
Paulette Dr
16200 BtnT 44021 2765 B7
Pauline Dr
400 LvpT 44280 3145 D7
Paulpine Rd
7800 SgHT 44067 3017 C7
Pau Pau Ct
6500 BDHT 44146 2887 D6
Pawnee Av
18500 CLEV 44119 2372 E5
19300 CLEV 44119 2373 A5
Pawnee Tr
13100 MDBH 44130 3012 D1
Paw Paw Lake Dr
10 SRSL 44073 2762 C5
Pawtucket Ln
100 PnvT 44077 2145 C4
Paxton Rd
100 ETLK 44095 2142 D5
800 CLEV 44108 2496 E5
2800 SRHT 44120 2627 C6
Payne Av
400 PNVL 44077 2040 B6
1300 CLEV 44114 2625 A2
3900 CLEV 44103 2625 C1
Payne Rd
18900 NsnT 44231 3027 C3
18900 PkmT 44231 3027 C3
Peach Blvd
800 WLBY 44094 2143 A4
Peach St
- VMLN 44089 2740 E4
10 OmsT 44138 2879 A4
Peach Tree Dr
11300 CsTp 44026 2502 C3
Peachtree Dr
10000 SGVL 44136 3011 C4
Peachtree Ln
10 PnvT 44077 2145 C3
22500 RKRV 44116 2621 A6
Pear Av
6800 CLEV 44102 2623 E6
6800 CLEV 44102 2624 A6
Pear St
33600 AVON 44011 2748 D2
Pearl Av
2700 LORN 44052 2745 D2
2700 LORN 44055 2745 D2
Pearl Ct
- CLEV 44113 2624 D6
Pearl Rd
10 BHIT 44212 3146 D6
10 BNWK 44212 3146 D6
10 BNWK 44136 3146 D6
10 SGVL 44136 3146 D6
3600 CLEV 44109 2754 D3
4500 CLEV 44144 2754 B6
5300 PRMA 44129 2753 E7
5300 PRMA 44129 2882 D1
5800 PMHT 44130 2882 D1
5800 PMHT 44129 2882 D1
5800 PRMA 44130 2882 D1
6600 MDBH 44130 2881 C6
6600 PMHT 44130 2881 C6
7400 MDBH 44130 3012 B1
7900 SGVL 44136 3012 B1
9000 SGVL 44136 3011 D6
12200 CdnT 44024 2255 A7
12400 HmbT 44024 2255 C7
Pearl Rd SR-3
3600 CLEV 44109 2754 D3
4500 CLEV 44144 2754 B6
5300 PRMA 44129 2753 E7
5300 PRMA 44129 2882 D1
Pearl Rd US-42
10 BHIT 44212 3146 D6
10 BNWK 44212 3146 D6
10 BNWK 44136 3146 D6
10 SGVL 44136 3146 D6
3600 CLEV 44109 2754 D3
4500 CLEV 44144 2754 B6
5300 PRMA 44129 2753 E7
5300 PRMA 44129 2882 D1
5800 PMHT 44130 2882 D1
5800 PMHT 44129 2882 D1
5800 PRMA 44130 2882 D1
6600 MDBH 44130 2881 C6
6600 PMHT 44130 2881 C6
7400 MDBH 44130 3012 B1
7900 SGVL 44136 3012 B1
9000 SGVL 44136 3011 D6
Pearl St
- EyrT 44035 2745 C7
10 PNVL 44077 2146 B1
100 AMHT 44001 2872 E2
400 BERA 44017 2880 C5
34100 NRDV 44039 2877 C2
S Pearl St
6000 EyrT 44035 2745 D6
6000 EyrT 44055 2745 D6
Pearldale Av
16200 CLEV 44135 2752 B3
Pearlview Dr
13800 SGVL 44136 3011 E7
14300 SGVL 44136 3146 E1
Pearse Av
4400 NBGH 44105 2755 C3
Pear Tree Dr
7800 CsTp 44026 2501 D4
Peartree Ln
6500 MNTR 44060 2143 E5
Pease Dr
2700 RKRV 44116 2751 C1
Pease Rd
14100 MPHT 44137 2886 A1
Peasley Rd
9000 BhmT 44001 2870 E5
9000 BhmT 44089 2870 E5
9000 BhmT 44001 2871 A5
9000 BhmT 44089 2871 A5
9200 BhmT 44001 2870 E7
Pebble Beach Ovl
30800 WTLK 44145 2749 A2
Pebble Beach Cove
9800 RMDV 44202 3020 E6
9800 RMDV 44202 3021 A6
Pebblebrook Dr
300 WBHL 44094 2374 E5
Pebble Brook Ln
6000 NOSD 44070 2879 B2
9500 SGVL 44136 3011 A4
Pebblebrook Ln
10 MDHL 44022 2759 E6
10 MDHL 44022 2760 A6
Pebblebrook Ovl
2200 WTLK 44145 2750 E2
Pebblebrook Tr
12600 NRYN 44133 3012 E2
Pebble Brooke Ct
7500 NCtT 44067 3153 E5
Pebble Cove
2200 WTLK 44145 2750 E1
11300 CcdT 44077 2146 C7
Pebble Creek Ct
8200 BbgT 44023 2890 E6
8200 BbgT 44023 2891 A7
Pebble Creek Dr
2200 TNBG 44087 3019 D6
Pebblecreek Dr
6300 INDE 44131 2884 C4
Pebble Creek Ln
5300 PryT 44077 2041 B7
5400 PryT 44077 2147 B1
Pebble Creek Pass
- BHIT 44212 3146 B7
Pebblehurst Ct
2100 PnvT 44077 2145 B6
Pecan Ct
3700 ORNG 44022 2759 D3
Pecan Dr
400 BERA 44017 2880 A5
7300 PRMA 44129 2882 D7
7300 PRMA 44130 2882 D7
Pecan Ovl
15500 MDBH 44130 2881 C5
Peck Av
6900 CLEV 44103 2495 E6
Peck Rd
10100 ManT 44255 3159 E6
10100 ShvT 44255 3159 E6
10300 MNTU 44255 3159 E6
Peckham Av
11600 HRM 44234 3161 A2
Peckham Rd
14400 BtnT 44021 2636 B7
14400 BtnT 44062 2636 B7
14400 BtnT 44062 2766 C1
14400 BtnT 44021 2766 C1
14400 BURT 44021 2636 B7
14400 BURT 44021 2766 C1
Peg Dr
- LORN 44052 2744 D5
Pekin Ct
9100 MNTR 44060 2144 E1
Pekin Rd
8500 RslT 44072 2632 B6
9300 NbyT 44072 2633 A6
9300 RslT 44072 2633 A6
9800 NbyT 44065 2633 C6
10900 NbyT 44065 2634 A6
11800 NbyT 44065 2635 A6
Pelham Dr
4600 BKLN 44144 2754 A6
5400 PRMA 44129 2883 A3
6800 PRMA 44129 2882 E3
7500 CsTp 44026 2501 C5
Pelham Pl
- AVON 44011 2747 E3
Pelican Cove
11300 CcdT 44077 2146 D6
11300 CcdT 44077 2254 D2
Pellett Dr
300 BYVL 44140 2619 B4
Pelley Dr
700 CLEV 44109 2754 E6
700 CLEV 44109 2755 A6
Pelret Pkwy
10 BERA 44017 2879 D6
Pelton Ct
1000 CLEV 44113 2624 E5
Pelton Rd
38100 WLBY 44094 2250 E4
38500 WLBY 44094 2251 A4
Pemberton Dr
5700 BKPK 44142 2881 D2
Pembridge Ct
100 SDLK 44054 2615 E4
Pembroke Ln
- AVON 44011 2618 B7
Pembroke Cove
400 BNWK 44212 3147 B7
Pembrook Ovl
20500 SGVL 44136 3146 B5
Pembrook Rd
900 CVHT 44121 2497 D6
Pendley Rd
600 WLWK 44095 2249 D5
Penfield Av
300 ELYR 44035 2874 D5
10500 GDHT 44125 2756 C7
Penfield Dr
8600 SgHT 44067 3017 E5
Penfield Ln
6000 SLN 44139 2889 D4
Penhurst Rd
1300 CLEV 44110 2372 E7
Penn Ct
1000 GFTN 44044 3142 B5
Pennant Ct
8300 CLEV 44102 2623 E6
Penney Pines Cir
17100 SGVL 44136 3147 A4
Pennfield Rd
900 CVHT 44121 2497 E6
Penniman Dr
10200 HmbT 44024 2380 E5
Pennington Dr
10 PnvT 44077 2145 D5
Pennington Rd
3500 SRHT 44120 2757 B2
Pennsylvania Av
100 ELYR 44035 3006 B3
1200 LORN 44052 2615 D6
5800 MPHT 44137 2886 C3
6600 CLEV 44103 2625 E1
Pennsylvania Ct
1700 LORN 44052 2615 D7
Pennsylvania St
800 AURA 44202 3021 A4
Penny Ln
17100 BbgT 44023 2890 B3
36500 CrlT 44035 3006 C2
Pennywhistle Cir
6900 CcdT 44077 2145 C7
Penrose Av
1800 CLEV 44106 2626 E1
1800 CLEV 44112 2626 E1
1800 ECLE 44112 2496 B3
1800 ECLE 44112 2626 E1
Penrose Ct
100 ELYR 44035 2746 A7
Pensacola Av
3900 CLEV 44109 2754 C4
Penshurst Dr
7000 CcdT 44060 2145 B7
24500 BHWD 44122 2628 D4
Peony Av
10700 CLEV 44111 2753 B2
Pepper Av
14600 CLEV 44110 2497 B2
Pepper Ct
10800 CcdT 44077 2146 A7
Pepper Dr
35900 SLN 44139 2889 B3
Peppercorn Ct
1400 BWHT 44147 3149 C4
Peppercorn Dr
25700 WTLK 44145 2620 B6
Peppercorn Ln
1200 BWHT 44147 3149 D5
Peppercorn Ter
1400 BWHT 44147 3149 C4
Peppercreek Dr
10 PRPK 44124 2629 E6
13700 SGVL 44136 3012 D5
Pepperdine Dr
100 ELYR 44035 2746 D6
Peppergrass Cir
16500 SGVL 44136 3147 A4
Pepper Hollow Ln
6500 MDHT 44124 2500 A6
Pepperidge Dr
100 GNVA 44041 1944 C6
Peppermill Ct
30600 NOSD 44070 2878 A4
Peppermill Run
8400 BbgT 44023 3022 A1
Peppermint Pl
11200 NRYN 44133 3013 B5
Pepper Ridge Dr
8900 BKLN 44144 2753 D3
Pepper Ridge Rd
10 PRPK 44124 2629 E5
10 PRPK 44124 2630 A5
Pepper Tree Ln
100 PnvT 44077 2145 C3
Pepperwood Ct
6100 MNTR 44060 2144 D4
Pepperwood Dr
500 BNWK 44212 3146 C7
16200 SGVL 44136 3147 B4
Pepperwood Ln
10 PRPK 44124 2629 C5
Percy Av
6500 CLEV 44127 2625 E6
Peregrine Dr
2200 AVON 44011 2747 E2
Perennial Ln
6700 MNTR 44060 2145 A6
Pergl Rd
27200 GNWL 44139 2888 A7
27200 GNWL 44139 3019 A1
Perham Dr
500 BERA 44017 3010 D1
Periwinkle Dr
10 OmsT 44138 2879 A4
Periwinkle Ln
4400 RDHT 44143 2498 C3
Periwinkle Wy
2200 AVON 44011 2747 E2
Perkins Av
3000 CLEV 44114 2625 C2
4000 CLEV 44103 2625 C2
Perkins Dr
8800 MNTR 44060 2252 C2
Perkins Rd
5400 BDHT 44146 2887 E1
S Perkins Rd
6000 BDHT 44146 2887 E4
Perl Ct
- BWHT 44134 3014 C3
- BWHT 44147 3014 C3
- PRMA 44134 3014 C3
3100 NRYN 44133 3014 C3
3100 NRYN 44147 3014 C3
Perry Cir
4400 SVHL 44131 3015 C1
Perry Ct
- CLEV 44114 2625 B1
100 ELYR 44035 2875 C5
Perry Dr
8500 RslT 44072 2632 A4
30800 BYVL 44140 2619 B5
35200 ETLK 44095 2142 B7
Perry St
500 VMLN 44089 2740 D5
Perry Park Rd
2800 PryT 44081 1939 E6
3300 PryT 44081 2041 E1
Pershing Av
3700 PRMA 44134 2883 B1
4200 CLEV 44105 2625 B7
4200 CLEV 44127 2625 B7
Pershing Dr
8000 BKVL 44141 3015 E4
Persimmon Dr
29900 WTLK 44145 2749 C6
Persimmon Ln
- AVON 44011 2748 C3
4800 NRYN 44133 3014 B4
Persons Ct
10 ELYR 44035 2874 D4
Perth Ln
200 HDHT 44143 2499 C1
Perth Rd
1700 MadT 44057 1941 D1
Peters Rd
16500 MdfT 44062 2638 D5
17400 MdfT 44062 2639 A5
17400 MstT 44062 2639 A5
Peterson Ln
- WTLK 44145 2620 E7
Petrarca Rd
2200 CLEV 44106 2626 C3
Pettibone Rd
7000 BbgT 44023 3021 C1
8300 BbgT 44023 3022 A1
26000 OKWD 44146 3018 E2
26200 OKWD 44146 3019 A2
27000 GNWL 44139 3019 A2
31200 SLN 44139 3019 D2
32900 SLN 44139 3020 A2
38600 SLN 44023 3021 C1
38600 SLN 44139 3021 C1
Phalanx Mills Herner Rd
3700 StnT 44491 3029 C7
4700 FnTp 44491 3029 C3
Pheasant Ct
12000 MsnT 44024 2504 D5
35400 BTVL 44022 2889 B3
Pheasant Dr
4700 LORN 44053 2743 B5
Pheasant Ln
100 HGVL 44073 2631 B6
8600 KTLD 44094 2377 C4
23200 WTLK 44145 2751 A2
Pheasant Run
100 MDHT 44124 2629 E2
Pheasant Tr
16700 SGVL 44136 3147 A2
Pheasant Run Cir
12000 NRYN 44133 3148 A1
Pheasant Run Dr
10 CNFL 44022 2761 B6
Pheasant Run Ln
8700 KDHL 44060 2252 C6
Pheasant Run Pl
9300 SGVL 44136 3011 C3
Pheasants Wk
5400 NOSD 44070 2878 C1
Pheasant View Ln
200 TroT 44234 2894 B6
Phelps Av
1300 LKWD 44107 2622 A5
Phelps St
100 PNVL 44077 2040 D7
Philena Av
3800 CLEV 44109 2754 C3
Philetus Av
6500 CLEV 44127 2625 E6
Philip Av
5000 MPHT 44137 2757 D7
Philip Pkwy
10200 STBR 44241 3156 C7
Phillip Ct
10 ELYR 44035 2875 A5
Phillips Av
11700 CLEV 44108 2496 D6
12500 ECLE 44112 2496 D6
29600 WKLF 44092 2374 B1
29900 WKLF 44092 2249 C7
Phillips Rd
- TpnT 44086 2150 E7
- TpnT 44086 2258 D1
17400 TmbT 44086 2151 A7
17400 TpnT 44086 2151 A7
Philomethian St
10 CNFL 44022 2761 A6
Phyllis Av
- LORN 44053 2743 D3
Piccadilly Sq
38300 WLBY 44094 2250 E1
Piccolo Pl
10 OmsT 44138 2879 A4
Pickands Ln
- BTNH 44108 2496 B3
Pickett Rd
3200 LORN 44053 2744 A3
3500 LORN 44053 2743 E3
Pickway Dr
6000 BKPK 44142 2881 C2
Pickwick St
100 NCtT 44067 3153 A3
Picone Ln
24600 BDHT 44146 2887 D2
Piedmont Ct
2500 WTLK 44145 2749 D3
Pierce Dr
19000 SGVL 44136 3146 D1
Pierce St
15900 MDFD 44062 2767 D2
Piercefield Dr
6300 MDHT 44124 2499 E6
Piermont Rd
1000 SELD 44121 2498 B6
Pierpont Av
9200 CLEV 44108 2496 B6
Pierson Dr
400 RDHT 44143 2498 E3
Pike Av
- LORN 44055 2745 C3
Pike Blvd
15300 BKPK 44142 2881 B1
Pike Dr
28100 ORNG 44022 2759 B5
Pikewood Manor Rd
- ELYR 44035 2874 E2
Pilgrim Av
16500 CLEV 44111 2622 B7
Pilgrim Dr
8800 BbgT 44023 2891 B6
9500 MNTR 44060 2253 A3
Pilgrim Rd
8500 BbgT 44023 2891 A6
Pilsen Av
5800 CLEV 44102 2624 A7
Pinckneya Dr
5100 NRYN 44133 3014 B4
Pine Av
- LORN 44055 2745 C4
Pine Cir
3800 NOSD 44070 2749 E5
Pine Ct
2800 PryT 44081 2041 D3
N Pine Ct
200 AURA 44202 3156 D1
S Pine Ct
300 AURA 44202 3156 D2
Pine Dr
- MNTR 44060 2251 B4
Pine Ln
5400 SLN 44139 2888 D1
S Pine Ln
4700 PryT 44081 2042 E3
Pine Ovl
4400 PRMA 44134 3014 B1
Pine Pt
7200 CcdT 44077 2146 C7
Pine St
10 GNVA 44041 1944 B4
100 ELYR 44035 2875 B6
300 BDHT 44146 2758 D7
7000 BbgT 44022 2761 A7
Pine Vw
- MDSN 44057 1941 E6
Pine Acres Ln
11300 CsTp 44026 2502 D2
Pinebark Pl
1600 TNBG 44087 3019 B7
Pine Branch Cir
33000 NRDV 44039 2877 D1
Pinebrook Cir
3200 PryT 44081 2041 E4
Pinebrook Dr
12500 NRYN 44133 3012 E3
12500 NRYN 44133 3013 A3
Pinebrook Ln
32300 PRPK 44124 2759 E2
Pine Cone Dr
7500 PRMA 44134 3014 B1
Pinecone Dr
5900 MNTR 44060 2145 A3
9200 MNTR 44060 2144 E3
Pine Cone Ovl
800 SgHT 44067 3152 B2
Pine Creek Ct
8200 BbgT 44023 2890 E7
8200 BbgT 44023 2891 A7
Pinecreek Ln
8500 SgHT 44067 3018 A5
8600 SgHT 44067 3017 E5
Pine Crest Dr
10 BTVL 44022 2889 E1
10 BTVL 44022 2890 A1
Pinecrest Dr
10 BDFD 44146 2887 B5
Pinecrest Pl
1100 WLBY 44094 2142 E5
Pinecrest Rd
9900 CcdT 44060 2253 C4
9900 CcdT 44077 2253 C4
Pine Forest Dr
3900 PRMA 44134 3014 B1
14000 NRYN 44133 3013 E7
14000 NRYN 44133 3149 A1
Pinegate Dr
10300 CdnT 44024 2378 D7
10300 CdnT 44024 2503 D1
Pinegrove Av
7800 PRMA 44129 2882 D1
Pine Hill Ct
4000 NRYN 44133 3014 B3
Pinehill Dr
5300 MONT 44060 2038 A7
5300 MONT 44060 2143 D1
Pine Hill Rd
1100 SgHT 44067 3017 A7
Pinehill Rd
7000 CcdT 44077 2145 E7
7100 CcdT 44077 2146 A7
7100 CcdT 44077 2254 A1
Pine Hill Tr
15100 MDBH 44130 2881 C7
Pine Hollow Blvd
800 ShfT 44055 2745 B6
Pine Hollow Cir
100 CRDN 44024 2505 A2
Pine Hollow Dr
8500 RslT 44072 2632 B4
Pine Hollow Pl
3300 PryT 44081 1940 D7
Pinehurst Av
- CrlT 44035 3006 D3
- ELYR 44035 3006 D3
Pinehurst Blvd
10 ETLK 44095 2142 C6
Pine Hurst Ct
7300 MDBH 44130 2881 C7
Pinehurst Dr
- AURA 44202 3156 B1
1700 EUCL 44117 2498 A2
7900 KTLD 44094 2376 E2
8000 PRMA 44130 2882 D7
11600 MsnT 44024 2504 D1
30800 WTLK 44145 2749 A2
32200 AVLK 44012 2618 C4
Pinehurst Rd
500 HDHT 44143 2499 C3
7400 MONT 44060 2143 D2
Pine Lakes Dr
13900 SGVL 44136 3012 C4
Pine Manor Dr
9600 CdnT 44024 2379 D3
Pine Meadow Pl
100 PnvT 44077 2041 A6
Pineneedle Dr
9200 MNTR 44060 2144 E4
9200 MNTR 44060 2145 A4
Pine Needle Tr
10100 SGVL 44136 3011 B4
Pine Ridge Ct
7300 MDBH 44130 2881 C7
Pineridge Dr
2100 WKLF 44092 2374 E3
Pine Ridge Ovl
4800 INDE 44131 2884 C7
Pine River Ct
7400 MDBH 44130 2881 C7
Pine River Dr
10 BTVL 44022 2889 D1
Pine Spring Dr
- MCDN 44056 3153 E2
- MCDN 44056 3154 A2
Pine Trails Cir
2800 HDSN 44236 3155 D6
2800 TwbT 44236 3155 D6
Pine Tree Ct
7400 MDBH 44130 2881 C7
Pine Tree Dr
8800 MCDN 44056 3018 C6
Pinetree Dr
6600 MNTR 44060 2144 A5
Pine Tree Ln
2200 TNBG 44087 3019 C6
Pine Tree Pl
11500 SGVL 44136 3012 C5
Pinetree Rd
30400 PRPK 44124 2759 D1
32900 PRPK 44124 2760 A1
Pinetree Rd SR-87
30400 PRPK 44124 2759 D1
Pinevalley Cir
- CcdT 44077 2253 E4
- CcdT 44077 2254 A4
Pine Valley Tr
14900 MDBH 44130 2881 C7
Pineview Cir
- NRDV 44039 2877 D7
300 BERA 44017 2880 A6
20600 SGVL 44136 3146 B2
Pineview Ct
6500 BSHT 44236 3153 B7
13400 MDBH 44130 2881 D5
Pine View Dr
4800 VMLN 44089 2741 A7
Pineview Dr
10 PnvT 44077 2040 E7
200 BERA 44017 2880 A6
6100 MDSN 44057 1941 E5
27200 WTLK 44145 2749 E4
27200 WTLK 44145 2750 A4
Pineview Ln
5800 WLBY 44094 2375 C2
Pineview Ovl
9200 BKVL 44141 3150 C1
Pine Villa Tr
- AURA 44202 3156 E3
Pineway Dr
- TpnT 44086 2259 A2
8200 ODFL 44138 2879 B6
Pinewood Av
- NRDV 44039 2877 D3
Pinewood Cir
1000 LNHT 44124 2499 A6
Pinewood Ct
- PRMA 44134 2883 E2
8700 MNTR 44060 2144 C4
Pinewood Dr
300 BYVL 44140 2619 D4
700 BSHT 44236 3153 B7
4900 SDLK 44054 2616 D3
7300 MDBH 44130 2881 C7
7300 MDBH 44130 3012 C1
15200 SGVL 44136 3146 B2
Pinewood St
100 ELYR 44035 3006 B1
Pinewood Tr
11600 CsTp 44026 2501 E3
Pinewoods Tr
- TpnT 44086 2259 A1
Pine Woods Wy
7200 OmsT 44138 2878 E5
Pinewood View Rd
700 SgHT 44067 3152 B2
Piney Hllw
13700 LryT 44077 2148 B4
Pinnacle Dr
100 BNWK 44212 3146 E6
Pinnacle Pkwy
2100 TNBG 44087 3155 A4
Pinnacle Park Dr
5500 SVHL 44131 2884 A1
Pin Oak Cir
10 NCtT 44067 3153 A2
5400 SFLD 44054 2616 E7
5400 SFLD 44054 2746 E1
5400 SFLD 44054 2747 A1
Pin Oak Ct
5500 INDE 44131 2884 D4
Pin Oak Dr
- LORN 44052 2615 D5
- LORN 44054 2615 D5
4700 VMLN 44089 2741 A5
8200 PRMA 44130 3013 D1
14300 SGVL 44136 3012 C4
Pinoak Dr
9000 ODFL 44138 3010 A1
Pin Oak Pkwy
- AVLK 44012 2618 A4
33500 AVLK 44012 2617 C5
Pinta St
17300 CLEV 44110 2497 D1
Pin Tail Dr
6700 BKVL 44141 3150 D2
N Pintail Dr
100 AbnT 44023 2892 A3
Pinto Ct
300 SgHT 44067 3017 E5
Pinyon Ln
4400 WTLK 44145 2749 C6
Pioneer Rd
15600 HtbT 44046 2637 C1
16000 HtbT 44046 2638 A1
16600 HtbT 44062 2638 D1
17100 HtbT 44062 2639 A1
17100 HtbT 44046 2639 A1
17100 WndT 44062 2639 A1
17100 WndT 44046 2639 A1
Pioneer Tr
2600 ManT 44202 3157 E3
2700 HDSN 44236 3155 D7
3300 ManT 44255 3158 A3
3900 ManT 44255 3159 A3
5400 HrmT 44255 3160 A3
5400 ManT 44255 3160 A3
5600 HrmT 44234 3160 B3
6600 HrmT 44234 3161 A4
6600 HrmT 44255 3161 A4
E Pioneer Tr
10 AURA 44202 3156 E1
10 AURA 44202 3157 B2
1200 ManT 44202 3157 E3
W Pioneer Tr
100 AURA 44202 3156 D1
Pioneers Creek Cir
17300 SGVL 44136 3147 A5
Pioneers Point Ln
6100 BKVL 44141 3016 C5
Pioneer Trail Dr
12600 NRYN 44133 3013 C6
Pipers Ct
5500 PRMA 44134 2883 E1
Pipes Ct
700 SgHT 44067 3152 C1
Pippen Cir
1400 BWHT 44147 3149 D4
Pirates Tr
10000 RMDV 44202 3020 D5
Pirates Cove
2900 RMDV 44202 3020 D5
Pirates Cove Dr
18000 SGVL 44136 3147 D4
Pitts Blvd
6400 NRDV 44039 2877 C3
Pittsburgh Av
2200 CLEV 44115 2625 B4
Pittsburgh Av SR-14
2200 CLEV 44115 2625 B4
Pittsburgh Av SR-43
2200 CLEV 44115 2625 B4
Pixley Ct
2100 CLEV 44109 2754 D3
Placid Curv
- SGVL 44136 3146 E1
Plainfield Av
6300 CLEV 44144 2753 E4
6300 CLEV 44144 2754 A4
7400 BKLN 44144 2753 E4
Plainfield Rd
1000 SELD 44121 2498 A7
Plains Ct
38500 WLBY 44094 2143 A4
Plains Rd
7700 MONT 44060 2143 E3
7900 MNTR 44060 2143 E3
8000 MNTR 44060 2144 A2
Plainview Ct
- ClbT 44028 3010 A4
Plane Av
17200 CLEV 44110 2497 D2
Plank Rd
7800 TpnT 44086 2257 B4
7800 TpnT 44064 2257 B4
8300 MtlT 44064 2257 D5
8400 MtlT 44086 2257 D5
8700 MtlT 44064 2382 E1
9000 MtlT 44064 2383 A4
10600 HtbT 44064 2508 E1
10600 HtbT 44064 2509 A1
10600 MtlT 44064 2508 E1
10600 MtlT 44064 2509 A1
11100 WndT 44064 2509 A1
Plank Rd SR-86
7800 TpnT 44086 2257 B4
7800 TpnT 44064 2257 B4
8300 MtlT 44064 2257 D5
8400 MtlT 44086 2257 D5
8700 MtlT 44064 2382 E1
9000 MtlT 44064 2383 A4
10600 HtbT 44064 2508 E1
10600 HtbT 44064 2509 A1
10600 MtlT 44064 2508 E1
11100 WndT 44064 2509 A1
Plant Ln
19400 BKPK 44142 2880 E3
Plant St
1200 LORN 44055 2745 B3
Plantation Dr
7700 BKVL 44141 3016 A3
Plantation Pl
- NRDV 44039 2877 A7
Planters Grove Ln
31000 WTLK 44145 2749 A1
Plas Ct
100 CrlT 44035 3006 C3
Plato Av
15200 CLEV 44110 2497 B2
Platt Av
7100 CLEV 44104 2625 E4
7300 CLEV 44104 2626 A4
Platten Av
8500 CLEV 44102 2623 D6
Players Club Dr
7200 CcdT 44077 2254 C1
Plaza Blvd
7800 MNTR 44060 2251 D3
Plaza Dr
- CRDN 44024 2379 E7
- WBHL 44092 2374 B5
10 CNFL 44022 2761 A5
1000 AMHT 44001 2872 E4
12200 PRMA 44130 2881 E2
12200 PRMA 44130 2882 A2
N Plaza Dr
9000 NHFD 44067 3018 B4
Pleasant Av
- GNVA 44041 1944 A3
500 PNVL 44077 2040 B6
5300 NRDV 44039 2748 D7
5400 NRDV 44039 2877 D1
7200 BERA 44017 2880 D6
Pleasant Dr
10 CNFL 44022 2761 A6
Pleasant Pl
2300 MadT 44057 1941 C3
Pleasant Run
2400 SVHL 44131 3015 B1
N Pleasant St
10 OBLN 44074 3138 E2
S Pleasant St
10 OBLN 44074 3138 E3
Pleasant Tr
24800 RDHT 44143 2498 C2
Pleasantdale Rd
1600 CLEV 44109 2754 D
Pleasant Hill Dr
7400 PRMA 44130 3013 A
Pleasant Lake Blvd
10300 PRMA 44130 3013 C

INDEX 37

Pleasant Ridge Pl

Cleveland Street Index

Rankin Rd

STREET Block City ZIP Map# Grid

Pleasant Ridge Pl
11500 SGVL 44136 3012 C6
Pleasantvale Ct
9100 MNTR 44060 2252 E3
Pleasant Valley Rd
37000 WBHL 44094 2375 D5
38000 WBHL 44094 2376 A5
E Pleasant Valley Rd
- INDE 44125 3016 C1
- INDE 44141 3016 C1
- VLVW 44125 3016 C1
100 SVHL 44131 3014 E1
100 SVHL 44131 3015 A1
4900 INDE 44131 3015 A1
7000 INDE 44131 3016 A1
W Pleasant Valley Rd
900 PRMA 44134 3014 C1
3600 PRMA 44134 2883 A7
4700 PRMA 44129 2882 E7
4700 PRMA 44134 2882 E7
4700 PRMA 44129 2883 A7
7300 PRMA 44130 2882 B7
12800 PRMA 44130 2881 E7
12900 MDBH 44130 2881 E7
Pleasantview Av
300 SDLK 44054 2616 E3
Pleasant View Blvd
2300 SVHL 44131 3015 B1
Pleasantview Dr
7500 PRMA 44134 3014 C1
9000 NCtT 44067 3153 A3
Pleasantview Tr
7800 CcdT 44060 2253 A3
Pleasantwood Dr
7200 INDE 44131 2884 C7
Plover Dr
- GnvT 44041 1944 D1
Plover St
12200 LKWD 44107 2623 A6
Plum Pth
21400 RKRV 44116 2621 C4
Plum St
100 FTHR 44077 2039 D5
Plumbrook Ct
32200 AVLK 44012 2618 C4
Plum Brook Ln
9600 SGVL 44136 3011 A4
Plum Creek Dr
14000 ClbT 44028 3009 C7
14500 ClbT 44028 3144 C1
Plum Creek Tr
17500 BbgT 44023 2891 B4
Plum Ridge Dr
11700 HRM 44234 3161 A1
Plumwood Dr
4200 NOSD 44070 2750 D6
Plumwood Ln
7600 SVHL 44131 3015 A1
Plymouth Av
2800 PRPK 44124 2629 D6
2900 RKRV 44116 2751 C1
8800 GDHT 44125 2756 B6
Plymouth Ct
300 BNWK 44212 3147 B7
Plymouth Dr
100 BYVL 44140 2619 A3
1000 GFTN 44044 3142 A4
4200 SELD 44121 2498 B5
5800 LORN 44053 2743 C6
Plymouth Ovl
1900 HkyT 44233 3148 B6
Plymouth Pl
10 AURA 44202 3157 A4
15300 ECLE 44112 2497 B5
Plymouth Rd
100 ETLK 44095 2142 D5
1300 CLEV 44109 2754 E4
Plymouth Row
17400 SGVL 44136 3147 A4
Pocono Dr
22800 RKRV 44116 2751 A1
Poe Av
3000 CLEV 44109 2754 C2
Poertner Dr
800 BERA 44017 2879 E6
N Point Dr
10 AVLK 44012 2618 D1
S Point Dr
100 AVLK 44012 2618 D1
W Point Dr
4500 FWPK 44126 2751 C4
7400 NRDV 44039 2877 B4
Pointe Dr
8700 BWHT 44147 3015 C6
Pointe Pkwy
4900 WVHT 44128 2758 D6
N Pointe Pkwy
5400 LORN 44053 2743 E6
Pointe Breeze
200 AbnT 44023 2892 A3
Point Overlook Pl
11600 SGVL 44136 3012 B6
Poland Ct
6600 CLEV 44105 2755 E3
Pole Av
1800 LORN 44052 2744 C1
3200 LORN 44053 2744 C3
3200 LORN 44052 2744 C3
Police Al
- PNVL 44077 2040 D7
Polk Ct
7000 MNTR 44060 2143 D6
Polo Club Dr
14200 SGVL 44136 3147 B1
E Polo Club Dr
- SGVL 44136 3147 B1
Pololei Dr
10 MadT 44057 1941 B5
Polonia Av
6800 CLEV 44105 2755 E3
Polo Park Dr
4100 MNTR 44060 2251 B5
4100 MNTR 44094 2251 B5
4100 WLBY 44094 2251 B5
4100 WLBY 44060 2251 B5
Pomeroy Av
16300 CLEV 44110 2497 C3
Pomeroy Blvd
15500 SGVL 44136 3147 B1
Pomona Dr
5900 PRMA 44130 2882 A3
Pomona Rd
1100 CVHT 44121 2498 A7
Pompano Ct
7700 PRMA 44134 3014 C2

Pompton Dr
27100 NOSD 44070 2879 A1
Ponciana Av
17400 CLEV 44135 2752 A5
18500 CLEV 44135 2751 E5
Pond Dr
10 RKRV 44116 2621 A5
N Pond Ln
10400 TNBG 44087 3020 A3
Pond Rd
12000 NbyT 44021 2764 E4
12000 NbyT 44065 2764 E4
12100 NbyT 44021 2765 A4
12300 BtnT 44021 2765 B5
Pond Run
400 AURA 44202 3156 D3
Ponderosa Ln
9400 ODFL 44138 3010 A1
Pondhaven Ct
1300 PnvT 44077 2041 A7
Pondside Pt
27000 OmsT 44138 2878 D5
Pontiac Av
800 PnvT 44077 2040 D2
Pontiac Dr
1700 EUCL 44117 2498 A2
Pontiac St
1500 ECLE 44112 2496 E6
1600 ECLE 44112 2497 A6
Pope Rd
12900 HrmT 44234 3025 D4
12900 TroT 44234 3025 D4
Popham Ln
32800 SLN 44139 3019 E2
Popham Pl
7200 SLN 44139 3019 E2
7200 SLN 44139 3020 A2
Poplar Av
- EUCL 44132 2374 A2
10 CLEV 44110 2372 C5
Poplar Ct
200 AURA 44202 3156 D1
Poplar Dr
1500 LORN 44053 2744 C4
6300 INDE 44131 2884 C4
38000 WLBY 44094 2250 E1
Poplar Ln
4500 NRYN 44133 3014 B6
7600 MNTR 44060 2251 D4
Poplar St
- VMLN 44089 2740 E4
400 ELYR 44035 2875 C4
35300 NRDV 44039 2877 A1
Port Av
7100 CLEV 44104 2625 E6
7300 CLEV 44104 2626 B4
Port Dr
36400 ETLK 44095 2142 D7
Portage Av
5700 CLEV 44127 2625 D7
Portage Dr
5200 VMLN 44089 2740 E5
5200 VMLN 44089 2741 A5
36000 ETLK 44095 2142 C7
N Portage Dr
- VMLN 44089 2740 E4
S Portage Dr
- VMLN 44089 2740 E4
Portage Rd
1600 LNHT 44124 2629 A1
Portage St
7300 SLN 44139 3020 E2
Port Cove
31800 AVLK 44012 2618 E2
Porter Rd
3900 WTLK 44145 2749 D5
4100 NOSD 44070 2749 E7
4100 NOSD 44145 2749 D5
4100 WTLK 44070 2749 D5
5300 NOSD 44070 2878 E1
Porter Creek Dr
300 BYVL 44140 2619 D4
Porter's Ln
19500 SGVL 44136 3146 D1
Portia Ct
100 ELYR 44035 3006 B3
Portland Av
- MPHT 44137 2757 E7
Portland Ct
- VmnT 44089 2740 A6
Portland Dr
200 VMLN 44089 2741 B4
Portland Rd
- WVHT 44128 2757 E6
Portlew Rd
11600 NbyT 44065 2764 C2
Portman Av
2100 CLEV 44109 2754 C6
Portman Rd
50600 BhmT 44001 2871 A7
51000 BhmT 44001 2870 C7
51000 BhmT 44889 2870 C7
51000 BhmT 44889 2871 A7
52300 HetT 44889 2870 C7
Port Royal Ct
7200 MNTR 44060 2143 C5
Portsmouth Dr
3000 BNWK 44212 3147 C7
Portsmouth Cove
3700 PRRY 44081 2042 B1
Portz Pkwy
34100 SLN 44139 2889 A6
Post Rd
100 PnvT 44077 2040 C4
2500 TNBG 44087 3020 A5
Postal Dr
9100 BWHT 44147 3015 B7
Postal Rd
5700 CLEV 44135 2880 D2
6100 BKPK 44142 2880 D2
6100 BKPK 44135 2880 D2
Potomac Av
13800 ECLE 44112 2497 A5
Potomac Dr
10 SRSL 44073 2762 B7
100 ELYR 44035 2873 E6
5300 BKVL 44141 3150 C3
9100 NRYN 44133 3013 C3
17700 SGVL 44136 3146 E1
Potomac Ln
10 ELYR 44035 2875 A3
Potter Ct
1900 CLEV 44113 2624 D6
Powell Av
1800 CVHT 44118 2627 D2

Powell Dr
300 BYVL 44140 2619 B4
Powell Rd
30100 WLWK 44095 2249 C6
Powers Blvd
5500 PRMA 44129 2882 E5
5500 PRMA 44129 2883 A5
Powers Rd
10 BDFD 44146 2886 E4
10 BDFD 44146 2887 C3
Praha Av
4400 CLEV 44127 2625 C6
Prairie Cross
7900 MCDN 44056 3154 B4
Prairie Mdws
- SGVL 44136 3011 C4
Prairie Dunes Ct
- SLN 44139 3020 E2
Prame Av
2100 CLEV 44109 2624 D7
Prasse Rd
4200 SELD 44121 2498 B7
Pratt Av
9300 CLEV 44105 2756 B3
Pratt Blvd
100 ELYR 44035 3006 B2
Pratt Ln
10200 TNBG 44087 3020 B4
Prayner Av
- MPHT 44146 2758 A7
5100 MPHT 44137 2758 A7
Preakness Dr
9400 NHFD 44067 3018 A3
Prebblebrook Ct
- AVLK 44012 2617 D2
Preble Av
8000 CLEV 44104 2626 A6
Prell Dr
9500 BWHT 44147 3149 D3
Prelog Ln
9000 KTLD 44094 2377 D7
Prentice Rd
10 PnvT 44077 2145 B4
Prentiss Rd
11700 NsnT 44231 3027 E6
Prescott Dr
8500 CsTp 44026 2632 B2
Preserve Ct
8400 MCDN 44056 3018 B7
Preserve Ln
100 MCDN 44056 3018 B7
100 NCtT 44056 3018 B7
100 NCtT 44067 3018 B7
Preserve Pl
8400 MCDN 44056 3018 B7
Presidential Pkwy
1900 TNBG 44087 3019 C6
Presler Ct
28000 WTLK 44145 2749 E3
Presley Av
7300 MNTR 44060 2252 B1
Prestige Woods Blvd
- AURA 44202 3157 B3
Preston Av
9500 CLEV 44102 2623 D5
Preston Pl
28000 WTLK 44145 2749 D2
W Preston Pl
28300 WTLK 44145 2749 D2
Preston Rd
18400 WVHT 44128 2757 E6
19800 WVHT 44128 2758 A6
Preston St
100 ELYR 44035 2875 C5
Preston Hill Ct
7800 MNTR 44060 2253 A3
Preston Valley Dr
9200 BKVL 44141 3016 D5
Prestwick Cross
4300 WTLK 44145 2749 A5
Prestwick Ln
5400 HDHT 44143 2499 B3
Preyer Av
1600 CVHT 44118 2627 B1
Price Rd
24600 BDHT 44146 2887 D2
Priday Av
20100 EUCL 44123 2373 A3
Priebe Av
16600 CLEV 44128 2757 C6
Priem Rd
8000 SGVL 44136 3011 A4
Primary Rd
19100 CLEV 44135 2751 E7
19100 CLEV 44135 2880 E1
Primavera Dr
5400 MNTR 44060 2144 E1
5500 MNTR 44060 2145 A1
Primrose Av
11000 CLEV 44108 2496 D6
Primrose Cir
10000 TNBG 44087 3019 B4
Primrose Ct
18900 AbnT 44023 3023 B3
Primrose Dr
300 MCDN 44056 3018 B6
800 SVHL 44131 2884 A4
7300 MONT 44060 2143 D3
Primrose Ln
2200 AVON 44011 2747 E2
8500 MCDN 44056 3018 B6
15000 MDFD 44062 2767 B2
26300 WTLK 44145 2750 A4
Prince Av
9100 CLEV 44105 2756 C2
Prince Charles Dr
1200 WTLK 44145 2620 D7
13600 NRYN 44133 3014 B7
Princess Ct
3400 BKVL 44141 3016 D5
Princess Anne Ct
4800 LORN 44052 2744 D4
Princeton Av
100 ELYR 44035 2875 B7
800 AMHT 44001 2743 E6
11600 CLEV 44105 2756 D3
Princeton Blvd
3700 SELD 44121 2497 E4
3800 SELD 44121 2498 A5
Princeton Cir
17700 SGVL 44136 3146 B3
Princeton Ct
6300 PMHT 44130 2882 C4
7400 MNTR 44060 2251 C1

Princeton Dr
4800 NRYN 44133 3014 A4
Princeton Pl
3600 WTLK 44145 2749 C4
7600 MDBH 44130 3012 D2
Princeton Rd
2400 CVHT 44118 2627 D5
11400 HtbT 44024 2507 B3
11400 HtbT 44046 2507 B3
12300 HtbT 44021 2507 B7
12300 HtbT 44021 2637 B1
12300 HtbT 44046 2637 B1
Princeton St
3000 MDSN 44057 1941 E6
Princewood Dr
7900 HDSN 44236 3155 C6
Prior Ct
2100 CLEV 44106 2626 D2
Priorway Dr
15500 NbyT 44073 2763 B4
Priscilla Av
2700 PRMA 44134 2883 C3
Pritchard Rd
9100 NsnT 44231 3027 E4
9100 NsnT 44231 3028 A4
Privacy Ln
12000 CsTp 44026 2502 A5
Private Dr
5900 PMHT 44130 2882 C2
14700 ECLE 44112 2497 B6
Privet Ln
10 NCtT 44067 3153 B4
Proctor Ct
11300 CLEV 44105 2756 D4
Proctor Rd
7700 LryT 44077 2256 C3
Production Dr
7300 MNTR 44060 2251 D1
Professor Av
2100 CLEV 44113 2624 E5
2300 CLEV 44113 2625 A5
Professor Rd
900 LNHT 44124 2498 D6
900 SELD 44124 2498 D6
900 SELD 44121 2498 D6
N Professor St
10 OBLN 44074 3138 D1
12300 NRsT 44074 3003 D7
12300 NRsT 44074 3138 D1
S Professor St
10 OBLN 44074 3138 D3
Pro Gram Pkwy
- GNVA 44041 1944 A4
Progress Dr
19300 SGVL 44136 3011 C5
Progress Pkwy
9200 MNTR 44060 2144 E2
9200 MNTR 44060 2145 A2
13700 NRYN 44133 3013 A7
Progressive Dr
- MAYF 44143 2499 E5
Project Av
3000 CLEV 44115 2625 C3
Promontory Plz
300 ETLK 44095 2250 C1
Prospect Av
1400 RKRV 44116 2621 E5
4000 CLEV 44103 2625 D2
W Prospect Av
10 CLEV 44113 2624 E3
10 CLEV 44115 2624 E3
Prospect Av E
10 CLEV 44115 2624 E3
1000 CLEV 44115 2625 C3
Prospect Rd
4200 CLEV 44103 2625 D3
8500 SGVL 44017 3011 B5
8500 SGVL 44136 3011 B5
14000 SGVL 44136 3146 B3
Prospect Rd SR-237
8500 SGVL 44136 3011 B5
8500 SGVL 44017 3011 B5
Prospect St
- AMHT 44001 2872 D2
- FTHR 44077 2039 C3
10 BERA 44017 2880 B7
10 CrlT 44044 3006 E5
200 BERA 44017 3011 B1
200 ELYR 44035 2875 C6
200 GNVA 44041 1944 C5
700 SGVL 44017 3011 B1
1200 ELYR 44035 3006 C2
1500 CrlT 44035 3006 C2
4600 MNTU 44255 3159 C6
8300 MNTR 44060 2252 A1
38200 WLBY 44094 2250 E5
Prospect St SR-237
10 BERA 44017 2880 B7
200 BERA 44017 3011 B1
700 SGVL 44017 3011 B1
E Prospect St
10 PNVL 44077 2040 A7
4700 MNTU 44255 3159 C6
N Prospect St
10 OBLN 44074 3138 D2
S Prospect St
10 OBLN 44074 3138 C3
W Prospect St
200 PNVL 44077 2040 A7
200 PNVL 44077 2145 E1
4400 MNTU 44255 3159 B6
Prosser Av
5500 CLEV 44103 2495 D7
Prosser St
10 OBLN 44074 3138 E2
Prouty Rd
10100 CcdT 44077 2145 D7
10500 CcdT 44077 2146 A7
Providence Ct
100 BTNH 44108 2496 E2
Providence Dr
2000 HkyT 44233 3148 B6
30400 PRPK 44124 2629 D6
Province Ct
5900 LORN 44053 2743 C6
Province Ln
9200 BKVL 44141 3016 D5
Provincetown Ct
1000 GFTN 44044 3142 A4
Provincetown Ln
30300 BYVL 44140 2619 B5
Ptarmigan Ct
8500 KTLD 44094 2377 B4
Public Sq
10 CLEV 44113 2624 E3

Public Sq
10 CLEV 44114 2624 E3
10 CLEV 44115 2624 E3
Public Sq US-20
10 CLEV 44114 2624 E3
10 CLEV 44115 2624 E3
Public Sq E
6600 INDE 44131 2884 E5
Public Sq W
6600 INDE 44131 2884 E5
Puddingstone Dr
7600 CsTp 44026 2501 D1
Pueblo Dr
3900 LORN 44053 2743 E2
Pugwash Cir
400 SgHT 44067 3017 D4
Pulaski Av
7900 CLEV 44103 2496 A6
8200 CLEV 44108 2496 A6
Pulaski St
100 BERA 44017 2880 B6
Pumpkin Ln
4400 BWHT 44147 3015 C5
Punderson Rd
15300 NbyT 44021 2764 E4
15300 NbyT 44021 2765 A3
15500 NbyT 44065 2764 E4
Pupule Cir
100 MadT 44057 1941 B6
Purdue Av
500 ELYR 44035 3006 C1
Purdue Ct
1300 PnvT 44077 2147 A1
Puritan Av
11600 CLEV 44105 2756 D4
11600 GDHT 44105 2756 D4
23700 EUCL 44123 2373 C3
Puritan Dr
7900 MNTR 44060 2143 E6
8000 MNTR 44060 2144 A6
Puritas Av
- FWPK 44126 2751 D4
13000 CLEV 44135 2753 B5
13900 CLEV 44135 2752 D5
18500 CLEV 44135 2751 D4
19900 FWPK 44135 2751 D4
Puritas Park Dr
4500 CLEV 44135 2751 E5
Purnell Av
19300 RKRV 44116 2621 D6
Puth Dr
34400 AVON 44011 2748 C2
Putnam Av
11600 CLEV 44105 2756 D3
Putnam Ct
9600 TNBG 44087 3020 A6
Putney Dr
700 BERA 44017 3010 E1
S Pyle-Amherst Rd
1000 NRsT 44074 3138 B3
1000 OBLN 44074 3138 B3
Pyle South Amherst Rd
7800 AhtT 44001 2872 C5
7800 AMHT 44001 2872 C5
10600 NRsT 44074 3003 B5
12300 NRsT 44074 3138 B2
12900 OBLN 44074 3138 B2
Pythias Av
15600 CLEV 44110 2372 C6

Q

Quail Cir
8600 KTLD 44094 2377 C3
Quail Ct
300 AMHT 44001 2743 E6
Quail Dr
300 ELYR 44035 2874 E2
10000 BKVL 44141 3151 D4
Quail Hllw
- AVON 44011 2747 D1
Quail Ln
10 HGVL 44073 2631 A5
Quail Ovl
13900 NRYN 44133 3014 C7
Quail Run
5400 NOSD 44070 2878 C1
Quail St
2000 LKWD 44107 2623 A6
Quail Hollow Cir
800 AVLK 44012 2618 C4
Quail Hollow Ct
45200 AhtT 44001 2873 B2
Quail Hollow Dr
7600 SVHL 44131 3015 B1
11300 CcdT 44077 2254 B2
19000 SGVL 44136 3147 A3
23200 WTLK 44145 2750 E2
Quail Hollow Ln
10 MDHL 44022 2760 C3
Quail Point Ln
8200 MNTR 44060 2144 A3
Quailridge Ct
8700 MCDN 44056 3018 B6
Quail Ridge Dr
10 BTVL 44022 2890 A1
14000 NRYN 44133 3148 A1
Quail Roost
200 MDHT 44124 2629 E2
Quail Run Dr
300 BWHT 44147 3014 D4
Quail Woods Dr
11700 CdnT 44024 2254 E5
12000 CdnT 44024 2255 A5
Quarry Dr
800 CVHT 44121 2498 A5
Quarry Ln
4800 RDHT 44143 2498 D4
6000 INDE 44131 2884 D4
N Quarry Ln
10 BERA 44017 2880 C7
S Quarry Ln
- MDBH 44017 3011 B2
- MDBH 44130 3011 B2
10 BERA 44130 3011 B2
10 BERA 44017 3011 B2
Quarry Rd
- ClbT 44028 3010 B4
7000 AhtT 44001 2872 A4
7000 AMHT 44001 2872 A4
8800 SAHT 44001 2872 A5
9200 NRsT 44001 3003 A2
10500 NRsT 44074 3003 A6
14600 PtfT 44074 3138 A5

N Quarry Rd
1000 AMHT 44001 2743 A7
1000 AMHT 44001 2872 B1
Quarry Ridge Rd
- ClbT 44028 3009 E3
Quarry Stone Ln
200 BERA 44017 3011 C1
Quartermane Cir
- MsnT 44024 2504 C5
35000 BTVL 44022 2889 B2
35000 SLN 44022 2889 B2
35000 SLN 44139 2889 B2
Quebec Av
9300 CLEV 44106 2626 C4
Queen Av
2500 CLEV 44113 2624 D6
Queen Ann Ct
4500 SELD 44121 2498 C5
Queen Ann Wy
5200 PryT 44077 2041 C7
Queen Anne Av
- LORN 44053 2744 D5
4100 LORN 44052 2744 D5
Queen Anne Cir
100 ELYR 44035 3006 D1
Queen Annes Gate
1200 WTLK 44145 2620 D7
Queen Anns Wy
21300 FWPK 44126 2751 B5
35200 AVON 44011 2748 B4
Queen Mary Dr
4500 SELD 44121 2498 C5
Queens Ct
10 ELYR 44035 2875 D5
1500 PnvT 44077 2041 B6
1500 WTLK 44145 2620 C7
Queens Hwy
5200 PRMA 44130 2753 B7
5400 PRMA 44130 2882 B1
5800 PMHT 44130 2882 B2
Queens Wy
6200 BKVL 44141 3150 D2
6500 NRYN 44133 3014 A4
6600 NRYN 44133 3013 E4
10000 AbnT 44023 2892 B3
Queensboro Dr
5100 RDHT 44143 2498 E3
5100 RDHT 44143 2499 A3
Queensbridge Ln
11700 NRYN 44133 3148 A5
N Queensferry Pl
7100 CcdT 44077 2146 A6
Queens Park Av
6500 MDHT 44124 2500 A7
Queenston Rd
2300 CVHT 44118 2627 D5
Queenswood Dr
400 BYVL 44140 2620 E5
500 BYVL 44140 2621 B4
Quentin Rd
300 ETLK 44095 2249 E3
16700 CLEV 44112 2497 C3
Quigley Rd
2800 CLEV 44113 2625 A7
Quill Ct
- GnvT 44041 1944 C2
Quilliams Rd
500 CVHT 44121 2497 E6
500 SELD 44121 2497 E4
600 CLEV 44121 2497 E4
Quimby Av
5500 CLEV 44103 2625 D1
Quincy Av
4000 CLEV 44104 2625 D4
7400 CLEV 44104 2626 A4
8500 CLEV 44106 2626 A4
Quincy St
100 ELYR 44035 2875 B6
Quinn Ct
- CLEV 44103 2496 A6
7000 CLEV 44103 2495 E6
Quinn Rd
18100 AbnT 44023 2892 A7
18100 AbnT 44023 3023 A1

R

Rabbit Run Dr
4000 BKLN 44144 2753 D3
16800 SGVL 44136 3146 E3
Rabun Ln
4400 RDHT 44143 2498 C4
Raccoon Tr
17000 SGVL 44136 3146 E2
17000 SGVL 44136 3147 A2
Raccoon Hill Dr
- KTLD 44094 2376 B5
Race Rd
7300 NRDV 44039 2876 C5
Race St
100 BERA 44017 3011 A1
200 BERA 44017 2880 A7
300 BERA 44017 2879 E7
Racebrook Rd
600 GSML 44040 2500 E4
Rachael Dr
- LrgT 44050 3140 C7
Rachel Ln
4700 RDHT 44143 2498 D4
Racoon Hill Dr
7200 KTLD 44094 2376 C4
Radcliff Rd
3500 CVHT 44121 2497 D6
Radcliffe Dr
1900 WTLK 44145 2750 B1
Radcliffe Rd
12900 CcdT 44024 2255 D5
12900 CcdT 44077 2255 D5
12900 HmbT 44077 2255 D5
12900 HmbT 44024 2255 D5
12900 LryT 44077 2255 D5
12900 LryT 44024 2255 D5
13100 HmbT 44024 2256 A5
13100 LryT 44024 2256 A5
13100 LryT 44077 2256 A5
13700 HmbT 44077 2256 A5
14600 LryT 44086 2256 C5
14600 LryT 44024 2256 C5
Rademaker Blvd
15200 BKPK 44142 2881 B2
Rader Ln
- CrlT 44044 3141 E3
- EatT 44044 3141 E3
Radford Dr
600 HDHT 44143 2499 A4

Radford Dr
600 RDHT 44143 2499 A4
Radio Ln
10 CLEV 44114 2625 B1
Radio Pl
10 PNVL 44077 2040 C5
Radley Dr
100 PnvT 44077 2147 A1
Radnor Rd
1700 CVHT 44118 2627 B1
5700 MDHT 44124 2629 C1
Rae Rd
5300 LNHT 44124 2499 A7
Ragall Pkwy
7500 MDBH 44130 3012 B2
Rail King Ct
9400 BbgT 44023 3022 D2
Railroad Pl
16700 BbgT 44023 2890 A1
Railroad St
- EyrT 44035 2745 D7
100 ELYR 44035 2874 E5
300 PNVL 44077 2040 B6
900 GFTN 44044 3142 A5
Railway Av
- CLEV 44113 2624 E5
- CLEV 44113 2625 A5
Rainbow Dr
10 PnvT 44077 2040 D2
100 AMHT 44001 2743 D7
14000 CLEV 44111 2752 D1
24000 NOSD 44070 2879 C2
24000 OmsT 44070 2879 C2
24000 OmsT 44138 2879 C2
Rainbow Ln
9300 NRYN 44133 3013 C3
Rainbow Rd
4400 SELD 44121 2628 C1
Rainbow End
300 AURA 44202 3156 D5
Rainier Ct
5500 PRMA 44134 2883 E1
Raintree Blvd
26100 ODFL 44138 3010 A2
Raintree Dr
11700 MsnT 44024 2503 B4
Raleigh Ct
- AURA 44202 3021 D6
Raleigh Dr
100 ELYR 44035 2874 B7
800 MAYF 44143 2500 A5
Ralph Av
2100 CLEV 44109 2754 C6
Ralston Dr
5500 PRMA 44129 2883 A5
Ramage Av
15200 MPHT 44137 2886 B3
Rambler Dr
4500 MNTR 44060 2039 A4
Rambler St E
41600 EyrT 44035 2874 D2
Rambler St W
41800 EyrT 44035 2874 D2
Ramblewood Ct
5100 SLN 44139 2759 E7
Ramblewood Dr
3800 RchT 44286 3150 B7
6200 MNTR 44060 2144 C4
Ramblewood Tr
1200 SELD 44121 2498 C7
Rambling Creek Tr
17400 BbgT 44023 2890 C4
Ramona Av
1200 LKWD 44107 2622 D4
Ramona Blvd
9300 CLEV 44104 2626 B7
Ramona Dr
15800 MDBH 44130 2881 B6
Ramona St
4100 WLBY 44094 2251 B5
Ramsay Rd
2600 BHWD 44122 2628 E5
Ramsey Av
15400 CLEV 44128 2757 B4
N Ramsgate Pl
7100 CcdT 44077 2146 A7
Ranch Dr
- WLBY 44094 2375 C1
Ranch Rd
- WLBY 44094 2250 C7
10 WLBY 44094 2375 C1
8600 CsTp 44026 2632 C1
23100 BHWD 44122 2628 C4
Ranchland Dr
1100 MDHT 44124 2499 C7
Ranchview Av
4300 NOSD 44070 2750 B6
W Ranchview Av
4300 NOSD 44070 2750 B6
Ranchview Dr
6100 INDE 44131 3015 D2
Ranchwood Dr
15000 SGVL 44136 3146 D1
Randall Ct
10 CRDN 44024 2380 A7
Randall Dr
4000 BNWK 44212 3146 D6
24600 NOSD 44070 2750 C6
N Randall Dr
4800 NRDL 44128 2758 B6
Randall Rd
500 ELYR 44035 2875 D3
1700 CLEV 44113 2624 B5
Randall St
1400 LORN 44052 2615 B6
Randolph Dr
6900 PRMA 44129 2882 E6
Randolph Ln
- AhtT 44001 2872 E6
Randolph Pkwy
20300 HIHL 44128 2758 A3
Randolph Rd
3400 CVHT 44121 2497 D5
6000 BDHT 44146 2887 D4
Random Rd
2000 CLEV 44106 2626 D2
Randy Rd
5800 BDHT 44146 2887 D3
Ranett Av
7600 HDSN 44236 3155 B7
Rangeview Dr
5600 SVHL 44131 2884 A1
Rankin Rd
22500 BDHT 44146 2887 B1

INDEX 38

Ranney Pkwy

W Ridgewood Dr

Cleveland Street Index

STREET Block	City	ZIP	Map#	Grid
Ranney Pkwy				
27100	WTLK	44145	2619	D6
Ransome Rd				
400	HDHT	44143	2499	B3
Rapids Rd				
14600	BtnT	44021	2766	A2
14600	BURT	44021	2766	A2
14900	BtnT	44021	2765	E3
16000	TrcT	44021	2765	D7
16000	TrcT	44021	2894	D1
17700	TrcT	44234	2894	D7
18300	TrcT	44234	3025	D1
Rashell Dr				
18900	WNHL	44146	3018	A2
Rathbun Av				
7100	CLEV	44105	2755	E4
Rauland Dr				
16700	WNHL	44146	3017	D2
Raven Cir				
-	ELYR	44035	3006	E3
Ravencrest Dr				
-	HGVL	44073	2631	B7
Ravenglass Blvd				
100	AMHT	44001	2872	D3
Ravenhill Dr				
700	SgHT	44067	3152	C2
Ravenna Rd				
900	CcdT	44077	2146	B4
900	PnvT	44077	2146	B4
7200	CcdT	44077	2254	D2
7600	HDSN	44236	3155	E7
7700	TwbT	44236	3155	E7
7800	TwbT	44087	3155	D5
8400	CcdT	44024	2254	D6
8400	CdnT	44024	2254	D6
8800	TNBG	44087	3155	D4
9000	CdnT	44024	2379	D2
9700	TNBG	44087	3155	A1
9800	TNBG	44087	3154	E1
9900	TNBG	44087	3019	D7
10000	CRDN	44024	2379	D2
11100	MsnT	44024	2505	B5
12500	MsnT	44024	2635	B1
13400	NbyT	44024	2635	B4
13700	NbyT	44065	2635	B4
13700	NbyT	44021	2635	B4
14200	NbyT	44021	2765	A1
14200	NbyT	44065	2765	A1
15400	NbyT	44021	2764	E6
15500	NbyT	44065	2764	E6
16300	AbnT	44021	2764	E6
16400	AbnT	44021	2893	D3
17900	AbnT	44234	2893	D7
18300	AbnT	44023	2893	D7
18300	AbnT	44023	3024	C3
18300	AbnT	44234	3024	C3
Ravenna Rd SR-44				
11100	MsnT	44024	2505	B5
12500	MsnT	44024	2635	B1
13400	NbyT	44024	2635	B4
13700	NbyT	44065	2635	B4
13700	NbyT	44021	2635	B4
14200	NbyT	44021	2765	A1
14200	NbyT	44065	2765	A1
15400	NbyT	44021	2764	E6
15500	NbyT	44065	2764	E6
16300	AbnT	44021	2764	E6
16400	AbnT	44021	2893	D3
17900	AbnT	44234	2893	D7
18300	AbnT	44023	2893	D7
18300	AbnT	44023	3024	C3
18300	AbnT	44234	3024	C3
Ravenna Rd SR-82				
9100	TNBG	44087	3155	A1
Ravenna Parkman Rd				
11900	NsnT	44231	3027	B5
Ravenna Parkman Rd SR-88				
11900	NsnT	44231	3027	B5
Ravenswood Dr				
6900	PMHT	44129	2882	D6
6900	PMHT	44130	2882	D6
6900	PRMA	44129	2882	D6
Ravenswood Ln				
8500	MCDN	44056	3018	B6
Ravenwood Dr				
-	BtnT	44021	2635	B5
-	NbyT	44021	2635	B5
-	NbyT	44065	2635	B5
12400	ClrT	44024	2635	B3
12400	MsnT	44024	2635	B3
Ravenwood Ln				
10400	CcdT	44077	2253	D1
Ravine Blvd				
5900	PRMA	44134	2883	D3
Ravine Dr				
-	MNTR	44060	2251	B4
300	AURA	44202	3156	D1
800	CVHT	44112	2497	C5
800	ECLE	44112	2497	C5
6700	MAYF	44040	2500	B4
E Ravine View Ct				
10400	NRYN	44133	3148	C4
W Ravine View Ct				
10400	NRYN	44133	3148	C3
Rawlings Av				
7500	CLEV	44104	2626	A5
Rawnsdale Rd				
3600	SRHT	44122	2757	E2
Ray Ct				
8700	TwbT	44087	3154	D2
Raymond Av				
9300	CLEV	44104	2756	B1
10600	GDHT	44125	2756	C7
Raymond Dr				
100	GNVA	44041	1944	C5
7600	MNTR	44060	2143	D4
12300	MsnT	44024	2503	E6
Raymond St				
15400	MPHT	44137	2757	B7
19800	MPHT	44137	2758	A7
Raymont Blvd				
3400	UNHT	44118	2627	D3
Raynham Dr				
7200	OKWD	44146	2887	E7
Raynor Dr				
100	BDFD	44146	2887	A3
Rays Ln				
100	MCDN	44056	3018	B7
Reading Av				
36100	WLBY	44094	2250	B6
Reamer St				
300	OBLN	44074	3138	C3
Reaser Ct				
100	ELYR	44035	2875	E6
Rebecca Dr				
-	MNTR	44060	2251	B4
Rebecca Ln				
-	BHIT	44212	3146	A6
Recher Av				
20700	EUCL	44119	2373	A5
Rechner Dr				
26300	WTLK	44145	2750	B3
Reckman Ct				
3200	NRYN	44133	3014	C3
Recreational Pk				
10	PNVL	44077	2040	B7
Redbay Ln				
4900	NRYN	44133	3014	B4
Red Bird Rd				
1500	MadT	44057	1843	A7
1600	MadT	44057	1942	A1
Redbridge Ln				
33900	SLN	44139	2889	A2
Redbud Pl				
1300	LORN	44053	2744	C4
Red Bush Ln				
1200	MCDN	44056	3153	E1
Red Delicious Ln				
10	AMHT	44001	2872	B1
Redding Rd				
4300	CLEV	44109	2754	E4
Reddington Av				
14100	MPHT	44137	2886	A2
Red Doe Cir				
2800	RHFD	44286	3150	D7
Redell Av				
7400	CLEV	44103	2626	A1
Red Fawn Pth				
400	AURA	44202	3156	C2
Redfern Rd				
3700	PRMA	44134	2883	B3
23200	ClbT	44028	3010	D3
23200	ClbT	44136	3010	D3
Red Fox Tr				
7500	HDSN	44236	3155	D7
17200	BbgT	44023	2890	D3
Red Fox Pass				
2400	WBHL	44094	2375	E3
Redhill Dr				
700	LORN	44052	2744	D4
Redman Av				
-	CLEV	44109	2754	E2
Red Maple Dr				
1300	PnvT	44077	2041	A7
Red Mill Cove				
3900	PRRY	44081	2042	B1
Red Oak Av				
33100	AVON	44011	2748	D6
Red Oak Dr				
-	CsTp	44026	2502	B5
2800	PryT	44081	2041	C3
6600	MNTR	44060	2144	E5
N Red Oak Dr				
16800	SGVL	44136	3147	A5
S Red Oak Dr				
16800	SGVL	44136	3147	A5
Red Oak Ln				
500	BYVL	44140	2620	C5
700	GNVA	44041	1944	D4
Red Oaks Dr				
-	BKVL	44141	3016	B4
Red Pine Dr				
10	PnvT	44077	2041	A7
Red Pine Wy				
4800	NRDV	44039	2748	D7
Red Raven Rd				
27900	PRPK	44124	2629	B4
N Redrock Dr				
16400	SGVL	44136	3147	A3
S Redrock Dr				
16400	SGVL	44136	3147	A4
Redtail Ct				
2500	TNBG	44087	3019	E7
8600	MCDN	44056	3018	A6
Red Tail Ln				
8900	KTLD	44094	2252	B7
Redwood Blvd				
32200	AVLK	44012	2618	C2
32800	AVLK	44012	2617	E2
Redwood Ct				
-	AhtT	44001	2872	E6
5700	MONT	44060	2143	E2
Redwood Dr				
400	BERA	44017	2880	A4
4400	PryT	44077	2041	C4
4900	SDLK	44054	2616	D3
5400	WLBY	44094	2375	A1
25900	ODFL	44138	3010	B1
Redwood Rd				
3200	CVHT	44118	2627	C2
19200	CLEV	44110	2372	E7
Reed Av				
400	PNVL	44077	2145	D1
8100	GDHT	44125	2756	A6
Reed Rd				
-	NOSD	44070	2750	E6
200	EatT	44028	3143	C2
9000	NRDV	44039	2877	C7
9000	NRDV	44039	3008	C1
9600	EatT	44028	3008	C1
9600	EatT	44039	3008	C1
12000	EatT	44028	3008	C7
12000	EatT	44044	3008	C7
Reedhurst Ln				
9400	MNTR	44060	2145	A7
Reeds Court Tr				
1800	WTLK	44145	2749	D1
Reef Rd				
5500	MONT	44060	2143	E1
5500	MONT	44060	2144	A1
Reese Rd				
18300	CLEV	44119	2372	E6
Reeve Rd				
900	ELYR	44035	2875	C3
Reeves Av				
1800	LORN	44052	2744	B1
3400	CLEV	44105	2755	B1
Reeves Rd				
2800	ETLK	44095	2250	E2
2800	WLBY	44095	2250	E2
2800	WLBY	44094	2250	E2
16600	PkmT	44062	2897	D1
17600	PkmT	44062	2898	A2
17800	FnTp	44062	2898	A2
Regal Dr				
6900	PRMA	44129	2882	E7
Regal Wy				
24500	WTLK	44145	2620	D7
Regalia Av				
11100	CLEV	44104	2626	D7
Regal Oaks Cir				
-	AURA	44202	3157	B3
Regal Ridge Cir				
7900	MCDN	44056	3154	B5
Regan Ct				
1900	HDSN	44236	3154	E7
Regan St				
4400	MNTU	44255	3159	B6
Regatta Dr				
300	AVLK	44012	2619	A2
Regatta Tr				
9800	RMDV	44202	3020	E5
Regency Cir				
29200	WTLK	44145	2749	C3
Regency Ct				
32300	AVLK	44012	2618	C3
Regency Dr				
-	PRMA	44134	2883	A6
5200	PRMA	44129	2883	A6
6900	PRMA	44129	2882	E6
7600	WNHL	44146	3018	A2
14400	SGVL	44136	3146	C1
Regency Pl				
-	WTLK	44145	2749	C2
Regency Woods Dr				
9000	KTLD	44094	2252	A7
9000	KTLD	44094	2377	B1
Regent Dr				
5300	SFLD	44054	2747	A1
Regent Rd				
3200	CLEV	44127	2625	E7
3400	CLEV	44127	2755	E1
29900	WKLF	44092	2249	C7
Regent Park Dr				
-	MsnT	44024	2635	A1
11500	MsnT	44024	2634	D1
Regents Wy				
15000	HmbT	44024	2382	A4
15000	MtlT	44024	2382	A4
Regina Av				
3100	LORN	44052	2744	D3
Regina Ct				
-	PryT	44081	1940	D7
Regina Dr				
200	BDFD	44146	2886	D3
600	VMLN	44089	2742	A5
Regina Ln				
7100	OmsT	44138	2879	B7
Rehwinkle Rd				
400	SgHT	44067	3152	D2
Reichert Rd				
9000	PRMA	44130	2882	C7
Reid Av				
500	LORN	44052	2614	D6
1700	LORN	44052	2744	E1
2600	LORN	44055	2744	E3
Reid Dr				
6700	PMHT	44130	2882	C5
Reindeer Av				
12300	GDHT	44125	2756	D6
Reinwald Rd				
3500	LORN	44053	2743	E3
3500	LORN	44053	2744	A3
Remington Av				
10500	CLEV	44108	2496	C4
Remington Cir				
27500	WTLK	44145	2619	E7
Remington Dr				
1500	WTLK	44145	2619	E7
9500	MNTR	44060	2253	A1
Remington Pt				
-	ManT	44202	3023	A7
Remora Blvd				
15300	BKPK	44142	2881	B1
Rena Ct				
25200	EUCL	44132	2373	D2
Renaissance Ct				
100	AbnT	44023	2892	B4
Renaissance Pkwy				
10	OmsT	44138	2879	A3
4300	WVHT	44022	2758	E5
26500	WVHT	44022	2759	A4
Renee Dr				
5400	HDHT	44143	2499	B4
5900	BKPK	44142	2881	C2
Renfield Rd				
900	CVHT	44121	2498	A5
Reno Av				
9100	CLEV	44105	2756	B2
Reno Dr				
11900	PRMA	44130	2882	A3
Renrock Rd				
2000	CVHT	44118	2627	B3
W Rental Rd				
-	CLEV	44135	2880	D1
Rental Car Access				
-	CLEV	44135	2751	D6
Renwood Av				
18600	EUCL	44119	2372	E4
19300	EUCL	44119	2373	A4
Renwood Dr				
5400	PRMA	44129	2883	A3
8200	PRMA	44129	2882	D3
Renwood Rd				
4400	SELD	44121	2628	C1
6600	INDE	44131	3015	D1
N Renwood Rd				
6900	INDE	44131	2884	E7
6900	INDE	44131	3015	E1
Republic Dr				
400	SgHT	44067	3017	D4
Reserve Av				
-	OBLN	44074	3138	D5
E Reserve Cir				
2000	AVON	44011	2617	E7
N Reserve Cir				
36400	AVON	44011	2617	E7
S Reserve Cir				
36400	AVON	44011	2617	E7
W Reserve Cir				
2000	AVON	44011	2617	E7
Reserve Cir N				
2000	LORN	44053	2744	A5
Reserve Cir S				
2000	LORN	44053	2744	A5
Reserve Ct				
2000	AVON	44011	2617	E7
10500	CLEV	44106	2626	C2
21000	FWPK	44126	2751	C1
Reserve Dr				
7200	WTHL	44094	2376	B3
Reserve Ln				
8600	MCDN	44056	3153	E1
12100	CsTp	44026	2502	A5
14200	MDBH	44130	2881	D7
Reserve Run				
9100	BKVL	44141	3150	C5
Reserve Tr				
400	SRSL	44073	2761	E5
Reserve Wy				
5200	SFLD	44054	2746	E4
33600	AVON	44011	2748	C4
Reservoir Dr				
-	PMHT	44130	2882	D3
Reservoir St				
10700	MNTU	44255	3159	C5
Resource Dr				
700	BNHT	44131	2884	C1
Restor Av				
18600	CLEV	44122	2757	E4
Retford Pkwy				
700	PnvT	44077	2040	E2
Reublin Ct				
600	ELYR	44035	2875	A4
Revely Av				
2000	LKWD	44107	2622	C6
Revere Av				
10900	CLEV	44105	2756	C2
Revere Cir				
14000	MDBH	44130	3012	C2
Revere Ct				
100	ELYR	44035	2873	E6
3600	CLEV	44109	2754	C3
10300	CcdT	44077	2145	D4
Revere Dr				
500	BYVL	44140	2619	D5
5400	NOSD	44070	2879	A1
6800	PMHT	44130	2882	C6
Revere Ln				
10	ELYR	44035	2875	A3
Revere Pl				
1800	LORN	44053	2744	B5
Revere Rd				
1800	CVHT	44118	2627	E2
Rex St				
16300	MPHT	44128	2757	C6
Rexford Av				
11800	CLEV	44105	2756	D1
27800	BYVL	44140	2619	E5
27800	BYVL	44140	2620	A5
Rexway Av				
3400	BHWD	44122	2758	C1
Rexwood Av				
12600	GDHT	44105	2756	E5
13600	GDHT	44105	2757	A5
14000	CLEV	44105	2757	A5
Rexwood Rd				
2100	CVHT	44118	2627	C3
Reyburn Rd				
1800	CLEV	44112	2497	D3
1900	ECLE	44112	2497	D3
2000	CVHT	44112	2497	D3
Reynolds Rd				
-	NsnT	44231	3028	E4
-	NsnT	44491	3028	E4
-	PkmT	44491	3028	E4
-	PkmT	44231	3028	E4
5800	MONT	44060	2143	C3
6100	MNTR	44060	2143	C6
7300	MNTR	44060	2251	C1
10000	PkmT	44491	3028	E4
10400	FnTp	44491	3029	A4
10400	NsnT	44491	3029	A4
10400	PkmT	44491	3029	A4
10400	StnT	44491	3029	A4
Reynolds Rd SR-306				
6200	MNTR	44060	2143	C6
7300	MNTR	44060	2251	C1
Reynosa Ct				
600	BERA	44017	3011	A1
Rhode Island Rd				
10	ELYR	44035	3006	A3
Rhodes Ct				
3200	CLEV	44109	2624	C7
3200	CLEV	44109	2754	C1
Rhonda Dr				
5900	NRDV	44039	2877	A2
Rhonda Ln				
-	LrgT	44050	3140	C7
Ribbonwood Ovl				
-	MDSN	44057	1942	A7
Rice Ct				
100	AhtT	44001	2872	A4
Rice Dr				
7700	MNTR	44060	2143	D3
Rice Rd				
7500	AhtT	44001	2872	A4
48000	AhtT	44001	2871	E4
48000	BhmT	44001	2871	E4
Rice Park Dr				
10	AVLK	44012	2488	B7
Richard Ct				
1000	WKLF	44092	2374	B1
Richard Dr				
9800	BKLN	44144	2753	C6
11200	PRMA	44130	2882	B1
15300	BKPK	44142	2881	B3
Richard Rd				
6600	BSHT	44236	3153	B7
7900	BWHT	44147	3014	D3
Richard St				
10	GNVA	44041	1944	B6
Richards Av				
25100	EUCL	44132	2373	D2
Richards Dr				
5300	MNTR	44060	2038	E7
13000	SGVL	44136	3011	C7
Richdale Dr				
16300	PkmT	44231	3028	A2
Richelieu Av				
4300	SDLK	44054	2616	B3
Rich Hills Dr				
8300	BWHT	44147	3015	C5
Richland Av				
100	AVLK	44012	2617	D2
2000	LKWD	44107	2622	E6
10100	GDHT	44125	2756	C6
Richland Rd				
-	BHWD	44122	2628	E5
Richmar Dr				
800	WTLK	44145	2620	A6
Richmond Av				
9100	CLEV	44105	2756	B3
Richmond Pl				
-	ECLE	44112	2497	B4
Richmond Rd				
100	EUCL	44117	2373	E6
100	EUCL	44143	2373	E6
100	RDHT	44143	2373	E6
300	RDHT	44143	2498	E2
800	LNHT	44124	2498	E6
800	PnvT	44077	2039	D6
1000	GDRV	44045	2039	D6
1000	PnvT	44045	2039	D6
1500	LNHT	44124	2628	E3
2100	BHWD	44122	2628	E3
3000	BHWD	44122	2758	E3
4100	HIHL	44122	2758	E4
4100	WVHT	44122	2758	E4
4500	WVHT	44128	2758	E4
4500	WVHT	44022	2758	E4
5000	BDHT	44146	2758	E4
5500	BDHT	44146	2888	A5
5500	SLN	44139	2888	A5
5800	OKWD	44146	2888	A1
6500	GNWL	44139	2888	A5
6800	GNWL	44146	2888	A5
7000	GNWL	44139	3019	A1
7000	OKWD	44146	3019	A1
25700	BDHT	44146	2887	E1
25700	BDHT	44146	2888	A1
25700	SLN	44146	2888	A1
27000	SLN	44139	2888	A1
Richmond Rd SR-87				
2900	BHWD	44122	2628	E6
3000	BHWD	44122	2758	E3
Richmond Rd SR-175				
100	EUCL	44117	2373	E6
100	EUCL	44143	2373	E6
100	RDHT	44143	2373	E6
300	RDHT	44143	2498	E2
800	LNHT	44124	2498	E6
1500	LNHT	44124	2628	E3
2100	BHWD	44122	2628	E3
3000	BHWD	44122	2758	E3
4100	HIHL	44122	2758	E4
4100	WVHT	44122	2758	E4
4500	WVHT	44128	2758	E4
4500	WVHT	44022	2758	E4
5000	BDHT	44146	2758	E4
25700	BDHT	44146	2887	E1
25700	BDHT	44146	2888	A1
25700	SLN	44146	2888	A1
27000	SLN	44139	2888	A1
Richmond Rd SR-283				
800	PnvT	44077	2039	D6
1000	GDRV	44045	2039	D6
1000	PnvT	44045	2039	D6
Richmond Sq				
10	EUCL	44143	2498	B2
Richmond St				
10	PNVL	44077	2040	A7
10	PNVL	44077	2146	B1
600	PNVL	44077	2039	E6
600	PnvT	44077	2039	E6
900	FTHR	44077	2039	E6
Richmond St SR-283				
10	PNVL	44077	2040	A7
600	PNVL	44077	2039	E7
600	PnvT	44077	2039	E7
Richmond St SR-535				
600	PNVL	44077	2039	E6
600	PnvT	44077	2039	E6
900	FTHR	44077	2039	E6
Richmond Bluffs Dr				
4800	RDHT	44143	2498	E1
Richmond Park East Dr				
400	RDHT	44143	2499	A3
Richmond Park West Dr				
400	RDHT	44143	2499	A2
Richner Av				
2600	TNBG	44087	3154	E1
2700	TNBG	44087	3155	B1
3900	CLEV	44113	2624	C7
Richwood Av				
5700	BKPK	44142	2881	D1
Richwood Dr				
7800	MONT	44060	2143	E1
Rickey Ln				
30000	WKLF	44092	2374	D2
Riddle Rd				
15400	RslT	44073	2761	C4
Rider Rd				
14400	BtnT	44021	2635	C7
14600	BtnT	44021	2765	C1
Ridge Ct				
9500	TNBG	44087	3019	C5
N Ridge Dr				
15500	RslT	44073	2762	C4
S Ridge Dr				
37100	AVON	44011	2747	D3
W Ridge Dr				
7900	BWHT	44147	3014	C3
14400	RslT	44072	2631	E7
Ridge Ln				
5400	SLN	44139	2888	D2
Ridge Rd				
10	HkyT	44233	3148	D7
3400	BKLN	44102	2753	E2
3400	BKLN	44144	2753	E2
3400	CLEV	44144	2753	E2
3400	CLEV	44102	2753	E2
5100	BKLN	44129	2753	E6
5100	CLEV	44129	2753	E6
5200	PRMA	44129	2753	E6
5400	PRMA	44129	2882	E1
7400	PRMA	44129	3013	E1
7400	PRMA	44134	3013	E1
7800	NRYN	44129	3013	E1
7800	NRYN	44133	3013	E4
14000	NRYN	44133	3148	D2
28700	WKLF	44092	2374	B4
33300	WLBY	44094	2375	A2
36800	WLBY	44094	2250	D7
Ridge Rd SR-3				
10	HkyT	44233	3148	D7
5400	PRMA	44129	2882	E1
7400	PRMA	44129	3013	E1
7400	PRMA	44134	3013	E1
7800	NRYN	44129	3013	E1
7800	NRYN	44133	3013	E4
14000	NRYN	44133	3148	D2
Ridge Rd SR-84				
28700	WKLF	44092	2374	B4
33300	WLBY	44094	2375	A2
36800	WLBY	44094	2250	D7
Ridge Rd SR-174				
37700	WLBY	44094	2250	D7
N Ridge Rd				
100	ShfT	44052	2745	A5
700	EyrT	44055	2745	A5
700	EyrT	44052	2745	A5
700	ShfT	44055	2745	A5
1200	PnvT	44077	2040	D5
1800	VMLN	44001	2871	A3
1900	PnvT	44077	2041	A4
1900	VMLN	44089	2871	A3
2100	ShfT	44035	2745	A5
2300	ShfT	44055	2746	B6
2400	PryT	44077	2041	A4
2400	PryT	44081	2041	A4
2400	VMLN	44001	2870	E3
2400	VMLN	44089	2870	E3
2500	BhmT	44089	2870	E3
3200	SFLD	44054	2746	B6
3200	SFLD	44035	2746	B6
3200	ShfT	44035	2746	B6
3200	ShfT	44054	2746	B6
3400	PryT	44081	1940	A7
4200	NPRY	44081	1940	A7
4200	PryT	44081	1940	E6
4700	NPRY	44081	1941	A5
4700	PryT	44081	1941	A5
5200	MadT	44057	1941	A5
5200	MadT	44081	1941	A5
6200	MadT	44057	1942	B4
7500	GnvT	44057	1943	A5
7500	MadT	44057	1943	A5
44800	AhtT	44001	2872	A2
44800	AMHT	44001	2872	A2
46100	AhtT	44001	2871	D2
46100	AMHT	44001	2871	D2
47100	BhmT	44001	2871	D2
N Ridge Rd SR-254				
2100	ShfT	44035	2745	E6
2100	ShfT	44055	2745	E6
2300	ShfT	44055	2746	B6
3200	SFLD	44035	2746	B6
3200	SFLD	44054	2746	B6
3200	ShfT	44054	2746	B6
3200	ShfT	44035	2746	B6
N Ridge Rd US-20				
1200	PnvT	44077	2040	D5
1900	PnvT	44077	2041	A4
2400	PryT	44077	2041	A4
2400	PryT	44081	2041	A4
3400	PryT	44081	1940	A7
3900	NPRY	44081	1940	A7
4700	NPRY	44081	1941	A5
4700	PryT	44081	1941	A5
5200	MadT	44057	1941	A5
5200	MadT	44081	1941	A5
6200	MadT	44057	1942	B4
7500	GnvT	44057	1943	A5
7500	MadT	44057	1943	A5
N Ridge Rd E				
1700	EyrT	44035	2745	B6
1700	EyrT	44055	2745	B6
1700	ShfT	44055	2745	B6
1800	LORN	44055	2745	B6
1900	ShfT	44035	2745	B6
4500	GnvT	44041	1944	E3
N Ridge Rd E US-20				
4500	GnvT	44041	1944	E3
N Ridge Rd W				
100	LORN	44053	2745	A5
100	ShfT	44053	2745	A5
100	ShfT	44052	2745	A5
200	LORN	44053	2744	D6
200	LORN	44052	2744	D6
200	ShfT	44052	2744	D6
200	ShfT	44053	2744	D6
1100	AhtT	44053	2744	C6
1100	AhtT	44001	2744	C6
5900	GnvT	44041	1943	D4
6700	GnvT	44057	1943	D4
44800	AMHT	44001	2744	C6
44800	AMHT	44053	2744	C6
45800	AhtT	44001	2873	A1
45800	AMHT	44001	2873	A1
N Ridge Rd W US-20				
5900	GnvT	44041	1943	D4
6700	GnvT	44057	1943	D4
S Ridge Rd				
2600	PryT	44077	2041	D6
2600	PryT	44081	2041	D6
2800	PryT	44081	2042	B5
4400	PRRY	44081	2042	E3
4500	PryT	44057	2042	E3
5000	MadT	44081	2043	A3
5000	MadT	44057	2043	A3
5000	PryT	44057	2043	A3
5000	PryT	44081	2043	A3
7100	MadT	44057	1942	E7
7100	MadT	44057	1943	A7
7100	MadT	44057	2044	D1
7800	HpfT	44057	1943	A7
S Ridge Rd SR-84				
2600	PryT	44077	2041	D6
2600	PryT	44081	2041	D6
2800	PryT	44081	2042	B5
4400	PRRY	44081	2042	E3
4500	PryT	44057	2042	E3
5000	MadT	44057	2043	A3
5000	MadT	44081	2043	A3
5000	PryT	44081	2043	A3
5000	PryT	44057	2043	A3
7100	MadT	44057	1942	E7
7100	MadT	44057	1943	A7
7100	MadT	44057	2044	D1
7800	HpfT	44057	1943	A7
S Ridge Rd E				
10	GNVA	44041	1944	C6
500	GnvT	44041	1944	D5
S Ridge Rd E SR-84				
10	GNVA	44041	1944	C6
500	GnvT	44041	1944	D5
S Ridge Rd W				
10	GNVA	44041	1944	A6
5500	HpfT	44041	1944	A6
5800	HpfT	44041	1943	E7
6800	HpfT	44057	1943	E7
S Ridge Rd W SR-84				
10	GNVA	44041	1944	A6
5500	HpfT	44041	1944	A6
5800	HpfT	44041	1943	E7
6800	HpfT	44057	1943	E7
W Ridge Rd				
-	ELYR	44035	2875	C1
1100	AhtT	44035	2744	E7
1100	AhtT	44035	2745	A7
6400	AhtT	44035	2874	A1
6400	EyrT	44035	2745	A7
6400	EyrT	44035	2874	A1
6900	AhtT	44035	2873	E3
6900	EyrT	44035	2873	E3
7900	ELYR	44035	2873	E4
8100	EyrT	44035	2874	A5
8300	ELYR	44035	2874	A7
8900	EyrT	44035	3005	A1
9200	ELYR	44035	3005	A1
9500	CrlT	44035	3005	A2
12100	CrlT	44074	3005	B7
Ridge St				
100	ELYR	44035	2875	B5
Ridgebrook Cir				
1800	LNHT	44122	2628	D3
Ridgebury Blvd				
4800	LNHT	44124	2498	D6
5000	LNHT	44124	2499	A6
5300	HDHT	44143	2499	A6
5300	LNHT	44143	2499	A6
5600	MDHT	44124	2499	C6
5600	MDHT	44143	2499	C6
6000	MAYF	44143	2499	D6
6300	MDHT	44124	2500	A6
Ridgebury Dr				
2000	PnvT	44077	2145	B6
Ridge Circle Ln				
100	ELYR	44035	2874	A6
Ridgecliff Cir				
11800	SGVL	44136	3011	E5
Ridgecliff Dr				
6700	SLN	44139	2889	B6
Ridge Creek Rd				
17300	SGVL	44136	3012	A7
Ridgecreek Tr				
10	MDHL	44022	2760	A6
Ridgecrest Dr				
10	PnvT	44077	2146	E2
10	PnvT	44077	2147	A2
10	SRSL	44073	2762	C6
Ridgedale Rd				
7900	NRYN	44133	3013	E3
Ridgefield Av				
7400	PRMA	44129	2882	E1
Ridgefield Rd				
1500	CVHT	44118	2627	B1
Ridgehill Rd				
1900	CLEV	44121	2497	E3
Ridgehills Dr				
28500	WBHL	44092	2374	B5
28500	WKLF	44092	2374	B5
Ridgehurst Dr				
1900	WKLF	44092	2374	E3
Ridgeland Av				
19400	CLEV	44135	2751	D4
Ridgeland Cir				
4200	CLEV	44135	2751	D4
Ridgeland Dr				
10	AMHT	44001	2873	A1
100	AhtT	44001	2873	A1
1900	AVON	44011	2617	E7
1900	AVON	44011	2747	E1
Ridgeland St				
4900	LORN	44055	2745	E5
4900	ShfT	44055	2745	E5
Ridgelawn Av				
100	PNVL	44077	2039	D7
100	PNVL	44077	2040	A6
Ridgeline Av				
18000	CLEV	44135	2752	A4
Ridgeline Ct				
19100	SGVL	44136	3146	E5
Ridge Line Dr				
9800	NRYN	44133	3014	A4
Ridgeline Dr				
24300	BDHT	44146	2887	D6
Ridge Meadow Ct				
1800	TNBG	44087	3019	C5
Ridgemore Av				
7100	CLEV	44144	2753	E3
Ridge Park Dr				
3300	BWHT	44147	3015	B5
Ridge Plaza Dr				
6700	NRDV	44039	2877	A2
Ridge Point Cir				
17000	SGVL	44136	3012	A6
Ridgeside Dr				
9300	MNTR	44060	2252	E1
9400	MNTR	44060	2253	A1
Ridgeton Dr				
16700	CLEV	44128	2757	C4
Ridgeton Rd				
17600	WVHT	44128	2757	D4
Ridgeview Blvd				
5700	NRDV	44039	2877	B2
Ridgeview Dr				
100	SVHL	44131	3014	E1
100	SVHL	44131	3015	A1
1600	WKLF	44092	2374	D1
4000	VMLN	44089	2741	C5
9300	MCDN	44056	3018	E5
Ridgeview Ln				
5700	WLBY	44094	2375	A2
Ridgeview Rd				
4000	CLEV	44144	2754	A4
6500	MDHT	44124	2630	A1
Ridgeview Tr				
9600	CcdT	44060	2253	B3
19000	BbgT	44023	3022	A3
Ridgewater Dr				
10500	CcdT	44077	2145	E5
Ridgeway Dr				
500	AURA	44202	3156	C2
6000	BDHT	44146	2887	D4
7700	MNTR	44060	2252	A2
Ridgeway Ln				
35400	WLBY	44094	2375	B2
Ridgewick Dr				
1500	WKLF	44092	2374	D1
Ridgewood Av				
1400	LKWD	44107	2623	A5
5400	PRMA	44129	2883	A1
6700	PRMA	44129	2882	E1
19000	WVHT	44122	2757	E3
19700	WVHT	44122	2758	A3
Ridgewood Ct				
1500	TNBG	44087	3019	B4
Ridgewood Dr				
300	ETLK	44095	2142	D7
9700	TNBG	44087	3019	C4
13300	SGVL	44136	3012	D5
15800	MDFD	44062	2767	D2
E Ridgewood Dr				
10	SVHL	44131	2883	E4
200	SVHL	44131	2884	A4
W Ridgewood Dr				
900	PRMA	44134	2883	D4

INDEX 39

W Ridgewood Dr — Cleveland Street Index — Roxanne Ln

STREET Block City ZIP Map# Grid

W Ridgewood Dr
3900 PRMA 44129 2883 A5
3900 PRMA 44134 2883 A5
6300 PRMA 44129 2882 C5
8500 PRMA 44129 2882 C5
8500 PMHT 44130 2882 C5
8500 PRMA 44130 2882 C5
Ridgewood Ln
5500 BKVL 44141 3150 C4
8300 RslT 44072 2762 A2
Ridgewood Rd
10 CNFL 44022 2761 C6
Ridgewood St
- LORN 44055 2745 E6
5000 ShfT 44055 2745 E6
Ridgewood Lakes Dr
6400 PRMA 44129 2882 E4
Ridpath Av
15000 CLEV 44110 2372 B7
Riedham Rd
3500 SRHT 44120 2757 C2
Riegelsberger Rd
35400 AVON 44011 2748 A4
Riester Av
6600 PRMA 44134 2883 B5
Rife Ct
15600 SRHT 44120 2757 B1
Riley Ct
12000 TNBG 44087 3020 B3
Riley Rd
1000 AURA 44202 3021 A7
1000 AURA 44202 3156 A1
W Rim Dr
23900 ClbT 44028 3010 B3
Rinard Rd
2300 CVHT 44118 2627 D4
Rindlewood Ln
14600 RslT 44072 2761 B1
Ringneck Cir
16900 SGVL 44136 3147 A3
Rio Av
1400 LKWD 44107 2622 A5
Rio Grande Tr
- ClrT 44024 2505 C6
Rio Vista Dr
6300 CcdT 44077 2146 D4
Ripley Rd
2900 CLEV 44120 2626 D7
8100 NRYN 44133 3013 C3
Rippling Brook Ln
7100 CcdT 44060 2145 B7
Risden Rd
5200 VmnT 44089 2740 A7
6200 VmnT 44089 2869 A1
Rita Dr
400 LvpT 44280 3145 D7
2700 LORN 44053 2744 A3
7200 INDE 44131 2884 D7
7200 INDE 44131 3015 D1
Ritchie Dr
500 BNWK 44212 3147 A7
Rivendell Rd
600 SgHT 44067 3152 C2
River Dr
- ETLK 44095 2250 C1
10 ELYR 44035 2875 A7
10 ETLK 44095 2142 B7
W River Dr
7900 RslT 44072 2631 E6
7900 RslT 44072 2632 A6
River Ln
3600 RKRV 44116 2751 B2
4100 FWPK 44126 2751 B2
River Rd
- WLBY 44094 2250 D7
10 HkyT 44133 3149 A6
10 HkyT 44233 3149 A6
10 NRYN 44133 3149 A6
1100 CLEV 44113 2624 C3
2100 WBHL 44094 2375 D1
2800 PryT 44077 2041 E7
2800 PryT 44081 2041 E7
2800 PryT 44081 2042 B6
2900 GSML 44040 2500 C1
2900 GSML 44094 2500 C1
2900 WBHL 44094 2500 C1
4200 PryT 44057 2042 B6
5000 MadT 44057 2043 B5
5000 PryT 44057 2043 B5
6000 MadT 44057 2044 A5
7300 ODFL 44138 2879 C5
7300 OmsT 44138 2879 C5
11000 MsnT 44024 2504 B5
17300 BbgT 44023 2890 A4
17300 BbgT 44139 2890 A4
17300 SLN 44139 2890 A4
River Rd SR-94
10 HkyT 44133 3149 A6
10 HkyT 44233 3149 A6
10 NRYN 44133 3149 A6
River Rd SR-174
- WLBY 44094 2250 D7
2100 WBHL 44094 2375 D1
2900 GSML 44040 2500 C1
2900 GSML 44094 2500 C1
2900 WBHL 44094 2500 C1
E River Rd
2000 SFLD 44054 2616 B7
2000 SFLD 44054 2746 B2
9500 CrlT 44035 3006 C2
9500 ELYR 44035 3006 C2
9800 ClbT 44028 3010 B3
14000 ClbT 44028 3145 A3
18000 LvpT 44028 3145 A3
29200 EatT 44035 3006 E3
E River Rd SR-252
9800 ClbT 44028 3010 B3
14000 ClbT 44028 3145 A3
18000 LvpT 44028 3145 A3
E River Rd N
9500 ODFL 44138 3010 C2
N River Rd W
5800 HpfT 44041 2045 E3
6700 HpfT 44057 2045 E3
N River Rd W SR-307
5800 HpfT 44041 2045 E3
6700 HpfT 44057 2045 E3
S River Rd W
6000 HpfT 44041 2045 D5
6800 HpfT 44057 2045 D5
W River Rd
10 ClbT 44280 3144 D7
10 LvpT 44280 3144 D7
10 VMLN 44089 2741 B7
200 BhmT 44089 2741 B7
600 VMLN 44089 2740 E5

W River Rd
700 VMLN 44089 2741 A6
1300 BhmT 44089 2870 B2
1500 ELYR 44035 2875 A1
2600 ELYR 44035 2746 A7
3100 ShfT 44035 2746 A7
3100 ShfT 44055 2746 A7
9800 ClbT 44028 3010 B2
9800 ClbT 44138 3010 B2
9800 ODFL 44138 3010 B2
12600 ClbT 44028 3009 E6
15100 ClbT 44028 3144 E1
W River Rd N
100 ELYR 44035 2874 E6
500 ELYR 44035 2875 A5
W River Rd S
100 ELYR 44035 2874 E7
800 ELYR 44035 3005 E3
2200 CrlT 44035 3005 E3
River St
10 CNFL 44022 2761 A6
10 MDSN 44057 2044 B2
100 GDRV 44045 2039 C5
700 PnvT 44045 2039 C6
4100 WLBY 44094 2250 E5
River St SR-174
4100 WLBY 44094 2250 E5
River St SR-283
600 GDRV 44045 2039 C6
700 PnvT 44045 2039 C6
River St SR-528
10 MDSN 44057 2044 B2
E River St
100 ELYR 44035 2875 B6
1000 ELYR 44035 3006 B1
1300 CrlT 44035 3006 B1
Riverbank Dr
4000 PryT 44057 2042 B7
4000 PryT 44081 2042 B7
River Beach Rd
11500 ManT 44255 3160 A2
Riverbed St
1200 CLEV 44113 2624 D3
River Bend Dr
38300 WLBY 44094 2250 E7
Rivercliff Dr
18500 FWPK 44126 2752 A2
Riverdale Ct
100 ELYR 44035 2875 B7
Riverdale Dr
300 RKRV 44116 2621 E4
400 ETLK 44095 2142 D7
6200 MadT 44057 2044 A5
River Edge Dr
2900 ShfT 44035 2746 B6
2900 ShfT 44055 2746 B6
3000 ELYR 44035 2746 B6
Riveredge Dr
10400 PRMA 44130 2753 B7
Riveredge Pkwy
10 BERA 44017 2880 B4
Riveredge Rd
3800 CLEV 44111 2752 A3
3900 CLEV 44135 2752 A3
Rivergate Dr
22100 RKRV 44116 2751 A2
River Glen Dr
14500 RslT 44072 2631 E7
14500 RslT 44072 2761 E1
24800 ClbT 44028 3010 B4
River Glen Rd
300 AURA 44202 3022 B6
River Industrial Rd
3400 LORN 44052 2615 C7
River Moss Rd
11500 SGVL 44136 3012 A5
River Mountain Dr
10 MDHL 44022 2760 C5
River Oaks Dr
2600 RKRV 44116 2621 B7
2600 RKRV 44116 2751 B1
9600 NRYN 44133 3013 A3
River Oaks Tr
7400 GSML 44040 2500 D4
River Ridge Ct
- CrlT 44044 3141 D2
38400 EatT 44044 3141 D2
River Ridge Dr
4100 CLEV 44109 2755 A4
River Ridge Rd
11600 SGVL 44136 3011 E5
River Rock Ln
10300 NRYN 44133 3148 B4
River Run Dr
900 MCDN 44056 3154 B5
River Run Ln
10200 NRYN 44133 3148 B4
Rivers Edge Dr E
18700 BbgT 44023 3021 E2
Rivers Edge Dr W
18700 BbgT 44023 3021 D2
Riverside Av
4300 CLEV 44102 2754 B2
4300 CLEV 44109 2754 B2
Riverside Blvd
400 ETLK 44095 2250 C1
Riverside Ct
100 ELYR 44035 2875 B6
Riverside Dr
10 BERA 44017 2880 C7
10 PnvT 44077 2040 D7
10 PnvT 44077 2146 D1
300 PNVL 44077 2146 D1
700 VMLN 44089 2741 A5
800 ELYR 44035 2875 A7
800 PnvT 44077 2147 A1
900 VMLN 44089 2741 A5
1000 ELYR 44035 3006 A1
1300 LKWD 44107 2622 A5
2300 CLEV 44111 2622 A6
2300 LKWD 44111 2622 A6
2500 PryT 44077 2041 C7
2600 LORN 44055 2746 B4
4900 WLBY 44094 2250 E7
5300 CLEV 44135 2880 E2
8300 RslT 44072 2632 A6
8900 BbgT 44023 3022 C3
Riverside Dr SR-84
400 PnvT 44077 2146 D2
800 PnvT 44077 2147 A1
2500 PryT 44077 2041 C7
Riverside Dr SR-237
1500 LKWD 44107 2622 A6
2300 CLEV 44111 2622 A6
2300 LKWD 44111 2622 A6

S Riverside Dr
7700 BbgT 44023 3021 D3
7700 BbgT 44202 3021 D3
Riverside Homes
100 ELYR 44035 3006 A1
Riverstone Dr
10 MDHL 44022 2760 C4
River Valley Blvd
17600 NRYN 44133 3148 A4
Riverview Av
19200 RKRV 44116 2621 D6
Riverview Ct
- GnvT 44041 1944 C1
10 BTVL 44022 2760 D7
Riverview Dr
900 MCDN 44056 3018 D7
18700 BbgT 44023 3022 C2
24700 ClbT 44028 3010 A2
N Riverview Dr
36200 ETLK 44095 2250 C2
S Riverview Dr
36200 ETLK 44095 2250 C3
Riverview Ln
2900 LORN 44055 2746 B4
Riverview Rd
- INDE 44125 2885 C7
- INDE 44131 2885 C7
- VLVW 44125 2885 C7
400 GSML 44040 2500 D2
5300 NRYN 44133 3149 A3
6900 BosT 44141 3152 B6
7200 INDE 44131 3016 D2
7200 INDE 44141 3016 D2
7500 BKVL 44141 3152 B6
7700 BKVL 44141 3016 D2
9000 BKVL 44141 3151 E1
River Walk Cir
17100 NRYN 44133 3149 B3
River Walk Rd
22200 RKRV 44116 2751 B1
Riverway Dr
17300 LKWD 44107 2622 A6
Riverwood Av
19300 RKRV 44116 2621 D6
Riverwood Dr
4600 PryT 44057 2042 E5
11000 CrlT 44044 3006 C6
11600 MsnT 44024 2503 C3
Riverwood Ln
9600 AbnT 44023 2763 A7
Riverwood Wy
8800 KTLD 44094 2251 E7
8800 KTLD 44094 2252 A7
Riviera Av
- AMHT 44001 2744 B7
Riviera Dr
21400 FWPK 44126 2751 B5
Riviera Ln
30800 WTLK 44145 2749 A3
Riviera Wy
- MCDN 44056 3154 A3
Riviera Ridge Rd
36800 WBHL 44094 2375 D3
Roadoan Rd
4300 BKLN 44144 2753 D6
Road to Happiness
800 VMLN 44089 2740 C5
Roanoke Av
2200 CLEV 44109 2754 C4
Roanoke Cir
6100 PRMA 44134 2883 E3
Roanoke Ct
27600 WTLK 44145 2619 E7
Roanoke Dr
1300 PRMA 44134 2883 E3
3000 VMLN 44089 2742 A5
Roanoke Rd
700 SELD 44121 2497 E5
800 CVHT 44121 2497 E5
Roanoke Wy
600 WTLK 44145 2619 E7
Robens Ct
100 CNFL 44022 2760 E7
Robert Av
3600 CLEV 44109 2624 B7
Robert Cir
4200 SELD 44121 2498 B6
Robert Ct
5500 NRDV 44039 2748 B7
5500 NRDV 44039 2877 B1
Robert Dr
6000 BKPK 44142 2881 B2
14300 MDBH 44130 2881 C6
21900 RKRV 44116 2751 B2
Robert Ln
10600 AbnT 44023 2892 E4
39600 CrlT 44035 3006 C2
Robert Pkwy
2800 BNWK 44212 3147 D6
Robert St
7700 PRMA 44134 3014 E2
29400 WKLF 44092 2374 B1
29900 WKLF 44092 2249 C7
Roberta Dr
31100 BYVL 44140 2619 A5
Robert Bishop Dr
- BHWD 44122 2758 D2
4300 HIHL 44122 2758 D3
Robertdale Rd
5800 OKWD 44146 2887 E3
Robert Donaldson Ct
6900 BKVL 44141 3016 A7
Roberts Av
20800 EUCL 44123 2373 A3
Roberts Ct
8700 ODFL 44138 2879 D7
Roberts Rd
33800 ETLK 44095 2249 E2
33800 LKLN 44095 2249 E2
34000 ETLK 44095 2250 A2
Roberts Run
300 BYVL 44140 2621 A5
Roberts St
- EyrT 44035 2874 C3
600 SDLK 44054 2616 A4
Robertson Av
11600 CLEV 44105 2756 D4
Robin Cir
6100 MAYF 44143 2499 D5
Robin Dr
200 BERA 44017 2880 D6
300 ELYR 44035 2874 E2
600 ETLK 44095 2250 D1
Robin Ln
400 MCDN 44056 3153 C2

Robin Ln
8000 BKVL 44141 3016 C3
8800 KTLD 44094 2252 C7
Robin St
2000 LKWD 44107 2623 A6
Robindale Dr
16000 SGVL 44136 3147 B2
Robindale St
1500 WKLF 44092 2374 C2
Robinhood Av
800 PnvT 44077 2040 D2
21000 FWPK 44126 2751 B5
Robin Hood Dr
4800 WLBY 44094 2250 C7
Robinhood Dr
400 AURA 44202 3021 C6
2400 PRMA 44134 2883 C7
2600 LORN 44053 2743 E2
5000 WLBY 44094 2250 C7
5000 WLBY 44094 2375 C1
13500 GDHT 44125 2885 E3
Robinia Dr
24300 BDHT 44146 2887 D3
Robin Park Blvd
10 OBLN 44074 3138 C2
Robinson Av
9600 GDHT 44125 2756 C5
Robinson Rd
8700 CdnT 44024 2254 E6
8700 CdnT 44024 2255 A7
9000 CdnT 44024 2380 A2
Robinwood Av
- AVLK 44012 2617 D2
400 SDLK 44054 2616 C4
1500 LKWD 44107 2622 D5
Robinwood Dr
4600 MNTR 44060 2038 E5
Robinwood Ln
- AbnT 44021 2893 C2
- AbnT 44023 2893 C2
7100 GSML 44040 2630 C2
Robinwood Ter
8300 MCDN 44056 3018 A5
Robley Ln
600 MAYF 44040 2500 B4
Robson Rd
11100 CrlT 44044 3006 D6
12500 CrlT 44044 3141 D1
38600 EatT 44044 3141 D1
Roc Ln
22800 OKWD 44146 2887 C7
Rochelle Av
14700 CLEV 44135 2752 C4
Rochelle Blvd
6600 PMHT 44130 2882 A4
Rochelle Dr
14000 MPHT 44137 2886 A3
Rochester Rd
2600 SRHT 44122 2628 D6
Rock Ct
1800 CVHT 44118 2627 B2
Rockcliff Dr
- LKWD 44111 2622 A6
- LKWD 44126 2622 A6
18900 LKWD 44116 2621 E7
18900 LKWD 44126 2621 E7
18900 RKRV 44126 2621 E7
18900 RKRV 44116 2621 E7
Rockcliffe Rd
- GDHT 44125 2885 A1
Rock Creek Cir
22200 SGVL 44136 3011 A4
Rock Creek Dr
600 AURA 44202 3021 B6
Rock Creek Rd
13900 HmbT 44024 2381 B2
14300 HmbT 44024 2256 D7
14800 HmbT 44024 2257 B5
14800 MtlT 44024 2257 B5
14800 MtlT 44064 2257 B5
14800 TpnT 44064 2257 B5
15600 TpnT 44086 2257 D3
16100 TpnT 44086 2258 B2
17500 TpnT 44086 2259 A2
17700 TmbT 44086 2259 A2
Rock Creek Rd SR-166
13900 HmbT 44024 2381 B2
14300 HmbT 44024 2256 D7
14800 HmbT 44024 2257 B5
14800 MtlT 44024 2257 B5
14800 MtlT 44064 2257 B5
14800 TpnT 44064 2257 B5
15600 TpnT 44086 2257 D3
16100 TpnT 44086 2258 B2
17500 TpnT 44086 2259 A2
17700 TmbT 44086 2259 A2
Rock Creek Run
400 AMHT 44001 2744 A7
Rockefeller Av
2400 CLEV 44115 2625 B5
Rockefeller Ln
8500 SgHT 44067 3017 C4
Rockefeller Rd
1300 WKLF 44092 2374 C2
2700 WBHL 44094 2374 D7
2700 WBHL 44092 2374 D7
Rocker St
- BbgT 44022 2890 A1
- CNFL 44022 2890 A1
7000 BbgT 44023 2890 A1
Rockfern Av
300 ELYR 44035 2874 D5
14300 CLEV 44111 2752 D2
Rockford Dr
32800 SLN 44139 2888 E2
32800 SLN 44139 2889 A2
Rockhaven Dr
5700 SVHL 44131 2884 A2
Rockhaven Rd
12200 MsnT 44024 2503 B7
12200 MsnT 44026 2503 B7
12800 MsnT 44026 2633 C1
13100 NbyT 44026 2633 C4
13500 NbyT 44072 2633 C4
Rockingham Rd
7300 MNTR 44060 2252 C1
Rocking Horse Tr
10400 KTLD 44094 2377 C6
Rockland Av
1400 RKRV 44116 2621 E6
18200 CLEV 44135 2752 A5
18500 CLEV 44135 2751 E5
Rockland Dr
4300 BKLN 44144 2753 E4

Rockledge Dr
300 BYVL 44140 2620 D4
6300 BKVL 44141 3016 A5
Rockledge Ln
- BHIT 44212 3146 B7
24800 RDHT 44143 2498 D1
Rock Ledge Wy
10300 NRYN 44133 3148 B4
Rocklyn Rd
2600 SRHT 44122 2628 C5
Rock Point Cir
5600 NRDV 44039 2877 E1
Rockport Av
3600 CLEV 44111 2752 C2
Rockport Ln
5800 FWPK 44126 2751 B6
6700 MNTR 44060 2145 A5
Rockside Pl
6000 INDE 44131 2884 D3
Rockside Rd
- INDE 44125 2885 C3
200 SVHL 44131 2883 E2
200 SVHL 44131 2884 B2
3700 INDE 44131 2884 B2
7300 INDE 44131 2885 C3
8000 VLVW 44125 2885 C3
11500 MsnT 44024 2504 C3
12500 GDHT 44125 2885 C3
13500 GDHT 44125 2886 A2
14000 MPHT 44137 2886 A2
17500 BDFD 44146 2886 D2
18200 BDFD 44137 2887 A2
18200 BDFD 44146 2887 A2
18200 MPHT 44137 2887 A2
23000 BDHT 44146 2887 C2
Rockside Woods Blvd
5800 INDE 44131 2884 D3
Rockspring Dr
8300 BbgT 44023 2891 A2
Rockway Av
1400 LKWD 44107 2622 B5
Rockwell Av
900 CLEV 44114 2624 E2
1300 CLEV 44114 2625 A2
Rockwell Ct
7400 MNTR 44060 2251 E1
Rockwood Ct
500 AVLK 44012 2618 B3
8700 MNTR 44060 2144 C4
Rockwood Dr
200 PNVL 44077 2040 B7
10500 KTLD 44094 2376 C6
Rockwood Ln
- CcdT 44077 2254 E4
Rockwood Rd
4600 GDHT 44105 2756 A6
4600 GDHT 44125 2756 A6
Rocky Pointe
29200 WTLK 44145 2749 C2
Rocky Ridge Dr
- WTLK 44145 2749 A2
Rocky River Dr
3100 CLEV 44111 2622 B7
3200 CLEV 44111 2752 A4
3900 CLEV 44135 2752 A4
4800 CLEV 44135 2751 E6
Rocky River Dr SR-237
3100 CLEV 44111 2622 B7
3200 CLEV 44111 2752 A4
3900 CLEV 44135 2752 A4
4800 CLEV 44135 2751 E6
N Rocky River Dr
10 BERA 44017 2880 C6
800 BERA 44142 2880 B5
800 BKPK 44142 2880 B5
N Rocky River Dr SR-237
800 BERA 44017 2880 C4
800 BERA 44142 2880 C4
800 BKPK 44142 2880 C4
S Rocky River Dr
10 BERA 44017 2880 C7
10 BERA 44017 3011 C1
20000 MDBH 44130 3011 C1
Rocky River Ovl
2300 RKRV 44116 2621 E6
2300 RKRV 44116 2622 A6
Rocky Top Cir
1100 MCDN 44056 3154 B4
Rodgers Dr
30000 WKLF 44092 2374 D2
Rodman Ct
900 CLEV 44110 2497 A3
Roe Blvd
6800 MadT 44057 1843 C6
Roe Ln
- SGVL 44136 3011 E7
Roedean Dr
9000 PRMA 44129 2753 D7
Roehl Av
3300 CLEV 44109 2624 C7
Roeper Rd
7600 PRMA 44134 3014 A1
Roger Dr
23300 EUCL 44123 2373 C2
Rogers Av
6500 CLEV 44127 2625 E6
Rogers Rd
- GSML 44040 2500 D1
- GSML 44094 2500 D1
- WBHL 44094 2500 D1
6400 CcdT 44077 2147 A5
36600 WBHL 44094 2375 D7
38200 WBHL 44094 2376 A7
Rokeby Rd
600 ETLK 44095 2249 E3
Roland Av
6100 CLEV 44127 2625 D6
Roland Dr
5300 GDHT 44125 2885 E1
5400 GDHT 44125 2886 A1
Roland Rd
800 LNHT 44124 2499 A5
Rollin Dr
9600 WTHL 44094 2376 C2
Rolling Av
5100 ShfT 44055 2745 C6
Rolling Acres Ct
6700 CcdT 44077 2145 D6
Rollingbrook Cir
9300 ODFL 44138 3009 D1
Rolling Brook Dr
18100 BbgT 44023 2891 A7
Rolling Brook Rd
8000 SgHT 44067 3017 D6

Rollingbrook Tr
- SLN 44139 3020 D2
Rolling Hills Dr
1700 TNBG 44087 3019 B5
3500 PRPK 44124 2759 D1
Rolling Meadow Ln
11800 NRYN 44133 3014 A6
Rolling Meadows Dr
- HrmT 44234 3161 B4
1300 BhmT 44089 2741 B7
1300 VMLN 44089 2741 B7
Rollingview Dr
4000 SVHL 44131 3015 B1
Rolliston Rd
3600 SRHT 44120 2757 C2
Roman Rd
- WTLK 44145 2620 D7
Romane Dr
1200 SgHT 44067 3017 A5
Rome Cir
1200 BWHT 44147 3149 E4
Rome Beauty Dr
800 AMHT 44001 2872 B1
Romeo Rd
5900 GnvT 44041 1943 E4
5900 GnvT 44041 1944 A4
Romford Rd
- HDHT 44143 2499 C5
Romilly Ovl
7100 PRMA 44129 2882 E6
Ronald Dr
4800 NRDV 44039 2877 B2
10700 PRMA 44130 3013 B1
30500 WLWK 44095 2249 D6
Ronan Rd
24200 BDHT 44146 2887 D3
Rondel Rd
800 CLEV 44110 2497 C2
Rook Cir
17600 CLEV 44112 2497 D3
Rookhill Cir
17700 CLEV 44112 2497 D3
Rookwood Cir
17700 CLEV 44112 2497 D3
Rookwood Rd
1900 CLEV 44112 2497 E3
Roosevelt Av
100 ELYR 44035 2875 C5
1600 LKWD 44107 2622 D6
2000 ShfT 44055 2745 E6
6800 MNTR 44060 2144 D7
Roosevelt Blvd
5200 NRDV 44039 2748 D7
5500 NRDV 44039 2877 D1
Roosevelt Ct
10 OBLN 44074 3138 D4
Roosevelt Dr
- GnvT 44041 1944 B2
- ODFL 44138 2879 C6
10 PNVL 44077 2145 D2
400 GNVA 44041 1944 B2
9000 NHFD 44067 3018 A4
Roosevelt Rd
30800 WKLF 44092 2374 E2
30800 WKLF 44092 2375 A2
Root Rd
400 LORN 44052 2615 D5
3800 NOSD 44070 2750 C6
6900 NRDV 44039 2877 A3
9000 NRDV 44039 3008 D1
9400 EatT 44035 3008 D1
9500 ClbT 44028 3008 D1
9500 EatT 44028 3008 D1
10600 ClbT 44028 3009 A4
18400 BbgT 44023 2890 A7
18400 BbgT 44023 3021 A1
Roryanna Dr
9300 CdnT 44024 2379 C2
Rosalee Av
900 ELYR 44035 2875 D3
Rosalie Av
1000 LKWD 44107 2622 C3
Rosalie Dr
13800 GDHT 44125 2757 A7
Rosalind Av
1700 ECLE 44112 2496 E7
1800 ECLE 44112 2497 A7
9200 CLEV 44106 2626 B1
Rosa Parks Dr
1300 CLEV 44106 2496 D7
Rosbough Dr
17500 MDBH 44130 2881 A6
Rose Av
- VmnT 44089 2740 C5
Rose Blvd
800 HDHT 44143 2499 C6
Rose Ct
3000 GnvT 44041 1944 E4
Rose Dr
400 BERA 44017 3011 A1
4000 BNWK 44212 3146 D7
Rose Ln
- AhtT 44001 2872 B2
10 LKWD 44107 2622 D4
Rose Rd
25600 WTLK 44070 2750 B4
25600 WTLK 44145 2750 B4
Rose St
33200 NRDV 44039 2877 D1
Roseann Dr
- AVON 44011 2748 C2
Rosebelle Av
5800 NRDV 44039 2877 A2
Rosebud Dr
8600 MNTR 44060 2252 C1
Rosebury Ct
100 MDHT 44124 2630 A1
Rosecliff Dr
5500 LORN 44053 2743 C6
Rosecliff Rd
17800 CLEV 44119 2372 D4
Rosecrest Dr
1600 LORN 44053 2744 C5
Rosedale Av
1700 ECLE 44112 2497 C4
6700 PMHT 44130 2882 B6
Rosedale Dr
6500 AhtT 44001 2873 C1
7200 CcdT 44060 2145 B7
7200 CcdT 44060 2253 B1
Rosedale Rd
3300 CVHT 44112 2497 D6
Rosehill Av
9800 CLEV 44104 2626 C5

Rose Hill Ln
27500 BYVL 44140 2619 E3
Roseland Av
19200 EUCL 44117 2497 E1
19600 EUCL 44117 2498 A1
20500 EUCL 44117 2373 A7
Roseland Dr
1300 MCDN 44056 3019 A6
Roseland Rd
17000 CLEV 44112 2497 C3
Roseland Wy
1500 WTLK 44145 2620 C7
Roselawn Av
38200 WLBY 44094 2250 E7
Roselawn Dr
7500 MNTR 44060 2252 E2
16200 BtnT 44021 2765 B7
Roselawn Rd
1100 LNHT 44124 2498 D6
1500 MDHT 44124 2499 D3
1500 MDHT 44124 2629 D1
3600 WDMR 44122 2759 B2
Roselum St
- MadT 44057 1942 B4
Rosemarie Ct
10900 CcdT 44077 2146 A6
Rosemary Av
15000 CLEV 44111 2752 C1
Rosemary Ln
- MNTR 44060 2039 A5
9100 MNTR 44060 2038 E5
Rosemere St
- ELYR 44035 3006 C2
9900 CrlT 44035 3006 C2
Rosemond Rd
3900 CVHT 44121 2498 A6
Rosemont Dr
6800 BKVL 44141 3150 E1
6800 BKVL 44141 3151 A1
Rosemont Rd
1800 ECLE 44112 2497 B6
Rosena Av
1400 MadT 44057 1843 B7
Roseside Dr
5200 PRMA 44134 2754 B7
Rosetta Dr
12700 MsnT 44026 2503 B7
12700 MsnT 44026 2633 B1
Roseville Ct
4400 CLEV 44127 2625 C6
Rosewood Av
10 NHFD 44067 3018 A4
100 NHFD 44067 3017 E4
1400 LKWD 44107 2622 C5
7500 GDHT 44105 2756 A5
7600 CLEV 44105 2756 A5
9700 CLEV 44125 2756 B5
32800 AVLK 44012 2618 A1
32900 AVLK 44012 2617 E1
Rosewood Cir
6800 INDE 44131 2884 E6
Rosewood Ct
- AhtT 44001 2872 E6
- MDBH 44130 2881 B4
4500 CLEV 44105 2756 B5
5300 SFLD 44054 2746 E1
Rosewood Dr
10 AVLK 44012 2617 D1
800 ELYR 44035 2875 E1
4900 SDLK 44054 2616 D4
9800 CdnT 44024 2380 A4
9900 CdnT 44024 2379 E4
Rosewood Ln
8500 MNTR 44060 2144 B4
13000 SGVL 44136 3012 D3
Rosewood Ovl
3100 NRYN 44133 3014 C5
Rosewood St
41300 EyrT 44035 2745 D6
Rosewood Tr
33500 WBHL 44094 2375 A6
Rosita Ln
24100 NOSD 44070 2750 D4
Roslyn Dr
19600 RKRV 44116 2621 D4
Ross Av
2700 NBGH 44105 2755 B3
14400 CLEV 44128 2757 A3
Ross Cir
26700 NOSD 44070 2750 A6
Ross Rd
6600 MadT 44057 2150 B1
6900 MadT 44057 2044 D7
7600 HpfT 44041 2151 B1
7600 HpfT 44057 2151 B1
7600 MadT 44057 2045 A7
7600 MadT 44057 2151 B1
Rosslyn Rd
11800 PMHT 44130 2882 A4
12900 PMHT 44130 2881 E4
Rossmoor Rd
2000 CVHT 44118 2627 D3
Rotary Dr
7100 WNHL 44146 2886 E7
Rothwood Av
- NCtT 44067 3153 A2
N Roundhead Dr
31700 SLN 44139 3019 E1
S Roundhead Dr
31700 SLN 44139 3019 E2
Roundhead Pl
32900 SLN 44139 3019 E1
Roundwood Rd
3000 HGVL 44022 2630 B7
3300 HGVL 44022 2760 B1
Rouse Av
7300 CLEV 44104 2625 E6
7300 CLEV 44104 2626 B4
Rousseau Dr
5600 PRMA 44129 2883 A7
6300 PRMA 44129 2882 E7
Rowan Dr
200 BERA 44017 2880 A5
Rowelyn Av
600 SDLK 44054 2616 B4
Rowelyn St
800 SDLK 44054 2616 B4
Rowena Av
15100 MPHT 44137 2886 B4
Rowland Rd
300 VMLN 44089 2741 C4
Rowley Av
1400 CLEV 44109 2624 D7
Roxanne Ln
- BHIT 44212 3145 E6

INDEX 40

Roxanne Ln — Cleveland Street Index — Scranton Ct

STREET Block City ZIP Map# Grid

Roxanne Ln
- BHIT 44212 3146 A6
Roxboro Av
14400 CLEV 44111 2622 D7
Roxboro Dr
15400 MDBH 44130 2881 C4
Roxboro Rd
- CVHT 44106 2626 E4
200 VMLN 44089 2741 D4
2300 CVHT 44106 2627 A4
Roxburghe Dr
4300 BKVL 44141 3150 D3
Roxbury Ct
10 BHWD 44122 2628 E4
Roxbury Rd
1800 ECLE 44112 2496 E7
9100 PMHT 44130 2882 C3
Roxbury Park Dr
31100 BYVL 44140 2619 A2
Roxford Rd
1800 ECLE 44112 2497 A6
Roy Av
7000 CLEV 44104 2625 E6
21900 BDHT 44146 2887 B1
Roy Dr
1000 LKWD 44107 2622 D3
Roy Rd
5400 HDHT 44143 2499 B4
Royal Blvd
- GDHT 44125 2756 E7
13600 GDHT 44125 2757 A7
Royal Ct
5700 WLBY 44094 2375 A2
Royal Dr
1100 AMHT 44001 2872 E4
Royal Pkwy
5800 PMHT 44130 2882 B2
Royal Rd
800 CLEV 44110 2497 C2
Royal St
5300 MPHT 44137 2886 B1
Royale Oak Ct
8600 MNTR 44060 2252 C2
Royal Forest Dr
27600 WTLK 44145 2749 E1
27600 WTLK 44145 2750 A1
Royal Haven Dr
8300 NRYN 44133 3013 D3
Royal Oak Blvd
300 RDHT 44143 2498 D1
Royal Oak Ct
3100 WTLK 44145 2749 B3
Royal Oak Dr
- MDFD 44062 2767 B3
10 AURA 44202 3022 A7
1000 SRSL 44073 2762 A6
1800 PnvT 44077 2041 A3
10400 SGVL 44136 3012 B5
Royal Oaks Cir
1700 HDSN 44236 3154 E6
Royal Portrush Dr
7200 SLN 44139 3020 E3
Royal Ridge Dr
7600 PRMA 44129 2882 D6
Royal Ridge Ln
14900 NRYN 44133 3148 E1
Royal St. George St
- AVON 44011 2748 C6
Royalton Rd
500 EatT 44044 3007 C7
2600 EatT 44044 3006 E6
2900 BWHT 44147 3014 B7
3600 NRYN 44133 3014 B7
3600 NRYN 44133 3013 D7
6200 NRYN 44133 3013 D7
11700 NRYN 44133 3012 D7
12800 SGVL 44133 3012 D7
12800 SGVL 44136 3012 D7
17800 SGVL 44136 3011 C7
22200 SGVL 44136 3010 D7
23000 ClbT 44028 3010 D7
23000 ClbT 44136 3010 D7
25000 ClbT 44028 3009 D7
26900 ClbT 44028 3008 D7
26900 EatT 44028 3008 D7
34700 EatT 44044 3008 A7
Royalton Rd SR-82
500 EatT 44044 3007 C7
2600 EatT 44044 3006 E6
2900 BWHT 44147 3014 B7
3600 NRYN 44133 3014 B7
6200 NRYN 44133 3013 D7
11700 NRYN 44133 3012 D7
12800 SGVL 44133 3012 D7
12800 SGVL 44136 3012 D7
17800 SGVL 44136 3011 C7
22200 SGVL 44136 3010 D7
23000 ClbT 44028 3010 D7
23000 ClbT 44136 3010 D7
25000 ClbT 44028 3009 D7
26900 ClbT 44028 3008 D7
26900 EatT 44028 3008 D7
34700 EatT 44044 3008 A7
E Royalton Rd
- BWHT 44141 3015 E7
100 BWHT 44147 3014 E7
3900 BWHT 44147 3015 A7
4000 BKVL 44147 3015 A7
4000 BKVL 44141 3015 A7
6900 BKVL 44141 3016 A7
E Royalton Rd SR-82
- BWHT 44141 3015 E7
100 BWHT 44147 3014 E7
500 BWHT 44147 3015 A7
2400 BKVL 44147 3015 A7
2400 BKVL 44141 3015 A7
6900 BKVL 44141 3016 A7
W Royalton Rd
1000 BWHT 44147 3014 D7
W Royalton Rd SR-82
1000 BWHT 44147 3014 D7
Royal Valley Dr
9200 NRYN 44133 3014 B4
Royalview Dr
7300 PRMA 44129 2882 D7
8300 PRMA 44130 2882 D7
30100 WLWK 44095 2249 C6
Royalview Ln
- SGVL 44136 3147 C1
Royalwood Rd
1100 BWHT 44147 3014 E6
3000 NRYN 44133 3014 C6
5700 NRYN 44133 3013 E6
Royal Woods Pl
30500 WTLK 44145 2749 B3
Roycroft Av
1400 LKWD 44107 2622 B5
Roycroft Dr
6500 PRMA 44129 2882 E4
Rozelle Av
1100 ECLE 44112 2496 E6
Ruble Ct
5000 CLEV 44104 2625 D4
Ruby Av
3000 CLEV 44109 2754 C5
Ruby Ln
4700 BHIT 44212 3146 B7
Rubyvale Rd
2400 UNHT 44118 2628 C4
Rudolph Av
9400 GDHT 44125 2885 B1
Rudwick Rd
1800 CLEV 44112 2497 D3
Rudy Dr
20600 SGVL 44136 3011 B5
Rudyard Rd
700 CLEV 44110 2497 C2
Rue St. Georges
1200 WTLK 44145 2620 D6
Rugby Ct
24000 BDHT 44146 2887 D4
Rugby Rd
- MDHT 44124 2629 C2
13400 CLEV 44110 2497 A3
Rugby St
1800 TwbT 44087 3154 C2
Ruggiero Cir
- MDBH 44130 3012 C2
Ruhr Dr
- PRMA 44130 3013 C2
Rumson Rd
3100 CVHT 44118 2497 C7
3400 CVHT 44121 2497 C7
Runn St
200 BERA 44017 2880 B6
Running Brook Dr
9000 PRMA 44130 3013 C1
Runny Meade Tr
- RsIT 44073 2761 C3
Runnymede Av
10200 GDHT 44125 2756 C6
Runnymede Blvd
3500 CVHT 44121 2497 D4
Ruple Pkwy
5800 BKPK 44142 2879 E2
6400 BKPK 44142 2880 A3
Ruple Rd
800 CLEV 44110 2497 C2
4100 SELD 44121 2498 B5
Rural Rd
600 ETLK 44095 2250 D2
Rush Rd
1500 WKLF 44092 2374 E1
Rush St
100 ELYR 44035 2874 E5
Rushleigh Rd
900 CVHT 44121 2497 E6
Rushmore Ct
25000 RDHT 44143 2498 C2
Rushmore Dr
400 RDHT 44143 2498 B2
Rushmore Wy
7000 CcdT 44077 2146 B7
Rushton Dr
8100 MNTR 44060 2144 A1
Rushton Rd
1600 SELD 44121 2628 C1
4500 SELD 44121 2498 C7
Rushwood Ln
7900 SgHT 44067 3017 C6
Rusnak Tr
1300 BWHT 44147 3015 A4
Russell Av
3700 PRMA 44134 2754 B7
3900 LORN 44055 2745 B4
3900 ShfT 44055 2745 B4
10000 GDHT 44125 2756 C6
24000 EUCL 44123 2373 D3
24700 EUCL 44132 2373 D3
Russell Ct
7000 CLEV 44103 2625 E1
Russell Dr
34000 SLN 44139 3020 A2
Russell Ln
- BKVL 44141 3016 D2
- INDE 44141 3016 D2
8000 CLEV 44144 2753 E2
14500 RsIT 44072 2631 E7
14500 RsIT 44072 2632 A7
14500 RsIT 44072 2762 A1
Russell Rd
1300 CLEV 44103 2495 E7
1300 CLEV 44103 2625 E1
15000 RsIT 44072 2761 C2
15000 RsIT 44073 2761 C2
15500 CNFL 44073 2761 B3
15500 CNFL 44022 2761 B3
23700 BYVL 44140 2620 E5
Russellhurst Dr
7800 KTLD 44094 2376 D1
Russet Dr
3400 BWHT 44147 3015 B5
Russett Woods Ct
600 AURA 44202 3156 B3
Russett Woods Ln
500 AURA 44202 3156 C3
Russia Rd
6100 SAHT 44074 3003 C3
6100 SAHT 44001 3003 C3
6300 NRsT 44001 3003 A3
6400 NRsT 44074 3003 A3
41300 CrlT 44035 3005 D3
43000 CrlT 44035 3004 E3
44500 NRsT 44035 3003 E3
46200 NRsT 44035 3003 E3
46200 NRsT 44074 3004 A3
Rust Dr
11400 CsTp 44026 2502 B2
Rustic Dr
3000 NRYN 44133 3014 C7
Rustic Hllw
18000 SGVL 44136 3146 E4
Rustic Ln
8200 LryT 44077 2256 C5
25600 WTLK 44145 2750 B3
Rustic Ovl
7000 SVHL 44131 2884 B7
Rustic Rd
4100 CLEV 44135 2752 A3
Rustic Tr
900 PRMA 44134 2883 E5
Rustic Hill Ln
200 AhtT 44001 2873 C1
Rutgers Ct
300 ELYR 44035 3006 C2
1000 PnvT 44077 2146 E1
Ruth Dr
- SVHL 44131 2884 B4
13400 SGVL 44136 3012 D6
Ruth St
10 GNVA 44041 1944 B5
200 BYVL 44140 2619 C3
7500 MNTR 44060 2252 B2
Ruth Ellen Dr
100 RDHT 44143 2374 A5
Rutherford Rd
1000 CVHT 44112 2497 C6
1000 CVHT 44118 2497 C6
Rutland Av
11400 CLEV 44108 2496 D3
Rutland Dr
500 HDHT 44143 2499 C3
7700 MNTR 44060 2143 D5
Rutland Rd
18900 PkmT 44231 3027 E4
Rutledge Av
7400 CLEV 44102 2623 E5
Ryan Dr
9600 MNTR 44060 2039 B7
14000 WNHL 44146 2886 A5
Rybak Av
13600 GDHT 44125 2885 E3
13600 GDHT 44125 2886 A3
Rydalmount Rd
1400 CVHT 44118 2497 D7
1400 CVHT 44118 2627 D1
Rydalwood Ln
10 MDHL 44022 2760 B2
Ryder Rd
11300 HRM 44234 3160 E3
11300 HrmT 44234 3160 E3
Rye Rd
21800 SRHT 44122 2628 B6
Rye Gate Dr
19300 NRYN 44133 3148 A5
Rye Gate St
300 BYVL 44140 2619 C4
Ryeland Dr
4100 BWHT 44147 3015 C5

S

Sable Ct
5200 MNTR 44060 2039 B7
Sable Rd
800 CLEV 44119 2372 D5
Sablewood Dr
10100 AbnT 44023 3023 B3
Sabol Ct
10 EatT 44044 3007 B5
Sackett Av
2300 CLEV 44109 2754 D1
Sacramento Av
13800 CLEV 44111 2752 E2
Saddle Ln
5500 SLN 44139 2888 B2
7500 MNTR 44060 2251 C4
Saddleback Ln
7400 GSML 44040 2500 D1
Saddle Brook Ln
1500 WTLK 44145 2619 D7
Saddlehorn Cir
- ClbT 44028 3010 C4
12400 SGVL 44136 3011 A6
Saddler Dr
- ELYR 44035 2874 C6
Saddler Rd
200 BYVL 44140 2619 C3
Saddlewood Dr
4900 SDLK 44054 2616 D3
Saddlewood Ln
11400 CcdT 44077 2254 C2
Safford St
10 MDSN 44057 2044 B1
Sagamore Av
7500 CLEV 44103 2626 A2
Sagamore Dr
1600 EUCL 44117 2497 E2
1600 EUCL 44117 2498 A3
Sagamore Rd
- SgHT 44067 3016 E2
- SgHT 44125 3016 E2
- VLVW 44125 3016 E2
- VLVW 44125 3017 A2
10 NHFD 44067 3018 A3
10 NHFD 44146 3018 A3
10 WNHL 44146 3018 A3
200 SgHT 44146 3017 D3
200 SgHT 44067 3017 D3
200 SgHT 44146 3018 A3
200 SgHT 44067 3018 A3
200 WNHL 44146 3017 D3
1100 PRMA 44134 2883 E7
N Sagamore Rd
19200 FWPK 44126 2751 E2
S Sagamore Rd
19100 FWPK 44126 2751 E2
Sagamore Hills Blvd
7600 SgHT 44067 3017 D7
7600 SgHT 44067 3152 D1
Sagewood Ln
700 AbnT 44023 2892 B5
Sailor Cir
12600 NRYN 44133 3147 E4
Sailors Cove
- AVLK 44012 2619 A2
Sailorway Dr
5400 VMLN 44089 2740 E7
5400 VMLN 44089 2741 A7
5500 VmnT 44089 2740 E7
Saint Albans Rd
3400 CVHT 44121 2497 D6
Saint Andrews
31300 WTLK 44145 2749 A6
Saint Andrews Dr
300 HDHT 44143 2499 D2
3200 PRMA 44134 3014 C2
E St. Andrews Dr
300 HDHT 44143 2499 D1
W St. Andrews Dr
300 HDHT 44143 2499 D1
Saint Andrews Ln
- AURA 44202 3021 E6
Saint Andrews Wy
11300 CcdT 44077 2146 D6
Saint Anthony Ln
16300 CLEV 44111 2752 B1
Saint Catherine Av
8800 CLEV 44104 2756 B1
Saint Charles Av
1100 LKWD 44107 2622 D4
Saint Charles Pl
5400 MNTR 44060 2144 E1
Saint Clair Av
4000 CLEV 44103 2495 C7
4000 CLEV 44114 2495 C7
4000 WLBY 44094 2250 C5
7300 CLEV 44103 2496 A6
7500 MNTR 44060 2251 D2
8700 CLEV 44108 2496 A6
13100 CLEV 44112 2496 D4
13100 ECLE 44112 2496 D4
13200 CLEV 44110 2496 D4
13200 ECLE 44110 2496 D4
14000 CLEV 44110 2497 B3
17600 CLEV 44110 2372 D7
18900 CLEV 44117 2372 D7
19400 CLEV 44117 2373 A6
19400 EUCL 44117 2373 A6
W St. Clair Av
10 CLEV 44113 2624 D3
10 CLEV 44114 2624 D3
Saint Clair Av NE
- CLEV 44114 2624 E2
1300 CLEV 44114 2625 A1
Saint Clair St
- WLBY 44094 2250 E3
100 ELYR 44035 2875 B5
N St. Clair St
400 PNVL 44077 2040 A6
900 PNVL 44077 2039 E5
1100 FTHR 44077 2039 D5
S St. Clair St
10 PNVL 44077 2040 B7
10 PNVL 44077 2146 B1
Saint Francis Dr
6000 SVHL 44131 2884 A3
Saint Francis St
- AVON 44011 2748 C5
Saint Ives
30100 WTLK 44145 2749 B3
Saint James Av
14500 CLEV 44135 2752 D4
Saint James Blvd
5100 LORN 44053 2744 B5
Saint James Ct
26800 ODFL 44138 3009 E1
Saint James Dr
7600 MNTR 44060 2143 D5
12700 ManT 44255 3023 C4
W St. James Pkwy
2400 CVHT 44106 2626 E4
Saint James Pl
17900 AbnT 44023 2892 E6
17900 AbnT 44023 2893 A6
Saint James St
2100 MadT 44057 1942 C2
13000 CLEV 44135 2752 E4
13000 CLEV 44135 2753 B5
N St. James St
2100 CVHT 44106 2627 A3
W St. James St
2500 CVHT 44106 2627 A4
Saint John Ct
7400 MNTR 44060 2143 C6
Saint John Dr
1500 MadT 44057 1843 A7
Saint John St
11800 CLEV 44111 2753 A3
Saint Joseph Blvd
11000 ManT 44255 3159 C4
Saint Joseph Dr
100 AMHT 44001 2872 E1
6000 SVHL 44131 2884 A3
Saint Lawrence Blvd
10 ETLK 44095 2142 D7
500 ETLK 44094 2142 D7
500 WLBY 44094 2142 D7
1400 WLBY 44095 2142 D7
Saint Lawrence Cir
300 SgHT 44067 3017 E4
Saint Mark St
10500 CLEV 44111 2753 B1
Saint Maron Blvd
34400 AVON 44011 2748 B5
Saint Maron Dr
- SVHL 44131 2884 A4
Saint Olga Av
2500 CLEV 44113 2625 A6
Saint Peters Wy
5300 MNTR 44060 2038 E7
5300 MNTR 44060 2144 E1
5400 MNTR 44060 2145 A1
Saint Petersburg Dr
3700 PRMA 44134 3014 B2
Saint Roccos Ct
3300 CLEV 44109 2624 C7
Saint Sharbel St
33600 AVON 44011 2748 C5
Saint Tikhon Av
2500 CLEV 44113 2625 A6
Salberry St
8500 BWHT 44147 3015 B5
Salem Av
800 ELYR 44035 2875 E2
6900 CLEV 44127 2755 E1
Salem Cir
7700 HDSN 44236 3155 B6
Salem Ct
10 AVLK 44012 2619 A2
10 BHWD 44122 2629 A4
10 HkyT 44233 3148 B6
Salem Dr
300 VMLN 44089 2741 B4
5300 LORN 44053 2743 C5
7600 HDSN 44236 3155 B7
30300 BYVL 44140 2619 B3
Salem Ln
500 BNWK 44212 3147 D7
Salem Pkwy
1700 WTLK 44145 2750 B1
Salem Rd
1900 PnvT 44077 2041 A4
N Salem Row
18200 SGVL 44136 3146 E4
S Salem Row
18400 SGVL 44136 3146 E4
Salida Rd
7300 MONT 44060 2143 D2
Salient Pl
300 ETLK 44095 2142 C7
Salisbury Dr
- CRDN 44024 2379 D7
7800 PRMA 44129 2882 D4
Salisbury Rd
3700 SELD 44121 2497 E5
3800 SELD 44121 2498 A5
20800 WVHT 44146 2758 A6
Sally Av
- CLEV 44135 2752 A6
Salt Lick Ct
5100 MNTR 44060 2039 A7
Samara Ct
13100 HmbT 44024 2380 E2
Samuel Dr
12700 ManT 44255 3023 C5
23600 EUCL 44143 2498 C1
Samuel St
10 MDSN 44057 2044 B1
100 ELYR 44035 2874 D3
Samuel Lord Dr
7300 BbgT 44023 2761 B7
Sanctuary Cir
- BKVL 44141 3150 D3
Sanctuary Dr
8200 KDHL 44060 2252 B7
Sand Ct
5500 PRMA 44134 2883 E1
Sandalhaven Dr
15100 MDBH 44130 2881 B5
Sandalwood Ct
2300 TNBG 44087 3019 E3
Sandalwood Dr
400 BYVL 44140 2621 A5
700 ELYR 44035 2875 E1
700 MAYF 44040 2500 A5
1700 AVON 44011 2617 D7
1900 AVON 44011 2747 D1
2200 TNBG 44087 3019 E3
2300 TNBG 44087 3020 A4
Sandalwood Ln
700 AbnT 44023 2892 B3
10200 TNBG 44087 3020 A4
20100 SGVL 44136 3146 C3
Sandalwood Rd
22000 BDHT 44146 2887 B1
Sandbridge Ct
7000 MNTR 44060 2145 A7
Sand Creek Cir
10900 SGVL 44136 3011 A5
Sanders Av
500 PNVL 44077 2040 A6
Sanders Ln
27700 NOSD 44070 2749 E5
Sandfield Dr
6300 BKPK 44142 2881 B4
Sandgate Dr
12000 CsTp 44026 2502 E4
Sandgate Rd
1700 MadT 44057 1941 D1
11800 CsTp 44026 2502 E4
Sandhurst Dr
300 HDHT 44143 2499 C2
6300 BKPK 44142 2881 A3
Sandhurst Rd
25000 BDHT 44146 2887 D4
San Diego Av
13400 CLEV 44111 2752 E2
Sandpiper Av
300 ELYR 44035 3006 D3
Sandpiper Ct
7000 CcdT 44077 2145 D7
Sandpiper Dr
5500 PRMA 44134 2883 E1
Sandpiper Ln
5900 NOSD 44070 2879 B2
Sandra Dr
500 BNWK 44212 3146 D7
Sandridge Dr
- AMHT 44001 2872 C1
Sands Av
- AMHT 44001 2744 B7
Sands Blvd
10 MadT 44057 1941 A5
Sandstone Blvd
200 AMHT 44001 2744 B6
200 AMHT 44053 2744 B6
Sandstone Dr
100 PnvT 44077 2041 A7
8000 SgHT 44067 3017 B5
Sandstone Ln
32800 NRDV 44039 2877 D1
Sandtrap Cir
300 PnvT 44077 2040 E4
Sandtree Ln
7100 MNTR 44060 2144 E7
Sandusky Av
9300 CLEV 44105 2756 C2
Sandusky St
600 VMLN 44089 2740 E5
Sandy Ln
10 CrlT 44035 3006 C2
3400 AVON 44011 2748 C4
22000 FWPK 44126 2751 A5
Sandy Hill Dr
26600 RDHT 44143 2373 E6
26600 RDHT 44143 2374 A6
Sandy Hill Rd
10 SgHT 44067 3017 E6
Sandy Hook Dr
4800 PRMA 44134 3014 A1
6600 PRMA 44134 3013 E1
Sandy Knoll Dr
35900 ETLK 44095 2250 B3
Sandy Oaks Tr
9000 CdnT 44024 2254 D7
Sandy Springs Dr
16900 NRYN 44133 3149 B4
San Fernando Cir
4300 INDE 44131 3015 C2
Sanford Av
16200 CLEV 44110 2497 C2
Sanford Dr
3700 PRMA 44134 3014 B2
Sanford St
10 PNVL 44077 2039 E6
10 PnvT 44077 2039 E6
200 PNVL 44077 2040 A6
1000 VMLN 44089 2741 A7
San Remo Ct
- MCDN 44056 3154 A3
Sansdan Ct
1700 PnvT 44077 2041 A3
Santa Clara Dr
27200 WTLK 44145 2620 A6
Santa Fe Ct
100 ELYR 44035 3006 D2
1000 GFTN 44044 3142 B5
Santa Fe Tr
- ClrT 44024 2505 C6
Santin Cir
10 BDFD 44146 2886 C5
Sapphire Ct
9000 PRMA 44130 3013 D1
Sarah Ct
9100 MNTR 44060 2038 E7
Sarah Lee Dr
7500 CcdT 44077 2254 E2
Saranac Dr
19800 FWPK 44126 2751 D2
Saranac Rd
14300 CLEV 44110 2497 A2
Sarasota Dr
3800 PRMA 44134 3014 B1
N Sarasota Dr
7500 PRMA 44134 3014 B1
Saratoga Av
2100 CLEV 44109 2754 C5
Saratoga Ct
10 BHWD 44122 2628 E3
Saratoga Dr
20700 FWPK 44126 2751 C4
Saratoga Rd
7400 MDBH 44130 3012 C1
Saratoga Tr
17700 SGVL 44136 3147 A4
19400 BNWK 44212 3147 A4
19400 BNWK 44136 3147 A4
Sassafras Cir
8900 NRYN 44133 3013 B3
Sassafras Dr
100 VmnT 44089 2869 D1
4600 PRMA 44129 2883 B7
15000 SGVL 44136 3012 B3
Sassafras Ln
30900 WTLK 44145 2749 B6
Saturn Dr
12300 NRYN 44133 3014 C6
Sauer Av
8600 CLEV 44102 2623 D6
Savage Rd
16600 BbgT 44023 2761 D7
16600 BbgT 44023 2890 D2
Savage St
100 BERA 44017 2880 A5
Savannah Av
13800 ECLE 44112 2497 A5
Savannah Dr
6400 MNTR 44060 2143 C4
Savannah Pkwy
1800 WTLK 44145 2619 B7
1800 WTLK 44145 2749 B1
Savoy Dr
3800 FWPK 44126 2752 A1
Sawgrass Cir
- NRYN 44133 3149 A3
Sawmill
- AVLK 44012 2618 D5
Sawmill Bnd
100 CRDN 44024 2505 B2
23600 ODFL 44138 3010 D2
Saw Mill Cir
4000 NOSD 44070 2750 D5
Sawmill Ct
7100 CcdT 44077 2145 D7
Sawmill Dr
- AVLK 44012 2618 D5
10000 HmbT 44024 2380 E5
10000 HmbT 44024 2381 A4
Sawtell Rd
3000 CLEV 44127 2625 D6
Sawyer Dr
- MNTR 44060 2038 B7
Saxe Av
9100 CLEV 44105 2756 B2
Saxon Dr
5500 GDHT 44125 2885 C1
8800 KTLD 44094 2251 D6
Saxton St
10 MDSN 44057 2044 B2
Saybrook Av
13100 GDHT 44105 2756 E5
13600 GDHT 44105 2757 A5
14100 CLEV 44105 2757 A5
Saybrook Dr
1100 MCDN 44056 3018 E7
8400 BKLN 44144 2753 D6
11000 CcdT 44077 2146 B6
Saybrook Ln
11300 AbnT 44023 2893 B1
Saybrook Rd
2200 UNHT 44118 2628 A5
Sayle Dr
29400 WBHL 44092 2374 D5
Saylor Dr
6200 BKPK 44142 2881 D4
Saywell Av
11300 CLEV 44108 2496 D6
Scarborough Ln
400 PnvT 44077 2145 B6
Scarborough Rd
2600 CVHT 44106 2627 A4
2600 CVHT 44118 2627 A4
E Scarborough Rd
3200 CVHT 44118 2627 C4
3500 UNHT 44118 2627 D4
Scarlet Dr
- SGVL 44136 3146 B1
Scarlet Oak Dr
5800 BDHT 44146 2887 D3
Scarlet Oak Ln
8600 PRMA 44130 3013 D2
Scarsdale Ln
600 RsIT 44073 2761 A3
Scenic Dr
10 OmsT 44138 2879 B4
Scenic Rd
4700 FnTp 44491 3029 D2
19100 RKRV 44116 2621 E5
Scenic St
1400 LKWD 44107 2622 A5
Scenic Park Dr
1500 LKWD 44107 2621 E5
Scenic Park Ovl
6500 MDBH 44130 2881 E5
Scenic Pointe
21700 SGVL 44136 3011 A5
Scenicview Dr
7500 INDE 44131 3015 D2
8500 BWHT 44147 3014 D5
Schaaf Dr
6200 BKPK 44142 2881 C4
Schaaf Ln
- BNHT 44131 2755 A7
E Schaaf Rd
10 BNHT 44131 2755 B7
1200 BNHT 44131 2884 D1
1400 INDE 44131 2884 D1
W Schaaf Rd
10 BNHT 44131 2755 A6
200 BNHT 44109 2755 A6
200 CLEV 44109 2755 A6
200 CLEV 44131 2755 A6
400 CLEV 44109 2754 E6
Schadden Rd
100 ELYR 44035 2875 A1
41100 ELYR 44035 2874 D1
41700 EyrT 44035 2874 D1
Schade Av
6100 CLEV 44103 2495 E7
Schady Rd
- ODFL 44138 3010 A1
- OmsT 44138 3010 A1
26800 ODFL 44138 2878 D7
26800 ODFL 44138 2879 A7
26800 OmsT 44138 2878 D7
26800 OmsT 44138 2879 A7
Schaefer Av
6500 CLEV 44103 2495 E7
Schaefer St
8800 MNTR 44060 2144 D7
Schaffer Dr
36500 NRDV 44039 2876 E3
Schell Av
2100 CLEV 44109 2754 D6
Schenely Av
17300 CLEV 44119 2372 D5
17800 CLEV 44119 2372 D5
Schiller Av
3500 CLEV 44109 2754 C5
4100 CLEV 44144 2754 C5
Schlather Ln
18900 RKRV 44116 2621 E6
Schneider Av
7100 CLEV 44102 2623 E7
Schneider Ct
35500 AVON 44011 2618 A6
Schoepf Rd
7100 NCtT 44067 3153 A5
Scholl Rd
2200 UNHT 44118 2627 E3
School Av
15200 CLEV 44110 2497 B2
School Dr
7400 BKLN 44144 2753 D5
School Ln
- CNFL 44022 2761 A4
School St
10 BERA 44017 2880 C6
100 ELYR 44035 2874 E5
1600 ShfT 44055 2745 C6
Schooner Ct
32500 AVLK 44012 2618 B3
Schooner Ln
400 NCtT 44067 3153 C5
Schooners Cove
7200 CcdT 44077 2146 D6
Schreiber Rd
11400 VLVW 44125 2885 D5
13700 GDHT 44125 2886 A4
13700 GDHT 44137 2886 A4
13700 MPHT 44137 2886 A4
Schuberts Al
10 OmsT 44138 2879 B4
Schustrich Rd
5500 HrmT 44255 3160 B6
5800 HrmT 44234 3160 D6
Schuyler Av
15000 CLEV 44111 2752 C2
Schwab Dr
10700 PRMA 44130 3013 B1
Schwartz Rd
28900 WTLK 44145 2749 C4
31500 AVON 44011 2749 A3
31500 AVON 44145 2749 A3
32300 AVON 44011 2748 E3
Science Park Dr
25700 BHWD 44122 2628 E7
25700 BHWD 44122 2629 A7
Scioto Av
13800 ECLE 44112 2497 A5
Scioto Ct
7400 SLN 44139 3020 E2
Scituata Ct
1000 GFTN 44044 3142 A4
Scotch Pine Ct
4100 PryT 44081 2042 E3
Scotch Pine Wy
- SGVL 44136 3011 C5
4700 NRDV 44039 2748 D6
Scotland Dr
6200 MadT 44057 1843 A7
7800 BbgT 44023 2890 D6
Scott Av
2000 ELYR 44035 3006 B2
Scott Blvd
24400 ODFL 44138 3010 C2
Scott Dr
6400 BKPK 44142 2880 E3
14400 SGVL 44136 3146 B1
Scott St
- PnvT 44077 2039 D7
Scottsdale Blvd
15500 SRHT 44120 2757 B2
17700 SRHT 44122 2757 E2
20000 SRHT 44122 2758 A2
Scottsdale Cir
7200 MNTR 44060 2144 D7
7300 MNTR 44060 2252 D1
Scottsdale Dr
4800 NRYN 44133 3014 A4
9200 BWHT 44147 3014 D7
9500 BWHT 44147 3149 D1
10400 SGVL 44136 3012 B5
Scottwood Av
11300 CLEV 44108 2496 D6
Scovill Av
5500 CLEV 44104 2625 D4
Scranton Ct
1800 CLEV 44109 2624 D7

INDEX 41
Scranton Rd
Cleveland Street Index
S Skyland Dr

STREET Block City ZIP Map# Grid

Scranton Rd
1800 CLEV 44113 2624 E5
3100 CLEV 44109 2624 D7
3200 CLEV 44109 2754 D1
Scranton Woods Tr
10700 NbyT 44065 2634 A7
Scupper Ln
10 NCtT 44067 3153 C4
Sea Pns
6000 MNTR 44060 2144 B3
Seabrooke Av
22300 EUCL 44123 2373 B2
Seabury Av
21000 FWPK 44126 2751 B5
Sea Ray Cove
3600 RMDV 44202 3020 E6
Seasdale Av
2200 CLEV 44109 2754 C4
Seaton Ct
- AMHT 44001 2872 E3
Seaton Pl
8400 MNTR 44060 2252 B2
Seaton Rd
3300 CVHT 44118 2497 D7
Seaward Wy
100 AVLK 44012 2618 E2
Sebastian Ct
5300 HDHT 44143 2499 A3
Sebert Av
6500 CLEV 44105 2755 E2
Sebor Rd
3100 SRHT 44120 2627 A7
Sebring Av
1300 MadT 44057 1843 C6
Seco Blvd
13500 BURT 44021 2766 A1
Second St
- MNTR 44060 2144 E7
Secondary Rd
5200 CLEV 44135 2751 E7
5200 CLEV 44135 2880 E1
Secretariat Ct
- AVON 44011 2747 B6
Sector Av
11700 CLEV 44111 2623 A7
Sector Dr
10 BDFD 44146 2886 D2
Sedalia Av
17600 CLEV 44135 2752 A3
Sederis Ln
500 ELYR 44035 2875 A7
Sedge Cir
35900 SLN 44139 3020 B1
Sedgefield Ovl
31500 SLN 44139 3019 D1
Sedgewick Ct
100 BNWK 44212 3147 B6
1100 NRYN 44133 3013 C5
Sedgewick Rd
- LNHT 44124 2498 E6
2800 SRHT 44120 2627 C6
N Sedgewick Rd
4700 LNHT 44124 2498 D6
S Sedgewick Rd
5000 LNHT 44124 2498 D6
Sedley Rd
24300 RDHT 44143 2373 C7
Seeley Rd
13100 LryT 44077 2041 C7
13100 LryT 44077 2147 C1
13300 LryT 44077 2148 A1
Seeley St
300 AMHT 44001 2872 C1
Seiberling Dr
100 SgHT 44067 3017 E5
100 SgHT 44067 3018 A5
Selby Cir
16200 SGVL 44136 3147 A3
Selfridge Pkwy
4100 HIHL 44128 2758 A3
Selhurst Rd
4300 NOSD 44070 2750 B6
Selig Dr
6300 INDE 44131 2884 D6
Selkirk Dr
6100 MadT 44057 1941 E1
Selkirk Rd
2700 BHWD 44122 2628 E5
2800 BHWD 44122 2629 A5
Sellers Av
11200 CLEV 44108 2496 D4
Selma Av
6500 CLEV 44127 2625 E6
Seltzer Wy
900 CLEV 44114 2624 E2
Selwick Dr
7400 PRMA 44129 2882 D6
Selworthy Ln
7100 SLN 44139 3019 D1
Selwyn Rd
800 CVHT 44112 2497 D5
Selzer Av
2100 CLEV 44109 2754 D3
Selzer Ct
- CLEV 44109 2754 D3
Seminary Ln
8500 CsTp 44026 2502 B7
Seminary St
10 BERA 44017 2880 C6
Seminole Av
9500 CLEV 44108 2496 B5
Seminole Ln
9000 MCDN 44056 3018 D6
Seminole Rd
19500 EUCL 44117 2497 E2
19500 EUCL 44117 2498 A2
Seminole St
6000 MONT 44060 2143 B4
6100 MNTR 44060 2143 B5
Seminole Wy
34100 SLN 44139 2889 A7
Semra Cir
7500 PRMA 44130 3013 D1
Seneca Av
100 ELYR 44035 2874 D5
2700 LORN 44052 2745 D3
2700 LORN 44055 2745 D3
16600 LKWD 44107 2622 B7
Seneca Blvd
1200 BWHT 44147 3014 E7
Seneca Ct
300 AVLK 44012 2618 D3
9800 BKVL 44141 3150 C4
14000 CLEV 44111 2752 D1
Seneca Dr
- WTLK 44145 2750 A2
1400 MadT 44057 1843 B7
27200 WTLK 44145 2749 E2
33300 SLN 44139 3019 E3
33300 SLN 44139 3020 A3
Seneca Pl
- NRDV 44039 2877 B6
5600 WLBY 44094 2375 A2
Seneca Rd
1900 EUCL 44117 2498 A2
6100 MNTR 44060 2143 B4
6600 MAYF 44143 2500 A5
Seneca Tr
6300 MNTR 44060 2143 B5
14400 MDBH 44130 2881 C7
Senlac Hills Dr
10 CNFL 44022 2761 A6
Sentinel Dr
4700 BKVL 44141 3150 C3
Sentry Ln
26800 WTLK 44145 2620 A6
Sequoia Ct
5800 MONT 44060 2143 E2
Sequoia Dr
5100 PRMA 44134 3014 A1
Sequoia Tr
29800 WTLK 44145 2749 C6
Serene Ct
9900 TNBG 44087 3019 C4
Serenity Ln
28800 WKLF 44092 2374 B4
E Serenity Ln
2000 LORN 44053 2744 B4
W Serenity Ln
2100 LORN 44053 2744 B4
Serio Dr
7400 INDE 44131 3015 D1
Service Ct
1700 EUCL 44117 2498 A2
Service Dr
10 ELYR 44035 3006 A3
Service Ln
3500 PryT 44081 1940 B7
Service Center Dr
6300 INDE 44131 2884 D6
Service Vehicles Access
- CLEV 44135 2751 E6
Sesquicentennial Dr
- PRMA 44130 2882 A7
Sesquicentennial Park Rd
- PMHT 44130 2882 A7
- PRMA 44130 2882 A7
Seth Paine Ct
7900 BKVL 44141 3016 A6
Seth Payne St
7900 BKVL 44141 3016 B3
Settlement Acres Dr
13300 BKPK 44130 2881 D3
13300 BKPK 44142 2881 D3
Settlers Ct
7600 MNTR 44060 2253 A2
Settlers Ln
28500 PRPK 44124 2629 B3
Settlers Psg
8100 BKVL 44141 3016 C5
Settlers Run
14400 SGVL 44136 3146 E1
Settlers Tr
17700 AbnT 44023 2893 B5
Settler's Wy
14000 SGVL 44136 3011 D7
14200 SGVL 44136 3146 D1
Settlers Reserve Ovl
1700 WTLK 44145 2749 D1
Settlers Reserve Wy
1600 WTLK 44145 2619 D7
1700 WTLK 44145 2749 D1
Settlers Ridge Rd
7100 GSML 44040 2500 C7
Seven Hills Blvd
6900 SVHL 44131 2884 B6
Seven Oaks Dr
1600 LNHT 44124 2628 E1
19000 SGVL 44136 3147 A5
Seven Pines Dr
5100 LORN 44053 2744 B5
Severance Cir
10 CVHT 44118 2497 D7
10 CVHT 44118 2627 E1
Severn Ln
1500 WKLF 44092 2374 E1
Severn Rd
3400 CVHT 44118 2627 E1
3700 CVHT 44121 2627 E1
Seville Av
15300 CLEV 44128 2757 B5
Seville Dr
26200 BHWD 44122 2629 A4
Sexton Ct
2700 BWHT 44147 3149 D5
Sexton Rd
4300 CLEV 44105 2756 B4
Seymour Av
2000 CLEV 44113 2624 C6
Shadeland Av
11500 CLEV 44108 2496 D3
Shadetree Tr
- AVON 44011 2617 E6
Shadley St
2700 ShvT 44241 3158 A7
Shadowbrook Cir
- AURA 44202 3156 D1
Shadowbrook Dr
7200 KTLD 44094 2376 B5
32200 SLN 44139 2759 E7
Shadow Hill Tr
9400 CsTp 44026 2502 E5
9500 CsTp 44026 2503 A5
Shadowood Dr
- NbyT 44065 2764 A2
Shadowrow Rd
800 WLBY 44094 2143 A4
Shadow Wood Cir
9800 AbnT 44023 2763 A7
Shady Dr
300 AMHT 44001 2872 D1
Shady Ln
100 PnvT 44077 2040 D2
400 ETLK 44095 2250 C1
2100 SVHL 44131 2884 B6
4600 FnTp 44491 3029 E3
7100 MNTR 44060 2144 D7
7600 NCtT 44067 3153 B2
9900 BKLN 44144 2753 C6
13200 CsTp 44026 2631 E3
13200 CsTp 44026 2632 A3
Shady Rd
37200 NRDV 44039 2876 D6
Shady Lake Dr
2700 VMLN 44089 2742 A5
Shady Lane Dr
8200 BWHT 44147 3014 E4
Shadylawn Dr
- AMHT 44001 2744 A7
100 AMHT 44001 2743 E7
Shady Moss Ln
4900 NRDV 44039 2748 E7
Shadyoak Blvd
11900 GDHT 44125 2885 E1
13500 GDHT 44125 2886 A1
Shady Pine Pl
3300 PryT 44081 1940 D7
Shady Ridge Ln
5000 BNHT 44131 2755 B7
Shadyside Av
5500 CLEV 44144 2754 A3
Shadyside Dr
- ETLK 44095 2250 C1
6100 VMLN 44089 2740 D5
Shadyway Rd
12800 GDHT 44125 2885 E3
Shadywood Ln
4000 WVHT 44122 2757 E3
9500 TNBG 44087 3019 B6
Shaffer Dr
1200 LORN 44053 2744 C6
Shagbark Tr
10 AURA 44202 3157 C1
21500 SGVL 44136 3011 A4
Shaker Blvd
10000 CLEV 44104 2626 C5
11600 CLEV 44120 2626 C5
13300 CLEV 44120 2627 C6
14000 SRHT 44120 2627 C6
18500 SRHT 44122 2627 C6
20200 SRHT 44122 2628 A6
24300 BHWD 44122 2628 D6
26000 BHWD 44122 2629 A6
27500 PRPK 44124 2629 A6
32700 PRPK 44124 2630 A6
34000 HGVL 44022 2630 B6
Shaker Blvd SR-87
10000 CLEV 44104 2626 C5
11600 CLEV 44120 2626 C5
13300 CLEV 44120 2627 C6
14000 SRHT 44120 2627 C6
18500 SRHT 44122 2627 C6
19500 SRHT 44122 2628 A6
24300 BHWD 44122 2628 D6
Shaker Dr
8800 NRDV 44039 2876 E7
10900 NRYN 44133 3013 B4
29300 WKLF 44092 2374 B1
Shaker Rd
2500 CVHT 44118 2627 D5
Shaker Sq
13100 CLEV 44120 2626 E5
Shakercrest Blvd
2700 BHWD 44122 2628 D6
Shakerwood Rd
19000 WVHT 44122 2757 E2
19700 WVHT 44122 2758 A2
Shakespeare Dr
600 BERA 44017 2880 B4
Shakespeare Ln
100 AVON 44011 2748 B2
Shakespeare Pkwy
1000 CLEV 44108 2496 B6
Shale Av
9900 CLEV 44104 2626 C5
Shale Brook Ct
10000 SGVL 44136 3011 A4
Shale Brook Wy
10100 SGVL 44136 3011 A4
Shamrock Av
11600 LNDL 44111 2753 B3
Shamrock Dr
7300 MONT 44060 2143 C2
Shandle Blvd
5600 MNTR 44060 2144 C2
Shandon Ct
20900 SGVL 44136 3146 B4
Shaner Dr
6900 WNHL 44146 2886 E6
6900 WNHL 44146 2887 A7
Shankland Rd
4700 WLBY 44094 2250 C7
Shannon Ct
14700 BURT 44021 2766 A1
Shannon Ln
6600 MNTR 44060 2145 A5
Shannon Rd
3400 CVHT 44118 2627 E1
Sharon Ct
2800 TNBG 44087 3020 A6
Sharon Dr
700 WTLK 44145 2620 D6
7600 MONT 44060 2143 D2
10400 PRMA 44130 2882 B1
18700 BbgT 44023 3021 D2
23200 NOSD 44070 2750 E4
Sharon Ln
22100 FWPK 44126 2751 A5
Sharondale Dr
900 AMHT 44001 2744 A6
1000 AMHT 44053 2744 A6
6200 SLN 44139 2889 B5
W Sharondale Dr
33300 SLN 44139 2889 A4
Sharonlee Dr
7300 MNTR 44060 2252 A1
Sharon Ln Dr
9300 NRYN 44133 3014 C4
Sharp Ln
8200 CsTp 44026 2502 A1
Sharp Rd
8800 OmsT 44138 2878 B7
8800 OmsT 44138 3009 B1
Sharpe Av
37200 WLBY 44094 2250 D5
Shasta Ct
15600 CLEV 44110 2372 C7
Shasta Dr
10500 CdnT 44024 2379 A6
Shaw Av
- KTLD 44094 2376 E1
1700 ECLE 44112 2497 A4
9100 KTLD 44094 2377 A1
12500 CLEV 44108 2496 E4
13100 ECLE 44112 2496 E4
17400 LKWD 44107 2622 A4
Shaw Dr
36000 NRDV 44039 2876 E7
Shaw Rd
- AbnT 44021 2894 B7
17900 AbnT 44234 2894 B7
17900 TroT 44234 2894 B7
17900 TroT 44021 2894 B7
18100 AbnT 44234 3025 B2
18100 TroT 44234 3025 B2
Shawn Dr
34800 NRDV 44039 2748 B7
Shawnee Av
18500 CLEV 44119 2372 E6
19700 CLEV 44119 2373 A6
20100 EUCL 44119 2373 A6
Shawnee Dr
4000 LORN 44055 2745 D4
5600 LNHT 44124 2629 B1
Shawnee Ln
500 BDFD 44146 2886 C5
Shawnee Rd
19000 EUCL 44117 2497 D1
Shawnee Tr
- WLBY 44094 2143 A4
10 AURA 44202 3157 A1
7000 MNTR 44060 2143 A4
7800 GTVL 44234 3161 E4
13600 MDBH 44130 2881 D6
Shawondassee Dr
10 TMLK 44095 2250 A1
Shaw View Av
1300 ECLE 44112 2497 B4
Shear St
10 ELYR 44035 2874 E5
Shearer Rd
7300 SgHT 44067 3152 D2
Shedd Rd
15000 BtnT 44021 2767 A7
15000 BtnT 44062 2767 A7
15000 MdfT 44062 2767 A7
15000 PkmT 44062 2767 A7
15000 TroT 44062 2767 A7
16700 MdfT 44062 2768 B7
16700 PkmT 44062 2768 B7
Sheerbrook Dr
1000 SRSL 44073 2761 E7
1000 SRSL 44073 2762 A7
Sheerwater Ln
38300 WLBY 44094 2142 E5
Sheffield Ct
300 ShfT 44055 2745 B6
Sheffield Rd
400 SDLK 44054 2616 B4
1300 SELD 44121 2498 B7
1400 SELD 44121 2628 B1
Sheffield Ter
100 BNWK 44212 3147 B6
1600 PnvT 44077 2040 E2
1700 PnvT 44077 2041 A2
Sheffield Edgewater Dr
100 SDLK 44054 2616 E2
Sheffield French Creek Rd
37300 AVON 44011 2747 B2
Shelbourne Ct
8700 CLEV 44106 2626 B3
Shelburne Dr
7600 MDBH 44130 3012 D2
Shelburne Rd
17400 CVHT 44118 2627 D5
18100 SRHT 44118 2627 E5
18100 SRHT 44120 2627 E5
19500 SRHT 44118 2628 A5
20200 SRHT 44122 2628 A5
Shelby Av
500 PNVL 44077 2040 A6
Shelby Ct
1000 GFTN 44044 3142 A4
Shelby Dr
16200 BKPK 44142 2881 B1
Sheldon Av
1800 ECLE 44112 2497 B5
Sheldon Blvd
13300 BKPK 44142 2881 D4
13300 MDBH 44142 2881 D4
13300 MDBH 44130 2881 D4
Sheldon Rd
5300 LNHT 44124 2499 A6
11500 ManT 44255 3159 D3
12000 ManT 44255 3024 E7
12200 ManT 44255 3025 A5
12900 AbnT 44255 3025 A5
15100 BKPK 44142 2881 B4
15100 MDBH 44142 2881 B4
15100 MDBH 44130 2881 B4
18000 MDBH 44130 2880 B4
18000 MDBH 44142 2880 B4
20000 BERA 44017 2880 B4
20000 BERA 44142 2880 B4
20000 BKPK 44142 2880 B4
Shelford Dr
7300 SLN 44139 3020 C2
Shelia Av
17900 CLEV 44111 2752 A3
Shelley Dr
3900 NOSD 44070 2750 B5
Shelley Pkwy
700 BERA 44017 2880 B4
Shelley Rd
2700 SRHT 44122 2628 B6
Shelly Av
33900 NRDV 44039 3008 C1
Shelly Dr
- LORN 44053 2744 B4
2900 SVHL 44131 3015 B2
6700 MadT 44057 1942 C2
Shelly Wy
6900 MadT 44057 1942 C2
Sheltered Cove
8200 MNTR 44060 2144 A3
Shelton Blvd
100 ETLK 44095 2142 D6
Shelton Ct
2700 MadT 44057 1942 E4
Shelton Dr
19500 CLEV 44110 2373 A7
Shenandoah Ct
7200 MNTR 44060 2143 B4
Shenandoah Dr
9100 NRYN 44133 3013 C4
9600 BKVL 44141 3150 D3
Shenandoah Ovl
1300 PRMA 44134 2883 E7
Shenandoah Rdg
19800 SGVL 44136 3146 C1
Shepard Ln
- NOSD 44070 2750 E7
- NOSD 44070 2879 E1
Shepard Rd
2800 PryT 44077 2041 D4
2800 PryT 44081 2041 D4
2800 PryT 44081 2042 A4
8200 MCDN 44056 3153 E2
8800 MCDN 44056 3018 E7
9000 MCDN 44056 3019 A6
9300 TNBG 44087 3019 A6
9900 TNBG 44056 3019 A4
Shepard Tr
9600 TNBG 44087 3019 A4
Shepard Hills Blvd
900 MCDN 44056 3018 D6
Shepherd Cir
- OBLN 44074 3139 A3
Sheraton Dr
3700 PRMA 44134 2883 B2
Sherborn Rd
6300 PMHT 44130 2882 A5
Sherborne Rd
24000 BDHT 44146 2887 D4
Sherbrook Dr
28900 WKLF 44092 2374 C4
Sherbrook Rd
1400 SELD 44121 2498 A7
1400 SELD 44121 2628 A1
Sherbrooke Av
- WTLK 44145 2620 C7
Sherbrooke Ovl
3800 BNWK 44212 3146 E7
18100 SGVL 44136 3146 E4
Sherbrooke Rd
- SRHT 44118 2628 A6
2700 SRHT 44122 2628 A6
Sherbrooke Valley Ct
2900 WBHL 44094 2376 A7
Sherbrook Park Dr
33800 SLN 44139 2889 A3
Sheri Dr
200 BNWK 44212 3146 D7
Sheridan Dr
1200 PRMA 44134 2883 E7
Sheridan Rd
1400 SELD 44121 2498 D7
1400 SELD 44121 2628 D1
Sheriff St
100 ELYR 44035 2874 D3
Sherman Av
7500 CLEV 44104 2626 A4
Sherman Dr
1200 PRMA 44134 2883 E7
Sherman Ln
9300 NRYN 44133 3013 C5
Sherman Rd
7000 CsTp 44026 2501 A5
7400 GSML 44040 2500 E5
7600 GSML 44040 2501 A5
8100 CsTp 44026 2502 A6
9200 CsTp 44026 2503 A5
9700 CsTp 44024 2503 A5
9700 MsnT 44024 2503 B5
9700 MsnT 44026 2503 A5
10700 MsnT 44024 2504 A5
Sherman St
400 ELYR 44035 2875 B7
400 GNVA 44041 1944 C5
1200 ELYR 44035 3006 B1
Sherri Dr
8700 MCDN 44056 3018 E7
W Sherri Dr
6800 MCDN 44056 3018 E7
Sherrie Ln
600 LORN 44053 2744 E6
Sherrington Rd
17900 SRHT 44122 2757 D1
Sherry Av
13300 CLEV 44135 2752 E4
Sherry Ln
300 BERA 44017 2880 A4
Sherwin Dr
2100 TNBG 44087 3019 E4
2400 TNBG 44087 3020 A4
Sherwin Rd
4300 WLBY 44094 2251 B6
Sherwood Av
800 ELYR 44035 2875 E2
Sherwood Blvd
1600 EUCL 44117 2373 C7
Sherwood Cir
13400 GDHT 44125 2885 E4
Sherwood Ct
10 BHWD 44122 2628 E3
400 PNVL 44077 2146 A3
Sherwood Dr
400 BYVL 44140 2619 C4
500 AURA 44202 3021 C6
700 MDSN 44057 2044 A3
800 MCDN 44056 3018 D7
2400 PRMA 44134 2883 C7
2500 LORN 44053 2743 E2
5200 FWPK 44126 2751 B5
5700 NOSD 44070 2878 D2
7400 MNTR 44060 2252 E1
14800 SGVL 44136 3146 C2
27400 WTLK 44145 2749 E4
34300 SLN 44139 2889 A2
Sherwood Ln
35700 WBHL 44094 2375 B3
Sherwood Rd
3700 SELD 44121 2497 E4
9300 CLEV 44104 2626 B5
Sherwood Tr
6600 NRYN 44133 3013 E5
9300 BKVL 44141 3150 D2
11600 CsTp 44026 2501 B3
Sheryl Dr
800 CLEV 44109 2754 E6
Shetland Cir
700 BERA 44017 3010 E2
700 BERA 44017 3011 A2
Shetland Ct
300 HDHT 44143 2499 C1
8800 KTLD 44094 2377 C6
Shilling Dr
- ELYR 44035 2874 B5
Shilling Rd
6600 HpfT 44041 2045 B7
Shillingham Wy
100 PnvT 44077 2145 C6
Shiloh Cir
1700 PRMA 44134 2883 D6
Shiloh Dr
12100 CsTp 44026 2502 B5
E Shiloh Dr
12200 CsTp 44026 2502 C5
N Shiloh Dr
8800 CsTp 44026 2502 C5
W Shiloh Dr
12100 CsTp 44026 2502 B5
Shiloh Pk
2500 WTLK 44145 2750 C2
Shiloh Rd
15200 CLEV 44110 2372 B7
Shinnecock Dr
- SLN 44139 3020 E2
Shinnecock Ln
- AURA 44202 3021 E5
Shipherd Av
9100 CLEV 44106 2496 B7
Shipherd Cir
10 OBLN 44074 3139 A3
Shire Ct
14500 RsIT 44072 2632 C7
14500 RsIT 44072 2762 C1
Shireen Dr
14300 SGVL 44136 3146 C1
Shirley Av
15200 MPHT 44137 2886 B4
26200 EUCL 44132 2373 E2
26800 EUCL 44132 2374 C2
Shirley Dr
4400 SELD 44121 2628 C1
Shirley Park Dr
13500 LryT 44077 2148 A4
Sholle Dr
10 BSHT 44236 3153 B6
E Shore Blvd
- LKLN 44095 2249 E2
10 ETLK 44095 2249 E2
10 TMLK 44095 2249 E1
10 TMLK 44095 2250 A1
35300 ETLK 44095 2250 B1
W Shore Blvd
400 SDLK 44054 2616 C4
S Shore Ct
500 VMLN 44089 2741 B5
W Shore Ct
15700 LKWD 44107 2622 C3
Shore Dr
200 ETLK 44095 2142 D6
4000 LORN 44053 2743 E2
5800 MadT 44057 1941 D1
5900 MadT 44057 1842 E7
11400 NbyT 44065 2764 C1
14500 NbyT 44065 2634 C7
W Shore Rd
10 AVLK 44012 2617 C1
Shoreacre Dr
1100 MadT 44057 1843 E6
Shore Acres Dr
14800 CLEV 44110 2372 B7
Shoreby Dr
10 BTNH 44108 2496 D2
Shore Center Dr
22400 EUCL 44123 2373 C2
Shoreham Dr
32500 WLWK 44095 2249 D3
36900 ETLK 44095 2142 D6
Shoreland Av
19200 RKRV 44116 2621 D6
E Shoreland Av
18400 RKRV 44116 2622 A6
18900 RKRV 44116 2621 E6
Shoreline Dr
4800 VMLN 44089 2741 A4
Shoreline Wy
5100 VMLN 44089 2741 A4
5200 VMLN 44089 2740 E4
Shoreview Av
24600 EUCL 44123 2373 E1
24800 EUCL 44132 2373 E1
26800 EUCL 44132 2374 C2
Short Rd
- TmbT 44041 2151 B5
- TmbT 44086 2151 B5
- TpnT 44086 2151 B5
Short St
- PNVL 44077 2040 A6
700 VMLN 44089 2740 E6
Short Court St
100 CRDN 44024 2380 A6
Shorthorn Dr
8500 SgHT 44067 3017 D5
Shortline Dr
10 OmsT 44138 2879 C4
Shoshone Tr
900 MCDN 44056 3018 D6
Shubert Dr
26700 WTLK 44145 2620 A7
Shupe Av
400 AMHT 44001 2872 D3
Shurmer Dr
23000 WVHT 44128 2758 C4
Shurmer Rd
16000 SGVL 44136 3147 A2
17000 SGVL 44136 3146 E2
Siam Av
3500 CLEV 44113 2624 C6
Sicily Ct
- NRDV 44039 3008 D1
Sidaway Av
6500 CLEV 44127 2625 E6
6900 CLEV 44104 2625 E6
Side Av
5700 CLEV 44102 2624 A6
Sidley Rd
5900 TpnT 44086 2150 E5
7100 TpnT 44086 2258 E1
Sidney Dr
26900 EUCL 44132 2373 E4
26900 EUCL 44132 2374 A4
Siegler Dr
6100 BKPK 44142 2880 E3
6100 BKPK 44142 2881 A3
26000 BHWD 44122 2629 A7
Sierra Dr
5400 WLBY 44094 2375 A1
Sierra Ovl
8300 PRMA 44130 3013 D1
Sigma Dr
- HDHT 44143 2499 B2
Signal Hl
10 AbnT 44023 2892 A4
Signature Dr
- SLN 44139 3020 E2
Signet Av
12300 CLEV 44120 2626 E7
Sikes Ln
2800 TNBG 44087 3020 B5
Silk Av
9500 CLEV 44102 2623 D5
Silktree Ln
30800 WTLK 44145 2749 B6
Silkwood Ln
6800 SLN 44139 2889 B7
Silmore
11800 CLEV 44108 2496 D3
Silsby Rd
3200 CVHT 44118 2627 C3
3400 UNHT 44118 2627 E3
3800 CLEV 44111 2752 C2
3800 UNHT 44118 2628 A3
4100 UNHT 44121 2628 A3
4200 UNHT 44118 2628 C3
E Silsby Rd
23300 BHWD 44122 2628 D3
Silver Cr
4500 BKVL 44141 3151 A2
Silver Ct
5900 MNTR 44060 2144 A3
Silver Dr
10 PNVL 44077 2145 E2
Silver Rd
13600 GDHT 44125 2756 E7
13600 GDHT 44125 2757 A7
Silver St
1300 WKLF 44092 2374 B2
Silver Ash Tr
7800 HpfT 44057 2045 A4
7800 MadT 44057 2045 A4
Silver Beech Ln
7500 MNTR 44060 2251 C4
Silverberry Ln
- HDSN 44236 3154 A6
Silvercreek Dr
8400 RsIT 44072 2632 A7
8400 RsIT 44072 2762 B1
Silverdale Av
2100 CLEV 44109 2754 C6
Silverdale Cir
1300 TNBG 44087 3019 B3
Silverdale Rd
4300 NOSD 44070 2750 A6
Silveridge Tr
2100 WTLK 44145 2749 B2
Silverleaf Dr
9700 NRYN 44133 3014 B3
Silvermound Dr
6600 MNTR 44060 2143 D5
Silver Springs Tr
10 SRSL 44073 2762 D6
Silverton Av
8700 CLEV 44102 2753 D1
Silverton St
- AVON 44011 2747 C2
Silvertree Ct
5700 MadT 44057 1941 D2
Simecek Dr
9200 TNBG 44087 3155 B1
Simich Dr
300 SVHL 44131 2884 A5
Simmons Pl
2000 MadT 44057 1941 D2
Simon Av
7900 CLEV 44103 2496 A6
7900 CLEV 44108 2496 A6
Simons Dr
500 BNWK 44212 3147 A7
Simsbury Ct
9600 TNBG 44087 3020 B6
Singer Av
100 GDRV 44045 2039 C6
400 PnvT 44077 2039 C6
Singer Av SR-283
100 GDRV 44045 2039 C6
400 PnvT 44077 2039 C6
Singer Dr
10100 STBR 44241 3157 A7
Singlefoot Tr
8600 KTLD 44094 2377 B3
Sinton Pl
2700 PRPK 44124 2629 C4
Sioux Ln
800 MCDN 44056 3018 D6
Sipple Av
100 AMHT 44001 2872 D1
Sir John Av
4200 NRYN 44133 3014 B7
Sir Richard Av
4200 NRYN 44133 3014 B7
Sir Robert Av
4200 NRYN 44133 3014 B7
Sir Roberts Ct
7400 MNTR 44060 2143 C6
Sisson Rd
14300 HmbT 44024 2381 D7
14400 HmbT 44024 2382 A7
14400 MltT 44024 2382 A7
Sites Rd
27900 BYVL 44140 2619 E4
Sittingbourne Dr
7000 CcdT 44060 2145 B7
Sittingbourne Ln
2400 BHWD 44122 2628 D4
Sivon Dr
10 PnvT 44077 2041 A4
Skeel Ct
- CLEV 44109 2754 B2
Skiff St
4000 WLBY 44094 2250 D5
Skinner Av
700 PNVL 44077 2039 E6
Skinner Rd
5000 ManT 44255 3159 D1
Skippers Cove
3700 RMDV 44202 3020 E5
Skyhaven Rd
7400 NCtT 44067 3153 C4
Skyland Dr
700 MCDN 44056 3018 E4
9500 MCDN 44056 3019 A4
S Skyland Dr
9400 MCDN 44056 3018 E5

INDEX 42
Skylane Dr
Cleveland Street Index
SR-3 Ridge Rd

STREET
Block City ZIP Map# Grid

Skylane Dr
300 NCtT 44067 3152 E3
300 NCtT 44067 3153 A3
4200 CLEV 44109 2755 A5
Skylark Ct
500 ELYR 44035 2875 D2
Skylark Dr
7400 PRMA 44130 2882 A7
7500 PRMA 44130 3013 A1
Skyline Dr
10 MDHL 44022 2760 D6
1700 RDHT 44143 2373 E6
5700 SVHL 44131 2884 A2
7900 BWHT 44147 3015 C3
26700 OmsT 44138 2879 A6
26800 OmsT 44138 2878 E6
36800 WBHL 44094 2375 D5
E Skyline Dr
1700 LORN 44053 2744 B3
N Skyline Dr
200 SVHL 44131 2883 D1
200 SVHL 44131 2884 A1
W Skyline Dr
2600 LORN 44053 2744 A3
Skyline Ln
8100 RslT 44073 2761 E2
Skylineview Dr
7700 CcdT 44060 2253 B2
Skytop Ln
35400 WLBY 44094 2375 B1
Skyview Dr
10 BNWK 44212 3147 A6
10 SVHL 44131 2883 E4
10 SVHL 44131 2884 A4
3800 BNWK 44212 3146 E6
5700 SLN 44139 2889 A3
Skyview Rd
300 CLEV 44109 2755 A5
Sladden Av
9400 GDHT 44125 2756 B5
9600 GDHT 44105 2756 B5
Slanes Ln
- BSHT 44236 3153 C6
Slater Dr
6000 BKPK 44142 2881 A2
Sleepy Hollow Dr
- WBHL 44094 2375 E7
100 AMHT 44001 2872 D4
7500 PRMA 44130 3013 A1
14600 RslT 44072 2762 E1
26700 WTLK 44145 2750 A1
Slife Rd
- CrlT 44044 3141 C1
39500 CrlT 44050 3140 E1
39500 CrlT 44050 3141 A1
Sloane Av
1300 LKWD 44107 2622 A5
Sloane Av SR-2
1300 LKWD 44107 2622 A5
Sloane Av SR-254
1300 LKWD 44107 2622 A5
Sloane Av US-20
1300 LKWD 44107 2622 A5
Smith Av
- BKPK 44142 2752 C7
3900 CLEV 44109 2754 C2
4600 ShfT 44052 2745 A5
23700 WTLK 44145 2750 D2
Smith Ct
10 ELYR 44035 2875 B6
600 RKRV 44116 2621 D5
1800 CLEV 44113 2624 D5
Smith Rd
5000 BKPK 44142 2752 C7
5200 BKPK 44142 2881 C1
6600 MDBH 44142 2881 C4
6600 MDBH 44130 2881 D6
9300 WTHL 44094 2376 A1
9400 WTHL 44094 2375 E3
Smith St
- PkmT 44234 2896 D7
10 OBLN 44074 3138 E4
Smithfield Dr
800 SgHT 44057 3152 B1
Smithfield Rd
29800 ORNG 44022 2759 C4
Smokerise Dr
8700 MCDN 44056 3018 D7
Smugglers Cove
3400 WLBY 44094 2250 D3
10300 RMDV 44202 3020 E5
Snavely Rd
400 RDHT 44143 2498 D3
Snell Dr
5300 MNTR 44060 2039 A7
5300 MNTR 44060 2145 A1
Snell Rd
23000 ClbT 44023 3010 E5
23000 ClbT 44136 3010 E5
Snow Rd
900 PRMA 44134 2883 D2
5400 PRMA 44129 2883 B2
6700 PRMA 44129 2882 E2
8500 PRMA 44130 2882 A2
8600 PMHT 44130 2882 E2
12000 NbyT 44021 2764 E6
12000 NbyT 44065 2764 E6
12000 NbyT 44021 2765 A6
12300 BtnT 44021 2765 B7
12900 PRMA 44130 2881 E2
13300 BKPK 44142 2881 E2
13300 BKPK 44130 2881 E2
16300 AbnT 44021 2765 B7
16300 TroT 44021 2765 B7
16300 TroT 44021 2894 B1
18000 BKPK 44142 2880 E2
Snowberry Ct
7600 MNTR 44060 2253 A2
Snowberry Ln
2400 PRPK 44124 2629 D4
Snowbird Cir
6400 MadT 44057 1942 A4
Snow Blossom Ln
4800 BKVL 44141 3150 B5
Snowflower Dr
21300 RKRV 44116 2621 C7
Snowshoe Tr
16400 BbgT 44023 2891 C1
Snowville Rd
7300 BKVL 44141 3151 B5
13100 BKVL 44141 3152 A5
W Snowville Rd
5000 BKVL 44141 3150 E5
6700 BKVL 44141 3151 A5

Snyder Av
2200 CLEV 44109 2754 D4
Snyder Rd
16100 SRSL 44073 2762 D7
16300 BbgT 44023 2762 D7
16300 BbgT 44023 2891 D1
18400 BbgT 44023 3022 D1
Sobieski Av
12100 CLEV 44135 2753 A4
Soika Av
11600 CLEV 44120 2626 D7
Solether Ln
10 CNFL 44022 2760 E5
Solon Blvd
6400 SLN 44139 2888 E6
Solon Rd
10 BDFD 44146 2887 A4
10 CNFL 44022 2760 E7
300 CNFL 44022 2889 D2
400 BTVL 44022 2889 D2
500 BDHT 44146 2887 D5
26300 OKWD 44146 2887 D5
26300 OKWD 44146 2888 C5
27000 SLN 44139 2888 C5
33400 SLN 44139 2889 A4
35700 SLN 44022 2889 D2
Solon Industrial Pkwy
29800 SLN 44139 2888 C7
Soltis Rd
16100 PkmT 44231 3027 D2
Som Center Rd
- MDHT 44040 2630 A2
- WLBY 44094 2250 A7
- WLBY 44095 2250 A7
200 MAYF 44143 2500 A2
400 ETLK 44095 2250 B2
700 MAYF 44040 2500 A6
1000 MDHT 44124 2500 A6
1500 MDHT 44124 2630 A2
1700 GSML 44040 2630 A2
1900 MDHT 44124 2630 A7
2400 HGVL 44022 2630 A4
2400 PRPK 44124 2630 A4
2500 WBHL 44094 2375 A7
2900 WBHL 44092 2375 A7
3000 WBHL 44092 2500 A2
3000 WBHL 44094 2500 A2
3300 HGVL 44022 2760 A2
3300 PRPK 44124 2760 A2
3500 PRPK 44022 2760 A2
3600 MDHL 44124 2760 A2
3600 MDHL 44022 2760 A2
4000 MDHL 44022 2759 E6
5000 SLN 44139 2759 E6
5100 SLN 44139 2760 A7
5200 SLN 44139 2889 A1
5200 WLBY 44094 2375 A7
7000 SLN 44139 3020 A3
Som Center Rd SR-91
- MDHT 44040 2630 A2
- WLBY 44094 2250 A7
- WLBY 44095 2250 A7
200 MAYF 44143 2500 A2
400 ETLK 44095 2250 B2
700 MAYF 44040 2500 A6
1000 MDHT 44124 2500 A6
1500 MDHT 44124 2630 A2
1700 GSML 44040 2630 A2
1900 MDHT 44124 2630 A7
2400 HGVL 44022 2630 A4
2400 PRPK 44124 2630 A4
2500 WBHL 44094 2375 A7
2900 WBHL 44092 2375 A7
3000 WBHL 44092 2500 A2
3000 WBHL 44094 2500 A2
3300 HGVL 44022 2760 A2
3300 PRPK 44124 2760 A2
3500 PRPK 44022 2760 A2
3600 MDHL 44124 2760 A2
3600 MDHL 44022 2760 A2
4000 MDHL 44022 2759 E6
5000 SLN 44139 2759 E6
5100 SLN 44139 2760 A7
5200 SLN 44139 2889 A1
5200 WLBY 44094 2375 A7
7000 SLN 44139 3020 A3
Somerdale Av
5700 BKPK 44142 2881 D2
Somers Cir
- GSML 44040 2630 B3
Somerset Av
9900 CLEV 44108 2496 B6
Somerset Ct
7200 NCtT 44067 3153 B4
Somerset Dr
10 HkyT 44233 3148 B6
400 CNFL 44022 2889 E1
3100 SRHT 44122 2628 A7
3200 BHWD 44122 2628 A7
6000 NOSD 44070 2878 C2
6600 BKVL 44141 3015 E3
8500 BWHT 44147 3014 D5
10500 HmbT 44024 2380 C6
11100 NRYN 44133 3013 A5
Somerset Ln
6600 SVHL 44131 2884 B5
Somerset Ovl
6800 BKVL 44141 3015 E3
Somerset Tr
11200 CcdT 44077 2146 C7
Somerton Rd
2900 CVHT 44118 2627 B2
Somerville Dr
7200 OKWD 44146 2887 E7
Somia Dr
2600 PRMA 44134 2883 C3
Somrack Dr
2300 WBHL 44094 2375 C3
Sonesta Av
200 ELYR 44035 3006 D2
Song Bird St
500 ELYR 44035 3006 D3
Sonny Dr
7700 WNHL 44146 3017 C2
Sonoma Ct
27800 WTLK 44145 2749 E1
Sonora Av
3200 CLEV 44114 2625 B1
Sonora Ct
600 BERA 44017 3011 A1
Sontag Ln
4800 MNTU 44255 3159 C5
Sophia Av
9200 CLEV 44104 2626 B6

Sorrel Ct
- GnvT 44041 1944 C1
Sorrelwood Ln
100 SRSL 44073 2761 D5
Sorrento Av
16000 CLEV 44128 2757 B4
Sotogrande Ct
- SLN 44139 3020 E2
Sourbrook Ln
32400 NRDV 44039 2748 E7
South Av
- SDLK 44054 2616 A5
3800 SDLK 44054 2615 E5
South Blvd
5200 MPHT 44137 2757 D6
5200 MPHT 44137 2886 D2
9700 AbnT 44023 3023 A2
9800 CLEV 44108 2496 B6
South Cir
10 BDFD 44146 2886 C5
South Ct
10100 BKVL 44141 3151 D4
30800 NOSD 44070 2878 B3
South Dr
- MNTR 44060 2251 B4
100 AVLK 44012 2618 E1
18000 SGVL 44136 3011 E3
South Ln
10 MDHL 44022 2760 C4
100 AhtT 44001 2872 B2
6800 WTHL 44094 2376 A2
23900 BDHT 44146 2887 C2
South Ovl
200 CRDN 44024 2505 A1
37600 SLN 44139 2889 D4
South Pk
2100 TwbT 44087 3154 D2
South Rd
10 BKVL 44141 3151 A4
South St
10 BbgT 44022 2761 A7
10 CNFL 44022 2761 A7
10 OBLN 44074 3138 D3
100 CRDN 44024 2380 A7
300 CRDN 44024 2505 A1
400 BNHT 44131 2884 A1
400 FTHR 44077 2039 D4
700 BNHT 44131 2883 E1
800 MsnT 44024 2505 A1
5100 VMLN 44089 2741 A5
5200 VMLN 44089 2740 E5
38200 WLBY 44094 2250 E6
South St SR-44
100 CRDN 44024 2380 A7
300 CRDN 44024 2505 A1
800 MsnT 44024 2505 A1
South St SR-60
5500 VMLN 44089 2740 E5
E South St
10 PNVL 44077 2146 B1
W South St
200 PNVL 44077 2146 A1
South Wy
7100 HDSN 44236 3154 A7
Southampton Dr
7500 NRYN 44133 3013 D5
Southbend Cir
21000 RKRV 44116 2621 C6
South Bend Dr
1600 RKRV 44116 2621 C6
Southbridge Blvd
500 BNWK 44212 3147 C7
Southbridge Cir
27600 WTLK 44145 2749 E4
Southbridge Ln
100 PnvT 44077 2145 B6
South Brook Tr
8800 BbgT 44023 2891 C4
South East Byp
- CrlT 44044 3006 E3
- EatT 44035 3006 E3
- EatT 44044 3006 E3
- EatT 44044 3007 A4
- ELYR 44035 2875 E7
- ELYR 44035 3006 E3
South East Byp SR-57
- CrlT 44044 3006 E3
- EatT 44035 3006 E3
- EatT 44035 3006 E3
- EatT 44044 3007 A4
- ELYR 44035 2875 E7
- ELYR 44035 3006 E3
South East Byp SR-301
- EatT 44035 3006 E3
- EatT 44044 3006 E3
- ELYR 44035 2875 E7
- ELYR 44035 3006 E3
South East Byp US-20
- EatT 44035 3006 E3
- EatT 44044 3006 E3
- ELYR 44035 2875 E7
- ELYR 44035 3006 E3
South Edgerton Rd
6900 BKVL 44141 3150 D3
Southern Av
12300 GDHT 44125 2756 D6
27700 NOSD 44070 2878 E2
Southern St
7800 HpfT 44057 1943 B7
7800 MadT 44057 1943 B7
Southfield Av
6300 CLEV 44144 2753 E4
6300 CLEV 44144 2754 A4
7400 BKLN 44144 2753 E4
Southgate Park Blvd
20500 MPHT 44137 2887 A1
Southgrove Rd
6300 MNTR 44060 2143 B4
Southham Cir
400 BERA 44017 3010 D1
South Hills Blvd
9000 BWHT 44147 3015 D7
Southington Blvd
300 PNVL 44077 2146 A3
Southington Dr
5400 PRMA 44129 2883 A4
6600 PRMA 44129 2882 E4
Southington Rd
2600 SRHT 44120 2627 B5
13500 CLEV 44120 2627 A6
Southland Av
16000 CLEV 44111 2752 B1
Southland Dr
6900 MDBH 44130 2881 E6
7400 MONT 44060 2143 D2

Southlane Dr
8400 BKLN 44144 2753 D5
Southpoint Dr
1700 CLEV 44109 2754 D1
South Point Tr
600 BERA 44017 3011 B2
Southpointe Pkwy
6700 BKVL 44141 3150 E5
Southporte
18500 SGVL 44136 3146 E1
Southridge Ct
8900 SgHT 44067 3017 D3
Southridge Dr
300 CLEV 44109 2755 A5
Southridge Rd
700 SgHT 44067 3017 C3
Southside Park Dr
7100 SLN 44139 3020 A1
Southview Av
13100 CLEV 44120 2756 E2
13600 CLEV 44120 2757 A2
Southview Ct
9600 SGVL 44136 3012 B4
Southview Dr
10 BDFD 44146 2887 A2
5000 VMLN 44089 2741 A7
Southview Ln
16500 SGVL 44136 3012 B4
Southway Ct
6500 BKPK 44142 2881 B4
Southway Dr
15400 BKPK 44142 2881 B4
Southwest Blvd
- WTLK 44145 2749 D5
Southwick Dr
10 BDFD 44146 2886 E3
Southwick Ln
- AURA 44202 3021 E7
Southwick Pl
31800 SLN 44139 2759 D7
Southwind Ct
11000 SGVL 44136 3011 A5
South Winds Dr
5700 MONT 44060 2143 E2
Southwood Av
13500 CLEV 44111 2752 E3
Southwood Dr
- ELYR 44035 3006 B3
300 CrlT 44035 3006 B3
2700 WTLK 44145 2750 A3
4600 BKLN 44144 2753 C6
4900 SDLK 44054 2616 D4
21100 FWPK 44126 2751 C1
Southwood Ln
26900 OmsT 44138 2878 E3
26900 OmsT 44138 2879 A3
Southwood Rd
10 PnvT 44077 2041 B3
2500 PryT 44077 2041 B3
7400 MNTR 44060 2252 C1
Southwood St
- EyrT 44035 2745 D7
Southwyck Dr
100 SRSL 44073 2761 E6
Sowinski Av
7900 CLEV 44103 2496 A7
8200 CLEV 44108 2496 A7
Sowul Dr
7100 CcdT 44077 2145 D7
7100 CcdT 44077 2253 D1
Spafford Ovl
700 SgHT 44067 3152 C1
Spafford Pl
7300 CLEV 44105 2755 E2
Spafford Rd
- BKPK 44142 2879 D3
6800 OmsT 44142 2879 D3
6900 OmsT 44138 2879 D3
7400 CLEV 44105 2755 E2
7400 CLEV 44105 2756 A2
Spanghurst Dr
7200 WNHL 44146 3017 D1
Spangler Rd
3300 CVHT 44112 2497 D6
Sparky Ln
- NOSD 44070 2750 A6
Sparrow Flight Dr
3000 SVHL 44131 3015 B1
Spatterdock Ln
34900 SLN 44139 3020 B1
35600 SLN 44139 2889 B7
Spaulding Ct
5000 LORN 44053 2743 C4
E Spaulding St
38200 WLBY 44094 2250 E5
W Spaulding St
37900 WLBY 44094 2250 D5
Spear Av
14300 CLEV 44120 2627 A7
Spear Rd
10900 CcdT 44077 2146 B7
10900 CcdT 44077 2254 A1
Spearhead Dr
9800 BKVL 44141 3150 C4
Speedway Ovlk
12600 ECLE 44112 2496 E6
Speidel Av
19900 FWPK 44126 2751 D2
Spencer Av
5300 CLEV 44103 2495 D7
Spencer Cir
3000 GnvT 44041 1944 E3
Spencer Cir W
3000 GnvT 44041 1944 E3
Spencer Ct
- NRDV 44039 2877 C7
Spencer Dr
1100 HRM 44234 3161 A2
2900 GnvT 44041 1944 E3
Spencer Ln
22200 FWPK 44126 2751 B5
Spencer Rd
3100 RKRV 44116 2751 B2
4100 FWPK 44126 2751 B2
5000 LNHT 44124 2498 E6
5100 LNHT 44124 2499 A7
Spencer St
12300 CrlT 44024 2505 C5
Spencer Park Dr
11700 ManT 44255 3160 A2
Sperry Cir
700 WTLK 44145 2620 D6
Sperry Dr
23700 WTLK 44145 2620 D6

Sperry Ln
15700 MDFD 44062 2767 C2
Sperry Rd
9100 KDHL 44060 2252 D7
9200 KDHL 44060 2377 E1
9200 KDHL 44060 2378 A1
9500 KTLD 44094 2378 A1
9600 KTLD 44094 2377 E4
10900 KTLD 44094 2502 D2
11100 CsTp 44026 2502 D5
13300 CsTp 44072 2632 E3
13500 NbyT 44072 2633 A4
13500 RslT 44072 2632 E3
13500 RslT 44072 2633 A4
14200 NbyT 44072 2633 B7
14200 NbyT 44065 2763 B1
14200 NbyT 44072 2763 B1
15000 BhmT 44089 2870 A6
15000 VmnT 44089 2869 E6
15000 VmnT 44089 2870 A6
16200 BhmT 44089 2870 B6
Sperrys Forge Ct
2000 WTLK 44145 2749 D1
Sperrys Forge Tr
1600 WTLK 44145 2619 D7
1600 WTLK 44145 2749 D1
Spiceberry Cir
11100 AbnT 44021 2893 A6
Spicebush Ln
500 AbnT 44023 2892 B5
35300 SLN 44139 2889 B7
Spicers Ln
800 SgHT 44067 3152 B2
Spilker Av
6400 CLEV 44103 2495 E6
Spillgate Trc
1100 BWHT 44147 3149 E5
Spinach Dr
6900 MNTR 44060 2144 A6
Spindlewood Ct
19500 NRYN 44133 3148 A5
Spindrift Dr
36500 ETLK 44095 2142 C7
Spinnaker Cir
19200 SGVL 44136 3146 E5
Spinnaker Ct
4600 MNTR 44060 2039 A5
Spinnaker Dr
32500 AVLK 44012 2618 A3
Spinnaker Run
10100 RMDV 44202 3020 D5
Spino Dr
1700 EUCL 44117 2498 C1
Spokane Av
3500 CLEV 44109 2754 B4
4700 CLEV 44144 2754 B4
Spottswood Dr
- LNHT 44124 2629 C3
Sprague Av
10700 CLEV 44108 2496 C4
Sprague Rd
10 BERA 44017 3011 B2
23000 ClbT 44017 3010 D2
23000 ClbT 44028 3010 D2
23000 ClbT 44138 3010 D2
23000 ODFL 44017 3010 D2
23000 ODFL 44138 3010 D2
26500 ClbT 44028 3009 B2
26500 ClbT 44138 3009 B2
26500 ODFL 44138 3009 B2
26500 OmsT 44138 3009 B2
27100 ClbT 44028 3008 E2
27100 ClbT 44138 3008 E2
27100 OmsT 44138 3008 E2
31600 EatT 44138 3008 E2
31600 EatT 44028 3008 E2
31600 EatT 44039 3008 E2
31600 NRDV 44039 3008 E2
31600 NRDV 44138 3008 E2
Sprague Rd SR-252
24400 ClbT 44028 3010 B2
24400 ClbT 44138 3010 B2
24400 ODFL 44138 3010 B2
E Sprague Rd
10 BWHT 44147 3014 E2
10 BWHT 44147 3014 E2
10 BWHT 44147 3015 B2
10 BWHT 44131 3015 B2
10 SVHL 44131 3014 E2
10 SVHL 44131 3015 B2
3600 INDE 44131 3015 C2
6900 BKVL 44141 3015 D2
6900 BKVL 44131 3015 D2
6900 BKVL 44131 3016 A2
6900 BKVL 44141 3016 A2
6900 INDE 44131 3016 A2
W Sprague Rd
200 BERA 44017 3011 A2
200 SGVL 44017 3011 A2
200 SGVL 44136 3011 A2
400 BERA 44017 3010 E2
400 SGVL 44017 3010 E2
400 SGVL 44136 3010 E2
900 BWHT 44134 3014 E2
900 BWHT 44147 3014 E2
900 PRMA 44134 3014 E2
3000 NRYN 44134 3014 A2
3000 PRMA 44134 3014 A2
7000 PRMA 44134 3013 E2
9000 NRYN 44133 3013 D2
9000 NRYN 44134 3013 D2
9000 PRMA 44130 3013 D2
9000 PRMA 44129 3013 D2
12000 NRYN 44130 3012 D2
12000 NRYN 44133 3012 D2
12000 PRMA 44130 3012 D2
13000 MDBH 44130 3012 D2
13000 SGVL 44130 3012 D2
13000 SGVL 44133 3012 D2
13000 SGVL 44136 3012 D2
Sprecher Av
12100 CLEV 44135 2753 A6
13000 CLEV 44135 2752 E6
Sprengel Av
14300 CLEV 44135 2752 C4
Spring Ct
13800 LryT 44077 2256 B5
Spring Dr
100 SRSL 44073 2761 D5
Spring Rd
400 CLEV 44109 2755 A5
900 CLEV 44109 2754 D5
4500 BNHT 44131 2755 A5
11400 CsTp 44026 2501 D2

Spring St
10 BERA 44017 2880 C6
10 ELYR 44035 2874 D3
10 OBLN 44074 3138 E3
10 OBLN 44074 3139 A2
100 AMHT 44001 2872 D2
W Spring St
13600 BURT 44021 2636 A7
W Spring St SR-87
13800 BURT 44021 2636 B7
Spring Bank Ln
- BTNH 44108 2496 B4
Spring Blossom Dr
7400 MNTR 44060 2143 C6
Springblossom Tr
13000 CsTp 44026 2631 B2
Springbrook Ct
10200 CcdT 44077 2253 D2
Springbrook Dr
300 BNHT 44131 2755 A7
Spring Creek Rd
10 NCtT 44067 3017 D7
100 SgHT 44067 3017 D7
Spring Crest Dr
4100 BKLN 44144 2753 D4
Springdale Av
7900 PRMA 44129 2882 E1
14700 MDFD 44062 2767 C2
18500 CLEV 44135 2751 E6
Springdale Ln
200 MDHL 44022 2759 D4
Springdale Rd
6600 MDBH 44130 2881 C4
N Springer Ct
10300 KTLD 44094 2376 E5
Springer Dr
8000 KTLD 44094 2376 E5
8000 KTLD 44094 2377 A5
Springfield Cir
20700 SGVL 44136 3146 B3
Springfield Dr
- AVON 44011 2747 A1
8000 NRYN 44133 3013 C7
Springfield Rd
4800 WVHT 44128 2758 E6
Spring Garden Av
1400 LKWD 44107 2622 B5
Spring Garden Rd
7400 PRMA 44129 2882 D2
Spring Grove Dr
1900 MadT 44057 1941 B1
5500 SLN 44139 2888 D3
Springhill Dr
10300 BKVL 44141 3151 B3
Springhill Rd
8600 MCDN 44056 3018 B6
Springhouse Ln E
9700 CcdT 44060 2145 B2
Springhouse Ln W
9700 CcdT 44060 2145 B7
Spring Lake Blvd
10 PnvT 44077 2041 B3
2400 PryT 44077 2041 B3
Springledge Rd
6900 SgHT 44067 3017 D7
Springmont Rd
200 SgHT 44067 3017 D7
Spring Pond Rd
300 SgHT 44067 3017 D6
Springside Ln
26900 ODFL 44138 3009 D1
32100 SLN 44139 2888 E2
32600 SLN 44139 2889 A2
Springside Ovl
- BKVL 44141 3150 B5
Springvale Cir
4100 AVON 44011 2748 C5
Springvale Dr
4400 WVHT 44128 2758 D5
Spring Valley Dr
8700 MNTR 44060 2144 C7
8800 BWHT 44147 3015 A6
14300 RslT 44072 2632 D7
N Spring Valley Park Dr
8500 BbgT 44023 3022 B2
S Spring Valley Park Dr
8400 BbgT 44023 3022 B2
Springview Dr
6700 INDE 44131 3015 E2
12100 NbyT 44021 2764 D3
12100 NbyT 44021 2765 A4
Spring View Rd
8200 SgHT 44067 3017 D6
Springway Rd
11200 MsnT 44024 2504 B3
Springwood Cir
10300 TNBG 44087 3019 B4
Springwood Ct
5700 MONT 44060 2143 E2
Springwood Dr
4800 BKLN 44144 2753 D6
5800 MONT 44060 2143 E2
Springwood Rd
10 NCtT 44067 3017 E7
100 SgHT 44067 3017 E7
6200 PMHT 44130 2882 D4
Spruce
- MNTR 44060 2144 E6
Spruce Av
- NRDV 44039 2877 D3
1200 CLEV 44113 2624 C3
Spruce Ct
- AVON 44011 2748 C3
2900 LORN 44052 2744 C2
Spruce Dr
200 BERA 44017 2880 A5
11200 CsTp 44026 2502 B1
20500 SGVL 44136 3146 B2
28300 NOSD 44070 2878 D3
Spruce Ln
- TpnT 44086 2259 A2
3000 HDSN 44236 3155 D6
3000 TwbT 44236 3155 D6
Spruce St
100 ELYR 44035 2874 D4
4300 BHIT 44212 3146 D7
35100 NRDV 44039 2877 B1
Sprucedale Rd
900 BWHT 44147 3015 A3
Spruce Pine Wy
4800 NRDV 44039 2748 D6
Spruce Pointe
12200 SGVL 44136 3011 A6

Spruce Run Dr
13200 NRYN 44133 3012 E7
Spruce Tree Ln
1200 AMHT 44001 2744 A7
Sprucewood St
4700 AVON 44011 2748 E6
Spyglass Dr
- ELYR 44035 3006 D3
Spyglass Hill Dr
17700 SGVL 44136 3147 E4
Square Dr
10 MDSN 44057 1942 B6
Square Circle Dr
10 MDSN 44057 1942 B6
Squire Dr
4600 SgHT 44067 3017 E4
Squire Ln
7000 RslT 44072 2631 C7
Squire Pl
10 BDFD 44146 2887 C3
Squire St
100 CrlT 44035 3005 E2
1600 ShfT 44055 2745 B5
Squires Ct
100 SAHT 44001 3003 D1
10300 CcdT 44077 2145 D4
Squires Rd
900 AURA 44202 3021 C4
24400 ClbT 44028 3145 B1
Squirrel Hollow Ln
16000 SGVL 44136 3146 E3
Squirrel Nest Dr
6400 LORN 44053 2743 B5
Squirrel Run Dr
18600 MDBH 44130 2880 E5
SR-2
- AhtT - 2744 D7
- AhtT - 2745 A7
- AMHT - 2743 E7
- AMHT - 2744 D7
- AMHT - 2871 E1
- AMHT - 2872 A1
- AVON - 2617 C7
- AVON - 2618 B7
- AVON - 2619 A6
- AVON - 2747 A1
- BhmT - 2870 A1
- BhmT - 2871 A1
- ELYR - 2746 B7
- ELYR - 2874 B1
- ELYR - 2875 B1
- EyrT - 2745 A7
- EyrT - 2874 B1
- LORN - 2744 D7
- PNVL - 2039 E7
- PNVL - 2040 B5
- PNVL - 2145 C1
- PnvT - 2039 E7
- PnvT - 2040 B5
- PnvT - 2041 A3
- PnvT - 2145 C1
- SFLD - 2746 B7
- SFLD - 2747 A1
- VMLN - 2870 A1
- VMLN - 2871 E1
- VmnT - 2869 E1
- VmnT - 2870 A1
SR-2 Cleveland Mem Shoreway
- CLEV - 2495 B7
- CLEV 44102 2623 E4
- CLEV - 2624 E1
- CLEV 44102 2624 B4
- CLEV 44113 2624 B4
- CLEV - 2625 A1
SR-2 Clifton Blvd
9200 CLEV 44102 2623 C5
11700 LKWD 44102 2623 C5
11700 LKWD 44107 2623 C5
13400 LKWD 44107 2622 B4
SR-2 W Clifton Blvd
1100 LKWD 44107 2622 A4
SR-2 Detroit Rd
- LKWD 44107 2621 D5
- RKRV 44107 2621 D5
19000 RKRV 44116 2621 D5
SR-2 Innerbelt Frwy
- CLEV - 2495 B7
SR-2 Lakeland Frwy
- BTNH - 2496 E2
- BTNH - 2497 B1
- CLEV - 2372 C7
- CLEV - 2373 B5
- CLEV - 2495 C7
- CLEV - 2496 A4
- CLEV - 2497 B1
- ETLK - 2249 D7
- ETLK - 2250 A6
- EUCL - 2373 B5
- EUCL - 2374 B1
- MNTR - 2143 E7
- MNTR - 2144 E2
- MNTR - 2145 A2
- MNTR - 2251 B2
- PNVL - 2145 B1
- PnvT - 2145 B1
- WKLF - 2249 D7
- WKLF - 2374 B1
- WLBY - 2250 A6
- WLBY - 2251 B2
- WLWK - 2249 D7
SR-2 Northwest Frwy
- RKRV - 2621 B6
- WTLK - 2619 A6
- WTLK - 2620 D6
- WTLK - 2621 B6
SR-2 Sloane Av
1300 LKWD 44107 2622 A4
SR-3 W 25th St
1400 CLEV 44113 2624 D7
3100 CLEV 44109 2624 D7
3200 CLEV 44109 2754 D2
SR-3 Pearl Rd
3600 CLEV 44109 2754 D2
4500 CLEV 44144 2754 C5
5000 CLEV 44129 2754 A7
5000 PRMA 44129 2754 A7
5000 PRMA 44109 2754 A7
5300 PRMA 44129 2753 E7
5300 PRMA 44129 2882 E4
SR-3 Ridge Rd
10 HkyT 44233 3148 D6
5400 PRMA 44129 2882 E1
7400 PRMA 44129 3013 E4
7400 PRMA 44134 3013 E4

INDEX 43

SR-3 Ridge Rd
Cleveland Street Index
SR-237 Front St

STREET
Block City ZIP Map# Grid

SR-3 Ridge Rd
7800 NRYN 44133 3013 E4
7800 NRYN 44129 3013 E4
14000 NRYN 44133 3148 D3
SR-8
- BSHT 44236 3153 D7
- CLEV 44115 2625 D4
- MCDN 44067 3018 B7
- MCDN 44056 3018 B7
- MCDN 44056 3153 B1
- NCtT 44056 3018 B7
- NCtT 44067 3018 B7
- NCtT 44067 3153 B1
- NCtT 44236 3153 D7
- NHFD 44067 3018 B7
- SgHT 44067 3018 B7
SR-8 Broadway Av
800 CLEV 44115 2625 A4
SR-8 Chagrin Blvd
15600 SRHT 44120 2757 B1
17700 SRHT 44122 2757 D1
19200 SRHT 44122 2758 A1
SR-8 Kinsman Rd
5500 CLEV 44104 2625 E5
7200 CLEV 44104 2626 B6
11300 CLEV 44120 2626 B6
12500 CLEV 44120 2756 E1
13500 CLEV 44120 2757 B1
15400 SRHT 44120 2757 B1
SR-8 Northfield Rd
- MPHT 44146 2758 B7
- WVHT 44146 2758 B6
10 BDFD 44146 2887 B7
3500 HIHL 44122 2758 B4
3500 SRHT 44122 2758 B4
3700 WVHT 44122 2758 B4
3900 HIHL 44128 2758 B4
3900 WVHT 44128 2758 B4
4300 NRDL 44128 2758 B4
5000 BDHT 44146 2758 B7
5000 MPHT 44137 2758 B7
5200 BDHT 44146 2887 B3
5200 MPHT 44137 2887 B3
6900 OKWD 44146 2887 B7
6900 WNHL 44146 2887 B7
7100 WNHL 44146 3018 B2
10100 NHFD 44067 3018 B2
10100 SgHT 44067 3018 B2
SR-8 Ontario St
1900 CLEV 44114 2624 E3
2000 CLEV 44115 2624 E3
2100 CLEV 44113 2624 E3
SR-8 Orange Av
1400 CLEV 44115 2625 A4
SR-8 Woodland Av
2500 CLEV 44115 2625 B4
4000 CLEV 44104 2625 C4
SR-10
- EatT - 3007 E1
- NRDV - 2877 E4
- NRDV - 3007 E1
- NRDV - 3008 A1
SR-10 Carnegie Av
- CLEV 44113 2624 E4
SR-10 Lorain Av
- FWPK 44126 2752 D2
2000 CLEV 44113 2624 D5
4500 CLEV 44102 2624 B6
6800 CLEV 44102 2623 D7
10000 CLEV 44111 2623 D7
10600 CLEV 44111 2753 B1
13200 CLEV 44111 2752 D2
SR-10 Lorain Rd
- NRDV 44039 2877 E4
18800 FWPK 44126 2752 A2
18900 FWPK 44126 2751 E2
22900 NOSD 44126 2751 E2
22900 NOSD 44070 2751 E2
23200 NOSD 44070 2750 E4
27200 NOSD 44070 2749 E7
28000 NOSD 44070 2878 B2
31200 NRDV 44070 2878 B2
31200 NRDV 44039 2878 B2
SR-14
- HDSN - 3155 D7
- MCDN - 3018 E4
- MCDN - 3019 A5
- OKWD - 3018 E4
- TNBG - 3019 A5
- TNBG - 3154 E2
- TNBG - 3155 D7
- TwbT - 3155 A2
SR-14 E 34th St
2700 CLEV 44115 2625 C5
SR-14 Broadway Av
- CLEV 44115 2625 B4
10 BDFD 44146 2886 E3
10 MPHT 44146 2886 C1
10 MPHT 44137 2886 C1
500 BDFD 44146 2887 C6
1500 OKWD 44146 2887 C6
3900 CLEV 44115 2625 C6
3900 CLEV 44127 2625 C6
5800 CLEV 44127 2755 E1
6300 CLEV 44105 2755 E1
7300 CLEV 44105 2756 A3
10100 CLEV 44125 2756 A3
10100 GDHT 44125 2756 A3
11900 GDHT 44105 2756 E6
13700 GDHT 44125 2757 B7
14100 MPHT 44125 2757 B7
14100 MPHT 44137 2757 B7
14300 GDHT 44128 2757 B7
14300 MPHT 44128 2757 B7
SR-14 Lee Rd
5300 MPHT 44137 2757 C7
5300 MPHT 44137 2886 C1
SR-14 Oakleaf Rd
- OKWD 44146 2887 C7
SR-14 Ontario St
2100 CLEV 44113 2624 E3
2100 CLEV 44115 2624 E3
SR-14 Outerbelt East Frwy
- OKWD - 2887 C7
- OKWD - 3018 C1
SR-14 Pittsburgh Av
2200 CLEV 44115 2625 B4
SR-17 Brookpark Rd
700 BNHT 44109 2754 D7
700 BNHT 44131 2754 D7
700 CLEV 44109 2754 D7
1100 CLEV 44134 2754 D7
1100 PRMA 44134 2754 D7
1100 PRMA 44109 2754 D7

SR-17 Brookpark Rd
5400 PRMA 44129 2754 A7
6000 CLEV 44129 2754 A7
6200 CLEV 44129 2753 B7
6200 PRMA 44129 2753 B7
7300 BKLN 44144 2753 B7
7300 PRMA 44144 2753 B7
10200 PRMA 44130 2753 B7
11700 CLEV 44135 2753 B7
11700 CLEV 44144 2753 B7
11700 PRMA 44135 2753 B7
13000 BKPK 44130 2752 D7
13000 BKPK 44135 2752 D7
13000 BKPK 44142 2752 D7
13000 CLEV 44135 2752 D7
13000 PRMA 44135 2752 D7
13000 PRMA 44130 2752 D7
18200 BKPK 44135 2751 E7
18200 BKPK 44142 2751 E7
18200 CLEV 44135 2751 E7
21100 FWPK 44126 2751 D7
23000 NOSD 44070 2750 E6
23000 NOSD 44126 2751 A6
23000 NOSD 44070 2751 A6
SR-17 Granger Rd
- INDE 44125 2884 E1
- VLVW 44131 2884 E1
5500 INDE 44131 2884 D1
7500 VLVW 44125 2884 E1
7500 VLVW 44125 2885 A1
7700 GDHT 44125 2885 A1
8900 GDHT 44125 2756 B7
13500 GDHT 44125 2757 D7
14000 MPHT 44137 2757 D7
SR-17 E Granger Rd
10 BNHT 44131 2755 A7
1200 BNHT 44131 2884 D1
1400 BNHT 44131 2884 D1
SR-17 W Granger Rd
- BNHT 44131 2754 E7
- BNHT 44109 2754 E7
- CLEV 44109 2754 E7
300 BNHT 44131 2755 B7
SR-17 Libby Rd
14400 MPHT 44137 2757 B7
19800 MPHT 44137 2758 A7
21800 BDHT 44146 2758 A7
SR-20
- EatT - 3006 B5
SR-21 Brecksville Rd
- CHHT 44125 2755 E7
- CHHT 44131 2755 E7
- INDE 44131 2755 E7
- INDE 44125 2755 E7
- VLVW 44125 2884 E2
- VLVW 44131 2884 E2
4700 RHFD 44286 3151 A6
5400 INDE 44131 2884 E2
7200 INDE 44131 3015 E1
7600 INDE 44131 3016 A3
7700 BKVL 44141 3016 A3
9000 BKVL 44141 3151 A2
SR-21 Willow Frwy
- CHHT - 2755 C1
- CLEV - 2625 C6
- CLEV - 2755 D6
- NBGH - 2755 C1
SR-43 E 34th St
2700 CLEV 44115 2625 C5
SR-43 Aurora Rd
21700 BDHT 44146 2758 B7
21700 MPHT 44146 2758 B7
23100 BDHT 44146 2887 C1
26200 BDHT 44146 2888 E4
27000 SLN 44139 2888 E4
33200 SLN 44139 2889 A5
37900 SLN 44139 3020 D1
39700 SLN 44139 3021 C5
40000 BbgT 44023 3021 C5
40000 BbgT 44139 3021 C5
SR-43 N Aurora Rd
10 AURA 44202 3021 E7
10 BbgT 44023 3021 A3
10 BbgT 44139 3021 A2
10 SLN 44139 3021 A2
1000 AURA 44023 3021 B3
SR-43 S Aurora Rd
10 AURA 44202 3156 E1
SR-43 Bartlett Rd
- BDHT 44146 2758 C7
SR-43 Broadway Av
- CLEV 44115 2625 B4
3900 CLEV 44127 2625 C6
5800 CLEV 44127 2755 E1
6300 CLEV 44105 2755 E1
7300 CLEV 44105 2756 A3
SR-43 S Chillicothe Rd
100 AURA 44202 3156 E1
10100 STBR 44241 3156 E7
SR-43 Miles Av
9100 CLEV 44105 2756 B3
13100 CLEV 44128 2756 E3
13600 CLEV 44105 2757 A3
13600 CLEV 44128 2757 A3
17600 WVHT 44128 2757 D5
SR-43 Miles Rd
17700 WVHT 44128 2757 E5
19400 NRDL 44128 2757 E5
19600 WVHT 44128 2758 B6
20000 NRDL 44128 2758 B6
SR-43 Mueti Dr
- BDHT 44146 2758 B7
- MPHT 44137 2758 B7
SR-43 Northfield Rd
- BDHT 44146 2758 B6
- MPHT 44146 2758 B6
- MPHT 44137 2758 B6
- WVHT 44146 2758 B6
4900 NRDL 44128 2758 B6
SR-43 Pittsburgh Av
2200 CLEV 44115 2625 B4
SR-44
- CcdT - 2145 E4
- CcdT - 2146 A6
- CcdT 44024 2254 B7
- CcdT 44077 2254 B3
- CdnT 44024 2254 B7
- CdnT 44024 2379 B1
- PNVL - 2145 D2
- PnvT - 2145 E4
SR-44 Center St
100 CRDN 44024 2379 E6
200 CRDN 44024 2380 A7
SR-44 N Hambden St
100 CRDN 44024 2380 A6

SR-44 Heisley Rd
- GDRV 44045 2039 B5
- GDRV 44077 2039 B5
- MNTR 44060 2039 B7
- MNTR 44060 2145 A1
- PnvT 44060 2039 B7
- PnvT 44077 2039 B7
- PnvT 44045 2039 B5
SR-44 Lakeland Frwy
- MNTR - 2145 B1
- PNVL - 2145 B1
- PnvT - 2145 B1
SR-44 Main St
100 CRDN 44024 2380 A6
10400 MNTU 44255 3159 C7
10900 ManT 44255 3159 C7
11900 ManT 44255 3024 C7
SR-44 Painesville Ravenna Rd
10300 MNTU 44255 3159 C7
10300 ShvT 44255 3159 B7
12400 ManT 44255 3024 C5
12800 AbnT 44255 3024 C4
SR-44 E Park St
100 CRDN 44024 2380 A6
SR-44 Ravenna Rd
11100 MsnT 44024 2505 A3
12500 MsnT 44024 2635 B1
13400 NbyT 44024 2635 B1
13700 NbyT 44065 2635 B7
13700 NbyT 44021 2635 B7
14200 NbyT 44021 2765 A2
14200 NbyT 44065 2765 A2
15400 NbyT 44021 2764 E5
15500 NbyT 44065 2764 E5
16300 AbnT 44021 2764 E5
16400 AbnT 44021 2893 E1
17900 AbnT 44234 2893 D7
18300 AbnT 44023 2893 D7
18300 AbnT 44023 3024 C2
18300 AbnT 44234 3024 C2
SR-44 South St
100 CRDN 44024 2380 A6
300 CRDN 44024 2505 A1
800 MsnT 44024 2505 A1
SR-44 Water St
100 CRDN 44024 2380 A6
SR-57
- ELYR 44035 2745 E7
- ELYR 44035 2875 A2
SR-57 E 28th St
100 LORN 44055 2745 A2
500 LORN 44052 2745 A2
SR-57 Broadway Av
300 LORN 44052 2614 E7
1500 LORN 44052 2744 E1
1900 LORN 44052 2745 A2
2300 LORN 44055 2745 A2
SR-57 Grafton Rd
2300 CrlT 44044 3006 E5
2300 EatT 44044 3006 E5
3000 EatT 44044 3141 E1
SR-57 Grafton-Eastern Rd
36000 GftT 44044 3142 D7
36700 GFTN 44044 3142 C7
SR-57 Grove Av
3700 LORN 44055 2745 E5
4800 ShfT 44055 2745 E5
SR-57 John F Kennedy Mem Pkwy
- ELYR 44035 2875 E4
SR-57 Lorain Blvd
1100 ELYR 44035 2874 E4
1800 ELYR 44035 2875 A2
2100 ELYR 44035 2874 E1
6000 EyrT 44035 2745 E7
6000 ShfT 44035 2745 E7
6000 ShfT 44055 2745 E7
6200 ELYR 44035 2745 E7
SR-57 Main St
300 EatT 44044 3141 E3
300 GFTN 44044 3141 E3
300 GFTN 44044 3142 D7
1100 GftT 44044 3142 D7
SR-57 South East Byp
- CrlT 44044 3006 E6
- EatT 44044 3006 E6
- EatT 44035 3006 E2
- EatT 44044 3007 A4
- ELYR 44035 2875 E6
- ELYR 44035 3006 E2
SR-57 Wooster-Avon Lake Rd
15500 GftT 44028 3142 E7
15500 GftT 44044 3142 E7
SR-58 Ashland-Oberlin Rd
500 NRsT 44074 3138 E4
500 OBLN 44074 3138 E4
14200 PtfT 44074 3138 E5
SR-58 Leavitt Rd
1200 LORN 44052 2614 B7
1200 LORN 44053 2614 B7
1300 LORN 44052 2744 A7
1300 LORN 44053 2744 A7
7400 AhtT 44001 2873 A3
7400 AMHT 44001 2873 A3
8000 AhtT 44035 2873 A5
SR-58 N Leavitt Rd
100 AMHT 44001 2744 A7
100 AMHT 44001 2873 A5
800 AMHT 44053 2744 A6
SR-58 S Leavitt Rd
100 AhtT 44001 2873 A1
100 AMHT 44001 2873 A1
SR-58 N Main St
10 OBLN 44074 3138 E2
SR-58 S Main St
10 OBLN 44074 3138 E2
SR-58 Oberlin-North Rd
8700 AhtT 44001 2873 A6
8700 AhtT 44035 2873 A6
9000 AhtT 44001 2872 E7
9000 AhtT 44035 2872 E7
9200 AhtT 44001 3003 E1
9200 AhtT 44035 3003 E1
9200 NRsT 44035 3003 E1
9200 NRsT 44074 3003 E1
10700 NRsT 44074 3003 E6
12400 OBLN 44074 3003 E6
12500 NRsT 44074 3138 E1
SR-60 Main St
600 VMLN 44089 2740 E7

SR-60 South St
5500 VMLN 44089 2740 E5
SR-60 State Rd
1400 VmnT 44089 2740 E7
1400 VmnT 44089 2869 E3
4700 FrnT 44889 2869 E3
4700 VmnT 44889 2869 E3
SR-60 State St
800 VMLN 44089 2740 E6
1200 VmnT 44089 2740 E7
SR-82
- HrmT 44234 3161 E4
- HrmT 44255 3161 E4
SR-82 Aurora Rd
3600 TwbT 44087 3155 E2
3600 TwbT 44087 3156 A2
SR-82 E Aurora Rd
10 NCtT 44067 3152 E1
10 NCtT 44067 3153 A1
300 MCDN 44056 3153 A1
1400 MCDN 44056 3154 B1
1600 TNBG 44087 3154 B1
2800 TNBG 44087 3155 B2
3500 TwbT 44087 3155 B2
SR-82 W Aurora Rd
10 NCtT 44067 3152 C1
100 SgHT 44067 3152 C1
900 SgHT 44067 3017 B7
1100 SgHT 44067 3016 E7
SR-82 Chippewa Rd
7300 BKVL 44141 3016 A7
SR-82 Garfield Rd
11400 HRM 44234 3161 A2
SR-82 E Garfield Rd
10 AURA 44202 3157 A1
1200 ManT 44202 3157 E1
SR-82 Ravenna Rd
9100 TNBG 44087 3155 C2
SR-82 Royalton Rd
500 EatT 44044 3007 B7
2600 EatT 44044 3006 E6
2900 BWHT 44147 3014 C7
3600 NRYN 44133 3014 C7
6200 NRYN 44133 3013 A7
11700 NRYN 44133 3012 E7
12800 SGVL 44133 3012 E7
12800 SGVL 44136 3012 E7
17800 SGVL 44136 3011 C7
22200 SGVL 44136 3010 D7
23000 ClbT 44028 3010 D7
23000 ClbT 44136 3010 D7
25000 ClbT 44028 3009 C7
26900 ClbT 44028 3008 D7
26900 EatT 44028 3008 D7
34700 EatT 44044 3008 D7
SR-82 E Royalton Rd
- BWHT 44141 3015 E7
100 BWHT 44147 3014 E7
500 BWHT 44147 3015 E7
2400 BKVL 44147 3015 E7
2400 BKVL 44141 3015 E7
6900 BKVL 44141 3016 A7
SR-82 W Royalton Rd
1000 BWHT 44147 3014 E7
SR-82 State St
7800 GTVL 44234 3161 E5
7800 HrmT 44234 3161 E5
SR-82 Twinsburg Warren Rd
10 AURA 44202 3156 E1
500 AURA 44202 3021 D7
500 AURA 44202 3156 C1
2600 AURA 44202 3157 D1
2600 ManT 44202 3157 D1
2600 ManT 44202 3158 A1
3000 ManT 44255 3158 A1
3700 ManT 44255 3159 C2
5300 ManT 44255 3160 C2
5500 HrmT 44255 3160 C2
7200 HrmT 44234 3161 E4
7200 HrmT 44255 3161 C4
SR-82 W Wakefield Rd
5700 HrmT 44234 3160 B2
5700 HrmT 44255 3160 A2
6500 HRM 44234 3160 E2
6600 HRM 44234 3161 B2
SR-82 Welshfield Limavle Rd S
11300 HRM 44234 3161 A3
11300 HrmT 44234 3161 A3
SR-83 Avon Belden Rd
800 AVON 44011 2618 A3
800 AVON 44012 2618 A3
2200 AVON 44011 2748 A1
4900 NRDV 44011 2748 A5
4900 NRDV 44039 2748 A5
5000 NRDV 44039 2877 A1
8900 NRDV 44039 3007 E2
8900 NRDV 44039 3008 A1
SR-83 Avon-Belden Center Rd
100 AVLK 44012 2488 A7
100 AVLK 44012 2618 A6
SR-83 Chester Rd
36500 AVON 44011 2618 A7
SR-83 Wooster-Avon Lake Rd
1600 EatT 44028 3142 E1
1600 EatT 44044 3142 E1
1600 GFTN 44044 3142 E1
1600 GFTN 44028 3142 E1
9700 EatT 44044 3007 E2
14700 GftT 44028 3142 E7
14700 GftT 44044 3142 E7
SR-84 Bank St
800 PNVL 44077 2146 A4
800 PnvT 44077 2146 A4
SR-84 Bishop Rd
2400 WKLF 44092 2374 B4
2700 WBHL 44092 2374 B5
SR-84 Chardon Rd
21000 EUCL 44117 2498 B1
23800 RDHT 44143 2498 B1
24400 RDHT 44143 2373 D7
26500 RDHT 44143 2374 A6
27200 WBHL 44092 2374 A6
SR-84 Johnnycake Ridge Rd
- MNTR 44094 2251 D3
10 PnvT 44077 2146 B3
7300 MNTR 44060 2251 D3
8000 MNTR 44060 2252 B2
8400 KDHL 44060 2252 B2
9300 MNTR 44060 2253 A2
9600 CcdT 44060 2253 A2

SR-84 Johnnycake Ridge Rd
9800 CcdT 44060 2145 C7
9800 CcdT 44077 2145 C7
10600 CcdT 44077 2146 A4
38200 WLBY 44094 2250 E6
38500 WLBY 44094 2251 D3
SR-84 E Main St
10 MDSN 44057 2044 B1
SR-84 W Main St
10 MDSN 44057 2044 A1
700 MDSN 44057 2043 E2
SR-84 Ridge Rd
28700 WKLF 44092 2374 B5
33300 WLBY 44094 2375 A3
36800 WLBY 44094 2250 D7
SR-84 S Ridge Rd
2600 PryT 44077 2041 D6
2600 PryT 44081 2041 D6
2800 PryT 44081 2042 A5
4400 PRRY 44081 2042 E3
4500 PryT 44057 2042 E3
5000 MadT 44057 2043 A3
5000 MadT 44081 2043 A3
5000 PryT 44081 2043 A3
5000 PryT 44057 2043 A3
7100 MadT 44057 1942 E7
7100 MadT 44057 1943 A7
7100 MadT 44057 2044 D1
7800 HpfT 44057 1943 B7
SR-84 S Ridge Rd E
10 GNVA 44041 1944 B6
500 GnvT 44041 1944 E5
SR-84 S Ridge Rd W
10 GNVA 44041 1944 B6
5500 HpfT 44041 1944 B6
5800 HpfT 44041 1943 C7
6800 HpfT 44057 1943 C7
SR-84 Riverside Dr
400 PnvT 44077 2146 D2
800 PnvT 44077 2147 B1
1400 PryT 44077 2147 B1
2500 PryT 44077 2041 C7
SR-84 S State St
400 PNVL 44077 2146 C2
700 PnvT 44077 2146 C2
SR-84 E Walnut Av
200 PNVL 44077 2146 C1
600 PnvT 44077 2146 C1
SR-86
- WndT 44064 2509 A2
- WndT 44099 2509 B2
SR-86 Painesville Warren Rd
- PnvT 44077 2146 C3
6100 CcdT 44077 2146 C4
11900 CcdT 44077 2147 B5
12200 LryT 44077 2147 B5
13000 LryT 44077 2255 E1
13000 LryT 44077 2256 D3
14100 LryT 44086 2256 D3
14500 LryT 44086 2257 B3
14500 TpnT 44086 2257 B3
SR-86 Plank Rd
7800 TpnT 44064 2257 B4
7800 TpnT 44086 2257 B4
8300 MtlT 44064 2257 D5
8400 MtlT 44086 2257 D6
8700 MtlT 44064 2382 E1
9000 MtlT 44064 2383 A4
10600 HtbT 44064 2508 E1
10600 HtbT 44064 2509 A2
10600 MtlT 44064 2508 E1
11100 WndT 44064 2509 A2
SR-86 N State St
10 PNVL 44077 2040 B7
SR-86 S State St
10 PNVL 44077 2040 B7
10 PNVL 44077 2146 C1
700 PnvT 44077 2146 C3
SR-87
- CLEV 44115 2625 D4
SR-87 Broadway Av
800 CLEV 44115 2625 A4
SR-87 Buckeye Rd
8400 CLEV 44104 2626 A5
SR-87 E Center St
13800 BURT 44021 2766 D2
SR-87 W Center St
13700 BURT 44021 2766 A1
SR-87 Chagrin Blvd
25600 BHWD 44122 2758 E1
26900 BHWD 44122 2759 C1
27000 ORNG 44122 2759 C1
27000 WDMR 44122 2759 C1
29000 ORNG 44124 2759 C1
29000 PRPK 44124 2759 C1
SR-87 E High St
15800 MDFD 44062 2767 D2
SR-87 W High St
15300 MDFD 44062 2767 B2
15400 MdfT 44062 2767 B2
SR-87 Kinsman Rd
4400 MstT 44062 2769 C2
7000 HGVL 44022 2761 B2
7100 RslT 44073 2761 B2
7300 RslT 44072 2761 B2
8200 RslT 44072 2762 D2
9600 NbyT 44072 2763 C2
9600 RslT 44072 2763 C2
9900 NbyT 44065 2763 C2
10500 NbyT 44065 2764 C2
11700 NbyT 44021 2764 C2
12000 NbyT 44021 2765 A1
12000 NbyT 44065 2765 A1
12400 BtnT 44021 2765 A1
13300 BtnT 44021 2766 A1
13600 BURT 44021 2766 A1
14100 BtnT 44062 2766 A1
15000 BtnT 44062 2767 A2
15100 MDFD 44062 2767 A2
15100 MdfT 44062 2767 A2
16200 MDFD 44062 2767 E2
16300 MDFD 44062 2768 A2
16400 MdfT 44062 2768 A2
17400 MdfT 44062 2769 C2
17400 MstT 44062 2769 C2
SR-87 Kirtland St
13800 BURT 44021 2636 B7
SR-87 Ontario St
1900 CLEV 44114 2624 E3
2000 CLEV 44115 2624 E3
2100 CLEV 44113 2624 E3
SR-87 Orange Av
1400 CLEV 44115 2625 A4

SR-87 E Park St
- BURT 44021 2636 B7
14600 BURT 44021 2766 B1
SR-87 W Park St
- BURT 44021 2636 A7
- BURT 44021 2766 A1
SR-87 Pinetree Rd
30400 PRPK 44124 2759 D1
SR-87 Richmond Rd
2900 BHWD 44122 2628 E7
3000 BHWD 44122 2758 E1
SR-87 Shaker Blvd
10000 CLEV 44104 2626 D5
11600 CLEV 44120 2626 D5
13300 CLEV 44120 2627 E6
14000 SRHT 44120 2627 B5
17400 SRHT 44122 2627 E6
19500 SRHT 44122 2628 D6
24300 BHWD 44122 2628 D6
SR-87 W Spring St
13800 BURT 44021 2636 B7
SR-87 Woodland Av
2500 CLEV 44115 2625 E4
4000 CLEV 44104 2625 E4
7500 CLEV 44104 2626 A4
SR-87 S Woodland Rd
32900 PRPK 44124 2759 D1
32900 PRPK 44124 2760 E2
33700 PRPK 44022 2760 E2
35200 HGVL 44022 2760 E2
35200 MDHL 44022 2760 E2
44000 HGVL 44022 2761 A2
SR-88 Greenville Rd NW
4400 FnTp 44491 2898 E5
4700 FnTp 44062 2898 C5
SR-88 Madison Rd
17700 PkmT 44062 2896 E7
SR-88 Main St
100 WFAR 44491 2898 E5
18200 PkmT 44062 2896 E7
18200 PkmT 44234 2896 E7
SR-88 McCall Rd
15600 NsnT 44231 3027 C2
15600 PkmT 44231 3027 C2
15900 PkmT 44234 3027 C2
SR-88 Nash Rd
16300 PkmT 44062 2896 E5
16300 PkmT 44062 2897 A5
16900 PkmT 44491 2897 E5
16900 PkmT 44062 2898 A5
16900 PkmT 44491 2898 A5
17800 FnTp 44491 2898 A5
17800 FnTp 44062 2898 A5
17800 FnTp 44491 2898 A5
SR-88 Nelson Parkman Rd
- PkmT 44231 3027 E1
- PkmT 44234 3027 E1
SR-88 Ravenna Parkman Rd
11900 NsnT 44231 3027 B7
SR-91 Darrow Rd
7300 HDSN 44236 3154 E7
7700 TwbT 44236 3154 E7
7900 TNBG 44236 3154 E7
7900 TNBG 44087 3154 E7
7900 TwbT 44087 3154 E7
8700 TNBG 44087 3155 A2
9700 TNBG 44087 3019 E5
9800 TNBG 44087 3020 A6
SR-91 Som Center Rd
- MDHT 44040 2630 A1
- WLBY 44094 2250 B4
- WLBY 44095 2250 B4
200 MAYF 44143 2500 A2
400 ETLK 44095 2250 B4
700 MAYF 44040 2500 A6
1000 MDHT 44124 2500 A6
1500 MDHT 44124 2630 A1
1700 GSML 44040 2630 A1
2400 HGVL 44022 2630 A1
2400 PRPK 44124 2630 A1
2500 WBHL 44094 2375 A5
2900 WBHL 44092 2375 A5
3000 WBHL 44092 2500 A2
3000 WBHL 44094 2500 A2
3300 HGVL 44022 2760 A2
3300 PRPK 44124 2760 A2
3500 PRPK 44022 2760 A2
3600 MDHL 44022 2760 A2
3600 MDHL 44124 2760 A2
4000 MDHL 44022 2759 E6
5000 SLN 44139 2759 E6
5100 SLN 44139 2760 A2
5200 SLN 44139 2889 A2
5200 WLBY 44094 2375 A1
7000 SLN 44139 3020 A1
SR-94 River Rd
10 HkyT 44133 3149 A5
10 HkyT 44233 3149 A6
10 NRYN 44133 3149 A5
SR-94 State Rd
4200 CLEV 44109 2754 C4
4900 CLEV 44134 2754 C4
5200 PRMA 44134 2754 C4
5300 PRMA 44134 2883 C1
7100 PRMA 44129 2883 B6
7400 PRMA 44134 3014 B1
7800 NRYN 44134 3014 B1
7900 NRYN 44133 3014 B1
14000 NRYN 44133 3149 A2
20000 HkyT 44233 3149 A6
20000 HkyT 44133 3149 A6
SR-113 Center Ridge Rd
19400 RKRV 44116 2621 E7
20500 RKRV 44116 2751 C1
20600 FWPK 44126 2751 C1
20600 FWPK 44116 2751 C1
21600 RKRV 44126 2751 C1
23000 WTLK 44145 2751 C1
23000 WTLK 44116 2751 C1
23200 WTLK 44145 2750 E1
27100 WTLK 44145 2749 D6
31400 NRDV 44039 2749 B6
31400 NRDV 44145 2749 B6
31700 NRDV 44039 2748 E7
31700 NRDV 44039 2877 A1
36000 NRDV 44039 2876 D4
39100 NRDV 44039 2875 E5
SR-113 Cleveland St
700 ELYR 44035 2875 E5
900 ELYR 44039 2875 E4
SR-113 John F Kennedy Mem Pkwy
- ELYR 44035 2874 D4

SR-113 John F Kennedy Mem Pkwy
- ELYR 44035 2875 B4
- EyrT 44035 2874 D4
SR-113 E Main St
100 SAHT 44001 2872 C7
300 AhtT 44001 2872 D7
SR-113 W Main St
100 SAHT 44001 2872 B7
400 SAHT 44001 3003 A1
SR-113 Milan Elyria Rd
42900 ELYR 44035 2873 D6
42900 EyrT 44035 2873 D6
42900 EyrT 44035 2874 A5
43000 AhtT 44001 2873 D6
46000 AhtT 44001 2873 D6
46100 AhtT 44001 2872 E6
SR-113 Wooster Rd
1500 RKRV 44116 2621 E6
2500 LKWD 44126 2621 E6
2500 RKRV 44126 2621 E6
SR-166
- TmbT 44084 2259 B2
- TmbT 44086 2259 B2
SR-166 Rock Creek Rd
13900 HmbT 44024 2381 C2
14300 HmbT 44024 2256 E7
14800 HmbT 44024 2257 C4
14800 MtlT 44024 2257 C4
14800 MtlT 44064 2257 C4
14800 TpnT 44064 2257 C4
15600 TpnT 44086 2257 C4
16100 TpnT 44086 2258 D2
17500 TpnT 44086 2259 C2
17700 TmbT 44086 2259 C2
SR-168 S Cheshire Rd
- BtnT 44021 2766 B2
14700 BURT 44021 2766 B1
SR-168 S Cheshire St
- BURT 44021 2766 B2
SR-168 High St
16000 PkmT 44062 2896 D7
16000 PkmT 44234 2896 D7
SR-168 Tavern Rd
14800 BtnT 44062 2766 E5
14800 BtnT 44021 2766 E5
14800 BURT 44021 2766 E5
16300 BtnT 44062 2767 A7
16300 BtnT 44021 2767 A7
16300 PkmT 44062 2896 B4
16300 PkmT 44021 2896 B4
16300 TroT 44021 2767 A7
16300 TroT 44021 2896 B4
16300 TroT 44062 2767 A7
16300 TroT 44062 2896 B4
17800 PkmT 44234 2896 B4
SR-174 Chagrin River Rd
- GSML 44094 2500 C1
- WBHL 44094 2500 C1
400 GSML 44040 2500 D2
1400 GSML 44040 2630 E1
SR-174 Ridge Rd
37700 WLBY 44094 2250 E7
SR-174 River Rd
- WLBY 44094 2250 D7
2100 WBHL 44094 2375 D2
2900 GSML 44040 2500 D2
2900 GSML 44094 2500 D2
2900 WBHL 44094 2500 D2
SR-174 River St
4100 WLBY 44094 2250 E6
SR-175 E 260th St
200 EUCL 44132 2373 E1
SR-175 Cannon Rd
27200 SLN 44139 2888 A2
27300 SLN 44146 2888 A2
SR-175 Richmond Rd
100 EUCL 44117 2373 E7
100 EUCL 44143 2373 E7
100 RDHT 44143 2373 E7
300 RDHT 44143 2498 E2
800 LNHT 44124 2498 E6
1500 LNHT 44124 2628 E5
2100 BHWD 44122 2628 E7
3000 BHWD 44122 2758 E1
4100 HIHL 44122 2758 E3
4100 WVHT 44122 2758 E3
4500 WVHT 44128 2758 E3
4500 WVHT 44022 2758 E6
5000 BDHT 44146 2758 E6
25700 BDHT 44146 2887 E1
25700 BDHT 44146 2888 A1
25700 SLN 44146 2888 A1
27000 SLN 44139 2888 A1
SR-176 Broadview Rd
4800 RchT 44286 3149 E6
4800 RchT 44286 3150 A7
5200 PRMA 44134 2754 D7
5300 PRMA 44134 2883 E2
5300 RchT 44233 3149 E6
5300 RchT 44286 3149 E6
5300 RchT 44147 3149 E6
6300 PRMA 44131 2883 E6
6300 SVHL 44131 2883 E6
7300 PRMA 44131 3014 E1
7300 PRMA 44134 3014 E1
7300 SVHL 44131 3014 E1
7900 BWHT 44147 3014 E1
9200 BWHT 44147 3149 E1
SR-176 Brookpark Rd
1500 CLEV 44134 2754 D7
1500 PRMA 44134 2754 D7
SR-176 Jennings Frwy
- CLEV - 2754 E1
- CLEV - 2755 A5
SR-237 W Bagley Rd
10 BERA 44017 2880 C6
SR-237 Berea Frwy
- BKPK - 2751 E7
- BKPK - 2880 D2
- CLEV - 2880 C6
- CLEV 44142 2880 C6
SR-237 Brookpark Rd
18200 BKPK 44135 2751 E7
18200 BKPK 44142 2751 E7
18200 BKPK 44135 2752 A7
18200 BKPK 44142 2752 A7
18200 CLEV 44135 2751 E7
18200 CLEV 44135 2752 A7
SR-237 W Clifton Blvd
1100 LKWD 44107 2622 A4
SR-237 Front St
200 BERA 44017 2880 C6

Cleveland Street Index

STREET Block City ZIP Map# Grid

SR-237 Henry St
10 BERA 44017 2880 B7
SR-237 Kolthoff Dr
6500 BERA 44142 2880 C4
6500 BKPK 44142 2880 C4
SR-237 Mulberry St
200 BERA 44017 2880 B6
SR-237 Prospect Rd
8500 SGVL 44017 3011 B2
8500 SGVL 44136 3011 B3
SR-237 Prospect St
10 BERA 44017 2880 B7
200 BERA 44017 3011 B2
700 SGVL 44017 3011 B2
SR-237 Riverside Dr
1500 LKWD 44107 2622 A5
2300 CLEV 44111 2622 A7
2300 LKWD 44111 2622 A7
SR-237 Rocky River Dr
3100 CLEV 44111 2622 B7
3200 CLEV 44111 2752 A4
3900 CLEV 44135 2752 A4
4800 CLEV 44135 2751 E6
SR-237 N Rocky River Dr
800 BERA 44017 2880 C4
800 BERA 44142 2880 C4
800 BKPK 44142 2880 C4
SR-252 Columbia Rd
10 LvpT 44028 3145 A5
10 LvpT 44280 3145 A5
300 BYVL 44140 2620 C6
300 LvpT 44280 3144 E7
600 WTLK 44145 2620 C6
1700 WTLK 44145 2750 C3
3200 NOSD 44070 2750 C3
3200 WTLK 44070 2750 C3
5900 NOSD 44070 2879 C1
6200 OmsT 44070 2879 C2
6200 OmsT 44138 2879 C2
6700 ODFL 44138 2879 C4
8400 ODFL 44138 3010 B3
SR-252 Great Northern Blvd
4500 NOSD 44070 2750 C6
5200 NOSD 44070 2879 C2
SR-252 Lorain Rd
24700 NOSD 44070 2750 C6
SR-252 Main St
7900 ODFL 44138 2879 C5
SR-252 E River Rd
9800 ClbT 44028 3010 C2
14000 ClbT 44028 3145 A2
18000 LvpT 44028 3145 A5
SR-252 Sprague Rd
24400 ClbT 44028 3010 B2
24400 ClbT 44138 3010 B2
24400 ODFL 44138 3010 B2
SR-254 Detroit Rd
- LKWD 44107 2621 D5
- RKRV 44107 2621 D5
- WTLK 44116 2621 B6
4700 SFLD 44035 2746 E5
4700 SFLD 44054 2746 E5
5300 AVON 44011 2747 A4
5300 SFLD 44011 2747 A4
5300 SFLD 44035 2747 A4
5300 SFLD 44054 2747 A4
19000 RKRV 44116 2621 D5
22900 WTLK 44145 2621 B6
23300 WTLK 44145 2620 B7
27300 WTLK 44145 2619 C7
30600 WTLK 44145 2749 A1
31400 AVON 44145 2749 A1
32200 AVON 44011 2748 B1
32200 AVON 44011 2749 A1
SR-254 N Ridge Rd
2100 ShfT 44035 2745 E6
2100 ShfT 44055 2745 E6
2300 ShfT 44055 2746 A6
3200 SFLD 44035 2746 C6
3200 SFLD 44054 2746 C6
3200 ShfT 44054 2746 C6
3200 ShfT 44035 2746 C6
SR-254 Sloane Av
1300 LKWD 44107 2622 A5
SR-282 Nelson Ledge Rd
- PkmT 44491 3028 B5
11500 NsnT 44231 3028 B5
12800 PkmT 44231 3028 B5
SR-283 Andrews Rd
5500 MONT 44060 2143 E1
SR-283 Lake Shore Blvd
500 PnvT 44077 2039 C6
600 PnvT 44060 2039 B7
7000 MNTR 44060 2143 B4
SR-283 Lake shore Blvd
7200 MNTR 44060 2143 B4
SR-283 Lake Shore Blvd
7700 MONT 44060 2143 E1
8000 MONT 44060 2144 B1
8100 MNTR 44060 2144 B1
9100 MNTR 44060 2038 E7
9300 MNTR 44060 2039 A7
13600 BTNH 44108 2497 A1
13600 BTNH 44110 2497 A1
13800 CLEV 44110 2372 C6
16900 CLEV 44119 2372 C6
18400 EUCL 44119 2372 C6
19500 EUCL 44119 2373 D1
19800 EUCL 44123 2373 D1
24800 EUCL 44132 2373 D1
25700 EUCL 44132 2248 E7
27200 EUCL 44132 2249 B6
28100 WLWK 44095 2249 B6
33000 ETLK 44095 2249 D4
33500 LKLN 44095 2249 D4
34400 TMLK 44095 2249 D4
34700 ETLK 44095 2250 B1
34700 TMLK 44095 2250 B1
35900 ETLK 44095 2142 C7
37900 WLBY 44094 2142 D5
37900 WLBY 44095 2142 D5
38400 WLBY 44094 2143 B4
38800 MNTR 44094 2143 B4
SR-283 Richmond Rd
800 PnvT 44077 2039 E7
1000 GDRV 44045 2039 C6
1000 PnvT 44045 2039 C6
SR-283 Richmond St
10 PNVL 44077 2040 A7
600 PNVL 44077 2039 E7
600 PnvT 44077 2039 E7
SR-283 River St
600 GDRV 44045 2039 C6

STREET Block City ZIP Map# Grid

SR-283 River St
700 PnvT 44045 2039 C6
SR-283 Singer Av
100 GDRV 44045 2039 C6
400 PnvT 44077 2039 C6
SR-291 Engle Rd
5000 BKPK 44142 2752 A7
5000 BKPK 44142 2881 A1
6600 MDBH 44130 2881 A6
7400 MDBH 44130 3012 A1
SR-291 Fowles Rd
16600 MDBH 44130 3012 B1
SR-301
- CrlT - 3006 B5
- EatT - 3006 B5
SR-301 Abbe Rd
100 SDLK 44054 2616 E6
400 ELYR 44035 2875 E2
600 SFLD 44054 2616 E6
800 ELYR 44035 2746 E6
2400 SFLD 44054 2746 E1
4900 SFLD 44035 2746 E6
SR-301 John F Kennedy Mem Pkwy
- ELYR 44035 2875 E4
SR-301 Lattasburg-Elyria Rd
11900 CrlT 44035 3005 E7
12000 CrlT 44050 3005 E7
12200 CrlT 44050 3140 E2
13800 LrgT 44050 3140 E6
SR-301 South East Byp
- EatT 44035 3006 E2
- EatT 44044 3006 E2
- ELYR 44035 2875 E6
- ELYR 44035 3006 E2
SR-305 E Wakefield Rd
6900 HRM 44234 3161 E2
7100 HrmT 44234 3161 E2
SR-306
- KTLD 44094 2251 C5
- WLBY 44094 2251 C5
SR-306 Broadmoor Rd
- WLBY 44060 2251 C5
- WLBY 44094 2251 C5
8000 MNTR 44060 2251 C3
SR-306 Chillicothe Rd
5000 SRSL 44073 2762 A4
8700 KTLD 44094 2251 D6
9100 KTLD 44094 2376 E2
9500 KTLD 44094 2377 A3
11000 KTLD 44094 2502 B5
11100 CsTp 44026 2502 B5
11100 CsTp 44094 2502 B5
12700 CsTp 44026 2632 A5
13400 CsTp 44072 2632 A5
13400 RslT 44072 2632 A5
14600 RslT 44072 2762 A4
15200 RslT 44073 2762 A4
15800 BbgT 44023 2762 A4
16400 BbgT 44023 2891 A1
18400 BbgT 44023 3022 A3
SR-306 N Chillicothe Rd
10 AURA 44202 3021 E7
200 AURA 44202 3022 A5
SR-306 S Chillicothe Rd
10 AURA 44202 3156 E1
SR-306 Reynolds Rd
6200 MNTR 44060 2143 C5
7300 MNTR 44060 2251 C3
SR-307 N River Rd W
5800 HpfT 44041 2045 D3
6700 HpfT 44057 2045 D3
SR-307 Warner Rd
6700 MadT 44057 2044 C3
6700 MDSN 44057 2044 C3
7200 HpfT 44057 2045 B3
7200 MadT 44057 2045 A3
SR-511 Cleveland Oberlin Rd
700 NRsT 44074 3139 B2
700 OBLN 44074 3139 B2
SR-511 E Lorain St
10 OBLN 44074 3138 E2
100 OBLN 44074 3139 A2
SR-511 W Lorain St
10 OBLN 44074 3138 E2
600 NRsT 44074 3138 B2
SR-511 Oberlin-Norwalk Rd
47000 NRsT 44074 3138 A2
SR-528 Chardon-Madison Rd
4400 MadT 44057 2044 B4
4400 MDSN 44057 2044 B4
5200 MadT 44057 2150 B3
5500 TpnT 44057 2150 B3
SR-528 Hubbard Rd
2700 MadT 44057 1942 B6
2700 MDSN 44057 1942 B6
SR-528 N Lake St
- MadT 44057 1942 B6
10 MDSN 44057 2044 B1
200 MDSN 44057 1942 B7
SR-528 Madison Rd
4300 MadT 44057 2044 B3
4300 MDSN 44057 2044 B3
5900 TpnT 44086 2150 B6
6700 TpnT 44086 2258 B2
8400 MtlT 44086 2258 B5
8600 MtlT 44064 2258 B5
8600 MtlT 44064 2383 B2
9800 HtbT 44064 2508 A4
11000 MtlT 44064 2508 A4
11400 HtbT 44046 2508 A4
12400 HtbT 44046 2638 A4
13200 HtbT 44062 2638 A4
13200 MdfT 44062 2638 A4
14300 MDFD 44062 2768 A1
14300 MdfT 44062 2768 A1
15900 MdfT 44062 2767 E7
16300 PkmT 44062 2767 E7
18300 PkmT 44062 2896 E1
SR-528 Main St
18200 PkmT 44062 2896 E7
18200 PkmT 44234 2896 E7
SR-528 W Main St
10 MDSN 44057 2044 B1
SR-528 River St
10 MDSN 44057 2044 B3
SR-528 Thompson Rd
- TpnT 44086 2150 B5

STREET Block City ZIP Map# Grid

SR-534
2100 HpfT 44041 1944 C7
2200 GNVA 44041 1944 C7
SR-534 N Broadway
10 GNVA 44041 1944 C4
SR-534 S Broadway
10 GNVA 44041 1944 B4
SR-534 N Broadway St
700 GNVA 44041 1944 C2
700 GnvT 44041 1944 C2
SR-534 S Broadway St
1200 GNVA 44041 1944 C6
SR-535 East St
600 FTHR 44077 2039 D4
SR-535 Fairport Nursery Rd
10 PnvT 44077 2040 C4
500 FTHR 44077 2039 D5
500 PnvT 44077 2039 D5
SR-535 Richmond St
600 PNVL 44077 2039 E6
600 PnvT 44077 2039 E6
900 FTHR 44077 2039 E6
SR-608 Concord-Hambden Rd
11500 CcdT 44077 2146 D7
11500 CcdT 44077 2254 E1
11900 CcdT 44077 2255 B4
12700 CcdT 44024 2255 D6
12700 HmbT 44024 2255 D6
12700 HmbT 44077 2255 D6
SR-608 Old State Rd
8400 HmbT 44024 2255 D6
8400 HmbT 44077 2255 C5
8800 HmbT 44024 2380 E1
8800 HmbT 44024 2381 A2
10900 ClrT 44024 2506 C2
10900 HmbT 44024 2506 C2
12400 ClrT 44021 2506 C2
12400 ClrT 44021 2636 E1
12800 ClrT 44021 2637 A2
13400 HtbT 44021 2637 A2
13500 MdfT 44021 2637 A2
13600 MdfT 44046 2637 A2
13700 MdfT 44062 2637 D7
14300 MDFD 44062 2767 D3
14300 MdfT 44062 2767 D3
SR-608 N State Av
14700 MDFD 44062 2767 D1
SR-608 S State Av
14900 MDFD 44062 2767 D2
15300 MdfT 44062 2767 D4
SR-611
- LORN 44053 2743 E2
SR-611 W 21st St
100 LORN 44052 2744 C1
3200 LORN 44053 2744 C1
3300 LORN 44053 2743 E2
SR-611 Colorado Av
1400 LORN 44052 2615 A7
3500 LORN 44054 2615 C7
3500 SFLD 44054 2615 C7
3600 SFLD 44054 2616 D7
5400 SFLD 44011 2617 A6
5400 SFLD 44054 2617 A6
37100 AVON 44011 2747 D1
38300 AVON 44011 2617 C7
SR-611 Henderson Dr
100 LORN 44052 2745 A1
1700 LORN 44052 2615 B7
SR-615 Center St
6300 MNTR 44060 2144 B4
7200 MNTR 44060 2252 B3
8300 KDHL 44060 2252 B3
SR-615 Chillicothe Rd
- KDHL 44060 2251 E6
- KTLD 44060 2251 E6
- KTLD 44060 2252 A6
- KTLD 44094 2252 A6
8400 KDHL 44060 2252 A6
8800 KTLD 44094 2251 E6
SR-615 Munson Rd
7700 MNTR 44060 2143 E3
7700 MONT 44060 2143 E3
8000 MNTR 44060 2144 A3
SR-633 Lloyd Rd
200 EUCL 44132 2249 A7
400 EUCL 44132 2374 B2
400 WKLF 44092 2374 B2
SR-640 Vine St
31000 WLWK 44095 2249 E5
32700 ETLK 44095 2249 E5
33700 ETLK 44095 2250 A5
36300 ETLK 44094 2250 D5
36300 WLBY 44094 2250 D5
SR-700 Burton Limaville Rd S
10000 FdmT 44255 3161 A7
10000 HrmT 44255 3161 A7
SR-700 S Cheshire Rd
- BtnT 44021 2766 B2
14700 BURT 44021 2766 B1
SR-700 S Cheshire St
- BURT 44021 2766 B2
SR-700 Claridon Troy Rd
14400 BtnT 44021 2766 B6
14400 BtnT 44062 2766 B6
15000 TroT 44021 2766 B6
16000 TroT 44021 2895 A2
17700 TroT 44234 2895 B7
18200 TroT 44234 3026 B2
SR-700 Garfield Rd
11400 HRM 44234 3161 A2
SR-700 Tavern Rd
14800 BtnT 44021 2766 B2
14800 BtnT 44062 2766 B2
14800 BURT 44021 2766 B2
SR-700 Welshfield Limavle Rd S
10300 HrmT 44234 3161 A7
10300 HrmT 44255 3161 A7
11300 HRM 44234 3161 A3
11900 HrmT 44234 3026 A7
11900 HrmT 44234 3161 A1
13000 TroT 44234 3026 A7
Stacy Ct
4800 RDHT 44143 2498 D4
Stacy Ln
7000 CsTp 44026 2501 A5
Stadium Dr
6900 BKVL 44141 3016 A6
Stafford Av
19200 MPHT 44137 2886 E1

STREET Block City ZIP Map# Grid

Stafford Av
19800 MPHT 44137 2887 A1
Stafford Dr
400 ELYR 44035 2875 D2
6000 NOSD 44070 2878 C2
6700 MDHT 44124 2630 A1
8400 SGVL 44136 3011 E3
Stafford Rd
8800 BbgT 44023 2891 C2
9400 AbnT 44023 2892 B2
9400 BbgT 44023 2892 B2
10600 AbnT 44023 2893 A2
11500 AbnT 44023 2893 C2
11800 AbnT 44021 2894 A1
12300 TroT 44021 2894 A1
Staffordshire Ct
6700 AbnT 44023 2893 B1
Stage Av
10 PNVL 44077 2039 E7
Stagecoach Dr
16200 PkmT 44231 3027 E2
16400 PkmT 44231 3028 A2
Stage I Rd
26700 RDHT 44143 2498 E1
26700 RDHT 44143 2499 A1
Staghorn Dr
24300 BDHT 44146 2887 D3
Stag Thicket Ln
16900 SGVL 44136 3146 E3
Stallion Ct
- AVON 44011 2747 B5
Stamford Av
7500 MNTR 44060 2251 C3
Stamford Ct
10100 SGVL 44136 3012 C4
Stamm Rd
10000 FdmT 44255 3160 E7
10000 HrmT 44255 3160 E7
Stanard Av
5300 CLEV 44103 2495 D7
Stanbury Rd
6000 PRMA 44129 2882 E4
Standish Av
2900 PRMA 44134 2883 C4
14800 MDFD 44062 2767 C2
Stanfield Dr
2400 PRMA 44134 2883 C6
12900 MsnT 44024 2634 E2
Stanford Av
100 ELYR 44035 2875 B7
3500 CLEV 44109 2754 C4
4100 LORN 44053 2744 A4
20400 FWPK 44126 2751 C2
Stanford Dr
2200 WKLF 44092 2374 C4
Stanford Rd
100 BERA 44017 2880 B7
5700 BosT 44067 3152 D6
5700 BosT 44141 3152 C6
5700 SgHT 44141 3152 D6
5700 SgHT 44067 3152 D6
6500 NCtT 44141 3152 D6
23300 SRHT 44122 2628 C6
Stanford St
1800 TwbT 44087 3154 C2
Stang Rd
- AhtT 44035 2873 C3
44100 EyrT 44035 2873 E3
Stanhope Rd
3700 SELD 44118 2628 A3
Stanley Av
5000 MPHT 44128 2757 B7
5000 MPHT 44137 2757 B7
Stanley Dr
13900 BtnT 44021 2635 C5
Stanley Ln
11200 TNBG 44087 3020 B4
Stanley Rd
12000 VmnT 44089 2869 A3
Stanmary Dr
200 BERA 44017 3011 C1
Stanridge Rd
10 CNFL 44022 2760 E5
10 CNFL 44022 2761 A5
Stansbury Dr
5000 SLN 44139 2759 E7
Stanwell Dr
800 HDHT 44143 2499 C6
Stanwich St
2700 ShvT 44241 3158 A7
Stanwood Rd
1900 ECLE 44112 2497 B5
Stapleton Dr
10500 SGVL 44136 3012 B4
Star Av
7400 CLEV 44103 2495 E7
7400 CLEV 44103 2496 A7
N Star Dr
12600 NRYN 44133 3147 E4
N Star Rd
9200 KTLD 44094 2376 E1
Starboard Dr
36400 ETLK 44095 2142 D7
Starboard Cove
31800 AVLK 44012 2618 E1
Starburst Rd
8100 MNTR 44060 2144 A3
Stardust Tr
10 AMHT 44001 2744 B7
Stark Dr
2700 WBHL 44094 2375 A6
6000 BKPK 44142 2881 D2
Stark St
400 SDLK 44054 2616 A4
Starkweather Av
700 CLEV 44113 2625 A6
800 CLEV 44113 2624 E6
Starlight Dr
10 SVHL 44131 2883 E6
100 SVHL 44131 2884 A6
4300 CLEV 44109 2755 A5
8800 MCDN 44056 3018 C6
Starling Ct
10 ELYR 44035 3006 D1
Starlite Dr
700 BERA 44017 3011 A2
6900 BKPK 44142 2881 D3
Starr Cir
1300 BWHT 44147 3149 D4
Starview Dr
300 BNWK 44212 3146 E7
Stary Dr
3800 PRMA 44134 3014 B1
N State Av
14700 MDFD 44062 2767 D1

STREET Block City ZIP Map# Grid

N State Av SR-608
14700 MDFD 44062 2767 D1
S State Av
14900 MDFD 44062 2767 D3
15300 MdfT 44062 2767 D3
S State Av SR-608
14900 MDFD 44062 2767 D3
15300 MdfT 44062 2767 D3
State Rd
10 HkyT 44133 3149 B6
10 HkyT 44233 3149 B6
10 NRYN 44133 3149 B6
1400 VmnT 44089 2740 E7
1400 VmnT 44089 2869 E1
4200 CLEV 44109 2754 C6
4700 FrnT 44889 2869 E6
4700 VmnT 44889 2869 E6
4900 CLEV 44134 2754 C6
5200 PRMA 44134 2754 C6
5300 PRMA 44134 2883 C3
7100 PRMA 44129 2883 B7
7400 PRMA 44134 3014 B1
7800 NRYN 44134 3014 A3
7900 NRYN 44133 3014 A3
State Rd SR-60
1400 VmnT 44089 2740 E7
1400 VmnT 44089 2869 E1
4700 FrnT 44889 2869 E6
4700 VmnT 44889 2869 E6
State Rd SR-94
4200 CLEV 44109 2754 C6
4900 CLEV 44134 2754 C6
5200 PRMA 44134 2754 C6
5300 PRMA 44134 2883 C3
7100 PRMA 44129 2883 B7
7400 PRMA 44134 3014 B1
7800 NRYN 44134 3014 A3
7900 NRYN 44133 3014 A3
14000 NRYN 44133 3149 A1
20000 HkyT 44233 3149 A5
20000 HkyT 44133 3149 A5
State St
- EyrT 44035 2745 C7
700 ELYR 44035 3006 A2
800 VMLN 44089 2740 E6
1100 GFTN 44044 3142 B5
1200 VmnT 44089 2740 E6
7800 GTVL 44234 3161 E5
7800 HrmT 44234 3161 E5
State St SR-60
800 VMLN 44089 2740 E6
1200 VmnT 44089 2740 E6
State St SR-82
7800 GTVL 44234 3161 E5
7800 HrmT 44234 3161 E5
N State St
300 PNVL 44077 2040 B6
900 PNVL 44077 2039 E5
N State St SR-86
10 PNVL 44077 2040 B7
S State St
10 PNVL 44077 2040 B7
10 PNVL 44077 2146 B1
700 PNVL 44077 2146 B1
S State St SR-84
400 PNVL 44077 2146 C1
700 PnvT 44077 2146 C1
S State St SR-86
10 PNVL 44077 2040 B7
10 PNVL 44077 2146 B1
700 PnvT 44077 2146 B1
Station Rd
10 ClbT 44028 3144 B7
10 ClbT 44280 3144 B7
10 LvpT 44280 3144 B7
11200 ClbT 44028 3009 C3
13000 BKVL 44141 3016 E7
13700 MdfT 44021 2637 A5
Station St
8300 MNTR 44060 2144 A7
32900 SLN 44139 2888 E5
Statten Ct
1500 PnvT 44077 2041 B5
Staunton Dr
1200 PRMA 44134 2883 D3
Staunton Rd
1700 CVHT 44118 2627 E2
2000 UNHT 44118 2627 E2
Stearns Rd
2000 CLEV 44106 2626 C2
5700 NOSD 44070 2878 C2
6700 NOSD 44138 2878 C2
6700 OmsT 44138 2878 C7
6800 OmsT 44070 2878 C5
Steel Av
- ShfT 44055 2745 D6
Steele Av
100 PNVL 44077 2146 C1
Steelton St
100 CrlT 44035 3005 E3
Steelwood Ln
7200 CsTp 44026 2631 B1
Steeple Chase
100 WBHL 44092 2374 B5
Steeple Chase Ct
- AVON 44011 2747 B6
Steeplechase Dr
8200 MNTR 44060 2251 C4
Steeplechase Run
100 NHFD 44067 3018 A3
Steep Rock Dr
400 SgHT 44067 3017 D5
Steinbeck Ct
6500 NRDV 44039 2877 D4
Steinway Av
9400 CLEV 44104 2626 B5
Steinway Blvd
15200 MPHT 44137 2886 B3
Stephanie Dr
8600 NRYN 44133 3014 A3
Stephanie Ln
5900 SLN 44139 2888 D3
Stephen Av
24300 EUCL 44123 2373 C3
24800 EUCL 44132 2373 C3
Stephen Rd
25000 OKWD 44146 3018 D2
Stephens Wy
- MsnT 44024 2503 E3
Sterling Av
10 PNVL 44077 2146 A1
5600 MPHT 44137 2886 C2
Sterling Cir
300 BERA 44017 2879 E7
300 BERA 44017 2880 A7

STREET Block City ZIP Map# Grid

Sterling Ct
9600 TNBG 44087 3020 B6
Sterling Rd
600 WKLF 44092 2249 A7
2900 LORN 44052 2615 C5
3500 LORN 44054 2615 D5
Sterling Wy
20300 SGVL 44136 3146 B1
Sterling Glen Ln
17700 AbnT 44023 2892 B5
Sterncrest Dr
10 MDHL 44022 2759 D5
10 ORNG 44022 2759 D5
Sterns Rd
400 OBLN 44074 3139 A1
Steven Blvd
300 RDHT 44143 2498 D2
Steven Dr
3600 SVHL 44131 2884 B4
Steven David Dr
7900 SGVL 44136 3011 A2
Stevens Blvd
100 LKLN 44095 2249 E3
400 ETLK 44095 2249 E3
33700 ETLK 44095 2250 A3
36300 WLBY 44094 2250 B4
Stevens St
4600 LORN 44053 2743 D2
Stevenson Rd
800 CLEV 44110 2497 C2
Stevenson St
5100 RDHT 44143 2498 E3
5100 RDHT 44143 2499 A3
Stewart Av
9000 CLEV 44108 2496 B5
Stewart Ct
25400 OKWD 44146 2887 D7
Stewart Dr
29300 NOSD 44070 2878 C2
Stewart St
10 OBLN 44074 3139 A3
Stick Rd
48600 BhmT 44001 2871 D7
Stickney Av
3500 CLEV 44109 2754 B5
4100 CLEV 44144 2754 B5
Stillbrooke Dr
14600 SGVL 44136 3146 E1
Stillman Rd
2000 CVHT 44118 2627 B3
Stillson Av
2900 CLEV 44105 2755 B1
Still Water Blvd
- ELYR 44035 3007 A2
Stillwater Dr
14900 RslT 44073 2761 E2
Stillwater Ln
30100 SLN 44139 2759 C7
30100 SLN 44139 2888 C1
Stillwell Rd
14500 ClrT 44024 2506 E5
14600 ClrT 44024 2507 B5
15200 HtbT 44024 2507 B5
15500 HtbT 44046 2507 B5
Stillwood Av
15700 CLEV 44111 2752 C1
Stilmore Rd
4000 SELD 44121 2628 A2
Stimson Ct
3100 CLEV 44109 2754 D4
Stirling Dr
- HDHT 44143 2499 C2
Stirling Rd
1600 MadT 44057 1843 A7
1600 MadT 44057 1942 A1
Stirrup Ct
8300 MNTR 44060 2251 D4
Stock Av
6400 CLEV 44102 2624 A7
Stockbridge Av
15500 CLEV 44128 2757 B3
Stockbridge Dr
12300 CsTp 44026 2501 C6
Stockbridge Rd
7900 MNTR 44060 2251 C4
Stockholm Rd
3200 SRHT 44120 2627 C7
Stocking Rd
7500 HpfT 44057 2151 A2
7500 HpfT 44086 2151 A2
7500 MadT 44057 2150 D2
7500 MadT 44057 2151 A2
7500 MadT 44086 2151 A2
7500 TmbT 44086 2151 A2
7500 TpnT 44057 2150 D2
7500 TpnT 44086 2150 D2
7500 TpnT 44086 2151 A2
17100 TpnT 44057 2150 D2
Stockton Av
19100 MPHT 44137 2886 E1
19800 MPHT 44137 2887 A1
Stockton Ln
17500 BbgT 44023 2891 D4
Stockwell St
10 PNVL 44077 2146 B2
Stockwood Dr
- SLN 44139 3020 C1
Stoer Rd
3500 SRHT 44122 2757 E2
Stokes Blvd
1900 CLEV 44106 2626 C2
10800 CLEV 44104 2626 D3
Stoltz Rd
400 HpfT 44041 2045 D7
800 HpfT 44041 2151 D2
Stone Av
5400 CLEV 44102 2624 A4
Stone Ct
1300 WTLK 44145 2620 B7
Stone Rd
- INDE 44125 2885 A6
7100 INDE 44131 2884 E5
7300 INDE 44131 2885 A5
9200 VLVW 44125 2885 C4
14400 NbyT 44065 2634 D7
14400 NbyT 44065 2764 D1
Stonebridge Ct
5200 SLN 44139 2759 C7
Stonebridge Dr
- AMHT 44001 2872 C1
200 SgHT 44067 3017 D5
Stone Canyon Ct
- HkyT 44233 3149 D6
Stonecreek Dr
10 CFIT 44022 2761 A4

STREET Block City ZIP Map# Grid

Stone Creek Ln
- CcdT 44077 2254 D3
1600 TNBG 44087 3019 B5
Stonecrest Dr
6300 BKPK 44142 2881 B4
Stonefield Dr
2200 AVON 44011 2747 A2
Stonefield Pl
39300 AVON 44011 2747 A1
Stonegate Cir
27900 WTLK 44145 2749 E4
Stonegate Dr
11500 MsnT 44024 2503 C3
Stoneham Rd
7300 GSML 44040 2630 D2
10900 PMHT 44130 2882 B3
Stonehaven Cir
- HDSN 44236 3154 A6
Stonehaven Dr
200 PNVL 44077 2146 C2
N Stonehaven Dr
300 HDHT 44143 2499 C2
S Stonehaven Dr
300 HDHT 44143 2499 C2
Stonehaven Rd
1600 MadT 44057 1842 E7
1700 MadT 44057 1941 E1
4000 SELD 44121 2628 A2
Stonehedge Dr
10100 CcdT 44077 2145 D7
14700 RslT 44072 2761 D1
23800 WTLK 44145 2750 D2
24100 NOSD 44070 2750 D2
24100 NOSD 44145 2750 D2
Stonehedge Wy
10 AMHT 44001 2872 C3
Stonehill Ln
10 MDHL 44022 2760 A2
Stone Hill Ovl
800 AURA 44202 3021 B6
Stonehinge Cir
10600 NRYN 44133 3014 A5
Stone Hollow Rd
9900 CcdT 44060 2253 C3
Stonelake Dr
1800 LNHT 44122 2628 D3
Stoneledge Dr
11100 ClrT 44024 2506 E2
Stoneleigh Rd
3600 CVHT 44121 2497 E4
Stone Mill Dr
9400 MNTR 44060 2253 A2
Stoneridge Rd
7800 MCDN 44056 3154 B5
16300 BbgT 44022 2761 B7
16300 BbgT 44023 2761 B7
Stoneridge Tr
13400 SGVL 44136 3147 D5
Stones Levee
400 CLEV 44113 2624 E4
Stone's Throw
2200 WTLK 44145 2750 C1
Stoneville Rd
5900 WndT 44099 2509 E3
Stonewood Ct
1000 WTLK 44145 2621 A7
1200 PnvT 44077 2041 A7
7300 MNTR 44060 2252 E1
Stonewood Dr
10 MDHL 44022 2760 A2
Stonewood Ln
6200 SLN 44139 2889 C5
Stonewood St
- AVON 44011 2747 D1
Stoney Ln
5400 PryT 44077 2041 B7
5400 PryT 44077 2147 B1
Stoney Brook Cir
1100 MCDN 44056 3154 B4
Stoney Brook Ct
18000 BbgT 44023 2890 E6
Stoney Brook Dr
8100 BbgT 44023 2890 E7
8100 BbgT 44023 2891 A6
32200 AVLK 44012 2618 C1
Stoneybrook Dr
8900 BWHT 44147 3015 A6
Stoneybrook Ln
7900 MNTR 44060 2251 E3
Stoney Brook Rd
600 SgHT 44067 3152 C1
Stoneybrook Rd
22900 NOSD 44070 2750 E3
22900 NOSD 44070 2751 A3
Stoney Creek Dr
3000 NRYN 44133 3014 B7
Stoney Creek Ln
9100 PMHT 44130 2882 C5
Stoneyridge Dr
2600 MadT 44057 1942 A3
Stoney Ridge Ln
600 RDHT 44143 2498 E4
Stoney Ridge Rd
2500 AVON 44011 2747 D2
4800 NRDV 44011 2747 C7
4800 NRDV 44039 2747 C7
4800 NRDV 44039 2876 D1
Stoney Run Cir
1700 BWHT 44147 3015 A7
Stoney Run Tr
10 BWHT 44147 3014 E7
10 BWHT 44147 3015 A7
Stoney Springs Dr
12700 ClrT 44024 2635 D1
13400 ClrT 44024 2636 A1
Stonington Dr
1500 HDSN 44236 3154 D7
Stonington Rd
9100 PMHT 44130 2882 C3
Stonybrook Dr
7300 MDBH 44130 2881 C7
7300 MDBH 44130 3012 C1
Stony Brook Ln
32500 SLN 44139 2888 E2
Stony Point Dr
17900 SGVL 44136 3147 C5
Storer Av
3300 CLEV 44109 2754 C1
4600 CLEV 44102 2754 A1
Stormes Dr
11400 PRMA 44130 3013 A2
Storrington Ovl
5500 PRMA 44134 2883 E1
Storrs St
400 PNVL 44077 2040 B6

STREET
Block City ZIP Map# Grid

Story Rd
3900 FWPK 44126 2752 A1
18800 FWPK 44126 2751 E1
18900 FWPK 44116 2751 E1
18900 RKRV 44116 2751 E1
18900 RKRV 44126 2751 E1
Storybook Ln
11800 CsTp 44026 2501 E4
Stoughton Av
9600 CLEV 44104 2626 B6
Stoughton Dr
19400 SGVL 44136 3146 C2
Stover Ln
8800 BKVL 44141 3016 B6
Stow Rd
7600 HDSN 44236 3155 C7
7900 TwbT 44236 3155 D6
8000 TwbT 44087 3155 D6
Stow Away Cove
400 AVLK 44012 2618 E3
Strandhill Rd
3500 SRHT 44122 2757 D2
3700 CLEV 44122 2757 D3
3700 CLEV 44128 2757 D3
Stratford Av
20500 RKRV 44116 2621 C5
Stratford Cir
6800 MNTR 44060 2143 E6
20600 SGVL 44136 3146 B1
Stratford Ct
- AURA 44202 3021 E6
10 BHWD 44122 2628 E4
900 MAYF 44143 2500 A5
900 STBR 44241 3156 D7
Stratford Dr
200 NHFD 44067 3018 B5
6100 PMHT 44130 2882 C4
7800 PRMA 44129 2882 D4
7900 NRYN 44133 3013 D7
30500 SLN 44139 2888 D2
Stratford Rd
10 PnvT 44077 2145 C5
200 CcdT 44077 2145 C5
2300 CVHT 44118 2627 B5
Stratford Tr
12900 CsTp 44026 2631 C2
Stratford Ridge Dr
11100 CdnT 44024 2379 B4
Strathalan Dr
6200 BDHT 44146 2887 D5
Strathaven Dr
5400 HDHT 44143 2499 B2
Strathavon Rd
3500 SRHT 44120 2757 C2
Strathmore Av
1700 ECLE 44112 2497 A5
Strathmore Dr
6500 VLVW 44125 2885 E5
6500 VLVW 44125 2886 A6
Stratton Ct
9800 CcdT 44060 2145 B7
Stratton Rd
3400 BHWD 44122 2758 C1
Strauss Dr
1800 WTLK 44145 2750 A1
Strawberry Ln
- MAYF 44094 2500 B1
- MAYF 44143 2500 B1
- MsnT 44026 2503 B6
- WBHL 44094 2375 B6
- WBHL 44094 2500 B1
5000 WLBY 44094 2250 C7
5000 WLBY 44094 2375 C1
26300 WTLK 44145 2750 A4
N Strawberry Ln
10 MDHL 44022 2760 A3
S Strawberry Ln
100 MDHL 44022 2760 A3
Strawbridge Ct
10 BHWD 44122 2629 B4
8600 MCDN 44056 3018 B7
Streator Pl
1000 LORN 44052 2614 E7
Strongsville Blvd
7900 SGVL 44136 3011 E2
17800 SGVL 44136 3012 A3
Strother Av
- PnvT 44077 2039 B6
Stroud Rd
6700 MDBH 44130 2881 C5
Struhar Dr
2400 RKRV 44116 2621 E7
Strumbly Dr
500 HDHT 44143 2499 A4
Strumbly Pl
38100 WLBY 44094 2250 E2
Stuart Ct
3100 NRYN 44133 3014 C3
Stuart Dr
800 SELD 44121 2498 C5
10400 CcdT 44077 2145 E6
Stuart Ln
8700 SgHT 44067 3017 E4
Stuart Rd
3600 CVHT 44112 2497 C6
Stubbins Rd
2600 RchT 44141 3151 B7
Stuble Ln
7200 WNHL 44146 3017 D1
Stuckey Ln
9700 CdnT 44024 2378 B6
Stumph Rd
5800 PMHT 44130 2882 A3
5800 PRMA 44130 2882 A3
Stump Hollow Ln
7300 RslT 44072 2631 B7
Sturbridge Ct
5300 SFLD 44054 2746 E4
Sturbridge Dr
500 HDHT 44143 2499 C3
6900 CcdT 44077 2146 C7
Sturbridge Ln
3400 BNWK 44212 3147 B6
27200 WTLK 44145 2620 A6
37300 WLBY 44094 2250 D3
Substation Rd
10 BHIT 44212 3146 B7
Success Blvd
- PryT 44081 2042 B1
Sudbury Dr
26400 NOSD 44070 2750 A5
Sudbury Rd
1700 GSML 44040 2630 D1
3600 SRHT 44120 2757 C2
Suffield Rd
6600 MDHT 44124 2630 A3
Suffolk Ln
2400 PRPK 44124 2629 C3
3000 BNWK 44212 3147 C7
15200 RslT 44073 2761 D4
Suffolk Rd
3900 SELD 44121 2498 A4
Sugar Ct
11100 NRYN 44133 3013 B4
Sugar Ln
600 ELYR 44035 2875 E7
600 ELYR 44035 3006 E1
Sugarbush Cir
400 BHIT 44212 3146 A7
9700 ODFL 44138 3010 E2
Sugarbush Dr
9100 MNTR 44060 2144 E5
Sugarbush Gln
100 CRDN 44024 2505 B2
Sugar Bush Ln
10 SRSL 44073 2762 A6
Sugarbush Ln
7100 RslT 44073 2761 B3
7700 GSML 44040 2500 E1
7700 GSML 44040 2501 A1
Sugarbush Tr
7500 HDSN 44236 3155 D7
Sugar Hill Tr
17300 BbgT 44023 2891 B3
Sugar Ridge Rd
36000 NRDV 44039 2877 A6
36300 NRDV 44039 2876 D5
39400 NRDV 44039 2875 E7
Sugar Sand Ln
7100 NOSD 44070 2878 A4
Sugar Tree Dr
8500 RslT 44072 2762 B3
Sugarwood Tr
10100 MsnT 44026 2503 C7
10100 MsnT 44026 2633 C1
E Sulgrave Ovl
2900 BHWD 44122 2628 D7
2900 SRHT 44122 2628 D7
W Sulgrave Ovl
2800 SRHT 44122 2628 D6
3000 BHWD 44122 2628 D6
Sulgrave Rd
2600 BHWD 44122 2628 D6
2600 SRHT 44122 2628 D6
Sullivan Dr
35000 NRDV 44039 2748 B7
Sullivan Rd
3700 TmbT 44084 2259 B5
3700 TmbT 44099 2259 B5
Sulphur Springs Dr
- BTVL 44022 2760 C7
- BTVL 44022 2889 C1
Sulzer Av
1400 EUCL 44132 2373 D5
Summer Ln
4800 BKLN 44144 2753 C6
Summer Rd
8300 MCDN 44056 3153 C1
8400 MCDN 44056 3018 C7
Summerdale Av
10300 GDHT 44125 2756 C6
Summerfield Rd
14400 UNHT 44118 2628 C4
Summer Hill Dr
7100 CcdT 44077 2145 E7
7100 CcdT 44077 2253 E1
Summerhill Dr
200 AURA 44202 3156 D4
34500 AVON 44011 2748 C5
Summerland Av
11800 CLEV 44111 2753 A3
22900 NOSD 44070 2750 E5
22900 NOSD 44070 2751 A5
Summerly Dr
1300 LORN 44053 2744 C5
Summer Place Dr
19600 SGVL 44136 3146 C2
Summers Rd
6100 HgvT 44099 2384 D5
6100 HgvT 44041 2384 D5
7000 HgvT 44064 2384 B5
11700 CsTp 44026 2501 E4
Summerset Dr
7700 WNHL 44146 3017 C2
11100 CrlT 44035 3005 D5
33900 SLN 44139 3020 A3
Summerset Ln
8800 ODFL 44138 3010 B1
Summersweet Tr
7900 SgHT 44067 3017 B5
Summer Wind Dr
6500 BKVL 44141 3150 B5
Summerwood Dr
- BWHT 44147 3015 A6
Summerwood Ln
5400 WLBY 44094 2375 A1
Summit
- CLEV 44113 2624 D2
- CLEV 44114 2624 D2
Summit Av
- GDHT 44125 2886 A3
10 NHFD 44067 3018 B3
1000 LKWD 44107 2622 C4
13900 MPHT 44137 2886 A3
Summit Blvd
1200 BWHT 44147 3014 E7
Summit Cir
5500 BKVL 44141 3015 E6
Summit Dr
- BtnT 44021 2635 E6
- MNTR 44060 2143 B7
1100 MDHT 44124 2499 C7
8200 BbgT 44023 2890 E2
8200 BbgT 44023 2891 A2
14700 NbyT 44065 2764 C1
Summit Ln
30500 PRPK 44124 2759 D1
Summit Ovl
5500 PRMA 44134 2883 E1
Summit Rd
- MsnT 44024 2504 D4
- RMDV 44202 3021 A4
5300 LNHT 44124 2629 A1
7300 BbgT 44023 3021 A2
7300 BbgT 44139 3021 A2
7300 SLN 44139 3021 A2
Summit St
4400 WLBY 44094 2250 E6
E Summit St
10 CNFL 44022 2761 A5
W Summit St
10 CNFL 44022 2760 E6
10 CNFL 44022 2761 A5
Summit Commerce Pk
1800 TNBG 44087 3154 E5
Summit Park Dr
10 INDE 44131 2884 C3
Summit Park Rd
3800 CVHT 44121 2497 E6
3800 CVHT 44121 2498 A6
Summitview Dr
7200 SVHL 44131 2884 A7
Sumner Av
900 CLEV 44115 2625 A3
Sumner Rd
7800 LryT 44086 2256 E4
8100 HmbT 44024 2256 E6
8100 LryT 44024 2256 E6
Sumner St
100 OBLN 44074 3138 E3
200 ELYR 44035 2875 C6
4500 SFLD 44054 2746 B2
45400 NRsT 44074 3139 A3
Sumpter Rd
18700 WVHT 44128 2757 E6
19800 WVHT 44128 2758 A6
Sun Av
- WKLF 44092 2374 A4
Sun Rd
- MtlT 44064 2383 C6
Sunbury Ovl
800 PNVL 44077 2040 A5
Suncliff Pl
17800 SGVL 44136 3011 E6
Sun Crest Ct
13400 SGVL 44136 3012 A7
Suncrest Ct
5500 PRMA 44134 2883 E1
Sunderland Dr
5500 PRMA 44129 2883 A3
6600 PRMA 44129 2882 D3
Sundew Ln
100 SRSL 44073 2761 E5
Sundown Tr
10000 NRYN 44133 3148 B5
Sunfish Cove
- AVON 44011 2748 C4
Sunflower Ct
7600 MNTR 44060 2143 D5
Sunflower Dr
100 BNWK 44212 3146 E6
Sunhaven Ovl
3200 PRMA 44134 3014 C1
Sunningdale Rd
1600 MDHT 44124 2629 D1
Sunny Ln
4700 BKLN 44144 2753 C6
Sunnycliff Av
9600 GDHT 44125 2885 B1
Sunnydale Dr
8200 BKVL 44141 3015 E5
Sunny Glen Av
16200 CLEV 44128 2757 C6
Sunny Hill Cir
4300 CLEV 44109 2754 E4
Sunnyhill Dr
22200 RKRV 44116 2751 A2
Sunny Lane Rd
5500 MPHT 44137 2886 B2
Sunnyside Av
14100 MDBH 44130 2881 D5
Sunnyside Dr
400 SAHT 44001 3003 D2
18200 CLEV 44110 2372 E7
Sunnyside Rd
400 VMLN 44089 2742 A6
1500 VMLN 44089 2871 A2
Sunnyslope Rd
5300 MPHT 44137 2887 A1
Sunnyvale Ct
9300 MNTR 44060 2252 E3
Sunnywood Dr
6200 SLN 44139 2889 B5
Sunnywood Ln
100 PnvT 44077 2146 D1
Sun Ray Dr
6100 PRMA 44134 2883 E3
Sun Ridge Cir
11700 MsnT 44024 2504 A4
Sunridge Cir
12300 SGVL 44136 3011 E6
Sun Ridge Ln
800 SRSL 44073 2762 C6
Sunrise Blvd
10 OmsT 44138 2879 C4
9500 NRYN 44133 3013 B5
Sunrise Ct
9300 MNTR 44060 2252 E1
Sunrise Dr
100 AMHT 44001 2743 D7
100 TroT 44234 2894 B6
Sunrise Ln
7800 RslT 44072 2631 D4
Sunrise Ovl
7400 MDBH 44130 3012 D1
7500 PRMA 44134 3014 C1
Sunrise Tr
10900 BKVL 44141 3016 C4
Sunrise Ridge Ln
- AbnT 44023 2892 A5
Sunset Av
- CLEV 44135 2751 E4
- CLEV 44135 2752 A4
500 SDLK 44054 2616 B4
6000 INDE 44131 2884 D5
Sunset Blvd
2300 LORN 44052 2744 B2
Sunset Ct
10 PnvT 44077 2040 D1
Sunset Dr
10 BERA 44017 2880 A7
10 SRSL 44073 2762 D6
400 AMHT 44001 2872 D2
600 MDSN 44057 2044 A2
1700 RDHT 44143 2373 E7
2100 WKLF 44092 2374 C3
5800 BDHT 44146 2887 E3
7000 MONT 44060 2143 B3
7000 MONT 44094 2143 B3
7000 WLBY 44094 2143 B3
9900 AbnT 44023 3023 B1
14600 NbyT 44065 2764 C1
15100 SGVL 44136 3147 A2
Sunset Dr
17000 BbgT 44023 2890 E3
19000 WVHT 44122 2757 E3
19700 WVHT 44122 2758 A3
24800 BYVL 44140 2620 D4
29200 WTLK 44145 2749 C1
36300 ETLK 44095 2142 C6
Sunset Ln
3000 MAYF 44094 2500 A1
3000 MAYF 44143 2500 A1
3000 WBHL 44094 2500 A1
5500 PRMA 44134 2883 E1
Sunset Ovl
4500 BKLN 44144 2753 C5
12300 NRYN 44133 3014 C6
24800 NOSD 44070 2879 C1
Sunset Rd
10 AVLK 44012 2488 C7
10 AVLK 44012 2618 C1
1100 MDHT 44124 2499 D7
6300 GDHT 44125 2885 D3
Sunset St
200 NHFD 44067 3017 E4
Sunset Tr
4500 BKLN 44144 2753 C5
Sunset Cove Cir
10 ETLK 44095 2142 B6
Sunshine Ct
1000 GFTN 44044 3142 B6
Sunshine Dr
10900 CdnT 44024 2254 A7
Sunstone Dr
7700 BKVL 44141 3016 D6
Sunview Av
14800 CLEV 44128 2757 A5
14800 GDHT 44128 2757 A5
Sunview Dr
1700 TNBG 44087 3019 C4
8500 BWHT 44147 3014 D5
Sunview Rd
1300 LNHT 44124 2499 B7
1400 LNHT 44124 2629 B1
Sun Vista Dr
7000 PRMA 44129 2882 E6
Sunwood Ovl
16400 SGVL 44136 3147 A5
Superior Av
- CLEV 44113 2624 D4
- ShfT 44055 2745 D6
4000 CLEV 44103 2625 C1
5100 CLEV 44103 2495 D7
7400 CLEV 44103 2496 A7
8400 CLEV 44106 2496 A7
8400 CLEV 44108 2496 A7
12500 ECLE 44112 2496 E7
Superior Av US-6
- CLEV 44113 2624 D4
4000 CLEV 44103 2625 C1
5100 CLEV 44103 2495 D7
7400 CLEV 44103 2496 A7
8400 CLEV 44106 2496 A7
8400 CLEV 44108 2496 A7
12500 ECLE 44112 2496 E7
Superior Av US-20
- CLEV 44113 2624 D4
Superior Av US-322
- CLEV 44113 2624 D4
W Superior Av
100 CLEV 44114 2624 E3
200 CLEV 44115 2624 D3
200 CLEV 44113 2624 D3
W Superior Av US-20
100 CLEV 44114 2624 E3
200 CLEV 44115 2624 D3
200 CLEV 44113 2624 D3
W Superior Av US-322
100 CLEV 44114 2624 E3
200 CLEV 44115 2624 D3
200 CLEV 44113 2624 D3
W Superior Av US-6
100 CLEV 44114 2624 E3
200 CLEV 44115 2624 D3
200 CLEV 44113 2624 D3
Superior Av E
10 CLEV 44114 2624 E3
1200 CLEV 44114 2625 B1
3800 CLEV 44103 2625 B1
Superior Av E US-6
10 CLEV 44114 2624 E3
1200 CLEV 44114 2625 B1
3800 CLEV 44103 2625 B1
Superior Av E US-20
10 CLEV 44114 2624 E3
Superior Av E US-322
10 CLEV 44114 2624 E3
1200 CLEV 44114 2625 A2
Superior Rd
13500 ECLE 44118 2497 A7
13900 ECLE 44112 2497 A7
14100 CVHT 44118 2627 D2
14100 ECLE 44112 2627 D2
14100 ECLE 44118 2627 D2
14700 UNHT 44118 2627 D2
Superior Park Dr
3300 CVHT 44118 2627 D2
Superior Viaduct
2200 CLEV 44113 2624 B3
Surf Av
2700 LORN 44053 2743 D2
Surfside Cir
1200 AURA 44202 3021 A5
3700 RMDV 44202 3020 E6
3700 RMDV 44202 3021 A5
N Surfside Cir
10000 AURA 44202 3021 A5
10000 RMDV 44202 3020 E5
10000 RMDV 44202 3021 A5
Surfside Ct
1200 AURA 44202 3021 A6
Surrey Cir
700 BERA 44017 3011 A2
24500 WTLK 44145 2750 D3
Surrey Ct
10 CcdT 44060 2145 B1
E Surrey Ct
3700 RKRV 44116 2751 E1
W Surrey Ct
3700 RKRV 44116 2751 E1
Surrey Dr
- AURA 44202 3157 A4
10 BNWK 44212 3146 E6
6200 NOSD 44070 2878 C3
Surrey Ln
10 CLEV 44110 2372 C5
10 GNVA 44041 1944 C7
Surrey Ln
7200 CsTp 44026 2501 B4
32500 AVLK 44012 2618 A1
Surrey Pl
1800 GSML 44040 2630 C2
Surrey Rd
2000 CVHT 44106 2626 E3
Surrey Downs Dr
14900 RslT 44072 2762 B2
Surry Dr
200 NCtT 44067 3152 E2
Susan Av
17700 CLEV 44111 2752 A3
Susan Ct
500 ETLK 44095 2142 E7
Susan Dr
15300 BKPK 44142 2881 B3
Susan Ln
10 HmbT 44024 2381 A3
S Sussex Ct
- AURA 44202 3021 C7
Sussex Dr
100 ELYR 44035 2874 A6
200 AURA 44202 3021 C6
9200 ODFL 44138 3010 A1
Sussex Pl
2200 MadT 44057 1942 B2
Sussex Rd
19600 SRHT 44122 2757 E1
19600 SRHT 44122 2758 A1
Sutcliffe Dr
400 BYVL 44140 2619 E5
Sutherland Av
6700 PMHT 44130 2882 B5
Sutherland Ct
6800 MNTR 44060 2143 D6
Sutherland Dr
300 HDHT 44143 2499 D2
Sutherland Rd
3500 SRHT 44122 2757 E2
Sutton Dr
6500 NOSD 44070 2878 C3
Sutton Ln
5500 WLBY 44094 2375 A1
Sutton Pl
- SRHT 44120 2627 B7
- SRHT 44120 2757 B1
6800 MDBH 44130 2881 B5
Sutton Rd
3200 SRHT 44120 2627 B7
3500 PRHT 44124 2759 A1
Suwanee Av
24900 OKWD 44146 2887 D7
Suwanee Dr
5800 MONT 44060 2143 C2
Suzanne Ln
6400 SLN 44139 2889 D5
Svec Av
13100 CLEV 44120 2756 E2
13100 CLEV 44120 2757 A2
Swaffield Rd
4200 SELD 44121 2498 B6
Swallow Dr
7900 MCDN 44056 3153 C2
Swan St
10 GNVA 44041 1944 B4
Swan Lake Blvd
14000 NRYN 44133 3014 A7
14000 NRYN 44133 3149 A1
Swanson Ct
10300 CcdT 44077 2145 D5
Sweeney Av
5100 CLEV 44127 2625 D6
Sweet Bay Ct
2500 BWHT 44147 3149 D4
Sweetbay Dr
6000 NRYN 44133 3014 C4
Sweet Bay Ln
- CLEV 44105 2756 B4
Sweet Birch Dr
5800 BDHT 44146 2887 D3
Sweetbriar Ct
32500 NRDV 44039 2748 E7
Sweetbriar Dr
1000 VMLN 44089 2740 E7
1000 VMLN 44089 2741 A6
26300 NOSD 44070 2750 A5
Sweetbriar Ln
13800 RslT 44072 2631 C6
Sweetgrass Cir
- AURA 44202 3021 B6
Sweetgum Tr
7900 CcdT 44060 2253 B3
Sweet Hollow Dr
7500 MNTR 44060 2253 A1
Sweetleaf Ln
10000 NRYN 44133 3014 B4
Sweet Spice Ct
12100 NRYN 44133 3013 B4
Sweet Valley Dr
8000 VLVW 44125 2885 A3
Sweetwater Dr
2500 BKVL 44141 3150 B3
Sweet West Rd
4100 MstT 44062 2639 E5
Swetland Blvd
4800 RDHT 44143 2373 E7
4800 RDHT 44143 2498 E1
Swetland Ct
5000 RDHT 44143 2498 D1
5000 RDHT 44143 2499 A1
Swetland Rd
6500 MadT 44057 1843 B6
Swift St
- CLEV 44113 2624 D6
Swine Creek Rd
16300 MdfT 44062 2768 A5
17500 PkmT 44062 2768 E7
17600 PkmT 44062 2769 A7
17600 PkmT 44062 2898 A1
17800 FnTp 44062 2898 A1
Swingos Ct
1800 CLEV 44115 2625 A3
Switzer Rd
23000 BKPK 44142 2879 E1
23000 BKPK 44142 2880 A1
Sycamore Cir
300 AVLK 44012 2618 C3
14000 SGVL 44136 3012 D4
Sycamore Ct
900 ETLK 44095 2250 B3
6300 INDE 44131 2884 C4
Sycamore Dr
- SFLD 44054 2746 A4
10 OmsT 44138 2879 B4
Sycamore Dr
10 PnvT 44077 2040 C2
400 AURA 44202 3021 C5
500 EUCL 44132 2374 A1
4600 LORN 44053 2744 C5
22200 FWPK 44126 2751 A6
Sycamore Ln
- AURA 44202 3021 C6
100 CrlT 44044 3006 D7
Sycamore Ovl
29900 WTLK 44145 2749 C6
Sycamore Rd
3100 CVHT 44118 2627 C1
6400 MNTR 44060 2143 E5
11600 MsnT 44024 2504 B3
Sycamore St
10 CLEV 44110 2372 C6
10 OBLN 44074 3138 B3
800 ELYR 44035 2875 D4
2000 CLEV 44113 2624 C3
35300 NRDV 44039 2877 A2
Sydenham Rd
20600 SRHT 44122 2628 A6
Sykora Rd
3500 CLEV 44105 2755 C1
Sylmar Dr
5700 BWHT 44147 3015 D4
Sylvan Av
1000 LKWD 44107 2622 C3
Sylvan Dr
29500 WLWK 44095 2249 B6
Sylvan Ln
9700 CcdT 44060 2145 B7
Sylvan Rd
- GnvT 44041 1944 E4
15800 RslT 44073 2761 D5
Sylvanhurst Ln
9700 MsnT 44026 2503 A6
Sylvanhurst Rd
3300 CVHT 44112 2497 D6
Sylvania Rd
1100 CVHT 44121 2498 A6
Sylvia Av
14000 CLEV 44110 2497 A1
Sylvia Ct
6200 BKPK 44142 2880 E3
Sylvia Dr
300 CRDN 44024 2380 B7
6100 BKPK 44142 2880 E3
8600 MNTR 44060 2144 C7
14500 BKPK 44142 2881 C3
34000 ETLK 44095 2249 E2
34100 ETLK 44095 2250 A2
Symphony St
10 OmsT 44138 2879 A4
Syracuse Av
18000 CLEV 44110 2372 D7
Syracuse Ct
200 ELYR 44035 3006 D2

T

Tabernacle St
- VMLN 44089 2741 A5
Tabor Av
14100 MPHT 44137 2886 A2
Tacoma Av
- ShfT 44055 2746 A5
2800 LORN 44055 2746 A3
10500 CLEV 44108 2496 C6
Taft Av
100 ELYR 44035 2875 A5
300 BDFD 44146 2887 B3
2000 ShfT 44055 2745 E6
12200 CLEV 44108 2496 E3
Taft St
7100 MNTR 44060 2143 C7
7300 MNTR 44060 2251 C1
Tait St
1400 LORN 44053 2744 A1
Talbot Av
- WLBY 44094 2250 C5
9300 CLEV 44106 2626 B1
Talbot Dr
10 BDFD 44146 2887 A3
6800 PRMA 44129 2882 E5
6800 PRMA 44129 2883 A6
Talbot Ln
4200 LORN 44055 2746 B4
Talford Av
15500 CLEV 44128 2757 C2
Talford Dr
800 SVHL 44131 2884 A3
Tall Oaks Dr
6000 MONT 44060 2143 C3
6100 MNTR 44060 2143 C3
Tall Oaks Tr
26900 OmsT 44138 2878 E4
Tallow Tree Dr
- MsnT 44024 2635 A1
12800 MsnT 44024 2634 D1
Tall Pines Dr
11600 MsnT 44024 2504 D1
Tall Timber Cir
12600 NRYN 44133 3013 C6
Tall Timbers Dr
5000 RchT 44286 3150 C6
Tall Tree Tr
2900 WBHL 44092 2374 C7
17300 BbgT 44023 2890 C3
Tallwood Ct
4200 NOSD 44070 2750 B5
10500 CcdT 44077 2145 E7
Tallwood Dr
25700 NOSD 44070 2750 B5
Tallyho Ct
33500 SLN 44139 3020 A1
Tallyho Dr
33100 SLN 44139 3019 E1
33300 SLN 44139 3020 A1
Tally Ho Ln
400 RDHT 44143 2498 E3
Talmadge Av
800 WKLF 44092 2249 B7
800 WKLF 44092 2374 B1
Tamalga Dr
4200 SELD 44121 2498 B6
Tamarac Blvd
1100 WLBY 44094 2142 E5
38000 WLBY 44094 2143 A5
Tamarack Dr
100 BERA 44017 2880 A7
3800 PRMA 44134 3014 B1
S Tamarack Dr
7500 PRMA 44134 3014 B2
Tamarack Tr
8500 BbgT 44023 3022 A1
9800 BKVL 44141 3150 B3
29800 WTLK 44145 2749 C6
Tamarin Ct
9500 MNTR 44060 2145 A7
Tamarind Dr
6500 BDHT 44146 2887 D6
Tamiami Dr
7500 PRMA 44134 3014 E1
Tamiami Tr
100 ClrT 44024 2505 C6
Tammany Ct
100 CcdT 44060 2145 B2
Tampa Av
1200 CLEV 44109 2754 C5
Tampico Ct
600 BERA 44017 3010 E1
Tanager Ct
5700 MNTR 44060 2144 E2
Tanager Dr
9500 HmbT 44024 2380 B2
Tanager Ovl
8000 BKVL 44141 3016 C3
Tanager Tr
10300 BKVL 44141 3016 C4
Tanbark Ln
19500 SGVL 44136 3011 D4
Tanbark Tr
9800 CcdT 44060 2253 B2
Tandem Ct
33300 SLN 44139 2889 A3
Tanglewood Ct
17400 BbgT 44023 2891 B4
32800 AVLK 44012 2618 A2
Tanglewood Dr
4600 LORN 44053 2744 C5
7100 INDE 44131 2884 E4
19100 NRYN 44133 3147 E5
Tanglewood Ln
- PRMA 44129 3013 D2
300 BYVL 44140 2619 B4
6300 SVHL 44131 2884 B4
Tanglewood Rd
9100 MCDN 44056 3018 E6
Tanglewood Sq
8500 BbgT 44023 2891 A5
Tanglewood Tr
8400 BbgT 44023 2891 B4
10700 CcdT 44077 2146 A4
Tanhollow Tr
1700 BWHT 44147 3149 D4
Tanner Av
9900 CLEV 44108 2496 B7
Tannery St
100 ELYR 44035 2875 B6
Tannery Wy
9700 ODFL 44138 3010 D1
Tappan Cir
800 VMLN 44089 2740 D6
Tappan Ovl
400 MDSN 44057 2044 A3
Tara-Lynn Dr
24600 NOSD 44070 2750 C4
Taras Dr
11300 NRYN 44133 3012 E5
Tarbell Av
10 BDFD 44146 2887 A4
6500 MadT 44057 1843 B7
Tarkington Av
16500 CLEV 44128 2757 C5
Tarlton Av
1500 CLEV 44109 2754 D4
Tarry Ln
100 ELYR 44035 2875 C2
900 AMHT 44001 2872 B2
Tarrymore Rd
17200 CLEV 44119 2372 D5
Tartan Ct
10 CNFL 44022 2761 B6
Tate Av
2000 CLEV 44109 2754 C5
Tatra Av
5000 MPHT 44137 2757 D7
Tattersall Ct
10 ELYR 44035 2874 D6
Tattersall Dr
7300 CsTp 44026 2501 C4
Taunton Av
7400 BKLN 44144 2753 E4
Tauton Dr
600 BERA 44017 3010 E1
Tavern Rd
14800 BtnT 44021 2766 B2
14800 BtnT 44062 2766 B2
14800 BURT 44021 2766 B2
16000 BtnT 44062 2767 A7
16000 BtnT 44021 2767 A7
16300 PkmT 44062 2896 B2
16300 PkmT 44021 2896 B2
16300 TroT 44021 2767 A7
16300 TroT 44062 2767 A7
16300 TroT 44021 2896 B2
16300 TroT 44062 2896 B2
17800 PkmT 44234 2896 C6
Tavern Rd SR-168
14800 BtnT 44021 2766 B2
14800 BtnT 44062 2766 B2
14800 BURT 44021 2766 B2
16000 BtnT 44021 2767 A7
16000 BtnT 44062 2767 A7
16300 PkmT 44021 2896 B2
16300 PkmT 44062 2896 B2
16300 TroT 44021 2767 A7
16300 TroT 44021 2896 B2
16300 TroT 44062 2767 A7
16300 TroT 44062 2896 B2
17800 PkmT 44234 2896 C6
Tavern Rd SR-700
14800 BtnT 44021 2766 B2
14800 BtnT 44062 2766 B2
14800 BURT 44021 2766 B2
Tawny Brook Ln
19400 SGVL 44136 3011 D5
Taylor Av
200 AhtT 44001 2872 E2
200 AMHT 44001 2872 E2
Taylor Ct
- SFLD 44054 2746 D4
4500 CLEV 44102 2624 B5
Taylor Ln
2500 TNBG 44087 3020 B4
4500 WVHT 44022 2758 E5
4500 WVHT 44128 2758 E5

INDEX 46
Taylor Pkwy
Cleveland Street Index
Truxton Pl

STREET Block City ZIP Map# Grid

Taylor Pkwy
37800 NRDV 44039 2876 C6
39100 NRDV 44039 2875 E6
39100 NRDV 44039 2876 A6
Taylor Pl
500 PNVL 44077 2040 A6
Taylor Rd
10 BDFD 44146 2887 A5
1700 ECLE 44112 2497 B4
5000 BDHT 44128 2758 C7
5600 LryT 44057 2148 B2
5600 LryT 44077 2148 B2
E Taylor Rd
10 BDFD 44146 2887 A5
N Taylor Rd
1800 ECLE 44112 2497 C5
2000 CVHT 44112 2497 C5
2300 CVHT 44121 2497 D6
2400 CVHT 44118 2497 D6
S Taylor Rd
1400 CVHT 44118 2497 D7
1400 CVHT 44118 2627 D1
2000 UNHT 44118 2627 D3
Taylor St
500 ELYR 44035 2875 D6
1300 ELYR 44039 2875 E6
25000 ODFL 44138 2879 C6
Taylor May Rd
8500 BbgT 44023 2891 B7
9300 AbnT 44023 2891 D7
9300 AbnT 44023 2892 A7
10900 AbnT 44023 2893 A6
11000 AbnT 44021 2893 B6
Taylors Mill Turn
1700 WTLK 44145 2749 E1
Taylor Wells Rd
11000 ClrT 44024 2506 A2
11000 HmbT 44024 2381 A7
11000 HmbT 44024 2506 A2
11700 ClrT 44024 2505 E5
12600 ClrT 44024 2635 E1
12700 BtnT 44024 2636 A2
12700 ClrT 44024 2636 A2
Tayport Dr
5400 SLN 44139 2888 E1
Teaberry Cir
100 SRSL 44073 2761 D5
Teal Ct
3400 RMDV 44202 3020 E4
4400 WTLK 44145 2749 B5
Teal Dr
- HmbT 44024 2381 E2
Teal Trc
100 MDHT 44124 2629 E2
Teal Cove
7000 CcdT 44077 2145 D7
Tea Rose Dr
7700 MNTR 44060 2252 E7
Teasel Ct
6700 SLN 44139 2889 B7
32000 AVLK 44012 2618 D4
Tecumseh Ct
10500 CLEV 44108 2496 C7
Tedman Ct
100 ELYR 44035 3006 B2
Tegam Wy
10 GNVA 44041 1944 B3
Telbir Av
19200 RKRV 44116 2621 D6
Telegraph Ln
4100 VMLN 44089 2741 C4
Telfair Av
16200 CLEV 44128 2757 C6
Telhurst Rd
4400 SELD 44121 2498 C7
Telling Dr
100 GNVA 44041 1944 D7
Temblethurst Rd
1800 SELD 44121 2628 B2
Temblett Av
11300 CLEV 44108 2496 D5
Temblett Ter
4400 SELD 44121 2628 C3
Temple Av
200 PnvT 44077 2039 B6
1500 MDHT 44124 2499 C4
1500 MDHT 44124 2629 C1
2000 LORN 44053 2744 B4
6800 CLEV 44127 2625 E7
Temple Ct
100 ELYR 44035 2875 B6
Temple Dr
19100 SGVL 44136 3146 D1
Tennessee Dr
100 ELYR 44035 3006 E2
Tenney St
100 AMHT 44001 2872 D2
900 AhtT 44001 2872 E2
Tennyson Av
3700 SDLK 44054 2615 E4
4000 SDLK 44054 2616 A3
Tennyson Ln
3900 NOSD 44070 2750 C5
Tennyson Rd
2600 CLEV 44104 2626 B5
Teresa Ct
3300 PryT 44081 1940 D7
Terminal Av
13000 CLEV 44135 2752 E4
13000 CLEV 44135 2753 B5
14300 CLEV 44135 2752 C4
Terminal Dr
- BKPK 44142 2880 E1
- CLEV 44135 2880 E1
7500 LORN 44053 2742 C6
Terminal Rd
- CLEV 44135 2880 D1
Ternes Ln
500 ELYR 44035 2875 E7
Terra Ln
- LORN 44053 2743 E7
100 AMHT 44001 2743 E7
100 AMHT 44001 2872 E1
900 AMHT 44053 2743 E7
Terrace Ct
10100 PRMA 44130 2882 C7
Terrace Dr
10 MdfT 44062 2768 B5
100 BDFD 44146 2887 A2
9800 TNBG 44087 3019 E4
27900 NOSD 44070 2878 E3
27900 NOSD 44138 2878 E3
Terrace Ln
100 BKLN 44144 2753 E5
Terrace Plz
500 WLWK 44095 2249 D5
Terrace Rd
13500 ECLE 44112 2497 A7
Terrace Park Dr
9000 MNTR 44060 2252 D1
Terre Dr
6300 BKPK 44142 2881 E4
Terrell Ct
400 RDHT 44143 2498 C3
Terrett Av
- CLEV 44113 2624 B5
Terry Ct
- EUCL 44132 2374 A4
17800 CLEV 44119 2372 D6
Tewksbury Ln
- ClrT 44024 2505 C2
8100 CcdT 44077 2253 C4
Texas Av
3700 ShfT 44055 2745 B4
7300 MNTR 44060 2143 C6
Thacker St
700 BERA 44017 2880 C4
Thackeray Av
5500 CLEV 44103 2625 D3
Thackeray Ct
8100 BWHT 44147 3015 B4
Thackeray Tr
400 RDHT 44143 2499 A3
Thames Av
- MPHT 44137 2886 D2
10 BDFD 44146 2886 D2
14500 CLEV 44110 2497 B1
Thames Dr
4600 NRYN 44133 3014 B3
Thatcher Dr
1300 PnvT 44077 2041 A6
Thatcher's Ln
14200 SGVL 44136 3146 D2
Thatchum Ln
7400 CcdT 44060 2253 D1
7400 CcdT 44077 2253 D1
Thayne Rd
1900 CVHT 44118 2627 D3
2000 UNHT 44118 2627 D3
The Bluffs
11600 SGVL 44136 3012 A6
The Burns
500 BERA 44017 2880 B4
The Capes Blvd
1000 PnvT 44077 2145 C4
Thelma Dr
300 SDLK 44054 2617 A3
Thelma St
33200 NRDV 44039 2877 D1
The Mall
100 BERA 44017 2880 B4
Theodore St
5100 MPHT 44137 2757 C7
Theota Av
- PRMA 44129 2882 D1
4500 PRMA 44134 2883 A1
5400 PRMA 44129 2883 A1
Theresa
- MNTR 44060 2144 E7
Theresa Ln
24500 NOSD 44070 2750 D5
Theresa St
33200 NRDV 44039 2748 D7
Thicket Ln
24400 ODFL 44138 2879 D7
Third St
- MNTR 44060 2144 E7
Thistle Ct
10200 BWHT 44147 3149 E4
Thistle Dr
7100 SLN 44139 3020 A1
Thistle Ln
7500 RsIT 44072 2631 D7
7600 RsIT 44072 2761 C1
Thistle Tr
300 MDHT 44124 2629 E2
Thistleridge Dr
900 MCDN 44056 3154 B5
Thistlewood Dr
6100 MNTR 44060 2143 D3
6100 MONT 44060 2143 D3
Thomas Ct
9100 MNTR 44060 2144 E1
Thomas Dr
10 MdfT 44062 2768 A5
Thomas St
10 OBLN 44074 3139 B2
5000 MPHT 44137 2757 D7
5300 MPHT 44137 2886 D1
15700 NbyT 44073 2763 B5
30000 WLWK 44095 2249 C6
Thomas Alva Dr
300 VMLN 44089 2741 C5
Thompson Av
14700 MDFD 44062 2767 D2
Thompson Blvd
14100 BKPK 44142 2881 D2
Thompson Dr
300 SAHT 44001 2872 C6
Thompson Rd
12400 VmnT 44089 2869 A3
15200 TpnT 44086 2149 B6
16100 TpnT 44086 2150 A5
17500 TmbT 44086 2151 A5
17500 TpnT 44086 2151 A5
Thompson Rd SR-528
- TpnT 44086 2150 B5
Thompson St
4100 PRRY 44081 2042 C3
Thompson-Rye Cir
10200 TNBG 44087 3020 A4
Thomson Cir
3200 RKRV 44116 2751 B2
Thor Ct
2500 PryT 44077 2041 B3
Thoreau Dr
5000 PRMA 44129 2883 A7
6300 PRMA 44129 2882 E7
Thoreau Rd
1200 LKWD 44107 2623 A4
Thorn Av
9600 CLEV 44108 2496 B6
Thornapple Dr
6600 MAYF 44040 2500 B4
6600 MAYF 44143 2500 B4
Thornapple Ln
3200 PRPK 44124 2760 A1
7200 SLN 44139 3020 A1
7800 RsIT 44072 2631 D7
Thornberry Ln
500 BHIT 44212 3146 D7
Thornbrook Av
6600 OmsT 44138 2879 B3
Thornbury Rd
5000 LNHT 44124 2498 E7
5000 LNHT 44124 2499 A7
Thorncliffe Blvd
7100 PRMA 44134 2883 D7
Thorne Av
8000 KTLD 44094 2376 E1
8000 KTLD 44094 2377 A1
Thorne Rd
3300 CVHT 44112 2497 D6
Thornfield Dr
39300 AVON 44011 2747 A2
Thorn Hill Dr
- ManT 44255 3159 A4
Thornhill Dr
700 CLEV 44108 2496 D5
1000 ECLE 44108 2496 D5
1000 ECLE 44112 2496 D5
Thornhill Ln
500 AURA 44202 3022 C7
Thornhope Rd
13200 CLEV 44135 2752 E5
Thornhurst Av
12500 GDHT 44105 2756 E4
13600 GDHT 44105 2757 A4
Thornhurst Dr
8000 NRYN 44133 3014 B3
Thornridge Av
19400 CLEV 44135 2751 D4
Thornridge Cir
4300 CLEV 44135 2751 D4
Thornsway Tr
- MAYF 44143 2500 B3
Thornton Av
- CLEV 44102 2623 B4
10900 GDHT 44125 2756 C7
Thornton Ct
- MCDN 44056 3153 D1
Thornton Dr
5400 PRMA 44129 2883 A3
7300 PRMA 44129 2882 D2
14700 NRYN 44133 3147 E1
Thorntree Dr
- BKVL 44141 3016 B5
3100 NRYN 44133 3014 C5
Thornwood Av
11400 CLEV 44108 2496 D6
Thornwood Blvd
700 ELYR 44035 2875 E1
Thornwood Rd
- VMLN 44089 2741 D5
Thorpe Rd
18000 AbnT 44023 2892 D7
18000 AbnT 44023 3023 D1
Thrasher Rd
12600 HrmT 44234 3025 D4
12800 TroT 44234 3025 D4
Thraves Rd
- MPHT 44137 2886 A2
12100 GDHT 44125 2885 D2
13600 GDHT 44125 2886 A2
Three Village Dr
5100 LNHT 44124 2628 E3
Throckley Av
15600 CLEV 44128 2757 C2
Thrush Av
10100 CLEV 44111 2753 B2
Thrush St
12200 LKWD 44107 2623 A6
Thunderbird Dr
5800 MONT 44060 2143 B3
6000 MPHT 44137 2886 A3
6100 MNTR 44060 2143 B3
Thurgood Av
3700 CLEV 44115 2625 C3
Thurman Av
2000 CLEV 44113 2624 E5
2300 CLEV 44113 2625 A5
Thwing Rd
10 CRDN 44024 2504 C1
10 MsnT 44024 2504 C1
9600 CdnT 44024 2378 B7
9600 CdnT 44094 2378 B7
9600 KTLD 44094 2378 B7
10000 CdnT 44024 2503 E1
10300 MsnT 44024 2503 E1
10800 CdnT 44024 2504 A1
Tibbetts Rd
10500 KTLD 44094 2376 D6
10500 KTLD 44094 2501 D1
Tibbitts St
10 GNVA 44041 1944 C5
W Tibbitts St
10 GNVA 44041 1944 B5
Tiber Ct
- MCDN 44056 3153 E6
- MCDN 44056 3154 A5
Tiber Dr
100 PNVL 44077 2146 B1
Tiber Pl
100 PNVL 44077 2146 B1
Tidewater Dr
37000 SLN 44139 3020 C2
Tiedeman Rd
4200 BKLN 44144 2753 C5
5200 PRMA 44144 2753 C5
5200 PRMA 44130 2753 C5
Tiffany Ct
- LNHT 44124 2629 C3
35400 AVON 44011 2748 B3
Tiffany Dr
8600 NRYN 44133 3014 B3
10400 CcdT 44077 2145 D7
10400 CcdT 44077 2253 D1
Tiffany Ln
10600 PMHT 44130 2882 B5
Tiffany Rdg
22500 RKRV 44116 2751 A1
Tiffin Ct
6100 MNTR 44060 2144 B3
Tilby Rd
7100 NRYN 44133 3013 D3
Tilden Av
100 CRDN 44024 2379 E7
Tilden Rd
13000 HrmT 44234 3026 A4
13000 TroT 44234 3026 A4
Tilden St
- VMLN 44089 2740 E5
12900 TroT 44234 2895 A7
18300 TroT 44234 3026 A1
Tillman Av
4600 CLEV 44102 2624 B4
Tillotson St
600 ELYR 44035 2875 A2
Timber Av
7700 TwbT 44236 3154 D5
Timber Ct
1700 TNBG 44087 3019 C3
Timber Ln
100 AURA 44202 3156 E3
700 GNVA 44041 1944 D4
7100 OmsT 44138 2878 E4
8100 CcdT 44077 2254 C5
10800 AbnT 44023 2892 E3
14700 MDBH 44130 2881 C7
14700 MDBH 44130 3012 C1
18800 FWPK 44126 2752 A1
30400 BYVL 44140 2619 B3
Timber Pt
11700 ManT 44255 3159 D2
Timber Tr
1000 GFTN 44044 3142 A3
1300 TwbT 44236 3154 C6
5900 NOSD 44070 2878 B2
8000 BKVL 44141 3016 B5
8200 BbgT 44023 3021 E3
8200 BbgT 44023 3022 A2
Timber Cove
25600 NOSD 44070 2750 B6
Timber Creek Cir
19100 SGVL 44136 3147 A5
Timbercreek Dr
10300 KTLD 44094 2376 B5
Timbercreek Rd
600 SgHT 44067 3152 C2
Timber Edge Dr
- NRDV 44039 2877 E7
4700 RchT 44286 3150 C7
Timber Edge Pl
11500 SGVL 44136 3012 C5
Timberidge Ct
9400 MNTR 44060 2145 A7
Timberidge Tr
300 GSML 44040 2500 E2
Timber Lake Dr
13900 SGVL 44136 3012 C4
Timberland Ln
1000 TNBG 44087 3019 A4
Timberlane Dr
100 ELYR 44035 2746 C7
300 AVLK 44012 2618 A2
6100 INDE 44131 3015 D2
23100 BHWD 44122 2628 C4
35400 SLN 44139 2889 B3
Timberlane Rd
23800 WVHT 44128 2758 C5
Timberlane St
10 NCtT 44067 3018 A7
Timberlane Tr
8900 NRYN 44133 3013 B3
Timber Lea Ct
1300 WTLK 44145 2620 D7
Timberline Dr
2500 WBHL 44094 2375 A4
16400 SGVL 44136 3147 A4
Timberline Tr
500 MAYF 44143 2500 B3
700 SgHT 44067 3152 C2
Timber Oak Ct
21300 SGVL 44136 3011 B5
Timber Ridge Dr
- MCDN 44056 3153 E1
- MCDN 44056 3154 A1
10 CNFL 44022 2760 E5
10 CNFL 44022 2761 A5
4400 INDE 44131 3015 C1
7900 NRYN 44133 3013 C2
15000 MDFD 44062 2767 B2
Timber Ridge Ln
35500 WLBY 44094 2375 B2
Timber View Dr
4600 VMLN 44089 2741 A7
Timberview Dr
800 AMHT 44001 2743 E7
800 AMHT 44001 2744 A7
4600 LORN 44053 2744 B5
34700 AVON 44011 2748 C4
Timberwood Dr
2700 BWHT 44147 3014 C5
Timeless Ln
6400 MadT 44057 1942 A3
Timothy Cir
32500 SLN 44139 2888 E2
Timothy Dr
7300 NRDV 44039 2877 C4
Timothy Ln
600 CLEV 44109 2755 A5
700 CLEV 44109 2754 E5
9100 KTLD 44094 2251 D7
10000 TNBG 44087 3020 B4
12200 BKVL 44141 3151 E4
Tina Ln
48200 AhtT 44001 2872 A2
Tinker Av
100 PNVL 44077 2146 A1
Tinkers Ct
27200 GNWL 44139 2888 B7
Tinkers Ln
700 SgHT 44067 3152 C1
2700 TNBG 44087 3155 A1
Tinkers Tr
100 CRDN 44024 2505 B2
200 AURA 44202 3156 D4
Tinkers Creek Dr
10 AURA 44202 3156 D4
Tinkers Creek Rd
10900 VLVW 44125 2885 D7
10900 VLVW 44125 2886 A6
14000 WNHL 44146 2886 A6
Tinkers Valley Dr
27000 GNWL 44139 2888 A7
Tinkers View Dr
1600 TNBG 44087 3019 C3
Tin Man Rd
- MNTR 44060 2144 D4
Tiny Ln
- VLVW 44125 2885 B2
Tioga Av
8300 CLEV 44105 2756 B4
Tioga Tr
500 WLBY 44094 2143 A4
Tiolki Ln
- GTVL 44234 3161 E5
- HrmT 44234 3161 E5
Tipperary Ln
9500 MNTR 44060 2145 A5
Titan Dr
3100 NRYN 44133 3014 C6
Titus Av
2200 CLEV 44109 2754 D1
Titus Hill Ln
- AVLK 44012 2617 E4
- AVLK 44012 2618 A4
Tiverton Rd
- CLEV 44110 2373 A7
Tobik Tr
6700 PMHT 44130 2882 C5
Todd Dr
5200 MadT 44057 1941 A4
5200 MadT 44081 1941 A4
Tokay Av
14100 MPHT 44137 2886 A2
Toledo Av
2700 LORN 44052 2745 A2
2800 LORN 44055 2745 A3
4100 ShfT 44052 2745 A4
4100 ShfT 44055 2745 A4
Toledo St
- VMLN 44089 2740 E5
Tolland Rd
3500 SRHT 44122 2757 E2
Tollis Pkwy
400 BWHT 44147 3014 D5
Tom Ln
4500 CLEV 44109 2754 E5
Tomahawk Dr
10 AVLK 44012 2618 E2
Tomahawk Ln
4200 VMLN 44089 2741 B6
Tompkins Av
8500 CLEV 44102 2623 D6
Tomson Dr
13100 SGVL 44136 3011 C7
Tonawanda Dr
2600 RKRV 44116 2621 A7
2600 RKRV 44116 2751 A1
Tonbridge Ct
6200 BDHT 44146 2887 D5
Tonsing Dr
11400 GDHT 44125 2885 D1
12200 GDHT 44125 2756 D7
Topaz Ln
600 BHIT 44212 3146 B7
Topaz St
34100 NRDV 44039 2748 C7
Topeka Av
13800 CLEV 44110 2497 A2
Topping Ln
3000 HGVL 44022 2630 B6
Topps Industrial Pk
4700 WLBY 44094 2250 B6
Top Rail Ln
8300 RsIT 44072 2762 A1
Torbenson Dr
1800 CLEV 44112 2497 D3
Torrance Av
8600 BKLN 44144 2753 D4
Torrington Av
2400 PRMA 44134 2883 B1
Torrington Rd
2800 SRHT 44120 2627 D7
2800 SRHT 44122 2627 D7
Tortugas Ln
9100 MNTR 44060 2144 E2
Torwood Ct
4300 CLEV 44109 2754 B2
Toscana Dr
- NRYN 44133 3014 C4
Tourelle Dr
6100 HDHT 44143 2499 D2
Tournament Dr
- AVLK 44012 2618 C4
Tower Blvd
700 LORN 44052 2744 D4
1200 LORN 44053 2744 D4
Tower Dr
20300 WNHL 44146 3018 A1
Tower Park Dr
8400 TwbT 44087 3154 C3
Town Centre Dr
7500 BWHT 44147 3150 A1
9000 BWHT 44147 3149 E1
Townley Rd
3500 SRHT 44122 2757 E2
Townline Rd
200 AURA 44202 3022 E7
200 AURA 44202 3157 E1
200 ManT 44202 3022 E7
200 ManT 44202 3157 E1
2100 MadT 44057 1941 A2
2100 MadT 44081 1941 A2
2100 NPRY 44081 1941 A2
3000 PryT 44081 1941 A7
3400 MadT 44057 2043 A1
3400 MadT 44081 2043 A1
3400 PryT 44081 2043 A1
12400 HtbT 44046 2509 A7
12400 HtbT 44046 2639 A1
12400 WndT 44046 2509 A7
12400 WndT 44099 2509 A7
12400 WndT 44046 2509 A7
12400 WndT 44046 2639 A1
12400 WndT 44099 2639 A1
Townmill Ct
300 PNVL 44077 2146 A2
Towns Ln
500 RDHT 44143 2498 C3
Townsend Av
7900 CLEV 44104 2626 A4
Townsend Ct
100 CcdT 44060 2145 B7
Townsend Rd
4700 RchT 44286 3150 D6
4700 RHFD 44286 3150 D6
5200 BKVL 44141 3150 D6
5200 RchT 44141 3150 D6
Towpath Dr
- VLVW 44125 2885 B3
Towpath Rd
600 BWHT 44147 3149 E4
600 BWHT 44147 3150 A4
Trabar Dr
2700 WBHL 44092 2374 C5
Track Av
4500 CLEV 44127 2625 D6
Track Rd
11700 NbyT 44065 2764 D1
Tracy Av
20100 EUCL 44123 2373 A4
Tracy Ln
10 TroT 44234 2894 B6
15100 SGVL 44136 3147 B1
31900 SLN 44139 2888 E2
Tracy Tr
9000 PRMA 44129 2882 C7
9000 PRMA 44130 2882 C7
Tradewinds Dr
- AVLK 44012 2618 E2
12700 NRYN 44133 3147 D4
13000 SGVL 44136 3147 D4
31900 AVLK 44012 2619 A2
Tradewinds Cove
3400 RMDV 44202 3020 D5
Trafalgar Av
15600 CLEV 44110 2372 C7
Trafalgar Sq
2600 WLBY 44094 2250 E1
Trail Run
8900 BKLN 44144 2753 D4
Trailard Dr
2300 WBHL 44094 2375 E3
Trail End
10 AURA 44202 3157 B1
Trail End Dr
700 AhtT 44001 2873 C2
Trails Lndg
15000 SGVL 44136 3147 C5
Trails Edge Ct
13400 SGVL 44136 3012 A7
Trails End
7500 BbgT 44023 2890 C4
Trails End Ct
4800 WTLK 44145 2749 A6
Trails End Dr
28600 SLN 44139 2888 B1
Trailside Dr
7300 SgHT 44067 3152 A1
Trailside Pl
18100 SGVL 44136 3011 E6
Trailwood Ct
8900 MNTR 44060 2144 D4
32500 SLN 44139 2759 E7
Trailwood Dr
300 PNVL 44077 2146 B2
1900 TNBG 44087 3019 D4
17500 HtbT 44046 2508 E6
17600 HtbT 44046 2509 A5
Train Av
1700 CLEV 44113 2624 D5
4300 CLEV 44102 2624 B7
Train Ct
- CLEV 44102 2624 A7
Tranquility Ln
4400 LORN 44053 2744 A4
Transit St
100 PNVL 44077 2039 E6
Transport Rd
2600 CLEV 44115 2625 B5
Transportation Blvd
5300 GDHT 44125 2756 C7
5300 GDHT 44125 2885 C1
Trapper Tr
19800 SGVL 44136 3146 C1
Trappers Tr
14800 RsIT 44072 2761 C1
Trask Rd
2600 TmbT 44084 2151 D7
2600 TmbT 44084 2259 D2
5400 LryT 44057 2148 D2
6200 LryT 44057 2149 A4
6200 LryT 44086 2148 E3
6200 LryT 44086 2149 A4
14600 TpnT 44057 2149 A4
14600 TpnT 44086 2149 A4
15200 TpnT 44057 2149 A4
Travelers Ln
- ELYR 44035 2875 A2
Traver Rd
3500 SRHT 44122 2758 A2
Travers Rd
1600 MadT 44057 1842 E7
Travis Dr
6100 HDHT 44143 2499 D4
Travis Ln
- MadT 44057 1844 A5
Traymore Av
5800 CLEV 44144 2754 A6
6000 BKLN 44144 2754 A6
6200 BKLN 44144 2753 E5
Traymore Blvd
100 ETLK 44095 2142 D5
Traymore Ct
6800 MNTR 44060 2143 D6
Traymore Dr
17400 BbgT 44023 2891 A4
Traymore Rd
2200 UNHT 44118 2628 A4
2600 UNHT 44118 2627 E5
Traynham Rd
3600 SRHT 44122 2758 A2
Treadway Av
1400 CLEV 44109 2754 D4
Treadway Blvd
200 SDLK 44054 2616 C4
Treadway Dr
13000 MsnT 44024 2635 A2
Treadwell Av
24900 EUCL 44117 2373 D6
Treasure Isle Dr
17800 SGVL 44136 3147 D4
Treat Rd
10 AURA 44202 3021 D4
19200 WNHL 44146 2887 A7
Trebec Av
20100 EUCL 44119 2373 A5
Trebisky Rd
400 RDHT 44143 2498 D4
500 SELD 44143 2498 D5
700 SELD 44121 2498 D5
Tree Ln
3300 NOSD 44070 2750 E4
Tree Fern Ct
1500 TNBG 44087 3019 C3
Treelawn Dr
7600 INDE 44131 3016 C2
7600 INDE 44141 3016 C2
Treeline Dr
6900 BKVL 44141 3151 A5
Tree Moss Ln
5600 NRDV 44039 2877 E2
Treeside Ln
500 AVLK 44012 2618 E4
Treetop Ct
- AURA 44202 3156 D1
5500 PRMA 44134 2883 E1
Treetops Ct
7600 NRYN 44133 3013 D7
Treetop Trail Dr
8600 BWHT 44147 3015 A6
Treetower Dr
8300 BbgT 44023 2891 A4
Treeworth Blvd
200 BWHT 44147 3015 C7
Tremaine Dr
27000 EUCL 44132 2374 A4
28000 WKLF 44092 2374 A4
Tremont Av
2300 CLEV 44113 2624 E5
2400 CLEV 44113 2625 A6
Tremont Rd
3800 CVHT 44121 2497 E6
Tremont St
400 ELYR 44035 2875 A6
Trent Av
4200 CLEV 44109 2624 B7
Trent Ct
- GnvT 44041 1944 C1
Trenton Av
7700 CLEV 44104 2626 A6
13900 SGVL 44136 3147 C5
Trenton Ct
3700 WTLK 44145 2749 C4
Trenton Ovl
13700 SGVL 44136 3147 D5
Trenton Pl
- WLBY 44094 2250 A7
- WLBY 44094 2375 A1
Trenton Sq
10 EUCL 44143 2498 B2
Trenton Tr
3900 BNWK 44212 3146 E7
7600 MDBH 44130 3012 D1
Tressa Av
3100 LORN 44052 2744 D3
Tressel St
100 BERA 44017 2880 C6
Trevitt Cir N
600 EUCL 44143 2498 B2
Trevitt Cir S
700 EUCL 44143 2498 B1
Trevitt Cir W
500 EUCL 44143 2498 B1
Trevor Ln
7000 PRMA 44129 2882 E6
Trian Ct
7400 MNTR 44060 2253 A1
Tricia Dr
24500 WTLK 44145 2750 C3
Trillium Dr
17400 BbgT 44023 2891 A4
Trillium Ln
9200 MNTR 44060 2144 E2
9300 MNTR 44060 2145 A1
Trillium Tr
19200 SGVL 44136 3011 D5
31300 PRPK 44124 2629 D7
Trimble Ct
8400 MNTR 44060 2144 B3
Trimble Pl
900 SgHT 44067 3152 B1
Trinity Ct
2700 AVON 44011 2748 D2
Trinity Rd
1600 MadT 44057 1842 E7
1700 MadT 44057 1941 E1
Trinter Rd
15500 BhmT 44089 2870 A4
15500 VmnT 44089 2869 E4
15500 VmnT 44089 2870 A4
Trish Ln
9100 HmbT 44024 2381 A1
Triskett Rd
11500 CLEV 44111 2753 A1
12500 CLEV 44111 2623 A7
13000 CLEV 44111 2622 E7
13000 CLEV 44111 2752 D1
Trivue Cir
9400 TNBG 44087 3019 D6
Troika Cir
400 SgHT 44067 3017 D5
Trolley Vw
10 OmsT 44138 2879 A3
Tropicana Av
100 AMHT 44001 2744 B7
Trotter Ct
- ClbT 44028 3010 D4
Trotter Ln
600 BERA 44017 3010 E2
1500 PnvT 44077 2041 B6
7200 MNTR 44060 2252 D1
9200 NHFD 44067 3018 A3
Trotters Ridge Ln
1400 WTLK 44145 2619 D7
Trotwood Dr
7300 CcdT 44077 2253 C1
Trotwood Park Dr
19300 SGVL 44136 3146 D1
Troubador Dr
200 SgHT 44067 3017 D5
Trowbridge Av
2500 CLEV 44109 2754 C1
Troy Ct
9600 MNTR 44060 2253 A3
Troy Ovl
6400 PRMA 44129 2883 A7
Troy Oaks Dr
100 TroT 44234 2894 B6
N Troy Oaks Dr
- TroT 44234 2894 B6
Truax Av
16700 CLEV 44111 2752 B3
Truman Av
29900 WKLF 44092 2249 C7
29900 WKLF 44092 2374 C1
Truman Ct
7300 MNTR 44060 2143 C7
Trumbull Av
3600 CLEV 44115 2625 C5
Trumbull Rd
6100 TmbT 44041 2151 E7
6100 TmbT 44084 2151 E7
6800 TmbT 44086 2151 B7
Trumpeter Blvd
5300 NRYN 44133 3149 A1
Truscon Av
5600 CLEV 44127 2625 D6
Truxton Pl
3200 AVON 44011 2747 E3

INDEX 47
Tryon Rd
Cleveland Street Index
Valley Villas Dr

STREET
Block City ZIP Map# Grid

Tryon Rd
24300 OKWD 44146 3018 D1
26200 OKWD 44146 3019 A1
Tuckahoe Av
14000 CLEV 44111 2752 D1
Tucker Ct
2900 TNBG 44087 3020 B5
Tuckmere Dr
10 PnvT 44077 2146 A3
Tucson Dr
11800 PRMA 44130 2882 A2
Tudor Av
10 BDFD 44146 2886 D2
14800 CLEV 44111 2752 C2
Tudor Cir
6000 NRYN 44133 3014 A5
6400 BKVL 44141 3150 D2
6600 NRYN 44133 3013 E5
Tudor Ct
6200 MAYF 44143 2500 A5
Tudor Dr
2200 CVHT 44106 2627 A3
28700 NOSD 44070 2749 D7
Tuland Av
13600 CLEV 44111 2622 E7
Tulane Ct
100 ELYR 44035 2746 D7
Tulip
- MNTR 44060 2144 E7
Tulip Ln
- MNTR 44060 2143 C3
8100 BbgT 44023 2890 E2
8200 BbgT 44023 2891 A2
16100 WNHL 44146 2886 C7
Tulip Tr
6500 INDE 44131 2884 E5
6500 INDE 44131 2885 A5
Tulip Wy
6300 CcdT 44077 2146 C5
Tullamore Rd
3100 CVHT 44118 2627 D3
3400 UNHT 44118 2627 D3
Tullis Dr
33400 AVON 44011 2748 D4
Tunbridge Dr
7000 CcdT 44060 2145 B7
Tunbridge Ln
24200 BHWD 44122 2628 D4
Tungsten Rd
- EUCL 44132 2373 D6
21600 EUCL 44117 2373 A6
25400 EUCL 44132 2373 E4
26900 EUCL 44132 2374 A4
Tupelo Dr
6600 BDHT 44146 2887 D6
Turkey Meadow Ln
17100 SGVL 44136 3147 A3
Turn Av
- CLEV 44102 2624 B6
Turnberry Ln
500 RDHT 44143 2498 C3
5400 HDHT 44143 2499 B3
Turnbridge Rd
28800 BYVL 44140 2619 D4
Turnburry Ct
31400 WTLK 44145 2749 A6
Turnbury Dr
5000 PryT 44057 2042 E4
5000 PryT 44057 2043 A4
Turnbury Rd
3500 PRPK 44124 2759 A1
Turner Blvd
1800 ELYR 44035 2874 A6
Turner Dr
10 AQLA 44024 2505 C4
Turner St
500 ELYR 44035 2874 E6
500 ELYR 44035 2875 A6
Turney Ct
100 PNVL 44077 2040 B7
Turney Rd
300 BDFD 44146 2886 C4
4200 CLEV 44105 2756 B4
4200 PryT 44057 2042 E4
4200 PryT 44081 2042 E4
4600 GDHT 44105 2756 B4
4600 GDHT 44125 2756 C7
5300 GDHT 44125 2885 E3
6200 GDHT 44125 2886 A3
6300 GDHT 44137 2886 A3
6300 MPHT 44137 2886 A3
Turning Leaf Tr
9800 BKVL 44141 3150 C5
Turtle Cr
2600 WTLK 44145 2749 A2
Turtle Tr
- WLBY 44094 2250 A7
N Turtle Tr
34800 WLBY 44094 2250 B7
S Turtle Tr
34800 WLBY 44094 2250 A7
34800 WLBY 44094 2375 A1
Turtleback Cove
- AVON 44011 2748 C4
Tuscany Dr
- MCDN 44056 3153 E5
- MCDN 44056 3154 A6
Tuscarawas St
200 ELYR 44035 2874 E5
Tuscora Av
11000 CLEV 44108 2496 D6
Tuttle Av
3400 CLEV 44111 2752 C2
Tuttle Ct
10 GNVA 44041 1944 B4
Tuttle Dr
31300 BYVL 44140 2619 A4
E Tuttle Park Rd
1800 MadT 44057 1941 D1
W Tuttle Park Rd
1800 MadT 44057 1941 D1
Tuxedo Av
200 BNHT 44109 2755 A7
200 CLEV 44109 2755 A7
300 BNHT 44131 2755 A7
700 BNHT 44131 2754 E7
900 PRMA 44134 2754 C7
Tweed Ln
5900 MadT 44057 1941 D1
Twelve Oaks Dr
9700 SGVL 44136 3012 B4
Twickenham Dr
2300 BHWD 44122 2628 D4
Twilight Dr
100 SVHL 44131 2884 A6
7700 MONT 44060 2143 D1
Twin Cir
3100 NOSD 44070 2750 D3
Twin Acre Ct
- MDHL 44022 2760 A2
Twinbrook Rd
8600 MNTR 44060 2144 C6
Twin Circle Dr
2100 TNBG 44087 3019 D6
Twin Creek Ct
8300 MNTR 44060 2144 B3
Twin Creeks Dr
200 AbnT 44023 2892 A3
Twin Hills Dr
8800 TNBG 44087 3154 E1
Twinky Ln
3000 CLEV 44113 2624 D7
Twin Lakes Dr
100 ELYR 44035 3005 B1
5800 PMHT 44130 2882 D2
5800 PMHT 44129 2882 D2
5800 PRMA 44129 2882 D2
30100 WKLF 44092 2374 D2
Twin Lakes Tr
7400 RslT 44073 2761 C4
Twin Mills Ln
11400 MsnT 44024 2503 E2
Twin Oaks Dr
7900 BWHT 44147 3014 C3
Twin Oaks Tr
11500 CdnT 44024 2254 C7
Twinsburg Rd
1200 MCDN 44056 3154 E5
1200 TwbT 44056 3154 E5
1200 TwbT 44087 3154 E5
1200 TwbT 44236 3154 E5
E Twinsburg Rd
10 NCtT 44067 3153 D5
10 NCtT 44236 3153 D5
800 MCDN 44056 3153 D5
800 MCDN 44056 3154 B5
W Twinsburg Rd
10 NCtT 44067 3153 A6
10 NCtT 44236 3153 A6
Twinsburg Warren Rd
10 AURA 44202 3156 D1
500 AURA 44202 3021 D7
500 AURA 44202 3156 A2
2600 AURA 44202 3157 E1
2600 ManT 44202 3157 E1
2600 ManT 44202 3158 B2
3000 ManT 44255 3158 B2
3700 ManT 44255 3159 A2
5300 ManT 44255 3160 A2
5500 HrmT 44255 3160 A2
7200 HrmT 44234 3161 C4
7200 HrmT 44255 3161 C4
Twinsburg Warren Rd SR-82
10 AURA 44202 3156 D1
500 AURA 44202 3021 D7
500 AURA 44202 3156 A2
2600 AURA 44202 3157 E1
2600 ManT 44202 3157 E1
2600 ManT 44202 3158 B2
3000 ManT 44255 3158 B2
3700 ManT 44255 3159 A2
5300 ManT 44255 3160 A2
5500 HrmT 44255 3160 A2
7200 HrmT 44234 3161 C4
7200 HrmT 44255 3161 C4
Tyler Av
13000 CLEV 44111 2752 E3
13000 CLEV 44111 2753 A3
Tyler Blvd
7400 MNTR 44060 2251 C2
7500 MNTR 44060 2143 D7
7900 MNTR 44060 2144 A6
Tyler Ct
- CLEV 44109 2754 D1
Tyler St
600 ELYR 44035 2874 E4
Tympani Harmony Cir
- OmsT 44138 2879 C4
Tyndall Rd
3800 UNHT 44118 2628 A5
Tyndall Falls Dr
25300 ODFL 44138 3010 C1
Tyronne Av
19300 EUCL 44119 2372 E5
19300 EUCL 44119 2373 A5

U

Udall Rd
12200 HrmT 44234 3026 D6
12200 HrmT 44234 3161 D1
12400 TroT 44231 3026 D4
12400 TroT 44234 3026 D4
19100 TroT 44234 3026 D4
19100 TroT 44231 3026 D4
Uhlin Dr
7100 MDBH 44130 2881 C6
Underwood Av
18500 CLEV 44119 2372 E6
Union Av
6400 CLEV 44105 2755 E1
6400 CLEV 44127 2755 E1
7300 CLEV 44105 2756 D1
7300 CLEV 44127 2756 D1
7900 CLEV 44104 2756 D1
11600 CLEV 44120 2756 D1
13500 CLEV 44120 2757 A1
Union Cir
24300 BHWD 44122 2628 D3
Union St
10 BDFD 44146 2887 A5
10 MDSN 44057 2044 B1
10 OBLN 44074 3138 D1
7700 MNTR 44060 2143 D3
38200 WLBY 44094 2250 E5
E Union St
100 GNVA 44041 1944 C5
W Union St
10 GNVA 44041 1944 B5
Unity Av
10000 CLEV 44102 2753 C1
10000 CLEV 44111 2753 C1
University Av
100 ELYR 44035 3006 C1
200 PNVL 44077 2145 E3
300 CcdT 44077 2145 E3
University Blvd
2500 UNHT 44118 2628 A5
20500 SRHT 44118 2628 A5
20500 SRHT 44122 2628 A5
University Pkwy
4200 UNHT 44118 2628 B4
University Rd
1000 CLEV 44113 2624 E5
University St
- BERA 44130 2880 D6
- MDBH 44130 2880 D6
200 BERA 44017 2880 D6
University Hospital Dr
2000 CLEV 44106 2626 D2
Unwin Rd
2300 CLEV 44104 2625 D3
Upland Ct
- CLEV 44109 2754 B3
Upland Rd
400 BYVL 44140 2620 D5
Upper Dr
- CLEV 44135 2880 D1
Upper Chelsea Dr
- MsnT 44024 2504 B2
Upper Forty Dr
- MAYF 44040 2500 C3
- MAYF 44143 2500 C3
Upper Terrace Dr
19700 EUCL 44117 2498 A2
Upper Valley Dr
19000 EUCL 44117 2497 E2
19200 EUCL 44117 2498 A2
Uppingham Rd
24200 BDHT 44146 2887 D4
Upson Ct
10100 TNBG 44087 3020 B4
Upton Av
14900 CLEV 44110 2372 B7
Urban Cir N
1700 LORN 44053 2744 B6
Urban Cir S
1700 LORN 44053 2744 B6
Urban Dr
4300 SELD 44121 2498 B6
Urban St
10 PnvT 44077 2145 D3
Urbana Rd
1600 CLEV 44112 2497 C3
Ursula Ct
30000 NOSD 44070 2878 C3
US-6
5600 HgvT 44041 2384 E3
5600 HgvT 44099 2384 E3
US-6 W 25th St
- CLEV 44113 2624 A4
US-6 Buckley Blvd
- CLEV 44113 2624 C4
US-6 Chardon Rd
- KTLD 44094 2378 A7
7000 KTLD 44094 2376 A5
7000 WBHL 44094 2376 A5
7900 KTLD 44094 2377 A6
9600 CdnT 44024 2378 A7
9600 CdnT 44094 2378 A7
10700 CdnT 44024 2379 A6
11100 CRDN 44024 2379 A6
21000 EUCL 44117 2498 C1
23800 RDHT 44143 2498 C1
24400 RDHT 44143 2373 D7
26500 RDHT 44143 2374 A6
27200 WBHL 44092 2374 A6
29600 WBHL 44094 2374 E6
33700 WBHL 44094 2375 A5
US-6 Cleveland Mem Shoreway
- CLEV 44102 2623 E4
- CLEV 44102 2624 A4
- CLEV 44113 2624 B4
US-6 Clifton Blvd
- RKRV 44107 2621 C5
- RKRV 44116 2621 C5
9200 CLEV 44102 2623 C5
11700 LKWD 44102 2623 C5
11700 LKWD 44107 2623 C5
13400 LKWD 44107 2622 B4
18000 LKWD 44107 2621 C5
US-6 Detroit Av
2400 CLEV 44113 2624 C4
US-6 E Erie Av
200 LORN 44052 2614 E6
800 LORN 44052 2615 A5
3500 LORN 44054 2615 D4
3500 SDLK 44054 2615 D4
US-6 W Erie Av
300 LORN 44052 2614 D6
2400 LORN 44053 2614 B7
2700 LORN 44053 2744 A1
3100 LORN 44053 2743 E1
6100 LORN 44053 2742 B5
US-6 E Erie Br
- LORN 44052 2614 D6
US-6 Euclid Av
13500 ECLE 44112 2497 E2
16300 CLEV 44112 2497 E2
18100 CLEV 44112 2497 E2
18900 EUCL 44117 2497 E2
19700 EUCL 44117 2498 A1
US-6 GAR Hwy
6600 HgvT 44064 2384 D3
6600 MtlT 44064 2384 D3
6700 HgvT 44064 2384 D3
6700 HgvT 44099 2384 D3
12500 HmbT 44024 2380 B6
13500 HmbT 44024 2381 A3
14900 HmbT 44024 2382 A3
14900 MtlT 44024 2382 A3
15200 MtlT 44064 2382 E3
16000 MtlT 44064 2383 A3
US-6 N Hambden St
100 CRDN 44024 2380 A6
US-6 Lake Rd
3500 SDLK 44054 2615 E4
3900 SDLK 44054 2616 A3
5400 SDLK 44054 2617 B2
5500 SDLK 44012 2617 B2
19200 RKRV 44116 2621 E5
22900 BYVL 44140 2621 A5
22900 BYVL 44116 2621 A5
23400 BYVL 44140 2620 A4
27500 BYVL 44140 2619 D3
31500 AVLK 44140 2619 D3
31700 AVLK 44012 2618 D1
31700 AVLK 44012 2619 D3
32100 AVLK 44012 2488 B7
32800 AVLK 44012 2487 E7
32900 AVLK 44012 2617 B2
US-6 W Lake Rd
12500 VmnT 44089 2740 A7
14200 VMLN 44089 2740 C6
US-6 Liberty Av
1800 VMLN 44053 2742 C4
1800 VMLN 44089 2742 C4
3300 VMLN 44089 2741 E5
5000 VMLN 44089 2740 B6
US-6 Main St
100 CRDN 44024 2380 A6
US-6 E Park St
100 CRDN 44024 2380 A6
US-6 Superior Av
- CLEV 44113 2624 D3
4000 CLEV 44103 2625 D1
5100 CLEV 44103 2495 D7
7400 CLEV 44103 2496 A7
8400 CLEV 44106 2496 A7
8400 CLEV 44108 2496 A7
12500 ECLE 44112 2496 E7
13200 ECLE 44112 2497 A7
US-6 W Superior Av
100 CLEV 44114 2624 E3
200 CLEV 44115 2624 E3
200 CLEV 44113 2624 E3
US-6 Superior Av E
10 CLEV 44114 2624 E2
1200 CLEV 44114 2625 A2
3800 CLEV 44103 2625 C1
US-6 Water St
100 CRDN 44024 2379 E6
100 CRDN 44024 2380 A6
600 CdnT 44024 2379 C6
US-20
- CrlT - 3005 E6
- CrlT - 3006 B5
- CrlT - 3139 E2
- CrlT - 3140 A1
- EatT - 3006 B5
- NRsT - 3139 E2
US-20 W 25th St
- CLEV 44113 2624 A4
US-20 Buckley Blvd
- CLEV 44113 2624 C4
US-20 Casement Av
400 PnvT 44077 2040 C6
US-20 Center Ridge Rd
19400 RKRV 44116 2621 E7
20500 RKRV 44116 2751 B1
20600 FWPK 44116 2751 B1
20600 FWPK 44126 2751 B1
21600 RKRV 44116 2751 B1
23000 WTLK 44116 2751 B1
23000 WTLK 44145 2751 B1
23200 WTLK 44145 2750 D1
27100 WTLK 44145 2749 E3
31400 NRDV 44039 2749 B6
31400 NRDV 44145 2749 B6
31700 NRDV 44039 2748 E7
31700 NRDV 44039 2877 D1
36000 NRDV 44039 2876 E4
39100 NRDV 44039 2875 E6
US-20 Cleveland St
700 ELYR 44035 2875 E5
900 ELYR 44039 2875 E4
US-20 Cleveland Mem Shoreway
- CLEV 44102 2623 E4
- CLEV 44102 2624 A4
- CLEV 44113 2624 B4
US-20 Clifton Blvd
9200 CLEV 44102 2623 C5
11700 LKWD 44102 2623 C5
11700 LKWD 44107 2623 C5
13400 LKWD 44107 2622 B4
US-20 W Clifton Blvd
1100 LKWD 44107 2622 A4
US-20 Detroit Av
2400 CLEV 44113 2624 C4
US-20 Detroit Rd
- LKWD 44107 2621 E6
- RKRV 44107 2621 E6
- RKRV 44116 2621 E6
US-20 Erie St
4000 WLBY 44094 2250 E5
US-20 E Erie St
10 PNVL 44077 2040 A7
800 PnvT 44077 2040 C6
US-20 W Erie St
10 PNVL 44077 2146 A1
US-20 Euclid Av
100 CLEV 44114 2624 E3
100 CLEV 44115 2624 E3
900 CLEV 44114 2625 B2
900 CLEV 44115 2625 B2
4000 CLEV 44103 2625 B2
7300 CLEV 44103 2626 C2
8500 CLEV 44106 2626 C2
12200 ECLE 44106 2626 C2
12200 CLEV 44112 2626 C2
12400 ECLE 44112 2626 C2
12600 ECLE 44112 2496 E7
13500 ECLE 44112 2497 E2
16300 CLEV 44112 2497 E2
18100 CLEV 44121 2497 E2
18900 EUCL 44117 2497 E2
19700 EUCL 44117 2498 A1
20700 EUCL 44117 2373 B7
25600 EUCL 44132 2373 E5
26000 EUCL 44143 2373 E5
27100 EUCL 44132 2374 A4
28300 WKLF 44092 2374 A4
30400 WLWK 44092 2374 D1
30700 WKLF 44092 2249 E7
30700 WKLF 44094 2249 E7
30700 WLBY 44094 2249 E7
30700 WLWK 44092 2249 E7
34000 WLBY 44094 2250 A7
US-20 Kipton East Rd
- NRsT 44074 3139 B4
45200 PtfT 44074 3138 E6
45200 PtfT 44074 3139 A5
US-20 E Main St
10 GNVA 44041 1944 C4
US-20 W Main St
10 GNVA 44041 1944 B4
1000 GnvT 44041 1944 A4
5900 GnvT 44041 1943 E4
US-20 Mentor Av
100 PNVL 44077 2146 A1
500 PNVL 44077 2145 E2
1100 PnvT 44077 2145 E2
2100 MNTR 44060 2145 A6
2100 PnvT 44060 2145 A6
7000 MNTR 44060 2251 B4
7000 WLBY 44060 2251 B4
7000 WLBY 44094 2251 B4
8000 MNTR 44060 2252 B1
8700 MNTR 44060 2144 E7
38100 WLBY 44094 2250 E5
38800 MNTR 44094 2251 B4
US-20 Public Sq
10 CLEV 44114 2624 E3
10 CLEV 44115 2624 E3
US-20 N Ridge Rd
1200 PnvT 44077 2040 E4
1900 PnvT 44077 2041 A4
2400 PryT 44077 2041 A4
2400 PryT 44081 2041 A4
3400 PryT 44081 1940 A7
3900 NPRY 44081 1940 A7
4700 NPRY 44081 1941 B5
4700 PryT 44081 1941 B5
5200 MadT 44057 1941 B5
5200 MadT 44081 1941 B5
6200 MadT 44057 1942 A4
7500 GnvT 44057 1943 B4
7500 MadT 44057 1943 A5
US-20 N Ridge Rd E
4500 GnvT 44041 1944 E3
US-20 N Ridge Rd W
5900 GnvT 44041 1943 B4
6700 GnvT 44057 1943 B4
US-20 Sloane Av
1300 LKWD 44107 2622 A4
US-20 South East Byp
- EatT 44035 3006 E3
- EatT 44044 3006 E3
- ELYR 44035 2875 E5
- ELYR 44035 3006 E3
US-20 Superior Av
- CLEV 44113 2624 D3
US-20 W Superior Av
100 CLEV 44114 2624 E3
200 CLEV 44115 2624 E3
200 CLEV 44113 2624 E3
US-20 Superior Av E
10 CLEV 44114 2624 A5
US-20 Wooster Rd
1500 RKRV 44116 2621 E6
2500 LKWD 44126 2621 E6
2500 RKRV 44126 2621 E6
US-42 W 25th St
1400 CLEV 44113 2624 D7
3100 CLEV 44109 2624 D7
3200 CLEV 44109 2754 D3
US-42 Pearl Rd
10 BHIT 44212 3146 D6
10 BNWK 44212 3146 D6
10 BNWK 44136 3146 D6
10 SGVL 44136 3146 D6
3600 CLEV 44109 2754 D2
4500 CLEV 44144 2754 C5
5000 CLEV 44129 2754 A7
5000 PRMA 44109 2754 A7
5000 PRMA 44129 2754 A7
5300 PRMA 44129 2753 E7
5300 PRMA 44129 2882 C3
5800 PMHT 44129 2882 C3
5800 PMHT 44130 2882 C3
5800 PRMA 44130 2882 C3
6600 MDBH 44130 2881 E5
6600 PMHT 44130 2881 E5
7400 MDBH 44130 3012 A2
7900 SGVL 44136 3012 A2
9000 SGVL 44136 3011 E3
US-301
- EatT - 3006 B5
US-322
- WndT 44046 2509 A6
5900 WndT 44099 2509 E6
US-322 E 13th St
1700 CLEV 44114 2625 A2
US-322 Chester Av
2200 CLEV 44114 2625 C2
4000 CLEV 44103 2625 E2
7300 CLEV 44103 2626 A2
8400 CLEV 44106 2626 A2
US-322 Detroit Av
2400 CLEV 44113 2624 C4
US-322 Euclid Av
10900 CLEV 44106 2626 C2
US-322 Mayfield Rd
2400 CVHT 44106 2626 E2
2400 CVHT 44106 2627 A2
2700 CVHT 44118 2627 A2
3200 CVHT 44118 2497 C7
3400 CVHT 44121 2497 C7
3800 CVHT 44121 2498 B7
3900 SELD 44121 2498 B7
4600 LNHT 44121 2498 B7
4600 LNHT 44124 2498 B7
5000 LNHT 44124 2499 B7
5700 MDHT 44124 2499 B7
6500 GSML 44040 2500 C7
6500 MDHT 44124 2500 C7
7000 CsTp 44026 2501 B7
7000 GSML 44040 2501 B7
8200 CsTp 44026 2502 D7
9500 CsTp 44026 2503 D7
9700 MsnT 44026 2503 D7
10100 MsnT 44024 2503 D7
10800 MsnT 44024 2504 C7
11400 CLEV 44106 2626 E2
11800 MsnT 44024 2505 A6
12400 ClrT 44024 2505 A6
13400 ClrT 44024 2506 C6
13900 ClrT 44021 2506 C6
14900 ClrT 44024 2507 C6
14900 ClrT 44021 2507 C6
15100 HtbT 44024 2507 C6
15100 HtbT 44021 2507 C6
15500 HtbT 44046 2507 C6
16000 HtbT 44046 2508 B6
17600 HtbT 44046 2509 D6
17700 WndT 44046 2509 D6
US-322 Superior Av
- CLEV 44113 2624 D3
US-322 W Superior Av
100 CLEV 44114 2624 E3
200 CLEV 44115 2624 E3
200 CLEV 44113 2624 E3
US-322 Superior Av E
10 CLEV 44114 2624 E2
1200 CLEV 44114 2625 A2
US-422
- AbnT - 2892 E6
- AbnT - 2893 C6
- AbnT 44234 2894 A6
- AbnT 44021 2894 A6
- BbgT - 2890 B5
- BbgT - 2891 D5
- BbgT - 2892 A6
- CLEV 44115 2625 C4
- ORNG - 2759 A7
- SLN - 2759 A7
- SLN - 2888 B1
- SLN - 2889 B4
- SLN - 2890 B5
- TroT 44021 2894 B5
- TroT 44234 2894 B5
- WVHT - 2758 E6
- WVHT - 2759 A7
US-422 Broadway Av
800 CLEV 44115 2625 A4
US-422 Chagrin Blvd
- BHWD 44122 2759 C1
15600 SRHT 44120 2757 B1
17700 SRHT 44122 2757 D1
19200 SRHT 44122 2758 B1
21100 BHWD 44122 2758 B1
21100 HIHL 44122 2758 B1
US-422 Kinsman Rd
5500 CLEV 44104 2625 E5
7200 CLEV 44104 2626 A6
11300 CLEV 44120 2626 A6
12500 CLEV 44120 2756 E1
13500 CLEV 44120 2757 B1
15400 SRHT 44120 2757 B1
US-422 Main Market Rd
12500 TroT 44021 2894 D5
12500 TroT 44234 2894 D5
13400 TroT 44021 2895 B5
13400 TroT 44234 2895 B5
14400 PkmT 44021 2896 B7
14400 PkmT 44021 3027 E1
14400 PkmT 44234 2896 B7
14400 PkmT 44234 3027 E1
14400 TroT 44021 2895 E7
14400 TroT 44021 2896 B7
14400 TroT 44234 2895 E7
14400 TroT 44234 2896 B7
16300 PkmT 44062 3027 E1
16300 PkmT 44062 3028 A1
16300 PkmT 44231 3027 E1
16300 PkmT 44231 3028 A1
16500 PkmT 44491 3028 C4
17000 PkmT 44231 3028 C4
US-422 Ontario St
1900 CLEV 44114 2624 E3
2000 CLEV 44115 2624 E3
2100 CLEV 44113 2624 E3
US-422 Orange Av
1400 CLEV 44115 2625 A4
US-422 Outerbelt East Frwy
- BHWD - 2758 E4
- BHWD - 2759 A2
- ORNG - 2758 E4
- ORNG - 2759 A2
- WVHT - 2758 E4
US-422 Parkman Rd NW
5100 StnT 44231 3029 A6
US-422 Warren Burton Rd
12300 NsnT 44231 3028 E6
12300 NsnT 44231 3029 B7
12300 StnT 44231 3029 B7
12800 PkmT 44491 3028 C4
12800 PkmT 44231 3028 C4
US-422 Woodland Av
2500 CLEV 44115 2625 B4
4000 CLEV 44104 2625 C4
Usher Rd
8200 ODFL 44138 2879 B7
8500 OmsT 44138 2879 B7
8800 OmsT 44138 3010 A1
9000 ODFL 44138 3010 A1
9200 ODFL 44138 3009 E2
9200 OmsT 44138 3009 E2
Utah Ct
4300 PryT 44081 2041 D3
Utica Av
1700 LORN 44052 2744 C1
5500 CLEV 44103 2625 D1
Utopia Av
- CLEV 44110 2497 B2
Uxbridge Dr
28500 WLWK 44095 2249 A6

V

Vahalla Dr
7300 SLN 44139 3020 E2
Vail Dr
9900 TNBG 44087 3020 A4
Vale Dr
200 BDFD 44146 2887 B4
4800 NRYN 44133 3014 A4
Valencia Cir
100 ORNG 44022 2759 A5
Valentine Av
1700 CLEV 44109 2754 D1
Valentine Rd
14500 LryT 44086 2256 E2
14500 LryT 44086 2257 B2
14500 TpnT 44086 2257 B2
Valerie Ct
800 ETLK 44095 2250 B3
Valerie Ln
7400 HDSN 44236 3155 B7
Valeside Ln
26900 OmsT 44138 2878 D5
Valewood Dr
1800 PRMA 44134 2883 D2
Vallevista Dr
6500 MDHT 44124 2500 A6
Valley Blvd
100 ELYR 44035 2875 C3
Valley Dr
700 AMHT 44001 2872 B3
8200 BbgT 44023 2890 E3
8200 BbgT 44023 2891 A3
N Valley Dr
3800 FWPK 44126 2751 E1
18700 FWPK 44126 2622 A7
18800 FWPK 44126 2752 A1
W Valley Dr
3800 FWPK 44126 2752 A1
Valley Ln
3000 NRYN 44133 3014 C3
5500 SLN 44139 2888 A2
8200 PRMA 44130 3013 D1
8800 BbgT 44023 3022 B3
12000 GDHT 44125 2885 C2
W Valley Ln
18500 FWPK 44126 2622 A7
Valley Pkwy
- BERA 44017 2880 A4
- BERA 44142 2880 A4
- BERA 44017 2880 B6
- BERA 44017 3011 C2
- BKPK 44142 2879 E3
- BKPK 44142 2880 A4
- BKPK 44017 2880 A4
- BKVL 44141 3016 D7
- CLEV 44111 2621 E7
- CLEV 44126 2621 E7
- CLEV 44111 2622 A7
- CLEV 44126 2622 A7
- CLEV 44111 2752 A1
- CLEV 44126 2752 A1
- FWPK 44111 2752 A1
- LKWD 44126 2621 E7
- LKWD 44111 2621 E7
- LKWD 44107 2621 E6
- LKWD 44107 2622 A7
- LKWD 44111 2622 A7
- LKWD 44116 2622 A7
- LKWD 44126 2622 A7
- LKWD 44107 2622 A5
- MDBH 44130 3011 C2
- OmsT 44142 2879 E3
- OmsT 44138 2879 E3
- RKRV 44107 2622 A5
- RKRV 44116 2622 A6
- SGVL 44136 3011 D3
- SGVL 44136 3012 C6
- WBHL 44094 2375 B5
2500 BKVL 44141 3150 B2
3300 NRYN 44133 3149 B2
4400 FWPK 44126 2752 A2
4600 FWPK 44126 2751 E3
5600 BKVL 44141 3151 A2
6300 NRYN 44133 3148 D2
11500 NRYN 44133 3147 E1
11500 SGVL 44133 3147 E1
11500 SGVL 44136 3147 E1
Valley Rd
3600 CLEV 44109 2754 D4
16100 NbyT 44021 2765 A7
16300 AbnT 44021 2765 A7
16300 AbnT 44021 2894 A2
16700 AbnT 44021 2893 E5
Valley Vw
- AVON 44011 2748 C5
Valley Belt Rd
900 BNHT 44131 2755 C7
5400 INDE 44131 2755 C7
5400 INDE 44131 2884 D1
Valley Brook Blvd
10 HkyT 44233 3148 B6
Valley Brook Cir
700 SgHT 44067 3152 C1
Valley Brook Dr
37900 WBHL 44094 2375 E7
Valleybrook Dr
4700 BKVL 44141 3150 B4
Valley Brook Ovl
200 HkyT 44233 3148 B7
Valley Creek Dr
900 ETLK 44095 2250 B4
16900 SGVL 44136 3012 A7
Valley Forge Cir
100 ELYR 44035 2873 E7
100 ELYR 44035 2874 A7
Valley Forge Dr
4300 FWPK 44126 2751 C4
9800 PMHT 44130 2882 C6
36700 SLN 44139 2889 C4
Valley Forge Ln
10 ELYR 44035 2875 B3
Valleypark Cir
2000 BWHT 44147 3014 E4
Valley Park Dr
900 BWHT 44147 3014 E4
Valley Parkway Dr
900 BWHT 44147 3149 E2
900 BWHT 44147 3150 A2
Valley Ranch Dr
6300 MPHT 44137 2886 A4
Valley Ridge Dr
36200 ETLK 44095 2250 C4
Valleyside Rd
4300 CLEV 44135 2751 E4
Valleyview
1200 BWHT 44147 3149 E5
Valleyview Av
15600 CLEV 44135 2752 B4
Valley View Cir
700 AURA 44202 3021 B6
Valleyview Ct
8000 NRYN 44133 3013 C2
E Valley View Ct
6000 MNTR 44060 2144 C3
W Valley View Ct
6000 MNTR 44060 2144 C3
Valley View Dr
2100 RKRV 44116 2622 A6
2100 WKLF 44092 2374 D3
5800 BKPK 44142 2879 E1
12300 CsTp 44026 2501 E6
12300 CsTp 44026 2502 A7
Valleyview Dr
300 PNVL 44077 2146 C1
3900 LORN 44053 2743 E2
9800 ClbT 44028 3010 C2
12100 NbyT 44021 2765 A4
36300 ETLK 44095 2142 D7
Valley View Ovl
8800 KTLD 44094 2377 C3
Valley View Rd
7500 HDSN 44236 3154 C7
8100 MCDN 44056 3154 C7
8500 MCDN 44056 3153 E2
10000 MCDN 44056 3018 B6
10400 NCtT 44067 3018 A6
10700 NCtT 44067 3017 D5
10700 SgHT 44067 3017 D5
12000 SgHT 44067 3016 E3
12000 SgHT 44125 3016 E3
Valleyview Tr
8200 NRYN 44133 3013 D2
Valley Villas Dr
7400 PRMA 44130 2882 D7
7700 PRMA 44130 3013 D1

STREET Block	City	ZIP	Map#	Grid
Valley Vista Dr				
7600	INDE	44131	3016	A2
12200	MsnT	44026	2503	B6
36100	ETLK	44095	2250	B3
Valley Woods Dr				
4300	INDE	44131	2884	C7
Valplast St				
15900	MDFD	44062	2767	D3
Van Aken Blvd				
2700	CLEV	44120	2627	A6
2800	SRHT	44120	2627	A6
15500	SRHT	44120	2757	B1
17700	SRHT	44122	2757	B1
18900	SRHT	44122	2758	A1
Van Buren Av				
300	ELYR	44035	2875	A4
Vanburen Ct				
7100	MNTR	44060	2143	D7
Van Buren Rd				
1800	ECLE	44112	2497	A6
E Vancey Dr				
6400	BKPK	44142	2880	C3
N Vancey Dr				
21000	BKPK	44142	2880	C3
W Vancey Dr				
6400	BKPK	44142	2880	C3
Vanda Av				
100	AVLK	44012	2618	D2
Vandalia Av				
4700	CLEV	44144	2754	A6
6000	BKLN	44144	2754	A6
6200	BKLN	44144	2753	E6
Vandemar St				
1300	CVHT	44121	2498	A7
Vanderbilt Ct				
100	ELYR	44035	3006	D2
Van Epps Av				
10	GNVA	44041	1944	C4
Van Epps Rd				
4900	BNHT	44131	2755	A6
5000	BNHT	44109	2755	A6
5000	CLEV	44109	2755	A6
5000	CLEV	44131	2755	A6
Van Ess Dr				
10	OmsT	44138	2879	A4
Van Oaks Dr				
600	AMHT	44001	2872	C2
2000	TNBG	44087	3019	D3
Van Pelt Rd				
1400	HpfT	44041	2045	D2
1900	HpfT	44041	1943	D7
Van Wert Av				
5700	BKPK	44142	2881	D1
Vardon Dr				
2400	LORN	44053	2743	E2
Varian Av				
6400	CLEV	44103	2495	E7
Vashti Av				
12400	CLEV	44108	2496	E4
Vassar Av				
200	ELYR	44035	3006	B1
2600	LORN	44053	2744	A4
Vassar Dr				
-	PnvT	44077	2147	A1
Vassar St				
1800	ECLE	44112	2497	A6
Vaughn Rd				
10200	FdmT	44255	3160	A7
10200	HrmT	44255	3160	A7
10200	ManT	44255	3160	A7
10200	ShvT	44255	3160	A7
11300	HrmT	44234	3160	A3
15600	BKVL	44141	3152	B4
Vega Av				
2500	CLEV	44113	2624	C6
Vegas Dr				
500	ETLK	44095	2250	A2
Velma Av				
6700	PRMA	44129	2753	E7
6700	PRMA	44129	2754	A7
14300	CLEV	44128	2757	A4
Velour Av				
14600	CLEV	44110	2497	B3
Venice Ct				
-	MCDN	44056	3154	A3
Vennicook Wy				
7500	HDSN	44236	3154	E6
Venning Ct				
5700	CLEV	44104	2625	D5
Ventnor Av				
-	CLEV	44135	2752	B5
Ventura Cir				
100	BNHT	44131	2755	B7
Venture Ln				
-	HmbT	44024	2380	D7
Venus Dr				
3900	BNWK	44212	3146	E7
9500	HmbT	44024	2381	C3
Vera Dr				
8200	BKVL	44141	3015	E5
8200	BWHT	44141	3015	E5
8200	BWHT	44147	3015	E5
Vera St				
22400	WVHT	44128	2758	C6
Vermilion Rd				
-	VMLN	44001	2870	E4
500	VMLN	44089	2741	C7
1500	BhmT	44089	2741	C7
1500	VMLN	44089	2870	D1
2300	BhmT	44089	2870	D2
3000	BhmT	44001	2870	E4
8000	BhmT	44001	2871	A4
8000	BhmT	44089	2871	A4
Vermont Av				
2400	CLEV	44113	2624	B3
2800	PryT	44077	2041	C4
2800	PryT	44081	2041	C4
Vermont Dr				
700	LORN	44052	2615	D5
Vermont Rd				
500	ELYR	44035	2875	D4
Vernon Av				
10600	GDHT	44125	2756	C6
Vernon Dr				
4500	NOSD	44070	2750	C6
16300	PkmT	44231	3027	E1
16300	PkmT	44231	3028	A1
Vernon Ln				
400	MCDN	44056	3018	B7
Vernon Rd				
2100	UNHT	44118	2628	A3
Vernondale Dr				
6100	PMHT	44130	2882	C3
Veron Ln				
2800	TNBG	44087	3020	A6
Verona Rd				
4000	SELD	44121	2628	A2
Versailles Dr				
10100	SGVL	44136	3012	C4
Versailles Pl				
-	MCDN	44056	3154	A3
Vesely Ct				
500	ETLK	44095	2142	E7
Vesta Av				
7900	NCtT	44067	3153	A1
Vestry Av				
2500	CLEV	44113	2624	C5
Vezber Dr				
2300	SVHL	44131	3015	B2
Via Lago Dr				
-	MCDN	44056	3154	A3
Vickie Ln				
5500	BDHT	44146	2887	C2
Vicksburg Dr				
1000	PRMA	44134	2883	E7
10600	PMHT	44130	2882	B2
Victor Av				
3000	CLEV	44127	2625	D6
Victor Dr				
34000	ETLK	44095	2249	E2
34100	ETLK	44095	2250	A2
Victoria Av				
1400	LKWD	44107	2622	D5
Victoria Cir				
-	INDE	44131	2884	E4
Victoria Ct				
14800	LKWD	44107	2622	C5
Victoria Dr				
5400	LORN	44053	2744	C5
7000	MNTR	44060	2144	D7
8400	BWHT	44147	3014	E4
16600	AbnT	44021	2893	C1
Victoria Ln				
5100	NOSD	44070	2750	B7
Victoria Rd				
1700	CLEV	44112	2497	C3
Victoria Lake Cir				
400	BHIT	44212	3146	A7
Victory Av				
3100	LORN	44055	2745	B3
Victory Blvd				
3900	CLEV	44111	2752	E3
3900	CLEV	44135	2752	E3
10400	NHFD	44067	3018	A4
Victory Dr				
1300	SELD	44121	2498	C7
Victory Ln				
13500	MsnT	44024	2634	D3
Vienna Dr				
9000	PRMA	44130	3013	C2
Vienna Pl				
8600	CLEV	44106	2626	B3
View Dr				
14400	NbyT	44065	2634	B7
14400	NbyT	44065	2764	B1
22600	EUCL	44143	2498	B3
22600	RDHT	44143	2498	B3
View Rd				
2200	CLEV	44109	2754	D2
Viewcrest Ct				
-	LORN	44053	2743	D4
Viewmount Dr				
7700	CcdT	44077	2253	D3
Viking Ct				
-	AVON	44011	2747	C2
Viking Pkwy				
30800	WTLK	44145	2619	A6
Vilamoura Dr				
-	AVON	44011	2748	C6
Villa Dr				
1300	SELD	44121	2498	B7
Villa Pl				
-	PryT	44081	1940	C7
Villa Angela Dr				
-	CLEV	44110	2372	C5
-	CLEV	44119	2372	C5
Villa Beach Dr				
10	CLEV	44110	2372	B6
Villa East Dr				
200	FTHR	44077	2039	D5
Village Cir				
700	MAYF	44040	2500	C4
Village Dr				
-	GTVL	44234	3161	E6
200	BWHT	44147	3014	E5
1200	WLBY	44094	2143	A5
7000	CcdT	44060	2145	B7
7000	CcdT	44077	2145	B7
Village Dr E				
300	SVHL	44131	3015	A2
Village Dr W				
200	SVHL	44131	3015	A2
Village Ln				
-	BHWD	44122	2628	E4
-	BHWD	44122	2629	A4
W Village Ln				
-	BHWD	44122	2628	E4
Village Pkwy				
700	SgHT	44067	3152	B1
Village Pl				
10	BHWD	44122	2628	E4
Village Tr				
-	MAYF	44040	2500	C4
800	GSML	44040	2500	C4
Village Circle Dr				
100	CNFL	44022	2761	A6
Village Club Dr				
600	SgHT	44067	3152	C1
Village Green Dr				
3000	WTLK	44145	2749	E3
20300	SGVL	44136	3011	C3
Village Park Dr				
10	OmsT	44138	2879	A4
Villa Grande Dr				
11200	NRYN	44133	3014	B6
Villa Lago Dr				
-	MCDN	44056	3154	A3
Villa Marina Ct				
8300	MNTR	44060	2144	B2
Villanova Cir				
100	ELYR	44035	2746	D7
Villas Dr				
-	NRYN	44133	3013	B5
Villaview Rd				
1000	CLEV	44119	2372	D7
16700	CLEV	44110	2372	D7
Ville Ct				
7300	PRMA	44129	2883	A7
Vincent Av				
600	CLEV	44114	2624	E3
4800	LORN	44055	2746	A5
4800	ShfT	44055	2746	A5
Vincent Dr				
2500	SVHL	44131	3015	B2
12700	CsTp	44026	2502	D7
12700	CsTp	44026	2632	D1
12700	ManT	44255	3023	C5
23700	NOSD	44070	2750	D3
Vincent Rd				
100	NHFD	44067	3018	A3
Vincent St				
100	CNFL	44022	2761	A6
Vine Av				
3000	LORN	44052	2745	C3
3000	LORN	44055	2745	C3
N Vine Av				
20600	EUCL	44119	2373	A5
Vine Ct				
2900	CLEV	44113	2624	B5
4500	CLEV	44102	2624	B5
22500	RKRV	44116	2751	A2
Vine St				
-	AVON	44011	2748	A2
100	FTHR	44077	2039	D4
100	GNVA	44041	1944	B4
5300	MPHT	44137	2757	C7
5300	MPHT	44137	2886	C1
31000	WLWK	44095	2249	E4
32700	ETLK	44095	2249	E4
33700	ETLK	44095	2250	B4
36300	ETLK	44094	2250	B4
36300	WLBY	44094	2250	B4
Vine St SR-640				
31000	WLWK	44095	2249	E4
32700	ETLK	44095	2249	E4
33700	ETLK	44095	2250	B4
36300	ETLK	44094	2250	B4
36300	WLBY	44094	2250	B4
E Vine St				
100	OBLN	44074	3138	E3
W Vine St				
10	OBLN	44074	3138	E3
Vineland Rd				
400	BYVL	44140	2620	D5
N Vinemount Ct				
7500	HDSN	44236	3154	C6
S Vinemount Ct				
7500	HDSN	44236	3154	C6
Vineshire Rd				
900	CVHT	44121	2497	E5
Vinewood Dr				
100	AVLK	44012	2617	E2
2000	PRMA	44134	2883	D2
29300	WKLF	44092	2374	B1
Vineyard Av				
7600	CLEV	44105	2756	A5
Vineyard Ct				
600	WTLK	44145	2620	A6
Vineyard Dr				
10	BNWK	44212	3146	E6
100	BWHT	44147	3014	E5
Vineyard Rd				
100	AVLK	44012	2488	C7
100	AVLK	44012	2618	C1
6900	INDE	44131	2884	D7
30000	WLWK	44095	2249	C7
Vintage Ct				
9300	MNTR	44060	2252	E2
Viola Av				
10	CLEV	44110	2372	C6
14300	CLEV	44111	2752	D3
Violet Av				
15000	CLEV	44135	2752	C5
Violet Ct				
2200	AVON	44011	2747	E1
Virginia Av				
10	CLEV	44110	2372	C5
100	ELYR	44035	3006	B3
1100	LKWD	44107	2622	C4
3300	CLEV	44109	2754	C2
5400	PRMA	44129	2883	A1
6700	PRMA	44129	2882	E1
22900	NOSD	44070	2750	E5
22900	NOSD	44070	2751	A5
Virginia Dr				
10	PnvT	44077	2040	D7
1500	AMHT	44001	2744	C6
4200	FWPK	44126	2751	E2
Virginia Rd				
3100	VMLN	44089	2742	A5
3200	VMLN	44089	2741	E5
3400	WDMR	44122	2759	A1
Vista Av				
8100	GDHT	44125	2756	A6
Vista Cir				
10	NOSD	44070	2879	A1
5600	WLBY	44094	2375	A2
Vista Ct				
100	ELYR	44035	2875	C3
100	NOSD	44070	2879	B1
Vista Dr				
-	NOSD	44070	2879	B1
7500	PRMA	44134	3014	B1
8900	NRYN	44133	3014	C4
11100	HrmT	44234	3161	A4
Vista Ln				
10	AURA	44202	3021	C7
8300	PRMA	44130	3013	D1
Vista Pointe Dr				
11300	ClrT	44024	2505	C2
Vista Ridge Cir				
-	HkyT	44233	3149	E6
Vita Ln				
29200	NOSD	44070	2878	B4
Vivian Av				
4700	CLEV	44127	2625	C7
Vivian Dr				
200	BERA	44017	3011	A2
900	GFTN	44044	3142	A4
Vivian St				
100	SAHT	44001	2872	C7
Voelker Av				
600	EUCL	44123	2373	C4
Vokes Dr				
33900	ETLK	44095	2250	A5
Vondracek Dr				
-	SLN	44139	2888	E4
Vorderman Av				
100	NHFD	44067	3018	A4
Vrooman Rd				
5000	PryT	44077	2041	C7
5000	PryT	44081	2041	C7
5300	LryT	44081	2041	C7
5300	LryT	44077	2147	D2
7600	GnvT	44057	1844	A6
7600	MadT	44057	1844	A6
Vulcan Ct				
9300	CLEV	44102	2623	D6
W				
Waban Rd				
10	TMLK	44095	2250	B2
Wabash Av				
1000	GFTN	44044	3142	B5
Wabash St				
-	EyrT	44035	2745	C7
Wacoka Dr				
10	ETLK	44095	2142	B6
Wade Av				
1900	CLEV	44113	2624	C6
Wade Ovl				
10	CLEV	44106	2626	C2
Wade St				
-	ELYR	44035	3006	B2
Wadena St				
1800	ECLE	44112	2496	E7
1800	ECLE	44112	2626	E1
Wade Park Av				
5800	CLEV	44103	2625	D1
7400	CLEV	44103	2626	A1
8400	CLEV	44106	2626	A1
12200	CLEV	44106	2496	E7
Wadsworth Av				
10500	GDHT	44125	2756	C6
Wadsworth Rd				
2600	SRHT	44122	2628	C6
Wagar Av				
1400	LKWD	44107	2622	B5
W Wagar Cir				
21000	RKRV	44116	2621	C7
Wagar Rd				
300	RKRV	44116	2621	C7
2600	RKRV	44116	2751	C1
Wagner Av				
7300	CLEV	44104	2625	E5
Wagner Ct				
10100	TNBG	44087	3019	D3
Wagon Wheel Dr				
33000	SLN	44139	2888	E3
33000	SLN	44139	2889	A3
Waikiki Dr				
10	MadT	44057	1941	B5
Wailele Dr				
10	MadT	44057	1941	B6
Wainfleet Av				
13100	CLEV	44135	2752	E5
Wainstead Av				
13400	CLEV	44111	2752	E3
Wainstead Dr				
7500	PRMA	44129	2882	D3
Wainwright Dr				
7300	NRDV	44039	2877	B4
Wainwright Ter				
9700	ODFL	44138	3010	E2
Waite Hill Rd				
-	WLBY	44094	2250	E7
6600	WTHL	44094	2375	E1
6600	WTHL	44094	2376	A1
9100	WTHL	44094	2250	E7
Wakefield Av				
5800	CLEV	44102	2624	A6
7000	CLEV	44102	2623	E6
Wakefield Cir				
20600	SGVL	44136	3146	B4
Wakefield Ct				
10	PNVL	44077	2146	B2
Wakefield Ln				
2500	WTLK	44145	2749	E2
E Wakefield Rd				
6900	HRM	44234	3161	D2
7100	HrmT	44234	3161	D2
E Wakefield Rd SR-305				
6900	HRM	44234	3161	D2
7100	HrmT	44234	3161	D2
W Wakefield Rd				
5700	HrmT	44234	3160	B2
5700	HrmT	44255	3160	B2
6500	HRM	44234	3160	B2
6600	HRM	44234	3161	A2
W Wakefield Rd SR-82				
5700	HrmT	44234	3160	B2
5700	HrmT	44255	3160	B2
6500	HRM	44234	3160	B2
6600	HRM	44234	3161	A2
Wakefield Run Blvd				
400	HkyT	44233	3149	D6
400	RchT	44233	3149	D6
4500	RchT	44286	3149	D6
Wake Robin Dr				
7400	HDSN	44236	3155	A7
7400	PRMA	44130	2882	D7
7400	PRMA	44130	3013	D1
16000	NbyT	44073	2763	B7
Wake Robin Rd				
4600	MNTR	44060	2038	D6
Walbrook Av				
2500	CLEV	44109	2754	C7
Waldamere Av				
4500	WLBY	44094	2250	D6
Walden Av				
15400	CLEV	44128	2757	C2
Walden Ct				
6000	MNTR	44060	2144	C3
Walden Dr				
-	AURA	44202	3156	C3
30900	WTLK	44145	2749	A1
Walden Rd				
2200	ECLE	44112	2497	C6
2300	CVHT	44118	2497	C6
Walden Oaks Dr				
12800	MsnT	44024	2634	C1
Waldensa Av				
29200	WKLF	44092	2374	D4
Waldmer Dr				
33900	ETLK	44095	2249	E2
34100	ETLK	44095	2250	A2
Waldo Rd				
-	CLEV	44110	2497	B3
Waldo Wy				
1000	TNBG	44087	3019	A4
Waldorf Dr				
10	PnvT	44077	2145	C4
Waldorf Pl				
6300	INDE	44131	2884	E4
Wales Av				
2700	PRMA	44134	2883	C3
Wales Ct				
4700	CLEV	44102	2624	B5
Walford Av				
9700	CLEV	44102	2753	C2
10000	CLEV	44111	2753	C2
Walford Rd				
4600	WVHT	44128	2758	D6
Walker Av				
8700	CLEV	44105	2756	B3
Walker Ovl				
-	INDE	44131	2885	A3
Walker Rd				
-	AVLK	44012	2619	A3
-	AVLK	44140	2619	A3
5100	SDLK	44054	2616	E3
5400	SDLK	44054	2617	C3
5500	SDLK	44012	2617	C3
30800	BYVL	44140	2619	A3
31700	AVLK	44012	2618	C3
32800	AVLK	44012	2617	C3
Walkers Ln				
8800	KTLD	44094	2377	C6
Walking Stick Wy				
13800	SGVL	44136	3147	C4
Wall St				
7000	INDE	44125	2885	A2
7000	INDE	44131	2885	A2
7300	VLVW	44125	2885	A2
Wallace Blvd				
5200	NRDV	44039	2748	C7
5200	NRDV	44039	2877	C2
Wallace Dr				
100	BERA	44017	3011	A1
300	BERA	44017	3010	E1
Wallace Ln				
2000	LORN	44053	2744	A1
Walleyford Dr				
400	BERA	44017	3010	E1
Wallingford Av				
11000	GDHT	44125	2756	D7
Wallingford Dr				
9200	TNBG	44087	3020	A6
Wallingford Gln				
300	RDHT	44143	2498	E1
Wallingford Rd				
3700	SELD	44121	2497	E4
3800	SELD	44121	2498	A4
Wallings Rd				
3000	BWHT	44147	3014	B5
3000	NRYN	44133	3014	B5
3000	NRYN	44147	3014	B5
5900	NRYN	44133	3013	E6
6500	BKVL	44141	3015	E3
7000	BKVL	44141	3016	A3
7100	NRYN	44133	3013	C6
E Wallings Rd				
100	BWHT	44147	3014	E3
100	BWHT	44147	3015	B3
W Wallings Rd				
900	BWHT	44147	3014	D4
2900	NRYN	44147	3014	D4
Wallu Dr				
100	NRsT	44001	3003	A1
100	SAHT	44001	3003	A1
Walmar Dr				
200	BYVL	44140	2619	A4
Walnut Av				
900	CLEV	44114	2624	C1
1600	CLEV	44114	2625	A2
4700	SFLD	44054	2746	C5
E Walnut Av				
10	PNVL	44077	2146	C1
600	PnvT	44077	2146	C1
E Walnut Av SR-84				
200	PNVL	44077	2146	C1
600	PnvT	44077	2146	C1
W Walnut Av				
10	PNVL	44077	2146	A2
600	PNVL	44077	2145	E2
Walnut Ct				
-	NRDV	44039	2877	A7
3500	LORN	44053	2744	C3
3700	ORNG	44022	2759	D2
32200	AVLK	44012	2618	C3
Walnut Dr				
100	AMHT	44001	2873	A1
300	BERA	44017	2880	A5
500	EUCL	44132	2374	A1
6700	MAYF	44040	2500	B4
17600	SGVL	44136	3146	C4
Walnut Ln				
1600	RKRV	44116	2621	C7
26100	NOSD	44070	2879	B2
Walnut St				
-	SAHT	44001	3003	C1
10	CNFL	44022	2761	A6
10	GNVA	44041	1944	C4
10	OBLN	44074	3138	E2
400	VMLN	44089	2741	A5
800	ELYR	44035	2874	D4
4600	MNTU	44255	3159	C5
5500	MONT	44060	2143	E1
Walnut Tr				
17500	BbgT	44023	2891	B5
Walnut Trc				
13400	MsnT	44024	2634	C3
13400	NbyT	44024	2634	C3
Walnut Creek Dr				
15200	SGVL	44136	3146	C1
Walnut Hill Dr				
12600	NRYN	44133	3012	E7
Walnut Hills Av				
3600	ORNG	44122	2759	A3
Walnut Point Dr				
-	WTLK	44145	2749	A2
W Walnut Ridge Dr				
10900	CsTp	44026	2501	B1
Walnutridge Rd				
10900	CsTp	44026	2501	C2
Walnut Ridge Tr				
500	AURA	44202	3021	C5
Walnutwood Dr				
7600	SVHL	44131	3015	A1
Walt Ct				
3600	CLEV	44111	2752	C2
Walter Av				
3700	PRMA	44134	2883	B1
Walter Rd				
2000	WTLK	44145	2750	D2
2700	NOSD	44070	2750	D3
2700	WTLK	44070	2750	D3
Walter Main Rd				
2100	GnvT	44041	1943	D7
2100	HpfT	44041	1943	D7
Walters Rd				
300	CNFL	44022	2761	B6
400	SRSL	44022	2761	B6
400	SRSL	44073	2761	B6
6900	BSHT	44236	3153	E7
6900	HDSN	44236	3153	E7
7500	MCDN	44056	3153	E2
7500	NCtT	44236	3153	E7
Walter Waite Ct N				
6700	BKVL	44141	3016	A6
Walter Waite Ct S				
6700	BKVL	44141	3016	A6
Walton Av				
1800	CLEV	44113	2624	C7
Walton Blvd				
2400	TNBG	44087	3020	A5
Walton Rd				
6900	WNHL	44146	2886	E7
7100	WNHL	44146	3017	E2
8400	SgHT	44067	3017	E5
Walvern Blvd				
15200	MPHT	44137	2886	B4
Walwick Ct				
700	BERA	44017	3011	B2
Walworth Av				
300	EUCL	44132	2373	D1
4500	CLEV	44113	2624	B6
5600	CLEV	44102	2624	A7
Wamelink Av				
9500	CLEV	44104	2626	B5
Wanaka Blvd				
35700	ETLK	44095	2142	B7
Wanda Av				
-	CLEV	44135	2753	A4
100	CrlT	44035	3005	E3
Wanda Dr				
5400	LORN	44053	2744	C6
Wandle Av				
10	BDFD	44146	2886	E3
10	BDFD	44146	2887	A3
Wandsworth Rd				
4000	SELD	44121	2628	A1
War Av				
6900	CLEV	44105	2755	E4
Warblers Roost				
6000	BKVL	44141	3016	C5
Ward Dr				
12400	CsTp	44026	2502	A7
Ward Rd				
7100	PRMA	44134	2883	C7
Warden Av				
100	ELYR	44035	2874	E3
Wareham Rd				
5900	PRMA	44129	2882	E3
5900	PRMA	44129	2883	A2
Warner Rd				
100	HkyT	44233	3147	E6
4200	CLEV	44105	2756	A5
4500	GDHT	44105	2756	A5
4600	GDHT	44125	2756	A5
4800	GDHT	44125	2755	E7
5200	VLVW	44125	2755	E7
5200	VLVW	44125	2884	E1
6700	MadT	44057	2044	D3
6700	MDSN	44057	2044	D3
7200	HpfT	44057	2045	A3
7200	MadT	44057	2045	A3
Warner Rd SR-307				
6700	MadT	44057	2044	D3
6700	MDSN	44057	2044	D3
7200	HpfT	44057	2045	A3
7200	MadT	44057	2045	A3
Warner Hollow Rd				
6100	WndT	44099	2509	E6
Warren Av				
100	ELYR	44035	2875	D6
1100	ELYR	44035	3006	D1
Warren Pkwy				
2400	TNBG	44087	3020	A4
9800	TNBG	44087	3019	D5
Warren Rd				
1100	LKWD	44107	2622	D6
3000	CLEV	44111	2622	D6
3200	CLEV	44111	2752	C1
29900	WKLF	44092	2249	C7
Warren Burton Rd				
12300	NsnT	44231	3028	D4
12300	NsnT	44231	3029	A6
12300	StnT	44231	3029	A6
12800	PkmT	44491	3028	D4
12800	PkmT	44231	3028	D4
Warren Burton Rd US-422				
12300	NsnT	44231	3028	D4
12300	NsnT	44231	3029	A6
12300	StnT	44231	3029	A6
12800	PkmT	44491	3028	D4
12800	PkmT	44231	3028	D4
Warrendale Rd				
3700	SELD	44118	2627	E2
3800	SELD	44118	2628	A2
8700	MNTR	44060	2144	C2
Warren Point Ln				
7500	HDSN	44236	3154	D6
Warrensville Center Rd				
10	BDFD	44146	2887	A3
1300	CVHT	44121	2498	A7
1300	SELD	44121	2498	A7
1500	CVHT	44121	2628	A4
1500	SELD	44121	2628	A4
1800	SELD	44118	2628	A4
2100	UNHT	44118	2628	A4
2100	UNHT	44121	2628	A4
2600	SRHT	44118	2628	A4
2600	SRHT	44122	2628	A4
3300	SRHT	44122	2758	A3
3700	WVHT	44122	2758	A3
3900	WVHT	44128	2758	A3
4000	HIHL	44128	2758	A3
4400	NRDL	44128	2758	A5
4800	WVHT	44146	2758	A5
5000	MPHT	44137	2758	A5
5300	MPHT	44137	2887	A3
Warrington Dr				
6700	NOSD	44070	2878	C3
Warrington Ln				
10	CcdT	44060	2145	B2
Warrington Rd				
2800	SRHT	44120	2627	B6
Warsaw Av				
6400	CLEV	44105	2755	D3
Warwick Dr				
100	ELYR	44035	2874	B7
700	SDLK	44054	2615	E6
5400	PRMA	44129	2883	A3
Warwick Ln				
10	RKRV	44116	2621	B6
7400	CsTp	44026	2631	C1
Warwick Rd				
2500	SRHT	44120	2627	A5
Warwickshire Ln				
33100	SLN	44139	2888	E7
33100	SLN	44139	2889	A7
Warwood Ct				
-	AhtT	44001	2872	E6
Wasatka Dr				
-	WLBY	44094	2143	A3
Wasatka St				
7000	MNTR	44060	2143	B3
Wascana Av				
2000	LKWD	44107	2622	E6
Washburn Rd				
12700	HrmT	44234	3025	D5
Washburne Rd				
5300	BDHT	44146	2887	C1
Washington Av				
100	ELYR	44035	2875	A5
100	LORN	44052	2614	D6
1100	LORN	44052	2744	D1
2500	CLEV	44113	2624	C4
3700	LORN	44052	2744	D3
4900	LORN	44053	2744	D5
5500	MNTR	44060	2144	A1
5500	MONT	44060	2144	A1
8000	NRYN	44133	3013	C5
16600	MPHT	44137	2886	C2
Washington Blvd				
10	CLEV	44110	2372	C5
1100	MDHT	44124	2499	D7
2800	CVHT	44118	2627	B2
3400	UNHT	44118	2627	D3
3600	SELD	44118	2627	E3
3800	UNHT	44118	2628	A3
14500	SRHT	44118	2628	B4
33600	NRDV	44039	2877	C2
Washington Cir				
300	OBLN	44074	3138	D3
Washington Ct				
700	BDFD	44146	2887	A4
3800	NBGH	44105	2755	B2
32700	SLN	44139	3019	E1
Washington Dr				
200	NHFD	44067	3017	E3
200	NHFD	44067	3018	A3
1000	GFTN	44044	3142	A3
Washington Sq				
-	EUCL	44143	2498	B2
Washington St				
100	CRDN	44024	2379	E6
300	AMHT	44001	2872	E1
400	VMLN	44089	2740	E6
500	AMHT	44001	2743	E7
600	BDFD	44146	2887	A4
11800	AbnT	44021	2893	D5
E Washington St				
10	CNFL	44022	2761	B6
10	PNVL	44077	2146	B1
400	SRSL	44022	2761	B6
400	SRSL	44073	2761	B6
500	BbgT	44023	2761	B6
500	BbgT	44073	2761	B6
7900	BbgT	44023	2890	E1
8300	BbgT	44023	2891	C3
9600	AbnT	44023	2892	C5
9600	BbgT	44023	2892	C5
10700	AbnT	44023	2893	B5
11400	AbnT	44021	2893	B5
W Washington St				
10	CNFL	44022	2760	E6
10	CNFL	44022	2761	B5
10	PNVL	44077	2146	A1
Washington Wy				
29600	WTLK	44145	2749	B4
Washington Park Blvd				
-	CLEV	44105	2755	C2
3900	NBGH	44105	2755	C2
W Wason Dr				
1400	STBR	44241	3157	A7
Water St				
10	CNFL	44022	2761	A5
10	ELYR	44035	2875	A6
10	FTHR	44077	2039	C3
10	GNVA	44041	1944	C3
100	CRDN	44024	2379	C6
100	CRDN	44024	2380	A6
600	CdnT	44024	2379	C6
1000	GFTN	44044	3142	B5
24600	ODFL	44138	2879	C5
Water St US-6				
100	CRDN	44024	2379	C6
100	CRDN	44024	2380	A6
600	CdnT	44024	2379	C6
Water St SR-44				
100	CRDN	44024	2380	A6
Waterbridge Dr				
5100	NRYN	44133	3149	B3
Waterbury Av				
5300	MPHT	44137	2886	C2
Waterbury Cir				
26400	NOSD	44070	2750	A5
Waterbury Dr				
300	ETLK	44095	2142	D7
400	BERA	44017	3010	E1
Waterbury Rd				
1400	LKWD	44107	2622	E5
Watercress Rd				
10800	SGVL	44136	3011	A4
Watercrest Av				
-	MPHT	44137	2887	A1
19000	MPHT	44137	2886	E1
Watercrest Dr				
16800	NRYN	44133	3149	B3
Waterfall Dr				
10	CrlT	44044	3006	E6
10	EatT	44044	3006	E6
Waterfall Rd				
10700	SGVL	44136	3010	E4
10700	SGVL	44136	3011	A4
Waterfall Tr				
7400	RslT	44073	2761	C4
Waterfall Wy				
2900	WTLK	44145	2749	A3
Waterford Ct				
-	AVLK	44012	2617	D3
Waterford Dr				
10	SRSL	44073	2762	B6
2900	TNBG	44087	3020	A4
15000	NRYN	44133	3147	E5
Waterford Ln				
10	BHWD	44122	2628	E4

INDEX 49
Waterford Ln — Cleveland Street Index — Wildflower Wy

STREET Block City ZIP Map# Grid

Waterford Ln
10 MNTR 44060 2145 A5
10 PnvT 44060 2145 A5
10 PnvT 44077 2145 A5
Waterford Pkwy
17600 SGVL 44136 3146 C4
Waterford Tr
9900 AbnT 44023 3023 B2
Waterford Wy
3200 AVON 44011 2748 B3
Waterfowl Ln
- ClrT 44024 2505 B7
12100 MsnT 44024 2505 A7
Waterfowl Wy
7200 CcdT 44077 2254 C1
Waterloo Rd
- CLEV 44110 2497 A1
15200 CLEV 44110 2372 B7
16200 CLEV 44119 2372 B7
S Waterloo Rd
16100 CLEV 44110 2372 D7
16100 CLEV 44110 2497 B1
16100 CLEV 44119 2372 D7
19000 CLEV 44119 2373 A6
Waterman Av
6100 CLEV 44127 2625 D6
Water Oaks Blvd
- CcdT 44077 2146 B6
Waterpepper Cir
6800 SLN 44139 2889 B7
Waters Dr
8200 MCDN 44056 3018 B7
8200 MCDN 44056 3153 B1
Waters Edge Dr
100 ELYR 44035 3006 D2
1900 AVON 44011 2749 A2
1900 AVON 44145 2749 A2
1900 WTLK 44145 2749 A2
Waterside Dr
- AVLK 44012 2617 D2
8500 SgHT 44067 3017 D5
26900 ODFL 44138 3009 D1
N Watling Wy
6100 MadT 44057 1842 E7
6200 MadT 44057 1942 A1
S Watling Wy
6100 MadT 44057 1941 E1
6200 MadT 44057 1942 A1
Watson Av
38800 NRDV 44039 2876 A4
Watson Ct
3500 LORN 44053 2743 E3
Watson Dr
- CrlT 44035 3006 A4
Watson Rd
20400 MPHT 44137 2758 A7
Watson St
10 PNVL 44077 2146 A1
Watt Rd
13800 RslT 44072 2632 D6
14400 RslT 44072 2762 D1
Watterson Av
12300 CLEV 44105 2756 E3
Waverly Ct
5800 CLEV 44102 2624 A5
Waverly Ln
10 SRSL 44073 2761 E6
Waverly Pl
100 LORN 44052 2614 B7
3900 SELD 44121 2498 A4
Waverly Rd
200 ETLK 44095 2249 E3
Waverly St
100 BERA 44017 2880 C7
100 ELYR 44035 2874 E5
Wa Wa Taysee St
4800 VMLN 44089 2741 A4
Waxberry Dr
6400 SVHL 44131 2884 A4
Way Av
9100 CLEV 44105 2756 C2
Wayland Av
11700 CLEV 44111 2753 A2
Wayland Way Rd
- NRDV 44039 2876 E7
- NRDV 44039 3007 E1
Wayne Av
1400 LKWD 44107 2622 A5
Wayne Ct
10100 CLEV 44106 2626 C3
24600 EUCL 44123 2373 D3
Wayne Dr
200 BERA 44017 2880 A7
16700 CLEV 44128 2757 C4
Wayne Ln
10 HmbT 44024 2381 A3
Wayne Rd
4100 ManT 44255 3159 A1
4200 ManT 44255 3024 B7
Wayne St
700 ELYR 44035 3006 A2
Wayne Tr
- VMLN 44089 2741 B6
Waynesboro Dr
1400 TwbT 44236 3154 C6
Waynoka Rd
2100 EUCL 44117 2498 A3
Wayside Av
- NCtT 44057 3153 B5
Wayside Dr
7000 MNTR 44060 2145 A7
Wayside Ln
28900 BYVL 44140 2619 D4
Wayside Rd
700 CLEV 44110 2497 C2
1600 CLEV 44112 2497 C2
Waywood Dr
11900 TNBG 44087 3019 D3
Weatherby Dr
6700 MNTR 44060 2143 D6
N Weatherby Dr
6600 MNTR 44060 2143 D5
Weathersfield Dr
7200 HDSN 44236 3154 C7
9800 CcdT 44060 2253 C2
Weathertop Ln
9700 AbnT 44023 2892 A1
Weathervane Ct
7600 CcdT 44060 2253 C2
Weathervane Dr
- MDFD 44062 2767 E1
9400 BbgT 44023 2891 E6
Weathervane Ln
10 BNWK 44212 3147 B6
Weatherwood Ln
2100 BWHT 44147 3149 C4
Weaver Dr
1500 AMHT 44001 2744 C7
Webb Rd
1000 LKWD 44107 2622 B4
4500 PryT 44081 2042 C5
Webb Cliff Dr
17800 LKWD 44107 2622 B5
Webber Rd
32700 AVLK 44012 2617 D4
32700 AVLK 44012 2618 A4
Weber Av
28900 WKLF 44092 2374 A2
Weber Rd
7600 MONT 44060 2143 D2
Weber Park Dr
22000 OKWD 44146 2887 C7
Webster Cir
2500 HDSN 44236 3155 C6
Webster Ct
200 PNVL 44077 2146 B1
3300 CLEV 44114 2625 C2
Webster Rd
7500 MDBH 44130 3012 B1
7900 SGVL 44130 3012 C3
7900 SGVL 44136 3012 C3
16300 MDBH 44130 2881 B7
30500 BYVL 44140 2619 B3
Wedgefield Ln
12200 CsTp 44026 2501 E5
Wedgewood Av
100 ELYR 44035 2875 E3
Wedgewood Ct
8500 OmsT 44138 2879 B7
Wedgewood Dr
500 AVLK 44012 2618 C4
5900 MONT 44060 2143 C3
6100 MNTR 44060 2143 C3
6400 BKPK 44142 2880 D3
6500 NOSD 44070 2878 B3
7900 CsTp 44026 2501 E5
30100 SLN 44139 2888 C1
Wedgewood Ln
15800 SGVL 44136 3146 B3
Wefel Av
7400 BKLN 44144 2753 E4
Welch Rd
1400 PnvT 44077 2041 A7
Welk Ct
- AMHT 44001 2872 E4
9100 MNTR 44060 2144 E1
Welk Rd
9800 CdnT 44024 2378 B5
Welland Dr
7100 MNTR 44060 2143 B7
Weller Rd
600 ELYR 44035 2875 A4
Wellesley Av
1800 ECLE 44112 2497 A6
5200 NOSD 44070 2749 C7
5400 NOSD 44070 2878 C1
Wellesley Blvd
10 CcdT 44077 2145 B6
10 PnvT 44077 2145 B6
Wellesley Cir
600 AVLK 44012 2618 D4
Wellesley Ln
11700 MsnT 44024 2503 E3
Wellfleet Dr
500 BYVL 44140 2619 C5
1000 GFTN 44044 3142 A4
7200 HDSN 44236 3154 E7
Wellingford Ct
33500 SLN 44139 2889 A2
Wellington Av
2400 PRMA 44134 2883 D3
Wellington Ct
7100 BSHT 44236 3153 E6
18100 SGVL 44136 3146 E4
Wellington Dr
4500 PryT 44081 2042 C5
11100 CdnT 44024 2379 B3
29500 NOSD 44070 2878 C3
Wellington Rd
- MDHT 44124 2629 B1
2400 CVHT 44118 2627 C5
5600 LNHT 44124 2629 B1
10000 ShvT 44241 3158 A7
Wellington St
10 BERA 44017 2880 B5
Wellman Rd
10200 STBR 44236 3156 A7
Wellmon St
600 BDFD 44146 2887 C4
Wellner Rd
31000 WLWK 44095 2249 D5
Wells Pl
200 EUCL 44132 2249 A7
Wells St
- WFAR 44491 2898 D5
Wells Fleet Cir
3000 WLBY 44094 2250 E2
Wellsley Pl
10 BNWK 44212 3147 B6
Wellswood Tr
12700 CsTp 44026 2501 B7
12700 CsTp 44026 2631 B1
Welshfield Limaville Rd S
10300 HrmT 44234 3161 A6
10300 HrmT 44255 3161 A6
11300 HRM 44234 3161 A6
11900 HrmT 44234 3026 A6
11900 HrmT 44234 3161 A1
13000 TroT 44234 3026 A6
Welshfield Limavle Rd S SR-82
11300 HRM 44234 3161 A6
11300 HrmT 44234 3161 A6
Welshfield Limavle Rd S SR-700
10300 HrmT 44234 3161 A6
10300 HrmT 44255 3161 A6
11300 HRM 44234 3161 A6
11900 HrmT 44234 3026 A6
11900 HrmT 44234 3161 A1
13000 TroT 44234 3026 A6
Welshire Dr
500 BYVL 44140 2619 D5
Welton Dr
15300 ECLE 44112 2497 B5
Wembley Ct
8400 BbgT 44023 2762 A7
8500 BbgT 44023 2761 E7
Wemple Rd
14700 CLEV 44110 2497 B3
14700 ECLE 44110 2497 B3
Wendell Av
4800 CLEV 44127 2625 C6
Wenden Ct
10 BTNH 44108 2496 E1
10 BTNH 44108 2497 A1
10 BTNH 44110 2497 A1
Wendover Dr
23100 BHWD 44122 2628 C4
Wendy Dr
3700 CLEV 44122 2757 D2
3900 CLEV 44128 2757 D2
12100 PRMA 44130 3013 A1
19600 MDBH 44130 2880 D5
Wendy Ln
600 ELYR 44035 2875 A7
Wengatz Dr
13100 MDBH 44130 3012 D1
Wengler Dr
5700 BKPK 44142 2881 B2
Wenhaven Dr
15400 RslT 44073 2761 E4
Wenso Rd
900 BDFD 44146 2887 B5
Wentworth Av
6400 BKPK 44142 2880 B3
7100 CLEV 44102 2623 E7
Wentworth Ln
7500 CcdT 44060 2253 B2
Wentworth Rd
10200 ShvT 44241 3158 A7
Werner Ct
2900 LORN 44052 2744 C3
Wesley Av
200 ELYR 44035 2875 E5
13000 CLEV 44111 2753 A2
13200 CLEV 44111 2752 E2
Wesley Dr
600 BERA 44017 2880 B4
7900 SGVL 44136 3012 D2
8400 PRMA 44129 2882 D2
8400 PRMA 44130 2882 D2
Wesleyan Ct
100 ELYR 44035 3006 B1
West Av
10 ELYR 44035 2875 A6
900 CLEV 44113 2624 B4
900 ELYR 44035 3006 A2
13000 CLEV 44111 2753 A3
13200 CLEV 44111 2752 E3
West Blvd
1900 CLEV 44102 2623 C6
3000 CLEV 44111 2623 C7
3200 CLEV 44111 2753 C1
3600 CLEV 44102 2753 C2
4000 BKLN 44144 2753 E3
5300 MPHT 44137 2886 C1
West Dr
- MNTR 44060 2251 B4
10 OmsT 44138 2879 A4
600 BNWK 44212 3146 E7
700 SDLK 44054 2616 A4
West Pk
- PkmT 44234 3027 E1
West Pl
200 PNVL 44077 2146 A2
West Rd
5700 MONT 44060 2143 D2
13400 NRsT 44074 3139 D4
13700 PtfT 44074 3139 C5
22900 BERA 44138 2879 E7
22900 ODFL 44017 2879 E7
24300 ODFL 44138 2879 D7
35300 EatT 44044 3008 A7
West Rd NW
4800 FnTp 44491 3029 E3
West St
- MadT 44057 1943 A7
- PkmT 44231 3027 E1
- PkmT 44234 3027 E1
10 BERA 44017 2880 A7
10 CNFL 44022 2761 A4
10 GNVA 44041 1944 A6
10 GnvT 44041 1944 A6
400 AMHT 44001 2872 D2
400 BERA 44017 2879 E7
2200 HpfT 44041 1944 A6
13600 BtnT 44021 2636 A7
13600 BtnT 44021 2766 A2
13600 BURT 44021 2636 A7
13600 BURT 44021 2766 A2
West Area Rd
- BKPK 44135 2751 A7
- BKPK 44142 2751 A7
- BKPK 44142 2880 A1
- CLEV 44135 2751 A7
Westborough Rd
10900 PMHT 44130 2882 B4
Westbourne Rd
4700 LNHT 44124 2498 D7
Westbridge Dr
200 BERA 44017 2880 B6
Westbrook Dr
100 EUCL 44132 2249 A6
4000 BKLN 44144 2753 D4
5800 BKPK 44142 2881 D2
Westbrook Wy
600 HDSN 44236 3153 E7
600 HDSN 44236 3154 A7
Westbrooke Ln
19100 SGVL 44136 3146 D4
Westburn Av
1900 CLEV 44112 2497 D4
1900 ECLE 44112 2497 D4
2100 CVHT 44112 2497 D4
Westbury Dr
500 PnvT 44077 2145 C5
Westbury Rd
3300 SRHT 44120 2627 B7
3300 SRHT 44120 2757 B1
Westchester Av
9800 CLEV 44108 2496 B6
Westchester Ct
1500 PnvT 44077 2041 B5
Westchester Dr
10 BNWK 44212 3147 A6
100 AMHT 44001 2872 D3
23200 NOSD 44070 2750 E3
Westchester Pkwy
27600 WTLK 44145 2619 E6
27600 WTLK 44145 2620 A6
Westchester Rd
21800 SRHT 44122 2628 B6
Westchester Tr
12700 CsTp 44026 2501 B7
12700 CsTp 44026 2631 B2
Westdale Av
15700 CLEV 44135 2752 B4
Westdale Dr
- PRMA 44130 2881 E7
- PRMA 44130 2882 A7
Westdale Rd
1400 SELD 44121 2498 B7
1400 SELD 44121 2628 B1
Westerham Rd
6000 MDHT 44124 2629 D1
Western Av
10000 CLEV 44102 2623 B7
10000 CLEV 44111 2623 B7
Western Pkwy
38100 WLBY 44094 2142 E6
38100 WLBY 44094 2143 A6
Westfield Av
16600 CLEV 44110 2497 C2
Westfield Cir
1000 PnvT 44077 2146 E2
Westfield Dr
8400 NRDV 44039 2876 E6
14600 NbyT 44065 2764 B1
Westfield Ln
10 RKRV 44116 2621 C7
18900 SGVL 44136 3147 A5
Westford Cir
- WTLK 44145 2619 C7
Westgate Mall
- FWPK 44126 2751 C1
- RKRV 44116 2751 C1
3000 FWPK 44116 2751 C1
Westhaven Ln
19900 RKRV 44116 2751 D1
19900 RKRV 44126 2751 D1
West Hemlock
2300 NPRY 44081 1940 D3
Westhill Blvd
1400 WTLK 44145 2620 D7
Westhill Dr
8000 BbgT 44023 2890 E3
8000 BbgT 44023 2891 A4
Westin Wy
- ELYR 44035 3007 A1
Westlake Av
1100 LKWD 44107 2622 B4
5400 PRMA 44129 2883 A1
6700 PRMA 44129 2882 E1
Westlake Dr
600 AMHT 44001 2872 C1
Westlake Village Ct
28600 WTLK 44145 2749 D4
Westlake Village Dr
28600 WTLK 44145 2749 D4
Westland Av
14500 CLEV 44111 2752 D1
14600 CLEV 44111 2622 D7
Westlawn Blvd
8700 ODFL 44138 2879 E7
Westlawn Dr
28200 NOSD 44070 2878 D3
29900 BYVL 44140 2619 C4
Westlawn Rd
5000 BDHT 44128 2758 D7
Westminister Dr
2200 LORN 44053 2744 B4
Westminster Av
35400 NRDV 44011 2748 A6
35400 NRDV 44039 2748 A6
Westminster Dr
5600 SLN 44139 2888 C2
5900 PRMA 44129 2882 D3
20500 SGVL 44136 3146 B4
29400 NOSD 44070 2878 B3
Westminster Ln
2600 WLBY 44094 2250 E1
Westminster Rd
2100 CVHT 44118 2627 B3
Westmont Av
- NOSD 44070 2749 C7
- NOSD 44070 2878 C1
Westmont Dr
- SFLD 44054 2746 D4
Westmoor Ln
20100 BERA 44017 2880 D5
20100 BERA 44130 2880 D5
Westmoor Rd
2200 RKRV 44116 2621 D6
8100 MNTR 44060 2251 C4
Weston Av
- WTLK 44145 2750 C2
Weston Ct
5500 WLBY 44094 2375 A1
Weston Rd
18000 CLEV 44121 2497 E3
Westover Av
19900 RKRV 44116 2751 D1
Westover Dr
10 SRSL 44073 2762 B6
Westover Rd
1300 CVHT 44118 2497 C7
Westown Blvd
27200 WTLK 44145 2749 E3
27200 WTLK 44145 2750 A3
Westpoint Pkwy
800 WTLK 44145 2620 D6
West Pointe Cir
100 CRDN 44024 2505 A1
Westport Av
- CLEV 44135 2752 A6
20100 EUCL 44123 2373 A4
Westport Dr
8400 MNTR 44060 2144 B5
Westridge Cir
11300 MsnT 44024 2634 B3
Westropp Av
14200 CLEV 44110 2372 A7
14800 CLEV 44110 2497 A1
Westview Av
15500 CLEV 44128 2757 B3
22100 BKPK 44142 2880 A3
Westview Ct
2300 LORN 44052 2744 B2
West View Dr
17600 BbgT 44023 2890 E5
Westview Dr
400 BDFD 44146 2887 A2
4400 NOSD 44070 2750 C6
6600 BKVL 44141 3150 E3
6600 BKVL 44141 3151 A3
9700 PRMA 44129 2753 C7
Westway Dr
19700 RKRV 44116 2621 C6
Westwind Ct
11000 SGVL 44136 3011 A5
Westwind Dr
100 AVLK 44012 2618 E2
Westwood
400 AhtT 44001 2872 A4
Westwood Av
400 BNWK 44212 3147 A7
1400 LKWD 44107 2622 C5
Westwood Dr
- ELYR 44035 3006 B3
- GnvT 44041 1944 C1
700 PNVL 44077 2146 B2
900 WLBY 44094 2142 E4
1300 LORN 44053 2744 C5
1600 TNBG 44087 3019 C4
6700 BKVL 44141 3150 E1
6700 BKVL 44141 3151 A1
9000 KTLD 44094 2252 A7
9300 MCDN 44056 3018 E5
14600 NbyT 44072 2763 A1
18700 SGVL 44136 3011 D7
22300 SGVL 44136 3010 E6
36200 NRDV 44039 2876 E5
36200 NRDV 44039 2877 A5
Westwood Ln
26900 OmsT 44138 2878 E3
26900 OmsT 44138 2879 A3
Westwood Rd
3700 UNHT 44118 2627 E3
10300 ClbT 44028 3010 D3
20800 FWPK 44126 2751 C2
22900 WTLK 44145 2750 D2
22900 WTLK 44145 2751 B2
28900 BYVL 44140 2619 D4
Westwood Park Blvd
20200 SGVL 44136 3011 C7
Wetherburn Wy
7400 HDSN 44236 3154 E7
Wethersfield Ct
4700 RDHT 44143 2498 D1
Wetmore St
100 GDRV 44045 2039 C6
200 PnvT 44045 2039 C6
200 PnvT 44077 2039 C6
Wetzel Av
3600 CLEV 44109 2754 B6
4800 CLEV 44144 2754 B6
Wexford Av
900 BNHT 44131 2754 E7
1100 PRMA 44134 2754 E7
Wexford Dr
- MsnT 44024 2504 B2
37300 SLN 44139 3020 C1
Weybridge Dr
28700 WTLK 44145 2749 D3
Weybridge Rd
2800 SRHT 44120 2627 C6
Weyburne Av
19300 CLEV 44135 2751 D5
Weymouth Cir
1500 WTLK 44145 2619 D7
Weymouth Dr
1900 HDSN 44236 3154 E7
6000 MNTR 44060 2144 B3
Weymouth Ln
16400 SGVL 44136 3147 A4
Weymouth Pl
10 AURA 44202 3157 A3
Weymouth Rd
2800 SRHT 44120 2627 A6
Whalers Cove
9300 MNTR 44060 2144 E6
9300 MNTR 44060 2145 A5
Wharton Dr
7300 RslT 44072 2631 B5
Wheat Ct
3300 CLEV 44113 2624 B5
4500 CLEV 44102 2624 B5
Wheatfield Dr
500 AURA 44202 3156 C4
Wheatfield Ln
9700 CcdT 44060 2145 B3
Wheatley Av
- LORN 44053 2743 D2
Wheaton Dr
- SFLD 44054 2746 E4
Wheeler Ct
8700 MNTR 44060 2144 C2
Wheeler Rd
10900 GTVL 44234 3161 E3
11200 HrmT 44234 3161 E3
14000 MPHT 44137 2886 A3
15700 LrgT 44050 3141 B6
Wheeler Creek Rd
3200 GnvT 44041 1943 D4
3900 GnvT 44041 1844 D6
Wheeler's Wy
19100 SGVL 44136 3011 D7
Wheeling St
- PNVL 44077 2040 A5
Wheelock Dr
10 BDFD 44146 2887 A4
Wheelock Rd
800 CLEV 44103 2496 A6
1000 CLEV 44108 2496 A6
Whetstone Cir
4900 BHIT 44212 3146 A7
Whippoorwill Av
1100 LKWD 44107 2622 E4
Whippoorwill Ln
8600 PRMA 44130 3013 D1
Whiskey Ln
11800 BKVL 44141 3151 D3
Whiskey Island Dr
2800 CLEV 44113 2624 A4
4600 CLEV 44102 2624 A4
Whispering Pt
3200 AVON 44011 2748 A4
Whispering Cove Cir
2200 WTLK 44145 2749 A2
Whispering Oaks Blvd
- PRMA 44129 2883 A5
Whispering Pines Cir
19300 SGVL 44136 3146 E5
Whispering Pines Dr
5700 LORN 44053 2744 E6
8200 RslT 44072 2631 E7
8200 RslT 44072 2632 A7
Whisperwood Ln
- AURA 44202 3022 E4
10 HGVL 44022 2631 A7
10 HGVL 44073 2631 A7
Whisperwood Ln
9700 AbnT 44023 2763 A7
14900 HGVL 44022 2761 A1
14900 HGVL 44073 2761 A1
Whistler Ct
5200 NRYN 44133 3149 A1
Whistlewood Wy
3700 PRRY 44081 2042 C1
Whitacre Cir
2500 BKVL 44141 3150 B3
Whitacre Ct
10 BDFD 44146 2887 C4
Whitaker Dr
7200 PRMA 44130 2882 C7
Whitaker Cove
- AVLK 44012 2617 D4
Whitby Av
7600 MNTR 44060 2251 D3
Whitby Rd
900 CVHT 44112 2497 D5
Whitcomb Rd
15900 CLEV 44110 2497 C2
White Av
5500 CLEV 44103 2625 D1
11000 CrlT 44035 3005 D4
White Ct
100 ELYR 44035 3006 B2
White Rd
2400 UNHT 44118 2628 C4
6400 MAYF 44092 2500 A1
6400 MAYF 44143 2500 A1
6400 WBHL 44092 2500 A1
8700 KTLD 44094 2252 C7
8800 KDHL 44060 2252 C7
8800 KDHL 44094 2252 C7
14900 BtnT 44062 2766 E3
26200 RDHT 44143 2374 A7
26600 WBHL 44092 2374 A7
White St
10 BERA 44017 2880 A5
White Angel Dr
4500 PryT 44081 1940 D7
White Ash Dr
1400 PnvT 44077 2041 A7
White Ash Tr
10300 TNBG 44087 3020 A3
White Bark Cir
4500 NRYN 44133 3014 B6
White Bark Dr
20200 SGVL 44136 3146 B2
White Birch Wy
100 NRsT 44001 3003 A1
100 SAHT 44001 3003 A1
White Cedar Pl
4100 PryT 44081 2041 D3
E Whitedove Ln
7000 MDBH 44130 2880 E5
N Whitedove Ln
18300 MDBH 44130 2880 E5
W Whitedove Ln
6900 MDBH 44130 2880 E5
White Fir Ln
17700 SGVL 44136 3146 E4
Whiteford Dr
5900 HDHT 44143 2499 D3
Whitehall Dr
10 BERA 44017 3011 B2
4400 SELD 44121 2498 C6
Whitehaven Av
5200 NOSD 44070 2749 C7
5200 NOSD 44070 2878 C1
Whitehaven Dr
7700 PRMA 44129 2882 D4
Whitehead Av
12600 CLEV 44105 2756 B3
Whitehead Rd
13200 CrlT 44050 3140 C4
14100 LrgT 44050 3140 C4
Whitehill Cir
27600 WTLK 44145 2619 E6
White Marsh Dr
2000 TNBG 44087 3019 E3
2300 TNBG 44087 3020 A4
Whitemarsh Ln
18400 SGVL 44136 3146 D4
Whitemarsh Wy
7400 HDSN 44236 3154 D6
White Oak Cir
15200 MDBH 44130 2881 C5
White Oak Ct
200 AURA 44202 3156 E1
4100 PryT 44081 2041 D3
White Oak Dr
200 ELYR 44035 2875 E4
5800 MNTR 44060 2144 C3
7500 SLN 44139 3019 E2
18600 AbnT 44023 3023 C2
Whiteoak Dr
8800 TNBG 44087 3154 D1
White Oak Ln
- NOSD 44070 2749 B7
- NOSD 44145 2749 B7
- TroT 44234 2894 B6
- WTLK 44145 2749 B7
- WTLK 44070 2749 B7
White Oak Rd
9000 KTLD 44094 2252 B7
White Oak Tr
3900 ORNG 44122 2759 C3
White Oak Wy
5600 NRDV 44039 2877 E1
White Oaks Cir
9100 BKVL 44141 3016 B4
N White Oaks Dr
16500 SGVL 44136 3147 A4
S White Oaks Dr
16500 SGVL 44136 3147 A4
Whitepine Ct
7600 MNTR 44060 2252 B2
White Pine Dr
5800 BDHT 44146 2887 D3
7500 CsTp 44026 2501 C5
White Pine St
4000 AVON 44011 2748 C4
White Pine Wy
4800 NRDV 44039 2748 D7
White Sands Blvd
7000 MadT 44057 1843 C6
Whitestone Ct
11800 NRYN 44133 3148 A5
White Swan Ct
5200 NRYN 44133 3149 A1
Whitetail Ct
3000 RHFD 44286 3150 D7
White Tail Dr
400 AURA 44202 3156 C2
Whitetail Dr
300 SRSL 44073 2762 A5
Whitetail Ln
10 BTVL 44022 2889 E1
Whitetail Run Ln
8600 KDHL 44060 2252 C6
White Tail Run Pl
7400 CcdT 44077 2254 C1
Whitethorn Av
5000 NOSD 44070 2750 A7
7800 CLEV 44103 2626 A1
Whitethorn Dr
5600 MONT 44060 2143 D1
Whitethorn Rd
3100 CVHT 44118 2627 C1
Whiteway Dr
26600 RDHT 44143 2373 E6
26600 RDHT 44143 2374 A6
Whitewood Dr
1800 MadT 44057 1942 A1
11100 NbyT 44065 2634 A4
Whitewood Pkwy
9400 TNBG 44087 3019 D6
Whitewood Rd
8200 BKVL 44141 3015 E5
8200 BKVL 44141 3016 A5
Whitfield Ln
4400 RDHT 44143 2498 C3
Whiting Dr
8300 CsTp 44026 2502 A5
Whitman Av
3100 CLEV 44113 2624 C5
Whitman Blvd
100 ELYR 44035 2875 D2
Whitmore Av
11200 CLEV 44108 2496 D5
Whitmore Ct
10 PnvT 44077 2040 E7
Whitney Av
6600 CLEV 44103 2625 E1
6800 CLEV 44103 2495 E7
Whitney Ln
8200 CcdT 44077 2253 D4
Whitney Rd
13000 SGVL 44133 3012 D3
13000 SGVL 44136 3012 D3
16700 MtlT 44064 2383 B5
16900 HgvT 44064 2384 A5
16900 MtlT 44064 2384 A5
18100 SGVL 44136 3011 E3
Whiton Rd
2600 UNHT 44118 2628 C5
Whittier Av
5500 CLEV 44103 2625 D1
Whittington Dr
7300 PRMA 44129 2882 D3
Whittlesay Ln
1000 RKRV 44116 2621 B6
Whittlesey Rd
48900 BhmT 44001 2871 D1
Whooper Ct
5200 NRYN 44133 3149 A1
Wichita Av
4000 CLEV 44109 2754 B5
4500 CLEV 44144 2754 B5
Wickens Pl
300 LORN 44052 2614 D6
Wickfield Av
19000 WVHT 44122 2757 E2
19700 WVHT 44122 2758 A2
Wickfield Dr
5800 PMHT 44130 2882 D2
Wickford Ct
17700 CLEV 44112 2497 D2
Wickford Rd
1600 CLEV 44112 2497 D2
Wickham Pl
1600 PnvT 44077 2040 E2
Wickland St
200 PNVL 44077 2146 A2
Wickley Ln
5500 BDHT 44146 2887 E2
Wicklow Dr
10 ETLK 44095 2142 B6
Wicklow Rd
2600 SRHT 44120 2627 A5
Widgeon Dr
10000 AbnT 44023 2892 B6
Wiese Rd
8200 BKVL 44141 3016 C5
Wight Oaks Dr
7000 WNHL 44146 2886 C7
Wilber Av
5400 PRMA 44129 2883 A2
6700 PRMA 44129 2882 E2
Wilbert Dr
10200 KTLD 44094 2377 B5
Wilbert Rd
1000 LKWD 44107 2622 E4
11300 MsnT 44024 2504 B2
Wilbur Av
10000 CLEV 44106 2626 C3
41100 EyrT 44035 2745 C6
Wilburn Dr
4500 SELD 44121 2498 C6
Wilcox Rd
4700 MstT 44062 2769 E1
Wildbrook Dr
500 BYVL 44140 2619 C5
Wild Cherry Ovl
3800 ORNG 44122 2759 B2
Wild Cherry Tr
3800 ORNG 44122 2759 B2
Wilder Av
800 ELYR 44035 2875 E2
Wilder Rd
9800 CdnT 44024 2379 A3
Wilderness Dr
7700 MNTR 44060 2253 A3
Wilderness Ln
5900 PMHT 44130 2882 B2
Wilderness Psg
9100 BbgT 44023 2891 D1
Wilderness Tr
24100 ODFL 44138 2879 D7
31000 WTLK 44145 2749 A2
Wildflower Cir
13500 RslT 44072 2631 D3
Wildflower Dr
2700 RKRV 44116 2621 C7
Wildflower Wy
10200 BWHT 44147 3149 E4

INDEX 50

Wilding Chase — Woodline Rd

Cleveland Street Index

STREET
Block City ZIP Map# Grid

Wilding Chase
10 CNFL 44022 2761 B4
Wild Oak Dr
5900 NOSD 44070 2878 A2
Wild Oak Pl
17400 BbgT 44023 2890 C4
Wildwood Av
6400 BKPK 44142 2880 B3
Wildwood Cir
1500 WTLK 44145 2619 B7
Wildwood Ct
5400 WLEY 44094 2375 A1
Wildwood Dr
1100 AMHT 44001 2743 D6
1100 VMLN 44089 2741 B6
7800 MNTR 44060 2252 D3
8800 NRYN 44133 3013 A3
9300 HmbT 44024 2380 D2
24100 EUCL 44123 2373 C2
24400 WTLK 44145 2750 C2
Wildwood Ln
19500 SGVL 44136 3146 C3
Wildwood Pl
100 ELYR 44035 2746 D7
Wildwood Tr
6600 MAYF 44143 2500 A3
10100 MsnT 44024 2503 C2
Wilkenson Cir
5400 MNTR 44060 2145 B1
Wilkes Ln
500 RDHT 44143 2498 C3
Wilks Ln
2700 WTLK 44145 2749 C2
Willard Av
10 BDFD 44146 2887 A2
8500 CLEV 44102 2623 D7
11600 GDHT 44125 2885 E1
Willard Ct
10 OBLN 44074 3138 E2
Willard Rd
100 AURA 44202 3157 A1
E Willard Rd
13900 RslT 44072 2631 E5
W Willard Rd
13900 RslT 44072 2631 D5
Willet Cir
5200 NOSD 44070 2749 D7
Willey Av
1600 CLEV 44113 2624 D5
William Cir
1500 PRMA 44134 2883 E5
William St
10 BDFD 44146 2887 B6
7600 MNTR 44060 2143 D4
Williams Av
11600 CLEV 44120 2626 D5
23200 EUCL 44123 2373 C2
Williams Ct
3400 AVON 44011 2748 E4
Williams Dr
- VMLN 44089 2741 B6
6300 BWHT 44147 3015 E5
25900 WTLK 44145 2750 B1
Williams Rd
6500 CcdT 44077 2147 A5
6900 CcdT 44077 2254 E1
6900 CcdT 44077 2255 A1
8400 HmbT 44024 2256 C7
8400 HmbT 44024 2381 C1
Williams St
- PnvT 44077 2039 C4
10 CNFL 44022 2761 A4
10 ELYR 44035 2875 C6
10 GDRV 44045 2039 C4
10 GDRV 44077 2039 C4
500 PNVL 44077 2040 A6
14500 MPHT 44137 2757 A7
Williamsburg
- AMHT 44001 2744 B6
- AMHT 44053 2744 B6
Williamsburg Ct
10 MDSN 44057 1942 B7
20300 BERA 44017 2880 C5
20300 BERA 44130 2880 C5
20300 MDBH 44130 2880 C5
Williamsburg Dr
300 AVLK 44012 2618 C2
500 HDHT 44143 2499 C3
2000 PRMA 44134 2883 D4
5500 LORN 44053 2744 B5
Williamsburg Ovl
18000 SGVL 44136 3146 E4
Williamson Av
11800 LKWD 44107 2623 B4
Williamston Av
4300 BKLN 44144 2753 D5
Williamstown Dr
4400 NOSD 44070 2750 A6
Willis St
10 BDFD 44146 2887 A4
Williston Dr
5500 PRMA 44129 2883 A6
Willman Av
15100 CLEV 44135 2752 C5
Willo Rd
33400 AVON 44011 2748 D2
Wil Lou Ln
6700 NRDV 44039 2877 C3
Willoughby Pkwy
38100 WLBY 44094 2142 E7
Willoughcroft Dr
4600 WLBY 44094 2250 D6
Willow Av
4300 LORN 44055 2746 A4
29600 WKLF 44092 2374 D3
Willow Bnd
1100 BWHT 44147 3149 E5
Willow Cir
400 AURA 44202 3156 D2
14400 SGVL 44136 3012 C4
32000 AVLK 44012 2618 D3
Willow Ct
10000 BKVL 44141 3151 D4
Willow Dr
- TNBG 44087 3019 D3
300 PNVL 44077 2146 B1
500 EUCL 44132 2374 A2
6400 INDE 44131 2884 C5
37100 ETLK 44095 2142 D6
Willow Frwy I-77
- BKVL - 3150 E3
- BWHT - 3015 D3
- CHHT - 2755 D5
- CLEV - 2625 C6
- CLEV - 2755 D5
- INDE - 2755 D5
- INDE - 2884 D6
- INDE - 3015 D1
- NBGH - 2755 D5
- RHFD - 3150 E3
Willow Frwy SR-21
- CHHT - 2755 D5
- CLEV - 2625 C6
- CLEV - 2755 D5
- NBGH - 2755 D5
Willow Ln
100 CNFL 44022 2761 A5
200 BERA 44017 2880 A5
3100 BHWD 44122 2628 E7
5300 SDLK 44054 2616 E2
5300 VMLN 44089 2740 E5
8400 LryT 44024 2256 A5
8500 HmbT 44024 2256 A5
9200 ODFL 44138 3010 A1
9700 CcdT 44060 2145 B7
21000 SGVL 44136 3011 B3
29200 WBHL 44092 2374 C7
30500 WLWK 44095 2249 C6
Willow Pkwy
4400 CHHT 44125 2755 D4
Willow St
400 BHIT 44212 3146 C7
1100 GFTN 44044 3142 B6
7200 SLN 44139 3020 E2
N Willow St
1000 GFTN 44044 3142 B6
Willow Wy
7200 OmsT 44138 2878 A4
30500 BYVL 44140 2619 B5
Willowbend Dr
100 MDSN 44057 1942 B6
Willowbrook Dr
10 OBLN 44074 3139 B2
3200 PRPK 44124 2629 E7
3200 PRPK 44124 2759 E1
4500 MNTR 44060 2038 E5
4900 CHHT 44125 2755 E6
7900 CsTp 44026 2501 E2
Willow Brook Ln
2000 HkyT 44233 3148 B6
32600 NRDV 44039 2877 E1
Willowbrook Cove
- AURA 44202 3021 C7
Willow Creek Dr
700 AMHT 44001 2872 B3
Willowdale Av
1800 CLEV 44109 2754 D2
Willowdale Dr
38800 WLBY 44094 2251 B5
Willow Haven Rd
10 CrlT 44035 3006 C3
Willow Hill Dr
11300 CsTp 44026 2501 D2
Willow Hollow Ct
800 AMHT 44001 2872 B3
Willowhurst Rd
1800 CLEV 44112 2497 D3
Willowick Dr
28900 WLWK 44095 2249 B7
33000 ETLK 44095 2249 E4
34000 LKLN 44095 2249 E3
Willow Lake Dr
- NRYN 44133 3148 E2
700 SgHT 44067 3017 C4
Willowmere Av
11100 CLEV 44108 2496 C5
Willowood Ct
1400 PnvT 44077 2041 A7
Willow Park Rd
500 ELYR 44035 2875 A4
Willow Run Dr
3600 WTLK 44145 2750 B4
7300 MNTR 44060 2143 C4
Willow Tree Ln
6600 GNWL 44139 2888 A7
Willow Wood Dr
16700 SGVL 44136 3147 A5
Willow Wood Ln
10 MDHL 44022 2760 C3
Willshire Dr
800 AMHT 44001 2743 E6
1000 AMHT 44001 2744 A6
Willshire Ln
12300 MsnT 44024 2503 C6
Willshire Rd
1300 LNHT 44124 2499 A7
Willson Dr
9000 BbgT 44023 3022 D1
Wilma Dr
14000 SGVL 44136 3012 D3
Wilmar Ct
3800 CVHT 44121 2498 A7
Wilmar Rd
1400 CVHT 44121 2498 A7
Wilmington Dr
10 PnvT 44077 2145 C4
14700 SGVL 44136 3146 E1
Wilmington Rd
4000 SELD 44121 2628 A2
Wilmore Av
20100 EUCL 44123 2373 A4
Wilmot St
100 GDRV 44045 2039 C5
Wilshire Ct
100 ELYR 44035 2875 E3
Wilson Av
38000 WLBY 44094 2250 E5
Wilson Ct
400 SgHT 44067 3017 D4
Wilson Dr
5400 MNTR 44060 2038 C7
5400 MNTR 44060 2144 C1
25400 ODFL 44138 2879 C6
Wilson Ln
2900 TNBG 44087 3020 B5
Wilson St
2100 ShfT 44055 2745 E6
2200 ShfT 44055 2746 A6
2400 LORN 44052 2615 C6
Wilson Mills Rd
- CRDN 44024 2504 C2
100 CRDN 44024 2379 D7
5100 RDHT 44143 2498 E5
5100 RDHT 44143 2499 B5
5300 HDHT 44143 2499 B5
6000 MAYF 44143 2499 B5
6400 MAYF 44143 2500 A5
6600 MAYF 44040 2500 B5
7000 CsTp 44026 2501 B4
7200 GSML 44040 2500 C4
8100 CsTp 44026 2502 A4
9500 CsTp 44026 2503 A4
9500 CsTp 44024 2503 A4
9600 MsnT 44024 2503 A4
10800 MsnT 44024 2504 A3
Wilton Av
13000 CLEV 44135 2752 E5
Wilton Ln
7500 NRYN 44133 3013 D5
Wilton Rd
1700 CVHT 44118 2627 B2
Wiltshire Dr
8600 MCDN 44056 3018 E7
8600 MCDN 44056 3153 E1
Wiltshire Rd
1500 HkyT 44133 3148 E5
1500 HkyT 44233 3148 E5
1500 NRYN 44133 3148 E5
2800 BWHT 44147 3149 B5
2800 HkyT 44147 3149 B5
2800 HkyT 44233 3149 B5
2800 NRYN 44133 3149 B5
2800 NRYN 44147 3149 B5
3700 MDHL 44022 2760 B3
Wimbledon Rd
23200 SRHT 44122 2628 C6
24400 BHWD 44122 2628 D6
Winagle Rd
12500 TroT 44234 3025 C1
Winchell Rd
900 AURA 44202 3022 D5
2600 ManT 44202 3022 D5
2600 ManT 44202 3023 A5
3500 SRHT 44122 2757 E2
3700 ManT 44255 3024 A5
5100 ManT 44255 3025 A4
5300 HrmT 44255 3025 A4
5700 HrmT 44234 3025 C4
6700 HrmT 44234 3026 A6
12300 CcdT 44024 2255 B4
12300 CcdT 44077 2255 B4
Winchester Av
10 CLEV 44110 2372 C5
1400 LKWD 44107 2623 A6
Winchester Ct
- AURA 44202 3021 D6
1600 WTLK 44145 2619 E7
10400 NRYN 44133 3013 E4
18000 SGVL 44136 3147 A4
Winchester Dr
1100 PRMA 44134 2883 E3
1500 WTLK 44145 2619 E7
6100 SVHL 44131 2884 A4
7200 SLN 44139 3020 A2
11500 MsnT 44024 2504 C1
Winchester Ln
300 BNWK 44212 3147 D7
Winchester Ovl
900 SVHL 44131 2884 A3
Winchester Pl
7200 CcdT 44077 2253 D1
Winchester Rd
1400 LNHT 44124 2499 C4
1400 LNHT 44124 2629 A1
Winchester Vly
9200 CsTp 44026 2632 E2
9200 CsTp 44026 2633 A2
Winckles St
100 ELYR 44035 2875 C5
N Wind Dr
27600 EUCL 44132 2249 A6
Windbrook Dr
100 ELYR 44035 2746 C7
Windburn Dr
10 MDHL 44022 2760 B2
Windcliff Rd
12100 SGVL 44136 3011 E5
Windermere Dr
900 WLBY 44094 2142 E4
1100 WLBY 44094 2143 C5
Windermere St
1800 ECLE 44112 2497 A6
Windham Ct
400 BWHT 44147 3149 E5
Windham Dr
8200 MNTR 44060 2252 A2
10400 PRMA 44130 2882 B2
Winding Tr
19300 SGVL 44136 3146 C1
Winding Wy
7300 BKVL 44141 3016 A6
7500 HDSN 44236 3155 B7
14700 NRYN 44133 3147 E1
Windingbrook Ln
11100 CsTp 44026 2502 C2
Winding Creek Ln
5900 NOSD 44070 2878 A3
Windingcreek Ln
1000 LNHT 44124 2498 E6
Winding Oak Dr
18500 MDBH 44130 2880 E5
N Winding Oak Dr
18600 MDBH 44130 2880 E5
Winding River Tr
10 BTVL 44022 2760 D7
Winding Trail Pl
7400 CcdT 44077 2254 C1
Windjammer Ct
- MadT 44057 1941 C1
Windjammer Tr
9900 RMDV 44202 3020 E5
Windjammer Cove
3600 RMDV 44202 3020 E5
Windmill Ct
- AVON 44011 2617 C7
Windmill Ln
1300 BWHT 44147 3149 E5
7000 CcdT 44060 2145 B2
Windmill Wy
1100 AVON 44011 2617 C7
Windmill Wy E
- AVON 44011 2617 C7
Windmill Wy N
1100 AVON 44011 2617 C7
Windmill Wy S
- AVON 44011 2617 C7
Windmill Point Rd
15500 HtbT 44024 2507 B4
15500 HtbT 44046 2507 B4
Windridge Dr
7900 BWHT 44147 3015 A5
Windrow Ln
1400 BWHT 44147 3149 D5
Windrush Ct
5500 PRMA 44134 2883 D1
Windrush Dr
10 MDHL 44022 2760 B2
600 WTLK 44145 2621 A6
Windrush Ln
10 BHWD 44122 2628 E4
Windsong Ct
3500 WTLK 44145 2750 A4
Windsong Tr
8300 CcdT 44077 2255 A5
Windsor Cir
1500 MDHT 44124 2630 B1
Windsor Ct
10 RKRV 44116 2621 B6
3900 LORN 44053 2743 E2
N Windsor Ct
3000 WTLK 44145 2749 C3
S Windsor Ct
3100 WTLK 44145 2749 C3
Windsor Ct N
34200 ETLK 44095 2250 A2
Windsor Ct S
34200 ETLK 44095 2250 A2
Windsor Dr
200 ELYR 44035 2875 D2
1600 MDHT 44124 2630 B1
8100 NRYN 44133 3013 D7
16000 SGVL 44136 3147 B2
28300 NOSD 44070 2878 D2
E Windsor Dr
9000 ODFL 44138 3009 E1
W Windsor Dr
9000 ODFL 44138 3009 E1
Windsor Ln
600 SgHT 44067 3152 C1
7200 MNTR 44060 2144 C7
Windsor Pl
200 NHFD 44067 3018 B4
Windsor Rd
3800 CVHT 44121 2497 E5
3800 CVHT 44121 2498 A5
S Windsor Rd
5800 WndT 44099 2639 E3
6500 WndT 44062 2639 D3
Windsor St
4200 WLBY 44094 2250 D5
Windsor Wy
8200 BWHT 44147 3014 C5
9500 TNBG 44087 3020 B6
Windstream Ln
4500 BKVL 44141 3150 E3
Windswept Cir
18100 BbgT 44023 2891 E6
Windswept Dr
9100 BKVL 44141 3015 C7
9100 BKVL 44141 3150 C1
Windward
- AVLK 44012 2618 B3
Windward Cir
300 AURA 44202 3156 D2
Windward Dr
300 ELYR 44035 2875 D1
700 AURA 44202 3156 C2
2200 WTLK 44145 2749 D1
36200 ETLK 44095 2142 C6
Windward Ln
10 AbnT 44023 2892 B6
Windward Rd
17700 CLEV 44119 2372 D4
Windward Wy
10 AbnT 44023 2892 A4
300 AVLK 44012 2618 E2
400 AVLK 44012 2619 A3
18400 SGVL 44136 3146 E4
Windward Hills Dr
6700 BKVL 44141 3016 A7
Windwood Wy
7100 OmsT 44138 2878 E4
Windy Hill Dr
10 WBHL 44094 2375 E7
2400 PRPK 44124 2629 C4
11700 MsnT 44024 2504 D7
Windy Hill Ln
37100 SLN 44139 2889 C5
Windy Hollow Ln
30700 NOSD 44070 2878 A2
Windy Lakes Cir
9500 BbgT 44023 2891 E6
Windy Willow Dr
6400 SLN 44139 2889 D5
Winesap Ct
2200 BWHT 44147 3149 D4
Winesap Dr
2200 BWHT 44147 3149 D4
Winesap Rd
600 AMHT 44001 2743 B7
Winfield Av
2200 RKRV 44116 2622 A6
7100 CLEV 44105 2755 E1
Winfield Dr
5400 MNTR 44060 2038 D7
5400 MNTR 44060 2144 D1
Winfield Park Dr
14600 NbyT 44072 2763 A1
Wing Rd
17000 AbnT 44023 2892 D3
Wingate Dr
11000 AbnT 44021 2893 A5
Wingate Rd
15300 MPHT 44137 2886 B2
Wingedfoot Dr
2300 WTLK 44145 2750 E2
23300 WTLK 44145 2751 A2
Winger Dr
3700 LORN 44053 2744 A4
Winona Cir
6700 MDBH 44130 2881 C4
Winona Rd
2000 EUCL 44117 2497 D1
Winrock Dr
- HRM 44234 3161 B1
Winsford Rd
3200 CVHT 44112 2497 D5
Winslow Av
1100 CLEV 44113 2624 C3
Winslow Ct
- SRHT 44120 2757 C1
Winslow Dr
- AURA 44202 3157 A4
Winslow Rd
17300 SRHT 44120 2757 E1
17700 SRHT 44122 2757 E1
19200 SRHT 44122 2758 B1
Winsor Dr
29900 BYVL 44140 2619 B4
Winsor Ter
10 CLEV 44103 2625 D2
Winsor Castle Ln
14400 SGVL 44136 3146 B1
Winsted Rd
7300 HDSN 44236 3154 D7
Winston Dr
30300 BYVL 44140 2619 B3
Winston Ln
6600 SLN 44139 2889 E6
Winston Rd
1000 SELD 44121 2498 B6
Winter Ln
4500 BKLN 44144 2753 C5
Winterberry Dr
7600 HDSN 44236 3155 C7
Winterberry Ln
10 MDHL 44022 2760 A5
9400 KDHL 44060 2253 A4
11400 MsnT 44024 2503 B2
30900 WTLK 44145 2749 A6
Winter Brook Dr
- AVON 44011 2748 C5
Wintergreen Dr
10000 CdnT 44024 2379 E4
12100 CdnT 44024 2380 A4
32200 SLN 44139 2759 E7
Wintergreen Hl
10 PnvT 44077 2146 D3
Wintergreen Ln
- MNTR 44060 2144 E7
Winterhaven Dr
6400 MadT 44057 1942 A3
Winterpark Dr
1600 PRMA 44134 3014 D2
Winthrop Ct
8200 MNTR 44060 2252 A2
Winthrop Dr
100 ELYR 44035 2746 D7
2900 PRMA 44134 2883 C4
Winthrop Rd
2800 SRHT 44120 2627 C6
10100 ShvT 44241 3157 E7
Winton Av
1400 LKWD 44107 2622 B5
Winton Park Dr
3800 NOSD 44070 2750 A5
Wire Av
7800 CLEV 44105 2756 A2
Wisconsin Cir
100 ELYR 44035 3006 D1
Wisner Rd
9100 CdnT 44024 2378 C1
10000 CdnT 44094 2378 A3
10000 KTLD 44094 2378 A3
10100 CdnT 44024 2378 A5
10100 CdnT 44094 2378 A5
10100 KTLD 44094 2378 A5
Wisteria Dr
8000 BbgT 44023 2890 E7
27900 NOSD 44070 2749 E6
Wisteria Wy
2200 AVON 44011 2747 E1
Wiswell Rd
7800 WndT 44099 2509 E6
7900 WndT 44099 2639 E2
Witch Hazel Ln
7100 SLN 44139 3020 B1
Wixford Ln
5300 MNTR 44060 2039 A7
5300 MNTR 44060 2145 A1
Woburn Av
3700 CLEV 44109 2754 B4
5300 CLEV 44144 2754 A4
6700 BKLN 44144 2753 E4
Woda Av
18200 CLEV 44122 2757 D2
Wolcott Dr
10 BSHT 44236 3153 C6
Wolf Av
7000 PRMA 44129 2882 E1
13300 GDHT 44125 2885 E1
13500 GDHT 44125 2886 A1
Wolf Ct
200 ELYR 44035 2875 B7
Wolf Dr
300 BWHT 44147 3014 E4
300 BWHT 44147 3015 A4
13200 SGVL 44136 3012 D3
Wolf Rd
6300 BKPK 44142 2881 C4
6400 BKPK 44130 2881 C4
6400 MDBH 44130 2881 C4
6400 MDBH 44142 2881 C4
23700 BYVL 44140 2620 D5
27400 BYVL 44140 2619 E4
Wolf Creek Ln
- GDHT 44125 2756 C6
Wolfpen Dr
10 SRSL 44073 2762 B7
Wolf Run Cir
16800 SGVL 44136 3146 E3
Wolverton Dr
4600 WVHT 44128 2758 C5
Wolzhaven Av
20700 SGVL 44136 3011 B4
Wondergrove Dr
100 EUCL 44132 2249 A7
Wonderlust Ct
10 PnvT 44077 2040 E7
Wonneta Pkwy
23700 WTLK 44145 2620 E7
Wood Av
2700 LORN 44052 2745 B2
2900 LORN 44055 2745 B3
3700 PRMA 44134 2883 B1
6500 INDE 44131 2884 D5
Wood Ovl
12000 NRYN 44133 3013 A5
Wood Rd
1500 CVHT 44121 2627 E1
1700 CVHT 44118 2627 E1
3300 MadT 44057 1941 B7
3300 MadT 44057 2043 B2
38300 WLBY 44094 2250 E2
38300 WLBY 44094 2251 A2
Wood St
- CrlT 44035 3006 A3
10 PNVL 44077 2146 B1
500 ELYR 44035 3006 A3
4400 WLBY 44094 2250 E6
23600 BDHT 44146 2887 C1
29500 WKLF 44092 2374 C3
35300 NRDV 44039 2877 A1
Woodacre Dr
2300 HDSN 44236 3155 B7
Wood Acre Tr
17100 AbnT 44023 2892 A3
17100 BbgT 44023 2891 E3
17100 BbgT 44023 2892 A3
Woodall Rd
30100 SLN 44139 2759 C7
W Woodall Rd
29100 SLN 44139 2759 C7
Woodberry Blvd
8100 BbgT 44023 2761 E7
8100 BbgT 44023 2762 A7
Woodberry Ln
12500 SGVL 44136 3011 A6
Woodbine Av
3000 CLEV 44113 2624 C5
Woodbine Cir
400 MAYF 44143 2500 B2
Woodbine Ovl
100 MDSN 44057 1942 B7
Woodbine St
35300 NRDV 44039 2877 B1
Woodbriar Cir
12300 SGVL 44136 3011 E6
Woodbridge Av
2500 CLEV 44109 2754 B1
Woodbridge Cir
100 CRDN 44024 2505 A2
Woodbridge Ct
8500 NRDV 44039 2877 D6
Woodbridge Gln
300 RDHT 44143 2498 E1
Woodbridge Ln
200 CRDN 44024 2505 A2
4500 BKVL 44141 3150 E2
Woodbridge Tr
700 SgHT 44067 3152 C2
Woodbridge Condominiums
1200 WLBY 44094 2143 A5
Woodbrook Av
15100 BDFD 44146 2886 B4
15100 MPHT 44137 2886 B4
Woodbury Av
15900 CLEV 44135 2752 B4
Woodbury Ct
9100 MNTR 44060 2252 E3
Woodbury Dr
6300 SLN 44139 2889 B6
14600 NbyT 44065 2764 C1
Woodbury Ln
1100 NRYN 44133 3013 C5
Woodbury Rd
2800 SRHT 44120 2627 B6
Woodbury St
100 ELYR 44035 2875 D5
Woodbury Hills Dr
4700 PRMA 44134 3014 A1
Woodchip Ln
9500 BWHT 44147 3149 D1
Woodchuck Cir
10 AhtT 44001 2744 C7
Woodchuck Ct
10400 TNBG 44087 3019 C3
Woodchuck Hllw
12000 CsTp 44026 2502 E5
Woodcreek Cir
3200 WTLK 44145 2749 E3
Wood Creek Dr
6700 MDBH 44130 2881 C5
15500 TpnT 44064 2257 C5
Woodcreek Dr
9700 CcdT 44060 2145 B7
Woodcrest Ct
100 ELYR 44035 2875 D1
Woodcrest Dr
9000 BKVL 44141 3016 A7
30800 ORNG 44022 2759 D6
E Woodcrest Dr
4800 ORNG 44022 2759 D6
W Woodcrest Dr
4800 ORNG 44022 2759 D6
Woodcrest Ln
13000 CsTp 44026 2631 C2
Woodcroft Ct
9500 KTLD 44094 2376 E2
Wood Duck Av
11200 CcdT 44077 2146 B7
Wood Duck Ct
7000 SLN 44139 3020 B1
Wooded Vw
6400 BSHT 44236 3153 B7
Woodfield Dr
32200 AVLK 44012 2618 C2
Woodfield Tr
21700 SGVL 44136 3011 A6
Woodford Av
10 ELYR 44035 2874 E7
17400 LKWD 44107 2622 B4
Woodford St
4600 MNTU 44255 3159 C5
Woodgate Cir
4100 WTLK 44145 2749 E5
Woodhaven Av
6300 CLEV 44144 2753 E4
6300 CLEV 44144 2754 A4
7400 BKLN 44144 2753 E4
Woodhaven Cir
- NRDV 44039 2877 D7
Woodhaven Ct
100 AURA 44202 3021 D7
Woodhaven Dr
- NbyT 44065 2633 E6
700 AMHT 44001 2872 E3
8800 OmsT 44138 2879 A7
18200 SGVL 44136 3146 D4
Woodhaven Pl
100 OBLN 44074 3138 C3
Woodhawk Dr
6300 MDHT 44124 2629 E2
6300 MDHT 44124 2630 A2
Woodhawk Ln
8600 KTLD 44094 2252 B7
Woodhill Ct
9400 CLEV 44104 2626 B6
Woodhill Dr
100 AMHT 44001 2872 E2
8200 TpnT 44064 2257 C5
8300 MtlT 44064 2257 C5
9100 KTLD 44094 2252 A7
23500 BKPK 44142 2879 E2
42800 EyrT 44035 2874 B2
N Woodhill Dr
100 AMHT 44001 2872 E1
500 AMHT 44001 2743 E7
Woodhill Rd
2300 CLEV 44106 2626 C4
2400 CLEV 44104 2626 C4
Woodhill St
5800 PryT 44077 2147 B2
Woodhill Street Ext
5800 PryT 44077 2147 B2
Wood Hollow Dr
10800 MsnT 44024 2504 A3
Woodhollow Dr
10 BNWK 44212 3146 E6
4200 ManT 44255 3024 A7
Wood Hollow Rd
8500 SgHT 44067 3017 E6
Woodhurst Av
1500 MDHT 44124 2499 D3
1500 MDHT 44124 2629 E1
Woodhurst Dr
9300 SGVL 44136 3011 C4
Woodie Gln
11200 CdnT 44024 2379 B4
Woodiebrook Rd
100 CRDN 44024 2505 A2
100 MsnT 44024 2505 A2
200 CRDN 44024 2504 D2
11300 MsnT 44024 2504 D2
Woodin Rd
11800 CdnT 44024 2379 E3
12000 CdnT 44024 2380 A3
12400 HmbT 44024 2380 A3
13300 HmbT 44024 2381 A3
Woodlake Dr
7400 WNHL 44146 3017 D1
10800 KTLD 44094 2378 A7
10800 KTLD 44094 2503 A1
Woodland Av
10 PnvT 44077 2145 D3
300 ELYR 44035 2874 D5
2100 CLEV 44115 2625 B4
4000 CLEV 44104 2625 B4
7000 BbgT 44023 2890 A1
7500 CLEV 44104 2626 A5
Woodland Av SR-8
2500 CLEV 44115 2625 B4
4000 CLEV 44104 2625 B4
Woodland Av SR-87
2500 CLEV 44115 2625 B4
4000 CLEV 44104 2625 B4
7500 CLEV 44104 2626 A5
Woodland Av US-422
2500 CLEV 44115 2625 B4
4000 CLEV 44104 2625 B4
Woodland Ct
500 SRSL 44073 2761 E5
1500 TNBG 44087 3019 B3
Woodland Dr
400 ETLK 44095 2250 C1
3900 VMLN 44089 2741 C5
5600 NRDV 44039 2877 E1
Woodland Pl
8800 MNTR 44060 2252 D2
N Woodland Rd
- SRHT 44118 2627 B5
- SRHT 44120 2627 B5
2900 CVHT 44118 2627 B5
25900 BHWD 44122 2628 E5
26100 BHWD 44122 2629 A4
27300 PRPK 44124 2629 B4
S Woodland Rd
- BHWD 44122 2629 B7
13200 CLEV 44120 2626 E6
13300 CLEV 44120 2627 A6
14000 SRHT 44120 2627 A6
18400 SRHT 44122 2627 D7
19800 SRHT 44122 2628 B7
24300 BHWD 44122 2628 E7
27700 PRPK 44124 2629 B7
29000 PRPK 44124 2759 C1
32900 PRPK 44124 2760 C2
33700 PRPK 44022 2760 C2
35200 HGVL 44022 2760 C2
35200 MDHL 44022 2760 C2
44000 HGVL 44022 2761 A2
S Woodland Rd SR-87
32900 PRPK 44124 2759 E1
32900 PRPK 44124 2760 C2
33700 PRPK 44022 2760 C2
35200 HGVL 44022 2760 C2
35200 MDHL 44022 2760 C2
44000 HGVL 44022 2761 A2
Woodland St
100 OBLN 44074 3138 D2
Woodland Trc
100 AURA 44202 3156 C1
Woodland Wy
36300 EatT 44035 3006 E4
Woodland Chase
1000 GFTN 44044 3142 A3
Woodlands Ln
6900 SLN 44139 2889 C7
Woodlands Tr
7700 CsTp 44026 2631 C1
Woodlane Dr
500 BYVL 44140 2620 C5
900 MAYF 44143 2499 D6
N Woodlane Dr
6100 MAYF 44143 2499 D5
S Woodlane Dr
6100 MAYF 44143 2499 D6
6200 MDHT 44124 2499 D6
Woodlawn Av
1800 CLEV 44106 2626 E1
1800 CLEV 44112 2626 E1
1800 ECLE 44112 2626 E1
33900 NRDV 44039 2877 C3
Woodlawn Cir
400 BERA 44017 2880 D5
Woodlawn Ct
17000 SGVL 44136 3146 C3
Woodlawn Dr
1000 MCDN 44056 3018 E5
2900 PRMA 44134 2883 C3
14300 NbyT 44065 2634 C7
Woodlawn St
100 GNVA 44041 1944 C3
Woodleaf Rd
16700 SGVL 44136 3012 A6
Woodleigh Rd
33000 PRPK 44124 2630 A7
Woodline Rd
24700 BDHT 44146 2887 D6

INDEX 51
Woodmere Dr — Cleveland Street Index — W 24th St

Cleveland Street Index

STREET
Block City ZIP Map# Grid

Woodmere Dr
100 WLWK 44095 2249 B7
500 BERA 44017 3011 A1
600 BWHT 44147 3014 E4
600 BWHT 44147 3015 A3
2200 CVHT 44106 2627 A3
17000 BbgT 44023 2890 E3
17000 BbgT 44023 2891 A3
24100 NOSD 44070 2750 D4
Woodmill Cir
5500 BKVL 44141 3016 B5
Woodmill Dr
2200 WTLK 44145 2749 D1
Wood Oak Cir
30300 WTLK 44145 2749 B3
Woodpark Dr
400 BYVL 44140 2619 E5
Woodpark Ln
3800 NOSD 44070 2749 E5
Woodpath Ct
1400 TwbT 44236 3154 D5
Wood Path Dr
29200 NOSD 44070 2878 C1
Woodpath Dr
7600 TwbT 44236 3154 C6
Woodpath Tr
3800 WTLK 44145 2750 B4
Woodridge Cir
400 BERA 44017 3010 E1
12100 SGVL 44136 3011 E6
Woodridge Ct
32600 NRDV 44039 2748 E7
Woodridge Dr
100 ELYR 44035 2875 D1
12000 NRYN 44133 3013 A5
12100 NRYN 44133 3012 E5
Woodridge Ln
8800 MNTR 44060 2038 D6
Wood Ridge Rd
300 AURA 44202 3156 C2
600 GNVA 44041 1944 D4
Woodridge Rd
100 VMLN 44089 2741 D4
3400 CVHT 44121 2497 D6
3800 CVHT 44121 2498 A6
Woodrow Av
10 BDFD 44146 2887 A4
600 WKLF 44092 2249 B7
1500 MDHT 44124 2499 D4
1500 MDHT 44124 2629 E1
3700 PRMA 44134 2883 B3
Woodruff Av
- AVLK 44012 2617 C2
Woodruff Ct
- MDBH 44130 2881 B4
2500 WTLK 44145 2749 C2
Woodruff Dr
400 SDLK 44054 2616 E3
1900 PnvT 44077 2145 B5
Woodruff Ln
9800 NbyT 44073 2763 B7
Woodrun Dr
- NRYN 44133 3149 A4
10600 SGVL 44136 3012 D5
Woodrush Cir
100 SRSL 44073 2761 D5
Woodsdale Ln
31700 SLN 44139 2759 E7
31700 SLN 44139 2888 E1
Woods Edge Ct
7900 CcdT 44060 2253 C3
Woodshire Dr
16600 SGVL 44136 3146 D3
Woods Hole
13100 MsnT 44024 2634 E2
Woodside Av
200 VMLN 44089 2741 E5
12300 CLEV 44108 2496 E5
38200 WLBY 44094 2250 E6
Woodside Cross N
18000 SGVL 44136 3146 D4
Woodside Cross S
18200 SGVL 44136 3146 D4
Woodside Ct
12200 SGVL 44136 3011 E6
Woodside Dr
100 CrlT 44035 3005 D5
300 SgHT 44067 3017 D4
1100 AMHT 44001 2873 A1
1100 RKRV 44116 2621 C5
3800 NOSD 44070 2750 D5
4000 NRYN 44133 3014 B3
12500 CsTp 44026 2502 A7
S Woodside Dr
12800 CsTp 44026 2502 A7
12800 CsTp 44026 2632 A1
Woodside Ln
24100 BHWD 44122 2628 D7
Woodside Rd
10 SRSL 44073 2761 C6
5400 MONT 44060 2037 E7
5400 MONT 44060 2143 E1
5900 HDHT 44143 2499 C4
Woodslee Ct
13500 CLEV 44111 2622 E7
Woodsmore Dr
5600 SLN 44139 2888 E2
Woodsong Dr
15000 MDFD 44062 2767 B2
Woodsong Wy
100 AbnT 44023 2892 B5
Woodspring Cir
32800 NRDV 44039 2877 D6
Woodstock Av
10800 CLEV 44104 2626 D4
20400 FWPK 44126 2751 C2
Woodstock Dr
100 AVLK 44012 2488 A7
100 AVLK 44012 2618 A1
3900 LORN 44053 2743 E2
Woodstock Rd
300 ETLK 44095 2249 D3
1600 GSML 44040 2630 C2
Woodstone Cir
- NRDV 44039 2877 D7
Woodstone Dr
8900 BKVL 44141 3016 D6
Woods Way Dr
9100 KTLD 44094 2252 A7
9100 KTLD 44094 2377 A1
Woodsway Ln
7800 RslT 44072 2631 D7
Wood Thrush Av
6900 CcdT 44077 2146 C7
Wood Thrush Dr
4300 PRMA 44134 2883 B5
Woodvale Ct
9200 MNTR 44060 2252 E3
Woodview Blvd
10600 PMHT 44130 2882 A6
Woodview Cir
21200 SGVL 44136 3011 B5
Wood View Dr
4900 VMLN 44089 2741 A7
Woodview Dr
- MCDN 44056 3018 D5
100 ELYR 44035 2875 D1
2500 BWHT 44147 3015 B4
3300 NOSD 44070 2750 E4
10000 CdnT 44024 2379 E4
Woodview Rd
800 CVHT 44121 2497 D5
Woodview Tr
400 AURA 44202 3021 C7
Woodwalk Dr
6700 BKVL 44141 3016 A7
Woodward Av
1400 LKWD 44107 2622 B5
1800 CVHT 44118 2627 B2
3700 LORN 44055 2745 D4
9700 CLEV 44106 2626 B2
Woodward Blvd
12000 GDHT 44125 2885 E1
13500 GDHT 44125 2886 A1
Woodway Av
3600 PRMA 44134 2754 B7
Woodway Dr
29300 WKLF 44092 2374 B1
Woodway Rd
23600 BHWD 44122 2628 D4
Woodwind Ct
8700 BWHT 44147 3015 A6
Woodworth Av
10 PnvT 44077 2040 C7
Woodworth Rd
13200 CLEV 44110 2496 E4
13200 ECLE 44110 2496 E4
13200 ECLE 44112 2496 E4
13400 CLEV 44110 2497 A4
13400 ECLE 44110 2497 A4
13400 ECLE 44112 2497 A4
Woodyard Rd
7300 HDSN 44236 3155 A7
Woolman Ct
5800 PRMA 44130 2882 A2
Wooster Cir
500 SgHT 44067 3017 D4
Wooster Ct
7300 MNTR 44060 2251 C1
Wooster Pkwy
7400 PRMA 44129 2882 E1
Wooster Rd
1500 RKRV 44116 2621 E7
2500 LKWD 44126 2621 E7
2500 RKRV 44126 2621 E7
3000 LKWD 44116 2621 E7
3100 RKRV 44116 2751 D2
3900 FWPK 44126 2751 D2
3900 RKRV 44126 2751 D2
Wooster Rd SR-113
1500 RKRV 44116 2621 E7
2500 LKWD 44126 2621 E7
2500 RKRV 44126 2621 E7
Wooster Rd US-20
1500 RKRV 44116 2621 E7
2500 LKWD 44126 2621 E7
2500 RKRV 44126 2621 E7
Wooster St
200 ELYR 44035 3006 A1
Wooster-Avon Lake Rd
1600 EatT 44028 3142 E5
1600 EatT 44044 3142 E5
1600 GFTN 44028 3142 E5
1600 GFTN 44044 3142 E5
9700 EatT 44044 3007 E3
14700 GftT 44028 3142 E5
14700 GftT 44044 3142 E5
Wooster-Avon Lake Rd SR-57
15500 GftT 44028 3142 E7
15500 GftT 44044 3142 E7
Wooster-Avon Lake Rd SR-83
1600 EatT 44028 3142 E5
1600 EatT 44044 3142 E5
1600 GFTN 44028 3142 E5
1600 GFTN 44044 3142 E5
9700 EatT 44044 3007 E3
14700 GftT 44028 3142 E5
14700 GftT 44044 3142 E5
Wooster Park Wy
19500 RKRV 44116 2621 D7
Worden Rd
- WKLF 44095 2249 B7
- WLWK 44095 2249 B7
800 WKLF 44092 2249 B7
900 WKLF 44092 2374 C1
Worley Av
6600 CLEV 44105 2755 E3
7500 CLEV 44105 2756 A2
Worlington Dr
7400 SLN 44139 3020 C2
Worrell Rd
2700 KTLD 44094 2376 A7
2700 WBHL 44094 2376 A7
3000 KTLD 44094 2501 A1
3000 WBHL 44094 2501 A1
Worthington Av
11700 CLEV 44111 2753 A3
Worthington Ct
6100 MNTR 44060 2144 B3
Worthington Park Dr
7900 SGVL 44136 3011 E2
Worton Blvd
1100 MDHT 44124 2499 D7
Worton Park Dr
800 MAYF 44143 2499 E5
Wren Av
6500 CLEV 44127 2625 E6
Wren Cir
100 ELYR 44035 2874 E2
Wren Ct
10 RKRV 44116 2621 C4
9000 MNTR 44060 2144 D1
Wren Dr
8000 MCDN 44056 3153 C2
Wren Rd
16500 BbgT 44023 2891 A1
Wrenford Ct
8500 MCDN 44056 3018 B6
Wrenford Rd
- SRHT 44118 2628 B5
1500 SELD 44121 2628 B1
2100 UNHT 44121 2628 B3
2300 UNHT 44118 2628 B3
2600 SRHT 44122 2628 B5
Wren Haven Dr
2000 HDSN 44236 3154 E6
2000 HDSN 44236 3155 A6
Wrens Ln
5500 WLBY 44094 2375 A1
Wrenwood Dr
10 ETLK 44095 2142 B6
7700 HrmT 44234 3161 E2
9600 KTLD 44094 2377 A3
11800 HRM 44234 3161 A1
Wright Av
1600 RKRV 44116 2621 E5
7200 OKWD 44146 2887 B7
7200 OKWD 44146 3018 B1
Wright Ct
9300 CLEV 44108 2496 B5
Wright Rd
7900 BWHT 44147 3015 C3
Wright St
37900 WLBY 44094 2250 D6
Wright Way Dr
- AhtT 44001 2872 E6
Wurst Ct
100 ELYR 44035 2875 B6
Wyandot Rd
8900 CsTp 44026 2632 D1
Wyandotte Av
1400 LKWD 44107 2622 E5
Wyandotte Rd
1900 EUCL 44117 2498 A2
Wyant Dr
9200 MNTR 44060 2252 E2
Wyatt Rd
4300 CLEV 44128 2757 C4
8100 BWHT 44147 3015 B4
15500 ECLE 44112 2497 B6
Wychwood Dr
10 MDHL 44022 2760 A2
Wye Rd
10200 MsnT 44026 2633 D1
Wyleswood Dr
100 BERA 44017 3011 A1
500 BERA 44017 3010 E1
700 BERA 44017 2879 D7
Wymore Av
1700 ECLE 44112 2497 A5
Wyncote Rd
4000 SELD 44121 2628 A2
Wyndemere Wy
35700 AVON 44011 2748 A3
Wynde Tree Dr
2300 SVHL 44131 3015 B2
Wyndgate Ct
2400 WTLK 44145 2749 C2
Wyndham Ln
- AURA 44202 3021 E7
Wyndtree Dr
10500 CcdT 44077 2145 E7
Wynewood Pl
100 CRDN 44024 2379 E7
100 CRDN 44024 2504 E1
Wynn Av
100 ELYR 44035 3006 E3
Wynn Rd
2000 UNHT 44118 2627 D3
Wynnewood Pl
20000 SGVL 44136 3146 C4
Wynwood Dr
1700 RKRV 44116 2621 A7
Wysteria Dr
- LORN 44053 2744 C4

X

Xavier Ct
- NRDV 44039 2877 B4
Xavier St
100 ELYR 44035 3006 D2
Xenia Ct
5600 CLEV 44102 2624 A7

Y

Yacht Club Dr
10 LKWD 44107 2621 E4
10 RKRV 44107 2621 E4
10 RKRV 44116 2621 E4
Yager Dr
13100 SGVL 44136 3011 C7
Yale Av
100 ELYR 44035 3006 C1
1500 MadT 44057 1843 B7
8800 CLEV 44108 2496 B5
Yale Dr
3900 LORN 44055 2745 E4
Yale Pl
1300 PnvT 44077 2147 A1
Yale St
8500 TwbT 44087 3154 D2
Yarish Rd
- GftT 44044 3141 E7
Yarmouth Ct
8500 SgHT 44067 3017 E5
Yarmouth Ln
500 BYVL 44140 2619 C5
Yarmouth Ovl
- MDBH 44130 2881 B4
Yarmouth Rd
1000 GFTN 44044 3142 A4
Yarrow Pl
11400 SGVL 44136 3011 A5
Yarrow Tr
22200 SGVL 44136 3011 A5
Yatchsmans Cove Dr
- ETLK 44095 2250 C3
Yeakel Av
9300 CLEV 44104 2626 B5
Yearling Dr
400 BERA 44017 3010 E2
400 BERA 44017 3011 A2
Yellowbrick Rd
8200 MNTR 44060 2144 A6
Yellow Springs Dr
6400 MadT 44057 1942 A3
Yellowstone Pkwy
8700 OmsT 44138 2879 A7
Yellowstone Rd
800 CVHT 44121 2497 E6
Yellowwood Dr
9500 MNTR 44060 2253 A3
9600 CcdT 44060 2253 A3
Yeoman Dr
25600 WTLK 44145 2750 B3
Yeshiva Ln
28500 WKLF 44092 2374 B4
Yoder Blvd
100 AVLK 44012 2618 C1
Yonkof Dr
8400 NRDV 44039 2877 D7
Yorick Av
15200 CLEV 44110 2497 B3
York Av
2800 CLEV 44113 2624 D6
York Blvd
12400 GDHT 44125 2885 E2
13600 GDHT 44125 2886 A2
York Cres
7100 NRDV 44039 2877 B4
York Ct
900 VMLN 44089 2740 D6
5700 WLBY 44094 2375 A2
York Dr
2900 LORN 44053 2743 E2
5700 LNHT 44124 2629 C3
York Rd
6300 PMHT 44130 2882 B7
7100 PRMA 44130 2882 B7
7400 PRMA 44130 3013 B2
7900 NRYN 44133 3013 C3
14300 NRYN 44133 3148 C1
York St
600 FTHR 44077 2039 D3
33400 AVLK 44012 2617 C2
York-Alpha Dr
9500 NRYN 44133 3013 B7
York-Delta Dr
12700 NRYN 44133 3013 B6
York Harbor Ln
1000 PnvT 44077 2145 C4
York Imperial Dr
10 AMHT 44001 2872 B1
Yorkshire Av
3700 PRMA 44134 2883 B3
Yorkshire Ct
100 ELYR 44035 2875 D5
Yorkshire Dr
8100 MNTR 44060 2144 A5
8200 BbgT 44023 3022 A2
Yorkshire Rd
2900 CVHT 44118 2627 C2
York-Theta Dr
9700 NRYN 44133 3013 B6
Yorktown Ct
7300 MNTR 44060 2251 C1
Yorktown Dr
6100 PRMA 44134 2883 D3
29800 WTLK 44145 2749 B4
Yorktown Ln
10 ELYR 44035 2875 A3
7500 MDBH 44130 3012 C1
Yorktown Ovl
18300 SGVL 44136 3146 E4
Yorktown Pl
200 VMLN 44089 2741 B4
Yorktown Rd
5700 LORN 44053 2743 C5
Yorkview Dr
8500 NRYN 44133 3013 C3
Yorkview Dr E
8500 NRYN 44133 3013 C3
Yorkview Dr W
8500 NRYN 44133 3013 C3
Yorkwood Ct
8800 MNTR 44060 2144 C4
Yosemite
- AbnT 44023 3023 A1
Yosemite Dr
2000 RDHT 44117 2373 D7
2000 RDHT 44143 2373 D7
24100 EUCL 44117 2373 D7
Young Dr
7300 WNHL 44146 3018 A1
Yunker Ct
100 CrlT 44035 3006 D4
Yvonne Dr
9300 NRYN 44133 3013 C3

Z

Zachary Tr
4600 BHIT 44212 3146 B6
Zanes Trc
100 ClrT 44024 2505 C6
Zaremba Dr
13300 BKPK 44130 2881 D4
13300 BKPK 44142 2881 D4
Zehman Ct
6200 BKPK 44142 2881 A3
Zehman Dr
6100 BKPK 44142 2881 A2
6200 BKPK 44142 2880 E3
Zelis Rd
11900 LNDL 44135 2753 B4
Zeller Ct
10 BERA 44017 2880 C5
Zeman Av
24500 EUCL 44123 2373 D2
24700 EUCL 44132 2373 D2
26800 EUCL 44132 2374 C2
Zenas Ct
2900 TNBG 44087 3020 B5
Zenith Dr
14600 NbyT 44065 2764 C1
Zimmer Av
9800 CLEV 44102 2623 D6
Zingales Rd
300 BDFD 44146 2886 D3
Zinnia Ct
6600 MNTR 44060 2143 D5
Zoar Ct
5600 CLEV 44102 2624 A7
Zoeter Av
6600 CLEV 44103 2625 E1
Zona Ln
7400 PRMA 44130 3013 A1
Zorn Ln
400 MAYF 44143 2500 B3
Zrolka Dr
- HtbT 44046 2508 A5
Zverina Ln
- SGVL 44136 3011 E7

#

1st Av
10 BERA 44017 2880 C4
10 BERA 44130 2880 C4
10 MDBH 44130 2880 C4
13300 ECLE 44112 2497 A6
1st Pl
400 ELYR 44035 2875 A6
7300 OKWD 44146 2887 C6
1st St
- BDHT 44146 2887 D1
- VMLN 44089 2741 A4
10 BDFD 44146 2887 A5
10 MadT 44057 1941 B5
10 ManT 44255 3158 B2
100 PNVL 44077 2146 A1
100 WFAR 44491 2898 E5
400 GNVA 44041 1944 C3
7200 MNTR 44060 2143 C3
8200 CLEV 44144 2753 D2
10700 MNTU 44255 3159 C6
26600 WTLK 44145 2620 A6
W 1st St
1000 LORN 44052 2614 D6
2nd Av
10 BERA 44017 2880 C5
6500 INDE 44131 2884 E5
13300 ECLE 44112 2497 A6
2nd St
- BDHT 44146 2887 D1
- VMLN 44089 2741 A5
10 ELYR 44035 2875 A6
10 MadT 44057 1941 B5
10 ManT 44255 3158 C2
100 FTHR 44077 2039 C3
100 PNVL 44077 2146 A1
100 WFAR 44491 2898 E5
400 GNVA 44041 1944 B3
8200 CLEV 44144 2753 D2
10600 MNTU 44255 3159 C5
27200 WTLK 44145 2620 A5
37200 WLBY 44094 2250 D5
E 2nd St
- CLEV 44114 2624 C2
2100 CLEV 44115 2624 C2
W 2nd St
- ELYR 44035 2875 A6
1200 LORN 44052 2614 C6
1600 CLEV 44113 2624 E3
3rd Av
10 BERA 44017 2880 C5
13300 ECLE 44112 2497 A5
3rd St
- BDHT 44146 2887 D1
10 MadT 44057 1941 B5
10 ManT 44255 3158 C2
100 FTHR 44077 2039 C3
100 PNVL 44077 2040 A7
200 ELYR 44035 2875 A6
300 GDRV 44045 2039 C6
400 GNVA 44041 1944 B3
8200 CLEV 44144 2753 D2
37700 WLBY 44094 2250 D5
E 3rd St
- CLEV 44115 2624 E3
1300 CLEV 44114 2624 C1
N 3rd St
300 WFAR 44491 2898 D4
S 3rd St
100 WFAR 44491 2898 D5
W 3rd St
- ELYR 44035 2874 E6
500 ELYR 44035 2875 A6
1000 CLEV 44113 2624 D2
1000 CLEV 44114 2624 D2
1900 CLEV 44113 2624 E4
2200 CLEV 44113 2625 A5
4th Av
10 BERA 44017 2880 C5
100 BERA 44130 2880 C5
13300 ECLE 44112 2497 A5
4th St
- BDHT 44146 2887 D1
10 MadT 44057 1941 B5
10 ManT 44255 3158 C2
100 FTHR 44077 2039 C3
100 WFAR 44491 2898 D5
200 ELYR 44035 2875 A7
400 GNVA 44041 1944 B3
8200 BKLN 44144 2753 D2
8200 CLEV 44144 2753 D2
E 4th St
100 ELYR 44035 2875 B7
2000 CLEV 44115 2624 E3
W 4th St
100 LORN 44052 2614 D6
1200 CLEV 44113 2624 D3
2500 CLEV 44113 2625 A6
4400 CLEV 44109 2755 A5
5100 BNHT 44131 2755 A7
5th Av
100 CRDN 44024 2379 E5
100 CRDN 44024 2380 A5
13300 ECLE 44112 2497 A5
E 5th Av
10 BERA 44017 2880 C5
W 5th Av
10 BERA 44017 2880 C5
5th St
- BDHT 44146 2887 D1
10 MadT 44057 1941 A5
100 ManT 44255 3158 C2
100 WFAR 44491 2898 D5
200 ELYR 44035 2875 A7
200 FTHR 44077 2039 C4
5100 VMLN 44089 2740 E4
5100 VMLN 44089 2741 A4
W 5th St
200 LORN 44052 2614 D6
2200 CLEV 44113 2625 A5
5000 BNHT 44131 2755 A7
5100 BNHT 44131 2884 A1
6th Av
- CLEV 44108 2496 E5
- CLEV 44112 2496 E5
- CRDN 44024 2379 E6
13200 ECLE 44112 2496 E5
13300 ECLE 44112 2497 A5
W 6th Ct
700 LORN 44052 2614 D7
6th St
700 BDHT 44146 2887 E1
200 ELYR 44035 2875 A7
200 FTHR 44077 2039 D4
200 ManT 44255 3158 C2
5100 VMLN 44089 2741 A4
5200 VMLN 44089 2740 E4
E 6th St
- LORN 44052 2614 E6
1200 CLEV 44114 2624 E2
2200 CLEV 44115 2624 E3
W 6th St
200 LORN 44052 2614 E7
400 ELYR 44035 2875 A7
1100 CLEV 44113 2624 D3
1200 LORN 44052 2614 C7
2100 CLEV 44113 2625 A5
4500 CLEV 44109 2755 A5
5000 BNHT 44131 2755 A7
5100 BNHT 44131 2884 A1
7th Av
100 CRDN 44024 2379 D5
W 7th Ct
900 LORN 44052 2614 D7
7th St
- BDHT 44146 2887 E1
200 ELYR 44035 2875 A7
200 FTHR 44077 2039 D4
200 ManT 44255 3158 C2
5100 VMLN 44089 2741 A4
5200 VMLN 44089 2740 E4
E 7th St
- CLEV 44115 2624 E3
W 7th St
1100 LORN 44052 2614 D7
2000 CLEV 44113 2624 E5
2000 CLEV 44113 2625 A6
5000 BNHT 44131 2754 E7
8th Av
200 ELYR 44035 2875 A7
8th St
100 ManT 44255 3158 C2
200 BDHT 44146 2887 E1
200 ELYR 44035 2875 A7
E 8th St
100 LORN 44052 2614 E7
W 8th St
400 ELYR 44035 2875 A7
1200 LORN 44052 2614 C7
2400 CLEV 44113 2625 A6
5000 BNHT 44131 2754 E7
5100 BNHT 44131 2883 E1
9th St
100 BDHT 44146 2887 D1
200 ELYR 44035 2875 A7
200 ManT 44255 3158 C2
E 9th St
200 LORN 44052 2614 E7
800 CLEV 44114 2624 E2
2000 CLEV 44115 2624 E2
2000 CLEV 44115 2625 C3
2600 CLEV 44113 2625 A4
W 9th St
- PRMA 44131 2883 E2
- PRMA 44134 2883 E2
- SVHL 44131 2883 E2
400 ELYR 44035 2875 A7
1100 CLEV 44113 2624 D2
1200 LORN 44052 2614 C7
2500 CLEV 44113 2624 E6
10th St
300 BDHT 44146 2887 E1
300 ELYR 44035 3006 A1
E 10th St
100 LORN 44052 2614 E7
W 10th St
200 LORN 44052 2614 E7
400 ELYR 44035 2875 A7
1200 CLEV 44113 2624 D3
1200 LORN 44052 2614 C7
2000 CLEV 44113 2624 E6
4300 CLEV 44109 2754 E5
5200 PRMA 44134 2754 E7
W 11th Ct
1000 CLEV 44109 2624 E7
W 11th Pl
- CLEV 44109 2624 E7
11th St
400 ELYR 44035 3006 A1
11th Street Al
- ELYR 44035 3006 A1
W 11th St
100 LORN 44052 2614 E7
400 ELYR 44035 3006 A1
1200 LORN 44052 2614 C7
2000 CLEV 44113 2624 E5
3100 CLEV 44109 2624 E7
4100 CLEV 44109 2754 E4
W 12th Pl
4000 CLEV 44109 2754 E4
12th St
400 ELYR 44035 3006 A1
E 12th St
1200 CLEV 44114 2624 E2
1500 CLEV 44114 2625 A2
2400 CLEV 44115 2625 A3
W 12th St
200 LORN 44052 2614 E7
1600 LORN 44052 2744 C1
2800 CLEV 44113 2624 E7
3100 CLEV 44109 2624 E7
4200 CLEV 44109 2754 E4
W 13th Pl
- CLEV 44109 2624 E7
- CLEV 44113 2624 E7
13th St
300 ELYR 44035 3006 A1
E 13th St
1300 CLEV 44114 2625 A2
E 13th St US-322
1700 CLEV 44114 2625 A2
W 13th St
200 LORN 44052 2614 E7
400 ELYR 44035 3006 A1
1100 LORN 44052 2744 D1
3700 CLEV 44109 2754 E2
14th St
300 ELYR 44035 3006 A1
E 14th St
100 LORN 44052 2614 E7
2000 CLEV 44114 2625 A3
2000 CLEV 44115 2625 A3
W 14th St
200 LORN 44052 2614 E7
400 ELYR 44035 3006 A1
1200 LORN 44052 2744 C1
2000 CLEV 44113 2624 E6
3100 CLEV 44109 2624 E6
3700 CLEV 44109 2754 E2
15th St
200 ELYR 44035 3006 A1
E 15th St
100 LORN 44052 2614 E7
100 LORN 44052 2744 E1
1800 CLEV 44114 2625 A2
W 15th St
200 LORN 44052 2744 E1
2200 CLEV 44113 2624 E5
3800 CLEV 44109 2754 E2
W 16th Pl
2300 CLEV 44113 2624 E5
16th St
200 CrlT 44035 3006 A1
200 ELYR 44035 3006 A1
600 ELYR 44035 3005 E1
E 16th St
100 LORN 44052 2744 E1
1100 CLEV 44114 2625 A1
W 16th St
200 LORN 44052 2744 E1
2900 CLEV 44113 2624 E7
3100 CLEV 44109 2624 E7
4100 CLEV 44109 2754 E3
5300 PRMA 44134 2754 E7
5300 PRMA 44134 2883 E1
W 17th Pl
3100 CLEV 44109 2624 D7
3800 CLEV 44109 2754 E3
17th St
100 LORN 44052 2744 E1
300 ELYR 44035 3006 A1
600 ELYR 44035 3005 E1
E 17th St
1200 CLEV 44114 2625 A2
W 17th St
1000 LORN 44052 2744 D1
2300 CLEV 44113 2624 D5
3100 CLEV 44109 2624 D7
3200 CLEV 44109 2754 D1
W 18th Pl
2400 CLEV 44113 2624 D6
3100 CLEV 44109 2624 D7
18th St
300 ELYR 44035 3006 A2
700 ELYR 44035 3005 E2
E 18th St
200 LORN 44052 2745 A1
1100 CLEV 44114 2625 A1
1900 CLEV 44115 2625 A2
W 18th St
100 LORN 44052 2744 E1
2000 CLEV 44113 2624 D5
3800 CLEV 44109 2754 D3
19th Av
- ShfT 44055 2745 B4
19th Ct
2000 LORN 44052 2744 B1
W 19th Pl
- CLEV 44109 2624 D7
2500 CLEV 44113 2624 D6
3200 CLEV 44109 2754 D1
19th St
700 ELYR 44035 3005 E2
E 19th St
200 LORN 44052 2745 A1
1700 CLEV 44114 2625 A2
2000 CLEV 44115 2625 B3
W 19th St
1300 LORN 44052 2744 C1
1900 CLEV 44113 2624 D5
3800 CLEV 44109 2754 D3
E 20th St
100 LORN 44052 2745 A1
1100 CLEV 44114 2625 A1
W 20th St
100 LORN 44052 2744 E1
1900 CLEV 44113 2624 D5
2300 LORN 44052 2744 B1
3800 CLEV 44109 2754 D3
W 21st Pl
- CLEV 44113 2624 D5
- CLEV 44109 2754 D2
E 21st St
200 LORN 44052 2745 A1
1300 CLEV 44114 2625 A2
2000 CLEV 44115 2625 B3
W 21st St
100 LORN 44052 2744 B1
3200 LORN 44053 2744 B1
3300 LORN 44053 2743 E2
3800 CLEV 44109 2754 D3
W 21st St SR-611
100 LORN 44052 2744 B1
3200 LORN 44053 2744 B1
3300 LORN 44053 2743 E2
W 22nd Av
3900 CLEV 44109 2754 D3
W 22nd Pl
3700 CLEV 44109 2754 D2
E 22nd St
200 LORN 44052 2745 A2
1100 CLEV 44114 2625 A1
2000 CLEV 44115 2625 B3
W 22nd St
200 LORN 44052 2744 E2
200 LORN 44052 2745 B1
1300 LORN 44052 2744 C2
1800 CLEV 44113 2624 D4
3900 CLEV 44109 2754 D3
W 23rd Pl
3200 CLEV 44109 2624 D7
3200 CLEV 44109 2754 D1
E 23rd St
100 LORN 44052 2745 A2
100 LORN 44055 2745 A2
1200 CLEV 44114 2625 A1
W 23rd St
100 LORN 44052 2744 E2
100 LORN 44052 2745 B2
100 LORN 44055 2745 B2
1700 LORN 44052 2744 B2
3800 CLEV 44109 2754 D3
W 24th Pl
- CLEV 44113 2624 D5
E 24th St
100 CLEV 44114 2625 B1
2300 CLEV 44115 2625 B3
W 24th St
1000 LORN 44052 2744 D2
1800 CLEV 44113 2624 D5
2100 LORN 44052 2744 B2

INDEX 52

W 24th St

Cleveland Street Index

E 93rd St

STREET Block	City	ZIP	Map#	Grid
W 24th St				
3800	CLEV	44109	2754	D3
5200	PRMA	44134	2754	D7
5300	PRMA	44134	2883	D1
W 25th Pl				
1200	LORN	44052	2744	C2
E 25th St				
300	LORN	44055	2745	A2
500	LORN	44052	2745	A2
1300	CLEV	44114	2625	B1
W 25th St				
100	LORN	44052	2745	A2
500	LORN	44052	2744	E2
100	LORN	44055	2745	A2
500	LORN	44052	2744	E2
1200	CLEV	44113	2624	C4
2000	LORN	44052	2744	B2
3100	CLEV	44109	2624	C4
3200	CLEV	44109	2754	D1
5200	PRMA	44134	2754	D7
W 25th St SR-3				
1400	CLEV	44113	2624	C4
3100	CLEV	44109	2624	C4
3200	CLEV	44109	2754	D1
W 25th St US-6				
-	CLEV	44113	2624	C4
W 25th St US-20				
-	CLEV	44113	2624	C4
W 25th St US-42				
1400	CLEV	44113	2624	C4
3100	CLEV	44109	2624	C4
3200	CLEV	44109	2754	D1
E 26th St				
100	LORN	44055	2745	A2
1100	CLEV	44114	2625	B1
3900	NEGH	44105	2755	B3
W 26th St				
200	LORN	44052	2744	E2
200	LORN	44055	2744	E2
200	LORN	44052	2745	B2
200	LORN	44055	2745	B2
1300	LORN	44052	2744	C2
1400	CLEV	44113	2624	C4
4600	CLEV	44109	2754	D6
5200	PRMA	44134	2754	D7
E 27th St				
200	LORN	44055	2745	A2
1500	CLEV	44114	2625	B2
4000	NBGH	44105	2755	B3
W 27th St				
200	LORN	44055	2745	B2
600	LORN	44052	2744	E2
600	LORN	44055	2744	E2
1900	LORN	44052	2744	B2
2500	CLEV	44113	2624	D6
4800	CLEV	44109	2754	D6
W 28th Pl				
2500	CLEV	44113	2624	D6
E 28th St				
100	LORN	44055	2745	B2
500	LORN	44052	2745	B2
2100	CLEV	44115	2625	B3
2300	LORN	44055	2746	A2
E 28th St SR-57				
100	LORN	44055	2745	B2
500	LORN	44052	2745	B2
W 28th St				
-	PRMA	44134	2883	D1
200	LORN	44055	2744	E2
200	LORN	44055	2745	A2
1300	CLEV	44113	2624	C4
1900	LORN	44052	2744	B2
4500	CLEV	44109	2754	D5
5200	PRMA	44134	2754	D7
E 29th St				
200	LORN	44055	2745	A2
2300	LORN	44055	2746	A2
3900	NBGH	44105	2755	B3
W 29th St				
-	CLEV	44109	2754	D1
200	LORN	44055	2744	E3
200	LORN	44055	2745	A2
800	LORN	44052	2744	D2
1300	CLEV	44113	2624	C4
4800	CLEV	44109	2754	C6
5600	PRMA	44134	2883	C1
E 30th St				
100	LORN	44055	2745	A3
1300	CLEV	44114	2625	B2
1500	LORN	44055	2745	C3
2000	CLEV	44115	2625	B2
2300	LORN	44055	2746	A3
W 30th St				
200	LORN	44055	2744	E3
200	LORN	44055	2745	B2
600	LORN	44052	2744	D3
1900	CLEV	44113	2624	C5
1900	LORN	44052	2744	B3
2800	CLEV	44113	2624	D7
3100	CLEV	44109	2624	D7
3200	CLEV	44109	2754	D1
31st Ct				
-	LORN	44055	2745	B3
W 31st Pl				
1600	CLEV	44113	2624	C5
3700	CLEV	44109	2754	D2
E 31st St				
100	LORN	44055	2745	A3
1300	CLEV	44114	2625	B1
1500	LORN	44055	2745	C3
2100	CLEV	44115	2625	C3
2300	LORN	44055	2746	B3
2800	SFLD	44055	2746	B3
4200	SFLD	44054	2746	B3
W 31st St				
-	CLEV	44109	2754	C5
200	LORN	44055	2744	E3
200	LORN	44055	2745	B2
2100	CLEV	44113	2624	C5
3100	CLEV	44109	2624	D7
3200	CLEV	44109	2754	D1
W 32nd Pl				
3700	CLEV	44109	2754	C2
E 32nd St				
100	LORN	44055	2745	A3
1300	CLEV	44114	2625	B1
1500	LORN	44055	2745	C3
2000	CLEV	44115	2625	C2
2200	LORN	44055	2745	E3
2300	LORN	44055	2746	A3
W 32nd St				
100	LORN	44055	2745	A3
200	LORN	44055	2744	E3
700	LORN	44052	2744	E3
1400	CLEV	44113	2624	C4
W 32nd St				
3100	CLEV	44109	2624	C7
3200	CLEV	44109	2754	C1
6200	PRMA	44134	2883	C4
W 33rd Pl				
-	CLEV	44113	2624	C5
3600	CLEV	44109	2754	C2
E 33rd St				
200	LORN	44055	2745	A3
1200	CLEV	44114	2495	B7
1500	LORN	44055	2745	C3
1700	CLEV	44114	2625	C2
2100	CLEV	44115	2625	C3
2200	LORN	44055	2745	E3
2300	LORN	44055	2746	A3
2800	CLEV	44115	2625	B5
W 33rd St				
-	CLEV	44113	2624	C4
-	CLEV	44134	2754	C7
100	LORN	44055	2745	A3
200	LORN	44055	2744	E3
700	LORN	44052	2744	E3
1300	LORN	44053	2744	C3
3100	CLEV	44109	2624	C7
3200	CLEV	44109	2754	C1
5200	PRMA	44134	2754	C7
5300	PRMA	44134	2883	C1
W 34th Pl				
3100	CLEV	44109	2624	C7
E 34th St				
100	LORN	44055	2745	A3
1300	CLEV	44114	2625	C1
1600	LORN	44055	2745	C3
2300	LORN	44055	2746	A3
2600	CLEV	44115	2625	B4
E 34th St SR-14				
2700	CLEV	44115	2625	C5
E 34th St SR-43				
2700	CLEV	44115	2625	C5
W 34th St				
100	LORN	44055	2745	A3
200	LORN	44055	2744	E3
700	LORN	44052	2744	E3
1300	LORN	44053	2744	C3
3300	CLEV	44109	2754	C1
E 35th Pl				
2300	CLEV	44115	2625	C4
E 35th St				
100	LORN	44055	2745	A3
2100	CLEV	44115	2625	C3
2200	LORN	44055	2745	E3
2300	LORN	44055	2746	A3
W 35th St				
100	LORN	44055	2745	A3
300	LORN	44055	2744	E3
1200	LORN	44052	2744	C3
1200	LORN	44053	2744	C3
3400	CLEV	44109	2754	C1
E 36th St				
200	LORN	44055	2745	C3
1100	ShfT	44055	2745	C3
1300	CLEV	44114	2625	C1
2300	CLEV	44115	2625	C3
W 36th St				
-	CLEV	44109	2624	C7
100	LORN	44052	2745	A3
100	LORN	44055	2745	A3
300	LORN	44052	2744	B3
300	LORN	44055	2744	B3
1700	LORN	44053	2744	B3
2100	CLEV	44113	2624	C6
3700	CLEV	44109	2754	C2
37th Ct				
-	LORN	44055	2745	C4
E 37th St				
1700	CLEV	44114	2625	C2
1700	LORN	44055	2745	D4
2100	CLEV	44115	2625	C3
2300	LORN	44055	2746	A3
E 37th Street Ovl				
-	LORN	44055	2746	A4
W 37th St				
100	LORN	44052	2745	A4
1000	LORN	44052	2744	D3
1300	LORN	44053	2744	C3
2300	CLEV	44113	2624	C6
2400	LORN	44053	2744	A3
3700	CLEV	44109	2754	C2
E 38th St				
100	LORN	44055	2745	A4
1100	CLEV	44114	2495	B7
1200	CLEV	44114	2625	B1
1700	LORN	44055	2745	C4
2100	CLEV	44115	2625	C3
2400	LORN	44055	2746	A4
3800	NBGH	44105	2755	C2
W 38th St				
200	LORN	44052	2745	A4
1100	LORN	44052	2744	D3
1400	CLEV	44113	2624	C4
2600	LORN	44053	2744	A3
3100	CLEV	44109	2624	C7
3200	CLEV	44109	2754	C1
39th Ct				
-	LORN	44055	2745	C4
E 39th Ct				
1800	LORN	44055	2745	D4
W 39th Pl				
3500	CLEV	44109	2754	C1
E 39th St				
-	LORN	44055	2745	C4
200	ShfT	44052	2745	A4
200	ShfT	44055	2745	A4
1500	CLEV	44114	2625	C1
2000	LORN	44055	2745	E4
2100	CLEV	44115	2625	C3
2400	LORN	44055	2746	A4
W 39th St				
100	LORN	44052	2745	A4
100	LORN	44055	2745	A4
100	ShfT	44055	2745	A4
100	ShfT	44052	2745	A4
1300	LORN	44052	2744	C4
1300	LORN	44053	2744	C4
3700	CLEV	44109	2754	C2
40th Ct				
-	LORN	44055	2745	C4
W 40th Pl				
2000	CLEV	44113	2624	C6
40th St				
-	LORN	44055	2745	C4
E 40th St				
1000	CLEV	44114	2495	C7
1300	CLEV	44103	2625	C4
1300	CLEV	44114	2625	C1
E 40th St				
1900	LORN	44055	2745	D4
2000	CLEV	44115	2625	C4
2300	CLEV	44104	2625	C4
2500	LORN	44055	2746	A4
3800	NBGH	44105	2755	C2
W 40th St				
1300	LORN	44052	2744	C4
1300	LORN	44053	2744	C4
2300	CLEV	44113	2624	C7
3100	CLEV	44109	2624	C7
3800	CLEV	44109	2754	C2
7600	PRMA	44134	3014	B1
W 41st Pl				
2600	CLEV	44113	2624	C7
E 41st St				
-	LORN	44055	2745	C4
300	ShfT	44052	2745	A4
300	ShfT	44055	2745	A4
1300	CLEV	44103	2495	C7
1300	CLEV	44103	2625	C1
2000	LORN	44055	2745	E4
2200	LORN	44055	2746	A4
3900	NBGH	44105	2755	C3
W 41st St				
1700	LORN	44053	2744	B4
2000	CLEV	44113	2624	C7
3100	CLEV	44109	2624	C7
3200	CLEV	44109	2754	C1
W 42nd Pl				
1100	LORN	44052	2744	D4
1900	CLEV	44113	2624	B6
E 42nd St				
-	CHHT	44105	2755	C3
200	ShfT	44052	2745	A4
200	ShfT	44055	2745	A4
1800	LORN	44055	2745	D4
2300	LORN	44055	2746	A4
3800	NBGH	44105	2755	C3
W 42nd St				
1800	LORN	44053	2744	B4
2000	CLEV	44113	2624	B6
3800	CLEV	44109	2754	B3
W 43rd Pl				
-	CLEV	44113	2624	B6
-	CLEV	44109	2754	B1
E 43rd St				
-	LORN	44055	2745	C5
100	ShfT	44052	2745	A4
100	ShfT	44055	2745	A4
1300	CLEV	44103	2495	C7
1300	CLEV	44103	2625	C1
2400	CLEV	44104	2625	C4
3800	NBGH	44105	2755	C2
W 43rd St				
-	CLEV	44113	2624	B6
1400	LORN	44053	2744	C4
3100	CLEV	44109	2624	B7
3200	CLEV	44109	2754	B1
5700	PRMA	44134	2883	B2
E 44th Pl				
3200	CLEV	44105	2625	C7
W 44th Pl				
-	CLEV	44109	2754	B2
44th St				
400	ShfT	44052	2745	A5
400	ShfT	44055	2745	A5
E 44th St				
3500	CLEV	44105	2755	C1
4000	NBGH	44105	2755	C3
W 44th St				
1200	LORN	44052	2744	C4
1200	LORN	44053	2744	C4
1700	CLEV	44113	2624	B7
3100	CLEV	44109	2624	B7
3200	CLEV	44109	2754	B1
5200	PRMA	44134	2754	B7
5500	PRMA	44134	2883	B1
W 45th Pl				
-	CLEV	44113	2624	B6
1000	LORN	44052	2744	D4
45th St				
-	LORN	44055	2745	D5
400	ShfT	44052	2745	A5
400	ShfT	44055	2745	A5
E 45th St				
-	CLEV	44127	2625	C7
1200	CLEV	44114	2495	C7
1300	CLEV	44103	2495	C7
1300	CLEV	44103	2625	C1
2600	CLEV	44104	2625	C4
2600	CLEV	44115	2625	C4
W 45th St				
1200	CLEV	44102	2624	B5
1200	CLEV	44113	2624	B5
3300	CLEV	44109	2754	B2
3500	CLEV	44102	2754	B2
4300	CLEV	44109	2754	B4
4400	CLEV	44144	2754	B5
4600	CLEV	44109	2754	B6
5200	PRMA	44134	2754	B7
5400	PRMA	44134	2883	B1
E 46th Pl				
-	CLEV	44105	2755	C2
W 46th Pl				
-	CLEV	44102	2624	B5
46th St				
200	ShfT	44052	2745	A5
500	ShfT	44055	2745	A5
E 46th St				
2000	CLEV	44103	2625	D3
2400	CLEV	44104	2625	D4
3400	CLEV	44105	2755	C1
W 46th St				
-	CLEV	44102	2624	B6
3100	CLEV	44109	2624	B7
3200	CLEV	44102	2754	B1
3200	CLEV	44109	2754	B1
5200	PRMA	44134	2754	B7
5700	PRMA	44134	2883	B2
E 47th Pl				
-	CLEV	44104	2625	C5
W 47th Pl				
3700	CLEV	44102	2754	B2
47th St				
100	ShfT	44052	2745	A5
400	ShfT	44055	2745	A5
E 47th St				
1300	CLEV	44103	2495	C7
1300	CLEV	44103	2625	D1
2700	CLEV	44104	2625	D5
3100	CLEV	44127	2625	C6
3500	CLEV	44105	2755	C1
W 47th St				
1700	CLEV	44102	2624	B5
W 47th St				
3300	CLEV	44102	2754	B1
4300	CLEV	44109	2754	B4
4300	CLEV	44144	2754	B4
4800	CLEV	44109	2754	B6
E 48th Pl				
1500	CLEV	44103	2625	D1
2700	CLEV	44104	2625	D5
W 48th Pl				
-	CLEV	44102	2624	B5
E 48th St				
200	ShfT	44052	2745	A5
500	ShfT	44055	2745	A5
3200	CLEV	44127	2625	C7
3600	CLEV	44105	2755	C1
W 48th St				
1400	CLEV	44102	2624	B5
3200	CLEV	44102	2754	B1
4000	CLEV	44144	2754	B4
5200	PRMA	44134	2754	B7
5500	PRMA	44134	2883	B1
E 49th Pl				
3100	CLEV	44127	2625	C7
49th St				
-	ELYR	44035	2875	A2
600	ELYR	44035	2874	E2
E 49th St				
-	NBGH	44105	2755	C6
1000	CLEV	44114	2495	C7
1300	CLEV	44103	2495	C7
1500	CLEV	44103	2625	D1
2500	CLEV	44104	2625	D4
3100	CLEV	44127	2625	C7
3300	CLEV	44127	2755	C2
3500	CLEV	44105	2755	C2
4000	CHHT	44105	2755	C2
4200	CHHT	44125	2755	C6
W 49th St				
1300	CLEV	44102	2624	B4
3300	CLEV	44102	2754	B1
4300	CLEV	44144	2754	B4
5200	PRMA	44134	2754	B7
E 50th Pl				
1600	CLEV	44103	2625	D1
W 50th Pl				
-	CLEV	44102	2624	B5
50th St				
41100	ELYR	44035	2874	E2
E 50th St				
2500	CLEV	44104	2625	D4
2900	CLEV	44127	2625	D6
3400	CLEV	44127	2755	C1
3600	CLEV	44105	2755	D2
W 50th St				
1400	CLEV	44102	2624	B5
3400	CLEV	44102	2754	B1
4000	CLEV	44144	2754	B3
5200	PRMA	44134	2754	B7
E 51st Pl				
2900	CLEV	44127	2625	D6
W 51st Pl				
-	CLEV	44102	2624	B7
-	CLEV	44102	2754	B1
51st St				
41500	EyrT	44035	2874	D2
E 51st St				
1300	CLEV	44103	2495	D7
2500	CLEV	44104	2625	D5
2900	CLEV	44127	2625	D6
3400	CLEV	44127	2755	D1
W 51st St				
3000	CLEV	44102	2624	B7
4400	CLEV	44144	2754	B5
5300	PRMA	44134	2754	B7
5300	PRMA	44134	2883	B1
E 52nd Pl				
3400	CLEV	44127	2755	D1
52nd St				
-	ELYR	44035	2874	E2
E 52nd St				
1300	CLEV	44103	2495	D7
3300	CLEV	44127	2625	D7
3300	CLEV	44127	2755	D1
3600	CLEV	44105	2755	D2
3900	NBGH	44105	2755	D3
W 52nd St				
1400	CLEV	44102	2624	B5
3200	CLEV	44102	2754	B1
4300	CLEV	44144	2754	B4
5200	PRMA	44134	2754	B7
E 53rd St				
1200	CLEV	44114	2495	C7
1300	CLEV	44103	2495	D7
3300	CLEV	44127	2625	D7
3300	CLEV	44127	2755	D1
3500	CLEV	44105	2755	D2
3900	NBGH	44105	2755	D3
W 53rd St				
1200	CLEV	44102	2624	B4
4400	CLEV	44144	2754	B5
E 54th Pl				
1500	CLEV	44103	2625	D1
E 54th St				
2900	CLEV	44127	2625	D6
3500	CLEV	44105	2755	D2
3900	NBGH	44105	2755	D3
W 54th St				
1300	CLEV	44102	2624	B4
3200	CLEV	44102	2754	A1
4500	CLEV	44144	2754	B5
5200	PRMA	44129	2754	A7
5200	PRMA	44134	2754	A7
5400	PRMA	44129	2883	A3
5400	PRMA	44134	2883	A3
E 55th St				
1000	CLEV	44103	2495	D6
1000	CLEV	44114	2495	D6
1600	CLEV	44103	2625	D2
2300	CLEV	44104	2625	D2
2800	CLEV	44127	2625	D6
3400	CLEV	44127	2755	D2
3500	CLEV	44105	2755	D2
3900	NBGH	44105	2755	D2
W 55th St				
1400	CLEV	44102	2624	A5
E 56th Pl				
1600	CLEV	44103	2625	D1
3200	CLEV	44127	2625	D7
E 56th St				
4000	CLEV	44105	2755	D3
W 56th St				
3000	CLEV	44102	2624	A7
3300	CLEV	44102	2754	A1
4300	CLEV	44144	2754	A4
E 57th St				
1400	CLEV	44103	2625	D1
2400	CLEV	44104	2625	D4
2900	CLEV	44127	2625	D6
3700	CLEV	44105	2755	D2
W 57th St				
1400	CLEV	44102	2624	A5
4300	CLEV	44144	2754	A4
E 58th St				
1200	CLEV	44103	2495	D7
3900	CLEV	44105	2755	D3
W 58th St				
1200	CLEV	44102	2624	A4
3400	CLEV	44102	2754	A1
3600	CLEV	44144	2753	E2
3600	CLEV	44144	2754	A2
W 59th Pl				
3300	CLEV	44102	2754	A1
E 59th St				
1200	CLEV	44103	2495	D7
1300	CLEV	44103	2625	D1
2400	CLEV	44104	2625	D4
2900	CLEV	44127	2625	D6
3500	CLEV	44105	2755	D2
W 59th St				
-	CLEV	44102	2624	A5
3300	CLEV	44102	2754	A1
4100	CLEV	44144	2754	A4
E 60th St				
-	CLEV	44103	2625	D1
1100	CLEV	44103	2495	D7
W 60th St				
3300	CLEV	44102	2754	A1
4300	CLEV	44144	2754	A4
5200	PRMA	44109	2754	A7
5200	PRMA	44129	2754	A7
5500	PRMA	44129	2883	A1
E 61st Pl				
2000	CLEV	44103	2625	D2
E 61st St				
1000	CLEV	44103	2495	D6
1400	CLEV	44103	2625	D1
2400	CLEV	44104	2625	D4
2800	CLEV	44127	2625	D6
3500	CLEV	44105	2755	D2
W 61st St				
1300	CLEV	44102	2624	A5
3500	CLEV	44102	2754	A1
4300	CLEV	44144	2754	A4
E 62nd St				
1000	CLEV	44103	2495	D6
2600	CLEV	44104	2625	D5
W 62nd St				
3500	CLEV	44102	2754	A1
4300	CLEV	44144	2754	A4
4400	BKLN	44144	2754	A4
E 63rd St				
800	CLEV	44103	2495	D6
1400	CLEV	44103	2625	E1
2400	CLEV	44104	2625	E4
2900	CLEV	44127	2625	D6
3500	CLEV	44105	2755	D2
W 63rd St				
3100	CLEV	44102	2624	A7
3500	CLEV	44102	2754	A1
3900	CLEV	44144	2754	A3
W 64th Pl				
1800	CLEV	44102	2624	A5
E 64th St				
900	CLEV	44103	2495	E6
2400	CLEV	44104	2625	E4
2800	CLEV	44127	2625	E6
3900	CLEV	44105	2755	E3
W 64th St				
1300	CLEV	44102	2624	A5
E 65th St				
1300	CLEV	44103	2495	E7
1300	CLEV	44103	2625	E1
2300	CLEV	44104	2625	E4
2900	CLEV	44127	2625	E6
3300	CLEV	44127	2755	E1
3700	CLEV	44105	2755	E2
W 65th St				
1200	CLEV	44102	2624	A5
3200	CLEV	44102	2754	A1
3500	CLEV	44102	2753	E2
E 66th Pl				
1000	CLEV	44103	2495	E6
E 66th St				
1000	CLEV	44103	2495	E6
1300	CLEV	44103	2625	E1
2400	CLEV	44104	2625	E4
2900	CLEV	44127	2625	E6
3300	CLEV	44127	2755	E1
3800	CLEV	44105	2755	E2
W 66th St				
3500	CLEV	44102	2753	E1
3500	CLEV	44102	2754	A2
4300	CLEV	44144	2754	A2
4400	BKLN	44144	2753	E5
W 67th Pl				
4400	BKLN	44144	2753	B5
4400	CLEV	44144	2753	B5
E 67th St				
800	CLEV	44103	2495	E6
2300	CLEV	44104	2625	E4
3000	CLEV	44127	2625	E6
3600	CLEV	44105	2755	E2
W 67th St				
1200	CLEV	44102	2624	A4
3500	CLEV	44102	2753	E1
5200	PRMA	44129	2754	A7
5500	PRMA	44129	2883	A1
E 68th Pl				
1700	CLEV	44103	2625	E1
W 68th Pl				
2100	CLEV	44102	2624	A3
E 68th St				
1000	CLEV	44103	2495	E6
1700	CLEV	44103	2625	E2
2700	CLEV	44104	2625	E5
3100	CLEV	44127	2625	E6
4000	CLEV	44105	2755	E3
W 68th St				
-	CLEV	44102	2624	A3
E 69th Pl				
900	CLEV	44103	2495	E6
1700	CLEV	44103	2625	E1
W 69th Pl				
4400	BKLN	44144	2753	E5
E 69th St				
1000	CLEV	44103	2495	E6
1800	CLEV	44103	2625	E2
2300	CLEV	44104	2625	E4
3400	CLEV	44127	2755	E1
E 69th St				
3600	CLEV	44105	2755	E2
W 69th St				
1200	CLEV	44102	2624	A4
2100	CLEV	44102	2623	E6
3500	CLEV	44102	2753	E1
E 70th St				
800	CLEV	44103	2495	E6
1500	CLEV	44103	2625	E1
2800	CLEV	44104	2625	E5
3300	CLEV	44127	2625	E7
3300	CLEV	44127	2755	E1
W 70th St				
-	CLEV	44102	2623	E7
1200	CLEV	44102	2624	A5
E 71st Pl				
2700	CLEV	44104	2625	E5
W 71st Pl				
4400	BKLN	44144	2753	E5
E 71st St				
1000	CLEV	44103	2495	E7
1400	CLEV	44103	2625	E2
2300	CLEV	44104	2625	E3
3400	CLEV	44127	2755	E1
3500	CLEV	44105	2755	E1
4300	CHHT	44105	2755	E5
4500	CHHT	44125	2755	E5
W 71st St				
1800	CLEV	44102	2623	E5
E 72nd Pl				
900	CLEV	44103	2495	E6
4900	CHHT	44125	2755	E6
E 72nd St				
600	CLEV	44103	2495	E5
600	CLEV	44103	2496	A4
1400	CLEV	44103	2625	E1
2800	CLEV	44104	2625	E5
3300	CLEV	44127	2625	E7
3300	CLEV	44127	2755	E1
3500	CLEV	44105	2755	E1
E 72th Pl				
2000	CLEV	44103	2625	E2
E 73rd Pl				
1200	CLEV	44103	2496	A7
3600	CLEV	44105	2755	E2
E 73rd St				
700	CLEV	44103	2496	A5
1600	CLEV	44103	2626	A1
1800	CLEV	44103	2625	E2
2500	CLEV	44104	2625	E4
3400	CLEV	44127	2756	A1
4200	CLEV	44105	2755	E4
W 73rd St				
1200	CLEV	44102	2623	E5
3200	CLEV	44102	2753	E1
E 74th St				
900	CLEV	44103	2496	A6
2100	CLEV	44103	2626	A3
2300	CLEV	44104	2626	A3
3500	CLEV	44105	2756	A1
4000	CLEV	44105	2755	E3
W 74th St				
1400	CLEV	44102	2623	E5
E 75th Pl				
-	CLEV	44104	2626	A6
1300	CLEV	44103	2496	A7
E 75th St				
800	CLEV	44103	2496	A6
1800	CLEV	44103	2626	A2
2500	CLEV	44104	2626	A4
3300	CLEV	44127	2756	A1
3500	CLEV	44105	2756	A1
W 75th St				
1400	CLEV	44102	2623	E5
E 76th Pl				
1300	CLEV	44103	2496	A7
E 76th St				
900	CLEV	44103	2496	A6
2100	CLEV	44103	2626	A3
2300	CLEV	44104	2626	A3
3400	CLEV	44127	2756	A1
3500	CLEV	44105	2756	A1
W 76th St				
1100	CLEV	44102	2623	E5
E 77th Pl				
-	CLEV	44127	2756	A1
E 77th St				
800	CLEV	44103	2496	A6
1600	CLEV	44103	2626	A1
2300	CLEV	44104	2626	A3
3600	CLEV	44105	2756	A2
W 77th St				
1400	CLEV	44102	2623	E5
E 78th Pl				
1300	CLEV	44103	2496	A7
E 78th St				
900	CLEV	44103	2496	A6
1600	CLEV	44103	2626	A1
2800	CLEV	44104	2626	A5
3400	CLEV	44127	2756	A1
3500	CLEV	44105	2756	A1
W 78th St				
-	NRYN	44133	3013	E2
1200	CLEV	44102	2623	E5
5200	PRMA	44129	2753	E7
5400	PRMA	44129	2882	E1
E 79th St				
700	CLEV	44103	2496	A6
1400	CLEV	44103	2626	A3
2300	CLEV	44104	2626	A4
3100	CLEV	44127	2626	A7
4000	CLEV	44105	2756	A3
W 79th St				
1300	CLEV	44102	2623	E5
5800	PRMA	44129	2882	E2
E 80th Pl				
-	CLEV	44104	2626	A5
W 80th Pl				
1400	CLEV	44102	2623	E5
E 80th St				
1300	CLEV	44103	2496	A7
1400	CLEV	44103	2626	A1
2500	CLEV	44104	2626	A4
3200	CLEV	44127	2626	A6
3500	CLEV	44105	2756	A1
W 80th St				
1300	CLEV	44102	2623	E5
E 81st Pl				
2100	CLEV	44103	2626	A3
E 81st St				
1300	CLEV	44103	2496	A7
1600	CLEV	44103	2626	A1
2500	CLEV	44104	2626	A4
3500	CLEV	44105	2756	A1
4800	GDHT	44125	2756	A6
W 81st St				
1400	CLEV	44102	2623	E5
E 82nd St				
600	CLEV	44103	2496	A5
1300	CLEV	44103	2626	A1
2300	CLEV	44104	2626	A4
3500	CLEV	44105	2756	A1
W 82nd St				
3100	CLEV	44102	2623	E7
3200	CLEV	44102	2753	E1
E 83rd Pl				
-	CLEV	44105	2756	A4
E 83rd St				
1100	CLEV	44103	2496	A7
2000	CLEV	44103	2626	A3
2100	CLEV	44106	2626	A3
2300	CLEV	44104	2626	A4
W 83rd St				
1200	CLEV	44102	2623	E5
5200	PRMA	44129	2753	D7
E 84th St				
1100	CLEV	44103	2496	A7
1100	CLEV	44108	2496	A7
1300	CLEV	44106	2496	A7
1600	CLEV	44103	2626	A1
1600	CLEV	44106	2626	A1
2100	CLEV	44103	2626	A4
2100	CLEV	44106	2626	A4
2300	CLEV	44104	2626	A4
4700	GDHT	44125	2756	B6
W 84th St				
-	NRYN	44133	3013	D2
1400	CLEV	44102	2623	E5
3200	CLEV	44102	2753	D1
5300	PRMA	44129	2753	D7
5400	PRMA	44129	2882	D1
E 85th St				
1100	CLEV	44103	2496	B7
1100	CLEV	44108	2496	B7
1300	CLEV	44106	2496	A7
1300	CLEV	44106	2626	A1
1800	CLEV	44103	2626	B2
2100	CLEV	44106	2626	B3
2200	CLEV	44104	2626	B3
4300	CLEV	44105	2756	B4
4600	GDHT	44105	2756	B5
4600	GDHT	44125	2756	B5
W 85th St				
1200	CLEV	44102	2623	D5
E 86th St				
-	CLEV	44103	2626	B1
1100	CLEV	44103	2496	B7
1100	CLEV	44108	2496	B7
1300	CLEV	44106	2496	B7
1600	CLEV	44106	2626	B1
2000	CLEV	44103	2626	B3
2100	CLEV	44106	2626	B3
2400	CLEV	44104	2626	B4
3900	CLEV	44105	2756	A3
4600	GDHT	44105	2756	B6
4600	GDHT	44125	2756	B6
W 86th St				
3100	CLEV	44102	2623	D7
3200	CLEV	44102	2753	D1
E 87th St				
-	CLEV	44103	2496	B7
1100	CLEV	44108	2496	B7
1700	CLEV	44106	2626	B2
2600	CLEV	44104	2626	B5
W 87th St				
1200	CLEV	44102	2623	D5
E 88th Pl				
1700	CLEV	44106	2626	B2
E 88th St				
700	CLEV	44103	2496	B5
700	CLEV	44108	2496	B5
1300	CLEV	44106	2496	B7
1400	CLEV	44106	2626	B1
3000	CLEV	44104	2626	B7
3400	CLEV	44104	2756	B1
3500	CLEV	44105	2756	B1
4600	GDHT	44105	2756	B6
4600	GDHT	44125	2756	B6
W 88th St				
3100	CLEV	44102	2623	D7
3200	CLEV	44102	2753	D1
E 89th Pl				
700	CLEV	44108	2496	B5
E 89th St				
1200	CLEV	44108	2496	B7
1300	CLEV	44106	2496	B7
1600	CLEV	44106	2626	B1
2400	CLEV	44104	2626	B4
3400	CLEV	44104	2756	B1
3900	CLEV	44105	2756	B3
W 89th St				
1200	CLEV	44102	2623	D5
E 90th Pl				
-	CLEV	44106	2626	B1
E 90th St				
700	CLEV	44108	2496	B5
1300	CLEV	44106	2496	B7
1600	CLEV	44106	2626	B1
2700	CLEV	44104	2626	B5
4600	GDHT	44105	2756	B6
4600	GDHT	44125	2756	B6
W 90th St				
1900	CLEV	44102	2623	D6
3200	CLEV	44102	2753	D1
E 91st St				
600	CLEV	44108	2496	B5
1300	CLEV	44106	2496	B7
1600	CLEV	44106	2626	B1
2800	CLEV	44104	2626	B7
3500	CLEV	44105	2756	B1
W 91st St				
1200	CLEV	44102	2623	D5
3200	CLEV	44102	2753	D1
E 92nd St				
-	CLEV	44105	2756	B3
600	CLEV	44108	2496	B5
1300	CLEV	44106	2496	B7
1400	CLEV	44106	2626	B1
2700	CLEV	44104	2626	B5
W 92nd St				
3100	CLEV	44102	2623	D7
E 93rd St				
700	CLEV	44108	2496	B5
1300	CLEV	44106	2496	B7
1600	CLEV	44106	2626	B1
2400	CLEV	44104	2626	B4
3400	CLEV	44104	2756	B2
3500	CLEV	44105	2756	B2
4600	GDHT	44105	2756	B6
4600	GDHT	44125	2756	B6

Cleveland Street Index

STREET Block | City | ZIP | Map# | Grid

W 93rd St
1200 CLEV 44102 2623 D5
E 94th St
600 CLEV 44108 2496 B4
1300 CLEV 44106 2496 B7
1500 CLEV 44106 2626 B1
3200 CLEV 44104 2626 B7
4100 CLEV 44105 2756 B3
4600 GDHT 44105 2756 B5
4600 GDHT 44125 2756 B5
5400 GDHT 44125 2885 B1
W 94th St
3100 CLEV 44102 2623 D7
3200 CLEV 44102 2753 D1
5600 PRMA 44129 2882 D1
E 95th St
600 CLEV 44108 2496 B5
1300 CLEV 44106 2496 B7
2100 CLEV 44106 2626 B3
3700 CLEV 44105 2756 B2
4800 GDHT 44125 2756 B6
W 95th St
1300 CLEV 44102 2623 D5
3300 CLEV 44102 2753 D1
W 96th Pl
- CLEV 44102 2623 D5
E 96th St
600 CLEV 44108 2496 B4
1500 CLEV 44106 2626 B1
2600 CLEV 44104 2626 B5
3800 CLEV 44105 2756 B2
4800 GDHT 44125 2756 B6
5500 GDHT 44125 2885 B1
W 96th St
2100 CLEV 44102 2623 D6
E 97th St
500 CLEV 44108 2496 B4
1800 CLEV 44106 2626 B2
2800 CLEV 44104 2626 B6
3800 CLEV 44105 2756 B2
4800 GDHT 44125 2756 B6
W 97th St
3100 CLEV 44102 2623 D7
3300 CLEV 44102 2753 D1
E 98th Pl
- CLEV 44108 2496 B6
4100 CLEV 44105 2756 C3
E 98th St
- CLEV 44105 2756 B2
1000 CLEV 44108 2496 B6
2800 CLEV 44104 2626 C5
3400 CLEV 44104 2756 C1
4200 CLEV 44105 2756 B4
5000 GDHT 44125 2756 C7
W 98th St
1400 CLEV 44102 2623 D6
3200 CLEV 44102 2753 D1
E 99th Pl
- CLEV 44108 2496 B7
2700 CLEV 44104 2626 C5
E 99th St
500 CLEV 44108 2496 B4
2800 CLEV 44104 2626 C5
3400 CLEV 44104 2756 C1
3800 CLEV 44105 2756 C2
4600 GDHT 44125 2756 C5
W 99th St
1900 CLEV 44102 2623 D6
3000 CLEV 44111 2623 D7
3200 CLEV 44102 2753 C1
E 100th Pl
- CLEV 44105 2756 C3
E 100th St
700 CLEV 44108 2496 B5
2000 CLEV 44106 2626 B3
2800 CLEV 44104 2626 C5
3700 CLEV 44105 2756 C2
5200 GDHT 44125 2756 C7
W 100th St
1900 CLEV 44102 2623 C6
3000 CLEV 44111 2623 C7
3200 CLEV 44102 2753 C1
3200 CLEV 44111 2753 C1
E 101st St
500 CLEV 44108 2496 B4
1800 CLEV 44106 2626 C2
W 101st St
2000 CLEV 44102 2623 C6
3000 CLEV 44111 2623 C7
E 102nd St
500 CLEV 44108 2496 C4
2000 CLEV 44106 2626 C3
2800 CLEV 44104 2626 C6
3300 CLEV 44104 2756 C1
4100 CLEV 44105 2756 C3
5200 GDHT 44125 2756 C7
W 102nd St
1200 CLEV 44102 2623 C5
3500 CLEV 44111 2753 C2
E 103rd St
- CLEV 44106 2496 C7
600 CLEV 44108 2496 C4
2100 CLEV 44106 2626 C3
2700 CLEV 44104 2626 C5
3300 CLEV 44104 2756 C1
3500 CLEV 44105 2756 C1
W 103rd St
1200 CLEV 44102 2623 C5
3100 CLEV 44111 2623 C7
3500 CLEV 44111 2753 C2
E 104th Pl
1100 CLEV 44108 2496 C7
E 104th St
2800 CLEV 44104 2626 C5
3300 CLEV 44104 2756 C1
3500 CLEV 44105 2756 C1
4500 GDHT 44125 2756 C5
W 104th St
1100 CLEV 44102 2623 C5
3100 CLEV 44111 2623 C7
3500 CLEV 44111 2753 C2
E 105th Pl
- CLEV 44105 2756 C3
E 105th St
400 BTNH 44108 2496 C6
400 CLEV 44108 2496 C6
1300 CLEV 44106 2496 C6
1400 CLEV 44106 2626 C1
3200 CLEV 44104 2626 C7
3300 CLEV 44104 2756 C1
3500 CLEV 44105 2756 C1
5200 GDHT 44125 2756 C7
W 105th St
1200 CLEV 44102 2623 C5
3100 CLEV 44111 2623 C7
3200 CLEV 44111 2753 C1
E 106th Pl
1100 CLEV 44108 2496 C7
E 106th St
500 CLEV 44108 2496 C4
1400 CLEV 44106 2496 C7
1400 CLEV 44106 2626 C1
2800 CLEV 44104 2626 C5
3300 CLEV 44104 2756 C1
3500 CLEV 44105 2756 C1
4800 GDHT 44125 2756 C6
W 106th St
1200 CLEV 44102 2623 C5
3000 CLEV 44111 2623 C7
3700 CLEV 44111 2753 C2
E 107th Pl
- CLEV 44108 2496 C4
E 107th St
600 CLEV 44108 2496 C4
1400 CLEV 44106 2496 C7
1400 CLEV 44106 2626 C1
4800 GDHT 44125 2756 C6
W 107th St
1400 CLEV 44102 2623 C5
3700 CLEV 44111 2753 C2
E 108th St
400 CLEV 44108 2496 C4
1400 CLEV 44106 2496 C7
1400 CLEV 44106 2626 C1
2800 CLEV 44104 2626 C5
3300 CLEV 44104 2756 C1
3500 CLEV 44105 2756 C1
4800 GDHT 44125 2756 C6
W 108th St
1200 CLEV 44102 2623 C5
E 109th St
400 CLEV 44108 2496 D4
1300 CLEV 44106 2496 C7
2000 CLEV 44106 2626 C3
2500 CLEV 44104 2626 C4
3700 CLEV 44105 2756 C2
4800 GDHT 44125 2756 C6
E 110th Ct
2500 CLEV 44104 2626 C4
E 110th St
400 CLEV 44108 2496 D4
1300 CLEV 44106 2496 D7
2400 CLEV 44104 2626 C5
3300 CLEV 44104 2756 C1
3500 CLEV 44105 2756 C1
4900 GDHT 44125 2756 C6
W 110th St
- CLEV 44102 2623 C4
3000 CLEV 44111 2623 B7
3200 CLEV 44111 2753 B1
E 111th St
1000 CLEV 44108 2496 D7
1300 CLEV 44106 2496 D7
1500 CLEV 44106 2626 D1
2500 CLEV 44104 2626 D4
4100 CLEV 44105 2756 C3
5300 GDHT 44125 2756 C7
5300 GDHT 44125 2885 C1
W 111th St
1200 CLEV 44102 2623 B5
3000 CLEV 44111 2623 B7
3200 CLEV 44111 2753 B1
E 112th St
400 CLEV 44108 2496 D4
1300 CLEV 44106 2496 D7
2600 CLEV 44104 2626 D5
3500 CLEV 44105 2756 D1
5100 GDHT 44125 2756 D7
W 112th St
1200 CLEV 44102 2623 B5
3100 CLEV 44111 2623 B7
3200 CLEV 44111 2753 B1
E 113th St
600 CLEV 44108 2496 D5
3300 CLEV 44104 2626 D7
3300 CLEV 44104 2756 D1
3500 CLEV 44105 2756 D1
5000 GDHT 44125 2756 D6
E 114th St
400 CLEV 44108 2496 D4
1400 CLEV 44106 2496 D7
1400 CLEV 44106 2626 D3
2600 CLEV 44104 2626 D5
3300 CLEV 44104 2756 D1
3500 CLEV 44105 2756 D1
5000 GDHT 44125 2756 D6
W 114th St
1200 CLEV 44102 2623 B5
2000 CLEV 44111 2623 B6
3200 CLEV 44111 2753 B1
E 115th St
400 CLEV 44108 2496 D4
1300 CLEV 44106 2496 D7
1500 CLEV 44106 2626 D1
2600 CLEV 44104 2626 D5
5000 GDHT 44125 2756 D6
W 115th St
1000 CLEV 44102 2623 B4
3100 CLEV 44111 2623 B7
3200 CLEV 44111 2753 B1
E 116th Pl
1700 CLEV 44106 2626 D1
E 116th St
1400 CLEV 44106 2496 D7
2700 CLEV 44104 2626 D5
2700 CLEV 44120 2626 D5
3300 CLEV 44104 2756 D1
3300 CLEV 44120 2756 D1
3500 CLEV 44105 2756 D1
W 116th St
1200 CLEV 44102 2623 B5
3100 CLEV 44111 2623 B7
3200 CLEV 44111 2753 D3
E 117th St
400 CLEV 44108 2496 D4
1300 CLEV 44106 2496 D7
1900 CLEV 44106 2626 D1
2700 CLEV 44120 2626 D5
3300 CLEV 44120 2756 D1
3500 CLEV 44105 2756 D1
5000 GDHT 44125 2756 D6
W 117th St
1100 CLEV 44102 2623 B7
1100 LKWD 44102 2623 B7
1100 LKWD 44107 2623 B7
2100 CLEV 44111 2623 B7
3200 CLEV 44111 2753 B1
W 118th Pl
- CLEV 44111 2623 B7
E 118th St
400 CLEV 44108 2496 D4
1400 CLEV 44106 2496 D7
1500 CLEV 44106 2626 D1
2700 CLEV 44120 2626 D5
3300 CLEV 44120 2756 D1
3500 CLEV 44105 2756 D1
W 118th St
3300 CLEV 44111 2753 B1
4400 CLEV 44135 2753 B5
E 119th St
1800 CLEV 44106 2626 D1
2700 CLEV 44120 2626 D5
3300 CLEV 44120 2756 D1
4100 CLEV 44105 2756 D4
5100 GDHT 44125 2756 D7
W 119th St
3100 CLEV 44111 2623 B7
3200 CLEV 44111 2753 D3
3900 LNDL 44135 2753 B3
E 120th St
400 CLEV 44108 2496 D4
1300 CLEV 44106 2496 D7
1800 CLEV 44106 2626 D1
2700 CLEV 44120 2626 D5
3500 CLEV 44105 2756 D2
5400 GDHT 44125 2885 D1
W 120th St
3000 CLEV 44111 2623 A7
3100 CLEV 44111 2753 A1
4000 LNDL 44135 2753 B3
E 121st St
2600 CLEV 44120 2626 E5
3300 CLEV 44120 2756 E1
3900 CLEV 44105 2756 D3
W 121st St
3000 CLEV 44111 2623 A7
3100 CLEV 44111 2753 D3
4200 CLEV 44135 2753 A4
E 122nd St
1500 CLEV 44106 2626 E1
2700 CLEV 44120 2626 E5
5400 GDHT 44125 2885 D1
W 122nd St
3400 CLEV 44111 2753 A1
4200 CLEV 44135 2753 A4
E 123rd St
300 CLEV 44108 2496 E4
1300 CLEV 44106 2496 D7
1800 CLEV 44106 2626 E1
2900 CLEV 44120 2626 E6
3300 CLEV 44120 2756 E1
3800 CLEV 44105 2756 E3
W 123rd St
3400 CLEV 44111 2753 A1
4300 CLEV 44135 2753 A4
E 124th Pl
1900 CLEV 44106 2626 E2
E 124th St
300 CLEV 44108 2496 E4
1300 CLEV 44106 2496 E7
1300 CLEV 44112 2496 E7
2400 CLEV 44120 2626 E4
3500 CLEV 44105 2756 E2
5300 GDHT 44125 2756 D7
5400 GDHT 44125 2885 D1
W 124th St
4600 CLEV 44135 2753 A6
E 125th St
400 CLEV 44108 2496 E4
1000 CLEV 44112 2496 E6
1000 ECLE 44112 2496 E6
1000 ECLE 44108 2496 E6
1200 CLEV 44106 2496 E6
2000 CLEV 44106 2626 E2
2700 CLEV 44120 2626 E5
3400 CLEV 44120 2756 E1
W 125th St
- CLEV 44135 2753 A3
3400 CLEV 44111 2753 A1
4500 CLEV 44135 2753 A5
E 126th St
400 CLEV 44108 2496 E4
1900 CLEV 44106 2626 E2
2400 CLEV 44120 2626 E4
3400 CLEV 44120 2756 E1
3700 CLEV 44105 2756 E2
4400 GDHT 44105 2756 E5
5100 GDHT 44125 2756 E7
W 126th St
3200 CLEV 44111 2623 A7
3200 CLEV 44111 2753 A1
4700 CLEV 44135 2753 A6
E 127th Pl
- CLEV 44108 2496 E4
E 127th St
400 CLEV 44108 2496 E5
2400 CLEV 44120 2626 E4
2400 SRHT 44120 2626 E4
3500 CLEV 44105 2756 E2
W 127th St
3200 CLEV 44111 2623 A7
3200 CLEV 44111 2753 A1
4100 CLEV 44135 2753 A4
E 128th St
500 CLEV 44108 2496 E4
2700 CLEV 44120 2626 E5
3400 CLEV 44120 2756 E1
4200 CLEV 44105 2756 E4
5100 GDHT 44125 2756 E7
5400 GDHT 44125 2885 E1
W 128th St
3200 CLEV 44111 2623 A7
3200 CLEV 44111 2753 A1
4400 CLEV 44135 2753 A5
E 129th St
400 CLEV 44108 2496 E4
1000 ECLE 44108 2496 E6
3500 CLEV 44105 2756 E1
5300 GDHT 44125 2885 E1
W 129th St
3200 CLEV 44111 2623 A7
3200 CLEV 44111 2753 A1
E 130th St
600 CLEV 44108 2496 E4
1000 ECLE 44108 2496 E5
2600 CLEV 44120 2626 E7
3400 CLEV 44120 2756 E1
3800 CLEV 44105 2756 E2
5700 GDHT 44125 2885 E2
W 130th St
10 BNWK 44212 3147 E6
10 BNWK 44233 3147 E6
10 HkyT 44233 3147 E6
3200 CLEV 44111 2622 E7
3200 CLEV 44111 2752 E1
3500 CLEV 44111 2753 A2
4000 CLEV 44135 2753 A2
4700 CLEV 44135 2752 E7
5000 PRMA 44135 2752 E7
5200 BKPK 44130 2752 E7
5200 BKPK 44142 2752 E7
5200 PRMA 44130 2752 E7
5300 BKPK 44142 2881 E2
5300 BKPK 44130 2881 E2
5300 PRMA 44130 2881 E2
6000 PMHT 44130 2881 E6
6400 MDBH 44130 2881 E6
7300 MDBH 44130 3012 E2
7300 PRMA 44130 3012 E2
7900 NRYN 44133 3012 E7
7900 SGVL 44133 3012 E7
7900 SGVL 44136 3012 E7
14200 NRYN 44133 3147 E2
14200 SGVL 44133 3147 E2
14200 SGVL 44136 3147 E2
E 131st St
100 CLEV 44108 2496 E3
300 CLEV 44112 2496 E3
300 ECLE 44112 2496 E3
600 CLEV 44108 2496 E5
1000 ECLE 44108 2496 E5
1000 ECLE 44112 2496 E5
3500 CLEV 44105 2756 E2
3500 CLEV 44120 2756 E2
4200 CLEV 44128 2756 E5
4300 GDHT 44105 2756 E5
4500 GDHT 44125 2756 E5
5300 GDHT 44125 2885 E1
W 131st St
3200 CLEV 44111 2752 E1
3300 CLEV 44111 2753 A1
4300 CLEV 44135 2752 E5
E 132nd St
- CLEV 44120 2756 E7
3100 CLEV 44120 2626 E7
5300 GDHT 44125 2756 E7
5300 GDHT 44125 2885 E1
W 132nd St
3300 CLEV 44111 2752 E1
3500 CLEV 44111 2753 A2
4300 CLEV 44135 2752 E4
E 133rd St
700 BTNH 44108 2496 E2
700 BTNH 44110 2496 E2
700 CLEV 44110 2496 E2
1200 ECLE 44112 2496 E4
1300 ECLE 44112 2497 A4
1400 ECLE 44112 2496 E6
3500 CLEV 44120 2756 E1
4200 CLEV 44105 2756 E4
5200 GDHT 44125 2756 E7
5400 GDHT 44125 2885 E1
W 133rd St
3400 CLEV 44111 2752 E1
4400 CLEV 44135 2752 E5
E 134th St
900 CLEV 44110 2497 A3
1300 ECLE 44112 2497 A4
3200 CLEV 44120 2626 E7
3400 CLEV 44120 2756 E4
4200 CLEV 44105 2756 E4
5300 GDHT 44125 2756 E7
5300 GDHT 44125 2885 E1
W 134th St
3500 CLEV 44111 2752 E2
4300 CLEV 44135 2752 E4
E 135th St
1400 ECLE 44112 2497 A4
3100 CLEV 44120 2627 A7
3200 CLEV 44120 2626 E7
3400 CLEV 44120 2756 E1
4100 CLEV 44105 2756 E3
4800 GDHT 44125 2756 E6
5300 GDHT 44125 2885 E1
W 135th St
3300 CLEV 44111 2752 E1
4600 CLEV 44135 2752 E5
E 136th St
600 CLEV 44110 2497 A1
3900 CLEV 44105 2757 A2
3900 CLEV 44120 2757 A2
4200 CLEV 44105 2756 E4
4300 GDHT 44105 2756 E4
4500 GDHT 44125 2756 E4
W 136th St
3000 CLEV 44111 2622 E3
3300 CLEV 44111 2752 E1
4400 CLEV 44135 2752 E5
E 137th St
800 CLEV 44110 2497 A2
1200 ECLE 44112 2497 A4
3100 CLEV 44120 2627 A7
3300 CLEV 44120 2757 A1
4200 CLEV 44105 2757 A4
W 137th St
3000 CLEV 44111 2622 E7
3300 CLEV 44111 2752 E1
3900 CLEV 44135 2752 E3
5000 BKPK 44142 2752 E7
E 138th Pl
800 CLEV 44110 2497 A3
E 138th St
700 CLEV 44110 2497 A3
3500 CLEV 44120 2757 A1
4000 CLEV 44105 2757 A3
5200 GDHT 44125 2757 A7
W 138th St
3000 CLEV 44111 2622 E7
3600 CLEV 44111 2752 E2
4300 CLEV 44135 2752 E4
E 139th St
- CLEV 44110 2497 A3
1300 ECLE 44112 2497 A4
3200 CLEV 44120 2627 A7
3500 CLEV 44120 2757 A1
4000 CLEV 44105 2757 A3
4300 GDHT 44105 2757 A4
5500 GDHT 44125 2886 A1
W 139th St
3000 CLEV 44111 2622 E7
3500 CLEV 44111 2752 E2
4300 CLEV 44135 2752 E4
5000 BKPK 44142 2752 D7
E 140th St
- GDHT 44125 2886 A3
- GDHT 44137 2886 A3
- MPHT 44137 2886 A3
400 BTNH 44110 2497 A1
400 CLEV 44110 2372 A7
400 CLEV 44110 2497 A1
3200 CLEV 44120 2627 A7
3200 SRHT 44120 2627 A7
3300 CLEV 44120 2757 A1
3900 CLEV 44128 2757 A2
3900 CLEV 44105 2757 A2
W 140th St
3000 CLEV 44111 2622 E7
3200 CLEV 44111 2752 E1
3900 CLEV 44135 2752 E2
5000 BKPK 44142 2752 D7
E 141st St
800 CLEV 44110 2497 A2
1200 ECLE 44112 2497 A4
3900 CLEV 44105 2757 A3
3900 CLEV 44128 2757 A3
4800 GDHT 44125 2757 A6
4800 GDHT 44128 2757 A6
5300 MPHT 44137 2757 A7
5300 MPHT 44137 2886 A1
W 141st St
3200 CLEV 44111 2622 E3
3200 CLEV 44111 2752 E1
E 142nd St
400 CLEV 44110 2372 A7
1200 ECLE 44112 2497 A4
3200 CLEV 44120 2627 A7
3300 CLEV 44120 2757 A1
3900 CLEV 44128 2757 A3
4600 GDHT 44125 2757 A5
W 142nd St
3100 CLEV 44111 2622 D7
3200 CLEV 44111 2752 D1
E 143rd St
400 CLEV 44110 2372 A7
500 CLEV 44110 2497 A1
1200 ECLE 44112 2497 A4
3200 CLEV 44120 2627 A7
3400 CLEV 44120 2757 A1
3900 CLEV 44128 2757 A3
4400 CLEV 44105 2757 A4
W 143rd St
3600 CLEV 44111 2752 D2
3900 CLEV 44135 2752 D2
E 144th St
800 CLEV 44110 2497 A2
1200 ECLE 44112 2497 A4
3500 CLEV 44120 2757 A1
3700 CLEV 44128 2757 A3
4500 GDHT 44128 2757 A5
W 144th St
3100 CLEV 44111 2622 D7
3400 CLEV 44111 2752 D1
4000 CLEV 44135 2752 D3
E 145th St
1000 CLEV 44110 2497 A3
1200 ECLE 44112 2497 B4
3200 CLEV 44120 2627 A7
3400 CLEV 44120 2757 A1
W 145th St
3400 CLEV 44111 2752 D1
4100 CLEV 44135 2752 D4
E 146th St
300 CLEV 44110 2372 B7
600 CLEV 44110 2497 B1
1200 ECLE 44112 2497 B4
3200 CLEV 44120 2627 A7
3200 SRHT 44120 2627 A7
3400 CLEV 44120 2757 A1
3700 CLEV 44128 2757 A2
5500 MPHT 44137 2886 A2
W 146th St
3000 CLEV 44111 2622 D7
3400 CLEV 44111 2752 D2
3900 CLEV 44135 2752 D3
E 147th St
300 CLEV 44110 2372 B7
500 CLEV 44110 2497 B1
3200 CLEV 44120 2627 A7
3400 CLEV 44120 2757 A1
3700 CLEV 44128 2757 A2
W 147th St
3500 CLEV 44111 2752 D2
4400 CLEV 44135 2752 D5
5000 BKPK 44142 2752 D7
5200 BKPK 44142 2881 D1
E 148th St
300 CLEV 44110 2372 B7
900 CLEV 44110 2497 B3
3900 CLEV 44128 2757 B3
W 148th St
3300 CLEV 44111 2752 D1
4300 CLEV 44135 2752 D4
5000 BKPK 44142 2752 D7
5200 BKPK 44142 2881 C1
E 149th St
300 CLEV 44110 2372 B7
800 CLEV 44110 2497 B2
3200 CLEV 44120 2627 B7
3400 CLEV 44120 2757 B1
3700 CLEV 44128 2757 B2
W 149th St
4400 CLEV 44135 2752 C5
5000 BKPK 44142 2752 C7
5200 BKPK 44142 2881 C1
E 150th St
200 CLEV 44110 2372 B7
800 CLEV 44110 2497 B2
3400 CLEV 44120 2757 B1
3900 CLEV 44128 2757 B3
W 150th St
3300 CLEV 44111 2752 C1
3900 CLEV 44135 2752 C1
5000 BKPK 44142 2752 C7
5200 BKPK 44142 2881 C1
E 151st St
200 CLEV 44110 2372 B7
3500 CLEV 44120 2757 B2
3700 CLEV 44128 2757 B2
W 151st St
3300 CLEV 44111 2752 C1
3900 CLEV 44135 2752 C3
5000 BKPK 44142 2752 C7
5200 BKPK 44142 2881 C1
E 152nd St
300 CLEV 44110 2372 B7
500 CLEV 44110 2497 B2
1200 ECLE 44110 2497 B2
1200 ECLE 44112 2497 B2
3400 CLEV 44120 2757 B1
W 152nd St
3400 CLEV 44111 2752 C1
4200 CLEV 44135 2752 C4
E 153rd Pl
- CLEV 44110 2497 B2
E 153rd St
800 CLEV 44110 2497 B2
3400 CLEV 44120 2757 B1
3700 CLEV 44128 2757 B2
W 153rd St
3000 CLEV 44111 2622 C7
4200 CLEV 44135 2752 C4
E 154th Pl
600 CLEV 44110 2497 B2
E 154th St
700 CLEV 44110 2497 B2
3400 CLEV 44120 2757 B1
3700 CLEV 44128 2757 B3
W 154th St
- CLEV 44135 2752 C4
E 155th St
700 CLEV 44110 2497 B2
3700 CLEV 44128 2757 B3
W 155th St
3200 CLEV 44111 2622 C7
3200 CLEV 44111 2752 C1
4200 CLEV 44135 2752 C4
E 156th St
10 CLEV 44110 2372 B6
600 CLEV 44110 2497 B1
4300 CLEV 44128 2757 B4
W 156th St
4300 CLEV 44135 2752 C4
E 157th Pl
700 CLEV 44110 2497 B1
E 157th St
400 CLEV 44110 2372 A6
600 CLEV 44110 2497 C1
W 157th St
3200 CLEV 44111 2622 C7
3300 CLEV 44111 2752 C1
4000 CLEV 44135 2752 C3
E 158th Pl
- CLEV 44110 2497 C1
E 158th St
400 CLEV 44110 2372 A6
4300 CLEV 44128 2757 B4
W 158th St
3300 CLEV 44111 2752 C1
4000 CLEV 44135 2752 C2
E 159th St
- CLEV 44110 2372 C6
600 CLEV 44110 2497 C1
W 159th St
3000 CLEV 44111 2622 C7
3400 CLEV 44111 2752 B1
E 160th St
300 CLEV 44110 2372 C7
600 CLEV 44110 2497 C1
4000 CLEV 44128 2757 B4
W 160th St
3000 CLEV 44111 2622 C7
3800 CLEV 44111 2752 C3
4000 CLEV 44135 2752 C3
E 161st St
200 CLEV 44110 2372 C7
3700 CLEV 44128 2757 C2
W 161st St
4000 CLEV 44135 2752 B3
5000 BKPK 44142 2752 B7
E 162nd St
300 CLEV 44110 2372 A6
600 CLEV 44110 2497 C1
4200 CLEV 44128 2757 C4
W 162nd St
3100 CLEV 44111 2622 B7
3200 CLEV 44111 2752 B1
4100 CLEV 44135 2752 B4
E 163rd St
300 CLEV 44110 2372 C7
600 CLEV 44110 2497 C1
4200 CLEV 44128 2757 C4
W 163rd St
4000 CLEV 44135 2752 B3
E 164th St
200 CLEV 44110 2372 C7
4200 CLEV 44128 2757 C4
W 164th St
5000 BKPK 44142 2752 B7
5000 BKPK 44142 2881 B1
E 165th St
300 CLEV 44110 2372 A6
700 CLEV 44110 2497 C1
W 165th St
3100 CLEV 44111 2622 B7
3200 CLEV 44111 2752 B1
E 166th St
700 CLEV 44110 2497 C1
W 166th St
4000 CLEV 44135 2752 B3
167th Pl
16600 CLEV 44128 2757 C4
E 167th St
1000 CLEV 44110 2372 C6
4200 CLEV 44128 2757 C4
W 167th St
4400 CLEV 44135 2752 B5
E 168th Pl
4200 CLEV 44128 2757 C4
E 168th St
1000 CLEV 44110 2372 C6
1300 CLEV 44110 2497 C1
W 168th St
3800 CLEV 44111 2752 B2
4100 CLEV 44135 2752 B4
E 169th St
1000 CLEV 44110 2372 D6
1000 CLEV 44119 2372 D6
3700 CLEV 44128 2757 C2
W 169th St
3600 CLEV 44111 2752 B2
E 170th Pl
4200 CLEV 44128 2757 C4
E 170th St
1100 CLEV 44110 2372 D7
1300 CLEV 44110 2497 D1
W 170th St
4400 CLEV 44135 2752 B5
E 171st St
1000 CLEV 44110 2372 D6
1000 CLEV 44119 2372 D6
1300 CLEV 44110 2497 D1
W 171st St
4300 CLEV 44135 2752 B4
E 172nd Pl
4200 CLEV 44128 2757 C4
E 172nd St
1100 CLEV 44110 2372 D7
1100 CLEV 44119 2372 D7
1400 CLEV 44110 2497 D1
W 172nd St
4400 CLEV 44135 2752 B5
E 173rd St
1100 CLEV 44119 2372 D7
1400 CLEV 44110 2497 D1
3700 CLEV 44128 2757 D2
W 173rd St
4300 CLEV 44135 2752 B4
E 174th Pl
4200 CLEV 44128 2757 D4
E 174th St
1000 CLEV 44119 2372 D6
1400 CLEV 44110 2497 D1
4500 CLEV 44128 2757 D5
W 174th St
4400 CLEV 44135 2752 B5
E 175th St
1100 CLEV 44119 2372 D7
1400 CLEV 44110 2497 D1
4000 CLEV 44128 2757 D3
E 176th St
- CLEV 44128 2757 D5
1000 CLEV 44119 2372 D6
1400 CLEV 44110 2497 D1
3800 CLEV 44128 2757 D3
W 176th St
3900 CLEV 44111 2752 A3
4300 CLEV 44135 2752 A4
E 177th Pl
4200 CLEV 44128 2757 D4
E 177th St
1000 CLEV 44119 2372 D6
3700 CLEV 44128 2757 D2
W 177th St
4400 CLEV 44135 2752 A5
E 178th St
900 CLEV 44119 2372 D6
4100 CLEV 44128 2757 D4
W 178th St
3700 CLEV 44111 2752 A2
E 179th St
900 CLEV 44119 2372 D6
1300 CLEV 44110 2372 D7
W 179th St
3700 CLEV 44111 2752 A2
W 180th St
4300 CLEV 44135 2752 A4
E 181st St
4100 CLEV 44128 2757 D4
4200 CLEV 44122 2757 D4
W 181st St
4300 CLEV 44135 2752 A4
W 182nd St
4200 CLEV 44135 2752 A4
E 183rd St
3700 CLEV 44122 2757 D2
4000 CLEV 44128 2757 D3
W 183rd St
4400 CLEV 44135 2752 A5
E 185th St
100 CLEV 44119 2372 E5
100 EUCL 44119 2372 E5
1300 CLEV 44110 2372 E7
1300 CLEV 44110 2497 E1
W 185th St
4400 CLEV 44135 2752 A5
4500 CLEV 44135 2751 E6
E 186th St
1200 CLEV 44110 2372 E7
4000 CLEV 44122 2757 D3
E 187th St
1200 CLEV 44110 2372 E7
4000 CLEV 44122 2757 E3
W 187th St
4200 CLEV 44135 2751 E4
E 188th St
- SRHT 44122 2757 E2
700 CLEV 44119 2372 E5
1200 CLEV 44110 2372 E7
3700 CLEV 44122 2757 E3
W 188th St
4700 CLEV 44135 2751 E6
189th St
- EUCL 44119 2372 E4
E 189th St
300 EUCL 44119 2372 E4
3800 CLEV 44122 2757 E2
W 189th St
4200 CLEV 44135 2751 E4
E 190th St
100 EUCL 44119 2372 E3
W 190th St
4500 CLEV 44135 2751 E5
E 191st St
100 EUCL 44119 2372 E3
1400 EUCL 44117 2497 E2
W 191st St
4200 CLEV 44135 2751 E4
E 192nd St
10 EUCL 44119 2372 E3
W 192nd St
1300 RKRV 44116 2621 E5
4200 FWPK 44126 2751 E2
4500 CLEV 44135 2751 E5
E 193rd St
500 EUCL 44119 2372 E4
600 CLEV 44119 2372 E5
1400 EUCL 44117 2497 E1
W 193rd St
4400 CLEV 44135 2751 E5
E 194th St
10 EUCL 44119 2372 E3
W 194th St
4300 CLEV 44135 2751 E4
4400 FWPK 44126 2751 E2
4700 CLEV 44135 2751 E6
E 195th St
200 EUCL 44119 2373 A4
1400 EUCL 44117 2497 E1
E 196th St
10 EUCL 44119 2372 E3
1400 EUCL 44117 2497 E1
W 196th St
3900 FWPK 44126 2751 E2
4600 CLEV 44135 2751 D5
E 197th St
10 EUCL 44119 2372 E3
10 EUCL 44119 2373 A3
700 CLEV 44119 2373 A5
W 197th St
4200 CLEV 44135 2751 D4

Street / Block	City	ZIP	Map#	Grid
W 198th St				
4700	CLEV	44135	2751	D6
E 199th St				
10	EUCL	44119	2372	E3
10	EUCL	44119	2373	A3
E 200th St				
-	CLEV	44117	2373	A6
-	EUCL	44117	2373	A6
10	EUCL	44119	2373	A3
10	EUCL	44123	2373	A3
600	CLEV	44119	2373	A4
W 200th St				
4800	CLEV	44135	2751	D6
E 201st St				
10	EUCL	44123	2373	A3
E 202nd St				
10	EUCL	44123	2373	A3
W 202nd St				
4200	FWPK	44126	2751	D2
4800	CLEV	44135	2751	D6
E 203rd Pl				
700	EUCL	44119	2373	A5
E 203rd St				
10	EUCL	44123	2373	A3
E 204th St				
200	EUCL	44123	2373	A3
1400	EUCL	44117	2498	A1
W 204th St				
3900	FWPK	44126	2751	D2
E 205th St				
10	EUCL	44123	2373	A3
700	EUCL	44119	2373	A5
E 206th St				
10	EUCL	44123	2373	A2
E 207th St				
10	EUCL	44123	2373	A2
800	EUCL	44119	2373	A5
E 208th St				
10	EUCL	44123	2373	A2
500	EUCL	44119	2373	A4
W 208th St				
4100	FWPK	44126	2751	C3
E 209th St				
10	EUCL	44123	2373	A2
800	EUCL	44119	2373	A5
E 210th St				
200	EUCL	44123	2373	A3
800	EUCL	44119	2373	A5
W 210th St				
3100	FWPK	44126	2751	C2
3100	RKRV	44116	2751	C2
E 211th St				
-	EUCL	44119	2373	A4
10	EUCL	44123	2373	A2
W 211th St				
4100	FWPK	44126	2751	C3
E 212th St				
10	EUCL	44123	2373	A2
700	EUCL	44119	2373	B5
1500	EUCL	44117	2373	B7
W 212th St				
3400	FWPK	44126	2751	C2
E 213th St				
10	EUCL	44123	2373	A2
500	EUCL	44119	2373	B4
900	EUCL	44123	2373	B4
W 213th St				
3400	FWPK	44126	2751	C2
E 214th St				
10	EUCL	44123	2373	B2
900	EUCL	44119	2373	B5
1500	EUCL	44117	2373	B7
W 214th St				
4400	FWPK	44126	2751	B3
E 215th St				
300	EUCL	44123	2373	B3
W 215th St				
4400	FWPK	44126	2751	B3
E 216th St				
200	EUCL	44123	2373	B2
800	EUCL	44119	2373	B5
E 217th St				
10	EUCL	44123	2373	B2
W 217th St				
4000	FWPK	44126	2751	B3
E 218th St				
200	EUCL	44123	2373	B2
800	EUCL	44119	2373	B5
E 219th St				
10	EUCL	44123	2373	B2
1300	EUCL	44117	2373	B7
W 219th St				
4000	FWPK	44126	2751	B3
E 220th St				
10	EUCL	44123	2373	B2
800	EUCL	44119	2373	B5
W 220th St				
3900	FWPK	44126	2751	B3
E 221st St				
10	EUCL	44123	2373	B1
1300	EUCL	44117	2373	B7
1900	EUCL	44117	2498	B1
W 221st St				
4400	FWPK	44126	2751	B4
E 222nd St				
200	EUCL	44123	2373	B4
800	EUCL	44119	2373	B4
1000	EUCL	44117	2373	B6
W 222nd St				
4200	FWPK	44126	2751	B3
E 223rd St				
-	EUCL	44117	2373	B5
800	EUCL	44123	2373	B5
1800	EUCL	44117	2373	B7
1800	EUCL	44117	2498	B1
W 223rd St				
3900	FWPK	44126	2751	B3
E 224th St				
10	EUCL	44123	2373	B1
900	EUCL	44117	2373	B5
900	EUCL	44123	2373	B5
1900	EUCL	44117	2498	B1
W 224th St				
3800	FWPK	44126	2751	A3
E 225th St				
10	EUCL	44123	2373	B1
900	EUCL	44117	2373	C5
900	EUCL	44123	2373	C5
1800	EUCL	44117	2373	B7
1800	EUCL	44117	2498	B1
W 225th St				
4400	FWPK	44126	2751	A4
E 226th St				
10	EUCL	44123	2373	B1
1900	EUCL	44117	2498	B1
W 226th St				
3800	FWPK	44126	2751	A3
E 227th St				
1700	EUCL	44117	2373	B7
1700	EUCL	44117	2498	B1
W 227th St				
3800	FWPK	44126	2751	A3
E 228th St				
100	EUCL	44123	2373	C2
900	EUCL	44117	2373	C4
1900	EUCL	44117	2498	C1
W 228th St				
4400	FWPK	44126	2751	A4
W 229th St				
3800	FWPK	44126	2751	A3
E 230th St				
800	EUCL	44117	2373	C4
800	EUCL	44123	2373	C4
1500	EUCL	44117	2373	C7
1500	EUCL	44117	2498	C1
W 230th St				
3000	NOSD	44070	2751	A3
W 231st St				
3000	NOSD	44070	2751	A3
E 232nd St				
200	EUCL	44123	2373	C2
1700	EUCL	44117	2498	C1
W 232nd St				
3600	NOSD	44070	2751	A4
E 233rd St				
10	EUCL	44123	2373	C1
1900	EUCL	44117	2498	C1
W 233rd St				
2700	NOSD	44070	2750	E3
E 234th St				
1700	EUCL	44117	2498	C1
E 235th St				
100	EUCL	44123	2373	C1
E 236th St				
700	EUCL	44123	2373	C4
1600	EUCL	44117	2373	C7
1600	EUCL	44117	2498	C1
E 237th St				
800	EUCL	44123	2373	C4
E 238th St				
10	EUCL	44123	2373	C1
1700	EUCL	44117	2373	C7
1700	EUCL	44117	2498	C1
E 239th St				
800	EUCL	44123	2373	C4
900	EUCL	44117	2373	C4
E 240th St				
500	EUCL	44123	2373	C2
1700	EUCL	44117	2373	D7
E 241st St				
300	EUCL	44123	2373	C2
E 242nd St				
10	EUCL	44123	2373	D1
E 243rd St				
200	EUCL	44123	2373	D1
1600	EUCL	44117	2373	D6
E 244th St				
200	EUCL	44123	2373	D1
E 245th St				
400	EUCL	44123	2373	D2
E 246th St				
200	EUCL	44123	2373	D1
E 248th St				
200	EUCL	44123	2373	D1
1400	EUCL	44117	2373	D5
E 249th St				
700	EUCL	44123	2373	D3
E 250th St				
200	EUCL	44132	2373	D1
800	EUCL	44123	2373	D3
1400	EUCL	44117	2373	D5
E 252nd St				
10	EUCL	44132	2373	D1
1400	EUCL	44117	2373	D5
E 253rd St				
400	EUCL	44132	2373	D2
E 254th St				
500	EUCL	44132	2373	D2
1500	EUCL	44117	2373	D5
1500	EUCL	44132	2373	D5
E 255th St				
200	EUCL	44132	2373	D1
E 256th St				
700	EUCL	44132	2373	D3
E 257th St				
200	EUCL	44132	2373	E1
E 258th St				
600	EUCL	44132	2373	E3
E 260th St				
100	EUCL	44132	2248	E7
200	EUCL	44132	2373	E1
E 260th St SR-175				
200	EUCL	44132	2373	E1
E 261st St				
600	EUCL	44132	2373	E2
E 262nd St				
200	EUCL	44132	2248	E7
200	EUCL	44132	2373	E1
E 263rd St				
700	EUCL	44132	2373	E2
E 264th St				
100	EUCL	44132	2248	E7
200	EUCL	44132	2373	E1
E 265th St				
100	EUCL	44132	2248	E7
E 266th St				
200	EUCL	44132	2248	E7
200	EUCL	44132	2373	E1
E 267th St				
10	EUCL	44132	2248	E7
E 270th St				
200	EUCL	44132	2248	E7
200	EUCL	44132	2373	E1
E 271st St				
200	EUCL	44132	2248	E7
300	EUCL	44132	2373	C1
300	EUCL	44132	2374	A1
E 272nd St				
100	EUCL	44132	2248	E7
100	EUCL	44132	2249	A7
400	EUCL	44132	2374	A1
E 273rd St				
300	EUCL	44132	2249	A7
E 274th St				
400	EUCL	44132	2374	A1
E 275th St				
400	EUCL	44132	2374	A1
E 276th St				
200	EUCL	44132	2249	A7
1200	EUCL	44132	2374	A4
E 279th St				
1200	EUCL	44132	2374	A3
E 280th St				
10	EUCL	44132	2249	A6
E 284th St				
200	WLWK	44095	2249	A6
E 285th St				
200	WLWK	44095	2249	A7
E 286th St				
100	WLWK	44095	2249	A6
1300	EUCL	44132	2374	A3
1300	WKLF	44092	2374	A3
E 288th St				
200	WLWK	44095	2249	B7
500	WKLF	44092	2249	B7
500	WKLF	44095	2249	B7
E 289th St				
100	WLWK	44095	2249	B6
1500	WKLF	44092	2374	B3
E 290th St				
1500	WKLF	44092	2374	C4
E 291st St				
100	WLWK	44095	2249	B6
1500	WKLF	44092	2374	B3
E 293rd St				
100	WLWK	44095	2249	B6
1400	WKLF	44092	2374	B2
E 294th St				
100	WLWK	44095	2249	B6
1500	WKLF	44092	2374	C2
E 296th St				
1500	WKLF	44092	2374	C2
E 298th St				
1500	WKLF	44092	2374	D2
E 300th St				
400	WLWK	44095	2249	C7
700	WKLF	44092	2249	C7
1300	WKLF	44092	2374	D1
E 302nd St				
700	WLWK	44095	2249	D7
E 305th St				
200	WLWK	44095	2249	C5
1000	WKLF	44092	2249	D7
1000	WLWK	44092	2249	D7
1000	WLWK	44092	2374	D1
E 307th St				
200	WLWK	44095	2249	C5
E 308th St				
200	WLWK	44095	2249	C5
E 309th St				
300	WLWK	44095	2249	C5
E 310th St				
200	WLWK	44095	2249	C5
E 312th St				
200	WLWK	44095	2249	C5
E 314th St				
100	WLWK	44095	2249	C4
E 315th St				
100	WLWK	44095	2249	C4
E 316th St				
100	WLWK	44095	2249	C4
E 317th St				
100	WLWK	44095	2249	C4
E 319th St				
300	WLWK	44095	2249	D5
E 320th St				
200	WLWK	44095	2249	D4
E 321st St				
400	WLWK	44095	2249	D5
E 322nd St				
200	WLWK	44095	2249	D4
E 323rd St				
200	WLWK	44095	2249	D4
E 324th St				
100	WLWK	44095	2249	D3
E 325th St				
-	WLWK	44095	2249	D3
326 Rd				
12900	EatT	44028	3008	D7
12900	EatT	44028	3143	D1
14300	GftT	44028	3143	D5
E 326th St				
200	WLWK	44095	2249	D4
E 327th St				
200	WLWK	44095	2249	D4
E 328th St				
200	WLWK	44095	2249	D4
E 329th St				
200	WLWK	44095	2249	E4
E 330th St				
200	WLWK	44095	2249	D4
1400	ETLK	44095	2249	E5
E 331st St				
200	ETLK	44095	2249	E4
E 332nd St				
300	ETLK	44095	2249	E3
E 337th St				
1100	ETLK	44095	2249	E4
E 340th St				
1200	ETLK	44095	2250	A4
E 341st St				
700	ETLK	44095	2250	A2
E 342nd St				
700	ETLK	44095	2250	A2
E 343rd St				
700	ETLK	44095	2250	A2
E 344th St				
700	ETLK	44095	2250	A2
E 345th St				
700	ETLK	44095	2250	A2
4800	WLBY	44094	2250	A7
E 346th St				
800	ETLK	44095	2250	A3
E 347th St				
700	ETLK	44095	2250	A2
E 348th St				
700	ETLK	44095	2250	A2
E 349th St				
600	ETLK	44095	2250	A2
E 351st St				
1100	ETLK	44095	2250	B4
E 353rd St				
700	ETLK	44095	2250	B2
E 354th St				
1100	ETLK	44095	2250	B4
E 355th St				
1400	ETLK	44095	2250	B5
4600	WLBY	44094	2250	B6
E 357th St				
1100	ETLK	44095	2250	B4
E 359th St				
1100	ETLK	44095	2250	B4
E 360th St				
1100	ETLK	44095	2250	B4
E 361st St				
-	WLBY	44094	2250	B5
-	WLBY	44095	2250	B5
1400	ETLK	44095	2250	B5
E 362nd St				
1100	ETLK	44095	2250	B4
E 363rd St				
1400	ETLK	44095	2250	B5
E 364th St				
3700	WLBY	44094	2250	B4
E 365th St				
1500	ETLK	44095	2250	C5
3700	WLBY	44094	2250	B4
E 367th St				
1400	ETLK	44095	2250	C5

INDEX 55

Airports

Cleveland Points of Interest Index

Buildings - Governmental

Airports

FEATURE NAME	Address City ZIP Code	MAP#	GRID
Burke Lakefront	CLEV, 44114	2495	B6
Casement	PnvT, 44077	2040	D6
Cleveland Hopkins International	CLEV, 44135	2751	C7
Columbia Station	ClbT, 44028	3009	A6
Concord Airpark	CcdT, 44077	2255	A1
Cuyahoga County	WBHL, 44092	2374	B7
Elyria	CrlT, 44035	3006	A4
Fairview	HrmT, 44234	3160	E3
Gates	PkmT, 44231	3027	B3
Lorain County Regional	NRsT, 44035	3004	D3
Lost Nation Municipal	MNTR, 44060	2143	B6

Beaches, Harbors & Water Rec

FEATURE NAME	Address City ZIP Code	MAP#	GRID
Bass Lake Club	11445 Lakeview Rd, MsnT, 44024	2504	C4
Beaver Park Marina	6101 W Erie Av, LORN, 44053	2743	B3
Chagrin Lagoon Yacht Club	35111 Halsey Dr, ETLK, 44095	2142	A7
Channel Park Marina	5300 Whiskey Island Dr, CLEV, 44113	2624	B4
Cleveland Yachting Club	200 Yacht Club Dr, RKRV, 44116	2621	E4
Commodore's Club	1785 Merwin Av, CLEV, 44113	2624	D4
East 55th Street Marina	5501 N Marginal Rd, CLEV, 44103	2495	C5
Edgewater Marina	6500 Cleveland Memorial Shorewa, CLEV, 44102	2624	A4
Emerald Necklace Marina	1500 Scenic Park Dr, LKWD, 44107	2621	E5
Fairport Harbor	5 Water St, FTHR, 44077	2039	C3
Fishing Pier	RKRV, 44116	2621	A5
Forest City Yacht Club	4301 N Marginal Rd, CLEV, 44114	2495	C6
Gordon Shore Boat Club	5401 S Marginal Rd, CLEV, 44114	2495	C6
Mentor Harbor Yachting Club	MONT, 44060	2037	E7
Mentor Lagoon	MNTR, 44060	2038	A7
Northeast Yacht Club	14021 Lake Shore Blvd, CLEV, 44110	2372	A7
Olde River Yacht Club	4900 Whiskey Island Dr, CLEV, 44113	2624	B4
Perkins Beach	CLEV, 44102	2623	E4
Whiskey Island Marina	2800 Whiskey Island Dr, CLEV, 44113	2624	B3

Buildings

FEATURE NAME	Address City ZIP Code	MAP#	GRID
Alcoa	1600 Harvard Av, CHHT, 44125	2755	A3
Avery Dennison	250 Chester St, PNVL, 44077	2040	A6
BF Goodrich Headquarters	9911 Brecksville Rd, BKVL, 44141	3151	A4
Coca-Cola Bottling	25000 Miles Rd, BDHT, 44146	2758	D7
EMI	1201 W 65th St, CLEV, 44102	2624	A4
Ford Motor Company	17601 Brookpark Rd, BKPK, 44142	2752	A7
GE Tungsten Products Plant	21800 Tungsten Rd, EUCL, 44117	2373	A6
Hewlett-Packard	15885 W Sprague Rd, SGVL, 44136	3012	B2
ndustrial Park	Curtis Blvd, ETLK, 44095	2249	E6
ndustrial Park	Morgan Ct, SGVL, 44136	3145	E2
ndustrial Park	Progress Dr, SGVL, 44136	3011	C5
.TV Steel	12610 Kirby Av, CLEV, 44108	2496	E3
ubrizol	29400 Lakeland Blvd, WKLF, 44092	2374	B2
Aentor Radio	1561 Lost Nation Rd, WLBY, 44094	2143	A5
lestle's	30003 Bainbridge Rd, SLN, 44139	2888	C2
'erry Nuclear Power Plant	10 Center Rd, NPRY, 44081	1940	C4
adiometer America	810 Sharon Dr, WTLK, 44145	2620	D6
ockefeller Building	614 W Superior Av, CLEV, 44113	2624	D3
ockwell	1 Allen Bradley Dr, MDHT, 44124	2629	D2
tein & Company	123 W Prospect Av, CLEV, 44113	2624	E3
toneco	900 Clark Av, CLEV, 44113	2625	A7
erminal Tower	50 Public Sq, CLEV, 44115	2624	E3
RW World Headquarters	1900 Richmond Rd, LNHT, 44124	2628	E2

Buildings - Governmental

FEATURE NAME	Address City ZIP Code	MAP#	GRID
mherst City Hall	206 S Main St, AMHT, 44001	2872	D2
mherst Township Hall	7530 Oberlin Rd, AhtT, 44035	2873	B3
nthony J Celebrezze Federal Building	1240 E 9th St, CLEV, 44114	2624	E2
quilla Village Hall	65 Turner Dr, AQLA, 44024	2505	C4
shtabula County Court West	117 W Main St, GNVA, 44041	1944	B4
uburn Township Hall	11010 E Washington St, AbnT, 44023	2893	A5
urora City Hall	130 S Chillicothe Rd, AURA, 44202	3156	E1
von City Hall	36080 Chester Rd, AVON, 44011	2618	B6
von Lake Town Hall	150 Avon-Belden Center Rd, AVLK, 44012	2488	A7
Bainbridge Township Town Hall	17826 Chillicothe Rd, BbgT, 44023	2891	A6
Bay Village City Hall	350 Dover Center Rd, BYVL, 44140	2620	A4
Beachwood City Hall	2700 Richmond Rd, BHWD, 44122	2628	D5
Bedford City Hall	65 Columbus Rd, BDFD, 44146	2887	A4
Bedford Heights City Hall	5661 Perkins Rd, BDHT, 44146	2887	E2
Bentleyville Village Hall	6253 Chagrin River Rd, BTVL, 44022	2889	D1
Berea City Hall	11 Berea Coms, BERA, 44017	2880	C7
Berea Municipal Court	11 Berea Coms, BERA, 44017	2880	B7
Bratenahl Village Hall	411 Bratenahl Rd, BTNH, 44108	2496	B3
Brecksville City Hall	9069 Brecksville Rd, BKVL, 44141	3016	A7
Broadview Heights City Hall	8938 Broadview Rd, BWHT, 44147	3014	E6
Brooklyn City Hall	7619 Memphis Av, BKLN, 44144	2753	D4
Brooklyn Heights Village Hall	345 Tuxedo Av, BNHT, 44131	2755	A7
Brook Park City Hall	6161 Engle Rd, BKPK, 44142	2881	A3
Brownhelm Township Hall	1940 N Ridge Rd, VMLN, 44001	2871	C2
Burton Township Hall	14821 Rapids Rd, BURT, 44021	2766	A1
Burton Village Hall	14588 W Park St, BURT, 44021	2636	A7
Carl B Stokes United States Court House	801 W Superior Av, CLEV, 44113	2624	D3
Carlisle Township Town Hall	11969 Lattasburg-Elyria Rd, CrlT, 44050	3005	E6
Chagrin Falls Town Hall	83 N Main St, CNFL, 44022	2761	A6
Chagrin Falls Village Hall	21 W Washington St, CNFL, 44022	2761	A6
Chardon Township Hall	9949 Mentor Rd, CdnT, 44024	2379	B4
Chardon Village Hall	111 Water St, CRDN, 44024	2380	A6
Chester Township Hall	12701 Chillicothe Rd, CsTp, 44026	2502	B7
Civic Center	Avon-Belden Center Rd, AVLK, 44012	2488	A7
Civic Center	5411 Turney Rd, GDHT, 44125	2756	D7
Civic Center	8500 Civic Center Blvd, MNTR, 44060	2144	C4
Civic Center	4575 Lake Rd, SDLK, 44054	2616	C3
Claridon Town Hall	13930 Mayfield Rd, ClrT, 44024	2506	B6
Cleveland City Hall	601 E Lakeside Av, CLEV, 44114	2624	E2
Cleveland Heights City Hall	40 Severance Cir, CVHT, 44118	2497	D7
Cleveland Heights Municipal Court	40 Severance Cir, CVHT, 44118	2497	D7
Cleveland Municipal Court	1200 Ontario St, CLEV, 44113	2624	D2
Columbia Town Hall	173914 Royalton Rd, ClbT, 44028	3009	E7
Cuyahoga County Administration Building	1219 Ontario St, CLEV, 44114	2624	D2
Cuyahoga County Appeals Court	1 W Lakeside Av, CLEV, 44113	2624	D2
Cuyahoga County Health District	1375 Euclid Av, CLEV, 44114	2625	A3
Cuyahoga County Jail	1215 W 3rd St, CLEV, 44113	2624	D3
Cuyahoga County Probate Court	1 W Lakeside Av, CLEV, 44113	2624	D3
Cuyahoga Heights Village Hall	4863 E 71st St, CHHT, 44125	2755	E6
East Cleveland City Hall	14340 Euclid Av, ECLE, 44112	2497	A6
East Cleveland Municipal Court	14340 Euclid Av, ECLE, 44112	2497	B6
Eastlake City Hall	35150 Lake Shore Blvd, ETLK, 44095	2250	B2
Eaton Township Town Hall	12043 Wooster-Avon Lake Rd, EatT, 44044	3007	E7
Elyria City Hall	328 Broad St, ELYR, 44035	2875	B6
Elyria Township Hall	41416 Griswold Rd, EyrT, 44035	2874	E1
Euclid City Hall	585 E 222nd St, EUCL, 44123	2373	B3
Euclid Municipal Court	555 E 222nd St, EUCL, 44123	2373	B3
Fairport Harbor Village Hall	220 3rd St, FTHR, 44077	2039	D3
Fairview Park City Hall	20777 Lorain Rd, FWPK, 44126	2751	D3
Federal Bureau of Investigation	1501 Lakeside Av E, CLEV, 44114	2624	E2
Federal Reserve Bank of Cleveland	1455 E 6th St, CLEV, 44114	2624	E2
Frank J Lausche State Office Building	615 W Superior Av, CLEV, 44113	2624	D3
Garfield Heights City Hall	5407 Turney Rd, GDHT, 44125	2885	D1
Garfield Heights Municipal Court	5555 Turney Rd, GDHT, 44125	2885	D1
Gates Mills Town Hall	1470 Chagrin River Rd, GSML, 44040	2500	E7
Geauga County Administration Building	231 Main St, CRDN, 44024	2380	A6
Geauga County General Health District	470 Center St, CRDN, 44024	2379	C5
Geauga County Jail	13205 Aquilla Rd, ClrT, 44024	2635	C2
Geneva City Hall	44 N Forest St, GNVA, 44041	1944	B3
Glenwillow Village Hall	29555 Pettibone Rd, GNWL, 44139	3019	B2
Grafton Correctional Institution	2500 Wooster-Avon Lake Rd, GFTN, 44044	3142	E4
Grafton Village Hall	960 Main St, GFTN, 44044	3142	B5
Grand River Village Hall	205 Singer Av, GDRV, 44045	2039	C6
Hambden Township Town Hall	13887 Gar Hwy, HmbT, 44024	2381	B3
Highland Heights City Hall	5827 Highland Rd, HDHT, 44143	2499	C3
Highland Hills Village Hall	3700 Northfield Rd, SRHT, 44122	2758	A2
Hiram Township Hall	11616 Garfield Rd, HRM, 44234	3161	A2
Hiram Village Hall	11617 Garfield Rd, HRM, 44234	3161	B2
Hunting Valley Village Hall	38252 Fairmount Blvd, HGVL, 44022	2630	D5
Huntsburg Town Hall	16534 Mayfield Rd, HtbT, 44046	2508	A6
Independence City Hall	6800 Brecksville Rd, INDE, 44131	2884	D6
Kirtland City Hall	9301 Chillicothe Rd, KTLD, 44094	2376	E1
Kirtland Hills Village Hall	8026 Chillicothe Rd, KDHL, 44060	2252	C3
Lake County Administration Building	105 Main St, PNVL, 44077	2040	B7
Lake County Court House	47 N Park Pl, PNVL, 44077	2040	B7
Lake County General Health District	33 Mill St, PNVL, 44077	2040	B7
Lake County Jail	104 E Erie St, PNVL, 44077	2040	B7
Lakeline Village Hall	33801 Lake Shore Blvd, LKLN, 44095	2249	E2
Lakewood City Hall	12650 Detroit Av, LKWD, 44107	2623	A5
Lakewood City Hall Annex	12805 Detroit Av, LKWD, 44107	2623	A5
Lakewood Municipal Court	12650 Detroit Av, LKWD, 44107	2623	A4
Leroy Town Hall	13639 Leroy Center Rd, LryT, 44077	2148	B6
Linndale Village Hall	4016 W 119th St, LNDL, 44135	2753	B3
Lorain City Hall	200 E Erie Br, LORN, 44052	2614	E6
Lorain Civic Center	617 Broadway Av, LORN, 44052	2614	E6
Lorain Correctional Institution	2075 Wooster-Avon Lake Rd, GFTN, 44028	3142	E3
Lorain County Administration Building	226 Middle Av, ELYR, 44035	2875	A7
Lorain County Common Pleas Court	308 2nd St, ELYR, 44035	2875	A6
Lorain County Domestic Relations Court	226 Middle Av, ELYR, 44035	2875	B6
Lorain County General Health District	9880 Murray Ridge Rd, ELYR, 44035	3005	C2
Lorain County Jail	9896 Murray Ridge Rd, ELYR, 44035	3005	C2
Lorain County Probate Court	226 Middle Av, ELYR, 44035	2875	A6
Lyndhurst City Hall	5301 Mayfield Rd, LNHT, 44124	2499	A7
Lyndhurst Municipal Court	5301 Mayfield Rd, LNHT, 44124	2499	A7
Macedonia City Hall	9691 Valley View Rd, MCDN, 44056	3153	D1
Madison Township Municipal Offices	2065 Hubbard Rd, MadT, 44057	1942	B2
Madison Village Hall	126 W Main St, MDSN, 44057	2044	A1
Mantua Township Hall	4122 Twinsburg Warren Rd, ManT, 44255	3159	A2
Mantua Village Hall	4736 E High St, MNTU, 44255	3159	C6
Maple Heights City Hall	5353 Lee Rd, MPHT, 44137	2886	C1
Mayfield Heights City Hall	6154 Mayfield Rd, MDHT, 44124	2499	D7
Mayfield Town Hall	6621 Wilson Mills Rd, MAYF, 44143	2500	A5
Mentor City Hall	8500 Civic Center Blvd, MNTR, 44060	2144	B4
Mentor Municipal Court	8500 Civic Center Blvd, MNTR, 44060	2144	B4
Mentor On The Lake Village Hall	5860 Andrews Rd, MONT, 44060	2143	D2
Middleburg Heights City Hall	15700 E Bagley Rd, MDBH, 44130	2881	B6
Middleburg Heights Court	15700 E Bagley Rd, MDBH, 44130	2881	B6
Middlefield Township Hall	15278 Madison Rd, MdfT, 44062	2768	A4
Middlefield Village Hall	14860 N State Av, MDFD, 44062	2767	D1
Moreland Hills Village Hall	4350 Som Center Rd, MDHL, 44022	2759	E5
Munson Township Hall	12210 Auburn Rd, MsnT, 44024	2504	A5
Newburgh Heights Village Hall	4000 Washington Park Blvd, NBGH, 44105	2755	C3
Newbury Town Hall	14899 Auburn Rd, NbyT, 44065	2764	A2
New Russia Township Hall	46268 Butternut Ridge Rd, NRsT, 44074	3003	D7
Northeast Pre-Release Center	2675 E 30th St, CLEV, 44115	2625	B4
Northfield Center Town Hall	9546 Brandywine Rd, NCtT, 44067	3152	E1
Northfield Village Hall	10455 Northfield Rd, NHFD, 44067	3018	A4
North Olmsted City Hall	5200 Dover Center Rd, NOSD, 44070	2750	A7
North Perry Village Hall	4449 Lockwood Rd, NPRY, 44081	1940	D3
North Randall City Hall	21937 Miles Rd, NRDL, 44128	2758	B6
North Ridgeville City Hall	7307 Avon Belden Rd, NRDV, 44039	2877	A4
North Royalton City Hall	13834 Ridge Rd, NRYN, 44133	3013	E7
Oakwood Village Court	24800 Broadway Av, OKWD, 44146	3018	D1
Oakwood Village Hall	24800 Broadway Av, OKWD, 44146	3018	D1
Oberlin City Hall	85 S Main St, OBLN, 44074	3138	E2
Olmsted Falls City Hall	26100 Bagley Rd, ODFL, 44138	2879	B6
Olmsted Town Hall	26900 Cook Rd, OmsT, 44138	2879	A4
Orange Village Hall	4600 Lander Rd, ORNG, 44022	2759	C5
Painesville City Hall	7 Richmond St, PNVL, 44077	2146	B1
Painesville Township Hall	55 Nye Rd, PnvT, 44077	2145	B4
Parkman Town Hall	16295 Main Market Rd, PkmT, 44234	3027	E1
Parma City Hall	6611 Ridge Rd, PRMA, 44129	2882	E5
Parma Heights City Hall	6281 Pearl Rd, PMHT, 44130	2882	B4
Parma Municipal Court	5750 W 54th St, PRMA, 44129	2883	B2
Pepper Pike City Hall	28000 Shaker Blvd, PRPK, 44124	2629	B6

Buildings - Governmental

Cemeteries

Cleveland Points of Interest Index

Cleveland Points of Interest Index

Cleveland Points of Interest Index

Cleveland Points of Interest Index

Parks & Recreation — **Parks & Recreation**

Cleveland Points of Interest Index

Parks & Recreation

Post Offices

Cleveland Points of Interest Index

Schools

Cleveland Points of Interest Index

Schools

Cleveland Points of Interest Index

Schools   **Cleveland Points of Interest Index**   **Shopping Centers**

Cleveland Points of Interest Index

Shopping Centers

FEATURE NAME Address City ZIP Code	MAP#	GRID
Westfield Shoppingtown SouthPark 500 Royalton Rd, SGVL, 44136	3012	A7
Westgate Mall 3211 Westgate Mall, FWPK, 44126	2751	C1
Westown Square Shopping Center 10604 Lorain Av, CLEV, 44111	2623	B7
Willoughby Commons Shopping Center Euclid Av, WLBY, 44094	2250	B6
Yorktown Shopping Center Pearl Rd, PMHT, 44130	2882	C3

Transportation

FEATURE NAME Address City ZIP Code	MAP#	GRID
Amtrak-Cleveland Station CLEV, 44114	2624	D2
Amtrak-Elyria Station ELYR, 44035	2875	C6
Greyhound-Cleveland CLEV, 44114	2625	A2
Greyhound-Maple Heights MPHT, 44137	2887	A1
RTA-East 34th-Campus Station CLEV, 44115	2625	B5
RTA-East 55th Station CLEV, 44127	2625	D6
RTA-East 79th Station CLEV, 44104	2626	A5
RTA-East 105th-Quincy Station CLEV, 44106	2626	C4
RTA-East 116th Station CLEV, 44104	2626	D5
RTA-West 3rd Street Station CLEV, 44114	2624	D2
RTA-West 25th-Ohio City Station CLEV, 44113	2624	D5
RTA-West 65th-Madison Station CLEV, 44102	2624	A6
RTA-West 117th-Madison Station CLEV, 44102	2623	B6
RTA-West 150th-Puritas Station CLEV, 44135	2752	C4
RTA-Ashby Station SRHT, 44120	2627	B7
RTA-Attleboro Station SRHT, 44120	2627	D6
RTA-Avalon Station SRHT, 44120	2757	C1
RTA-Belvoir Station SRHT, 44122	2628	B6
RTA-Brookpark Station CLEV, 44135	2752	A7
RTA-Cleveland Hopkins Intl Airport CLEV, 44135	2880	E1
RTA-Courtland Station SRHT, 44122	2627	E6
RTA-Coventry Station SRHT, 44120	2627	A5
RTA-Drexmore Station CLEV, 44120	2627	A5
RTA-Eaton Station SRHT, 44120	2627	D6
RTA-Euclid Station CLEV, 44106	2626	E1
RTA-Farnsleigh Station SRHT, 44122	2758	A1
RTA-Flats East Bank Station CLEV, 44113	2624	D3
RTA-Green Station SRHT, 44122	2628	C6
RTA-Kenmore Station SRHT, 44122	2757	D1
RTA-Lee Station SRHT, 44120	2627	C6
RTA-Lynnfield Station SRHT, 44122	2757	D1
RTA-North Coast Station CLEV, 44114	2624	E2
RTA-Onaway Station SRHT, 44120	2627	B7
RTA-Settlers Landing Station CLEV, 44113	2624	D3
RTA-Shaker Square Station CLEV, 44120	2626	E5
RTA-South Harbor Station CLEV, 44114	2624	E1
RTA-Southington Station SRHT, 44120	2627	B5
RTA-South Woodland Station CLEV, 44120	2627	A6
RTA-S Park Station SRHT, 44120	2627	B5
RTA-Superior Station ECLE, 44112	2496	E7
RTA-Tower City-Public Square Station CLEV, 44113	2624	E3
RTA-Triskett Station CLEV, 44111	2622	E7
RTA-University Circle Station CLEV, 44106	2626	D3
RTA-Warrensville Station SRHT, 44122	2628	A6
RTA-West Blvd-Cudell Station CLEV, 44102	2623	C5
RTA-West Green Station SRHT, 44122	2628	B6
RTA-West Park Station CLEV, 44111	2752	D2
RTA-Windermere Station ECLE, 44112	2497	A6
RTA-Woodhill Station CLEV, 44104	2626	C5

Visitor Information

FEATURE NAME Address City ZIP Code	MAP#	GRID
AAA 12628 Chillicothe Rd, CsTp, 44026	2502	A7
Amherst Chamber of Commerce 480 Park Av, AMHT, 44001	2872	E2
Aurora Chamber of Commerce 173 S Chillicothe Rd, AURA, 44202	3156	E1
Beachwood Chamber of Commerce 24500 Chagrin Blvd, BHWD, 44122	2758	D1
Bedford Chamber of Commerce 33 S Park Av, BDFD, 44146	2887	A4
Bedford Heights Chamber of Commerce 24816 Aurora Rd, BDHT, 44146	2887	D1
Berea Chamber of Commerce 173 Front St, BERA, 44017	2880	C6
Brecksville Chamber of Commerce 4450 Oakes Rd, BKVL, 44141	3150	C1
Broadview Heights Chamber of Commerce 8191 Broadview Rd, BWHT, 44147	3014	E3
Burton Chamber of Commerce 14590 E Park St, BURT, 44021	2766	B1
Canal Visitors Center Hillside Rd, VLVW, 44125	2885	C7

Visitor Information

FEATURE NAME Address City ZIP Code	MAP#	GRID
Carlisle Visitor Center 12882 Diagonal Rd, CrlT, 44050	3140	C1
Chagrin Valley Chamber of Commerce 13 N Franklin St, CNFL, 44022	2761	A6
Chardon Area Chamber of Commerce 112 E Park St, CRDN, 44024	2380	A6
Cleveland Chamber of Commerce 50 Public Sq, CLEV, 44115	2624	E3
Cuyahoga Valley Chamber of Commerce 6596 Brecksville Rd, INDE, 44131	2884	D5
East Cleveland Chamber of Commerce 1801 Charles Rd, ECLE, 44112	2497	B5
Eastlake Chamber of Commerce 35150 Lake Shore Blvd, ETLK, 44095	2250	B2
Euclid Chamber of Commerce 21935 Lake Shore Blvd, EUCL, 44123	2373	B2
Garfield Heights Chamber of Commerce 5284 E 98th St, GDHT, 44125	2756	B7
Geauga County Historical Society 14653 E Park St, BURT, 44021	2766	B1
Geneva Area Chamber of Commerce 866 E Main St, GNVA, 44041	1944	D3
Heights Regional Chamber of Commerce 2490 Lee Blvd, CVHT, 44118	2627	C1
Lakewood Chamber of Commerce 14701 Detroit Av, LKWD, 44107	2622	D5
Lorain County Chamber of Commerce 6100 Broadway Av, LORN, 44053	2745	A6
Madison-Perry Area Chamber of Commerce 33 E Main St, MDSN, 44057	2044	B1
Mayfield Area Chamber of Commerce 1280 Som Center Rd, MDHT, 44124	2500	A7
Mentor Area Chamber of Commerce 7547 Mentor Av, MNTR, 44060	2251	C3
Middleburg Heights Chamber of Commerce 16000 E Bagley Rd, MDBH, 44130	2881	B6
Middlefield Chamber of Commerce 14909 S State Av, MDFD, 44062	2767	C2
Nordonia Hills Chamber of Commerce 9880 N Freeway Dr, MCDN, 44056	3018	C1
North Olmsted Chamber of Commerce 25045 Lorain Rd, NOSD, 44070	2750	C6
North Ridgeville Chamber of Commerce 34845 Lorain Rd, NRDV, 44039	2877	B7
North Royalton Chamber of Commerce 13737 State Rd, NRYN, 44133	3014	A7
Oberlin Area Chamber of Commerce 20 E College St, OBLN, 44074	3138	D2
Painesville Area Chamber of Commerce 391 W Washington St, PNVL, 44077	2146	A1
Parma Area Chamber of Commerce 5255 Regency Dr, PRMA, 44129	2883	A5
Rocky River Chamber of Commerce 20525 Detroit Rd, RKRV, 44116	2621	D6
Seven Hills Chamber of Commerce 5733 Skyline Dr, SVHL, 44131	2884	A1
Solon Chamber of Commerce 33595 Bainbridge Rd, SLN, 44139	2889	A4
Strongsville Chamber of Commerce 18829 Royalton Rd, SGVL, 44136	3011	E7
Twinsburg Chamber of Commerce 9044 Church St, TNBG, 44087	3154	E1
Vermilion Chamber of Commerce 5495 Liberty Av, VMLN, 44089	2740	E5
Visitor Center 1170 Old River Rd, CLEV, 44113	2624	C3
Visitor Center 50 Public Sq, CLEV, 44115	2624	E3
Visitor Center Chillicothe Rd, KTLD, 44094	2251	D6
West Shore Chamber of Commerce 24600 Center Ridge Rd, WTLK, 44145	2750	D1
Wickliffe Area Chamber of Commerce 28855 Euclid Av, WKLF, 44092	2374	A3
Willoughby Area Chamber of Commerce 25 W Spaulding St, WLBY, 44094	2250	E5
Willowick Chamber of Commerce 30435 Lake Shore Blvd, WLWK, 44095	2249	B5

RAND MCNALLY

Thank you for purchasing this Rand McNally Street Guide!
Our goal is to provide you with the information you need.

Please complete the information below so we will be able to serve you better in the future. We value your comments and suggestions for improvements and feedback on corrections. This information can also be e-mailed to: **consumeraffairs@randmcnally.com.** *(This information is for internal use ONLY and will not be distributed or sold to any external third party.)*

Missing pages? Maybe not... Please refer to page A for further explanation.

Street Guide Title: **Cleveland**
Cuyahoga, Geauga, Lake, and portions of Lorain County

ISBN# 0-528-99908-7   **Edition Year: 2004**

2ND FOLD LINE

Today s Date: _____

1. Your Name: _____ Title: _____

2. Address ☐ Business ☐ Personal: _____

3. City/State/Zip: _____

4. Phone Number: _____ E-mail address: _____

5. Age Group: ☐ 18 – 24   ☐ 25-31   ☐ 32-40   ☐ 41- 50   ☐ 51+

6. Company name: _____

7. Type of business: _____

8. Where did you purchase this Street Guide? (store name & location) _____

9. How often do you purchase an updated Street Guide?   ☐ Annually   ☐ Every 2 Years   ☐ Other _____

10. How often do you use it?   ☐ Daily   ☐ Weekly   ☐ Monthly   ☐ Other _____

11. What do you use your Street Guide for?

    ☐ Find Address   ☐ Find Unincorporated Areas   ☐ Navigation   ☐ Identifying Routes   ☐ Other _____

12. Do you use it for: ☐ Business   ☐ Personal   ☐ Both

13. If you have used the Digital Edition software:

1ST FOLD LINE

    What features do you use? _____

    How often do you use it?   ☐ Daily   ☐ Weekly   ☐ Monthly   ☐ Other _____

14. What information would you add/correct in this Street Guide to better meet your needs?

    Map Page # _____   Grid # _____   Index Page # _____

    ☐ Street Name Missing   ☐ Street Name Misspelled   ☐ Street Information Incorrect

    ☐ Incorrect Location for Point of Interest   ☐ Index Error   ☐ Other

    _____

    _____

15. Please provide any additional comments and suggestions you have: _____

    _____

    _____

16. Would you like to receive information about updated editions and special offers from Rand McNally?   ☐ Yes   ☐ No

TAPE SHUT

CUT ALONG DOTTED LINE

ri

BUSINESS REPLY MAIL
FIRST-CLASS MAIL   PERMIT NO. 388   CHICAGO IL

POSTAGE WILL BE PAID BY ADDRESSEE

CONSUMER AFFAIRS
RAND MCNALLY
PO BOX 7600
CHICAGO IL 60680-9915

RAND McNALLY

You'll never need to ask for directions again with these Rand McNally products!

- EasyFinder® Laminated Maps
- Folded Maps
- Street Guides
- Road Atlas
- Motor Carriers' Road Atlas

get directions at
randmcnally.com